HAESE MATHEMATICS

Specialists in mathematics

Mathematics
for the international student
MYP 5 (Extended)
10ᴱ

Michael Haese
Sandra Haese
Mark Humphries
Edward Kemp
Pamela Vollmar

for use with
IB Middle Years
Programme

MATHEMATICS FOR THE INTERNATIONAL STUDENT 10E
MYP 5 (Extended)

Michael Haese   B.Sc.(Hons.), Ph.D.
Sandra Haese   B.Sc.
Mark Humphries   B.Sc.(Hons.)
Edward Kemp   B.Sc., M.A.
Pamela Vollmar   B.Sc.(Hons.), PGCE.

Published by Haese Mathematics
152 Richmond Road, Marleston, SA 5033, AUSTRALIA
Telephone: +61 8 8210 4666, Fax: +61 8 8354 1238
Email: info@haesemathematics.com.au
Web: www.haesemathematics.com.au

National Library of Australia Card Number & ISBN 978-1-921972-53-9

© Haese & Harris Publications 2014

First Edition   2014
Reprinted   2015, 2016 (twice), 2017, 2018

Cartoon artwork by John Martin. Artwork by Brian Houston and Gregory Olesinski.

Cover design by Piotr Poturaj.

Typeset in Australia by Deanne Gallasch and Charlotte Frost. Typeset in Times Roman 10.

Computer software by Adrian Blackburn, Ashvin Narayanan, Tim Lee, Seth Pink, William Pietsch, Brett Laishley, Nicole Szymanczyk and Linden May.

Production work by Gregory Olesinski, Katie Richer, Anna Rijken, and Ryan Quinlan.

Printed in China by Prolong Press Limited.

The textbook has been developed independently of the International Baccalaureate Organization (IBO). The textbook is in no way connected with, or endorsed by, the IBO.

This book is copyright. Except as permitted by the Copyright Act (any fair dealing for the purposes of private study, research, criticism or review), no part of this publication may be reproduced, stored in a retrieval system, or transmitted in any form or by any means, electronic, mechanical, photocopying, recording or otherwise, without the prior permission of the publisher. Enquiries to be made to Haese Mathematics.

Copying for educational purposes: Where copies of part or the whole of the book are made under Part VB of the Copyright Act, the law requires that the educational institution or the body that administers it has given a remuneration notice to Copyright Agency Limited (CAL). For information, contact the Copyright Agency Limited.

Acknowledgements: Maps that have been provided by OpenStreetMap are available freely at www.openstreetmap.org. Licensing terms can be viewed at www.openstreetmap.org/copyright. While every attempt has been made to trace and acknowledge copyright, the authors and publishers apologise for any accidental infringement where copyright has proved untraceable. They would be pleased to come to a suitable agreement with the rightful owner.

Disclaimer: All the internet addresses (URLs) given in this book were valid at the time of printing. While the authors and publisher regret any inconvenience that changes of address may cause readers, no responsibility for any such changes can be accepted by either the authors or the publisher.

FOREWORD

MYP 5 (Extended) has been designed and written for the IB Middle Years Program (MYP) Mathematics framework. The textbook covers the Extended content outlined in the framework.

This book may also be used as a general textbook at about 10th Grade level in classes where students complete a rigorous course in preparation for the study of mathematics at a high level in their final two years of high school. We have developed this book independently of the International Baccalaureate Organization (IBO) in consultation with experienced teachers of IB Mathematics. The text is not endorsed by the IBO.

It is not our intention that each chapter be worked through in full. Teachers must select carefully, according to the abilities and prior knowledge of their students, to make the most efficient use of time and give as thorough coverage of content as possible.

Each chapter begins with an Opening Problem, offering an insight into the application of the mathematics that will be studied in the chapter. Important information and key notes are highlighted, while worked examples provide step-by-step instructions with concise and relevant explanations. Discussions, Activities, Investigations, Puzzles, and Research exercises are used throughout the chapters to develop understanding, problem solving, and reasoning, within an interactive environment.

Four additional chapters are available online:

> Chapter 26: Counting and probability
> Chapter 27: Circles and ellipses
> Chapter 28: Matrices
> Chapter 29: Linear programming

Students who are preparing for Further Mathematics HL at IB Diploma level are encouraged to complete Chapters 27 and 28.

We understand the emphasis that the IB MYP places on the six Global Contexts, and in response there are online links to ideas for projects and investigations to help busy teachers (see p. 6).

Frequent use of the interactive online features should nurture a much deeper understanding and appreciation of mathematical concepts. The inclusion of our *Self Tutor* software (see p. 4) is intended to help students who have been absent from classes or who experience difficulty understanding the material.

The book contains many problems to cater for a range of student abilities and interests, and efforts have been made to contextualise problems so that students can see the practical applications of the mathematics they are studying.

We welcome your feedback. Email: info@haesemathematics.com.au
> Web: www.haesemathematics.com.au

PMH, SHH, MH, EK, PV

ACKNOWLEDGEMENTS

The authors and publishers would like to thank all those teachers who have read proofs and offered advice and encouragement.

ONLINE FEATURES

There are a range of interactive features which are available online.

With the purchase of a new hard copy textbook, you will gain 15 months subscription to our online product. This subscription can be renewed annually for a small fee.

COMPATIBILITY

For iPads, tablets, and other mobile devices, the interactive features may not work. However, the electronic version of the textbook and additional chapters can be viewed online using any of these devices.

REGISTERING

You will need to register to access the online features of this textbook.

Visit www.haesemathematics.com.au/register and follow the instructions. Once you have registered, you can:
- activate your electronic textbook
- use your account to make additional purchases.

To activate your electronic textbook, contact Haese Mathematics. On providing proof of purchase, your electronic textbook will be activated. **It is important that you keep your receipt as proof of purchase.**

For general queries about registering and licence keys:
- Visit our Frequently Asked Questions page: www.haesemathematics.com.au/faq.asp
- Contact Haese Mathematics: info@haesemathematics.com.au

ONLINE VERSION OF THE TEXTBOOK

The entire text of the book can be viewed online, allowing you to leave your textbook at school.

The online text contains the four additional chapters:
- **Chapter 26: Counting and probability**
- **Chapter 27: Circles and ellipses**
- **Chapter 28: Matrices**
- **Chapter 29: Linear programming**

SELF TUTOR

Self tutor is an exciting feature of this book.

The ◀) Self Tutor icon on each worked example denotes an active online link.

> Simply 'click' on the ◀) Self Tutor (or anywhere in the example box) to access the worked example, with a teacher's voice explaining each step necessary to reach the answer.
>
> Play any line as often as you like. See how the basic processes come alive using movement and colour on the screen.

For example:

Example 7 **Self Tutor**

Find x given:

Click here

The angles given are opposite angles of a cyclic quadrilateral.

$$\therefore \quad x + (x+36) = 180$$
$$\therefore \quad 2x + 36 = 180$$
$$\therefore \quad 2x = 144$$
$$\therefore \quad x = 72$$

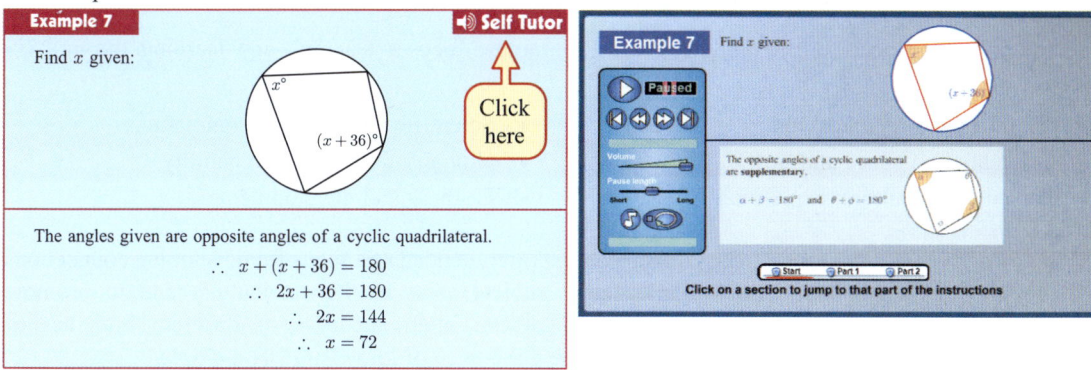

See **Chapter 19**, **Deductive geometry**, p. 424

INTERACTIVE LINKS

Throughout your electronic textbook, you will find interactive links to:

- Graphing software
- Statistics packages
- Geometry packages
- Games
- Demonstrations
- Printable pages

CLICK ON THESE ICONS ONLINE

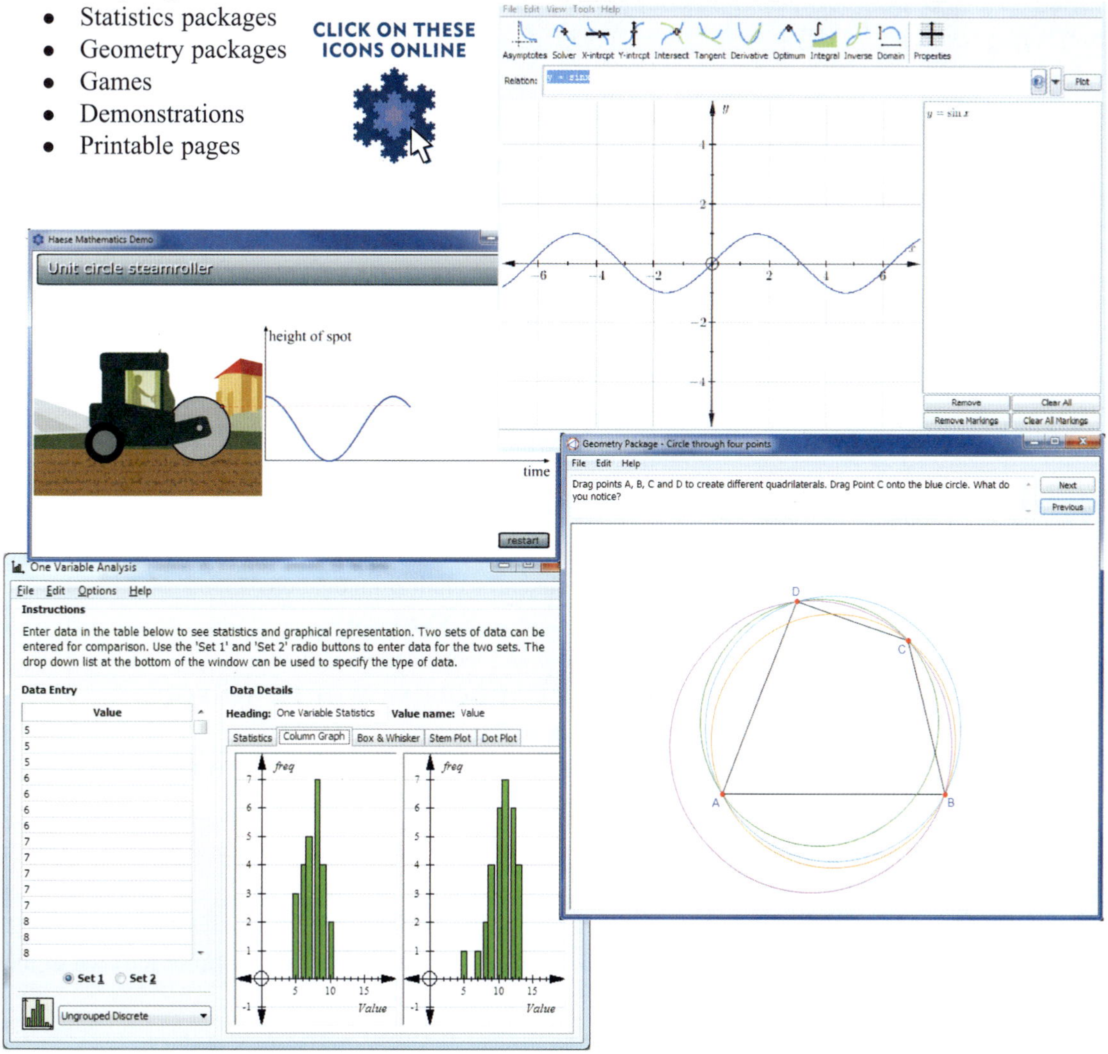

GLOBAL CONTEXTS

The International Baccalaureate Middle Years Programme focuses teaching and learning through six Global Contexts:

- Identities and relationships
- Orientation in space and time
- Personal and cultural expression
- Scientific and technical innovation
- Globalisation and sustainability
- Fairness and development

Click on the heading to access the online link.

The Global Contexts are intended as a focus for developing connections between different subject areas in the curriculum, and to promote an understanding of the interrelatedness of different branches of knowledge and the coherence of knowledge as a whole.

Global context click here

How much time do we have?

Statement of inquiry:	Collecting and interpreting data can help us to understand our place in the world.
Global context:	Identities and relationships
Key concept:	Relationships
Related concepts:	Change, Representation
Objectives:	Knowing and understanding, Applying mathematics in real-life contexts
Approaches to learning:	Communication, Self-management

The available projects are:

Chapter 8:	Transformation Geometry p. 162	**TRANSFORMING ART** Personal and cultural expression
Chapter 9:	Statistics p. 203	**AIR PASSENGER NUMBERS** Orientation in space and time
Chapter 13:	Probability p. 283	**HOW MUCH TIME DO WE HAVE?** Identities and relationships
Chapter 18:	Exponential functions and logarithms p. 406	**HOW DO WE MEASURE THE MAGNITUDE OF AN EARTHQUAKE?** Scientific and technical innovation
Chapter 21:	Advanced trigonometry	**COORDINATE SYSTEMS** Scientific and technical innovation
Chapter 23:	Bivariate statistics p. 509	**WHAT IS A DOLLAR WORTH TO YOU?** Fairness and development
Chapter 25:	Introduction to calculus p. 539	**MODELLING POPULATION GROWTH** Globalisation and sustainability

Each project contains a series of questions, divided into:

- Factual questions (green)
- Conceptual questions (blue)
- Debatable questions (red).

The projects are also accompanied by the general descriptor and a task-specific descriptor for each of the relevant assessment criteria, to help teachers assess the unit of work.

TABLE OF CONTENTS

Extension questions and exercises are marked in red

Summary of measurement facts	10
Summary of circle properties	12
Graphics calculator instructions	12

1 INDICES — 13
- A Index laws — 14
- B Rational indices — 17
- C Scientific notation (standard form) — 20
-    Review set 1A — 25
-    Review set 1B — 26

2 SETS AND VENN DIAGRAMS — 27
- A Number sets — 28
- B Interval notation — 30
- C Subsets and complement — 31
- D Venn diagrams — 33
- E Union and intersection — 36
- F Numbers in regions — 39
- G Problem solving with Venn diagrams — 41
- H The algebra of sets — 43
-    Review set 2A — 44
-    Review set 2B — 45

3 ALGEBRAIC EXPANSION AND FACTORISATION — 47
- A Revision of expansion laws — 48
- B Further expansion — 51
- C The binomial expansion — 52
- D Revision of factorisation — 54
- E Factorising expressions with four terms — 55
- F Factorising quadratic trinomials — 56
- G Factorisation of $ax^2 + bx + c$, $a \neq 1$ — 58
- H Miscellaneous factorisation — 60
-    Review set 3A — 61
-    Review set 3B — 62

4 RADICALS AND SURDS — 63
- A Radicals — 64
- B Simplest radical form — 68
- C Adding and subtracting radicals — 68
- D Multiplications involving radicals — 70
- E Division by radicals — 72
- F Equality of surds — 74
-    Review set 4A — 77
-    Review set 4B — 78

5 PYTHAGORAS' THEOREM — 79
- A Pythagoras' theorem — 80
- B The converse of Pythagoras' theorem — 85
- C Pythagorean triples — 86
- D Problem solving using Pythagoras — 88
- E Circle problems — 92
- F 3-dimensional problems — 96
-    Review set 5A — 98
-    Review set 5B — 100

6 COORDINATE GEOMETRY — 103
- A The distance between two points — 105
- B Midpoints — 108
- C Gradient — 109
- D Parallel and perpendicular lines — 113
- E The equation of a line — 117
- F Perpendicular bisectors — 123
- G Distance from a point to a line — 125
- H 3-dimensional coordinate geometry — 127
-    Review set 6A — 128
-    Review set 6B — 129

7 CONGRUENCE AND SIMILARITY — 131
- A Congruent triangles — 132
- B Proof using congruence — 135
- C Similarity — 139
- D Areas and volumes — 144
-    Review set 7A — 149
-    Review set 7B — 151

8 TRANSFORMATION GEOMETRY — 153
- A Translations — 155
- B Reflections — 158
- C Rotations — 160
- D Dilations — 163
-    Review set 8A — 168
-    Review set 8B — 169

9 STATISTICS — 171
- A Discrete data — 173
- B Continuous data — 177
- C Measuring the centre — 179
- D Cumulative data — 185
- E Measuring the spread — 188
- F Box-and-whisker plots — 191
- G Standard deviation — 195
- H The normal distribution — 200
-    Review set 9A — 203
-    Review set 9B — 205

10 ALGEBRAIC FRACTIONS — 207
- A Evaluating algebraic fractions — 208
- B Simplifying algebraic fractions — 209
- C Multiplying and dividing algebraic fractions — 213
- D Adding and subtracting algebraic fractions — 215
- E Equations with algebraic fractions — 219
-    Review set 10A — 220
-    Review set 10B — 221

11 QUADRATIC EQUATIONS — 223
- A Equations of the form $x^2 = k$ — 224
- B Solution by factorisation — 226
- C Completing the square — 229
- D The quadratic formula — 232
- E Problem solving — 234
- F Quadratic equations with $\Delta < 0$ — 238
- G The sum and product of the roots — 240
-    Review set 11A — 241
-    Review set 11B — 242

12 TRIGONOMETRY — 243
- A Trigonometric ratios — 245
- B Problem solving using trigonometry — 249
- C True bearings — 253
- D 3-dimensional problem solving — 256
- E Supplementary angles — 260
- F The area of a triangle — 262
- G The sine rule — 264
- H The cosine rule — 267
- I Problem solving using the sine and cosine rules — 271
-    Review set 12A — 273
-    Review set 12B — 275

13 PROBABILITY — 277
- A Experimental probability — 279
- B Probabilities from tabled data — 280
- C Sample space — 283
- D Theoretical probability — 285
- E Compound events — 289
- F Conditional probability — 295
- G Mutually exclusive and independent events — 298
-    Review set 13A — 300
-    Review set 13B — 302

14 FORMULAE — 305
- A Formula construction — 306
- B Substituting into formulae — 310
- C Rearranging formulae — 312
- D Rearrangement and substitution — 315
- E Predicting formulae — 319
-    Review set 14A — 320
-    Review set 14B — 321

15 RELATIONS AND FUNCTIONS — 323
- A Relations — 324
- B Functions — 327
- C Function notation — 328
- D Composite functions — 332
- E Inverse functions — 333
- F The modulus function — 336
- G Where functions meet — 338
-    Review set 15A — 339
-    Review set 15B — 341

16 NUMBER SEQUENCES — 343
- A Number sequences — 344
- B Arithmetic sequences — 347
- C Geometric sequences — 350
- D Series — 353
- E Arithmetic series — 353
- F Geometric series — 356
-    Review set 16A — 359
-    Review set 16B — 359

17 VECTORS — 361
- A Directed line segment representation — 362
- B Vector equality — 364
- C Vector addition — 365
- D Vector subtraction — 368
- E Vectors in component form — 370
- F Scalar multiplication — 376
- G Parallelism of vectors — 377
- H The scalar product of two vectors — 379
- I 3-dimensional vectors — 382
-    Review set 17A — 385
-    Review set 17B — 386

18 EXPONENTIAL FUNCTIONS AND LOGARITHMS — 387
- A Exponential functions — 388
- B Graphs of exponential functions — 389
- C Growth and decay — 394
- D Compound interest — 397
- E Depreciation — 399
- F Exponential equations — 401
- G Logarithms — 403
-    Review set 18A — 409
-    Review set 18B — 410

19 DEDUCTIVE GEOMETRY — 411
- A Circle theorems — 412

B	Further circle theorems	415	
C	Geometric proof	420	
D	Cyclic quadrilaterals	423	
	Review set 19A	428	
	Review set 19B	429	

20 QUADRATIC FUNCTIONS — 431

A	Quadratic functions	432
B	Graphs of quadratic functions	434
C	Axes intercepts	441
D	Axis of symmetry	447
E	Vertex	449
F	Quadratic optimisation	451
	Review set 20A	453
	Review set 20B	454

21 ADVANCED TRIGONOMETRY — 455

A	Radian measure	456
B	The unit circle	458
C	The relationship between $\sin\theta$ and $\cos\theta$	461
D	The multiples of $30°$ and $45°$	463
E	Trigonometric functions	465
F	Simplifying trigonometric expressions	472
G	Trigonometric equations	474
H	Negative and complementary angle formulae	476
I	Compound angle formulae	477
	Review set 21A	479
	Review set 21B	480

22 INEQUALITIES — 481

A	Interval notation	482
B	Linear inequalities	484
C	Sign diagrams	486
D	Non-linear inequalities	490
	Review set 22A	491
	Review set 22B	492

23 BIVARIATE STATISTICS — 493

A	Scatter plots	494
B	Correlation	496
C	Measuring correlation	499
D	Line of best fit	503
	Review set 23A	510
	Review set 23B	511

24 POLYNOMIALS — 513

A	Polynomials	514
B	Polynomial operations	515
C	The Remainder theorem	520
D	The Factor theorem	522
	Review set 24A	523
	Review set 24B	524

25 INTRODUCTION TO CALCULUS — 525

A	Tangents	526
B	Limits	529
C	The derivative function	531
D	Rules for differentiation	534
E	Stationary points	536
F	Areas under curves	539
G	Integration	541
H	The definite integral	544
	Review set 25A	546
	Review set 25B	547

26 COUNTING AND PROBABILITY — 549 ONLINE

A	The product and sum principles
B	Permutations
C	Factorial notation
D	Combinations
E	Probabilities using permutations and combinations
	Review set 26A
	Review set 26B

27 CIRCLES AND ELLIPSES — 550 ONLINE

A	Circles
B	Ellipses
	Review set 27A
	Review set 27B

28 MATRICES — 551 ONLINE

A	Matrix structure
B	Matrix operations and definitions
C	Matrix multiplication
D	The inverse of a 2×2 matrix
E	Simultaneous linear equations
	Review set 28A
	Review set 28B

29 LINEAR PROGRAMMING — 552 ONLINE

A	Feasible regions
B	Constructing constraints
C	Linear programming
	Review set 29A
	Review set 29B

ANSWERS — 553

INDEX — 615

SUMMARY OF MEASUREMENT FACTS

PERIMETER FORMULAE

The distance around a closed figure is its **perimeter**.

For some shapes we can derive a formula for perimeter. The formulae for the most common shapes are given below:

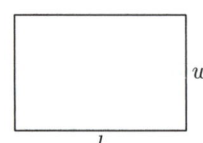
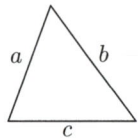
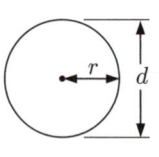

The length of an arc is a fraction of the circumference of a circle.

square	rectangle	triangle	circle	arc
$P = 4l$	$P = 2(l+w)$	$P = a+b+c$	$C = 2\pi r$ or $C = \pi d$	$l = \left(\frac{\theta}{360}\right)2\pi r$

AREA FORMULAE

Shape	Figure	Formula
Rectangle	rectangle with width and length	Area = length × width
Triangle	triangle with base and height	Area = $\frac{1}{2}$ base × height
Parallelogram	parallelogram with base and height	Area = base × height
Trapezium or Trapezoid	trapezium with parallel sides a and b, height h	Area = $\left(\frac{a+b}{2}\right) \times h$
Circle	circle with radius r	Area = πr^2
Sector	sector with radius r and angle θ	Area = $\left(\frac{\theta}{360}\right) \times \pi r^2$

SURFACE AREA FORMULAE

RECTANGULAR PRISM

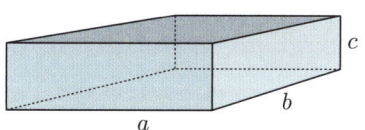

$A = 2(ab+bc+ac)$

SPHERE

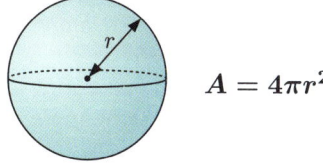

$A = 4\pi r^2$

CYLINDER

Hollow cylinder

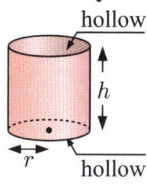

$A = 2\pi rh$
(no ends)

Open can

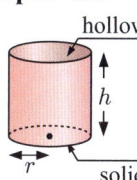

$A = 2\pi rh + \pi r^2$
(one end)

Solid cylinder

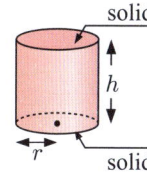

$A = 2\pi rh + 2\pi r^2$
(two ends)

CONE

Open cone

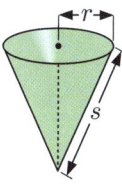

$A = \pi rs$
(no base)

Solid cone

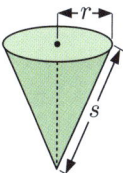

$A = \pi rs + \pi r^2$
(solid)

VOLUME FORMULAE

Solids of uniform cross-section

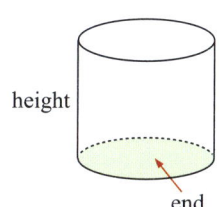

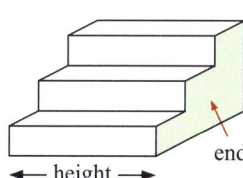

**Volume of uniform solid
= area of end × height**

Pyramids and cones

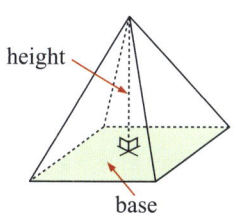

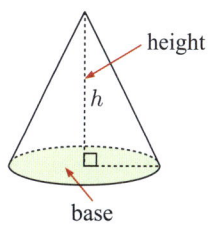

**Volume of a pyramid or cone
$= \frac{1}{3}$(area of base × height)**

Spheres

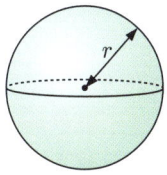

Volume of a sphere $= \frac{4}{3}\pi r^3$

SUMMARY OF CIRCLE PROPERTIES

Click on the appropriate icon to revisit these well known theorems.

Theorem	Statement	Diagram	
Angle in a semi-circle	The angle in a semi-circle is a right angle.		$A\hat{B}C = 90°$ **GEOMETRY PACKAGE**
Chords of a circle	The perpendicular from the centre of a circle to a chord bisects the chord.		$AM = BM$ **GEOMETRY PACKAGE**
Radius-tangent	The tangent to a circle is perpendicular to the radius at the point of contact.		$O\hat{A}T = 90°$ **GEOMETRY PACKAGE**
Tangents from an external point	Tangents from an external point are equal in length.		$AP = BP$ **GEOMETRY PACKAGE**

GRAPHICS CALCULATOR INSTRUCTIONS

Graphics calculator instruction booklets are available for the **Casio fx-9860G Plus**, **Casio fx-CG20**, **TI-84 Plus**, and the **TI-*n*spire**. Click on the relevant icon below.

CASIO fx-9860G Plus  **CASIO fx-CG20**  **TI-84 Plus**  **TI-*n*spire**

When additional calculator help may be needed, specific instructions are available from icons within the text.

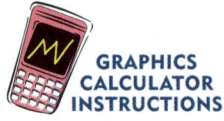
GRAPHICS CALCULATOR INSTRUCTIONS

Chapter 1

Indices

Contents:
- **A** Index laws
- **B** Rational indices
- **C** Scientific notation (standard form)

OPENING PROBLEM

Approximately 58 400 000 vehicles cross the Sydney Harbour Bridge each year.

Things to think about:

a Can you write this number in the form $a \times 10^k$ where $1 \leqslant a < 10$ and k is an integer?

b Can you use the number in this form to estimate how many vehicles cross the bridge:

  i each day
  ii over 10 years?

INDEX NOTATION

We often deal with numbers that are repeatedly multiplied together, such as $5 \times 5 \times 5$. We can use **indices** or **exponents** to conveniently represent such expressions.

Using **index notation**, we represent $5 \times 5 \times 5$ as 5^3, which reads "5 to the power 3". We say that 5 is the **base**, and 3 is the **index** or **power** or **exponent**.

If n is a positive integer, then a^n is the product of n factors of a.

$$a^n = \underbrace{a \times a \times a \times a \times \ldots \times a}_{n \text{ factors}}$$

A INDEX LAWS

In previous years we have seen the following **index laws**:

If the bases a and b are both positive, and the indices m and n are integers, then:

$a^m \times a^n = a^{m+n}$	To **multiply** numbers with the **same base**, keep the base and **add** the indices.
$\dfrac{a^m}{a^n} = a^{m-n}$	To **divide** numbers with the same base, keep the base and **subtract** the indices.
$(a^m)^n = a^{mn}$	When **raising** a **power** to a **power**, keep the base and **multiply** the indices.
$(ab)^n = a^n b^n$	The power of a product is the product of the powers.
$\left(\dfrac{a}{b}\right)^n = \dfrac{a^n}{b^n}$	The power of a quotient is the quotient of the powers.
$a^0 = 1, \quad a \neq 0$	Any non-zero number raised to the power of zero is 1.
$a^{-n} = \dfrac{1}{a^n}$	and in particular, $a^{-1} = \dfrac{1}{a}$.

INDICES (Chapter 1)   15

Example 1   ◀◈ Self Tutor

Express in simplest form with a prime number base:

   a 9^4 **b** 4×2^p **c** $\dfrac{3^x}{9^y}$ **d** 25^{x-1}

a 9^4	**b** 4×2^p	**c** $\dfrac{3^x}{9^y}$	**d** 25^{x-1}
$= (3^2)^4$	$= 2^2 \times 2^p$	$= \dfrac{3^x}{(3^2)^y}$	$= (5^2)^{x-1}$
$= 3^{2 \times 4}$	$= 2^{2+p}$	$= \dfrac{3^x}{3^{2y}}$	$= 5^{2(x-1)}$
$= 3^8$		$= 3^{x-2y}$	$= 5^{2x-2}$

EXERCISE 1A

1 Simplify using the index laws:

   a $3^2 \times 3^5$ **b** $x^6 \times x^3$ **c** $x^5 \times x^n$ **d** $t^3 \times t^4 \times t^5$

   e $\dfrac{7^9}{7^5}$ **f** $\dfrac{x^7}{x^3}$ **g** $\dfrac{t^6}{t^x}$ **h** $t^{3m} \div t$

   i $(5^3)^2$ **j** $(t^4)^3$ **k** $(y^3)^m$ **l** $(a^{3m})^4$

2 Express in simplest form with a prime number base:

   a 121 **b** 32 **c** 81 **d** 4^2

   e 25^2 **f** $7^t \times 49$ **g** $3^a \div 9$ **h** $8^p \div 4$

   i $\dfrac{7^n}{7^{n-2}}$ **j** $\dfrac{9}{3^x}$ **k** $(25^t)^2$ **l** $16^{k-3} \times 2^{-k}$

   m $\dfrac{4^a}{2^b}$ **n** $\dfrac{8^x}{16^y}$ **o** $\dfrac{125^{x+1}}{5^{x-1}}$ **p** $\dfrac{27^{a+2}}{3^a \times 9^a}$

Example 2   ◀◈ Self Tutor

Remove the brackets of:

   a $(2x)^3$ **b** $\left(\dfrac{3c}{b}\right)^4$

a $(2x)^3$	**b** $\left(\dfrac{3c}{b}\right)^4$
$= 2^3 \times x^3$	$= \dfrac{3^4 \times c^4}{b^4}$
$= 8x^3$	$= \dfrac{81c^4}{b^4}$

Each factor within the brackets is raised to the power outside them.

3 Remove the brackets of:

   a $(xy)^2$ **b** $(ab)^3$ **c** $(xyz)^2$ **d** $(3b)^3$

   e $(5a)^4$ **f** $(10xy)^5$ **g** $\left(\dfrac{p}{q}\right)^2$ **h** $\left(\dfrac{m}{n}\right)^3$

i $\left(\dfrac{x}{3}\right)^4$ **j** $\left(\dfrac{5}{z}\right)^3$ **k** $\left(\dfrac{2a}{b}\right)^4$ **l** $\left(\dfrac{3x}{4y}\right)^3$

4 Simplify the following expressions using one or more of the index laws:

a $4b^2 \times 2b^3$ **b** $\dfrac{a^6 b^3}{a^4 b}$ **c** $3ab^2 \times 2a^3$ **d** $\dfrac{5x^3 y^2}{15xy}$

e $\left(\dfrac{a^2}{5b}\right)^3$ **f** $\dfrac{24t^6 r^4}{15t^6 r^2}$ **g** $\dfrac{(4c^3 d^2)^2}{c^2 d}$ **h** $\dfrac{10k^7}{(2k)^5}$

Example 3   Self Tutor

Simplify, giving your answers in simplest rational form:

a 7^0 **b** 3^{-2} **c** $3^0 - 3^{-1}$ **d** $\left(\dfrac{5}{3}\right)^{-2}$

Notice that $\left(\dfrac{a}{b}\right)^{-2} = \left(\dfrac{b}{a}\right)^2$

a $7^0 = 1$

b $3^{-2} = \dfrac{1}{3^2} = \dfrac{1}{9}$

c $3^0 - 3^{-1} = 1 - \dfrac{1}{3} = \dfrac{2}{3}$

d $\left(\dfrac{5}{3}\right)^{-2} = \left(\dfrac{3}{5}\right)^2 = \dfrac{9}{25}$

5 Simplify, giving your answers in simplest rational form:

a 3^0 **b** 6^{-1} **c** 4^{-1} **d** 5^0
e 4^2 **f** 4^{-2} **g** 5^3 **h** 5^{-3}
i 7^2 **j** 7^{-2} **k** 10^3 **l** 10^{-3}

6 Simplify, giving your answers in simplest rational form:

a $\left(\dfrac{1}{2}\right)^0$ **b** $\dfrac{5^4}{5^4}$ **c** $2t^0$ **d** $(2t)^0$

e 7^0 **f** 3×4^0 **g** $\dfrac{5^3}{5^5}$ **h** $\dfrac{2^6}{2^{10}}$

i $\dfrac{x^4}{x^9}$ **j** $\left(\dfrac{3}{8}\right)^{-1}$ **k** $\left(\dfrac{2}{3}\right)^{-1}$ **l** $\left(\dfrac{1}{5}\right)^{-1}$

m $2^0 + 2^1$ **n** $5^0 - 5^{-1}$ **o** $3^0 + 3^1 - 3^{-1}$ **p** $\left(\dfrac{1}{3}\right)^{-2}$

q $\left(\dfrac{2}{3}\right)^{-3}$ **r** $\left(1\tfrac{1}{2}\right)^{-3}$ **s** $\left(\dfrac{4}{5}\right)^{-2}$ **t** $\left(2\tfrac{1}{2}\right)^{-2}$

7 Write the following without brackets or negative indices:

a $(3b)^{-1}$ **b** $3b^{-1}$ **c** $7a^{-1}$ **d** $(7a)^{-1}$

e $\left(\dfrac{1}{t}\right)^{-2}$ **f** $\left(\dfrac{3x}{y}\right)^{-1}$ **g** $(5t)^{-2}$ **h** $(5t^{-2})^{-1}$

i xy^{-1} **j** $(xy)^{-1}$ **k** xy^{-3} **l** $(xy)^{-3}$

m $(3pq)^{-1}$ **n** $3(pq)^{-1}$ **o** $3pq^{-1}$ **p** $\dfrac{(xy)^3}{y^{-2}}$

q $(5x^{-2}y^3)^3$ **r** $\left(\dfrac{c}{2d^3}\right)^{-2}$ **s** $\left(\dfrac{3r^{-3}}{t}\right)^{-2}$ **t** $\left(\dfrac{2p}{5q^{-2}}\right)^{-3}$

8 Use the index laws to show that, for positive a and b, and integer n:

    a $\dfrac{1}{a^{-n}} = a^n$ **b** $\left(\dfrac{a}{b}\right)^{-n} = \dfrac{b^n}{a^n}$

9 The units for speed *kilometres per hour* can be written as km/h or km h^{-1}.
Write these units in index form:

    a m/s   **b** cubic metres/hour

    c square centimetres per second   **d** cubic centimetres per minute

    e grams per second   **f** kilogram metres per second

    g metres per second per second.

10 Find the smaller of 2^{125} and 3^{75} without a calculator.
    Hint: $2^{125} = (2^5)^{25}$

11 Order the following numbers from smallest to largest: 2^{90}, 3^{60}, 5^{36}, 10^{24}.

B   RATIONAL INDICES

A **rational** number is a number which can be written in the form $\dfrac{p}{q}$ where p and q are integers. The integers themselves are rational numbers, since for example $2 = \dfrac{2}{1}$.

The index laws can be applied not just to integer indices, but to rational indices in general. This helps to give meaning to values such as $5^{\frac{1}{2}}$ and $7^{\frac{1}{3}}$.

In previous years we have established that: $a^{\frac{1}{2}} = \sqrt{a}$ and $a^{\frac{1}{3}} = \sqrt[3]{a}$.

In general, $a^{\frac{1}{n}} = \sqrt[n]{a}$ where $\sqrt[n]{a}$ is called the *n*th root of *a*.

Example 4   ◀)) **Self Tutor**

Simplify:

    a $49^{\frac{1}{2}}$ **b** $27^{\frac{1}{3}}$ **c** $49^{-\frac{1}{2}}$ **d** $27^{-\frac{1}{3}}$

a $49^{\frac{1}{2}}$ $= \sqrt{49}$ $= 7$	**b** $27^{\frac{1}{3}}$ $= \sqrt[3]{27}$ $= 3$	**c** $49^{-\frac{1}{2}}$ $= \dfrac{1}{49^{\frac{1}{2}}}$ $= \dfrac{1}{\sqrt{49}}$ $= \frac{1}{7}$	**d** $27^{-\frac{1}{3}}$ $= \dfrac{1}{27^{\frac{1}{3}}}$ $= \dfrac{1}{\sqrt[3]{27}}$ $= \frac{1}{3}$

INVESTIGATION 1 — RATIONAL INDICES

This Investigation will help you discover the meaning of numbers raised to rational indices of the form $\frac{m}{n}$ where $m, n \in \mathbb{Z}$, $n \neq 0$.

For example, what does $8^{\frac{2}{3}}$ mean?

What to do:

1. Use the rule $(a^m)^n = a^{mn}$ to simplify $(8^2)^{\frac{1}{3}}$ and $\left(8^{\frac{1}{3}}\right)^2$.

2. Simplify:
   a $(8^2)^{\frac{1}{3}} = \sqrt[3]{8^2} = \ldots\ldots$
   b $\left(8^{\frac{1}{3}}\right)^2 = \left(\sqrt[3]{8}\right)^2 = \ldots\ldots$

3. Hence write $a^{\frac{m}{n}}$ in two different forms.

From the **Investigation** you should have discovered that $\quad a^{\frac{m}{n}} = \left(\sqrt[n]{a}\right)^m = \sqrt[n]{a^m}$.

When dealing with indices of this form, it is often easiest to write the base number as a prime raised to a power. We simplify the result using the index laws.

Example 5

Evaluate without using a calculator:

a $8^{\frac{4}{3}}$
b $32^{-\frac{2}{5}}$

a $8^{\frac{4}{3}}$
$= (2^3)^{\frac{4}{3}}$
$= 2^{3 \times \frac{4}{3}}$
$= 2^4$
$= 16$

b $32^{-\frac{2}{5}}$
$= (2^5)^{-\frac{2}{5}}$
$= 2^{5 \times -\frac{2}{5}}$
$= 2^{-2}$
$= \frac{1}{4}$

EXERCISE 1B

1. Evaluate without using your calculator:

   a $16^{\frac{1}{2}}$
   b $16^{-\frac{1}{2}}$
   c $25^{\frac{1}{2}}$
   d $25^{-\frac{1}{2}}$
   e $8^{\frac{1}{3}}$
   f $8^{-\frac{1}{3}}$
   g $(-8)^{\frac{1}{3}}$
   h $(-8)^{-\frac{1}{3}}$
   i $81^{\frac{1}{4}}$
   j $81^{-\frac{1}{4}}$
   k $32^{\frac{1}{5}}$
   l $32^{-\frac{1}{5}}$

2. Evaluate if possible:

   a $(-1)^{\frac{1}{2}}$
   b $(-1)^{\frac{1}{3}}$
   c $(-27)^{-\frac{1}{3}}$
   d $(-64)^{-\frac{1}{2}}$

INDICES (Chapter 1) 19

3 Write the following in index form:

a $\sqrt{10}$
b $\dfrac{1}{\sqrt{10}}$
c $\sqrt[3]{15}$
d $\dfrac{1}{\sqrt[3]{15}}$

e $\sqrt[4]{19}$
f $\dfrac{1}{\sqrt[4]{19}}$
g $\sqrt[5]{13}$
h $\dfrac{1}{\sqrt[5]{13}}$

4 Evaluate without using a calculator:

a $8^{\frac{2}{3}}$
b $4^{\frac{3}{2}}$
c $4^{\frac{5}{2}}$
d $8^{\frac{5}{3}}$

e $16^{\frac{3}{4}}$
f $9^{\frac{3}{2}}$
g $9^{-\frac{3}{2}}$
h $4^{-\frac{1}{2}}$

i $32^{\frac{1}{5}}$
j $32^{\frac{2}{5}}$
k $32^{\frac{3}{5}}$
l $16^{-\frac{3}{4}}$

m $8^{-\frac{2}{3}}$
n $27^{-\frac{4}{3}}$
o $25^{-\frac{3}{2}}$

5 Write the following as powers of 2:

a $\sqrt{8}$
b $\sqrt[3]{32}$
c $\sqrt[4]{4}$
d $\sqrt[3]{16}$

e $\dfrac{1}{\sqrt[4]{8}}$
f $\dfrac{1}{\sqrt[3]{16}}$
g $\dfrac{1}{\sqrt[7]{8}}$
h $\dfrac{1}{\sqrt[5]{64}}$

i $8\sqrt{2}$
j $4\sqrt{32}$
k $\dfrac{2}{\sqrt[3]{4}}$
l $\dfrac{4\sqrt{32}}{8}$

6 Write the following as powers of 3:

a $\sqrt[3]{9}$
b $\sqrt{27}$
c $\dfrac{1}{\sqrt[4]{27}}$
d $\dfrac{1}{\sqrt[5]{81}}$

e $9\sqrt{3}$
f $3\sqrt{27}$
g $\dfrac{9}{\sqrt[5]{3}}$
h $\dfrac{\sqrt[3]{81}}{9}$

7 Write with a prime number base:

a $\sqrt[3]{25}$
b $\sqrt[4]{32}$
c $\sqrt[5]{125}$
d $\sqrt[7]{121}$

e $\dfrac{1}{\sqrt[3]{49}}$
f $\sqrt[5]{64}$
g $\dfrac{1}{\sqrt[7]{625}}$
h $\dfrac{1}{\sqrt[6]{243}}$

i $16\sqrt{8}$
j $25\sqrt{125}$
k $\dfrac{13}{\sqrt[3]{169}}$
l $\dfrac{81}{\sqrt{27}}$

8 Use your calculator to evaluate, rounded to 3 significant figures where necessary:

a $25^{\frac{3}{2}}$
b $27^{\frac{2}{3}}$
c $8^{\frac{7}{3}}$
d $9^{\frac{2}{5}}$

e $10^{\frac{3}{7}}$
f $15^{\frac{5}{3}}$
g $10^{\frac{2}{7}}$
h $18^{\frac{7}{3}}$

i $16^{\frac{3}{11}}$
j $146^{\frac{4}{9}}$
k $4^{-\frac{5}{2}}$
l $27^{-\frac{5}{3}}$

m $15^{-\frac{2}{5}}$
n $53^{-\frac{3}{7}}$
o $3^{-\frac{7}{5}}$

9 Without using your calculator, evaluate $\dfrac{\sqrt[3]{9} \times \sqrt[4]{27}}{\sqrt[12]{243}}$.

GAME

This game can be played by 2 players.

$\frac{1}{4}$	5	3	$\frac{1}{3}$	2	4	$\frac{1}{8}$	2	$\frac{4}{5}$
2	9	4	$\frac{2}{5}$	$\frac{2}{3}$	81	3	$-\frac{1}{2}$	81
32	-3	$\frac{1}{27}$	125	$\frac{1}{16}$	64	$\frac{1}{2}$	243	5
4	3	$\frac{1}{8}$	-2	3	32	7	$\frac{3}{4}$	2
5	0	2	$\frac{1}{2}$	$-\frac{2}{3}$	1	6	2	36
49	25	$\frac{1}{2}$	-3	0	-2	64	7	$\frac{1}{5}$
25	$\frac{1}{81}$	-4	27	2	-3	5	4	27
-1	6	$-\frac{1}{3}$	16	-2	$\frac{1}{16}$	3	125	$\frac{1}{2}$
$\frac{1}{25}$	16	343	$\frac{1}{2}$	5	3	1	9	$\frac{1}{5}$

PRINTABLE BOARD

What to do:

- Taking alternate turns, each player selects 3 squares on the board to create a statement of the form $a^b = c$.
  For example, the shaded squares can be used to create the statement $3^4 = 81$. These squares are then crossed out and cannot be used again.
- The last player who is able to make a valid selection is the winner.

Single player variant:

- Try to use all 81 squares in 27 selections.

C   SCIENTIFIC NOTATION (STANDARD FORM)

Observe the pattern:

$$\begin{array}{l}
10\,000 = 10^4 \\
1000 = 10^3 \\
100 = 10^2 \\
10 = 10^1 \\
1 = 10^0 \\
\frac{1}{10} = 10^{-1} \\
\frac{1}{100} = 10^{-2} \\
\frac{1}{1000} = 10^{-3}
\end{array}$$

(÷10 between each, exponent decreases by 1)

As we divide by 10, the **exponent** or **power** of 10 decreases by one.

We can use this pattern to simplify the writing of very large and very small numbers.

For example,
$$5\,000\,000$$
$$= 5 \times 1\,000\,000$$
$$= 5 \times 10^6$$

and
$$0.000\,003$$
$$= \frac{3}{1\,000\,000}$$
$$= 3 \times \frac{1}{1\,000\,000}$$
$$= 3 \times 10^{-6}$$

> **Scientific notation** involves writing any given number as *a number between 1 inclusive and 10*, multiplied by a *power of 10*. The result has the form
> $$a \times 10^k \quad \text{where} \quad 1 \leqslant a < 10 \quad \text{and } k \text{ is an integer.}$$

Example 6 🔊 Self Tutor

Write in scientific notation:
a $23\,600\,000$ **b** $0.000\,023\,6$

a $23\,600\,000$
$= 2.36 \times 10^7$

b $0.000\,023\,6$
$= 2.36 \times 10^{-5}$

Remember that $10^{-3} = \dfrac{1}{10^3}$.

Example 7 🔊 Self Tutor

Write as an ordinary decimal number:
a 2.57×10^4 **b** 7.853×10^{-3}

a 2.57×10^4
$= 2.5700 \times 10\,000$
$= 25\,700$

b 7.853×10^{-3}
$= 0007.853 \div 10^3$
$= 0.007\,853$

EXERCISE 1C

1 Write using scientific notation:
  a 230   **b** 53 900   **c** 0.0361   **d** 0.006 80
  e 3.26   **f** 0.5821   **g** 361 000 000   **h** 0.000 001 674

2 Write as an ordinary decimal number:
  a 2.3×10^3 **b** 2.3×10^{-2} **c** 5.64×10^5 **d** 7.931×10^{-4}
  e 9.97×10^0 **f** 6.04×10^7 **g** 4.215×10^{-1} **h** 3.621×10^{-8}

3 Express the following quantities using scientific notation:
  a There are approximately 4 million red blood cells in a drop of blood.
  b The thickness of a coin is about 0.0008 m.
  c Earth's radius is about 6.38 million metres.
  d A Rubik's Cube has approximately 43 252 000 000 000 000 000 possible arrangements.

4 Express the following quantities as ordinary decimal numbers:

   a The Amazon River is approximately 6.99×10^6 m long.
   b A piece of paper is about 1.8×10^{-2} cm thick.
   c A test tube holds 3.2×10^7 bacteria.
   d A mushroom weighs 8.2×10^{-6} tonnes.

Example 8   ◀) Self Tutor

Simplify, writing your answer in scientific notation:

   a $(3 \times 10^4) \times (8 \times 10^3)$ **b** $\dfrac{2 \times 10^{-3}}{5 \times 10^{-8}}$

---

a $(3 \times 10^4) \times (8 \times 10^3)$
 $= 24 \times 10^{4+3}$
 $= (2.4 \times 10^1) \times 10^7$
 $= 2.4 \times 10^8$

b $\dfrac{2 \times 10^{-3}}{5 \times 10^{-8}}$
 $= \tfrac{2}{5} \times 10^{-3-(-8)}$
 $= 0.4 \times 10^5$
 $= (4 \times 10^{-1}) \times 10^5$
 $= 4 \times 10^4$

5 Simplify the following, writing your answers in scientific notation:

   a $(3 \times 10^3) \times (2 \times 10^7)$
   b $(4 \times 10^3) \times (7 \times 10^5)$
   c $(8 \times 10^{-4}) \times (7 \times 10^{-5})$
   d $(9 \times 10^{-5}) \times (6 \times 10^{-2})$
   e $(3 \times 10^5)^2$
   f $(4 \times 10^7)^2$
   g $(2 \times 10^{-3})^4$
   h $(5 \times 10^{-3})^3$
   i $(6 \times 10^{-1}) \times (4 \times 10^3) \times (5 \times 10^{-4})$
   j $(6 \times 10^{-3})^2 \times (8 \times 10^{11})$
   k $(4 \times 10^3)^{-1}$
   l $(5 \times 10^{-4})^{-2}$

6 Simplify the following, writing your answers in scientific notation:

   a $\dfrac{8 \times 10^6}{4 \times 10^3}$
   b $\dfrac{9 \times 10^{-3}}{3 \times 10^{-1}}$
   c $\dfrac{4 \times 10^6}{2 \times 10^{-2}}$
   d $\dfrac{2.5 \times 10^{-4}}{(5 \times 10^7)^2}$
   e $\dfrac{(8 \times 10^{-2})^2}{2 \times 10^{-6}}$
   f $\dfrac{(5 \times 10^{-3})^{-2}}{(2 \times 10^4)^{-1}}$

7 **a** How many times larger is 3×10^{11} than 3×10^8?

   b **i** Which is smaller, 5×10^{-16} or 5×10^{-21}?
       ii By how many times is it smaller than the other number?
   c How many times larger is 4×10^6 than 8×10^{-5}?

INDICES (Chapter 1) 23

Example 9 ◀) Self Tutor

Use your calculator to find:

a $(2.58 \times 10^7) \times (1.5 \times 10^6)$

b $\dfrac{6.5 \times 10^{-2}}{1.04 \times 10^5}$

GRAPHICS CALCULATOR INSTRUCTIONS

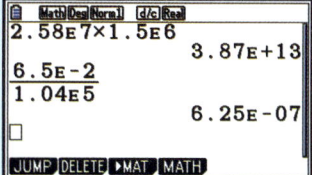

a $(2.58 \times 10^7) \times (1.5 \times 10^6) = 3.87 \times 10^{13}$

b $\dfrac{6.5 \times 10^{-2}}{1.04 \times 10^5} = 6.25 \times 10^{-7}$

---

8 Calculate the following, giving each answer in scientific notation. The decimal part should be rounded to 3 significant figures.

a $(4.7 \times 10^5) \times (8.53 \times 10^7)$

b $(2.7 \times 10^{-3}) \times (9.6 \times 10^{14})$

c $\dfrac{3.4 \times 10^7}{4.8 \times 10^{15}}$

d $\dfrac{7.3 \times 10^{-7}}{1.5 \times 10^4}$

e $(2.83 \times 10^3)^2$

f $(5.96 \times 10^{-5})^2$

g $\dfrac{(3.56 \times 10^4)^2}{8.05 \times 10^{-5}}$

h $\dfrac{2.9 \times 10^2}{(7.62 \times 10^7)^3}$

9 Answer the **Opening Problem** on page 14.

10 Use your calculator to answer the following:

a A rocket travels in space at 4×10^5 km h^{-1}. Assuming 1 year ≈ 365.25 days, how far will it travel in:

  i 30 days   **ii** 20 years?

b A bullet travelling at an average speed of 2×10^3 km h^{-1} hits a target 500 m away. Find the time of the bullet's flight, in seconds.

c Mars has volume 1.31×10^{21} m^3 whereas Pluto has volume 4.93×10^{19} m^3.
How many times bigger is Mars than Pluto?

d Microbe C has mass 2.63×10^{-5} grams whereas microbe D has mass 8×10^{-7} grams.

  i Which microbe is heavier?
  ii How many times heavier is it, than the other microbe?

11 The table alongside shows the land areas of the Canadian provinces (shaded green) and territories (shaded purple).

    a Find the total land area of Canada.

    b Place the *provinces* in order, from largest to smallest.

    c How many times larger is:

        i Quebec than Manitoba

        ii Nunavut than Prince Edward Island?

    d What percentage of the land area of Canada, is included in Nova Scotia?

	Land area (km^2)
Ontario	9.2×10^5
Quebec	1.4×10^6
Nova Scotia	5.3×10^4
New Brunswick	7.1×10^4
Manitoba	5.5×10^5
British Columbia	9.3×10^5
Prince Edward Island	5.7×10^3
Saskatchewan	5.9×10^5
Alberta	6.4×10^5
Newfoundland and Labrador	3.7×10^5
Northwest Territories	1.2×10^6
Yukon	4.7×10^5
Nunavut	1.9×10^6

HISTORICAL NOTE

The ancient Indians explored the concept of expressing very large and very small numbers. In the *Lalitavistara Sutra*, a Sanskrit text dating from around the 4th century, it is written that the Buddha gave a description of the size of an atom.

In terms of the length of a finger bone, the Buddha stated that:

".... each was the length of

seven grains of barley, each of which was the length of
seven mustard seeds, each of which was the length of
seven poppy seeds, each of which was the length of
seven particles of dust stirred up by a cow, each of which was the length of
seven specks of dust disturbed by a ram, each of which was the length of
seven specks of dust stirred up by a hare, each of which was the length of
seven specks of dust carried away by the wind, each of which was the length of
seven tiny specks of dust, each of which was the length of
seven minute specks of dust, each of which was the length of
seven particles of the first atoms."

What to do:

1 Assuming a finger bone is 4 cm long, use the Buddha's description to estimate the length of an atom, in metres. Write your answer in scientific notation.

2 Research the size of a carbon atom. How accurate is the estimate in **1**?

REVIEW SET 1A

1 Simplify using the index laws:

    a $k^5 \times k^3$ **b** $\dfrac{p^6}{p}$ **c** $(m^6)^8$

2 Remove the brackets of:

    a $(3w)^2$ **b** $(2x^2y)^3$ **c** $\left(\dfrac{a}{b}\right)^6$ **d** $\left(\dfrac{1}{5n}\right)^3$

3 Simplify, giving answers in simplest rational form:

    a 7^{-1} **b** $\left(\tfrac{4}{3}\right)^{-1}$ **c** $11^0 - 11^{-1}$ **d** $\left(1\tfrac{3}{4}\right)^{-2}$

4 Write using scientific notation:

    a $59\,000$ **b** 0.009 **c** $6\,085\,000$ **d** $0.000\,007\,71$

5 Evaluate without using a calculator:

    a $49^{\frac{1}{2}}$ **b** $64^{-\frac{1}{3}}$ **c** $125^{\frac{4}{3}}$ **d** $27^{-\frac{2}{3}}$

6 Write as an ordinary decimal number:

    a 6.23×10^5 **b** 3.008×10^{-4} **c** 4.597×10^0

7 Write with a prime number base:

    a $\sqrt[5]{16}$ **b** $\dfrac{1}{\sqrt[3]{9}}$ **c** $\dfrac{625}{\sqrt{5}}$ **d** $8\sqrt{32}$

8 Use your calculator to evaluate the following correct to 3 significant figures:

    a $\sqrt[3]{20}$ **b** $\dfrac{1}{\sqrt[6]{100}}$ **c** $10^{\frac{5}{4}}$ **d** $15^{-\frac{3}{7}}$

9 Write without brackets or negative indices:

    a $(mn)^{-2}$ **b** mn^{-2} **c** $\left(\dfrac{x}{5y^2}\right)^{-3}$

10 Simplify the following, writing your answers in scientific notation:

    a $(6 \times 10^5) \times (3 \times 10^6)$ **b** $(8 \times 10^9) \times (5 \times 10^{-4})$

    c $\dfrac{9 \times 10^{-5}}{6 \times 10^3}$ **d** $(8 \times 10^7)^{-1}$

11 Write the answers to the following in scientific notation:

    a The speed of light in a vacuum is about 2.998×10^8 m s^{-1}.
        Assuming 1 year ≈ 365.25 days, determine how far light travels in:

        i 1 hour   **ii** 1 day   **iii** 1 year.

    b How long does it take for light to travel:

        i 1 m   **ii** 1 cm   **iii** 1 mm?

    c In air, light travels at 2.989×10^8 m s^{-1} and sound travels at 343.2 m s^{-1}. How many times faster is light than sound?

REVIEW SET 1B

1 Express in simplest form with a prime number base:

    a 8^2 **b** $\dfrac{25^x}{125}$ **c** $\dfrac{49^{k+3}}{7^{k-1}}$

2 Simplify using one or more of the index laws:

    a $5c^3 \times 3c^4$ **b** $\dfrac{14x^5 y^2}{2x^2 y}$ **c** $\left(\dfrac{3p}{q^{-3}}\right)^2$

3 Evaluate $27^{\frac{4}{3}}$ without using a calculator.

4 Write without brackets or negative indices: **a** $\left(\dfrac{a}{b}\right)^{-2}$ **b** $\left(\dfrac{3a^{-1}}{2b^2}\right)^{-3}$

5 **a** Write using index notation: **i** $\sqrt[3]{13}$ **ii** $\dfrac{1}{\sqrt[5]{40}}$

    b Use your calculator to evaluate $\dfrac{1}{\sqrt[5]{40}}$ correct to 3 significant figures.

6 Simplify the following, writing your answers in scientific notation:

    a $(7 \times 10^5) \times (3 \times 10^9)$ **b** $\dfrac{2.7 \times 10^{-4}}{4.5 \times 10^7}$ **c** $\dfrac{8 \times 10^7}{2 \times 10^{-3}}$

7 Write the following as powers of 2:

    a $\sqrt[4]{8}$ **b** $\dfrac{1}{\sqrt[5]{16}}$ **c** $\dfrac{4}{\sqrt{32}}$

8 How many times larger is 3.5×10^{11} than 5×10^9?

9 Find the smaller of 2^{60} and 7^{20} without using a calculator.

10 The table alongside shows the diameters of the planets in the solar system.

    a Find the diameter of Saturn in:
        i kilometres   **ii** centimetres.
    b Find the radius of Venus.
    c Write the planets in order of size, from smallest to largest.
    d How many times greater is the diameter of:
        i Uranus than Mercury
        ii Jupiter than Mars?

Planet	Diameter
Mercury	4.88×10^6 m
Venus	1.21×10^7 m
Earth	1.27×10^7 m
Mars	6.79×10^6 m
Jupiter	1.40×10^8 m
Saturn	1.21×10^8 m
Uranus	5.11×10^7 m
Neptune	4.95×10^7 m

11 **a** Write $(\sqrt[5]{7} \times \sqrt[4]{7})^{20}$ as a power of 7.

    b Hence, show that $\sqrt[5]{7} \times \sqrt[4]{7} = 7^{\frac{9}{20}}$.

    c Use the index laws to show that $\sqrt[m]{a} \times \sqrt[n]{a} = a^{\frac{m+n}{mn}}$.

    d Hence, write $\sqrt[3]{11} \times \sqrt[5]{11}$ as a power of 11.

Chapter 2

Sets and Venn diagrams

Contents:
- **A** Number sets
- **B** Interval notation
- **C** Subsets and complement
- **D** Venn diagrams
- **E** Union and intersection
- **F** Numbers in regions
- **G** Problem solving with Venn diagrams
- **H** The algebra of sets

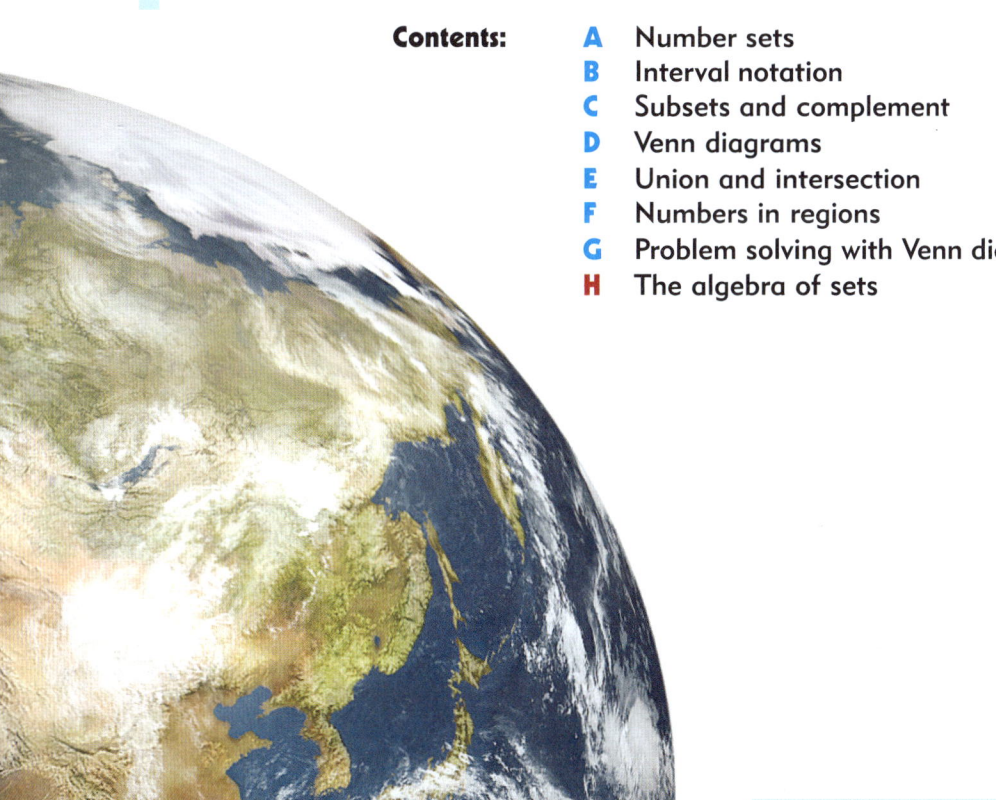

OPENING PROBLEM

A city has two newspapers, The Sun and The Advertiser. 56% of the people read The Sun and 71% of the people read The Advertiser. 18% read neither newspaper.

Things to think about:
- **a** How can we represent this information on a diagram?
- **b** What percentage of the people read:
  - **i** both of the newspapers
  - **ii** at least one of the newspapers
  - **iii** The Sun, but not The Advertiser
  - **iv** exactly one of the two newspapers?

A NUMBER SETS

SET NOTATION

A **set** is a collection of numbers or objects.

For example:
- if V is the set of all vowels, then $V = \{\text{vowels}\} = \{a, e, i, o, u\}$
- if E is the set of all even numbers, then $E = \{\text{even numbers}\} = \{2, 4, 6, 8, 10, 12, \ldots\}$.

We use the symbol $\in$ to mean *is an element of* and $\notin$ to mean *is not an element of*.

So, for the set $E = \{2, 4, 6, 8, 10, 12, \ldots\}$, we can say $6 \in E$ but $11 \notin E$.

The set $\{\ \}$ or $\varnothing$ is called the **empty set** and contains no elements.

COUNTING ELEMENTS OF SETS

The number of elements in set S is written $n(S)$.

A set which contains a finite number of elements is called a **finite set**.

A set which contains an infinite number of elements is called an **infinite set**.

For example:
- the set of vowels V has 5 elements. V is a finite set, and $n(V) = 5$
- the set of even numbers E is an infinite set.

SPECIAL NUMBER SETS

Following is a list of some special number sets you should be familiar with:

- $\mathbb{N} = \{0, 1, 2, 3, 4, 5, 6, 7, \ldots\}$ is the set of all **natural** or **counting numbers**.

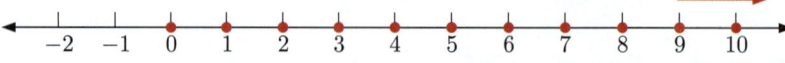

- $\mathbb{Z} = \{0, \pm 1, \pm 2, \pm 3, \pm 4, ...\}$ is the set of all **integers**.

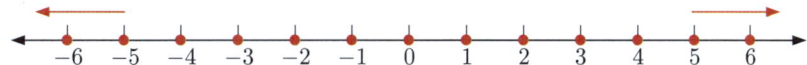

- $\mathbb{Z}^+ = \{1, 2, 3, 4, 5, 6, 7, ...\}$ is the set of all **positive integers**.

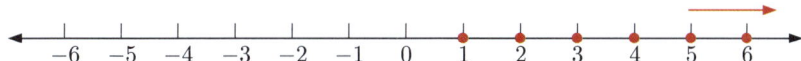

- $\mathbb{Q}$ is the set of all **rational numbers**, or numbers which can be written in the form $\frac{p}{q}$ where p and q are integers, $q \neq 0$.

For example: $\frac{15}{4}$, $10\ (= \frac{10}{1})$, $0.5\ (= \frac{1}{2})$, and $-\frac{3}{8}$ are all rational numbers.

We cannot represent the rational numbers on a number line, because there are infinitely many of them, and in between them are **irrational numbers** which cannot be written in rational form.

For example:
- Radicals or surds such as $\sqrt{2}$ and $\sqrt{7}$ are irrational.
- $\pi \approx 3.14159265$ is an irrational number.
- Decimal numbers which neither terminate nor recur are irrational.

- $\mathbb{R}$ is the set of all **real numbers**, which are all numbers which can be placed on the number line.

$\mathbb{R}$ includes all rational and irrational numbers.

$\frac{2}{0}$ and $\sqrt{-2}$ are not real numbers because we cannot write them in decimal form or place them on a number line.

Example 1 ◀)) Self Tutor

Show that $0.\overline{36}$, which is $0.36363636....$, is a rational number.

Let $x = 0.\overline{36} = 0.36363636....$
$\therefore\ 100x = 36.363636.... = 36 + x$
$\therefore\ 99x = 36$
$\therefore\ x = \frac{36}{99} = \frac{4}{11}$

So, $0.\overline{36}$ is actually the rational number $\frac{4}{11}$.

The bar indicates that the decimal number is recurring.

EXERCISE 2A

1 Write using set notation:
   a 8 is an element of set P.
   b k is not an element of set S.
   c 14 is not an element of the set of all odd numbers.
   d There are 9 elements in set Y.

2 True or false?

   a $3 \in \mathbb{Z}^+$ **b** $6 \in \mathbb{Z}$ **c** $\frac{3}{4} \in \mathbb{Q}$ **d** $\sqrt{2} \notin \mathbb{Q}$

   e $-\frac{1}{4} \notin \mathbb{Q}$ **f** $2\frac{1}{3} \in \mathbb{Z}$ **g** $0.3684 \in \mathbb{R}$ **h** $\frac{1}{0.1} \in \mathbb{Z}$

3 Determine whether each of the following numbers is rational, irrational, or neither:

   a 8 **b** -8 **c** $2\frac{1}{3}$ **d** $-3\frac{1}{4}$ **e** $\sqrt{3}$

   f $\sqrt{-3}$ **g** $\sqrt{400}$ **h** 9.176 **i** $\frac{1}{0}$ **j** $\pi - \pi$

4 For each of the following sets:

   i list the elements of the set
   ii determine whether the set is finite or infinite
   iii if the set is finite, find the number of elements in the set.

   a $A = \{\text{factors of } 6\}$ **b** $B = \{\text{multiples of } 6\}$ **c** $C = \{\text{factors of } 17\}$
   d $D = \{\text{multiples of } 17\}$ **e** $E = \{\text{prime numbers less than } 20\}$
   f $F = \{\text{composite numbers between } 10 \text{ and } 30\}$

5 Show that each of the following numbers is rational:

   a $0.\overline{7}$ **b** $0.\overline{41}$ **c** $0.\overline{324}$

6 Explain why 0.527 is a rational number.

7 Explain why $0.\overline{9} \in \mathbb{Z}$.

8 Give examples to show that these statements are false:

   a The sum of two irrationals is irrational.
   b The product of two irrationals is irrational.

B   INTERVAL NOTATION

To avoid having to list all members of a set, we often use a general description of its members. We often describe a set of all values of x with a particular property.

The notation $\{x \mid \ldots\ldots\}$ is used to describe "the set of all x such that ......".

For example:

- $\{x \mid -3 < x \leqslant 2, \ x \in \mathbb{R}\}$
  reads "the set of all real x such that x lies between minus 3 and 2, including 2".
  We can represent the set on a number line as: an open circle indicates -3 is not included   a closed circle indicates 2 is included

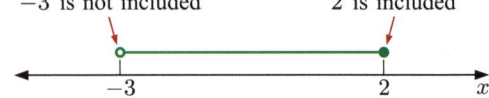

  Unless stated otherwise, we *assume* we are dealing with *real* numbers. Thus, the set can also be written as $\{x \mid -3 < x \leqslant 2\}$.

- $\{x \mid -5 < x < 5, \ x \in \mathbb{Z}\}$
  reads "the set of all integers x such that x lies between minus 5 and 5".
  We can represent the set on a number line as:

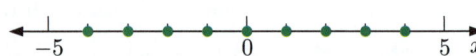

Example 2

Write using interval notation:

a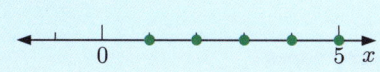

b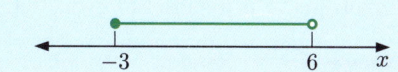

a $\{x \mid 1 \leqslant x \leqslant 5,\ x \in \mathbb{N}\}$
   or $\{x \mid 1 \leqslant x \leqslant 5,\ x \in \mathbb{Z}\}$

b $\{x \mid -3 \leqslant x < 6\}$

EXERCISE 2B

1 Explain the meaning of:

- a $\{x \mid x > 4\}$
- b $\{x \mid x \leqslant 5,\ x \in \mathbb{Z}\}$
- c $\{y \mid 0 < y < 8\}$
- d $\{x \mid 1 \leqslant x \leqslant 4,\ x \in \mathbb{Z}\}$
- e $\{t \mid 2 < t < 7,\ t \in \mathbb{R}\}$
- f $\{n \mid n \leqslant 3 \text{ or } n > 6\}$

2 Write using interval notation:

a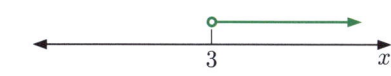

b

c

d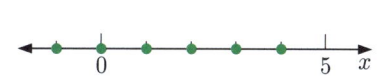

e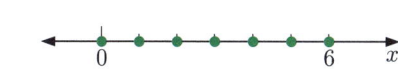

f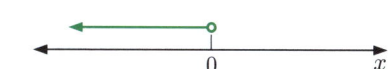

3 Represent each of the following number sets on a number line:

- a $\{x \mid 4 \leqslant x < 8,\ x \in \mathbb{N}\}$
- b $\{x \mid -5 < x \leqslant 4,\ x \in \mathbb{Z}\}$
- c $\{x \mid -3 < x \leqslant 5,\ x \in \mathbb{R}\}$
- d $\{x \mid x > -5,\ x \in \mathbb{Z}\}$
- e $\{x \mid x \leqslant 6\}$
- f $\{x \mid -5 \leqslant x \leqslant 0\}$

4 Write in interval notation:

- a the set of all real numbers greater than 7
- b the set of all integers between -8 and 15
- c the set of all rational numbers between 4 and 6, including 4.

C SUBSETS AND COMPLEMENT

In this section we consider some other important terms relating to sets.

SUBSETS

Suppose A and B are two sets. A is a **subset** of B if every element of A is also an element of B. We write $A \subseteq B$.

For example:
- If $E = \{\text{even numbers}\}$ then $E \subseteq \mathbb{Z}$.
- The empty set $\varnothing$ is a subset of every set.

Example 3 ◀)) Self Tutor

Suppose $A = \{1, 2, 3, 4, 5, 6, 7\}$, $B = \{2, 3, 5\}$, and $C = \{3, 5, 8\}$.

Decide whether B or C are subsets of A.

Every element of B is also an element of A, so $B \subseteq A$.

The element 8 of C is not an element of A, so $C \nsubseteq A$.

$\nsubseteq$ reads "is not a subset of".

THE COMPLEMENT OF A SET

If we are given a problem involving sets, the **universal set** U is the set of all elements under consideration.

For example, we might be only interested in integers, or only positive integers.

The complement of A, denoted A', is the set of all elements of U which are *not* in A.
$$A' = \{x \mid x \notin A, \ x \in U\}$$

Example 4 ◀)) Self Tutor

Suppose $U = \{x \mid x \leqslant 12, \ x \in \mathbb{Z}^+\}$. Find the complement of:

a $A = \{\text{even numbers in } U\}$ **b** $B = \{\text{prime numbers in } U\}$

a $A' = \{\text{odd numbers in } U\}$
    $= \{1, 3, 5, 7, 9, 11\}$

b $B' = \{1, 4, 6, 8, 9, 10, 12\}$

EXERCISE 2C

1 For each of the following sets A and B, decide whether $A \subseteq B$:
  a $A = \{2, 5, 6\}$, $B = \{1, 2, 3, 4, 5, 6, 7, 8\}$
  b $A = \{4, 8, 11, 12\}$, $B = \{2, 4, 6, 8, 10, 12, 14, 16\}$
  c $A = \varnothing$, $B = \{1, 4, 7, 10\}$
  d $A = \{5, 10, 15, 20, 25, 30\}$, $B = \{10, 15, 20\}$
  e $A = \{6, 7, 8\}$, $B = \mathbb{N}$

2 Are the following statements true or false?
  a $\mathbb{Z} \subseteq \mathbb{R}$ **b** $\mathbb{Z}^+ \subseteq \mathbb{Z}$ **c** $\{\frac{1}{3}, \sqrt{2}, 5\} \subseteq \mathbb{Q}$
  d $\mathbb{N} \subseteq \mathbb{Q}$ **e** $\mathbb{R} \subseteq \mathbb{Z}$ **f** $\mathbb{Z}^+ \subseteq \mathbb{N}$

3 Suppose $A = \{1, 2, 3, 4, 5, 6, 7, 8\}$, $B = \{3, 6, 9\}$, and $C = \{4, 7\}$. Decide whether B or C are subsets of A.

4 Suppose $P = \{$prime numbers less than $10\}$, $Q = \{$multiples of 3 less than $20\}$, $R = \{3, 5, 7\}$, and $S = \{$multiples of 6 less than $20\}$. Decide whether the following statements are true or false:
   a $P \subseteq Q$ **b** $R \subseteq P$ **c** $R \subseteq S$ **d** $S \subseteq Q$

5 Suppose $U = \{x \mid x \leqslant 9,\ x \in \mathbb{Z}^+\}$. Find the complement of:
   a $A = \{2, 5, 6\}$
   b $B = \{$prime numbers in $U\}$
   c $C = \{$odd numbers in $U\}$
   d $D = \{$multiples of 4 in $U\}$
   e $E = \varnothing$
   f $F = \{x \mid x < 3,\ x \in \mathbb{Z}^+\}$.

6 Suppose $U = \{$letters of the English alphabet$\}$. Find the complement of:
   a $P = \{$C, F, J, M, P, U, Y, Z$\}$
   b $Q = \{$consonants$\}$
   c $R = \{$letters in the word HOSPITAL$\}$
   d $S = \{$letters after J in the alphabet$\}$.

7 Suppose $U = \{x \mid x \leqslant 15,\ x \in \mathbb{Z}^+\}$, $A = \{x \mid 5 \leqslant x < 13,\ x \in \mathbb{Z}^+\}$, and $B = \{x \mid 6 < x < 10,\ x \in \mathbb{Z}^+\}$.
   a Write down A' and B'.
   b True or false?
      i $A \subseteq B$ **ii** $B \subseteq A$ **iii** $A' \subseteq B'$ **iv** $B' \subseteq A'$

D   VENN DIAGRAMS

A **Venn diagram** consists of a universal set U represented by a rectangle, and subsets within it that are generally represented by circles.

Example 5   ◀) Self Tutor

Consider the set $S = \{2, 4, 6, 7\}$ within the universal set $U = \{x \mid x \leqslant 10,\ x \in \mathbb{Z}^+\}$.
   a Draw a Venn diagram to show S.
   b List the elements of the complement set S'.
   c Find: **i** $n(S)$ **ii** $n(S')$ **iii** $n(U)$

a
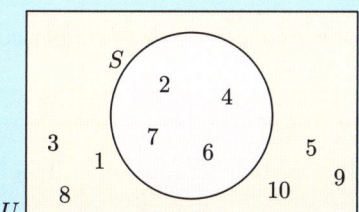

b $S' = \{1, 3, 5, 8, 9, 10\}$
c **i** $n(S) = 4$
   ii $n(S') = 6$
   iii $n(U) = 10$

For sets which are subsets of other sets, we can place circles within circles.

For example, this Venn diagram displays real numbers, rational numbers, integers, and natural numbers:

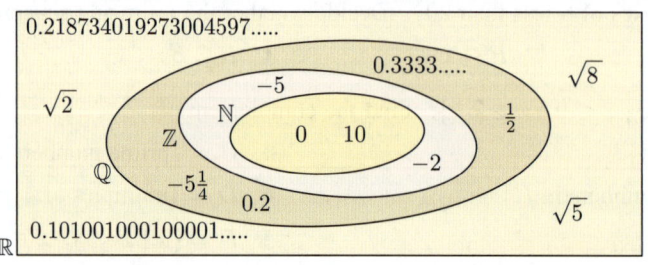

Example 6

Illustrate the following numbers on a Venn diagram:

$\sqrt{3}, 8\frac{1}{2}, -2, 7.1, 16, 0.115$

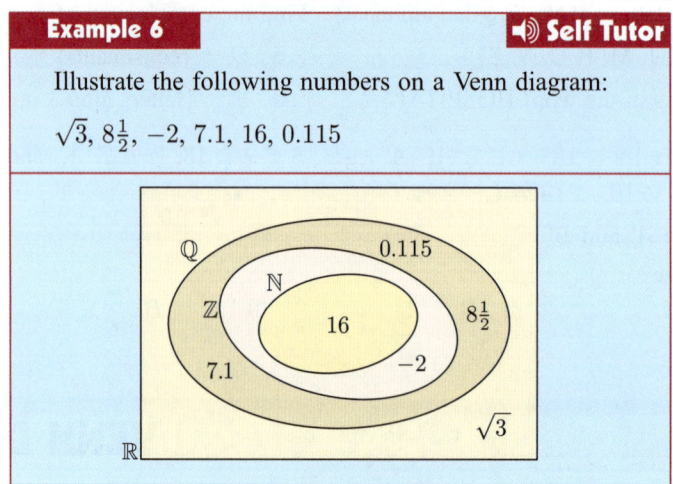

For two sets which have elements in common, we use circles which overlap.

Example 7

Consider $U = \{x \mid 0 \leqslant x \leqslant 12,\ x \in \mathbb{Z}\}$, $A = \{2, 3, 5, 7, 11\}$, and $B = \{1, 3, 6, 7, 8\}$.

Illustrate A and B on a Venn diagram.

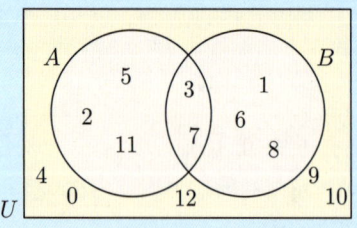

3 and 7 are in both A and B, so the circles representing A and B must overlap.

We place 3 and 7 in the overlap, then fill in the rest of A and the rest of B.

The remaining elements of U are placed outside the two circles.

EXERCISE 2D

1. Suppose $U = \{x \mid x \leqslant 8,\ x \in \mathbb{Z}^+\}$ and $A = \{$prime numbers $\leqslant 8\}$.
   a. Show set A on a Venn diagram.
   b. List the set A'.
   c. Find: i $n(A)$ ii $n(A')$ iii $n(U)$

2 Suppose U = {letters of the English alphabet} and
V = {letters of the English alphabet which are vowels}.

    a Show these sets on a Venn diagram.   **b** List the set V'.

    c Find: **i** $n(V)$ **ii** $n(V')$ **iii** $n(U)$

3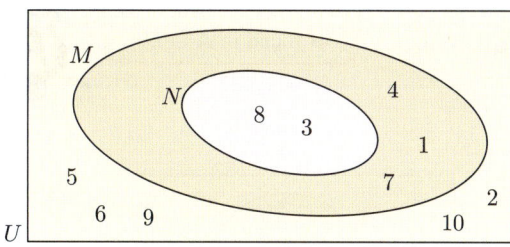

    a List the elements of:

        i U **ii** N **iii** M

    b Find $n(N)$ and $n(M)$.

    c Is $M \subseteq N$?

4 Illustrate A and B on a Venn diagram if:

    a $U = \{1, 2, 3, 4, 5, 6\}$, $A = \{1, 2, 3, 4\}$, $B = \{3, 4, 5, 6\}$

    b $U = \{4, 5, 6, 7, 8, 9, 10\}$, $A = \{6, 7, 9, 10\}$, $B = \{5, 6, 8, 9\}$

    c $U = \{3, 4, 5, 6, 7, 8, 9\}$, $A = \{3, 5, 7, 9\}$, $B = \{4, 6, 8\}$

5 Suppose the universal set is $U = \mathbb{R}$, the set of all real numbers.

$\mathbb{Q}$, $\mathbb{Z}$, and $\mathbb{N}$ are all subsets of $\mathbb{R}$.

    a Copy the given Venn diagram and label the sets U, $\mathbb{Q}$, $\mathbb{Z}$, and $\mathbb{N}$.

    b Place these numbers on the Venn diagram:

        $\frac{2}{3}$, $\sqrt{7}$, $0.\overline{4}$, -1, $-8\frac{1}{3}$, 0, 4, and

        $\alpha = 0.564\,105\,923\,6\,....$ which does not terminate or recur.

    c Shade the region representing the set of irrationals $\mathbb{Q}'$.

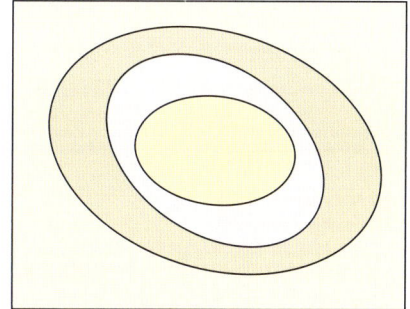

6 Show the following information on a Venn diagram:

    a U = {triangles}, E = {equilateral triangles}, I = {isosceles triangles}

    b U = {quadrilaterals}, P = {parallelograms}, R = {rectangles}

7 Suppose $U = \{x \mid x \leqslant 30,\ x \in \mathbb{Z}^+\}$,

              A = {prime numbers $\leqslant 30$},

              B = {multiples of $5 \leqslant 30$},

    and C = {odd numbers $\leqslant 30$}.

Use the Venn diagram shown to display the elements of the sets.

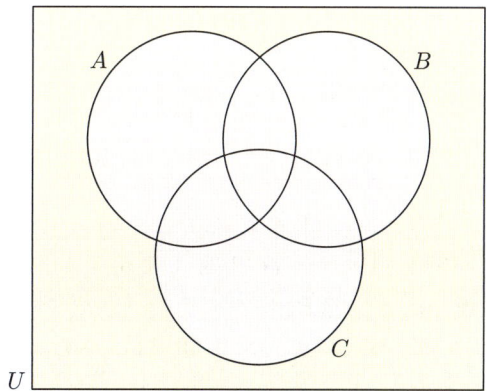

E UNION AND INTERSECTION

If A and B are two sets, then
- $A \cap B$ is the **intersection** of A and B, and consists of all elements which are in **both A and B**
- $A \cup B$ is the **union** of A and B, and consists of all elements which are in A **or** B (or both).

Every element in A and every element in B is found in $A \cup B$.

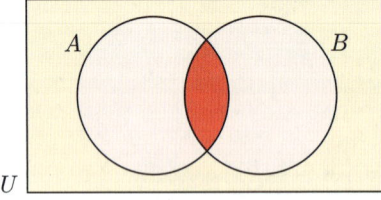

$A \cap B$ is shaded red.

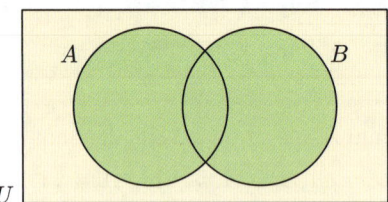

$A \cup B$ is shaded green.

For example, the Venn diagram alongside shows
$A = \{2, 3, 4, 7\}$ and $B = \{1, 3, 7, 8, 10\}$.

We can see that $A \cap B = \{3, 7\}$
and $A \cup B = \{1, 2, 3, 4, 7, 8, 10\}$.

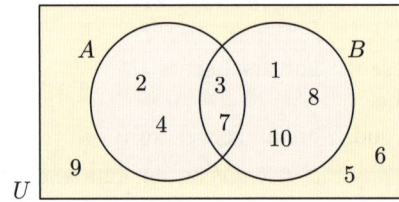

Example 8   ◀)) Self Tutor

Suppose $U = \{\text{positive integers} \leqslant 12\}$, $A = \{\text{primes} \leqslant 12\}$, and $B = \{\text{factors of } 12\}$.
- **a** List the elements of the sets A and B.
- **b** Show the sets A, B, and U on a Venn diagram.
- **c** List the elements in: **i** A' **ii** $A \cap B$ **iii** $A \cup B$
- **d** Find: **i** $n(A \cap B)$ **ii** $n(A \cup B)$ **iii** $n(B')$

a $A = \{2, 3, 5, 7, 11\}$ and $B = \{1, 2, 3, 4, 6, 12\}$

b

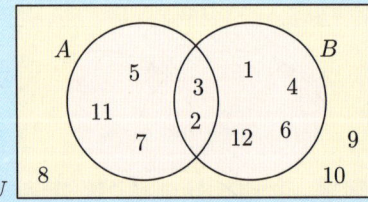

c **i** $A' = \{1, 4, 6, 8, 9, 10, 12\}$ **ii** $A \cap B = \{2, 3\}$
   iii $A \cup B = \{1, 2, 3, 4, 5, 6, 7, 11, 12\}$

d **i** $n(A \cap B) = 2$ **ii** $n(A \cup B) = 9$
   iii $B' = \{5, 7, 8, 9, 10, 11\}$, so $n(B') = 6$

Two sets are **disjoint** or **mutually exclusive** if they have no elements in common.
If A and B are disjoint then $A \cap B = \varnothing$.

EXERCISE 2E.1

1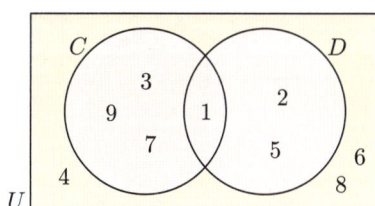

a List the elements of set:
  i C ii D iii U
  iv $C \cap D$ v $C \cup D$
b Find:
  i $n(C)$ ii $n(D)$ iii $n(U)$
  iv $n(C \cap D)$ v $n(C \cup D)$

2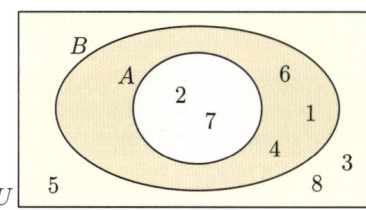

a List the elements of set:
  i A ii B iii U
  iv $A \cap B$ v $A \cup B$
b Find:
  i $n(A)$ ii $n(B)$ iii $n(U)$
  iv $n(A \cap B)$ v $n(A \cup B)$

3 Consider $U = \{x \mid x \leqslant 12, \ x \in \mathbb{Z}^+\}$, $A = \{2, 7, 9, 10, 11\}$, and $B = \{1, 2, 9, 11, 12\}$.
  a Show these sets on a Venn diagram.
  b List the elements of: i $A \cap B$ ii $A \cup B$ iii B'
  c Find: i $n(A)$ ii $n(B')$ iii $n(A \cap B)$ iv $n(A \cup B)$

4 If A is the set of all factors of 36 and B is the set of all factors of 63, find:
  a $A \cap B$ b $A \cup B$

5 If $X = \{A, B, D, M, N, P, R, T, Z\}$ and $Y = \{B, C, M, T, W, Z\}$, find:
  a $X \cap Y$ b $X \cup Y$

6 Suppose $U = \{x \mid x \leqslant 30, \ x \in \mathbb{Z}^+\}$, $A = \{\text{factors of } 30\}$, and $B = \{\text{prime numbers} \leqslant 30\}$.
  a Find: i $n(A)$ ii $n(B)$ iii $n(A \cap B)$ iv $n(A \cup B)$
  b Show that $n(A \cup B) = n(A) + n(B) - n(A \cap B)$.

7 Simplify:
  a $X \cap Y$ for $X = \{1, 3, 5, 7\}$ and $Y = \{2, 4, 6, 8\}$
  b $A \cup A'$ for any set $A \in U$.
  c $A \cap A'$ for any set $A \in U$.

USING VENN DIAGRAMS TO ILLUSTRATE REGIONS

We can use a Venn diagram to help illustrate the union or intersection of regions.

Shaded regions of a Venn diagram can be used to verify **set identities**. These are equations involving sets which are true for *all* sets.

Examples of set identities include:

$$A \cup A' = U \qquad\qquad A \cap A' = \varnothing$$
$$(A \cup B)' = A' \cap B' \qquad\qquad (A \cap B)' = A' \cup B'$$

Example 9   Self Tutor

On separate Venn diagrams, shade the region representing:

a in A or in B but not in both   **b** $A' \cap B$

a 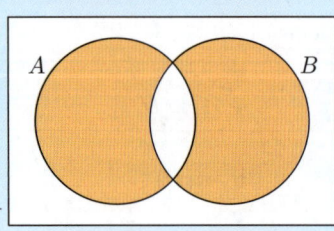   **b**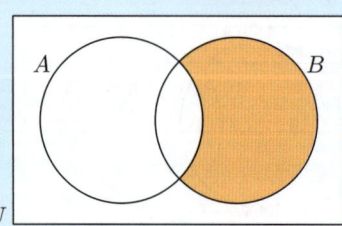

EXERCISE 2E.2

1 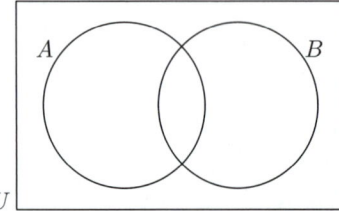   On separate Venn diagrams, shade regions for:

   a $A \cap B$ **b** $A \cap B'$
   c $A' \cup B$ **d** $A \cup B'$
   e $A' \cap B$ **f** $A' \cap B'$

    PRINTABLE VENN DIAGRAMS (OVERLAPPING)

2 Describe in words, the shaded region of:

   a 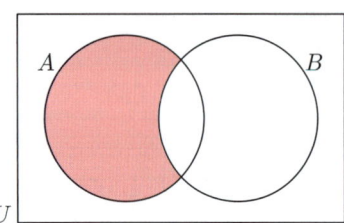   **b**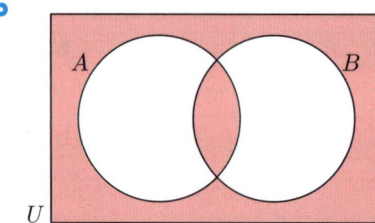

3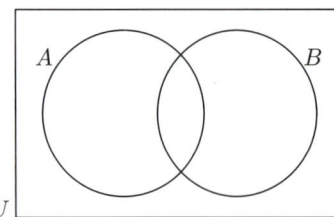

   a On separate Venn diagrams, shade regions for:

   i $A \cup B$ **ii** $(A \cup B)'$ **iii** $A' \cap B'$
   iv $A \cap B'$ **v** $(A \cap B)'$ **vi** $A' \cup B'$
   vii $(A' \cup B')'$

   b Hence verify that:

   i $(A \cap B)' = A' \cup B'$ **ii** $(A \cup B)' = A' \cap B'$

4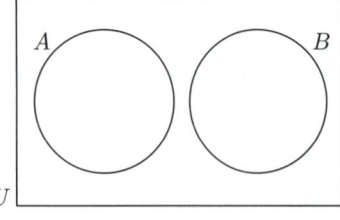

   Suppose A and B are two disjoint sets. Shade on separate Venn diagrams:

   a A **b** B'
   c $A \cup B$ **d** $A' \cap B$
   e $(A \cap B)'$

    PRINTABLE VENN DIAGRAMS (DISJOINT)

5 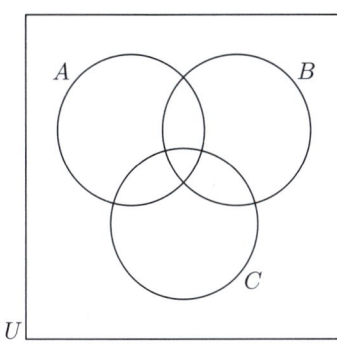 This Venn diagram consists of three intersecting sets.

  a Shade on separate Venn diagrams:

    i A **ii** B'
    iii $B \cap C$ **iv** $A \cup B$
    v $A \cap B \cap C$ **vi** $A \cup B \cup C$
    vii $(A \cap B \cap C)'$ **viii** $(B \cap C) \cup A$
    ix $(A \cup B) \cap C$ **x** $(A \cap C) \cup (B \cap C)$
    xi $(A \cap B) \cup C$ **xii** $(A \cup C) \cap (B \cup C)$

PRINTABLE VENN DIAGRAMS (3 SETS)

  b Verify that:

    i $A \cup (B \cap C) = (A \cup B) \cap (A \cup C)$
    ii $A \cap (B \cup C) = (A \cap B) \cup (A \cap C)$

Click on the icon to practise shading regions representing various subsets. You can practise with both two and three intersecting sets.

VENN DIAGRAMS

F   NUMBERS IN REGIONS

We have seen that there are four regions on a Venn diagram which contains two overlapping sets A and B.

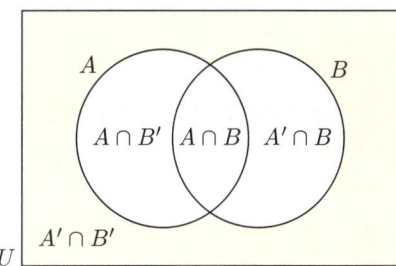

There are many situations where we are only interested in the **number of elements** of U that are in each region. We do not need to show all the elements on the diagram, so instead we write the number of elements in each region in brackets.

Example 10   ◀)) Self Tutor

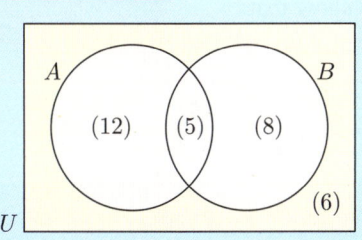

In the Venn diagram given, (5) means that there are 5 elements in the set $A \cap B$.

How many elements are there in:

  a A **b** B' **c** $A \cup B$
  d A, but not B **e** B, but not A **f** neither A nor B?

  a $n(A) = 12 + 5 = 17$ **b** $n(B') = 12 + 6 = 18$
  c $n(A \cup B) = 12 + 5 + 8 = 25$ **d** $n(A$, but not $B) = 12$
  e $n(B$, but not $A) = 8$ **f** $n($neither A nor $B) = 6$

Example 11   🔊 Self Tutor

Given $n(U) = 25$, $n(P) = 10$, $n(Q) = 12$, and $n(P \cap Q) = 3$, find:
a $n(P \cup Q)$
b $n(P, \text{but not } Q)$

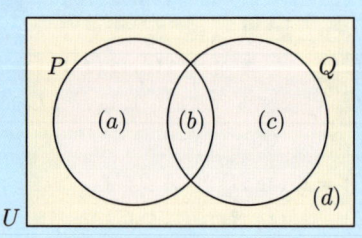

We see that $b = 3$ {as $n(P \cap Q) = 3$}
$ a + b = 10$ {as $n(P) = 10$}
$ b + c = 12$ {as $n(Q) = 12$}
$ a + b + c + d = 25$ {as $n(U) = 25$}
$\therefore \; b = 3$, $a = 7$, and $c = 9$
$\therefore \; 7 + 3 + 9 + d = 25$
$\therefore \; d = 6$

a $n(P \cup Q) = a + b + c = 19$
b $n(P, \text{but not } Q) = a = 7$

EXERCISE 2F

1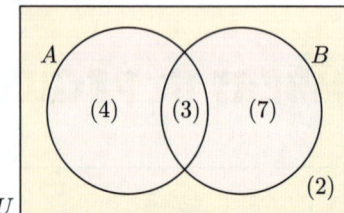

How many elements are there in:
a B
b A'
c $A \cup B$
d A, but not B
e B, but not A
f neither A nor B?

2 In the Venn diagram below, (a) means that there are a elements in that region.

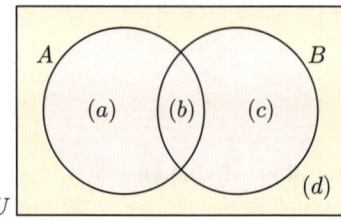

a Write an expression for:
   i $n(A)$ **ii** $n(B)$
   iii $n(A \cap B)$ **iv** $n(A \cup B)$

b Show that:
   i $n(A \cup B) = n(A) + n(B) - n(A \cap B)$
   ii $n(A \cap B) = n(A) + n(B) - n(A \cup B)$
   iii if A and B are disjoint, then $n(A \cup B) = n(A) + n(B)$.

3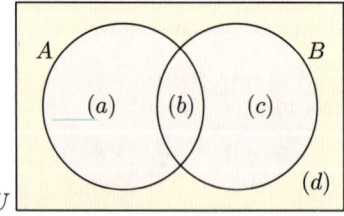

Use the Venn diagram to show that:
a $n(A \cap B') = n(A) - n(A \cap B)$
b $n(A \cup B') = n(U) - n(A' \cap B)$

4 Given $n(U) = 20$, $n(A) = 12$, $n(B) = 13$, and $n(A \cap B) = 8$, find:
a $n(A \cup B)$
b $n(B, \text{but not } A)$

5 Given $n(U) = 28$, $n(M) = 14$, $n(M \cap N) = 3$, and $n(M \cup N) = 18$, find:
a $n(N)$
b $n((M \cup N)')$

G PROBLEM SOLVING WITH VENN DIAGRAMS

Example 12

The Venn diagram alongside illustrates the number of people in a sporting club who play tennis (T) and hockey (H).

Determine the number of people:

a in the club
b who play hockey
c who play both sports
d who play neither sport
e who play at least one sport.

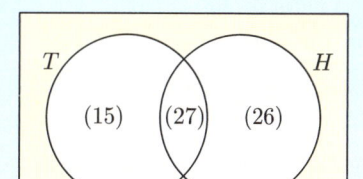

a $n(U) = 15 + 27 + 26 + 7 = 75$
There are 75 people in the club.

b $n(H) = 27 + 26 = 53$
53 people play hockey.

c $n(T \cap H) = 27$
27 people play both sports.

d $n(T' \cap H') = 7$
7 people play neither sport.

e $n(T \cup H) = 15 + 27 + 26 = 68$
68 people play at least one sport.

EXERCISE 2G

1 The Venn diagram alongside illustrates the number of students in a particular class who study French (F) and Spanish (S).

Determine the number of students:

a in the class
b who study both subjects
c who study at least one of the subjects
d who only study Spanish.

2 In a survey at a resort, people were asked whether they went sailing (S) or fishing (F) during their stay.

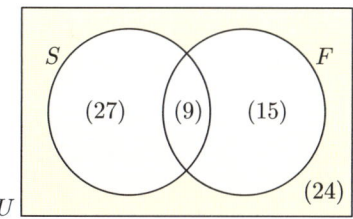

Use the Venn diagram to determine the number of people:

a in the survey
b who did both activities
c who did neither activity
d who did exactly one of the activities.

3 In a class of 30 students, 19 study Physics, 17 study Chemistry, and 15 study both subjects. Determine the number of students who study:
    a at least one of the subjects   **b** Physics, but not Chemistry
    c exactly one of the subjects   **d** neither subject.

4 In a class of 40 students, 19 play tennis, 20 play netball, and 8 play neither sport. Determine the number of students in the class who:
    a do not play netball   **b** play at least one of the sports
    c play exactly one of the sports   **d** play netball, but not tennis.

5 In a class of 25 students, 15 play hockey, 16 play basketball, and 4 play neither sport. Determine the number of students who play:
    a both sports   **b** hockey but not basketball.

6 In a class of 40 students, 34 like bananas, 22 like pineapples, and 2 dislike both fruits. Find the number of students who:
    a like both fruits   **b** like at least one fruit.

7 In a class of 40 students, 23 have dark hair, 18 have brown eyes, and 26 have dark hair, brown eyes or both. How many students have:
    a dark hair and brown eyes   **b** neither dark hair nor brown eyes
    c dark hair but not brown eyes?

8 Answer the **Opening Problem** on page **28**.

9 In a circle of music lovers, 14 people play the piano or violin, 8 people are piano players, and 5 people play both instruments. Find the number of violin players.

10 64% of students at a school study a language, and 79% study Mathematics. Every student studies at least one of these subjects. What percentage of students study both a language and Mathematics?

11 Our team scored well in the interschool athletics carnival. Each person was allowed to participate in one running and one jumping event. We gained 8 places in running events. 5 of us gained a place in both running and jumping events, and 14 of us gained exactly one place. In total, how many places were gained by the team?

12 At a certain school there are 90 students studying for their IB diploma. They all study at least one of the subjects Physics, French, or History. 50 are studying Physics, 60 are studying French, and 55 are studying History. 30 students are studying both Physics and French, while 10 students are studying both French and History but not Physics. 20 students are studying all three subjects.
    a Construct a Venn diagram to illustrate this information.
    b How many students are studying both Physics and History, but not French?
    c How many students are studying at least two of the three subjects?

13 In a school of 405 pupils, a survey on sporting activities shows that 251 pupils play tennis, 157 play hockey, and 111 play softball. There are 45 pupils who play both tennis and hockey, 60 who play hockey and softball, and 39 who play tennis and softball. What conclusion may be drawn about the number of students who participate in all three sports?

H   THE ALGEBRA OF SETS

For the set of real numbers $\mathbb{R}$, we can write laws for the operations $+$ and $\times$:

For any real numbers a, b, and c:
- **commutative** $a + b = b + a$ and $ab = ba$
- **identity**   Identity elements 0 and 1 exist such that
  $a + 0 = 0 + a = a$ and $a \times 1 = 1 \times a = a$.
- **associativity** $(a + b) + c = a + (b + c)$ and $(ab)c = a(bc)$
- **distributive** $a(b + c) = ab + ac$

The following are the **laws for the algebra of sets** under the operations $\cup$ and $\cap$:

For any subsets A, B, and C of the universal set U:
- **commutative** $A \cap B = B \cap A$ and $A \cup B = B \cup A$
- **associativity** $A \cap (B \cap C) = (A \cap B) \cap C$ and
  $A \cup (B \cup C) = (A \cup B) \cup C$
- **distributive** $A \cup (B \cap C) = (A \cup B) \cap (A \cup C)$ and
  $A \cap (B \cup C) = (A \cap B) \cup (A \cap C)$
- **identity** $A \cup \varnothing = A$ and $A \cap U = A$
- **complement** $A \cup A' = U$ and $A \cap A' = \varnothing$
- **domination** $A \cup U = U$ and $A \cap \varnothing = \varnothing$
- **idempotent** $A \cap A = A$ and $A \cup A = A$
- **DeMorgan's** $(A \cap B)' = A' \cup B'$ and $(A \cup B)' = A' \cap B'$
- **involution** $(A')' = A$

We have already used Venn diagrams to verify the distributive laws.

EXERCISE 2H

1 With the aid of Venn diagrams, explain why the following laws are valid:
  a the *commutative* laws $A \cap B = B \cap A$ and $A \cup B = B \cup A$
  b the *idempotent* laws $A \cap A = A$ and $A \cup A = A$
  c the *associative* laws $A \cap (B \cap C) = (A \cap B) \cap C$ and $A \cup (B \cup C) = (A \cup B) \cup C$
  d the *complement* law $(A')' = A$.

2 Use the laws for the algebra of sets to show that:
  a $A \cup (B \cup A') = U$
  b $A \cap (B \cap A') = \varnothing$
  c $A \cup (B \cap A') = A \cup B$
  d $(A' \cup B')' = A \cap B$
  e $(A \cup B) \cap (A' \cap B') = \varnothing$
  f $(A \cup B) \cap (C \cup D) = (A \cap C) \cup (A \cap D) \cup (B \cap C) \cup (B \cap D)$.

REVIEW SET 2A

1. Explain why 1.3 is a rational number.

2. Is $\sqrt{4000} \in \mathbb{Q}$?

3. Let P be the set of all prime numbers between 20 and 40.
   - **a** Is $37 \in P$?
   - **b** Find $n(P)$.

4. Write a statement describing the meaning of $S = \{t \mid -1 \leqslant t < 3\}$.

5. Write using interval notation: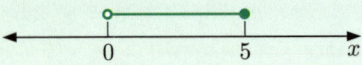

6. For each of the following sets P and Q, decide whether $P \subseteq Q$:
   - **a** $P = \{5, 6, 7, 8\}$, $Q = \{1, 2, 3, 4, 5, 6, 7\}$
   - **b** $P = \{$multiples of 4 between 10 and 30$\}$, $Q = \{$even numbers between 0 and 40$\}$

7. Suppose $U = \{x \mid x \leqslant 10,\ x \in \mathbb{Z}^+\}$. Find the complement of:
   - **a** $A = \{3, 7, 9\}$
   - **b** $B = \{$composite numbers in $U\}$.

8. Suppose $U = \{x \mid x \leqslant 12,\ x \in \mathbb{Z}^+\}$ and $A = \{$multiples of $3 \leqslant 12\}$.
   - **a** Show A on a Venn diagram.
   - **b** List the set A'.
   - **c** Find $n(A')$.

9. True or false?
   - **a** $\mathbb{N} \subseteq \mathbb{Z}^+$
   - **b** $\mathbb{Q} \subseteq \mathbb{Z}$

10.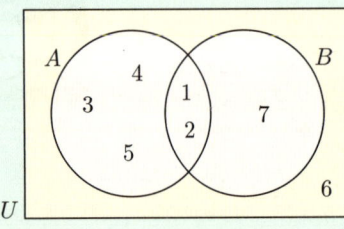
    - **a** List the elements of set:
      - **i** A
      - **ii** B
      - **iii** U
      - **iv** $A \cup B$
      - **v** $A \cap B$
    - **b** Find:
      - **i** $n(A)$
      - **ii** $n(B)$
      - **iii** $n(A \cup B)$

11. Consider $U = \{x \mid x \leqslant 10,\ x \in \mathbb{Z}^+\}$, $P = \{2, 3, 5, 7\}$, and $Q = \{2, 4, 6, 8\}$.
    - **a** Show these sets on a Venn diagram.
    - **b** List the elements of:
      - **i** $P \cap Q$
      - **ii** $P \cup Q$
      - **iii** Q'
    - **c** Find:
      - **i** $n(P')$
      - **ii** $n(P \cap Q)$
      - **iii** $n(P \cup Q)$
    - **d** Is $P \cap Q \subseteq P$?

12. Describe in words the shaded region:
    - **a**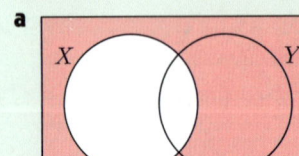
    - **b**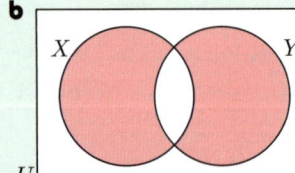
    - **c**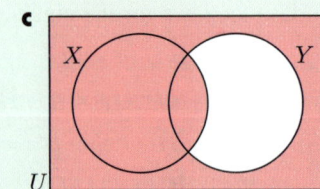

13 How many elements are there in:
  a A
  b B
  c $A \cup B$
  d neither A nor B?

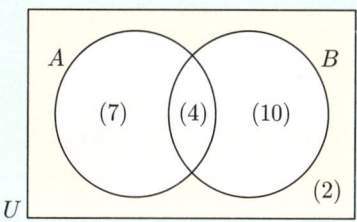

14 400 families were surveyed. It was found that 90% had a TV set, and 60% had a computer. Every family had at least one of these items. How many families had both a TV set and a computer?

REVIEW SET 2B

1 Is $-2 \in \mathbb{Z}^+$?

2 Show that $0.\overline{51}$ is a rational number.

3 Sketch the number set $\{x \mid x \leqslant 3 \text{ or } x > 7, \ x \in \mathbb{R}\}$.

4 For each of the following sets:
  i list the elements of the set
  ii determine whether the set is finite or infinite
  iii if the set is finite, find the number of elements in the set.

  a $A = \{\text{factors of } 15\}$
  b $B = \{\text{multiples of } 8\}$
  c $C = \{\text{odd numbers between 30 and 50}\}$
  d $D = \{\text{prime numbers less than } 30\}$

5 Suppose $P = \{3, 4, 5, 6, 7, 8, 9, 10, 11\}$, $Q = \{4, 9, 10\}$, and $R = \{5, 6, 12\}$. Decide whether Q and R are subsets of P.

6 Suppose $U = \{x \mid x \leqslant 12, \ x \in \mathbb{Z}^+\}$ and $A = \{\text{prime numbers less than } 12\}$. Find:
  a A
  b A'
  c $n(A)$
  d $n(A')$
  e $n(U)$

7 Illustrate these numbers on a Venn diagram like the one shown:
$-1, \sqrt{2}, 2, 3.1, \pi, 4.\overline{2}$

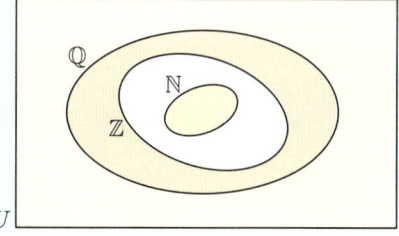

8 Show this information on a Venn diagram:
  a $U = \{10, 11, 12, 13, 14, 15\}$, $A = \{10, 12, 14\}$, $B = \{11, 12, 13\}$
  b $U = \{\text{quadrilaterals}\}$, $S = \{\text{squares}\}$, $R = \{\text{rectangles}\}$

9 If A is the set of all factors of 24 and B is the set of all factors of 18, find:
  a $A \cap B$
  b $A \cup B$

10 On separate Venn diagrams like the one shown, shade the region representing:

  a B'
  b in A and in B
  c $(A \cup B)'$

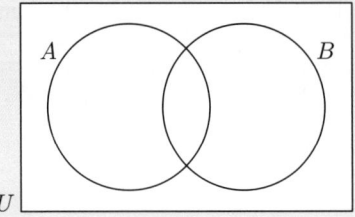

11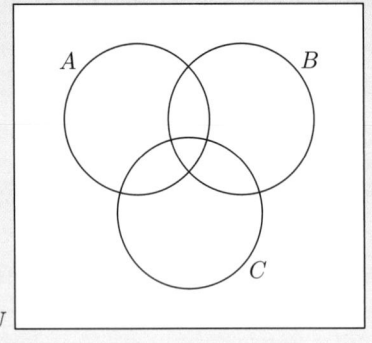

Using separate Venn diagrams like the one shown, shade regions to verify that $(A \cap B) \cup C = (A \cup C) \cap (B \cup C)$.

12 Given $n(U) = 30$, $n(A) = 14$, $n(B) = 10$, and $n(A \cap B) = 6$, find:

  a $n(A \cup B)$
  b $n(B,\ \text{but not}\ A)$

13 In a certain town, three newspapers are published. 20% of the population read A, 16% read B, 14% read C, 8% read A and B, 5% read A and C, 4% read B and C, and 2% read all 3 newspapers. What percentage of the population read:

  a none of the papers
  b at least one of the papers
  c exactly one of the papers
  d either A or B
  e A only?

14 Use the laws for the algebra of sets to show that $A \cap (B \cup A') = A \cap B$.

Chapter 3

Algebraic expansion and factorisation

Contents:
- **A** Revision of expansion laws
- **B** Further expansion
- **C** The binomial expansion
- **D** Revision of factorisation
- **E** Factorising expressions with four terms
- **F** Factorising quadratic trinomials
- **G** Factorisation of $ax^2 + bx + c$, $a \neq 1$
- **H** Miscellaneous factorisation

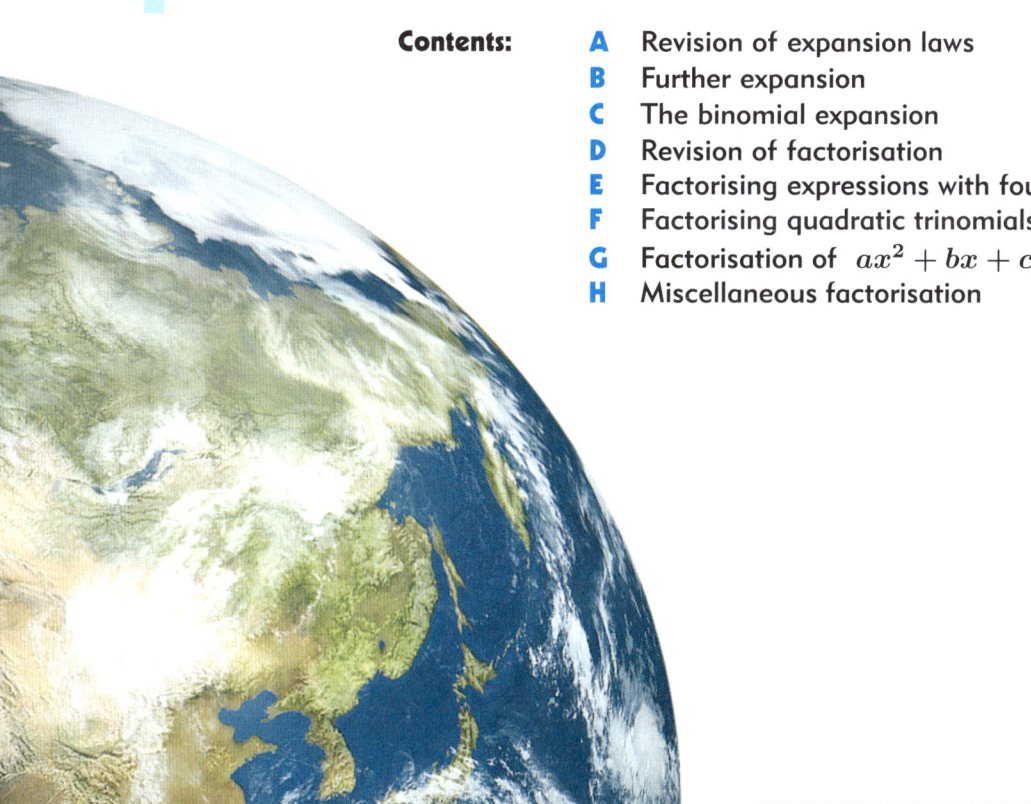

OPENING PROBLEM

Jody showed her friend Leanne a trick for performing multiplications of 2 digit numbers, such as 42×83:

Step 1: Multiply the digits in the units column.
$2 \times 3 = 6$

Step 2: Multiply the digits along the diagonals, then add the results.
$(4 \times 3) + (8 \times 2) = 28$, so we write 8 and carry the 2.

Step 3: Multiply the digits in the tens column.
$4 \times 8 = 32$, adding the 2 gives 34.

So, $42 \times 83 = 3486$.

Things to think about:

Can you use algebra to explain why this trick works?

The study of **algebra** is vital for many areas of mathematics. We need it to manipulate equations, solve problems for unknown variables, and also to develop higher level mathematical theories.

In this chapter we revise the **expansion** of expressions which involve brackets, and the reverse process which is called **factorisation**.

A   REVISION OF EXPANSION LAWS

In this section we revise the laws for expanding algebraic expressions.

DISTRIBUTIVE LAW

$$a(b+c) = ab + ac$$

Example 1   🔊 Self Tutor

Expand the following:

a $2(3x - 1)$ b $-3x(x + 2)$

a $2(3x - 1)$
    $= 2 \times 3x + 2 \times (-1)$
    $= 6x - 2$

b $-3x(x + 2)$
    $= -3x \times x + -3x \times 2$
    $= -3x^2 - 6x$

THE PRODUCT $(a+b)(c+d)$

$$(a+b)(c+d) = ac + ad + bc + bd$$

Example 2

Expand and simplify:

a $(x+4)(x-3)$
b $(2x-5)(-x+3)$

a $(x+4)(x-3)$
$= x \times x + x \times (-3) + 4 \times x + 4 \times (-3)$
$= x^2 - 3x + 4x - 12$
$= x^2 + x - 12$

b $(2x-5)(-x+3)$
$= 2x \times (-x) + 2x \times 3 - 5 \times (-x) - 5 \times 3$
$= -2x^2 + 6x + 5x - 15$
$= -2x^2 + 11x - 15$

DIFFERENCE OF TWO SQUARES

$$(a+b)(a-b) = a^2 - b^2$$

Example 3

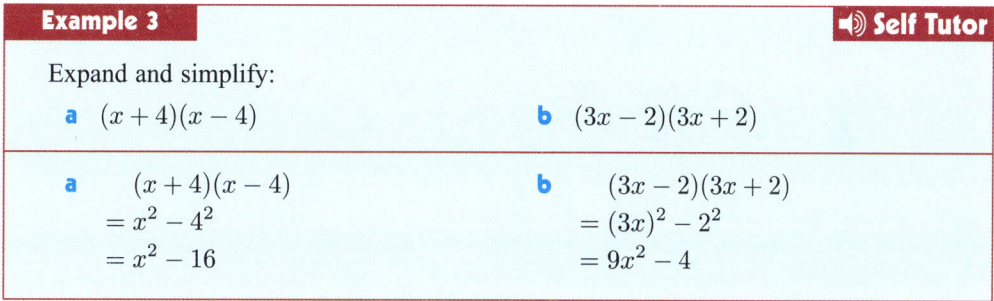

PERFECT SQUARES EXPANSION

$$(a+b)^2 = a^2 + 2ab + b^2$$

Example 4

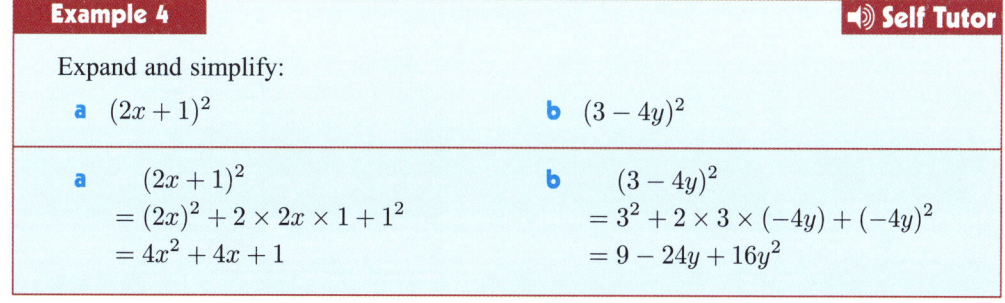

EXERCISE 3A

1 Expand and simplify:
- **a** $3(2x+5)$
- **b** $4x(x-3)$
- **c** $-2(3+x)$
- **d** $-3x(x+y)$
- **e** $2x(x^2-1)$
- **f** $-x(1-x^2)$
- **g** $-ab(b-a)$
- **h** $x^2(x-3)$
- **i** $3(a^2+3a+1)$
- **j** $5(x^2-3x+2)$
- **k** $-4(2c^2-3c-7)$
- **l** $2a(3a^2-5a+1)$

2 Expand and simplify:
- **a** $2(x+3)+5(x-4)$
- **b** $2(3-x)-3(4+x)$
- **c** $x(x+2)+2x(1-x)$
- **d** $x(x^2+2x)-x^2(2-x)$
- **e** $a(a+b)-b(a-b)$
- **f** $x^2(6-x)+3x(x-4)$

3 Expand and simplify:
- **a** $(x+2)(x+5)$
- **b** $(x-3)(x+4)$
- **c** $(x+5)(x-3)$
- **d** $(x-2)(x-10)$
- **e** $(2x+1)(x-3)$
- **f** $(3x-4)(2x-5)$
- **g** $(2x+y)(x-y)$
- **h** $(x+3)(-2x-1)$
- **i** $(x+2y)(-x-1)$

4 Expand and simplify:
- **a** $(x+3)(x-1)+3(x-5)$
- **b** $(x+7)(x-5)+(x+1)(x+4)$
- **c** $(2x+3)(x-2)-(x+1)(x+6)$
- **d** $(4t-3)(t+1)-(2t-1)(2t+5)$
- **e** $(4x-1)(3-x)+(2x-3)(3x-2)$
- **f** $5(3x-4)(x+2)-(7-x)(8-5x)$

5 Expand and simplify:
- **a** $(x+7)(x-7)$
- **b** $(3+a)(3-a)$
- **c** $(5-x)(5+x)$
- **d** $(2x+1)(2x-1)$
- **e** $(4-3y)(4+3y)$
- **f** $(3x-4z)(4z+3x)$

6 Expand and simplify:
- **a** $(x+3)(x-3)-(x+6)(x-6)$
- **b** $(5p-2)(5p+2)-p(3p-1)$
- **c** $(3y-z)(3y+z)-(2y+3z)(2y-3z)$
- **d** $(10-x^2)(10+x^2)-(10-3x^2)(10+3x^2)$

7 Expand and simplify:
- **a** $(x+5)^2$
- **b** $(2x+3)^2$
- **c** $(7+x)^2$
- **d** $(3x+4)^2$
- **e** $(5+x^2)^2$
- **f** $(3x^2+2)^2$
- **g** $(5x+3y)^2$
- **h** $(2x^2+7y)^2$
- **i** $(x^3+8x)^2$

8 Expand and simplify:
- **a** $(x-3)^2$
- **b** $(2-x)^2$
- **c** $(3x-1)^2$
- **d** $(6-5p)^2$
- **e** $(2x-5y)^2$
- **f** $(ab-2)^2$
- **g** $(x^2-5)^2$
- **h** $(4x^2-3y)^2$
- **i** $(-x^2-y^2)^2$

9 Use the diagram alongside to show that $(a-b)^2 = a^2 - 2ab + b^2$.

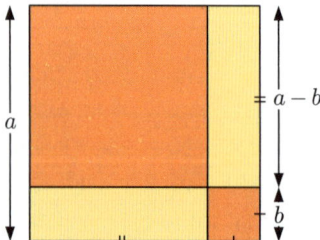

10 Expand and simplify:

    a $(x+9)^2 + (x-2)^2$ **b** $(3x+1)^2 - (2x-3)^2$ **c** $(x+8)^2 - (x+2)(x-5)$

    d $(5-p)^2 + (p^2-4)^2$ **e** $(3x^2-1)^2 - 4(1-x)^2$ **f** $(5x+y^2)^2 - x(x^2-y)^2$

B   FURTHER EXPANSION

When expressions containing more than two terms are multiplied together, we can still use the distributive law to expand the brackets. Each term in the first set of brackets is multiplied by each term in the second set of brackets.

If there are 2 terms in the first brackets and 3 terms in the second brackets, there will be $2 \times 3 = 6$ terms in the expansion. However, when we simplify by collecting like terms, the final answer may contain fewer terms.

Example 5   ◀) Self Tutor

Expand and simplify: $(x+3)(x^2+2x+4)$

$(x+3)(x^2+2x+4)$

$= x^3 + 2x^2 + 4x$ {$x \times$ each term in 2nd bracket}

$ + 3x^2 + 6x + 12$ {$3 \times$ each term in 2nd bracket}

$= x^3 + 5x^2 + 10x + 12$ {collecting like terms}

Each term in the first bracket is multiplied by each term in the second bracket.

EXERCISE 3B

1 Expand and simplify:

    a $(x+2)(x^2+x+4)$ **b** $(x+3)(x^2+2x-3)$ **c** $(x+3)(x^2+2x+1)$

    d $(x+1)(2x^2-x-5)$ **e** $(2x+3)(x^2+2x+1)$ **f** $(2x-5)(x^2-2x-3)$

    g $(x+5)(3x^2-x+4)$ **h** $(4x-1)(2x^2-3x+1)$

Example 6   ◀) Self Tutor

Expand and simplify: $(x+1)(x-3)(x+2)$

$(x+1)(x-3)(x+2)$

$= (x^2 - 3x + x - 3)(x+2)$ {expanding first two factors}

$= (x^2 - 2x - 3)(x+2)$ {collecting like terms}

$= x^3 + 2x^2 - 2x^2 - 4x - 3x - 6$ {expanding remaining factors}

$= x^3 - 7x - 6$ {collecting like terms}

2 Expand and simplify:

    a $(x+4)(x+3)(x+2)$ **b** $(x-3)(x-2)(x+4)$ **c** $(x-3)(x-2)(x-5)$

    d $(2x-3)(x+3)(x-1)$ **e** $(4x+1)(3x-1)(x+1)$ **f** $(2-x)(3x+1)(x-7)$

    g $(x-2)(4-x)(3x+2)$ **h** $(x+3)^3$ **i** $(x-2)^3$

3 State how many terms you would obtain by expanding:

a $(a+b)(c+d)$
b $(a+b+c)(d+e)$
c $(a+b)(c+d+e)$
d $(a+b+c)(d+e+f)$
e $(a+b)(c+d)(e+f)$
f $(a+b+c)(d+e)(f+g)$

4 Expand and simplify:

a $(x^2+3x+1)(x^2-x+3)$
b $(2x^2+x-1)(x^2+3x-2)$
c $(3x^2+x-4)(2x^2-3x+1)$
d $(x^2-3x+2)(x+5)(x-3)$

C THE BINOMIAL EXPANSION

Consider $(a+b)^n$ where n is a positive integer.

$a+b$ is called a **binomial** as it contains two terms.

The **binomial expansion** of $(a+b)^n$ is obtained by writing the expression without brackets.

INVESTIGATION 1 THE BINOMIAL EXPANSION OF $(a+b)^3$

In this Investigation we discover the binomial expansion of $(a+b)^3$.

What to do:

1 Find a large potato and cut it to obtain a 4 cm by 4 cm by 4 cm cube.

2 By making 3 cuts parallel to the cube's surfaces, divide the cube into 8 rectangular prisms as shown.

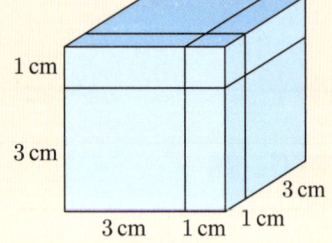

3 How many prisms are:

a 3 by 3 by 3
b 3 by 3 by 1
c 3 by 1 by 1
d 1 by 1 by 1?

4 Now instead of the 4 cm × 4 cm × 4 cm potato cube, suppose you had a cube with edge length $(a+b)$ cm.

a Explain why the volume of the cube is given by $(a+b)^3$.
b Suppose you made cuts so each edge was divided into a cm and b cm. How many prisms would be:

i a by a by a
ii a by a by b
iii a by b by b
iv b by b by b?

DEMO

c By adding the volumes of the 8 rectangular prisms, find an expression for the total volume. Hence write down the binomial expansion of $(a+b)^3$.

Another method of finding the binomial expansion of $(a+b)^3$ is to expand the brackets:

$$(a+b)^3 = (a+b)^2(a+b)$$
$$= (a^2+2ab+b^2)(a+b)$$
$$= a^3+a^2b+2a^2b+2ab^2+ab^2+b^3$$
$$= a^3+3a^2b+3ab^2+b^3$$

$$(a+b)^3 = a^3+3a^2b+3ab^2+b^3.$$

The binomial expansion of $(a+b)^3$ can be used to expand other perfect cubes.

Example 7 ◀) Self Tutor

Expand and simplify using the rule $(a+b)^3 = a^3 + 3a^2b + 3ab^2 + b^3$:

a $(x+4)^3$ **b** $(3x-2)^3$

a We substitute $a = x$ and $b = 4$.
$\therefore \ (x+4)^3 = x^3 + 3 \times x^2 \times 4 + 3 \times x \times 4^2 + 4^3$
$= x^3 + 12x^2 + 48x + 64$

b We substitute $a = (3x)$ and $b = (-2)$.
$\therefore \ (3x-2)^3 = (3x)^3 + 3 \times (3x)^2 \times (-2) + 3 \times (3x) \times (-2)^2 + (-2)^3$
$= 27x^3 - 54x^2 + 36x - 8$

Notice the use of brackets.

EXERCISE 3C

1 Use the binomial expansion of $(a+b)^3$ to expand and simplify:

    a $(x+1)^3$ **b** $(x+3)^3$ **c** $(x+5)^3$ **d** $(x+y)^3$
    e $(x-1)^3$ **f** $(x-5)^3$ **g** $(x-4)^3$ **h** $(x-y)^3$
    i $(2+y)^3$ **j** $(2x+1)^3$ **k** $(3x+1)^3$ **l** $(2y+3x)^3$
    m $(2-y)^3$ **n** $(2x-1)^3$ **o** $(3x-1)^3$ **p** $(2y-3x)^3$

2 By expanding and simplifying $(a+b)^3(a+b)$, show that
$(a+b)^4 = a^4 + 4a^3b + 6a^2b^2 + 4ab^3 + b^4$.

3 Use the binomial expansion $(a+b)^4 = a^4 + 4a^3b + 6a^2b^2 + 4ab^3 + b^4$ to expand and simplify:

    a $(x+y)^4$ **b** $(x+1)^4$ **c** $(x+2)^4$ **d** $(x+3)^4$
    e $(x-y)^4$ **f** $(x-1)^4$ **g** $(x-2)^4$ **h** $(2x-1)^4$

4 Consider:
$(a+b)^1 = \quad\quad\quad\quad\quad\quad\quad a + b$
$(a+b)^2 = \quad\quad\quad\quad\quad a^2 + 2ab + b^2$
$(a+b)^3 = \quad\quad\quad a^3 + 3a^2b + 3ab^2 + b^3$
$(a+b)^4 = a^4 + 4a^3b + 6a^2b^2 + 4ab^3 + b^4$

The expressions on the right hand side of each identity contain the coefficients:

$$\begin{array}{ccccccccc} & & & & 1 & & 1 & & \\ & & & 1 & & 2 & & 1 & \\ & & 1 & & 3 & & 3 & & 1 \\ & 1 & & 4 & & 6 & & 4 & & 1 \end{array}$$

This triangle of numbers is called **Pascal's triangle**.

    a Predict the next two rows of Pascal's triangle, and explain how you found them.
    b Hence, write down the binomial expansion for:
       i $(a+b)^5$ **ii** $(a-b)^5$ **iii** $(a+b)^6$ **iv** $(a-b)^6$
    c   **i** Expand and simplify $(x-2)^5$.
       ii Check your answer by substituting $x = 1$ into your expansion.

D REVISION OF FACTORISATION

Factorisation is the process of writing an expression as a **product** of its **factors**.

Factorisation is the reverse process of expansion, so we use the expansion laws in reverse.

FACTORISING WITH COMMON FACTORS

If every term in an expression has the same common factor, then we can place this factor in front of a set of brackets. We use the reverse of the distributive law for expansion.

Example 8 Self Tutor

Fully factorise:

a $6x^2 + 4x$

b $-4(a+1) + (a+2)(a+1)$

a $6x^2 + 4x$
$= 2 \times 3 \times x \times x + 2 \times 2 \times x$
$= 2x(3x+2)$

b $-4(a+1) + (a+2)(a+1)$
$= (a+1)[-4 + (a+2)]$
$= (a+1)(a-2)$

DIFFERENCE OF TWO SQUARES FACTORISATION

$$\boldsymbol{a^2 - b^2 = (a+b)(a-b)}$$

Example 9 Self Tutor

Fully factorise:

a $4 - 9y^2$

b $9a - 16a^3$

a $4 - 9y^2$
$= 2^2 - (3y)^2$
$= (2+3y)(2-3y)$

b $9a - 16a^3$
$= a(9 - 16a^2)$
$= a(3^2 - (4a)^2)$
$= a(3+4a)(3-4a)$

PERFECT SQUARES FACTORISATION

$$\boldsymbol{a^2 + 2ab + b^2 = (a+b)^2}$$
$$\boldsymbol{a^2 - 2ab + b^2 = (a-b)^2}$$

Example 10 Self Tutor

Factorise:

a $4x^2 + 4x + 1$

b $8x^2 - 24x + 18$

a $4x^2 + 4x + 1$
$= (2x)^2 + 2 \times 2x \times 1 + 1^2$
$= (2x+1)^2$

b $8x^2 - 24x + 18$
$= 2(4x^2 - 12x + 9)$
$= 2((2x)^2 - 2 \times 2x \times 3 + 3^2)$
$= 2(2x-3)^2$

EXERCISE 3D

1 Fully factorise:
- **a** $x^2 - 5x$
- **b** $2x^2 + 6x$
- **c** $4x - 2xy$
- **d** $3ab - 6b$
- **e** $2x^2 + 8x^3$
- **f** $-6x^2 + 12x$
- **g** $x^3 + x^2$
- **h** $3ab^2 - 9a^2b$

2 Fully factorise:
- **a** $3(x+5) + x(x+5)$
- **b** $a(b+3) - 5(b+3)$
- **c** $x(x+4) + x + 4$
- **d** $x(x+2) + (x+2)(x+5)$
- **e** $a(c-d) + b(c-d)$
- **f** $y(2+y) - y - 2$
- **g** $ab(x-1) + c(x-1)$
- **h** $a(x+2) - x - 2$
- **i** $(x-3)^2 + x - 3$
- **j** $(x+5)^2 + 3x + 15$
- **k** $2(x-2)^2 + 4x - 8$
- **l** $(x+y)^3 - x - y$

3 Fully factorise:
- **a** $x^2 - 16$
- **b** $64 - x^2$
- **c** $9x^2 - 1$
- **d** $49 - 4x^2$
- **e** $y^2 - 4x^2$
- **f** $4a^2 - 25b^2$
- **g** $81x^2 - 16y^2$
- **h** $4x^4 - y^2$
- **i** $9a^2b^2 - 16$
- **j** $(x+3)^2 - 4$
- **k** $(3x-2)^2 - 16$
- **l** $(2x-5)^2 - (x-4)^2$

4 Fully factorise:
- **a** $2x^2 - 8$
- **b** $3y^2 - 27$
- **c** $2 - 18x^2$
- **d** $4x - 9x^3$
- **e** $a^3b - ab^3$
- **f** $50 - 2x^2y^2$
- **g** $9b^3 - 4b$
- **h** $x^5 - xy^4$

5 Factorise:
- **a** $x^2 + 4x + 4$
- **b** $x^2 - 10x + 25$
- **c** $9x^2 + 30x + 25$
- **d** $x^2 - 8x + 16$
- **e** $4x^2 + 28x + 49$
- **f** $x^2 - 20x + 100$

6 Factorise:
- **a** $-9x^2 + 6x - 1$
- **b** $3x^2 + 18x + 27$
- **c** $-18x^2 + 12x - 2$
- **d** $2x^2 - 50$
- **e** $2x^2 - 16x + 32$
- **f** $-3x^2 - 18x - 27$

E FACTORISING EXPRESSIONS WITH FOUR TERMS

Some expressions with four terms do not have an overall common factor, but can be factorised by pairing the four terms.

For example,
$$ab + ac + bd + cd$$
$$= a(b+c) + d(b+c) \quad \text{\{factorising each pair separately\}}$$
$$= (b+c)(a+d) \quad \text{\{removing common factor } (b+c)\text{\}}$$

Example 11 ◀) Self Tutor

Factorise: $3ab + d + 3ad + b$.

$3ab + d + 3ad + b$
$= 3ab + b + 3ad + d$ {putting terms containing b together}
$= b(3a+1) + d(3a+1)$ {factorising each pair}
$= (3a+1)(b+d)$ {$(3a+1)$ is a common factor}

Sometimes we need to reorder the terms first.

EXERCISE 3E

1 Factorise:
- **a** $2a + 2 + ab + b$
- **b** $4d + ac + ad + 4c$
- **c** $ab + 6 + 2b + 3a$
- **d** $mn + 3p + np + 3m$
- **e** $2xy - 5 + 10y - x$
- **f** $6a - bc - 2ac + 3b$

Example 12 — Self Tutor

Factorise:
- **a** $x^2 + 2x + 5x + 10$
- **b** $x^2 + 3x - 4x - 12$

a $\underbrace{x^2 + 2x}_{} + \underbrace{5x + 10}_{}$
$= x(x+2) + 5(x+2)$ {factorising each pair}
$= (x+2)(x+5)$ {$(x+2)$ is a common factor}

b $\underbrace{x^2 + 3x}_{} \underbrace{- 4x - 12}_{}$
$= x(x+3) - 4(x+3)$ {factorising each pair}
$= (x+3)(x-4)$ {$(x+3)$ is a common factor}

2 Factorise:
- **a** $x^2 + 2x + 4x + 8$
- **b** $x^2 + 3x + 7x + 21$
- **c** $x^2 + 5x + 4x + 20$
- **d** $2x^2 + x + 6x + 3$
- **e** $3x^2 + 2x + 12x + 8$
- **f** $20x^2 + 12x + 5x + 3$

3 Factorise:
- **a** $x^2 - 4x + 5x - 20$
- **b** $x^2 - 7x + 2x - 14$
- **c** $x^2 - 3x - 2x + 6$
- **d** $x^2 - 5x - 3x + 15$
- **e** $x^2 + 7x - 8x - 56$
- **f** $2x^2 + x - 6x - 3$
- **g** $3x^2 + 2x - 12x - 8$
- **h** $4x^2 - 3x - 8x + 6$
- **i** $9x^2 + 2x - 9x - 2$

F FACTORISING QUADRATIC TRINOMIALS

A **quadratic trinomial** is an algebraic expression of the form $ax^2 + bx + c$ where x is a variable and a, b, c are constants, $a \neq 0$.

Consider the expansion of the product $(x+2)(x+5)$:

$(x+2)(x+5) = x^2 + 5x + 2x + 2 \times 5$ {using FOIL}
$= x^2 + [5+2]x + [2 \times 5]$
$= x^2 + [\text{sum of 2 and 5}]x + [\text{product of 2 and 5}]$
$= x^2 + 7x + 10$

$$x^2 + px + q = (x+a)(x+b)$$

where a and b are two numbers whose sum is p, and whose product is q.

So, if we want to factorise the quadratic trinomial $x^2 + 7x + 10$ into $(x + ...)(x + ...)$ we must find two numbers to fill the vacant places which have a *sum* of 7 and a *product* of 10. The numbers are 2 and 5, so $x^2 + 7x + 10 = (x+2)(x+5)$.

Example 13

Factorise:

a $x^2 - 7x + 12$
b $x^2 - 2x - 15$

a We need two numbers with sum -7 and product 12.
The numbers are -3 and -4.
$\therefore \quad x^2 - 7x + 12 = (x-3)(x-4)$

b We need two numbers with sum -2 and product -15.
The numbers are -5 and 3.
$\therefore \quad x^2 - 2x - 15 = (x-5)(x+3)$

EXERCISE 3F

1 Fully factorise:

a $x^2 + 3x + 2$
b $x^2 + 5x + 6$
c $x^2 - x - 6$
d $x^2 + 3x - 10$
e $x^2 + 4x - 21$
f $x^2 + 8x + 16$
g $x^2 - 14x + 49$
h $x^2 + 3x - 28$
i $x^2 - 11x + 24$
j $x^2 + 15x + 44$
k $x^2 - x - 56$
l $x^2 - 18x + 81$
m $x^2 - 4x - 32$
n $x^2 + 4x - 45$
o $x^2 - 4x - 96$
p $x^2 + 4x - 96$

Example 14

Fully factorise by first removing a common factor:

a $3x^2 + 6x - 72$
b $77 + 4x - x^2$

a $3x^2 + 6x - 72$
$= 3(x^2 + 2x - 24)$ {3 is a common factor}
$= 3(x+6)(x-4)$ {sum = 2, product = -24
$\therefore$ the numbers are 6 and -4}

b $77 + 4x - x^2$
$= -x^2 + 4x + 77$ {writing in descending powers of x}
$= -1(x^2 - 4x - 77)$ {-1 is a common factor}
$= -(x-11)(x+7)$ {sum = -4, product = -77
$\therefore$ the numbers are -11 and 7}

2 Fully factorise by first removing a common factor:

a $2x^2 + 10x + 8$
b $3x^2 - 21x + 18$
c $2x^2 + 14x + 24$
d $5x^2 - 30x - 80$
e $4x^2 - 8x - 12$
f $3x^2 - 42x + 99$
g $2x^2 - 2x - 180$
h $3x^2 - 6x - 24$
i $2x^2 + 18x + 40$
j $x^3 - 7x^2 - 8x$
k $4x^2 - 24x + 36$
l $3x^2 + 18x - 81$
m $2x^2 - 44x + 240$
n $x^3 - 3x^2 - 28x$
o $x^4 + 2x^3 + x^2$

3 Fully factorise:

a $-x^2 - 3x + 54$
b $-x^2 - 7x - 10$
c $-x^2 - 10x - 21$
d $4x - x^2 - 3$
e $-4 + 4x - x^2$
f $3 - x^2 - 2x$

4 Fully factorise:

  a $-x^2 + 2x + 48$
  b $6x - x^2 - 9$
  c $30x - 3x^2 - 63$
  d $-2x^2 + 4x + 126$
  e $20x - 2x^2 - 50$
  f $-x^3 + x^2 + 2x$

5 Given that $x^2 + bx + c = (x+m)(x+n)$, factorise $x^2 - bx + c$.

G FACTORISATION OF $ax^2 + bx + c$, $a \neq 1$

In this section we will learn how to factorise quadratic trinomials where the coefficient of x^2 is not 1, and we cannot remove a common factor.

Consider the quadratic trinomial $4x^2 + 11x + 6$.

Using the FOIL rule, we observe that
$$(4x+3)(x+2)$$
$$= 4x^2 + 8x + 3x + 6$$
$$= 4x^2 + 11x + 6$$

We will now *reverse* the process to factorise $4x^2 + 11x + 6$:

$$4x^2 + 11x + 6$$
$$= 4x^2 + 8x + 3x + 6 \quad \{\text{'splitting' the middle term}\}$$
$$= (4x^2 + 8x) + (3x + 6) \quad \{\text{grouping in pairs}\}$$
$$= 4x(x+2) + 3(x+2) \quad \{\text{factorising each pair separately}\}$$
$$= (4x+3)(x+2) \quad \{\text{completing the factorisation}\}$$

But how do we know how to correctly 'split' the middle term? How do we know that $11x$ should be written as $8x + 3x$ rather than $6x + 5x$ or $10x + x$?

INVESTIGATION 2 'SPLITTING' THE MIDDLE TERM

Consider the general quadratic trinomial $ax^2 + bx + c$.

Suppose we 'split' the middle term into $px + qx$, so $ax^2 + bx + c = ax^2 + px + qx + c$.

What to do:

1 Explain why $p + q = b$.

2 Show that $ax^2 + bx + c = x(ax + p) + (qx + c)$.

3 We can only factorise this expression further if the two terms have a common factor. This means that $ax + p = k(qx + c)$ for some k.

  a By equating coefficients, show that $kq = a$ and $kc = p$.
  b Hence, show that $pq = ac$.

This tells us that factorisation by 'splitting' the middle term only works if we can choose p and q such that $p + q = b$ and $pq = ac$.

4 Since $pq = ac$, we let $q = \dfrac{ac}{p}$. When we 'split' the middle term, we therefore either

write $ax^2 + px + \dfrac{ac}{p}x + c$ or $ax^2 + \dfrac{ac}{p}x + px + c$.

Show that factorising gives the result $\left(x + \dfrac{c}{p}\right)(ax + p)$ in either case.

ALGEBRAIC EXPANSION AND FACTORISATION (Chapter 3) 59

The following procedure is used to factorise $ax^2 + bx + c$ by 'splitting' the middle term:

Step 1: Find two numbers p and q whose sum is b and whose product is ac.

Step 2: Replace bx by $px + qx$.

Step 3: Complete the factorisation.

Example 15   Self Tutor

Factorise:

a $3x^2 + 17x + 10$ **b** $6x^2 - 11x - 10$

a For $3x^2 + 17x + 10$, $ac = 3 \times 10 = 30$ and $b = 17$.
We need two numbers with sum 17 and product 30. These are 2 and 15.
$\therefore \ 3x^2 + 17x + 10 = 3x^2 + 2x + 15x + 10$
$= x(3x + 2) + 5(3x + 2)$
$= (3x + 2)(x + 5)$

b For $6x^2 - 11x - 10$, $ac = 6 \times -10 = -60$ and $b = -11$.
We need two numbers with sum -11 and product -60. These are -15 and 4.
$\therefore \ 6x^2 - 11x - 10 = 6x^2 - 15x + 4x - 10$
$= 3x(2x - 5) + 2(2x - 5)$
$= (2x - 5)(3x + 2)$

EXERCISE 3G

1 Consider the quadratic trinomial $3x^2 + 7x + 2$.

 a Factorise the expression by 'splitting' the middle term into:
  i $+6x + x$ **ii** $+x + 6x$

 b Are your factorisations in **a** equivalent?

2 Fully factorise:

 a $2x^2 + 5x + 3$ **b** $2x^2 + 13x + 18$ **c** $7x^2 + 9x + 2$ **d** $3x^2 + 13x + 4$
 e $3x^2 + 8x + 4$ **f** $3x^2 + 16x + 21$ **g** $8x^2 + 14x + 3$ **h** $21x^2 + 17x + 2$
 i $6x^2 + 5x + 1$ **j** $6x^2 + 19x + 3$ **k** $10x^2 + 17x + 3$ **l** $14x^2 + 37x + 5$

3 Consider the quadratic trinomial $4x^2 + 4x - 3$.

 a Factorise the expression by 'splitting' the middle term into:
  i $+6x - 2x$ **ii** $-2x + 6x$

 b Are your factorisations in **a** equivalent?

4 Fully factorise:

 a $2x^2 - 9x - 5$ **b** $3x^2 + 5x - 2$ **c** $3x^2 - 5x - 2$ **d** $2x^2 + 3x - 2$
 e $2x^2 + 3x - 5$ **f** $5x^2 - 8x + 3$ **g** $11x^2 - 9x - 2$ **h** $2x^2 - 3x - 9$
 i $3x^2 - 17x + 10$ **j** $5x^2 - 13x - 6$ **k** $3x^2 + 10x - 8$ **l** $2x^2 + 17x - 9$
 m $2x^2 + 9x - 18$ **n** $15x^2 + x - 2$ **o** $21x^2 - 62x - 3$

Example 16

Fully factorise: $-5x^2 - 7x + 6$

We remove -1 as a common factor first.

$-5x^2 - 7x + 6$
$= -1[5x^2 + 7x - 6]$
$= -[5x^2 + 10x - 3x - 6]$
$= -[5x(x+2) - 3(x+2)]$
$= -[(x+2)(5x-3)]$
$= -(x+2)(5x-3)$

For $5x^2 + 7x - 6$, $ac = -30$ and $b = 7$.
The two numbers with product -30 and sum 7 are 10 and -3.

5 Fully factorise by first removing -1 as a common factor:

   a $-3x^2 - x + 14$ **b** $-5x^2 + 11x - 2$ **c** $-4x^2 - 9x + 9$
   d $-9x^2 + 12x - 4$ **e** $-8x^2 - 14x - 3$ **f** $-12x^2 + 16x + 3$

6 **a** Show that $(3x+5)^2 - (2x-3)^2 = 5x^2 + 42x + 16$ by expanding the LHS.
   b Factorise $5x^2 + 42x + 16$ by 'splitting' the middle term.
   c Factorise $(3x+5)^2 - (2x-3)^2$ using the difference of two squares.

H   MISCELLANEOUS FACTORISATION

In the following **Exercise** you will need to determine which factorisation method to use.

This flowchart may prove useful:

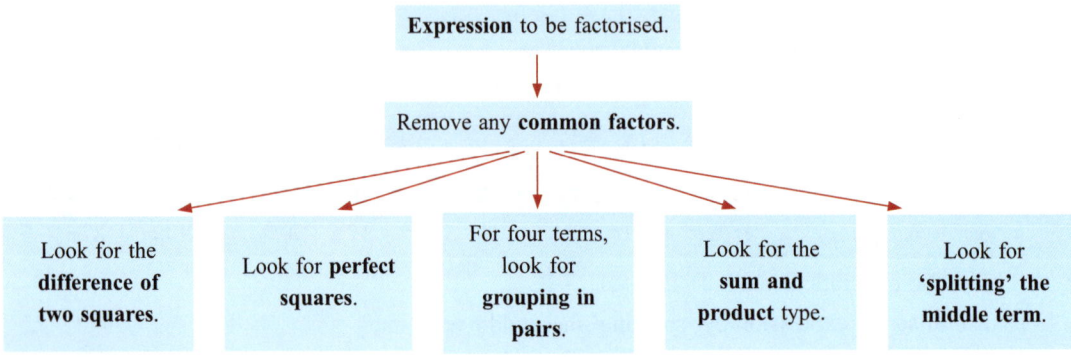

EXERCISE 3H

1 Fully factorise:

   a $3x^2 + 2x$ **b** $x^2 - 81$ **c** $2p^2 + 8$ **d** $3b^2 - 75$
   e $2x^2 - 32$ **f** $n^4 - 4n^2$ **g** $x^2 - 8x - 9$ **h** $d^2 + 6d - 7$
   i $x^2 + 8x - 9$ **j** $4t + 8t^2$ **k** $4x^2 + 12x + 5$ **l** $2g^2 - 12g - 110$
   m $4a^2 - 9d^2$ **n** $5a^2 - 5a - 10$ **o** $2c^2 - 8c + 6$ **p** $2x^2 + 17x + 21$
   q $d^4 + 2d^3 - 3d^2$ **r** $x^3 + 4x^2 + 4x$

2 Fully factorise:

a $7x - 35y$
b $2g^2 - 8$
c $-5x^2 - 10x$
d $m^2 + 3mp$
e $a^2 + 8a + 15$
f $m^2 - 6m + 9$
g $5x^2 + 5xy - 5x^2y$
h $xy + 2x + 2y + 4$
i $y^2 + 5y - 9y - 45$
j $2x^2 + 10x + x + 5$
k $3y^2 - 147$
l $6x^2 - 29x - 5$
m $4c^2 - 1$
n $3x^2 + 3x - 36$
o $2bx - 6b + 10x - 30$
p $12x^2 + 13x + 3$
q $-2x^2 - 6 + 8x$
r $16x^2 + 8x + 1$
s $4x^2 - 2x^3 - 2x$
t $(a+b)^2 - 9$
u $12x^2 - 38x + 6$

REVIEW SET 3A

1 Use the diagram alongside to show that $a(b+c) = ab + ac$.

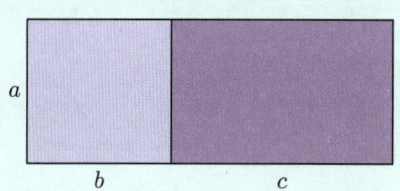

2 Expand and simplify:

a $(x+5)(x-6)$
b $(2x+5)(3x-1)$
c $(x+3)(x+2) - (2x-1)(x-6)$

3 Fully factorise:

a $7x^2 - 4x$
b $x^3 + 5x^2 - 6x$
c $x(x-8) + 5(x-8)$

4 Expand and simplify:

a $(x+5)(x-2)(x+1)$
b $(2x-3)(x^2+4x+2)$

5 Fully factorise:

a $16 - 9m^2$
b $x^3 - 81x$
c $(x+7)^2 - 25$

6 Expand and simplify:

a $(t+7)(t-7)$
b $(2y+5)(2y-5)$
c $(2m-5n)^2$

7 Fully factorise:

a $2x^2 + 20x + 50$
b $2b - dc + 2d - bc$

8 Use the binomial expansion of $(a+b)^3$ to expand and simplify:

a $(2k+3)^3$
b $(r-4t)^3$

9 Fully factorise:

a $x^2 + 7x - 18$
b $3x^2 - 9x - 30$
c $64 - 2x^2 + 8x$

10 Fully factorise:

a $8x^2 + 10x + 3$
b $5x^2 - 13x + 6$
c $-9x^2 + 3x + 2$

11 a Show that $(2x+9)^2 - (x-3)^2 = 3x^2 + 42x + 72$ by expanding the LHS.
  b Factorise $3x^2 + 42x + 72$ by first taking out a common factor.
  c Factorise $(2x+9)^2 - (x-3)^2$ using the difference of two squares.

12
  a Write down the binomial expansion of:
   i $(a+b)^2$ **ii** $(a+b)^3$ **iii** $(a+b)^4$ **iv** $(a+b)^5$
  b In $(a+b)^2 = a^2 + 2ab + b^2$, the sum of the coefficients of the expansion is $1+2+1=4$. Find the sum of the coefficients in the expansion of:
   i $(a+b)^3$ **ii** $(a+b)^4$ **iii** $(a+b)^5$
  c What do you suspect is the sum of the coefficients in the expansion of $(a+b)^n$?
  d Prove your result by letting $a=b=1$.

REVIEW SET 3B

1 Expand and simplify:
  a $5(4x-5)$ **b** $-4x(x-3)$ **c** $2(x+6) + x(3x-7)$

2 Expand and simplify:
  a $x(x^2-3) + 5(x-4)$ **b** $(a+b)(a-b) - (a+2b)(a-2b)$

3 Fully factorise:
  a $2x^2 - 98$ **b** $(3x+1)^2 - (x-4)^2$

4 Answer the **Opening Problem** on page **48**.
  Hint: The 2 digit number with digit form 'ab' represents the value $10a+b$.

5 Fully factorise:
  a $x^2 + 3x - 54$ **b** $3x^2 + 24x + 48$

6 How many terms would you obtain by expanding $(a+b+c+d)(e+f)(g+h)$?

7 Expand and simplify:
  a $(3x^2 - 5)^2$ **b** $(2a-b)^3$

8 Fully factorise:
  a $x^2 - 5x - 66$ **b** $2x^2 + 20x - 78$ **c** $4x^2 - 8x - 21$

9 Expand and simplify: $(x^2 - x + 4)(x^2 + 2x + 3)$

10 Fully factorise:
  a $-x^2 + x + 12$ **b** $-6x^2 - 5x + 50$

11 Consider factorising the expression $6x^2 + 17x + 12$.
  a Explain why the middle term $17x$ should be 'split' into $9x$ and $8x$.
  b Factorise $6x^2 + 17x + 12$ by writing $17x$ as $9x + 8x$.
  c Now factorise $6x^2 + 17x + 12$ by writing $17x$ as $8x + 9x$. Check that you get the same answer as in **b**.

12
  a Use your calculator to find:
   i 23^2 and 27^2 **ii** 18^2 and 32^2 **iii** 11^2 and 39^2 **iv** 14^2 and 36^2.
  b If a and b are two integers whose sum is 50, what can we say about the last 2 digits of the squares a^2 and b^2?
  c Prove that your answer to **b** is correct.
   Hint: Write b in terms of a, then find the difference between the two squares.

Chapter 4

Radicals and surds

Contents:
- **A** Radicals
- **B** Simplest radical form
- **C** Adding and subtracting radicals
- **D** Multiplications involving radicals
- **E** Division by radicals
- **F** Equality of surds

OPENING PROBLEM

Pamela's students claim that since an irrational number cannot be written as a fraction, it cannot be placed on a number line.

To demonstrate that an irrational length can be represented, and therefore placed on a number line, Pamela draws this figure.

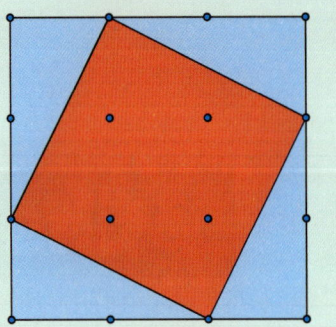

Things to think about:

a Find:
  i the area of the large square
  ii the total area of the blue triangles.
b Using your answers to **a**, find the area of the red square.
c Hence explain why the side length of the red square is $\sqrt{5}$ units.
d What is the perimeter of the red square?

A RADICALS

In **Chapter 1** we encountered values such as $\sqrt{3}$, $\sqrt{5}$, and $\sqrt[3]{8}$. These numbers are known as *radicals*.

> A **radical** is a number that is written using the radical sign $\sqrt{}$.

Radicals occur frequently in mathematics, often as solutions to equations involving squared terms. We will see a typical example of this in **Chapter 5** when we study Pythagoras' theorem.

SQUARE ROOTS

> The **square root of** a, written $\sqrt{a}$, is the *positive* solution of the equation $x^2 = a$.
>
> $\sqrt{a}$ is the *positive* number which obeys the rule $\sqrt{a} \times \sqrt{a} = a$.

For example, $\sqrt{2} \times \sqrt{2} = 2$, $\sqrt{3} \times \sqrt{3} = 3$, $\sqrt{4} \times \sqrt{4} = 4$, and so on.

We know that the square of any real number is non-negative. This means that:

> $\sqrt{a}$ is real only if $a \geqslant 0$.

HIGHER ROOTS

In this course we will concentrate mainly on square roots, but it is important to understand that other radicals exist. For example:

> The **cube root of** a, written $\sqrt[3]{a}$, satisfies the rule $\left(\sqrt[3]{a}\right)^3 = a$.
> If $a > 0$ then $\sqrt[3]{a} > 0$.
> If $a < 0$ then $\sqrt[3]{a} < 0$.

We can define higher roots in a similar way.

RATIONAL AND IRRATIONAL RADICALS

In **Chapter 2** we saw that the set of **real numbers** $\mathbb{R}$ can be divided into the set of **rational numbers** $\mathbb{Q}$, and the set of **irrational numbers** $\mathbb{Q}'$.

Remember that:

An **irrational number** is a real number which cannot be written in the form $\dfrac{p}{q}$, where p and q are integers, $q \neq 0$.

Radical numbers may be rational or irrational. An irrational radical is called a surd.

Examples of rational radicals include:

$$\sqrt{4} = 2 = \tfrac{2}{1}$$

$$\sqrt{\tfrac{9}{16}} = \sqrt{\left(\tfrac{3}{4}\right)^2} = \tfrac{3}{4}$$

Two examples of surds are $\sqrt{2} \approx 1.414\,214$
and $\sqrt{3} \approx 1.732\,051$.

If the number under the radical sign can be written as a perfect square, then the radical is rational.

HISTORICAL NOTE

When the Golden Age of the Greeks was past, the writings of the Greeks were preserved, translated into Arabic and extended by Arabic mathematicians in the regions currently known as Iraq and Iran and also in Moslem Spain. The word *surd* came about because of an error in translation.

The Greek word *alogos* meaning 'irrational', or 'without reason', was translated as the Arabic word *asamm* which means 'irrational', but also means 'deaf'. Thus rational and irrational numbers were called 'audible' and 'inaudible' numbers respectively by the Arabic mathematician **Al-Khwarizmi**, from Persia, around 825 AD.

This later led to the Arabic word *asamm* meaning 'deaf' or 'dumb' for irrational numbers being translated into Latin as *surdus* meaning 'deaf' or 'mute'. The European mathematician, Gherardo of Cremona (c. 1150), adopted the word surd.

The origin of the root symbol $\sqrt{}$ is not clear. Some sources suggest that the symbol was first used by Arabic mathematicians. It is believed that the modern square root symbol developed from the letter r which is the first letter in the Latin word radix, meaning 'root', from which we get the word *radical*.

SIMPLIFYING RADICALS

In previous years we have established that:

- $\sqrt{a} \times \sqrt{b} = \sqrt{a \times b}$ for $a \geqslant 0,\ b \geqslant 0$
- $\dfrac{\sqrt{a}}{\sqrt{b}} = \sqrt{\dfrac{a}{b}}$ for $a \geqslant 0,\ b > 0$

Example 1

Simplify:

a $(\sqrt{5})^2$ **b** $\left(\dfrac{1}{\sqrt{5}}\right)^2$

a $(\sqrt{5})^2$
$= \sqrt{5} \times \sqrt{5}$
$= 5$

b $\left(\dfrac{1}{\sqrt{5}}\right)^2$
$= \dfrac{1}{\sqrt{5}} \times \dfrac{1}{\sqrt{5}}$
$= \tfrac{1}{5}$

Example 2

Simplify:

a $(2\sqrt{5})^3$ **b** $-2\sqrt{5} \times 3\sqrt{5}$

a $(2\sqrt{5})^3$
$= 2\sqrt{5} \times 2\sqrt{5} \times 2\sqrt{5}$
$= 2 \times 2 \times 2 \times \sqrt{5} \times \sqrt{5} \times \sqrt{5}$
$= 8 \times 5 \times \sqrt{5}$
$= 40\sqrt{5}$

b $-2\sqrt{5} \times 3\sqrt{5}$
$= -2 \times 3 \times \sqrt{5} \times \sqrt{5}$
$= -6 \times 5$
$= -30$

EXERCISE 4A

1 Simplify:

- **a** $(\sqrt{7})^2$
- **b** $(\sqrt{13})^2$
- **c** $(\sqrt{15})^2$
- **d** $(\sqrt{24})^2$
- **e** $(\sqrt{2})^3$
- **f** $(\sqrt{2})^4$
- **g** $(\sqrt{2})^5$
- **h** $\left(\dfrac{1}{\sqrt{2}}\right)^2$
- **i** $\left(\dfrac{1}{\sqrt{3}}\right)^2$
- **j** $\left(\dfrac{2}{\sqrt{11}}\right)^2$
- **k** $\left(\dfrac{\sqrt{3}}{\sqrt{17}}\right)^2$
- **l** $\left(\sqrt{\dfrac{2}{23}}\right)^2$

2 Simplify:

- **a** $(\sqrt[3]{2})^3$
- **b** $(\sqrt[3]{-5})^3$
- **c** $\left(\dfrac{1}{\sqrt[3]{5}}\right)^3$

3 Simplify:

- **a** $4\sqrt{3} \times \sqrt{3}$
- **b** $3\sqrt{2} \times \sqrt{2}$
- **c** $\sqrt{5} \times 6\sqrt{5}$
- **d** $3\sqrt{2} \times 4\sqrt{2}$
- **e** $-2\sqrt{3} \times 5\sqrt{3}$
- **f** $3\sqrt{5} \times (-2\sqrt{5})$
- **g** $-2\sqrt{2} \times (-3\sqrt{2})$
- **h** $(3\sqrt{2})^2$
- **i** $(3\sqrt{2})^3$
- **j** $(4\sqrt{3})^2$
- **k** $(4\sqrt{3})^3$
- **l** $(2\sqrt{2})^4$
- **m** $\sqrt{5} \times (3\sqrt{5})^2$
- **n** $-2\sqrt{3} \times (5\sqrt{3})^2$
- **o** $(2\sqrt{2})^3 \times (-7\sqrt{2})$

RADICALS AND SURDS (Chapter 4)

Example 3

Write in simplest form:

a $\sqrt{3} \times \sqrt{2}$ **b** $2\sqrt{5} \times 3\sqrt{2}$

a $\sqrt{3} \times \sqrt{2}$
$= \sqrt{3 \times 2}$
$= \sqrt{6}$

b $2\sqrt{5} \times 3\sqrt{2}$
$= 2 \times 3 \times \sqrt{5} \times \sqrt{2}$
$= 6 \times \sqrt{5 \times 2}$
$= 6\sqrt{10}$

With practice you should not need the middle steps.

4 Simplify:

a $\sqrt{2} \times \sqrt{5}$ **b** $\sqrt{3} \times \sqrt{7}$ **c** $\sqrt{3} \times \sqrt{11}$
d $\sqrt{7} \times \sqrt{7}$ **e** $\sqrt{3} \times 2\sqrt{3}$ **f** $2\sqrt{2} \times (-\sqrt{5})$
g $3\sqrt{3} \times 2\sqrt{2}$ **h** $2\sqrt{3} \times 3\sqrt{5}$ **i** $\sqrt{2} \times \sqrt{3} \times \sqrt{5}$
j $\sqrt{3} \times \sqrt{2} \times 2\sqrt{2}$ **k** $-3\sqrt{2} \times (\sqrt{2})^3$ **l** $(3\sqrt{2})^3 \times (\sqrt{3})^3$

Example 4

Simplify: **a** $\dfrac{\sqrt{32}}{\sqrt{2}}$ **b** $\dfrac{\sqrt{12}}{2\sqrt{3}}$

a $\dfrac{\sqrt{32}}{\sqrt{2}}$
$= \sqrt{\dfrac{32}{2}}$
$= \sqrt{16}$
$= 4$

b $\dfrac{\sqrt{12}}{2\sqrt{3}}$
$= \tfrac{1}{2}\sqrt{\dfrac{12}{3}}$ {using $\dfrac{\sqrt{a}}{\sqrt{b}} = \sqrt{\dfrac{a}{b}}$}
$= \tfrac{1}{2}\sqrt{4}$
$= \tfrac{1}{2} \times 2$
$= 1$

5 Simplify:

a $\dfrac{\sqrt{8}}{\sqrt{2}}$ **b** $\dfrac{\sqrt{2}}{\sqrt{8}}$ **c** $\dfrac{\sqrt{18}}{\sqrt{2}}$ **d** $\dfrac{\sqrt{2}}{\sqrt{18}}$
e $\dfrac{\sqrt{20}}{\sqrt{5}}$ **f** $\dfrac{\sqrt{5}}{\sqrt{20}}$ **g** $\dfrac{\sqrt{27}}{\sqrt{3}}$ **h** $\dfrac{\sqrt{18}}{\sqrt{3}}$
i $\dfrac{\sqrt{3}}{\sqrt{30}}$ **j** $\dfrac{\sqrt{50}}{\sqrt{2}}$ **k** $\dfrac{2\sqrt{6}}{\sqrt{24}}$ **l** $\dfrac{5\sqrt{75}}{\sqrt{3}}$

6 Simplify:

a $\sqrt{\dfrac{1}{25}}$ **b** $\sqrt{\dfrac{16}{9}}$ **c** $\sqrt{3\tfrac{1}{16}}$ **d** $\sqrt{20\tfrac{1}{4}}$

7 a Prove that $\sqrt{a}\sqrt{b} = \sqrt{ab}$ for all positive numbers a and b.
   Hint: Consider $(\sqrt{a}\sqrt{b})^2$ and $(\sqrt{ab})^2$.

b Prove that $\dfrac{\sqrt{a}}{\sqrt{b}} = \sqrt{\dfrac{a}{b}}$ for $a \geqslant 0$ and $b > 0$.

8 **a** Is $\sqrt{9} + \sqrt{16} = \sqrt{9+16}$? Is $\sqrt{25} - \sqrt{16} = \sqrt{25-16}$?

    b Are $\sqrt{a} + \sqrt{b} = \sqrt{a+b}$ and $\sqrt{a} - \sqrt{b} = \sqrt{a-b}$ possible laws for radicals?

B   SIMPLEST RADICAL FORM

A radical is in **simplest form** when the number under the radical sign is the smallest possible integer.

Example 5   ◀) Self Tutor

Write $\sqrt{28}$ in simplest radical form.

4 is the largest perfect square factor of 28.

$\sqrt{28}$
$= \sqrt{4 \times 7}$
$= \sqrt{4} \times \sqrt{7}$
$= 2\sqrt{7}$

EXERCISE 4B

1 Write in simplest radical form:

    a $\sqrt{24}$ **b** $\sqrt{50}$ **c** $\sqrt{54}$ **d** $\sqrt{40}$

    e $\sqrt{56}$ **f** $\sqrt{63}$ **g** $\sqrt{52}$ **h** $\sqrt{44}$

    i $\sqrt{60}$ **j** $\sqrt{90}$ **k** $\sqrt{96}$ **l** $\sqrt{68}$

    m $\sqrt{175}$ **n** $\sqrt{162}$ **o** $\sqrt{128}$ **p** $\sqrt{700}$

2 Write in simplest radical form:

    a $\sqrt{\frac{5}{9}}$ **b** $\sqrt{\frac{18}{4}}$ **c** $\sqrt{\frac{12}{16}}$ **d** $\sqrt{\frac{75}{36}}$

3 Write in simplest radical form $a + b\sqrt{n}$ where $a, b \in \mathbb{Q}$, $n \in \mathbb{Z}$:

    a $\dfrac{4 + \sqrt{8}}{2}$ **b** $\dfrac{6 - \sqrt{12}}{2}$ **c** $\dfrac{4 + \sqrt{20}}{4}$ **d** $\dfrac{8 - \sqrt{32}}{4}$

    e $\dfrac{12 + \sqrt{72}}{6}$ **f** $\dfrac{18 + \sqrt{27}}{6}$ **g** $\dfrac{14 - \sqrt{60}}{8}$ **h** $\dfrac{5 - \sqrt{200}}{10}$

C   ADDING AND SUBTRACTING RADICALS

We can add and subtract 'like' radicals in the same way as we do 'like' terms in algebra.

For example:

- just as $3a + 2a = 5a$, $3\sqrt{2} + 2\sqrt{2} = 5\sqrt{2}$
- just as $6b - 4b = 2b$, $6\sqrt{3} - 4\sqrt{3} = 2\sqrt{3}$.

Example 6

Simplify:

a $3\sqrt{2} - 4\sqrt{2}$ **b** $5\sqrt{3} + 2\sqrt{5} - \sqrt{3} + 7\sqrt{5}$

a $\quad 3\sqrt{2} - 4\sqrt{2}$
$\quad = -1\sqrt{2}$
$\quad = -\sqrt{2}$

b 'like' radicals: $5\sqrt{3} + 2\sqrt{5} - \sqrt{3} + 7\sqrt{5}$
$\quad = 4\sqrt{3} + 9\sqrt{5}$

We write the whole number first, then the radical. So, we write $4\sqrt{3}$ not $\sqrt{3}4$.

EXERCISE 4C

1 Simplify:

   a $3\sqrt{2} + 7\sqrt{2}$ **b** $11\sqrt{3} - 8\sqrt{3}$ **c** $6\sqrt{5} - 7\sqrt{5}$

   d $-\sqrt{10} + 2\sqrt{10}$ **e** $\sqrt{6} + 7\sqrt{6} - 3\sqrt{6}$ **f** $9\sqrt{15} - 4\sqrt{15} - 11\sqrt{15}$

2 Simplify:

   a $5\sqrt{2} - \sqrt{3} + \sqrt{2} - \sqrt{3}$ **b** $4\sqrt{7} + 5\sqrt{6} + 3\sqrt{7} - 2\sqrt{6}$

   c $9\sqrt{10} - 5\sqrt{5} + 8\sqrt{5} - \sqrt{10}$ **d** $11\sqrt{3} - 8\sqrt{13} + \sqrt{13} - 13\sqrt{3}$

   e $\sqrt{7} + 5\sqrt{11} + 9\sqrt{7} - 4\sqrt{7}$ **f** $-6\sqrt{14} - 3\sqrt{14} - 2\sqrt{6} + 10\sqrt{14}$

   g $14 + 6\sqrt{17} - 8\sqrt{17} - 3$ **h** $-8 - \sqrt{15} + 7\sqrt{15} - 13$

Example 7

Simplify: $\dfrac{\sqrt{7}}{2} + \dfrac{\sqrt{7}}{3}$

$\dfrac{\sqrt{7}}{2} + \dfrac{\sqrt{7}}{3} \quad \{\text{LCD} = 6\}$

$= \dfrac{\sqrt{7} \times 3}{2 \times 3} + \dfrac{\sqrt{7} \times 2}{3 \times 2}$

$= \dfrac{3\sqrt{7}}{6} + \dfrac{2\sqrt{7}}{6}$

$= \dfrac{3\sqrt{7} + 2\sqrt{7}}{6}$

$= \dfrac{5\sqrt{7}}{6}$

3 Simplify:

   a $\dfrac{\sqrt{5}}{3} + \dfrac{\sqrt{5}}{4}$ **b** $\dfrac{\sqrt{6}}{2} - \dfrac{\sqrt{6}}{7}$ **c** $\dfrac{5\sqrt{3}}{6} + \dfrac{\sqrt{3}}{8}$

   d $\dfrac{2\sqrt{11}}{9} - \dfrac{8\sqrt{11}}{15}$ **e** $\dfrac{\sqrt{10}}{2} + \dfrac{\sqrt{10}}{3} + \dfrac{\sqrt{10}}{4}$ **f** $\sqrt{2} + \dfrac{5\sqrt{2}}{14} - \dfrac{7\sqrt{2}}{4}$

4 Show that:

   a $\sqrt{20} + \sqrt{5} = \sqrt{45}$ **b** $\sqrt{147} - \sqrt{75} = \sqrt{12}$

5 Answer the **Opening Problem** on page **64**.

D MULTIPLICATIONS INVOLVING RADICALS

The rules for expanding expressions containing radicals are identical to those for ordinary algebra.

$$a(b+c) = ab + ac$$
$$(a+b)(c+d) = ac + ad + bc + bd$$
$$(a+b)^2 = a^2 + 2ab + b^2$$
$$(a+b)(a-b) = a^2 - b^2$$

Example 8 ◀)) Self Tutor

Expand and simplify:

a $\sqrt{2}(\sqrt{2} + \sqrt{3})$ **b** $\sqrt{3}(6 - 2\sqrt{3})$

a $\sqrt{2}(\sqrt{2} + \sqrt{3})$
    $= \sqrt{2} \times \sqrt{2} + \sqrt{2} \times \sqrt{3}$
    $= 2 + \sqrt{6}$

b $\sqrt{3}(6 - 2\sqrt{3})$
    $= \sqrt{3} \times 6 + \sqrt{3} \times (-2\sqrt{3})$
    $= 6\sqrt{3} - 6$

With practice you should not need all of the steps.

EXERCISE 4D

1 Expand and simplify:

   a $\sqrt{2}(\sqrt{5} + \sqrt{2})$ **b** $\sqrt{2}(3 - \sqrt{2})$ **c** $\sqrt{3}(\sqrt{3} + 1)$
   d $\sqrt{3}(1 - \sqrt{3})$ **e** $\sqrt{7}(7 - \sqrt{7})$ **f** $\sqrt{5}(2 - \sqrt{5})$
   g $\sqrt{11}(2\sqrt{11} - 1)$ **h** $\sqrt{6}(1 - 2\sqrt{6})$ **i** $\sqrt{3}(\sqrt{3} + \sqrt{2} - 1)$
   j $2\sqrt{3}(\sqrt{3} - \sqrt{5})$ **k** $2\sqrt{5}(3 - \sqrt{5})$ **l** $3\sqrt{5}(2\sqrt{5} + \sqrt{2})$

Example 9 ◀)) Self Tutor

Expand and simplify:

a $-\sqrt{2}(\sqrt{2} + 3)$ **b** $-\sqrt{3}(7 - 2\sqrt{3})$

a $-\sqrt{2}(\sqrt{2} + 3)$
    $= -\sqrt{2} \times \sqrt{2} + -\sqrt{2} \times 3$
    $= -2 - 3\sqrt{2}$

b $-\sqrt{3}(7 - 2\sqrt{3})$
    $= -\sqrt{3} \times 7 + -\sqrt{3} \times (-2\sqrt{3})$
    $= -7\sqrt{3} + 6$

2 Expand and simplify:

   a $-\sqrt{2}(3 - \sqrt{2})$ **b** $-\sqrt{2}(\sqrt{2} + \sqrt{3})$ **c** $-\sqrt{2}(4 - \sqrt{2})$
   d $-\sqrt{3}(1 + \sqrt{3})$ **e** $-\sqrt{3}(\sqrt{3} + 2)$ **f** $-\sqrt{5}(2 + \sqrt{5})$
   g $-(\sqrt{2} + 3)$ **h** $-\sqrt{5}(\sqrt{5} - 4)$ **i** $-(3 - \sqrt{7})$
   j $-\sqrt{11}(2 - \sqrt{11})$ **k** $-(\sqrt{3} - \sqrt{7})$ **l** $-2\sqrt{2}(1 - \sqrt{2})$
   m $-3\sqrt{3}(5 - \sqrt{3})$ **n** $-7\sqrt{2}(\sqrt{2} + \sqrt{6})$ **o** $(-\sqrt{2})^3(3 - \sqrt{2})$

Example 10

Expand and simplify: $(3 - \sqrt{2})(4 + 2\sqrt{2})$

$(3 - \sqrt{2})(4 + 2\sqrt{2})$
$= 12 + 3 \times 2\sqrt{2} + (-\sqrt{2}) \times 4 + (-\sqrt{2}) \times 2\sqrt{2}$ {FOIL rule}
$= 12 + 6\sqrt{2} - 4\sqrt{2} - 4$
$= 8 + 2\sqrt{2}$

3 Expand and simplify:

- **a** $(1 + \sqrt{2})(2 + \sqrt{2})$
- **b** $(2 + \sqrt{3})(2 + \sqrt{3})$
- **c** $(\sqrt{3} + 2)(\sqrt{3} - 1)$
- **d** $(4 - \sqrt{2})(3 + \sqrt{2})$
- **e** $(1 + \sqrt{3})(1 - \sqrt{3})$
- **f** $(5 + \sqrt{7})(2 - \sqrt{7})$
- **g** $(\sqrt{5} + 2)(\sqrt{5} - 3)$
- **h** $(2\sqrt{2} + \sqrt{3})(\sqrt{2} - \sqrt{3})$
- **i** $(4 - \sqrt{2})(3 - \sqrt{2})$

Example 11

Expand and simplify:
- **a** $(\sqrt{3} + 2)^2$
- **b** $(\sqrt{3} - \sqrt{7})^2$

a $(\sqrt{3} + 2)^2$
$= (\sqrt{3})^2 + 2 \times \sqrt{3} \times 2 + 2^2$
$= 3 + 4\sqrt{3} + 4$
$= 7 + 4\sqrt{3}$

b $(\sqrt{3} - \sqrt{7})^2$
$= (\sqrt{3})^2 + 2 \times \sqrt{3} \times (-\sqrt{7}) + (-\sqrt{7})^2$
$= 3 - 2\sqrt{21} + 7$
$= 10 - 2\sqrt{21}$

4 Expand and simplify:

- **a** $(1 + \sqrt{2})^2$
- **b** $(2 - \sqrt{3})^2$
- **c** $(\sqrt{3} + 2)^2$
- **d** $(1 + \sqrt{5})^2$
- **e** $(\sqrt{2} - \sqrt{3})^2$
- **f** $(5 - \sqrt{2})^2$
- **g** $(\sqrt{2} + \sqrt{7})^2$
- **h** $(4 - \sqrt{6})^2$
- **i** $(\sqrt{6} - \sqrt{2})^2$
- **j** $(\sqrt{5} + 2\sqrt{2})^2$
- **k** $(\sqrt{5} - 2\sqrt{2})^2$
- **l** $(6 + \sqrt{8})^2$
- **m** $(5\sqrt{2} - 1)^2$
- **n** $(3 - 2\sqrt{2})^2$
- **o** $(1 + 3\sqrt{2})^2$

5 Use the binomial expansion for $(a + b)^3$ to write the following in simplest radical form:

- **a** $(3 + \sqrt{7})^3$
- **b** $(\sqrt{3} - \sqrt{2})^3$

Example 12

Expand and simplify:
- **a** $(3 + \sqrt{2})(3 - \sqrt{2})$
- **b** $(2\sqrt{3} - 5)(2\sqrt{3} + 5)$

a $(3 + \sqrt{2})(3 - \sqrt{2})$
$= 3^2 - (\sqrt{2})^2$
$= 9 - 2$
$= 7$

b $(2\sqrt{3} - 5)(2\sqrt{3} + 5)$
$= (2\sqrt{3})^2 - 5^2$
$= (4 \times 3) - 25$
$= 12 - 25$
$= -13$

Did you notice that these answers are **integers**?

6 Expand and simplify:

a $(4+\sqrt{3})(4-\sqrt{3})$ b $(5-\sqrt{2})(5+\sqrt{2})$ c $(\sqrt{5}-2)(\sqrt{5}+2)$

d $(\sqrt{7}+4)(\sqrt{7}-4)$ e $(3\sqrt{2}+2)(3\sqrt{2}-2)$ f $(2\sqrt{5}-1)(2\sqrt{5}+1)$

g $(5-3\sqrt{3})(5+3\sqrt{3})$ h $(2-4\sqrt{2})(2+4\sqrt{2})$ i $(1+5\sqrt{7})(1-5\sqrt{7})$

7 Expand and simplify:

a $(\sqrt{3}+\sqrt{2})(\sqrt{3}-\sqrt{2})$ b $(\sqrt{7}+\sqrt{11})(\sqrt{7}-\sqrt{11})$ c $(\sqrt{x}-\sqrt{y})(\sqrt{y}+\sqrt{x})$

d $(3\sqrt{2}+\sqrt{3})(3\sqrt{2}-\sqrt{3})$ e $(3\sqrt{3}+\sqrt{7})(3\sqrt{3}-\sqrt{7})$ f $(2\sqrt{5}-3\sqrt{2})(3\sqrt{2}+2\sqrt{5})$

E DIVISION BY RADICALS

When an expression involves division by a radical, we can write the expression with an **integer denominator** which does **not** contain radicals.

If the denominator contains a simple radical such as $\sqrt{a}$ then we use the rule $\sqrt{a} \times \sqrt{a} = a$.

For example, consider $\dfrac{6}{\sqrt{3}}$.

Since $\dfrac{\sqrt{3}}{\sqrt{3}} = 1$, we can multiply $\dfrac{6}{\sqrt{3}}$ by $\dfrac{\sqrt{3}}{\sqrt{3}}$ without changing its value.

$$\dfrac{6}{\sqrt{3}} = \dfrac{6}{\sqrt{3}} \times \dfrac{\sqrt{3}}{\sqrt{3}}$$
$$= \dfrac{6 \times \sqrt{3}}{\sqrt{3} \times \sqrt{3}}$$
$$= \dfrac{6\sqrt{3}}{3} \quad \{\text{since } \sqrt{a} \times \sqrt{a} = a\}$$
$$= 2\sqrt{3}$$

This process is called "rationalising the denominator".

Example 13   ◀)) Self Tutor

Express with integer denominator:

a $\dfrac{7}{\sqrt{3}}$ b $\dfrac{10}{\sqrt{5}}$ c $\dfrac{10}{2\sqrt{2}}$

a $\dfrac{7}{\sqrt{3}}$
$= \dfrac{7}{\sqrt{3}} \times \dfrac{\sqrt{3}}{\sqrt{3}}$
$= \dfrac{7\sqrt{3}}{3}$

b $\dfrac{10}{\sqrt{5}}$
$= \dfrac{10}{\sqrt{5}} \times \dfrac{\sqrt{5}}{\sqrt{5}}$
$= \dfrac{10\sqrt{5}}{5}$
$= 2\sqrt{5}$

c $\dfrac{10}{2\sqrt{2}}$
$= \dfrac{10}{2\sqrt{2}} \times \dfrac{\sqrt{2}}{\sqrt{2}}$
$= \dfrac{10\sqrt{2}}{4}$
$= \dfrac{5\sqrt{2}}{2}$

Now suppose the denominator has the form $a + b\sqrt{c}$.

The **radical conjugate** of $a + b\sqrt{c}$ is $a - b\sqrt{c}$.

The product of the radical conjugates is $(a + b\sqrt{c})(a - b\sqrt{c}) = a^2 - (b\sqrt{c})^2$
$= a^2 - b^2 c$

which does not involve a radical.

So, given a denominator of the form $a + b\sqrt{c}$, we multiply the fraction by $\dfrac{a - b\sqrt{c}}{a - b\sqrt{c}}$.

Example 14 ◀)) Self Tutor

Express $\dfrac{1}{3 + 5\sqrt{2}}$ with integer denominator.

$\dfrac{1}{3 + 5\sqrt{2}} = \left(\dfrac{1}{3 + 5\sqrt{2}}\right)\left(\dfrac{3 - 5\sqrt{2}}{3 - 5\sqrt{2}}\right)$

$= \dfrac{3 - 5\sqrt{2}}{3^2 - (5\sqrt{2})^2}$ {using $(a+b)(a-b) = a^2 - b^2$}

$= \dfrac{3 - 5\sqrt{2}}{9 - 50}$

$= \dfrac{5\sqrt{2} - 3}{41}$

We are really multiplying by one, which does not change the value of the original expression.

EXERCISE 4E

1 Express with integer denominator:

a $\dfrac{1}{\sqrt{2}}$
b $\dfrac{2}{\sqrt{2}}$
c $\dfrac{4}{\sqrt{2}}$
d $\dfrac{\sqrt{3}}{\sqrt{2}}$
e $\dfrac{\sqrt{7}}{3\sqrt{2}}$

f $\dfrac{1}{\sqrt{3}}$
g $\dfrac{3}{\sqrt{3}}$
h $\dfrac{4}{\sqrt{3}}$
i $\dfrac{\sqrt{7}}{\sqrt{3}}$
j $\dfrac{\sqrt{11}}{4\sqrt{3}}$

k $\dfrac{1}{\sqrt{5}}$
l $\dfrac{3}{\sqrt{5}}$
m $\dfrac{15}{\sqrt{5}}$
n $\dfrac{\sqrt{3}}{\sqrt{5}}$
o $\dfrac{125}{2\sqrt{5}}$

p $\dfrac{\sqrt{10}}{\sqrt{2}}$
q $\dfrac{1}{2\sqrt{3}}$
r $\dfrac{2\sqrt{2}}{\sqrt{3}}$
s $\dfrac{15}{2\sqrt{5}}$
t $\dfrac{1}{(\sqrt{2})^3}$

2 Express with integer denominator:

a $\dfrac{1}{3 - \sqrt{5}}$
b $\dfrac{1}{2 + \sqrt{3}}$
c $\dfrac{1}{4 - \sqrt{11}}$
d $\dfrac{\sqrt{2}}{5 + \sqrt{2}}$

e $\dfrac{\sqrt{3}}{3 + \sqrt{3}}$
f $\dfrac{5}{2 - 3\sqrt{2}}$
g $\dfrac{-\sqrt{5}}{3 + 2\sqrt{5}}$
h $\dfrac{3 - 2\sqrt{7}}{2 + 3\sqrt{7}}$

3 Write in the form $a + b\sqrt{2}$ where $a, b \in \mathbb{Q}$:

a $\dfrac{4}{2 - \sqrt{2}}$
b $\dfrac{-5}{1 + \sqrt{2}}$
c $\dfrac{1 - \sqrt{2}}{1 + \sqrt{2}}$
d $\dfrac{\sqrt{2} - 2}{3 - \sqrt{2}}$

e $\dfrac{\frac{1}{\sqrt{2}}}{1 - \frac{1}{\sqrt{2}}}$
f $\dfrac{1 + \frac{1}{\sqrt{2}}}{1 - \frac{1}{\sqrt{2}}}$
g $\dfrac{1}{1 - \frac{\sqrt{2}}{3}}$
h $\dfrac{\frac{\sqrt{2}}{2} + 1}{1 - \frac{\sqrt{2}}{4}}$

Example 15

Write $\dfrac{\sqrt{3}}{1-\sqrt{3}} - \dfrac{1-2\sqrt{3}}{1+\sqrt{3}}$ in simplest form.

$$\dfrac{\sqrt{3}}{1-\sqrt{3}} - \dfrac{1-2\sqrt{3}}{1+\sqrt{3}} = \left(\dfrac{\sqrt{3}}{1-\sqrt{3}}\right)\left(\dfrac{1+\sqrt{3}}{1+\sqrt{3}}\right) - \left(\dfrac{1-2\sqrt{3}}{1+\sqrt{3}}\right)\left(\dfrac{1-\sqrt{3}}{1-\sqrt{3}}\right)$$

$$= \dfrac{\sqrt{3}+3}{1-3} - \dfrac{1-\sqrt{3}-2\sqrt{3}+6}{1-3}$$

$$= \dfrac{\sqrt{3}+3}{-2} - \dfrac{7-3\sqrt{3}}{-2}$$

$$= \dfrac{\sqrt{3}+3-7+3\sqrt{3}}{-2}$$

$$= \dfrac{-4+4\sqrt{3}}{-2}$$

$$= \dfrac{-4}{-2} + \dfrac{4\sqrt{3}}{-2}$$

$$= 2 - 2\sqrt{3}$$

4 Write in simplest form:

a $\dfrac{1+\sqrt{2}}{1-\sqrt{2}} + \dfrac{1-\sqrt{2}}{1+\sqrt{2}}$

b $\dfrac{2+\sqrt{5}}{2-\sqrt{5}} - \dfrac{\sqrt{5}}{2+\sqrt{5}}$

c $\dfrac{4-\sqrt{3}}{3-2\sqrt{2}} - \dfrac{2\sqrt{3}}{3+2\sqrt{2}}$

5 **a** Suppose a and b are positive integers. Show that $(\sqrt{a}+\sqrt{b})(\sqrt{a}-\sqrt{b})$ is also an integer.

b Write with an integer denominator:

i $\dfrac{4}{\sqrt{7}+\sqrt{2}}$

ii $\dfrac{2\sqrt{5}}{\sqrt{5}-\sqrt{2}}$

iii $\dfrac{\sqrt{3}+2\sqrt{13}}{\sqrt{3}-\sqrt{13}}$

6 Write $\sqrt{\dfrac{3+2\sqrt{2}}{3-2\sqrt{2}}}$ in the form $a+b\sqrt{2}$ where $a, b \in \mathbb{Q}$.

7 If $\dfrac{1}{\sqrt{3}} - \dfrac{1}{\sqrt{2}} = p$, find $\sqrt{6}$ in terms of p.

8 If $x = \sqrt{5} - \sqrt{3}$, find x^2 and hence show that $x^4 - 16x^2 + 4 = 0$.
You have just shown that one solution of $x^4 - 16x^2 + 4 = 0$ is $x = \sqrt{5} - \sqrt{3}$.

9 Suppose $u_n = \dfrac{1}{\sqrt{5}}\left[\left(\dfrac{1+\sqrt{5}}{2}\right)^n - \left(\dfrac{1-\sqrt{5}}{2}\right)^n\right]$. Evaluate u_n for $n = 1, 2, 3, 4, 5,$ and 6.

F EQUALITY OF SURDS

We have discussed how irrational radicals such as $\sqrt{2}$, $\sqrt{3}$, $\sqrt{5}$, and $\sqrt{6}$ are also known as **surds**. In this section we develop a theorem for the equality of surds which does *not* hold for rational radicals.

Following is the traditional **proof by contradiction** that $\sqrt{2}$ is an irrational number.

Proof: Suppose $\sqrt{2}$ is rational.

$\therefore \ \sqrt{2} = \dfrac{p}{q}$ where p and q are integers, $q \neq 0$, and where all common factors of p and q have been cancelled.

Now $2 = \dfrac{p^2}{q^2}$ {squaring both sides}

$\therefore \ p^2 = 2q^2$
$\therefore \ p^2$ is even {as it has a factor of 2 and q^2 is an integer}
$\therefore \ p$ is even. .... (1)

$\therefore$ we can write $p = 2k$ where k is some integer

$\therefore \ (2k)^2 = 2q^2$
$\therefore \ 2q^2 = 4k^2$
$\therefore \ q^2 = 2k^2$ where k^2 is an integer.

$\therefore \ q^2$ is even and so q is even .... (2)

From (1) and (2) we have a contradiction to our supposition, since if both p and q are even then they share a common factor of 2.

$\therefore$ the supposition is false, and hence $\sqrt{2}$ must be irrational.

An immediate consequence of $\sqrt{2}$ being irrational is:

> If a, b, c, and d are rational, and $a + b\sqrt{2} = c + d\sqrt{2}$, then $a = c$ and $b = d$.

Proof: Suppose a, b, c, and d are rational. Assume that $b \neq d$.

So, $a + b\sqrt{2} = c + d\sqrt{2}$ gives
$a - c = (d - b)\sqrt{2}$ .... (1)
$\therefore \ \dfrac{a-c}{d-b} = \sqrt{2}$ where the LHS exists as $b \neq d$.

However, this result is impossible as the LHS is rational and the RHS is irrational.

Thus the assumption is false, and so $b = d$.

$\therefore$ using (1), $a - c = 0$, and so $a = c$.

THEOREM FOR EQUALITY OF SURDS

> Suppose $\sqrt{k}$ is irrational, and that a, b, c, and d are rational.
> If $a + b\sqrt{k} = c + d\sqrt{k}$ then $a = c$ and $b = d$.

We can easily show by counter-example that this theorem does not hold for rational radicals.

For example, $1 + 4\sqrt{4} = 3 + 3\sqrt{4}$ but $1 \neq 3$ and $4 \neq 3$.

Example 16

Solve for x and y given that they are rational:

a $x + y\sqrt{2} = 5 - 6\sqrt{2}$

b $(x + y\sqrt{2})(3 - \sqrt{2}) = -2\sqrt{2}$

a Since $\sqrt{2}$ is irrational,
$x = 5$ and $y = -6$.

b $(x + y\sqrt{2})(3 - \sqrt{2}) = -2\sqrt{2}$

$\therefore\ x + y\sqrt{2} = \dfrac{-2\sqrt{2}}{3 - \sqrt{2}}$

$= \left(\dfrac{-2\sqrt{2}}{3 - \sqrt{2}}\right)\left(\dfrac{3 + \sqrt{2}}{3 + \sqrt{2}}\right)$

$= \dfrac{-6\sqrt{2} - 4}{9 - 2}$

$= \dfrac{-4 - 6\sqrt{2}}{7}$

$= -\dfrac{4}{7} - \dfrac{6}{7}\sqrt{2}$

$\therefore$ since $\sqrt{2}$ is irrational, $x = -\dfrac{4}{7}$ and $y = -\dfrac{6}{7}$.

Example 17

Find rationals a and b such that $(a + 2\sqrt{2})(3 - \sqrt{2}) = 5 + b\sqrt{2}$.

$(a + 2\sqrt{2})(3 - \sqrt{2}) = 5 + b\sqrt{2}$

$\therefore\ 3a - a\sqrt{2} + 6\sqrt{2} - 4 = 5 + b\sqrt{2}$

$\therefore\ (3a - 4) + (6 - a)\sqrt{2} = 5 + b\sqrt{2}$

$\therefore$ since $\sqrt{2}$ is irrational, $3a - 4 = 5$ and $6 - a = b$

$\therefore\ 3a = 9$

$\therefore\ a = 3$ and hence $b = 6 - 3 = 3$

EXERCISE 4F

1 Solve for x and y given that they are rational:

a $x + y\sqrt{2} = 3 + 2\sqrt{2}$

b $15 - 4\sqrt{2} = x + y\sqrt{2}$

c $-x + y\sqrt{2} = 11 - 3\sqrt{2}$

d $x + y\sqrt{2} = 6$

e $x + y\sqrt{2} = -3\sqrt{2}$

f $x + y\sqrt{2} = 0$

2 Solve for x and y given that they are rational:

a $(x + y\sqrt{2})(2 - \sqrt{2}) = 1 + \sqrt{2}$

b $(x + y\sqrt{2})(3 + \sqrt{2}) = 1$

c $(2 - 3\sqrt{2})(x + y\sqrt{2}) = \sqrt{2}$

d $(x + y\sqrt{2})(3 - \sqrt{2}) = -4\sqrt{2}$

3 Find rationals a and b such that:

a $(a + \sqrt{2})(2 - \sqrt{2}) = 4 - b\sqrt{2}$

b $(a + 3\sqrt{2})(3 - \sqrt{2}) = 6 + b\sqrt{2}$

c $(a + b\sqrt{2})^2 = 33 + 20\sqrt{2}$

d $(a + b\sqrt{2})^2 = 41 - 24\sqrt{2}$

4 Find $\sqrt{11 - 6\sqrt{2}}$.   **Hint:** $\sqrt{2}$ is never negative.

5 a Write $\sqrt{11+4\sqrt{6}}$ in the form $a\sqrt{2}+b\sqrt{3}$ where $a, b \in \mathbb{Q}$.

b Can $\sqrt{11+4\sqrt{6}}$ be written in the form $a+b\sqrt{6}$ where $a, b \in \mathbb{Q}$? Explain your answer.

INVESTIGATION — CONTINUED SQUARE ROOTS

$X = \sqrt{2+\sqrt{2+\sqrt{2+\sqrt{2+\sqrt{2+....}}}}}$ is an example of a **continued square root**.

Some continued square roots can be simplified to integers.

What to do:

1 Use your calculator to find, correct to 6 decimal places:

  a $\sqrt{2}$ **b** $\sqrt{2+\sqrt{2}}$ **c** $\sqrt{2+\sqrt{2+\sqrt{2}}}$

  d $\sqrt{2+\sqrt{2+\sqrt{2+\sqrt{2}}}}$ **e** $\sqrt{2+\sqrt{2+\sqrt{2+\sqrt{2+\sqrt{2}}}}}$

2 Continue the process and hence predict the value of X.

3 Use algebra to find the value of X.
   Hint: Find X^2 in terms of X.

4 Work your algebraic solution in **3** backwards to find a continued square root whose value is 3.

REVIEW SET 4A

1 Simplify:

  a $(3\sqrt{2})^2$ **b** $-2\sqrt{3} \times 4\sqrt{3}$ **c** $3\sqrt{2} - \sqrt{8}$

  d $(\sqrt[3]{-27})^3$ **e** $(5\sqrt{3})^3 \times (\sqrt{2})^4$ **f** $\sqrt{\frac{81}{256}}$

2 Write in simplest radical form:

  a $\sqrt{48}$ **b** $\sqrt{864}$

3 Simplify:

  a $2\sqrt{3} + 6\sqrt{5} - 3\sqrt{3} - 4\sqrt{5}$ **b** $\frac{\sqrt{6}}{3} - \frac{\sqrt{6}}{4} + \frac{2\sqrt{6}}{5}$

4 Expand and simplify:

  a $2\sqrt{3}(4-\sqrt{3})$ **b** $(3-\sqrt{7})^2$ **c** $(2-\sqrt{3})(2+\sqrt{3})$

  d $(3+2\sqrt{5})(2-\sqrt{5})$ **e** $(4-\sqrt{2})(3+2\sqrt{2})$ **f** $(\sqrt{7}+3\sqrt{8})^2$

5 Express with integer denominator:

  a $\frac{8}{\sqrt{2}}$ **b** $\frac{15}{\sqrt{3}}$ **c** $\frac{\sqrt{3}}{4+\sqrt{2}}$ **d** $\frac{5}{6-2\sqrt{3}}$

6 Write $\sqrt{\frac{1}{7}}$ in the form $k\sqrt{7}$.

7 Use the binomial expansion for $(a+b)^3$ to write $(5+\sqrt{2})^3$ in the form $a + b\sqrt{2}$ where $a, b \in \mathbb{Z}$.

8 Write in the form $a + b\sqrt{3}$ where $a, b \in \mathbb{Q}$:

   a $\dfrac{\frac{\sqrt{3}}{2} + 1}{1 - \frac{\sqrt{3}}{2}}$ **b** $\dfrac{2+\sqrt{3}}{2-\sqrt{3}} - \dfrac{2\sqrt{3}}{2+\sqrt{3}}$

9 Write with integer denominator: $\dfrac{2\sqrt{5} - \sqrt{7}}{\sqrt{5} + 2\sqrt{7}}$

10 Find $x, y \in \mathbb{Q}$ such that $(3 + x\sqrt{5})(\sqrt{5} - y) = -13 + 5\sqrt{5}$.

REVIEW SET 4B

1 Simplify:

   a $2\sqrt{3} \times 3\sqrt{5}$ **b** $(2\sqrt{5})^2$ **c** $5\sqrt{2} - 7\sqrt{2}$

   d $-\sqrt{2}(2 - \sqrt{2})$ **e** $(\sqrt{3})^4$ **f** $\sqrt{3} \times \sqrt{5} \times \sqrt{15}$

2 Write $\sqrt{75}$ in simplest radical form.

3 Write in simplest radical form $a + b\sqrt{n}$ where $a, b \in \mathbb{Q}, n \in \mathbb{Z}$:

   a $\dfrac{3 + \sqrt{24}}{2}$ **b** $\dfrac{8 - \sqrt{72}}{4}$

4 Expand and simplify:

   a $(5 - \sqrt{3})(5 + \sqrt{3})$ **b** $-(2 - \sqrt{5})^2$

   c $2\sqrt{3}(\sqrt{3} - 1) - 2\sqrt{3}$ **d** $(2\sqrt{2} - 5)(1 - \sqrt{2})$

5 Express with integer denominator:

   a $\dfrac{14}{\sqrt{2}}$ **b** $\dfrac{\sqrt{2}}{1 - \sqrt{3}}$ **c** $\dfrac{\sqrt{2}}{1 + 3\sqrt{2}}$ **d** $\dfrac{-5}{5 - 2\sqrt{3}}$

6 Use the binomial expansion $(a+b)^4 = a^4 + 4a^3b + 6a^2b^2 + 4ab^3 + b^4$ to write $(\sqrt{2} + \sqrt{3})^4$ in simplest radical form.

7 Write in the form $a + b\sqrt{5}$ where $a, b \in \mathbb{Q}$:

   a $\dfrac{1 - \frac{1}{\sqrt{5}}}{2\sqrt{5} + \frac{1}{\sqrt{5}}}$ **b** $\dfrac{3 - \sqrt{5}}{3 + \sqrt{5}} - \dfrac{4}{3 - \sqrt{5}}$ **c** $\sqrt{\dfrac{3 - \sqrt{5}}{3 + \sqrt{5}}}$

8 Write in simplest form:

   a $\dfrac{2 - \sqrt{2}}{1 + \sqrt{2}} - \dfrac{1 + \sqrt{2}}{1 - \sqrt{2}}$ **b** $\dfrac{2 + \sqrt{3}}{1 + 2\sqrt{3}} + \dfrac{-2\sqrt{3}}{1 - 2\sqrt{3}}$

9 Write $\sqrt{\dfrac{3\sqrt{2} + 1}{3\sqrt{2} - 1}}$ in the form $a\sqrt{b} + c\sqrt{d}$.

10 Find $p, q \in \mathbb{Q}$ such that $(p + 3\sqrt{7})(5 + q\sqrt{7}) = 9\sqrt{7} - 53$.

Chapter 5

Pythagoras' theorem

Contents:
- **A** Pythagoras' theorem
- **B** The converse of Pythagoras' theorem
- **C** Pythagorean triples
- **D** Problem solving using Pythagoras
- **E** Circle problems
- **F** 3-dimensional problems

OPENING PROBLEM

Sven has challenged Jill to a swimming race in a lake. Both swimmers will swim from A to B, but each needs to touch a buoy along the way. Sven thinks he is a very good swimmer, so he will swim to buoy C on his way to B. Jill will swim to buoy D, as shown.

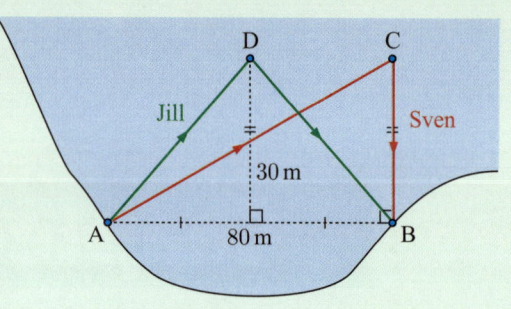

Things to think about:

a How far will Sven swim?

b How far will Jill swim?

c How much further will Sven swim than Jill?

A   PYTHAGORAS' THEOREM

A **right angled triangle** is a triangle which has a right angle as one of its angles.

The side opposite the right angle is called the **hypotenuse**, and is the **longest** side of the triangle.

The other two sides are called the **legs** of the triangle.

Around 500 BC, the Greek mathematician **Pythagoras** discovered a rule which connects the lengths of the sides of right angled triangles.

PYTHAGORAS' THEOREM

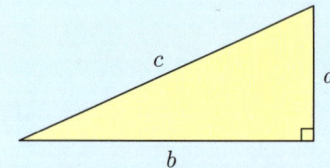

In a right angled triangle with hypotenuse c and legs a and b, $c^2 = a^2 + b^2$.

GEOMETRY PACKAGE

RESEARCH

The Persian mathematician **Al-Nayrīzī** (865 - 922 AD) came from Nayriz, Iran. Around 900 AD, he used the tiling arrangement shown to prove Pythagoras' theorem.

Research the method of **five-piece dissection** he used for his proof.

In geometric form, **Pythagoras' theorem** states that:

In any right angled triangle, the area of the square on the hypotenuse is equal to the sum of the areas of the squares on the other two sides.

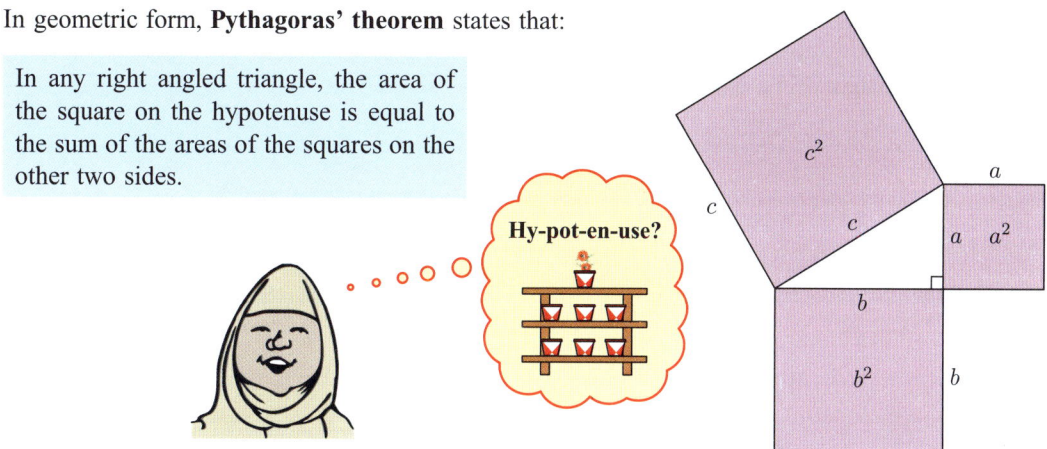

We can use Pythagoras' theorem to find unknown side lengths in right angled triangles.

Example 1 ◀) Self Tutor

Find the length of the hypotenuse in:

[triangle with legs 2 cm and 3 cm]

Let the hypotenuse have length x cm.

$\therefore x^2 = 3^2 + 2^2$ {Pythagoras}
$\therefore x^2 = 9 + 4$
$\therefore x^2 = 13$
$\therefore x = \sqrt{13}$ {as $x > 0$}

The hypotenuse is $\sqrt{13}$ cm long.

If $x^2 = k$, then $x = \pm\sqrt{k}$, but we reject $-\sqrt{k}$ as lengths must be positive!

EXERCISE 5A

1 Find the length of the hypotenuse of each of the following triangles, leaving your answer in simplest radical form where appropriate:

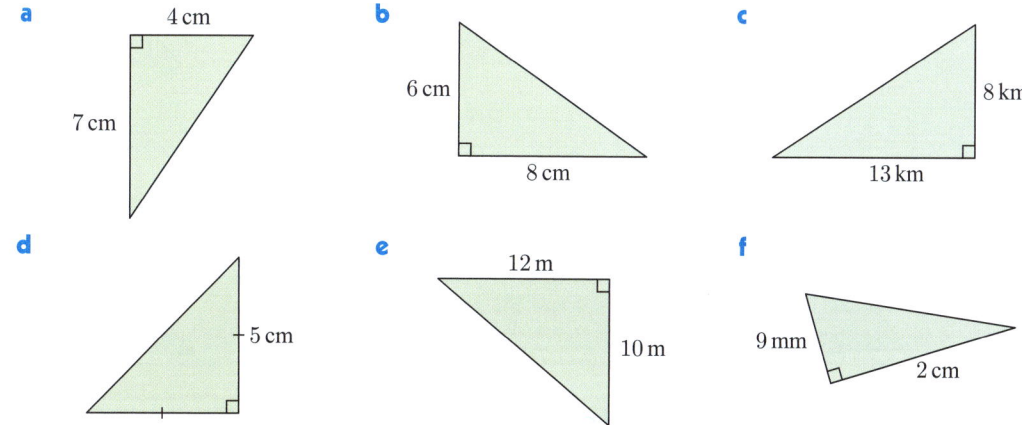

Example 2 ◀)) Self Tutor

Find the length of the third side of the triangle.

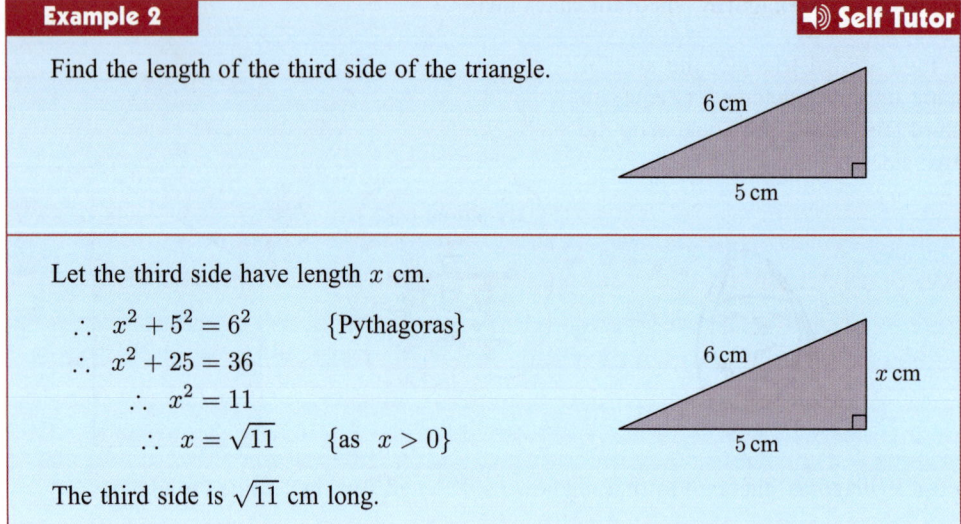

Let the third side have length x cm.

$\therefore\ x^2 + 5^2 = 6^2$ {Pythagoras}
$\therefore\ x^2 + 25 = 36$
$\therefore\ x^2 = 11$
$\therefore\ x = \sqrt{11}$ {as $x > 0$}

The third side is $\sqrt{11}$ cm long.

2 Find the length of the third side of each of the following right angled triangles. Where appropriate, leave your answer in simplest radical form.

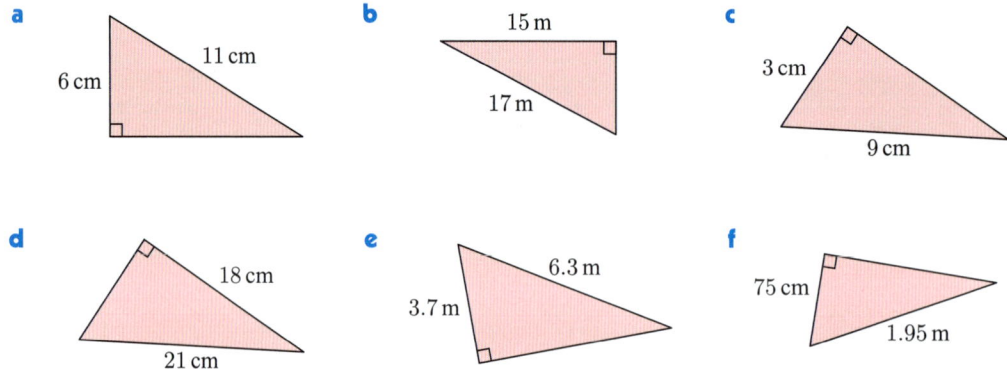

3 Find the length of the unknown side of each of the following right angled triangles. Give your answer to 1 decimal place where appropriate.

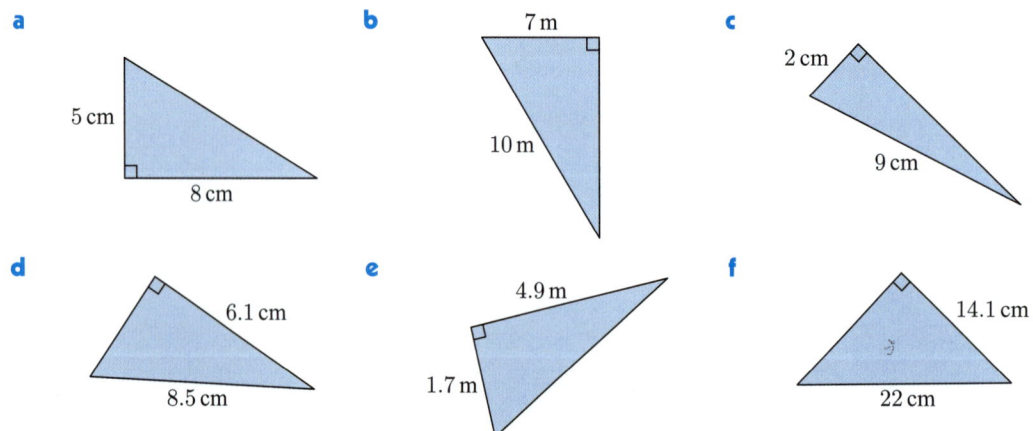

4 Find x in each of the following:

a 3 cm, $\sqrt{2}$ cm, x cm

b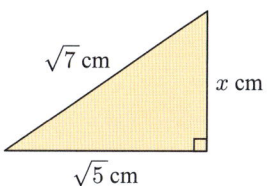

c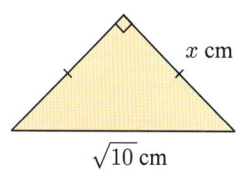

d x cm, $2\sqrt{2}$ cm, $3\sqrt{3}$ cm

e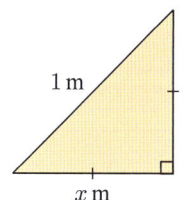

f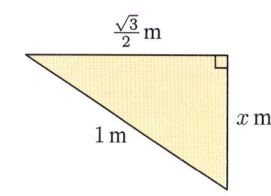

Example 3

Find x:

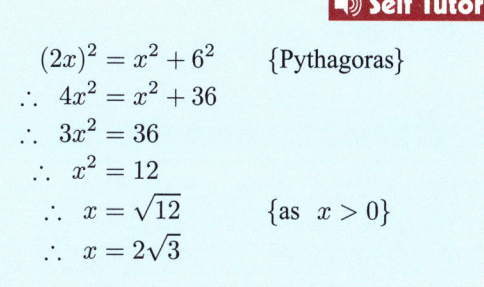

$(2x)^2 = x^2 + 6^2$ {Pythagoras}

$\therefore \ 4x^2 = x^2 + 36$

$\therefore \ 3x^2 = 36$

$\therefore \ x^2 = 12$

$\therefore \ x = \sqrt{12}$ {as $x > 0$}

$\therefore \ x = 2\sqrt{3}$

5 Find the value of x:

a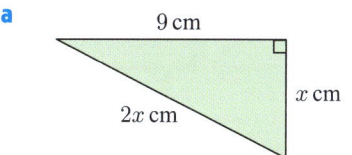

b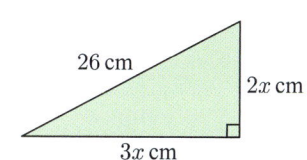

c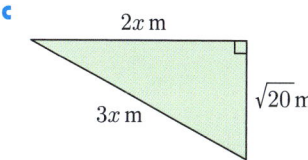

Example 4

Find the values of the unknowns:

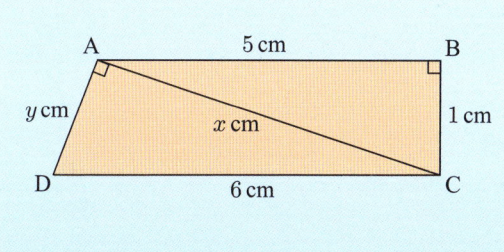

In triangle ABC, the hypotenuse is x cm.

$\therefore \ x^2 = 5^2 + 1^2$ {Pythagoras}

$\therefore \ x^2 = 26$

$\therefore \ x = \sqrt{26}$ {as $x > 0$}

In triangle ACD, the hypotenuse is 6 cm.

$\therefore \ y^2 + (\sqrt{26})^2 = 6^2$ {Pythagoras}

$\therefore \ y^2 + 26 = 36$

$\therefore \ y^2 = 10$

$\therefore \ y = \sqrt{10}$ {as $y > 0$}

6 Find the values of the unknowns:

a 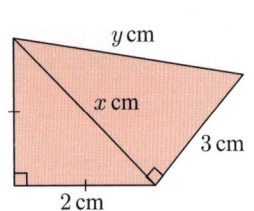 b 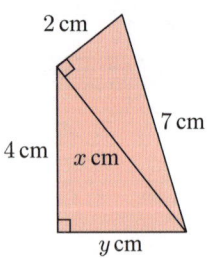 c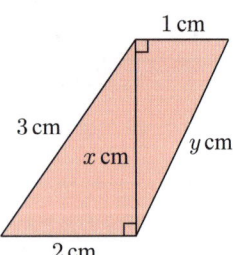

7 Find x:

a 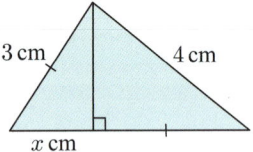 b 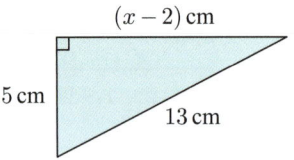 c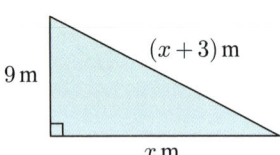

8 Find the length of [AC]:

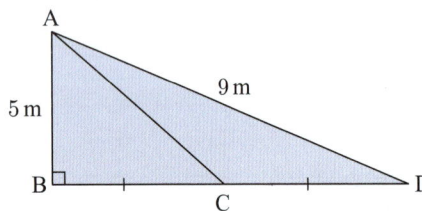

9 Use the figure below to show that $\sqrt{2} + \sqrt{8} = \sqrt{18}$.

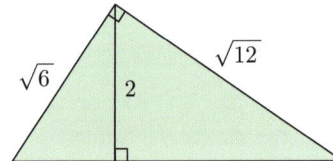

10 Find the distance AB in each of the following figures:

a 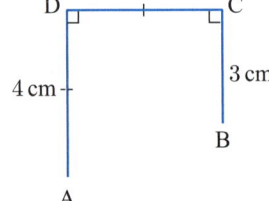 b 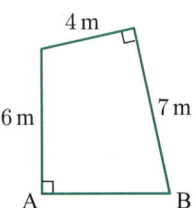 c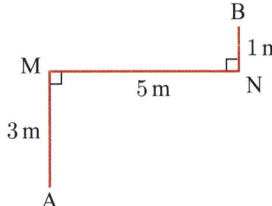

INVESTIGATION — PRESIDENT GARFIELD'S PROOF

Prior to being President of the United States, **James Garfield** used the diagram alongside to prove Pythagoras' theorem. When he found this proof he was so pleased he gave cigars out to his many friends.

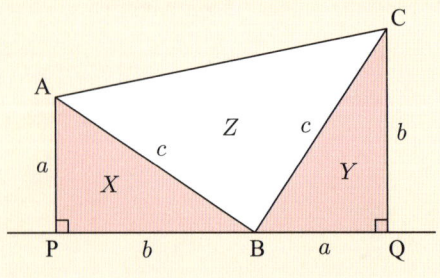

What to do:

1. Two identical right angled triangles, ABP and BCQ, are placed on a line. What can you deduce about $\widehat{ABC}$? Explain your answer.

2. Find the areas of triangles X, Y, and Z. Hence, express area X + area Y + area Z in simplest form.

3 The combined regions X, Y, and Z form a trapezium. Find:
  a the average length of the parallel sides
  b the distance between the parallel sides
  c the area of the trapezium in terms of a and b.

4 Use your results from **2** and **3 c** to find a relationship between a, b, and c.

B THE CONVERSE OF PYTHAGORAS' THEOREM

If we know all of the side lengths of a triangle, we can use the **converse of Pythagoras' theorem** to test whether the triangle is right angled.

GEOMETRY PACKAGE

If a triangle has sides of length a, b, and c units where $a^2 + b^2 = c^2$, then the triangle is right angled.

Example 5   ◀) Self Tutor

Is a triangle with side lengths 6 cm, 8 cm, and 5 cm right angled?

The two shorter sides have lengths 5 cm and 6 cm.

Now $5^2 + 6^2 = 25 + 36 = 61$, but $8^2 = 64$.

$\therefore$ $5^2 + 6^2 \neq 8^2$, and hence the triangle is not right angled.

The hypotenuse would be the longest side!

EXERCISE 5B

1 The following figures are not drawn to scale. Which of the triangles are right angled?

a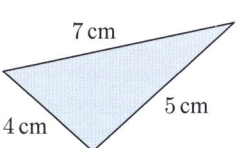

b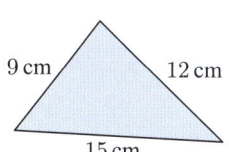

c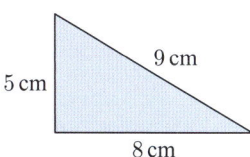

d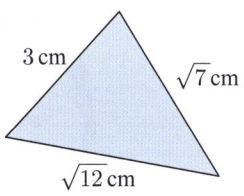

e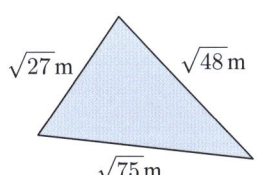

f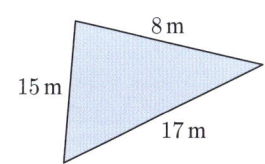

2 The following triangles are not drawn to scale. If any of them is right angled, identify the right angle.

a 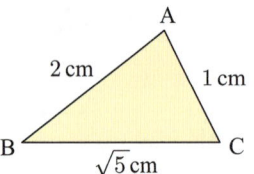 **b** 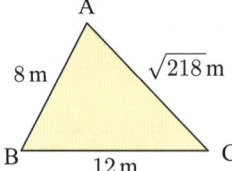 **c**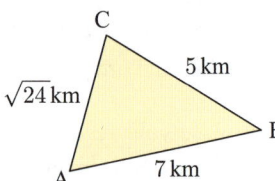

d 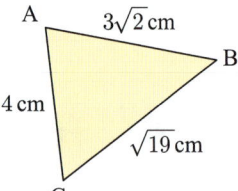 **e** 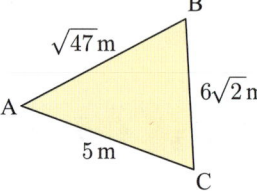 **f**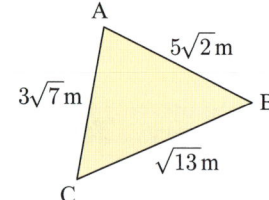

3 Find x:

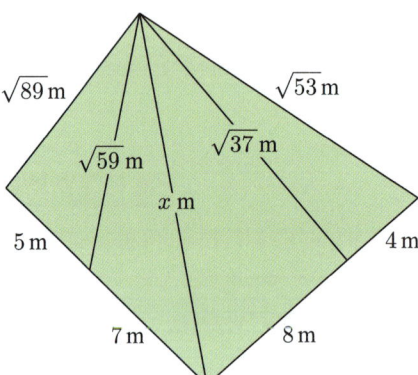

C PYTHAGOREAN TRIPLES

The set of positive integers $\{a,\ b,\ c\}$ where $a < b < c$ is a **Pythagorean triple** if it obeys the rule $a^2 + b^2 = c^2$.

For example, $\{3,\ 4,\ 5\}$ is a Pythagorean triple because $3^2 + 4^2 = 5^2$.

Other examples of Pythagorean triples include $\{5,\ 12,\ 13\}$ and $\{8,\ 15,\ 17\}$.

Pythagorean triples correspond to right angled triangles with sides of integer length.

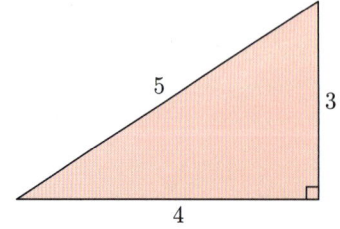

Example 6

Determine whether the following sets of numbers are Pythagorean triples:

a $\{5, 8, 9\}$ **b** $\{6, 8, 10\}$ **c** $\{2, 3, \sqrt{13}\}$

a $\quad 5^2 + 8^2 = 25 + 64 = 89$
and $\quad 9^2 = 81$
Since $\quad 5^2 + 8^2 \neq 9^2$, $\{5, 8, 9\}$ is not a Pythagorean triple.

b $\quad 6^2 + 8^2 = 36 + 64 = 100$
and $\quad 10^2 = 100$
Since $\quad 6^2 + 8^2 = 10^2$, $\{6, 8, 10\}$ is a Pythagorean triple.

c $\{2, 3, \sqrt{13}\}$ is not a Pythagorean triple, as these numbers are not all positive integers.

Example 7

Find k given that $\{9, k, 15\}$ is a Pythagorean triple.

$9^2 + k^2 = 15^2$
$\therefore \quad 81 + k^2 = 225$
$\therefore \quad k^2 = 144$
$\therefore \quad k = 12 \qquad \{\text{as } k > 0\}$

Pythagorean triples are always written in ascending order.

EXERCISE 5C

1 Determine whether the following are Pythagorean triples:
   a $\{15, 20, 25\}$ **b** $\{5, 6, 7\}$ **c** $\{14, 48, 50\}$
   d $\{1, 6, \sqrt{37}\}$ **e** $\{20, 48, 52\}$ **f** $\{-15, 8, 17\}$

2 Find k given that the following are Pythagorean triples:
   a $\{12, 16, k\}$ **b** $\{k, 24, 26\}$ **c** $\{14, k, 50\}$
   d $\{8, k, k+2\}$ **e** $\{20, k, k+8\}$ **f** $\{k, 60, k+50\}$

3 **a** Given that $\{a, b, c\}$ is a Pythagorean triple and k is a positive integer, show that $\{ka, kb, kc\}$ is also a Pythagorean triple.
   b Use the multiples $k = 2, 3, 4,$ and 5 to construct new Pythagorean triples from these Pythagorean triples:
      i $\{3, 4, 5\}$ **ii** $\{5, 12, 13\}$

4 **a** Given that $\{a, b, c\}$ and $\{d, e, f\}$ are Pythagorean triples, show that $\{be - ad, bd + ae, cf\}$ is also a Pythagorean triple.
   b Given that $\{3, 4, 5\}$ and $\{8, 15, 17\}$ are Pythagorean triples, use **a** to construct a new Pythagorean triple. Use technology to check your answer.

5 **a** For each of these values of n, show that $\{2n+1,\ 2n^2+2n,\ 2n^2+2n+1\}$ is a Pythagorean triple:

    i $n=1$ **ii** $n=2$ **iii** $n=3$ **iv** $n=4$

  b Prove that $\{2n+1,\ 2n^2+2n,\ 2n^2+2n+1\}$ is a Pythagorean triple for all $n \in \mathbb{Z}^+$.

    Hint: Let $a = 2n+1$, $b = 2n^2+2n$, and $c = 2n^2+2n+1$, then simplify $c^2 - b^2 = (2n^2+2n+1)^2 - (2n^2+2n)^2$ using the *difference of two squares* factorisation.

PUZZLE — PYTHAGOREAN TRIPLE SEQUENCES

Consider a sequence of numbers such that any two consecutive numbers are members of a Pythagorean triple.

For example, one such sequence is 6, 10, 24, 18.

With underbraces: $\{6, 8, 10\}$, $\{10, 24, 26\}$, $\{18, 24, 30\}$

What to do:

1 Create a sequence of 6 numbers with this property, which starts with 3 and ends with:

    a 6   **b** 50   **c** 75.

2 Find the shortest such sequence you can, that starts with 3 and ends with 1000.

    $\boxed{3}$, ... ? ...., $\boxed{1000}$

D   PROBLEM SOLVING USING PYTHAGORAS

Right angled triangles occur in many practical problems. In these situations we can apply Pythagoras' theorem to help find unknown side lengths. The problem solving method involves the following steps:

> *Step 1*: Draw a neat, clear diagram of the situation.
> *Step 2*: Mark known lengths and right angles on the diagram.
> *Step 3*: Use a symbol such as x to represent the unknown length.
> *Step 4*: Apply Pythagoras' theorem to the right angled triangle.
> *Step 5*: Solve the equation.
> *Step 6*: Where necessary, write your answer in sentence form.

The following special figures contain right angled triangles:

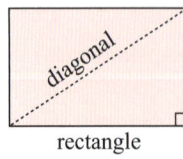
rectangle

In a **rectangle**, right angles exist between adjacent sides. We can construct a diagonal to form a right angled triangle.

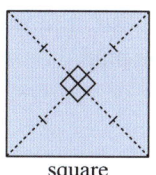 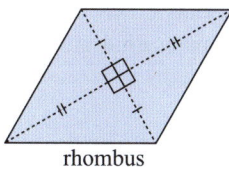

In a **square** and a **rhombus**, the diagonals bisect each other at right angles.

square   rhombus

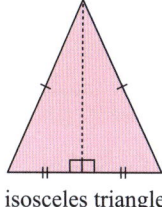 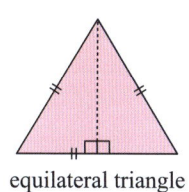

In an **isosceles triangle** and an **equilateral triangle**, the altitude bisects the base at right angles.

isosceles triangle   equilateral triangle

Example 8 ◀)) Self Tutor

A rhombus has diagonals of length 6 cm and 8 cm. Find the length of its sides.

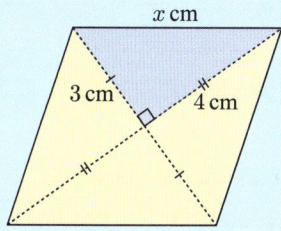

The diagonals of a rhombus bisect at right angles.

Let each side of the rhombus have length x cm.

$\therefore\ x^2 = 3^2 + 4^2$ {Pythagoras}

$\therefore\ x^2 = 25$

$\therefore\ x = 5$ {as $x > 0$}

The sides are 5 cm long.

EXERCISE 5D

1 A rectangle has sides of length 8 cm and 3 cm. Find the length of its diagonals.

2 The longer side of a rectangle is three times the length of the shorter side. The length of the diagonal is 10 cm. Find the dimensions of the rectangle.

3 A rectangle with diagonals of length 20 cm has sides in the ratio 2 : 1. Find the:

  a perimeter   **b** area of the rectangle.

4 A rhombus has sides of length 6 cm. One of its diagonals is 10 cm long. Find the length of the other diagonal.

5 A square has diagonals of length 10 cm. Find the length of its sides.

6 A rhombus has diagonals of length 8 cm and 10 cm. Find its perimeter.

7 To check that his set square was right angled, Roger measured its sides. The two shorter sides were 8 cm and 11.55 cm long, and the longest side was 14.05 cm long. Is the set square right angled?

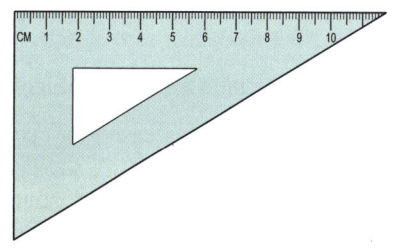

8 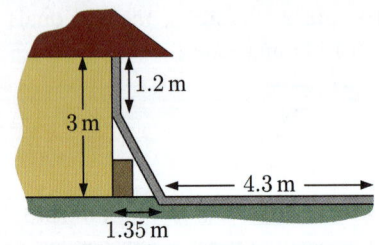 A drain pipe runs down the wall of a house, then out to the road as shown. Find the length of the pipe.

Example 9 ◀)) Self Tutor

A man and his son both leave point A at the same time. The man rides his bicycle due east at 16 km h^{-1}. The son rides his bicycle due south at 20 km h^{-1}. How far apart are they after 4 hours?

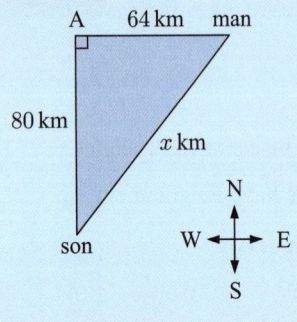

After 4 hours, the man has travelled $4 \times 16 = 64$ km, and his son has travelled $4 \times 20 = 80$ km.

Let the distance between them be x km.

Thus $x^2 = 64^2 + 80^2$ {Pythagoras}

$\therefore x^2 = 10\,496$

$\therefore x = \sqrt{10\,496}$ {as $x > 0$}

$\therefore x \approx 102$

$\therefore$ they are about 102 km apart after 4 hours.

9 A yacht sails 5 km due west and then 8 km due south. How far is it from its starting point?

10 Pirate Captain William Hawk left his hat on Treasure Island. He sailed 18 km northeast through the Forbidden Strait, then 11 km southeast to his home before realising it was missing. He sent his parrot to fetch the hat and return it to the boat. How far did the parrot need to fly?

11 Two runners set off from town A at the same time. One runs due east to town B, and the other runs due south to town C at twice the speed of the first. They both arrive at their destinations two hours later. Given that B and C are 50 km apart, find the average speed of each runner.

12 Answer the **Opening Problem** on page 80.

13 A highway runs east-west between two towns B and C that are 25 km apart. Town A lies 15 km directly north of B. A straight road is built from A to meet the highway at D. Given that D is equidistant from A and C, find the position of D on the highway.

PYTHAGORAS' THEOREM (Chapter 5)

Example 10   Self Tutor

An equilateral triangle has sides of length 6 cm. Find its area.

The altitude bisects the base at right angles.

$\therefore \ a^2 + 3^2 = 6^2$ {Pythagoras}
$\therefore \ a^2 + 9 = 36$
$\therefore \ a^2 = 27$
$\therefore \ a = \sqrt{27}$ {as $a > 0$}

Area $= \frac{1}{2} \times$ base $\times$ height
$= \frac{1}{2} \times 6 \times \sqrt{27}$
$= 3\sqrt{27}$ cm^2
≈ 15.6 cm^2

So, the area is about 15.6 cm^2.

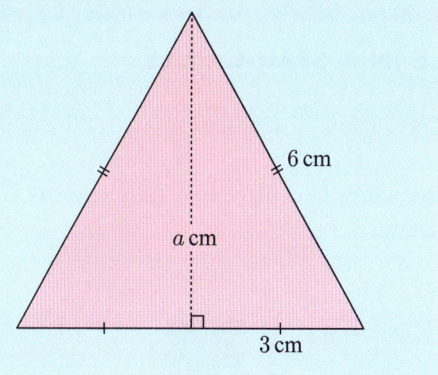

14 An equilateral triangle has sides of length 12 cm. Find the length of one of its altitudes.

15 An isosceles triangle has equal sides of length 8 cm and a base of length 6 cm. Find the area of the triangle.

16 An equilateral triangle has area $16\sqrt{3}$ cm^2. Find the length of its sides.

17 An extension ladder rests 4 m up a wall. If the ladder is extended a further 0.8 m without moving its feet, then it will now rest 1 m further up the wall. How long is the extended ladder?

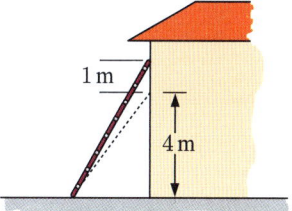

18 A rectangular piece of paper, 10 cm by 25 cm, is folded so that a pair of diagonally opposite corners coincide. Find the length of the crease.

ACTIVITY   ALTITUDES

An **altitude** of a triangle is a line which is perpendicular to one side of the triangle, and which passes through the opposite vertex. Every triangle has three altitudes.

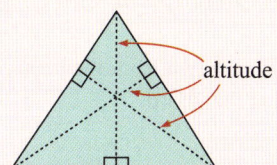

Can you use Pythagoras' theorem to find the lengths of the three altitudes of this triangle?

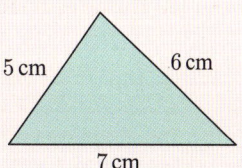

E CIRCLE PROBLEMS

There are also certain properties of circles which involve right angles. They are described in the following theorems:

ANGLE IN A SEMI-CIRCLE

The angle in a semi-circle is a right angle.

No matter where C is placed on the circle, $\widehat{ACB}$ is always a right angle.

DEMO

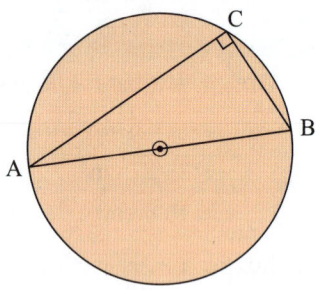

Example 11 — Self Tutor

A circle has diameter [XY] of length 13 cm. Z is a point on the circle such that XZ is 5 cm. Find the length YZ.

From the angle in a semi-circle theorem, $\widehat{XZY}$ is a right angle.

Let the length YZ be x cm.

$\therefore\ 5^2 + x^2 = 13^2$ {Pythagoras}

$\therefore\ x^2 = 169 - 25 = 144$

$\therefore\ x = \sqrt{144}$ {as $x > 0$}

$\therefore\ x = 12$

So, YZ has length 12 cm.

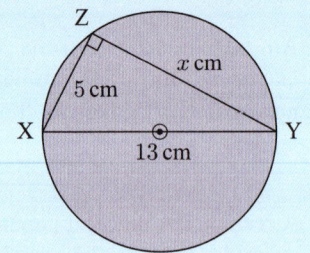

A CHORD OF A CIRCLE

The line drawn from the centre of a circle at right angles to a chord, bisects the chord.

The construction of radii from the centre of the circle to the end points of the chord produces an isosceles triangle. The above property then follows from the **isosceles triangle theorem**.

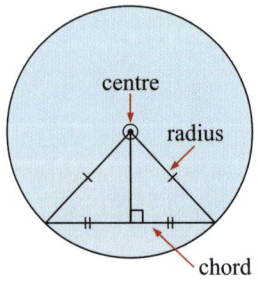

Example 12

A circle with radius 8 cm has a chord of length 10 cm.
Find the shortest distance from the centre of the circle to the chord.

The shortest distance is the 'perpendicular distance'. The line drawn from the centre of a circle, perpendicular to a chord, bisects the chord.

$\therefore$ AB = BC = 5 cm

In $\triangle$AOB, $5^2 + x^2 = 8^2$ {Pythagoras}
$\therefore x^2 = 64 - 25 = 39$
$\therefore x = \sqrt{39}$ {as $x > 0$}
$\therefore x \approx 6.24$

So, the shortest distance is about 6.24 cm.

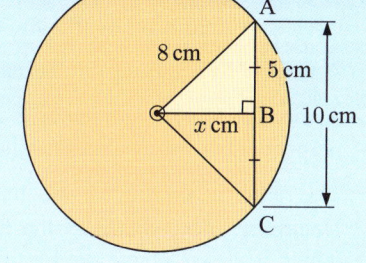

TANGENT-RADIUS PROPERTY

A tangent to a circle and a radius at the point of contact meet at right angles.

Notice that we can now form a right angled triangle.

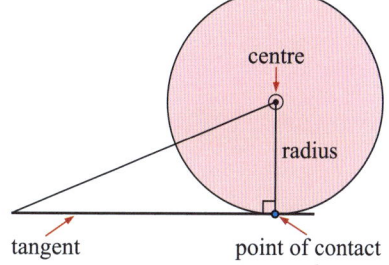

Example 13

A tangent of length 10 cm is drawn to a circle with radius 7 cm. How far is the centre of the circle from the end point of the tangent?

Let the distance be d cm.
$\therefore d^2 = 7^2 + 10^2$ {Pythagoras}
$\therefore d^2 = 149$
$\therefore d = \sqrt{149}$ {as $d > 0$}
$\therefore d \approx 12.2$

The centre is about 12.2 cm from the end point of the tangent.

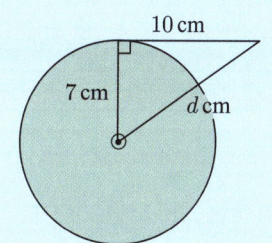

EXERCISE 5E

1. A circle has diameter [AB] of length 10 cm. C is a point on the circle such that AC is 8 cm. Find the length BC.

2. A rectangle with side lengths 11 cm and 6 cm is inscribed in a circle. Find the radius of the circle.

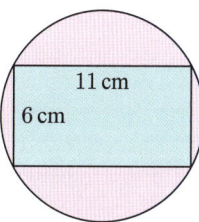

3 A circle with radius 4 cm has a chord of length 3 cm. Find the shortest distance from the centre of the circle to the chord.

4 A chord of length 6 cm is 3 cm from the centre of a circle. Find the radius of the circle.

5 A chord is 5 cm from the centre of a circle of radius 8 cm. Find the length of the chord.

6 A circle has radius 3 cm. A tangent is drawn to the circle from point P, which is 9 cm from the circle's centre. How long is the tangent?

7 A tangent of length 12 cm has end point 16 cm from the circle's centre. Find the radius of the circle.

8 A circular table of diameter 2 m is placed in the corner of a room so that its edges touch two perpendicular walls. Find the shortest distance from the corner of the room to the edge of the table.

9 The radius of the Earth is about 6400 km. Determine the distance to the horizon from a rocket which is 40 km above the Earth's surface.

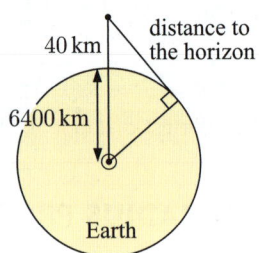

10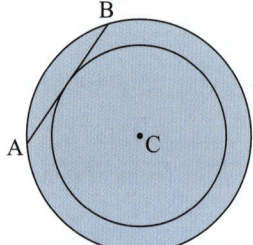

C is the centre of two circles with radii 7 cm and 5 cm. [AB] is a chord of the larger circle, and a tangent of the smaller circle.

Find the length of [AB].

Example 14 🔊 Self Tutor

Two circles have a common tangent with points of contact A and B which are 7 cm apart. The radii of the circles are 4 cm and 2 cm respectively. Find the distance between the centres.

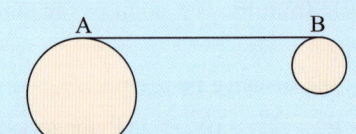

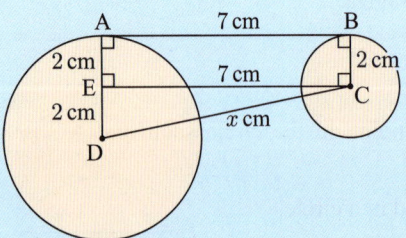

For centres C and D, we draw [BC], [AD], [CD], and [CE] ∥ [AB].

∴ ABCE is a rectangle.

∴ CE = 7 cm   {as CE = AB}
and DE = 4 − 2 = 2 cm

Let the distance between the centres be x cm.

∴ $x^2 = 2^2 + 7^2$ {Pythagoras in △DEC}

∴ $x^2 = 53$

∴ $x = \sqrt{53}$ {as $x > 0$}

∴ $x \approx 7.28$

The distance between the centres is about 7.28 cm.

11 A and B are the centres of two circles with radii 4 m and 3 m respectively. The illustrated common tangent has length 10 m.
Find the distance between the centres to the nearest millimetre.

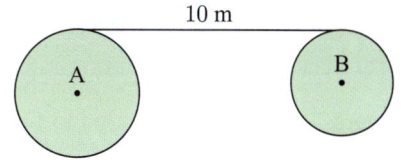

12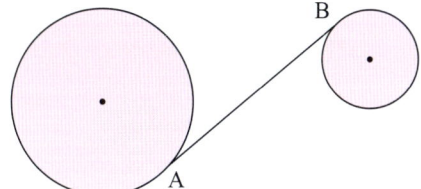

The illustration shows two circles of radii 4 cm and 2 cm respectively. The distance between the two centres is 8 cm. Find the length of the common tangent [AB].

13 In the given figure, AB = 1 cm and AC = 3 cm. Find the radius of the circle.

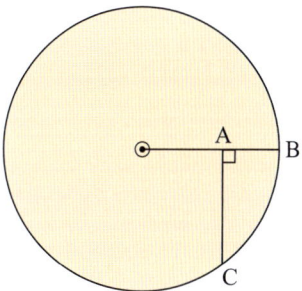

14 In the given figure, the largest circle has radius 12 cm.
  a Find the radius of:
   i the medium circles
   ii the smallest circles.
  b What fraction of the largest circle is occupied by the four inner circles?

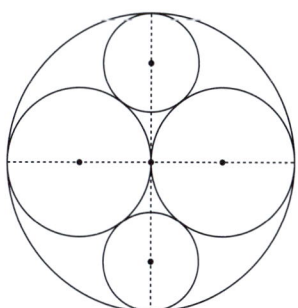

15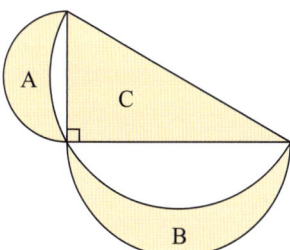

Show that   Area A + Area B = Area C.

F 3-DIMENSIONAL PROBLEMS

Pythagoras' theorem is often used to find lengths in **3-dimensional** problems.

Example 15

A 50 m rope is attached inside an empty cylindrical wheat silo of diameter 12 m as shown. How high is the silo?

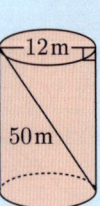

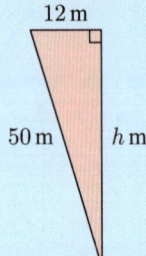

Let the height be h m.

$\therefore\ h^2 + 12^2 = 50^2$ {Pythagoras}
$\therefore\ h^2 + 144 = 2500$
$\therefore\ h^2 = 2356$
$\therefore\ h \approx 48.5$ {as $h > 0$}

The wheat silo is about 48.5 m high.

Sometimes we need to apply Pythagoras' theorem *twice*.

Example 16

A room is 6 m by 4 m, and has a height of 3 m. Find the distance from a corner point on the floor to the opposite corner point on the ceiling.

The required distance is AD. We join [BD].

In $\triangle$BCD, $x^2 = 4^2 + 6^2$ {Pythagoras}
In $\triangle$ABD, $y^2 = x^2 + 3^2$ {Pythagoras}

$\therefore\ y^2 = 4^2 + 6^2 + 3^2$
$\therefore\ y^2 = 61$
$\therefore\ y \approx 7.81$ {as $y > 0$}

$\therefore$ the distance is about 7.81 m.

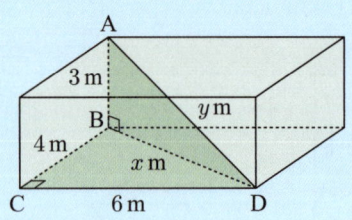

EXERCISE 5F

1 A cone has a slant height of 17 cm, and a base radius of 8 cm. How high is the cone?

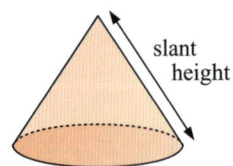

2 Find the length of the longest nail that could fit entirely within a cylindrical can with radius 3 cm and height 8 cm.

3 A 20 cm nail just fits inside a cylindrical can. Three identical spherical balls need to fit entirely within the can. What is the maximum radius each ball could have?

4 A cube has sides of length 3 cm. Find the length of a diagonal of the cube.

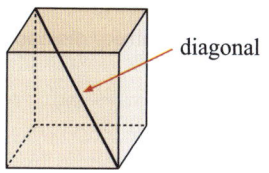

5 A room is 5 m by 3 m, and has a height of 3.5 m. Find the distance from a corner point on the floor to the opposite corner of the ceiling.

6 A rectangular box has internal dimensions 2 cm by 3 cm by 2 cm. Find the length of the longest toothpick that can be placed within the box.

7 Can an 8.5 m long piece of timber be stored in a rectangular shed which is 6 m by 5 m by 2 m high?

Example 17 ◀) Self Tutor

A pyramid of height 40 m has a square base with edges of length 50 m. Determine the length of the slant edges.

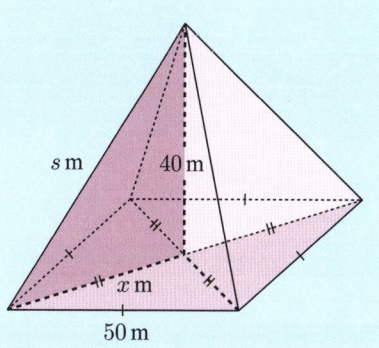

Let a slant edge have length s m.

Let half a diagonal have length x m.

Using

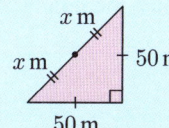

$(2x)^2 = 50^2 + 50^2$ {Pythagoras}

$\therefore 4x^2 = 5000$

$\therefore x^2 = 1250$

Using

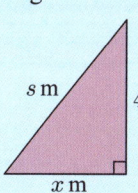

$s^2 = x^2 + 40^2$ {Pythagoras}

$\therefore s^2 = 1250 + 1600$

$\therefore s^2 = 2850$

$\therefore s \approx 53.4$ {as $s > 0$}

Each slant edge is about 53.4 m long.

8 An Egyptian Pharaoh wishes to build a square-based pyramid with all edges of length 100 m. Its apex will be directly above the centre of its base. How high, to the nearest metre, will the pyramid reach above the desert sands?

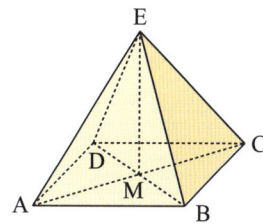

9 A symmetrical square-based pyramid has height 10 cm and slant edges of length 15 cm. Find the dimensions of its square base.

10 In the office building alongside, the entrance is at E. A radio antenna at A, the centre of the roof, receives security signals from the door E.
Find the direct distance between the entrance and the antenna.

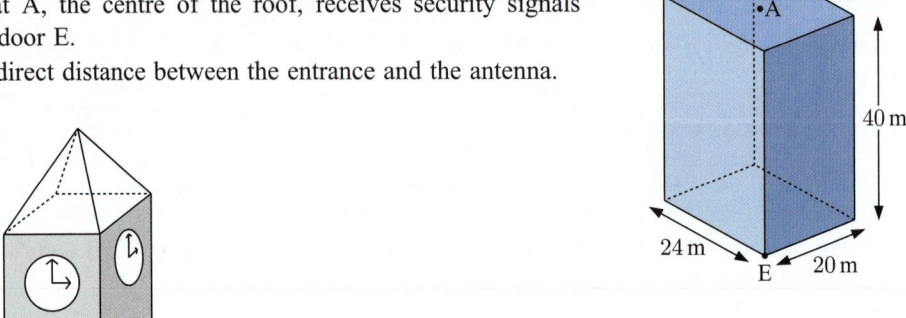

11 A clock tower has the dimensions shown. The slant edges of the pyramid are 7.5 m long. Find the height of the tower, to the nearest cm.

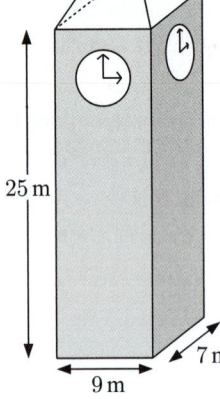

12 An aircraft hangar is semi-cylindrical with diameter 40 m and length 50 m. A helicopter places a cable across the top of the hangar, and one end is pinned to the corner at A. The cable is then pulled tight and pinned at the opposite corner B. Determine the length of the cable, to the nearest cm.

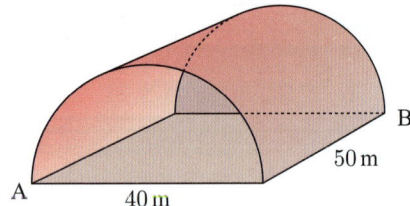

REVIEW SET 5A

1 Find the length of the unknown side in each of the following triangles:

a 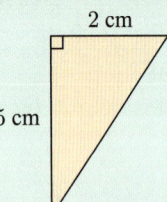   b 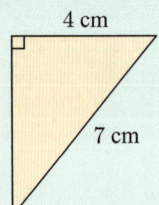   c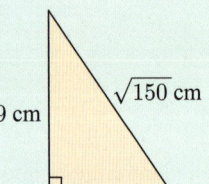

2 Determine whether $\{5, 11, 13\}$ is a Pythagorean triple.

3 Is this triangle right angled? Explain your answer.

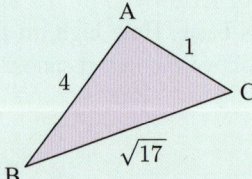

4 Find the values of the unknowns:

a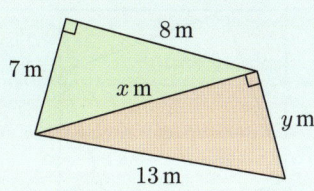

b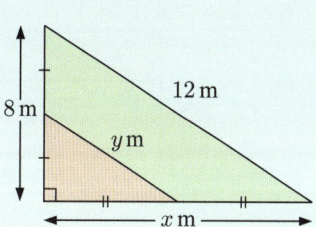

5 Use the figure alongside to show that $\sqrt{2} + \sqrt{18} = \sqrt{32}$.

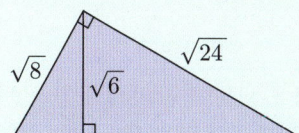

6 A softball diamond has sides of length 30 m. Determine the distance a fielder must throw the ball from second base to reach home base.

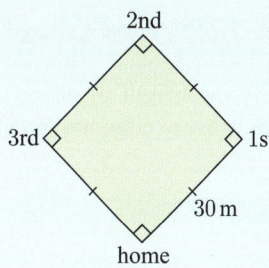

7 a Find the value of k such that $\{15,\ k,\ k+3\}$ is a Pythagorean triple.

b i For any integer $k > 2$, show that $\{4k,\ k^2 - 4,\ k^2 + 4\}$ is a Pythagorean triple.
  ii Find the Pythagorean triple which results when $k = 5$.

8 A rectangle has diagonals 15 cm long, and one side is 8 cm long. Find the perimeter of the rectangle.

9 A circle has a chord of length 10 cm. The shortest distance from the circle's centre to the chord is 5 cm. Find the radius of the circle.

10 Find x:

a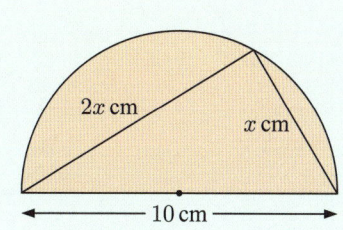

b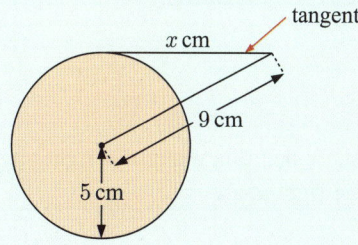

11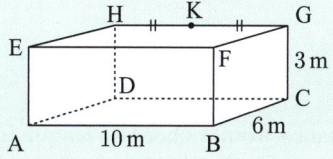

A room is 10 m by 6 m by 3 m.
Find the shortest distance from:
  a E to K
  b A to K.

12 Consider the two squares below.

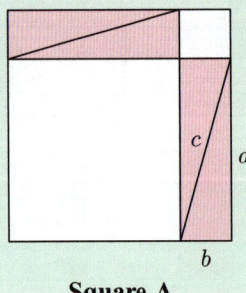 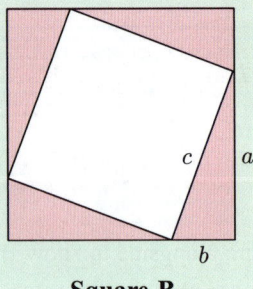

    Square A   Square B

In each square, the 4 shaded right angled triangles have legs a and b, and hypotenuse c.

a Show that the squares have the same area.

b Find an expression for the unshaded area in: **i** square A **ii** square B.

c Hence, prove Pythagoras' theorem.

13 Find the height of an equilateral triangular pyramid in which every edge has length 1 m.

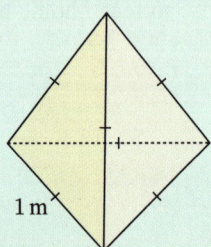

REVIEW SET 5B

1 Find the value of x in the following:

a 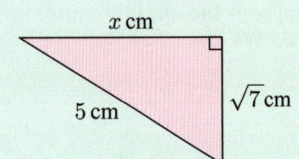   **b**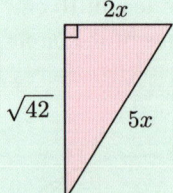

2 Show that this triangle is right angled, and identify which is the right angle.

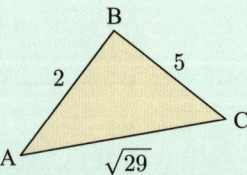

3 Find k given that $\{12, k, 37\}$ is a Pythagorean triple.

4 The diameter of a circle is 20 cm. Find the shortest distance from a chord of length 16 cm to the centre of the circle.

5 Find the distance AB in the following figures:

a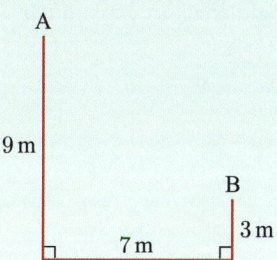

b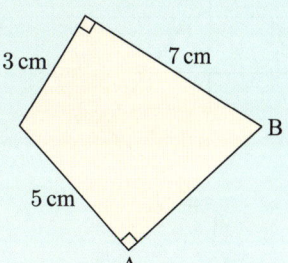

6 A rectangular gate is twice as wide as it is high. It is held in shape by a diagonal strut 3.2 m long. Find the height of the gate to the nearest millimetre.

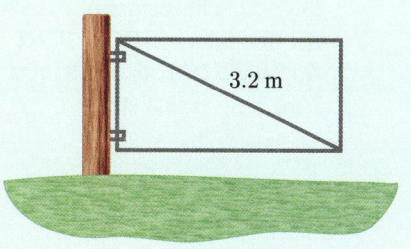

7 A 15 m ladder reaches twice as far up a vertical wall as the base is out from the wall. How far up the wall does the ladder reach?

8 Can a wooden beam 10.5 m long be placed in a rectangular shed 8 m by 7 m by 3 m?

9 Two circles have a common tangent with points of contact X and Y.
The radii of the circles are 4 cm and 5 cm respectively, and the distance between the centres is 10 cm.
Find the length of the common tangent [XY].

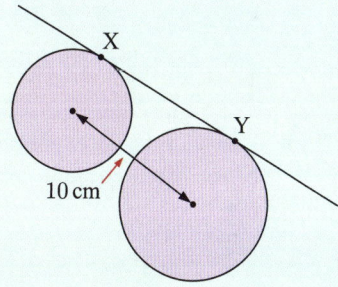

10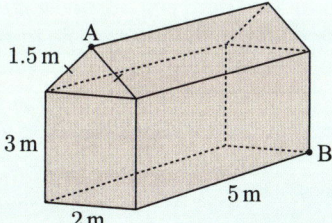

A barn has the dimensions given.
Find the shortest distance from A to B.

11 Consider a regular octagon with side length s.
The interior angles of a regular octagon are $135°$.

    a Find AB in terms of s.

    b Find the area of:

        i a red triangle

        ii a green rectangle.

    c Hence, show that the area of a regular octagon with side length s is $(2 + 2\sqrt{2})s^2$.

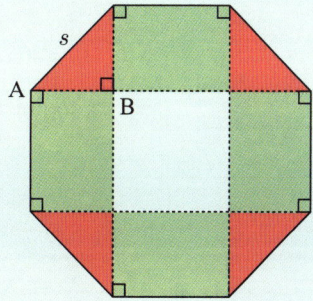

12 **a**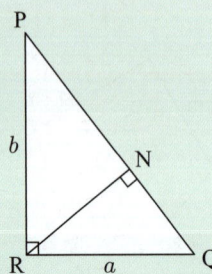

  i Find the length of [PQ].
  ii Use triangle areas to explain why
  $$RN = \frac{ab}{\sqrt{a^2 + b^2}}.$$

b All edges of a square-based pyramid are 200 m long. O is the centre of base ABCD and M is the midpoint of [BC]. [ON] is a small shaft from face BCE to the King's chamber at O. How long is this shaft?

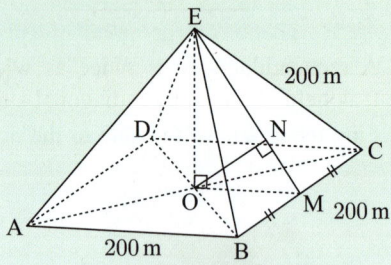

13 Two circles are inscribed inside a semi-circle with radius r as shown.

  a Find the radius of the red circle in terms of r.
  b Let x be the radius of the green circle.
   i Show that
   $$\left(\frac{r}{2}+x\right)^2 - \left(\frac{r}{2}-x\right)^2 = (r-x)^2 - x^2.$$
   ii Hence, find an expression for the radius of the green circle in terms of r.

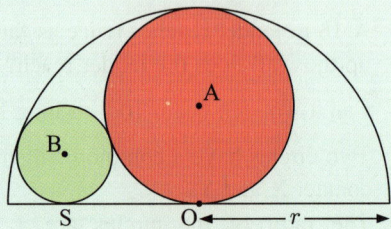

Chapter 6

Coordinate geometry

Contents:
- **A** The distance between two points
- **B** Midpoints
- **C** Gradient
- **D** Parallel and perpendicular lines
- **E** The equation of a line
- **F** Perpendicular bisectors
- **G** Distance from a point to a line
- **H** 3-dimensional coordinate geometry

OPENING PROBLEM

The towns Artville, Branton, and Carden are joined by straight roads. On a road map Artville is at $(-3, 8)$, Branton is at $(7, 2)$, and Carden is at $(5, -3)$. The grid units are kilometres.

Things to think about:

a How far is it from Artville to Branton?

b What point is halfway between Branton and Carden?

c Are any of the roads perpendicular to each other?

d **i** Can you find the *equation* of the road connecting Artville and Carden?

   ii Does the point $(2, 1)$ lie on this road?

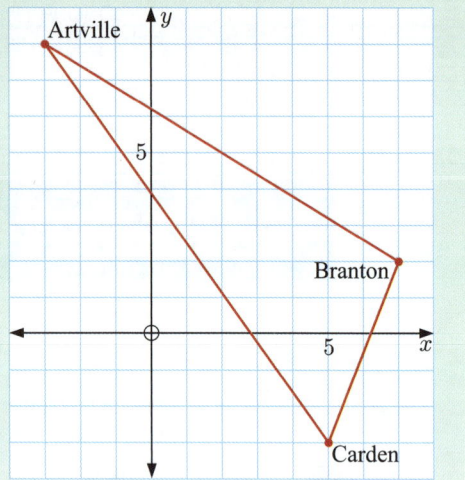

HISTORICAL NOTE

History shows that the two Frenchmen **René Descartes** and **Pierre de Fermat** arrived at the idea of **analytical geometry** at about the same time. Descartes' work *La Geometrie* was published first, in 1637, while Fermat's *Introduction to Loci* was not published until after his death.

Today, they are considered the co-founders of this important branch of mathematics which links algebra and geometry.

The initial approaches used by these mathematicians were quite opposite.

René Descartes

Pierre de Fermat

Descartes began with a line or curve and then found the equation which described it. Fermat, to a large extent, started with an equation and investigated the shape of the curve it described.

Analytical geometry and its use of coordinates enabled **Isaac Newton** to later develop another important branch of mathematics called **calculus**. Newton humbly stated: *"If I have seen further than Descartes, it is because I have stood on the shoulders of giants."*

The **number plane** consists of two perpendicular axes which intersect at the **origin**, O.

The x-**axis** is horizontal and the y-**axis** is vertical.

The axes divide the number plane into four **quadrants**.

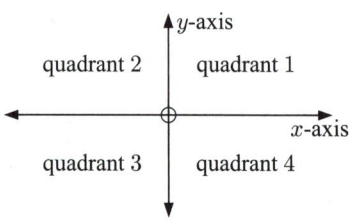

The number plane is also known as either the **2-dimensional plane**, or the **Cartesian plane** after **René Descartes**.

The position of any point in the number plane can be specified in terms of an **ordered pair** of numbers (x, y), where:

- x is the **horizontal step** from O, and is the x-coordinate of the point
- y is the **vertical step** from O, and is the y-coordinate of the point.

DEMO

A   THE DISTANCE BETWEEN TWO POINTS

Suppose we want to find the distance d between the points A(1, 3) and B(4, 1).

By drawing line segments [AC] and [BC] along the grid lines, we form a right angled triangle with hypotenuse [AB].

$\therefore \ d^2 = 2^2 + 3^2$ {Pythagoras}
$\therefore \ d^2 = 13$
$\therefore \ d = \sqrt{13}$ {as $d > 0$}

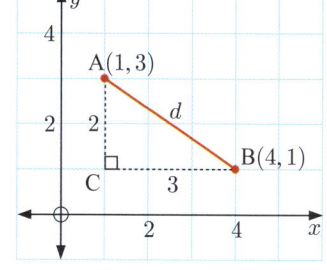

So, the distance between A and B is $\sqrt{13}$ units.

While this approach is effective, it is time-consuming because a diagram is needed.

To make the process quicker, we can develop a formula.

To go from $A(x_1, y_1)$ to $B(x_2, y_2)$, we find the

x-step $= x_2 - x_1$
and y-step $= y_2 - y_1$.

Using Pythagoras' theorem,

$(AB)^2 = (x\text{-step})^2 + (y\text{-step})^2$
$\therefore \ AB = \sqrt{(x\text{-step})^2 + (y\text{-step})^2}$
$\therefore \ d = \sqrt{(x_2 - x_1)^2 + (y_2 - y_1)^2}.$

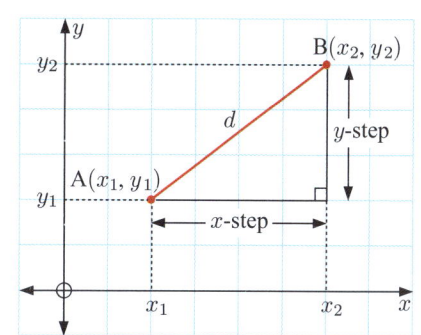

The distance d between two points (x_1, y_1) and (x_2, y_2) is given by
$$d = \sqrt{(x_2 - x_1)^2 + (y_2 - y_1)^2}.$$

Example 1   ◀) Self Tutor

Find the distance between A(−2, 1) and B(3, 4).

A(−2, 1)   B(3, 4) $AB = \sqrt{(3 - -2)^2 + (4 - 1)^2}$
 ↑ ↑   ↑ ↑ $= \sqrt{5^2 + 3^2}$
 x_1 y_1 x_2 y_2 $= \sqrt{25 + 9}$
                       $= \sqrt{34}$ units

The distance formula saves us having to graph the points each time we want to find a distance.

Example 2

Consider the triangle formed by the points A(1, 2), B(2, 5), and C(4, 1).
  a Use the distance formula to classify the triangle as equilateral, isosceles, or scalene.
  b Determine whether the triangle is right angled.

a $AB = \sqrt{(2-1)^2 + (5-2)^2}$ $AC = \sqrt{(4-1)^2 + (1-2)^2}$
$\quad\quad = \sqrt{1^2 + 3^2}$ $\quad\quad = \sqrt{3^2 + (-1)^2}$
$\quad\quad = \sqrt{10}$ units $\quad\quad = \sqrt{10}$ units

$BC = \sqrt{(4-2)^2 + (1-5)^2}$
$\quad\quad = \sqrt{2^2 + (-4)^2}$
$\quad\quad = \sqrt{20}$ units

Since AB = AC, the triangle is isosceles.

b The shortest sides are [AB] and [AC].
Now $AB^2 + AC^2 = 10 + 10$
$\quad\quad\quad\quad\quad\quad = 20$
$\quad\quad\quad\quad\quad\quad = BC^2$

Using the converse of Pythagoras' theorem, the triangle is right angled. The right angle is at A, opposite the longest side.

EXERCISE 6A

1 Find the distance between:
  a A(3, 1) and B(5, 3)
  b C(−1, 2) and D(6, 2)
  c O(0, 0) and P(−2, 4)
  d E(8, 0) and F(2, −3)
  e G(0, −2) and H(0, 5)
  f I(2, 0) and J(0, −1)
  g R(1, 2) and S(−2, 3)
  h W(1, −1) and Z($\frac{1}{2}$, −2).

2 In the map below, the grid lines are 10 km apart.

Find the direct distance between:
  a Dalgety Bay and Edinburgh
  b Coatbridge and Dalgety Bay
  c Coatbridge and Edinburgh.

3 Use the distance formula to classify triangle ABC as either equilateral, isosceles, or scalene:
  a A(3, −1), B(1, 8), C(−6, 1)
  b A(1, 0), B(3, 1), C(4, 5)
  c A(−1, 0), B(2, −2), C(4, 1)
  d A($\sqrt{2}$, 0), B(−$\sqrt{2}$, 0), C(0, −$\sqrt{5}$)
  e A($\sqrt{3}$, 1), B(−$\sqrt{3}$, 1), C(0, −2)
  f A(a, b), B(−a, b), C(0, 2)

4 Determine whether the following triangles are right angled. If there is a right angle, state the vertex where it occurs.
  a A(−2, −1), B(3, −1), C(3, 3)
  b A(−1, 2), B(4, 1), C(4, −5)
  c A(1, −2), B(3, 0), C(−3, 2)
  d A(3, −4), B(−2, −5), C(−1, 1)

Example 3 — Self Tutor

Find b given that A(3, −2) and B(b, 1) are $\sqrt{13}$ units apart.
Explain your result using a diagram.

From A to B, x-step $= b - 3$
y-step $= 1 - -2 = 3$

$\therefore \sqrt{(b-3)^2 + 3^2} = \sqrt{13}$
$\therefore (b-3)^2 + 9 = 13$ {squaring both sides}
$\therefore (b-3)^2 = 4$
$\therefore b - 3 = \pm 2$
$\therefore b = 3 \pm 2$
$\therefore b = 5$ or 1

Point B could be at two possible locations:
(5, 1) or (1, 1).

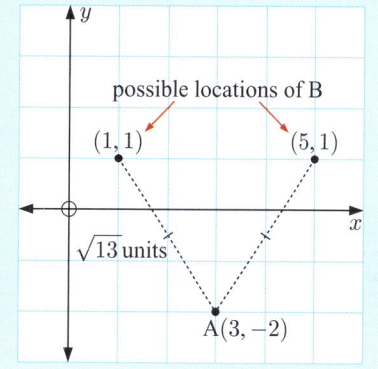

5 For each of the cases below, find a and explain the result using a diagram:
  a P(2, 3) and Q(a, −1) are 4 units apart
  b P(−1, 1) and Q(a, −2) are 5 units apart
  c X(a, a) is $\sqrt{8}$ units from the origin
  d A(0, a) is equidistant from P(3, −3) and Q(−2, 2).

6 a Find the relationship between x and y if the point P(x, y) is always:
  i 3 units from O(0, 0)
  ii 2 units from A(1, 3).
  b Illustrate and describe the set $\{(x, y) \mid x^2 + y^2 = 1\}$.

7 P is at (−5, 9), Q is at (1, 2), and R is on the x-axis.
Given that triangle PQR is isosceles, find the possible coordinates of R.

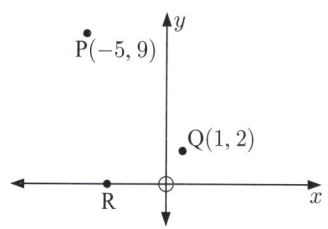

B MIDPOINTS

The **midpoint** of line segment [AB] is the point which lies midway between points A and B.

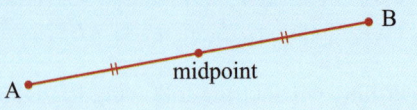

Consider the points A$(-1, -2)$ and B$(6, 4)$. From the diagram we see that the midpoint of [AB] is M$(2\frac{1}{2}, 1)$.

The x-coordinate of M is the *average* of the x-coordinates of A and B.

∴ the x-coordinate of M $= \dfrac{-1 + 6}{2} = \dfrac{5}{2} = 2\frac{1}{2}$

The y-coordinate of M is the *average* of the y-coordinates of A and B.

∴ the y-coordinate of M $= \dfrac{-2 + 4}{2} = 1$

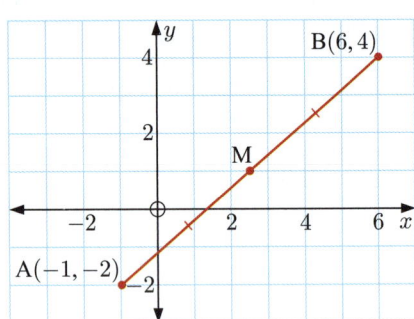

If A(x_1, y_1) and B(x_2, y_2) are two points, then the **midpoint** of [AB] has coordinates $\left(\dfrac{x_1 + x_2}{2}, \dfrac{y_1 + y_2}{2}\right)$.

DEMO

Example 4 🔊 Self Tutor

Find the midpoint of [AB] given A$(-1, 3)$ and B$(4, 7)$.

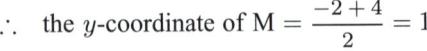

The x-coordinate of the midpoint $= \dfrac{x_1 + x_2}{2} = \dfrac{-1 + 4}{2} = \dfrac{3}{2} = 1\frac{1}{2}$

The y-coordinate of the midpoint $= \dfrac{y_1 + y_2}{2} = \dfrac{3 + 7}{2} = 5$

So, the midpoint is $(1\frac{1}{2}, 5)$.

EXERCISE 6B

1 Find the coordinates of the midpoint of the line segment joining:

   a $(8, 1)$ and $(2, 5)$ **b** $(2, -3)$ and $(0, 1)$ **c** $(3, 0)$ and $(0, 6)$
   d $(-1, 4)$ and $(1, 4)$ **e** $(5, -3)$ and $(-1, 0)$ **f** $(5, 9)$ and $(-3, -4)$.

Example 5 🔊 Self Tutor

M is the midpoint of [AB]. A is $(1, 3)$ and M is $(4, -2)$. Find the coordinates of B.

Suppose B has coordinates (a, b).

∴ $\dfrac{a + 1}{2} = 4$ and $\dfrac{b + 3}{2} = -2$

∴ $a + 1 = 8$ and $b + 3 = -4$

∴ $a = 7$ and $b = -7$

∴ B is $(7, -7)$.

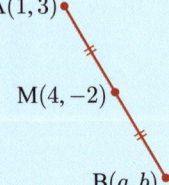

Example 6

Suppose A is $(-2, 4)$ and M is $(3, 1)$, where M is the midpoint of [AB]. Use *equal steps* to find the coordinates of B.

x-step: $-2 \xrightarrow{+5} 3 \xrightarrow{+5} 8$

y-step: $4 \xrightarrow{-3} 1 \xrightarrow{-3} -2$

$\therefore$ B is $(8, -2)$.

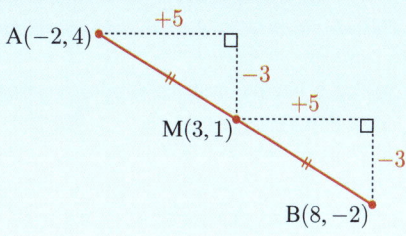

2 M is the midpoint of [AB]. Find the coordinates of B for:

  a A$(6, 4)$ and M$(3, -1)$
  b A$(-5, 0)$ and M$(0, -1)$
  c A$(3, -2)$ and M$(1\frac{1}{2}, 2)$
  d A$(-1, -2)$ and M$(-\frac{1}{2}, 2\frac{1}{2})$
  e A$(7, -3)$ and M$(0, 0)$
  f A$(3, -1)$ and M$(0, -\frac{1}{2})$.

Check your answers using the *equal steps* method given in **Example 6**.

3 [AB] is a diameter of a circle with centre C. If A is $(3, -2)$ and B is $(-1, -4)$, find the coordinates of C.

4 [PQ] is a diameter of a circle with centre $(3, -\frac{1}{2})$. If Q is $(-1, 2)$, find the coordinates of P.

5 The diagonals of parallelogram PQRS bisect each other at X. Find the coordinates of S.

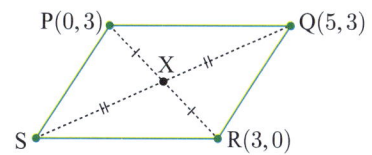

6 Triangle ABC has vertices A$(-1, 3)$, B$(1, -1)$, and C$(5, 2)$. Find the length of the line segment from A to the midpoint of [BC].

7 A, B, C, and D are four points on the same straight line. The distances between successive points are equal, as shown. If A is $(1, -3)$, C is $(4, a)$, and D is $(b, 5)$, find the values of a and b.

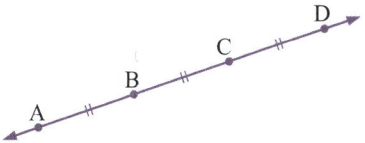

8 The midpoints of the sides of a triangle are $(5, 4)$, $(8, 5)$, and $(6, 0)$. Find the coordinates of the vertices of the triangle.

C GRADIENT

Consider the lines shown:

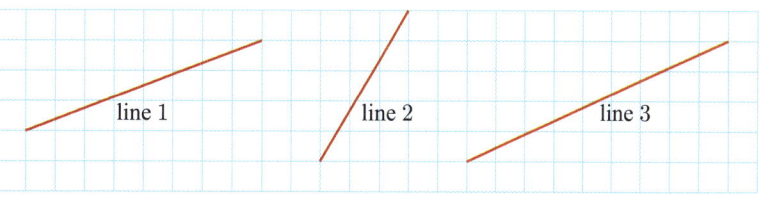

110 COORDINATE GEOMETRY (Chapter 6)

We can see that line 2 rises much faster than the other two lines, so line 2 is steepest.

However, most people would find it hard to tell which of lines 1 and 3 is steeper just by looking at them. We therefore need a more precise way to measure the steepness of a line.

> The **gradient** of a line is a measure of its steepness.

To calculate the gradient of a line, we first choose any two distinct points on the line. We can move from one point to the other by making a positive **horizontal step** followed by a **vertical step**.

The gradient is calculated by dividing the vertical step by the horizontal step.

$$\text{The gradient of a line} = \frac{\text{vertical step}}{\text{horizontal step}} \quad \text{or} \quad \frac{y\text{-step}}{x\text{-step}}.$$

If the line is sloping upwards, then both steps are positive, so the line has a **positive gradient**.

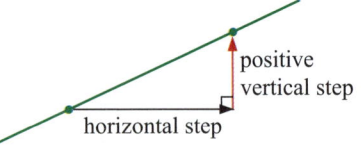

If the line is sloping downwards, the horizontal step is positive and the vertical step is negative, so the line has a **negative gradient**.

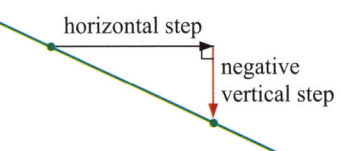

Example 7 ◀)) Self Tutor

Find the gradient of each line segment:

a gradient = $\frac{3}{2}$

b gradient = $\frac{-2}{5} = -\frac{2}{5}$

c gradient = $\frac{0}{3} = 0$

d gradient = $\frac{3}{0}$ which is undefined

COORDINATE GEOMETRY (Chapter 6)

From the previous **Example**, we can see that:

- The gradient of all **horizontal** lines is **0**, since the vertical step is 0.
- The gradient of all **vertical** lines is **undefined**, since the horizontal step is 0.

Example 8 ◀) Self Tutor

Draw a line with gradient $-\frac{2}{3}$, through the point $(2, 4)$.

Plot the point $(2, 4)$.

gradient $= -\frac{2}{3} = \frac{-2}{3}$ ← y-step, x-step

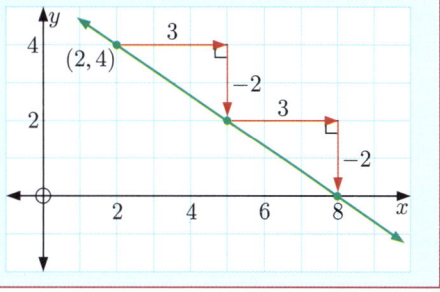

Use a positive x-step.

EXERCISE 6C.1

1 Find the gradient of each line segment:

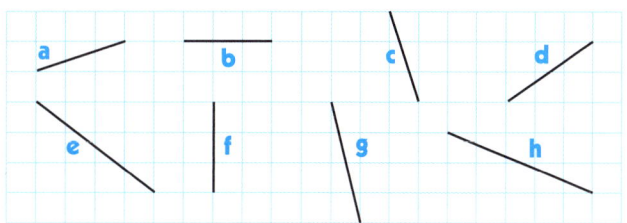

2 On grid paper, draw a line segment with gradient:

   a $\frac{3}{4}$ **b** $-\frac{1}{2}$ **c** 2 **d** -3 **e** 0 **f** $-\frac{2}{5}$

3 Draw a line with gradient $\frac{1}{2}$, through the point $(3, -1)$.

4 Draw a line with gradient $-\frac{3}{4}$, through the point $(-1, 3)$.

5 On the same set of axes, draw lines through $(2, 3)$ with gradients $\frac{1}{3}$, $\frac{3}{4}$, 2, and 4.

6 On the same set of axes, draw lines through $(-1, 2)$ with gradients 0, $-\frac{2}{5}$, -2, and -5.

THE GRADIENT FORMULA

The **gradient** of the line through (x_1, y_1) and (x_2, y_2) is $\dfrac{y_2 - y_1}{x_2 - x_1}$.

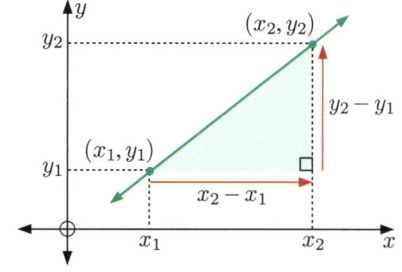

Example 9

Find the gradient of the line through $(3, -2)$ and $(6, 4)$.

$(3, -2)$ $(6, 4)$
$\uparrow\uparrow$ $\uparrow\uparrow$
$x_1\ y_1$ $x_2\ y_2$

gradient $= \dfrac{y_2 - y_1}{x_2 - x_1}$

$= \dfrac{4 - -2}{6 - 3}$

$= \dfrac{6}{3}$

$= 2$

EXERCISE 6C.2

1 Use the gradient formula to find the gradient of the line through $A(-2, -3)$ and $B(5, 1)$. Plot the line segment [AB] on a set of axes to illustrate your answer.

2 Find the gradient of the line segment joining:

- **a** $(2, 3)$ and $(7, 4)$
- **b** $(5, 7)$ and $(1, 6)$
- **c** $(1, -2)$ and $(3, 6)$
- **d** $(5, 5)$ and $(-1, 5)$
- **e** $(3, -1)$ and $(3, -4)$
- **f** $(5, -1)$ and $(-2, -3)$
- **g** $(-5, 2)$ and $(2, 0)$
- **h** $(0, -1)$ and $(-2, -3)$
- **i** $(-1, 7)$ and $(11, -9)$.

Example 10

Find t given that the line segment joining $(5, -2)$ and $(9, t)$ has gradient $\frac{2}{3}$.

The line segment joining $(5, -2)$ and $(9, t)$ has gradient $= \dfrac{t - -2}{9 - 5} = \dfrac{t + 2}{4}$.

$\therefore \dfrac{t+2}{4} = \dfrac{2}{3}$

$\therefore 3(t+2) = 8$

$\therefore 3t + 6 = 8$

$\therefore 3t = 2$

$\therefore t = \frac{2}{3}$

3 Find t given that the line segment joining:

- **a** $(-3, 5)$ and $(4, t)$ has gradient 2
- **b** $(5, t)$ and $(10, 12)$ has gradient $-\frac{1}{2}$
- **c** $(3, -6)$ and $(t, -2)$ has gradient 3
- **d** $(t, 9)$ and $(4, 7)$ has gradient $-\frac{3}{5}$
- **e** $(2, 5)$ and (t, t) has gradient $\frac{4}{7}$
- **f** $(t, 2t)$ and $(-3, 12)$ has gradient $-\frac{1}{4}$.

4 The gradient of [PQ] is $\frac{3}{2}$, and the gradient of [QR] is $-\frac{3}{4}$. Find the coordinates of R.

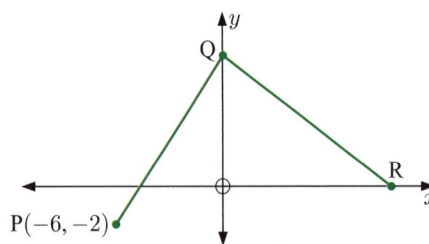

5 $A(x_1, y_1)$, $B(x_2, y_2)$, and $C(x_3, y_3)$ are three points such that the gradient of [AB] is 7, the gradient of [BC] is 1, and $AB = BC$.

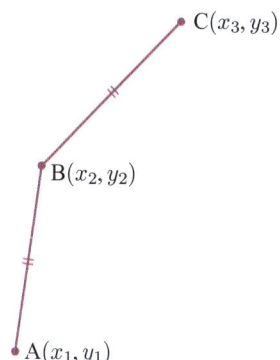

  a Use the gradient formula to show that $(y_2 - y_1)^2 = 49(x_2 - x_1)^2$ and $(y_3 - y_2)^2 = (x_3 - x_2)^2$.

  b Use **a** and the distance formula to show that $x_3 - x_2 = 5(x_2 - x_1)$.

  c Hence, find the gradient of [AC].

D   PARALLEL AND PERPENDICULAR LINES

PARALLEL LINES

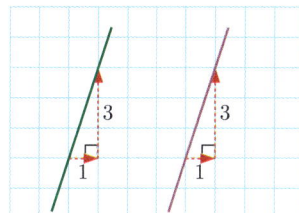

The given lines are parallel, and both of them have a gradient of 3.

- If two lines are **parallel**, then they have **equal gradient**.
- If two lines have **equal gradient**, then they are **parallel**.

PERPENDICULAR LINES

INVESTIGATION   PERPENDICULAR LINES

Consider two lines l_1 and l_2 which intersect at right angles at point $P(X, Y)$.

If l_1 and l_2 are not horizontal or vertical, then both lines will cut the y-axis. We suppose line l_1 cuts the y-axis at $A(0, a)$, and line l_2 cuts the y-axis at $B(0, b)$.

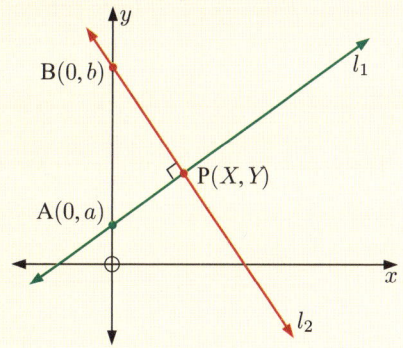

What to do:

1 Explain why $(AP)^2 + (BP)^2 = (AB)^2$.

2 Hence show that $X^2 + (Y - a)^2 + X^2 + (Y - b)^2 = (b - a)^2$.

3 By expanding the brackets and simplifying, show that $Y^2 - (a + b)Y + ab = -X^2$.

4 Hence show that $\dfrac{Y - a}{X} \times \dfrac{Y - b}{X} = -1$.

5 Explain the significance of the result in **4**.

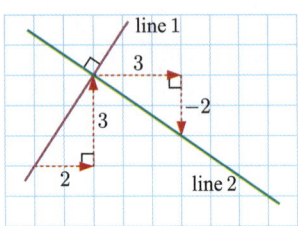

Line 1 and line 2 are perpendicular.

Line 1 has gradient $\frac{3}{2}$.

Line 2 has gradient $\frac{-2}{3} = -\frac{2}{3}$.

We see that the gradients are *negative reciprocals* of each other, and their product is $\frac{3}{2} \times -\frac{2}{3} = -1$.

For lines which are not horizontal or vertical:
- if the lines are **perpendicular**, then their gradients are **negative reciprocals**.
- if the gradients are **negative reciprocals**, then the lines are **perpendicular**.

DEMO

Example 11   ◀) Self Tutor

Find the gradient of all lines perpendicular to a line with a gradient of:

a $\frac{2}{7}$ b -5

a The negative reciprocal of $\frac{2}{7}$ is $-\frac{7}{2}$.

∴ the gradient of any perpendicular line is $-\frac{7}{2}$.

b The negative reciprocal of $-5 = \frac{-5}{1}$ is $\frac{1}{5}$.

∴ the gradient of any perpendicular line is $\frac{1}{5}$.

The negative reciprocal of $\frac{a}{b}$ is $-\frac{b}{a}$.

EXERCISE 6D.1

1 Find the gradient of all lines perpendicular to a line with a gradient of:

a $\frac{1}{2}$ b $\frac{2}{5}$ c 3 d 7

e $-\frac{2}{5}$ f $-\frac{7}{2}$ g $-1\frac{1}{3}$ h -1

2 The gradients of two lines are listed below. Which of the line pairs are perpendicular?

a $\frac{1}{3}, 3$ b $5, -5$ c $\frac{3}{7}, -2\frac{1}{3}$ d $4, -\frac{1}{4}$

e $6, -\frac{5}{6}$ f $\frac{2}{3}, -\frac{3}{2}$ g $\frac{p}{q}, \frac{q}{p}$ h $\frac{a}{b}, -\frac{b}{a}$

3 Consider the hexagon alongside.

   a Calculate the gradient of each side of the hexagon.

   b Which sides are:

       i parallel   ii perpendicular?

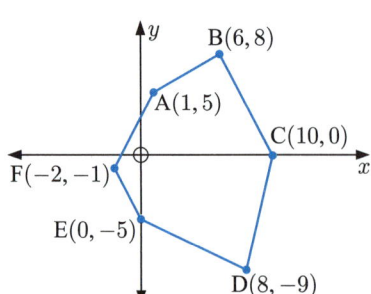

4 Find the value of k:

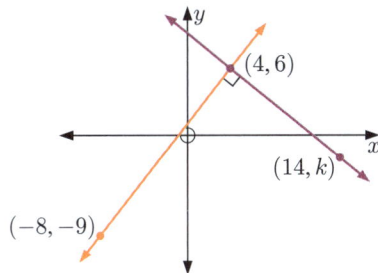

5 Consider the points A(1, 4), B(−1, 0), C(6, 3), and D(t, −1). Find t if:
  a [AB] is parallel to [CD]
  b [AC] is parallel to [DB]
  c [AB] is perpendicular to [CD]
  d [AD] is perpendicular to [BC].

6 Consider the points P(1, 5), Q(5, 7), and R(3, 1).
  a Show that triangle PQR is isosceles.
  b Find the midpoint M of [QR].
  c Use gradients to verify that [PM] is perpendicular to [QR].
  d Draw a sketch to illustrate what you have found.

7 For the points A(−1, 1), B(1, 5), and C(5, 1), M is the midpoint of [AB], and N is the midpoint of [BC].
  a Show that [MN] is parallel to [AC].
  b Show that [MN] is half the length of [AC].

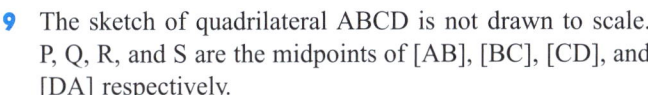

8 Consider the points A(1, 3), B(6, 3), C(3, −1), and D(−2, −1).
  a Use the distance formula to show that ABCD is a rhombus.
  b Find the midpoints of [AC] and [BD].
  c Show that [AC] and [BD] are perpendicular.
  d Draw a sketch to illustrate your findings.

9 The sketch of quadrilateral ABCD is not drawn to scale. P, Q, R, and S are the midpoints of [AB], [BC], [CD], and [DA] respectively.
  a Find the coordinates of:
    i P **ii** Q **iii** R **iv** S.
  b Find the gradient of:
    i [PQ] **ii** [QR] **iii** [RS] **iv** [SP].
  c What can be deduced about quadrilateral PQRS?

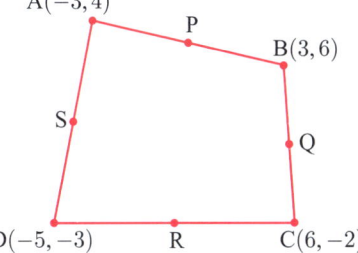

10 S(s, 8) lies on a semi-circle as shown.
  a Find s.
  b Find the gradient of:
    i [PS] **ii** [SQ].
  c Hence show that angle PSQ is a right angle.

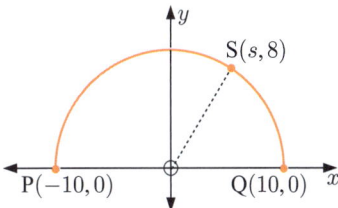

COLLINEAR POINTS

Three or more points are **collinear** if they lie on the same straight line.

Consider the three collinear points A, B, and C, which all lie on the line l.

gradient of [AB] = gradient of [BC] = gradient of l

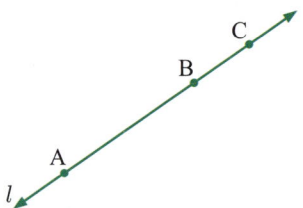

Three points A, B, and C are **collinear** if gradient of [AB] = gradient of [BC].

Example 12 ◉ Self Tutor

Show that the points A(1, −1), B(6, 9), and C(3, 3) are collinear.

Gradient of [AB] $= \frac{9 - -1}{6 - 1} = \frac{10}{5} = 2.$ Gradient of [BC] $= \frac{3 - 9}{3 - 6} = \frac{-6}{-3} = 2.$

∴ [AB] is parallel to [BC], and point B is common to both line segments.

∴ A, B, and C are collinear.

EXERCISE 6D.2

1. Determine whether the following sets of points are collinear:
   a A(1, 2), B(4, 6), and C(−4, −4)
   b P(−6, −6), Q(−1, 0), and R(4, 6)
   c R(5, 2), S(−6, 5), and T(0, −4)
   d A(0, −2), B(−1, −5), and C(3, 7).

2. Find c given that these three points are collinear:
   a A(−4, −2), B(0, 2), and C(c, 5)
   b P(3, −2), Q(4, c), and R(−1, 10).

3. The points A(−2, −7), B(0, −3), C(6, 1), and D(2, −5) form a kite.
   a Find the midpoint M of [BD].
   b Show that A, M, and C are collinear.
   c Show that [AC] is perpendicular to [BD].

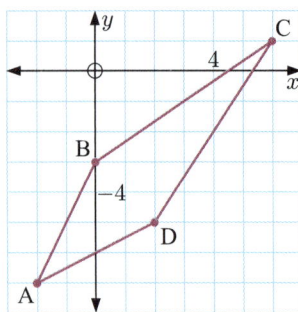

PUZZLE — THE MISSING SQUARE

Stephanie presents the following puzzle to her friend Courtney:

"I can arrange these four shapes to form a right angled triangle which is 13 units long and 5 units high."

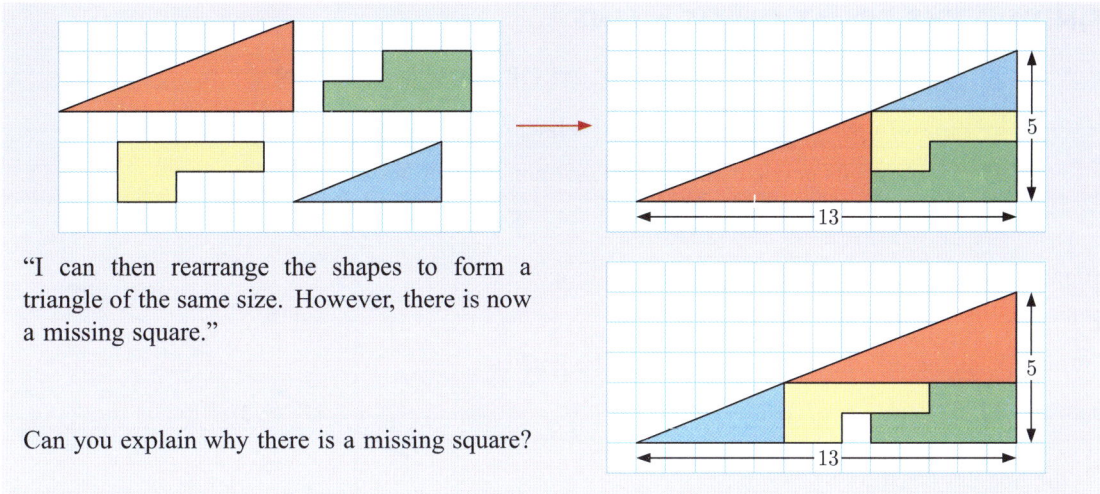

"I can then rearrange the shapes to form a triangle of the same size. However, there is now a missing square."

Can you explain why there is a missing square?

E THE EQUATION OF A LINE

The **equation of a line** is a rule which connects the x and y-coordinates of **all** points on the line.

The equation of a line is commonly written in either **gradient-intercept form** or in **general form**.

GRADIENT-INTERCEPT FORM

$y = mx + c$ is called the **gradient-intercept form** of an equation of a line.

The line with equation $y = mx + c$ has gradient m and y-intercept c.

For example, the line with equation $y = 2x - 3$ has gradient 2 and y-intercept -3.

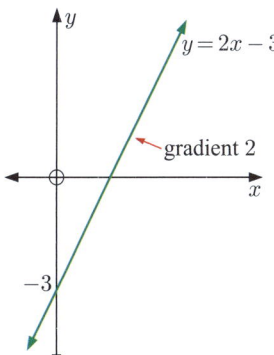

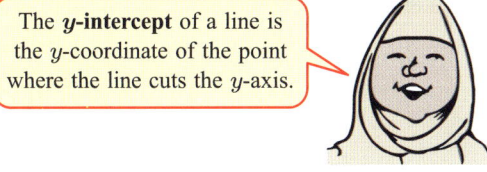

The **y-intercept** of a line is the y-coordinate of the point where the line cuts the y-axis.

GENERAL FORM

$Ax + By = C$ is called the **general form** of the equation of a line.

For example, the equations $2x + 3y = 5$ and $x - 6y = -7$ are in general form.

Equations in general form are usually written with a positive coefficient of x.

FINDING THE EQUATION OF A LINE

If we are given enough information about a line, we can determine its equation.

> To determine the equation of a line, we need to know either:
> - its gradient and at least one point which lies on the line, or
> - two points which lie on the line.

Suppose that a line has gradient $\frac{1}{2}$, and passes through the point $(2, 3)$.

For any point (x, y) which lies on the line, the gradient between $(2, 3)$ and (x, y) is $\frac{y - 3}{x - 2}$.

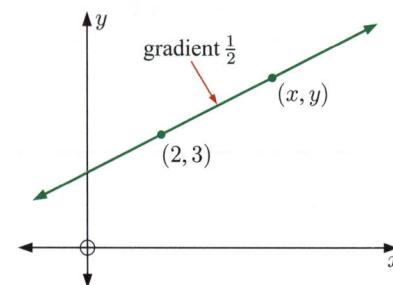

∴ the line has equation $\frac{y - 3}{x - 2} = \frac{1}{2}$

which can be written as $y - 3 = \frac{1}{2}(x - 2)$.

We can rearrange this to find the equation of the line in either gradient-intercept form or general form:

Gradient-intercept form

$y - 3 = \frac{1}{2}(x - 2)$
∴ $y - 3 = \frac{1}{2}x - 1$
∴ $y = \frac{1}{2}x + 2$

General form

$y - 3 = \frac{1}{2}(x - 2)$
∴ $2(y - 3) = 1(x - 2)$
∴ $2y - 6 = x - 2$
∴ $x - 2y = -4$

> If a straight line has gradient m and passes through (a, b), then it has equation
> $$\frac{y - b}{x - a} = m \quad \text{or} \quad y - b = m(x - a).$$
> We can rearrange the equation into either **gradient-intercept form** or **general form**.

Example 13 ◀)) Self Tutor

Find, in *gradient-intercept form*, the equation of the line with gradient 5 that passes through $(-1, 3)$.

The equation of the line is $\quad y - 3 = 5(x - -1)$
∴ $y - 3 = 5(x + 1)$
∴ $y - 3 = 5x + 5$
∴ $y = 5x + 8$

We are given the gradient and a point which lies on the line.

EXERCISE 6E.1

1 Find, in *gradient-intercept form*, the equation of the line with:

   a gradient 2, passing through $(1, 3)$ **b** gradient -1, passing through $(-1, 2)$

   c gradient $\frac{2}{3}$, passing through $(-3, 1)$ **d** gradient $-\frac{4}{5}$, passing through $(4, -2)$

   e gradient $-\frac{3}{4}$, passing through $(6, -5)$.

Example 14

Find, in *general form*, the equation of the line with gradient $\frac{3}{4}$ that passes through $(5, -2)$.

The equation of the line is $\quad y - -2 = \frac{3}{4}(x - 5)$
$\therefore \quad 4(y + 2) = 3(x - 5)$
$\therefore \quad 4y + 8 = 3x - 15$
$\therefore \quad 3x - 4y = 23$

2 Find, in *general form*, the equation of the line with:

   a gradient 4, passing through $(3, 5)$
   b gradient $-\frac{3}{5}$, passing through $(-2, 1)$
   c gradient $\frac{1}{3}$, passing through $(1, 4)$
   d gradient $-\frac{3}{4}$, passing through $(0, 6)$
   e gradient $\frac{2}{7}$, passing through $(-5, -5)$.

Example 15

Find, in *gradient-intercept form*, the equation of the line which passes through A$(1, 3)$ and B$(-2, 5)$.

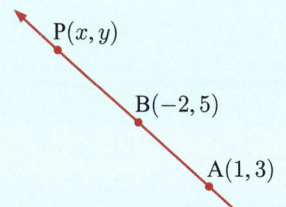

The line has gradient $= \dfrac{5-3}{-2-1} = \dfrac{2}{-3} = -\dfrac{2}{3}$,

and passes through the point A$(1, 3)$.

$\therefore$ the equation of the line is

$$y - 3 = -\tfrac{2}{3}(x - 1)$$
$$\therefore \quad y - 3 = -\tfrac{2}{3}x + \tfrac{2}{3}$$
$$\therefore \quad y = -\tfrac{2}{3}x + \tfrac{11}{3}$$

We could use *either* A or B as the point which lies on the line.

3 Find, in *gradient-intercept form*, the equation of the line which passes through:

   a A$(8, 4)$ and B$(5, 1)$
   b A$(5, -1)$ and B$(4, 0)$
   c A$(-2, 4)$ and B$(-3, -2)$
   d P$(-4, 6)$ and Q$(2, 9)$
   e M$(-1, -2)$ and N$(5, -4)$
   f R$(2, -4)$ and S$(7, -7)$.

4 Find, in *general form*, the equation of each of the following lines:

a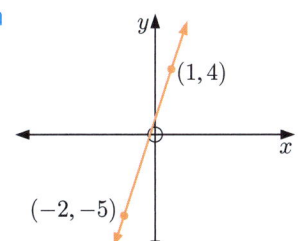

b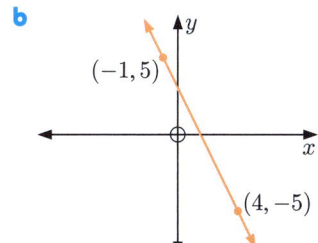

c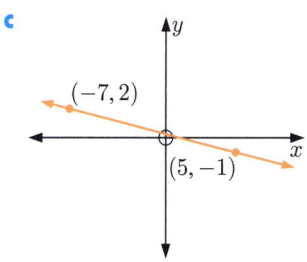

d

(−1, −5), passes through 2 on x-axis

e

(−4, −3) and (5, −3)

f

(2, 4) and (2, −2)

5 **a** Find, in general form, the equation of the line through A(−3, 5) and B(2, 1).
  b Show that the point C(12, −7) also lies on this line.

6 Find the equation of the line which:
  a cuts the x-axis at 5 and the y-axis at −2
  b cuts the x axis at −1, and passes through (−3, 4)
  c is parallel to a line with gradient 2, and passes through the point (−1, 4)
  d is perpendicular to a line with gradient $\frac{3}{4}$, and cuts the x-axis at 5
  e is perpendicular to a line with gradient −2, and passes through (−2, 3).

7 **a** Find the gradient of line 1.
  b Hence, find the equation of line 2.

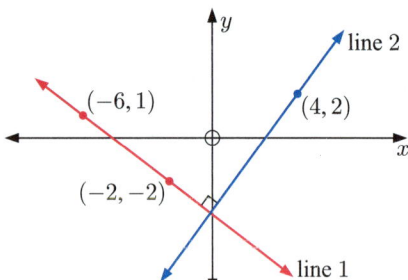

8 Find the equation of the line through (−1, 7), which is parallel to the line through (−3, −4) and (2, 3).

9 Find the equation of the line through (2, 0), which is perpendicular to the line through (−5, 3) and (4, −3).

10 **a** Find, in gradient-intercept form, the equation of line 2.
  b Hence, find the y-intercept of line 2.

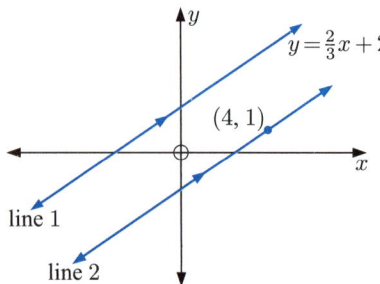

11 Lines l_1 and l_2 are perpendicular to each other, and intersect at (−2, 5). The equation of l_1 is $y = 3x + 11$. Find, in general form, the equation of l_2.

12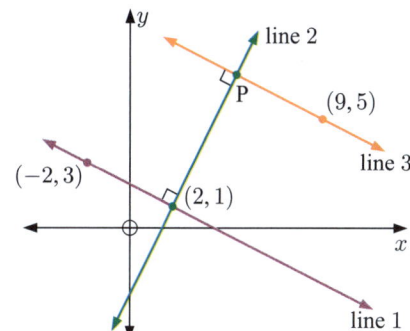

a Find, in gradient-intercept form, the equation of:
  i line 1   **ii** line 2   **iii** line 3.

b Show that the coordinates of P are $(5, 7)$.

13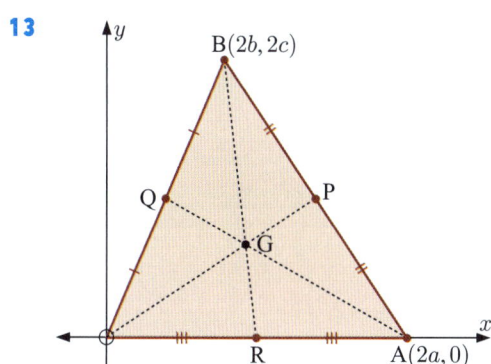

A **median** of a triangle is a line segment from a vertex to the midpoint of the opposite side.

a Show that [OP] has equation $cx - (a+b)y = 0$.

b Show that [AQ] has equation $cx - (b-2a)y = 2ac$.

c Prove that the third median [BR] passes through the point of intersection G of medians [OP] and [AQ].

FINDING THE GENERAL FORM OF A LINE QUICKLY

If a line has gradient $\frac{3}{4}$, its equation has the form $\quad y = \frac{3}{4}x + c$

$$\therefore \quad 4y = 3x + 4c$$

$$\therefore \quad 3x - 4y = C \quad \text{for some constant } C.$$

Similarly, if a line has gradient $-\frac{3}{4}$, its equation has the form $\quad 3x + 4y = C$.

- The equation of a line with gradient $\dfrac{A}{B}$ has the general form $\quad Ax - By = C$.

- The equation of a line with gradient $-\dfrac{A}{B}$ has the general form $\quad Ax + By = C$.

The constant term C is obtained by substituting the coordinates of any point which lies on the line.

Example 16   ◀)) Self Tutor

Find the equation of the line:

a with gradient $\frac{3}{4}$, which passes through $(5, -2)$

b with gradient $-\frac{3}{4}$, which passes through $(1, 7)$.

a The equation is $\quad 3x - 4y = 3(5) - 4(-2)$
$$\therefore \quad 3x - 4y = 23$$

b The equation is $\quad 3x + 4y = 3(1) + 4(7)$
$$\therefore \quad 3x + 4y = 31$$

With practice you can write down the equation very quickly.

EXERCISE 6E.2

1 Find the equation of the line:
   a through $(4, 1)$ with gradient $\frac{1}{2}$
   b through $(-2, 5)$ with gradient $\frac{2}{3}$
   c through $(5, 0)$ with gradient $\frac{3}{4}$
   d through $(3, -2)$ with gradient 3
   e through $(1, 4)$ with gradient $-\frac{1}{3}$
   f through $(2, -3)$ with gradient $-\frac{3}{4}$
   g through $(3, -2)$ with gradient -2
   h through $(0, 4)$ with gradient -3.

2 Find the gradient of the line with equation:
   a $2x + 3y = 8$
   b $3x - 7y = 11$
   c $6x - 11y = 4$
   d $5x + 6y = -1$
   e $3x + 6y = -1$
   f $15x - 5y = 17$

3 Explain why:
   a any line parallel to $3x + 5y = 2$ has the form $3x + 5y = C$
   b any line perpendicular to $3x + 5y = 2$ has the form $5x - 3y = C$.

4 Find the equation of the line which is:
   a parallel to the line $3x + 4y = 6$ and which passes through $(2, 1)$
   b perpendicular to the line $5x + 2y = 10$ and which passes through $(-1, -1)$
   c perpendicular to the line $x - 3y + 6 = 0$ and which passes through $(-4, 0)$
   d parallel to the line $x - 3y = 11$ and which passes through $(0, 0)$.

5 $2x - 3y = 6$ and $6x + ky = 4$ are two straight lines.
   a Write down the gradient of each line.
   b Find k such that the lines are parallel.
   c Find k such that the lines are perpendicular.

6 Answer the **Opening Problem** on page 104.

Example 17

A circle has centre $(2, 3)$. Find the equation of the tangent to the circle with point of contact $(-1, 5)$.

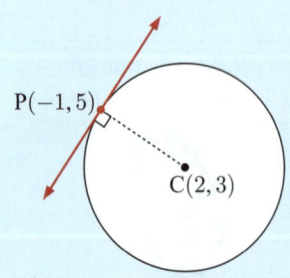

The gradient of [CP] is $\dfrac{5-3}{(-1)-2} = \dfrac{2}{-3}$

$= -\dfrac{2}{3}$

$\therefore$ the gradient of the tangent at P is $\frac{3}{2}$

$\therefore$ the equation of the tangent is

$$3x - 2y = 3(-1) - 2(5)$$

which is $\quad 3x - 2y = -13$.

The tangent is perpendicular to the radius at the point of contact.

7 Find the equation of the tangent to the circle:

  a with centre $(0, 2)$ if the point of contact is $(-1, 5)$

  b with centre $(0, 0)$ if the point of contact is $(3, -2)$

  c with centre $(3, -1)$ if the point of contact is $(-1, 1)$

  d with centre $(2, -2)$ if the point of contact is $(5, -2)$.

8

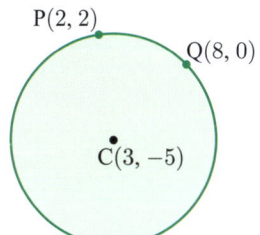

  a Find the equation of the tangent to the circle at:

    i P   **ii** Q.

  b Show that the point $R(\frac{11}{2}, \frac{5}{2})$ lies on both tangents.

  c Show that $PR = QR$.

F   PERPENDICULAR BISECTORS

If A and B are two points, the **perpendicular bisector** of [AB] is the line perpendicular to [AB], passing through the midpoint of [AB].

The perpendicular bisector of [AB] divides the number plane into two regions. On one side of the line are points that are closer to A than to B, and on the other side are points that are closer to B than to A.

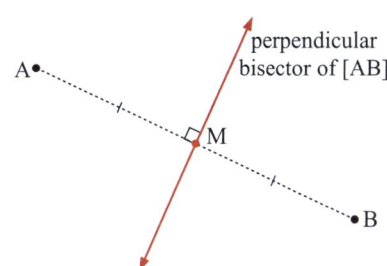

Points on the perpendicular bisector of [AB] are **equidistant** from A and B.

Example 18   ◀) Self Tutor

Given $A(-1, 2)$ and $B(3, 4)$, find the equation of the perpendicular bisector of [AB].

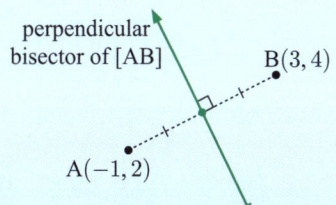

M is $\left(\dfrac{-1+3}{2}, \dfrac{2+4}{2}\right)$ or $(1, 3)$.

The gradient of [AB] is $\dfrac{4-2}{3--1} = \dfrac{2}{4} = \dfrac{1}{2}$

$\therefore$ the gradient of the perpendicular bisector is $-\dfrac{2}{1}$

$\therefore$ the equation of the perpendicular bisector is $2x + y = 2(1) + (3)$

which is $2x + y = 5$.

EXERCISE 6F

1 Find the equation of the perpendicular bisector of [AB] for:

    a A(3, −3) and B(1, −1)   **b** A(1, 3) and B(−3, 5)

    c A(3, 1) and B(−3, 6)   **d** A(4, −2) and B(4, 4).

2 Suppose A is (−1, −4) and B is (3, 2).

    a Find the equation of the perpendicular bisector of [AB].

    b Show that C(−5, 3) lies on the perpendicular bisector.

    c Show that C is equidistant from A and B.

3 Two Post Offices are located at P(3, 8) and Q(7, 2) on a Council map. Find the equation of the line which should form the boundary between the two regions serviced by the Post Offices.

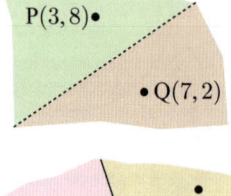

4 The **Voronoi** diagram alongside shows the location of three Post Offices and the corresponding regions of closest proximity. The Voronoi edges are the perpendicular bisectors of [AB], [BC], and [CA] respectively. Find:

    a the equations of the Voronoi edges

    b the coordinates of the point where the Voronoi edges meet.

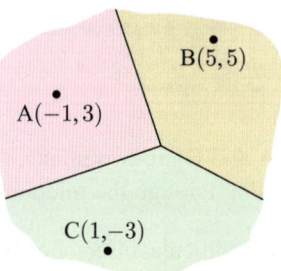

5 Consider the points $A(x_1, y_1)$ and $B(x_2, y_2)$. Show that the equation of the perpendicular bisector of [AB] is $(x_2 - x_1)x + (y_2 - y_1)y = \dfrac{(x_2^2 + y_2^2) - (x_1^2 + y_1^2)}{2}$.

6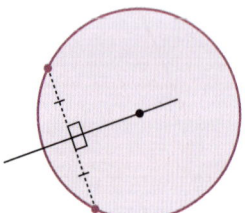

The perpendicular bisector of a chord of a circle, passes through its centre.

Find the centre of a circle passing through points P(5, 7), Q(7, 1), and R(−1, 5).

Hint: Find the perpendicular bisectors of [PQ] and [QR], and solve them simultaneously.

7 Triangle ABC has the vertices shown.

    a Find the coordinates of P, Q, and R, the midpoints of [AB], [BC], and [AC] respectively.

    b Find the equation of the perpendicular bisector of:

        i [AB]   **ii** [BC]   **iii** [AC]

    c Find the coordinates of X, the point of intersection of the perpendicular bisector of [AB] and the perpendicular bisector of [BC].

    d Does X lie on the perpendicular bisector of [AC]?

    e What does your result from **d** suggest about the perpendicular bisectors of the sides of a triangle?

    f What is special about the point X in relation to the vertices of triangle ABC?

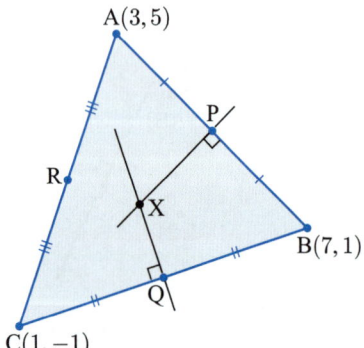

COORDINATE GEOMETRY (Chapter 6) 125

G DISTANCE FROM A POINT TO A LINE

When we talk about the distance from a point to a line, we actually mean the *shortest* distance from the point to the line.

Suppose N is the foot of the perpendicular from P to the line l.

If M is any point on the line other than at N, then triangle MNP is right angled with hypotenuse [MP], and so MP $\geqslant$ NP.

Hence NP is the shortest distance from P to line l.

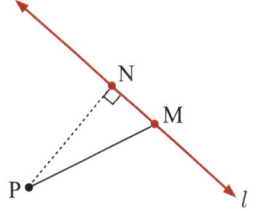

> The distance from a point P to a line l is the distance from P to N, where N is the point on l such that [NP] is perpendicular to l.

FINDING THE DISTANCE

To find the shortest distance from a point P to a line l we follow these steps:

Step 1: Find the gradient of the line l, and hence the gradient of [NP].
Step 2: Find the equation of the line segment [NP].
Step 3: Find the coordinates of N by solving simultaneously the equations of line l and line segment [NP].
Step 4: Find the distance NP using the distance formula.

Example 19   ◀)) Self Tutor

Find the distance from P(7, −4) to the line with equation $2x + y = 5$.

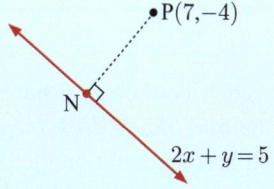

Step 1: The gradient of $2x + y = 5$ is $-\frac{2}{1}$

∴ the gradient of [NP] is $\frac{1}{2}$

Step 2: The equation of [NP] is

$$x - 2y = (7) - 2(-4)$$

which is $x - 2y = 15$

Step 3: We now solve simultaneously: $\begin{cases} 2x + y = 5 & \text{.... (1)} \\ x - 2y = 15 & \text{.... (2)} \end{cases}$

$$\begin{array}{rl} 4x + 2y = 10 & \{(1) \times 2\} \\ x - 2y = 15 & \{(2)\} \\ \hline \text{Adding,} \quad 5x \quad = 25 & \\ \therefore \quad x \quad = 5 & \end{array}$$

When $x = 5$, $2(5) + y = 5$
∴ $10 + y = 5$
∴ $y = -5$

∴ N is (5, −5).

Step 4: NP $= \sqrt{(7-5)^2 + (-4--5)^2}$
$= \sqrt{2^2 + 1^2}$
$= \sqrt{5}$ units

EXERCISE 6G

1 Find the distance from:
   a $(7, -4)$ to $y = 3x - 5$
   b $(-6, 0)$ to $y = 3 - 2x$
   c $(8, -5)$ to $y = -2x - 4$
   d $(-10, 9)$ to $y = -4x + 3$
   e $(-2, 8)$ to $3x - y = 6$
   f $(1, 7)$ to $4x - 3y = 8$.

2 Find the distance between the following pairs of parallel lines:
   a $y = 3x + 2$ and $y = 3x - 8$
   b $3x + 4y = 4$ and $3x + 4y = -16$

   Hint: Find any point on one of the lines, then find the distance from this point to the other line.

3 A straight water pipeline passes through two points with map references $(3, 2)$ and $(7, -1)$. The shortest spur pipe from the pipeline to the farm at $P(9, 7)$ is [NP].
   a Find the coordinates of N.
   b Find the length of the pipeline [NP] given that the grid reference scale is 1 unit $\equiv 0.5$ km.

4 a For the diagram alongside, write *two* expressions for the area of the shaded triangle. Hence show that $d = \dfrac{ab}{\sqrt{a^2 + b^2}}$.

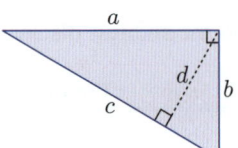

b The **modulus** of x is $|x|$. It is the *size* of x, ignoring its sign, and can be defined by $|x| = \sqrt{x^2}$.
A property of modulus is that $|xy| = |x||y|$ for all real numbers x, y.

$|x|$ is never negative.

Consider the shortest distance d from a point (h, k) to the line $Ax + By + C = 0$.
Point P is the point on the line with y-coordinate k.
Point Q is the point on the line with x-coordinate h.
Show that:

   i the distance $a = \dfrac{|Ah + Bk + C|}{|A|}$

   ii the distance $b = \dfrac{|Ah + Bk + C|}{|B|}$

   iii the distance $d = \dfrac{|Ah + Bk + C|}{\sqrt{A^2 + B^2}}$.

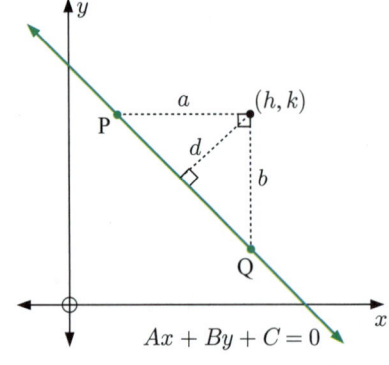

3-DIMENSIONAL COORDINATE GEOMETRY

In 3-dimensional coordinate geometry, we specify an origin O, and three mutually perpendicular axes called the X-axis, the Y-axis, and the Z-axis.

3D-POINT PLOTTER

Any point in space can then be specified using an ordered triple in the form (x, y, z).

We generally suppose that the Y and Z-axes are in the plane of the page, and the X-axis is coming out of the page as shown.

The point $(2, 3, 4)$ is found by starting at the origin $O(0, 0, 0)$, moving 2 units along the X-axis, 3 units in the Y-direction, and then 4 units in the Z-direction.

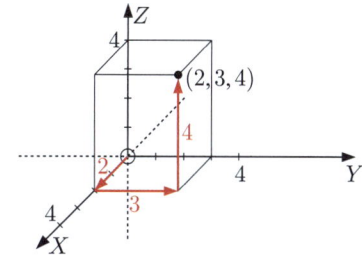

We see that $(2, 3, 4)$ is located on the corner of a rectangular prism opposite O.

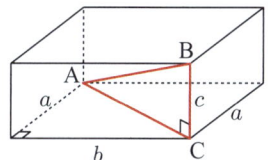

Now consider the rectangular prism illustrated, in which A is opposite B.

$$AC^2 = a^2 + b^2 \qquad \{\text{Pythagoras}\}$$
$$\text{and} \quad AB^2 = AC^2 + c^2 \qquad \{\text{Pythagoras}\}$$
$$\therefore \quad AB^2 = a^2 + b^2 + c^2$$
$$\therefore \quad AB = \sqrt{a^2 + b^2 + c^2} \quad \{AB > 0\}$$

Suppose A is (x_1, y_1, z_1) and B is (x_2, y_2, z_2).

- The **distance** $AB = \sqrt{(x_2 - x_1)^2 + (y_2 - y_1)^2 + (z_2 - z_1)^2}$.

- The **midpoint** of [AB] is $\left(\dfrac{x_1 + x_2}{2}, \dfrac{y_1 + y_2}{2}, \dfrac{z_1 + z_2}{2}\right)$.

Example 20   ◀)) Self Tutor

Consider $A(3, -1, 2)$ and $B(-1, 2, 4)$. Find:

a the distance AB **b** the midpoint of [AB].

a $AB = \sqrt{(-1 - 3)^2 + (2 - -1)^2 + (4 - 2)^2}$
$= \sqrt{(-4)^2 + 3^2 + 2^2}$
$= \sqrt{16 + 9 + 4}$
$= \sqrt{29}$ units

b The midpoint is $\left(\dfrac{3 + -1}{2}, \dfrac{-1 + 2}{2}, \dfrac{2 + 4}{2}\right)$,

which is $(1, \tfrac{1}{2}, 3)$.

EXERCISE 6H

1 On separate axes, plot the points:

PRINTABLE 3-D PLOTTER PAPER

- **a** $(4, 0, 0)$
- **b** $(0, 2, 0)$
- **c** $(0, 0, -3)$
- **d** $(1, 2, 0)$
- **e** $(2, 0, 4)$
- **f** $(0, 3, -1)$
- **g** $(2, 2, 2)$
- **h** $(2, -1, 3)$
- **i** $(4, 1, 2)$
- **j** $(-2, 2, 3)$
- **k** $(-1, 1, -1)$
- **l** $(-3, 2, -1)$

2 For these pairs of points find:
    i the distance AB   **ii** the midpoint of [AB].

- **a** A$(2, 3, -4)$ and B$(0, -1, 2)$
- **b** A$(0, 0, 0)$ and B$(2, -4, 4)$
- **c** A$(1, 1, 1)$ and B$(3, 3, 3)$
- **d** A$(-1, 2, 4)$ and B$(4, -1, 3)$

3 Find the nature of triangle ABC given that:
- **a** A is $(3, -3, 6)$, B is $(6, 2, 4)$, and C is $(4, -1, 3)$
- **b** A is $(1, -2, 2)$, B is $(-8, 4, 17)$, and C is $(3, 6, 0)$.

4 Find k if the distance from P$(1, 2, 3)$ to Q$(k, 1, -1)$ is 6 units.

5 Find the relationship between x, y, and z if the point P(x, y, z):
- **a** is always 2 units from O$(0, 0, 0)$
- **b** is always 4 units from A$(1, 2, 3)$.

Comment on your answer in each case.

6 Illustrate and describe these sets:
- **a** $\{(x, y, z) \mid y = 2\}$
- **b** $\{(x, y, z) \mid x = 1, y = 2\}$
- **c** $\{(x, y, z) \mid x^2 + y^2 = 1, z = 0\}$
- **d** $\{(x, y, z) \mid x^2 + y^2 + z^2 = 4\}$
- **e** $\{(x, y, z) \mid 0 \leqslant x \leqslant 2, 0 \leqslant y \leqslant 2, z = 3\}$
- **f** $\{(x, y, z) \mid 0 \leqslant x \leqslant 2, 0 \leqslant y \leqslant 2, 0 \leqslant z \leqslant 1\}$.

REVIEW SET 6A

1 Find the midpoint of the line segment joining A$(-2, 3)$ to B$(-4, 3)$.

2 Find the distance from C$(-3, -2)$ to D$(0, 5)$.

3 Find the gradient of all lines perpendicular to a line with gradient $\frac{2}{3}$.

4 K$(-3, 2)$ and L$(3, m)$ are $\sqrt{52}$ units apart. Find m.

5 Find t given that the line joining $(-1, t)$ and $(5, -3)$ has gradient $\frac{4}{3}$.

6 Show that A$(1, -2)$, B$(4, 4)$, and C$(5, 6)$ are collinear.

7 Find the equation of the line:
- **a** with gradient -2 and y-intercept 7
- **b** passing through $(-1, 3)$ and $(2, 1)$
- **c** parallel to a line with gradient $\frac{3}{2}$, and passing through $(5, 0)$.

8 Find the equation of the line:

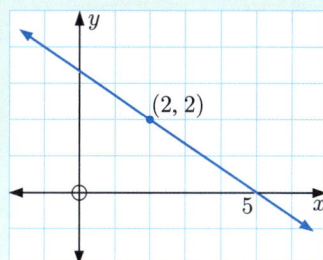

9 Find the value of a:

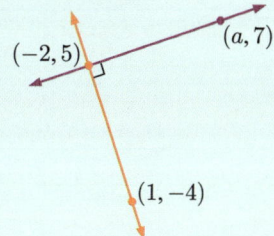

10 Consider the points A(-3, 1), B(1, 4), and C(4, 0).
   a Show that triangle ABC is right angled and isosceles.
   b Find the midpoint X of [AC].
   c Use gradients to verify that [BX] is perpendicular to [AC].

11 **a** Find, in general form, the equation of line 1.
   b Point P has x-coordinate 3, and is equidistant from A and B. Find the coordinates of P.
   c Find the equation of line 2, which is perpendicular to line 1, and passes through P.
   d **i** Find the midpoint M of [AB].
      ii Show that M lies on line 2.

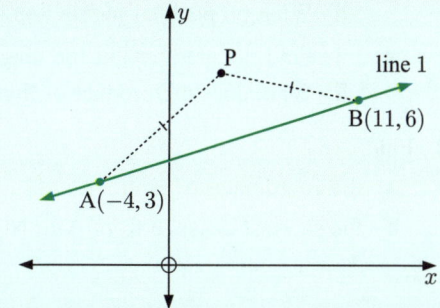

12 Find the equation of the:
   a tangent to the circle with centre $(-1, 2)$ at the point $(3, 1)$
   b perpendicular bisector of [AB] for A(2, 6) and B(5, -2).

13 Find the shortest distance from A(3, 5) to the line with equation $3x + 2y = 6$.

14 For P(-1, 2, 3) and Q(1, -2, -3), find:
   a the distance PQ
   b the midpoint of [PQ].

15 The distance between P(1, 3, -1) and Q(2, 1, k), is $\sqrt{30}$ units. Find k.

REVIEW SET 6B

1 Consider the points S(7, -2) and T(-1, 1).
   a Find the distance ST.
   b Determine the midpoint of [ST].

2 Find, in general form, the equation of the line passing through P(-3, 2) and Q(3, -1).

3 **a** Find the gradient of all lines perpendicular to a line with gradient $-\frac{1}{2}$.
   b Determine whether the line $2x + y = 3$ is perpendicular to a line with gradient $-\frac{1}{2}$.

4 X(-2, 3) and Y(a, -1) are $\sqrt{17}$ units apart. Find the value of a.

5 Find b given that A(-6, 2), B(b, 0), and C(3, -4) are collinear.

6 Determine the equation of the line:

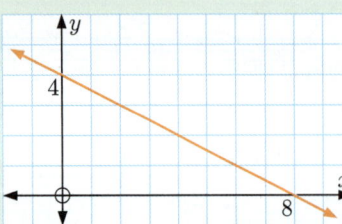

7 Find the equation of line 2.

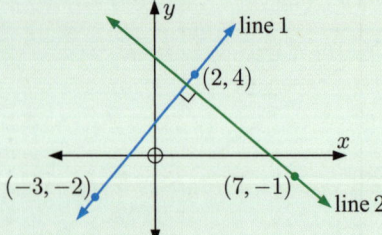

8 Find, in gradient-intercept form, the equation of the line passing through $(1, -2)$ and $(3, 4)$.

9 $A(-3, 2)$, $B(2, 3)$, $C(4, -1)$, and $D(-1, -2)$ are the vertices of quadrilateral ABCD.

   a **i** Find the gradient of each side of the quadrilateral.
       ii What can you deduce about quadrilateral ABCD?

   b **i** Find the midpoints of the diagonals [AC] and [BD].
       ii What property of parallelograms does this check?

   c **i** Find the gradients of the diagonals [AC] and [BD].
       ii What does the product of these gradients tell us about quadrilateral ABCD?

10 Find:

   a the coordinates of point N

   b the shortest distance from A to N.

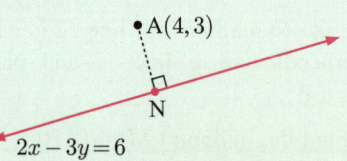

11 [AB] is a diameter of a circle with centre $(1, -1)$.
A has coordinates $(-3, 2)$.

   a Find the radius of the circle.

   b Find the equation of the tangent at A.

   c Find the coordinates of B.

   d Find the equation of the tangent at B.

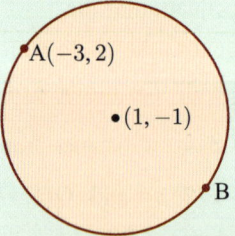

12 **a** Show that the perpendicular bisector of [OB] has equation $bx + cy = b^2 + c^2$.

   b Show that the perpendicular bisector of [AB] has equation $(a - b)x - cy = a^2 - b^2 - c^2$.

   c Prove that the perpendicular bisector of [OA] passes through the point of intersection of the other two perpendicular bisectors of △OAB.

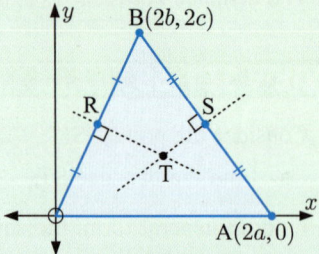

13 Find the distance between the parallel lines $2x + y = -5$ and $2x + y = 7$.

14 How far is $A(-1, -2, 5)$ from the origin O?

15 $P(x, y, z)$ is equidistant from $(-1, 1, 0)$ and $(2, 0, 0)$. Deduce that $y = 3x - 1$.

Chapter 7

Congruence and similarity

Contents:
- **A** Congruent triangles
- **B** Proof using congruence
- **C** Similarity
- **D** Areas and volumes

CONGRUENCE AND SIMILARITY

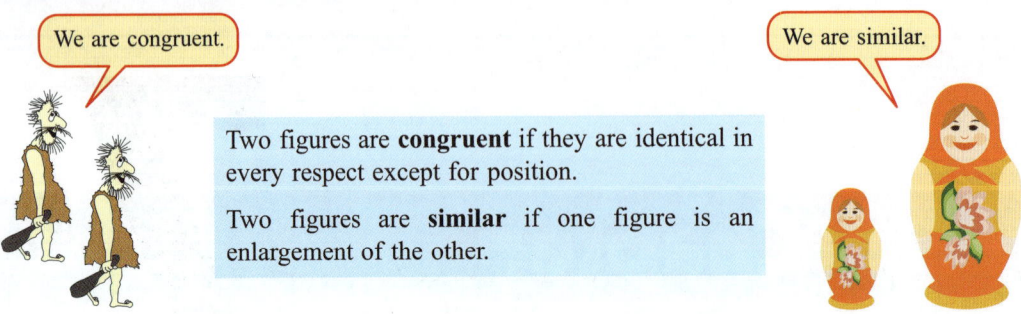

Two figures are **congruent** if they are identical in every respect except for position.

Two figures are **similar** if one figure is an enlargement of the other.

OPENING PROBLEM

In an art gallery, a security camera is being installed along the wall [AB], to view the opposite wall [CD].

Peter is wondering which location for the camera along [AB] maximises the viewing region on the opposite wall.

"It doesn't matter," says Linda, "no matter where the camera is placed, the size of the viewing region will be the same."

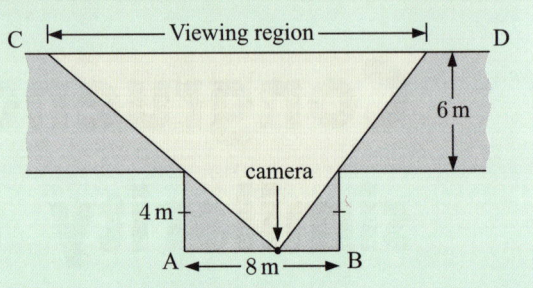

Things to think about:

Can you use similar triangles to determine whether Linda is correct?

 # CONGRUENT TRIANGLES

Two triangles are **congruent** if they are identical in every respect except for position.

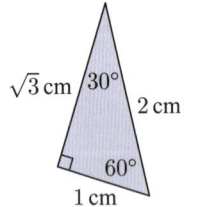
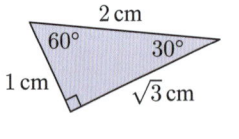

The triangles alongside are congruent.

They have identical side lengths and angles.

If we are given sufficient information about a triangle, there will be only one way in which it can be drawn. Any two triangles which have this information in common must be **congruent**.

TESTS FOR TRIANGLE CONGRUENCE

There are four acceptable tests for the congruence of two triangles.

CONGRUENCE AND SIMILARITY (Chapter 7) 133

Two triangles are **congruent** if one of the following is true:

- All corresponding sides are equal in length. (**SSS**)

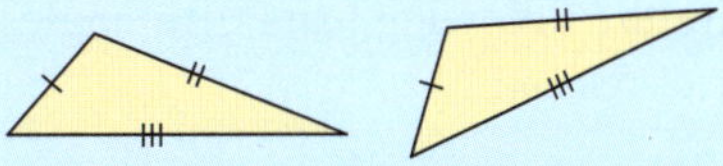

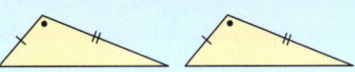

- Two sides and the **included** angle are equal. (**SAS**)

- Two angles and a pair of **corresponding sides** are equal. (**AAcorS**)

- For right angled triangles, the hypotenuses and one other pair of sides are equal. (**RHS**)

The information we are given will help us decide which congruence test to use. The diagrams in the following Exercise are sketches only and are *not* drawn to scale. However, the information marked on them is correct.

Example 1 — Self Tutor

Are the following pairs of triangles congruent? If so, state the congruence relationship and give a brief reason.

a triangles ABC and PQR (with R,B matching one tick, A,Q matching two ticks, C,P matching three ticks)

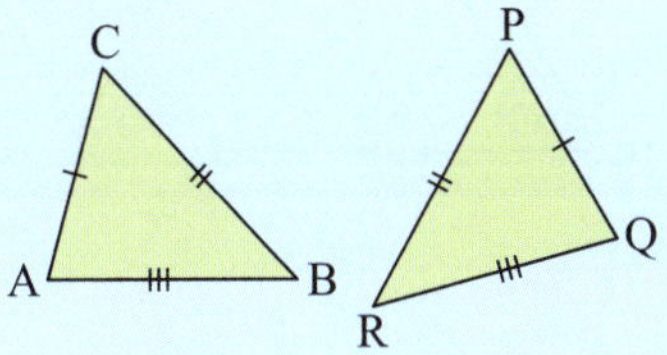

b triangles ABC (right-angled at A) and KLM (right-angled at L)

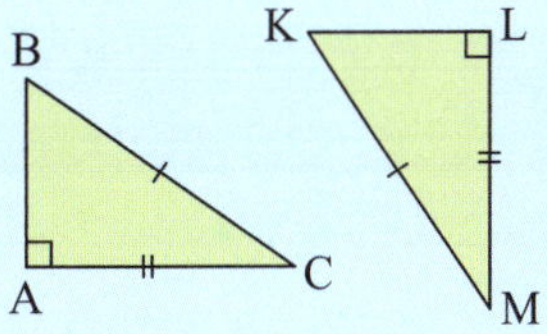

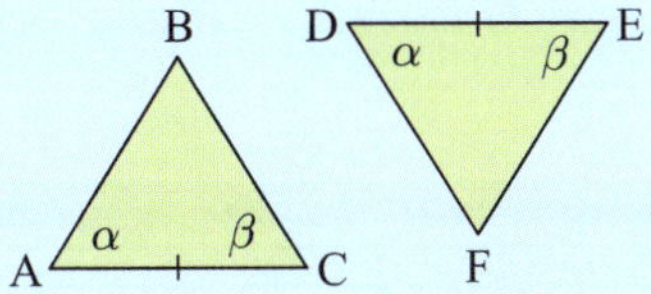

c triangles ABC and DEF (angles α at A and F, β at C and E)

d triangles ABC and XYZ (angles α at B and X, β at C and Y)

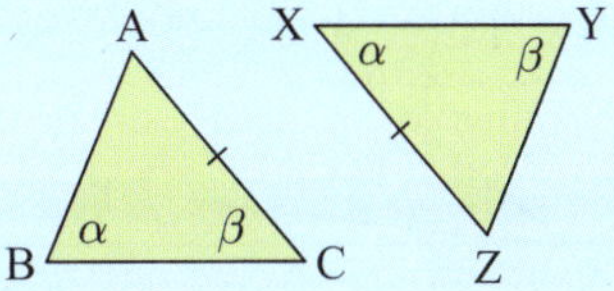

a $\triangle ABC \cong \triangle QRP$ {SSS}

b $\triangle ABC \cong \triangle LKM$ {RHS}

c $\triangle ABC \cong \triangle DFE$ {AAcorS}

d The two angles α and β are common, but although AC equals XZ, these sides are *not* corresponding. [AC] is opposite α whereas [XZ] is opposite β.
So, the triangles are not congruent.

$\cong$ reads "is congruent to".

When we describe congruent triangles, we label the vertices in corresponding positions in the same order. In **Example 1** part **a** above, A and Q are opposite two tick marks, B and R are opposite one tick mark, and C and P are opposite three tick marks. So we write $\triangle ABC \cong \triangle QRP$, not $\triangle ABC \cong \triangle PQR$.

134   CONGRUENCE AND SIMILARITY   (Chapter 7)

EXERCISE 7A

1 Are the following pairs of triangles congruent? If so, state the congruence relationship and give a brief reason.

a, b, c, d, e, f, g, h, i, j

2 For the following groups of triangles, determine which two triangles are congruent. Give reasons for your answers. The triangles are not drawn to scale, but contain correct information.

a

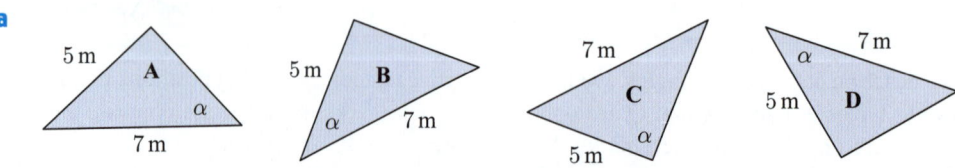

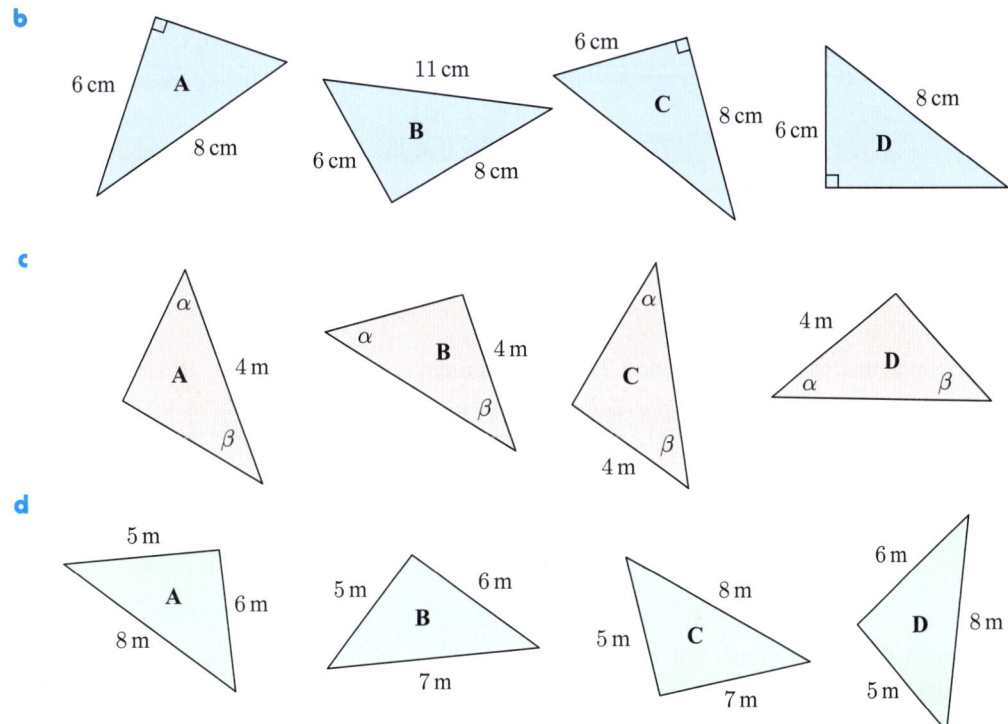

B PROOF USING CONGRUENCE

Once we have proven that two triangles are congruent, we can deduce that the remaining corresponding sides and angles of the triangles are equal. We can therefore use congruence to prove facts about geometric figures.

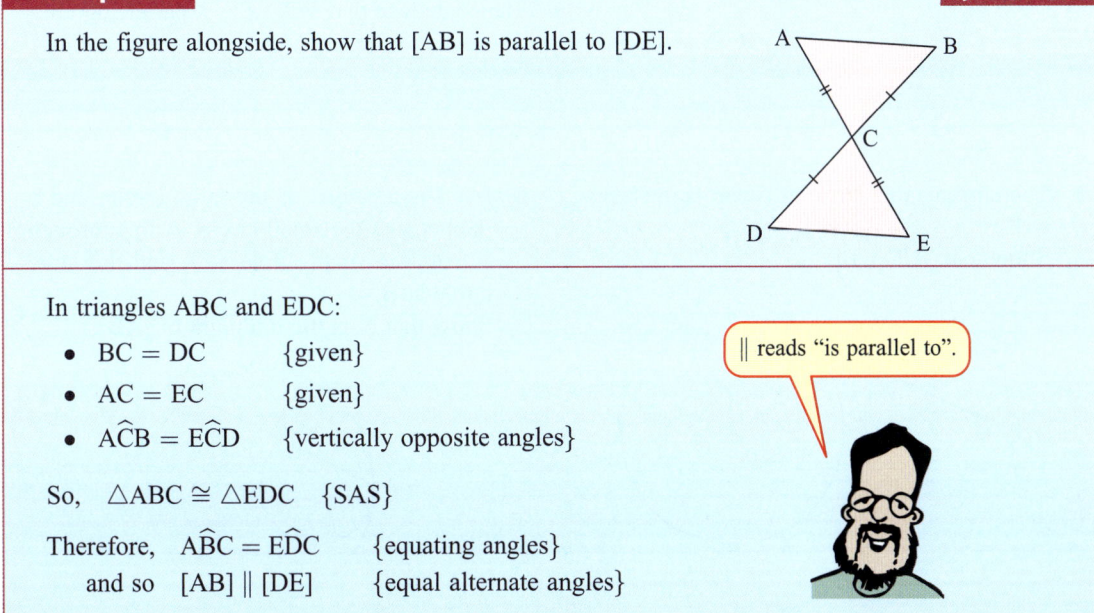

EXERCISE 7B

1 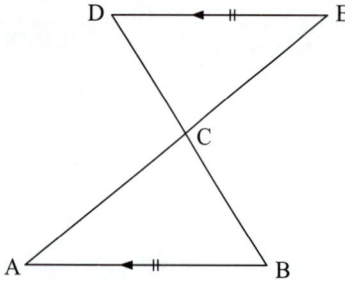 In the given figure, [DE] is parallel to [AB] and DE = AB.
Show that the triangles are congruent.

2 **a** Show that triangles ABD and CBD are congruent.

  b Given that $A\hat{B}D = 47°$ and $B\hat{A}D = 82°$, find the size of:

  i $C\hat{B}D$ **ii** $C\hat{D}B$.

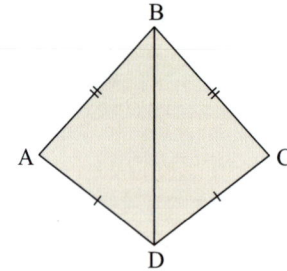

3 Consider the quadrilateral ABCD alongside. [AB] is parallel to [DC], and [AD] is parallel to [BC].

  a Use congruence to show that the opposite sides are equal in length.

  b Hence, show that the diagonals of a parallelogram bisect each other.

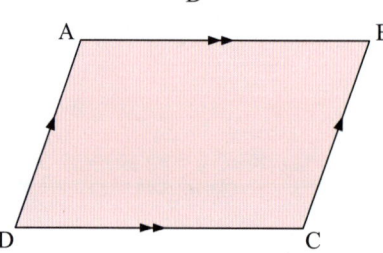

4 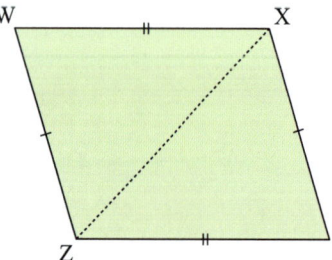 WXYZ is a quadrilateral with opposite sides equal. [XZ] is added to the figure.

  a Show that the two triangles created are congruent.

  b Hence deduce that WXYZ is a parallelogram.

5 The tangents to a circle at A and B intersect at P.
Show that AP = BP.

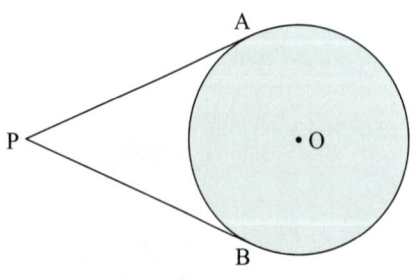

6 [AC] is a radius of the large circle, and a diameter of the small circle. A line through A cuts the small circle at X and the large circle at B.
Show that X is the midpoint of [AB].

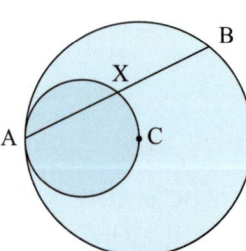

7 Triangle ABC is isosceles, with AB = AC. The angle bisectors of B and C are drawn, meeting the triangle at P and Q respectively. Show that AP = AQ.

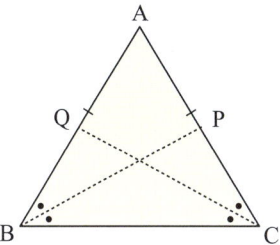

8 The perpendicular bisectors of a triangle's edges meet at a point called the **circumcentre** of the triangle.
Prove that the circumcentre is equidistant from each vertex of the triangle.

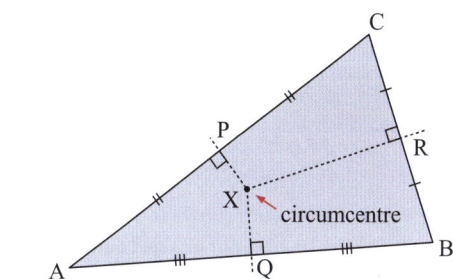

9 ABCD is a rectangle. Equilateral triangles are drawn from each side of the rectangle, with apexes W, X, Y, and Z.
Show that WXYZ is a rhombus.

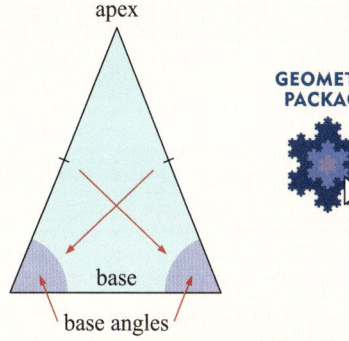

INVESTIGATION 1   THE ISOSCELES TRIANGLE THEOREM AND ITS CONVERSES

THE ISOSCELES TRIANGLE THEOREM

In an isosceles triangle:
- the base angles are equal
- the line joining the apex to the midpoint of the base bisects the vertical angle and meets the base at right angles.

CONVERSES OF THE ISOSCELES TRIANGLE THEOREM

With many theorems there are converses which we can use in problem solving. We have already seen one example in the converse to Pythagoras' theorem.

The isosceles triangle theorem has these converses:

Converse 1: If a triangle has two equal angles then it is isosceles.

Converse 2: The angle bisector of the apex of an isosceles triangle bisects the base at right angles.

Converse 3: The perpendicular bisector of the base of an isosceles triangle passes through its apex.

What to do:

1 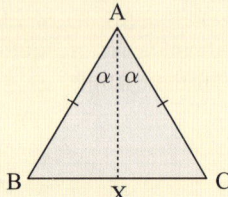 Triangle ABC is isosceles. The angle bisector at A meets [BC] at X. Prove *Converse 2* by using congruence to show that [AX] is perpendicular to [BC].

2 Sam wants to prove *Converse 1*.

  a Suppose Sam draws a line from the apex to the midpoint of the base. Can he use congruence to prove *Converse 1*?

  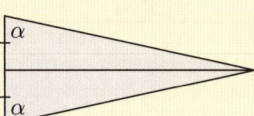

  b Sam now decides to begin by drawing the perpendicular from the apex to the base. Can he now use congruence to prove *Converse 1*?

  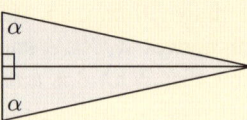

3 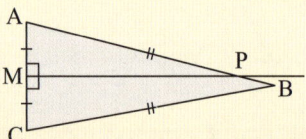 Mustafa is trying to prove *Converse 3*. He draws the perpendicular bisector of the base so that it does not pass through vertex B, but instead meets [AB] at some other point P. By joining [CP], help Mustafa complete his proof.

INVESTIGATION 2 — THE MIDPOINT THEOREM

In triangle ABC, M is the midpoint of [AB], and N is the midpoint of [AC].

The **midpoint theorem** states that the line [MN] is parallel to [BC], and half its length.

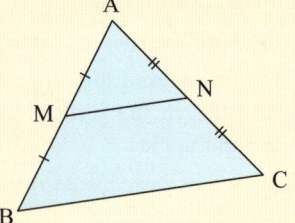

Proving the midpoint theorem

What to do:

Suppose we extend [MN], and draw a line through C parallel to [AB]. We let these lines meet at D.

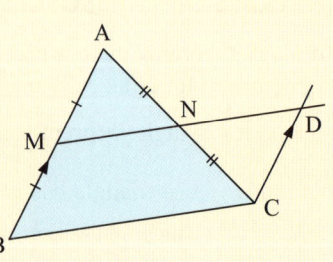

1 Show that triangles AMN and CDN are congruent.

2 Hence show that:
  a MN = DN
  b BM = CD.

3 Show that BCDM is a parallelogram.

4 Hence, show that:
  a [MN] is parallel to [BC]
  b MN = $\frac{1}{2}$BC.

Using the midpoint theorem

What to do:

1 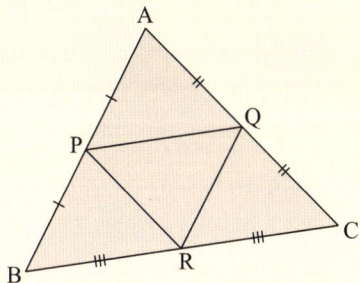 In the diagram alongside, P, Q, and R are the midpoints of [AB], [AC], and [BC] respectively. Use the midpoint theorem to show that the four small triangles are all congruent.

2 For any quadrilateral ABCD, let W, X, Y, and Z be the midpoints of [AB], [BC], [CD], and [DA] respectively. Use the midpoint theorem to show that WXYZ is a parallelogram.

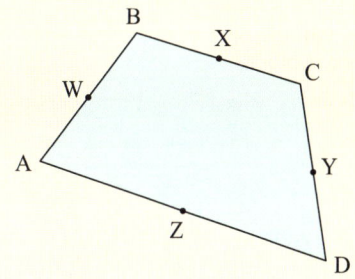

C SIMILARITY

> Two figures are **similar** if one is an enlargement of the other, regardless of orientation.

If two figures are similar then their corresponding sides are **in proportion**. The lengths of their sides will be increased (or decreased) by the **same ratio** from one figure to the next. This ratio is called the **enlargement factor**.

Consider the enlargement below for which the enlargement factor k is 1.5.

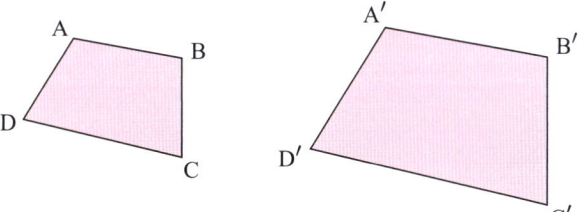

Since $k = 1.5$, $\dfrac{A'B'}{AB} = \dfrac{B'C'}{BC} = \dfrac{C'D'}{CD} = \dfrac{D'A'}{DA} = \dfrac{B'D'}{BD} = ... = 1.5$.

When a figure is enlarged or reduced, the size of its angles does not change. The figures are therefore **equiangular**.

> Two figures are **similar** if:
> - the figures are **equiangular** and
> - the corresponding sides are in the **same ratio**.

SIMILAR TRIANGLES

When we are dealing with triangles, if either of the above conditions is true, then the other condition must also be true. Therefore, when testing for similar triangles, we only need to check that *one* of the conditions is true.

> Two triangles are similar if *either*:
> - they are equiangular   *or*   • their side lengths are in the same ratio.

If we can show that two of the angles in one triangle are equal in size to two of the angles in another triangle, then the remaining angles must also be equal, since the angles in each triangle sum to 180°.

Once we have established that two triangles are similar, we can use the fact that corresponding sides are in the same ratio to find unknown lengths.

Example 3

Show that the following figures possess similar triangles:

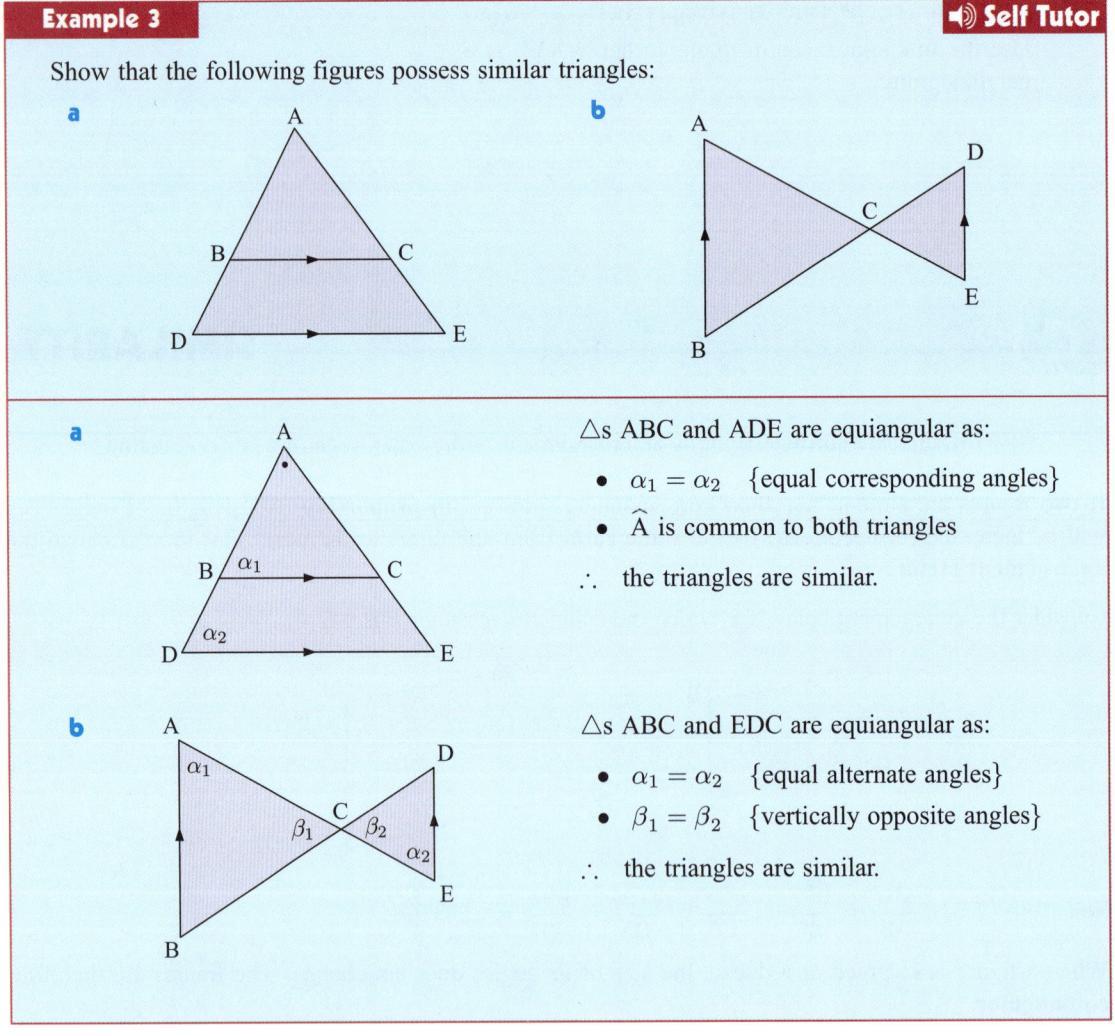

△s ABC and ADE are equiangular as:
- $\alpha_1 = \alpha_2$ {equal corresponding angles}
- $\widehat{A}$ is common to both triangles

∴ the triangles are similar.

△s ABC and EDC are equiangular as:
- $\alpha_1 = \alpha_2$ {equal alternate angles}
- $\beta_1 = \beta_2$ {vertically opposite angles}

∴ the triangles are similar.

EXERCISE 7C

1 Show that the following figures possess similar triangles:

a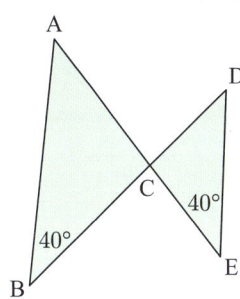

b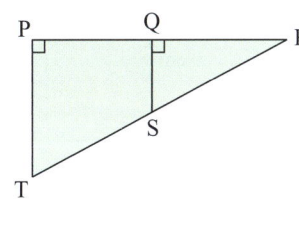

c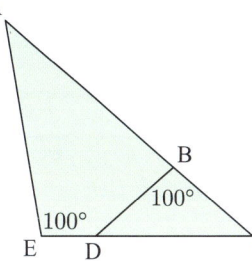

d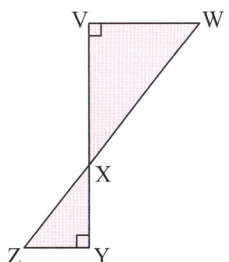

e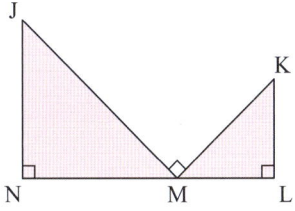

f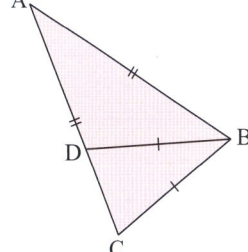

Example 4

Establish that a pair of triangles is similar, and hence find x:

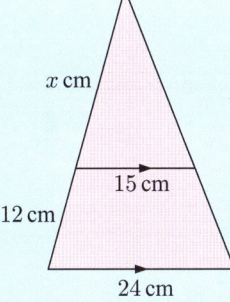

We label the vertices and angles of the figure so that we can easily refer to them.

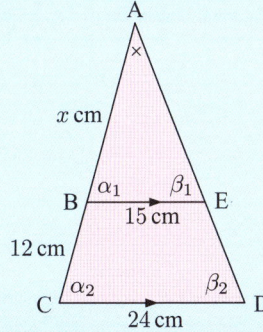

$\triangle$s ABE and ACD are equiangular since

$\alpha_1 = \alpha_2$ and $\beta_1 = \beta_2$ {corresponding angles}

$\therefore$ $\triangle$s ABE and ACD are similar.

Corresponding sides must be in the same ratio.

$\therefore \dfrac{AC}{AB} = \dfrac{CD}{BE}$

$\therefore \dfrac{x+12}{x} = \dfrac{24}{15}$

$\therefore 1 + \dfrac{12}{x} = \dfrac{8}{5}$

$\therefore \dfrac{12}{x} = \dfrac{3}{5}$

$\therefore \dfrac{x}{12} = \dfrac{5}{3}$

$\therefore x = 20$

2 For the following figures, establish that a pair of triangles is similar, and hence find x:

a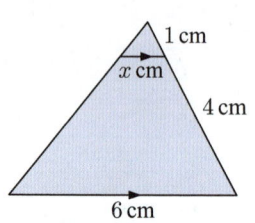

b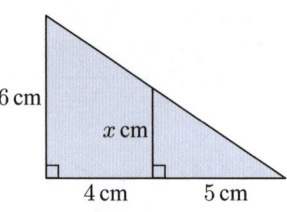

c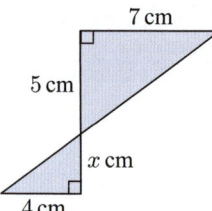

d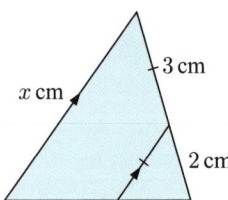

e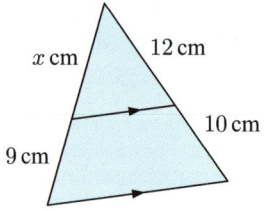

f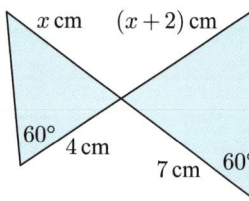

g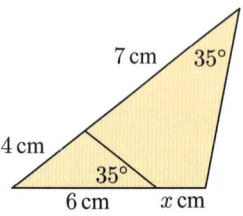

h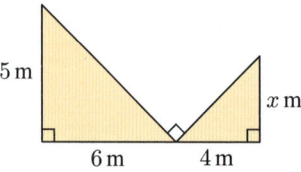

i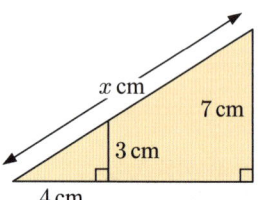

Example 5 ◀) Self Tutor

An electric light post E is directly opposite a mail box M on the other side of a straight road. Taj walks 30 metres along the road away from E to point T.

Kanvar is 4 metres away from M at point S, so that E, M, and S are in a straight line. Kanvar walks 6 metres parallel to the road in the opposite direction to Taj, to K. Now T, M, and K are in a straight line.

Find the width of the road.

Let the width of the road be x m.

△s TEM and KSM are equiangular as:

- $\hat{TEM} = \hat{KSM} = 90°$
- $\hat{EMT} = \hat{SMK}$ {vertically opposite angles}

∴ △s TEM and KSM are similar.

Corresponding sides must be in the same ratio.

∴ $\dfrac{EM}{SM} = \dfrac{TE}{KS}$

∴ $\dfrac{x}{4} = \dfrac{30}{6}$

∴ $x = 5 \times 4 = 20$

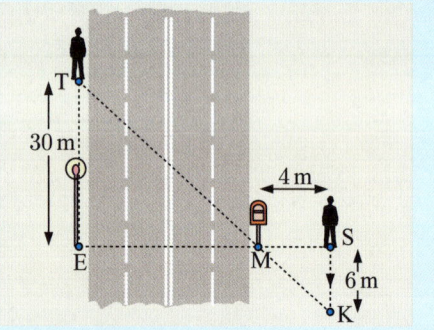

So, the road is 20 metres wide.

3 A boy who is 1.6 m tall stands 8.1 m from the base of an electric light pole. He casts a shadow 2.4 m long. How high above the ground is the light globe?

4 A 3.5 m ladder leans on a 2.4 m high fence. One end is on the ground and the other end touches a vertical wall 2.9 m from the ground.
How far is the bottom of the ladder from the fence?

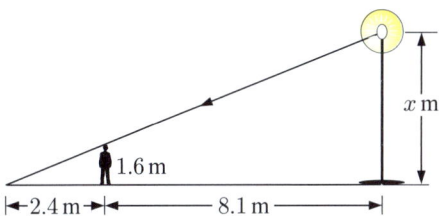

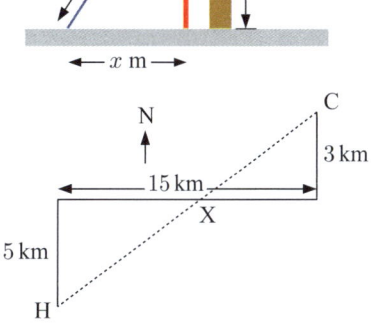

5 A hospital H receives a report about a serious road accident at C. An ambulance reaches the scene by travelling 5 km north, 15 km east, then 3 km north. A helicopter travels directly from H to C. Their paths intersect at X.
Find the distance from the hospital to X.

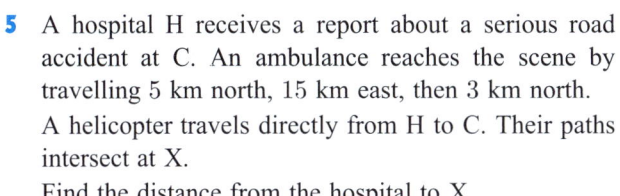

6 Two surveyors estimate the height of a nearby hill. One stands 5 m away from the other on horizontal ground holding a measuring stick vertically. The other surveyor finds a "line of sight" to the top of the hill, and observes that this line passes the vertical stick at a height of 2.4 m. They measure the distance from the stick to the top of the hill to be 1500 m using laser equipment.
Find, correct to the nearest metre, their estimate for the height of the hill.

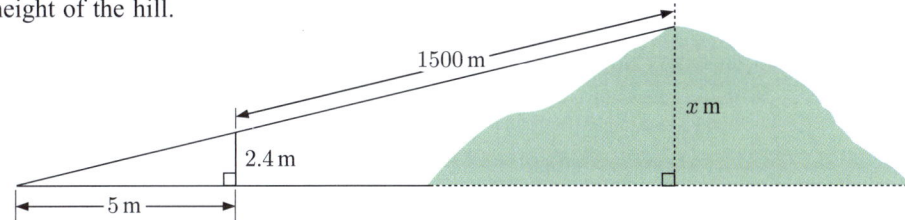

7 Mitchell pushes a coin of diameter 3 cm into a cone with diameter 9 cm and height 12 cm. How far into the cone can Mitchell push the coin before it gets stuck?

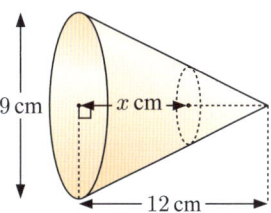

8 Answer the **Opening Problem** on page **132**.

9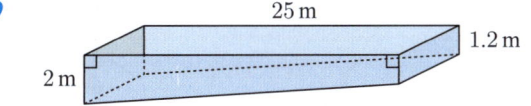

A swimming pool is 1.2 m deep at one end, and 2 m deep at the other end. The pool is 25 m long. Isaac jumps into the pool 10 m from the shallow end. How deep is the pool at this point?

10 It is safe to let go of the flying fox shown alongside when you are 3 m above the ground. How far can you travel along the flying fox before letting go?

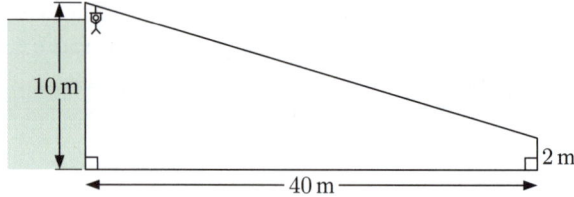

11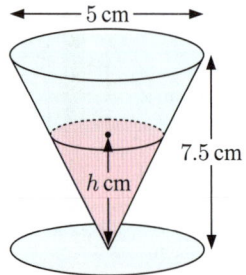

The conical medicine glass alongside is filled with 20 mL of medicine.
To what height does the medicine level rise?

ACTIVITY — THE SHOEMAKER'S KNIFE

The shaded area alongside is called an **arbelos**, a Greek word meaning "shoemaker's knife". It is formed by drawing two smaller semi-circles inside a large semi-circle.

Archimedes showed that if a line is drawn from P perpendicular to [AB], meeting the arbelos again at Q, then the area of the arbelos is equal to the area of the circle with diameter [PQ].

Can you use similarity to prove this fact?

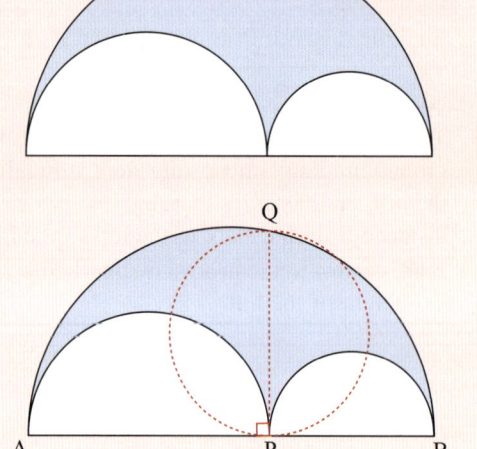

D   AREAS AND VOLUMES

Triangle **A** has base b cm and height h cm.

Suppose it is enlarged with scale factor k to produce a *similar* triangle **B**.

    Area of triangle **B**
$= \frac{1}{2}(kb)(kh)$
$= k^2(\frac{1}{2}bh)$
$= k^2 \times$ area of triangle **A**.

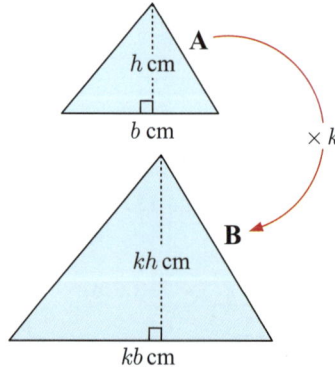

If $k > 1$, we have an enlargement. If $0 < k < 1$, we have a reduction.

This suggests that:

> If a figure is enlarged with scale factor k to produce a similar figure, then
> the new area $= k^2 \times$ the old area.

Example 6

For the following similar figures, find x:

a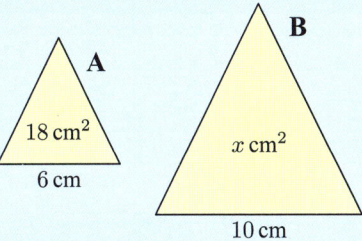

b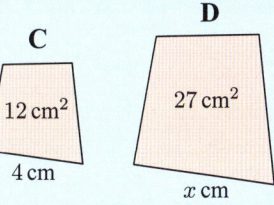

a A is enlarged with scale factor k to give B.
$\therefore\ k = \frac{10}{6} = \frac{5}{3}$
Area of B $= k^2 \times$ area of A
$\therefore\ x = (\frac{5}{3})^2 \times 18$
$\therefore\ x = 50$

b C is enlarged with scale factor k to give D.
Area of D $= k^2 \times$ area of C
$\therefore\ 27 = k^2 \times 12$
$\therefore\ \frac{9}{4} = k^2$
$\therefore\ k = \frac{3}{2}$ {as $k > 0$}
Since the sides are in the same ratio,
$x = \frac{3}{2} \times 4$
$\therefore\ x = 6$

VOLUME

The cylinder **A** has radius r cm and height h cm. Suppose it is enlarged with scale factor k to produce a *similar* cylinder **B**.

The radius of cylinder **B** will be kr, and its height will be kh.

Volume of cylinder **B**
$= \pi(kr)^2(kh)$
$= \pi(k^2r^2)(kh)$
$= k^3(\pi r^2 h)$
$= k^3 \times$ volume of cylinder **A**.

This suggests that:

> If a 3-dimensional figure is enlarged with scale factor k to produce a similar figure, then
> the new volume $= k^3 \times$ the old volume.

Example 7

For the following similar figures, find x:

a
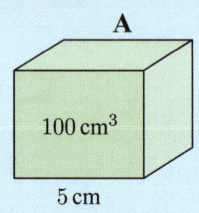
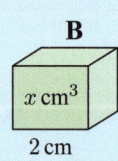

b
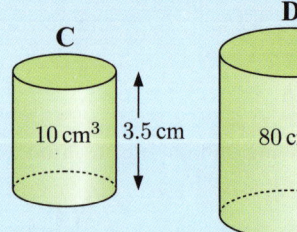

a A is reduced with scale factor k to give **B**.
$\therefore \ k = \frac{2}{5}$
Volume of **B** $= k^3 \times$ volume of **A**
$\therefore \ x = (\frac{2}{5})^3 \times 100$
$\therefore \ x = 6.4$

b C is enlarged with scale factor k to give **D**.
Volume of **D** $= k^3 \times$ volume of **C**
$\therefore \ 80 = k^3 \times 10$
$\therefore \ 8 = k^3$
$\therefore \ k = 2$
So, $x = 2 \times 3.5$
$\therefore \ x = 7$

EXERCISE 7D

1 For each pair of similar figures, find x:

a
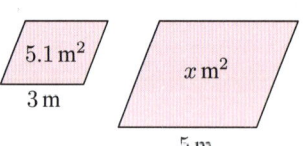

b
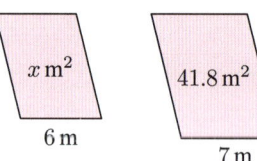

c
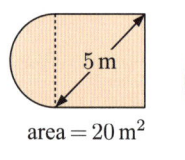

d
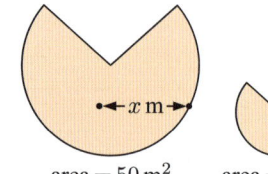

e
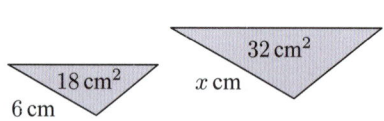

f
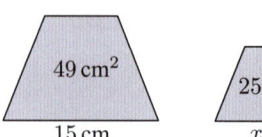

2 For each pair of similar figures, find x:

a
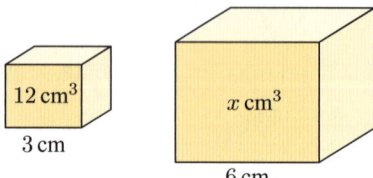

b
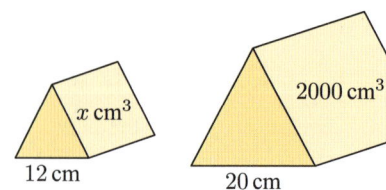

c

2.2 m, volume = 1.6 m³ ; 1 m, volume = x m³

d

5 cm, 24 cm³ ; x cm, 81 cm³

e

648 cm³, x cm ; 375 cm³, 11 cm

f

67 m³, 4 m ; 350 m³, x m

3

Triangle with A, B, C; D on AC with BD; E below with ED. BC = 5 cm, DE = 2 cm.

The area of △BCD is 6.4 cm². Find the area of:
  a △ACE   **b** quadrilateral ABDE.

4

P, Q, R with PQ = 5 m, QR = 4 m; T on PR with QT, PT = 6 m, TS = x m; angle α at T and at R.

  a Find the value of x.
  b Quadrilateral QRST has area 22 m². Find the area of △PQT.

5 Rhombuses **A** and **B** are similar.
Given that each side of **A** is 13.5 cm long, find the perimeter of **B**.

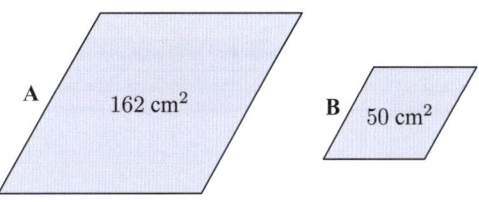

A: 162 cm²   B: 50 cm²

6 The *density* of an object is its ratio of mass to volume. Objects made of the same material have the same density, so their mass is in proportion to their volume.
  a What will happen to the mass of a sphere if its radius is:
    i doubled   **ii** increased by 20%?
  b What will happen to the mass of a cylinder if its radius and height are both:
    i halved   **ii** increased by 50%?
  c Two similar cones made from the same material have surface areas 192 cm² and 75 cm². The volume of the larger cone is 200 cm³. The mass of the smaller cone is 320 g.
    i Find the volume of the smaller cone.   **ii** Find the mass of the larger cone.

7 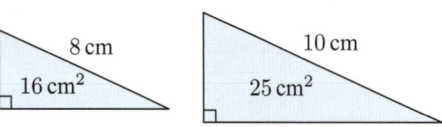 In parallelogram PQRS, M is the midpoint of [PQ]. Show that the red area is 4 times larger than the blue area.

8 Determine whether each of the pairs of figures below are similar.

  a   **b**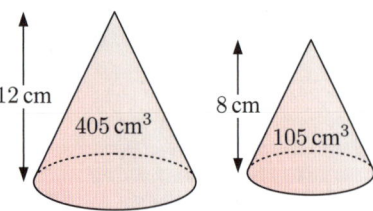

9 A scale model is made of a 300 year old sailing ship. The model is a 1 : 200 reduction of the original. Find:

  a the height of the mast in the model if the original mast was 20 m high
  b the area of a sail in the model if the original sail was 120 m²
  c the height and radius of a keg in the model if the original was 1.2 m high and 0.9 m in diameter
  d the capacity of the water tank in the model if the capacity of the original was 10 000 litres.

10 A glassware company manufactures cylindrical drinking glasses in six different sizes. Their heights and capacities are given below. Which two of the glasses are similar?

A 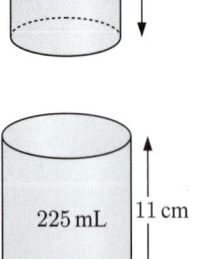 **B** 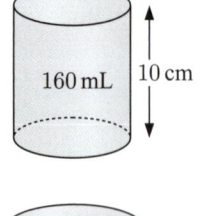 **C**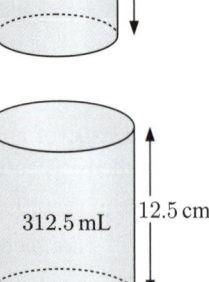

D **E** 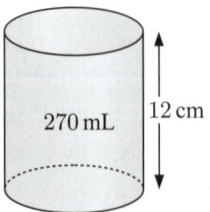 **F**

CONGRUENCE AND SIMILARITY (Chapter 7) 149

REVIEW SET 7A

1 In each set of three triangles, two are congruent. State which pair is congruent giving a reason for your answer. The triangles are not drawn to scale, but contain correct information.

   a   A   B   C

   b   A   B   C

2 Consider the quadrilateral ABCD.

   a Show that triangles ABC and CDA are congruent.
   b Hence deduce that ABCD is a parallelogram.

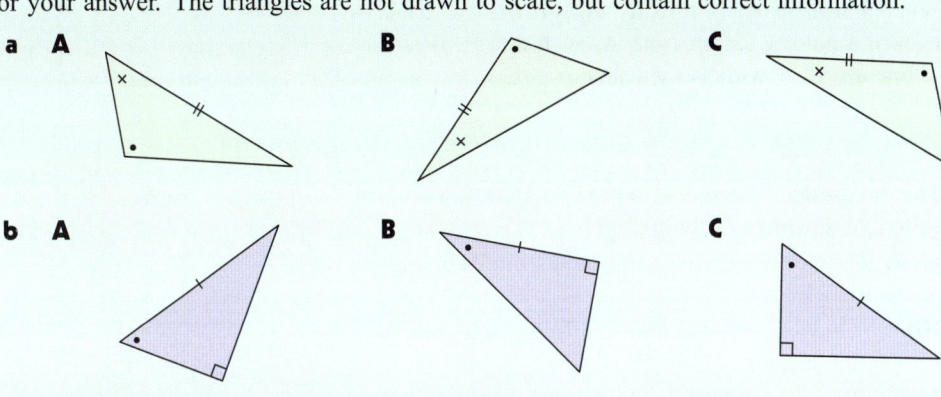

3 Show that the following figures possess similar triangles.

   a 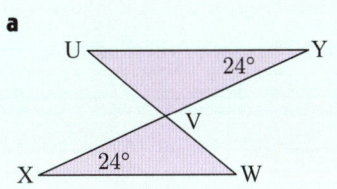   b 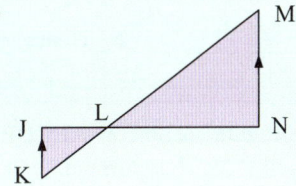   c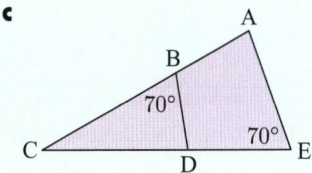

4 In each of the following figures, establish that a pair of triangles is similar, and hence find x:

   a 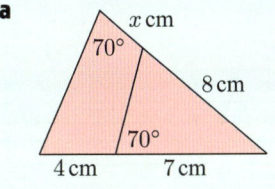   b 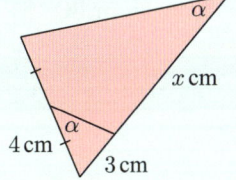   c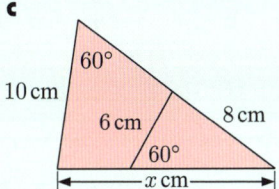

5 △ABC has an area of 15 cm².

   a Find the area of △CDE.
   b Find the area of PQED.

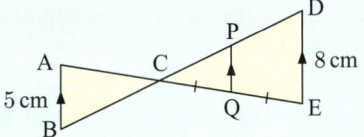

6
Triangle ABC is isosceles, with AB = AC.
[PQ] is parallel to [BC].
Show that CP = BQ.

7 A, B, and C are pegs on the bank of a canal which has parallel straight sides. C and D are directly opposite each other. AB = 30 m and BC = 140 m.
When I walk from A directly away from the bank, I reach a point E, 25 m from A, such that E, B, and D line up. How wide is the canal?

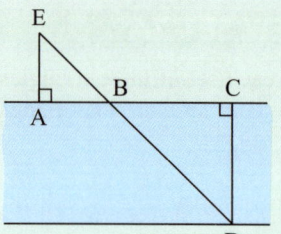

8 The three angle bisectors of a triangle meet at a point called the **incentre** of the triangle.
Show that the incentre is equidistant from each edge of the triangle.
Hint: Draw a perpendicular line from each edge to the incentre.

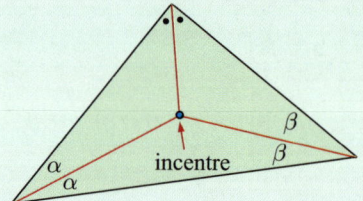

9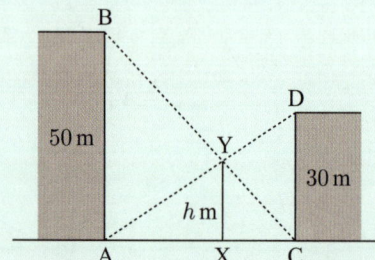

The vertical walls of two buildings are 50 m and 30 m tall. A vertical flagpole [XY] stands between the buildings such that B, Y, and C are collinear, and A, Y, and D are collinear.

a Show that $\dfrac{h}{50} + \dfrac{h}{30} = 1$.

b Hence, find the height of the flagpole.

10 When the diagonals of the regular pentagon ABCDE are drawn, a smaller pentagon PQRST is formed.

a Explain why all of the angles marked • are of equal size.

b Hence show that the interior angles of PQRST are of equal size.

c Hence show that PQRST is a regular pentagon.

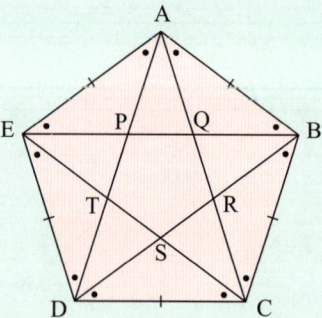

11 A sphere of lead with radius 10 cm is melted into 125 identical smaller spheres. Find the radius of each new sphere.

12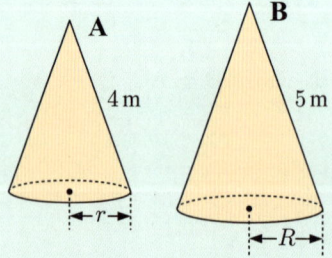

The slant heights of two similar cones are 4 m and 5 m respectively.

a Find the ratio $R : r$.

b Find the ratio of the surface areas for the curved part of each figure.

c Find the ratio of the volumes of the cones.

REVIEW SET 7B

1 Are these triangles congruent? If so, state the congruence relationship and give a brief reason.

a 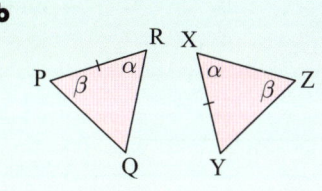   **b**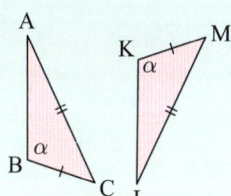

c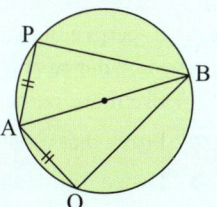

2 [AB] is a diameter of the circle.
   a Show that the figure contains congruent triangles.
   b What other facts can then be deduced about the figure?

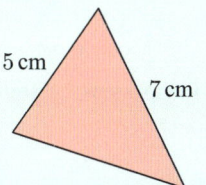

3 The figures alongside are similar. Find x.

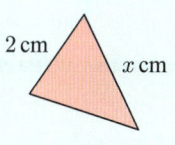

4 In the following figures, establish that a pair of triangles is similar, then find x:

a 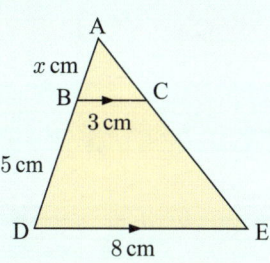   **b**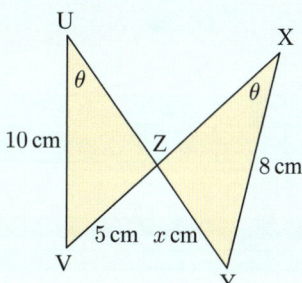

5 Triangle BCD has area 8 m^2, and quadrilateral ABDE has area 12 m^2.
Find the length of [AE].

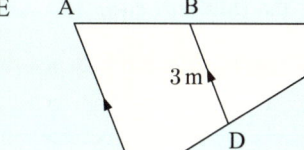

6 PQRS is a kite, with PQ = PS and QR = SR. M and N are the midpoints of [PQ] and [PS] respectively. Prove that triangle MNR is isosceles.

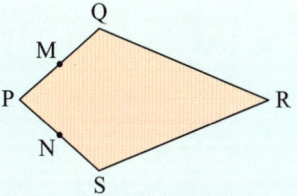

7 For the following similar figures, find x.

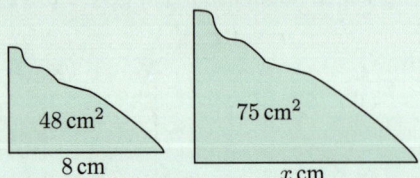

8 The cylinders below are made from the same material, so their densities are the same. Determine whether the cylinders are similar.

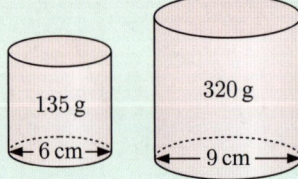

9 In $\triangle PQR$, M is the midpoint of [QR]. [MX] is drawn perpendicular to [PQ], and [MY] is drawn perpendicular to [PR].
Suppose these perpendiculars are equal in length.
  a Prove that $\triangle MQX$ is congruent to $\triangle MRY$.
  b Hence, prove that $\triangle PQR$ is isosceles.

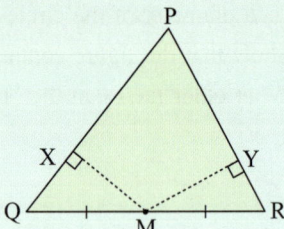

10 In a measuring cup set, the $\frac{1}{2}$ cup measure is 6 cm wide. The set also contains a 1 cup measure and a $\frac{1}{3}$ cup measure, both of which are similar in shape to the $\frac{1}{2}$ cup measure. Find the width of:
  a the 1 cup measure
  b the $\frac{1}{3}$ cup measure.

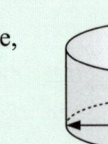

11

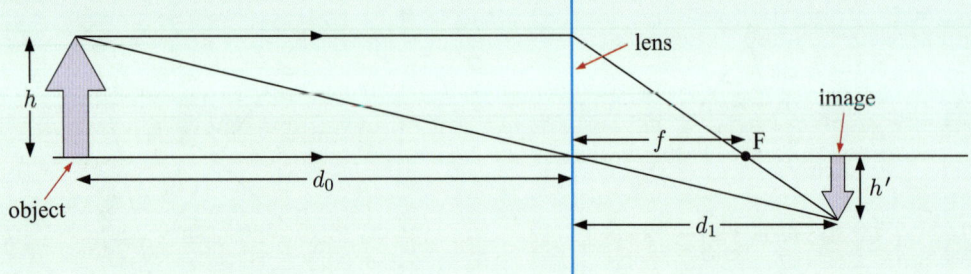

In optics, the **thin lens equation** states that $\dfrac{1}{f} = \dfrac{1}{d_0} + \dfrac{1}{d_1}$, where:

  f is the distance between the lens and the focal point F
  d_0 is the distance between the object and the lens
  d_1 is the distance between the image and the lens.

  a Use similar triangles to show that: **i** $\dfrac{h'}{h} = \dfrac{d_1}{d_0}$ **ii** $\dfrac{h'}{h} = \dfrac{d_1 - f}{f}$
  b Hence, show that $\dfrac{1}{f} = \dfrac{1}{d_0} + \dfrac{1}{d_1}$.

Chapter 8

Transformation geometry

Contents:
- **A** Translations
- **B** Reflections
- **C** Rotations
- **D** Dilations

OPENING PROBLEM

Consider the green triangle on the illustrated plane.

a What transformation would map the triangle onto:
  i triangle A   **ii** triangle B
  iii triangle C   **iv** triangle D?

b What single transformation would map triangle A onto triangle C?

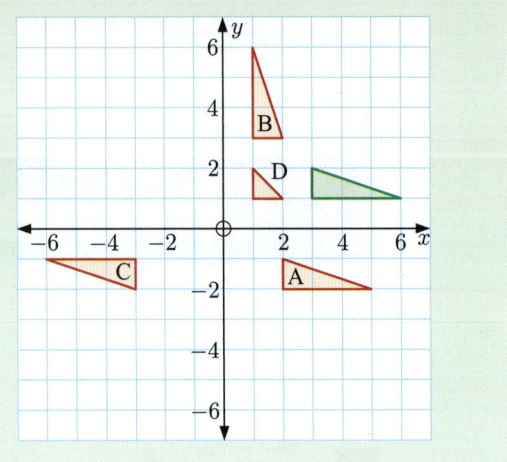

TRANSFORMATIONS

A change in the size, shape, orientation, or position of a figure is called a **transformation**.

Many trees, plants, flowers, animals, and insects are **symmetrical** in some way. Such symmetry results from a reflection, so we can describe symmetry using transformations.

Reflections, rotations, translations, and dilations are all examples of transformations. We can describe these transformations mathematically using **transformation geometry**.

The original figure is called the **object** and the new figure is called the **image**.

We will consider the following **transformations**:

- **Translations**, where every point moves a fixed distance in a given direction
- **Reflections** or mirror images
- **Rotations** about a point through a given angle
- **Dilations** (enlargements and reductions) of three kinds:
  ▸ with centre the origin
  ▸ vertical, with x-axis fixed
  ▸ horizontal, with y-axis fixed.

Here are some examples:

- **a translation**

  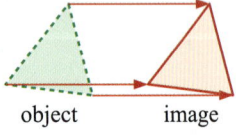

- **reflection**

  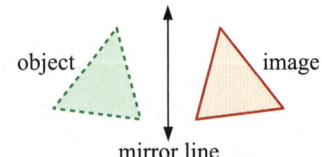

TRANSFORMATION GEOMETRY (Chapter 8) 155

- rotation about O through angle θ

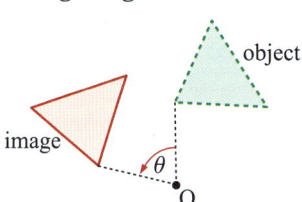

- an enlargement

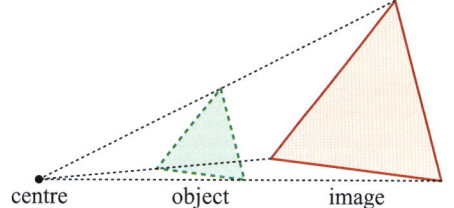

DEMO

A TRANSLATIONS

A **translation** moves a figure from one place to another. Every point on the figure moves the same distance in the same direction.

If P(x, y) is **translated** h units in the x-direction and k units in the y-direction, then the image point P$'$ has coordinates $(x + h, y + k)$.

We write P(x, y) $\xrightarrow{\binom{h}{k}}$ P$'(x + h, y + k)$

where P$'$ is called the **image** of the object P, and $\binom{h}{k}$ is called the **translation vector**.

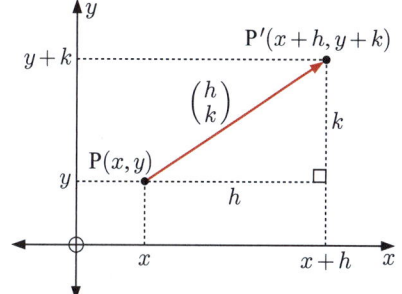

Example 1 ◀)) Self Tutor

Triangle OAB with vertices O$(0, 0)$, A$(2, 3)$, and B$(-1, 2)$ is translated $\binom{3}{2}$.

Find the image vertices and illustrate the object and image.

O$(0, 0)$ $\xrightarrow{\binom{3}{2}}$ O$'(3, 2)$

A$(2, 3)$ $\xrightarrow{\binom{3}{2}}$ A$'(5, 5)$

B$(-1, 2)$ $\xrightarrow{\binom{3}{2}}$ B$'(2, 4)$

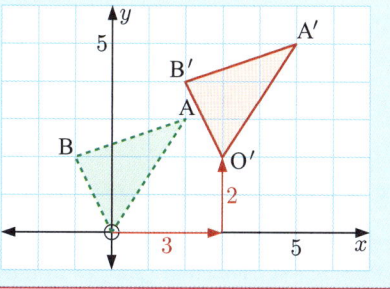

When we translate point A, we label its image A$'$.

EXERCISE 8A.1

1 Find the image point when:

a $(2, -1)$ is translated $\binom{3}{4}$

b $(5, 2)$ is translated $\binom{-1}{4}$.

2 Find the translation vector which translates the point:
  a (3, −2) to (3, 1)
  b (−1, 7) to (4, 2).

3 What point has image (−3, 2) under the translation $\begin{pmatrix} -3 \\ 1 \end{pmatrix}$?

4 Find the translation vector which maps:
  a A onto E
  b E onto A
  c A onto C
  d C onto A
  e B onto E
  f D onto E
  g E onto C
  h E onto D
  i D onto B
  j A onto D.

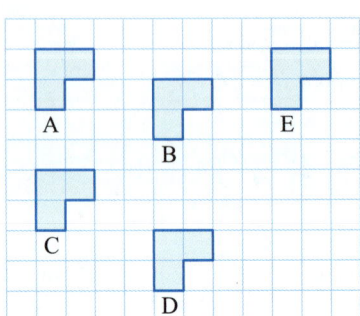

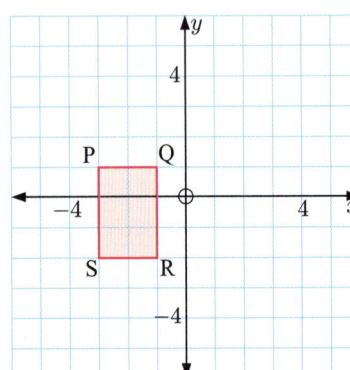

PQRS is a rectangle.
  a State the coordinates of P, Q, R, and S.
  b Copy the rectangle, and translate it $\begin{pmatrix} 5 \\ 1 \end{pmatrix}$.
  c State the coordinates of the image vertices P′, Q′, R′, and S′.

PRINTABLE DIAGRAM

6 Triangle ABC has vertices A(−1, 3), B(4, 1), and C(0, −2).
  a Draw triangle ABC on a set of axes.
  b Translate the figure $\begin{pmatrix} 4 \\ -2 \end{pmatrix}$.
  c State the coordinates of the image vertices A′, B′, and C′.
  d Find the distance each point has moved.

7 What single transformation is equivalent to a translation of $\begin{pmatrix} 2 \\ 1 \end{pmatrix}$ followed by a translation of $\begin{pmatrix} 3 \\ 4 \end{pmatrix}$?

TRANSLATION OF LINES AND CURVES

We have seen that when a point P(x, y) is translated $\begin{pmatrix} h \\ k \end{pmatrix}$ to the image point P′(x', y'), the image coordinates are given by the equations $\begin{cases} x' = x + h \\ y' = y + k \end{cases}$. We call these the **transformation equations** for the translation.

Rearranging the transformation equations, we find that $x = x' - h$ and $y = y' - k$.

If we are given the equation of a line or curve to be translated $\begin{pmatrix} h \\ k \end{pmatrix}$, we can substitute these expressions to find the equation of the resulting image. When we make the substitution, we leave off the dashes, since we do not need them in the final answer.

Example 2

Find the image equation when $2x - 3y = 6$ is translated $\begin{pmatrix} -1 \\ 2 \end{pmatrix}$.

Check your result by graphing.

The transformation equations are
$x' = x - 1$ and $y' = y + 2$
$\therefore \ x = x' + 1$ and $y = y' - 2$

So, we replace x by $(x + 1)$ and y by $(y - 2)$.

The image equation is
$2(x + 1) - 3(y - 2) = 6$
$\therefore \ 2x + 2 - 3y + 6 = 6$
$\therefore \ 2x - 3y = -2$

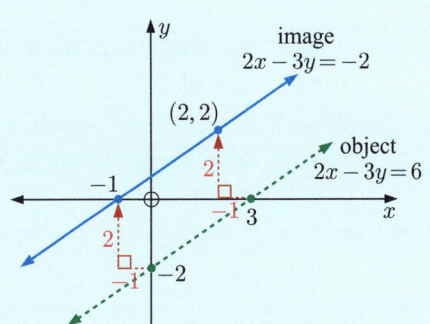

The image line is parallel to the object line.

EXERCISE 8A.2

1 Find the equation of the image line when:

a $y = 2x + 3$ is translated $\begin{pmatrix} -1 \\ 2 \end{pmatrix}$

b $y = \frac{1}{3}x + 2$ is translated $\begin{pmatrix} 3 \\ 0 \end{pmatrix}$

c $y = -x + 2$ is translated $\begin{pmatrix} 2 \\ 3 \end{pmatrix}$

d $y = -\frac{1}{2}x$ is translated $\begin{pmatrix} -2 \\ -5 \end{pmatrix}$

e $3x + 2y = 8$ is translated $\begin{pmatrix} -1 \\ 3 \end{pmatrix}$

f $x = 4$ is translated $\begin{pmatrix} 2 \\ 1 \end{pmatrix}$

g $2x - y = 6$ is translated $\begin{pmatrix} -3 \\ 0 \end{pmatrix}$

h $y = 5$ is translated $\begin{pmatrix} 2 \\ -5 \end{pmatrix}$.

2 Find the image equations of the following, and if possible give your answers in the form $y = f(x)$. Use the transformation geometry package to check your answers.

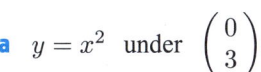

TRANSFORMATION GEOMETRY

a $y = x^2$ under $\begin{pmatrix} 0 \\ 3 \end{pmatrix}$

b $y = -2x^2$ under $\begin{pmatrix} 3 \\ 2 \end{pmatrix}$

c $xy = 5$ under $\begin{pmatrix} -4 \\ 1 \end{pmatrix}$

d $xy = -8$ under $\begin{pmatrix} 3 \\ -2 \end{pmatrix}$

e $y = 2^x$ under $\begin{pmatrix} 0 \\ -3 \end{pmatrix}$

f $y = 3^{-x}$ under $\begin{pmatrix} 2 \\ 0 \end{pmatrix}$

B REFLECTIONS

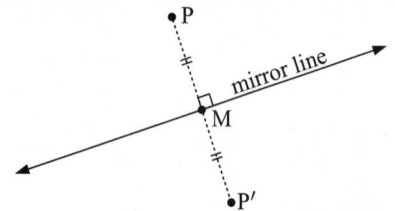

When $P(x, y)$ is **reflected** in the **mirror line** to become $P'(x', y')$, the mirror line perpendicularly bisects [PP']. This means that $PM = P'M$.

We will concentrate on the following reflections:

$\mathbf{M}_x$ the reflection in the x-axis
$\mathbf{M}_y$ the reflection in the y-axis
$\mathbf{M}_{y=x}$ the reflection in the line $y = x$
$\mathbf{M}_{y=-x}$ the reflection in the line $y = -x$.

Example 3

Find the image of the point $(3, 1)$ in:

  a $\mathbf{M}_x$ **b** $\mathbf{M}_y$ **c** $\mathbf{M}_{y=x}$ **d** $\mathbf{M}_{y=-x}$

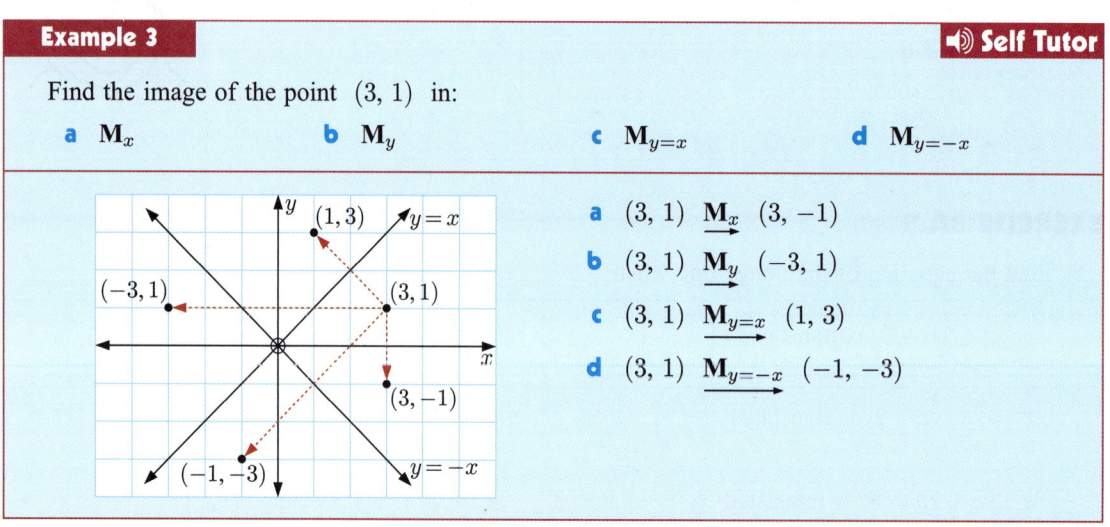

The diagram in **Example 3** is useful for deducing the transformation equations for the four basic reflections.

For example, for $(3, 1) \xrightarrow{\mathbf{M}_{y=x}} (1, 3)$ we can see that in general $(x, y) \xrightarrow{\mathbf{M}_{y=x}} (y, x)$.

$\therefore\ x' = y$ and $y' = x$

Reflection	Transformation equations
$(x, y) \xrightarrow{\mathbf{M}_x} (x, -y)$	$x' = x$ and $y' = -y$
$(x, y) \xrightarrow{\mathbf{M}_y} (-x, y)$	$x' = -x$ and $y' = y$
$(x, y) \xrightarrow{\mathbf{M}_{y=x}} (y, x)$	$x' = y$ and $y' = x$
$(x, y) \xrightarrow{\mathbf{M}_{y=-x}} (-y, -x)$	$x' = -y$ and $y' = -x$

If you forget these or want to check any of them, choose a point such as $(3, 1)$.

Example 4

Find the image equation of $2x - 3y = 8$ reflected in the y-axis.
Check your result by graphing.

The transformation equations are

$x' = -x$ and $y' = y$

$\therefore\ x = -x'$ and $y = y'$

So, we replace x by $(-x)$ and leave y as is.

The image equation is $2(-x) - 3(y) = 8$

$\therefore\ -2x - 3y = 8$

$\therefore\ 2x + 3y = -8$

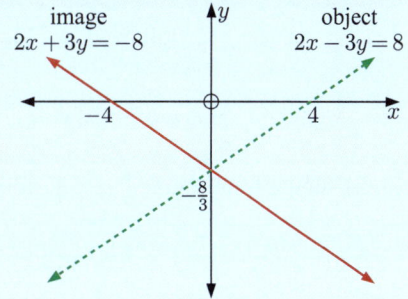

EXERCISE 8B

1 Copy and reflect in the given line:

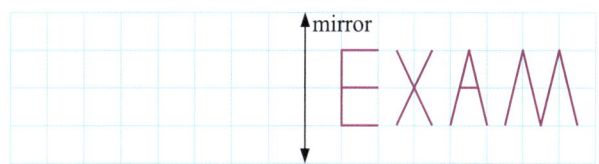

2 Find, by graphical means, the image of the point $(4, -1)$ under:

   a M_x **b** M_y **c** $M_{y=x}$ **d** $M_{y=-x}$.

3 Find, by graphical means, the image of the point $(-1, -3)$ under:

   a M_x **b** M_y **c** $M_{y=x}$ **d** $M_{y=-x}$.

4 Copy the graph given. Reflect T in:

   a the x-axis and label it U

   b the y-axis and label it V

   c the line $y = -x$ and label it W.

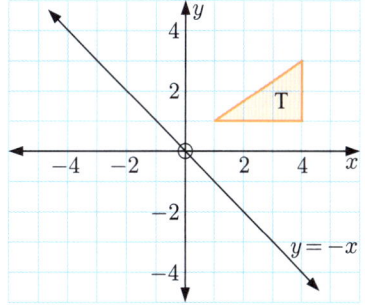

5 Find the image equation of:

   a $y = 2x + 3$ under M_x **b** $y = x^2$ under M_x

   c $y = \dfrac{5}{x}$ under M_y **d** $y = 2^x$ under $M_{y=x}$

   e $2x + 3y = 4$ under $M_{y=-x}$ **f** $x^2 + y^2 = 4$ under M_x

   g $y = -x^2$ under M_x **h** $2x - 3y = 4$ under M_y

   i $x = 3$ under $M_{y=-x}$ **j** $y = 2x^2$ under $M_{y=x}$

160 TRANSFORMATION GEOMETRY (Chapter 8)

6 Find the image of:

DEMO

   a $(2, 3)$ under M_x followed by translation $\begin{pmatrix} -1 \\ 2 \end{pmatrix}$

   b $(4, -1)$ under $M_{y=-x}$ followed by translation $\begin{pmatrix} 4 \\ 3 \end{pmatrix}$

   c $(-1, 5)$ under M_y followed by M_x followed by translation $\begin{pmatrix} 2 \\ -4 \end{pmatrix}$

   d $(3, -2)$ under $M_{y=x}$ followed by translation $\begin{pmatrix} 3 \\ 4 \end{pmatrix}$

   e $(4, 3)$ under translation $\begin{pmatrix} 1 \\ -4 \end{pmatrix}$ followed by M_x

   f $(-2, 5)$ under $M_{y=-x}$ followed by translation $\begin{pmatrix} -3 \\ 1 \end{pmatrix}$.

7 Consider the line $y = 2x + 3$.

   a Find the equation of the image when the line is translated $\begin{pmatrix} 3 \\ -2 \end{pmatrix}$.

   b If the resulting image is reflected using M_x, find the equation of the reflected image.

   c Draw the three lines on the same set of axes, clearly labelling each line.

8 Consider the curve $y = 3^x$.

   a Find the equation of the image when the curve is reflected using M_y.

   b If the resulting image is translated $\begin{pmatrix} -4 \\ 1 \end{pmatrix}$, find the equation of the translated image.

   c Draw the three curves on the same set of axes, clearly labelling each curve.

C   ROTATIONS

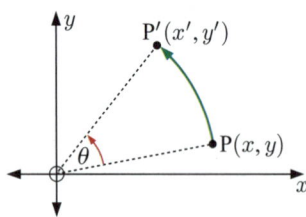

If $P(x, y)$ is moved under a **rotation** about O through an angle of θ to a new position $P'(x', y')$, then $OP = OP'$ and $\widehat{POP'} = \theta$.

O is the only point which does not move under such a rotation.

Positive θ is measured **anticlockwise**.

We use $\mathbf{R}_\theta$ to indicate a rotation about O through an angle of $\theta°$.

We will concentrate on the following rotations:

Rotation	Transformation equations
$(x, y) \xrightarrow{\mathbf{R}_{90}} (-y, x)$	$x' = -y$ and $y' = x$
$(x, y) \xrightarrow{\mathbf{R}_{-90}} (y, -x)$	$x' = y$ and $y' = -x$
$(x, y) \xrightarrow{\mathbf{R}_{180}} (-x, -y)$	$x' = -x$ and $y' = -y$

Example 5   ◁)) Self Tutor

Find the image of the point $(3, 1)$ under: **a** $\mathbf{R}_{90}$ **b** $\mathbf{R}_{-90}$ **c** $\mathbf{R}_{180}$

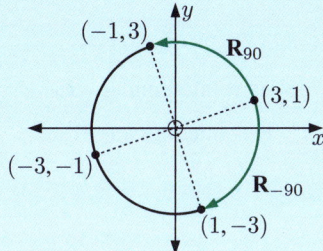

a $(3, 1) \xrightarrow{\mathbf{R}_{90}} (-1, 3)$ anticlockwise

b $(3, 1) \xrightarrow{\mathbf{R}_{-90}} (1, -3)$ clockwise

c $(3, 1) \xrightarrow{\mathbf{R}_{180}} (-3, -1)$

Example 6   ◁)) Self Tutor

Find the image equation of the line $2x - 3y = -6$ under a clockwise rotation about O through $90°$. Check your result by graphing.

The transformation equations are $x' = y$ and $y' = -x$
$$\therefore \quad x = -y' \quad \text{and} \quad y = x'$$

So, we replace x by $(-y)$ and y by (x).

The image equation is $2(-y) - 3(x) = -6$
$$\therefore \quad -2y - 3x = -6$$
$$\therefore \quad 3x + 2y = 6$$

Check:

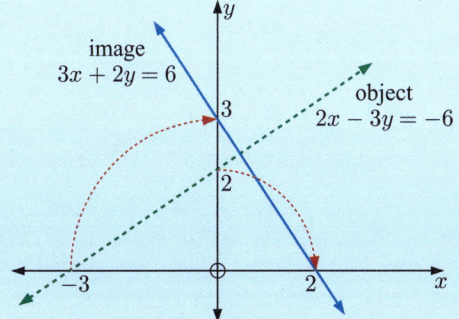

The object and image are perpendicular.

EXERCISE 8C

1 Find the image of the point $(-2, 3)$ under:
  a R_{90}
  b R_{-90}
  c R_{180}

2 Find the image of the point $(4, -1)$ under:
  a R_{90}
  b R_{-90}
  c R_{180}

3 Triangle ABC has vertices A(2, 4), B(4, 1), and C(2, 1). It is rotated anticlockwise through 90° about O.
  a Draw triangle ABC and its image $A'B'C'$.
  b Write down the coordinates of A', B', and C'.

4 Triangle PQR with P(3, −2), Q(1, 4), and R(−1, 1) is rotated about O through 180°.
  a Draw triangle PQR and its image $P'Q'R'$.
  b Write down the coordinates of P', Q', and R'.

5 Find the image equation when:
  a $3x - 4y = 7$ is rotated under R_{-90}
  b $y = -3$ is rotated under R_{90}
  c $x = 7$ is rotated under R_{180}
  d $y = x^2$ is rotated under R_{180}
  e $2x + 3y = 12$ is rotated under R_{-90}.

6 Find the image of:
  a $(2, 3)$ under R_{90} followed by M_x
  b $(-2, 5)$ under $M_{y=-x}$ followed by R_{-90}
  c $(-3, -1)$ under $M_{y=x}$ followed by R_{180}
  d $(4, -2)$ under R_{90} followed by translation $\begin{pmatrix} -2 \\ -3 \end{pmatrix}$

7 Find the image of:
  a $x - y = 8$ under $M_{y=-x}$ followed by translation $\begin{pmatrix} 4 \\ -1 \end{pmatrix}$
  b $x + 2y = -4$ under R_{-90} followed by translation $\begin{pmatrix} 2 \\ -5 \end{pmatrix}$
  c $x + y = 1$ under R_{90} followed by $M_{y=x}$ followed by translation $\begin{pmatrix} 3 \\ 1 \end{pmatrix}$.

Global context

click here

Transforming art

Statement of inquiry: Understanding form and shape enhances creativity.
Global context: Personal and cultural expression
Key concept: Form
Related concepts: Pattern, Space
Objectives: Investigating patterns, Communication
Approaches to learning: Thinking

TRANSFORMATION GEOMETRY (Chapter 8)   163

DILATIONS

A **dilation** is an enlargement or reduction.

DILATIONS WITH CENTRE THE ORIGIN

Suppose $P(x, y)$ moves to $P'(x', y')$ such that P' lies on the line (OP), and $OP' = kOP$.

We call this a **dilation** with centre O and **scale factor** k.

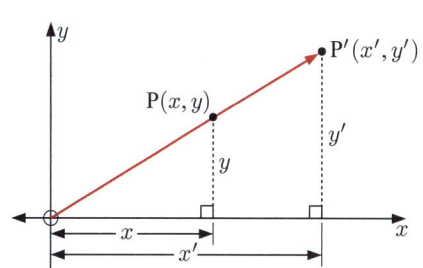

From the similar triangles

$$\frac{x'}{x} = \frac{y'}{y} = \frac{OP'}{OP} = k$$

$$\therefore \quad x' = kx \text{ and } y' = ky$$

$k = \dfrac{OP'}{OP}$ is a ratio of distances, so k is positive.

The **transformation equations** for a **dilation** with **centre** $O(0, 0)$ and **scale factor** k are: $\begin{cases} x' = kx \\ y' = ky. \end{cases}$

Example 7   ◀)) Self Tutor

Consider the triangle ABC with vertices $A(1, 1)$, $B(4, 1)$, and $C(1, 4)$ under a dilation with centre O and scale factor   **a** $k = 2$ **b** $k = \frac{1}{2}$.

Draw the image of $\triangle ABC$ under each dilation.

a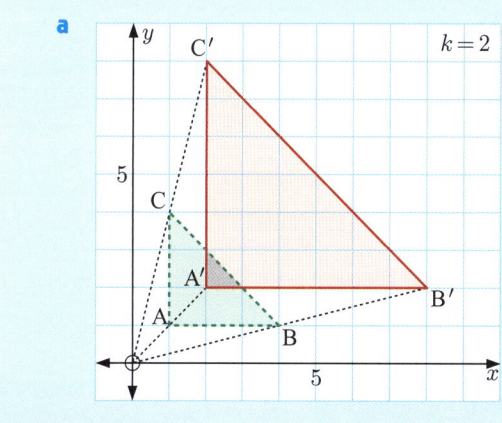

b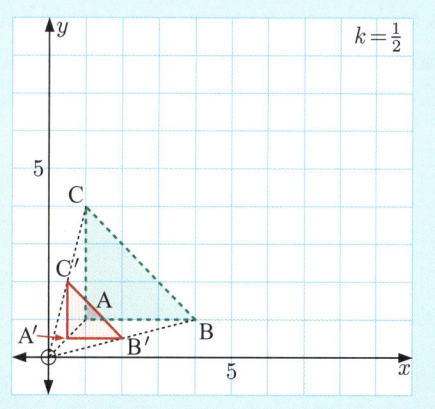

We can see from the examples above that:

If $k > 1$, the image is an **enlargement** of the object.
If $0 < k < 1$, the image is a **reduction** of the object.

> **DISCUSSION**   **NEGATIVE SCALE FACTORS**
>
> - Do we need to consider negative scale factors?
> - What combination of transformations would be equivalent to a dilation with centre O and scale factor $k = -2$?
> - If we allowed negative scale factors, what would this say about the *uniqueness* of describing a series of transformations?

Example 8   🔊 Self Tutor

Find the equation of the image when $y = x^2$ is dilated with centre O and scale factor 3. Illustrate your answer.

Since $k = 3$, the transformation equations are
$$x' = 3x \text{ and } y' = 3y$$
$$\therefore x = \frac{x'}{3} \text{ and } y = \frac{y'}{3}$$

So, we replace x by $\left(\frac{x}{3}\right)$ and y by $\left(\frac{y}{3}\right)$.

The image equation is $\frac{y}{3} = \left(\frac{x}{3}\right)^2$

$$\therefore \frac{y}{3} = \frac{x^2}{9}$$

$$\therefore y = \tfrac{1}{3}x^2$$

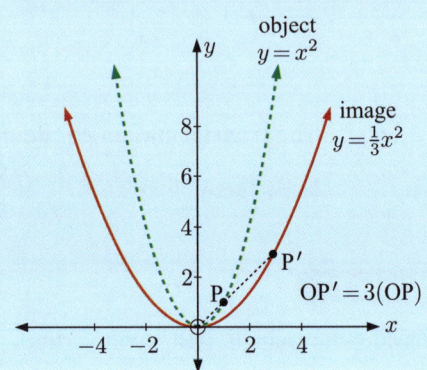

VERTICAL DILATIONS WITH FIXED x-AXIS

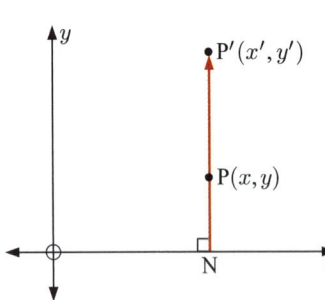

For a vertical dilation with fixed x-axis, we stretch the figure in the vertical direction only.

Suppose $P(x, y)$ moves to $P'(x', y')$ such that P' lies on the line through $N(x, 0)$ and P, and $NP' = kNP$.

We call this a **vertical dilation** with scale factor k.

For a **vertical dilation** with **scale factor** k, the **transformation equations** are:
$$\begin{cases} x' = x \\ y' = ky \end{cases}$$

Example 9

Consider the triangle ABC with A(1, 1), B(5, 1), and C(1, 4) under a vertical dilation with scale factor **a** $k = 2$ **b** $k = \frac{1}{2}$.

Draw the image of $\triangle$ABC under each dilation.

a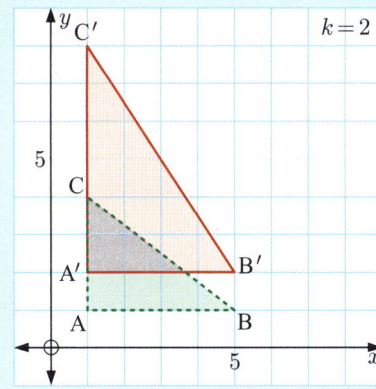

b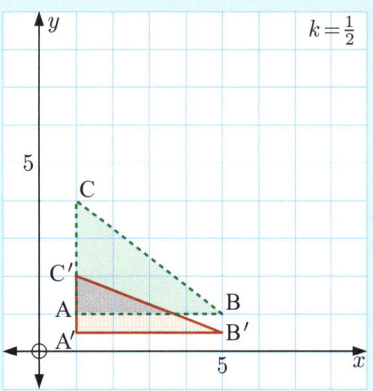

HORIZONTAL DILATIONS WITH FIXED y-AXIS

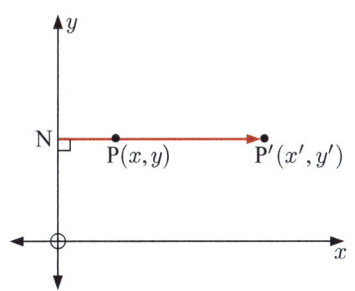

For a horizontal dilation with fixed y-axis, we stretch the figure in the horizontal direction only.

Suppose P(x, y) moves to P$'(x', y')$ such that P$'$ lies on the line through N$(0, y)$ and P, and NP$' = k$NP.

We call this a **horizontal dilation** with scale factor k.

For a **horizontal dilation** with **scale factor** k, the **transformation equations** are: $\begin{cases} x' = kx \\ y' = y. \end{cases}$

Example 10

Consider the triangle ABC with A(1, 1), B(5, 1), and C(1, 4) under a horizontal dilation with scale factor **a** $k = 2$ **b** $k = \frac{1}{2}$.

Draw the image of $\triangle$ABC under each dilation.

a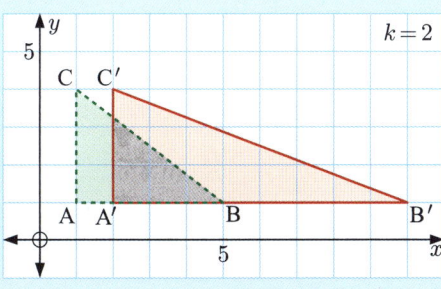

b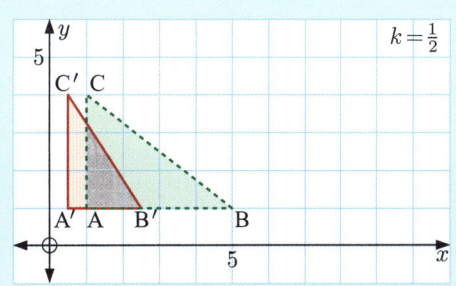

Example 11

Find the image of a circle with centre O and radius 3 units, under a horizontal dilation with scale factor 2.

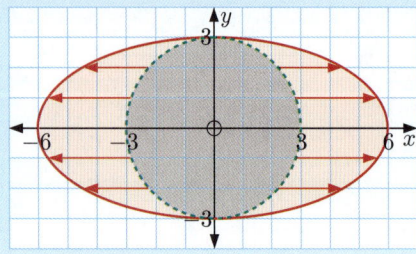

$x' = 2x$ and $y' = y$

$\therefore$ the horizontal distances from the y-axis are doubled whilst the y-values remain the same.

The image is an ellipse.

EXERCISE 8D

1 Find the image of:
   a $(2, 3)$ under a dilation with centre O and scale factor 3
   b $(-1, 4)$ under a dilation with centre O and scale factor $\frac{1}{3}$
   c $(3, -1)$ under a vertical dilation with scale factor 4
   d $(4, 5)$ under a vertical dilation with scale factor 2
   e $(-2, 1)$ under a horizontal dilation with scale factor $\frac{1}{2}$
   f $(3, -4)$ under a horizontal dilation with scale factor $\frac{3}{2}$.

2 Find the image equation of:
   a $y = 2x + 3$ under a dilation with centre O and scale factor 2
   b $y = -x^2$ under a dilation with centre O and scale factor $\frac{1}{2}$
   c $y = 2x^2$ under a horizontal dilation with scale factor 4
   d $xy = 2$ under a horizontal dilation with scale factor 2
   e $y = -x + 2$ under a vertical dilation with scale factor 3
   f $y = 2^x$ under a vertical dilation with scale factor 2.

3 Sketch the image of a circle with centre O and radius 2 units under:
   a a dilation with centre O and scale factor $\frac{3}{2}$
   b a vertical dilation with scale factor $\frac{3}{2}$
   c a horizontal dilation with scale factor $\frac{3}{2}$.

4 a Describe the single transformation which maps the object rectangle OABC onto the image rectangle OA$'$B$'$C$'$.

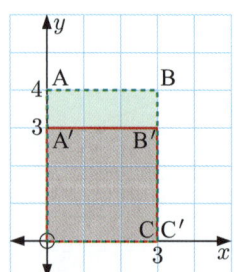

b 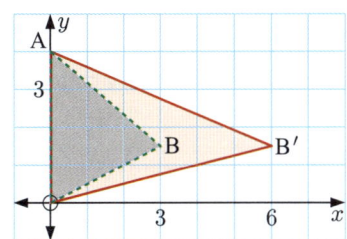 Describe the single transformation which maps the object triangle OAB onto the image triangle OAB'.

c ABCD is mapped onto A'B'C'D'. Describe the single transformation which has occurred.

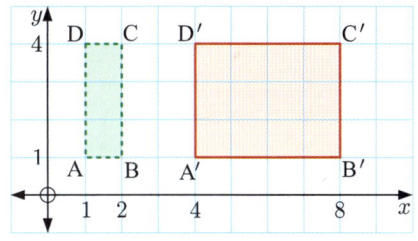

d 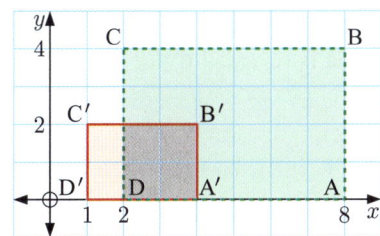 ABCD is mapped onto A'B'C'D'. Describe the single transformation which has occurred.

DISCUSSION — INVARIANT POINTS

Invariant points are points which do not move under a transformation.

What points would be invariant under a:

- translation
- reflection
- rotation
- dilation?

INVESTIGATION — LINEAR TRANSFORMATIONS

A **linear transformation** transforms a point $P(x, y)$ to $P'(x', y')$ using transformation equations of the form $\begin{cases} x' = ax + by \\ y' = cx + dy \end{cases}$ where a, b, c, and d are real numbers.

For example, consider the **unit square** with vertices $O(0, 0)$, $A(1, 0)$, $B(1, 1)$, and $C(0, 1)$.

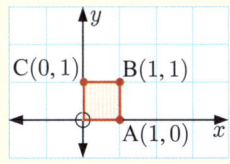

If we perform the linear transformation
$\begin{cases} x' = 3x + y \\ y' = x + 2y \end{cases}$

then $O(0, 0) \rightarrow O'(0, 0)$
  $A(1, 0) \rightarrow A'(3, 1)$
  $B(1, 1) \rightarrow B'(4, 3)$
  $C(0, 1) \rightarrow C'(1, 2)$.

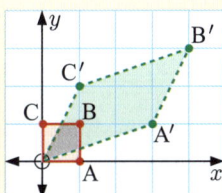

Notice that:
- OABC is labelled anticlockwise and O'A'B'C' is also labelled anticlockwise. In this case we say that the **sense** of the object has been **preserved**. Otherwise, we would say the sense was **reversed**.
- O'A'B'C' has area 5 units^2.
  So, the area of the image $= 5 \times$ the area of the object.

What to do:

1 Determine the effect that each linear transformation has on the unit square's sense and area:

   a $\begin{cases} x' = 2x + y \\ y' = x + 2y \end{cases}$
   b $\begin{cases} x' = x + y \\ y' = x - y \end{cases}$
   c $\begin{cases} x' = 2x \\ y' = 2y \end{cases}$

   d $\begin{cases} x' = 2x \\ y' = y \end{cases}$
   e $\begin{cases} x' = x - 3y \\ y' = x + y \end{cases}$
   f $\begin{cases} x' = -2x + y \\ y' = 3x + 2y \end{cases}$

2 Consider the general linear transformation $\begin{cases} x' = ax + by \\ y' = cx + dy. \end{cases}$

   a Show that sense is preserved if $ad - bc > 0$, and is reversed if $ad - bc < 0$.
   b If $k = |ad - bc|$ is the modulus or absolute value of $ad - bc$, show that the area of the image $= k \times$ the area of the object.
   c Explain what happens in the case $ad - bc = 0$.

REVIEW SET 8A

1 Find the image point when:

   a $(-4, 3)$ is translated $\begin{pmatrix} 5 \\ -3 \end{pmatrix}$
   b $(-1, -6)$ is translated $\begin{pmatrix} -2 \\ 4 \end{pmatrix}$.

2 Find the image equation of:

   a $3x - 2y = 6$ under $\begin{pmatrix} -1 \\ 4 \end{pmatrix}$
   b $y = 2$ under $\begin{pmatrix} -4 \\ 1 \end{pmatrix}$
   c $2x + y = 5$ under $\begin{pmatrix} 2 \\ 3 \end{pmatrix}$
   d $y = 2x^2$ under $\begin{pmatrix} 2 \\ -5 \end{pmatrix}$.

3 Find the image of:

   a $(2, -5)$ under $\mathbf{M}_y$
   b $(-3, 6)$ under $\mathbf{M}_{y=x}$
   c $(-1, 5)$ under $\mathbf{R}_{-90}$
   d $(3, -5)$ under $\mathbf{R}_{90}$.

4 Find the equation of the image of:

   a $y = 3x + 2$ under $\mathbf{M}_y$
   b $y = 3x^2$ under $\mathbf{M}_x$
   c $y = 3^x$ under $\mathbf{M}_{y=x}$
   d $xy = 6$ under $\mathbf{M}_{y=-x}$.

5 Find the image of:

   a $(5, 1)$ under $\mathbf{R}_{180}$ followed by the translation $\begin{pmatrix} 2 \\ 3 \end{pmatrix}$
   b $(-2, 4)$ under $\mathbf{M}_y$ followed by $\mathbf{M}_x$.

6 Consider the line $2x + y = 6$.
  a Rotate the line under R_{90}.
  b Translate the resulting image $\begin{pmatrix} 3 \\ -1 \end{pmatrix}$.
  c Draw the three lines on the same set of axes, clearly labelling each line.

7 Find the image of:
  a $(2, -1)$ under a dilation with centre O and scale factor 2
  b $(3, 5)$ under a vertical dilation with scale factor 4
  c $(-4, -7)$ under a horizontal dilation with scale factor 2.

8 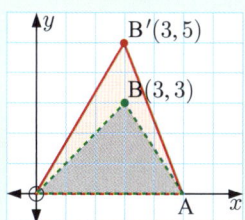 The triangle OAB is mapped onto OAB'. Describe the transformation which has occurred.

9 Find the image equation of:
  a $y = 3x + 2$ under a dilation with centre O and scale factor 3
  b $2x - 5y = 10$ under a vertical dilation with scale factor 2
  c $y = -2x + 1$ under a horizontal dilation with scale factor $\frac{1}{2}$
  d $y = x^2 - 3x + 5$ under a reflection in the x-axis
  e $x^2 + y^2 = 4$ under the translation $\begin{pmatrix} 5 \\ -2 \end{pmatrix}$.

10 Answer the **Opening Problem** on page 154.

11 Sketch the image of a circle with centre O and radius 4 units under a dilation with centre O and scale factor $\frac{1}{2}$.

REVIEW SET 8B

1 Find the image of $(3, -2)$ under a reflection in:
  a the x-axis
  b the y-axis
  c the line $y = -x$.

2 Find the image of $(3, -7)$ under:
  a a translation of $\begin{pmatrix} 2 \\ -4 \end{pmatrix}$ followed by a reflection in the y-axis
  b a reflection in the x-axis followed by a reflection in the line $y = -x$.

3 Find the image of $(2, -5)$ under:
  a R_{90}
  b R_{-90}
  c R_{180}.

4 Find the image of:
  a $(3, -2)$ under M_x
  b $(5, -4)$ under $M_{y=-x}$
  c $(-2, -5)$ under R_{180}
  d $(-2, 7)$ under R_{-90}

5 Find the image equation of:

   a $5x - 2y = 8$ under the translation $\begin{pmatrix} 3 \\ -2 \end{pmatrix}$

   b $y = -x^2$ under the translation $\begin{pmatrix} -2 \\ 5 \end{pmatrix}$

   c $xy = -4$ under the translation $\begin{pmatrix} 1 \\ -2 \end{pmatrix}$

   d $x^2 + y^2 = 9$ under the translation $\begin{pmatrix} -3 \\ -4 \end{pmatrix}$

6 Find the equation of the image of:

   a $3x - 4y = 8$ under $\mathbf{M}_{y=x}$ **b** $xy = -12$ under $\mathbf{R}_{180}$

   c $2x + 3y = 9$ under $\mathbf{R}_{90}$ **d** $y = -2x^2$ under $\mathbf{M}_x$

7 Find the image of:

   a $(3, -7)$ under $\mathbf{M}_y$ followed by the translation $\begin{pmatrix} 2 \\ -6 \end{pmatrix}$

   b $(3, -2)$ under $\mathbf{M}_{y=-x}$ followed by $\mathbf{R}_{-90}$.

8 Find the image of:

   a $(3, 5)$ under a dilation with centre O and scale factor 3

   b $(-2, 3)$ under a horizontal dilation with scale factor 2

   c $(-5, -3)$ under a vertical dilation with scale factor $\frac{1}{2}$.

9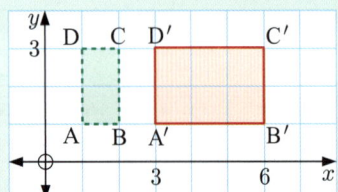

The object ABCD is mapped onto the image A'B'C'D'.

Describe the single transformation which has occurred.

10 Find the image equation of:

   a $y = -2x + 1$ under a vertical dilation with scale factor 3

   b $y = 2 - 5x$ under a horizontal dilation with scale factor $\frac{1}{3}$

   c $2x - 6y = 7$ under a dilation with centre O and scale factor 2

   d $y = 2x^2 - 3x - 1$ under $\mathbf{R}_{90}$

   e $x^2 + y^2 = 8$ under the translation $\begin{pmatrix} -3 \\ -4 \end{pmatrix}$.

Chapter 9

Statistics

Contents:
- **A** Discrete data
- **B** Continuous data
- **C** Measuring the centre
- **D** Cumulative data
- **E** Measuring the spread
- **F** Box-and-whisker plots
- **G** Standard deviation
- **H** The normal distribution

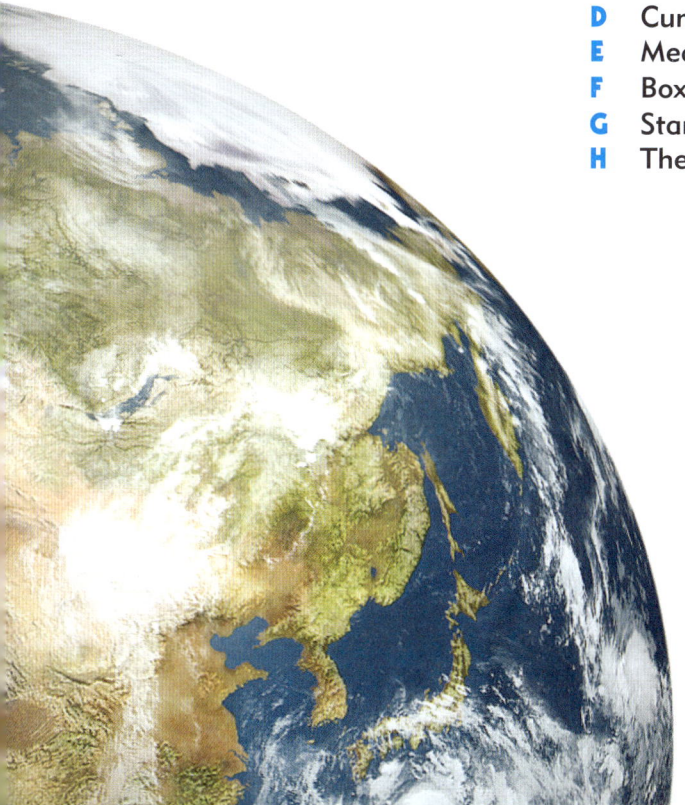

OPENING PROBLEM

Roland owns 2 hotels, one in New York and one in Miami. He wants to find out whether there is a difference in the number of nights guests stay at the hotels.

He therefore inspects the last 40 reservations placed for each hotel, and records the number of nights the guests stayed.

New York

2 3 1 2 4 2 6 3 4 5
8 3 1 3 4 2 1 2 4 5
3 6 2 3 2 1 3 6 2 4
8 1 5 7 2 1 8 5 3 2

Miami

2 4 4 5 3 6 2 3 1 7
2 3 4 3 5 6 5 2 4 7
3 2 8 1 7 3 1 2 5 6
4 5 6 4 5 4 8 1 3 7

Things to think about:

a What is the best way to organise this data?

b How can the data be displayed?

c What is the most common length of stay at each hotel?

d How can Roland best measure:
  i the average length of stay for each hotel
  ii the spread of each data set?

e Can a reliable conclusion be drawn from the data? What factors could affect the reliability of the conclusion?

f How could Roland improve the accuracy of his investigation?

HISTORICAL NOTE

Florence Nightingale (1820-1910) was a British nurse in Turkey during the Crimean War. She worked in very difficult conditions, with overcrowding, poor sanitation, little food, and few basic supplies. Nightingale provided a statistical argument for the British government to provide improved facilities. By the time the war ended in 1856, the hospitals were well-run and efficient, with mortality rates no greater than civilian hospitals in England. Nightingale had earned an extraordinary reputation, along with the label "the lady with the lamp".

Florence Nightingale

After returning from the war, Nightingale compiled vast tables of statistics about how many soldiers died, where and why. Many of her findings shocked her. She discovered that in peacetime, soldiers in England died at twice the rate of civilians, even though they were strong young men. She recognised that the problems with the military health service extended far beyond the hospitals during war-time. The statistics also made Nightingale realise that poor sanitation had been the principal cause of most of the deaths in Turkey. Work conducted in March 1855 by the Turkish Sanitary Commission led to a dramatic decrease in deaths due to disease. However, Nightingale worried that Queen Victoria would not properly consider the data presented in the tables, so she found ways to present the data in charts, to persuade the Queen of the need for action.

Nightingale's best-known chart was a variation of a pie graph called the **polar area diagram**. It showed the number of deaths each month and their causes. Each month is represented as a twelfth of a circle. Months with more deaths were shown with longer wedges, and the area of each wedge represented the number of deaths in that month from wounds, disease, or other causes. Nightingale used blue wedges to represent disease, red wedges for wounds, and black wedges for other causes. Using this diagram, Nightingale illustrated the dramatic effect of the Sanitary Commission's work in 1855, as the wedges were far smaller in the following months.

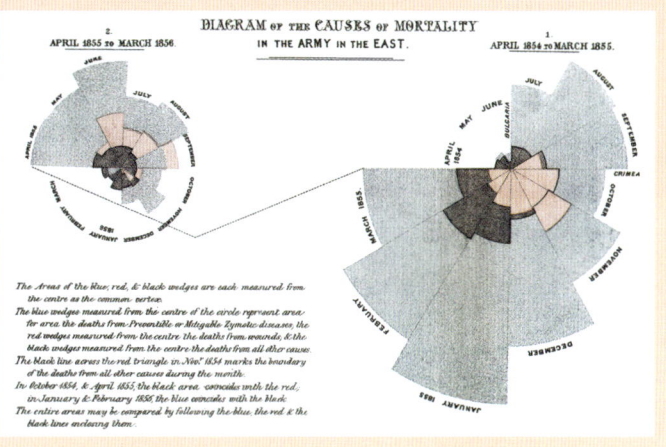

Nightingale's work had a lasting effect. By the end of the century, Army mortality was lower than civilian mortality. She wrote, "To understand God's thoughts we must study statistics, for these are the measure of his purpose."

In **statistics** we collect and analyse data to give us an understanding of the world around us.

Most nations conduct a census at regular intervals to gain information about their populations. The United Nations gives assistance to developing countries to help them with census procedures, so that accurate and comparable worldwide statistics can be collected.

DISCRETE DATA

A **discrete variable** takes exact number values, and is often a result of **counting**.

For example, in the **Opening Problem**, the *number of nights stayed* is a discrete variable. It can only take an exact value such as 1, 2, 3, 4, 5, ...

ORGANISATION AND DISPLAY OF DISCRETE DATA

A **tally and frequency table** can be used to organise numerical data.

The data can then be displayed using a **column graph** or **dot plot**.

For the New York hotel data, we have:

Tally and frequency table

Nights	Tally	Frequency
1							6
2										10
3									8
4						5
5						4
6					3
7			1
8					3

Column graph

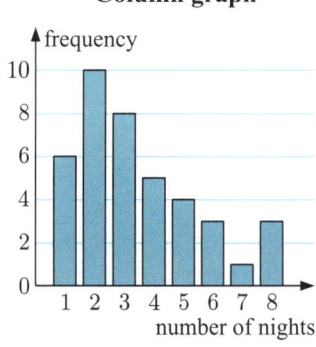

Dot plot

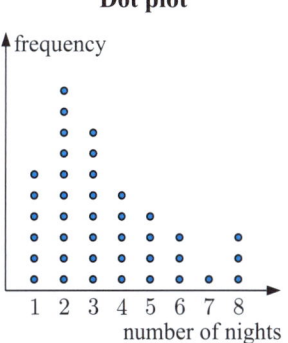

DESCRIBING THE DISTRIBUTION OF THE DATA SET

Many data sets show **symmetry** or **partial symmetry** about the **mode**, which is the most frequently occurring value.

If we place a curve over the column graph alongside, we see that this curve shows symmetry. We say that we have a **symmetrical distribution**.

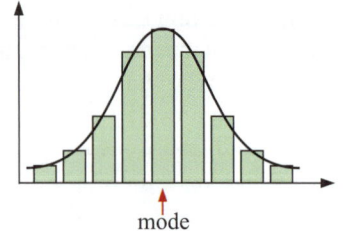

The distribution for the New York hotel data is shown alongside. It is said to be **positively skewed** because, by comparison with the symmetrical distribution, it has been 'stretched' on the right or positive side of the mode.

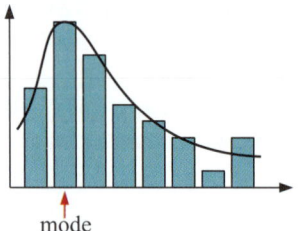

So, we have:

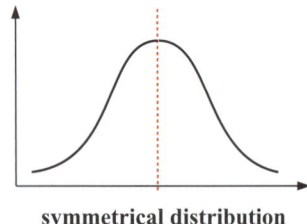
symmetrical distribution

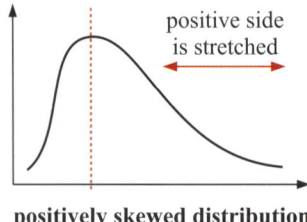
positively skewed distribution

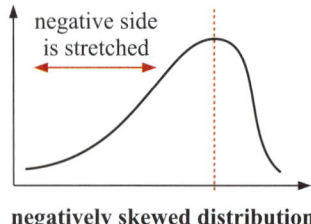
negatively skewed distribution

OUTLIERS

> **Outliers** are data values that are either much larger or much smaller than the general body of data. Outliers appear separated from the body of data on a frequency graph.

For example, in the data set   3, 1, 7, 6, 8, 18, 2, 6, 7, 7,   the data value 18 is an outlier. If outliers are genuine pieces of data, then they should be included in an analysis of the whole data set. However, if outliers occur due to human recording error, they should not be included when the data is analysed.

GROUPED DISCRETE DATA

In situations where there are lots of different numerical values recorded, it may not be practical to use an ordinary tally and frequency table, or to display the data using a dot plot or column graph. Instead, we group the data into **class intervals**.

For example, a local hardware store is studying the number of people visiting the store at lunch time. Over 30 consecutive weekdays they recorded the data:

37, 30, 17, 13, 46, 23, 40, 28, 38, 24, 23, 22, 18, 29, 16, 35, 24, 18, 24, 44, 32, 54, 31, 39, 32, 38, 41, 38, 24, 32.

In this case, we group the data into class intervals of length 10. The tally and frequency table is shown alongside.

Number of people	Tally	Frequency
10 to 19	|||||	5
20 to 29	||||| ||||	9
30 to 39	||||| |||||		11
40 to 49	||||	4
50 to 59			1
	Total	30

We can now use this table to draw a column graph for the data. However, we must remember that the individual data values are no longer seen.

EXERCISE 9A

1 A randomly selected sample of shoppers was asked, "How many times did you shop at a supermarket in the past week?" A column graph was constructed for the results.

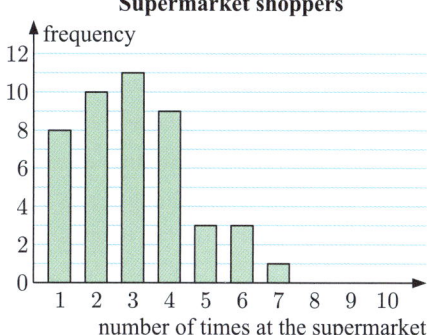

Supermarket shoppers

  a How many shoppers gave data in the survey?

  b How many of the shoppers shopped once or twice?

  c What percentage of the shoppers shopped more than four times?

  d Describe the distribution of the data.

2 Employees of a company were asked how many times they left the office on business appointments during one week. The following dot plot was constructed from the data:

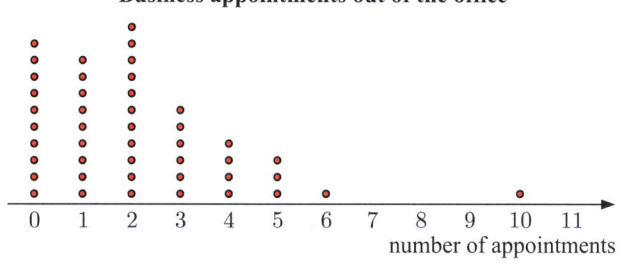

Business appointments out of the office

  a How many employees did not leave the office?

  b What percentage of the employees left the office more than 5 times?

  c Describe the distribution of the data.

  d How would you describe the data value '10'?

3 20 students were asked "How many TV sets do you have in your household?" The following data was collected:

        2 1 0 3 1 2 1 3 4 0 0 2 2 0 1 1 0 1 0 1

  a Construct a dot plot to display the data.

  b How would you describe the distribution of the data? Are there any outliers?

  c How many households had no TV sets?

  d What percentage of the households had three or more TV sets?

4 The number of toothpicks in a box is stated as 50, but the actual number of toothpicks has been found to vary. To investigate this, the number of toothpicks in a box was counted for a sample of 60 boxes. The results were:

50 52 51 50 50 51 52 49 50 48 51 50 47 50 52 48 50 49 51 50
49 50 52 51 50 50 52 50 53 48 50 51 50 50 49 48 51 49 52 50
49 49 50 52 50 51 49 52 52 50 49 50 49 51 50 50 51 50 53 48

a Use a tally and frequency table to organise this data.
b Display the data using a column graph.
c Describe the distribution of the data.
d What percentage of the boxes contained exactly 50 toothpicks?

5 Consider the data for the Miami hotel in the **Opening Problem** on page **172**.
a Organise the data in a tally and frequency table.
b Draw a column graph of the data.
c Are there any outliers?
d Describe the distribution of the data.
e Compare your column graph with that for the New York hotel on page **173**. In which hotel do guests generally stay longer?

6 The data below are the test scores (out of 100) for a Science test for 50 students.

92 29 78 67 68 58 80 89 92
69 66 56 88 81 70 73 63 55
67 64 62 74 56 75 90 56 47
59 64 89 39 51 87 89 76 59
72 80 95 68 80 64 53 43 61
71 38 44 88 62

a Construct a tally and frequency table for this data using class intervals 20 - 29, 30 - 39, ..., 90 - 100.
b What percentage of the students scored 80 or more for the test?
c What percentage of students scored less than 50 for the test?
d Copy and complete the following:
More students had a test score in the interval ...... than in any other interval.
e Describe the distribution of the data.

7 A test score out of 60 marks is recorded for a group of 45 students:

34 37 44 51 53 39 33 58 40 42 43 43 47 37 35
41 43 48 50 55 44 44 52 54 59 39 31 29 44 57
45 34 29 27 18 49 41 42 37 42 43 43 45 34 51

a Organise the data in a tally and frequency table, using the test score ranges 15 - 19, 20 - 24, and so on.
b Draw a column graph for the data.
c Describe the distribution of the data.
d An A is awarded to students who scored 50 or more in the test. What percentage of students scored an A?

B CONTINUOUS DATA

A **continuous variable** takes values within a certain continuous range, and is usually a result of **measuring**.

When data is recorded for a continuous variable, there will be many different values. The data is therefore organised using **class intervals**. A **frequency histogram** is used to display the data.

A histogram is similar to a column graph, but because the data is continuous, the columns are joined together.

An example is given alongside.

The **modal class** is the class of values that appears most often. On a histogram, the modal class has the highest column.

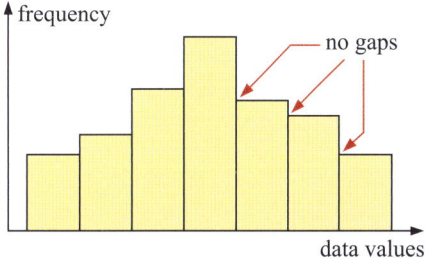

Example 1

The weights of parcels sent on a given day from a post office were, in kilograms:

  4.07   1.63   3.52   2.91   3.24   3.47   5.29   4.63
  3.11   2.85   3.76   4.92   3.44   1.39   2.58   2.22

a Organise the data into class intervals.
b Draw a frequency histogram to display the data.
c Find the modal class.
d Describe the distribution of the data.
e Over the next month, 564 parcels are sent from the post office. Estimate the number which weigh more than 4 kg.

a The lowest weight recorded was 1.39 kg and the highest was 5.29 kg, so we will use class intervals of 1 kg.
We suppose w is the weight of a parcel.

Weight w (kg)	Frequency
$1 \leqslant w < 2$	2
$2 \leqslant w < 3$	4
$3 \leqslant w < 4$	6
$4 \leqslant w < 5$	3
$5 \leqslant w < 6$	1

b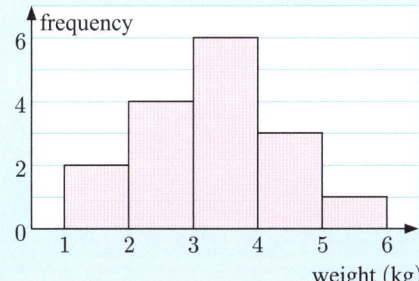

Distribution of parcel weights

c The modal class is $3 \leqslant w < 4$ kg.
d The distribution is approximately symmetrical.
e Of the 16 parcels sent on the one day, $\frac{4}{16} = \frac{1}{4}$ of them weighed more than 4 kg.
∴ for the next month we expect
$\frac{1}{4} \times 564 = 141$ parcels to weigh more than 4 kg.

EXERCISE 9B

1 A frequency table for the weights w of players in a volleyball squad is given alongside.

Weight w (kg)	Frequency
$75 \leqslant w < 80$	2
$80 \leqslant w < 85$	5
$85 \leqslant w < 90$	8
$90 \leqslant w < 95$	7
$95 \leqslant w < 100$	5
$100 \leqslant w < 105$	1

  a Explain why *weight* is a continuous variable.
  b Construct a frequency histogram to display the data.
  c Find and interpret the modal class.
  d Describe the distribution of the data.

2 A plant inspector takes a random sample of seedlings from a nursery, and measures their height h in millimetres.
The results are shown in the table alongside.

Height h (mm)	Frequency
$20 \leqslant h < 40$	4
$40 \leqslant h < 60$	17
$60 \leqslant h < 80$	15
$80 \leqslant h < 100$	8
$100 \leqslant h < 120$	2
$120 \leqslant h < 140$	4

  a How many of the seedlings are 100 mm or more?
  b What percentage of the seedlings are between 60 and 80 mm?
  c Represent the data on a frequency histogram.
  d Find the modal class.
  e Describe the distribution of the data.
  f There are 857 seedlings in the nursery. Estimate the number of seedlings which measure:
    i less than 100 mm   **ii** between 40 and 100 mm.

3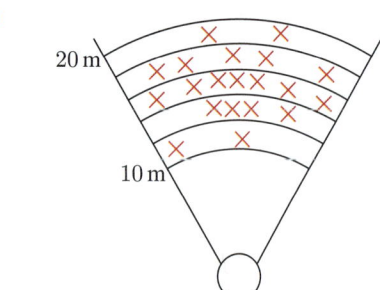

During a training session, Daniel performed 20 throws of the shot put. The results of the throws are shown alongside.

  a Organise the data into class intervals.
  b Draw a histogram to display the data.
  c Find the modal class.
  d Describe the distribution of the data.

4 A group of athletics students obtained the following times, in seconds, for running 200 metres:

    26.57   25.22   27.09   26.44   24.13   27.83   25.72   26.40
    23.12   27.44   24.76   25.09   28.70   26.13   23.94   27.23
    26.35   28.91   26.30   27.02   24.19   25.27   27.45   26.45
    27.40   27.22   25.88   23.50   26.49   27.19   28.37   25.17
    28.08   26.80   28.14   26.82   27.66   25.41   24.89   27.92

  a Organise the data into class intervals.
  b What percentage of the students obtained a time faster than 25 seconds?
  c Draw a histogram to display the data.
  d Find the modal class.
  e Describe the distribution of the data.

MEASURING THE CENTRE

We can get a better understanding of a data set if we can locate the **middle** or **centre** of the data, and get an indication of its **spread**. Knowing one of these without the other is often of little use.

There are three statistics that are used to measure the **centre** of a data set. These are:
the **mean**, the **median**, and the **mode**.

THE MEAN

The **mean** $\bar{x}$ of a data set is the statistical name for its arithmetic average.

$$\text{mean} = \frac{\text{the sum of the data values}}{\text{the number of data values}}$$

or $\bar{x} = \dfrac{\sum x}{n}$ where $\sum x$ is the sum of the data.

$\bar{x}$ is read 'x bar'.
$\sum$ is read 'the sum of all'.

The mean is not necessarily a member of the data set.

THE MEDIAN

The **median** is the *middle value* of an ordered data set.

The median splits an ordered data set in halves. Half of the data are less than or equal to the median, and half are greater than or equal to it.

If there are n data, the median is the $\left(\dfrac{n+1}{2}\right)$th data value.

We *order* a data set by listing it from smallest to largest.

For example:

If $n = 13$, $\dfrac{n+1}{2} = 7$ so the median is the 7th ordered data value.

If $n = 14$, $\dfrac{n+1}{2} = 7.5$ so the median is the average of 7th and 8th ordered data values.

If there is an even number of data values, the median is not necessarily a member of the data set.

THE MODE

The **mode** is the most frequently occurring value in the data set.

If there are two values which occur most frequently, we say the data set is **bimodal**.

If a data set has more than two modes, we do not use the mode as a measure of the centre of the data set.

Example 2

The number of small aeroplanes flying into a remote airstrip over a 15-day period is given below:

$$5\ 7\ 0\ 3\ 4\ 6\ 4\ 0\ 5\ 3\ 6\ 9\ 4\ 2\ 8$$

For this data set, find the: **a** mean **b** median **c** mode.

a mean $= \dfrac{5+7+0+3+4+6+4+0+5+3+6+9+4+2+8}{15}$ $\leftarrow \dfrac{\sum x}{n}$

$= \dfrac{66}{15}$

$= 4.4$ aeroplanes

b The ordered data set is: ~~0~~ ~~0~~ ~~2~~ ~~3~~ ~~3~~ ~~4~~ ~~4~~ $\boxed{4}$ ~~5~~ ~~5~~ ~~6~~ ~~6~~ ~~7~~ ~~8~~ ~~9~~

Since $n = 15$, $\dfrac{n+1}{2} = 8$

∴ the median is the 8th data value

∴ the median $= 4$ aeroplanes.

c 4 is the score which occurs the most often

∴ the mode $= 4$ aeroplanes.

Equal or approximately equal values of the mean, mode, and median *may* indicate a *symmetrical distribution* of data. However, we should always check using a graph before calling a data set symmetric.

EXERCISE 9C.1

1 For each of the following data sets, find the:

   i mean   **ii** median   **iii** mode.

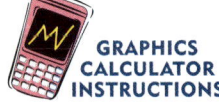
GRAPHICS CALCULATOR INSTRUCTIONS

   a 12, 17, 20, 24, 30, 30, 42
   b 8, 8, 8, 10, 11, 11, 12, 12, 16, 20, 20, 24
   c 7.9, 8.5, 9.1, 9.2, 9.9, 10.0, 11.1, 11.2, 11.2, 12.6, 12.9
   d 427, 423, 415, 405, 445, 433, 442, 415, 435, 448, 429, 427, 403, 430, 446, 440, 425, 424, 419, 428, 441

2 Consider the following two data sets:
   Data set A: 5, 6, 6, 7, 7, 7, 8, 8, 9, 10, 12
   Data set B: 5, 6, 6, 7, 7, 7, 8, 8, 9, 10, 20

   a Find the mean for both *Data set A* and *Data set B*.
   b Find the median for both *Data set A* and *Data set B*.
   c Explain why the mean of *Data set A* is less than the mean of *Data set B*.
   d Explain why the median of *Data set A* is the same as the median of *Data set B*.

3 The selling price of nine houses are:
   $158 000, $290 000, $290 000, $1.1 million, $900 000,
   $395 000, $925 000, $420 000, $760 000

   a Find the mean, median, and modal selling prices.
   b Explain why the mode is an unsatisfactory measure of the middle in this case.
   c Is the median a satisfactory measure of the middle of this data set?

4 The following raw data is the daily rainfall (to the nearest millimetre) for the month of February 2014 in a city in China:

0, 4, 1, 0, 0, 0, 2, 9, 3, 0, 0, 0, 8, 27, 5, 0, 0, 0, 0, 8, 1, 3, 0, 0, 15, 1, 0, 0

a Find the mean, median, and mode for the data.
b Explain why the **i** median **ii** mode is not a suitable measure of centre for this data.
c Identify any outliers in the data set. Do you think the outliers are errors or genuine data? Should they be removed before finding the measures of centre? Explain your answer.

5 A basketball team scored 38, 52, 43, 54, 41, and 36 points in their first six matches.

a Find the mean number of points scored for the first six matches.
b What score does the team need to shoot in their next match to maintain the same mean score?
c The team scores only 20 points in their seventh match. Find the mean number of points scored for the seven matches.
d The team scores 42 points in their eighth and final match.
  i Will their previous mean score increase or decrease?
  ii Find the mean score for all eight matches.

Example 3   ◀) Self Tutor

Each student in a class of 20 is assigned a number between 1 and 10 to indicate his or her fitness. The results are: 7, 9, 8, 8, 10, 9, 8, 7, 8, 6, 9, 5, 6, 8, 9, 7, 7, 8, 10, 8

Group the data in a table, and hence calculate the:

a mean   **b** median   **c** mode.

a

Score	Tally	Number of students	Product
5	|	1	5
6	||	2	12
7	||||	4	28
8	⊬⊬ ||	7	56
9	||||	4	36
10	||	2	20
Total		20	157

The mean score

$= \dfrac{\text{total of scores}}{\text{number of scores}}$

$= \dfrac{157}{20}$

$= 7.85$

b There are 20 scores, so the median is the average of the 10th and 11th ordered scores.

Score	Number of students	
5	1	← 1st student
6	2	← 2nd and 3rd student
7	4	← 4th, 5th, 6th, and 7th student
8	7	← 8th, 9th, **10th, 11th**, 12th, 13th, 14th student
9	4	
10	2	

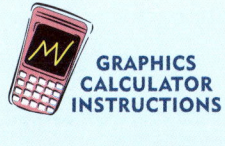
GRAPHICS CALCULATOR INSTRUCTIONS

The 10th and 11th students both scored 8, so the median = 8.

c Looking down the 'number of students' column, the highest frequency is 7. This corresponds to a score of 8, so the mode = 8.

STATISTICS PACKAGE

6 3 coins were tossed simultaneously 40 times, and the number of heads for each toss was recorded.

Calculate the:
  a mode
  b median
  c mean.

Number of heads	Frequency
0	6
1	16
2	14
3	4
Total	40

7 The frequency column graph gives the value of donations for an overseas aid organisation, collected in a particular street.

  a Construct a frequency table from the graph.
  b Determine the total number of donations.
  c Find the:
    i mean   **ii** median   **iii** mode.
  d Which of the measures of centre can be found easily from the graph only?

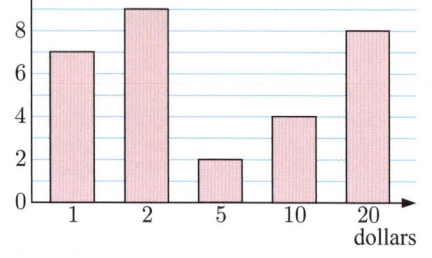

8 Hui breeds ducks. The number of ducklings surviving for each pair after one month is recorded in the table.

  a Calculate the:
    i mean   **ii** mode   **iii** median.
  b Is the data skewed?
  c How does the skewness of the data affect the measures of the middle of the distribution?

Number of survivors	Frequency
0	1
1	2
2	5
3	9
4	20
5	30
6	9
Total	76

9 Consider the **Opening Problem** on page **172**.
  a For each data set, find the: **i** mean   **ii** mode   **iii** median.
  b At which hotel do guests generally stay longer?

Example 4 🔊 **Self Tutor**

Linda has taken four Mathematics tests so far this year. Each test has been out of 20 marks, and her average mark has been 15.

What mark does Linda need in the 5th test to raise her average to 16?

Average mark $= \dfrac{\text{sum of marks}}{4} = 15$

$\therefore$ sum of marks $= 15 \times 4 = 60$

Let Linda's mark for the 5th test be x.

$\therefore$ we require $\dfrac{60 + x}{5} = 16$

$\therefore \ 60 + x = 80$

$\therefore \ x = 20$

So, Linda needs a mark of 20 in the 5th test.

10 Jackie has played 8 games of netball this season, scoring an average of 17 goals per game. How many goals does she need to score in the next game to increase her average to 18?

11 A sample of 12 measurements has a mean of 8.5, and a sample of 20 measurements has a mean of 7.5. Find the mean of all 32 measurements.

12  On Saturday, Derek picked pears from 32 trees. He picked an average of 17 pears per tree. On Sunday he picked some more pears, averaging 12 pears per tree. Over the whole weekend he picked an average of 14 pears per tree. How many trees did Derek pick from on Sunday?

13 Find x if:
   a 7, 15, 6, 10, 4, and x have a mean of 9
   b 10, x, 15, 20, x, x, 17, 7, and 15 have a mean of 12.

14 The mean, median, and mode of seven numbers are 8, 7, and 6 respectively. Two of the numbers are 8 and 10. The smallest of the numbers is 4. Find the largest of the numbers.

15 Consider four numbers a, b, c, and d. The mean of a and b is 7, the mean of b and c is 10, and the mean of c and d is 9. Find the mean of a and d.

DISCUSSION

Develop at least two examples to show how the measures of centre are affected by outliers.

Which of the measures of centre is most affected by the presence of an outlier?

Which of the measures of centre are unaffected by the presence of an outlier?

ESTIMATING THE MEAN OF GROUPED DATA

When data is presented in **class intervals**, the actual data values are not known. This makes it impossible to calculate the exact mean of the data set.

To *estimate* the mean of the data, we use the **midpoint** of an interval to represent all of the scores within the interval.

For example, if we have the interval $50 \text{ km} \leqslant d < 100 \text{ km}$, we *estimate* that all of the data in that interval corresponds to the distance 75 km.

Example 5 🔊 Self Tutor

The transport department collected data regarding the distance each of its trams travelled in one day. This is shown in the table.

Estimate the mean distance travelled by the trams.

Distance d (km)	Frequency
$50 \leqslant d < 100$	10
$100 \leqslant d < 150$	15
$150 \leqslant d < 200$	16
$200 \leqslant d < 250$	9

Distance d (km)	Frequency	Interval midpoint	Product
$50 \leqslant d < 100$	10	75	750
$100 \leqslant d < 150$	15	125	1875
$150 \leqslant d < 200$	16	175	2800
$200 \leqslant d < 250$	9	225	2025
Total	50		7450

$\therefore$ mean
$= \dfrac{\text{sum of data values}}{\text{the number of data values}}$
$\approx \dfrac{7450}{50}$
≈ 149 km

EXERCISE 9C.2

1 The daily maximum temperatures for Manila over a one year period are given below.

Maximum temperature t (°C)	Frequency
$24 \leqslant t < 26$	1
$26 \leqslant t < 28$	8
$28 \leqslant t < 30$	32
$30 \leqslant t < 32$	107
$32 \leqslant t < 34$	174
$34 \leqslant t < 36$	43

Estimate the mean maximum temperature.

2 Nick served a tennis ball 200 times. The speeds of the serves are summarised in the table alongside.

  a Find the modal class of the data.
  b If possible, find the:
    i number of serves faster than 170 km h^{-1}
    ii number of serves slower than 162 km h^{-1}
    iii percentage of serves between 155 km h^{-1} and 175 km h^{-1}.
  c Estimate the mean speed of the serves.

Speed s (km h^{-1})	Frequency
$150 \leqslant s < 155$	18
$155 \leqslant s < 160$	28
$160 \leqslant s < 165$	35
$165 \leqslant s < 170$	43
$170 \leqslant s < 175$	41
$175 \leqslant s < 180$	35

3 The table alongside shows the number of runs scored by Clive during his team's cricket season.

  a How many times did Clive bat?
  b How many times did Clive score at least 20 runs?
  c Estimate the mean number of runs scored by Clive.

Number of runs	Frequency
0 - 9	3
10 - 19	4
20 - 29	9
30 - 39	5
40 - 49	2

4 The male and female Year 10 students of a school were asked how long they slept for last night. The responses are shown below.

Male

Time slept, t (hours)	Frequency
$4 \leqslant t < 5$	6
$5 \leqslant t < 6$	10
$6 \leqslant t < 7$	13
$7 \leqslant t < 8$	9
$8 \leqslant t < 9$	7

Female

Time slept, t (hours)	Frequency
$4 \leqslant t < 5$	4
$5 \leqslant t < 6$	8
$6 \leqslant t < 7$	10
$7 \leqslant t < 8$	11
$8 \leqslant t < 9$	8

  a Draw a histogram to display each data set.
  b Describe the distribution of each data set.
  c Estimate the mean of each data set.
  d Which group do you suspect slept on average for longer? Comment on the reliability of your answer.

5 The amounts of petrol bought in one hour by customers at a service station are shown below, in litres:

    41.59 33.09 37.21 58.85 47.20 26.01 31.12 41.11 56.21 43.59
    31.77 44.56 23.15 46.67 44.43 58.55 40.09 37.51 43.72 27.56
    28.90 36.82 47.19 59.23 39.08 47.81 29.95 55.91 34.11 44.75
    46.12 27.09 57.85 33.13 51.05 34.80 56.14 47.33 51.91 57.76
    37.10 52.39 48.52 41.08 22.09 49.91 38.10 58.77 25.87 39.21

Suppose the amount of petrol is p litres.

  a Find the mean $\overline{p}$ of the data.
  b **i** Organise the data into the class intervals $20 \leqslant p < 30$, $30 \leqslant p < 40$, $40 \leqslant p < 50$, and $50 \leqslant p < 60$.
     ii Use these intervals to estimate the mean of the data.
  c **i** Organise the data into the class intervals $20 \leqslant p < 25$, $25 \leqslant p < 30$, $30 \leqslant p < 35$, ..., $55 \leqslant p < 60$.
     ii Use these intervals to estimate the mean of the data.

  d Compare the estimates of the mean in **b** and **c** with the actual mean found in **a**.
  e In general, would you expect the use of larger or smaller intervals to produce a more accurate estimate of the mean? Explain your answer.

D   CUMULATIVE DATA

It is sometimes useful to know the number or proportion of scores that lie above or below a particular value. To determine this we construct a **cumulative frequency table**, and draw a **cumulative frequency graph**.

The **cumulative frequency** gives a *running total* of the number of data less than a particular value.

Example 6

The table summarises the weights of 60 male rugby players.

a Construct a cumulative frequency table for the data.
b Represent the data on a cumulative frequency graph.
c Use your graph to estimate the:
  i median weight
  ii number of men weighing less than 83 kg
  iii number of men weighing more than 102 kg.

Weight w (kg)	Frequency
$75 \leqslant w < 80$	3
$80 \leqslant w < 85$	11
$85 \leqslant w < 90$	12
$90 \leqslant w < 95$	14
$95 \leqslant w < 100$	13
$100 \leqslant w < 105$	4
$105 \leqslant w < 110$	2
$110 \leqslant w < 115$	1

a

Weight w (kg)	Frequency	Cumulative frequency
$75 \leqslant w < 80$	3	3
$80 \leqslant w < 85$	11	14 ← this is $3 + 11$
$85 \leqslant w < 90$	12	26 ← there are $3 + 11 + 12 = 26$ players who weigh less than 90 kg
$90 \leqslant w < 95$	14	40
$95 \leqslant w < 100$	13	53
$100 \leqslant w < 105$	4	57
$105 \leqslant w < 110$	2	59
$110 \leqslant w < 115$	1	60

b

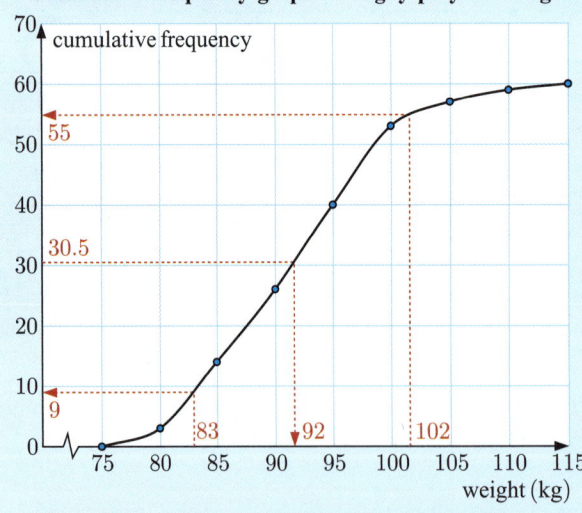

c **i** The median is the average of the 30th and 31st weights.
Reading from the graph, the median ≈ 92 kg.
  ii There are 9 men who weigh less than 83 kg.
  iii There are $60 - 55 = 5$ men who weigh more than 102 kg.

STATISTICS PACKAGE

EXERCISE 9D

1 The cumulative frequency graph alongside shows the lengths of trout caught during a fishing competition.

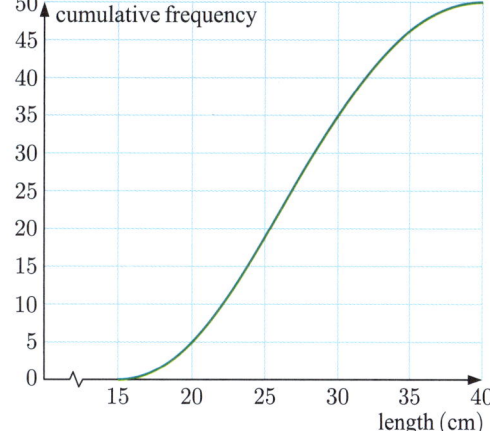

  a How many trout were caught during the competition?

  b How many of the trout were:

   i shorter than 20 cm

   ii longer than 30 cm?

  c Estimate the median length of trout caught.

2 In an examination, a group of students achieved the percentages shown in the table.

  a Construct a cumulative frequency table for the data.

  b Draw a cumulative frequency graph of the data.

  c Use your graph to estimate:

   i the median examination mark

   ii the number of students who scored less than 65%

   iii the mark required to be awarded a credit, given that this is awarded to the top 25% of students.

Score x (%)	Frequency
$10 \leqslant x < 20$	1
$20 \leqslant x < 30$	3
$30 \leqslant x < 40$	6
$40 \leqslant x < 50$	15
$50 \leqslant x < 60$	14
$60 \leqslant x < 70$	28
$70 \leqslant x < 80$	18
$80 \leqslant x < 90$	11
$90 \leqslant x < 100$	4

3

Time t (min)	Frequency
$30 \leqslant t < 35$	7
$35 \leqslant t < 40$	13
$40 \leqslant t < 45$	18
$45 \leqslant t < 50$	25
$50 \leqslant t < 55$	12
$55 \leqslant t < 60$	5

In a running race, the times of 80 competitors were recorded. They are summarised in the table shown.

  a Construct a cumulative frequency table for the data.

  b Draw a cumulative frequency graph of the data.

  c Use your graph to estimate:

   i the median time

   ii the number of runners whose time was less than 38 minutes

   iii the time in which the fastest 30 runners completed the course.

4 The table alongside is a summary of the distance a baseball was thrown by a number of students.

  a Estimate the mean distance the ball was thrown.

  b Draw a cumulative frequency graph of the data.

  c Use your graph to estimate:

   i the median distance thrown by the students

   ii the number of students who threw the ball less than 35 m

   iii the distance required to be in the top 20% of students.

Distance d (m)	Frequency
$20 \leqslant d < 30$	2
$30 \leqslant d < 40$	6
$40 \leqslant d < 50$	26
$50 \leqslant d < 60$	12
$60 \leqslant d < 70$	3
$70 \leqslant d < 80$	1

E MEASURING THE SPREAD

Knowing the middle of a data set can be quite useful, but for a more complete picture of the data set we also need to know its **spread** or **variation**.

Three commonly used statistics that indicate the spread of a set of data are:
- the **range**
- the **interquartile range**
- the **standard deviation**.

THE RANGE

The **range** is the difference between the **maximum** data value and the **minimum** data value.

range = maximum data value − minimum data value

Example 7

Find the range of the data set: 5, 3, 8, 4, 9, 7, 5, 6, 2, 3, 6, 8, 4.

range = maximum data value − minimum data value = 9 − 2 = 7

THE INTERQUARTILE RANGE

The median divides an ordered data set in halves. By finding the median of each half, we divide the original data into **quartiles**.

The **lower quartile** is the median of the lower half, and is 25% of the way through the ordered data set.

The **upper quartile** is the median of the upper half, and is 75% of the way through the ordered data set.

The data set is therefore divided into quarters by the lower quartile Q_1, the median Q_2, and the upper quartile Q_3.

The **interquartile range** is the range of the middle half (50%) of the data.

interquartile range = upper quartile − lower quartile

or $IQR = Q_3 − Q_1$

Example 8

For the data set   6, 7, 3, 7, 9, 8, 5, 5, 4, 6, 6, 8, 7, 6, 6, 5, 4, 5, 6,   find the:
- **a** median
- **b** lower and upper quartiles
- **c** interquartile range.

The ordered data set is: 3̶ 4̶ 4̶ 5̶ 5̶ 5̶ 5̶ 6̶ 6̶ |6| 6̶ 6̶ 6̶ 7̶ 7̶ 7̶ 8̶ 8̶ 9̶   {19 data values}

a Since $n = 19$, $\dfrac{n+1}{2} = \dfrac{19+1}{2} = 10$

∴ the median is the 10th data value, which is 6.

b As the median is a data value, we ignore it and split the remaining data into two groups.

3̶ 4̶ 4̶ 5̶ |5| 5̶ 5̶ 6̶ 6̶   6̶ 6̶ 6̶ 7̶ |7| 7̶ 8̶ 8̶ 9̶

Q_1 = median of lower half = 5 Q_3 = median of upper half = 7

c $IQR = Q_3 − Q_1 = 2$

STATISTICS (Chapter 9) 189

Example 9

For the data set 9, 8, 2, 3, 7, 6, 5, 4, 5, 4, 6, 8, 9, 5, 5, 5, 4, 6, 6, 8, find the:

a median b lower and upper quartiles c interquartile range.

The ordered data set is:

2 3 4 4 4 5 5 5 5 | 5 6 | 6 6 6 7 8 8 8 9 9   {20 data values}

a Since $n = 20$, $\dfrac{n+1}{2} = \dfrac{21}{2} = 10.5$

∴ the median $= \dfrac{\text{10th value} + \text{11th value}}{2} = \dfrac{5+6}{2} = 5.5$

b As the median is not a data value, we split the original data into two equal groups of 10.

2 3 4 4 | 4 5 | 5 5 5 5   6 6 6 6 | 7 8 | 8 8 9 9
           ↓   ↓
∴ $Q_1 = 4.5$ ∴ $Q_3 = 7.5$

c IQR $= Q_3 - Q_1 = 3$

You can use the **statistics package** or your **calculator** to find the measures of spread of a data set.

STATISTICS PACKAGE

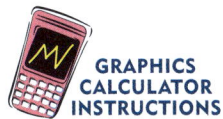
GRAPHICS CALCULATOR INSTRUCTIONS

EXERCISE 9E

1 For each of the following data sets, make sure the data is ordered and then find:

  i the range   ii the median
  iii the lower and upper quartiles   iv the interquartile range.

  a 5, 6, 6, 6, 7, 7, 7, 8, 8, 8, 8, 9, 9, 9, 9, 9, 10, 10, 11, 11, 11, 12, 12
  b 11, 13, 16, 13, 25, 19, 20, 19, 19, 16, 17, 21, 22, 18, 19, 17, 23, 15
  c 23.8, 24.4, 25.5, 25.5, 26.6, 26.9, 27, 27.3, 28.1, 28.4, 31.5

2 While Jarrod was eating a bag of mandarins, he counted the number of seeds in each. The numbers he counted were:

  3 4 7 11 2 6 3 14 10 6 9

Calculate the range and interquartile range of the data.

3 The table alongside shows the number of tows performed by a tow truck driver each day over a 45 day period.
Find the:

  a mean   b median
  c range   d interquartile range.

Number of tows	Frequency
3	2
4	5
5	6
6	9
7	12
8	8
9	3

4 Kylie and Chris were asked to listen to 20 songs, and give each a rating out of 20. The results are shown below.

Kylie						Chris			
14	11	16	8	10		15	11	9	12	16
7	10	5	20	13		14	10	14	9	17
12	3	19	6	11		18	13	12	12	16
4	15	10	19	16		11	12	18	14	10

  a Find the:
   i median   **ii** range
   iii interquartile range   of each data set.
  b In general, who gave the higher ratings?
  c Who had the greater variation in their ratings?

5 The Year 6 and Year 10 students at a school were asked how many times they visited their grandparents in the last month. The results are shown in the graphs below.

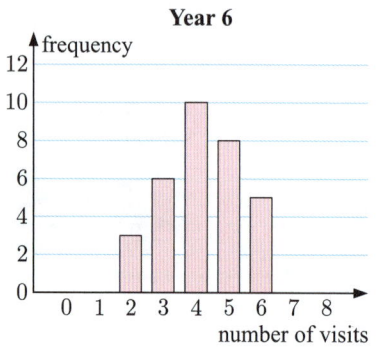 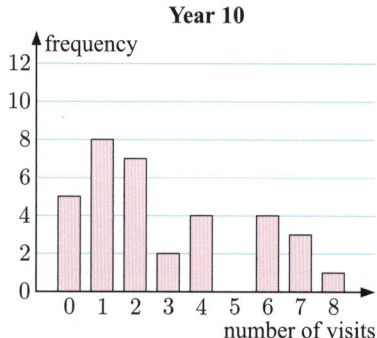

  a For each data set, find the:
   i median   **ii** range   **iii** interquartile range.
  b Which class:
   i generally visited their grandparents more often
   ii had greater variation in their number of visits?

6 In one month, Milton made 40 phone calls. The cumulative frequency graph alongside shows the lengths of the calls.
Using the graph, estimate the:
  a median
  b lower quartile
  c upper quartile
  d interquartile range   of the data.

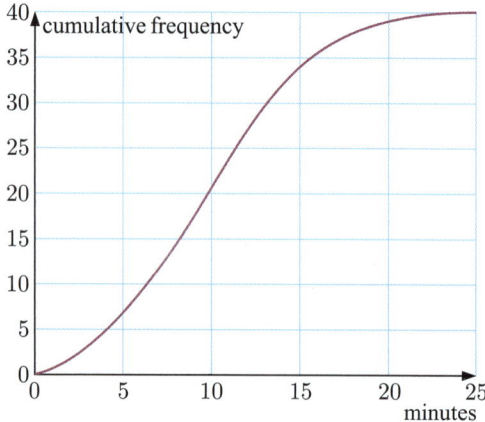

F BOX-AND-WHISKER PLOTS

A **box-and-whisker plot** is a visual display of some of the descriptive statistics of a data set. It shows:

- the minimum value   (min)
- the lower quartile   (Q_1)
- the median   (Q_2)
- the upper quartile   (Q_3)
- the maximum value   (max)

These five numbers form the **five-number summary** of a data set.

For **Example 9**, the five-number summary and corresponding box-and-whisker plot are:

minimum = 2
$Q_1 = 4.5$
median = 5.5
$Q_3 = 7.5$
maximum = 9

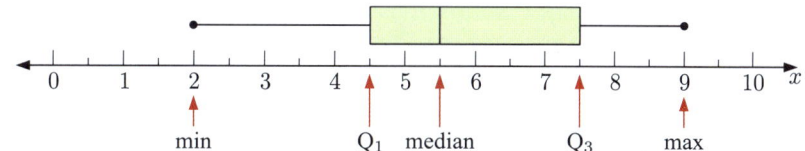

Notice that:
- the rectangular box represents the 'middle' half of the data set
- the lower whisker represents the 25% of the data with the lowest values
- the upper whisker represents the 25% of the data with the highest values.

Example 10   ◀) Self Tutor

Consider the data set: 5 1 6 8 1 7 4 5 6 11 3 4 4 2 5 5

a Construct the five-number summary for the data.
b Draw a box-and-whisker plot for the data.
c Find the   i range   ii interquartile range.
d Find the percentage of data values less than 4.

a The ordered data set is:

1 1 2 [3 4 4 4 |5 5 5 5 |6 6] 7 8 11   {16 data values}

$Q_1 = 3.5$ median = 5 $Q_3 = 6$

The five-number summary is: $\begin{cases} \text{min} = 1 & Q_1 = 3.5 \\ \text{median} = 5 & Q_3 = 6 \\ \text{max} = 11 \end{cases}$

b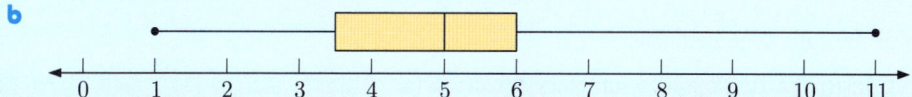

c i range = max − min   ii IQR = $Q_3 - Q_1$
      = 11 − 1   = 6 − 3.5
      = 10   = 2.5

STATISTICS PACKAGE

d 25% of the data values are less than 4.

STATISTICS PACKAGE

EXERCISE 9F.1

1

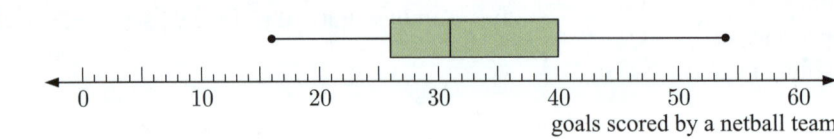

goals scored by a netball team

    a This box-and-whisker plot summarises the goals scored by a netball team. Find the:
        i median   **ii** maximum value   **iii** minimum value
        iv upper quartile   **v** lower quartile.
    b Calculate:
        i the range   **ii** the interquartile range.

2

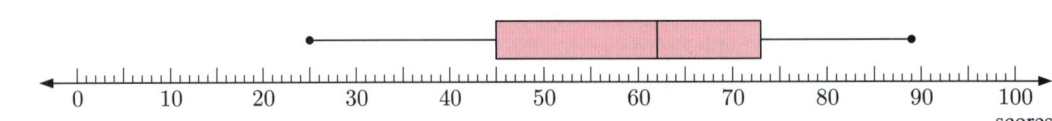

scores

The box-and-whisker plot shown summarises the points scored by a basketball team in their matches during a season.

    a Copy and complete the following statements about their results:
        i The highest score was ...... points.
        ii The lowest score was ...... points.
        iii Half of the scores were greater than or equal to ...... points.
        iv The top 25% of the scores were at least ...... points.
        v The middle half of the scores were between ...... and ...... points.
    b Find the range of the data set.
    c Find the interquartile range of the data set.

3 For each of the following data sets:
        i Construct a five-number summary for the data.
        ii Draw a box-and-whisker plot for the data.
        iii Find the range.
        iv Find the interquartile range.
    a 5, 5, 10, 9, 4, 2, 8, 6, 5, 8, 6, 7, 9, 6, 10, 3, 11
    b 7, 0, 4, 6, 8, 8, 9, 5, 6, 8, 8, 8, 9, 8, 1, 8, 3, 7, 2, 7, 4, 5, 9, 4

4 The weight, in kilograms, of a particular brand of bags of firewood is stated to be 20 kg. However, some bags weigh more than this and some weigh less. A sample of bags is carefully weighed, and the measurements are given in the ordered stem-and-leaf plot shown.

Stem	Leaf
18	8
19	5 7 7 8 8 9
20	1 1 1 2 2 5 6 8
21	0 1 1 2 4 6
22	3

20 | 5   represents   20.5 kg

- **a** Locate the median, upper and lower quartiles, and maximum and minimum weights for the sample.
- **b** Draw a box-and-whisker plot for the data.
- **c** Find: **i** the interquartile range   **ii** the range.
- **d** Copy and complete the following statements about the distribution of weights for the bags of firewood in this sample:
    - **i** Half of the bags of firewood weighed at least ...... kg.
    - **ii** ......% of the bags weighed less than 20 kg.
    - **iii** The weights of the middle 50% of the bags were spread over ...... kg.
    - **iv** The lightest 25% of the bags weighed ...... kg or less.
- **e** Is the distribution of weights in this sample symmetrical, or positively or negatively skewed?

ACTIVITY 1

Click on the icon to practice matching box-and-whisker plots with their graphs.

GAME

PARALLEL BOX-AND-WHISKER PLOTS

If we have two data sets that we want to compare, we can draw a box-and-whisker plot for each data set on the same scale. This is known as a **parallel box-and-whisker plot**. It can be drawn horizontally or vertically.

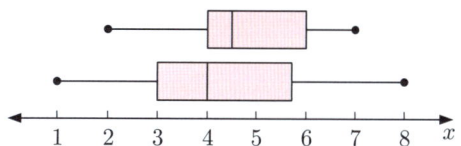

Parallel box-and-whisker plots enable us to make a *visual comparison* of the statistics and distributions of two data sets.

Example 11   ◀) Self Tutor

An office worker has the choice of travelling to work by car or bus. He has collected data giving the travel times from recent journeys using both of these methods. He is interested to know which type of transport is the quickest to get him to work, and which is the most reliable.

Car (minutes):   13 14 18 18 19 21 22 22 24 25 27 28 30 33 43
Bus (minutes):   16 16 16 17 17 18 18 18 20 20 21 21 23 28 30

- **a** Draw a parallel box-and-whisker plot for the data sets.
- **b** Hence, determine which method of transport is:
    - **i** quicker   **ii** more reliable.

a We first construct the five-number summary for each data set.

Car: min = 13 $Q_1 = 18$ median = 22 $Q_3 = 28$ max = 43
Bus: min = 16 $Q_1 = 17$ median = 18 $Q_3 = 21$ max = 30

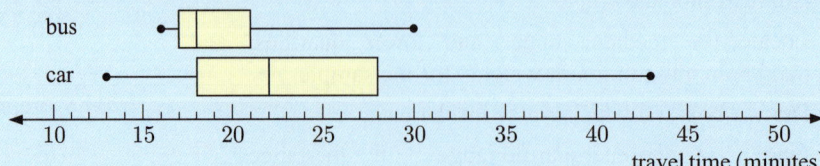

b **i** Looking at the parallel box-and-whisker plot, the bus travel times are generally lower than the car travel times. So, the bus is generally quicker.

ii The car travel times have greater spread than the bus travel times. So, the bus is also more reliable.

EXERCISE 9F.2

1 This parallel box-and-whisker plot compares the times students in Year 10 and Year 12 spend on homework over a one week period.

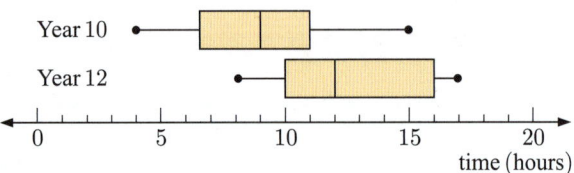

  a Find the five-number summaries for each year group.
  b For each group, determine the:
   i range
   ii interquartile range.

2 Barramundi is a species of fish caught in the tropical waters of northern Australia and Indonesia. Alongside is a parallel box-and-whisker plot of the lengths of barramundi caught in Indonesian and Australian waters.

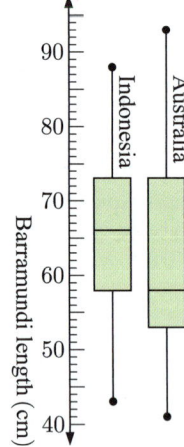

  a For each region, find the:
   i greatest length   **ii** shortest length
   iii range   **iv** interquartile range.
  b The legal length for a barramundi to be kept is 58 cm. What percentage of fish caught were of legal length in:
   i Indonesia   **ii** Australia?
  c Copy and complete:
   i The fish caught in ...... generally have greater length.
   ii The fish caught in ...... have greater length variability.

3 Consider the **Opening Problem** on page 172.
  a Construct the five-number summary for each data set.
  b Draw a parallel box-and-whisker plot to display the data sets.
  c Describe the distribution of each data set.
  d Determine the hotel in which the guests generally stay longer.

4 The heights, in centimetres, of boys and girls in a Year 10 class are:

Boys: 165 171 169 169 172 171 171 180 168 168 166 168 170
165 171 173 187 181 175 174 165 167 163 160 169 167
172 174 177 188 177 185 167 160

Girls: 162 171 156 166 168 163 170 171 177 169 168 165 156
159 165 164 154 171 172 166 152 169 170 163 162 165
163 168 155 175 176 170 166

  a Find the five-number summary for each of the data sets.

  b Draw a parallel box-and-whisker plot to display the data sets.

  c Compare and comment on the distribution of the data.

5 Samples of lobster were caught in two adjacent bays on the coast of California. The following data shows the average weights in pounds for the two bays over a 20 day catching period.

Bay 1: 2.6 2.5 2.7 2.4 2.9 2.7 2.6 2.7 2.8 2.5
2.7 2.6 2.8 2.6 2.5 2.8 2.5 2.4 2.7 2.3

Bay 2: 2.7 3.0 2.6 2.9 2.7 2.8 2.9 2.6 2.7 2.7
2.9 3.1 2.6 2.7 2.7 2.8 3.2 2.7 2.8 2.8

  a Find the five-number summary for each of the data sets.

  b Construct a parallel box-and-whisker plot to display the data sets.

  c Compare and comment on the distributions of the data.

G STANDARD DEVIATION

The problem with the range and the IQR as measures of spread is that both only use two data values in their calculation. A preferred measure of spread is the **standard deviation**, which indicates the degree to which the data values *deviate* from the mean. The advantage of the standard deviation is that it uses all of the data values. However, the IQR is more reliable if the distribution is considerably skewed.

Consider the data set 2, 3, 5, 9, 11. The mean of the data set is 6. For each data value x, we can find the **deviation** $x - \overline{x}$ from the mean $\overline{x}$. The deviations are shown in the table alongside.

x	$x - \overline{x}$
2	-4
3	-3
5	-1
9	3
11	5

If we take the average of these deviations, the result will always be zero. However, we get a much more meaningful result if instead, we square the deviations to form a set of positive values, and then take their average:

$$\frac{(-4)^2 + (-3)^2 + (-1)^2 + 3^2 + 5^2}{5} = \frac{60}{5} = 12$$

Finally, since we squared the deviations, we take the square root of this value to convert back to the original units. This gives us the standard deviation $= \sqrt{12} \approx 3.46$.

> For a sample of n data with mean $\overline{x}$, the **standard deviation** $s = \sqrt{\dfrac{\sum(x - \overline{x})^2}{n}}$.

If most of the data values are close to the mean $\bar{x}$, then the deviations $x - \bar{x}$ will be small. This will result in a lower standard deviation.

Example 12

A greengrocer purchases oranges from two different wholesalers. He takes five random crates from each wholesaler, and counts the number of blemished oranges in each:

| Sunblessed | 4 | 16 | 14 | 8 | 8 |
| Valencia Star | 9 | 12 | 11 | 10 | 13 |

Find the mean and standard deviation for each data set, and hence compare the wholesale suppliers.

Sunblessed:

x	$x - \bar{x}$	$(x - \bar{x})^2$
4	-6	36
16	6	36
14	4	16
8	-2	4
8	-2	4
Total		96

$$\bar{x} = \frac{4 + 16 + 14 + 8 + 8}{5} = 10$$

$$s = \sqrt{\frac{\sum(x - \bar{x})^2}{n}} = \sqrt{\frac{96}{5}} \approx 4.38$$

Valencia Star:

x	$x - \bar{x}$	$(x - \bar{x})^2$
9	-2	4
12	1	1
11	0	0
10	-1	1
13	2	4
Total		10

$$\bar{x} = \frac{9 + 12 + 11 + 10 + 13}{5} = 11$$

$$s = \sqrt{\frac{\sum(x - \bar{x})^2}{n}} = \sqrt{\frac{10}{5}} \approx 1.41$$

The *Sunblessed* oranges generally have less blemishes, but the *Valencia Star* oranges have less variability.

We often use technology to find the standard deviation, especially when there are a large number of data values.

Example 13

Find the standard deviation of the data set:

16 11 9 15 14 22 18 17 22 12 16 10

Casio fx-CG20

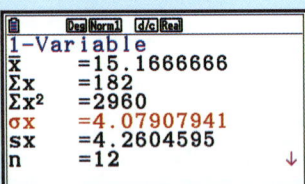

TI-84 Plus

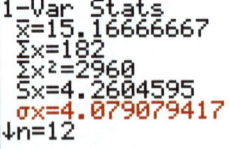

TI-*n*spire

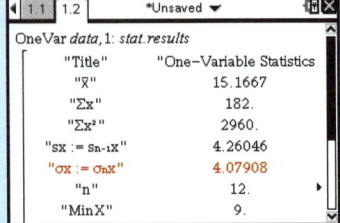

GRAPHICS CALCULATOR INSTRUCTIONS

So, the standard deviation $s \approx 4.08$.

Make sure you use the population standard deviation σ_x.

EXERCISE 9G.1

1 Without using technology, find the standard deviation of the following data sets:

    a 5, 8, 9, 10   **b** 3, 5, 11, 13, 18

2   **a** Find the standard deviation of the data set: 4, 7, 8, 10, 11, 32

    b Identify and remove the outlier, then recalculate the standard deviation.

    c What effect does the outlier have on the standard deviation?

3 Consider the following two samples:

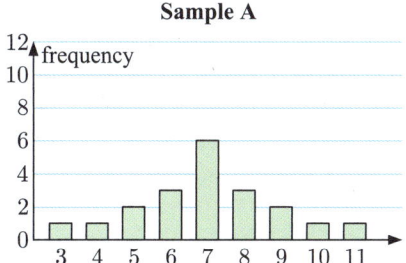 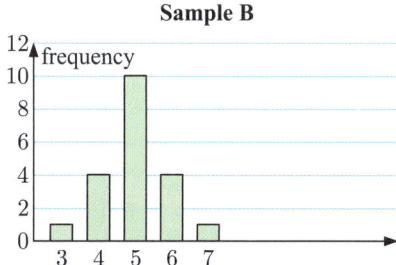

    a By looking at the graphs, which distribution has the wider spread?

    b Find the mean of each sample.

    c For each sample, find:

        i the range   **ii** the interquartile range   **iii** the standard deviation.

    d Explain why s provides a better measure of spread than the other two measures.

4 Brothers Kento and Dongming were each given 80 chocolate eggs. They both ate their eggs over a period of 10 days. The number of eggs eaten by the brothers each day were:

Kento	9	7	6	7	8	10	6	9	10	8
Dongming	15	10	13	8	12	3	9	5	3	2

    a Explain why the mean of each data set will be the same.

    b Find the IQR of each data set.

    c Use technology to find the standard deviation of each data set.

    d Which brother had the most variation in the number of eggs eaten each day?

5 Two baseballers compare their batting performances for a ten game stretch. Their numbers of safe hits per game were:

Mickey	5	4	1	0	5	4	0	5	4	2
Julio	1	2	3	3	3	4	6	2	3	3

    a Show that each baseballer has the same mean and range.

    b Whose performance do you suspect is more variable?

    c Check your answer to **b** by finding the standard deviation for each data set.

    d Does the range or the standard deviation give a better indication of variability?

6 Finnley and Florence each perform a nightly comedy show during an arts festival. The attendance for their shows each night is:

Finnley	23	21	26	27	19	24	28	26	30	15	23	17	25	18
Florence	10	19	22	7	13	8	24	16	5	31	20	7	35	27

a Find the mean of each data set.
b Find the standard deviation of each data set.
c Who had more people attending their shows?
d Who had the greater variation in attendance?

DISCUSSION

Is it reasonable to compare the standard deviation of two data sets if the data sets are not of equal size?

ACTIVITY 2 — THE STOP WATCH CHALLENGE

In this Activity, we will find out who in your class is best at timing 1 second.

You will need: A stop watch or the software provided.

STOP WATCH

What to do:

1 Start the timer, then attempt to stop the timer on exactly 1 second.

2 Repeat this process 30 times, and record your results. A sample set of results is shown alongside.

3 Find the mean and standard deviation of your results.

Sample results

1.09	0.96	0.96	1.15	1.02	1.01
0.92	0.97	0.96	0.95	1.05	0.91
1.09	1.01	1.04	0.91	0.97	1.01
0.98	1.03	0.96	1.01	0.98	1.03
1.02	1.01	0.98	0.97	1.02	1.01

4 As a class, study the results of all the students.

a Was it more common for students to average less than one second, or more than one second?

b Discuss methods for determining whether one result is 'better' than another. For example, given the results shown alongside, would you say that Ian or Hayley performed better?

	Mean	Standard deviation
Ian	1.01	0.087
Hayley	0.97	0.036

c Hence determine which student performed best in the challenge.

STATISTICS (Chapter 9) 199

STANDARD DEVIATION FOR GROUPED DATA

For grouped data, the standard deviation $s = \sqrt{\dfrac{\sum f(x - \overline{x})^2}{\sum f}}$,

where x is **any score**, $\overline{x}$ is the **mean**, and f is the **frequency** of each score.

Example 14
◀)) Self Tutor

Find the standard deviation for the data set:

Score	0	1	2	3	4
Frequency	1	2	4	2	1

x	f	fx	$x - \overline{x}$	$(x - \overline{x})^2$	$f(x - \overline{x})^2$
0	1	0	−2	4	4
1	2	2	−1	1	2
2	4	8	0	0	0
3	2	6	1	1	2
4	1	4	2	4	4
Total	10	20			12

$\overline{x} = \dfrac{\sum fx}{\sum f} = \dfrac{20}{10} = 2$

$s = \sqrt{\dfrac{\sum f(x - \overline{x})^2}{\sum f}}$

$= \sqrt{\dfrac{12}{10}}$

≈ 1.10

Example 15
◀)) Self Tutor

The weights of 25 calves were measured, and the results in kilograms are summarised in the table shown.

a Estimate the standard deviation by using interval midpoints.

b Can the range of the data be found? Explain your answer.

Weight w (kg)	Frequency
$50 \leqslant w < 60$	1
$60 \leqslant w < 70$	3
$70 \leqslant w < 80$	9
$80 \leqslant w < 90$	6
$90 \leqslant w < 100$	4
$100 \leqslant w < 110$	2

a

Weight w (kg)	Centre of class (x)	Frequency	fx	$f(x - \overline{x})^2$
$50 \leqslant w < 60$	55	1	55	676
$60 \leqslant w < 70$	65	3	195	768
$70 \leqslant w < 80$	75	9	675	324
$80 \leqslant w < 90$	85	6	510	96
$90 \leqslant w < 100$	95	4	380	784
$100 \leqslant w < 110$	105	2	210	1152
Totals		25	2025	3800

$\overline{x} = \dfrac{\sum fx}{\sum f} \approx \dfrac{2025}{25} \approx 81$

$s = \sqrt{\dfrac{\sum f(x - \overline{x})^2}{\sum f}} \approx \sqrt{\dfrac{3800}{25}} \approx 12.3$

b Since the data has been grouped in classes, we do not know the smallest and largest data values. Consequently, the range cannot be found.

EXERCISE 9G.2

1 Find the standard deviation of the test results:

Test score x	10	11	12	13	14	15
Frequency f	4	6	7	2	3	2

2 The contents of 60 boxes of chocolates were counted, and the results tabulated below:

Number of chocolates	25	26	27	28	29	30	31	32
Frequency	1	5	7	13	12	12	8	2

Find the mean and standard deviation of the distribution.

3 The lengths of 30 trout were measured to the nearest cm. The following data was obtained:

Length l (cm)	$30 \leqslant l < 32$	$32 \leqslant l < 34$	$34 \leqslant l < 36$	$36 \leqslant l < 38$	$38 \leqslant l < 40$	$40 \leqslant l < 42$	$42 \leqslant l < 44$
Frequency	1	1	3	7	11	5	2

Estimate the mean length and the standard deviation of the lengths.

4 The weekly wages of 90 department store workers are given alongside:
Estimate the mean wage and the standard deviation of the wages.

Wage (€)	Number of workers
380 - 389.99	5
390 - 399.99	16
400 - 409.99	27
410 - 419.99	16
420 - 429.99	12
430 - 439.99	8
440 - 449.99	4
450 - 459.99	2

H THE NORMAL DISTRIBUTION

The normal distribution is the most important distribution for a continuous random variable, and lies at the heart of statistics. Many observable quantities have distributions that are normal or approximately normal. The graphs of these distributions will be approximately **bell-shaped**.

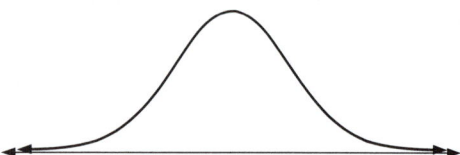

Some examples are:
- the heights of 16 year old boys
- the lengths of adult sharks
- scores on tests taken by a large population
- the life times of batteries
- the volumes of liquid in soft drink cans
- the lengths of cilia on a cell
- yields of corn or wheat

A TYPICAL NORMAL DISTRIBUTION

A large sample of cockle shells was collected and the maximum distance across each shell was measured. Click on the video clip icon to see how a histogram of the data is built up.

Now click on the demo icon to observe the effect of changing the class interval lengths for normally distributed data.

VIDEO CLIP

DEMO

HOW THE NORMAL DISTRIBUTION ARISES

Example 1:

Consider the apples harvested from an apple tree. They do not all have the same weight. This variation may be due to genetic factors, different times when the flowers were fertilised, different amounts of sunlight reaching the leaves and fruit, different weather conditions, and so on.

The result is that much of the fruit will have weights centred about the mean weight, and there will be fewer apples that are much heavier or much lighter than this mean.

Example 2:

In the manufacturing of 50 mm nails, machines are set to produce nails of average length 50 mm. However, there is always minor variation due to random errors in the manufacturing process. A small standard deviation of 0.3 mm, say, may be observed, but once again a bell-shaped distribution models the situation.

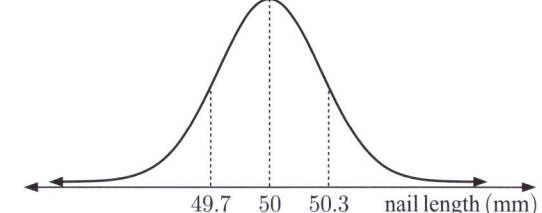

THE SIGNIFICANCE OF STANDARD DEVIATION

If a large sample from a typical bell-shaped data distribution is taken, what percentage of the data values would lie between $\bar{x} - s$ and $\bar{x} + s$?

Click on the icon and try to answer this question. Repeat the sampling many times to improve the accuracy of your estimate.

DEMO

Now try to determine the percentage of data values which would lie between $\bar{x} - 2s$ and $\bar{x} + 2s$ and between $\bar{x} - 3s$ and $\bar{x} + 3s$.

It can be shown that:

> For any measured variable from any population that is normally distributed, no matter the values of the mean $\bar{x}$ and standard deviation s:
> - approximately **68%** of the population will measure between $\bar{x} - s$ and $\bar{x} + s$
> - approximately **95%** of the population will measure between $\bar{x} - 2s$ and $\bar{x} + 2s$
> - approximately **99.7%** of the population will measure between $\bar{x} - 3s$ and $\bar{x} + 3s$.

The proportion of data values that lie within different ranges relative to the mean are shown below:

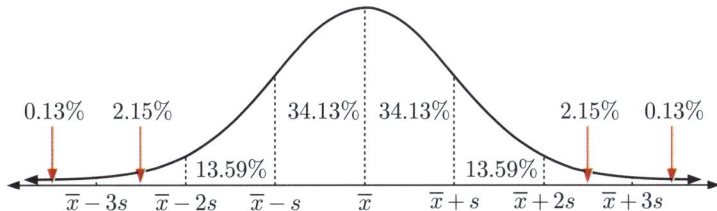

Example 16

A sample of 200 cans of peaches was taken from a warehouse and the contents of each can measured for net weight. The sample mean was 486 g with standard deviation 6.2 g. State the proportion of cans that will lie in the given range, and what this range is, in g:

a within 1 standard deviation of the mean
b within 3 standard deviations of the mean.

For a manufacturing process such as this, the distribution of net weights is approximately normal.

a About 68% of the cans would be expected to have contents between 486 ± 6.2 g, which is between 479.8 g and 492.2 g.

b Nearly all of the cans would be expected to have contents between $486 \pm 3 \times 6.2$ g, which is between 467.4 g and 504.6 g.

EXERCISE 9H

1 A sample of overcoats was taken from the manufacturer and each overcoat weighed. The sample mean was 2.864 kg with standard deviation 0.023 kg. State the proportion of overcoats that will lie in the given range, and what this range is, in kg:

  a within 1 standard deviation of the mean
  b within 2 standard deviations of the mean
  c within 3 standard deviations of the mean.

2 Five hundred Year 10 students sat for a Mathematics examination. Their marks were approximately normally distributed with mean 75 and standard deviation 8.

  a Copy and complete this bell-shaped curve, assigning scores to the markings on the horizontal axis:

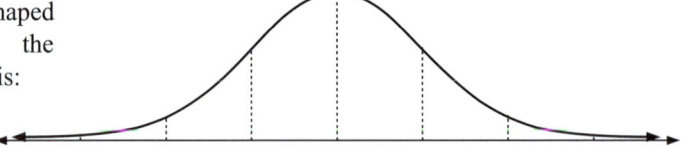

  b How many students would you expect to have scored:
   i more than 83
   ii less than 59
   iii between 67 and 91?

3 A sample of 300 bottles of soft drink was taken from a production line and the contents of each bottle measured for net volume. The sample mean was 377 mL with standard deviation 1.5 mL.

  a Represent this information on a bell-shaped curve.
  b How many bottles in the sample would you expect to have contents
   i between 374 and 380 mL
   ii more than 375.5 mL?
  c What proportion of bottles in the production line would you expect to have contents less than 375.5 mL?

4 The mean height of players in a basketball competition is 181 cm. If the standard deviation is 4 cm, what percentage of the players are likely to be:

  a taller than 189 cm
  b taller than 177 cm
  c between 169 cm and 189 cm
  d shorter than 185 cm?

5 The mean average rainfall of Charlesville in August is 68 mm with standard deviation 8 mm. Over a 40 year period, how many times would you expect there to be less than 52 mm of rainfall during August in Charlesville?

Global context	Air passenger numbers	
click here	*Statement of inquiry*:	Analysing data can help us to identify changes over time.
	Global context:	Orientation in space and time
	Key concept:	Logic
	Related concepts:	Quantity, Change
	Objectives:	Communicating, Applying mathematics in real-life contexts
	Approaches to learning:	Communication, Self-management

REVIEW SET 9A

1 Describe the data distribution shown:

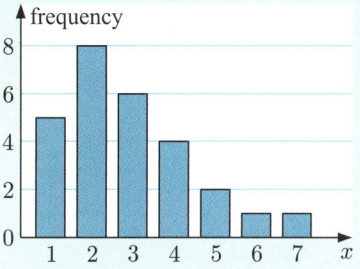

2 A class of 20 students was asked "How many bedrooms are there in your house?" The following data was collected:

3 2 3 2 2 4 3 4 2 3 2 1 2 2 3 2 4 2 3 2

  a Is the data discrete or continuous?   **b** Are there any outliers in the data?

  c Construct a dot plot to display the data.

3 Consider the set of data: 17 14 9 12 23 14 12 18 9 15 6 14 21 13 10

  a Find the:

    i mode   **ii** mean   **iii** median   **iv** range

    v upper and lower quartiles   **vi** interquartile range.

  b Draw a box-and-whisker plot to display the data.

4 The masses of eggs in a carton marked '50 g eggs' are recorded alongside.

Mass m (g)	Frequency
$48 \leqslant m < 49$	1
$49 \leqslant m < 50$	1
$50 \leqslant m < 51$	16
$51 \leqslant m < 52$	4
$52 \leqslant m < 53$	3

  a Construct a frequency histogram for the data.

  b What is the modal class? Explain what this means.

  c Describe the distribution of the data.

  d Estimate the mean mass of an egg in the carton.

5 The scores out of 100 for an exam are displayed in the box-and-whisker plot below.

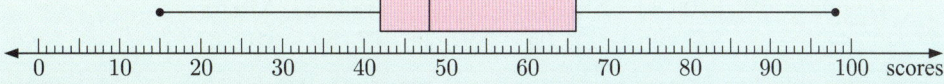

  a State the: **i** median score   **ii** maximum score   **iii** minimum score

    iv upper quartile   **v** lower quartile.

  b Calculate the: **i** range   **ii** interquartile range of scores.

6 Nine scores have an average of 8. Scores of x and $x + 1$ are added, and these increase the average to 9. Find x.

7 The given parallel box-and-whisker plot represents the 100-metre swim times for the members of a swimming squad.

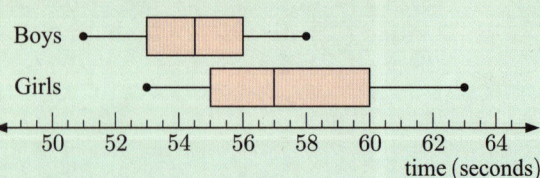

Copy and complete the following:

a Comparing the median swim times for girls and boys shows that, in general, the ...... swim ...... seconds faster than the ......

b The range of the girls' swim times is ...... seconds compared to the range of ...... seconds for the boys.

c The fastest 25% of the boys swim as fast as or faster than ...... % of the girls.

d ...... % of the boys swim faster than 60 seconds whereas ...... % of the girls swim faster than 60 seconds.

8

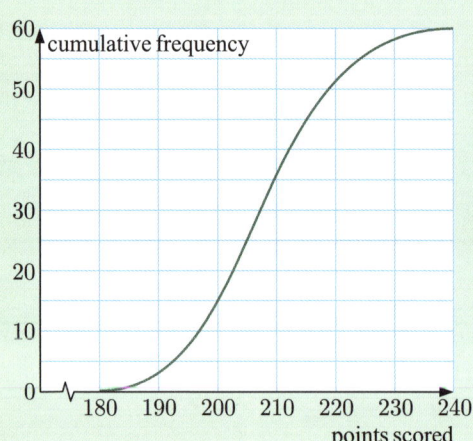

The cumulative frequency graph illustrates the points scored by competitors in a ski aerials competition.

a How many competitors took part in the competition?

b What percentage of competitors scored less than 200 points?

c Estimate the median score.

9 The Davis and Douglas families kept a record of the amount they spent at the supermarket each week for 10 weeks:

Davis:	$102.50	$115.95	$107.60	$122.15	$131.05
	$111.15	$120.50	$127.55	$100.95	$113.40
Douglas:	$109.80	$86.75	$94.50	$129.75	$72.05
	$133.05	$121.05	$97.60	$73.80	$105.35

a Use technology to find the mean and standard deviation of each data set.

b Which family generally spent more at the supermarket each week?

c Which family had the greater variation in the amount they spent each week?

10 The weights, in kilograms, of the three month old chickens in a hen house were:

0.8   0.7   1.0   0.9   0.9   0.8   0.9   1.0   1.0   0.8

  a Find the mean and standard deviation of the weights.

  b In the next three months, the weights of the chickens doubled. Find the new mean and standard deviation.

  c Comment, in general terms, on your findings from **a** and **b**.

11 The lengths of newborn babies at a hospital were recorded over a one month period. The results are shown in the table.

  a Display the data using a frequency histogram.

  b How many babies were 52 cm or more?

  c What percentage of babies had lengths in the interval $50 \text{ cm} \leqslant l < 53 \text{ cm}$?

  d Draw a cumulative frequency graph for the data.

  e Use your graph to estimate the:

   i median length

   ii number of babies with length less than 51.5 cm.

Length l (cm)	Frequency
$48 \leqslant l < 49$	1
$49 \leqslant l < 50$	3
$50 \leqslant l < 51$	9
$51 \leqslant l < 52$	10
$52 \leqslant l < 53$	16
$53 \leqslant l < 54$	4
$54 \leqslant l < 55$	5
$55 \leqslant l < 56$	2

12 The weights of apples in an orchard are normally distributed with mean 150 g and standard deviation 11 g. In a carton of 400 apples, how many would you expect to weigh more than 139 g?

REVIEW SET 9B

1 As punishment for misbehaving, a class of students had to pick up litter during recess. The table shows the number of litter pieces picked up by the students.

  a How many students were in the class?

  b For this data, find the:

   i mean   **ii** mode   **iii** median.

  c Draw a dot plot to display the data.

  d Describe the distribution of the data.

Pieces of litter	Frequency
6	1
7	3
8	2
9	6
10	7
11	8
12	5

2 For the data set alongside, find the:

  a mean   **b** median   **c** mode.

13   16   15   17   14   13   13   15   16   14
16   14   15   15   15   13   17   14   12   14

3 A sample of 15 measurements has a mean of 14.2, and a sample of 10 measurements has a mean of 12.6. Find the mean of the combined sample of 25 measurements.

4 The numbers of people at a judo class each week were:

10   8   10   9   7   11   9   11   10
10   9   8   9   9   11   8   10   9
10   11   10   7   9   11   10   8

  a Draw a column graph to display the data.

  b Describe the distribution of the data.

5 The data below show how many people used the swimming pool at a gym each day over 40 days:

22	37	54	31	43	47	65	60	51	42
34	30	26	38	45	55	49	32	49	53
68	47	32	45	58	37	42	53	41	59
64	51	37	23	25	41	30	28	34	53

    a Organise the data into a tally and frequency table, grouping the data appropriately.

    b Draw a column graph for the data.

    c On what percentage of the days did at least 50 people use the pool?

6 Draw a box-and-whisker plot to display the following data set:

    5 7 8 9 12 15 15 17 19 20 22

7 A class consists of 30 students. The mean height of students in the class is 172 cm. The mean height of the males is 176 cm, and the mean height of the females is 166 cm. How many males are in the class?

8 Find the interquartile range of the following data set:

    21 39 27 43 51 37 18 31 44

9 The table alongside shows the prices of houses listed for sale in a particular suburb.

    a How many houses are listed for sale in the suburb?

    b Estimate the mean house price.

Price p ($\$ \times 1000$)	Frequency
$250 \leqslant p < 300$	3
$300 \leqslant p < 350$	6
$350 \leqslant p < 400$	11
$400 \leqslant p < 450$	7
$450 \leqslant p < 500$	5

10 Find the standard deviation of:

    a 4 7 11 12 15 19 20 27

    b

Score	1	2	3	4
Frequency	2	5	10	9

11 The students at a touch typing course were tested to see how many words they could correctly type in one minute. The test was given both before and after the practice modules in the course.

    Before: 47 52 32 41 37 39 42 27 36 41 33 29 36 40 25

    After: 59 67 42 49 52 60 59 48 53 62 55 44 50 48 47

    a Construct a five-number summary for each data set.

    b Draw a parallel box-and-whisker plot to display the data.

    c Did the course improve the typing speeds of the students? Explain your answer.

12 The life of a clock battery is found to be normally distributed with mean 35.4 weeks and standard deviation 6.8 weeks.

In a batch of 500 batteries, find the number that you would expect to last:

    a at least 42.2 weeks

    b less than 21.8 weeks

    c between 35.4 and 49 weeks.

Chapter 10

Algebraic fractions

Contents:
- **A** Evaluating algebraic fractions
- **B** Simplifying algebraic fractions
- **C** Multiplying and dividing algebraic fractions
- **D** Adding and subtracting algebraic fractions
- **E** Equations with algebraic fractions

OPENING PROBLEM

To participate in a tennis league, each team must pay $150 in court fees, and a $60 team registration fee. The court fees are shared equally between the players in the team, and the registration fee is shared equally between the players and the team coach.

Suppose a team has x players.

Things to think about:

a Can you write the amount that each player must pay as a single fraction involving x?

b How much must each player pay if the team has:
  i 4 players
  ii 5 players?

Algebraic fractions are fractions which contain at least one variable or unknown.

The variable may be in the numerator, the denominator, or both the numerator and denominator.

For example, $\dfrac{x}{7}$, $\dfrac{-2}{5-y}$, and $\dfrac{x+2y}{1-y}$ are all algebraic fractions.

A EVALUATING ALGEBRAIC FRACTIONS

To **evaluate** an algebraic fraction, we replace the variables with their known values. We then give our answer in simplest form.

Example 1

If $a = 2$, $b = -3$, and $c = -5$, evaluate:

a $\dfrac{a-b}{c}$

b $\dfrac{a-c-b}{b-a}$

a $\dfrac{a-b}{c}$
$= \dfrac{2-(-3)}{(-5)}$
$= \dfrac{2+3}{-5}$
$= \dfrac{5}{-5}$
$= -1$

b $\dfrac{a-c-b}{b-a}$
$= \dfrac{2-(-5)-(-3)}{(-3)-2}$
$= \dfrac{2+5+3}{-3-2}$
$= \dfrac{10}{-5}$
$= -2$

EXERCISE 10A

1 If $a = 3$, $b = 2$, and $c = 6$, evaluate:

a $\dfrac{c}{2}$
b $\dfrac{c}{a}$
c $\dfrac{a}{c}$
d $\dfrac{c}{b-a}$
e $\dfrac{a+c}{b}$

f $\dfrac{ab}{c}$
g $\dfrac{a^2}{b}$
h $\dfrac{c^2}{a}$
i $\dfrac{ab^2}{c}$
j $\dfrac{(ab)^2}{c}$

2 If $a = 2$, $b = -3$, and $c = -4$, evaluate:

   a $\dfrac{c}{a}$ **b** $\dfrac{a}{c}$ **c** $\dfrac{-1}{b}$ **d** $\dfrac{c^2}{a}$ **e** $\dfrac{c}{a+b}$

   f $\dfrac{a-c}{2b}$ **g** $\dfrac{b}{c-a}$ **h** $\dfrac{a-c}{a+c}$ **i** $\dfrac{c-a}{b^2}$ **j** $\dfrac{a^2}{c-b}$

B   SIMPLIFYING ALGEBRAIC FRACTIONS

We have observed previously that number fractions can be simplified by cancelling common factors.

For example, $\dfrac{15}{35} = \dfrac{3 \times \cancel{5}^1}{7 \times \cancel{5}_1} = \dfrac{3}{7}$ where the common factor 5 is cancelled.

The same principle can be applied to algebraic fractions.

> If the numerator and denominator of an algebraic fraction are both written in factored form and common factors are found, we can simplify by **cancelling the common factors**.

For example, $\dfrac{6bc}{3c} = \dfrac{{}^2\cancel{6} \times b \times \cancel{c}^1}{{}_1\cancel{3} \times \cancel{c}_1}$ {3 and c are common factors}

$\qquad\qquad\quad = \dfrac{2b}{1}$ {after cancellation}

$\qquad\qquad\quad = 2b$

Fractions such as $\dfrac{3xy}{7z}$ cannot be simplified since the numerator and denominator do not have any common factors.

> To simplify algebraic expressions:
> - factorise the numerator and the denominator
> - cancel any common factors
> - simplify the result.

DISCUSSION

Discuss what is wrong with the cancellation $\dfrac{x + \cancel{4}^2}{\cancel{2}_1} = \dfrac{x+2}{1} = x + 2$.

Example 2   🔊 Self Tutor

Simplify: **a** $\dfrac{a^2}{2a}$ **b** $\dfrac{6a^2 b}{3b}$ **c** $\dfrac{a+b}{a}$

a $\dfrac{a^2}{2a}$

$= \dfrac{a \times \cancel{a}^1}{2 \times \cancel{a}_1}$

$= \dfrac{a}{2}$

b $\dfrac{6a^2 b}{3b}$

$= \dfrac{{}^2\cancel{6} \times a \times a \times \cancel{b}^1}{{}_1\cancel{3} \times \cancel{b}_1}$

$= \dfrac{2 \times a \times a}{1}$

$= 2a^2$

c $\dfrac{a+b}{a}$ cannot be simplified as $a+b$ is a sum, not a product.

EXERCISE 10B.1

1 Simplify:

a $\dfrac{2a}{4}$ b $\dfrac{4m}{2}$ c $\dfrac{6a}{a}$ d $\dfrac{6a}{2a}$ e $\dfrac{2a^2}{a}$

f $\dfrac{2x^3}{2x}$ g $\dfrac{2x^3}{x^2}$ h $\dfrac{2x^3}{x^3}$ i $\dfrac{2a^2}{4a^3}$ j $\dfrac{8m^2}{4m}$

k $\dfrac{4a^2}{a^2}$ l $\dfrac{6t}{3t^2}$ m $\dfrac{4d^2}{2d}$ n $\dfrac{ab^2}{2ab}$ o $\dfrac{4ab^2}{6a^2b}$

2 Simplify if possible:

a $\dfrac{2t}{2}$ b $\dfrac{2+t}{2}$ c $\dfrac{xy}{x}$

d $\dfrac{x+y}{x}$ e $\dfrac{ac}{bc}$ f $\dfrac{a+c}{b+c}$

g $\dfrac{2a^2}{4a}$ h $\dfrac{5a}{9b}$ i $\dfrac{14c}{8d}$

We can cancel common factors but not terms.

Example 3 🔊 Self Tutor

Simplify: a $\dfrac{(-4b)^2}{2b}$ b $\dfrac{18}{3(c-1)}$

a $\dfrac{(-4b)^2}{2b}$

$= \dfrac{(-4b) \times (-4b)}{2 \times b}$

$= \dfrac{{}^{8}\cancel{16} \times b \times \cancel{b}^{1}}{{}_{1}\cancel{2} \times \cancel{b}_{1}}$

$= 8b$

b $\dfrac{18}{3(c-1)}$

$= \dfrac{\cancel{18}^{6}}{{}_{1}\cancel{3}(c-1)}$

$= \dfrac{6}{c-1}$

---

3 Simplify:

a $\dfrac{(2a)^2}{a^2}$ b $\dfrac{(4n)^2}{8n}$ c $\dfrac{(-a)^2}{a}$ d $\dfrac{a^2}{(-a)^2}$

e $\dfrac{(-2a)^2}{4}$ f $\dfrac{(-3n)^2}{6n}$ g $\dfrac{2b}{(2b^2)^2}$ h $\dfrac{(3k^2)^2}{18a^3}$

4 Simplify:

a $\dfrac{4(x+5)}{2}$ b $\dfrac{2(n+5)}{12}$ c $\dfrac{7(b+2)}{14}$ d $\dfrac{6(k-2)}{8}$

e $\dfrac{15}{3(t-1)}$ f $\dfrac{10}{25(k+4)}$ g $\dfrac{4}{12(x-3)}$ h $\dfrac{20(p+4)}{12}$

ALGEBRAIC FRACTIONS   (Chapter 10)   211

Example 4

Simplify:

a $\dfrac{(2x+3)(x+4)}{5(2x+3)}$ **b** $\dfrac{12(x+4)^2}{3(x+4)}$

a $\dfrac{{}^1(2x+3)(x+4)}{5(2x+3)_1}$

$= \dfrac{(x+4)}{5}$

$= \dfrac{x+4}{5}$

b $\dfrac{12(x+4)^2}{3(x+4)}$

$= \dfrac{{}^4\cancel{12}(x+4)(x+4)^1}{{}_1\cancel{3}(x+4)_1}$

$= 4(x+4)$

5 Simplify:

a $\dfrac{(x+4)(x+2)}{9(x+4)}$ **b** $\dfrac{12(a-3)}{(a-3)(a+1)}$ **c** $\dfrac{(x+y)(x-y)}{3(x-y)}$

d $\dfrac{(x+y)^2}{x+y}$ **e** $\dfrac{2(x+2)}{(x+2)^2}$ **f** $\dfrac{(a+5)^2}{3(a+5)}$

g $\dfrac{2xy(x-y)}{6x(x-y)}$ **h** $\dfrac{5(y+2)(y-3)}{15(y+2)}$ **i** $\dfrac{x(x+1)(x+2)}{3x(x+2)}$

j $\dfrac{3(b-4)}{6(b-4)^2}$ **k** $\dfrac{8(p+q)^2}{12(p+q)}$ **l** $\dfrac{24(r-2)}{15(r-2)^2}$

m $\dfrac{x^2(x+2)}{x(x+2)(x-1)}$ **n** $\dfrac{(x+2)^2(x+1)}{4(x+2)}$ **o** $\dfrac{2(x+2)^2(x-1)^2}{8x(x+2)}$

FACTORISATION AND SIMPLIFICATION

It is often necessary to **factorise** either the numerator or denominator before simplification can take place. To do this we use the rules for factorisation that we have seen previously.

Example 5

Simplify:

a $\dfrac{3a+9}{3}$ **b** $\dfrac{4a+12}{8}$

a $\dfrac{3a+9}{3}$

$= \dfrac{{}^1\cancel{3}(a+3)}{{}_1\cancel{3}}$

$= a+3$

b $\dfrac{4a+12}{8}$

$= \dfrac{{}^1\cancel{4}(a+3)}{{}_2\cancel{8}}$

$= \dfrac{a+3}{2}$

EXERCISE 10B.2

1 Simplify by factorising:

a $\dfrac{2x+4}{2}$ **b** $\dfrac{3x-6}{3}$ **c** $\dfrac{3x+6}{6}$ **d** $\dfrac{4x-20}{8}$

e $\dfrac{4y+12}{12}$ **f** $\dfrac{6x-30}{4}$ **g** $\dfrac{ax+bx}{x}$ **h** $\dfrac{ax+bx}{cx+dx}$

2 Simplify, if possible:

a $\dfrac{4x+6}{6}$ b $\dfrac{4x+6}{5}$ c $\dfrac{6a-3}{2}$ d $\dfrac{6a-3}{3}$

e $\dfrac{6a+2}{4}$ f $\dfrac{3b+9}{2}$ g $\dfrac{3b+9}{6}$ h $\dfrac{8b-12}{6}$

Example 6 🔊 Self Tutor

Simplify by factorising:

a $\dfrac{ab+ac}{b+c}$ b $\dfrac{6x^2-6xy}{3x-3y}$

a $\dfrac{ab+ac}{b+c}$
$= \dfrac{a(b+c)}{b+c}$ ← HCF is a
$= \dfrac{a(b+c)^1}{(b+c)_1}$
$= a$

b $\dfrac{6x^2-6xy}{3x-3y}$
$= \dfrac{6x(x-y)}{3(x-y)}$ ← HCF is $6x$, HCF is 3
$= \dfrac{{}^2\cancel{6} \times x \times (x-y)^1}{{}_1\cancel{3} \times (x-y)_1}$
$= 2x$

---

3 Simplify by factorising:

a $\dfrac{3x+6}{4x+8}$ b $\dfrac{5x-15}{3x-9}$ c $\dfrac{ax+bx}{a+b}$ d $\dfrac{16x-8}{20x-10}$

e $\dfrac{a+b}{ay+by}$ f $\dfrac{ax+bx}{ay+by}$ g $\dfrac{4x^2+8x}{x+2}$ h $\dfrac{3x^2+9x}{x+3}$

i $\dfrac{5x^2-5xy}{7x-7y}$ j $\dfrac{9b^2-9ab}{12b-12a}$ k $\dfrac{6x^2-18x}{9x-27}$ l $\dfrac{6a+6b}{8a^3+4a^2b}$

Example 7 🔊 Self Tutor

Simplify: a $\dfrac{6a-6b}{b-a}$ b $\dfrac{xy^2-xy}{1-y}$

$b-a = -1(a-b)$ is a useful rule.

a $\dfrac{6a-6b}{b-a}$
$= \dfrac{6(a-b)^1}{-1(a-b)_1}$
$= -6$

b $\dfrac{xy^2-xy}{1-y}$
$= \dfrac{xy(y-1)^1}{-1(y-1)_1}$
$= -xy$

---

4 Simplify:

a $\dfrac{2x-2y}{y-x}$ b $\dfrac{3x-3y}{2y-2x}$ c $\dfrac{m-n}{n-m}$ d $\dfrac{r-2s}{4s-2r}$

e $\dfrac{3r-6s}{2s-r}$ f $\dfrac{2x-2}{x-x^2}$ g $\dfrac{ab^2-ab}{2-2b}$ h $\dfrac{4x^2-4x}{2-2x}$

Example 8

Simplify:

a $\dfrac{x^2 - 1}{x^2 + 3x + 2}$

b $\dfrac{6x^2 + 10x - 4}{18x^2 + 3x - 3}$

a $\dfrac{x^2 - 1}{x^2 + 3x + 2}$

$= \dfrac{(x-1)(x+1)^1}{(x+2)(x+1)_1}$

$= \dfrac{x - 1}{x + 2}$

b $\dfrac{6x^2 + 10x - 4}{18x^2 + 3x - 3}$

$= \dfrac{2(3x^2 + 5x - 2)}{3(6x^2 + x - 1)}$

$= \dfrac{2(3x-1)^1(x+2)}{3(3x-1)_1(2x+1)}$

$= \dfrac{2(x+2)}{3(2x+1)}$

5 Simplify:

a $\dfrac{x^2 - 1}{x - 1}$ **b** $\dfrac{x^2 - 1}{x + 1}$ **c** $\dfrac{x^2 - 1}{1 - x}$ **d** $\dfrac{x + 2}{x^2 - 4}$

e $\dfrac{a^2 - b^2}{a + b}$ **f** $\dfrac{a^2 - b^2}{b - a}$ **g** $\dfrac{2x + 2}{x^2 - 1}$ **h** $\dfrac{9 - x^2}{3x - x^2}$

i $\dfrac{3x^2 - 3y^2}{2xy - 2y^2}$ **j** $\dfrac{2b^2 - 2a^2}{a^2 - ab}$ **k** $\dfrac{4xy - y^2}{16x^2 - y^2}$ **l** $\dfrac{4x(x - 4)}{16 - x^2}$

6 Simplify:

a $\dfrac{x^2 - x - 2}{x - 2}$ **b** $\dfrac{x + 3}{x^2 - 2x - 15}$ **c** $\dfrac{2x^2 + 2x}{x^2 - 4x - 5}$

d $\dfrac{x^2 - 4}{x^2 + 4x + 4}$ **e** $\dfrac{x^2 - x - 12}{x^2 - 5x + 4}$ **f** $\dfrac{x^2 + 2x + 1}{1 - x^2}$

g $\dfrac{x^2 - x - 20}{x^2 + 7x + 12}$ **h** $\dfrac{2x^2 + 5x + 2}{2x^2 + 7x + 3}$ **i** $\dfrac{3x^2 + 7x + 2}{6x^2 - x - 1}$

j $\dfrac{8x^2 + 2x - 1}{4x^2 - 5x + 1}$ **k** $\dfrac{12x^2 - 5x - 3}{6x^2 + 5x + 1}$ **l** $\dfrac{15x^2 + 17x - 4}{5x^2 + 9x - 2}$

PUZZLE

Click on the icon to load a dynamic puzzle for algebraic fractions.

C   MULTIPLYING AND DIVIDING ALGEBRAIC FRACTIONS

Variables are used in algebraic fractions to represent unknown numbers. We can treat algebraic fractions in the same way that we treat numerical fractions, since they are in fact *representing* numerical fractions.

The rules for multiplying and dividing algebraic fractions are identical to those used with numerical fractions.

MULTIPLICATION

To **multiply** two or more fractions, we multiply the numerators to form the new numerator, and we multiply the denominators to form the new denominator.

$$\frac{a}{b} \times \frac{c}{d} = \frac{a \times c}{b \times d} = \frac{ac}{bd}$$

We can then cancel any common factors, and write our answer in simplest form.

Example 9

Simplify:
a $\dfrac{3}{m} \times \dfrac{m}{6}$ **b** $\dfrac{3}{m} \times m^2$

a $\dfrac{3}{m} \times \dfrac{m}{6}$

$= \dfrac{{}^1\cancel{3} \times \cancel{m}^1}{{}_1\cancel{m} \times \cancel{6}_2}$

$= \dfrac{1}{2}$

b $\dfrac{3}{m} \times m^2$

$= \dfrac{3}{m} \times \dfrac{m^2}{1}$

$= \dfrac{3 \times m^2}{m \times 1}$

$= \dfrac{3 \times m \times \cancel{m}^1}{\cancel{m}_1}$

$= 3m$

DIVISION

To **divide** by a fraction, we multiply by its **reciprocal**. The reciprocal is obtained by swapping the numerator and denominator.

$$\frac{a}{b} \div \frac{c}{d} = \frac{a}{b} \times \frac{d}{c} = \frac{ad}{bc}$$

Example 10

Simplify:
a $\dfrac{4}{n} \div \dfrac{2}{n^2}$ **b** $\dfrac{3}{a} \div 2$

a $\dfrac{4}{n} \div \dfrac{2}{n^2}$

$= \dfrac{4}{n} \times \dfrac{n^2}{2}$

$= \dfrac{4 \times n^2}{n \times 2}$

$= \dfrac{{}^2\cancel{4} \times n \times \cancel{n}^1}{{}_1\cancel{n} \times \cancel{2}_1}$

$= 2n$

b $\dfrac{3}{a} \div 2$

$= \dfrac{3}{a} \times \dfrac{1}{2}$

$= \dfrac{3 \times 1}{a \times 2}$

$= \dfrac{3}{2a}$

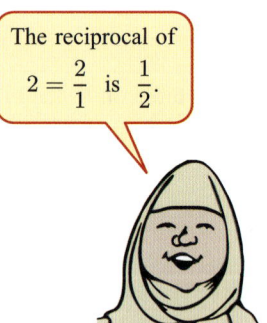

The reciprocal of $2 = \dfrac{2}{1}$ is $\dfrac{1}{2}$.

EXERCISE 10C

1 Simplify:

a $\dfrac{x}{2} \times \dfrac{y}{5}$ **b** $\dfrac{a}{2} \times \dfrac{3}{a}$ **c** $\dfrac{a}{2} \times a$ **d** $\dfrac{a}{4} \times \dfrac{2}{3a}$

e $\dfrac{c}{5} \times \dfrac{1}{c}$ **f** $\dfrac{c}{5} \times \dfrac{c}{2}$ **g** $\dfrac{a}{b} \times \dfrac{c}{d}$ **h** $\dfrac{a}{b} \times \dfrac{b}{a}$

i $\dfrac{1}{m^2} \times \dfrac{m}{2}$ **j** $\dfrac{m}{2} \times \dfrac{4}{m}$ **k** $\dfrac{a}{x} \times \dfrac{x}{b}$ **l** $m \times \dfrac{4}{m}$

m $\dfrac{3}{m^2} \times m$ **n** $\left(\dfrac{a}{b}\right)^2$ **o** $\left(\dfrac{2}{x}\right)^2$ **p** $\dfrac{1}{a} \times \dfrac{a}{b} \times \dfrac{b}{c}$

2 Simplify:

a $\dfrac{a}{2} \div \dfrac{a}{3}$ **b** $\dfrac{2}{a} \div \dfrac{2}{3}$ **c** $\dfrac{3}{4} \div \dfrac{4}{x}$ **d** $\dfrac{3}{x} \div \dfrac{4}{x}$

e $\dfrac{2}{n} \div \dfrac{1}{n}$ **f** $\dfrac{c}{5} \div 5$ **g** $\dfrac{c}{5} \div c$ **h** $m \div \dfrac{2}{m}$

i $m \div \dfrac{m}{2}$ **j** $1 \div \dfrac{m}{n}$ **k** $\dfrac{3}{g} \div 4$ **l** $\dfrac{3}{g} \div \dfrac{9}{g^2}$

m $\dfrac{4}{x} \div \dfrac{x^2}{2}$ **n** $\dfrac{2}{x} \div \dfrac{6}{x^3}$ **o** $\dfrac{a}{b} \div \dfrac{a^2}{b}$ **p** $\dfrac{a^2}{5} \div \dfrac{a}{3}$

Example 11   🔊 **Self Tutor**

Simplify:

a $\dfrac{y^2 - y}{y - 2} \times \dfrac{3y - 6}{4y - 4}$ **b** $\dfrac{5m - 20}{4} \div \dfrac{2m - 8}{3}$

a $\quad \dfrac{y^2 - y}{y - 2} \times \dfrac{3y - 6}{4y - 4}$

$= \dfrac{y(y - 1)^1}{y - 2_1} \times \dfrac{3(y - 2)^1}{4(y - 1)_1}$

$= \dfrac{3y}{4}$

b $\quad \dfrac{5m - 20}{4} \div \dfrac{2m - 8}{3}$

$= \dfrac{5m - 20}{4} \times \dfrac{3}{2m - 8}$

$= \dfrac{5(m - 4)^1}{4} \times \dfrac{3}{2(m - 4)_1}$

$= \dfrac{15}{8}$

---

3 Simplify:

a $\dfrac{x^2 + 3x}{x - 2} \times \dfrac{5}{2x + 6}$ **b** $\dfrac{t - 5}{t^2 + t} \times \dfrac{4t + 4}{3t - 15}$ **c** $\dfrac{4a - 28}{a} \div \dfrac{a - 7}{5}$

d $\dfrac{6k - 2}{k + 2} \times \dfrac{2k^2 + 4k}{9k - 3}$ **e** $\dfrac{x^2 - 2x}{x + 5} \div \dfrac{8 - 4x}{2x + 10}$ **f** $\dfrac{m^2 - 4m}{10m - 2} \div \dfrac{m^2 - 16}{3m + 12}$

D   ADDING AND SUBTRACTING ALGEBRAIC FRACTIONS

The rules for addition and subtraction of algebraic fractions are identical to those used with numerical fractions.

To **add** two or more fractions, we obtain the *lowest common denominator* and then add the resulting numerators.

$$\dfrac{a}{c} + \dfrac{b}{c} = \dfrac{a + b}{c}$$

To **subtract** two or more fractions, we obtain the *lowest common denominator* and then subtract the resulting numerators.

$$\dfrac{a}{c} - \dfrac{d}{c} = \dfrac{a - d}{c}$$

To find the lowest common denominator of numerical fractions, we look for the **lowest common multiple of the denominators**.

For example:
- when finding $\dfrac{3}{2} + \dfrac{5}{3}$, the lowest common denominator is 6
- when finding $\dfrac{5}{6} + \dfrac{4}{9}$, the lowest common denominator is 18.

The same method is used when there are variables in the denominator.

For example:
- when finding $\dfrac{2}{a} + \dfrac{3}{b}$, the lowest common denominator is ab
- when finding $\dfrac{2}{x} + \dfrac{4}{5x}$, the lowest common denominator is $5x$
- when finding $\dfrac{5}{6x} + \dfrac{4}{9y}$, the lowest common denominator is $18xy$.

Example 12 — Self Tutor

Simplify: **a** $\dfrac{x}{2} + \dfrac{3x}{4}$ **b** $\dfrac{a}{3} - \dfrac{2a}{5}$

a $\dfrac{x}{2} + \dfrac{3x}{4}$ {LCD = 4}

$= \dfrac{x \times 2}{2 \times 2} + \dfrac{3x}{4}$

$= \dfrac{2x}{4} + \dfrac{3x}{4}$

$= \dfrac{2x + 3x}{4}$

$= \dfrac{5x}{4}$

b $\dfrac{a}{3} - \dfrac{2a}{5}$ {LCD = 15}

$= \dfrac{a \times 5}{3 \times 5} - \dfrac{2a \times 3}{5 \times 3}$

$= \dfrac{5a}{15} - \dfrac{6a}{15}$

$= \dfrac{5a - 6a}{15}$

$= -\dfrac{a}{15}$

EXERCISE 10D

1 Simplify by writing as a single fraction:

a $\dfrac{a}{2} + \dfrac{a}{3}$ **b** $\dfrac{b}{5} - \dfrac{b}{10}$ **c** $\dfrac{c}{4} + \dfrac{3c}{2}$

d $\dfrac{d}{2} - \dfrac{3}{5}$ **e** $\dfrac{5}{8} + \dfrac{x}{12}$ **f** $\dfrac{x}{7} - \dfrac{x}{2}$

g $\dfrac{a}{3} + \dfrac{b}{4}$ **h** $\dfrac{t}{3} - \dfrac{5t}{9}$ **i** $\dfrac{m}{7} + \dfrac{2m}{21}$

j $\dfrac{5d}{6} - \dfrac{d}{3}$ **k** $\dfrac{3p}{5} - \dfrac{2p}{7}$ **l** $\dfrac{2t}{9} + \dfrac{4t}{15}$

m $\dfrac{7k}{8} - \dfrac{11k}{18}$ **n** $\dfrac{m}{2} + \dfrac{m}{3} + \dfrac{m}{6}$ **o** $\dfrac{a}{2} - \dfrac{a}{3} + \dfrac{a}{4}$

p $\dfrac{x}{4} - \dfrac{x}{3} + \dfrac{x}{6}$ **q** $\dfrac{z}{2} - \dfrac{z}{5} + \dfrac{z}{4}$ **r** $2q - \dfrac{q}{3} + \dfrac{2q}{7}$

Example 13

Simplify: a $\dfrac{4}{a} + \dfrac{3}{b}$ b $\dfrac{5}{x} - \dfrac{4}{3x}$

a $\dfrac{4}{a} + \dfrac{3}{b}$ {LCD = ab}

$= \dfrac{4 \times b}{a \times b} + \dfrac{3 \times a}{b \times a}$

$= \dfrac{4b}{ab} + \dfrac{3a}{ab}$

$= \dfrac{4b + 3a}{ab}$

b $\dfrac{5}{x} - \dfrac{4}{3x}$ {LCD = $3x$}

$= \dfrac{5 \times 3}{x \times 3} - \dfrac{4}{3x}$

$= \dfrac{15}{3x} - \dfrac{4}{3x}$

$= \dfrac{15 - 4}{3x}$

$= \dfrac{11}{3x}$

2 Simplify:

a $\dfrac{7}{a} + \dfrac{3}{b}$
b $\dfrac{3}{a} + \dfrac{2}{c}$
c $\dfrac{4}{a} + \dfrac{5}{d}$
d $\dfrac{2a}{m} - \dfrac{a}{n}$

e $\dfrac{a}{x} + \dfrac{b}{2x}$
f $\dfrac{3}{a} - \dfrac{1}{2a}$
g $\dfrac{4}{x} - \dfrac{1}{xy}$
h $\dfrac{5}{x} + \dfrac{6}{5x}$

i $\dfrac{11}{3z} - \dfrac{3}{4z}$
j $\dfrac{a}{b} + \dfrac{c}{d}$
k $\dfrac{3}{a} + \dfrac{a}{2}$
l $\dfrac{x}{y} + \dfrac{2}{3}$

m $\dfrac{8}{p} - \dfrac{2}{5}$
n $\dfrac{x}{6y} + \dfrac{2x}{9y}$
o $\dfrac{1}{8t} - \dfrac{3}{5t}$
p $\dfrac{5}{2x} + \dfrac{3}{x^2}$

Example 14

Simplify: a $\dfrac{b}{3} + 1$ b $\dfrac{a}{4} - a$

a $\dfrac{b}{3} + 1$

$= \dfrac{b}{3} + \dfrac{3}{3}$

$= \dfrac{b + 3}{3}$

b $\dfrac{a}{4} - a$

$= \dfrac{a}{4} - \dfrac{a \times 4}{1 \times 4}$

$= \dfrac{a}{4} - \dfrac{4a}{4}$

$= \dfrac{-3a}{4}$

$= -\dfrac{3a}{4}$

3 Simplify by writing as a single fraction:

a $\dfrac{x}{2} + 1$
b $\dfrac{y}{3} - 1$
c $\dfrac{a}{2} + a$
d $\dfrac{b}{4} - 3$

e $\dfrac{x}{2} - 4$
f $2 + \dfrac{a}{3}$
g $x - \dfrac{x}{5}$
h $2 + \dfrac{1}{x}$

i $5 - \dfrac{2}{x}$
j $a + \dfrac{2}{a}$
k $\dfrac{3}{b} + b$
l $\dfrac{1}{x^2} - 2x$

Example 15

Write as a single fraction: a $\dfrac{x}{6} + \dfrac{x-2}{3}$ b $\dfrac{x+1}{2} - \dfrac{x-2}{3}$

a $\dfrac{x}{6} + \dfrac{x-2}{3}$ {LCD = 6}

$= \dfrac{x}{6} + \dfrac{2}{2}\left(\dfrac{x-2}{3}\right)$

$= \dfrac{x}{6} + \dfrac{2(x-2)}{6}$

$= \dfrac{x + 2(x-2)}{6}$

$= \dfrac{x + 2x - 4}{6}$

$= \dfrac{3x - 4}{6}$

b $\dfrac{x+1}{2} - \dfrac{x-2}{3}$ {LCD = 6}

$= \dfrac{3}{3}\left(\dfrac{x+1}{2}\right) - \dfrac{2}{2}\left(\dfrac{x-2}{3}\right)$

$= \dfrac{3(x+1)}{6} - \dfrac{2(x-2)}{6}$

$= \dfrac{3(x+1) - 2(x-2)}{6}$

$= \dfrac{3x + 3 - 2x + 4}{6}$

$= \dfrac{x + 7}{6}$

---

4 Write as a single fraction, and hence simplify:

a $\dfrac{x}{2} + \dfrac{x+1}{3}$ b $\dfrac{x-1}{4} - \dfrac{x}{2}$ c $\dfrac{2x}{3} + \dfrac{x+3}{4}$

d $\dfrac{x+1}{2} + \dfrac{x-1}{3}$ e $\dfrac{x-1}{3} + \dfrac{1-2x}{4}$ f $\dfrac{2x+3}{2} + \dfrac{2x-3}{3}$

g $\dfrac{x}{3} + \dfrac{x+1}{4}$ h $\dfrac{3x+2}{4} + \dfrac{x}{2}$ i $\dfrac{x}{6} + \dfrac{3x-1}{5}$

j $\dfrac{a+b}{3} + \dfrac{b-a}{2}$ k $\dfrac{x+1}{5} + \dfrac{2x-1}{4}$ l $\dfrac{x+1}{7} + \dfrac{3-x}{2}$

m $\dfrac{x}{6} - \dfrac{2-x}{5}$ n $\dfrac{2x-1}{5} - \dfrac{x}{4}$ o $\dfrac{x}{8} - \dfrac{1-x}{4}$

p $\dfrac{x}{5} - \dfrac{2-x}{10}$ q $\dfrac{x-1}{5} - \dfrac{2x-7}{3}$ r $\dfrac{1-3x}{4} - \dfrac{2x+1}{3}$

Example 16

Write as a single fraction: a $\dfrac{1}{x} + \dfrac{2}{x-1}$ b $\dfrac{2}{x-1} - \dfrac{3}{x+1}$

a $\dfrac{1}{x} + \dfrac{2}{x-1}$ {LCD = $x(x-1)$}

$= \dfrac{1}{x}\left(\dfrac{x-1}{x-1}\right) + \left(\dfrac{2}{x-1}\right)\dfrac{x}{x}$

$= \dfrac{1(x-1) + 2x}{x(x-1)}$

$= \dfrac{x - 1 + 2x}{x(x-1)}$

$= \dfrac{3x - 1}{x(x-1)}$

b $\dfrac{2}{x-1} - \dfrac{3}{x+1}$ {LCD = $(x-1)(x+1)$}

$= \left(\dfrac{2}{x-1}\right)\left(\dfrac{x+1}{x+1}\right) - \left(\dfrac{3}{x+1}\right)\left(\dfrac{x-1}{x-1}\right)$

$= \dfrac{2(x+1) - 3(x-1)}{(x-1)(x+1)}$

$= \dfrac{2x + 2 - 3x + 3}{(x-1)(x+1)}$

$= \dfrac{-x + 5}{(x-1)(x+1)}$ or $\dfrac{5 - x}{(x-1)(x+1)}$

5 Simplify:

a $\dfrac{3}{x} + \dfrac{4}{x+1}$
b $\dfrac{5}{x+2} - \dfrac{3}{x}$
c $\dfrac{4}{x+1} - \dfrac{3}{x-1}$

d $3 + \dfrac{1}{x+2}$
e $\dfrac{1}{x} + \dfrac{4}{x-4}$
f $\dfrac{2}{x+3} - 4$

g $\dfrac{x+1}{x-1} + \dfrac{x}{x+1}$
h $\dfrac{5}{x} + \dfrac{6}{x-2}$
i $\dfrac{2}{x+2} - \dfrac{4}{x+1}$

j $\dfrac{x}{x-1} + \dfrac{4}{2x+1}$
k $\dfrac{5}{x-1} + \dfrac{x-2}{x+3}$
l $\dfrac{x}{x+5} - \dfrac{x}{x-3}$

m $\dfrac{1}{x} + \dfrac{1}{x+1} + \dfrac{1}{x+2}$
n $\dfrac{2}{x} - \dfrac{5}{x+3} + \dfrac{3}{x-4}$
o $\dfrac{x}{x-1} - \dfrac{1}{x} + \dfrac{x}{x+1}$

6 Answer the **Opening Problem** on page **208**.

7 Write as a single fraction:

a $\dfrac{2}{x(x+1)} + \dfrac{1}{x+1}$
b $\dfrac{2x}{x-3} + \dfrac{4}{(x+2)(x-3)}$

c $\dfrac{3}{(x-2)(x+3)} + \dfrac{x}{x+3}$
d $\dfrac{x+5}{x-2} - \dfrac{63}{(x-2)(x+7)}$

8 Simplify:

a $\dfrac{\frac{x}{x-2} - 3}{x-3}$
b $\dfrac{\frac{3x}{x+4} - 1}{x-2}$
c $\dfrac{\frac{x^2}{x+2} - 1}{x+1}$

d $\dfrac{\frac{x^2}{2-x} + 9}{x-3}$
e $\dfrac{\frac{1}{x^2} - \frac{1}{4}}{x-2}$
f $\dfrac{\frac{x-3}{x^2} - \frac{1}{16}}{x-4}$

9 Simplify each of the following expressions. Hence write down a value of x for which the expression is zero, and the values of x for which it is undefined.

a $\dfrac{2x}{x+1} - \dfrac{4}{(x-1)(x+1)}$
b $\dfrac{6}{(x+2)(x+5)} + \dfrac{x}{x+2}$

E EQUATIONS WITH ALGEBRAIC FRACTIONS

To solve equations involving algebraic fractions, we:

- write all fractions with the same **lowest common denominator (LCD)**, and then
- **equate numerators**.

Example 17   Self Tutor

Solve for x: $\dfrac{6}{x} = \dfrac{2}{3}$

$\dfrac{6}{x} = \dfrac{2}{3}$ {LCD $= 3x$}

$\therefore \dfrac{3 \times 6}{3 \times x} = \dfrac{2 \times x}{3 \times x}$ {to achieve a common denominator}

$\therefore 18 = 2x$ {equating numerators}

$\therefore x = 9$ {dividing both sides by 2}

Write the fractions with the same LCD then equate numerators.

Example 18

Solve for x: $\dfrac{5}{x+2} = \dfrac{2}{x-1}$

$\dfrac{5}{x+2} = \dfrac{2}{x-1}$ {LCD $= (x+2)(x-1)$}

$\therefore \dfrac{5 \times (x-1)}{(x+2) \times (x-1)} = \dfrac{2 \times (x+2)}{(x-1) \times (x+2)}$ {to achieve a common denominator}

$\therefore 5(x-1) = 2(x+2)$ {equating numerators}

$\therefore 5x - 5 = 2x + 4$ {expanding brackets}

$\therefore 3x - 5 = 4$ {subtracting $2x$ from both sides}

$\therefore 3x = 9$ {adding 5 to both sides}

$\therefore x = 3$ {dividing both sides by 3}

EXERCISE 10E

1 Solve for x:

a $\dfrac{3}{x} = \dfrac{1}{5}$ b $\dfrac{3}{x} = \dfrac{2}{3}$ c $\dfrac{2}{7} = \dfrac{5}{x}$ d $\dfrac{1}{2x} = \dfrac{4}{3}$

e $\dfrac{7}{3x} = -\dfrac{4}{5}$ f $\dfrac{x-3}{x} = \dfrac{3}{5}$ g $\dfrac{x+5}{2x} = -\dfrac{8}{5}$ h $\dfrac{x-1}{4x} = \dfrac{5}{6}$

2 Solve for x:

a $\dfrac{2}{x} = \dfrac{8}{x+6}$ b $\dfrac{3}{x} = \dfrac{5}{x-6}$ c $\dfrac{1}{x+1} = \dfrac{7}{x-1}$

d $\dfrac{10}{x-3} = \dfrac{7}{x+6}$ e $\dfrac{8}{2x+3} = \dfrac{9}{x-1}$ f $\dfrac{5}{3x-2} = \dfrac{4}{x-3}$

REVIEW SET 10A

1 If $p = 5$, $q = -3$, and $r = 6$, evaluate:

a $\dfrac{r}{q}$ b $\dfrac{p-q}{p+q}$ c $\dfrac{\sqrt{p^2 - 16}}{r - q}$ d $\dfrac{p + 2q - 2r}{r^2 - p^2}$

2 Simplify:

a $\dfrac{(2t)^2}{6t}$ b $\dfrac{16a + 8b}{6a + 3b}$ c $\dfrac{x(x-4)}{3(x-4)}$ d $\dfrac{8}{4x + 8}$

3 Simplify:

a $\dfrac{2x + 6}{x^2 - 9}$ b $\dfrac{x^2 + 4x + 4}{x^2 + 2x}$ c $\dfrac{3x^2 - 6x}{3x^2 - 5x - 2}$

4 Simplify:

a $\dfrac{2a - 2b}{b - a}$ b $\dfrac{5x - 15}{3x - x^2}$ c $\dfrac{16 - x^2}{2x - 8}$

5 Simplify:

a $\dfrac{a}{b} \times \dfrac{b}{3}$ b $\dfrac{a}{b} \div \dfrac{b}{3}$ c $\dfrac{a}{b} + \dfrac{b}{3}$ d $\dfrac{a}{b} - \dfrac{b}{3}$

6 Simplify:

a $\dfrac{7x-14}{x} \times \dfrac{3}{x-2}$ b $\dfrac{t^2-3t}{6t+6} \times \dfrac{t+1}{4t-12}$

7 Simplify:

a $\dfrac{9}{n} \div 6$ b $\dfrac{7}{3x-6} \div \dfrac{x+5}{x^2-2x}$

8 Write as a single fraction:

a $\dfrac{2x}{3} + \dfrac{x}{4}$ b $2 + \dfrac{x}{7}$ c $\dfrac{x}{4} - 1$ d $\dfrac{x}{2} + \dfrac{x}{4} - \dfrac{x}{3}$

9 Simplify:

a $\dfrac{x}{3} + \dfrac{x-1}{4}$ b $\dfrac{x+2}{3} - \dfrac{2-x}{6}$ c $\dfrac{2x+1}{5} - \dfrac{x-1}{10}$

10 Simplify:

a $\dfrac{1}{x+1} + \dfrac{2}{x-2}$ b $\dfrac{5}{x-1} - \dfrac{4}{x+1}$ c $\dfrac{1}{x^2} + \dfrac{1}{x+1}$

11 Solve for x: $\dfrac{6}{x} = \dfrac{5}{11-x}$

12 a Write as a single fraction: i $a - \dfrac{9}{a}$ ii $1 - \dfrac{a}{3}$

b Hence simplify $\left(a - \dfrac{9}{a}\right) \div \left(1 - \dfrac{a}{3}\right)$.

c Evaluate $\left(a - \dfrac{9}{a}\right) \div \left(1 - \dfrac{a}{3}\right)$ for:

i $a = 1$ ii $a = 3$ iii $a = 5$

REVIEW SET 10B

1 If $m = -4$, $n = 3$, and $p = 6$, evaluate:

a $\dfrac{p}{m+n}$ b $\dfrac{p-2n}{m+n}$ c $\dfrac{p-m}{\sqrt{m^2+n^2}}$

2 Simplify:

a $\dfrac{(3x)^2}{6x^3}$ b $\dfrac{3a+6b}{3}$ c $\dfrac{(x+2)^2}{x^2+2x}$

3 Simplify:

a $\dfrac{a+b}{3b+3a}$ b $\dfrac{2x^2-8}{x+2}$ c $\dfrac{x^2-6x+9}{4x-12}$

4 Simplify:

a $\dfrac{m}{n} \times \dfrac{2}{n}$ b $\dfrac{m}{n} \div \dfrac{2}{n}$ c $m^2 \div \dfrac{n}{m}$

5 Simplify:

a $\dfrac{3}{x} + \dfrac{5}{2x}$ b $\dfrac{6}{y} - \dfrac{a}{b}$ c $\dfrac{8}{3x} + \dfrac{1}{4x}$

6 Simplify:

   a $\dfrac{3x}{7} - \dfrac{x}{14}$ **b** $\dfrac{4}{3x} + \dfrac{3}{x^2}$

7 Write as a single fraction:

   a $5 + \dfrac{x}{2}$ **b** $3 - \dfrac{y}{x}$ **c** $1 + \dfrac{x}{2} + \dfrac{y}{3}$

8 Simplify:

   a $\dfrac{y^2 - 5y}{y+2} \times \dfrac{3}{2y-10}$ **b** $\dfrac{9-3x}{4x+16} \div \dfrac{x^2-3x}{x+4}$

9 Simplify:

   a $\dfrac{x}{4} - \dfrac{2-x}{8}$ **b** $\dfrac{x+5}{2} + \dfrac{2x+1}{5}$ **c** $\dfrac{3-x}{6} - \dfrac{2x}{9}$

10 Simplify:

   a $\dfrac{2}{x-1} - \dfrac{3}{x+2}$ **b** $\dfrac{1}{x-1} - \dfrac{2}{x^2}$ **c** $\dfrac{x}{x+2} - \dfrac{2}{x} + \dfrac{x}{x+3}$

11 a Evaluate $(x+y) \div \left(\dfrac{1}{x} + \dfrac{1}{y}\right)$ for:

      i $x=3,\ y=4$ **ii** $x=5,\ y=10$

   b In terms of x and y, what do you suspect $(x+y) \div \left(\dfrac{1}{x} + \dfrac{1}{y}\right)$ simplifies to?

   c Prove your answer to **b** is correct by first writing $\dfrac{1}{x} + \dfrac{1}{y}$ as a single fraction.

   d Hence, state the value of $\dfrac{41}{\frac{1}{21} + \frac{1}{20}}$.

12 Solve for x: $\dfrac{4}{x-1} + \dfrac{x+4}{x} = 1$

Chapter 11

Quadratic equations

Contents:
- **A** Equations of the form $x^2 = k$
- **B** Solution by factorisation
- **C** Completing the square
- **D** The quadratic formula
- **E** Problem solving
- **F** Quadratic equations with $\Delta < 0$
- **G** The sum and product of the roots

OPENING PROBLEM

A square garden gazebo is surrounded by 4 semi-circles of lawn as shown.

For a wedding, quarter circles of flowers are planted in each corner of the gazebo. The lawn covers 4 times as much area as the flower beds.

Suppose the flower beds are x metres apart as shown.

Things to think about:

a Explain why the radius of each flower bed is $\left(5 - \dfrac{x}{2}\right)$ metres.

b Hence, show that $x^2 - 20x + 50 = 0$.

c By solving this equation, can you find the distance between the flower beds?

In the past we have solved many equations of the form $ax + b = 0$, $a \neq 0$. These are called **linear equations**, and have *only one* solution.

For example, $3x - 2 = 0$ is a linear equation which has the solution $x = \frac{2}{3}$.

A **quadratic equation** is an equation which can be written in the form $ax^2 + bx + c = 0$, where a, b, and c are constants, $a \neq 0$.

A quadratic equation may have *two*, *one*, or *zero* real solutions.

For example: $x^2 + 3x - 10 = 0$ is a quadratic equation.

If $x = 2$, $x^2 + 3x - 10$ If $x = -5$, $x^2 + 3x - 10$
$\qquad\qquad\quad = 2^2 + 3 \times 2 - 10 \qquad\qquad\qquad\qquad = (-5)^2 + 3 \times (-5) - 10$
$\qquad\qquad\quad = 4 + 6 - 10 \qquad\qquad\qquad\qquad\qquad\; = 25 - 15 - 10$
$\qquad\qquad\quad = 0 \qquad\qquad\qquad\qquad\qquad\qquad\qquad = 0$

$x = 2$ and $x = -5$ both satisfy the equation $x^2 + 3x - 10 = 0$, so we say that they are both **solutions** or **roots** of the equation.

In contrast, the quadratic equation $x^2 + 2x + 1 = 0$ has only the one solution $x = -1$, and the quadratic equation $x^2 + 1 = 0$ has no real solutions.

A   EQUATIONS OF THE FORM $x^2 = k$

Consider the equation $x^2 = 7$.

If $x = \sqrt{7}$, then $x^2 = (\sqrt{7})^2$
$\qquad\qquad\qquad\quad\; = 7$

If $x = -\sqrt{7}$, then $x^2 = (-\sqrt{7})^2$
$\qquad\qquad\qquad\qquad\; = (-\sqrt{7}) \times (-\sqrt{7})$
$\qquad\qquad\qquad\qquad\; = 7$

$\pm\sqrt{7}$ is read as 'plus or minus the square root of 7'.

So, the solutions of $x^2 = 7$ are $x = \pm\sqrt{7}$.

QUADRATIC EQUATIONS (Chapter 11)

If $x^2 = k$ then $\begin{cases} x = \pm\sqrt{k} & \text{if } k > 0 \\ x = 0 & \text{if } k = 0 \\ \text{there are \textbf{no real solutions}} & \text{if } k < 0. \end{cases}$

Example 1 — Self Tutor

Solve for x:

a $2x^2 + 1 = 15$ **b** $2 - 3x^2 = 8$

a $2x^2 + 1 = 15$
$\therefore 2x^2 = 14$ {subtracting 1 from both sides}
$\therefore x^2 = 7$ {dividing both sides by 2}
$\therefore x = \pm\sqrt{7}$

b $2 - 3x^2 = 8$
$\therefore -3x^2 = 6$ {subtracting 2 from both sides}
$\therefore x^2 = -2$ {dividing both sides by -3}

which has no real solutions as x^2 cannot be < 0.

Example 2 — Self Tutor

Solve for x:

a $(x-3)^2 = 16$ **b** $(x+2)^2 = 11$

a $(x-3)^2 = 16$
$\therefore x - 3 = \pm\sqrt{16}$
$\therefore x - 3 = \pm 4$
$\therefore x = 3 \pm 4$
$\therefore x = 7$ or -1

b $(x+2)^2 = 11$
$\therefore x + 2 = \pm\sqrt{11}$
$\therefore x = -2 \pm \sqrt{11}$

For equations of the form $(x \pm a)^2 = k$ we do not expand the LHS.

EXERCISE 11A

1 Solve for x:

a $x^2 - 10 = 90$ **b** $2x^2 = 50$ **c** $5x^2 = 20$
d $6x^2 = 54$ **e** $5x^2 = -45$ **f** $7x^2 = 0$
g $3x^2 - 2 = 25$ **h** $4 - 2x^2 = 12$ **i** $4x^2 + 2 = 10$

2 Solve for x:

a $(x-1)^2 = 9$ **b** $(x+4)^2 = 16$ **c** $(x+2)^2 = -1$
d $(x-4)^2 = 5$ **e** $(x-6)^2 = -4$ **f** $(x+2)^2 = 0$
g $(2x-5)^2 = 0$ **h** $(3x+2)^2 = 4$ **i** $(3x+1)^2 = 81$
j $(2x+1)^2 = 48$ **k** $(3-2x)^2 = 7$ **l** $\frac{1}{3}(2x+3)^2 = 2$

3 Solve for x by first eliminating the algebraic fractions:

   a $\dfrac{x}{4} = \dfrac{1}{x}$ **b** $\dfrac{5}{x} = \dfrac{x}{2}$ **c** $\dfrac{x}{8} = \dfrac{2}{x}$

4 Solve for x:

   a $(x+1)^2 = (3-x)^2$ **b** $(2x-1)^2 = (2-3x)^2$

B   SOLUTION BY FACTORISATION

For quadratic equations which are not of the form $x^2 = k$, we need an alternative method of solution. One method is to **factorise** the quadratic and then apply the **Null Factor law**.

The **Null Factor law** states that:

> When the product of two or more numbers is zero, then *at least one* of them must be zero.
>
> So, if $ab = 0$ then $a = 0$ or $b = 0$.

To solve quadratic equations by factorisation, we follow these steps:

> *Step 1:*   If necessary, rearrange the equation so one side is **zero**.
>
> *Step 2:*   **Fully factorise** the other side (usually the LHS).
>
> *Step 3:*   Apply the **Null Factor law**.
>
> *Step 4:*   **Solve** the resulting linear equations.

Example 3   🔊 Self Tutor

Solve for x: $x^2 = 3x$

$$x^2 = 3x$$
$$\therefore \; x^2 - 3x = 0 \quad \text{\{making the RHS = 0\}}$$
$$\therefore \; x(x-3) = 0 \quad \text{\{factorising the LHS\}}$$
$$\therefore \; x = 0 \; \text{or} \; x-3 = 0 \quad \text{\{Null Factor law\}}$$
$$\therefore \; x = 0 \; \text{or} \; 3$$

If $a \times b = 0$ then either $a = 0$ or $b = 0$.

WARNING ON INCORRECT CANCELLING

Let us reconsider the equation $x^2 = 3x$ from **Example 3**.

We notice that there is a common factor of x on both sides.

If we cancel x from both sides, we will have $\dfrac{x^2}{x} = \dfrac{3x}{x}$ and thus $x = 3$.

Consequently, we will 'lose' the solution $x = 0$.

From this example we conclude that:

> We must never cancel a variable that is a common factor from both sides of an equation unless we know that the factor cannot be zero.

Example 4

Solve for x: $\quad x^2 + 3x = 28$

$$x^2 + 3x = 28$$
$\therefore \ x^2 + 3x - 28 = 0 \quad$ {making the RHS $= 0$}
$\therefore \ (x+7)(x-4) = 0 \quad$ {the numbers $+7$ and -4 have sum 3 and product -28}
$\therefore \ x+7 = 0 \ $ or $\ x - 4 = 0 \quad$ {Null Factor law}
$\qquad \therefore \ x = -7 \ $ or $\ 4$

Check: If $\ x = -7$, then $\ x^2 + 3x = (-7)^2 + 3(-7) = 49 - 21 = 28 \ \checkmark$
$\qquad\quad$ If $\ x = 4$, $\ $ then $\ x^2 + 3x = 4^2 + 3(4) = 16 + 12 = 28 \ \checkmark$

Example 5

Solve for x: $\quad 5x^2 = 3x + 2$

$$5x^2 = 3x + 2$$
$\therefore \ 5x^2 - 3x - 2 = 0 \quad$ {making the RHS $= 0$}

We need two numbers with sum -3 and product -10. These are -5 and $+2$.

$\therefore \ 5x^2 - 5x + 2x - 2 = 0 \quad$ {'splitting' the middle term}
$\therefore \ 5x(x-1) + 2(x-1) = 0$
$\therefore \ (x-1)(5x+2) = 0$
$\therefore \ x - 1 = 0 \ $ or $\ 5x + 2 = 0 \quad$ {Null Factor law}
$\qquad \therefore \ x = 1 \ $ or $\ -\frac{2}{5}$

EXERCISE 11B

1 Solve for x:

  a $\ x^2 - 7x = 0$ **b** $\ x^2 - 5x = 0$ **c** $\ x^2 = 8x$

  d $\ x^2 = 4x$ **e** $\ 3x^2 + 6x = 0$ **f** $\ 2x^2 + 5x = 0$

  g $\ 4x^2 - 3x = 0$ **h** $\ 4x^2 = 5x$ **i** $\ 3x^2 = 9x$

2 Solve for x:

  a $\ x^2 + 3x + 2 = 0$ **b** $\ x^2 - 3x + 2 = 0$ **c** $\ x^2 - 10x + 25 = 0$

  d $\ x^2 + 5x + 6 = 0$ **e** $\ x^2 + 6 = 5x$ **f** $\ x^2 + 7x = -6$

  g $\ x^2 + 14 = -9x$ **h** $\ x^2 + 11x = -30$ **i** $\ x^2 = 15 - 2x$

  j $\ x^2 + 4x = 12$ **k** $\ x^2 = 11x - 24$ **l** $\ x^2 = 14x - 49$

3 Solve for x:

  a $\ 2x^2 + 18x + 36 = 0$ **b** $\ -x^2 - 11x - 28 = 0$ **c** $\ 3x^2 + 6x = 24$

  d $\ 2x^2 + 2x = 24$ **e** $\ 4x^2 + 24 = 20x$ **f** $\ 5x^2 + 20 = 20x$

  g $\ 3x^2 = 3x + 18$ **h** $\ -x^2 = 7x - 60$ **i** $\ 140 + 6x = 2x^2$

  j $\ 2x^2 - 5x + 2 = 0$ **k** $\ 3x^2 + 8x - 3 = 0$ **l** $\ 3x^2 + 17x + 20 = 0$

  m $\ 2x^2 + 5x = 3$ **n** $\ 2x^2 + 5 = 11x$ **o** $\ 2x^2 + 7x + 5 = 0$

4 Solve for x:

a $3x^2 + 13x + 4 = 0$
b $5x^2 - 6 = 13x$
c $2x^2 + 17x = 9$
d $2x^2 = 3x + 5$
e $3x^2 = 8 - 2x$
f $2x^2 = 18 - 9x$
g $-6x^2 + 17x + 3 = 0$
h $-2x^2 - 5x + 12 = 0$
i $12x^2 - 22x + 6 = 0$
j $9x^2 + 6x - 48 = 0$
k $28x^2 - 8 = 2x$
l $36x^2 + 39x = 12$

5 Solve for x:

a $x(x+5) + 2(x+6) = 0$
b $x(1+x) + x = 3$
c $(x-1)(x+9) = 8x$
d $3x(x+2) - 5(x-3) = 17$
e $4x(x+1) = -1$
f $2x(x-6) = x - 20$
g $x(8-x) + 20 = -13$
h $(8x+1)(x-2) = 13 - x$

Example 6   ◀)) Self Tutor

Solve for x: $\dfrac{x-2}{x} = \dfrac{6+x}{2}$

$\dfrac{x-2}{x} = \dfrac{6+x}{2}$ {LCD $= 2x$}

$\therefore \dfrac{2 \times (x-2)}{2 \times x} = \dfrac{x \times (6+x)}{x \times 2}$ {to achieve a common denominator}

$\therefore 2(x-2) = x(6+x)$ {equating numerators}

$\therefore 2x - 4 = 6x + x^2$

$\therefore x^2 + 4x + 4 = 0$

$\therefore (x+2)^2 = 0$

$\therefore x + 2 = 0$

$\therefore x = -2$

Check: If $x = -2$ then

LHS $= \dfrac{(-2) - 2}{(-2)} = \dfrac{-4}{-2} = 2$

and   RHS $= \dfrac{6 + (-2)}{2} = \dfrac{4}{2} = 2$ ✓

---

6 Solve for x:

a $\dfrac{x+1}{4} = \dfrac{1}{2x}$
b $\dfrac{x+4}{2} = \dfrac{6}{x}$
c $\dfrac{x+2}{x} = x$
d $\dfrac{x-1}{x+2} = \dfrac{2}{x}$
e $\dfrac{x}{1+2x} = \dfrac{1}{3x}$
f $\dfrac{3x+1}{2x} = x + 2$

Example 7   ◀)) Self Tutor

Solve for x: $\dfrac{1}{x} + \dfrac{4}{x+6} = 1$

$\dfrac{1}{x} + \dfrac{4}{x+6} = \dfrac{1}{1}$ {LCD $= x(x+6)$}

$\therefore \dfrac{1 \times (x+6)}{x \times (x+6)} + \dfrac{4 \times x}{(x+6) \times x} = \dfrac{1 \times x(x+6)}{1 \times x(x+6)}$ {to achieve a common denominator}

$\therefore x + 6 + 4x = x(x+6)$ {equating numerators}

$\therefore 5x + 6 = x^2 + 6x$

$\therefore 0 = x^2 + x - 6$

$\therefore (x+3)(x-2) = 0$

$\therefore x = -3$ or 2

7 Solve for x:

a $\dfrac{2}{x} + \dfrac{3}{x+2} = 1$
b $\dfrac{5}{x} + \dfrac{x}{x-6} = 2$
c $\dfrac{4}{x+1} + \dfrac{3}{x+3} = -1$

d $\dfrac{5}{x+2} - \dfrac{6}{x-1} = -2$
e $\dfrac{4}{x-2} + \dfrac{3}{x-1} = 3$
f $\dfrac{x}{x-2} - \dfrac{x+3}{x} = -5$

g $\dfrac{1}{x+3} + \dfrac{1}{x-3} = x$
h $\dfrac{4}{x+2} - \dfrac{2}{x+1} = x$

8 Solve for x:

a $x^4 - 5x^2 + 4 = 0$
b $x^4 - 7x^2 + 12 = 0$
c $x^4 = 4x^2 + 5$

Hint: Treat these as quadratics in the variable x^2.

9 Solve for x:

a $x^3 - 10x^2 = 39x$
b $3x^4 - 24x^3 + 48x^2 = 0$
c $2x^6 + 88x^2 = 30x^4$

10 Solve for x:

a $\sqrt{x+2} = x$
b $\sqrt{x+13} - \sqrt{7-x} = 2$

C COMPLETING THE SQUARE

Some quadratic equations, such as $x^2 + 4x - 7 = 0$, cannot be solved using the factorisation methods already practised. This is because the solutions are irrational.

Instead, we use a method called **completing the square**.

We can solve $x^2 + 4x - 7 = 0$ if we can rearrange it so there is a perfect square on the left hand side.

$x^2 + 4x - 7 = 0$
$\therefore \; x^2 + 4x = 7$
$\therefore \; x^2 + 4x + 4 = 7 + 4$
$\therefore \; (x+2)^2 = 11$
$\therefore \; x + 2 = \pm\sqrt{11}$
$\therefore \; x = -2 \pm \sqrt{11}$

We add 4 to both sides to 'complete' a perfect square on the LHS.

The process of creating a **perfect square** on the left hand side is called **completing the square**.

From our previous study of perfect squares, we observe that:

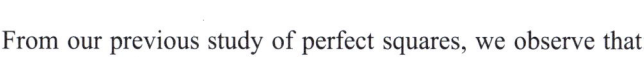

and in general that $(x+a)^2 = x^2 + 2ax + a^2$.

To complete a perfect square, the number we must add to both sides is found by **halving the coefficient of x, then squaring this value**.

Example 8

For each of the following equations:
- **i** Find what must be added to both sides of the equation to create a perfect square on the LHS.
- **ii** Write the equation in the form $(x+p)^2 = k$.

a $x^2 + 8x = -5$ **b** $x^2 - 6x = 13$

a **i** In $x^2 + 8x = -5$, half the coefficient of x is $\frac{8}{2} = 4$.
So, we add 4^2 to both sides.

ii The equation becomes $x^2 + 8x + 4^2 = -5 + 4^2$
$\therefore (x+4)^2 = -5 + 16$
$\therefore (x+4)^2 = 11$

b **i** In $x^2 - 6x = 13$, half the coefficient of x is $\frac{-6}{2} = -3$.
So, we add $(-3)^2 = 3^2$ to both sides.

ii The equation becomes $x^2 - 6x + 3^2 = 13 + 3^2$
$\therefore (x-3)^2 = 13 + 9$
$\therefore (x-3)^2 = 22$

We keep the equation balanced by adding the same number to both sides of the equation.

Example 9

Solve for x by completing the square, leaving answers in simplest radical form:

a $x^2 + 2x - 2 = 0$ **b** $x^2 - 5x + 3 = 0$

a $x^2 + 2x - 2 = 0$
$\therefore x^2 + 2x = 2$ {moving the constant term to the RHS}
$\therefore x^2 + 2x + 1^2 = 2 + 1^2$ {adding $(\frac{2}{2})^2 = 1^2$ to both sides}
$\therefore (x+1)^2 = 3$
$\therefore x + 1 = \pm\sqrt{3}$
$\therefore x = -1 \pm \sqrt{3}$

b $x^2 - 5x + 3 = 0$
$\therefore x^2 - 5x = -3$ {moving the constant term to the RHS}
$\therefore x^2 - 5x + (\frac{5}{2})^2 = -3 + (\frac{5}{2})^2$ {adding $(\frac{-5}{2})^2 = (\frac{5}{2})^2$ to both sides}
$\therefore (x - \frac{5}{2})^2 = -3 + \frac{25}{4}$
$\therefore (x - \frac{5}{2})^2 = \frac{13}{4}$
$\therefore x - \frac{5}{2} = \pm\sqrt{\frac{13}{4}}$
$\therefore x = \frac{5}{2} \pm \frac{\sqrt{13}}{2}$
$\therefore x = \frac{5 \pm \sqrt{13}}{2}$

If $(x-a)^2 = k$ where $k > 0$, then $x = a \pm \sqrt{k}$.

EXERCISE 11C

1 For each of the following equations:

    i Find what must be added to both sides of the equation to create a perfect square on the LHS.

    ii Write each equation in the form $(x+p)^2 = k$.

  a $x^2 + 2x = 5$ **b** $x^2 - 2x = -7$ **c** $x^2 + 6x = 2$

  d $x^2 - 6x = -3$ **e** $x^2 + 10x = 1$ **f** $x^2 - 8x = 5$

  g $x^2 + 12x = 13$ **h** $x^2 + 5x = -2$ **i** $x^2 - 7x = 4$

2 Solve for x by completing the square, leaving answers in simplest radical form:

  a $x^2 - 4x + 1 = 0$ **b** $x^2 - 2x - 2 = 0$ **c** $x^2 - 4x - 3 = 0$

  d $x^2 + 2x - 1 = 0$ **e** $x^2 + 4x + 1 = 0$ **f** $x^2 + 6x + 3 = 0$

  g $x^2 + 3x + 2 = 0$ **h** $x^2 + 8x + 14 = 0$ **i** $x^2 - 3x - 1 = 0$

Example 10   ◀)) Self Tutor

Solve for x by completing the square: $x^2 - 4x + 6 = 0$

$x^2 - 4x + 6 = 0$

$\therefore x^2 - 4x = -6$ {moving the constant term to the RHS}

$\therefore x^2 - 4x + 2^2 = -6 + 2^2$ {adding $(-\frac{4}{2})^2 = 2^2$ to both sides}

$\therefore (x-2)^2 = -2$

which is impossible as $(x-2)^2$ cannot be < 0.

$\therefore$ no real solutions exist.

If $(x-a)^2 = k$ where $k < 0$, then there are no real solutions.

3 If possible, solve for x by completing the square:

  a $x^2 + 2x + 4 = 0$ **b** $x^2 - 5x + 6 = 0$ **c** $x^2 - 6x + 11 = 0$

  d $x^2 + x - 1 = 0$ **e** $x^2 + 5x - 2 = 0$ **f** $x^2 - 7x + 13 = 0$

Example 11   ◀)) Self Tutor

Solve the equation $3x^2 + 6x - 2 = 0$ by completing the square.

$3x^2 + 6x - 2 = 0$

$\therefore x^2 + 2x - \frac{2}{3} = 0$ {dividing both sides by 3}

$\therefore x^2 + 2x = \frac{2}{3}$

$\therefore x^2 + 2x + 1^2 = \frac{2}{3} + 1^2$ {adding $(\frac{2}{2})^2 = 1^2$ to both sides}

$\therefore (x+1)^2 = \frac{5}{3}$

$\therefore x + 1 = \pm\sqrt{\frac{5}{3}}$

$\therefore x = -1 \pm \frac{\sqrt{5}}{\sqrt{3}} \times \frac{\sqrt{3}}{\sqrt{3}}$ {writing the RHS with integer denominator}

$\therefore x = \frac{-3 \pm \sqrt{15}}{3}$

4 Solve by completing the square:

    a $2x^2 + 4x - 1 = 0$ **b** $3x^2 - 12x + 7 = 0$ **c** $5x^2 - 10x + 3 = 0$

    d $2x^2 + 12x - 5 = 0$ **e** $2x^2 - 2x + 3 = 0$ **f** $3x^2 + 3x - 1 = 0$

5   **a** Solve by completing the square: $x^2 + bx + c = 0$

    b Under what conditions does the equation $x^2 + bx + c = 0$ have:

        i two real solutions   **ii** one real solution   **iii** no real solutions?

HISTORICAL NOTE — BABYLONIAN ALGEBRA

The mathematics used by the **Babylonians** was recorded on clay tablets in cuneiform. One such tablet which has been preserved is called *Plimpton 322*, written around 1600 BC.

The Ancient Babylonians were able to solve difficult equations using the rules we use today, such as transposing terms, multiplying both sides by like quantities to remove fractions, and factorisation.

They could, for example, add $4xy$ to $(x-y)^2$ to obtain $(x+y)^2$.

Plimpton 322

This was all achieved without the use of letters for unknown quantities. Instead, they often used words for the unknown.

Consider the following example from about 4000 years ago:

Problem: *"I have subtracted the side of my square from the area and the result is 870. What is the side of the square?"*

Solution: Take half of 1, which is $\frac{1}{2}$, and multiply $\frac{1}{2}$ by $\frac{1}{2}$ which is $\frac{1}{4}$.

Add this to 870 to get $870\frac{1}{4}$. This is the square of $29\frac{1}{2}$.

Now add $\frac{1}{2}$ to $29\frac{1}{2}$ and the result is 30, the side of the square.

Using our modern symbols, the equation is $x^2 - x = 870$, and one of the solutions is $x = \sqrt{(\frac{1}{2})^2 + 870} + \frac{1}{2} = 30$.

D   THE QUADRATIC FORMULA

Many quadratic equations cannot be solved easily by factorisation, and completing the square is rather tedious. Consequently, the **quadratic formula** has been developed.

If $ax^2 + bx + c = 0$ where $a \neq 0$, then $x = \dfrac{-b \pm \sqrt{b^2 - 4ac}}{2a}$.

Proof: If $ax^2 + bx + c = 0$

then $x^2 + \dfrac{b}{a}x + \dfrac{c}{a} = 0$ {dividing each term by a, as $a \neq 0$}

$\therefore\ x^2 + \dfrac{b}{a}x = -\dfrac{c}{a}$

$\therefore\ x^2 + \dfrac{b}{a}x + \left(\dfrac{b}{2a}\right)^2 = -\dfrac{c}{a} + \left(\dfrac{b}{2a}\right)^2$ {completing the square on the LHS}

$\therefore\ \left(x + \dfrac{b}{2a}\right)^2 = -\dfrac{c}{a}\left(\dfrac{4a}{4a}\right) + \dfrac{b^2}{4a^2}$

$\therefore\ \left(x + \dfrac{b}{2a}\right)^2 = \dfrac{b^2 - 4ac}{4a^2}$

$\therefore\ x + \dfrac{b}{2a} = \pm\sqrt{\dfrac{b^2 - 4ac}{4a^2}}$

$\therefore\ x = -\dfrac{b}{2a} \pm \dfrac{\sqrt{b^2 - 4ac}}{2a}$

$\therefore\ x = \dfrac{-b \pm \sqrt{b^2 - 4ac}}{2a}$

The quantity $b^2 - 4ac$ under the square root sign is called the **discriminant**.

The symbol **delta** Δ is used to represent the discriminant, so $\Delta = b^2 - 4ac$.

The quadratic formula becomes $x = \dfrac{-b \pm \sqrt{\Delta}}{2a}$ where Δ replaces $b^2 - 4ac$.

Δ must be $\geqslant 0$ for a quadratic equation to have real solutions.

If $\Delta > 0$, the quadratic equation has two distinct real solutions.

If $\Delta = 0$, the quadratic equation has one real solution, which is $x = -\dfrac{b}{2a}$.

Example 12   ◀)) Self Tutor

Solve for x:

a $x^2 - 2x - 2 = 0$ **b** $2x^2 + 3x - 4 = 0$

a $x^2 - 2x - 2 = 0$ has
$a = 1,\ b = -2,\ c = -2$

$\therefore\ x = \dfrac{-(-2) \pm \sqrt{(-2)^2 - 4(1)(-2)}}{2(1)}$

$\therefore\ x = \dfrac{2 \pm \sqrt{4 + 8}}{2}$

$\therefore\ x = \dfrac{2 \pm \sqrt{12}}{2}$

$\therefore\ x = \dfrac{2 \pm 2\sqrt{3}}{2}$

$\therefore\ x = 1 \pm \sqrt{3}$

b $2x^2 + 3x - 4 = 0$ has
$a = 2,\ b = 3,\ c = -4$

$\therefore\ x = \dfrac{-3 \pm \sqrt{3^2 - 4(2)(-4)}}{2(2)}$

$\therefore\ x = \dfrac{-3 \pm \sqrt{9 + 32}}{4}$

$\therefore\ x = \dfrac{-3 \pm \sqrt{41}}{4}$

EXERCISE 11D

1 Solve the following equations using: **i** factorisation **ii** the quadratic formula.
- **a** $x^2 + 6x + 8 = 0$
- **b** $x^2 - 10x + 25 = 0$
- **c** $3x^2 - 7x - 6 = 0$

2 Use the quadratic formula to solve for x:
- **a** $x^2 + x - 5 = 0$
- **b** $x^2 - 5x + 5 = 0$
- **c** $x^2 - 4x - 1 = 0$
- **d** $3x^2 + 5x - 1 = 0$
- **e** $-2x^2 + x + 7 = 0$
- **f** $5x^2 - 8x + 1 = 0$
- **g** $x^2 + 1 = 3x$
- **h** $2x^2 = 2x + 3$
- **i** $9x^2 = 6x + 1$
- **j** $7x^2 = 5x + 1$
- **k** $3x^2 + 2x = 2$
- **l** $25x^2 + 1 = 20x$

3 Use the quadratic formula to solve for x:
- **a** $(x+2)(x-1) = 5$
- **b** $(x+1)^2 = 3 - x^2$
- **c** $\dfrac{x-1}{x} = \dfrac{x}{3}$
- **d** $x + \dfrac{1}{x+2} = 4$
- **e** $3x - \dfrac{4}{x+1} = 10$
- **f** $\dfrac{x+2}{x-1} = \dfrac{3x}{x+1}$

E PROBLEM SOLVING

When practical problems are converted into algebraic form, a quadratic equation may result. To solve these problems, follow these steps:

> *Step 1:* Carefully **read the question** until you understand the problem. A **sketch** may be useful.
> *Step 2:* Decide on the **unknown** quantity and label it x, say.
> *Step 3:* Use the information given to write an **equation**.
> *Step 4:* **Solve** the equation.
> *Step 5:* **Check** that any solutions satisfy the equation and are reasonable.
> *Step 6:* Write your answer to the question in **sentence form**.

Example 13 ◀) Self Tutor

The sum of a number and its square is 42. Find the number.

Let the number be x. Therefore its square is x^2.

$$x + x^2 = 42$$
$$\therefore x^2 + x - 42 = 0 \quad \{\text{rearranging}\}$$
$$\therefore (x+7)(x-6) = 0 \quad \{\text{factorising}\}$$
$$\therefore x = -7 \text{ or } x = 6$$

So, the number is -7 or 6.

Check: The sum of -7 and its square is $-7 + (-7)^2 = -7 + 49 = 42$ ✓
The sum of 6 and its square is $6 + 6^2 = 6 + 36 = 42$ ✓

EXERCISE 11E

1 The sum of a number and its square is 110. Find the number.

2 When 24 is subtracted from the square of a number, the result is five times the original number. Find the number.

3 The sum of two numbers is 6, and the sum of their squares is 28. Find these numbers exactly.

4 Two numbers differ by 7, and the sum of their squares is 29. Find the numbers.

Example 14   Self Tutor

A rectangle has length 5 cm greater than its width, and its area is 84 cm². Find the dimensions of the rectangle.

Let the width of the rectangle be x cm.

∴ the length of the rectangle is $(x+5)$ cm.

Now area $= 84$ cm²
∴ $x(x+5) = 84$
∴ $x^2 + 5x = 84$
∴ $x^2 + 5x - 84 = 0$
∴ $(x+12)(x-7) = 0$
∴ $x = -12$ or 7

But $x > 0$ as lengths must be positive, so $x = 7$.

∴ the rectangle is 7 cm by 12 cm.

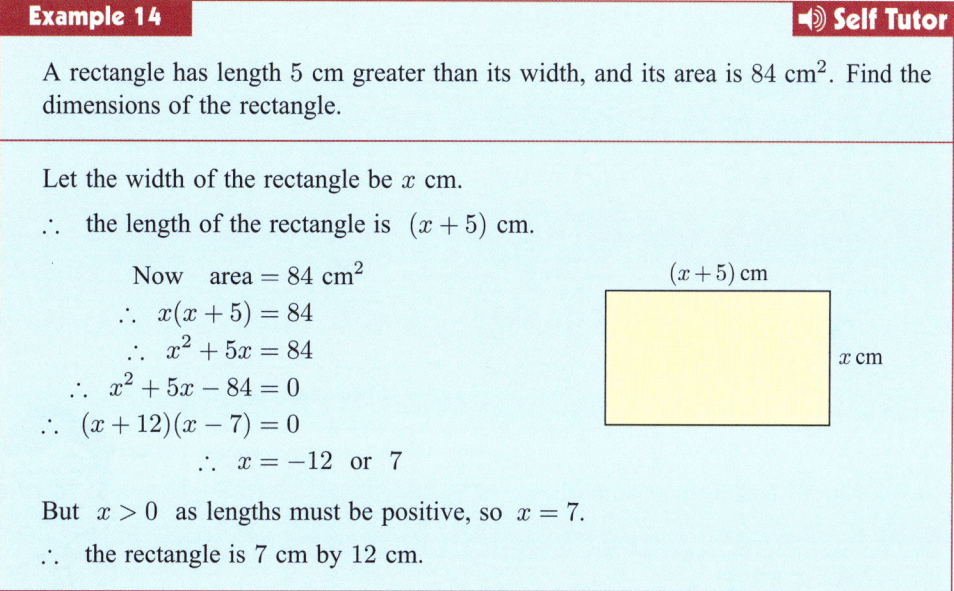

5 A rectangle has length 4 cm greater than its width. Find its width given that its area is 96 cm².

6 The base of a triangle is 4 m longer than its altitude. The area of the triangle is 70 m². Find the triangle's altitude.

7 A rectangular enclosure is made from 60 m of fencing. The area enclosed is 216 m². Find the dimensions of the enclosure.

8 A rectangular garden bed was built against an existing brick wall. 24 m of edging was used to enclose 60 m². Find the dimensions of the garden bed to the nearest centimetre.

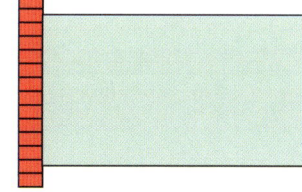

9 A right angled triangle has sides 3 cm and 8 cm respectively less than its hypotenuse. Find the length of the hypotenuse to the nearest millimetre.

10 ABCD is a rectangle in which AB = 21 cm.
The square AXYD is removed and the remaining rectangle has area 80 cm².
Find the length of [BC].

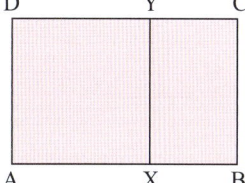

Example 15

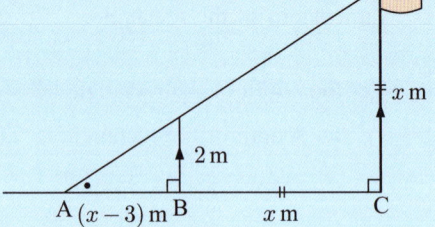

Given that [AB] is 3 m shorter than [BC], find the height of the flagpole.

Let the height of the flagpole be x m.

∴ BC = x m and AB = $(x-3)$ m

The triangles are equiangular, so they are similar.

∴ $\dfrac{x}{2} = \dfrac{(x-3)+x}{x-3}$

∴ $x(x-3) = 2(2x-3)$

∴ $x^2 - 3x = 4x - 6$

∴ $x^2 - 7x + 6 = 0$

∴ $(x-1)(x-6) = 0$

∴ $x = 1$ or 6

But $x - 3 > 0$ as lengths must be positive

∴ $x = 6$

So, the flagpole is 6 m high.

If two angles of two triangles are equal, then the third angles must also be equal.

11 Find x in:

a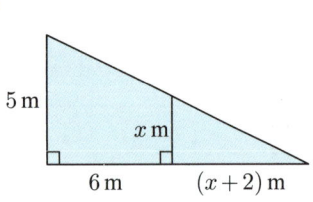

b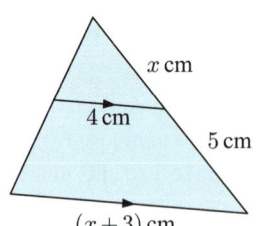

c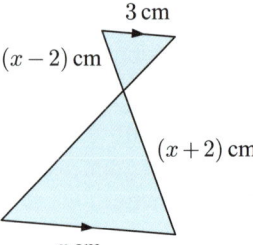

d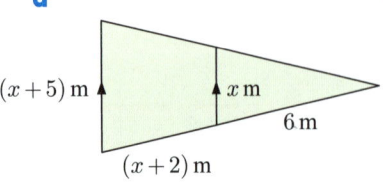

e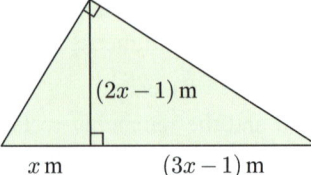

f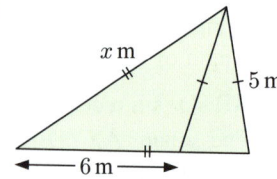

12 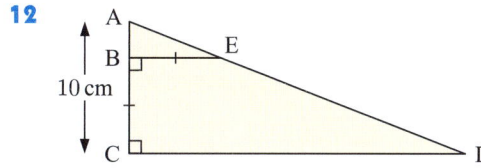 In the figure alongside, [BC] is the same length as [BE], and [CD] is 3 cm more than twice the length of [BE].
Find the length of [BE].

13 A, B, C, and D are posts on the banks of a 20 m wide canal. A and B are 2 m apart, and OA = CD.
Find the exact distance between C and D.

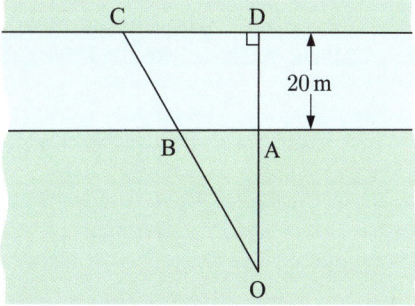

14 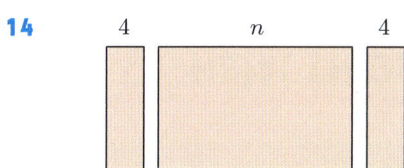 A theatre contains a central block of seats with n seats per row. Blocks on either side contain 4 seats per row. The number of rows is 5 less than the total number of seats per row. In total there are 126 seats in the theatre. Find the value of n.

15 The numerator of a fraction is 3 less than the denominator. If the numerator is increased by 6 and the denominator is increased by 5, the fraction is doubled in value. Find the original fraction.

16 At a fruit market, John bought some oranges for a total of $20. When Jenny visited a different stall, she bought 10 more oranges than John for the same total amount. Given that the difference in price per orange was 10 cents, how many oranges did John purchase?

17 The sum of a number and its reciprocal is $2\frac{1}{12}$. Find the number.

18 Two numbers have a sum of 4, and the sum of their reciprocals is 8. Find the numbers.

19 A sheet of cardboard is 15 cm long and 10 cm wide. It is to be made into an open box with base area 66 cm², by cutting out equal squares from the four corners and then bending the edges upwards.
Find the size of the squares to be cut out.

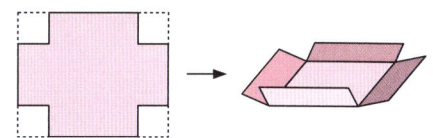

20 Answer the **Opening Problem** on page 224.

21 A circular magnet has an inner radius of x cm, an outer radius 2 cm larger, and its depth is the same as the inner radius. The total volume of the magnet is 120π cm³. Find x.

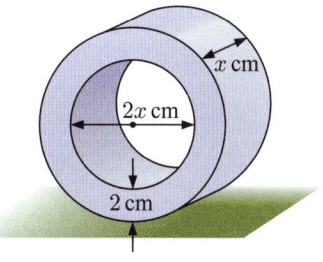

22 A rectangular swimming pool is 12 m long by 6 m wide. It is surrounded by a pavement of uniform width. The area of the pavement is $\frac{7}{8}$ of the area of the pool.

  a If the pavement is x m wide, show that the area of the pavement is $(4x^2 + 36x)$ m^2.
  b Hence, show that $4x^2 + 36x - 63 = 0$.
  c How wide is the pavement?

23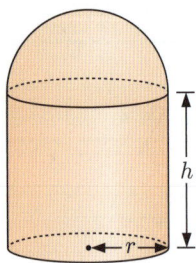

A takeaway milkshake container is cylindrical, with a hemispherical lid on top.
The height h of the container is 7 cm greater than its base radius r.
The surface area of the container and lid is 96π cm^2.
Find the base radius of the container.

F QUADRATIC EQUATIONS WITH $\Delta < 0$

Previously in this chapter, we determined that:

If $ax^2 + bx + c = 0$, $a \neq 0$ and $a, b, c \in \mathbb{R}$, then the **solutions** are $x = \dfrac{-b \pm \sqrt{\Delta}}{2a}$ where $\Delta = b^2 - 4ac$ is known as the **discriminant**.

We also observed that if $\Delta \geqslant 0$, the quadratic equation has real solutions.

It is in fact possible to find solutions for the case where $\Delta < 0$, but the solutions are not real numbers!

In 1572, Rafael Bombelli defined the **imaginary number** $i = \sqrt{-1}$. It is called 'imaginary' because we cannot place it on a number line. With i defined, we can write down solutions for quadratic equations with $\Delta < 0$. They are called *complex* solutions because they include a real and an imaginary part.

Any number of the form $a + bi$ where a and b are real and $i = \sqrt{-1}$, is called a **complex number**.

Example 16 ◀)) Self Tutor

Write in terms of i:
  a $\sqrt{-5}$
  b $\sqrt{-16}$

  a $\sqrt{-5} = \sqrt{5 \times -1}$
    $= \sqrt{5} \times \sqrt{-1}$
    $= i\sqrt{5}$

  b $\sqrt{-16} = \sqrt{16 \times -1}$
    $= \sqrt{16} \times \sqrt{-1}$
    $= 4i$

If the coefficient of i is a square root, we write the i first.

QUADRATIC EQUATIONS (Chapter 11) 239

Example 17 *Self Tutor*

Solve for x:
a $x^2 = -9$
b $x^2 = -13$

a $x^2 = -9$
$\therefore x = \pm\sqrt{-9}$
$\therefore x = \pm\sqrt{9}\sqrt{-1}$
$\therefore x = \pm 3i$

b $x^2 = -13$
$\therefore x = \pm\sqrt{-13}$
$\therefore x = \pm\sqrt{13}\sqrt{-1}$
$\therefore x = \pm i\sqrt{13}$

EXERCISE 11F

1 Write in terms of i:
  a $\sqrt{-2}$
  b $\sqrt{-25}$
  c $\sqrt{-11}$
  d $\sqrt{-81}$

2 Solve for x:
  a $x^2 = -3$
  b $x^2 = -4$
  c $x^2 = -14$
  d $x^2 + 7 = 0$
  e $3x^2 = -48$
  f $2x^2 + 15 = 3$

Example 18 *Self Tutor*

Solve for x:
a $x^2 + 2x + 2 = 0$
b $2x^2 - x + 3 = 0$

a $x^2 + 2x + 2 = 0$ has $a = 1,\ b = 2,\ c = 2$
$\therefore x = \dfrac{-2 \pm \sqrt{2^2 - 4(1)(2)}}{2(1)}$
$\therefore x = \dfrac{-2 \pm \sqrt{4 - 8}}{2}$
$\therefore x = \dfrac{-2 \pm \sqrt{-4}}{2}$
$\therefore x = \dfrac{-2 \pm \sqrt{-1}\sqrt{4}}{2}$
$\therefore x = \dfrac{-2 \pm 2i}{2}$
$\therefore x = -1 \pm i$

b $2x^2 - x + 3 = 0$ has $a = 2,\ b = -1,\ c = 3$
$\therefore x = \dfrac{-(-1) \pm \sqrt{(-1)^2 - 4(2)(3)}}{2(2)}$
$\therefore x = \dfrac{1 \pm \sqrt{1 - 24}}{4}$
$\therefore x = \dfrac{1 \pm \sqrt{-23}}{4}$
$\therefore x = \dfrac{1 \pm \sqrt{-1}\sqrt{23}}{4}$
$\therefore x = \dfrac{1 \pm i\sqrt{23}}{4}$

$\Delta < 0$, so the solutions are imaginary.

3 Without solving them, decide whether these equations have two real solutions, one real solution, or imaginary solutions.
  a $3x^2 + 5x - 1$
  b $x^2 - 4x + 4 = 0$
  c $2x^2 - 3x + 5 = 0$

4 Solve for x:
  a $x^2 + x + 2 = 0$
  b $x^2 - 3x + 6 = 0$
  c $x^2 + 4x + 13 = 0$
  d $2x^2 - x + 5 = 0$
  e $-x^2 + 2x - 17 = 0$
  f $3x^2 + 5 = 3x$

G THE SUM AND PRODUCT OF THE ROOTS

We have now seen that any real quadratic equation has 2 (not necessarily distinct) solutions, and that these solutions may be real or imaginary.

> A real quadratic equation takes the form
> $ax^2 + bx + c = 0$
> where $a \neq 0$, $a, b, c \in \mathbb{R}$

The solutions of an equation are also called its **roots**.

We can easily find the sum and product of the roots of a quadratic equation without finding the roots themselves.

> If the quadratic equation $ax^2 + bx + c = 0$ has roots p and q, then:
> - the **sum** of the roots $p + q = -\dfrac{b}{a}$
> - the **product** of the roots $pq = \dfrac{c}{a}$.

Proof:

If p and q are the roots of $ax^2 + bx + c = 0$,

then $ax^2 + bx + c = a(x - p)(x - q)$
$= a(x^2 - [p + q]x + pq)$

$\therefore x^2 + \dfrac{b}{a}x + \dfrac{c}{a} = x^2 - [p + q]x + pq$

Equating coefficients,

$p + q = -\dfrac{b}{a}$ and $pq = \dfrac{c}{a}$.

Example 19   ◀)) Self Tutor

Find the sum and product of the roots of $2x^2 + 5x - 3 = 0$.

$2x^2 + 5x - 3 = 0$ has $a = 2$, $b = 5$, $c = -3$.

$\therefore$ the sum of the roots is $-\dfrac{b}{a} = -\dfrac{5}{2}$, and the product of the roots is $\dfrac{c}{a} = -\dfrac{3}{2}$.

EXERCISE 11G

1. **a** Find the sum and product of the roots of $3x^2 - 7x + 2 = 0$.
   b Check your answer by solving the quadratic equation.

2. **a** Find the sum and product of the roots of $x^2 + 2x - 4 = 0$.
   b Check your answer by solving the quadratic equation.

3. Find the sum and product of the roots of:
   a $2x^2 - 6x + 1 = 0$ **b** $5x^2 + 4x - 10 = 0$ **c** $-4x^2 + x - 6 = 0$

4 $\frac{1}{2}$ is one of the roots of $6x^2 + x - 2 = 0$. Find the other root without solving the equation directly.

5 **a** Find the sum and product of the roots of $x^2 + 4x + 5 = 0$.
   b Check your answer by solving the quadratic equation.
      Hint: $i = \sqrt{-1}$ and so $i^2 = -1$.

REVIEW SET 11A

1 Solve for x: **a** $-x^2 + 11 = 0$ **b** $7 - 2x^2 = -25$

2 Solve for x: **a** $(x-4)^2 = 25$ **b** $(x+1)^2 - 1 = 0$

3 Solve for x:
   a $x^2 - 4x - 21 = 0$ **b** $4x^2 - 25 = 0$ **c** $6x^2 - x - 2 = 0$

4 Solve for x:
   a $3x^2 - 6x - 72 = 0$ **b** $5x^2 + 30x + 45 = 0$ **c** $4x^2 - 18x + 8 = 0$

5 Solve by completing the square: $x^2 + 6x + 4 = 0$

6 Solve for x:
   a $x^2 + 24x = 11$ **b** $(x+6)(x-3) = 10x$ **c** $10x^2 - 6 = 11x$

7 The sum of a number and its reciprocal is $2\frac{1}{6}$. Find the number.

8 Use the quadratic formula to solve for x:
   a $2x^2 - 3x - 2 = 0$ **b** $3x^2 + 4x - 5 = 0$ **c** $\dfrac{x+4}{x-2} = \dfrac{5x}{x-1}$

9 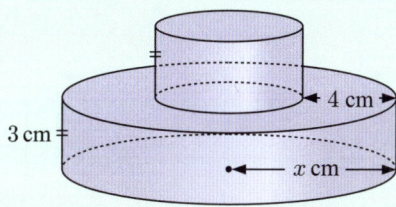 The volume of the solid alongside is 174π cm^3. Find x.

10 A straight length of wire is 20 cm long. It is bent at right angles to form the two shorter sides of a right angled triangle.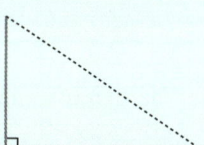
   a If the triangle's area is 30 cm^2, find:
      i the length of each side
      ii the triangle's perimeter.
   b Is it possible for a right angled triangle with shorter sides made from a 20 cm length of wire to have an area of 51 cm^2? Explain your answer.

11 Solve for x: $\dfrac{1}{x-3} + \dfrac{3}{x+1} = 1$

12 Solve for x: **a** $x^2 + 6 = 5$ **b** $x^2 + 5x + 9 = 0$

13 Find the sum and product of the roots of $3x^2 - 12x + 1 = 0$.

REVIEW SET 11B

1. Solve for x: **a** $8 - 3x^2 = -10$ **b** $2x^2 - 5 = -3$

2. Solve for x: **a** $(x+3)^2 - 19 = 0$ **b** $(3x-1)^2 = 17$

3. Solve for x: **a** $x^2 - 8x - 33 = 0$ **b** $8x^2 + 2x - 3 = 0$

4. Solve by completing the square: $x^2 - 2x = 100$

5. Solve for x: **a** $x^2 - 45 = 4x$ **b** $6x^2 + 26x = 20$

6. Solve for x: **a** $\dfrac{x}{5} = \dfrac{7}{x}$ **b** $\dfrac{x}{3-2x} = \dfrac{x+1}{3-x}$

7. The hypotenuse of a right angled triangle is one centimetre more than twice the length of the shortest side. The other side is 7 cm longer than the shortest side. Find the length of each side of the triangle.

8. Use the quadratic formula to solve:

    a $2x^2 + 2x - 1 = 0$ **b** $\dfrac{1}{x} - \dfrac{1}{1-x} = 2$

9. A group of friends hires a bus for a day for $480, agreeing to share the cost equally. At the last minute, two more people decide to go on the trip, and as a result each person pays $8 less.
   How many people go on the trip and how much does each person pay?

10. In the flag alongside, the area of the red stripes is 700 cm². Find the width of the red stripes.

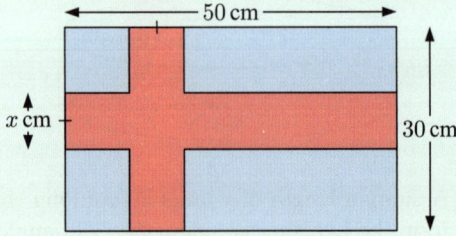

11. The sum of a number and its reciprocal is 5.

    a Show that $\dfrac{5 + \sqrt{21}}{2}$ is a possible value for the number.

    b Check your answer by simplifying $\dfrac{5 + \sqrt{21}}{2} + \dfrac{2}{5 + \sqrt{21}}$.

12. Solve for x: **a** $4x^2 + 20 = 0$ **b** $x^2 + 6x + 18 = 0$

13. $\tfrac{3}{4}$ is one of the roots of $8x^2 + 6x - 9 = 0$. Find the other root without solving the quadratic equation directly.

Chapter 12

Trigonometry

Contents:
- **A** Trigonometric ratios
- **B** Problem solving using trigonometry
- **C** True bearings
- **D** 3-dimensional problem solving
- **E** Supplementary angles
- **F** The area of a triangle
- **G** The sine rule
- **H** The cosine rule
- **I** Problem solving using the sine and cosine rules

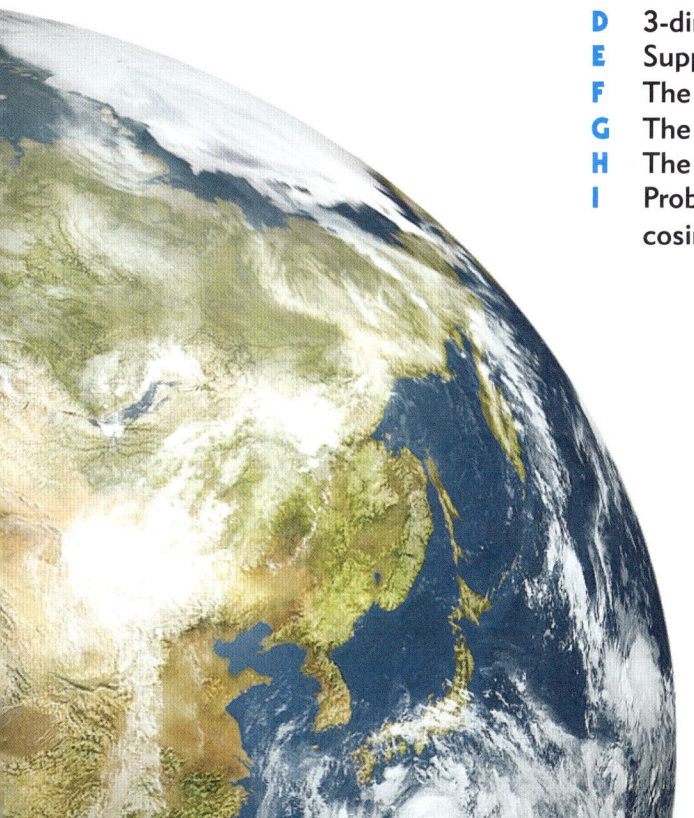

OPENING PROBLEM

A surveyor is standing on horizontal ground, and wishes to find the height of a mountain on the other side of a lake. He uses a theodolite to accurately measure:

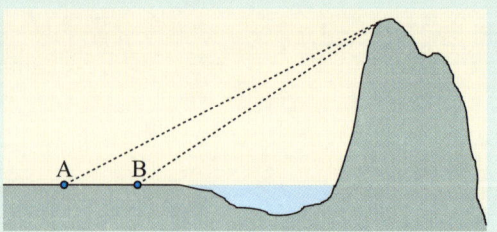

- the angle of elevation from the horizontal ground at A up to the top of the mountain, to be 33.7°
- the angle of elevation from the horizontal ground at B up to the top of the mountain, to be 41.6°
- the distance from A to B to be 400 m.

Things to think about:

a Can you draw a labelled diagram of the situation showing all information given?
b Can you solve this problem using right angled triangle trigonometry?
c Can you solve this problem faster using the sine or cosine rules?

Trigonometry is a branch of mathematics that deals with the relationship between the side lengths and angles of triangles.

We can apply trigonometry in engineering, astronomy, architecture, navigation, surveying, the building industry, and in many other branches of applied science.

HISTORICAL NOTE — ASTRONOMY AND TRIGONOMETRY

The Greek astronomer **Hipparchus** (140 BC) is credited with being the founder of trigonometry. To aid his astronomical calculations, he produced a table of numbers in which the lengths of chords of a circle were related to the length of the radius.

Ptolemy, another great Greek astronomer of the time, extended this table in his major published work *Almagest*, which was used by astronomers for the next 1000 years. In fact, much of Hipparchus' work is known through the writings of Ptolemy. These writings found their way to Hindu and Arab scholars.

Aryabhata, a Hindu mathematician in the 5th and 6th Century AD, constructed a table of the lengths of half-chords of a circle with radius one unit. This was the first table of **sine** values.

In the late 16th century, **Georg Joachim de Porris**, also known as **Rheticus**, produced comprehensive and remarkably accurate tables of all six trigonometric ratios, three of which you will learn about in this chapter. These involved a tremendous number of tedious calculations, all without the aid of calculators or computers.

Rheticus was the only student of **Nicolaus Copernicus**, and helped his tutor publish his work *De revolutionibus orbium coelestium* (On the Revolutions of the Heavenly Spheres).

Nicolaus Copernicus

A TRIGONOMETRIC RATIOS

In previous years we have defined the following basic trigonometric ratios for right-angled triangles:

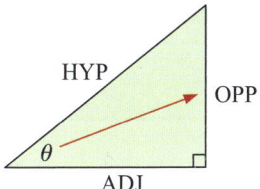

$$\sin\theta = \frac{\text{OPP}}{\text{HYP}}, \quad \cos\theta = \frac{\text{ADJ}}{\text{HYP}}, \quad \tan\theta = \frac{\text{OPP}}{\text{ADJ}}$$

We can use these ratios to find unknown side lengths and angles in right angled triangles.

INVESTIGATION 1 — COMPLEMENTARY ANGLES

Two angles are **complementary** if their sum is 90°. We say that θ and $(90° - \theta)$ are **complements** of each other.

PRINTABLE WORKSHEET

Your task is to determine whether a relationship exists between the sines and cosines of an angle and its complement.

What to do:

1 Use your calculator to complete a table like the one shown. Include some angles of your choice.

θ	$\sin\theta$	$\cos\theta$	$90° - \theta$	$\sin(90° - \theta)$	$\cos(90° - \theta)$
17°			73°		
38°					
59°					

2 Write down your observations from the tabled values.

3 Use the figure alongside to prove that your observations are true for all angles θ where $0° < \theta < 90°$.

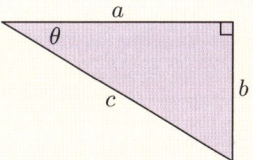

4 Find a relationship between $\tan\theta$ and $\tan(90° - \theta)$.

FINDING SIDE LENGTHS

Suppose we are given the angles of a right angled triangle, and the length of a side. We can use the trigonometric ratios to find the other side lengths.

> *Step 1*: Redraw the figure and mark on it HYP, OPP, and ADJ relative to a given angle.
> *Step 2*: Choose an appropriate trigonometric ratio, and construct an equation.
> *Step 3*: Solve the equation to find the unknown side length.

Example 1 ◀) Self Tutor

Find x, rounded to 3 significant figures:

a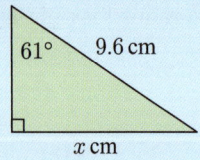

b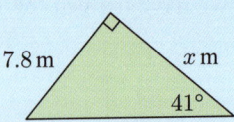

a The relevant sides are OPP and HYP, so we use the *sine* ratio.

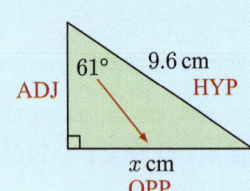

$$\sin 61° = \frac{x}{9.6} \quad \{\sin \theta = \frac{\text{OPP}}{\text{HYP}}\}$$
$$\therefore \sin 61° \times 9.6 = x \quad \{\text{multiplying both sides by } 9.6\}$$
$$\therefore x \approx 8.40 \quad \{\text{calculator}\}$$

b The relevant sides are OPP and ADJ, so we use the *tangent* ratio.

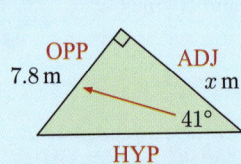

$$\tan 41° = \frac{7.8}{x} \quad \{\tan \theta = \frac{\text{OPP}}{\text{ADJ}}\}$$
$$\therefore x \times \tan 41° = 7.8 \quad \{\text{multiplying both sides by } x\}$$
$$\therefore x = \frac{7.8}{\tan 41°} \quad \{\text{dividing both sides by } \tan 41°\}$$
$$\therefore x \approx 8.97 \quad \{\text{calculator}\}$$

EXERCISE 12A.1

1 Construct a trigonometric equation connecting the angle with the sides given:

a 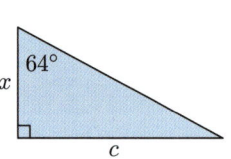   b 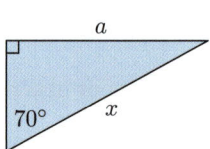   c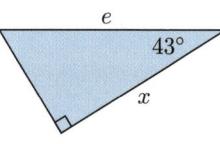

d 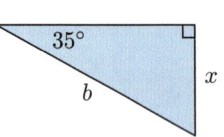   e 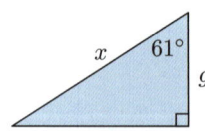   f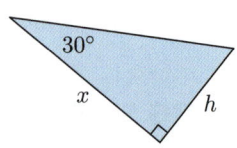

2 Find x, rounded to 2 decimal places:

a 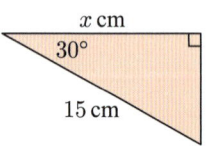   b 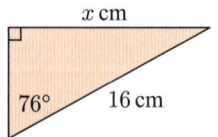   c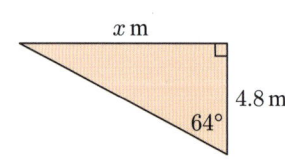

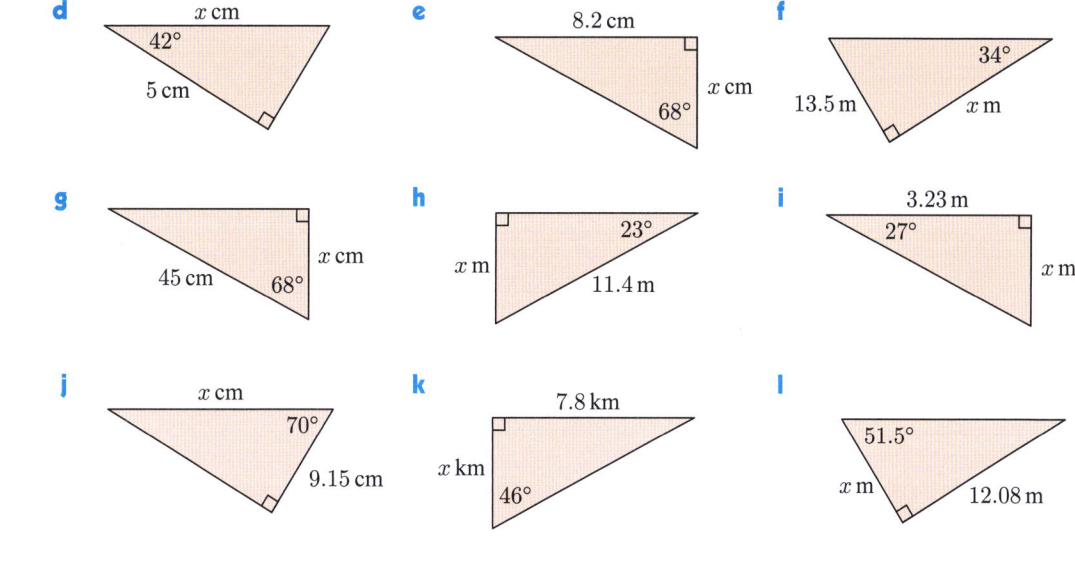

3 Find *all* the unknown angles and sides of:

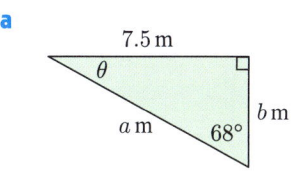 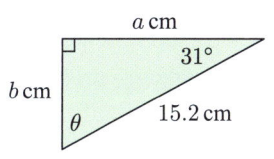 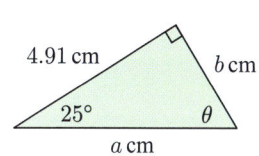

4 Find the perimeter of triangle ABC.

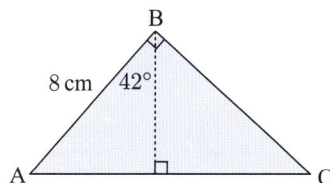

FINDING ANGLES

If we know two side lengths of a right angled triangle, we can use trigonometry to find the angles.

In the right angled triangle shown, $\sin \theta = \frac{3}{5}$.

We say that θ is the **inverse sine** of $\frac{3}{5}$, and write $\theta = \sin^{-1}(\frac{3}{5})$.

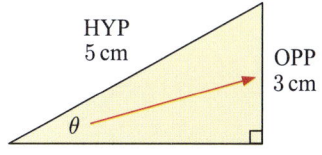

We can use a calculator to evaluate inverse sines. Click on the icon for instructions.

For the right angled triangle above, we find $\theta \approx 36.9°$.

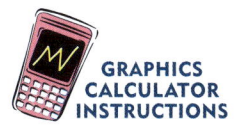
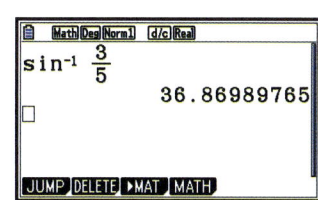

We define **inverse cosine** and **inverse tangent** in a similar way.

Example 2

Find the measure of the angle marked θ:

a (triangle with 7 m adjacent, 4 m opposite, angle θ)

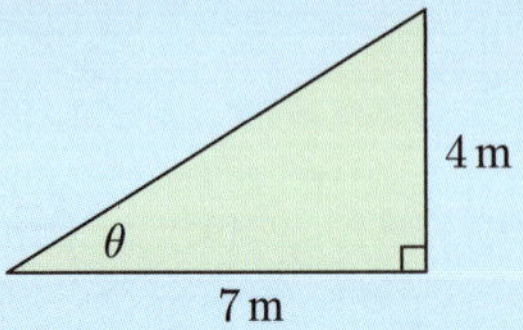

b (triangle with 5.92 km hypotenuse, 2.67 km adjacent, angle θ)

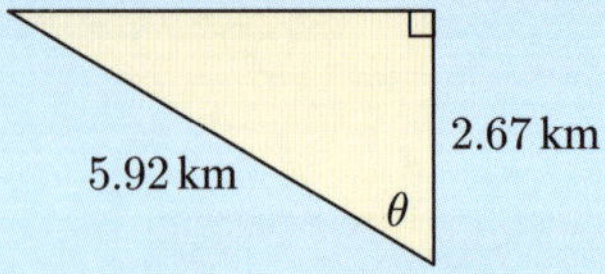

a

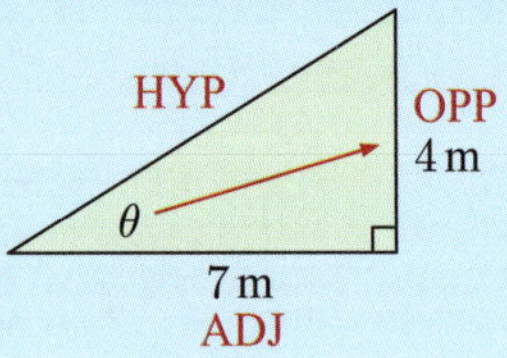

$\tan \theta = \frac{4}{7}$ $\{\tan \theta = \frac{\text{OPP}}{\text{ADJ}}\}$

$\therefore \theta = \tan^{-1}\left(\frac{4}{7}\right)$

$\therefore \theta \approx 29.7°$ {calculator}

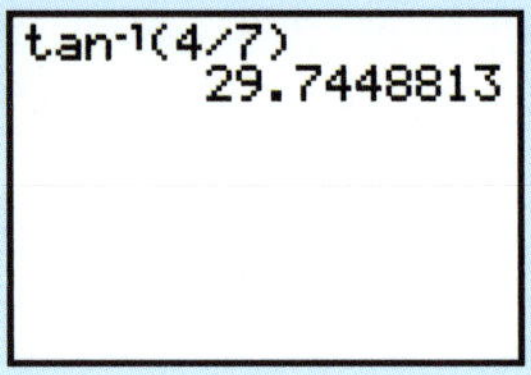

b

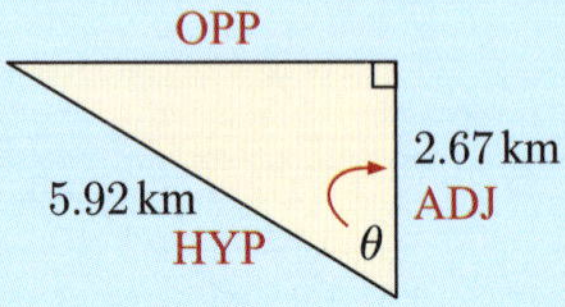

$\cos \theta = \frac{2.67}{5.92}$ $\{\cos \theta = \frac{\text{ADJ}}{\text{HYP}}\}$

$\therefore \theta = \cos^{-1}\left(\frac{2.67}{5.92}\right)$

$\therefore \theta \approx 63.2°$ {calculator}

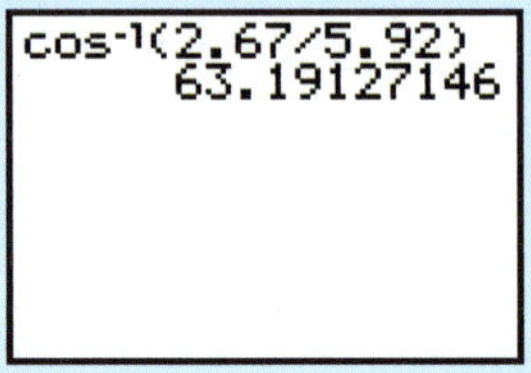

EXERCISE 12A.2

1 Find the measure of the angle marked θ:

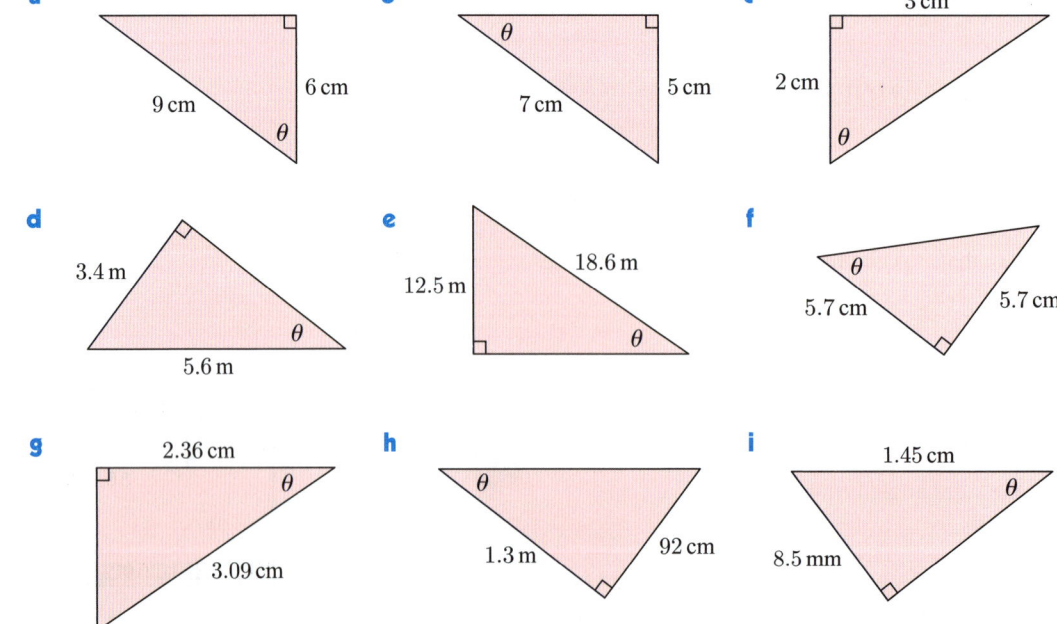

2 Find, using trigonometry, all the unknown sides and angles in the following triangles. Check your answers for x using Pythagoras' theorem.

a 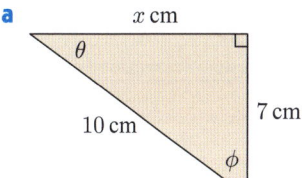 **b** 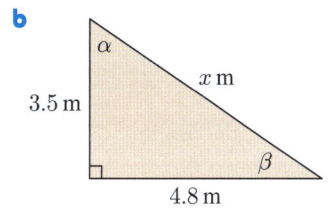 **c**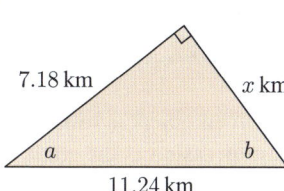

3 Consider the triangle alongside.

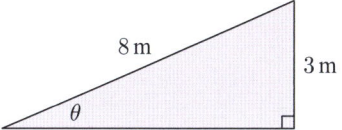

   a Copy and complete, stating exact values:
      i $\sin\theta = \ldots\ldots$ **ii** $\cos\theta = \ldots\ldots$
      iii $\tan\theta = \ldots\ldots$

   b Use each of these equations to find θ. Check that you get the same answer each time.

B   PROBLEM SOLVING USING TRIGONOMETRY

The trigonometric ratios can be used to solve a wide variety of problems involving right angled triangles. When solving these problems it is important to follow the steps below:

- Draw a **diagram** to illustrate the situation.
- Mark on the diagram the **unknown** angle or side that needs to be calculated. We often use x for a length and θ for an angle.
- Locate a **right angled triangle** in your diagram.
- Write an **equation** connecting an angle and two sides of the triangle using an appropriate trigonometric ratio.
- **Solve** the equation to find the unknown.
- **Write** your answer in sentence form.

When solving problems using trigonometry, we often use:

- the properties of isosceles triangles

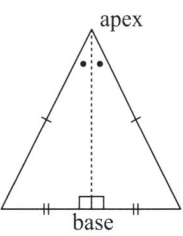

- the properties of circles and tangents

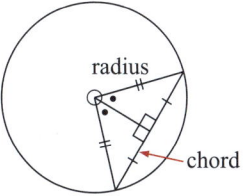 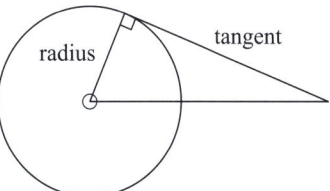

- angles of elevation and depression.

ANGLES OF ELEVATION AND DEPRESSION

When an object is **higher** than an observer, the **angle of elevation** is the angle from the horizontal **up** to the object.

When an object is **lower** than an observer, the **angle of depression** is the angle from the horizontal **down** to the object.

If the angle of elevation from A to B is θ, then the angle of depression from B to A is also θ.

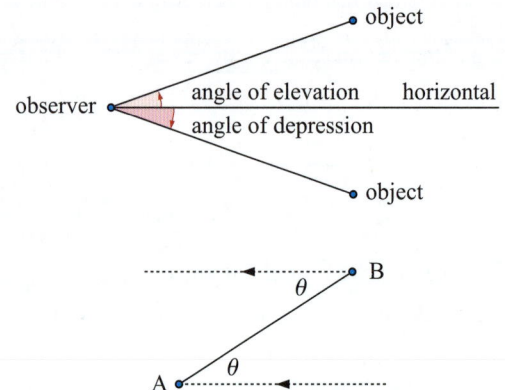

Example 3

The roof alongside has a pitch of 16°. Find the length of the horizontal beam.

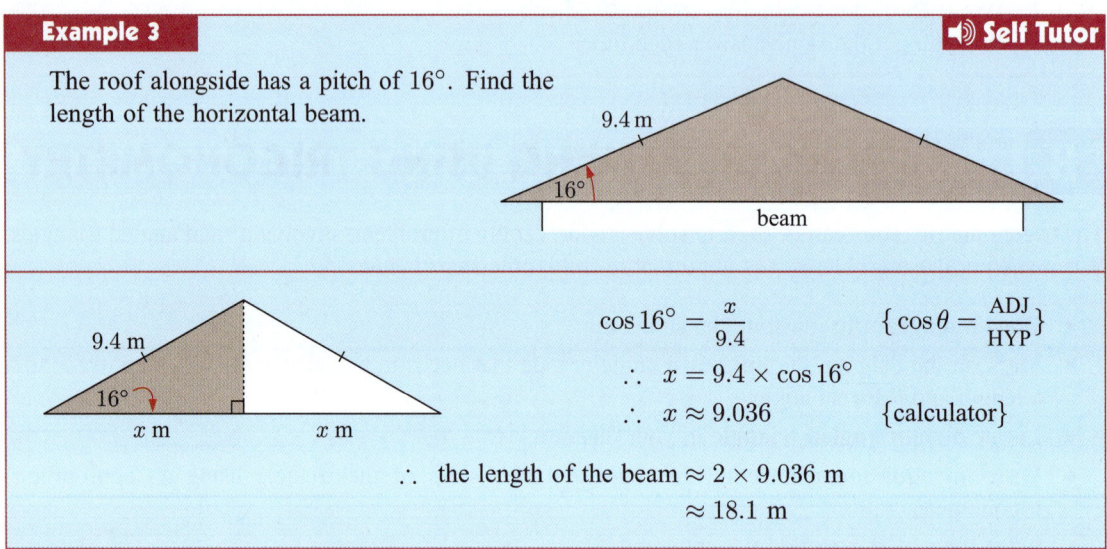

$$\cos 16° = \frac{x}{9.4}$$

$\therefore\ x = 9.4 \times \cos 16°$ $\{\cos\theta = \frac{\text{ADJ}}{\text{HYP}}\}$

$\therefore\ x \approx 9.036$ {calculator}

$\therefore\ $ the length of the beam $\approx 2 \times 9.036$ m

≈ 18.1 m

EXERCISE 12B

1 From a point 235 m from the base of a cliff, the angle of elevation to the cliff top is 25°. Find the height of the cliff.

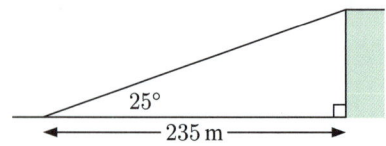

2 A 5 m ladder reaches 4.2 m up a wall. What angle does the ladder make with the wall?

3 The angle of elevation from a row boat to the top of a lighthouse 25 m above sea-level is 6°. Calculate the horizontal distance from the boat to the lighthouse.

4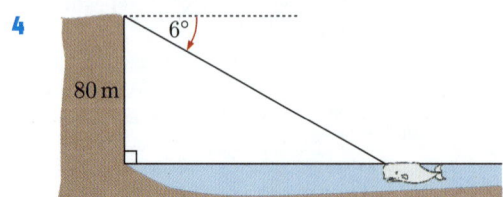

From a vertical cliff 80 m above sea level, a whale is observed at an angle of depression of 6°.

Find the distance between the observer at the top of the cliff, and the whale.

5 A train travelling up an incline of 4° travels a horizontal distance of 4 km. How much altitude has the train gained?

6 At the entrance to a building there is a ramp for wheelchair access. The length of the ramp is 5 metres, and it rises to a height of 0.6 metres. Find the angle θ that the ramp makes with the ground.

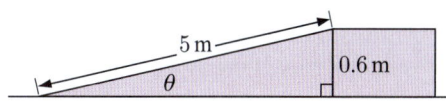

7 A goal post was hit by lightning and snapped in two. The top of the post is now resting 15 m from its base, at an angle of 25°. Find the height of the goal post before it snapped.

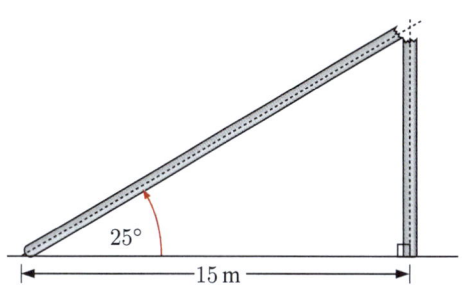

Example 4   ◄)) **Self Tutor**

A point P is 9.5 cm from the centre C of a circle with radius 2 cm.

Find the angle between [PC] and the tangent to the circle from P.

$\sin \theta = \dfrac{2}{9.5}$ $\quad \{\sin \theta = \dfrac{\text{OPP}}{\text{HYP}}\}$

$\therefore \theta = \sin^{-1}\left(\dfrac{2}{9.5}\right)$

$\therefore \theta \approx 12.2°$ {calculator}

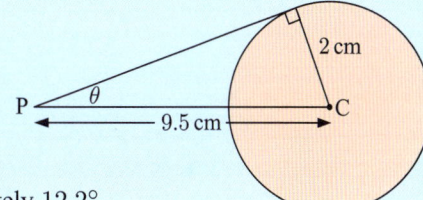

The angle between [PC] and the tangent is approximately 12.2°.

---

8 A tangent from point P to a circle of radius 4 cm is 10 cm long. Find the angle between the tangent and the line joining P to the centre of the circle.

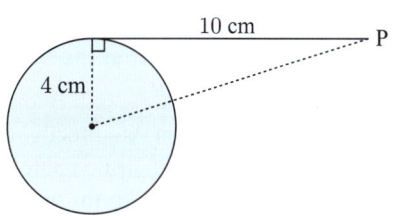

9 A rhombus has sides of length 10 cm, and the angle between two adjacent sides is 76°. Find the length of the longer diagonal of the rhombus.

10 [AB] is a chord of a circle with centre O and radius 5 cm. [AB] has length 8 cm. Find the size of $\widehat{AOB}$.

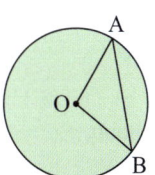

11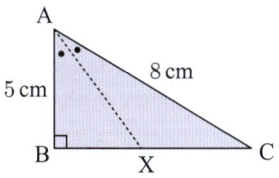

In triangle ABC, the angle bisector at A meets [BC] at X. Is X the midpoint of [BC]? If not, what is the distance between X and the midpoint?

12 In an isosceles triangle, the equal sides are $\frac{2}{3}$ of the length of the base. Determine the measure of the base angles.

13 An isosceles triangle is drawn with base angles 24° and base 28 cm. Find the base angles of the isosceles triangle with the same base length but with treble the area.

14 The angle of elevation from a marker on level ground to the top of a building 100 m high is 22°. Find the distance:

    a from the marker to the base of the building

    b the marker must be moved towards the building so that the angle of elevation becomes 40°.

15 An observer notices an aeroplane flying directly overhead. Two minutes later the aeroplane is at an angle of elevation of 27°. Assuming the aeroplane is travelling with constant speed and altitude, what will be its angle of elevation after another two minutes?

16 A surveyor standing on a horizontal plain can see a volcano in the distance. The angle of elevation to the top of the volcano is 23°. If the surveyor moves 750 m closer, the angle of elevation is now 37°. Determine the height of the volcano above the plain.

17 Find the shortest distance between the two parallel lines using:

    a trigonometry   **b** areas.

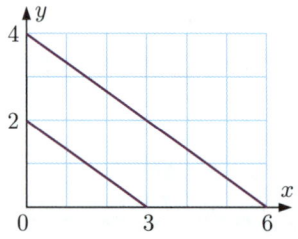

INVESTIGATION 2   HIPPARCHUS AND THE UNIVERSE

Hipparchus was a Greek astronomer and mathematician born in Nicaea in the 2nd century BC. He is considered among the greatest astronomers of all time.

Part 1: How Hipparchus measured the distance to the moon

Consider two points A and B on the Earth's equator. The moon is directly overhead A. From B the moon is just visible, since [MB] is a tangent to the Earth and is therefore perpendicular to [BC]. Angle BCM is the difference in longitude between A and B, which Hipparchus calculated to be approximately 89°.

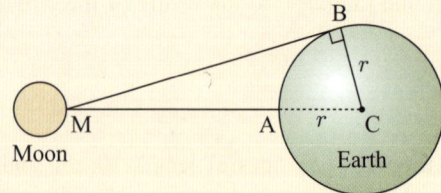

What to do:

1 Given $r = 6378$ km and $\widehat{BCM} = 89°$, estimate the distance from the centre of the Earth C to the moon.

2 Now calculate the distance AM *between* the Earth and the moon.

3 In calculating just one distance between the Earth and the moon, Hipparchus was assuming that the orbit of the moon was circular. In fact it is not. Research the shortest and longest distances to the moon. How were these distances determined? How do they compare with the distance obtained using Hipparchus' method?

Part 2: How Hipparchus measured the radius of the moon

From point A on the Earth's surface, the angle between an imaginary line to the centre of the moon and a tangent to the moon is about $0.25°$.

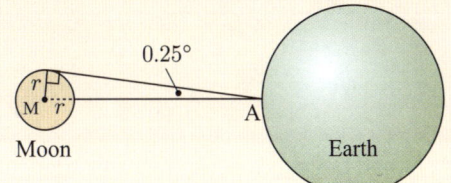

The average distance from the Earth to the moon is about $384\,403$ km.

What to do:

1 Confirm from the diagram that $\sin 0.25° = \dfrac{r}{r + 384\,403}$.

2 Solve this equation to find r, the radius of the moon.

3 Research the actual radius of the moon, and if possible find out how it was calculated. Compare your answer in **2** to the actual radius.

C   TRUE BEARINGS

We can describe a direction by comparing it with the **true north direction**. We call this a **true bearing**.

Imagine you are standing at point A, facing north. You turn **clockwise** through an angle until you face B. The **bearing of B from A** is the angle through which you have turned.

So, the bearing of B from A is the clockwise measure of the angle between the 'north' line through A, and [AB].

In the diagram alongside, the bearing of B from A is $72°$ from true north. We write this as $72°T$ or $072°$.

To find the **bearing of A from B**, we place ourselves at point B, face north, then turn clockwise until we face A. The true bearing of A from B is $252°$.

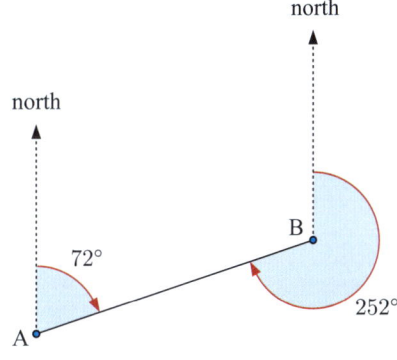

Note:
- A true bearing is always written using three digits. For example, we write $072°$ rather than $72°$.
- The bearing of A from B, and the bearing of B from A, always differ by $180°$. You should be able to explain this using angle pair properties for parallel lines.

EXERCISE 12C

1 Draw diagrams to represent bearings from O of:

   a $136°$ **b** $240°$ **c** $051°$ **d** $327°$

2 Write the bearing of Q from P in each diagram:

   a 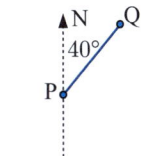   **b** 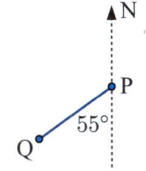   **c**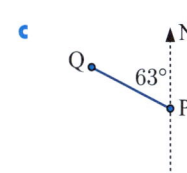

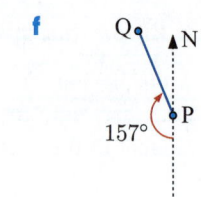

d P, 48°, Q (N at P) **e** P, 45°, Q (N at P) **f** Q, 157°, P (N at P)

3 A, B, and C are the checkpoints of a triangular orienteering course. Find the bearing of:

  a B from A   **b** C from B   **c** B from C
  d C from A   **e** A from B   **f** A from C.

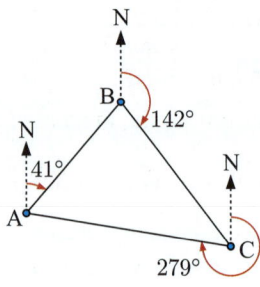

4 Find the bearing of:

  a B from A   **b** A from B
  c C from A   **d** A from C
  e C from B   **f** B from C.

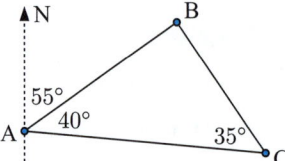

Example 5   ◀)) Self Tutor

Starting from A, a motorbike travels 7 km east to B, then 3 km south to C. Find the bearing of C from A.

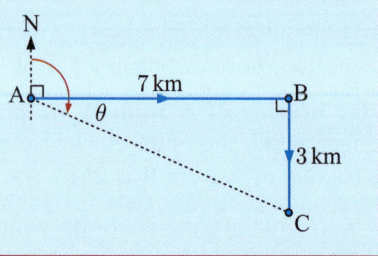

$\tan \theta = \frac{3}{7}$ $\{\tan \theta = \frac{\text{OPP}}{\text{ADJ}}\}$

$\therefore \theta = \tan^{-1}(\frac{3}{7})$

$\therefore \theta \approx 23.2°$

So, the bearing of C from A $\approx 90° + 23.2°$

$\approx 113°$

5 A bush-walker walks 14 km east and then 9 km north. Find the bearing of his finishing point from his starting point.

6 Starting from A, a truck travels 10 km north to B, then 13 km west to C. Find the bearing of C from A.

7 A kayaker paddles due west for 1.5 km. He then turns due south and paddles a further 800 m.

  a Draw a diagram of the situation.
  b How far is the kayaker from his starting point?
  c In what direction must he travel to return to his starting point?

8 Runners A and B leave the same point at the same time. Runner A runs at 10 km h^{-1} due north. Runner B runs at 12 km h^{-1} due east. Find the distance and bearing of runner B from runner A after 30 minutes.

Example 6

A rally driver travels on a bearing of 145° for 28.5 km.
How far east of the starting position is the rally driver?

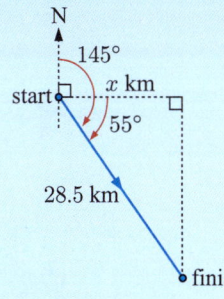

$$\cos 55° = \frac{x}{28.5} \quad \{\cos\theta = \frac{\text{ADJ}}{\text{HYP}}\}$$

$$\therefore \quad x = 28.5 \times \cos 55°$$

$$\therefore \quad x \approx 16.3$$

The driver is about 16.3 km east of his starting position.

9 A ship sails for 60 km on a bearing 040°. How far north of its starting point is the ship?

10 An athlete ran for $2\frac{1}{2}$ hours in the direction 164° at a speed of 14 km h^{-1}.

   a Draw a fully labelled diagram of the situation.
   b Find the distance travelled by the athlete.
   c How far **i** east **ii** south of the starting point is the athlete?

11 A hiker walks in the direction 215° and stops when she is 2 km south of her starting point. How far did she walk?

12 An aeroplane travels on a bearing of 295° until it is 200 km west of its starting point. How far has it travelled on this bearing?

Example 7

An aeroplane departs A and flies on a 143° course for 368 km to B. It then changes direction to a 233° course and flies a further 472 km to C. Find:

   a the distance of C from A   **b** the bearing of C from A.

$\widehat{ABN} = 180° - 143° = 37°$ {cointerior angles}
$\therefore \widehat{ABC} = 360° - 37° - 233°$
$\quad\quad\quad = 90°$ {angles at a point}

a $AC^2 = 368^2 + 472^2$ {Pythagoras}
$\therefore AC = \sqrt{368^2 + 472^2}$ {as $AC > 0$}
$\quad\quad\quad \approx 598.5$

So, C is about 598.5 km from A.

b To find the bearing of C from A, we first need to find θ.

Now $\tan\theta = \frac{472}{368}$ $\{\tan\theta = \frac{\text{OPP}}{\text{ADJ}}\}$

$\therefore \theta = \tan^{-1}(\frac{472}{368})$

$\therefore \theta \approx 52.1°$

The bearing of C from A is $143° + 52.1° \approx 195°$.

In some bearings problems we use the properties of parallel lines to find angles.

13 A cyclist departs point R and rides on a straight road for 2.3 km in the direction 197°. She then changes direction and rides for 1.8 km in the direction 107° to point S.
  a Draw a fully labelled sketch of this situation.
  b Find the distance between R and S.
  c Find the bearing of S from R.

14 An orienteering competitor travels 3 km in the direction 024°, and then 2 km in the direction 114°. Find the distance and bearing of the finishing point from the starting point.

15 A fishing trawler sails from port P in the direction 313° for 10 km, and then in the direction 043° for 32 km. Calculate:
  a the distance and bearing of the trawler from P
  b the direction in which the trawler must sail in order to return to P.

D 3-DIMENSIONAL PROBLEM SOLVING

Right angled triangles occur frequently in 3-dimensional figures. We can use Pythagoras' theorem and trigonometry to find unknown angles and lengths.

Example 8 ◀) Self Tutor

A cube has sides of length 10 cm. Find the angle between the diagonal [AB] and the edge [BC].

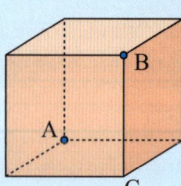

Let AC = x cm.

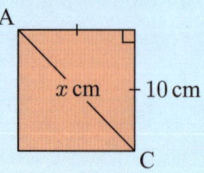

Using Pythagoras, $x^2 = 10^2 + 10^2$
$\therefore x^2 = 200$
$\therefore x = \sqrt{200}$

The required angle is $A\hat{B}C$. We let this angle be θ.

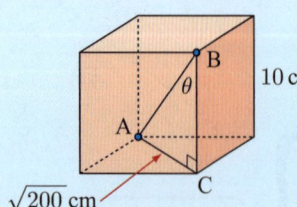

$\tan \theta = \frac{\sqrt{200}}{10}$ $\{\tan \theta = \frac{\text{OPP}}{\text{ADJ}}\}$

$\therefore \theta = \tan^{-1}\left(\frac{\sqrt{200}}{10}\right)$

$\therefore \theta \approx 54.7°$

The angle between the diagonal [AB] and the edge [BC] is about 54.7°.

EXERCISE 12D.1

1 The figure alongside is a cube with sides of length 15 cm. Find:

   a EG
   b $\widehat{AGE}$.

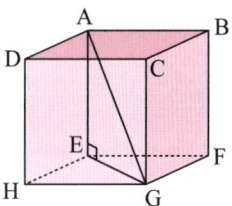

2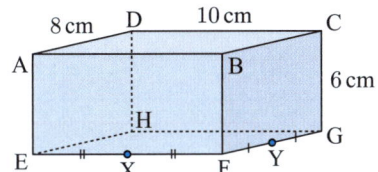

The figure alongside is a rectangular prism. X and Y are the midpoints of [EF] and [FG] respectively. Find:

   a HX
   b $\widehat{DXH}$
   c HY
   d $\widehat{DYH}$.

3 In the triangular prism below, find:

   a DF
   b $\widehat{AFD}$.

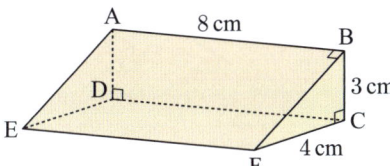

4 [AB] and [BC] are wooden support struts on a crate. Find the total length of wood required to make the two struts.

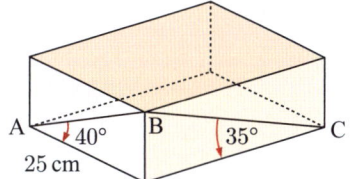

5 All edges of a square-based pyramid are 12 m in length.
   a Find the angle between a slant edge and a base diagonal.
   b Show that this angle is the same for any square-based pyramid with all edge lengths equal.

6 Each side of a tent is fixed to the ground by ropes as shown. The peg is 1.5 m from the side of the tent. Find the angle θ between the ropes.

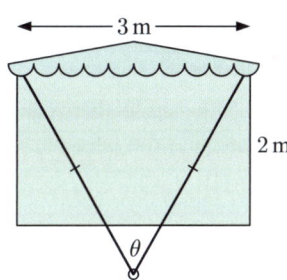

PROJECTIONS

Consider a wire frame in the shape of a cube, as shown. Imagine a light source shining down directly on this cube from above.

The shadow cast by wire [AG] would be [EG]. This is called the **projection** of [AG] onto the base plane EFGH.

Similarly, the projection of [BG] onto the base plane is [FG].

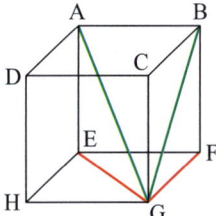

Example 9 **Self Tutor**

Find the projection of the following onto the base plane TUVW:

a [PU] **b** [PW]
c [QV] **d** [QX].

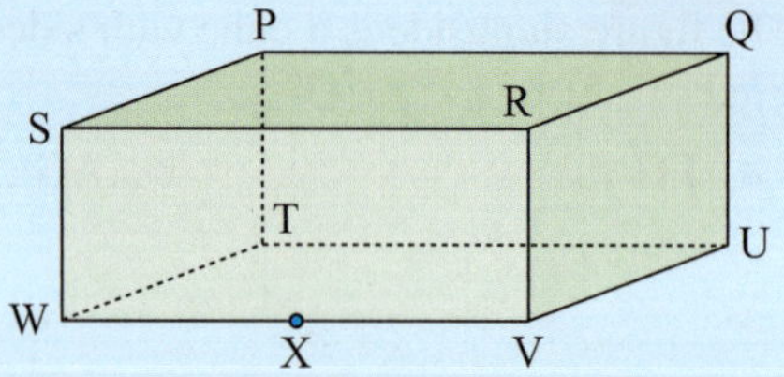

a The projection of [PU] onto the base plane is [TU].

b The projection of [PW] onto the base plane is [TW].

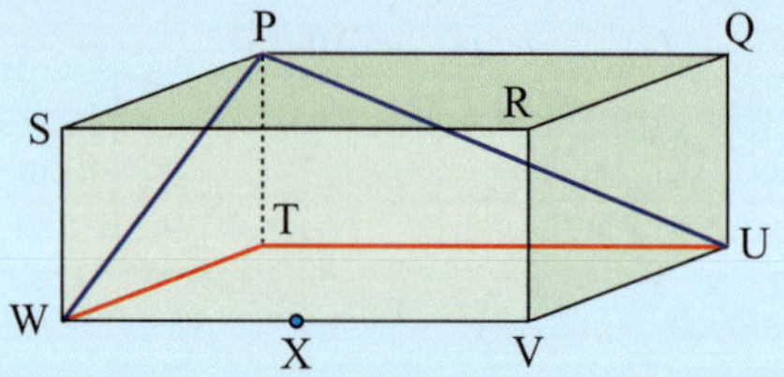

c The projection of [QV] onto the base plane is [UV].

d The projection of [QX] onto the base plane is [UX].

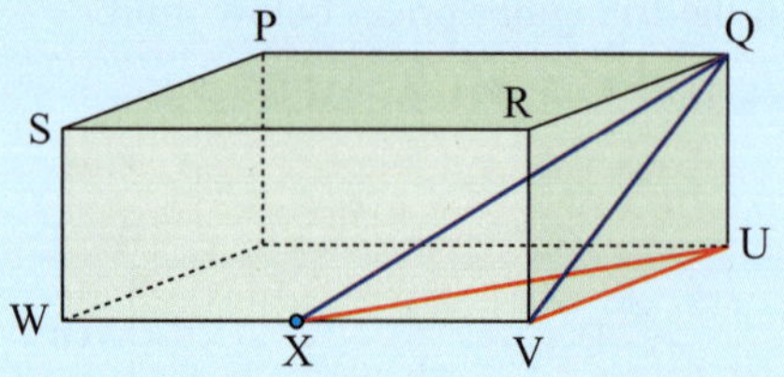

THE ANGLE BETWEEN A LINE AND A PLANE

The angle between a line and a plane is the angle between the line and its projection on the plane.

Example 10 **Self Tutor**

Name the angle between the following line segments and the base plane EFGH:

a [AH] **b** [AG].

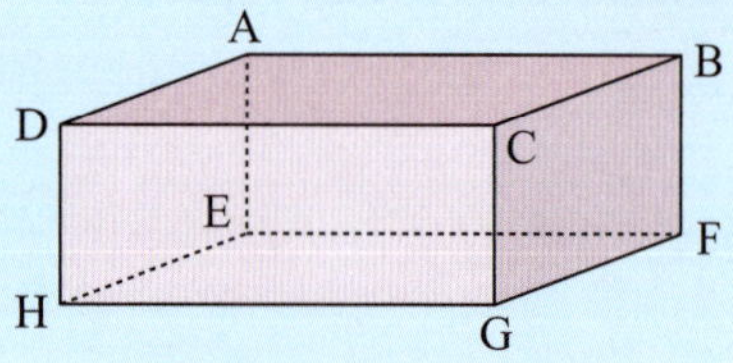

a The projection of [AH] onto the base plane EFGH is [EH]

$\therefore$ the required angle is $A\widehat{H}E$.

b The projection of [AG] onto the base plane EFGH is [EG]

$\therefore$ the required angle is $A\widehat{G}E$.

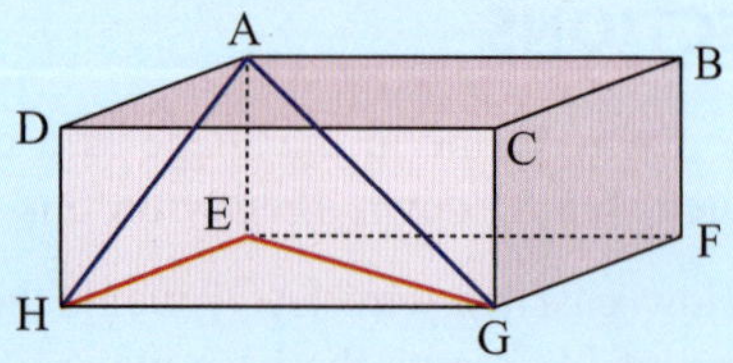

Example 11

Find the angle between the following line segments and the base plane EFGH:

a [DG] **b** [BH]

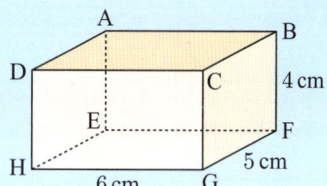

a The required angle is $D\hat{G}H$.

$\tan \theta = \frac{4}{6}$ $\{\tan \theta = \frac{\text{OPP}}{\text{ADJ}}\}$

$\therefore \theta = \tan^{-1}\left(\frac{4}{6}\right)$

$\therefore \theta \approx 33.69°$

The angle is about $33.7°$.

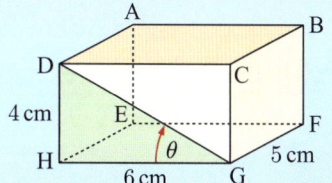

b The required angle is $B\hat{H}F$.

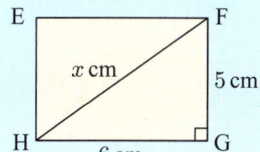

Let $HF = x$ cm.
Using Pythagoras,
$x^2 = 6^2 + 5^2$
$\therefore x^2 = 61$
$\therefore x = \sqrt{61}$

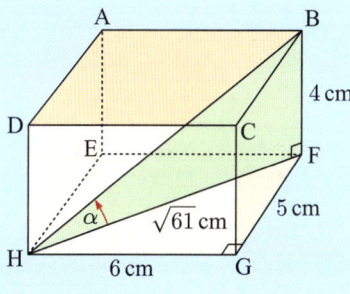

$\tan \alpha = \frac{4}{\sqrt{61}}$ $\{\tan \alpha = \frac{\text{OPP}}{\text{ADJ}}\}$

$\therefore \alpha = \tan^{-1}\left(\frac{4}{\sqrt{61}}\right)$

$\therefore \alpha \approx 27.12°$

The angle is about $27.1°$.

EXERCISE 12D.2

1 Find the following projections onto the base planes of the given figures:

a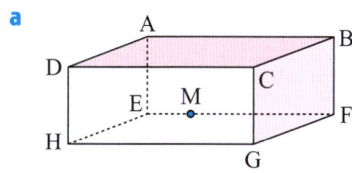

　　i [CF]
　　ii [DG]
　　iii [DF]
　　iv [CM]

b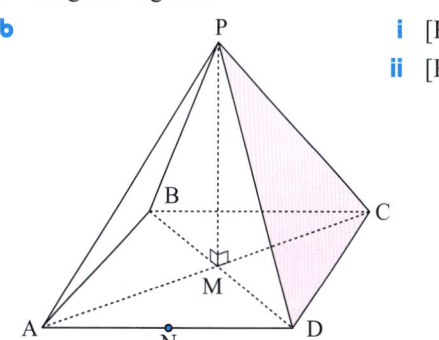

　　i [PA]
　　ii [PN]

c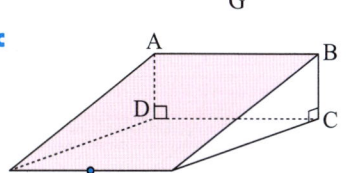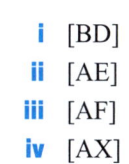

　　i [BD]
　　ii [AE]
　　iii [AF]
　　iv [AX]

2 For each of the following figures, name the angle between the given line segment and the base plane:

a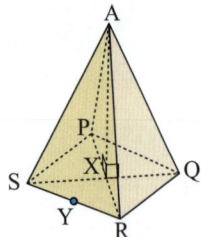
  i [BG]
  ii [BH]
  iii [DF]
  iv [AX]

b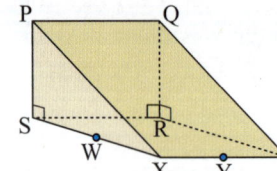
  i [PZ]
  ii [QY]
  iii [PW]
  iv [QW]

c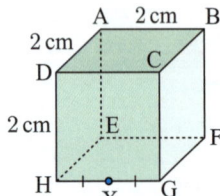
  i [AS]
  ii [AY]

3 For each of the following figures, find the angle between the given line segments and the base plane:

a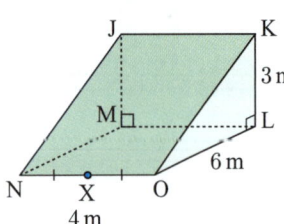
  i [DG]
  ii [AG]
  iii [CX]
  iv [BX]

b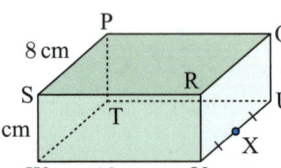
  i [SV]
  ii [SU]
  iii [PX]

c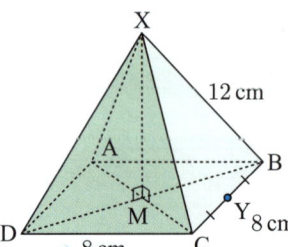
  i [JN]
  ii [JO]
  iii [KO]

d
  i [XB]
  ii [XY]

E   SUPPLEMENTARY ANGLES

Two angles are **supplementary** if their sum is 180°.

In this section we consider the sine and cosine of obtuse angles, and in particular the relationship between the sines and cosines of supplementary angles.

Consider the circle of radius 1 unit with its centre at the origin O. This circle is called the **unit circle**. It has equation $x^2 + y^2 = 1$.

Suppose P lies on the circle so that [OP] makes angle θ with the positive x-axis. θ is always measured in the anticlockwise direction.

For any acute angle θ, notice that $\cos \theta = \dfrac{a}{1} = a$ and $\sin \theta = \dfrac{b}{1} = b$.

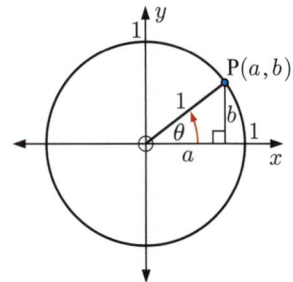

In fact, for any angle θ:

> The x-coordinate of P is called the **cosine** of angle θ, written $\cos\theta$.
>
> The y-coordinate of P is called the **sine** of angle θ, written $\sin\theta$.

For any point $P(\cos\theta, \sin\theta)$ on the unit circle,

$$OP = \sqrt{(\cos\theta - 0)^2 + (\sin\theta - 0)^2} = 1$$
$$\therefore \quad \sqrt{\cos^2\theta + \sin^2\theta} = 1$$

Squaring both sides, we find:

$$\cos^2\theta + \sin^2\theta = 1 \quad \text{for all } \theta.$$

Now consider an acute angle θ, and its supplement which is the obtuse angle $(180° - \theta)$.

The point P′ corresponding to angle $(180° - \theta)$ is the reflection of $P(\cos\theta, \sin\theta)$ in the y-axis.

$\therefore$ the coordinates of P′ are $(-\cos\theta, \sin\theta)$.

But P′ has coordinates $(\cos(180° - \theta), \sin(180° - \theta))$.

We therefore conclude that:

$$\cos(180° - \theta) = -\cos\theta$$
$$\sin(180° - \theta) = \sin\theta$$

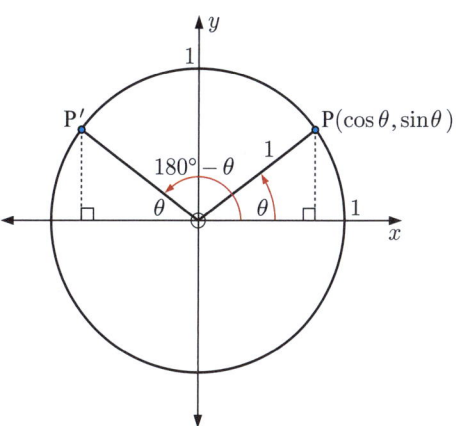

EXERCISE 12E

1 Copy and complete the following table, giving answers correct to four decimal places:

θ	$\cos\theta$	$\sin\theta$	$\cos(180° - \theta)$	$\sin(180° - \theta)$
18°				
27°				
53°				
62°				
80°				
125°				

Make sure your calculator is in degrees mode.

For each value of θ, check that:
- $\cos^2\theta + \sin^2\theta = 1$
- $\cos(180° - \theta) = -\cos\theta$
- $\sin(180° - \theta) = \sin\theta$

2 Use your calculator to find the coordinates of P and Q, rounded to 3 decimal places.

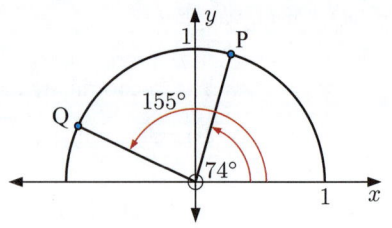

3 Find the obtuse angle which has the same sine as:
   a 26°   **b** 45°   **c** 69°   **d** 86°

4 Find the acute angle which has the same sine as:
   a 98°   **b** 127°   **c** 156°   **d** 168°

5 Find the obtuse angle whose cosine is the negative of:
   a cos 26°   **b** cos 45°   **c** cos 69°   **d** cos 86°

6 Find the acute angle whose cosine is the negative of:
   a cos 98°   **b** cos 127°   **c** cos 156°   **d** cos 168°

F THE AREA OF A TRIANGLE

We can use trigonometry to find the area of a triangle if we are given the lengths of **two sides**, as well as the **included angle** between the sides.

Consider triangle ABC in which the sides opposite angles A, B, and C are labelled a, b, and c respectively.

Suppose N lies on [BC] such that [AN] is perpendicular to [BC].

In $\triangle$ANC, $\sin C = \dfrac{h}{b}$

$\therefore\ h = b \sin C$

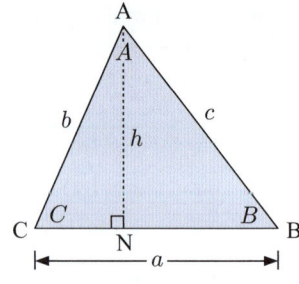

Since the area of $\triangle$ABC $= \frac{1}{2}ah$, we find: **Area $= \dfrac{1}{2}ab \sin C$**

If the altitudes from B and C were drawn, we could also show that the area is $\frac{1}{2}bc \sin A$ or $\frac{1}{2}ac \sin B$.

> The **area of a triangle** is
>
> *a half of the product of two sides and the sine of the included angle.*

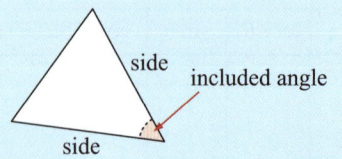

Example 12

Find the area of triangle ABC.

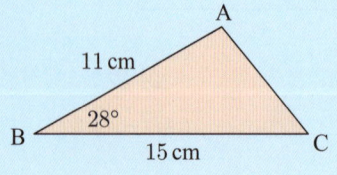

Area $= \frac{1}{2}ac \sin B$
$= \frac{1}{2} \times 15 \times 11 \times \sin 28°$
≈ 38.7 cm²

EXERCISE 12F

1 Find the area of:

a 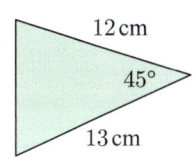 b 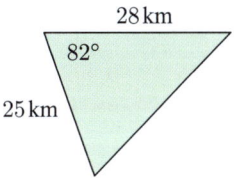 c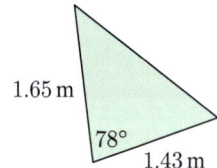

2 The proof of the area formula given above assumes that the included angle C is acute. Use the diagram alongside to prove that the formula is also true in the case where C is obtuse.

Hint: $\sin(180° - C) = \sin C$

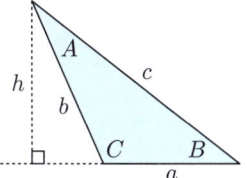

3 Find the area of:

a 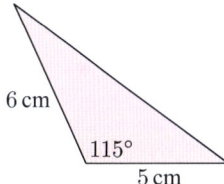 b 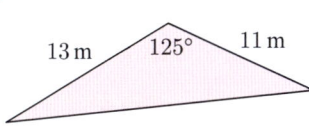 c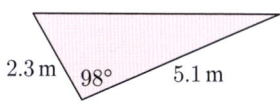

4 Find the area of:

a 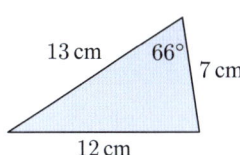 b 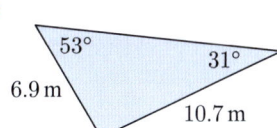 c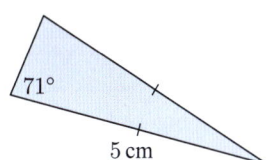

5 Find the area of a parallelogram with sides 6.4 cm and 8.7 cm, and one interior angle 64°.

6 Triangle ABC has area 150 cm². Find the value of x.

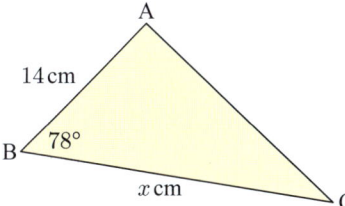

7 Triangle XYZ has area 80 cm². Find the length of the equal sides.

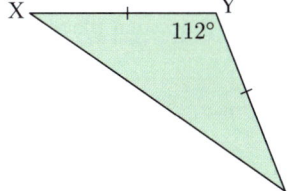

8 [AB] is the diameter of a circle with centre O and radius r. Show that the shaded triangles have equal area.

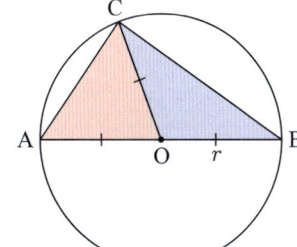

9 **a** Find the area of triangle ABC using:
   i angle A **ii** angle C

   b Hence, show that $\dfrac{\sin A}{a} = \dfrac{\sin C}{c}$.

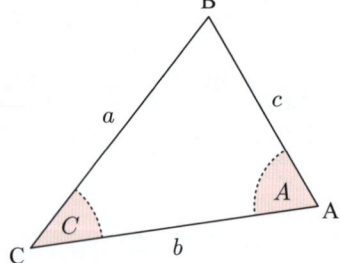

G THE SINE RULE

The **sine rule** is a set of equations which connects the lengths of the sides of any triangle with the sines of the opposite angles.

In any triangle ABC with sides a, b, and c units, and opposite angles A, B, and C respectively,

$$\dfrac{\sin A}{a} = \dfrac{\sin B}{b} = \dfrac{\sin C}{c} \quad \text{or} \quad \dfrac{a}{\sin A} = \dfrac{b}{\sin B} = \dfrac{c}{\sin C}.$$

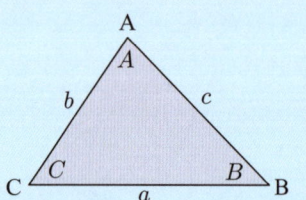

Proof:

The area of any triangle ABC is given by $\tfrac{1}{2}bc\sin A = \tfrac{1}{2}ac\sin B = \tfrac{1}{2}ab\sin C$.

Dividing each expression by $\tfrac{1}{2}abc$ gives $\dfrac{\sin A}{a} = \dfrac{\sin B}{b} = \dfrac{\sin C}{c}$.

GEOMETRY PACKAGE

FINDING SIDES

If we are given two angles and one side of a triangle, we can use the sine rule to find another side length.

Example 13 *Self Tutor*

Find x, rounded to 2 decimal places:

[Triangle with A at top-left with angle 113°, B at bottom-left with angle 41°, C at right; AC = 18 m, BC = x m]

Using the sine rule, $\dfrac{x}{\sin 113°} = \dfrac{18}{\sin 41°}$

$\therefore x = \dfrac{18 \times \sin 113°}{\sin 41°}$

$\therefore x \approx 25.26$

We use the form $\dfrac{a}{\sin A} = \dfrac{b}{\sin B}$ so that the unknown is in the numerator.

EXERCISE 12G.1

1 Find x, rounded to 2 decimal places:

a 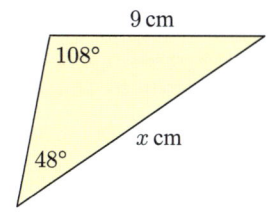 **b** 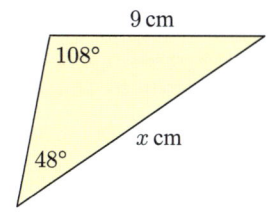 **c**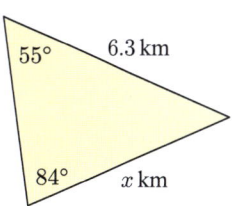

(Triangle a: 15 cm, 32°, 46°, x cm)
(Triangle b: 9 cm, 108°, 48°, x cm)
(Triangle c: 55°, 6.3 km, 84°, x km)

2 Find x:

a 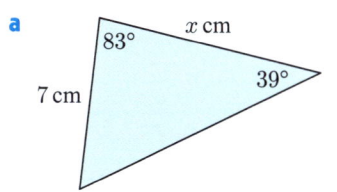 **b** 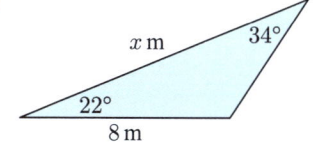 **c**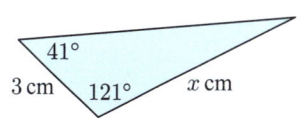

(a: 83°, 39°, 7 cm, x cm)
(b: 34°, 22°, 8 m, x m)
(c: 41°, 121°, 3 cm, x cm)

3 Find the area of this triangle.

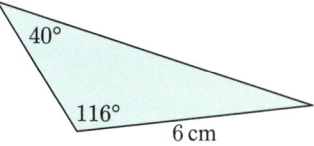

(40°, 116°, 6 cm)

4 Find *all* unknown sides and angles of:

a 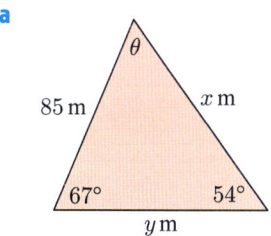 **b** 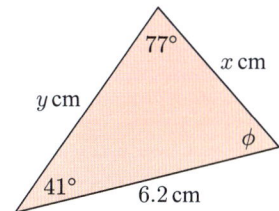 **c**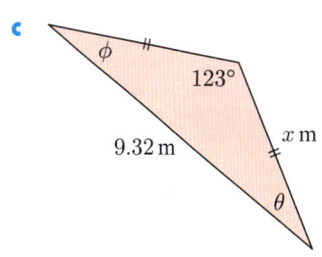

(a: θ, 85 m, 67°, 54°, y m, x m)
(b: 77°, ϕ, 41°, 6.2 cm, x cm, y cm)
(c: ϕ, 123°, 9.32 m, θ, x m)

FINDING ANGLES

Finding angles using the sine rule is more complicated than finding sides because there may be two possible answers.

In **Section E**, we saw that $\sin(180° - \theta) = \sin\theta$. This means that an equation of the form $\sin\theta = k$ has two solutions, $\theta = \sin^{-1} k$ and $\theta = 180° - \sin^{-1} k$.

We must examine both of the possible solutions to see whether each is feasible. Sometimes there is information in the question which enables us to **reject** one of the solutions.

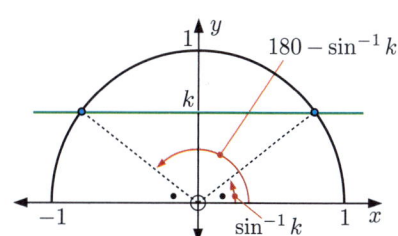

Example 14

In triangle ABC, AB = 12 cm, AC = 8 cm, and angle B measures 28°. Find, rounded to 1 decimal place, the measure of angle C.

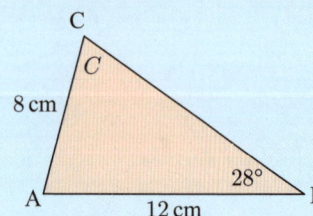

$$\frac{\sin C}{12} = \frac{\sin 28°}{8} \quad \text{\{sine rule\}}$$

$$\therefore \sin C = \frac{12 \times \sin 28°}{8}$$

Now $\sin^{-1}\left(\dfrac{12 \times \sin 28°}{8}\right) \approx 44.8°$

This is called the "ambiguous case".

Since the angle at C could be acute or obtuse, $C \approx 44.8°$ or $(180 - 44.8)°$

$$\therefore C \approx 44.8° \text{ or } 135.2°$$

In this case there is insufficient information to determine the actual shape of the triangle.

The validity of the two answers in the above **Example** can be demonstrated by a simple construction.

Step 1: Draw [AB] of length 12 cm, and construct an angle of 28° at B.

Step 2: From A, draw an arc of radius 8 cm.

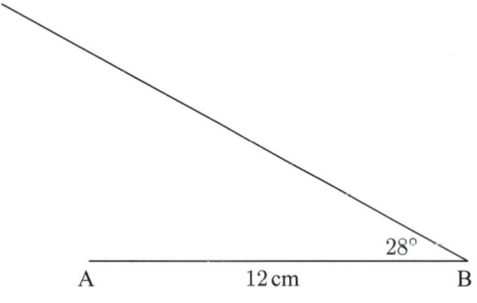
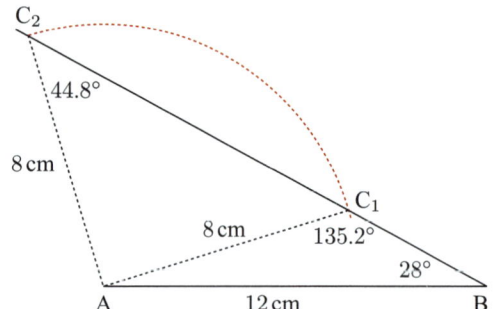

Example 15

In triangle KLM, $L\widehat{K}M$ measures 52°, LM = 158 m, and KM = 128 m. Find the measure of angle L.

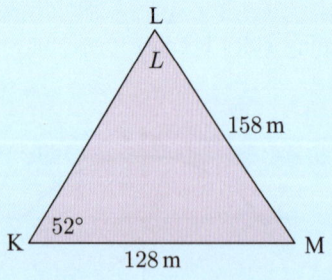

$$\frac{\sin L}{128} = \frac{\sin 52°}{158} \quad \text{\{sine rule\}}$$

$$\therefore \sin L = \frac{128 \times \sin 52°}{158}$$

Now $\sin^{-1}\left(\dfrac{128 \times \sin 52°}{158}\right) \approx 39.7°$

$\therefore$ since L could be acute or obtuse,

$$L \approx 39.7° \text{ or } (180 - 39.7)° \approx 140.3°$$

However, we can reject $L \approx 140.3°$ as $140.3° + 52° > 180°$ which is impossible.

$\therefore$ the angle $L \approx 39.7°$.

EXERCISE 12G.2

1 In triangle ABC, AB = 10 cm, BC = 7 cm, and CÂB measures 42°.

   a Find the two possible values for AĈB.

   b Draw a diagram to illustrate the two possible triangles.

2 In triangle PQR, PQ = 10 cm, QR = 12 cm, and RP̂Q measures 42°.

   a Show that there is only one possible value for PR̂Q, and state its measure.

   b Draw a diagram to demonstrate that only one triangle can be drawn from the information given.

3 The following diagrams are not drawn to scale, but the information on them is correct. Find the value of θ:

a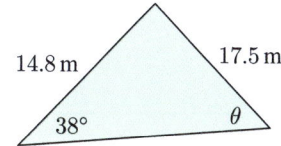

b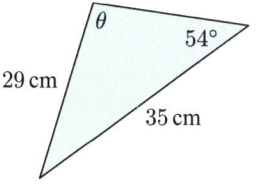

There may be two possible solutions.

c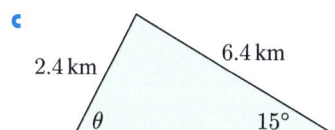

d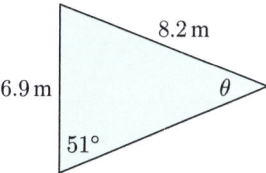

4 In triangle ABC, find the measure of:

   a angle A if $a = 12.6$ cm, $b = 15.1$ cm, and AB̂C = 65°

   b angle B if $b = 38.4$ cm, $c = 27.6$ cm, and AĈB = 43°

   c angle C if $a = 5.5$ km, $c = 4.1$ km, and BÂC = 71°.

H THE COSINE RULE

The **cosine rule** relates the three sides of a triangle and one of its angles.

Consider triangle ABC with side lengths a, b, and c as shown.

Using Pythagoras' theorem in $\triangle$BCN,

$$a^2 = h^2 + (c-x)^2$$
$$\therefore \ a^2 = h^2 + c^2 - 2cx + x^2$$

In $\triangle$ACN, $b^2 = h^2 + x^2$ and so $h^2 = b^2 - x^2$

Thus, $a^2 = (b^2 - x^2) + c^2 - 2cx + x^2$

$$\therefore \ a^2 = b^2 + c^2 - 2cx$$

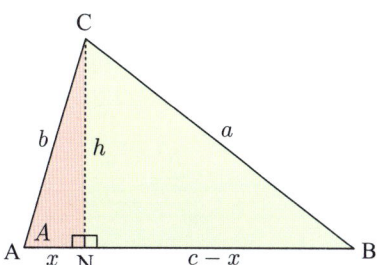

In $\triangle$ACN, $\cos A = \dfrac{x}{b}$ and so $x = b \cos A$

$$\therefore \ a^2 = b^2 + c^2 - 2bc \cos A$$

In any triangle ABC with sides a, b, and c units, and opposite angles A, B, and C respectively,

$$a^2 = b^2 + c^2 - 2bc \cos A$$
$$b^2 = a^2 + c^2 - 2ac \cos B$$
$$c^2 = a^2 + b^2 - 2ab \cos C.$$

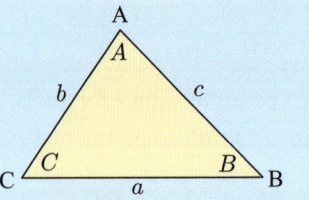

GEOMETRY PACKAGE

ACTIVITY

Prove the **cosine rule** $a^2 = b^2 + c^2 - 2bc \cos A$ in the case where A is obtuse.

Hint: $\cos(180° - A) = -\cos A$

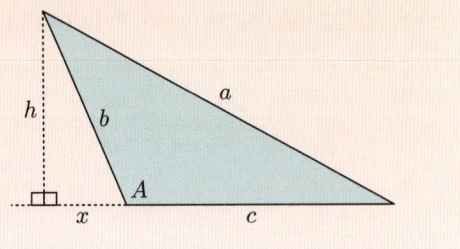

If we are given two sides of a triangle and the included angle, we can use the cosine rule to find the third side.

Example 16
Self Tutor

Find, correct to 2 decimal places, the length of [BC].

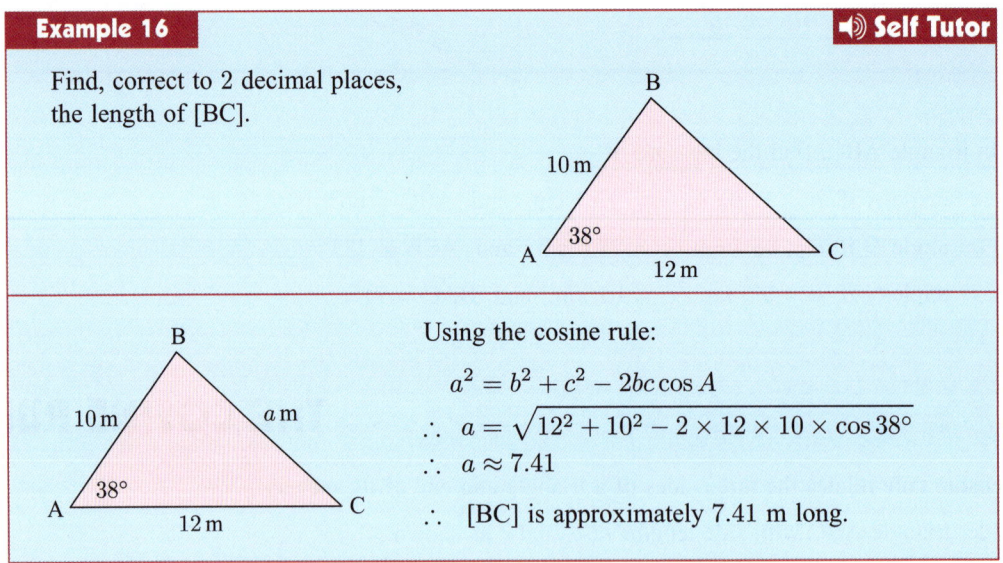

Using the cosine rule:
$$a^2 = b^2 + c^2 - 2bc \cos A$$
$$\therefore a = \sqrt{12^2 + 10^2 - 2 \times 12 \times 10 \times \cos 38°}$$
$$\therefore a \approx 7.41$$
$$\therefore \text{[BC] is approximately 7.41 m long.}$$

If we know all three side lengths of a triangle, we can use the cosine rule to find any of the angles. To do this, we rearrange the original cosine rule formulae:

$$\cos A = \frac{b^2 + c^2 - a^2}{2bc}, \quad \cos B = \frac{a^2 + c^2 - b^2}{2ac}, \quad \cos C = \frac{a^2 + b^2 - c^2}{2ab}$$

Example 17

Find the measure of angle C in the given figure.

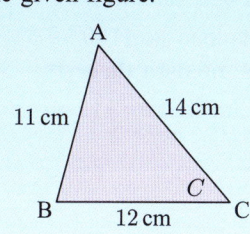

$$\cos C = \frac{a^2 + b^2 - c^2}{2ab}$$

$\therefore \cos C = \dfrac{12^2 + 14^2 - 11^2}{2 \times 12 \times 14}$

$\therefore \cos C = \dfrac{219}{336}$

$\therefore C = \cos^{-1}\left(\dfrac{219}{336}\right)$

$\therefore C \approx 49.3°$

EXERCISE 12H

1 Find the length of the remaining side in the triangle:

a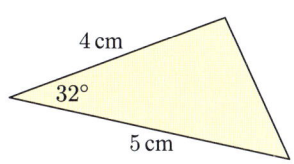

b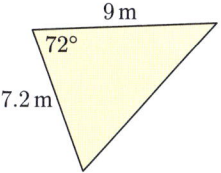

c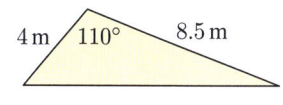

d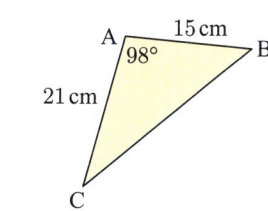

e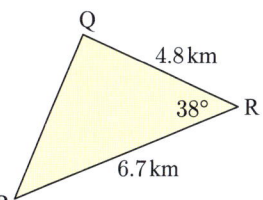

f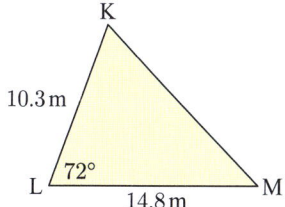

2 Find θ, rounded to 1 decimal place:

a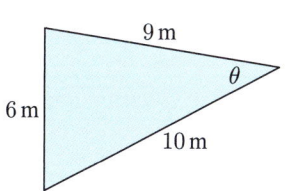

b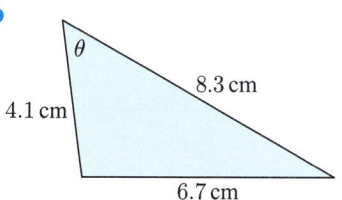

c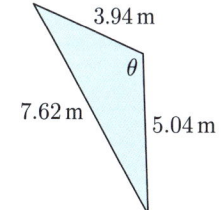

3 Find the measure of all angles of the triangle:

a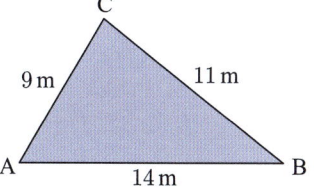

b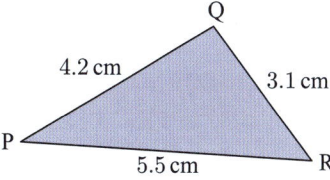

4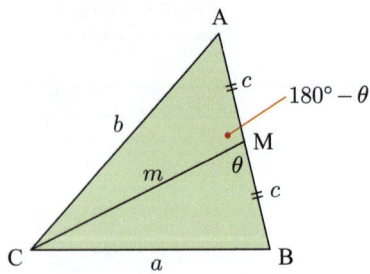

a Use the cosine rule in $\triangle BCM$ to find $\cos\theta$ in terms of a, c, and m.

b Use the cosine rule in $\triangle ACM$ to find $\cos(180° - \theta)$ in terms of b, c, and m.

c Use the fact that $\cos(180° - \theta) = -\cos\theta$ to prove **Apollonius' median theorem**:
$a^2 + b^2 = 2m^2 + 2c^2$.

d Find x in the following:

i 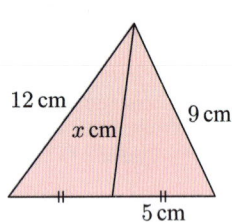   **ii**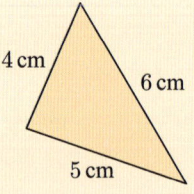

5 In triangle ABC, $AB = 10$ cm, $AC = 9$ cm, and $\widehat{ABC} = 60°$. Let $BC = x$ cm.

a Use the cosine rule to show that x is a solution of $x^2 - 10x + 19 = 0$.

b Solve this equation for x.

c Use a scale diagram and a compass to explain why there are two possible values of x.

INVESTIGATION 3   ANGLE SIZES

If we know the side lengths of a triangle, can we tell which angles are the largest and smallest?

What to do:

1 In the triangle alongside, calculate the size of the angle opposite:

  a the 4 cm side   **b** the 5 cm side

  c the 6 cm side.

Record your results in a table like the one shown.

Side length	Opposite angle
4 cm	
5 cm	
6 cm	

2 Fill in a similar table for the following triangles:

a 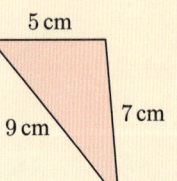   **b**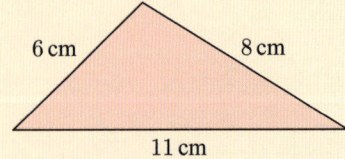

3 In each of your tables, compare the lengths of the sides with the sizes of their opposite angles. What do you notice?

4 To prove your result, consider the sides a and b of a triangle, with opposite angles A and B respectively.

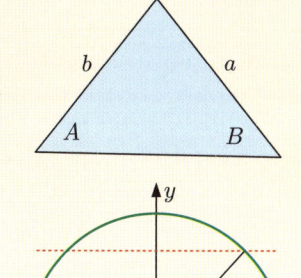

a Use the sine rule to show that $\dfrac{a}{b} = \dfrac{\sin A}{\sin B}$.

b Hence, show that if $a > b$, then $\sin A > \sin B$.

c Use the unit circle to show that if $\sin A > \sin B$, then $A > B$.

  Hint: The sum of A and B must not exceed 180°.

d Use **b** and **c** to show that if $a > b$, then $A > B$.

I   PROBLEM SOLVING USING THE SINE AND COSINE RULES

When using trigonometry to solve problems, you should draw a diagram of the situation. The diagram should be reasonably accurate, and all important information should be clearly marked on it.

Example 18   ◀) Self Tutor

A triangular property is bounded by two roads and a long, straight drain. Find:

a the area of the property in hectares

b the length of the drain boundary.

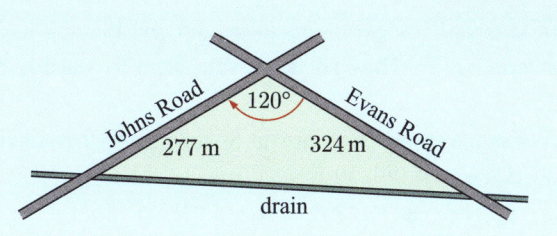

a Area $= \tfrac{1}{2} \times 277 \times 324 \times \sin 120°$

$\approx 38\,862$ m^2

≈ 3.89 ha   {1 ha = 10 000 m^2}

b Let the drain boundary be x m long.

$\therefore x^2 = 277^2 + 324^2 - 2 \times 277 \times 324 \times \cos 120°$ {cosine rule}

$\therefore x = \sqrt{277^2 + 324^2 - 2 \times 277 \times 324 \times \cos 120°}$

$\therefore x \approx 521$

The drain boundary is approximately 521 m long.

EXERCISE 12I

1 Two farm houses A and B are 10.3 km apart. A third farm house C is located such that $\widehat{BAC} = 83°$ and $\widehat{ABC} = 59°$. How far is C from A?

2 A roadway is horizontal from A to B, then rises up a 12° incline from B to C.
How far is it directly from A to C?

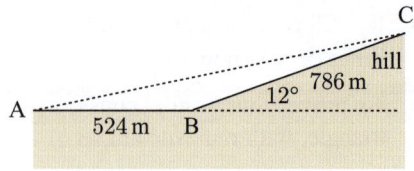

3 Sharon drives a golf ball 253 m from the tee T to point X on the fairway. X is 93 m from the flag, and $X\hat{F}T$ is 39°.
Find the angle θ that Sharon's drive was off line.

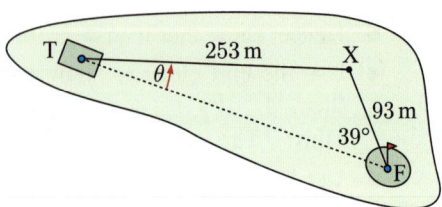

4 Hazel's property is triangular with the dimensions shown.

  a Find the measure of the angle at A, rounded to 2 decimal places.

  b Find the area of Hazel's property, to the nearest hectare.

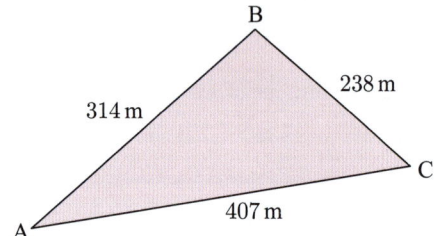

Example 19   ◀)) Self Tutor

A ship sails 58 km on the bearing 072°. Once it has passed a reef, it turns and sails 41 km on the bearing 158°. How far is the ship from its starting point?

We suppose the ship starts at S, sails to A, then changes direction and sails to F.

$S\hat{A}N = 180° - 72° = 108°$ {co-interior angles}

$\therefore S\hat{A}F = 360° - 158° - 108°$
$= 94°$ {angles at a point}

Let $SF = x$ km.

Using the cosine rule, $x^2 = 58^2 + 41^2 - 2 \times 58 \times 41 \times \cos 94°$

$\therefore x = \sqrt{58^2 + 41^2 - 2 \times 58 \times 41 \times \cos 94°}$

$\therefore x \approx 73.3$

The ship is about 73.3 km from its starting point.

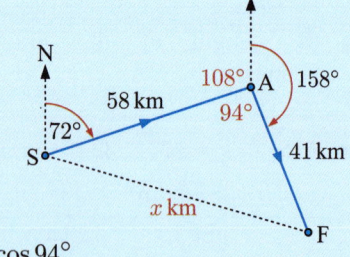

5 Fred walks 83 m in the direction 111°, and then 78 m in the direction 214°. How far is Fred from his starting point?

6 A boat travels 13 km in the direction 138°, and then a further 11 km in the direction 067°. Find the distance and bearing of the boat from its starting point.

7 Mount X is 9 km from Mount Y, on a bearing 146°. Mount Z is 14 km from Mount X, and on a bearing 072° from Mount Y. Find the bearing of X from Z.

8 X is 20 km north of Y. A mobile telephone mast M is to be placed 15 km from Y so the bearing of M from X is 140°.
   a Draw a sketch to show the two possible positions where the mast could be placed.
   b Calculate the distance of each of these positions from X.

9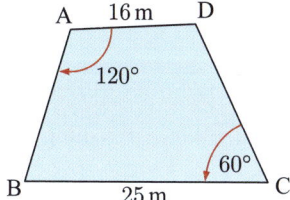
   The quadrilateral ABCD represents David's garden plot. AD = 16 m, BC = 25 m, and [DC] is 5 m longer than [AB]. A fence runs around the entire boundary of the plot. How long is the fence?

10 In the given triangle, X is 5 m from each of the vertices. Find the length of each side of the triangle.

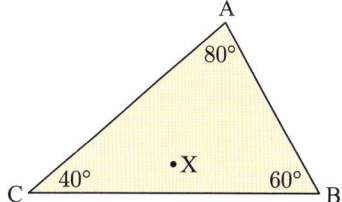

11 The angles of a triangle measure 104°, 51°, and 25°. The perimeter of the triangle is 10 m. Find, rounded to 2 decimal places, the length of each side of the triangle.

REVIEW SET 12A

1 Find the value of x:

   a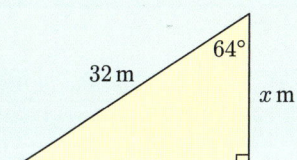

   b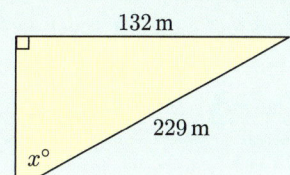

2 Find the measure of all unknown sides and angles in triangle CDE.

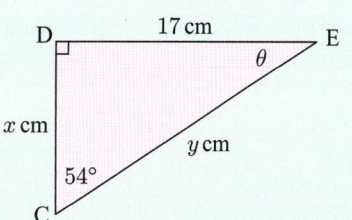

3 The shadow of a cathedral is 85 m in length. The angle of elevation from the end of the shadow to the top of the steeple is 33°. Find the height of the cathedral.

4 Find the bearing of Q from P in the following diagrams:

a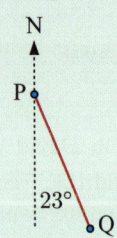
b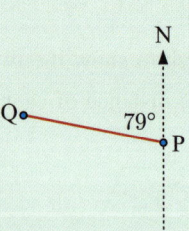

5 A taxi travels 8 km south, then 3 km west. Find the bearing of the taxi's finishing point from its starting point.

6 Find the measure of:
  a $B\widehat{G}F$ **b** $A\widehat{G}E$

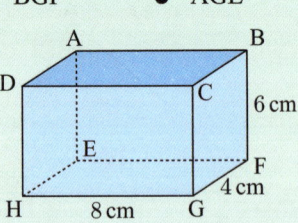

7 Use your calculator to find the coordinates of P and Q, rounded to 3 decimal places.

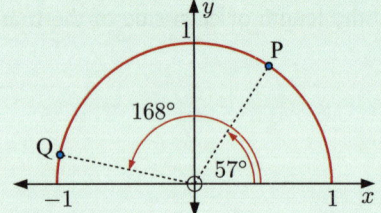

8 Laura is at the top of a scenic lookout. Her friends Ariel and Briannah are at ground level, and are 50 m apart.

The angle of depression from L to A is 36°, and the angle of depression from L to B is 29°.

  a Find the angle of elevation from B to L.
  b Find the height of the lookout.
  c The girls' car is at C, at an angle of depression of 20° from L. How far is the car from Ariel?

9 **a** Find the area of triangle ABC, to the nearest m².
   b Find the length of side [BC] rounded to 1 decimal place.

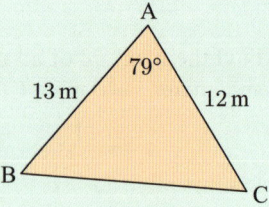

10 Find the value of x:

  a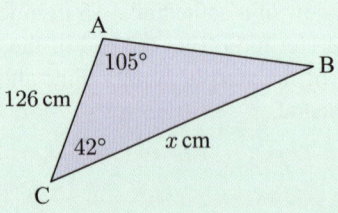
  b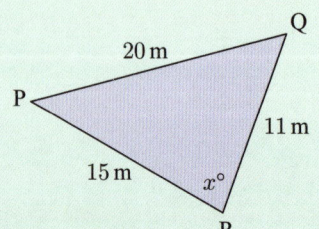

11 Stuart swam 200 m in the direction 124°, then 150 m in the direction 156°. Find the distance and bearing of Stuart from his starting point.

12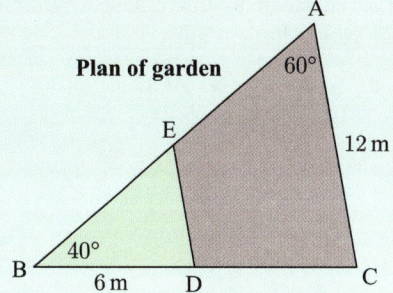

In the given plan view, AC = 12 m, $\widehat{BAC} = 60°$, and $\widehat{ABC} = 40°$.

D is a post 6 m from corner B, E is a tap, and triangle BDE is a lawn with area 13.5 m².

a Calculate the length DC.
b Calculate the length BE.
c Find the area of quadrilateral ACDE.

13 X is a point inside triangle PQR. It is 3 cm from P, and 4 cm from Q. How far is X from R?

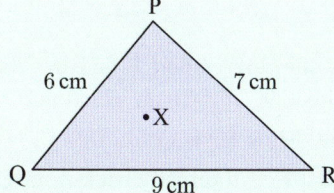

REVIEW SET 12B

1 Find the measure of the angle marked θ:

a 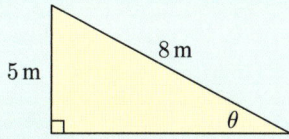 **b**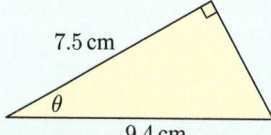

2 Find the value of x, rounding your answer to 2 decimal places:

a 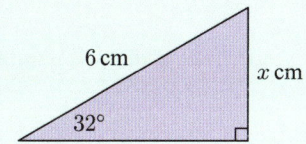 **b**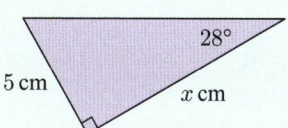

3 Find the measure of all unknown sides and angles in triangle KLM.

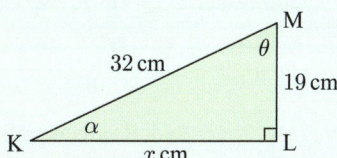

4 Point P is 13 cm from the centre of a circle. The tangent from P to the circle is 11 cm long. Find the angle between the tangent and the line from P to the centre of the circle.

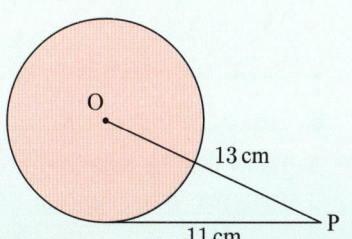

5 An aeroplane takes off at an angle of 22° to the horizontal runway. At the time when it has flown 500 m, what is the altitude of the plane? Give your answer correct to the nearest metre.

6 Find the bearing of:
 a P from Q **b** R from Q
 c R from P.

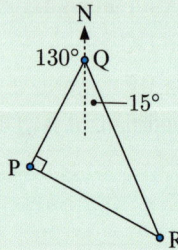

7 The edges of a square-based pyramid are all 20 cm long. Find:
 a $A\hat{D}M$ **b** $A\hat{C}D$.

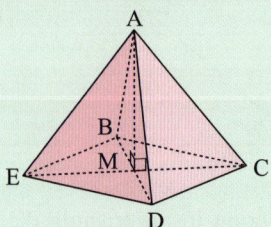

8 A ship leaves port P and travels for 50 km in the direction 181°. It then sails 60 km in the direction 271° to an island port Q.
 a How far is Q from P?
 b To sail directly back from Q to P, in what direction must the ship sail?

9 Find the obtuse angle:
 a which has the same sine as 38°
 b whose cosine is the negative of $\cos 52°$.

10 Find the area of this triangle.

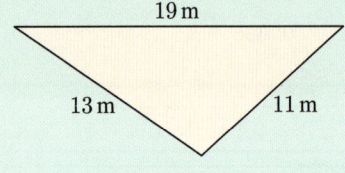

11 Find the distance between A and C.

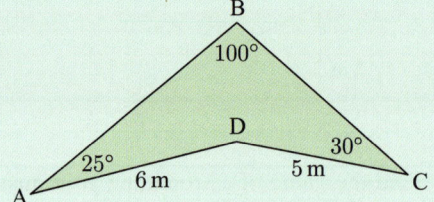

12 Triangle ABC has AB = 12 m, BC = 10 m, and $B\hat{A}C = 40°$. Find the two possible values for $A\hat{C}B$.

13 A surveyor at point A measures 200 m in the direction 138° to point B. From B the surveyor then measures 150 m in the direction 256° to point C.
 a How far is C from A?
 b What is the bearing of C from A?

14 Ports P, Q, and R are equally spaced along the coast. A boat B is 4 km from P, and 2 km from Q.
 a Show that $\cos B\hat{Q}P = \frac{13}{20}$.
 b Hence, find $\cos B\hat{Q}R$.
 c Show that the boat is $\sqrt{42}$ km from port R.

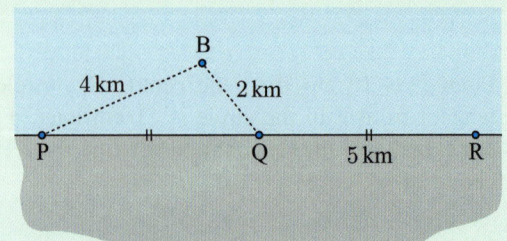

Chapter 13
Probability

Contents:
- **A** Experimental probability
- **B** Probabilities from tabled data
- **C** Sample space
- **D** Theoretical probability
- **E** Compound events
- **F** Conditional probability
- **G** Mutually exclusive and independent events

OPENING PROBLEM

When Karla dropped some metal nuts she noticed that they finished either on their ends or on their sides. She was interested to know how likely it was that a nut would finish on its end. So, she tossed a nut 200 times, and found that it finished on its end 137 times.

Her friend Sam repeated the experiment, and the nut finished on its end 145 times.

Things to think about:

a What would Karla's best estimate be of the chance or probability that the nut will finish on its end?

b What would Sam's estimate be?

c How can we obtain a better estimate of the chance of an end occurring?

d Hilda said that the best estimate would be obtained when the nut is tossed thousands of times. Do you agree with Hilda?

side   end

Consider these statements:

"The Wildcats will probably beat the Tigers on Saturday."
"It is unlikely that it will rain today."
"I will probably make the team."

Each of these statements indicates a **likelihood** or **chance** of a particular event happening.

We can indicate the likelihood of an event happening in the future by using a percentage.

> 0%   indicates the event **will not occur**.
> 100% indicates the event **is certain to occur**.

All events can therefore be assigned a percentage between 0% and 100% inclusive.

A number close to 0% indicates the event is **unlikely** to occur, whereas a number close to 100% means that it is **highly likely** to occur.

In mathematics, we usually write probabilities as either decimals or fractions rather than percentages.

> An **impossible** event has 0% chance of happening, and is assigned the probability 0.
>
> A **certain** event has 100% chance of happening, and is assigned the probability 1.
>
> All other events can be assigned a probability between 0 and 1.

Probabilities are usually determined by either:

- observing the results of an experiment (experimental probability),   or
- using arguments of symmetry (theoretical probability).

HISTORICAL NOTE

- **Girolamo Cardano** (1501 to 1576) admitted in his autobiography that he gambled "not only every year, but .... every day, and with the loss at once of thought, of substance, and of time". He wrote a handbook on gambling, with tips on cheating and how to detect it. His book included discussion on equally likely events, frequency tables for dice probabilities, and expectations.
- **Pierre-Simon Laplace** (1749 - 1827) once described the theory of probability as "nothing but common sense reduced to calculation".
- **Blaise Pascal** (1623 - 1662) invented the first mechanical digital calculator. Pascal and his friend **Pierre de Fermat** (1601 - 1665) were the first to develop probability theory as we know it today. Pascal also developed the syringe and the hydraulic press, and he wrote a large number of articles on Christian beliefs and ethics.

Girolamo Cardano

A   EXPERIMENTAL PROBABILITY

In experiments involving chance, we use the following terms to describe what we are doing and the results we are obtaining:

- The **number of trials** is the total number of times the experiment is repeated.
- The **outcomes** are the different results possible for one trial of the experiment.
- The **frequency** of a particular outcome is the number of times that this outcome is observed.
- The **relative frequency** of an outcome is the frequency of that outcome divided by the total number of trials. It can be expressed as a fraction, a decimal, or a percentage.

For example, suppose a tin can is tossed in the air 250 times, and it comes to rest on an end 29 times. We say:

- the number of trials is 250
- the outcomes are *ends* and *sides*
- the frequency of *ends* is 29, and of *sides* is 221
- the relative frequency of *ends* $= \frac{29}{250} = 0.116$
- the relative frequency of *sides* $= \frac{221}{250} = 0.884$.

EXPERIMENTAL PROBABILITY

Sometimes the only way of estimating the probability of a particular event occurring is by experimentation.

Tossing a tin can is one such example. The **relative frequencies** from an experiment can be used to estimate the probabilities of the corresponding events.

The larger the number of trials, the more accurate the estimate will be.

Example 1

Larissa took 43 shots at a netball goal, and scored 29 times. Estimate the probability that Larissa will miss with her next shot.

From 43 shots, Larissa scored 29 times and missed 14 times.

$\therefore$ P(misses next shot) $\approx \frac{14}{43}$

≈ 0.326

Experimental probabilities are usually written as decimals.

EXERCISE 13A

1. Clem fired 200 arrows at a target and hit the target 168 times. Estimate the probability that Clem will hit the target with his next shot.

2. Ivy has free-range hens. Out of the first 123 eggs that they laid, she found that 11 had double-yolks. Estimate the probability that the next egg laid will have a double-yolk.

3. Jackson leaves for work at the same time each day. Over a period of 227 working days, he had to wait for a train at the railway crossing on 58 days. Estimate the probability that Jackson will not have to wait for a train tomorrow.

4. Ravi has a circular spinner marked P, Q, and R. When the spinner was twirled 417 times, it finished on P 138 times, and on Q 107 times. Estimate the probability that the next spin will finish on R.

5. Answer the **Opening Problem** on page 278.

B   PROBABILITIES FROM TABLED DATA

If we are given a table of frequencies then we use **relative frequencies** to estimate the probabilities of the events.

$$\text{relative frequency} = \frac{\text{frequency}}{\text{number of trials}}$$

Example 2

A marketing company surveys 80 people to discover what brand of shoe cleaner they use. The results are shown in the table alongside.

Estimate the probability that a randomly selected community member uses:
  a Brite
  b Cleano or No scuff.

Brand	Frequency
Shine	27
Brite	22
Cleano	20
No scuff	11

a P(Brite) $\approx \frac{22}{80} \approx 0.275$

b P(Cleano or No scuff) $\approx \frac{20 + 11}{80} \approx 0.388$

PROBABILITIES FROM TWO-WAY TABLES

Two-way tables are tables comparing two variables. They usually result from a survey.

For example, the Year 10 students in a small school were asked whether they were good at mathematics. The results are summarised in the following two-way table:

	Boy	Girl
Good at mathematics	17	19
Not good at mathematics	8	9

← 9 girls were not good at mathematics.

In this case the variables are *ability in mathematics* and *gender*.

We can use two-way tables to estimate probabilities.

Example 3

To investigate the breakfast habits of teenagers, a survey was conducted amongst some students from a high school. The results are shown alongside.

	Male	Female
Regularly eats breakfast	87	53
Does not regularly eat breakfast	68	92

Use this table to estimate the probability that a randomly selected student from the school:

a is male **b** is male *and* regularly eats breakfast
c is female *or* regularly eats breakfast.

We extend the table to include totals:

	Male	Female	Total
Regularly eats breakfast	87	53	140
Does not regularly eat breakfast	68	92	160
Total	155	145	300

a There are 155 males amongst the 300 students surveyed.

$\therefore$ P(male) $\approx \frac{155}{300} \approx 0.517$

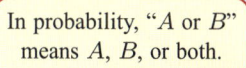

In probability, "A or B" means A, B, or both.

b 87 of the 300 students are male and regularly eat breakfast.

$\therefore$ P(male *and* regularly eats breakfast) $\approx \frac{87}{300} \approx 0.29$

c $53 + 92 + 87 = 232$ out of the 300 are female or regularly eat breakfast.

$\therefore$ P(female *or* regularly eats breakfast) $\approx \frac{232}{300} \approx 0.773$

EXERCISE 13B

1 A marketing company surveyed people to discover which brand of soap they use. The results of the survey are given alongside.

  a How many people were surveyed?
  b Estimate the probability that a randomly selected person uses:
    i Just Soap **ii** Indulgence or Silktouch.

Brand	Frequency
Silktouch	125
Super	107
Just Soap	93
Indulgence	82

2 This table shows the flavour of ice creams sold in a café one afternoon.

Flavour	Frequency
Chocolate	21
Strawberry	17
Lemon	4
Vanilla	15

  a How many ice creams were sold?

  b Estimate the probability that the next ice cream sold will be:

    i strawberry   **ii** chocolate or vanilla.

3

Councillor	Frequency
Mr Tony Trimboli	216
Mrs Andrea Sims	72
Mrs Sara Chong	238
Mr John Henry	
Total	

Results from a poll for a local Council election are shown in the table. It is known that 600 people were surveyed in the poll.

  a Copy and complete the table.

  b Estimate the probability that a randomly selected person from this electorate will vote for:

    i John Henry   **ii** a female councillor.

4 310 students at a high school in South Africa were surveyed on the question "Do you like watching rugby on TV?". The results are shown in the two-way table.

	Like	Dislike
Junior students	87	38
Senior students	129	56

  a Copy and complete the table to include 'totals'.

  b Estimate the probability that a randomly selected student:

    i likes watching rugby on TV and is a junior student

    ii likes watching rugby on TV and is a senior student

    iii dislikes watching rugby on TV.

  c Find the total of the probabilities found in **b**. Explain your answer.

5 A random selection of students in a youth club were asked whether they wore glasses, contact lenses, or neither. The results were further categorised by gender.

	Glasses	Contact lenses	Neither
Male	15	6	26
Female	14	8	31

  a How many students were surveyed?

  b Estimate the probability that a randomly chosen student in the club:

    i wears glasses   **ii** is female and wears contact lenses

    iii is male and wears neither   **iv** is female or wears glasses.

6 The table alongside describes the types of cars advertised for sale in a newspaper.

Estimate the probability that a randomly selected car for sale:

	Manual	Automatic
Hatchback	26	27
Sedan	30	39
4WD	9	16

  a is a sedan   **b** is a manual hatchback

  c is automatic, but not a sedan.

7 A random selection of hotels in Paris are given a gold star rating for quality, and a green star for environmental friendliness.

Estimate the probability that a randomly selected Paris hotel is given:

- **a** 2 gold stars and 4 green stars
- **b** 3 gold stars or higher
- **c** the same number of gold stars as green stars
- **d** more green stars than gold stars.

Green star

Gold star	★	★★	★★★	★★★★
★	5	2	1	1
★★	4	10	4	3
★★★	2	8	13	8
★★★★	1	7	9	4

8 The table alongside gives the age distribution of inmates in a prison on December 31, 2011.

A new prisoner entered the prison on January 1, 2012. Estimate the probability that:

- **a** the prisoner was male
- **b** the prisoner was aged from 17 to 19
- **c** the prisoner was 19 or under and was female
- **d** the prisoner was aged from 30 to 49 and was male.

Age distribution of prison inmates

Age	Female	Male	Total
15	0	6	6
16	5	23	28
17 - 19	26	422	448
20 - 24	41	1124	1165
25 - 29	36	1001	1037
30 - 34	32	751	783
35 - 39	31	520	551
40 - 49	24	593	617
50 - 59	16	234	250
60+	5	148	153
Total	216	4822	5038

Global context

How much time do we have?

Statement of inquiry: Collecting and interpreting data can help us to understand our place in the world.

Global context: Identities and relationships

Key concept: Relationships

Related concepts: Change, Representation

Objectives: Knowing and understanding, Applying mathematics in real-life contexts

Approaches to learning: Communication, Self-management

C SAMPLE SPACE

A **sample space** is the set of all possible outcomes of an experiment.

Possible ways of representing sample spaces are:
- listing them
- using a 2-dimensional grid
- using a tree diagram
- using a Venn diagram.

Example 4

When two coins are tossed, the possible outcomes are:

two heads   head and tail   tail and head   two tails

Represent the sample space for tossing two coins using:
- **a** a list
- **b** a 2-D grid
- **c** a tree diagram.

We let H represent a 'head' and T represent a 'tail'.

a {HH, HT, TH, TT}

b 2-D grid with coin 1 on horizontal axis (H, T) and coin 2 on vertical axis (H, T), showing four points.

c Tree diagram:
- coin 1: H → coin 2: H, T
- coin 1: T → coin 2: H, T

Example 5

Illustrate, using a tree diagram, the possible outcomes when drawing two marbles from a bag containing red, green, and yellow marbles.

Let R be the event of getting a red,
G be the event of getting a green, and
Y be the event of getting a yellow.

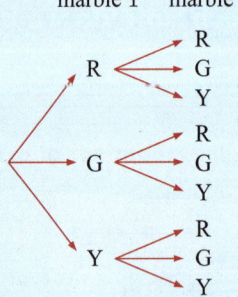

Each branch of the tree diagram represents a possible outcome.

EXERCISE 13C

1 List the sample space for the following:
  - **a** twirling a square spinner labelled A, B, C, D
  - **b** the genders of a 2-child family
  - **c** the order in which 4 blocks A, B, C, and D can be lined up
  - **d** the 8 different 3-child families.
  - **e** tossing a coin   **i** twice   **ii** three times   **iii** four times.

2 Use a 2-dimensional grid to illustrate the sample space for:
  - **a** rolling a die and tossing a coin simultaneously
  - **b** rolling two dice

c rolling a die and spinning a spinner with sides A, B, C, D

d twirling two square spinners, one labelled A, B, C, D, and the other 1, 2, 3, 4.

3 Illustrate on a tree diagram the sample space for:

a tossing a 5-cent and 10-cent coin simultaneously

b tossing a coin and twirling an equilateral triangular spinner labelled A, B, and C

c twirling two equilateral triangular spinners labelled 1, 2, 3, and X, Y, Z respectively

d drawing two tickets from a hat containing pink, blue, and white tickets

e selecting bag A or bag B, then drawing a ball from that bag.

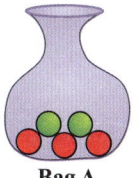
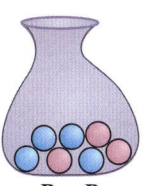

Bag A   Bag B

4 Draw a Venn diagram to show a class of 20 students in which 7 study History and Geography, 10 study History, and 15 study Geography.

D THEORETICAL PROBABILITY

Once we have represented the sample space of an experiment, we can use it to calculate probabilities.

If a sample space has n outcomes which are **equally likely** to occur when the experiment is performed once, then each outcome has probability $\frac{1}{n}$ of occurring.

An **event** occurs when we obtain an outcome with a particular property or feature.

When the outcomes of an experiment are equally likely, the probability of an event E occurring is given by:

$$P(E) = \frac{\text{number of outcomes corresponding to } E}{\text{number of outcomes in the sample space}}$$

Example 6

Suppose three coins are tossed simultaneously. Find the probability of getting:

a three heads   **b** at least one head.

The possible outcomes are:

{HHH, HHT, HTH, THH, TTH, THT, HTT, TTT}.

There are 8 possible outcomes.

a P(three heads) = $\frac{1}{8}$ ← three heads only occurs in the outcome HHH
← 8 possible outcomes

b P(at least one head) = $\frac{7}{8}$ ← all outcomes except TTT contain at least one head
← 8 possible outcomes

EXERCISE 13D

1 The three letters O, D, and G are placed at random in a row. Find the probability of:
   a spelling DOG
   b O appearing first
   c O not appearing first
   d spelling DOG or GOD.

2 Determine the probability that a randomly selected 3-child family consists of:
   a all boys
   b all girls
   c boy, then girl, then girl
   d two girls and a boy
   e a girl for the eldest
   f at least one boy.

3 Four friends Alex, Bodi, Claire, and Daniel sit randomly in a row. Determine the probability that:
   a Alex is on one of the ends
   b Claire and Daniel are on the ends
   c Bodi is on an end, and Claire is seated next to him
   d Alex and Claire sit next to each other.

Example 7   🔊 Self Tutor

A die has the numbers 0, 0, 1, 1, 4, and 5. It is rolled twice.
 a Illustrate the possible outcomes using a 2-dimensional grid.
 b Hence find the probability of getting:
    i a total of 5
    ii two numbers which are the same.

a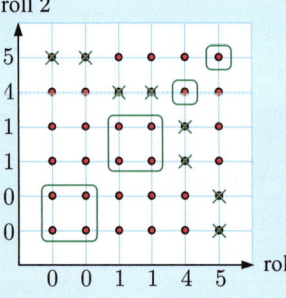

b There are $6 \times 6 = 36$ possible outcomes.

   i P(total of 5)
      $= \frac{8}{36}$ {those with a $\times$}
      $= \frac{2}{9}$

   ii P(same numbers)
      $= \frac{10}{36}$ {those circled}
      $= \frac{5}{18}$

---

4 a Draw a grid to illustrate the sample space when a 10-cent and a 50-cent coin are tossed simultaneously.
   b Hence, determine the probability of getting:
      i   two heads
      ii two tails
      iii exactly one head
      iv at least one head.

5 A coin and a pentagonal spinner with sectors 1, 2, 3, 4, and 5 are tossed and spun respectively.
   a Draw a grid to illustrate the sample space of possible outcomes.
   b Use your grid to determine the chance of getting:
      i   a head and a 4
      ii a tail and an odd number
      iii an even number
      iv a tail or a 3.

6 **a** Use a grid to display the possible outcomes when a pair of dice is rolled.

   b Hence, determine the probability of:

   i one die showing a 4 and the other a 5
   ii both dice showing the same number
   iii at least one of the dice showing a 3
   iv either a 4 or 6 being displayed
   v both dice showing even numbers
   vi the sum of the numbers being 7.

7 A die has the numbers 1, 2, 2, 2, 5, and 6. It is rolled twice.

   a Draw a grid to illustrate the possible outcomes.
   b Hence, find the probability of getting:

   i a 2 and a 5
   ii a total of 7
   iii numbers which are the same
   iv at least one 6
   v at least one prime number
   vi numbers whose product is at least 5.

8 The spinners shown are spun once, and the numbers spun are multiplied together.

 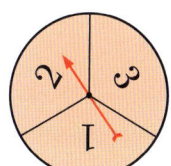

   a Find the probability that the result is:

   i 9
   ii 6
   iii greater than 5
   iv prime.

   b Is the result more likely to be even or odd?

Example 8   🔊 **Self Tutor**

In a library group of 50 readers, 31 like science fiction, 20 like detective stories, and 12 dislike both.

a Draw a Venn diagram to represent this information.
b If a reader is randomly selected, find the probability that he or she:
   i likes science fiction and detective stories
   ii likes exactly one of science fiction and detective stories.

a Let S represent readers who like science fiction, and D represent readers who like detective stories.

We are given that $a + b = 31$
$$b + c = 20$$
$$a + b + c = 50 - 12 = 38$$
$$\therefore c = 38 - 31 = 7$$
$$\therefore b = 13 \text{ and } a = 18$$

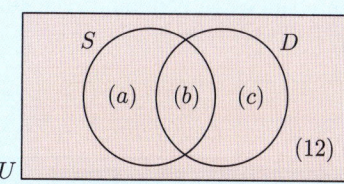

b **i** P(likes both) $= \frac{13}{50}$

ii P(likes exactly one) $= \frac{18 + 7}{50}$
$$= \tfrac{1}{2}$$

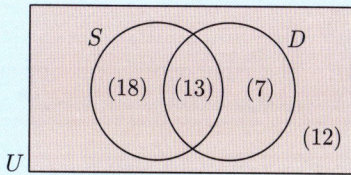

9 The Venn diagram shows the sports played by the students in a Year 10 class.

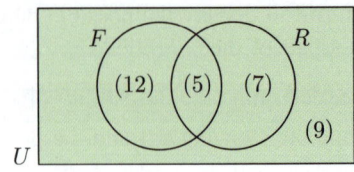

$F \equiv$ football
$R \equiv$ rugby

  a How many students are in the class?

  b A student is chosen at random. Find the probability that the student:

    i plays football   **ii** plays both sports

    iii plays football or rugby   **iv** plays exactly one of these sports.

10 In a class of 24 students, 10 study Biology, 12 study Chemistry, and 5 study neither Biology nor Chemistry.

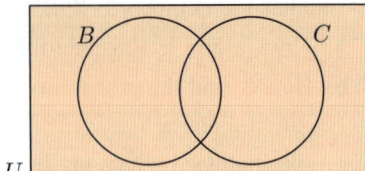

  a Copy and complete the Venn diagram.

  b Find the probability that a student picked at random from the class studies:

    i Chemistry, but not Biology

    ii both Chemistry and Biology.

11 50 tourists went on a 'thrill seekers' holiday. 40 went white-water rafting, 21 went paragliding, and each tourist did at least one of these activities.

Find the probability that a randomly selected tourist:

  a participated in both activities   **b** went white-water rafting but not paragliding.

PUZZLE   THE DICE PROBLEM

Suppose we roll a pair of standard dice, and find the sum of the numbers rolled.

We can use a 2-dimensional grid to find the probability of obtaining each sum:

Sum	2	3	4	5	6	7	8	9	10	11	12
Probability	$\frac{1}{36}$	$\frac{2}{36}$	$\frac{3}{36}$	$\frac{4}{36}$	$\frac{5}{36}$	$\frac{6}{36}$	$\frac{5}{36}$	$\frac{4}{36}$	$\frac{3}{36}$	$\frac{2}{36}$	$\frac{1}{36}$

Can you find another way to label 2 dice with positive whole numbers, so that the sum probabilities are the same as those given above?

Hint: The same number can appear more than once on a die, and numbers greater than 6 can be used.

E COMPOUND EVENTS

We will now look at calculating probabilities for **combined events**, which are also called **compound events**. We will consider both **independent events** and **dependent events**.

INDEPENDENT EVENTS

Two events are **independent** if the occurrence of each event does not affect the occurrence of the other.

For example, suppose the spinners alongside are spun simultaneously.

Let A be the event *the first spinner lands on red*, and B be the event *the second spinner lands on an even number*.

Whether A occurs or not does not affect the probability of B occurring. Likewise, whether B occurs or not does not affect the probability of A occurring. Therefore, A and B are independent events.

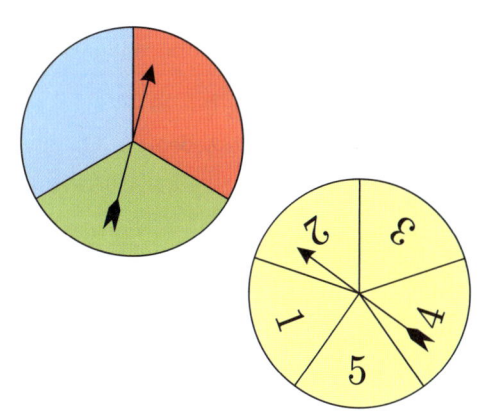

Now, we know that $P(A) = \frac{1}{3}$, and $P(B) = \frac{2}{5}$.

By listing each of the possible outcomes, we can see that $P(A \text{ and } B) = \frac{2}{15}$.

$$\{R1, \mathbf{R2}, R3, \mathbf{R4}, R5, G1, G2, G3, G4, G5, B1, B2, B3, B4, B5\}$$

We notice that $\frac{2}{15} = \frac{1}{3} \times \frac{2}{5}$, so $P(A \text{ and } B) = P(A) \times P(B)$.

If two events A and B are **independent**, then $P(A \text{ and } B) = P(A) \times P(B)$.

Example 9   ◀) Self Tutor

A coin is tossed and a die rolled simultaneously. Find the probability that a tail and a '2' result.

'Getting a tail' and 'rolling a 2' are independent events.

∴ P(a tail **and** a '2') = P(a tail) × P(a '2')
$= \frac{1}{2} \times \frac{1}{6}$
$= \frac{1}{12}$

This rule can be extended to any number of independent events.

For example: If A, B, and C are all independent events, then
$$P(A \text{ and } B \text{ and } C) = P(A) \times P(B) \times P(C).$$

EXERCISE 13E.1

1. A die is rolled, and the spinner alongside is spun. Find the probability of obtaining:

    a a '5' and a green

    b an even number and a non-red.

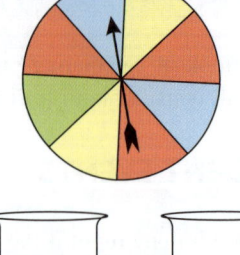

2. A disc is selected from each of the containers alongside. Find the probability of selecting:

    a a red disc from **A** and a green disc from **B**

    b a blue disc from both containers.

A   **B**

3. A school has two photocopiers. On any one day, machine A has an 8% chance of having a paper jam, and machine B has a 12% chance of having a paper jam.
Determine the probability that, on any one day, both machines will:

    a have paper jams   b work uninterrupted.

4. A boy and a girl were each asked what day of the week they were born. Find the probability that:

    a the boy was born on a Monday and the girl was born on a Wednesday

    b the boy was born on a weekend, but the girl was not

    c both children were born on a weekday.

5. Each day, Steve attempts the easy, medium, and hard crosswords in the newspaper. He has probability 0.84 of completing the easy crossword, probability 0.59 of completing the medium crossword, and probability 0.11 of completing the hard crossword.
Find the probability that, on any given day, Steve will:

    a complete all 3 crosswords

    b leave all 3 crosswords incomplete

    c complete the easy and medium crosswords, but not the hard crossword

    d complete the medium crossword, but not the other two crosswords.

6. A drawing pin was tossed into the air 600 times. It landed on its back 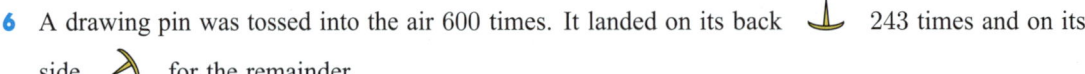 243 times and on its side   for the remainder.

    a Estimate the probability that, when tossed once, this drawing pin will land on its:

        i back   ii side.

    b Suppose the drawing pin is tossed twice. Estimate the probability that:

        i it lands on its back both times   ii it lands on its side both times.

7. A biased coin is flipped 200 times. It lands on heads 143 times, and on tails for the remainder. If the coin is flipped 3 times, estimate the probability of getting:

    a all heads   b all tails.

Example 10

A marble is selected at random from each of the bags alongside.

a Draw a tree diagram to display the possible outcomes.

b Find the probability of obtaining a green marble and a yellow marble.

Bag A

Bag B

a Let G represent a green marble,
Y represent a yellow marble, and
R represent a red marble.

*If 2 or more branches satisfy the event, the probabilities are **added**.*

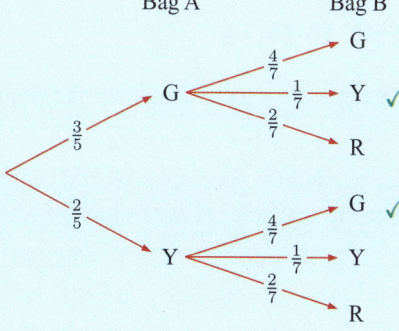

b P(a green and a yellow)
= P(GY or YG)   {branches marked ✓}
= $\frac{3}{5} \times \frac{1}{7} + \frac{2}{5} \times \frac{4}{7}$
= $\frac{11}{35}$

8 Each of the spinners alongside is spun once.

a Copy and complete this tree diagram for the possible outcomes:

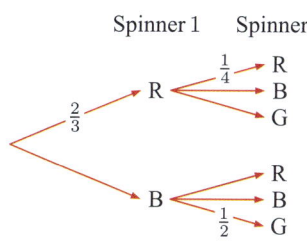

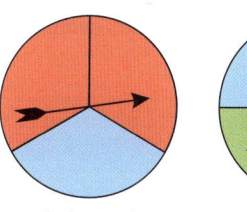
Spinner 1

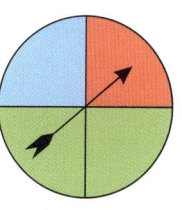
Spinner 2

b Find the probability that:
  i the spinners land on the same colour
  ii the spinners land on different colours
  iii exactly one of the spinners lands on blue.

9 A ticket is selected at random from each of the boxes alongside.

a Draw a tree diagram to display the possible outcomes.

b Find the probability of obtaining:
  i a blue ticket and a green ticket
  ii two tickets of the same colour
  iii exactly one pink ticket.

c Find the sum of the probabilities in **b**. Explain your result.

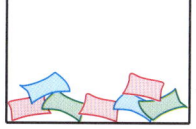
Box A

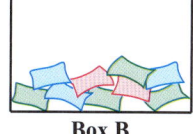
Box B

10 Sharon, Christine, and Keith have agreed to meet at a restaurant for lunch. Sharon has probability 0.8 of being on time, Christine has probability 0.7 of being on time, and Keith has probability 0.4 of being on time.

    a Draw a tree diagram to display the possible outcomes.

    b Determine the probability that at least 2 people will arrive on time.

DEPENDENT EVENTS

Dependent events are events for which the occurrence of one event *does affect* the occurrence of the other event.

Suppose a bag contains 5 blue discs and 3 yellow discs. One disc is selected at random, and put to one side. A second disc is then selected from the bag.

Let A be the event that the *first* disc is blue, and B be the event that the *second* disc is blue.

Now, if A occurs, then $\quad P(B) = \dfrac{4}{7} \quad \begin{matrix}\leftarrow \text{ 4 blue discs remaining} \\ \leftarrow \text{ 7 discs left to choose from}\end{matrix}$

However, if A does not occur, then $\quad P(B) = \dfrac{5}{7} \quad \begin{matrix}\leftarrow \text{ 5 blue discs remaining} \\ \leftarrow \text{ 7 discs left to choose from}\end{matrix}$

The occurrence of A *does* affect the probability of B occurring. Therefore A and B are **dependent events**.

The rule for finding compound event probabilities for dependent events is different from the rule for independent events.

If A and B are dependent events, then $\quad P(A \text{ and } B) = P(A) \times P(B \text{ given that } A \text{ has occurred})$.

Example 11 ◀)) Self Tutor

A fruit bowl contains 3 apples and 5 oranges. Callan selects a piece of fruit at random, and eats it. His sister Michelle then selects a piece of fruit for herself.

Find the probability that:

    a both pieces of fruit selected are apples

    b Callan selects an orange and Michelle selects an apple.

a   P(both are apples)

= P(Callan selects an apple *and* Michelle selects an apple)

= P(Callan selects an apple)

       × P(Michelle selects an apple *given* that Callan selects an apple)

$= \dfrac{3}{8} \times \dfrac{2}{7} \quad \begin{matrix}\leftarrow \text{ 2 apples remaining} \\ \leftarrow \text{ 7 pieces of fruit to choose from}\end{matrix}$

$= \dfrac{6}{56}$

$= \dfrac{3}{28}$

b P(Callan selects an orange *and* Michelle selects an apple)

= P(Callan selects an orange)

$\qquad$ × P(Michelle selects an apple *given* that Callan selects an orange)

= $\frac{5}{8} \times \frac{3}{7}$ ← 3 apples remaining
← 7 pieces of fruit to choose from

= $\frac{15}{56}$

EXERCISE 13E.2

1 A bucket contains 2 orange, 5 white, and 3 yellow ping pong balls. Two balls are selected at random from the bucket, the second being selected without replacing the first. Find the probability that:

a both balls are orange **b** the first ball is yellow, and the second ball is white.

2 Two cards are selected, without replacement, from a standard deck of 52 cards. Find the probability that:

a both of the cards are red

b the first card is a club, and the second card is a diamond

c both of the cards are aces.

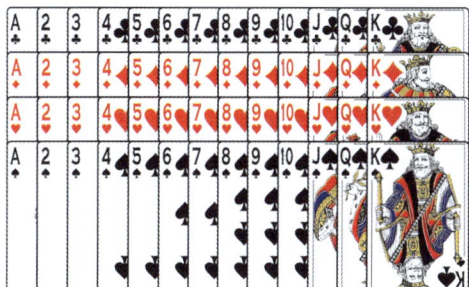

Example 12 ◀)) Self Tutor

A container holds 3 banana iceblocks, 4 chocolate iceblocks, and 2 raspberry iceblocks. George randomly selects an iceblock from the container and eats it. His brother Oliver then randomly selects an iceblock from the container.

a Draw a tree diagram to display the possible outcomes.

b Find the probability that the brothers selected the same type of iceblock.

a Let B represent a banana iceblock,
C represent a chocolate iceblock, and
R represent a raspberry iceblock.

George has 9 iceblocks to choose from. Oliver has only 8 iceblocks to choose from.

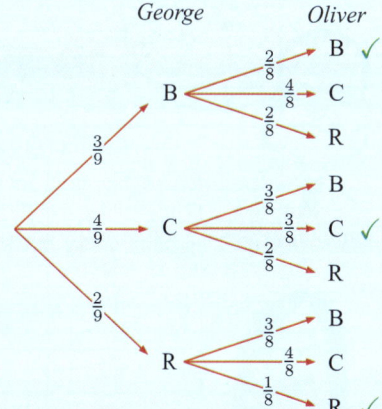

b P(brothers selected the same type of iceblock)

= P(BB or CC or RR) {those marked ✓}

= $\frac{3}{9} \times \frac{2}{8} + \frac{4}{9} \times \frac{3}{8} + \frac{2}{9} \times \frac{1}{8}$

= $\frac{20}{72}$

= $\frac{5}{18}$

3 A drawer contains 5 blue pens, 3 red pens, and 2 green pens. A pen is selected at random from the drawer and put to one side. A second pen is then selected at random from the drawer.
   a Draw a tree diagram to display the possible outcomes.
   b Find the probability that:
      i the selected pens are the same colour
      ii exactly one of the pens is green.

4 Matt is the best player in his lacrosse team. He has an injured knee, and has only a 60% chance of playing the next game. The team has a 70% chance of winning the next game if Matt plays, but only a 45% chance of winning if he does not play.
   a Represent this information on a tree diagram.
   b Find the probability that the team will win the next game.

5 In a netball team, the Goal Shooter takes 65% of the team's shots, and scores 70% of the time. The Goal Attack takes the remainder of the shots, and scores 60% of the time.
   Find the probability that the team will score with their next shot.

6 A fair coin is tossed. If the result is heads, one marble is selected from the bag alongside. If the result is tails, two marbles are selected, without replacement. Find the probability that at least one red marble will be selected.

7 The spinner below is used to select box A, B, or C. Two discs are then randomly selected without replacement from that box.

 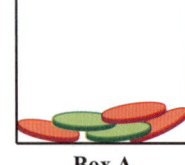 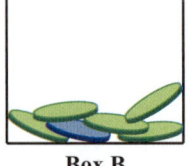 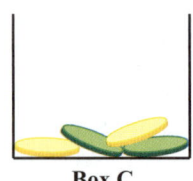

Box A   Box B   Box C

Find the probability that exactly one green disc is selected.

8 A coin is selected at random from pot A and placed in pot B. Then, a coin is selected at random from pot B and placed in pot A. Finally, a coin is selected at random from pot A. Find the probability that this coin is gold.

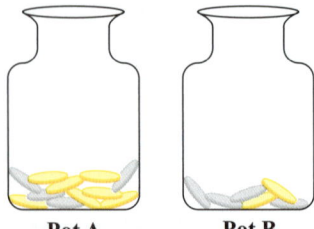

9 Jill and Mandy are considering whether to go to a party. If their friend Donna does *not* go, the probability that Jill will attend is 0.4, and the probability that Mandy will attend is 0.6. If Donna *does* go to the party, Jill and Mandy's probabilities will increase to 0.5 and 0.7 respectively.
   The probability that Donna will go to the party is 0.8. Find the probability that exactly two of the three friends will attend.

10 A frog is in the middle of a 3×3 arrangement of squares. Each time the frog jumps, it lands with equal probability on one of the adjacent squares (either horizontally, vertically, or diagonally). Find the probability that, after 3 jumps, the frog is on:

   a the middle square   **b** a corner square

   c an edge square that is not a corner square.

F   CONDITIONAL PROBABILITY

We are often interested in the probability of an event occurring *given* that another event occurs.

For example:

"Given that it is raining, what is the probability of Newcastle winning?"

"Given that George likes sausages, what is the probability that he also likes steak?"

"Given that Mae has to pick up her son on the way, what is the probability that she will be late?"

If A and B are events, then $P(A \mid B)$ means "the probability of A occurring given that B has occurred".

$A \mid B$ is read as 'A given B'.

Venn diagrams, two-way tables, and 2-dimensional grids are useful for answering questions involving conditional probability.

Example 13   ◆) Self Tutor

In a group of 25 students, 15 like milk (M), and 17 like iced coffee (C). Two students like neither, and 9 students like both.

One student is randomly selected from the class. Find the probability that the student:

   a likes milk   **b** likes milk given that he or she likes iced coffee.

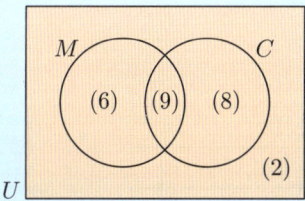

a 15 of the 25 students like milk.

    $\therefore \ P(M) = \frac{15}{25} = \frac{3}{5}$

b Of the 17 who like iced coffee, 9 also like milk.

    $\therefore \ P(M \mid C) = \frac{9}{17}$

EXERCISE 13F

1 In a class of 25 students, 19 have fair hair, 15 have blue eyes, and 22 have fair hair, blue eyes, or both. A child is selected at random. Find the probability that the child has:
   a fair hair and blue eyes
   b blue eyes, given that the child has fair hair.

2 A French examination has an aural part and a written part. When 30 students sit for the examination, 25 pass aural, 26 pass written, and 3 fail both parts. Determine the probability that a randomly selected student:
   a passed written, given that they passed aural
   b failed written, given that they passed aural.

3
28 members of a youth group went bushwalking. 23 got sunburn, 8 got blisters, and 5 got both sunburn and blisters. Determine the probability that a randomly selected person:
   a got blisters or sunburn
   b got blisters, given that the person was sunburnt
   c was sunburnt, given that the person did not get blisters.

4 In a small town there are 3 supermarkets: P, Q, and R. 60% of the population shop at P, 36% shop at Q, and 34% shop at R. 18% shop at P and Q, 15% shop at P and R, 4% shop at Q and R, and 2% shop at all 3 supermarkets. A person is selected at random.
Determine the probability that the person shops at:
   a none of the supermarkets
   b P, given that the person shops at at least one supermarket
   c R, given that the person shops at P or Q or both
   d Q, given that the person shops at exactly one supermarket.

Example 14   ◀) Self Tutor

A restaurant owner collected the following data from his customers one night:

		Dine in	Takeaway	Delivery
Amount spent	Less than $20	12	17	9
	At least $20	31	15	13

Find the probability that a randomly selected customer:
a spent at least $20
b spent less than $20, given that they had their meal delivered
c dined in, given that they spent less than $20.

		Dine in	Takeaway	Delivery	Total
Amount spent	Less than $20	12	17	9	38
	At least $20	31	15	13	59
	Total	43	32	22	97

a P(spent at least $20) = $\frac{59}{97}$

b Of the 22 customers who had their meal delivered, 9 spent less than $20.

  $\therefore$ P(spent less than \$20 | delivered) $= \frac{9}{22}$

  c Of the 38 customers who spent less than $20, 12 dined in.

  $\therefore$ P(dined in | spent less than \$20) $= \frac{12}{38} = \frac{6}{19}$

5 Lee's soccer team played 37 games this season. Their results are shown in the two-way table alongside.

Find the probability that a randomly selected game was:

	Win	Draw	Lose
Home	11	5	3
Away	6	8	4

  a won
  b won, given that it was at home
  c at home, given that it was won.

6 The Year 10 students at a school were asked how many people and pets lived in their house. The results are shown alongside.

Find the probability that a randomly selected student's house has:

		\multicolumn{4}{c}{Number of people}
		2	3	4	5+
Number of pets	0	4	6	7	3
	1	4	11	12	6
	2	2	9	11	7
	3+	1	5	7	5

  a 2 pets, given that it has 4 people
  b 3 people, given that it has at least 2 pets
  c at most 1 pet, given that it has at least 4 people.

Example 15   ◀)) Self Tutor

A pair of dice is rolled. Given that at least one of the dice shows a 6, find the probability that the sum of the rolls is 10.

Let A be the event "the sum of the rolls is 10".

Let B be the event "at least one of the dice shows a 6".

Of the 11 outcomes in B {those highlighted}, 2 of the outcomes are also in A {those with a ×}.

$\therefore$ P$(A \mid B) = \frac{2}{11}$

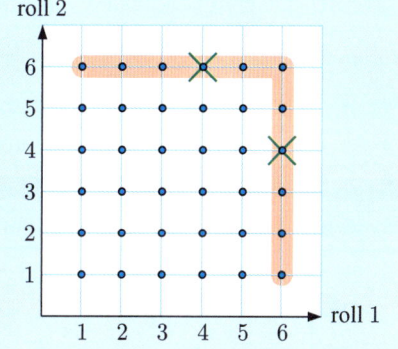

7 A pair of dice is rolled.

  a Given that both of the dice show less than 5, find the probability that the sum of the rolls is 6.
  b Given that the sum of the rolls is 8, find the probability that at least one of the dice shows a 3.

8 Suppose each spinner alongside is spun once.
Given that exactly one of the spins is green, find the probability that the result of spinner 2 is green.

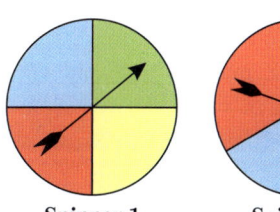

Spinner 1   Spinner 2

9 A card is selected at random from each of the bags shown.

    a Find the probability that the card drawn from bag A is a 4.

    b You are told that the sum of the selected cards is 5.

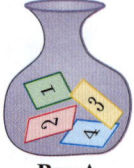

Bag A   Bag B

        i Do you think this increases or decreases the probability that the card drawn from bag A is a 4? Explain your answer.

        ii Find the probability that the card drawn from bag A is a 4, given that the sum of the selected cards is 5.

G   MUTUALLY EXCLUSIVE AND INDEPENDENT EVENTS

MUTUALLY EXCLUSIVE EVENTS

> Two events are **mutually exclusive** or **disjoint** if they have no common outcomes.
>
> If A and B are mutually exclusive events then $P(A \text{ and } B) = 0$.

For example, suppose we select a card at random from a normal pack of 52 playing cards. Consider these events:

Event X: the card is a heart   *Event Y:* the card is an ace   *Event Z:* the card is a 7

Notice that:

- X and Y have a common outcome, the Ace of hearts
- X and Z have a common outcome, the 7 of hearts
- Y and Z do not have a common outcome, so they are mutually exclusive.

The events Y and Z are shown on the 2-dimensional grid below:

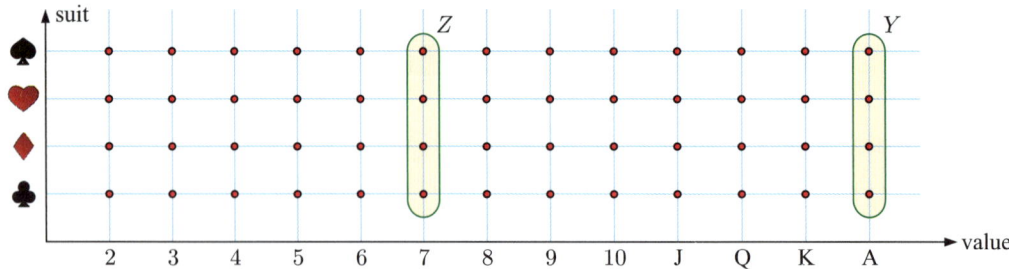

Notice that $P(Y \text{ or } Z) = \frac{8}{52}$ and $P(Y) + P(Z) = \frac{4}{52} + \frac{4}{52} = \frac{8}{52}$.

> If two events A and B are **mutually exclusive**, then
> $$P(A \text{ or } B) = P(A) + P(B)$$

Now consider the events X and Z, which are *not* mutually exclusive since they have a common outcome: the 7 of hearts.

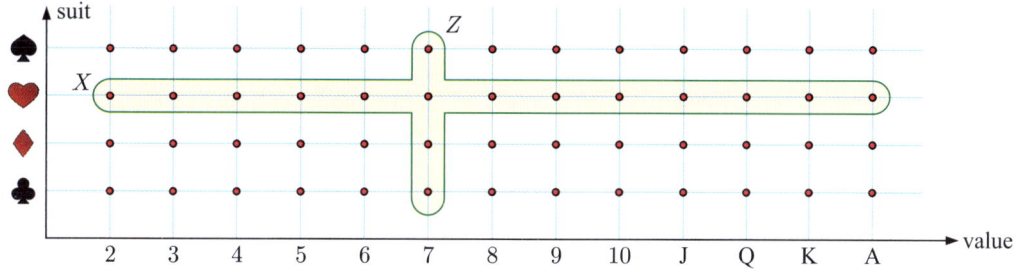

Notice that $P(X \text{ or } Z) = \frac{16}{52}$ and $P(X) + P(Z) = \frac{13}{52} + \frac{4}{52} = \frac{17}{52}$.

These values are not the same, since when we find $P(X) + P(Z)$ the common outcome is counted *twice*.

Actually, $P(X \text{ or } Z) = P(X) + P(Z) - P(X \text{ and } Z)$.

If two events A and B are **not mutually exclusive** then

$P(A \text{ or } B) = P(A) + P(B) - P(A \text{ and } B)$.

Notice the similarity to
$n(A \cup B) = n(A) + n(B) - n(A \cap B)$.

Example 16 ◀)) Self Tutor

Suppose $P(A) = 0.2$, $P(B) = 0.6$, and $P(A \text{ and } B) = 0.1$.
a Are A and B mutually exclusive events? Explain your answer.
b Find $P(A \text{ or } B)$.

a A and B are *not* mutually exclusive, since $P(A \text{ and } B) \neq 0$.
b $P(A \text{ or } B) = P(A) + P(B) - P(A \text{ and } B)$
$= 0.2 + 0.6 - 0.1$
$= 0.7$

INDEPENDENT EVENTS

In **Section E**, we saw that two events are **independent** if the occurrence of each event does not affect the occurrence of the other.

If A and B are independent events, then $P(A \text{ and } B) = P(A) \times P(B)$.

Example 17 ◀)) Self Tutor

Suppose $P(X) = 0.6$ and $P(Y) = 0.2$. Find $P(X \text{ and } Y)$ given that X and Y are:
a mutually exclusive **b** independent.

a If X and Y are mutually exclusive, then $P(X \text{ and } Y) = 0$.
b If X and Y are independent, then $P(X \text{ and } Y) = P(X) \times P(Y)$
$= 0.6 \times 0.2$
$= 0.12$

EXERCISE 13G

1 An ordinary die with faces 1, 2, 3, 4, 5, and 6 is rolled once. Consider these events:

    A: rolling a 1 B: rolling a 3
    C: rolling an odd number D: rolling an even number
    E: rolling a prime number F: rolling a result greater than 3.

List the pairs of events which are mutually exclusive.

2 A coin and an ordinary die are tossed and rolled simultaneously.

   a Draw a grid showing the 12 possible outcomes.
   b Let A be the event 'tossing a head' and B be the event 'rolling a 5'.
      i Are A and B mutually exclusive? Explain your answer.
     ii Find P(A or B) and P(A and B).
    iii Check that P(A or B) = P(A) + P(B) − P(A and B).

3 Suppose $P(A) = 0.7$, $P(B) = 0.2$, and $P(A \text{ and } B) = 0.15$.

   a Are A and B mutually exclusive events? Explain your answer.
   b Find P(A or B).

4 Suppose $P(X) = 0.3$ and $P(X \text{ or } Y) = 0.7$. Given that X and Y are mutually exclusive, find $P(Y)$.

5 Suppose $P(C) = 0.6$ and $P(D) = 0.7$. Explain why C and D are not mutually exclusive.

6 Let $P(A) = 0.4$ and $P(B) = 0.25$. Find P(A and B) given that A and B are:

   a mutually exclusive   **b** independent.

7 X and Y are independent events such that $P(X) = 0.5$ and $P(Y) = 0.3$. Find P(X or Y).

8 A and B are independent events such that $P(A \text{ or } B) = 0.9$ and $P(A \text{ and } B) = 0.4$. Find $P(A)$ and $P(B)$ given that $P(A) > P(B)$.

REVIEW SET 13A

1 Donna kept records of the number of clients she interviewed over consecutive days.

   a For how many days did Donna keep records?
   b Estimate the probability that tomorrow Donna will interview:
      i no clients
     ii four or more clients
    iii less than three clients.

Number of clients	Frequency
0	1
1	6
2	12
3	8
4	6
5	3
6	0
7	2

2 A coin and a pentagonal spinner with sides labelled A, B, C, D, and E are tossed and spun simultaneously. Illustrate the possible outcomes using a 2-dimensional grid.

3 When a box of drawing pins was dropped onto the floor, 49 pins landed on their backs, and 32 landed on their sides. Estimate, to 2 decimal places, the probability of a drawing pin landing:

   a on its back   **b** on its side.

back   side

4 A wheel numbered 1 to 20 is spun.
Find the probability that the result is:
  a 13
  b a multiple of 3
  c greater than 11.

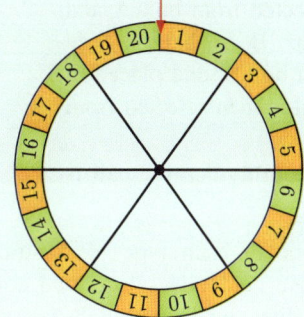

5 On a particular day, 500 people visited a carnival. 300 people rode the Ferris wheel, and 350 people rode the roller coaster. Each person rode at least one of these attractions.
  a Display this information on a Venn diagram.
  b Find the probability that a randomly chosen person:
   i rode the Ferris wheel, but not the roller coaster
   ii rode the roller coaster, given that they rode the Ferris wheel.

6 A bag contains 4 green and 3 red marbles. Two marbles are randomly selected from the bag, the first being put to one side before the second is drawn. Determine the probability that:
  a both are green
  b they are different in colour.

7 A chess piece is placed on a random square of an 8×8 chess board. A second piece is then placed at random on one of the unoccupied squares.
Find the probability that:
  a the two pieces lie on the same row
  b the pieces lie on the same row or column.

8 Brothers Paul, Cameron, and Bruce play in the same rugby team. Their probabilities of getting injured during the season are 0.4, 0.3, and 0.2 respectively. What is the most likely number of injured brothers during the season?

9 A married couple own a large car and a small car. Glen uses the small car 30% of the time. When he goes to the shops, the probability that he can park in the car park is 80% if he has the small car, and 60% if he has the large car.
Find the probability that, on a given day, Glen is able to park in the shop's car park.

10 The two-way table alongside describes the books on Elizabeth's bookshelf.
  a How many books are on Elizabeth's bookshelf?

	Biography	Novel	Reference
Softcover	3	22	6
Hardcover	5	7	4

  b Find the probability that a randomly selected book is:
   i a softcover book
   ii a hardcover reference book
   iii a novel, given that it has a hard cover.

11 A ball is selected from box A and placed in box B. A ball is then selected from box B, and placed in box C. A ball is then selected from box C.
Find the probability that the ball is blue.

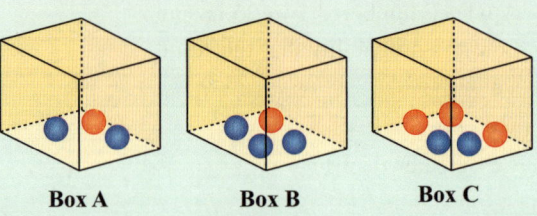

Box A   Box B   Box C

12 Tyson has one of each type of Australian coin in his pocket. He randomly selects two coins from his pocket, replacing the first coin before selecting the second.

20 cents   10 cents   5 cents

2 dollars   1 dollar   50 cents

  a Draw a 2-dimensional grid to display the possible outcomes.
  b Find the probability that:
    i both coins are silver
    ii at least one of the coins is the 50 cent coin
    iii the value of the coins is at least 65 cents.
  c Given that the value of the coins is at least 65 cents, find the probability that at least one of the coins is gold.

13 Let $P(A) = 0.2$ and $P(B) = 0.7$. Find $P(A \text{ and } B)$ given that A and B are:
  a mutually exclusive   **b** independent.

REVIEW SET 13B

1 Pierre conducted a survey to determine the ages of people walking through a shopping mall. The results are shown in the table alongside. Estimate the probability that the next person Pierre meets in the shopping mall will be:

Age	Frequency
0 - 19	22
20 - 39	43
40 - 59	39
60+	14

  a between 20 and 39 years of age
  b less than 40 years of age   **c** at least 20 years of age.

2 Use a tree diagram to illustrate the sample spaces for the following:
  a Bags A, B, and C contain green and yellow tickets. A bag is selected and then a ticket taken from it.
  b Martina and Justine play tennis. The first to win three sets wins the match.

3 The two-way table alongside shows the results from asking the question "Do you like the school uniform?".
If a student is randomly selected from these year groups, estimate the probability that the student:

	Likes	Dislikes
Year 8	129	21
Year 9	108	42
Year 10	81	69

  a likes the school uniform
  b dislikes the school uniform
  c is in Year 8 and dislikes the uniform.

4 The digits 1, 6, and 9 are placed in random order to create a 3 digit number. Find the probability that this number will be a perfect square.

5 A farmer fences his rectangular property into 9 rectangular paddocks as shown.

A paddock is selected at random. Find the probability that it has:
  a no fences on the boundary of the property
  b one fence on the boundary of the property
  c two fences on the boundary of the property.

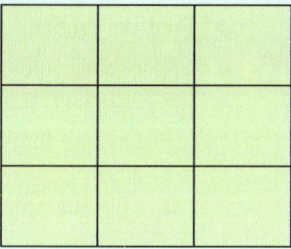

6 A paper plate is tossed in the air 50 times. It lands face up 37 times, and lands face down 13 times.
  a Estimate the probability that the paper plate will land face up next time it is thrown.
  b If the plate is tossed in the air three times, estimate the probability that the plate will land face down on all three occasions.

7 Bag X contains three white and two red marbles. Bag Y contains one white and three red marbles. A bag is randomly chosen, and two marbles are drawn from it.
  a Illustrate the given information on a tree diagram.
  b Determine the probability of drawing two marbles of the same colour.

8 A knife block contains 6 knives of different sizes. Each knife fits exactly into its specific hole, and will also fit into the holes of larger knives.

Suppose a knife is chosen at random, and a hole in the knife block is chosen at random. Find the probability that the knife will fit in the hole.

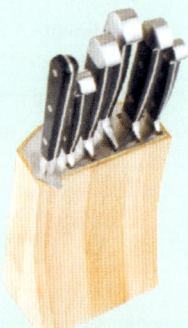

9 Matthew is taking a mathematics test. There is a 2% chance that his calculator will not work. If his calculator works, Matthew has a 70% probability of passing the test. If his calculator does not work, Matthew has a 55% probability of passing the test.
Find the probability that Matthew passes the test.

10 The spinners alongside are each spun once. Given that the spins are the same colour, find the probability that they are both red.

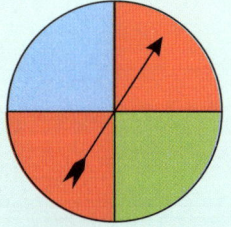 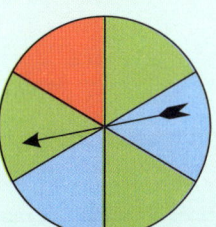

11 Events A, B, and C are all mutually exclusive with each other.
$P(A \text{ or } B) = 0.5$, $P(B \text{ or } C) = 0.75$, and $P(A \text{ or } C) = 0.55$. Find the probability of each event occurring.

12 Shelley draws 3 cards without replacement from the container alongside. She will win a prize if all 3 cards are the same colour.

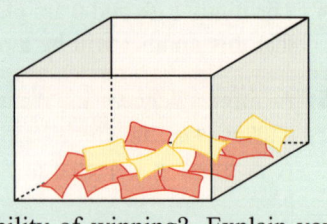

   a Find the probability that Shelley will win a prize.

   b Suppose the rules change so that Shelley now draws her cards *with* replacement.

      i Do you think this increases or decreases her probability of winning? Explain your answer.

      ii Find the probability of Shelley winning.

13 In a weightlifting competition, 3 competitors are given one chance to lift a weight of their choosing. The table alongside shows the weights chosen by each competitor, and their probability of lifting it.

Competitor	Weight	Probability
Ihor	210 kg	0.5
Ruslan	225 kg	0.4
Behdad	240 kg	0.3

The winner is the competitor who successfully lifts the greatest weight. If nobody lifts their weight, the competition is a tie.

   a Find the probability that:

      i Ihor   **ii** Ruslan   **iii** Behdad

   will win the competition.

   b Ihor is considering increasing his weight to 230 kg, so he is lifting more than Ruslan.

   However, the probability that he can lift this weight is only 0.34.

   Would this strategy increase or decrease Ihor's probability of winning the competition?

Chapter 14

Formulae

Contents:
- **A** Formula construction
- **B** Substituting into formulae
- **C** Rearranging formulae
- **D** Rearrangement and substitution
- **E** Predicting formulae

OPENING PROBLEM

In Gaelic football games, each goal is worth 3 points.

While watching a football game, Josh noticed something unusual about Mayo's score.

Mayo had scored 2 goals and 6 points, which is a total of 12 points, but he also recognised that $2 \times 6 = 12$.

Josh wondered whether there were other football scores with this property.

Things to think about:
  a For a score of g goals and p points to have this property, can you explain why $3g + p = gp$?
  b Can you *rearrange* this formula to make p the subject?
  c By *substituting* different values for g, can you find other scores which have this property?

A **formula** is an equation which connects two or more variables.

For example, the formula $s = \dfrac{d}{t}$ relates the three variables *speed* (s), *distance travelled* (d), and *time taken* (t).

We usually write a formula with one variable on its own on the left hand side. The other variable(s) and constants are written on the right hand side.

The variable on its own is called the **subject** of the formula. We say this variable is written *in terms of* the other variables.

A FORMULA CONSTRUCTION

When we try to construct a formula to connect related variables, we often start with numerical examples. They are useful to help us understand the situation before we generalise the result.

Example 1

Write a formula for the amount A in a person's bank account if initially the balance was:
  a $5000, and $200 was withdrawn each week for 10 weeks
  b $5000, and $200 was withdrawn each week for w weeks
  c $5000, and x was withdrawn each week for w weeks
  d B, and x was withdrawn each week for w weeks.

  a $A = 5000 - 200 \times 10$
  b $A = 5000 - 200 \times w$
     $\therefore A = 5000 - 200w$
  c $A = 5000 - x \times w$
     $\therefore A = 5000 - xw$
  d $A = B - x \times w$
     $\therefore A = B - xw$

We do not simplify the amount in **a** because we want to see how the formula is put together.

EXERCISE 14A

1 Write a formula for the amount A in a bank account if the initial balance was:
- **a** $2000, and then $150 was deposited each week for 8 weeks
- **b** $2000, and then $150 was deposited each week for w weeks
- **c** $2000, and then d was deposited each week for w weeks
- **d** P, and then d was deposited each week for w weeks.

2 Write a formula for the total cost £C of hiring a plumber given a fixed call-out fee of:
- **a** £40, plus £60 per hour for 5 hours of work
- **b** £40, plus £60 per hour for t hours of work
- **c** £40, plus £x per hour for t hours of work
- **d** £F, plus £x per hour for t hours of work.

3 In a multiple choice mathematics competition, students are awarded 3 points for each question answered correctly, and penalised 1 point for each question answered incorrectly. Write a formula for the number of points P scored by a student who:
- **a** answers 15 questions and gets 10 of them correct
- **b** answers 20 questions and gets c of them correct
- **c** answers a questions and gets c of them correct.

4 A musical recital consists of performances by a number of musicians, with a short break between each performance. Write a formula for the duration D minutes of a recital consisting of:
- **a** 4 performances of 6 minutes each, with a 2 minute break between performances
- **b** 5 performances of m minutes each, with a 3 minute break between performances
- **c** 8 performances of m minutes each, with a b minute break between performances
- **d** p performances of m minutes each, with a b minute break between performances.

5 A rectangular paddock is fenced into a rectangular array of yards so that each yard is connected by a gate to each adjacent yard. A 2×3 arrangement of yards is shown alongside.

Find a formula for the number of gates G for:
- **a** a 2×3 arrangement
- **b** a 3×5 arrangement
- **c** a 4×4 arrangement
- **d** an $m \times n$ arrangement.

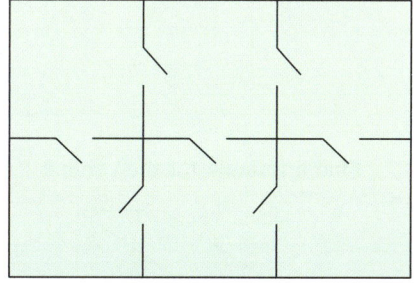

Example 2

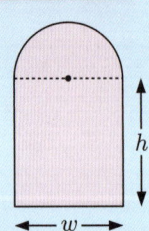

The illustrated door consists of a semi-circle and a rectangle. Find a formula for the area of the door in terms of the width w and height h of the rectangular part.

The area of a rectangle = height × width
$$= hw$$

The radius of the semi-circle is $\frac{w}{2}$.

∴ the area of the semi-circle $= \frac{1}{2} \times$ (area of full circle)
$$= \frac{1}{2} \times \pi r^2$$
$$= \frac{1}{2} \times \pi \times \left(\frac{w}{2}\right)^2$$
$$= \frac{1}{2} \times \pi \times \frac{w^2}{4}$$
$$= \frac{1}{8}\pi w^2$$

∴ the total area is $A = hw + \frac{1}{8}\pi w^2$

We can use known geometric formulae to help construct formulae for more complicated shapes.

6 Find a formula for the area A of each of the shaded regions:

a
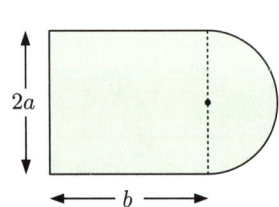

b
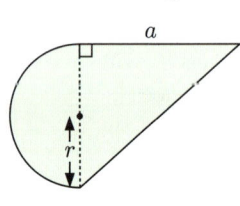

c
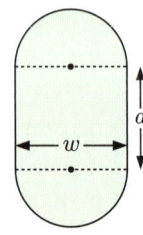

d
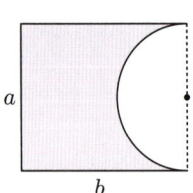

e
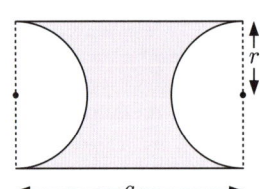

f
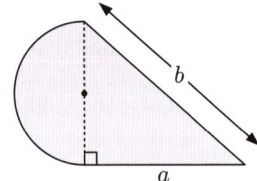

7 Find a formula for the volume V of each of the following objects:

a
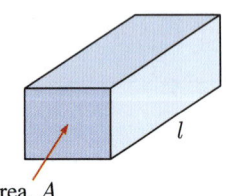

b
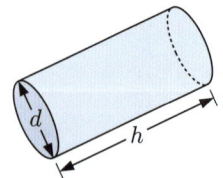

c
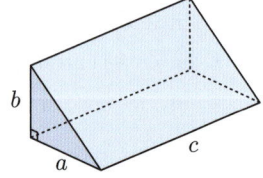

8 Find a formula for the surface area A of each of the following:

a 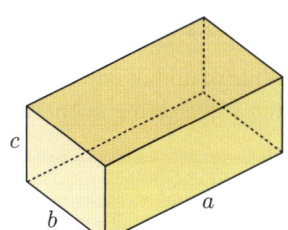   **b** 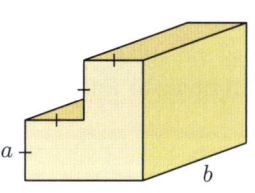   **c**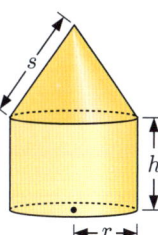

9 A cylindrical pipe has outside radius R, inside radius r, and length l. Show that the volume of concrete used to make the pipe is given by
$$V = \pi l (R+r)(R-r).$$

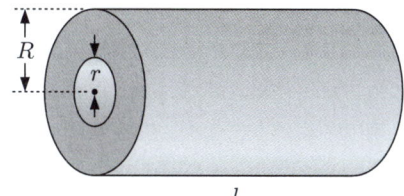

INVESTIGATION — DIMENSIONAL ANALYSIS

When we construct a formula, it is good to check that:
- We only ever add or subtract variables of the same kind.
  For example, it does not make sense to add a length variable to a time variable.
- The dimensions on the LHS must match the dimensions on the RHS.

If either of these things is not true then we know the formula must be incorrect.

For example, consider the speed formula $s = \dfrac{d}{t}$ where s is the speed, d is the distance travelled in metres, and t is the time taken in seconds.

The dimensions on the RHS are $\dfrac{\text{m}}{\text{s}} = \text{m} \div \text{s}$, so the units of speed must be m/s or $\text{m}\,\text{s}^{-1}$.

What to do:

1 The formula for the density of a solid is $D = \dfrac{M}{V}$, where M is the mass of the solid in kg and V is the volume of the solid in m^3.
Determine the units of density.

2 When a solid object is dropped, it falls with gravity according to the formula $D = \tfrac{1}{2}gt^2$, where D is the distance fallen in metres, g is the Earth's gravitational constant, and t is the time in seconds.
Determine the units of the Earth's gravitational constant.

3 In **Exercise 14A** question **9** we showed that if a cylindrical pipe has outside radius R, inside radius r, and length l, then its volume is given by $V = \pi l (R+r)(R-r)$.
Explain why this formula is dimensionally correct.

B SUBSTITUTING INTO FORMULAE

Suppose a formula contains two or more variables, and we know the value of all but one of them. We can **substitute** the known values into the formula to find the corresponding value of the unknown variable.

> *Step 1*: Write down the formula.
> *Step 2*: State the values of the known variables.
> *Step 3*: Substitute the known values into the formula to form a one variable equation.
> *Step 4*: Solve the equation for the unknown variable.

Example 3   ◀)) Self Tutor

When a stone is dropped from a cliff, the total distance fallen after t seconds is given by the formula $D = \frac{1}{2}gt^2$ metres, where $g = 9.8$ m/s². Find:
- **a** the distance fallen after 4 seconds
- **b** the time, to the nearest $\frac{1}{100}$th second, taken for the stone to fall 200 metres.

a $D = \frac{1}{2}gt^2$ where $g = 9.8$ and $t = 4$
$\therefore D = \frac{1}{2} \times 9.8 \times 4^2 = 78.4$
$\therefore$ the stone has fallen 78.4 metres.

b $D = \frac{1}{2}gt^2$ where $D = 200$ and $g = 9.8$
$\therefore \frac{1}{2} \times 9.8 \times t^2 = 200$
$\therefore 4.9t^2 = 200$
$\therefore t^2 = \frac{200}{4.9}$
$\therefore t = \sqrt{\frac{200}{4.9}}$ {t must be positive}
$\therefore t \approx 6.39$
$\therefore$ the time taken is about 6.39 seconds.

EXERCISE 14B

1 The formula for finding the circumference C of a circle with radius r is $C = 2\pi r$. Find:
- **a** the circumference of a circle of radius 4.2 cm
- **b** the radius of a circle with circumference 112 cm
- **c** the diameter of a circle with circumference 400 metres.

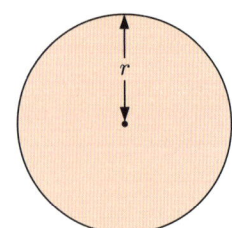

2 When a stone is dropped from the top of a cliff, the distance fallen after t seconds is given by the formula $D = \frac{1}{2}gt^2$ metres, where $g = 9.8$ m/s². Find:
- **a** the distance fallen in the first 2 seconds
- **b** the time taken for the stone to fall 100 metres.

3 The area A of a circle with radius r is $A = \pi r^2$. Find:
  a the area of a circle with radius 6.4 cm
  b the radius of a circular swimming pool which has an area of 160 m².

4 The volume of a cylinder with radius r and height h is given by $V = \pi r^2 h$. Find: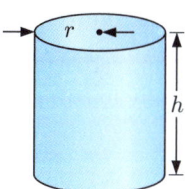
  a the volume of a cylindrical tin can with radius 8 cm and height 21.2 cm
  b the height of a cylinder with radius 6 cm and volume 120 cm³
  c the radius, in mm, of a copper pipe with volume 470 cm³ and length 6 m.

5 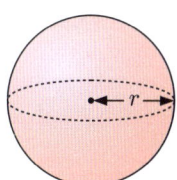 The formula for the surface area A of a sphere with radius r is $A = 4\pi r^2$. Find:
  a the surface area of a sphere with radius 7.5 cm
  b the radius, in cm, of a spherical balloon which has a surface area of 2 m².

6 The *period* or time taken for one complete swing of a simple pendulum is given approximately by $T = \frac{1}{5}\sqrt{l}$ seconds, where l is the length of the pendulum in centimetres. Find: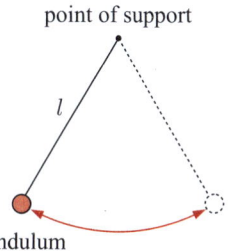
  a the time for one complete swing of a pendulum with length 45 cm
  b the length of a pendulum which has a period of 1.8 seconds.

ACTIVITY — PIZZA PRICING

Luigi's Pizza Parlour has a 'Seafood Special' pizza advertised this week.

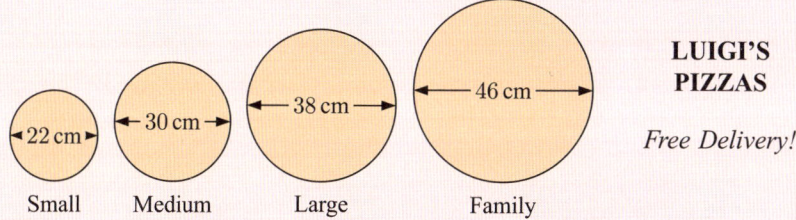

"Seafood Special"
Small   €8.00
Medium   €10.60
Large   €14.00
Family   €18.20

LUIGI'S PIZZAS — Free Delivery!

Sasha, Enrico, and Bianca each attempted to find Luigi's formula for the price €P of each pizza size. The formulae they worked out for a pizza of radius r cm were:

Sasha: $P = \dfrac{17r - 27}{20}$ Enrico: $P = \sqrt{\dfrac{33r - 235}{2}}$ Bianca: $P = 5 + \dfrac{r^2}{40}$.

What to do:

1 Investigate the suitability of each formula.

2 Luigi is introducing a Party size pizza of diameter 54 cm. What do you think his price will be?

REARRANGING FORMULAE

In the formula $D = xt + p$, D is expressed in terms of the other variables, x, t, and p. We say that D is the **subject** of the formula.

We can rearrange a formula to make one of the other variables the subject. However, we must do this carefully to ensure that the formula is still true.

> We **rearrange** formulae using the same processes which we use to solve equations. Anything we do to one side we must also do to the other.

Example 4

Make y the subject of:

a $2x + 3y = 12$ **b** $x = 5 - cy$

a $2x + 3y = 12$
$\therefore 3y = 12 - 2x$ {subtracting $2x$ from both sides}
$\therefore y = \dfrac{12 - 2x}{3}$ {dividing both sides by 3}
$\therefore y = 4 - \tfrac{2}{3}x$

b $x = 5 - cy$
$\therefore x + cy = 5$ {adding cy to both sides}
$\therefore cy = 5 - x$ {subtracting x from both sides}
$\therefore y = \dfrac{5 - x}{c}$ {dividing both sides by c}

EXERCISE 14C

1 Make y the subject of:
   a $2x + 5y = 10$ **b** $3x + 4y = 20$ **c** $2x - y = 8$
   d $2x + 7y = 14$ **e** $5x + 2y = 20$ **f** $2x - 3y = -12$

2 Make x the subject of:
   a $p + x = r$ **b** $xy = z$ **c** $3x + a = d$
   d $5x + 2y = d$ **e** $ax + by = p$ **f** $y = mx + c$
   g $2 + tx = s$ **h** $p + qx = m$ **i** $6 = a + bx$

3 Make y the subject of:
   a $z = t - 5y$ **b** $c - 2y = p$ **c** $a - 3y = t$
   d $n - ky = 5$ **e** $a - by = n$ **f** $p = a - ny$

FORMULAE (Chapter 14) 313

Example 5

Make z the subject of $c = \dfrac{m}{z}$.

$c = \dfrac{m}{z}$

$\therefore cz = m$ {multiplying both sides by z}

$\therefore z = \dfrac{m}{c}$ {dividing both sides by c}

4 Make z the subject of:

   a $az = \dfrac{b}{c}$ **b** $\dfrac{a}{z} = d$ **c** $\dfrac{3}{d} = \dfrac{2}{z}$

   d $\dfrac{z}{2} = \dfrac{a}{z}$ **e** $\dfrac{b}{z} = \dfrac{z}{n}$ **f** $\dfrac{m}{z} = \dfrac{z}{a-b}$

5 Make:

   a a the subject of $F = ma$ **b** r the subject of $C = 2\pi r$

   c d the subject of $V = ldh$ **d** K the subject of $A = \dfrac{b}{K}$

   e h the subject of $A = \dfrac{bh}{2}$ **f** T the subject of $I = \dfrac{PRT}{100}$

6 The surface area of a cylinder with radius r and height h is given by $A = 2\pi r^2 + 2\pi rh$.

Rearrange this formula to make h the subject.

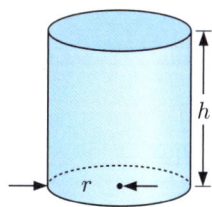

Example 6

Make t the subject of $s = \tfrac{1}{2}gt^2$, given that $t > 0$.

$\tfrac{1}{2}gt^2 = s$ {rewriting with t^2 on the LHS}

$\therefore gt^2 = 2s$ {multiplying both sides by 2}

$\therefore t^2 = \dfrac{2s}{g}$ {dividing both sides by g}

$\therefore t = \sqrt{\dfrac{2s}{g}}$ {as $t > 0$}

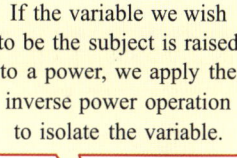

If the variable we wish to be the subject is raised to a power, we apply the inverse power operation to isolate the variable.

7 Make:

   a r the subject of $A = \pi r^2$, $r > 0$ **b** x the subject of $N = \dfrac{x^5}{a}$

   c k the subject of $M = 5k^3$ **d** x the subject of $D = \dfrac{n}{x^3}$

   e x the subject of $y = 4x^2 - 7$ **f** Q the subject of $P^2 = Q^2 + R^2$

Example 7

Make x the subject of $T = \dfrac{a}{\sqrt{x}}$.

$T = \dfrac{a}{\sqrt{x}}$

$\therefore T^2 = \left(\dfrac{a}{\sqrt{x}}\right)^2$ {squaring both sides}

$\therefore T^2 = \dfrac{a^2}{x}$

$\therefore T^2 x = a^2$ {multiplying both sides by x}

$\therefore x = \dfrac{a^2}{T^2}$ {dividing both sides by T^2}

8 Make:

a a the subject of $d = \dfrac{\sqrt{a}}{n}$

b l the subject of $T = \tfrac{1}{5}\sqrt{l}$

c a the subject of $c = \sqrt{a^2 - b^2}$

d d the subject of $\dfrac{k}{a} = \dfrac{5}{\sqrt{d}}$

e l the subject of $T = 2\pi\sqrt{\dfrac{l}{g}}$

f b the subject of $A = 4\sqrt{\dfrac{a}{b}}$

Example 8

Make x the subject of $ax + 3 = bx + d$.

$ax + 3 = bx + d$

$\therefore ax - bx = d - 3$ {writing terms containing x on the LHS}

$\therefore x(a - b) = d - 3$ {x is a common factor on the LHS}

$\therefore x = \dfrac{d - 3}{a - b}$ {dividing both sides by $(a - b)$}

If the variable we wish to be the subject appears more than once, we will need factorisation or expansion.

9 Make x the subject of:

a $3x + a = bx + c$
b $ax = c - bx$
c $mx + a = nx - 2$
d $8x + a = -bx$
e $a - x = b - cx$
f $rx + d = e - sx$

Example 9

Make x the subject of $T = \dfrac{a}{x - b}$.

$T = \dfrac{a}{x - b}$

$\therefore T(x - b) = a$ {multiplying both sides by $(x - b)$}

$\therefore Tx - Tb = a$

$\therefore Tx = a + Tb$ {adding Tb to both sides}

$\therefore x = \dfrac{a + Tb}{T}$ {dividing both sides by T}

10 Make:

a a the subject of $P = \dfrac{2}{a+b}$

b r the subject of $T = \dfrac{8}{q+r}$

c q the subject of $A = \dfrac{B}{p-q}$

d x the subject of $A = \dfrac{3}{2x+y}$

e y the subject of $M = \dfrac{4}{x^2+y^2}$, $y > 0$

Example 10   ◀)) **Self Tutor**

Make x the subject of $y = \dfrac{3x+2}{x-1}$.

$y = \dfrac{3x+2}{x-1}$

$\therefore y(x-1) = 3x+2$ {multiplying both sides by $(x-1)$}

$\therefore xy - y = 3x + 2$ {expanding the brackets}

$\therefore xy - 3x = y + 2$ {writing the terms containing x on the LHS}

$\therefore x(y-3) = y+2$ {x is a common factor}

$\therefore x = \dfrac{y+2}{y-3}$

---

11 Make x the subject of:

a $y = \dfrac{x}{x+1}$

b $y = \dfrac{x-3}{x+2}$

c $y = \dfrac{3x-1}{x+3}$

d $y = \dfrac{4x-1}{2-x}$

e $y = \dfrac{3x+7}{3-2x}$

f $y = 1 + \dfrac{2}{x-3}$

g $y = -2 + \dfrac{5}{x+4}$

h $y = -3 - \dfrac{6}{x-2}$

i $\dfrac{y}{x-2} = 5 + \dfrac{2}{2-x}$

12 In a carnival sideshow, William is given two attempts to hole a golf putt. If he succeeds with either attempt then he wins a prize. Given that William has probability p of missing each putt, the expected number of games he needs to play in order to win a prize is $N = \dfrac{1}{1-p^2}$.

Rearrange this formula to make p the subject.

D REARRANGEMENT AND SUBSTITUTION

In the section on formula substitution, the known variables were replaced by numbers, and we then solved an equation to find the unknown.

In situations when we need to perform this process several times, it is quicker to **rearrange** the formula first, and then **substitute**.

Example 11

The volume of a cone is given by $V = \frac{1}{3}\pi r^2 h$, where r is the base radius and h is the height.

a Rearrange this formula to make r the subject.
b Hence, find the base radius of a cone with:
  i height 6 cm and volume 100 cm^3
  ii height 10 cm and volume 200 cm^3
  iii height 15 cm and volume 150 cm^3.

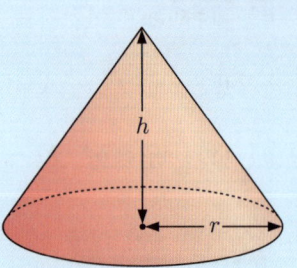

a
$V = \frac{1}{3}\pi r^2 h$
$\therefore\ 3V = \pi r^2 h$ {multiplying both sides by 3}
$\therefore\ \dfrac{3V}{\pi h} = r^2$ {dividing both sides by πh}
$\therefore\ r = \sqrt{\dfrac{3V}{\pi h}}$ {as r must be positive}

b
i When $h = 6$ and $V = 100$, $r = \sqrt{\dfrac{3 \times 100}{\pi \times 6}} = \sqrt{\dfrac{50}{\pi}} \approx 3.99$
So, the base radius is approximately 3.99 cm.

ii When $h = 10$ and $V = 200$, $r = \sqrt{\dfrac{3 \times 200}{\pi \times 10}} = \sqrt{\dfrac{60}{\pi}} \approx 4.37$
So, the base radius is approximately 4.37 cm.

iii When $h = 15$ and $V = 150$, $r = \sqrt{\dfrac{3 \times 150}{\pi \times 15}} = \sqrt{\dfrac{30}{\pi}} \approx 3.09$
So, the base radius is approximately 3.09 cm.

EXERCISE 14D

1 The area of a sector with radius r and angle θ is given by the formula $A = \dfrac{\theta}{360} \times \pi r^2$.

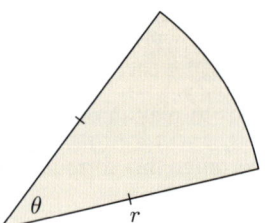

  a Rearrange this formula to make θ the subject.
  b Hence, find the angle of a sector with:
    i radius 3 cm and area 5 cm^2
    ii radius 7 cm and area 45 cm^2
    iii radius 8.5 cm and area 135 cm^2.

2 a Make a the subject of the formula $K = \dfrac{d^2}{2ab}$.
  b Find the value of a when:
    i $K = 112$, $d = 24$, $b = 2$
    ii $K = 400$, $d = 72$, $b = 0.4$

3 The height of a bush after t years is given by the formula $H = 1 + \sqrt{t}$ metres.
  a Rearrange this formula to make t the subject.
  b How long will it take for the bush to reach a height of:
    i 2 m   **ii** 3 m   **iii** 3.5 m?

4 The formula for the volume V of a sphere with radius r is $V = \frac{4}{3}\pi r^3$.

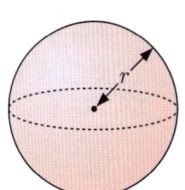

   a Make r the subject of the formula.
   b Find the radius of a sphere which has volume:
       i 40 cm³   ii 800 cm³   iii 1 000 000 cm³.

5 An object with constant acceleration a m/s² travels s m. Its initial speed is u m/s and its final speed is v m/s. The variables are connected by the formula $v^2 - u^2 = 2as$.
   a Rearrange the formula to make v the subject, where $v \geq 0$.
   b Find the final speed of an object which travels:
       i 100 m with initial speed 5 m/s and constant acceleration 2 m/s²
       ii 1.5 km with initial speed 10 m/s and constant acceleration 0.9 m/s².

6 The *winning percentage* of a tennis player who has won w matches and lost l matches is given by the formula $P = \dfrac{w}{w+l} \times 100\%$.
   a Find the winning percentage of a player who has won 10 matches and lost 7 matches.
   b Rearrange the formula to make w the subject.
   c This year Mary has lost 15 matches, with a winning percentage of 37.5%. How many matches has she won?
   d Over his career, Claude has won 84 matches and lost 49 matches. His aim is to increase his winning percentage to 65%. How many consecutive matches must he win to reach his target?

7 The surface area of a rectangular prism with dimensions a units by b units by c units is given by the formula $A = 2(ab + ac + bc)$.

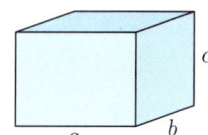

   a Make c the subject of the formula.
   b Hence, find c in the following:
       i surface area = 180 cm²   ii surface area = 102 cm²   iii surface area = 531 cm²

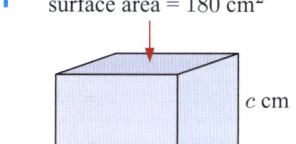
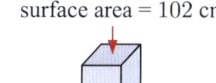
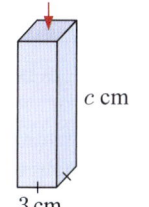
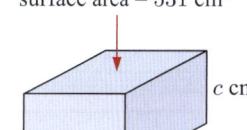

8 Consider two objects with masses m_1 kg and m_2 kg, which are d m apart. The gravitational force between the objects is given by the formula

$$F = G\frac{m_1 m_2}{d^2} \text{ Newtons}$$

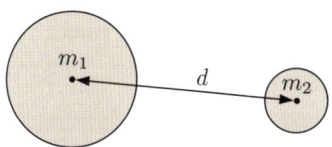

where $G \approx 6.67 \times 10^{-11}$ is the universal gravitational constant.
   a The Earth has mass 5.97×10^{24} kg, and the Moon has mass 7.35×10^{22} kg. Given that the Earth and the Moon are approximately 3.82×10^8 m apart, find the gravitational force between them. Give your answer in scientific notation.
   b Rearrange the formula so that d is the subject.

c **i** The Sun has mass 1.99×10^{30} kg. Given that the gravitational force between the Sun and the Earth is 3.54×10^{22} N, find the distance between the Sun and the Earth.

ii Two planets each have mass 2.32×10^{26} kg, and the gravitational force between them is 1.76×10^{14} N. Find the distance between the planets.

9 Consider a square-based pyramid whose edges are all s units long.

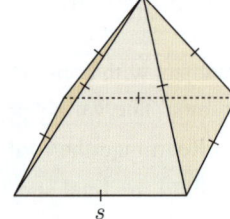

a Show that the surface area of the pyramid is given by $A = s^2(1 + \sqrt{3})$.

b Rearrange this formula to show that $s = \sqrt{\dfrac{A}{2}(\sqrt{3} - 1)}$.

c Find the side length if the pyramid has surface area:

i 50 cm² **ii** 150 cm² **iii** 600 cm².

10 Answer the **Opening Problem** on page **306**.

11 The **coefficient of restitution** of a ball gives a measure of how 'bouncy' the ball is.
It is given by the formula

$$C = \sqrt{\dfrac{h}{H}}$$

where H is the drop height and h is the bounce height.

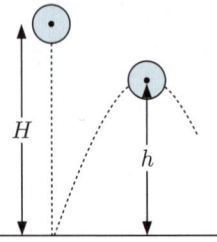

a Find the coefficient of restitution for the following balls:

i 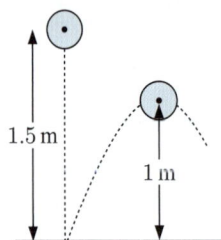 1.5 m, 1 m

ii 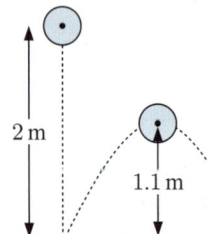 2 m, 1.1 m

b Rearrange the formula to make h the subject.

c The coefficients of restitution for several balls dropped onto the pavement are shown alongside.
Find how high each of these balls would bounce when dropped onto the pavement from a height of 5 metres.

Tennis ball	0.728
Golf ball	0.858
Marble	0.657
Superball	0.893

12 According to Einstein's theory of relativity, the mass of a particle is given by the formula

$$m = \dfrac{m_0}{\sqrt{1 - \left(\dfrac{v}{c}\right)^2}}$$

where m_0 is the mass of the particle at rest,
v is the speed of the particle, and
c is the speed of light.

a Make v the subject of the formula.

b Find the speed necessary to increase the mass of a particle to three times its rest mass, which is $3m_0$. Give the value for v as a fraction of c.

c A cyclotron increased the mass of an electron to $30m_0$. At what speed was the electron travelling, given that $c \approx 3 \times 10^8$ m/s?

E PREDICTING FORMULAE

We can often predict a formula for a general situation by examining simple cases and looking for a pattern.

For example, the set of even numbers is $\{2, 4, 6, 8, 10, 12, ...\}$.

We observe that: the 1st term is 2×1
                   the 2nd term is 2×2
                   the 3rd term is 2×3, and so on.

We see from the pattern that the 13th term will be 2×13.

So, we generalise by saying that "the nth even number is $2n$".

The coefficient 2 in $2n$ indicates that the terms increase by 2 each time n is increased by 1.

Example 12   Self Tutor

Examine the matchstick pattern:

How many matches are needed to make:

a the first diagram   b the second diagram   c the third diagram
d the 4th diagram   e the nth diagram?

a 3 matches   b 5 matches   c 7 matches

d The fourth diagram is , which contains 9 matches.

e So far, the sequence is $\{3, 5, 7, 9, ...\}$.   We are adding 2 matches each time, so the formula must involve $2n$.
   The expression $2n$ would generate the set $\{2, 4, 6, 8, ...\}$, whereas our sequence is always 1 more than these values.
   $\therefore$ there are $2n + 1$ matches in the nth diagram.
   Check: If $n = 1$, $2(1) + 1 = 3$ ✓
              If $n = 2$, $2(2) + 1 = 5$ ✓
              If $n = 3$, $2(3) + 1 = 7$ ✓

EXERCISE 14E

1 Examine the matchstick pattern:

   How many matchsticks make up the:
   a 1st, 2nd, 3rd, 4th, and 5th diagrams   b 10th diagram   c nth diagram?

2 Examine the matchstick pattern:

   How many matchsticks make up the:
   a 1st, 2nd, 3rd, 4th, and 5th diagrams   b 10th diagram   c nth diagram?

3 **a** Find:
      i $1+3$ **ii** $1+3+5$
      iii $1+3+5+7$ **iv** $1+3+5+7+9$

    b If S_n is the sum of the first n positive odd numbers, then $S_1 = 1$, $S_2 = 4$, and $S_3 = 9$. Find a formula for S_n.

4 **a** Find:
      i $1+2$ **ii** $1+2+4$
      iii $1+2+4+8$ **iv** $1+2+4+8+16$

    b Find a formula for the sum of the first n terms of the number set $\{1, 2, 4, 8, 16, ...\}$.

5 Consider the pattern:
$$S_1 = \frac{1}{1 \times 2}, \quad S_2 = \frac{1}{1 \times 2} + \frac{1}{2 \times 3}, \quad S_3 = \frac{1}{1 \times 2} + \frac{1}{2 \times 3} + \frac{1}{3 \times 4}, \quad ....$$

    a Find the values of S_1, S_2, S_3, and S_4.

    b Write down the value of: **i** S_{10} **ii** S_n.

6 Consider the pattern: $S_1 = 1^2$, $S_2 = 1^2 + 2^2$, $S_3 = 1^2 + 2^2 + 3^2$, ...

    a Check that the formula $S_n = \dfrac{n(n+1)(2n+1)}{6}$ is correct for $n = 1, 2, 3$, and 4.

    b Assuming the formula in **a** is always true, find the sum of $1^2 + 2^2 + 3^2 + 4^2 + 5^2 + ... + 100^2$, which is the sum of the squares of the first one hundred integers.

REVIEW SET 14A

1 **a** A trough is initially empty. Write a formula for the volume of water V in the trough if:
      i six 8-litre buckets of water are poured into it
      ii n 8-litre buckets of water are poured into it
      iii n l-litre buckets of water are poured into it.

    b A trough initially contains 25 L of water. Write a formula for the volume of water V in the trough if n buckets of water, each containing l litres, are poured into it.

2 The average speed of an object which travels d km in t hours is given by the formula $s = \dfrac{d}{t}$ km/h.

    a Find the average speed of a truck which travels 540 km in 6 hours.

    b Find the distance travelled by an aeroplane which flies for $6\frac{1}{2}$ hours at an average speed of 600 km/h.

3 Find a formula for the surface area A of the solid alongside.

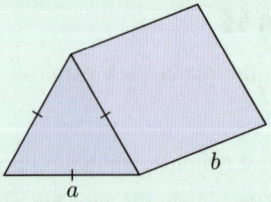

4 Make x the subject of:
     a $mx + n = 3p$ **b** $\dfrac{7}{y} = \dfrac{5}{x}$

5 Make k the subject of:
     a $T = \sqrt{k - l^2}$ **b** $P = 2k^2 - r$, $k < 0$

6 The length of the diagonal in the rectangular prism shown is given by $L = \sqrt{a^2 + b^2 + c^2}$.

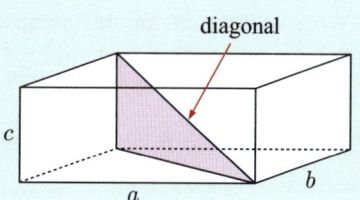

   a Find the length of the diagonal in a 2 cm by 6 cm by 9 cm rectangular prism.

   b Rearrange the formula to make c the subject.

   c A rectangular prism has an 8 cm by 12 cm base, and a diagonal of length 17 cm. Find the height of the rectangular prism.

7 Make x the subject of the formula $y = \dfrac{2x - 3}{x - 2}$.

8 The electric current in a circuit with voltage E volts, resistance r ohms, and load resistance R ohms, is given by the formula $I = \dfrac{E}{r + R}$ amperes.

   a Find the current in a circuit with voltage 24 V, resistance 0.5 ohms, and load resistance 2.5 ohms.

   b Rearrange the formula to make r the subject.

   c Find the resistance of a circuit with current 1.5 amperes, voltage 7.725 V, and load resistance 5 ohms.

9 For the following matchstick pattern, find the number of matches M in the:

   a 1st, 2nd, and 3rd diagram   **b** nth diagram.

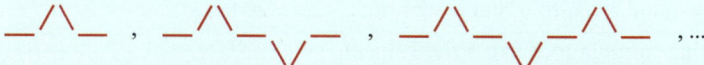

10 **a** Find: **i** $1 + 2$ **ii** $1 + 2 + 3$ **iii** $1 + 2 + 3 + 4$

    b Find: **i** $1^3 + 2^3$ **ii** $1^3 + 2^3 + 3^3$ **iii** $1^3 + 2^3 + 3^3 + 4^3$

    c Suppose S_n is the sum of the first n positive integers, and C_n is the sum of the first n positive perfect cubes. Predict a formula for C_n in terms of S_n.

11 To convert temperatures from degrees Fahrenheit (°F) to Kelvin (K), we use the formula $K = \frac{5}{9}(F - 32) + 273.15$.

   a Convert the following temperatures to Kelvin, correct to 1 decimal place:

     i 50°F   **ii** −130°F   **iii** 150°F

   b Rearrange the formula to make F the subject.

   c Convert the following temperatures to degrees Fahrenheit:

     i 313.15 K   **ii** 0 K   **iii** 200 K

REVIEW SET 14B

1 Write a formula for the bill $B at a restaurant if there is a charge of:

   a $15 for corkage, plus $25 per person for 5 people

   b $c for corkage, plus $25 per person for p people

   c $c for corkage, plus $m per person for p people.

2 Write a formula for the number of edge pieces E (excluding corner pieces) in a:

   a 3×5 jigsaw puzzle

   b 4×8 jigsaw puzzle

   c $m \times n$ jigsaw puzzle.

3 Given that $M = p - qr$, find:

   a M when $p = 19$, $q = -3$, and $r = 6$

   b r when $M = -2$, $p = 14$, and $q = 2$.

4 Find a formula for the volume V of the solid of uniform cross-section shown.

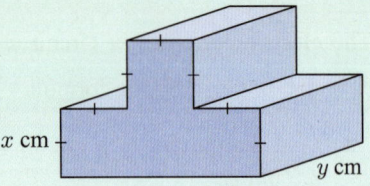

5 Make a the subject of: **a** $B = ad - f$ **b** $\dfrac{Q}{\sqrt{a}} = \dfrac{t}{3}$

6 Make h the subject of $G = \sqrt{\dfrac{5}{h+1}}$.

7 Amy is trying to find pairs of numbers which have the same sum and product. In other words, she is looking for number pairs a and b such that $ab = a + b$.

   a Rearrange this formula to make b the subject.

   b Find b given that $a = 3$. Check your answer by finding the sum and product of the numbers.

8 Make x the subject of $y = \dfrac{4x - 3}{3x + 2}$.

9 Examine the matchstick pattern:

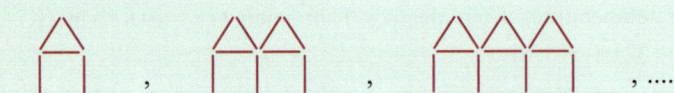

How many matchsticks make up the nth diagram?

10 **a** Find: **i** $2 + 4$ **ii** $2 + 4 + 6$

             iii $2 + 4 + 6 + 8$ **iv** $2 + 4 + 6 + 8 + 10$

   b Hence write a formula for the sum of the first n positive even numbers.

11 The kinetic energy of an object with mass m kg which is moving with speed v m/s, is given by the formula $E = \tfrac{1}{2}mv^2$ joules, $v \geqslant 0$.

   a Find the kinetic energy of a person with mass 80 kg moving at 5 m/s.

   b Rearrange the formula to make v the subject.

   c A running wombat with mass 25 kg has 800 joules of kinetic energy. Find the speed of the wombat.

Chapter 15
Relations and functions

Contents:
- **A** Relations
- **B** Functions
- **C** Function notation
- **D** Composite functions
- **E** Inverse functions
- **F** The modulus function
- **G** Where functions meet

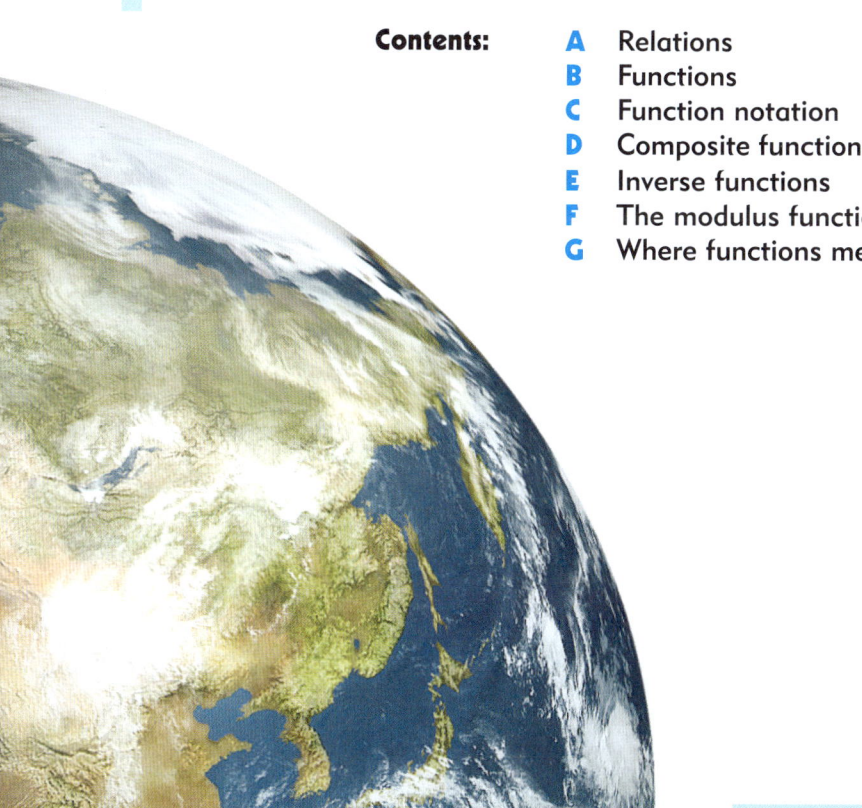

When two variables are connected, we often use a **relation** or a **function** to describe the relationship.

OPENING PROBLEM

Fernando and Gerard are competing in a cycling race. The graph alongside shows how far Fernando is ahead of Gerard after x minutes.

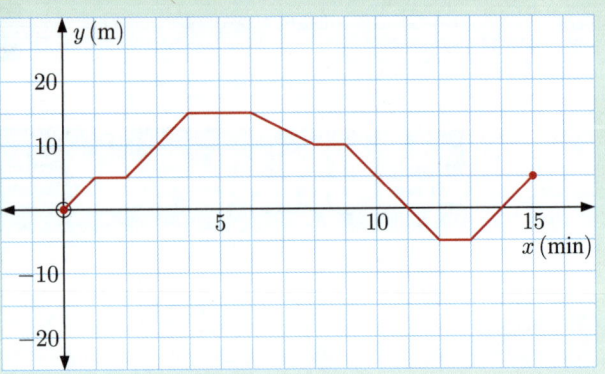

Things to think about:

a For what values of x are there corresponding values of y?

b For what values of y are there corresponding values of x?

c What is the value of y when $x = 3$? How can we write this using function notation?

d What are the values of x for which $y = 10$?

A RELATIONS

Sue-Ellen wants to send a parcel to a friend. The cost of posting the parcel a fixed distance is determined by the weight of the parcel, as shown in the table.

For example, it will cost $8.00 to post a parcel weighing at least 2 kg but less than 5 kg. It will therefore cost $8.00 to post a parcel weighing 2 kg or 3.6 kg or 4.955 kg.

Weight w (kg)	Cost $C
$1 \leqslant w < 2$	$5.00
$2 \leqslant w < 5$	$8.00
$5 \leqslant w < 10$	$12.00
$10 \leqslant w < 15$	$16.00
$15 \leqslant w < 20$	$20.00

We can illustrate the postal charges on a graph.

An end point that is included has a filled in circle.

An end point that is not included has an open circle.

There is a *relationship* between the variables *weight* and *cost*, so the table of costs is an example of a **relation**.

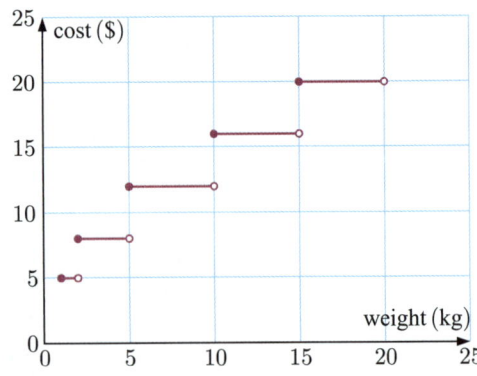

A relation may be a finite number of ordered pairs, for example $\{(2, 8), (3, 8), (4, 8), (5, 12)\}$, or an infinite number of ordered pairs, such as the relation between the variables *weight* and *cost* in the postal charges above.

> A **relation** is any set of points which connects two variables.

The following are examples of relations:

- The set of 8 points represented by the dots is a relation.
  There is no equation connecting the variables x and y in this case.

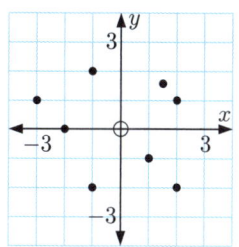

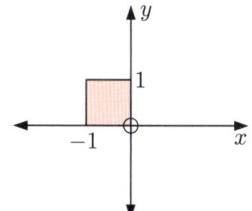

The set of all points on and within the illustrated square is a relation. It is the set of all points (x, y) such that $-1 \leqslant x \leqslant 0$ and $0 \leqslant y \leqslant 1$.

- The set of all points on this parabola is a relation.
  It is the set of all points (x, y) lying on the curve $y = -x^2 + 6x - 5$.

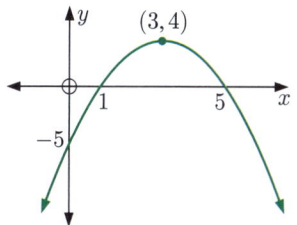

DOMAIN AND RANGE

The **domain** of a relation is the set of possible values that x may have.
The **range** of a relation is the set of possible values that y may have.

The domain and range of a relation are often described using **interval notation**.

Consider the following examples:

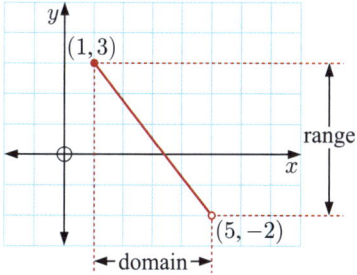

The domain consists of all real x such that $1 \leqslant x < 5$. We write this as:

$$\{x \mid 1 \leqslant x < 5\}.$$

    ↑   ↖
the set of all   such that

The range is $\{y \mid -2 < y \leqslant 3\}$.

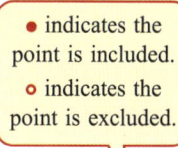
• indicates the point is included.
◦ indicates the point is excluded.

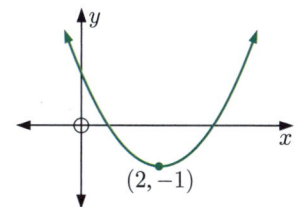

The domain is $\{x \mid x \in \mathbb{R}\}$.
The range is $\{y \mid y \geqslant -1\}$.

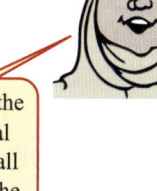
$\mathbb{R}$ represents the set of all real numbers, or all numbers on the number line.

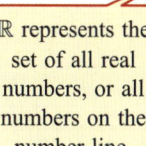

Example 1

For each of the following graphs, state the domain and range:

a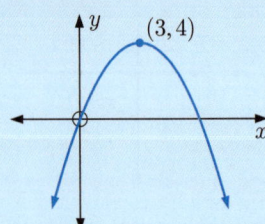
b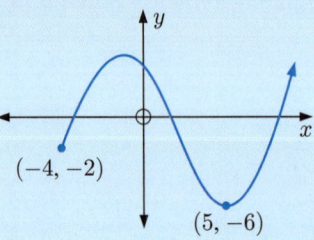
c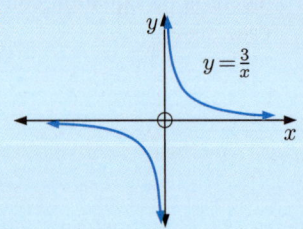

a Domain is $\{x \mid x \in \mathbb{R}\}$.
  Range is $\{y \mid y \leqslant 4\}$.

b Domain is $\{x \mid x \geqslant -4\}$.
  Range is $\{y \mid y \geqslant -6\}$.

c Domain is $\{x \mid x \neq 0\}$.
  Range is $\{y \mid y \neq 0\}$.

EXERCISE 15A

1 For each of the following graphs, state the domain and range:

a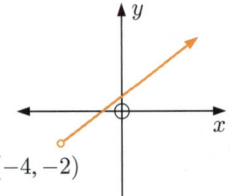
b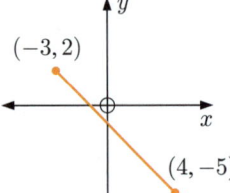
c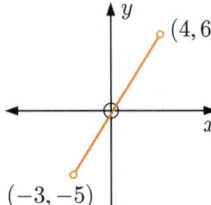

d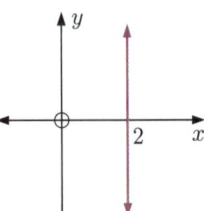
e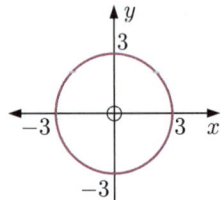
f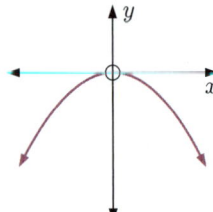

g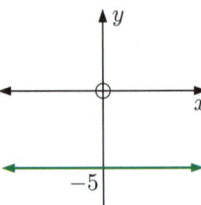
h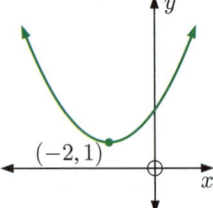
i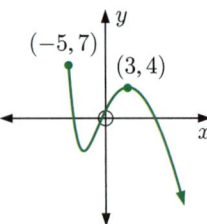

j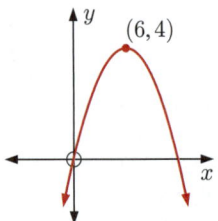
k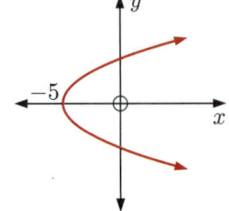
l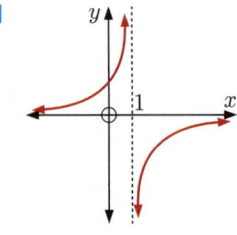

2 State the domain and range of:

a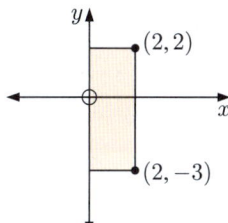
b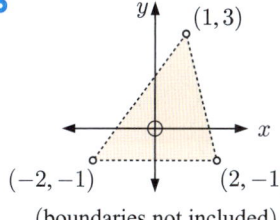
(boundaries not included)
c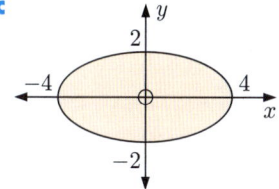

B FUNCTIONS

A **function** is a relation in which no two different ordered pairs have the same first member.

The grid alongside shows the set of points:
$\{(-1, 3), (2, 2), (-1, -2), (3, 2), (4, -1)\}$.

The two circled points $(-1, -2)$ and $(-1, 3)$ have the same first member, so the set of points is a relation but not a function.

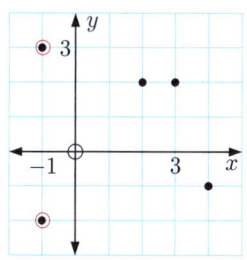

GEOMETRIC TEST FOR FUNCTIONS: "VERTICAL LINE TEST"

Suppose we draw all possible vertical lines on the graph of a relation.
- If each line cuts the graph at most once, then the relation is a function.
- If *any* line cuts the graph more than once, then the relation is *not* a function.

Example 2   ◀)) **Self Tutor**

Which of these relations are functions?

a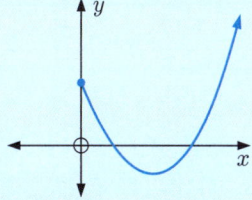
b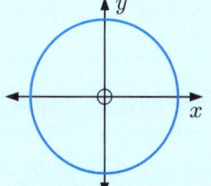

a Every vertical line we could draw cuts the graph only once.
∴ the relation is a function.

b This vertical line cuts the graph twice.
∴ the relation is not a function.

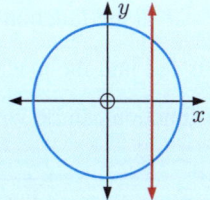

EXERCISE 15B

1 Which of the following sets of ordered pairs are functions? Give reasons for your answers.
   a $\{(1, 1), (2, 2), (3, 3), (4, 4)\}$
   b $\{(-1, 2), (-3, 2), (3, 2), (1, 2)\}$
   c $\{(2, 5), (-1, 4), (-3, 7), (2, -3)\}$
   d $\{(3, -2), (3, 0), (3, 2), (3, 4)\}$
   e $\{(-7, 0), (-5, 0), (-3, 0), (-1, 0)\}$
   f $\{(0, 5), (0, 1), (2, 1), (2, -5)\}$

2 Use the vertical line test to determine which of the following relations are functions:

a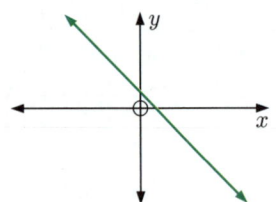
b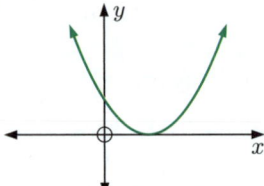
c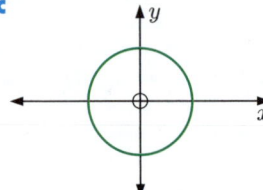
d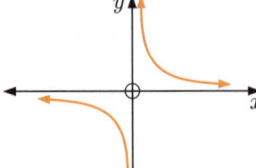
e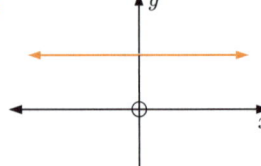
f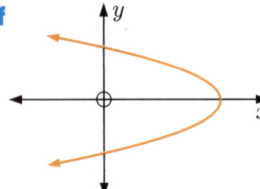
g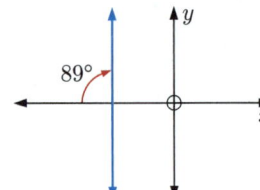
h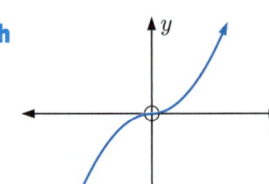
i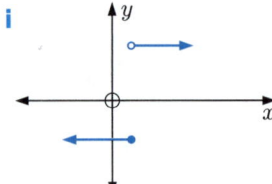

3 Will the graph of a straight line always be a function? Explain your answer.

C FUNCTION NOTATION

We sometimes use a 'function machine' to illustrate how functions behave.

For example, the machine alongside has been programmed to perform a particular function. Whatever number is fed into the machine, the machine will double the number and then subtract 1.

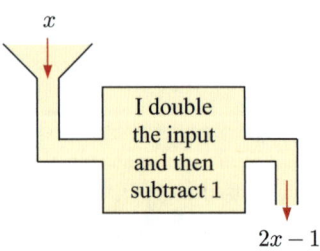

If f is used to represent this particular function, we can write:

   f is the function that will convert x into $2x - 1$.

If 3 is fed into the machine, $2(3) - 1 = 5$ comes out.

This function can be written as: $f : x \mapsto 2x - 1$

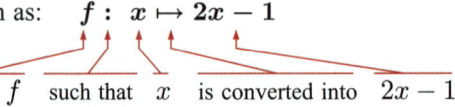

function f such that x is converted into $2x - 1$

We can also write this function as $f(x) = 2x - 1$

For any function f, the value of the function when $x = a$ is given by $f(a)$.

For $f(x) = 2x - 1$, $f(2) = 2(2) - 1 = 3$.

This indicates that the point $(2, 3)$ lies on the graph of the function.

Likewise, $f(-4) = 2(-4) - 1 = -9$.

This indicates that the point $(-4, -9)$ also lies on the graph.

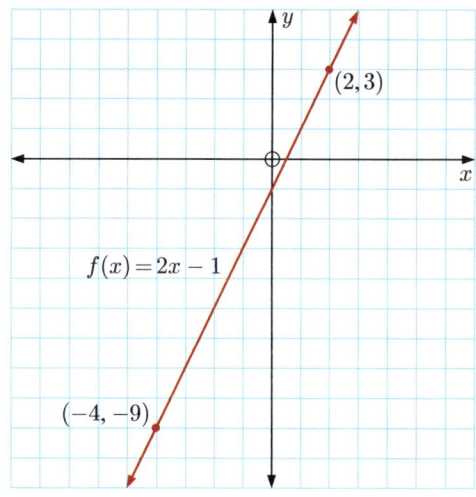

Note that:
- $f(x)$ is read as "f of x", and is the value of the function at any value of x.
- f is the function which converts x into $f(x)$, so $f : x \mapsto f(x)$.
- $f(x)$ is sometimes called the **image** of x.

Example 3 ◀) Self Tutor

For $f : x \mapsto 3x^2 - 4x$, find the value of:

a $f(2)$ **b** $f(-5)$

$f(x) = 3x^2 - 4x$

a $f(2)$
$= 3(2)^2 - 4(2)$ {replacing x by (2)}
$= 3 \times 4 - 8$
$= 4$

b $f(-5)$
$= 3(-5)^2 - 4(-5)$ {replacing x by (-5)}
$= 3(25) + 20$
$= 95$

Example 4 ◀) Self Tutor

For $f(x) = 4 - 3x - x^2$, find in simplest form:

a $f(-x)$ **b** $f(x+2)$

a $f(-x) = 4 - 3(-x) - (-x)^2$ {replacing x by $(-x)$}
$= 4 + 3x - x^2$

b $f(x+2) = 4 - 3(x+2) - (x+2)^2$ {replacing x by $(x+2)$}
$= 4 - 3x - 6 - [x^2 + 4x + 4]$
$= -x^2 - 7x - 6$

EXERCISE 15C.1

1. For $f : x \mapsto 2x + 3$, find:
   a $f(0)$
   b $f(2)$
   c $f(-1)$
   d $f(-5)$
   e $f(-\frac{1}{2})$

2. For $g(x) = -5x + 3$, find:
   a $g(1)$
   b $g(4)$
   c $g(-2)$
   d $g(-x)$
   e $g(x + 4)$

3. For $f(x) = 2x^2 - 3x + 2$, find:
   a $f(0)$
   b $f(3)$
   c $f(-4)$
   d $f(-x)$
   e $f(x + 1)$

4. For $P : x \mapsto 4x^2 + 4x - 3$, find:
   a $P(3)$
   b $P(-1)$
   c $P(\frac{1}{2})$
   d $P(x - 3)$
   e $P(2x)$

5. Consider the function $R(x) = \dfrac{2x - 3}{x + 2}$.
   a Evaluate: i $R(0)$ ii $R(1)$ iii $R(-\frac{1}{2})$
   b Find a value of x such that $R(x)$ does not exist.
   c Find $R(x - 2)$ in simplest form.
   d Find x such that $R(x) = -5$.

6. The value of a car t years after purchase is given by $V(t) = 28\,000 - 4000t$ dollars.
   a Find $V(4)$, and state what this value means.
   b Find t when $V(t) = 8000$, and explain what this represents.
   c Find the original purchase price of the car.

7. The graph of $y = f(x)$ is shown alongside.
   a Find:
      i $f(2)$
      ii $f(3)$
   b Find the value of x such that $f(x) = 4$.

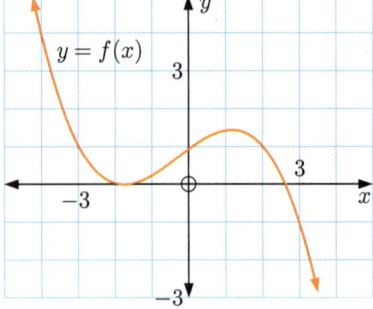

8.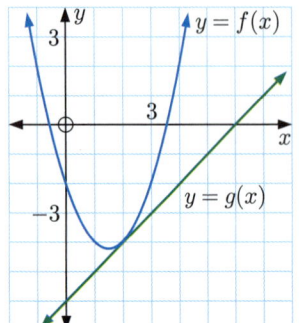

Consider the graphs of $y = f(x)$ and $y = g(x)$ shown.
   a Find:
      i $f(4)$ ii $g(0)$ iii $g(5)$
   b Find the *two* values of x such that $f(x) = -2$.
   c Find the value of x such that $f(x) = g(x)$.
   d Show that $g(x) = x - 6$.

9 Draw a graph of $y = f(x)$ such that $f(-2) = 5$, $f(1) = 0$, and $f(4) = 3$.

10 The graph of $y = f(x)$ is a straight line passing through $(-3, -5)$ and $(1, 7)$.
  a Draw the graph of $y = f(x)$.
  b Find $f(-3)$ and $f(1)$.
  c Find $f(x)$.

THE DOMAIN OF A FUNCTION

To find the domain of a function, we need to consider what values of the variable make the function undefined.

For example:

- the domain of $f(x) = \sqrt{x}$ is $\{x \mid x \geqslant 0, \ x \in \mathbb{R}\}$, since $\sqrt{x}$ has meaning only when $x \geqslant 0$.
- the domain of $f(x) = \dfrac{1}{\sqrt{x-1}}$ is $\{x \mid x > 1, \ x \in \mathbb{R}\}$ since, when $x - 1 = 0$ we are 'dividing by zero', and when $x - 1 < 0$, $\sqrt{x-1}$ is undefined.

Example 5 ◀)) **Self Tutor**

Find the domain of:

a $f(x) = \dfrac{2}{\sqrt{x+3}}$ **b** $f(x) = \sqrt{x} + \sqrt{5-x}$

a $f(x) = \dfrac{2}{\sqrt{x+3}}$ is defined when $x + 3 > 0$
$\therefore \ x > -3$
So, the domain of $f(x)$ is $\{x \mid x > -3, \ x \in \mathbb{R}\}$.

b $f(x) = \sqrt{x} + \sqrt{5-x}$ is defined when $x \geqslant 0$ and $5 - x \geqslant 0$
$\therefore \ x \geqslant 0$ and $x \leqslant 5$
So, the domain of $f(x)$ is $\{x \mid 0 \leqslant x \leqslant 5, \ x \in \mathbb{R}\}$.

EXERCISE 15C.2

1 Find the domain of:

  a $f(x) = 2x$
  b $f(x) = \dfrac{1}{x}$
  c $f(x) = \dfrac{1}{x-3}$
  d $f(x) = \dfrac{1}{(x-1)(x+2)}$
  e $f(x) = \dfrac{x}{x^2-9}$
  f $f(x) = \dfrac{3}{x^2-5x+4}$

2 Find the domain of:

  a $f(x) = \sqrt{x-2}$
  b $f(x) = \sqrt{3-x}$
  c $f(x) = \sqrt{x} + \sqrt{2-x}$
  d $f(x) = \dfrac{1}{\sqrt{x}}$
  e $f(x) = \dfrac{1}{\sqrt{x}} + \dfrac{1}{\sqrt{x+2}}$
  f $f(x) = \dfrac{1}{x\sqrt{4-x}}$

Check your answers using the graphing package.

GRAPHING PACKAGE

D COMPOSITE FUNCTIONS

Sometimes functions are built up in two or more stages.

For example, consider $f(x) = 2\sqrt{x}$.

Using the techniques studied in **Section C**, $f(x+3) = 2\sqrt{x+3}$. {replacing x by $(x+3)$}

If we let $g(x) = x + 3$, then $f(g(x)) = 2\sqrt{x+3}$.

So, the function $f(g(x)) = 2\sqrt{x+3}$ is *composed* of $f(x) = 2\sqrt{x}$ and $g(x) = x + 3$.

> Given $f : x \mapsto f(x)$ and $g : x \mapsto g(x)$, the **composite function** of f and g will convert x into $f(g(x))$.

Example 6 ◀)) Self Tutor

If $f(x) = 3x + 2$ and $g(x) = x^2 + 4$, find in simplest form:

a $f(g(x))$ **b** $g(f(x))$

a $f(g(x))$
$= f(x^2 + 4)$
$= 3(x^2 + 4) + 2$
$= 3x^2 + 12 + 2$
$= 3x^2 + 14$

b $g(f(x))$
$= g(3x + 2)$
$= (3x + 2)^2 + 4$
$= 9x^2 + 12x + 4 + 4$
$= 9x^2 + 12x + 8$

To find $f(g(x))$ we look at the f function. Whenever we see x we replace it by $g(x)$ within brackets.

From the previous **Example**, we can see that in general, $f(g(x)) \neq g(f(x))$.

Example 7 ◀)) Self Tutor

If $f(x) = 2x - 1$, find:

a $f(f(x))$ **b** $f(f(5))$

a $f(f(x))$
$= f(2x - 1)$
$= 2(2x - 1) - 1$
$= 4x - 2 - 1$
$= 4x - 3$

b $f(f(5))$
$= 4(5) - 3$ {using **a**}
$= 17$

EXERCISE 15D

1 If $f(x) = 3x - 4$ and $g(x) = 2 - x$, find in simplest form:

a $f(g(x))$ **b** $g(f(x))$ **c** $f(f(x))$ **d** $g(g(x))$

2 If $f(x) = \sqrt{x}$ and $g(x) = 4x - 3$, find in simplest form:

a $f(g(x))$ **b** $g(f(x))$ **c** $f(g(7))$ **d** $g(f(4))$

3 Find two functions f and g such that:

   a $f(g(x)) = \sqrt{x-3}$ **b** $f(g(x)) = (x+5)^3$ **c** $f(g(x)) = \dfrac{5}{x+7}$

   d $g(f(x)) = \dfrac{1}{\sqrt{3-4x}}$ **e** $g(f(x)) = 3^{x^2}$ **f** $g(f(x)) = \left(\dfrac{x+1}{x-1}\right)^2$

4 Suppose $f(x) = 3x + 1$ and $g(x) = x^2 + 2x$.
   a Find $f(g(x))$.   **b** Find x such that $f(g(x)) = 10$.

5 Suppose $f(x) = 4x + 1$ and $g(x) = \dfrac{1}{x+2}$.
   a Find $f(g(x))$.   **b** Find $f(g(-1))$.
   c Find x such that $f(g(x)) = 3$.

6 Suppose $f(x) = 2x + 5$ and $g(x) = \dfrac{x-5}{2}$.
   a Find:
      i $f(4)$ **ii** $g(13)$ **iii** $g(17)$ **iv** $f(6)$.
   b Find $f(g(x))$ and $g(f(x))$.
   c Find:
      i $f(g(3))$ **ii** $g(f(-7))$.

E   INVERSE FUNCTIONS

The operations of $+$ and $-$, and $\times$ and $\div$, are **inverse operations** since one 'undoes' the other.

In the same way, some functions have **inverse functions** which 'undo' each other.

> For a function f which converts x to $f(x)$, the **inverse function** f^{-1} converts $f(x)$ back to x.
> The inverse function satisfies $f(f^{-1}(x)) = x$ and $f^{-1}(f(x)) = x$.

For a given function f, an inverse function f^{-1} only exists if, for any value of $f(x)$, there is only *one* corresponding value of x.

INVESTIGATION 1   INVERSE FUNCTIONS

In this Investigation we explore inverse functions, how they relate to composite functions, and also how they relate to transformations.

What to do:

1 Consider $f(x) = 3x + 2$ which has graph $y = 3x + 2$.
   a Interchange x and y and then make y the subject of this new equation. Let this function be $g(x)$.
   b Hence show that $f(3) = 11$ and $g(11) = 3$.
   c From **b**, notice that $g(11) = g(f(3)) = 3$. Show that $f(g(3)) = 3$ also.
   d Prove that $f(g(x)) = x$ and $g(f(x)) = x$.
   e Graph $y = f(x)$ and $y = g(x)$ on the same set of axes. What do you notice?

2 Consider $f(x) = 3 - 4x$ which has graph $y = 3 - 4x$.

   a Interchange x and y and then make y the subject of this new equation. Hence find the inverse function $f^{-1}(x)$.

   b Show that $f(f^{-1}(x)) = f^{-1}(f(x)) = x$.

   c Graph $y = f(x)$ and $y = f^{-1}(x)$ on the same set of axes. What do you notice?

From the **Investigation** you should have found that:

- $f^{-1}(x)$ can be found algebraically by interchanging x and y and then making y the subject of the resulting formula. The new y is $f^{-1}(x)$.
- $y = f^{-1}(x)$ is the reflection of $y = f(x)$ in the line $y = x$.

Example 8   ◀ Self Tutor

Consider $f(x) = \tfrac{1}{2}x - 1$.

  a Find $f^{-1}(x)$.   **b** Check that $f(f^{-1}(x)) = f^{-1}(f(x)) = x$.

  c Sketch $y = f(x)$, $y = f^{-1}(x)$, and $y = x$ on the same set of axes.

a $y = \tfrac{1}{2}x - 1$ has inverse function $x = \tfrac{1}{2}y - 1$ {interchanging x and y}

$$\therefore\ 2x = y - 2$$
$$\therefore\ y = 2x + 2$$
$$\therefore\ f^{-1}(x) = 2x + 2$$

b $f(f^{-1}(x)) = f(2x + 2)$ $f^{-1}(f(x)) = f^{-1}(\tfrac{1}{2}x - 1)$
$\phantom{f(f^{-1}(x))} = \tfrac{1}{2}(2x + 2) - 1$ $= 2(\tfrac{1}{2}x - 1) + 2$
$\phantom{f(f^{-1}(x))} = x + 1 - 1$ $= x - 2 + 2$
$\phantom{f(f^{-1}(x))} = x$ $= x$

c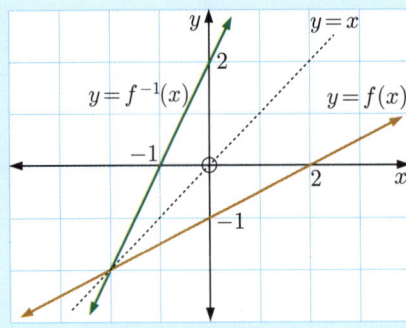

$y = f^{-1}(x)$ is a reflection of $y = f(x)$ in the line $y = x$.

EXERCISE 15E

1 For each of the following functions:

    i Find $f^{-1}(x)$.

    ii Sketch $y = f(x)$, $y = f^{-1}(x)$, and $y = x$ on the same set of axes.

    a $f(x) = x + 3$ **b** $f(x) = 2x + 5$ **c** $f(x) = \dfrac{3 - 2x}{4}$

2 Copy the following graphs and draw the graph of each inverse function:

a 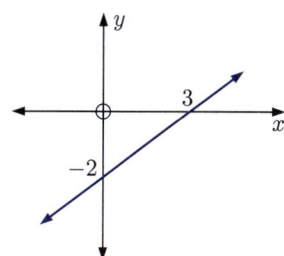 b 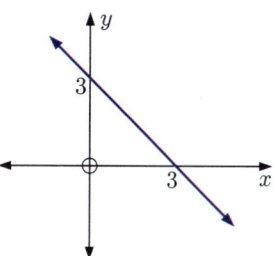 c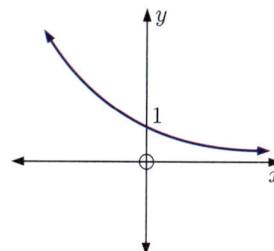

3 Consider $f(x) = 2x + 7$.
  a Find $f^{-1}(x)$.
  b Check that $f(f^{-1}(x)) = f^{-1}(f(x)) = x$.

4 Consider $f(x) = \dfrac{2x+1}{x+3}$.
  a Find $f^{-1}(x)$.
  b Check that $f(f^{-1}(x)) = f^{-1}(f(x)) = x$.

5 Consider $g(x) = \dfrac{x}{x-5}$.
  a Find $g^{-1}(x)$.
  b Check that $g(g^{-1}(x)) = x$ and $g^{-1}(g(x)) = x$.
  c Find $g(6)$ and $g^{-1}(1)$.

6 a Sketch the graph of $y = x^2$ and reflect it in the line $y = x$.
  b Does $f(x) = x^2$ have an inverse function? Explain your answer.
  c Does $f(x) = x^2$, $x \geqslant 0$ have an inverse function? Explain your answer.

7 The **horizontal line test** says that *'for a function to have an inverse function, no horizontal line can cut it more than once'*.
  a Explain why this is a valid test for the existence of an inverse function.
  b Which of the following functions have an inverse function?

  i 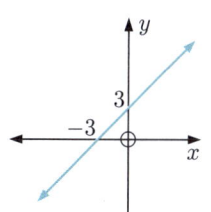 ii 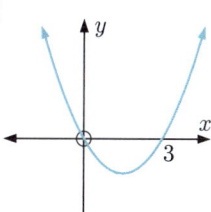 iii iv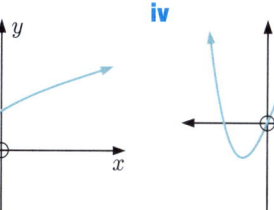

8 a Explain why $f(x) = x^2 - 2x + 5$ is a function but does not have an inverse function.
  b Explain why $f(x) = x^2 - 2x + 5$, $x \geqslant 1$ has an inverse function.
  c Show that the inverse function of **b** is $f^{-1}(x) = 1 + \sqrt{x-4}$.
    Hint: Swap x and y, then use the quadratic formula to solve for y in terms of x.

F THE MODULUS FUNCTION

MODULUS

The **modulus** or **absolute value** of a real number is its size, ignoring its sign. We denote the modulus of x by $|x|$.

For example, the modulus of 7 is 7, and the modulus of -7 is also 7, so we write $|7| = 7$ and $|-7| = 7$.

Example 9 ◀)) Self Tutor

If $a = -7$ and $b = 3$, find:
a $|a + b|$ **b** $|ab|$

a $|a + b|$
$= |-7 + 3|$
$= |-4|$
$= 4$

b $|ab|$
$= |-7 \times 3|$
$= |-21|$
$= 21$

Perform all operations inside the modulus signs before actually finding the modulus.

GEOMETRIC DEFINITION OF MODULUS

$|x|$ is the distance of x from 0 on the number line. Because the modulus is a distance, it cannot be negative.

If $x > 0$:

If $x < 0$:

For example: $|-7| = |7| = 7$

ALGEBRAIC DEFINITION OF MODULUS

INVESTIGATION 2 ALGEBRAIC DEFINITION OF MODULUS

What to do:

1 Suppose $y = \begin{cases} x & \text{if } x \geqslant 0 \\ -x & \text{if } x < 0. \end{cases}$

a Copy and complete the table of values:

x	-10	-8	-2	0	$\frac{1}{2}$	3	5	7
y								

b Plot the points from the table and hence graph $y = \begin{cases} x & \text{if } x \geqslant 0 \\ -x & \text{if } x < 0. \end{cases}$

2 Copy and complete:

x	-10	-8	-2	0	$\frac{1}{2}$	3	5	7
$\sqrt{x^2}$								

3 What can you conclude from **1** and **2**?

From the **Investigation**, you should have found that: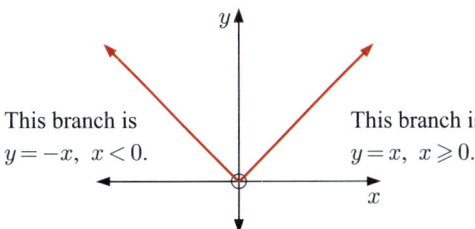

$y = |x|$ has graph:

This branch is
$y = -x, \ x < 0$.

This branch is
$y = x, \ x \geqslant 0$.

To draw graphs involving $|x|$, we must consider the cases $x \geqslant 0$ and $x < 0$ separately, so that we can write the function without the modulus sign.

Example 10   ◀) Self Tutor

Draw the graph of $f(x) = x + 2|x|$.

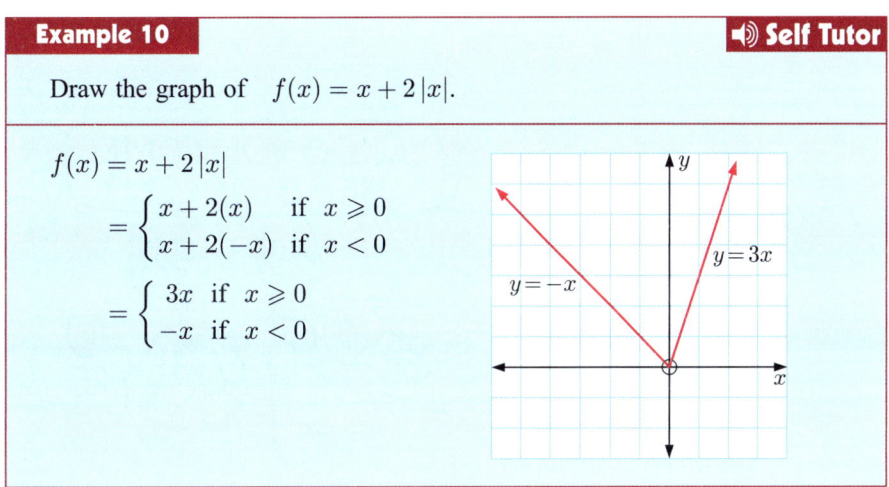

$f(x) = x + 2|x|$

$= \begin{cases} x + 2(x) & \text{if } x \geqslant 0 \\ x + 2(-x) & \text{if } x < 0 \end{cases}$

$= \begin{cases} 3x & \text{if } x \geqslant 0 \\ -x & \text{if } x < 0 \end{cases}$

EXERCISE 15F

1 If $x = -4$, find the value of:

    a $|x + 6|$ **b** $|x - 6|$ **c** $|2x + 3|$ **d** $|7 - x|$

    e $|x - 7|$ **f** $|x^2 - 6x|$ **g** $|6x - x^2|$ **h** $\dfrac{|x|}{x + 2}$

2 If $a = 5$ and $b = -2$, find the value of:

    a $|a + b|$ **b** $|ab|$ **c** $|b - a|$ **d** $|a| + b$

    e $|3a + b|$ **f** $\dfrac{|b - 8|}{a}$ **g** $\left|\dfrac{a}{b}\right|$ **h** $\dfrac{|b^2|}{|a|}$

3 **a** Copy and complete:

x	9	3	0	-3	-9
x^2					
$|x|^2$					

b What can you conclude from **a**?

4 By replacing $|x|$ with x for $x \geqslant 0$ and $(-x)$ for $x < 0$, write the following functions without the modulus sign. Hence, graph each function:

a $f(x) = -|x|$ **b** $f(x) = |x| + x$ **c** $f(x) = |x| + 2$

d $f(x) = x - 2|x|$ **e** $f(x) = 3|x| + 1$ **f** $f(x) = 5 - |x|$

g $f(x) = |x|^2 - 4$ **h** $f(x) = \dfrac{|x|}{x}$ **i** $f(x) = \sqrt{|x|}$

5 **a** Use technology to graph:

  i $y = |(x-2)(x-4)|$ **ii** $y = |x(x-3)|$

b Explain how these functions are related to $y = (x-2)(x-4)$ and $y = x(x-3)$.

GRAPHING PACKAGE

G WHERE FUNCTIONS MEET

We often draw the graphs of two functions on the same set of axes, and are interested in finding where the functions meet.

To find the points of intersection of the graphs of $y = f(x)$ and $y = g(x)$, we solve the equation $f(x) = g(x)$.

The solutions of this equation give us the x-coordinates of the intersection points.

The y-coordinates can then be found by substituting the x-coordinates into one of the functions.

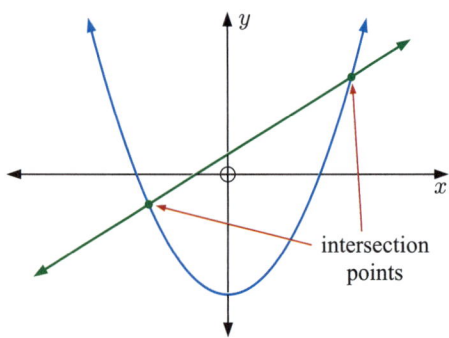

Example 11

Find the coordinates of the points of intersection of the graphs with equations
$y = x^2 - x + 3$ and $y = 2x + 7$.

The graphs meet when $x^2 - x + 3 = 2x + 7$
$\therefore x^2 - 3x - 4 = 0$
$\therefore (x+1)(x-4) = 0$
$\therefore x = -1$ or 4

Substituting into $y = 2x + 7$: when $x = -1$, $y = 2(-1) + 7 = 5$
when $x = 4$, $y = 2(4) + 7 = 15$

$\therefore$ the graphs meet at $(-1, 5)$ and $(4, 15)$.

EXERCISE 15G

1. Find the coordinates of the point of intersection of the graphs with equations:

   a $y = 5x - 1$ and $y = 2x + 5$
   b $y = 12 - x$ and $y = 3x + 7$
   c $y = \dfrac{1}{x}$ and $y = \dfrac{2}{x+5}$
   d $y = x^2 - x + 3$ and $y = x^2 + 5x - 3$.

2. Find the coordinates of the point(s) of intersection of the graphs with equations:

   a $y = x^2 + 2x - 1$ and $y = x + 5$
   b $y = \dfrac{2}{x}$ and $y = x - 1$
   c $y = 3x^2 + 4x - 1$ and $y = x^2 - 3x - 4$
   d $y = \dfrac{1}{x}$ and $y = 5x - 4$.

3. Use a **graphing package** or a **graphics calculator** to find the coordinates, correct to 2 decimal places, of the points of intersection of the graphs with equations:

   a $y = x^2 + 3x + 1$ and $y = 2x + 2$
   b $y = x^2 - 5x + 2$ and $y = \dfrac{3}{x}$
   c $y = -x^2 - 2x + 5$ and $y = x^2 + 7$
   d $y = x^2 - 1$ and $y = x^3$.

GRAPHING PACKAGE

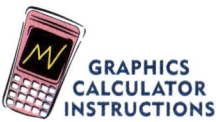
GRAPHICS CALCULATOR INSTRUCTIONS

REVIEW SET 15A

1. Find the domain and range of the following relations:

   a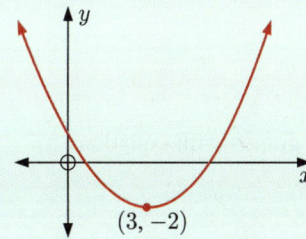
   $(3, -2)$

   b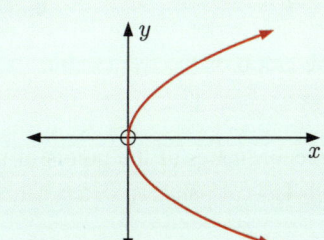

2 For $f(x) = 3x - x^2$, find:
   a $f(2)$
   b $f(-1)$
   c $f(x-3)$

3 Determine whether the following sets of ordered pairs are functions:
   a $\{(-3, 5), (1, 7), (-1, 7), (2, 5)\}$
   b $\{(-4, -5), (-1, 3), (5, 4), (0, 3), (-1, 2)\}$

4 Consider the function $g(x) = x^2 + 2x$. Find:
   a $g(2)$
   b $g(3x)$
   c x such that $g(x) = 15$.

5 Determine whether the following relations are functions:
   a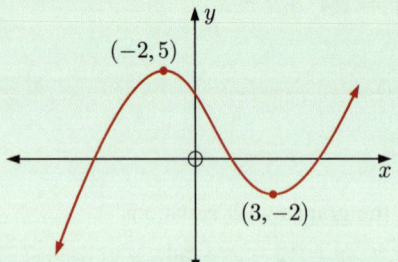
   b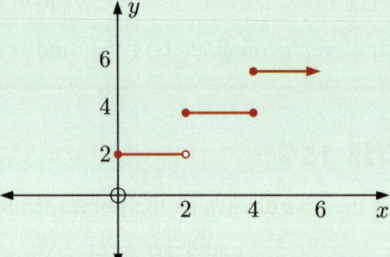

6 Draw a graph of $y = f(x)$ such that $f(-3) = 2$, $f(1) = -4$, and $f(4) = 5$.

7 Answer the **Opening Problem** on page 324.

8 If $f(x) = \sqrt{x}$ and $g(x) = 5x - 3$, find in simplest form:
   a $f(g(x))$
   b $g(f(x))$
   c $g(g(x))$

9 Consider the function $f(x) = \dfrac{x+2}{7}$.
   a Find $f^{-1}(x)$.
   b Check that $f(f^{-1}(x)) = f^{-1}(f(x)) = x$.
   c Sketch $y = f(x)$, $y = f^{-1}(x)$, and $y = x$ on the same set of axes.

10 Suppose $g(x) = \dfrac{x+4}{x}$.
   a Find $g^{-1}(x)$.
   b Check that $g(g^{-1}(x)) = g^{-1}(g(x)) = x$.
   c Find $g(2)$ and $g^{-1}(3)$.

11 If $x = -3$, find the value of:
   a $|x - 4|$
   b $|x| - 4$
   c $|x^2 + 3x|$

12 Draw the graph of $y = f(x)$ for:
   a $f(x) = |x| + 3x$
   b $f(x) = 2|x| - 4$

13 Find the coordinates of the points of intersection of the graphs with equations $y = x^2 + 4x - 2$ and $y = 2x + 1$.

REVIEW SET 15B

1 Find the domain and range of the following relations:

a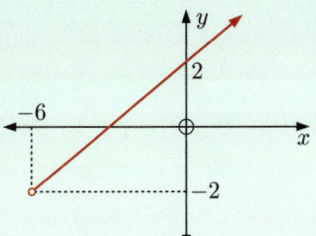

b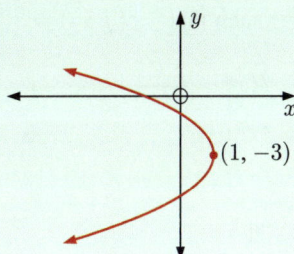

2 Determine whether the following relations are functions:

a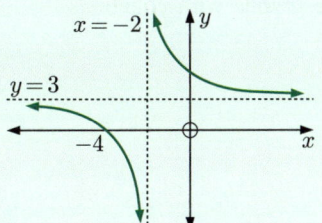

b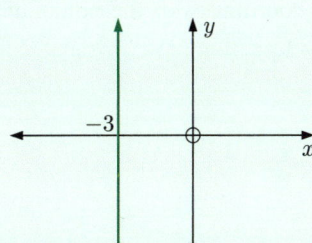

3 For $f(x) = 5x - x^2$, find:

   a $f(-3)$ **b** $f(-x)$ **c** $f(x+1)$

4 Find the domain of:

   a $f(x) = \dfrac{1}{x+4}$ **b** $f(x) = \dfrac{x}{x^2 + 4x - 5}$ **c** $f(x) = \sqrt{x} + \sqrt{6-x}$

5 The graph of $y = f(x)$ is a straight line passing through $(-1, 5)$ and $(3, -3)$.

   a Draw the graph of $y = f(x)$.   **b** Find $f(-1)$ and $f(3)$.
   c Find $f(x)$.   **d** Find $f^{-1}(x)$.

6 If $f(x) = 2x + 1$ and $g(x) = 7 - x$, find in simplest form:

   a $f(g(x))$ **b** $g(f(x))$ **c** $f(g(-2))$

7 Copy the following graphs, and draw the graph of each inverse function:

a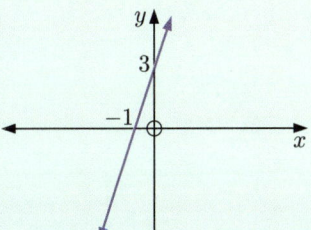

b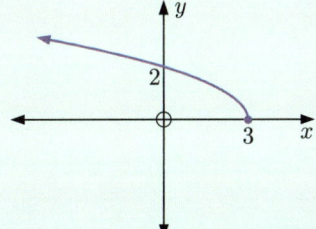

8 If $a = -4$ and $b = 9$, find the value of:

   a $|ab|$ **b** $|2a - b| + a$ **c** $\dfrac{|a^2 - b|}{|a|}$

9 Suppose $f(x) = 3x - 1$ and $g(x) = \dfrac{1}{x-4}$.

   a Find $f(g(x))$.   **b** Find $f(g(5))$.

   c Find x such that $f(g(x)) = -\frac{1}{2}$.

10 Consider $f(x) = \dfrac{x+1}{x-2}$.

   a Find $f^{-1}(x)$.   **b** Check that $f(f^{-1}(x)) = f^{-1}(f(x)) = x$.

   c Find $f^{-1}(4)$.

11 Draw the graph of:

   a $f(x) = 7 - |x|$ **b** $f(x) = \dfrac{x}{|x|} + 3$

12 Find the coordinates of the points of intersection of the graphs with equations $y = \dfrac{3}{x}$ and $y = 2x - 1$.

Chapter 16

Number sequences

Contents:
- **A** Number sequences
- **B** Arithmetic sequences
- **C** Geometric sequences
- **D** Series
- **E** Arithmetic series
- **F** Geometric series

OPENING PROBLEM

Jasmine is attempting to cycle 2000 km in 30 days to raise money for charity. She cycled 40 km on the first day, and each day she will cycle 2 km further than the day before.

Things to think about:
- **a** How far will Jasmine cycle on the:
  - **i** 2nd day
  - **ii** 10th day
  - **iii** 20th day?
- **b** How far will Jasmine have cycled in total after:
  - **i** 2 days
  - **ii** 10 days
  - **iii** 20 days?
- **c** Can we find the answers to **a** and **b** without having to calculate the distance cycled on each of the days?
- **d** Will Jasmine achieve her goal of cycling 2000 km in 30 days?

In this chapter, we will study **number sequences**. We will see that, for certain types of sequences, there are rules which allow us to find any member of the sequence. We can also calculate the sum of the members of the sequence without having to add all the members individually.

A — NUMBER SEQUENCES

Consider the illustrated pattern of balls:

The first layer has just one blue ball.
The second layer has three pink balls.
The third layer has five black balls.
The fourth layer has seven green balls.

If we let u_n represent the number of balls in the nth layer, then $u_1 = 1$, $u_2 = 3$, $u_3 = 5$, and $u_4 = 7$.

The pattern could be continued forever, generating the **sequence** of numbers:
1, 3, 5, 7, 9, 11, 13, 15, 17, ...

The string of dots indicates that the pattern continues forever.

> A **number sequence** is an ordered list of numbers defined by a rule.
>
> The numbers in a sequence are called the **terms** of the sequence.

We will look at three ways of describing a number sequence.

(1) Using **words**.

The sequence for the pattern of balls can be described as "starting at 1, and increasing by 2 each time".

(2) Using an **explicit formula**, which gives the nth term of the sequence u_n in terms of n.

The explicit formula for the pattern of balls is $u_n = 2n - 1$. u_n is called the **nth term** or the **general term**.

We can use this formula to find, for example, the 10th term of the sequence, which is $u_{10} = 2(10) - 1 = 19$.

(3) Using a **recursive formula**, which gives the nth term of the sequence in terms of one or more of the preceding terms.

The recursive formula for the pattern of balls is $u_1 = 1$, $u_n = u_{n-1} + 2$ for $n \geqslant 2$.

So, we have $u_1 = 1$
$u_2 = u_1 + 2 = 1 + 2 = 3$
$u_3 = u_2 + 2 = 3 + 2 = 5$, and so on.

In a recursive formula, at least one initial term must be defined.

EXERCISE 16A

1 Consider the number sequence $2, 4, 7, 11, 16, 22, \ldots$. Find:

   a u_2 **b** u_5 **c** $u_1 + u_2 + u_3$.

2 Write down the first five terms of the sequence:

   a starting at 3, and increasing by 4 each time
   b starting at 40, and decreasing by 5 each time
   c whose nth term is the nth prime number.

3 Describe the sequence $5, 8, 11, 14, 17, 20, \ldots$ using:

   a words   **b** a recursive formula.

4 Describe the sequence $1, 4, 9, 16, 25, 36, \ldots$ using:

   a words   **b** an explicit formula.

5 Find the 5th term of the sequence with explicit formula:

   a $u_n = 3n + 4$ **b** $u_n = 54 - 7n$ **c** $u_n = 3 \times 2^n$ **d** $u_n = n^2 + 2$

6 Consider the sequence with explicit formula $u_n = 50 - n^2$. Find:

   a the 6th term   **b** the sum of the first 3 terms
   c the first term of the sequence which is negative.

7 Find the first four terms of the sequence with recursive formula:

   a $u_1 = 7$, $u_n = u_{n-1} + 3$, $n \geqslant 2$ **b** $u_1 = 25$, $u_n = u_{n-1} - 4$, $n \geqslant 2$
   c $u_1 = 5$, $u_n = 3 \times u_{n-1}$, $n \geqslant 2$ **d** $u_1 = 100$, $u_n = \dfrac{u_{n-1}}{2}$, $n \geqslant 2$
   e $u_1 = 3$, $u_n = 2 \times u_{n-1} - 1$, $n \geqslant 2$ **f** $u_1 = 4$, $u_n = 10 - u_{n-1}$, $n \geqslant 2$
   g $u_1 = 3$, $u_2 = 4$, $u_n = u_{n-1} \times u_{n-2}$, $n \geqslant 3$

INVESTIGATION 1 — THE FIBONACCI SEQUENCE

Perhaps the most famous example of a recursive relationship is that which generates the **Fibonacci sequence**:

$$1,\ 1,\ 2,\ 3,\ 5,\ 8,\ 13,\ 21,\ 34,\ 55,\ ....$$

The sequence starts with two 1s, and after that each term is obtained by adding the two terms preceding it:

$$1 + 1 = 2$$
$$1 + 2 = 3$$
$$2 + 3 = 5$$
$$3 + 5 = 8$$
$$\vdots$$

Leonardo Fibonacci

We can hence write down a **recursive formula** for the sequence:
$u_1 = u_2 = 1$, $u_n = u_{n-1} + u_{n-2}$ for $n \geqslant 3$.

Check: If $n = 3$, $u_3 = u_2 + u_1 = 1 + 1 = 2$ ✓
If $n = 4$, $u_4 = u_3 + u_2 = 2 + 1 = 3$ ✓
If $n = 5$, $u_5 = u_4 + u_3 = 3 + 2 = 5$ ✓

Leonardo Fibonacci (1170 - 1250) noticed that the sequence $1, 1, 2, 3, 5, 8, ...$ occurred frequently in the natural world.

For example, he noticed that flowers of particular species have the same number of petals, and that these numbers are often members of the Fibonacci sequence.

3 petals	lily, iris
5 petals	buttercup
8 petals	delphinium
13 petals	cineraria
21 petals	aster
34 petals	pyrethrum

Fibonacci also observed the number sequence in:
- the number of leaves arranged about the stem in plants
- the seed patterns of a sunflower
- the seed pattern on a pine cone.

The recursive formula is very useful for dealing with the Fibonacci sequence because its explicit formula is very complicated. In fact, it is not obvious from the explicit formula

$$u_n = \frac{1}{\sqrt{5}}\left[\left(\frac{1+\sqrt{5}}{2}\right)^n - \left(\frac{1-\sqrt{5}}{2}\right)^n\right], \quad n = 1, 2, 3, 4, 5, ...$$

that the sequence generated will be integers.

What to do:

1 Show that the explicit formula is correct for $n = 1$ and $n = 2$.

2 Use the recursive formula to find the next five terms of the Fibonacci sequence after 55.

3 Can you see a pattern of even and odd numbers in the Fibonacci sequence? Do you think the 100th term of the sequence will be even or odd?

4 Research other occurrences of the Fibonacci sequence in nature.

B   ARITHMETIC SEQUENCES

An **arithmetic sequence** is a sequence in which each term differs from the previous one by the same fixed number. We call this number the **common difference**.

For example:

- the sequence 1, 5, 9, 13, 17, ... is arithmetic with common difference 4, since
  $5 - 1 = 4$
  $9 - 5 = 4$
  $13 - 9 = 4$, and so on.
- the sequence 42, 37, 32, 27, ... is arithmetic with common difference -5, since
  $37 - 42 = -5$
  $32 - 37 = -5$
  $27 - 32 = -5$, and so on.

THE GENERAL TERM OF AN ARITHMETIC SEQUENCE

Notice in the sequence 1, 5, 9, 13, 17, ... that $u_1 = 1$
$u_2 = 1 + 4 \qquad = 1 + 1(4)$
$u_3 = 1 + 4 + 4 \qquad = 1 + 2(4)$
$u_4 = 1 + 4 + 4 + 4 = 1 + 3(4)$, and so on.

For an **arithmetic sequence** with **first term** u_1 and **common difference** d, the **general term** or **nth term** is $u_n = u_1 + (n-1)d$.

Example 1 ◀)) **Self Tutor**

Consider the sequence 3, 9, 15, 21, 27, ...
 a Show that the sequence is arithmetic.
 b Find a formula for the general term u_n.
 c Find the 100th term of the sequence.
 d Is **i** 489 **ii** 1592 a member of the sequence?

---

a $9 - 3 = 6$, $15 - 9 = 6$, $21 - 15 = 6$, $27 - 21 = 6$
Assuming that the pattern continues, consecutive terms differ by 6.
$\therefore$ the sequence is arithmetic with $u_1 = 3$ and common difference $d = 6$.

b $u_n = u_1 + (n-1)d$
$\therefore u_n = 3 + 6(n-1)$
$\therefore u_n = 6n - 3$

c $u_{100} = 6(100) - 3$
$= 597$

d **i** Let $u_n = 489$
$\therefore\ 6n - 3 = 489$
$\therefore\ 6n = 492$
$\therefore\ n = 82$
$\therefore\ 489$ is the 82nd term of the sequence.

ii Let $u_n = 1592$
$\therefore\ 6n - 3 = 1592$
$\therefore\ 6n = 1595$
$\therefore\ n = 265\frac{5}{6}$
But n must be an integer, so 1592 is not a term of the sequence.

EXERCISE 16B

1 Determine whether the following sequences are arithmetic:
   a 2, 5, 8, 11, 14, ...
   b 5, 9, 13, 18, 22, ...
   c 29, 23, 16, 10, 4, ...
   d 11, 4, −3, −10, −17, ...

2 Find the unknowns given that the following sequences are arithmetic:
   a 4, 10, □, 22, 28, ...
   b 13, 20, 27, □, 41, ...
   c 19, □, 11, 7, △, ...
   d 22, □, 4, △, −14, ...

3 Write down the first term u_1 and common difference d for the arithmetic sequence of numbers given by:
   a the green arrow
   b the blue arrow
   c the purple arrow
   d the red arrow.

4 Consider the sequence 4, 11, 18, 25, 32, ...
   a Show that the sequence is arithmetic.
   b Find a formula for the general term u_n.
   c Find the 30th term of the sequence.
   d Is 340 a member of the sequence?
   e Is 738 a member of the sequence?

5 Consider the sequence 67, 63, 59, 55, ...
   a Show that the sequence is arithmetic.
   b Find a formula for the general term u_n.
   c Find the 60th term of the sequence.
   d Is −143 a member of the sequence?
   e Is 85 a member of the sequence?

6 An arithmetic sequence is defined by $u_n = 11n - 7$.
   a Find u_1 and d.
   b Find the 37th term.
   c What is the least term of the sequence which is greater than 250?

Example 2

Find k given that $k + 5$, -1, and $2k - 1$ are consecutive terms of an arithmetic sequence.

Since the terms are consecutive,

$-1 - (k + 5) = (2k - 1) - (-1)$ {equating common differences}
$\therefore\ -1 - k - 5 = 2k - 1 + 1$
$\therefore\ -k - 6 = 2k$
$\therefore\ -6 = 3k$
$\therefore\ k = -2$

7 Find k given the consecutive terms of an arithmetic sequence:

   a 31, k, 13 **b** k, 8, $k + 11$ **c** $k + 2$, $2k + 3$, 17

8   **a** Find k given that $k - 1$, 13, and $3k + 3$ are consecutive terms of an arithmetic sequence.
    b Write down the next two terms of the sequence.

Example 3

Find the general term u_n for an arithmetic sequence given that $u_3 = 4$ and $u_7 = -24$.

$u_3 = u_1 + 2d = 4$ .... (1)
and $u_7 = u_1 + 6d = -24$ .... (2)
$\therefore\ -4d = 28$ {(1) − (2)}
$\therefore\ d = -7$

Substituting into (1), $u_1 + 2(-7) = 4$
$\therefore\ u_1 - 14 = 4$
$\therefore\ u_1 = 18$

Thus $u_n = 18 + (n - 1)(-7)$ Check:
$\therefore\ u_n = 18 - 7n + 7$ $u_3 = 25 - 7(3) = 4$ ✓
$\therefore\ u_n = 25 - 7n$ $u_7 = 25 - 7(7) = -24$ ✓

9 Find the general term u_n for an arithmetic sequence given that:

  a $u_4 = 37$ and $u_{10} = 67$ **b** $u_5 = -10$ and $u_{12} = -38$
  c $u_4 = -4$ and $u_{15} = 29$ **d** $u_{10} = -16$ and $u_6 = -13$.

10 An arithmetic sequence has $u_3 = 10$ and $u_{11} = 58$.

  a Find the general term for the sequence.   **b** Find the 30th term of the sequence.

GEOMETRIC SEQUENCES

A sequence is **geometric** if each term can be obtained from the previous one by multiplying by the same non-zero constant. This constant is called the **common ratio**.

For example: 2, 6, 18, 54, ... is a geometric sequence with common ratio 3, since

$$2 \times 3 = 6 \quad \text{and} \quad 6 \times 3 = 18 \quad \text{and} \quad 18 \times 3 = 54.$$

THE GENERAL TERM OF A GEOMETRIC SEQUENCE

Notice in the sequence 2, 6, 18, 54, ... that
$$u_1 = 2$$
$$u_2 = 2 \times 3$$
$$u_3 = 2 \times 3 \times 3 = 2 \times 3^2$$
$$u_4 = 2 \times 3 \times 3 \times 3 = 2 \times 3^3, \text{ and so on.}$$

For a **geometric sequence** with **first term** u_1 and **common ratio** r, the **general term** or **nth term** is $u_n = u_1 r^{n-1}$.

r is called the common ratio because $\dfrac{u_{n+1}}{u_n} = r$ for all n.

Example 4   ◀)) Self Tutor

Consider the sequence 16, 8, 4, 2, 1, ...
a Show that the sequence is geometric.
b Find the general term u_n.
c Find the 10th term as a fraction.

a $\frac{8}{16} = \frac{1}{2}$, $\frac{4}{8} = \frac{1}{2}$, $\frac{2}{4} = \frac{1}{2}$, $\frac{1}{2} = \frac{1}{2}$

Assuming the pattern continues, consecutive terms have a common ratio of $\frac{1}{2}$.
∴ the sequence is geometric with $u_1 = 16$ and $r = \frac{1}{2}$.

b $u_n = u_1 r^{n-1}$ ∴ $u_n = 16 \times \left(\frac{1}{2}\right)^{n-1}$

c $u_{10} = 16 \times \left(\frac{1}{2}\right)^9 = \dfrac{2^4}{2^9} = \dfrac{1}{2^5} = \dfrac{1}{32}$

EXERCISE 16C

1 Determine whether the following sequences are geometric:
   a 5, 10, 20, 40, ...
   b 4, 12, 36, 72, ...
   c 45, 15, 5, $\frac{5}{3}$, ...
   d 1, −4, 16, 64, ...

2 Write down the common ratio for these geometric sequences:
   a 2, 10, 50, 250, ...
   b 60, 30, 15, 7.5, ...
   c 3, −6, 12, −24, ...
   d 4000, −400, 40, −4, ...

3 For the geometric sequence with first two terms given, find b and c:
   a 3, 6, b, c, ...
   b 8, 2, b, c, ...
   c 15, −5, b, c, ...

4 **a** Show that the sequence $1, 3, 9, 27, ...$ is geometric.
   b Find the general term u_n.   **c** Find the 10th term of the sequence.

5 **a** Show that the sequence $40, -20, 10, -5, ...$ is geometric.
   b Find the general term u_n.   **c** Find the 12th term as a fraction.

6 **a** Show that the sequence $16, -4, 1, -0.25, ...$ is geometric.
   b Find the 8th term as a decimal.

7 Find the general term of the geometric sequence: $3, 3\sqrt{2}, 6, 6\sqrt{2}, ...$

Example 5   🔊 Self Tutor

$k - 1$, $k + 2$, and $3k$ are consecutive terms of a geometric sequence.
Find the possible values of k.

Equating common ratios gives $\dfrac{3k}{k+2} = \dfrac{k+2}{k-1}$

$\therefore \ 3k(k-1) = (k+2)^2$

$\therefore \ 3k^2 - 3k = k^2 + 4k + 4$

$\therefore \ 2k^2 - 7k - 4 = 0$

$\therefore \ (k-4)(2k+1) = 0$

$\therefore \ k = 4 \text{ or } -\tfrac{1}{2}$

Check: If $k = 4$,   the terms are: $3, 6, 12$. ✓ $\{r = 2\}$
       If $k = -\tfrac{1}{2}$, the terms are: $-\tfrac{3}{2}, \tfrac{3}{2}, -\tfrac{3}{2}$. ✓ $\{r = -1\}$

---

8 Find k given the consecutive terms of a geometric sequence:
   a $k, 2, 6$ **b** $4, 6, k$ **c** $k, 2\sqrt{2}, k^2$
   d $3, k, 27$ **e** $k, 3k, 10k + 7$ **f** $k, k + 4, 8k + 2$

Example 6   🔊 Self Tutor

A geometric sequence has $u_2 = -5$ and $u_5 = 40$. Find its general term.

$u_2 = u_1 r = -5$ .... (1)

and $u_5 = u_1 r^4 = 40$ .... (2)

$\therefore \ \dfrac{u_1 r^4}{u_1 r} = \dfrac{40}{-5}$ $\{(2) \div (1)\}$

$\therefore \ r^3 = -8$

$\therefore \ r = \sqrt[3]{-8}$

$\therefore \ r = -2$

Substituting into (1), $u_1(-2) = -5$

$\therefore \ u_1 = \tfrac{5}{2}$

Thus $u_n = \tfrac{5}{2} \times (-2)^{n-1}$

9 Find the general term u_n of the geometric sequence which has:

  a $u_3 = 16$ and $u_4 = 48$
  b $u_3 = 32$ and $u_6 = -4$
  c $u_2 = 10$ and $u_4 = 250$
  d $u_3 = 3$ and $u_7 = \frac{3}{4}$.

10 A geometric sequence has general term u_n with $u_3 = 48$ and $u_7 = 3$. Find u_{12}.

INVESTIGATION 2 — SEQUENCES IN FINANCE

Arithmetic and geometric sequences are observed in financial calculations such as simple interest, compound interest, and depreciation.

What to do:

1 $1000 is invested at a **simple interest** rate of 7% per year with the interest paid at the end of each year. For the case of simple interest, interest is only paid on the amount originally invested.

After 1 year, the value is 1000×1.07 {to increase by 7% we multiply by 107%}
After 2 years, the value is 1000×1.14 {an increase of $2 \times 7\% = 14\%$ on the original}

  a Find the value of the investment at the end of:
    i 3 years   **ii** 4 years   **iii** 5 years.
  b Do the amounts form an arithmetic sequence, geometric sequence, or neither? Explain your answer.
  c Write an explicit formula for the sequence.
  d Write a recursive formula for the sequence.

2 $6000 is invested at a fixed rate of 7% p.a. **compound interest** over a lengthy period. Interest is paid at the end of each year. For the case of compound interest, interest is paid on the current value of the investment.

After 1 year, the value is 6000×1.07
After 2 years, the value is   ($6000 \times 1.07) \times 1.07 = \$6000 \times (1.07)^2$

  a Explain why the amount after 3 years is given by $\$6000 \times (1.07)^3$.
  b Write down, in the same form, the amount after:
    i 4 years   **ii** 5 years   **iii** 6 years.
  c Do the amounts at the end of each year form an arithmetic sequence, geometric sequence, or neither? Explain your answer.
  d Write an explicit formula for the sequence.
  e Write a recursive formula for the sequence.

3 A photocopier originally cost $12 000 and it depreciates in value by 20% each year.
After one year, its value is $\$12\,000 \times 0.8$.

  a Find its value at the end of:
    i two years   **ii** three years.
  b Do the resulting annual values form an arithmetic sequence, or a geometric sequence?
  c Give an explicit formula for the value at the end of the nth year.
  d Give a recursive formula for the value.

D SERIES

A **series** is the sum of the terms of a sequence.

For a finite sequence $u_1, u_2, u_3, ..., u_n$ with n terms, the corresponding series is $u_1 + u_2 + u_3 + ... + u_n$.

The sum of this series is $S_n = u_1 + u_2 + u_3 + ... + u_n$.

For example, consider the sequence $1, 3, 6, 10, 15$, which has 5 terms. The corresponding series is $1 + 3 + 6 + 10 + 15$, and the sum of the series is $S_5 = 35$.

EXERCISE 16D

1 Consider the sequence $3, 5, 8, 11, 19$. Find:
   a u_3 **b** S_3 **c** u_5 **d** S_5.

2 For each of the following sequences, find:
   i the first 4 terms of the sequence   **ii** S_4.
   a $u_n = 2n + 3$
   b $u_n = n^2 - 6$
   c $u_n = 7 \times 2^{n-1}$
   d $u_1 = 3, \ u_n = 3 \times u_{n-1} - 4, \ n \geqslant 2$

3 A sequence has $S_5 = 21$ and $S_6 = 33$. Find the value of u_6.

4 Consider a sequence with general term $u_n = \dfrac{1}{n(n+1)}$. Let S_n be the sum of the first n terms of the sequence.
   a Find the values of S_1, S_2, S_3, and S_4 as fractions.
   b Hence conjecture the value of $\dfrac{1}{1 \times 2} + \dfrac{1}{2 \times 3} + \dfrac{1}{3 \times 4} + \dfrac{1}{4 \times 5} + ... + \dfrac{1}{100 \times 101}$.

E ARITHMETIC SERIES

An **arithmetic series** is the sum of the terms of an arithmetic sequence.

Consider the arithmetic sequence $5, 10, 15, ..., 90, 95, 100$. The first term is $u_1 = 5$ and the last term is $u_{20} = 100$.

The sum of the terms of this sequence is $S_{20} = 5 + 10 + 15 + ... + 90 + 95 + 100$
However, we can also write $S_{20} = 100 + 95 + 90 + ... + 15 + 10 + 5$
                                                             {reversing the terms}

Adding these equations gives $2 \times S_{20} = \underbrace{105 + 105 + 105 + ... + 105 + 105 + 105}_{20 \text{ of these}}$

$\therefore \ 2 \times S_{20} = 20 \times 105$

$\therefore \ S_{20} = \frac{20}{2} \times 105 = 1050$

The sum of a finite arithmetic series with first term u_1, common difference d, and last term u_n, is

$$S_n = \frac{n}{2}(u_1 + u_n)$$

or $S_n = \dfrac{n}{2}(2u_1 + (n-1)d)$ {using $u_n = u_1 + (n-1)d$}

Example 7

An arithmetic series has 8 terms. The first term is 3 and the last term is 17. Find the sum of the series.

The series is arithmetic with $u_1 = 3$ and $u_8 = 17$.

Now $S_n = \dfrac{n}{2}(u_1 + u_n)$

$\therefore\ S_8 = \dfrac{8}{2}(3 + 17)$
$= 80$

Example 8

Find the sum of $1 + 5 + 9 + 13 + ...$ to 30 terms.

The series is arithmetic with $u_1 = 1$, $d = 4$, and $n = 30$.

Now $S_n = \dfrac{n}{2}(2u_1 + (n-1)d)$

$\therefore\ S_{30} = \dfrac{30}{2}(2 \times 1 + 29 \times 4)$
$= 1770$

Example 9

Find the sum of $6 + 10 + 14 + 18 + ... + 102$.

The series is arithmetic with $u_1 = 6$, $d = 4$, and $u_n = 102$.

First we need to find n.

$u_n = 102$
$\therefore\ u_1 + (n-1)d = 102$
$\therefore\ 6 + 4(n-1) = 102$
$\therefore\ 4n = 100$
$\therefore\ n = 25$

Now $S_n = \dfrac{n}{2}(u_1 + u_n)$

$\therefore\ S_{25} = \dfrac{25}{2}(6 + 102)$
$= 1350$

EXERCISE 16E

1 Find the value of $5 + 8 + 11 + 14 + 17 + 20$:
   a by adding the terms directly
   b using $S_n = \dfrac{n}{2}(u_1 + u_n)$
   c using $S_n = \dfrac{n}{2}(2u_1 + (n-1)d)$.

2 An arithmetic series has 12 terms. The first term is 10 and the last term is 65. Find the sum of the series.

3 An arithmetic series has 20 terms. The first term is 30 and the last term is -8. Find the sum of the series.

4 Find the sum of:

    a $3 + 7 + 11 + 15 + ...$ to 10 terms
    b $40 + 35 + 30 + 25 + ...$ to 15 terms
    c $8 + 11 + 14 + 17 + ...$ to 50 terms
    d $-6 + 3 + 12 + 21 + ...$ to 40 terms
    e $21 + 19 + 17 + 15 + ...$ to 60 terms
    f $7 + 1 + (-5) + (-11) + ...$ to 30 terms
    g $5 + 5\frac{1}{2} + 6 + 6\frac{1}{2} + ...$ to 25 terms
    h $20 + 19\frac{1}{2} + 19 + 18\frac{1}{2} + ...$ to 50 terms.

5 An arithmetic sequence has $S_1 = 4$ and $S_2 = 11$. Find S_{40}.

6 Consider the series $4 + 9 + 14 + 19 + ... + 119$.

    a How many terms are in the series?
    b Find the sum of the series.

7 Find the sum of:

    a $7 + 9 + 11 + 13 + ... + 55$
    b $10 + 13 + 16 + 19 + ... + 100$
    c $87 + 83 + 79 + 75 + ... + 15$
    d $-5 + 1 + 7 + 13 + ... + 109$
    e $12 + 7 + 2 + (-3) + ... + (-58)$
    f $6 + 7\frac{1}{2} + 9 + 10\frac{1}{2} + ... + 30$

8 **a** Show that the sum of the first n multiples of 4 is $2n(n + 1)$.
    b Hence, find $4 + 8 + 12 + 16 + ... + 80$.

9 Jim is saving money to buy a car. He puts €20 in the bank in the first week, then €25 in the second week, then €30 in the third week, and so on.

    a How much will Jim put into the bank in the 10th week?
    b How much money will Jim have saved in total after 20 weeks?

10 The arrangement of numbers alongside is called a 3×3 **magic square**. The numbers from 1 to 9 are placed so that the numbers in each row, column, and main diagonal all add up to the same number, known as the **magic constant**. For a 3×3 magic square, the magic constant is 15.

An $n \times n$ magic square contains the numbers from 1 to n^2.

    a Find, in terms of n, the magic constant for an $n \times n$ magic square.
    b Check that your formula is correct for $n = 3$.
    c Find the magic constant for an 8×8 magic square.

2	7	6
9	5	1
4	3	8

DISCUSSION

Is it possible to find the sum of an infinite arithmetic series?

F GEOMETRIC SERIES

A **geometric series** is the sum of the terms of a geometric sequence.

For example: $1, 2, 4, 8, 16, ..., 1024$ is a geometric sequence.

$1 + 2 + 4 + 8 + 16 + ... + 1024$ is a geometric series.

If we are adding the first n terms of a geometric sequence, we say we have a **finite geometric series**.

If we are adding all of the terms of a geometric sequence which goes on and on forever, we say we have an **infinite geometric series**.

SUM OF A FINITE GEOMETRIC SERIES

The sum of the first n terms of a geometric series is

$$S_n = u_1 + u_1 r + u_1 r^2 + u_1 r^3 + ... + u_1 r^{n-1}$$

For a finite geometric series with $r \neq 1$,

$$S_n = \frac{u_1(r^n - 1)}{r - 1} \quad \text{or} \quad S_n = \frac{u_1(1 - r^n)}{1 - r}.$$

Proof:

If $S_n = u_1 + u_1 r + u_1 r^2 + u_1 r^3 + ... + u_1 r^{n-2} + u_1 r^{n-1}$ $(*)$

then $r S_n = (u_1 r + u_1 r^2 + u_1 r^3 + u_1 r^4 + ... + u_1 r^{n-1}) + u_1 r^n$

$\therefore \ r S_n = (S_n - u_1) + u_1 r^n$ {from $(*)$}

$\therefore \ r S_n - S_n = u_1 r^n - u_1$

$\therefore \ S_n(r - 1) = u_1(r^n - 1)$

$\therefore \ S_n = \dfrac{u_1(r^n - 1)}{r - 1} \quad \text{or} \quad \dfrac{u_1(1 - r^n)}{1 - r} \quad$ provided $r \neq 1$.

Example 10   🔊 Self Tutor

Find the sum of:

a $3 + 6 + 12 + 24 + ...$ to 10 terms

b $8 - 4 + 2 - 1 + ...$ to 7 terms.

a The series is geometric with $u_1 = 3$ and $r = 2$.

$S_n = \dfrac{u_1(r^n - 1)}{r - 1}$

$\therefore \ S_{10} = \dfrac{3(2^{10} - 1)}{2 - 1}$

$= 3069$

b The series is geometric with $u_1 = 8$ and $r = -\frac{1}{2}$.

$S_n = \dfrac{u_1(1 - r^n)}{1 - r}$

$\therefore \ S_7 = \dfrac{8(1 - (-\frac{1}{2})^7)}{1 - (-\frac{1}{2})}$

$= \dfrac{8(\frac{129}{128})}{\frac{3}{2}}$

$= \dfrac{43}{8}$

EXERCISE 16F.1

1 Find $5 + 10 + 20 + 40 + 80 + 160$:

  a by adding the terms directly

  b using $S_n = \dfrac{u_1(r^n - 1)}{r - 1}$.

2 Find the sum of:

  a $1 + 3 + 9 + 27 + ...$ to 8 terms
  b $2 + 10 + 50 + 250 + ...$ to 10 terms
  c $24 + 12 + 6 + 3 + ...$ to 9 terms
  d $1 + \sqrt{2} + 2 + 2\sqrt{2} + ...$ to 12 terms
  e $4 - 8 + 16 - 32 + ...$ to 10 terms
  f $81 - 27 + 9 - 3 + ...$ to 8 terms
  g $11\sqrt{11} + 11 + \sqrt{11} + 1 + ...$ to 9 terms
  h $16 - 4 + 1 - \frac{1}{4} + ...$ to 10 terms.

3 A geometric series has $S_1 = 2$ and $S_2 = 8$.

  a Find the first term u_1 and the common ratio r.
  b Find the sum of the first 10 terms of the series.

4 A geometric series has first term u_1 and common ratio $r = -1$.

  Show that $S_n = \begin{cases} u_1 & \text{if } n \text{ is odd} \\ 0 & \text{if } n \text{ is even} \end{cases}$.

5 Doug is marooned on a desert island with only 2000 mL of fresh water.

He drinks 500 mL on the first day, but realises he will soon run out of water if he drinks that much each day. He decides that each day he will drink $\frac{3}{4}$ of the amount he drank the previous day.

  a How much water will Doug drink on the:

  i 5th day **ii** 10th day **iii** 15th day?

  b Describe what happens to the amount of water Doug drinks each day.

  c How much water will Doug have drunk in total after:

  i 10 days **ii** 20 days **iii** 30 days?

  d Do you think Doug will ever run out of water? Explain your answer.

SUM OF AN INFINITE GEOMETRIC SERIES

An **infinite geometric series** is the sum of the terms of a geometric sequence which continues indefinitely.

Examples of infinite geometric series include $2 + 8 + 32 + 128 + ...$ and $10 + 5 + 2\frac{1}{2} + 1\frac{1}{4} + ...$

If $r > 1$ or $r < -1$, the terms in the series get larger and larger. The sum of the series becomes infinitely large, and cannot be found. We say that the series **diverges**.

If $-1 < r < 1$, the terms in the series get smaller and smaller, and the sum of the series **converges** to a finite value.

Consider $S_n = \dfrac{u_1(1 - r^n)}{1 - r}$ as n gets very large.

For $-1 < r < 1$, r^n approaches zero, so S_n approaches the value $\dfrac{u_1}{1 - r}$.

> If $-1 < r < 1$, the sum of an infinite geometric series with first term u_1 and common ratio r is $S = \dfrac{u_1}{1-r}$.

Example 11

Find the sum of $2 + 1 + \frac{1}{2} + \frac{1}{4} + ...$

This is an infinite geometric series with $u_1 = 2$ and $r = \frac{1}{2}$.

$-1 < r < 1$, so the series converges, and the sum is $S = \dfrac{u_1}{1-r}$

$$= \dfrac{2}{1 - \frac{1}{2}}$$

$$= 4$$

EXERCISE 16F.2

1 Decide whether the following infinite geometric series will converge or diverge:

   a $7 + 14 + 28 + 56 + ...$
   b $6 + 3 + 1\frac{1}{2} + \frac{3}{4} + ...$
   c $1 - \sqrt{3} + 3 - 3\sqrt{3} + ...$
   d $80 - 8 + 0.8 - 0.08 + ...$

2 Consider the infinite geometric series $9 + 6 + 4 + \frac{8}{3} + ...$
   a Find: i S_5 ii S_{10} iii S_{20}.
   b Predict the sum of the infinite geometric series.
   c Check your answer to **b** by finding the sum $S = \dfrac{u_1}{1-r}$.

3 Find the sum of:
   a $16 + 8 + 4 + 2 + ...$
   b $1 + \frac{1}{5} + \frac{1}{25} + \frac{1}{125} + ...$
   c $36 - 12 + 4 - \frac{4}{3} + ...$
   d $32 + 24 + 18 + \frac{27}{2} + ...$
   e $72 - 12 + 2 - \frac{1}{3} + ...$
   f $0.6 + 0.06 + 0.006 + 0.0006 + ...$

4 Consider a rectangle with area 1 unit^2.
   The rectangle is divided into thirds, with one third coloured blue, and another third coloured red. The rectangle is then rotated $90°$, and the process is repeated on the remaining unshaded third.
   Suppose this process continues indefinitely.

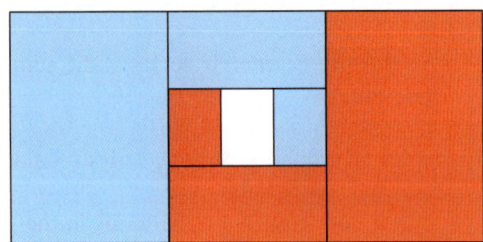

   a Show that the total blue shaded area $= \frac{1}{3} + \frac{1}{9} + \frac{1}{27} + ...$
   b Explain why the blue shaded area $=$ red shaded area.
   c Hence, explain why $\frac{1}{3} + \frac{1}{9} + \frac{1}{27} + ... = \frac{1}{2}$.
   d Check this fact using $S = \dfrac{u_1}{1-r}$.

DEMO

5 **a** Without evaluating either sum, explain why $8 - 4 + 2 - 1 + \frac{1}{2} - \frac{1}{4} + ... = 4 + 1 + \frac{1}{4} + ...$
   b Verify this fact by evaluating each sum.

6 Find the sum of $5 + \frac{5}{\sqrt{2}} + \frac{5}{2} + \frac{5}{2\sqrt{2}} + ...$, giving your answer in the form $a + b\sqrt{2}$, $a, b \in \mathbb{Z}$.

REVIEW SET 16A

1 Write down the first five terms of the sequence:
   a starting at 8, and increasing by 5 each time
   b starting at 19, and decreasing by 7 each time
   c whose nth term is the nth cubic number.

2 Find the first four terms of the sequence with recursive formula $u_1 = 2$, $u_n = 2u_{n-1} + 4$, $n \geqslant 2$.

3 Find the unknowns given that the following sequences are arithmetic:
   a 9, 17, □, 33, 41, ...
   b 27, □, 15, △, 3, ...

4 Find k given that $k - 2$, $2k - 1$, and $4k - 6$ are consecutive terms of an arithmetic sequence.

5 Write down the common ratio for these geometric sequences:
   a 250, 200, 160, 128, ...
   b 4, −12, 36, −108, ...

6 Find the general term u_n of the geometric sequence with $u_4 = 24$ and $u_7 = -192$.

7 Consider the sequence defined by $u_n = n^2 + 2n$. Find:
   a the first 4 terms of the sequence
   b S_4.

8 Find the sum of:
   a $21 + 25 + 29 + 33 + ...$ to 20 terms
   b $40 + 34 + 28 + 22 + ...$ to 30 terms.

9 Find the sum of:
   a $5 + 20 + 80 + 320 + ...$ to 10 terms
   b $18 - 12 + 8 - \frac{16}{3} + ...$ to 9 terms.

10 Find the sum of:
   a $25 + 5 + 1 + \frac{1}{5} + ...$
   b $24 - 12 + 6 - 3 + ...$

REVIEW SET 16B

1 Find the 8th term of the sequence with explicit formula:
   a $u_n = 61 - 4n$
   b $u_n = n^2 - 10$

2 Consider the sequence $-6, -2, 2, 6, ...$
   a Show that the sequence is arithmetic.
   b Find a formula for the general term u_n.
   c Find the 100th term of the sequence.
   d Find the largest term that is less than 500.

3 **a** Show that the sequence $64, -32, 16, -8, 4, ...$ is geometric.
   b Find the 16th term of the sequence as a fraction.

4 **a** Find the first 5 terms of the sequence defined by the recursive formula
$u_1 = 5$, $u_n = 12 - u_{n-1}$, $n \geqslant 2$.

b Hence, state the value of u_{100}.

5 An arithmetic series has 15 terms. The first term is -10, and the last term is 32. Find the sum of the series.

6 Find the general term u_n for the arithmetic sequence with $u_3 = 24$ and $u_{11} = -36$.

7 Find the sum of:

a $6 + 11 + 16 + 21 + ... + 101$
b $80 + 73 + 66 + 59 + ...$ to 20 terms
c $17 + 14 + 11 + 8 + ... + (-31)$
d $16 + 24 + 36 + 54 + ...$ to 10 terms.

8 $2k + 7$, $1 - k$, and $k - 7$ are consecutive terms of a geometric sequence.

a Find the possible values of k.
b For each possible value of k, find the corresponding common ratio.

9 A geometric series has $S_1 = 6$ and $S_2 = 3$.

a Find the first term u_1 and the common ratio r.
b Find the sum of the first 10 terms.

10 Answer the **Opening Problem** on page **344**.

11 The equilateral triangle ABC has sides of length 2 cm. Another equilateral triangle is formed inside it by joining the midpoints of each side. This process continues indefinitely, as shown in the diagram. Find the total length of the lines drawn.

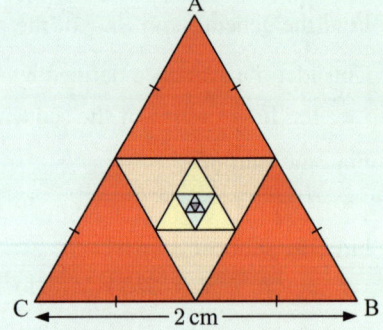

Chapter 17

Vectors

Contents:
- **A** Directed line segment representation
- **B** Vector equality
- **C** Vector addition
- **D** Vector subtraction
- **E** Vectors in component form
- **F** Scalar multiplication
- **G** Parallelism of vectors
- **H** The scalar product of two vectors
- **I** 3-dimensional vectors

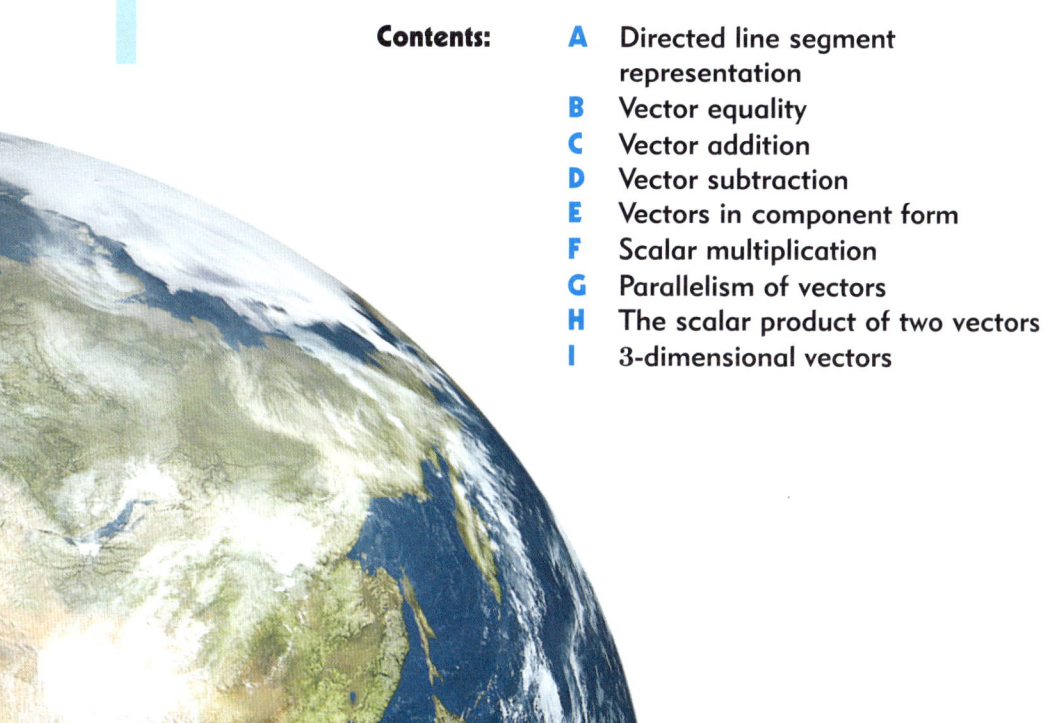

OPENING PROBLEM

Ian can swim in a swimming pool at a speed of 3 km h^{-1}. However, today he needs to swim directly across a river which is flowing at a constant speed of 2 km h^{-1} to his right.

Things to think about:

a Can you draw a diagram to illustrate the situation?

b Can you describe the effect the current in the river will have on the speed and direction in which Ian swims?

c How can we accurately find Ian's speed and direction, if he *aims* to swim directly across the river?

d In what direction must Ian face so that he *does* swim directly across the river?

VECTORS AND SCALARS

> Quantities which only have magnitude are called **scalars**.
>
> Quantities which have both magnitude and direction are called **vectors**.

To solve the **Opening Problem**, we need to consider not only the *speed* of Ian and the current, but also their *directions*.

Velocity is a vector quantity which includes both **speed** *and* **direction**.

Other examples of vector quantities include acceleration, force, displacement, and momentum.

For example, when using force we consider how hard we push an object, and what direction we push it in.

A DIRECTED LINE SEGMENT REPRESENTATION

Consider a bus which is travelling at 100 km h^{-1} to the south-east. We can represent the motion of the bus using an arrow on a scale diagram.

The **length of the arrow** represents the size or magnitude of the velocity. The **arrowhead** shows the direction of travel.

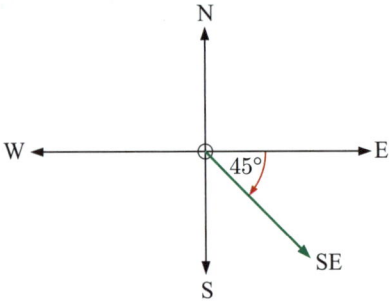

Scale: 1 cm represents 50 km h^{-1}

VECTORS (Chapter 17)

NOTATION

- The vector from O to A can be written as
  $\overrightarrow{OA}$ or **a** or $\vec{a}$.

  bold used in textbooks

  used by students

  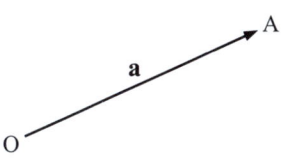

  The **magnitude** or **length** of the vector can be written as
  $|\overrightarrow{OA}|$ or OA or $|\mathbf{a}|$ or $|\vec{a}|$.

- $\overrightarrow{AB}$ is the vector which **emanates** from A and **terminates** at B. $\overrightarrow{AB}$ is the **position vector** of B relative to A.

  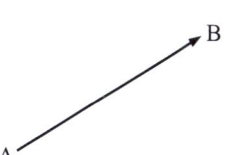

Example 1 ◀)) Self Tutor

On a scale diagram, draw a vector representing a velocity of 40 m s^{-1} on the bearing $075°$.

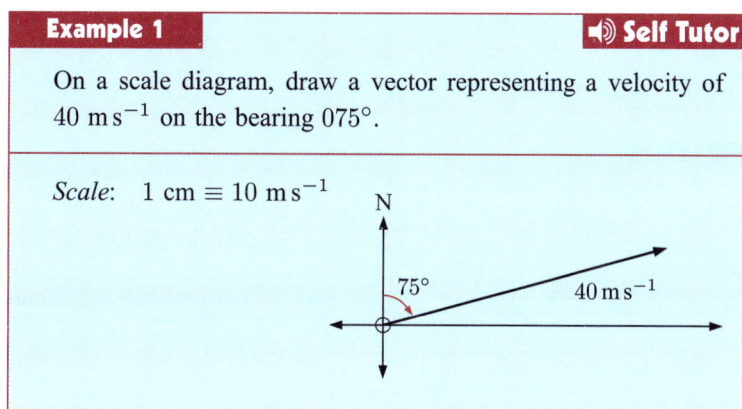

EXERCISE 17A

1. Using a scale of 1 cm represents 10 units, draw a vector which represents:
   a. a velocity of 40 km h^{-1} to the south-west
   b. a velocity of 35 m s^{-1} to the north
   c. a displacement of 25 m in the direction $120°$
   d. an aeroplane taking off at an angle of $12°$ to the runway, with speed 60 m s^{-1}.

2. If 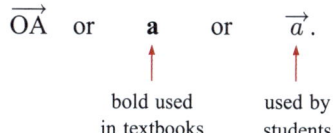 represents a force of 45 Newtons due east, draw a directed line segment to represent a force of:
   a. 75 N due west
   b. 60 N south-west.

3. On a scale diagram, draw a vector representing:
   a. a velocity of 60 km h^{-1} in a north-easterly direction
   b. a momentum of 45 kg m s^{-1} in the direction $250°$
   c. a displacement of 25 km on the bearing $055°$
   d. an aeroplane taking off at an angle of $10°$ to the runway, with speed 90 km h^{-1}.

B VECTOR EQUALITY

EQUAL VECTORS

> Two vectors are **equal** if they have the same magnitude *and* direction.

Equal vectors are **parallel** and in the same direction, and are **equal in length**.

This means that arrows representing equal vectors are translations of one another.

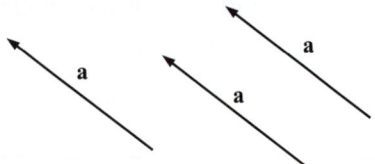

THE ZERO VECTOR

> The **zero vector**, **0**, is a vector of length 0. It is the only vector with no direction.

When we write the zero vector by hand, we usually write $\vec{0}$.

NEGATIVE VECTORS

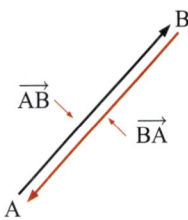

$\overrightarrow{AB}$ and $\overrightarrow{BA}$ have the same length but opposite directions.

We say that $\overrightarrow{BA}$ is the **negative** of $\overrightarrow{AB}$ and write $\overrightarrow{BA} = -\overrightarrow{AB}$.

Given the vector **a** shown, we can draw the vector −**a**.

a and −**a** are parallel and equal in length, but are opposite in direction.

Example 2 ◀)) Self Tutor

ABCD is a parallelogram in which $\overrightarrow{AB} = \mathbf{a}$ and $\overrightarrow{BC} = \mathbf{b}$.

Find vector expressions for:

a $\overrightarrow{BA}$ **b** $\overrightarrow{CB}$ **c** $\overrightarrow{AD}$ **d** $\overrightarrow{CD}$

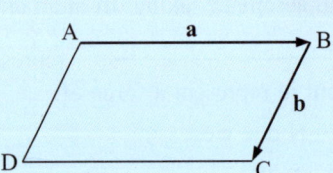

a $\overrightarrow{BA} = -\mathbf{a}$ {the negative vector of $\overrightarrow{AB}$}

b $\overrightarrow{CB} = -\mathbf{b}$ {the negative vector of $\overrightarrow{BC}$}

c $\overrightarrow{AD} = \mathbf{b}$ {parallel to and the same length as $\overrightarrow{BC}$}

d $\overrightarrow{CD} = -\mathbf{a}$ {parallel to and the same length as $\overrightarrow{BA}$}

EXERCISE 17B

1 State the vectors which are:
   a equal in magnitude
   b parallel
   c in the same direction
   d equal
   e negatives of one another.

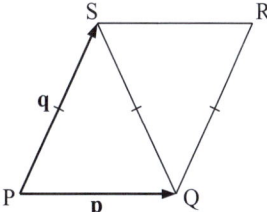

2 The figure alongside consists of two isosceles triangles with [PQ] ∥ [SR], $\vec{PQ} = \mathbf{p}$, and $\vec{PS} = \mathbf{q}$.
Which of the following statements are true?

   a $\vec{RS} = \mathbf{p}$ **b** $\vec{QR} = \mathbf{q}$ **c** $\vec{QS} = \mathbf{q}$
   d QS = PS   **e** $\vec{PS} = -\vec{RQ}$

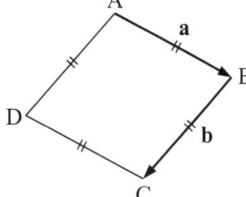

3 ABCD is a rhombus. Let $\vec{AB} = \mathbf{a}$ and $\vec{BC} = \mathbf{b}$.
Which of the following statements are true?

   a $\vec{AD} = \mathbf{b}$ **b** $\vec{CD} = \mathbf{a}$
   c $\vec{DC} = \mathbf{b}$ **d** $|\mathbf{a}| = |\mathbf{b}|$
   e $|\vec{DA}| = -|\mathbf{b}|$ **f** $|-\mathbf{a}| = |-\mathbf{b}|$

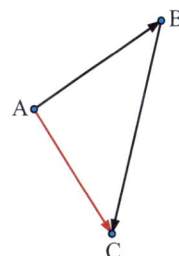

C   VECTOR ADDITION

Suppose we have three towns A, B, and C.

A trip from A to B, followed by a trip from B to C, is equivalent to a trip from A to C.

This can be expressed in vector form as the sum $\vec{AB} + \vec{BC} = \vec{AC}$, where the + sign could mean *'followed by'*.

After considering diagrams like the one above, we can define vector addition geometrically:

> To add **a** and **b**:   *Step 1:*   Draw **a**.
> *Step 2:*   At the arrowhead end of **a**, draw **b**.
> *Step 3:*   Join the beginning of **a** to the arrowhead end of **b**. This is vector **a** + **b**.

So, given  we have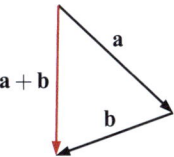

DEMO

Example 3

Find a single vector which is equal to:

a $\vec{AB} + \vec{BE}$
b $\vec{DC} + \vec{CA} + \vec{AE}$
c $\vec{CB} + \vec{BD} + \vec{DC}$

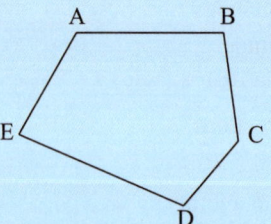

a $\vec{AB} + \vec{BE} = \vec{AE}$ {as shown}
b $\vec{DC} + \vec{CA} + \vec{AE} = \vec{DE}$
c $\vec{CB} + \vec{BD} + \vec{DC} = \vec{CC} = \mathbf{0}$ {zero vector}

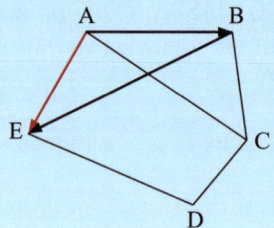

THE ZERO VECTOR

Having defined vector addition, we are now able to state that:

> The **zero vector**, **0**, is a vector of length 0.
>
> For any vector **a**: $\mathbf{a} + \mathbf{0} = \mathbf{0} + \mathbf{a} = \mathbf{a}$
> $\mathbf{a} + (-\mathbf{a}) = (-\mathbf{a}) + \mathbf{a} = \mathbf{0}$

Example 4

Sonya can swim at 3 km h^{-1} in calm water. She swims in a river where the current is 1 km h^{-1} in an easterly direction. Find the resultant velocity if Sonya swims:

a with the current
b against the current
c northwards, across the river.

Scale: 1 cm ≡ 1 km h^{-1}

The velocity vector of the river is

a Sonya's velocity vector is

The net result is **r** + **s**.

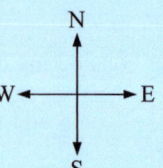

∴ Sonya swims at 4 km h^{-1} to the east.

b Sonya's velocity vector is

The net result is **r** + **s**.

∴ Sonya swims at 2 km h^{-1} to the west.

c

Sonya's velocity vector is $\mathbf{s}$ and the net result is $\mathbf{r} + \mathbf{s}$.

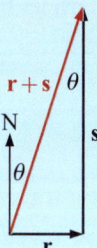

$\therefore \ |\mathbf{r} + \mathbf{s}| = \sqrt{10} \approx 3.16$

Now $\tan\theta = \frac{1}{3}$, so $\theta = \tan^{-1}(\frac{1}{3})$
$\approx 18.4°$

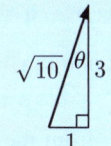

$\therefore$ Sonya swims at about 3.16 km h^{-1} in the direction $018.4°$.

EXERCISE 17C

1 Copy the given vectors $\mathbf{p}$ and $\mathbf{q}$ and show how to construct $\mathbf{p} + \mathbf{q}$:

a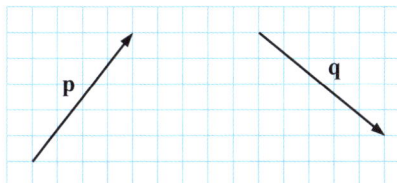

b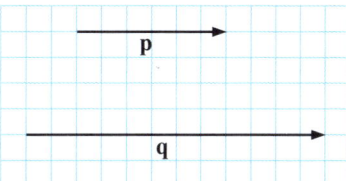

c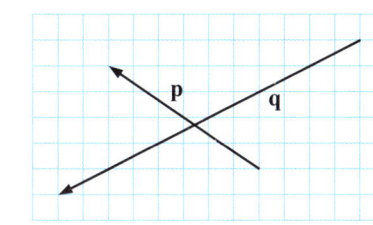

d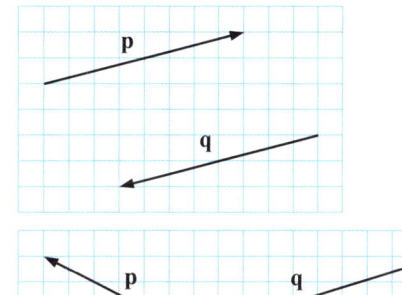

e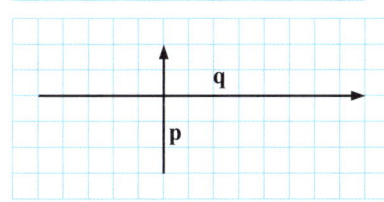

f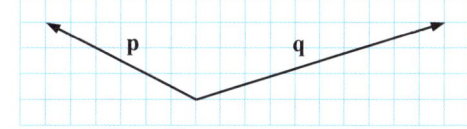

2 Find a single vector which is equal to:

    a $\overrightarrow{QR} + \overrightarrow{RS}$ **b** $\overrightarrow{PQ} + \overrightarrow{QR}$

    c $\overrightarrow{PS} + \overrightarrow{SR} + \overrightarrow{RQ}$ **d** $\overrightarrow{PR} + \overrightarrow{RQ} + \overrightarrow{QS}$

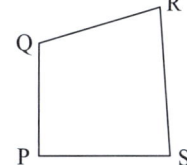

3 **a** Consider the vectors:

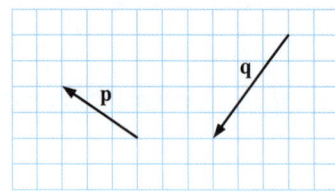

Use vector diagrams to find: **i** p + q **ii** q + p

b For any two vectors **p** and **q**, is **p** + **q** = **q** + **p**? Explain your answer.

4 Consider an aeroplane trying to fly at 500 km h^{-1} due north. Find the actual speed and direction of the aeroplane if a gale of 100 km h^{-1} is blowing:

a from the south **b** from the north **c** from the west.

5 A vessel is trying to travel east at 10 km h^{-1}. Find its actual speed and direction if there is a current of 10 km h^{-1}:

a from the east **b** from the west **c** from the south.

6 An aircraft flying at 400 km h^{-1} due east encounters a 60 km h^{-1} wind from the north. Find the resultant new speed and direction of the aircraft.

7 A ship travelling at 23 knots on a course 124° encounters a current of 4 knots in the direction 214°. Find the resultant new speed and direction of the ship.

D VECTOR SUBTRACTION

To subtract one vector from another, we simply **add its negative**.

$$\mathbf{a} - \mathbf{b} = \mathbf{a} + (-\mathbf{b}).$$

For example, given

 we have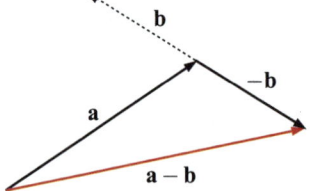

DEMO

Example 5   ◀) Self Tutor

Given

find **s** − **t**.

Example 6

For points P, Q, R, and S, simplify the following vector expressions:

a $\vec{QR} - \vec{SR}$

b $\vec{QR} - \vec{SR} - \vec{PS}$

a $\vec{QR} - \vec{SR}$
$= \vec{QR} + \vec{RS}$ {as $\vec{RS} = -\vec{SR}$}
$= \vec{QS}$

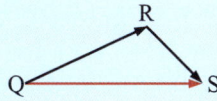

b $\vec{QR} - \vec{SR} - \vec{PS}$
$= \vec{QR} + \vec{RS} + \vec{SP}$
$= \vec{QP}$

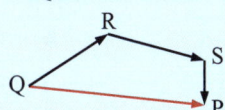

Example 7

Xiang Zhu is about to fire an arrow at a target. In still conditions, the arrow would travel at 18 m s^{-1}. Today, however, there is a wind blowing at 6 m s^{-1} from the left, directly across the arrow's path.

a In what direction should Zhu fire the arrow?

b What will be its actual speed?

Suppose Zhu is at Z and the target is at T. Let **a** be the arrow's velocity in still conditions, **w** be the velocity of the wind, and **x** be the vector $\vec{ZT}$.

$\quad\quad \mathbf{a} + \mathbf{w} = \mathbf{x}$
$\therefore \quad \mathbf{a} + \mathbf{w} - \mathbf{w} = \mathbf{x} - \mathbf{w}$
$\therefore \quad \mathbf{a} = \mathbf{x} - \mathbf{w}$

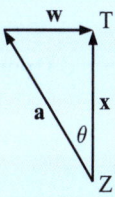

a Now $|\mathbf{a}| = 18 \text{ m s}^{-1}$ and $|\mathbf{w}| = 6 \text{ m s}^{-1}$

$\therefore \sin\theta = \frac{6}{18} = \frac{1}{3}$

$\therefore \theta = \sin^{-1}\left(\frac{1}{3}\right) \approx 19.47°$

$\therefore$ Zhu should fire about 19.5° to the left of the target.

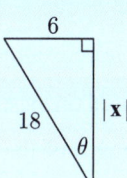

b By Pythagoras' theorem, $|\mathbf{x}|^2 + 6^2 = 18^2$

$\therefore |\mathbf{x}| = \sqrt{18^2 - 6^2} \approx 16.97 \text{ m s}^{-1}$

$\therefore$ the arrow will travel at about 17.0 m s^{-1}.

EXERCISE 17D

1 For the following vectors **p** and **q**, show how to construct $\mathbf{p} - \mathbf{q}$:

a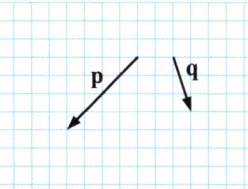

b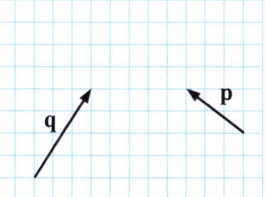

c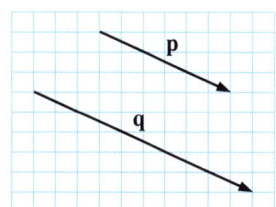

d 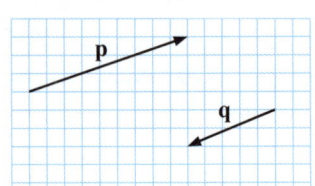   **e** 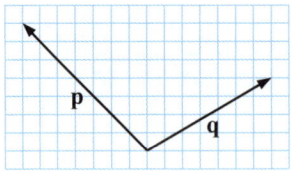   **f**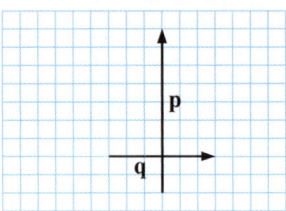

2 For points P, Q, R, and S, simplify the following vector expressions:
   a $\vec{QR} + \vec{RS}$
   b $\vec{PS} - \vec{RS}$
   c $\vec{RS} + \vec{SR}$
   d $\vec{RS} + \vec{SP} + \vec{PQ}$
   e $\vec{QP} - \vec{RP} + \vec{RS}$
   f $\vec{RS} - \vec{PS} - \vec{QP}$

3 An aeroplane needs to fly due north at a speed of 500 km h^{-1}. However, it is affected by a 40 km h^{-1} wind blowing constantly from the west. In what direction should it aim, and at what speed?

4 A motorboat wishes to travel north-west to a safe haven before an electrical storm arrives. In still water the boat can travel at 30 km h^{-1}. However, a strong current is flowing at 10 km h^{-1} from the north-east.
   a In what direction must the boat head?
   b At what speed will the boat actually travel?

5 Answer the **Opening Problem** on page 362.

E   VECTORS IN COMPONENT FORM

So far we have examined vectors in their geometric representation.

We have used arrows where:
- the **length** of the arrow represents size or magnitude
- the **arrowhead** indicates direction.

However, we can also represent vectors by describing the horizontal and vertical steps required to go from the starting point to the finishing point.

The **component form** of a vector is $\begin{pmatrix} x\text{-step} \\ y\text{-step} \end{pmatrix}$.

The x-step is positive if we move to the right, and negative if we move to the left.

The y-step is positive if we move upwards, and negative if we move downwards.

For example:

-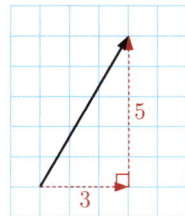

  We move 3 units to the right and 5 units upwards, so the vector is $\begin{pmatrix} 3 \\ 5 \end{pmatrix}$.

-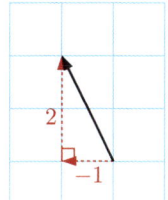

  We move 1 unit to the left and 2 units upwards, so the vector is $\begin{pmatrix} -1 \\ 2 \end{pmatrix}$.

THE VECTOR BETWEEN TWO POINTS

The position vector of point $A(a_1, a_2)$ relative to the origin $O(0, 0)$ is $\overrightarrow{OA} = \begin{pmatrix} x\text{-step} \\ y\text{-step} \end{pmatrix} = \begin{pmatrix} a_1 \\ a_2 \end{pmatrix}$.

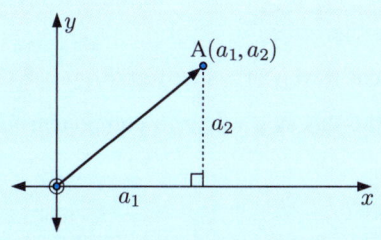

The position vector of $B(b_1, b_2)$ relative to $A(a_1, a_2)$ is $\overrightarrow{AB} = \begin{pmatrix} x\text{-step} \\ y\text{-step} \end{pmatrix} = \begin{pmatrix} b_1 - a_1 \\ b_2 - a_2 \end{pmatrix}$.

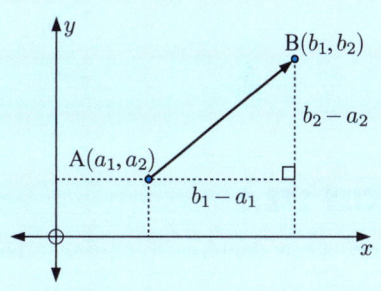

Example 8

Given the points $A(2, -3)$ and $B(4, 2)$, find:

a $\overrightarrow{AB}$ **b** $\overrightarrow{BA}$.

a $\overrightarrow{AB} = \begin{pmatrix} 4 - 2 \\ 2 - -3 \end{pmatrix} = \begin{pmatrix} 2 \\ 5 \end{pmatrix}$

b $\overrightarrow{BA} = \begin{pmatrix} 2 - 4 \\ -3 - 2 \end{pmatrix} = \begin{pmatrix} -2 \\ -5 \end{pmatrix}$

From this **Example**, we notice that $\overrightarrow{BA} = -\overrightarrow{AB}$.

VECTOR EQUALITY

Two vectors are equal if and only if their x-components are equal *and* their y-components are equal.

$$\begin{pmatrix} p \\ q \end{pmatrix} = \begin{pmatrix} r \\ s \end{pmatrix} \quad \text{if and only if} \quad p = r \quad \text{and} \quad q = s.$$

Example 9 ◀)) Self Tutor

Find k given that $\begin{pmatrix} k^2 \\ k-1 \end{pmatrix} = \begin{pmatrix} 9 \\ -4 \end{pmatrix}$.

We have $k^2 = 9$ and $k - 1 = -4$.

The only value of k which satisfies both equations is $k = -3$.

Example 10 ◀)) Self Tutor

A car travels at a speed of 20 m s^{-1} in the direction 125°.

Write this as a vector in component form.

Sketch:

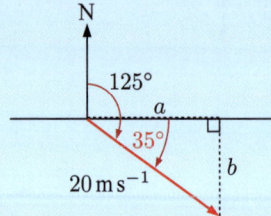

$\cos 35° = \dfrac{a}{20}$, so $a = 20 \times \cos 35° \approx 16.4$

$\sin 35° = \dfrac{b}{20}$, so $b = 20 \times \sin 35° \approx 11.5$

$\therefore$ the vector is $\begin{pmatrix} a \\ -b \end{pmatrix} \approx \begin{pmatrix} 16.4 \\ -11.5 \end{pmatrix}$

EXERCISE 17E.1

1 Draw arrow diagrams to represent the vectors:

   a $\begin{pmatrix} 4 \\ 2 \end{pmatrix}$ **b** $\begin{pmatrix} 0 \\ 3 \end{pmatrix}$ **c** $\begin{pmatrix} -2 \\ 5 \end{pmatrix}$ **d** $\begin{pmatrix} 3 \\ 4 \end{pmatrix}$

2 Write the illustrated vectors in component form:

a 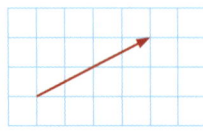   **b** 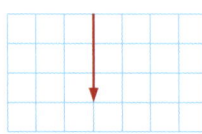   **c**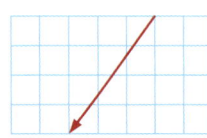

d 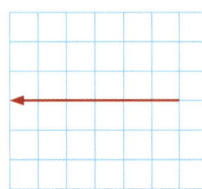   **e** 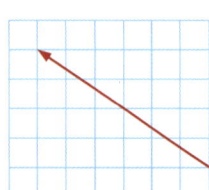   **f**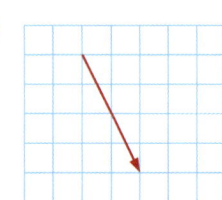

3 Given the points A(3, 4), B(−1, 2), and C(2, −1), find:

a $\overrightarrow{OA}$ **b** $\overrightarrow{AB}$ **c** $\overrightarrow{CO}$ **d** $\overrightarrow{BC}$ **e** $\overrightarrow{CA}$

4 Find k given that:

a $\begin{pmatrix} k+2 \\ k^2 \end{pmatrix} = \begin{pmatrix} 4 \\ 4 \end{pmatrix}$ **b** $\begin{pmatrix} 2 \\ k+1 \end{pmatrix} = \begin{pmatrix} k^2+1 \\ 0 \end{pmatrix}$ **c** $\begin{pmatrix} 3 \\ k^2+6 \end{pmatrix} = \begin{pmatrix} k^2-2k \\ 5k \end{pmatrix}$

5 Use an arrow diagram to help write each of the following vectors in component form:

a a velocity of 60 m s^{-1} in the direction 120°

b a displacement of 15 km in the direction 221°

c an aeroplane on the runway takes off at an angle of 9° and a speed of 160 km h^{-1}.

VECTOR ADDITION

Consider the addition of vectors $\mathbf{a} = \begin{pmatrix} a_1 \\ a_2 \end{pmatrix}$ and $\mathbf{b} = \begin{pmatrix} b_1 \\ b_2 \end{pmatrix}$.

The horizontal step for $\mathbf{a} + \mathbf{b}$ is $a_1 + b_1$,

and the vertical step for $\mathbf{a} + \mathbf{b}$ is $a_2 + b_2$.

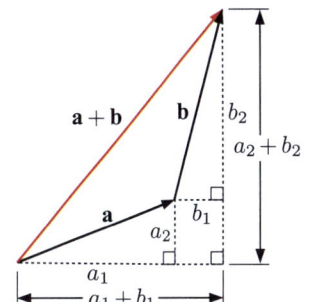

If $\mathbf{a} = \begin{pmatrix} a_1 \\ a_2 \end{pmatrix}$ and $\mathbf{b} = \begin{pmatrix} b_1 \\ b_2 \end{pmatrix}$ then $\mathbf{a} + \mathbf{b} = \begin{pmatrix} a_1 + b_1 \\ a_2 + b_2 \end{pmatrix}$.

Example 11 ◀)) Self Tutor

Given $\mathbf{a} = \begin{pmatrix} 2 \\ 5 \end{pmatrix}$ and $\mathbf{b} = \begin{pmatrix} 1 \\ -3 \end{pmatrix}$, find $\mathbf{a} + \mathbf{b}$.

Check your answer graphically.

$\mathbf{a} + \mathbf{b} = \begin{pmatrix} 2 \\ 5 \end{pmatrix} + \begin{pmatrix} 1 \\ -3 \end{pmatrix}$

$= \begin{pmatrix} 2+1 \\ 5+-3 \end{pmatrix}$

$= \begin{pmatrix} 3 \\ 2 \end{pmatrix}$

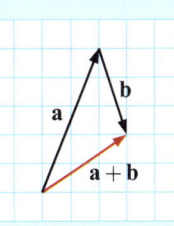

NEGATIVE VECTORS

For the vector $\mathbf{a} = \begin{pmatrix} 5 \\ 2 \end{pmatrix}$, we notice that $-\mathbf{a} = \begin{pmatrix} -5 \\ -2 \end{pmatrix}$.

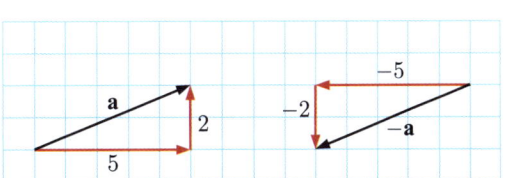

If $\mathbf{a} = \begin{pmatrix} a_1 \\ a_2 \end{pmatrix}$ then $-\mathbf{a} = \begin{pmatrix} -a_1 \\ -a_2 \end{pmatrix}$.

ZERO VECTOR

The zero vector is $\mathbf{0} = \begin{pmatrix} 0 \\ 0 \end{pmatrix}$.

> For any vector $\mathbf{a}$:
>
> $\mathbf{a} + \mathbf{0} = \mathbf{0} + \mathbf{a} = \mathbf{a}$
>
> $\mathbf{a} + (-\mathbf{a}) = (-\mathbf{a}) + \mathbf{a} = \mathbf{0}$

VECTOR SUBTRACTION

To subtract one vector from another, we **add its negative**.

If $\mathbf{a} = \begin{pmatrix} a_1 \\ a_2 \end{pmatrix}$ and $\mathbf{b} = \begin{pmatrix} b_1 \\ b_2 \end{pmatrix}$ then $\mathbf{a} - \mathbf{b} = \mathbf{a} + (-\mathbf{b})$

$$= \begin{pmatrix} a_1 \\ a_2 \end{pmatrix} + \begin{pmatrix} -b_1 \\ -b_2 \end{pmatrix}$$

$$= \begin{pmatrix} a_1 - b_1 \\ a_2 - b_2 \end{pmatrix}$$

> If $\mathbf{a} = \begin{pmatrix} a_1 \\ a_2 \end{pmatrix}$ and $\mathbf{b} = \begin{pmatrix} b_1 \\ b_2 \end{pmatrix}$ then $\mathbf{a} - \mathbf{b} = \begin{pmatrix} a_1 - b_1 \\ a_2 - b_2 \end{pmatrix}$.

Example 12

Given $\mathbf{p} = \begin{pmatrix} 3 \\ -2 \end{pmatrix}$ and $\mathbf{q} = \begin{pmatrix} 1 \\ 4 \end{pmatrix}$ find:

a $\mathbf{p} - \mathbf{q}$ **b** $\mathbf{q} - \mathbf{p}$

a $\mathbf{p} - \mathbf{q} = \begin{pmatrix} 3 \\ -2 \end{pmatrix} - \begin{pmatrix} 1 \\ 4 \end{pmatrix}$

$= \begin{pmatrix} 3 - 1 \\ -2 - 4 \end{pmatrix}$

$= \begin{pmatrix} 2 \\ -6 \end{pmatrix}$

b $\mathbf{q} - \mathbf{p} = \begin{pmatrix} 1 \\ 4 \end{pmatrix} - \begin{pmatrix} 3 \\ -2 \end{pmatrix}$

$= \begin{pmatrix} 1 - 3 \\ 4 - -2 \end{pmatrix}$

$= \begin{pmatrix} -2 \\ 6 \end{pmatrix}$

THE MAGNITUDE OF A VECTOR

By the theorem of Pythagoras,

If $\mathbf{a} = \begin{pmatrix} a_1 \\ a_2 \end{pmatrix}$, the **magnitude** or **length** of $\mathbf{a}$ is $|\mathbf{a}| = \sqrt{a_1^2 + a_2^2}$.

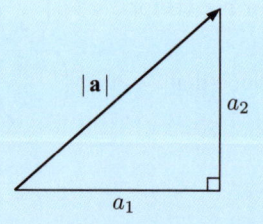

Example 13

Find the length of: **a** $\begin{pmatrix} 5 \\ 2 \end{pmatrix}$ **b** $\begin{pmatrix} -4 \\ 3 \end{pmatrix}$

a The length of $\begin{pmatrix} 5 \\ 2 \end{pmatrix}$
$= \sqrt{5^2 + 2^2}$
$= \sqrt{25 + 4}$
$= \sqrt{29}$ units

b The length of $\begin{pmatrix} -4 \\ 3 \end{pmatrix}$
$= \sqrt{(-4)^2 + 3^2}$
$= \sqrt{16 + 9}$
$= 5$ units

EXERCISE 17E.2

1 Given $\mathbf{a} = \begin{pmatrix} 2 \\ -3 \end{pmatrix}$, $\mathbf{b} = \begin{pmatrix} 3 \\ -1 \end{pmatrix}$, and $\mathbf{c} = \begin{pmatrix} -2 \\ -3 \end{pmatrix}$, find:

  a $\mathbf{a} + \mathbf{b}$ **b** $\mathbf{b} + \mathbf{a}$ **c** $\mathbf{b} + \mathbf{c}$ **d** $\mathbf{c} + \mathbf{b}$
  e $\mathbf{a} + \mathbf{c}$ **f** $\mathbf{c} + \mathbf{a}$ **g** $\mathbf{a} + \mathbf{a}$ **h** $\mathbf{b} + \mathbf{a} + \mathbf{c}$

2 Given $\mathbf{m} = \begin{pmatrix} 3 \\ 4 \end{pmatrix}$ and $\mathbf{n} = \begin{pmatrix} 1 \\ -2 \end{pmatrix}$, find:

  a $\mathbf{m} + \mathbf{n}$ **b** $-\mathbf{m}$ **c** $-\mathbf{n}$

3 Given $\mathbf{p} = \begin{pmatrix} -1 \\ 3 \end{pmatrix}$, $\mathbf{q} = \begin{pmatrix} -2 \\ -3 \end{pmatrix}$, and $\mathbf{r} = \begin{pmatrix} 3 \\ -4 \end{pmatrix}$, find:

  a $\mathbf{p} - \mathbf{q}$ **b** $\mathbf{q} - \mathbf{r}$ **c** $\mathbf{p} + \mathbf{q} - \mathbf{r}$
  d $\mathbf{p} - \mathbf{q} - \mathbf{r}$ **e** $\mathbf{q} - \mathbf{r} - \mathbf{p}$ **f** $\mathbf{r} + \mathbf{q} - \mathbf{p}$

4 a Given $\overrightarrow{AB} = \begin{pmatrix} 1 \\ 4 \end{pmatrix}$ and $\overrightarrow{AC} = \begin{pmatrix} -2 \\ 1 \end{pmatrix}$, find $\overrightarrow{BC}$.

  b Given $\overrightarrow{AB} = \begin{pmatrix} -3 \\ 2 \end{pmatrix}$, $\overrightarrow{BD} = \begin{pmatrix} 0 \\ 4 \end{pmatrix}$, and $\overrightarrow{CD} = \begin{pmatrix} 1 \\ -3 \end{pmatrix}$, find $\overrightarrow{AC}$.

5 Find the length of each of these vectors:

  a $\begin{pmatrix} 1 \\ 4 \end{pmatrix}$ **b** $\begin{pmatrix} 6 \\ 0 \end{pmatrix}$ **c** $\begin{pmatrix} 3 \\ -2 \end{pmatrix}$ **d** $\begin{pmatrix} -1 \\ -5 \end{pmatrix}$ **e** $\begin{pmatrix} -4 \\ 2 \end{pmatrix}$ **f** $\begin{pmatrix} -6 \\ -1 \end{pmatrix}$

6 For each of the following pairs of points, find: **i** $\overrightarrow{AB}$ **ii** the distance AB.

  a A(3, 5) and B(1, 2) **b** A(-2, 1) and B(3, -1)
  c A(3, 4) and B(0, 0) **d** A(11, -5) and B(-1, 0)

7 Prove that for any two vectors $\mathbf{a}$ and $\mathbf{b}$, $\mathbf{a} + \mathbf{b} = \mathbf{b} + \mathbf{a}$.

  Hint: Let $\mathbf{a} = \begin{pmatrix} a_1 \\ a_2 \end{pmatrix}$ and $\mathbf{b} = \begin{pmatrix} b_1 \\ b_2 \end{pmatrix}$.

F SCALAR MULTIPLICATION

Numbers such as 1 and -2 are called *scalars* because they have size but no direction.

$2\mathbf{a}$ and $-2\mathbf{a}$ are examples of multiplying a vector by a scalar.

$2\mathbf{a}$ is a short way to write $\mathbf{a} + \mathbf{a}$, and similarly $-2\mathbf{a} = (-\mathbf{a}) + (-\mathbf{a})$

For we have 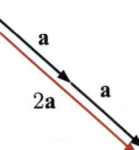 and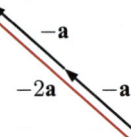

So, $2\mathbf{a}$ has the same direction as $\mathbf{a}$ and is twice as long as $\mathbf{a}$, and

$-2\mathbf{a}$ is in the opposite direction to $\mathbf{a}$ and is twice as long as $\mathbf{a}$.

Example 14   ◀)) Self Tutor

Given $\mathbf{r} = \begin{pmatrix} 3 \\ 2 \end{pmatrix}$ and $\mathbf{s} = \begin{pmatrix} 2 \\ -2 \end{pmatrix}$, find geometrically:

a $2\mathbf{r} + \mathbf{s}$ **b** $\mathbf{r} - 2\mathbf{s}$

a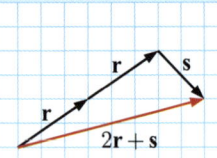

$2\mathbf{r} + \mathbf{s} = \begin{pmatrix} 8 \\ 2 \end{pmatrix}$.

b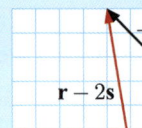

$\mathbf{r} - 2\mathbf{s} = \begin{pmatrix} -1 \\ 6 \end{pmatrix}$.

In component form:

If k is a scalar then $k \begin{pmatrix} a \\ b \end{pmatrix} = \begin{pmatrix} ka \\ kb \end{pmatrix}$.

Each component is multiplied by k.

We can now check the results of **Example 14** using the component form:

In **a**, $2\mathbf{r} + \mathbf{s} = 2\begin{pmatrix} 3 \\ 2 \end{pmatrix} + \begin{pmatrix} 2 \\ -2 \end{pmatrix}$

$= \begin{pmatrix} 6 \\ 4 \end{pmatrix} + \begin{pmatrix} 2 \\ -2 \end{pmatrix}$

$= \begin{pmatrix} 8 \\ 2 \end{pmatrix}$

In **b**, $\mathbf{r} - 2\mathbf{s} = \begin{pmatrix} 3 \\ 2 \end{pmatrix} - 2\begin{pmatrix} 2 \\ -2 \end{pmatrix}$

$= \begin{pmatrix} 3 \\ 2 \end{pmatrix} - \begin{pmatrix} 4 \\ -4 \end{pmatrix}$

$= \begin{pmatrix} -1 \\ 6 \end{pmatrix}$

Example 15

Sketch any two vectors **p** and **q** such that:

a $\mathbf{p} = 2\mathbf{q}$
b $\mathbf{p} = -\frac{1}{2}\mathbf{q}$.

Let **q** be   a 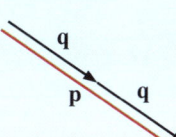   b

EXERCISE 17F

1 Given $\mathbf{r} = \begin{pmatrix} 2 \\ 3 \end{pmatrix}$ and $\mathbf{s} = \begin{pmatrix} 4 \\ -2 \end{pmatrix}$, find using   **i** geometry   **ii** component form:

a $2\mathbf{r}$
b $-3\mathbf{s}$
c $\frac{1}{2}\mathbf{r}$
d $\mathbf{r} - 2\mathbf{s}$

e $3\mathbf{r} + \mathbf{s}$
f $2\mathbf{r} - 3\mathbf{s}$
g $\frac{1}{2}\mathbf{s} + \mathbf{r}$
h $\frac{1}{2}(2\mathbf{r} + \mathbf{s})$

2 Sketch any two vectors **p** and **q** such that:

a $\mathbf{p} = \mathbf{q}$
b $\mathbf{p} = -\mathbf{q}$
c $\mathbf{p} = 3\mathbf{q}$
d $\mathbf{p} = \frac{3}{4}\mathbf{q}$
e $\mathbf{p} = -\frac{3}{2}\mathbf{q}$

3 If **a** is any vector, prove that:

a $|k\mathbf{a}| = |k||\mathbf{a}|$
b $\dfrac{1}{|\mathbf{a}|}\mathbf{a}$ is a vector of length 1 in the direction of **a**.

Hint: Let $\mathbf{a} = \begin{pmatrix} a_1 \\ a_2 \end{pmatrix}$.

G PARALLELISM OF VECTORS

Two vectors are **parallel** ⇔ one is a scalar multiple of the other.

⇔ means "if and only if".

This statement means both:

- if one vector is a scalar multiple of another then the two vectors are parallel
- if two vectors are parallel then one vector is a scalar multiple of the other.

If **a** is parallel to **b** then we write **a** ∥ **b**.

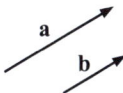

- If $\mathbf{a} = k\mathbf{b}$ for some non-zero scalar k, then **a** ∥ **b**.
- If **a** ∥ **b** there exists a non-zero scalar k such that $\mathbf{a} = k\mathbf{b}$.

Example 16

The vectors $\begin{pmatrix} 12 \\ t \end{pmatrix}$ and $\begin{pmatrix} 3 \\ -2 \end{pmatrix}$ are parallel. Find t.

The vectors are parallel, so $\begin{pmatrix} 12 \\ t \end{pmatrix} = k \begin{pmatrix} 3 \\ -2 \end{pmatrix}$ for some k.

$\therefore\ 12 = 3k$ and $t = -2k$

$\therefore\ k = 4$

$\therefore\ t = -2(4) = -8$

Consider the vectors $\mathbf{a} = \begin{pmatrix} 6 \\ 3 \end{pmatrix}$ and $\mathbf{b} = \begin{pmatrix} 2 \\ 1 \end{pmatrix}$. Notice that $\begin{pmatrix} 6 \\ 3 \end{pmatrix} = 3 \begin{pmatrix} 2 \\ 1 \end{pmatrix}$, so $\mathbf{a} = 3\mathbf{b}$.

$\therefore\ \mathbf{a} \parallel \mathbf{b}$.

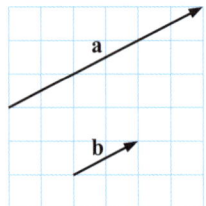

Notice also that $|\mathbf{a}| = \sqrt{36 + 9}$
$= \sqrt{45}$
$= 3\sqrt{5}$
$= 3\,|\mathbf{b}|$.

Consider the vector $k\mathbf{a}$ which is parallel to $\mathbf{a}$.

- If $k > 0$ then $k\mathbf{a}$ has the same direction as $\mathbf{a}$.
- If $k < 0$ then $k\mathbf{a}$ has the opposite direction to $\mathbf{a}$.
- The length of $k\mathbf{a}$ is the **modulus** of k times the length of $\mathbf{a}$. $|k\mathbf{a}| = |k|\,|\mathbf{a}|$

Example 17

What two facts can be deduced about $\mathbf{p}$ and $\mathbf{q}$ if:

a $\mathbf{p} = 5\mathbf{q}$ **b** $\mathbf{q} = -\tfrac{3}{4}\mathbf{p}$?

a $\mathbf{p} = 5\mathbf{q}$

$\therefore\ \mathbf{p}$ is parallel to $\mathbf{q}$ and $|\mathbf{p}| = |5|\,|\mathbf{q}| = 5\,|\mathbf{q}|$

$\therefore\ \mathbf{p}$ is 5 times longer than $\mathbf{q}$, and they have the same direction.

b $\mathbf{q} = -\tfrac{3}{4}\mathbf{p}$

$\therefore\ \mathbf{q}$ is parallel to $\mathbf{p}$ and $|\mathbf{q}| = |-\tfrac{3}{4}|\,|\mathbf{p}| = \tfrac{3}{4}|\mathbf{p}|$

$\therefore\ \mathbf{q}$ is $\tfrac{3}{4}$ as long as $\mathbf{p}$, but has the opposite direction.

EXERCISE 17G

1 Find the scalar t given that the following pairs of vectors are parallel:

a $\begin{pmatrix} 20 \\ t \end{pmatrix}$ and $\begin{pmatrix} -5 \\ 3 \end{pmatrix}$ **b** $\begin{pmatrix} 3 \\ 2 \end{pmatrix}$ and $\begin{pmatrix} 9 \\ t \end{pmatrix}$

c $\begin{pmatrix} -4 \\ 1 \end{pmatrix}$ and $\begin{pmatrix} t \\ -5 \end{pmatrix}$ **d** $\begin{pmatrix} 5 \\ 2 \end{pmatrix}$ and $\begin{pmatrix} t \\ -4 \end{pmatrix}$

2 Find a such that $\begin{pmatrix} 3 \\ a \end{pmatrix}$ and $\begin{pmatrix} 5a+2 \\ 8 \end{pmatrix}$ are parallel.

3 Consider the points A(1, 5), B(3, 8), C(5, 11), and D(−3, t). Find the value of t such that [AB] ∥ [DC].

4 What two facts can be deduced about **p** and **q** if:

    a $\mathbf{p} = 2\mathbf{q}$ **b** $\mathbf{p} = \tfrac{1}{2}\mathbf{q}$ **c** $\mathbf{p} = -3\mathbf{q}$ **d** $\mathbf{p} = -\tfrac{1}{3}\mathbf{q}$?

5 Using vector methods only, show that P(−2, 5), Q(3, 1), R(2, −1), and S(−3, 3), form the vertices of a parallelogram.

6 Use vector methods to find the remaining vertex of parallelogram ABCD:

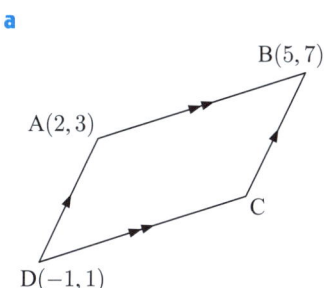
a

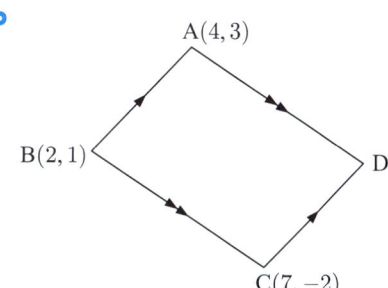
b

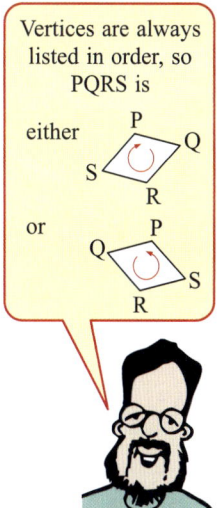
Vertices are always listed in order, so PQRS is either [P Q S R] or [Q P R S]

H   THE SCALAR PRODUCT OF TWO VECTORS

If $\mathbf{a} = \begin{pmatrix} a_1 \\ a_2 \end{pmatrix}$ and $\mathbf{b} = \begin{pmatrix} b_1 \\ b_2 \end{pmatrix}$, the **scalar product** or **dot product** of **a** and **b** is defined as $\mathbf{a} \bullet \mathbf{b} = a_1 b_1 + a_2 b_2$.

Example 18   ◀)) Self Tutor

Find: **a** $\begin{pmatrix} 4 \\ 3 \end{pmatrix} \bullet \begin{pmatrix} 2 \\ -3 \end{pmatrix}$ **b** $\begin{pmatrix} -7 \\ 4 \end{pmatrix} \bullet \begin{pmatrix} 1 \\ 5 \end{pmatrix}$

a $\begin{pmatrix} 4 \\ 3 \end{pmatrix} \bullet \begin{pmatrix} 2 \\ -3 \end{pmatrix}$ **b** $\begin{pmatrix} -7 \\ 4 \end{pmatrix} \bullet \begin{pmatrix} 1 \\ 5 \end{pmatrix}$

$= 4(2) + 3(-3)$ $= -7(1) + 4(5)$

$= -1$ $= 13$

The scalar product is important for determining the angle between two vectors.

If two vectors $\mathbf{a} = \begin{pmatrix} a_1 \\ a_2 \end{pmatrix}$ and $\mathbf{b} = \begin{pmatrix} b_1 \\ b_2 \end{pmatrix}$ make an angle θ between them,

then $\cos\theta = \dfrac{\mathbf{a} \bullet \mathbf{b}}{|\mathbf{a}||\mathbf{b}|}$.

Proof:

Given two vectors $\mathbf{a} = \begin{pmatrix} a_1 \\ a_2 \end{pmatrix}$ and $\mathbf{b} = \begin{pmatrix} b_1 \\ b_2 \end{pmatrix}$,

we can translate either of the vectors so that both emanate from the same point.

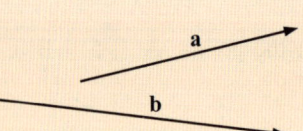

Let the angle between the two vectors be θ.

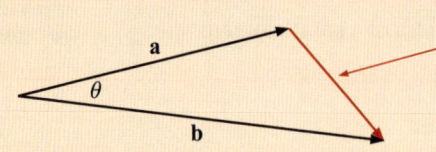

This vector is $-\mathbf{a} + \mathbf{b} = \mathbf{b} - \mathbf{a}$ and has length $|\mathbf{b} - \mathbf{a}|$.

Using the cosine rule, $|\mathbf{b} - \mathbf{a}|^2 = |\mathbf{a}|^2 + |\mathbf{b}|^2 - 2|\mathbf{a}||\mathbf{b}|\cos\theta$

But $\mathbf{b} - \mathbf{a} = \begin{pmatrix} b_1 \\ b_2 \end{pmatrix} - \begin{pmatrix} a_1 \\ a_2 \end{pmatrix} = \begin{pmatrix} b_1 - a_1 \\ b_2 - a_2 \end{pmatrix}$

$\therefore (b_1 - a_1)^2 + (b_2 - a_2)^2 = a_1^2 + a_2^2 + b_1^2 + b_2^2 - 2|\mathbf{a}||\mathbf{b}|\cos\theta$

$\therefore b_1^2 - 2a_1 b_1 + a_1^2 + b_2^2 - 2a_2 b_2 + a_2^2 = a_1^2 + a_2^2 + b_1^2 + b_2^2 - 2|\mathbf{a}||\mathbf{b}|\cos\theta$

$\therefore 2|\mathbf{a}||\mathbf{b}|\cos\theta = 2a_1 b_1 + 2a_2 b_2$

$\therefore |\mathbf{a}||\mathbf{b}|\cos\theta = a_1 b_1 + a_2 b_2$

$\therefore \cos\theta = \dfrac{\mathbf{a} \bullet \mathbf{b}}{|\mathbf{a}||\mathbf{b}|}$

Example 19 ◀) Self Tutor

For the vectors $\mathbf{p} = \begin{pmatrix} 3 \\ 1 \end{pmatrix}$ and $\mathbf{q} = \begin{pmatrix} 2 \\ -1 \end{pmatrix}$, find:

a $\mathbf{p} \bullet \mathbf{q}$ **b** the angle between $\mathbf{p}$ and $\mathbf{q}$.

a $\mathbf{p} \bullet \mathbf{q}$
$= \begin{pmatrix} 3 \\ 1 \end{pmatrix} \bullet \begin{pmatrix} 2 \\ -1 \end{pmatrix}$
$= 6 + -1$
$= 5$

b $\cos\theta = \dfrac{\mathbf{p} \bullet \mathbf{q}}{|\mathbf{p}||\mathbf{q}|}$

$\therefore \cos\theta = \dfrac{5}{\sqrt{9+1}\sqrt{4+1}}$

$\therefore \cos\theta = \dfrac{5}{\sqrt{10}\sqrt{5}}$

$\therefore \cos\theta = \dfrac{5}{5\sqrt{2}}$

$\therefore \cos\theta = \dfrac{1}{\sqrt{2}}$

$\therefore \theta = 45°$

The angle between $\mathbf{p}$ and $\mathbf{q}$ is $45°$.

If $\mathbf{a}$ and $\mathbf{b}$ are perpendicular, the angle θ between them is $90°$. In this case $\cos\theta = 0$ and so $\mathbf{a} \bullet \mathbf{b} = 0$.

$\mathbf{a}$ is perpendicular to $\mathbf{b}$ if $\mathbf{a} \bullet \mathbf{b} = 0$.

VECTORS (Chapter 17)

Example 20

The two vectors $\mathbf{a} = \begin{pmatrix} 2 \\ -5 \end{pmatrix}$ and $\mathbf{b} = \begin{pmatrix} t \\ -3 \end{pmatrix}$ are perpendicular. Find t.

$\mathbf{a} \perp \mathbf{b}$ reads '$\mathbf{a}$ is perpendicular to $\mathbf{b}$'.

Since $\mathbf{a} \perp \mathbf{b}$, $\quad \mathbf{a} \bullet \mathbf{b} = 0$

$\therefore \begin{pmatrix} 2 \\ -5 \end{pmatrix} \bullet \begin{pmatrix} t \\ -3 \end{pmatrix} = 0$

$\therefore 2t + 15 = 0$

$\therefore t = -\frac{15}{2}$

Example 21

Find the measure of $\widehat{ACB}$ for $A(3, -1)$, $B(2, 0)$, and $C(-1, 4)$.

$\overrightarrow{CA} = \begin{pmatrix} 4 \\ -5 \end{pmatrix}$ and $\overrightarrow{CB} = \begin{pmatrix} 3 \\ -4 \end{pmatrix}$

Now $\cos \theta = \dfrac{\overrightarrow{CA} \bullet \overrightarrow{CB}}{|\overrightarrow{CA}||\overrightarrow{CB}|}$

$\therefore \cos \theta = \dfrac{12 + 20}{\sqrt{16 + 25}\sqrt{9 + 16}}$

$\therefore \cos \theta = \dfrac{32}{5\sqrt{41}}$

$\therefore \theta = \cos^{-1}\left(\dfrac{32}{5\sqrt{41}}\right) \approx 1.79°$

So, the measure of $\widehat{ACB}$ is about $1.79°$.

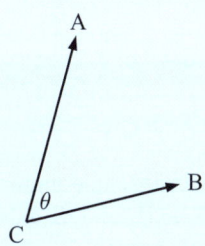

EXERCISE 17H

1 Find:

  a $\begin{pmatrix} 2 \\ 5 \end{pmatrix} \bullet \begin{pmatrix} 1 \\ 3 \end{pmatrix}$ **b** $\begin{pmatrix} 3 \\ -4 \end{pmatrix} \bullet \begin{pmatrix} -5 \\ 0 \end{pmatrix}$ **c** $\begin{pmatrix} -8 \\ 5 \end{pmatrix} \bullet \begin{pmatrix} -2 \\ -6 \end{pmatrix}$

2 Show that $\begin{pmatrix} 1 \\ -4 \end{pmatrix}$ is perpendicular to $\begin{pmatrix} 8 \\ 2 \end{pmatrix}$.

3 For the vectors $\mathbf{p}$ and $\mathbf{q}$, find: **i** $\mathbf{p} \bullet \mathbf{q}$ **ii** the angle between $\mathbf{p}$ and $\mathbf{q}$.

  a $\mathbf{p} = \begin{pmatrix} 1 \\ 3 \end{pmatrix}$, $\mathbf{q} = \begin{pmatrix} 2 \\ 1 \end{pmatrix}$ **b** $\mathbf{p} = \begin{pmatrix} 2 \\ 4 \end{pmatrix}$, $\mathbf{q} = \begin{pmatrix} 1 \\ 2 \end{pmatrix}$

  c $\mathbf{p} = \begin{pmatrix} 2 \\ -4 \end{pmatrix}$, $\mathbf{q} = \begin{pmatrix} 2 \\ 1 \end{pmatrix}$ **d** $\mathbf{p} = \begin{pmatrix} -1 \\ 4 \end{pmatrix}$, $\mathbf{q} = \begin{pmatrix} 3 \\ 2 \end{pmatrix}$

  e $\mathbf{p} = \begin{pmatrix} 3 \\ 4 \end{pmatrix}$, $\mathbf{q} = \begin{pmatrix} -5 \\ 12 \end{pmatrix}$ **f** $\mathbf{p} = \begin{pmatrix} 1 \\ -4 \end{pmatrix}$, $\mathbf{q} = \begin{pmatrix} -3 \\ 2 \end{pmatrix}$

4 Find t given that:

a $\begin{pmatrix} t \\ 3 \end{pmatrix}$ is perpendicular to $\begin{pmatrix} 1 \\ -2 \end{pmatrix}$
b $\begin{pmatrix} -2 \\ t \end{pmatrix}$ is perpendicular to $\begin{pmatrix} 6 \\ t \end{pmatrix}$
c $\begin{pmatrix} t+2 \\ t \end{pmatrix}$ is perpendicular to $\begin{pmatrix} -4 \\ 3 \end{pmatrix}$
d $\begin{pmatrix} 2 \\ t^2 \end{pmatrix}$ is perpendicular to $\begin{pmatrix} t+4 \\ -3 \end{pmatrix}$.

5 Find the measure of:

a $\widehat{ABC}$ given $A(-1, -2)$, $B(2, 4)$, and $C(3, -1)$
b $\widehat{BAC}$ given $A(4, 1)$, $B(3, -3)$, and $C(-1, 6)$
c $\widehat{PQR}$ given $R(2, 2)$, $P(-1, 5)$, and $Q(3, -4)$
d $\widehat{KML}$ given $K(4, 2)$, $L(3, 7)$, and $M(5, -1)$.

6 Consider the points $A(3, 2)$, $B(-1, 3)$, and $C(k, -4)$. Find k such that $\widehat{ABC}$ is a right angle.

7 Find the measure of all angles of triangle PQR, given:

a $P(-2, 4)$, $Q(3, -1)$, and $R(1, 0)$
b $P(4, 1)$, $Q(-1, 3)$, and $R(2, -1)$.

I — 3-DIMENSIONAL VECTORS

In **Chapter 6**, we specified three mutually perpendicular axes, called the X-axis, Y-axis, and Z-axis, in order to describe points in 3-dimensional space.

We can do the same thing to describe vectors in three dimensions.

Any vector in 3-dimensional space can be described using a set of three numbers $\begin{pmatrix} x \\ y \\ z \end{pmatrix}$, where x, y, and z are the steps in the X, Y, and Z directions respectively.

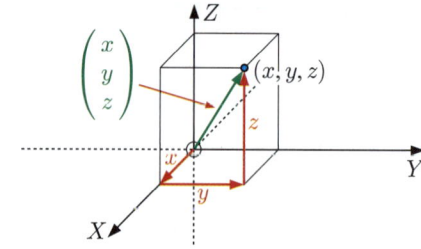

The rules we have seen for dealing with vectors in two dimensions extend readily to vectors in three dimensions.

- The position vector of point $A(a_1, a_2, a_3)$ relative to the origin $O(0, 0, 0)$ is $\overrightarrow{OA} = \begin{pmatrix} a_1 \\ a_2 \\ a_3 \end{pmatrix}$.

- The position vector of point $B(b_1, b_2, b_3)$ relative to $A(a_1, a_2, a_3)$ is $\overrightarrow{AB} = \begin{pmatrix} b_1 - a_1 \\ b_2 - a_2 \\ b_3 - a_3 \end{pmatrix}$.

- $\begin{pmatrix} a \\ b \\ c \end{pmatrix} = \begin{pmatrix} p \\ q \\ r \end{pmatrix}$ if and only if $a = p$, $b = q$, and $c = r$.

- The zero vector is $\mathbf{0} = \begin{pmatrix} 0 \\ 0 \\ 0 \end{pmatrix}$.

- The vector $\mathbf{a} = \begin{pmatrix} a_1 \\ a_2 \\ a_3 \end{pmatrix}$ has magnitude $|\mathbf{a}| = \sqrt{a_1^2 + a_2^2 + a_3^2}$.

- Given $\mathbf{a} = \begin{pmatrix} a_1 \\ a_2 \\ a_3 \end{pmatrix}$ and $\mathbf{b} = \begin{pmatrix} b_1 \\ b_2 \\ b_3 \end{pmatrix}$:

  ▸ $\mathbf{a} + \mathbf{b} = \begin{pmatrix} a_1 + b_1 \\ a_2 + b_2 \\ a_3 + b_3 \end{pmatrix}$ ▸ $\mathbf{a} - \mathbf{b} = \begin{pmatrix} a_1 - b_1 \\ a_2 - b_2 \\ a_3 - b_3 \end{pmatrix}$

  ▸ $k\mathbf{a} = \begin{pmatrix} ka_1 \\ ka_2 \\ ka_3 \end{pmatrix}$ for any scalar k

  ▸ the scalar product of $\mathbf{a}$ and $\mathbf{b}$ is $\mathbf{a} \bullet \mathbf{b} = a_1 b_1 + a_2 b_2 + a_3 b_3$

  ▸ if θ is the angle between $\mathbf{a}$ and $\mathbf{b}$, then $\cos \theta = \dfrac{\mathbf{a} \bullet \mathbf{b}}{|\mathbf{a}||\mathbf{b}|}$.

Example 22 ◀) Self Tutor

Consider the points A(2, 5, 1), B(-2, 6, -4), and C(4, 0, 3). Find:

a $\overrightarrow{AB}$ **b** the coordinates of D such that $\overrightarrow{AB} = \overrightarrow{CD}$.

a $\overrightarrow{AB} = \begin{pmatrix} -2 - 2 \\ 6 - 5 \\ -4 - 1 \end{pmatrix} = \begin{pmatrix} -4 \\ 1 \\ -5 \end{pmatrix}$

b Let D have coordinates (x, y, z).

Now $\overrightarrow{CD} = \overrightarrow{AB}$

$\therefore \begin{pmatrix} x - 4 \\ y - 0 \\ z - 3 \end{pmatrix} = \begin{pmatrix} -4 \\ 1 \\ -5 \end{pmatrix}$

$\therefore x - 4 = -4$, $y - 0 = 1$, and $z - 3 = -5$

$\therefore x = 0$, $y = 1$, and $z = -2$

The coordinates of D are $(0, 1, -2)$.

EXERCISE 17I

1 Consider the points A(3, 5, 2), B(-1, 4, 0), C(0, 6, -2), and D(-1, 4, -3). Find:

  a $\overrightarrow{OA}$ **b** $\overrightarrow{AB}$ **c** $\overrightarrow{DC}$ **d** $\overrightarrow{CB}$

2 Consider the points P(2, -1, 3), Q(0, 5, -6), and R(1, -1, -4). Find:

  a $\overrightarrow{PQ}$ **b** the coordinates of S such that $\overrightarrow{PQ} = \overrightarrow{RS}$.

Example 23

Let $\mathbf{a} = \begin{pmatrix} 5 \\ -1 \\ 3 \end{pmatrix}$ and $\mathbf{b} = \begin{pmatrix} -2 \\ 2 \\ 6 \end{pmatrix}$. Find:

a $|\mathbf{a}|$ **b** $3\mathbf{a} - \mathbf{b}$ **c** the angle between $\mathbf{a}$ and $\mathbf{b}$.

a $|\mathbf{a}| = \sqrt{5^2 + (-1)^2 + 3^2}$
$= \sqrt{25 + 1 + 9}$
$= \sqrt{35}$ units

c Let θ be the angle between $\mathbf{a}$ and $\mathbf{b}$.

Now $\cos\theta = \dfrac{\mathbf{a} \bullet \mathbf{b}}{|\mathbf{a}||\mathbf{b}|}$

$\therefore \cos\theta = \dfrac{-10 - 2 + 18}{\sqrt{35}\sqrt{4 + 4 + 36}}$

$\therefore \cos\theta = \dfrac{6}{\sqrt{35}\sqrt{44}}$

$\therefore \theta = \cos^{-1}\left(\dfrac{6}{\sqrt{35}\sqrt{44}}\right) \approx 81.2°$

The angle between $\mathbf{a}$ and $\mathbf{b}$ is about $81.2°$.

b $3\mathbf{a} - \mathbf{b}$
$= 3\begin{pmatrix} 5 \\ -1 \\ 3 \end{pmatrix} - \begin{pmatrix} -2 \\ 2 \\ 6 \end{pmatrix}$
$= \begin{pmatrix} 15 \\ -3 \\ 9 \end{pmatrix} - \begin{pmatrix} -2 \\ 2 \\ 6 \end{pmatrix}$
$= \begin{pmatrix} 17 \\ -5 \\ 3 \end{pmatrix}$

3 Let $\mathbf{a} = \begin{pmatrix} 2 \\ 0 \\ 3 \end{pmatrix}$ and $\mathbf{b} = \begin{pmatrix} -1 \\ 5 \\ -2 \end{pmatrix}$. Find:

  a $4\mathbf{a}$ **b** $-2\mathbf{b}$ **c** $\mathbf{a} + \mathbf{b}$
  d $\mathbf{a} - \mathbf{b}$ **e** $3\mathbf{a} + \mathbf{b}$ **f** $\mathbf{a} - 5\mathbf{b}$

4 Find the magnitude of:

  a $\begin{pmatrix} 2 \\ -1 \\ -2 \end{pmatrix}$ **b** $\begin{pmatrix} -4 \\ 0 \\ 7 \end{pmatrix}$ **c** $\begin{pmatrix} 3 \\ -6 \\ 4 \end{pmatrix}$

5 Show that $\begin{pmatrix} 6 \\ -1 \\ 4 \end{pmatrix}$ is perpendicular to $\begin{pmatrix} 5 \\ 2 \\ -7 \end{pmatrix}$.

6 Find t given that $\begin{pmatrix} t^2 - 1 \\ -4 \\ 1 \end{pmatrix}$ is parallel to $\begin{pmatrix} -6 \\ 8 \\ 2t + 2 \end{pmatrix}$.

7 Find the angle between $\mathbf{a} = \begin{pmatrix} 5 \\ -4 \\ 2 \end{pmatrix}$ and $\mathbf{b} = \begin{pmatrix} -1 \\ 0 \\ 6 \end{pmatrix}$.

8 Find the measure of all angles of triangle PQR with vertices P(6, 0, −1), Q(4, 3, 3), and R(−2, 3, −1).

REVIEW SET 17A

1 Using a scale of 1 cm represents 10 units, sketch a vector to represent:

   a an aeroplane taking off at an angle of $8°$ to the runway with a speed of 60 m s^{-1}

   b a displacement of 45 m in the direction $060°$.

2 For the given vectors **p**, **q**, and **r**, show how to construct:

   a $\mathbf{p} + \mathbf{r}$ **b** $\mathbf{r} - \mathbf{q} - \mathbf{p}$

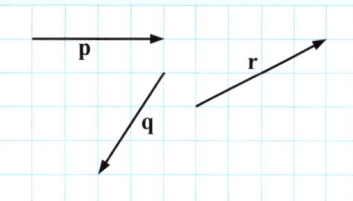

3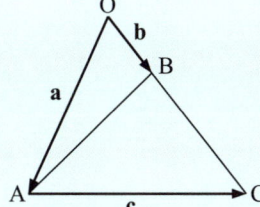

In the figure alongside, $\overrightarrow{OA} = \mathbf{a}$, $\overrightarrow{OB} = \mathbf{b}$, and $\overrightarrow{AC} = \mathbf{c}$.

Find, in terms of **a**, **b**, and **c**:

   a $\overrightarrow{CA}$ **b** $\overrightarrow{AB}$ **c** $\overrightarrow{OC}$ **d** $\overrightarrow{BC}$

4 For points A, B, C, and D, simplify the following vector expressions:

   a $\overrightarrow{AB} + \overrightarrow{BD}$ **b** $\overrightarrow{BC} - \overrightarrow{DC}$ **c** $\overrightarrow{AB} - \overrightarrow{CB} + \overrightarrow{CD} - \overrightarrow{AD}$

5 A yacht is moving at 10 km h^{-1} in a south-easterly direction. It encounters a 3 km h^{-1} current from the north. Find the resultant speed and direction of the yacht.

6 What can be deduced about vectors **a** and **b** if $\mathbf{a} = \frac{1}{3}\mathbf{b}$?

7 Suppose $\mathbf{p} = \begin{pmatrix} 4 \\ 3 \end{pmatrix}$, $\mathbf{q} = \begin{pmatrix} 3 \\ -5 \end{pmatrix}$, and $\mathbf{r} = \begin{pmatrix} 0 \\ -4 \end{pmatrix}$. Find:

   a $2\mathbf{p} + \mathbf{q}$ **b** $\mathbf{p} - \mathbf{q} - \mathbf{r}$ **c** the length of **q**.

8 Find the value of k such that $\begin{pmatrix} 2 \\ -3 \end{pmatrix}$ and $\begin{pmatrix} k \\ 6 \end{pmatrix}$ are:

   a parallel   **b** perpendicular.

9 Use vectors to find the remaining vertex of parallelogram ABCD.

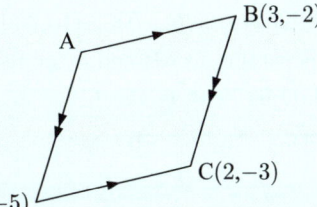

10 For the vectors $\mathbf{p} = \begin{pmatrix} 1 \\ 2 \end{pmatrix}$ and $\mathbf{q} = \begin{pmatrix} 3 \\ -2 \end{pmatrix}$, find:

   a $\mathbf{p} \bullet \mathbf{q}$ **b** the angle between **p** and **q**.

11 Find the measure of $C\widehat{B}A$ for A(1, 2), B(−2, 3), and C(0, −4).

12 Consider the points P(7, −1, 2) and Q(4, −3, −1). Find:

a $\overrightarrow{PQ}$

b the distance PQ.

REVIEW SET 17B

1 What can be said about vectors **p** and **q** if:

a $|\mathbf{p}| = |\mathbf{q}|$

b $\mathbf{p} = 2\mathbf{q}$?

2 How are $\overrightarrow{AB}$ and $\overrightarrow{BA}$ related?

3 A pilot wishes to fly his aeroplane due east at a speed of 200 km h^{-1}. However, his flight is affected by a wind blowing constantly at 40 km h^{-1} from the south.

a In what direction must he face the aeroplane?

b What would be his speed in still conditions?

4 Find:

a $\begin{pmatrix} 2 \\ 5 \end{pmatrix} \bullet \begin{pmatrix} -4 \\ -3 \end{pmatrix}$

b $\begin{pmatrix} -4 \\ -1 \end{pmatrix} \bullet \begin{pmatrix} 6 \\ -3 \end{pmatrix}$

5 For $\mathbf{m} = \begin{pmatrix} 3 \\ -1 \end{pmatrix}$ and $\mathbf{n} = \begin{pmatrix} 2 \\ 4 \end{pmatrix}$ find:

a $\mathbf{m} - 2\mathbf{n}$

b $|\mathbf{m} + \mathbf{n}|$.

6 Find the value of t such that $\begin{pmatrix} 2 \\ t \end{pmatrix}$ and $\begin{pmatrix} -3 \\ 4 \end{pmatrix}$ are:

a perpendicular

b parallel.

7 Consider the points P(4, 7), Q(8, 4), R(7, 0), and S(−1, t). Find t given that [PQ] ∥ [SR].

8 For A(−1, 1) and B(2, −3), find:

a $\overrightarrow{AB}$

b the distance AB.

9 Find k given that $\begin{pmatrix} k \\ k^2 + 3k \end{pmatrix} = \begin{pmatrix} k^2 - 2 \\ 10 \end{pmatrix}$.

10 For P(1, 4), Q(−2, 5), and R(−1, −2), find the measure of $Q\hat{R}P$.

11 In the given figure, $\overrightarrow{AB} = \mathbf{p}$ and $\overrightarrow{BC} = \mathbf{q}$. $\overrightarrow{DC}$ is parallel to $\overrightarrow{AB}$ and twice its length. Find, in terms of **p** and **q**:

a $\overrightarrow{DC}$

b $\overrightarrow{AC}$

c $\overrightarrow{AD}$.

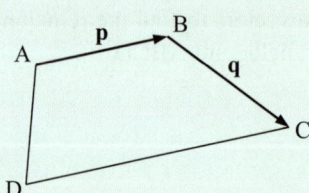

12 Let $\mathbf{a} = \begin{pmatrix} -4 \\ 1 \\ -1 \end{pmatrix}$ and $\mathbf{b} = \begin{pmatrix} 2 \\ -7 \\ 3 \end{pmatrix}$. Find:

a $5\mathbf{a}$

b $2\mathbf{b} - \mathbf{a}$

c the angle between **a** and **b**.

Chapter 18

Exponential functions and logarithms

Contents:
- **A** Exponential functions
- **B** Graphs of exponential functions
- **C** Growth and decay
- **D** Compound interest
- **E** Depreciation
- **F** Exponential equations
- **G** Logarithms

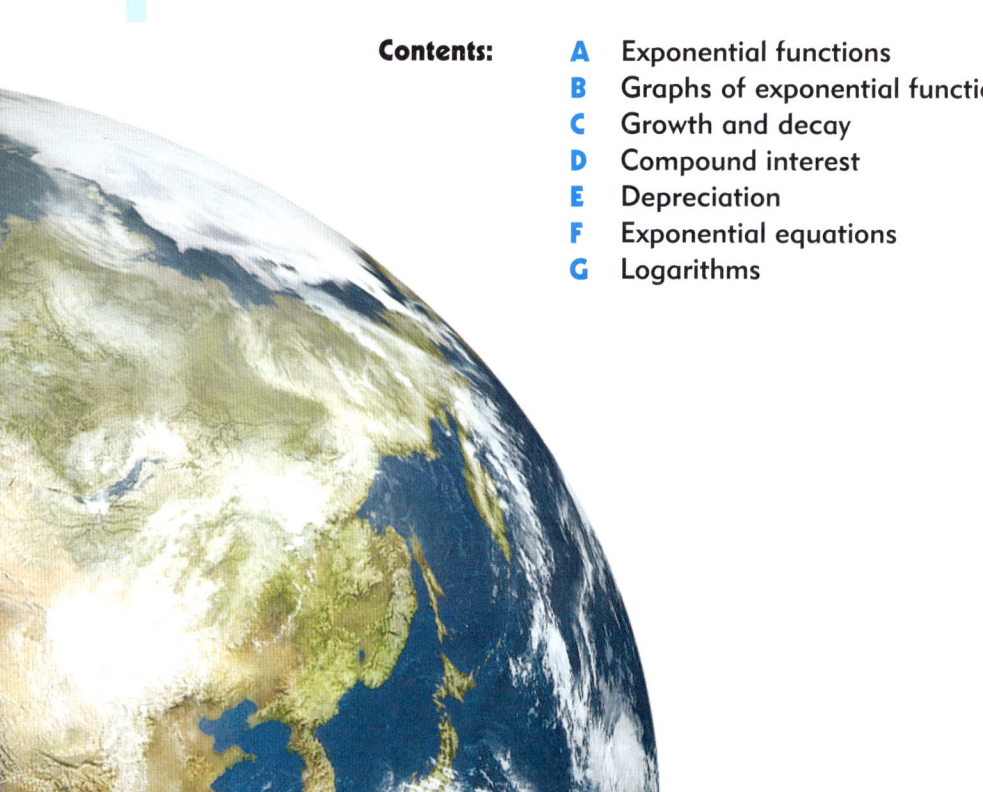

OPENING PROBLEM

A lotus plant initially covers an area of 40 cm². The area it covers increases by 20% each week.

Things to think about:

a Does the area covered by the plant increase by a constant amount each week?

b Can you explain why the area covered by the lotus plant after n weeks is given by the function $A(n) = 40 \times 1.2^n$ cm²?

c What does the graph of $A(n)$ look like?

d What area is covered by the lotus plant after 3 weeks?

e How long will it take for the plant to cover an area of 100 cm²?

When a quantity increases or decreases by a **fixed percentage** each time period, the quantity can be described using an **exponential function**.

In this chapter, we will study exponential functions and their graphs. We will also solve **exponential equations** using algebraic methods, technology, and **logarithms**.

A   EXPONENTIAL FUNCTIONS

An **exponential function** is a function in which the variable occurs as part of the index or exponent.

Examples of exponential functions are $f(x) = 3^x$, $g(x) = 2^{x-4}$, and $h(x) = 6 + 5^{-x}$.

Example 1   🔊 Self Tutor

For the function $f(x) = 3 - 2^{-x}$, find:

a $f(0)$ b $f(3)$ c $f(-x)$

a $f(0) = 3 - 2^0$
       $= 3 - 1$
       $= 2$

b $f(3) = 3 - 2^{-3}$
       $= 3 - \frac{1}{8}$
       $= 2\frac{7}{8}$

c $f(-x) = 3 - 2^{-(-x)}$
         $= 3 - 2^x$

EXERCISE 18A

1 Determine whether the following are exponential functions:

   a $f(x) = 7^x$ b $f(x) = x^4$ c $f(x) = 5 - 3^{x-2}$

   d $f(x) = 10 \times 2^{\frac{x}{2}}$ e $f(x) = 9x - x^6$ f $f(x) = -2 - 5^{3x}$

2 For the function $f(x) = 3^x + 2$, find:

   a $f(0)$ b $f(2)$ c $f(-1)$ d $f(2x)$

3 For the function $f(x) = 5^{-x} - 3$, find:
  a $f(0)$ **b** $f(1)$ **c** $f(-2)$ **d** $f(-x)$

4 For the function $g(x) = 3^{x-2}$, find:
  a $g(0)$ **b** $g(4)$ **c** $g(-1)$ **d** $g(x+5)$

B GRAPHS OF EXPONENTIAL FUNCTIONS

GRAPHS OF THE FORM $f(x) = a^x$, $a > 0$, $a \neq 1$

We can draw graphs of exponential functions using a table of values.

For example, the graph of $f(x) = 2^x$ is shown alongside.

x	-3	-2	-1	0	1	2	3
y	$\frac{1}{8}$	$\frac{1}{4}$	$\frac{1}{2}$	1	2	4	8

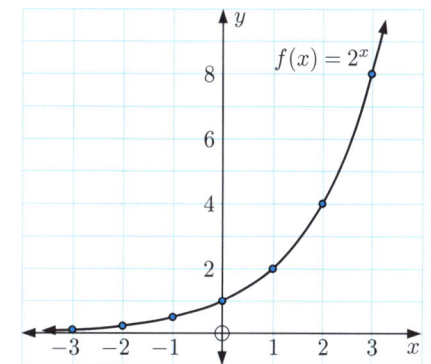

Notice that:
- the y-intercept of the function is 1
- the graph lies entirely above the y-axis
- as the values of x get smaller, the values of y get closer and closer to zero, but never actually reach zero. We say that the line $y = 0$ is a **horizontal asymptote** of the function.

$a^0 = 1$ for all $a \neq 0$.

INVESTIGATION 1 GRAPHS OF THE FORM $f(x) = a^x$, $a > 0$, $a \neq 1$

What to do:

1 Use the **graphing package** or your **graphics calculator** to draw the graph of:

  a $f(x) = 1.3^x$ **b** $f(x) = 2^x$ **c** $f(x) = 3^x$ **d** $f(x) = 5^x$
  e $f(x) = 0.8^x$ **f** $f(x) = \left(\frac{1}{2}\right)^x$ **g** $f(x) = 0.3^x$ **h** $f(x) = 0.1^x$

GRAPHING PACKAGE

GRAPHICS CALCULATOR INSTRUCTIONS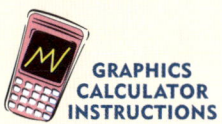

2 What do you notice about:
  a the y-intercept of each graph **b** the horizontal asymptote of each graph?

3 For the graph of $f(x) = a^x$, what effect does a have on:
  a whether the graph is increasing or decreasing
  b the steepness of the graph?

In the previous **Investigation** you should have made the following discoveries:

For all exponential functions of the form $f(x) = a^x$, $a > 0$, $a \neq 1$:
- The y-intercept is 1, since $f(0) = a^0 = 1$.
- The graph has the horizontal asymptote $y = 0$.
- If $a > 1$, the graph is **increasing**.
- If $0 < a < 1$, the graph is **decreasing**.

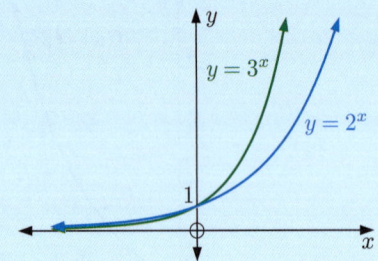
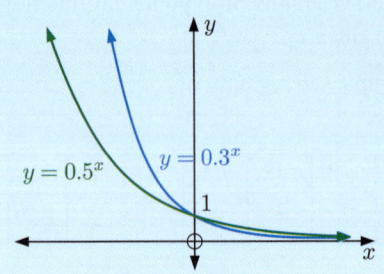

- The graph of $f(x) = a^x$ becomes steeper as a moves further away from 1.

EXERCISE 18B.1

1 Use a table of values from $x = -3$ to $x = 3$ to help sketch each of the following exponential functions:
  a $f(x) = 3^x$
  b $f(x) = 4^x$
  c $f(x) = \left(\frac{1}{2}\right)^x$
  d $f(x) = \left(\frac{1}{3}\right)^x$

2 Use technology to graph the following functions on the same set of axes:
  a $y = 5^x$
  b $y = 1.8^x$
  c $y = 0.7^x$
  d $y = \left(\frac{2}{5}\right)^x$

3 Match each function with the correct graph:
  a $y = 3.6^x$
  b $y = 0.9^x$
  c $y = 1.5^x$
  d $y = \left(\frac{1}{4}\right)^x$
  e $y = \left(\frac{2}{3}\right)^x$
  f $y = \left(\frac{5}{2}\right)^x$

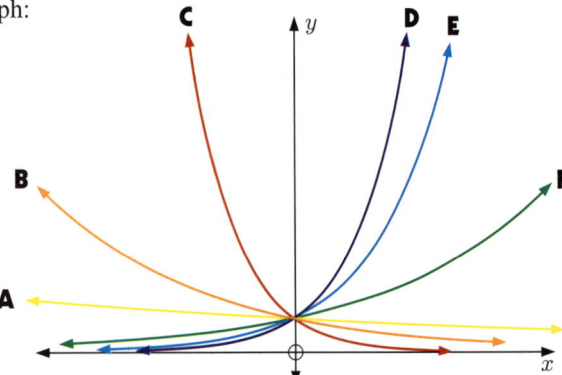

USING TRANSFORMATIONS TO GRAPH EXPONENTIAL FUNCTIONS

To graph more complicated exponential functions, we apply **transformations** to graphs of the form $y = a^x$.

INVESTIGATION 2 — TRANSLATING $y = a^x$

What to do:

1. **a** Use the **graphing package** or your **graphics calculator** to draw the graph of:

   i $y = 3^x$ **ii** $y = 3^x + 2$

   iii $y = 3^x - 4$

   b For each graph in **a**, find the y-intercept and the equation of the horizontal asymptote.

   c What transformation is needed to graph $y = 3^x + k$ from $y = 3^x$?

2. **a** Draw the graph of:

   i $y = 2^x$ **ii** $y = 2^{x-1}$ **iii** $y = 2^{x+4}$

   b What transformation is needed to graph $y = 2^{x-k}$ from $y = 2^x$?

INVESTIGATION 3 — DILATING $y = a^x$

What to do:

1. **a** Use the **graphing package** or your **graphics calculator** to draw the graph of:

   i $y = 4^x$ **ii** $y = 2 \times 4^x$ **iii** $y = \frac{1}{3} \times 4^x$

   b Find the y-intercept of each graph in **a**.

   c What transformation is needed to graph $y = k \times 4^x$ from $y = 4^x$?

2. **a** Draw the graph of:

   i $y = 3^x$ **ii** $y = 3^{\frac{x}{2}}$ **iii** $y = 3^{2x}$

   b What transformation is needed to graph $y = 3^{\frac{x}{k}}$ from $y = 3^x$?

INVESTIGATION 4 — REFLECTING $y = a^x$

What to do:

1. Use the **graphing package** or your **graphics calculator** to draw the graph of:

   a $y = 5^x$ **b** $y = -5^x$ **c** $y = 5^{-x}$

   d $y = \left(\frac{1}{2}\right)^x$ **e** $y = -\left(\frac{1}{2}\right)^x$ **f** $y = \left(\frac{1}{2}\right)^{-x}$

2. What transformation is needed to graph:

   a $y = -a^x$ from $y = a^x$ **b** $y = a^{-x}$ from $y = a^x$?

From the **Investigations** you should have found that:

- Graphs of the form $y = a^x + k$ are obtained by translating $y = a^x$ by $\begin{pmatrix} 0 \\ k \end{pmatrix}$.
  ▸ If $k > 0$, the graph moves upwards.   ▸ If $k < 0$, the graph moves downwards.
- Graphs of the form $y = a^{x-k}$ are obtained by translating $y = a^x$ by $\begin{pmatrix} k \\ 0 \end{pmatrix}$.
  ▸ If $k > 0$, the graph moves right.   ▸ If $k < 0$, the graph moves left.
- Graphs of the form $y = k \times a^x$ are obtained by vertically dilating $y = a^x$ with scale factor k.
  ▸ If $k > 1$, the graph moves away from the x-axis.
  ▸ If $0 < k < 1$, the graph moves towards the x-axis.
- Graphs of the form $y = a^{\frac{x}{k}}$ are obtained by horizontally dilating $y = a^x$ with scale factor k.
  ▸ If $k > 1$, the graph moves away from the y-axis.
  ▸ If $0 < k < 1$, the graph moves towards the y-axis.
- Graphs of the form $y = -a^x$ are obtained by reflecting $y = a^x$ in the x-axis.
- Graphs of the form $y = a^{-x}$ are obtained by reflecting $y = a^x$ in the y-axis.

Example 2   ◀)) Self Tutor

Sketch the graph of:

a $y = 2^x + 3$ **b** $y = 3^{x-4}$

a The graph of $y = 2^x + 3$ is found by translating $y = 2^x$ upwards by 3 units.

b The graph of $y = 3^{x-4}$ is found by translating $y = 3^x$ to the right by 4 units.

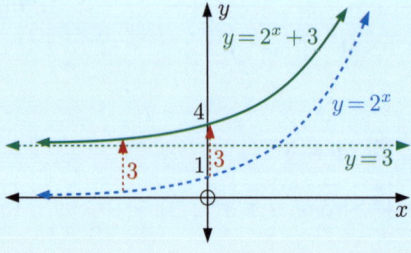
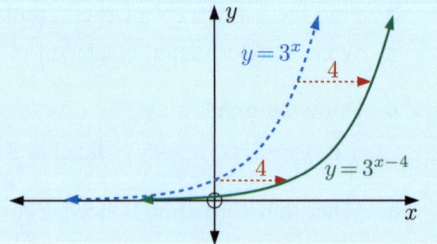

EXERCISE 18B.2

1 For each of the following functions:
  i sketch the graph
  ii state the equation of the horizontal asymptote
  iii find the range
  iv find the y-intercept.

  a $y = 2^x - 1$ **b** $y = 3^x + 2$ **c** $y = \left(\tfrac{1}{2}\right)^x - 3$

2 Sketch the graph of:

  a $y = 2^{x-3}$ **b** $y = 5^{x+2}$ **c** $y = \left(\tfrac{1}{3}\right)^{x-1}$

Example 3

Sketch the graph of:

a $y = 2 \times 3^x$

b $y = 2^{\frac{x}{3}}$

a The graph of $y = 2 \times 3^x$ is found by vertically dilating $y = 3^x$ with scale factor 2.

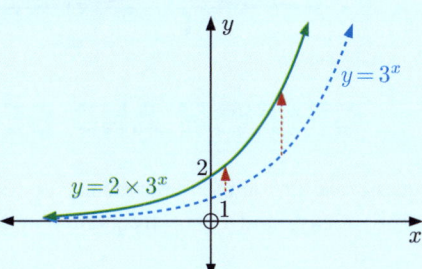

b The graph of $y = 2^{\frac{x}{3}}$ is found by horizontally dilating $y = 2^x$ with scale factor 3.

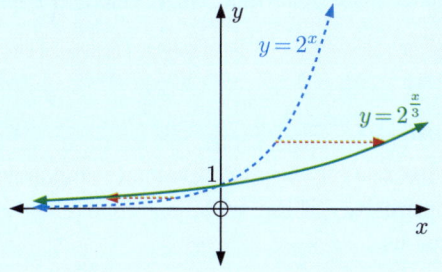

3 Sketch the graph of:

a $y = 3 \times 2^x$
b $y = \frac{1}{2} \times 5^x$
c $y = 4 \times \left(\frac{1}{2}\right)^x$

4 Sketch the graph of:

a $y = 5^{\frac{x}{2}}$
b $y = 2^{3x}$
c $y = \left(\frac{2}{3}\right)^{2x}$

Example 4

Sketch the graph of:

a $y = -4^x$

b $y = 3^{-x}$

a The graph of $y = -4^x$ is found by reflecting $y = 4^x$ in the x-axis.

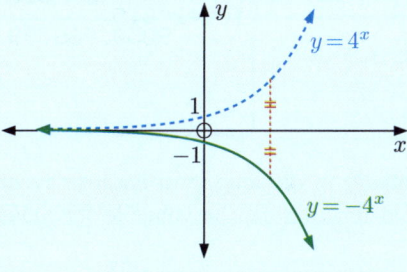

b The graph of $y = 3^{-x}$ is found by reflecting $y = 3^x$ in the y-axis.

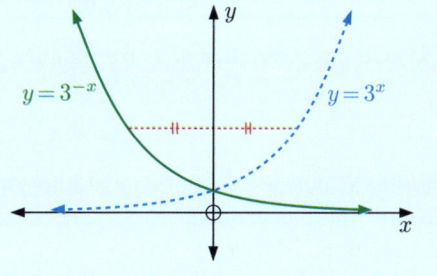

5 Sketch the graph of:

a $y = -2^x$
b $y = -5^x$
c $y = -\left(\frac{1}{3}\right)^x$

6 Sketch the graph of:

a $y = 4^{-x}$
b $y = 2^{-x}$
c $y = \left(\frac{1}{3}\right)^{-x}$

7 Consider the graph of $f(x) = 3^x$ alongside.

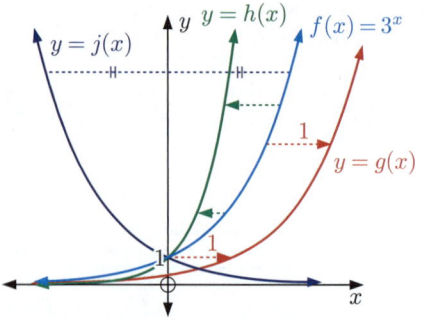

  a $y = g(x)$ is found by translating $y = f(x)$ 1 unit to the right. Show that $g(x) = \frac{1}{3} \times 3^x$.

  b $y = h(x)$ is found by horizontally stretching $y = f(x)$ with scale factor $\frac{1}{2}$. Show that $h(x) = 9^x$.

  c $y = j(x)$ is found by reflecting $y = f(x)$ in the y-axis. Show that $j(x) = \left(\frac{1}{3}\right)^x$.

C GROWTH AND DECAY

In this section we will examine situations where quantities are either increasing or decreasing exponentially. These situations are known as **growth** and **decay**, and occur frequently in the world around us.

> An exponential function of the form $f(x) = k \times a^x$ exhibits:
> - **growth** if $a > 1$
> - **decay** if $0 < a < 1$.

GROWTH

Under favourable conditions, a population of rabbits will grow exponentially.

Suppose the population is initially 100 rabbits, and the population doubles every month. The population after t months can be described by the exponential function $P = 100 \times 2^t$.

We can use this relationship to answer questions about the rabbit population. For example:

TI-84 Plus

- To find the population after 3 months, we substitute $t = 3$ and find $P = 100 \times 2^3$
  $= 800$ rabbits.

- To find the population after $6\frac{1}{2}$ months, we substitute $t = 6.5$ and find $P = 100 \times 2^{6.5}$
  ≈ 9051 rabbits.

Clearly, the population cannot continue to grow exponentially in the long term because eventually the rabbits will run out of food. Nevertheless, an exponential function can be valuable for modelling the population in the short term.

Example 5   ◀)) Self Tutor

During a locust plague, the area of land eaten n weeks after the initial observation, is given by $A = 8000 \times 1.4^n$ hectares.

  a Find the size of the area initially eaten.
  b Find the size of the area eaten after: **i** 4 weeks   **ii** 7 weeks.

c Use **a** and **b** to sketch the graph of A against n.

a Initially, $n = 0$ ∴ $A = 8000 \times 1.4^0$
$= 8000$ hectares

b i When $n = 4$,
$A = 8000 \times 1.4^4$
$\approx 30\,700$ ha

  ii When $n = 7$,
$A = 8000 \times 1.4^7$
$\approx 84\,300$ ha

c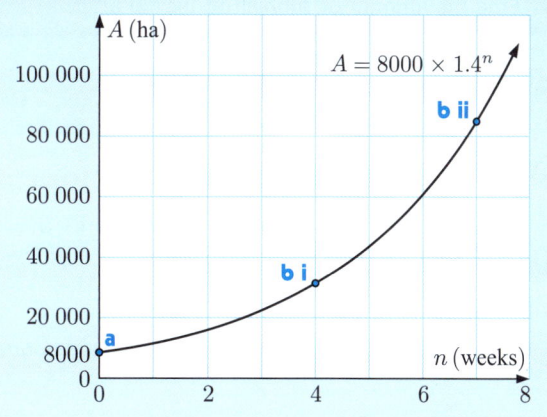

EXERCISE 18C.1

1 A local zoo starts a breeding program to ensure the survival of a species of mongoose. Using results from a previous program, the expected population in n years' time is given by $P = 40 \times 1.15^n$.

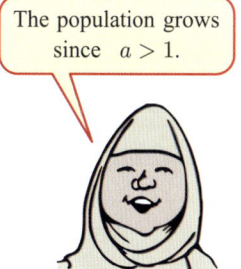

The population grows since $a > 1$.

  a What is the initial population purchased by the zoo?
  b Find the expected population after:
   i 3 years   **ii** 10 years   **iii** 30 years.
  c Sketch the graph of P against n using **a** and **b**.

2 In Tasmania, a reserve is set aside for the breeding of echidnas. The expected population after t years is given by $P = 50 \times 1.26^t$.

  a What is the initial breeding colony size?
  b Find the expected colony size after:
   i 3 years   **ii** 9 years   **iii** 20 years.
  c Graph P against t using **a** and **b**.

3 In Uganda, the number of breeding females in an endangered population of gorillas is G_0. Biologists predict that the number of breeding females G in n years' time will grow according to $G = G_0 \times 1.01^n$.

  a There are currently 28 breeding females in the colony. Find G_0.
  b Predict the number of breeding females after:
   i 5 years   **ii** 10 years   **iii** 20 years.
  c Sketch the graph of G against n using **a** and **b**.

4 A tip contains 3000 tonnes of rubbish. The amount of rubbish in the tip increases by 5% each year.

  a Explain why the amount of rubbish in the tip after n years is given by $A(n) = 3000 \times 1.05^n$.

  b Find the amount of rubbish in the tip after:

  i 5 years **ii** 10 years.

  c Sketch the graph of A against n.

DECAY

When the value of a variable decreases exponentially over time, we call it **decay**.

Examples of decay include:
- cooling of a cup of tea or coffee
- radioactive decay
- the drop in current when an electrical appliance is turned off.

Example 6   ◀)) **Self Tutor**

The current I flowing through the electric circuit in a fan, t milliseconds after it is switched off, is given by $I = 320 \times 0.7^t$ milliamps.

  a Find the initial current in the circuit.

  b Find the current after: **i** 4 milliseconds   **ii** 10 milliseconds.

  c Sketch the graph of I against t using **a** and **b**.

a When $t = 0$, $I = 320 \times 0.7^0$
$= 320$ milliamps

b **i** When $t = 4$,
$I = 320 \times 0.7^4$
≈ 76.8 milliamps

   ii When $t = 10$,
$I = 320 \times 0.7^{10}$
≈ 9.04 milliamps

c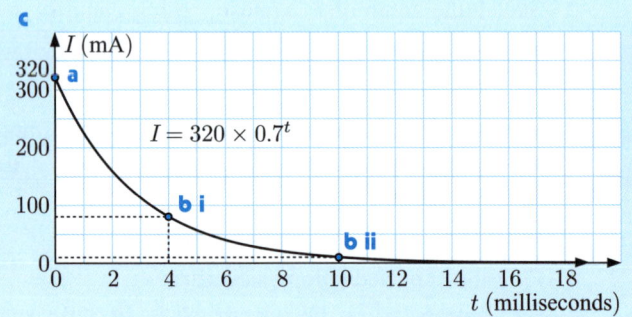

EXERCISE 18C.2

1 Boiling water is left in a pot to cool. After t minutes, its temperature is given by $T = 100 \times 0.84^t$ °C.

  a Find the initial temperature of the water.

  b Find the water temperature after:

  i 2 minutes   **ii** 10 minutes   **iii** 20 minutes.

  c Graph T against t using **a** and **b**.

The function decays since $0 < a < 1$.

2 The weight of radioactive material in an ore sample after t years is given by
$W = 2.3 \times 0.96^t$ grams.
  a Find the initial weight.
  b Find the weight after: **i** 20 years   **ii** 40 years   **iii** 60 years.
  c Sketch the graph of W against t using **a** and **b**.
  d What is the percentage loss in weight from $t = 0$ to $t = 20$?

3 There are currently 500 possums in a section of bushland. The population is expected to fall by 8% each year.
  a Write an exponential function for the expected possum population P after t years.
  b Find the expected possum population after:
     i 1 year   **ii** 5 years   **iii** 10 years.
  c Sketch the graph of P against t.

D COMPOUND INTEREST

When you place money in a bank, you are in effect lending the money to the bank. The bank in turn uses your money to lend to other people. The bank pays you **interest** to encourage your custom, and they charge interest to borrowers at a higher rate. This is how the bank makes money.

When you place money in a bank, the value in your account is called your **balance**. After a period of time, the interest is automatically added to your account. When this happens, the next lot of interest will be calculated on the higher balance. This creates a **compounding** effect on the interest as you are getting **interest on interest**.

> **Compound interest** is calculated as a percentage of the total amount at the end of the previous time period.

Consider an investment of €1000 with compound interest of 6% p.a. paid each year.

After year	Interest paid	Account balance
0	-	€1000.00
1	6% of €1000.00 = €60.00	€1000.00 + €60.00 = €1060.00
2	6% of €1060.00 = €63.60	€1060.00 + €63.60 = €1123.60
3	6% of €1123.60 = €67.42	€1123.60 + €67.42 = €1191.02

Notice the increasing amount of interest each year.

Each year, the account balance becomes $(100\% + 6\%)$ or 106% of its previous value.

∴ the value after 3 years $= €1000 \times 1.06 \times 1.06 \times 1.06$
$= €1000 \times (1.06)^3$
$= €1191.02$

This suggests that if the money is left in the account for n years, it will amount to €1000 × $(1.06)^n$.

The **annual multiplier** is $(1 + i)$, where i is the annual interest rate expressed as a decimal.

These observations lead to the **compound interest formula**:

$$F_v = P_v(1+i)^n$$

where F_v is the **future value**
P_v is the **present value** or amount initially invested
i is the **annual interest rate** as a decimal
n is the **number of years of investment**.

> Compound interest is an example of exponential growth!

Example 7 ◀) Self Tutor

a Find the future value when $5000 is invested at 8% p.a. compound interest for 2 years.
b How much interest is earned?

> The interest earned is $F_v - P_v$

a $F_v = P_v(1+i)^n$
$\therefore F_v = 5000 \times (1 + 0.08)^2$
$= 5000 \times (1.08)^2$
$= \$5832$

b Interest earned
$= \$5832 - \$5000$
$= \$832$

EXERCISE 18D

1 Copy and complete the table to find the future value when €8000 is invested at 5% p.a. compound interest.

After year	Interest paid	Future value
0	-	€8000
1	5% of €8000 = €400	
2		
3		

2 a Find the future value when £40 000 is invested at 10% p.a. compound interest for 3 years.
  b How much interest is earned?

3 a Find the future value of a ¥ 50 000 investment at 8% p.a. compounding yearly over 3 years.
  b How much interest is earned?

Example 8 ◀) Self Tutor

I am able to invest at 8.5% p.a. compounding annually. How much should I invest now to achieve a future value of $10 000 in 4 years' time?

$F_v = P_v(1+i)^n$
$\therefore 10\,000 = P_v \times (1 + 0.085)^4$ $\{8.5\% = 0.085\}$
$\therefore 10\,000 = P_v \times (1.085)^4$
$\therefore \dfrac{10\,000}{(1.085)^4} = P_v$
$\therefore P_v = 7215.74$ $\{Calculator:\ 10\,000\ \boxed{\div}\ 1.085\ \boxed{\wedge}\ 4\ \boxed{\text{ENTER}}\ \}$

I should invest $7215.74 now.

4 I can invest money at a fixed rate of 7.5% p.a. compounding annually. How much money must I invest now to produce $20 000 for a holiday in 4 years' time?

5 What initial investment is required to produce a maturing amount of 15 000 euros in 5 years' time, given a fixed interest rate of 5.5% p.a. compounding annually?

Example 9 — Self Tutor

An investment of £3000 has grown to £3752 after 4 years. Find the annual compound interest rate.

$$P_v(1+i)^n = F_v$$
$$\therefore\ 3000(1+i)^4 = 3752$$
$$\therefore\ (1+i)^4 = \frac{3752}{3000}$$
$$\therefore\ 1+i = \sqrt[4]{\frac{3752}{3000}} \quad \{\text{finding the fourth root of both sides}\}$$
$$\therefore\ i = \sqrt[4]{\frac{3752}{3000}} - 1$$
$$\therefore\ i \approx 0.0575$$

The annual interest rate is approximately 5.75%.

6 An investment of $4000 has grown to $4855 after 5 years. Find the annual compound interest rate.

7 Julian invested £8500, and three years later his account balance was £9686.
  a How much interest did Julian earn?
  b Find the annual compound interest rate.

E DEPRECIATION

Depreciation describes how items diminish in value over time.

Motor cars, office furniture, computers, and many other items decrease in value as they age. We call this process **depreciation**.

Items usually depreciate because they become damaged and imperfect through use and time, or because their technology becomes superseded.

The following table shows how a computer bought for $1500 depreciates by 20% each year. Items are depreciated on their **reduced value** each year. This creates a compounding effect similar to what we saw with interest in the previous section.

Age (years)	Depreciation	Value
0	-	$1500
1	20% of $1500 = $300	$1500 − $300 = $1200
2	20% of $1200 = $240	$1200 − $240 = $ 960
3	20% of $960 = $192	$960 − $192 = $ 768

At the end of each year, the computer is only worth $100\% - 20\% = 80\%$ of its previous value. Thus, we multiply by 0.8.

Its value after 1 year is $\quad V_1 = \$1500 \times 0.8$,
$\qquad$ after 2 years is $\quad V_2 = V_1 \times 0.8 = \$1500 \times (0.8)^2$,
$\qquad$ and after 3 years is $\quad V_3 = V_2 \times 0.8 = \$1500 \times (0.8)^3$.

This suggests that after n years, the value will be $V_n = \$1500 \times (0.8)^n$.

Depreciation is an example of exponential decay!

The **depreciation formula** is:

$$F_v = P_v(1-i)^n$$

where $\quad F_v \quad$ is the **future value** after n years
$\qquad P_v \quad$ is the **original purchase price** or **present value**
$\qquad i \quad$ is the **annual depreciation rate** as a decimal
$\qquad n \quad$ is the **number of years**.

Example 10 ◀) Self Tutor

Photocopiers depreciate in value by 15% per year. Suppose a photocopier was purchased for $18 500.

a Find the value of the photocopier after 5 years.

b By how much has its value depreciated?

a $P_v = 18\,500$ $\qquad$ Now $F_v = P_v(1-i)^n$
$\quad i = 0.15$ $\qquad\qquad \therefore\ F_v = 18\,500\,(1 - 0.15)^5$
$\quad n = 5$ $\qquad\qquad\qquad\ \ = 18\,500(0.85)^5$
$\qquad\qquad\qquad\qquad\qquad\ \ \approx \$8208.55$

b Depreciation $= \$18\,500 - \$8208.55 = \$10\,291.45$

Depreciation is $P_v - F_v$

EXERCISE 18E

1 A car was purchased for $32 500, and its value depreciated annually by 16%. Find the value of the car after 10 years.

2 A motorbike was purchased for £8495, and its value depreciated at 12% each year.

a Copy and complete the following table:

Number of years owned	Depreciation or annual loss in value	Value after n years
0	-	£8495
1	£1019.40	£7475.60
2		
3		
4		

b The motorbike is used for a delivery service, and so the depreciation each year can be claimed as a tax deduction. How much can be 'claimed' during the 4th year?

c Find the value of the motorbike at the end of the 8th year.

3 Kevin bought a truck for $38 500. It depreciated at a rate of 20% p.a.

  a Find the truck's value after 3 years. **b** By how much has it lost value?

4 A cabin cruiser was bought for €120 000 in April 2005, and was sold for €45 000 in April 2013. Find the annual rate of depreciation of the boat.

F EXPONENTIAL EQUATIONS

An **exponential equation** is an equation in which the unknown occurs as part of the index or exponent.

For example: $2^x = 8$ and $30 \times 3^x = 7$ are both exponential equations.

To solve exponential equations, we try to write both sides of the equation with the **same base**. We can then **equate indices**.

$$\text{If } a^x = a^k, \text{ then } x = k.$$

Example 11

Solve for x:

a $2^x = 32$ **b** $3^{x-2} = \frac{1}{9}$

a $2^x = 32$
$\therefore 2^x = 2^5$
$\therefore x = 5$ {equating indices}

b $3^{x-2} = \frac{1}{9}$
$\therefore 3^{x-2} = 3^{-2}$
$\therefore x - 2 = -2$ {equating indices}
$\therefore x = 0$

Example 12

Solve for x:

a $6 \times 3^x = 54$ **b** $4^{x-1} = \left(\frac{1}{2}\right)^{1-3x}$

a $6 \times 3^x = 54$
$\therefore 3^x = 9$
$\therefore 3^x = 3^2$
$\therefore x = 2$ {equating indices}

b $4^{x-1} = \left(\frac{1}{2}\right)^{1-3x}$
$\therefore (2^2)^{x-1} = (2^{-1})^{1-3x}$
$\therefore 2^{2x-2} = 2^{3x-1}$
$\therefore 2x - 2 = 3x - 1$ {equating indices}
$\therefore -2 + 1 = 3x - 2x$
$\therefore x = -1$

EXERCISE 18F

1 Solve for x:

a $3^x = 3$
b $3^x = 9$
c $2^x = 8$
d $5^x = 1$
e $3^x = \frac{1}{3}$
f $5^x = \frac{1}{5}$
g $2^x = \frac{1}{16}$
h $5^{x+2} = 25$
i $2^{x+2} = \frac{1}{4}$
j $3^{x-1} = \frac{1}{27}$
k $2^{x-1} = 32$
l $3^{1-2x} = \frac{1}{27}$
m $4^{2x+1} = \frac{1}{2}$
n $9^{x-3} = 3$
o $\left(\frac{1}{2}\right)^{x-1} = 2$
p $\left(\frac{1}{3}\right)^{2-x} = 9$

2 Solve for x:

a $5 \times 2^x = 40$
b $6 \times 2^{x+2} = 24$
c $3 \times \left(\frac{1}{2}\right)^x = 12$
d $4 \times 5^x = 500$
e $54 \times 3^{x+2} = 2$
f $7 \times \left(\frac{1}{3}\right)^x = 63$
g $2^{2-5x} = 4^x$
h $5^{x-1} = \left(\frac{1}{25}\right)^x$
i $9^{x-2} = \left(\frac{1}{3}\right)^{3x-1}$
j $2^x \times 4^{2-x} = 8$
k $3^{x+1} \times 9^{-x} = \left(\frac{1}{3}\right)^{x+1}$
l $2^{x^2 - 2x} = 8$

3 Consider the rabbit population described on page **394**, which is given by the function $P = 100 \times 2^t$ after t months. How long will it take for the rabbit population to reach 3200?

4 Solve for x:

a $\dfrac{3^{2x+1}}{3^x} = 9^x$
b $\dfrac{25^x}{5^{x+4}} = 25^{1-x}$
c $\dfrac{4^x}{2^{x+2}} = \dfrac{2^{x+1}}{8^x}$
d $\dfrac{5^{2x-5}}{125^x} = \dfrac{25^{1-2x}}{5^{x+2}}$
e $\dfrac{4^x}{8^{2-x}} = 2^x \times 4^{x-1}$
f $\dfrac{9^{2x}}{27^{2-x}} = \dfrac{81^{3x+1}}{3^{1-2x}}$

INVESTIGATION 5 — SOLVING EXPONENTIAL EQUATIONS GRAPHICALLY

Consider the exponential equation $3^x = 6$. We cannot easily write 6 as a power of 3, so we cannot solve this equation by equating indices. However, since $3^1 = 3$ and $3^2 = 9$, the solution for x must lie between 1 and 2.

We can solve this equation graphically using either a **graphics calculator** or the **graphing package**.

GRAPHING PACKAGE

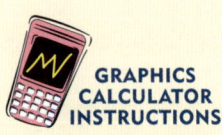
GRAPHICS CALCULATOR INSTRUCTIONS

What to do:

1 Draw the graphs of $y = 3^x$ and $y = 6$ on the same set of axes.

2 Find the coordinates of the point of intersection of the graphs.

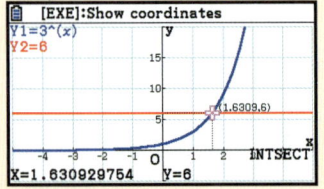
Casio fx-CG20

3 Solve for x, rounded to 3 decimal places:

a $3^x = 10$
b $3^x = 30$
c $3^x = 100$
d $2^x = 12$
e $5^x = 40$
f $7^x = 42$

G LOGARITHMS

The **logarithm** of a positive number is the power that 10 must be raised to in order to obtain the number.

For example, we know that $1000 = 10^3$. Since 10 must be raised to the power 3 to obtain 1000, the logarithm of 1000 is 3. We write $\log 1000 = 3$.

Similarly, $\frac{1}{10} = 10^{-1}$, so $\log\left(\frac{1}{10}\right) = -1$.

HISTORICAL NOTE — THE INVENTION OF LOGARITHMS

It is easy to take modern technology, such as the electronic calculator, for granted. Until electronic computers became affordable in the 1980s, a "calculator" was a *profession*, literally someone who would spend their time performing calculations by hand. They used mechanical calculators and technology such as logarithms. They often worked in banks, but sometimes for astronomers and other scientists.

The logarithm was invented by **John Napier** (1550 - 1617) and first published in 1614 in a Latin book which translates as *Description of the Wonderful Canon of Logarithms*. John Napier was the 8th Lord of Merchiston, which is now part of Edinburgh, Scotland. Napier wrote a number of other books on many subjects including religion and mathematics. One of his other inventions was a device for performing long multiplication which is now called "Napier's Bones". Other calculators, such as slide rules, used logarithms as part of their design. Napier also popularised the use of the decimal point in mathematical notation.

John Napier

In Napier's time, mathematicians did not use the same notation a^b for indices, nor did they make use of the general concept of a function as described in this course. It was therefore impossible for Napier to explain logarithms as we have done. Instead, Napier's definition was based on the continuous movement of two points.

To enable people to actually use logarithms, he calculated tables of numbers by hand to seven places of decimals. This took him many years of work. To find the logarithm of a particular number, you would look it up in the table. Although this seems awkward to us, it is much quicker to use tables than calculate multiplication, division, and square roots by hand.

Logarithms were an extremely important development and they had an immediate effect on the seventeenth century scientific community. **Johannes Kepler** used Napier's tables to assist with his calculations. This helped him develop his laws of planetary motion. Without logarithms these calculations would have taken many years. Kepler published a letter congratulating and acknowledging Napier. Kepler's laws gave **Sir Isaac Newton** important evidence to support his theory of universal gravitation. 200 years later, **Laplace** said that logarithms "by shortening the labours, doubled the life of the astronomer".

The logarithms of values such as 1000 and $\frac{1}{10}$ can be found by hand because it is easy to write these values as power of 10. The logarithms of most values, however, can only be found using a calculator.

For example, using a calculator we can see that $\log 47 \approx 1.672$.

This means that $10^{1.672} \approx 47$.

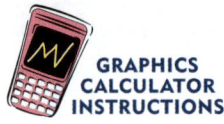
GRAPHICS CALCULATOR INSTRUCTIONS

TI-84 Plus
```
log(47)
        1.672097858
10^1.672
        46.98941086
```

EXERCISE 18G.1

1 Without using a calculator, find:

    a $\log 100$ **b** $\log 100\,000$ **c** $\log \left(\frac{1}{100}\right)$ **d** $\log 10$

    e $\log 0.0001$ **f** $\log 1$ **g** $\log \sqrt{10}$ **h** $\log 10\sqrt{10}$

2 Use your calculator to find, rounded to 3 decimal places:

    a $\log 28$ **b** $\log 5$ **c** $\log 300$

    d $\log 0.4$ **e** $\log 800$ **f** $\log 90$

    g $\log 0.07$ **h** $\log 4000$ **i** $\log(-6)$

Before calculating these values, try to estimate what the answer will be.

3   **a** Use your calculator to find $\log 70$.

     b Hence, write 70 as a power of 10.

4 Explain why it is impossible to find the logarithm of a negative number.

5 Copy and complete:

     a $\log x$ is positive if x is ......   **b** $\log x$ is negative if x is ......

LOGARITHM LAWS

In the following **Investigation**, we will discover some **logarithm laws** which can be used to simplify logarithmic expressions.

INVESTIGATION 6   LOGARITHM LAWS

What to do:

1   **a** Use your calculator to find:

     i $\log 2 + \log 6$ **ii** $\log 12$ **iii** $\log 7 + \log 9$ **iv** $\log 63$

     v $\log 5 + \log 11$ **vi** $\log 55$ **vii** $\log 4 + \log 8$ **viii** $\log 32$

   b Use $10^{1.699} \approx 50$ and $10^{0.903} \approx 8$ to:

     i find $\log 50$ **ii** find $\log 8$

     iii write 400 as a power of 10   **iv** find $\log 400$.

   c Copy and complete: $\log(ab) = \log a$ ...... $\log b$.

2   **a** Use your calculator to find:

     i $\log 15 - \log 3$ **ii** $\log 5$ **iii** $\log 56 - \log 8$ **iv** $\log 7$

     v $\log 2 - \log 13$ **vi** $\log\left(\frac{2}{13}\right)$ **vii** $\log 11 - \log 7$ **viii** $\log\left(\frac{11}{7}\right)$

b Use $10^{2.176} \approx 150$ and $10^{0.778} \approx 6$ to:
  i find $\log 150$
  ii find $\log 6$
  iii write 25 as a power of 10
  iv find $\log 25$.

c Copy and complete: $\log\left(\dfrac{a}{b}\right) = \log a \, \ldots\ldots \, \log b$.

3 a Use your calculator to find:
  i $\log(2^3)$
  ii $3 \log 2$
  iii $\log(7^4)$
  iv $4 \log 7$
  v $\log(6^{-2})$
  vi $-2 \log 6$
  vii $\log(5^{-3})$
  viii $-3 \log 5$

b Use $10^{0.602} \approx 4$ to:
  i find $\log 4$
  ii write 64 as a power of 10
  iii find $\log 64$.

c Copy and complete: $\log(a^n) = \ldots\ldots$

You should have discovered the following **logarithm laws** which are true for all positive values of a and b:

- $\log(ab) = \log a + \log b$
- $\log\left(\dfrac{a}{b}\right) = \log a - \log b$
- $\log(a^n) = n \log a$, where n is real.

These laws are closely related to the index laws!

Example 13 ◀) Self Tutor

Simplify, without using a calculator:

a $\log 2 + \log 7$
b $\log 6 - \log 3$
c $\dfrac{\log 49}{\log\left(\frac{1}{7}\right)}$

a $\log 2 + \log 7$
$= \log(2 \times 7)$
$= \log 14$

b $\log 6 - \log 3$
$= \log\left(\dfrac{6}{3}\right)$
$= \log 2$

c $\dfrac{\log 49}{\log\left(\frac{1}{7}\right)}$
$= \dfrac{\log 7^2}{\log 7^{-1}}$
$= \dfrac{2 \log 7}{-1 \log 7}$
$= -2$

EXERCISE 18G.2

1 Write as a single logarithm in the form $\log k$:

a $\log 6 + \log 5$
b $\log 10 - \log 2$
c $\log 77 + \log\left(\dfrac{1}{7}\right)$
d $2 \log 2 + \log 3$
e $\log 5 - 2 \log 2$
f $\tfrac{1}{2} \log 4 - \log 2$
g $\log 2 + \log 3 + \log 5$
h $\log 20 + \log(0.2)$
i $-\log 2 - \log 3$
j $3 \log\left(\dfrac{1}{8}\right)$
k $4 \log 2 + 3 \log 5$
l $6 \log 2 - 3 \log 5$

2 Without using a calculator, simplify:

a $\dfrac{\log 8}{\log 2}$
b $\dfrac{\log 9}{\log 3}$
c $\dfrac{\log 32}{\log 64}$
d $\dfrac{\log 5}{\log\left(\frac{1}{5}\right)}$

e $\dfrac{\log(0.5)}{\log 2}$
f $\dfrac{\log 125}{\log\left(\frac{1}{25}\right)}$
g $\dfrac{\log 2^b}{\log 8}$
h $\dfrac{\log 4}{\log 2^a}$

3 Without using a calculator, show that:

a $\log\sqrt{5} = \tfrac{1}{2}\log 5$
b $\log\sqrt[3]{2} = \tfrac{1}{3}\log 2$
c $\log\left(\dfrac{1}{\sqrt{3}}\right) = -\tfrac{1}{2}\log 3$

4 a Use a calculator to find, rounded to 3 decimal places:
   i $\log 5$ ii $\log 5000$
b Use the logarithm laws to show that $\log 5000 = \log 5 + 3$.

5 Use the logarithm laws to show that $\log 10^x = x$.

6 Write as a single logarithm:

a $2 + \log 6$
b $1 - \log 2$
c $\log 80 - 1$
d $1 + 2\log 5$
e $2\log 30 - 2$
f $3 + \log 2 + \log 7$

7 a Use a calculator to find, rounded to 3 decimal places:
   i $\log 13$ ii $\log\left(\dfrac{1}{13}\right)$ iii $\log 250$ iv $\log\left(\dfrac{1}{250}\right)$
b Use the logarithm laws to show that $\log\left(\dfrac{1}{x}\right) = -\log x$.

8 Simplify without using a calculator: $\dfrac{4\log\sqrt{8} - 3\log(\frac{1}{2})}{3 - 6\log\sqrt{5}}$

PUZZLE

Click on the icon to print a set of game squares, and cut them out.

Arrange the squares into a 4×3 rectangle so that adjoining edges have the same value.

PRINTABLE SQUARES

Global context

click here

How do we measure the magnitude of an earthquake?

Statement of inquiry: Mathematics is a powerful tool for measuring natural phenomena.

Global context: Scientific and technical innovation

Key concept: Relationships

Related concepts: Model, Measurement

Objectives: Communicating, Applying mathematics in real-life contexts

Approaches to learning: Thinking, Research

USING LOGARITHMS TO SOLVE EXPONENTIAL EQUATIONS

We cannot solve exponential equations such as $2^x = 7$ by writing both sides with the same base, but we have seen that we can solve these equations graphically. Another option is to take the logarithm of both sides of the equation, and then apply the logarithm laws to find the solution.

Example 14 — Self Tutor

Solve for x: $\quad 2^x = 7$

$2^x = 7$
$\therefore \log 2^x = \log 7 \quad$ {taking the log of both sides}
$\therefore x \log 2 = \log 7 \quad$ {$\log(a^n) = n \log a$}
$\therefore x = \dfrac{\log 7}{\log 2}$
$\therefore x \approx 2.81 \quad$ {technology}

Casio fx-CG20

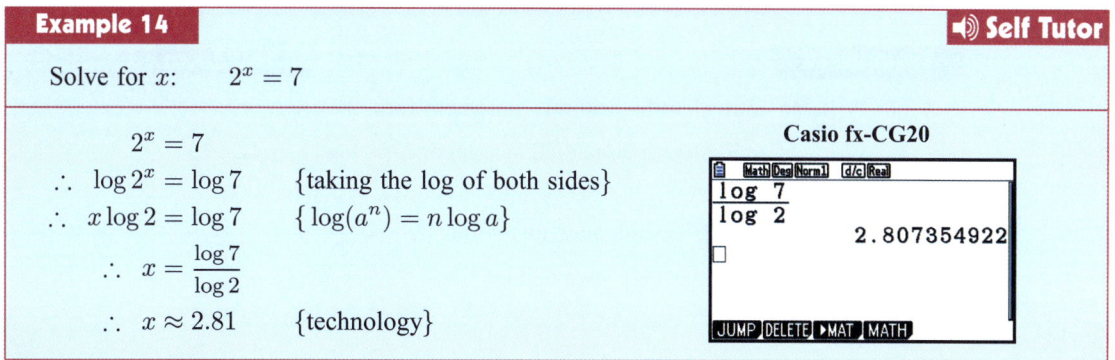

EXERCISE 18G.3

1 Solve for x using logarithms, giving answers to 4 significant figures:

- **a** $2^x = 3$
- **b** $2^x = 10$
- **c** $2^x = 400$
- **d** $3^x = 0.0075$
- **e** $5^x = 1000$
- **f** $6^x = 0.836$
- **g** $1.1^x = 1.86$
- **h** $1.25^x = 3$
- **i** $0.87^x = 0.001$
- **j** $0.7^x = 0.21$
- **k** $1.085^x = 2$
- **l** $0.997^x = 0.5$

2 Solve for x:

- **a** $5 \times 2^x = 70$
- **b** $4 \times 5^x = 1200$
- **c** $80 \times 1.1^x = 90$
- **d** $30 \times 0.9^x = 15$
- **e** $200 \times 0.5^x = 30$
- **f** $60 \times 0.99^x = 50$

3 The weight of bacteria in a culture t hours after it has been established, is given by $W = 2.5 \times 1.03^t$ grams.
At what time will the weight reach:

- **a** 4 grams
- **b** 15 grams?

4 A cube of ice has sides of length 5 cm. As it melts, its volume decreases by 15% each minute.

- **a** Write an exponential function for the volume V cm^3 of the block of ice after t minutes.
- **b** Find the volume of the block of ice after 2 minutes.
- **c** How long will it take for the volume of the block of ice to reduce to 50 cm^3?

5 Answer the **Opening Problem** on page **388**.

LOGARITHMS IN OTHER BASES

In the definition of logarithm we have used so far, we consider the power that 10 must be raised to in order to obtain a given number. More completely, this is called a **logarithm in base 10**.

However, we can also talk about logarithms in bases other than 10.

The **logarithm in base a of b** is the power that a must be raised to in order to get b. It is written $\log_a b$.

For logarithms in base 10, we have seen that $1000 = 10^3$, so $\log 1000 = 3$.

Using logarithms in base 2, we can see that $8 = 2^3$, so $\log_2 8 = 3$.

Example 15 ◀) Self Tutor

a Write an equivalent logarithmic statement for $2^5 = 32$.
b Write an equivalent exponential statement for $\log_7 \left(\frac{1}{7}\right) = -1$.

a From $2^5 = 32$, we deduce that $\log_2 32 = 5$.
b From $\log_7 \left(\frac{1}{7}\right) = -1$, we deduce that $7^{-1} = \frac{1}{7}$.

EXERCISE 18G.4

1 Write an equivalent logarithmic statement for:

   a $2^3 = 8$ **b** $3^2 = 9$ **c** $5^{-1} = \frac{1}{5}$ **d** $2^5 = 32$

   e $7^0 = 1$ **f** $3^{-4} = \frac{1}{81}$ **g** $2^{-6} = \frac{1}{64}$ **h** $2^{\frac{1}{2}} = \sqrt{2}$

2 Write an equivalent exponential statement for:

   a $\log_{10} 1000 = 3$ **b** $\log_2 16 = 4$

   c $\log_3 \left(\frac{1}{3}\right) = -1$ **d** $\log_4 1 = 0$

   e $\log_7 \left(\frac{1}{49}\right) = -2$ **f** $\log_{\frac{1}{7}} \left(\frac{1}{49}\right) = 2$

   g $\log 100 = 2$ **h** $\log_{\sqrt{5}} 25 = 4$

If no base is specified, it is assumed we are working in base 10.

Example 16 ◀) Self Tutor

Find:
a $\log_3 81$ **b** $\log_4 2$

a $81 = 3^4$, so $\log_3 81 = 4$.
b $2 = 4^{\frac{1}{2}}$, so $\log_4 2 = \frac{1}{2}$.

To find $\log_a b$, write b with base a.

3 Write 125 with base 5, and hence find $\log_5 125$.

4 Write $\frac{1}{36}$ with base 6, and hence find $\log_6 \left(\frac{1}{36}\right)$.

5 Find:

   a $\log_3 9$ **b** $\log_2 64$ **c** $\log_2 \sqrt{2}$ **d** $\log_4 \sqrt{2}$

   e $\log_3 3\sqrt{3}$ **f** $\log_6 1$ **g** $\log_8 8$ **h** $\log_8 \left(\frac{1}{8}\right)$

   i $\log_{\frac{1}{8}} \left(\frac{1}{8}\right)$ **j** $\log_{\sqrt{2}} \left(\frac{1}{\sqrt{2}}\right)$ **k** $\log_2 \left(\frac{1}{\sqrt{2}}\right)$ **l** $\log_8 \left(\frac{1}{\sqrt{2}}\right)$

REVIEW SET 18A

1 Consider the function $f(x) = 3^x - 1$. Find:
   a $f(0)$ **b** $f(3)$ **c** $f(-1)$ **d** $f(2x)$

2 Use technology to help sketch the following on the same set of axes:
   a $y = 2.7^x$ **b** $y = 1.6^x$ **c** $y = 0.8^x$

3 Use transformations to sketch the graph of:
   a $y = -3^x$ **b** $y = 2^x + 5$

4 The weight of a radioactive substance remaining after t years is given by $W = 1000 \times (0.98)^t$ grams.
   a Find the initial weight present.
   b Find the weight after:
      i 10 years   **ii** 50 years   **iii** 100 years.
   c Graph W against t using **a** and **b** only.

5 £120 000 is invested at 7.4% p.a. compound interest for 5 years.
   a Find the future value of the investment.   **b** How much interest is earned?

6 Solve for x without using a calculator:
   a $27^x = 3$ **b** $8^{x+1} = 16^{4-x}$ **c** $4^{x+1} = \left(\frac{1}{8}\right)^x$
   d $8 \times 2^{x+1} = 4$ **e** $3 \times 25^{3-x} = 15$ **f** $\dfrac{3^{x+2}}{9^{3-x}} = \dfrac{27^{1-2x}}{3^{2x}}$

7 The population of a colony of seals after t years is given by $P = 50 \times 3^t$.
   a Find the population after 2 years.
   b How long will it take for the population to reach 4050?

8 **a** Use your calculator to find $\log 80$.   **b** Hence, write 80 as a power of 10.

9 Without using a calculator, find: **a** $\log\left(\dfrac{1}{\sqrt{10}}\right)$ **b** $\log 100\sqrt{10}$

10 Without using a calculator, simplify:
   a $\log 4 + \log 2$ **b** $\log 45 - 2\log 3$ **c** $\dfrac{\log 16}{\log 2}$ **d** $\dfrac{\log 9^b}{\log 27}$

11 Danielle writes an online blog. The number of people following her blog after t weeks is given by $N(t) = 10 \times 1.3^t$.
   a How many people are following Danielle's blog:
      i initially   **ii** after 4 weeks
      iii after 8 weeks?
   b Sketch the graph of N against t.
   c How long will it take for Danielle's blog to have 200 followers?

12 **a** Write $\dfrac{1}{\sqrt{5}}$ as a power of 5.   **b** Hence, find $\log_5 \dfrac{1}{\sqrt{5}}$.

REVIEW SET 18B

1 **a** Explain why $f(x) = 5^{x-2}$ is an exponential function.
   b What transformation can be applied to $y = 5^x$ to obtain $y = f(x)$?

2 Suppose $P(x) = 2 \times 3^{-x}$. Find:
   a $P(0)$
   b $P(2)$
   c $P(x+4)$

3 Sketch the graph of:
   a $y = 2^{x+2}$
   b $y = 5^{-x}$

4 Find the range of the function $y = 3^x - 2$.

5 Kelly has started taking Spanish lessons. The number of Spanish words she knows after n weeks is given by $W(n) = 2 \times 1.9^n$.
   a How many Spanish words does Kelly know:
      i before she starts the lessons
      ii after 3 weeks
      iii after 5 weeks?
   b Sketch the graph of W against n.

6 A new caravan worth $15 000 depreciates at 16% p.a. Find the caravan's value in 5 years' time.

7 Use your calculator to find $\log 700$, rounded to 2 decimal places.

8 Find x without using your calculator:
   a $5^{1-x} = 125$
   b $9^x = 27^{2-2x}$
   c $16^{x+1} = 32^{2-x}$

9 Write as a single logarithm:
   a $\frac{1}{2} \log 25 + \log 11$
   b $2 + \log 4$
   c $3 - \log 5 - \log 8$

10 **a** Use your calculator to find the value of $(\log 5)^2 + \log 50 \times \log 2$.
   b Prove this result algebraically by simplifying $(1+\log 5)(1-\log 5)$ in two different ways.

11 Solve using logarithms:
   a $1.5^x = 9$
   b $200 \times 0.6^x = 10$

12 Find:
   a $\log_3 \sqrt{3}$
   b $\log_2 \left(\frac{1}{16}\right)$

Chapter 19
Deductive geometry

Contents:
- **A** Circle theorems
- **B** Further circle theorems
- **C** Geometric proof
- **D** Cyclic quadrilaterals

OPENING PROBLEM

Market gardener Joe has four long straight pipes of different lengths. He places the pipes on the ground, and joins them with rubber hose to form a garden bed in the shape of a quadrilateral. A sprinkler which casts water in semi-circles of diameter equal to the length of a pipe is placed at the midpoint of each pipe.

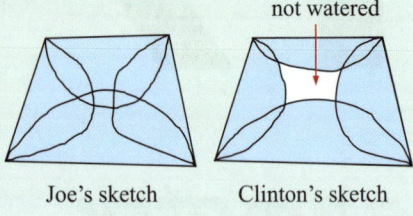

Joe's sketch   Clinton's sketch

Joe draws a rough sketch of the watering system, and decides that his sprinklers will water the whole of the garden. His son Clinton is sceptical of his father's idea, and draws his own sketch which suggests that there will be an unwatered patch in the centre.

Things to think about:

a By drawing an accurate diagram of this situation, can you determine whether Joe or Clinton is correct?

b Can you prove that your answer is true using geometric theorems?

The geometry of triangles, quadrilaterals, and circles has been used for at least 3000 years in art, design, and architecture. Many amazing discoveries have been made by mathematicians and non-mathematicians who were simply drawing figures with rulers and compasses.

A   CIRCLE THEOREMS

In geometry, we use logical reasoning to prove that certain observations about geometrical figures are true. We do this using special results called **theorems**.

CIRCLE THEOREMS

You should be familiar with the following **circle theorems**:

Name of theorem	Statement	Diagram
Angle in a semi-circle	The angle in a semi-circle is a right angle.	$A\widehat{B}C = 90°$
Chords of a circle	The perpendicular from the centre of a circle to a chord bisects the chord.	$AM = BM$

DEDUCTIVE GEOMETRY (Chapter 19)

Name of theorem	Statement	Diagram
Radius-tangent	The tangent to a circle is perpendicular to the radius at the point of contact.	$\widehat{OAT} = 90°$ 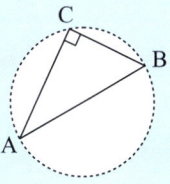
Tangents from an external point	Tangents from an external point are equal in length.	$AP = BP$ 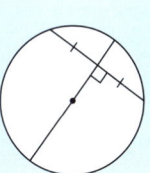

Two useful **converses** are:

- If line segment [AB] subtends a right angle at C, then the circle through A, B, and C has diameter [AB].

- The perpendicular bisector of a chord of a circle passes through its centre.

Example 1   ◀) Self Tutor

Find x, giving brief reasons for your answer.

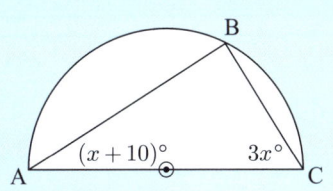

$\widehat{ABC}$ measures $90°$ {angle in a semi-circle}
$\therefore\ (x+10) + 3x + 90 = 180$ {angles in a triangle}
$\therefore\ 4x + 100 = 180$
$\therefore\ 4x = 80$
$\therefore\ x = 20$

EXERCISE 19A

1 Find x, giving brief reasons for your answers:

a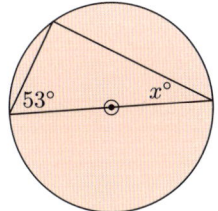

b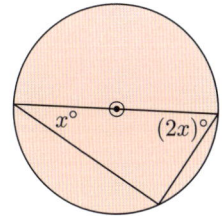

c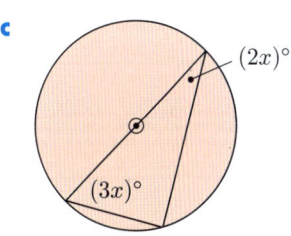

Example 2

In the figure alongside, find a and b.

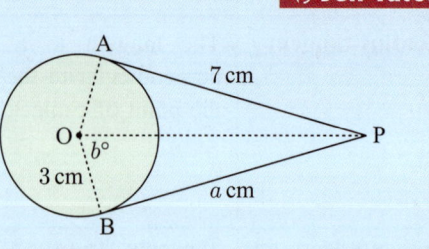

AP = BP   {tangents from an external point}
∴ $a = 7$

Now, $\widehat{OBP} = 90°$ {radius-tangent theorem}

∴ in △OBP, $\tan b° = \frac{7}{3}$

∴ $b = \tan^{-1}(\frac{7}{3})$

∴ $b \approx 66.8$

---

2 Find a and b in the following figures:

a 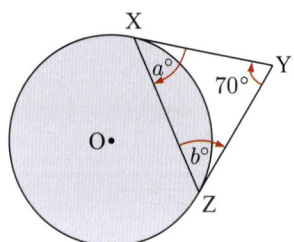   **b** 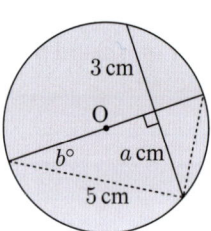   **c**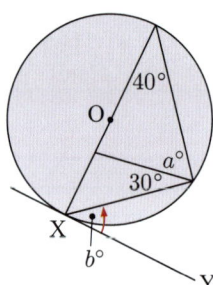

3 a Find x.
   b Hence, find the diameter of the circle.

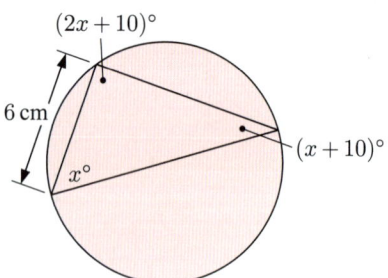

4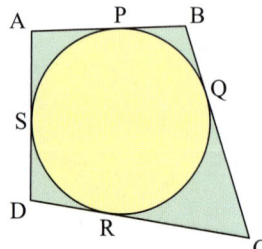

A circle is drawn, and four tangents to it are constructed as shown.

Deduce that   AB + CD = BC + AD.

5 The chord [AB] is equal in length to the radius of the circle. Find the length of [XY].

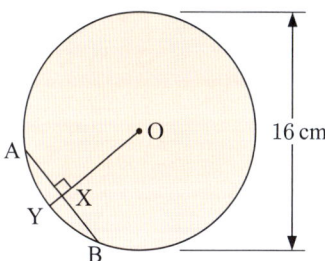

6 [AB] is the perpendicular bisector of the chord [CD].
Find the diameter of the circle.

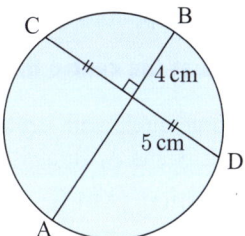

7 A circle touches the three sides of the triangle as shown. Find the radius of the circle.

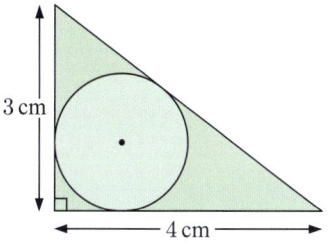

8 A circle is inscribed in a right angled triangle. The radius of the circle is 3 cm, and [BC] has length 8 cm.
Find the perimeter of the triangle ABC.

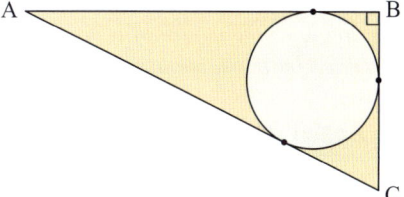

B   FURTHER CIRCLE THEOREMS

Before we can explore additional circle theorems, we need some more terminology for describing the parts of a circle.

Any continuous part of a circle is called an **arc**.

If the arc is less than half the circle, it is called a **minor arc**.

If the arc is greater than half the circle, it is called a **major arc**.

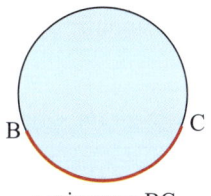
a minor arc BC

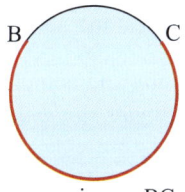
a major arc BC

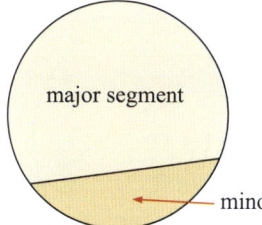

A chord divides the interior of a circle into two regions called **segments**. The larger region is called a **major segment**, and the smaller region is called a **minor segment**.

In the diagram opposite:

- the minor arc BC **subtends** the angle BAC, where A is on the circle
- the minor arc BC also subtends angle BOC at the centre of the circle.

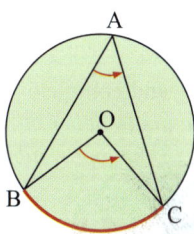

INVESTIGATION 1 — FURTHER CIRCLE THEOREMS

The use of the **geometry package** is recommended, but this Investigation can also be done using a ruler, compass, and protractor.

Part 1: Angle at the centre theorem

1. Draw a large circle with centre O. Mark on it points A, B, and P.

2. Join [AO], [BO], [AP], and [BP].

3. Measure angles AOB and APB. What do you notice?

4. Repeat the above steps with another circle.

5. Copy and complete:
   "The angle at the centre of a circle is ...... the angle on the circle subtended by the same arc."

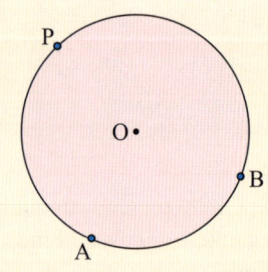

Part 2: Angles subtended by the same arc theorem

1. Draw a circle with centre O. Mark on it points A, B, C, and D.

2. Join [AC], [BC], [AD], and [BD].

3. Measure angles ACB and ADB. What do you notice?

4. Repeat the above steps with another circle.

5. Copy and complete:
   "Angles subtended by an arc on the circle are ...... in size."

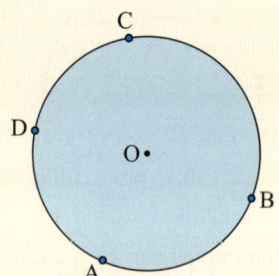
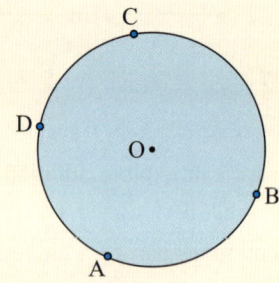

Part 3: Angle between a tangent and a chord theorem

1. Draw a circle and mark on it points A, B, and C.

2. Draw tangent TAS at A, and join [AB], [BC], and [CA].

3. Measure angles BAS and ACB. What do you notice?

4. Repeat the above steps with another circle.

5. Copy and complete:
   "The angle between a tangent and a chord at the point of contact is ...... to the angle subtended by the chord in the alternate ......"

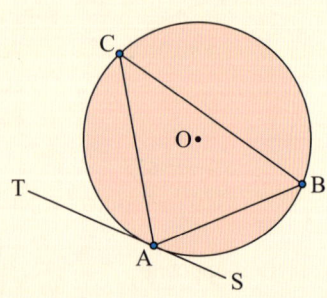

From the **Investigation** you should have discovered the following theorems:

Name of theorem	Statement	Diagram
Angle at the centre	The angle at the centre of a circle is twice the angle on the circle subtended by the same arc.	$A\hat{O}B = 2 \times A\hat{C}B$
Angles subtended by the same arc	Angles subtended by an arc on the circle are equal in size.	$A\hat{D}B = A\hat{C}B$
Angle between a tangent and a chord	The angle between a tangent and a chord at the point of contact is equal to the angle subtended by the chord in the alternate segment.	$B\hat{A}S = A\hat{C}B$

Note:
- The following diagrams show other cases of **the angle at the centre theorem**. These cases can be shown using the **geometry package**.

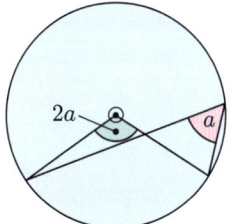 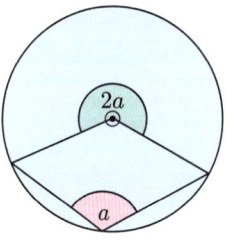 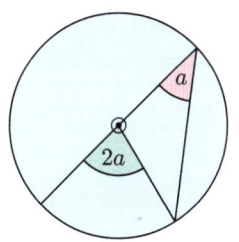 

GEOMETRY PACKAGE

- The **angle in a semi-circle theorem** is a special case of the angle at the centre theorem.

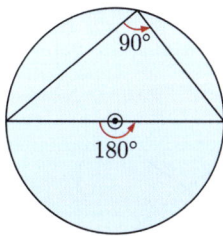

Example 3

Find x:

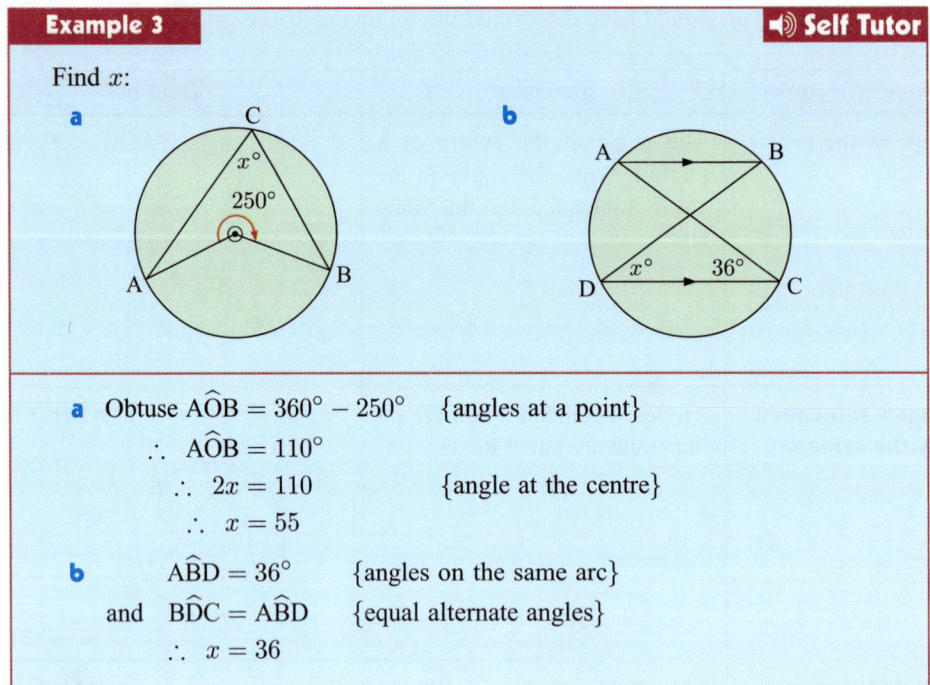

a Obtuse $\widehat{AOB} = 360° - 250°$ {angles at a point}
∴ $\widehat{AOB} = 110°$
∴ $2x = 110$ {angle at the centre}
∴ $x = 55$

b $\widehat{ABD} = 36°$ {angles on the same arc}
and $\widehat{BDC} = \widehat{ABD}$ {equal alternate angles}
∴ $x = 36$

EXERCISE 19B

1 Find, giving reasons, the value of x:

a **b** **c**

d **e** **f**

2 Find, giving reasons, the value of each pronumeral:

a 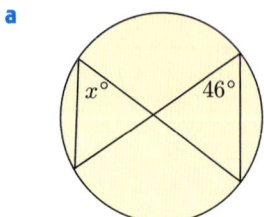 **b** 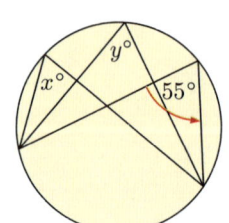 **c**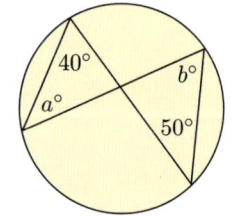

DEDUCTIVE GEOMETRY (Chapter 19) 419

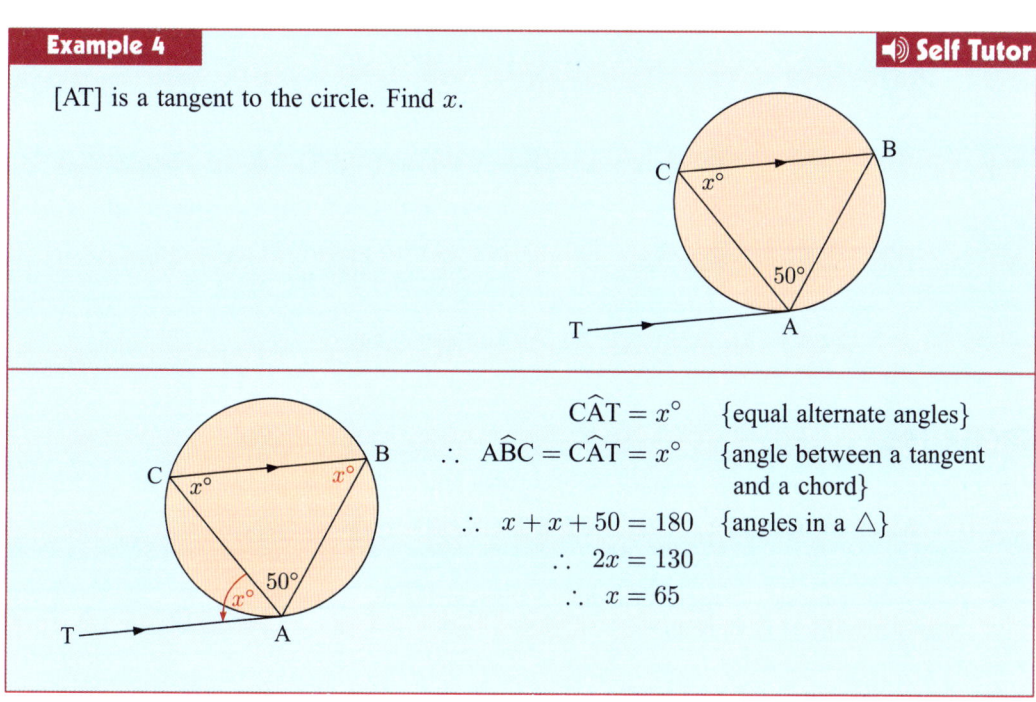

Example 4

[AT] is a tangent to the circle. Find x.

$\widehat{CAT} = x°$ {equal alternate angles}

$\therefore \widehat{ABC} = \widehat{CAT} = x°$ {angle between a tangent and a chord}

$\therefore x + x + 50 = 180$ {angles in a $\triangle$}

$\therefore 2x = 130$

$\therefore x = 65$

3 In each diagram, C is the point of contact of tangent [CT]. Find x, giving reasons:

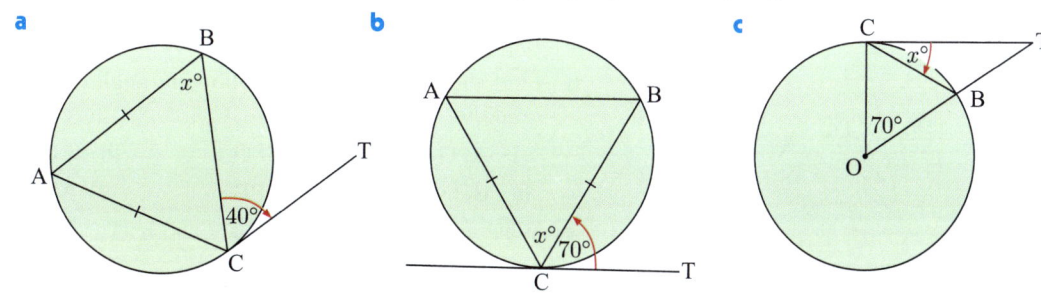

GEOMETRIC PROOF

The circle theorems and other geometric facts can be formally **proven** using mathematical tools we already possess, such as the isosceles triangle theorem and congruence.

Example 5

Use the given figure to prove the *angle in a semi-circle theorem*.

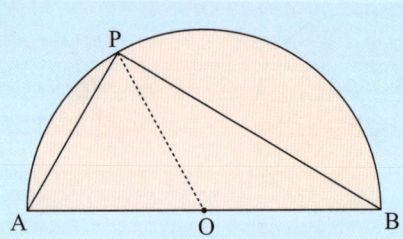

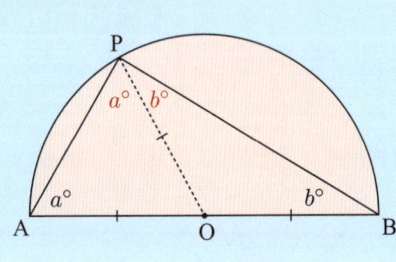

Let $P\hat{A}O = a°$ and $P\hat{B}O = b°$.
Now $OA = OP = OB$ {equal radii}

∴ △s OAP and OBP are isosceles.

∴ $O\hat{P}A = a°$ and $B\hat{P}O = b°$ {isosceles △s}
Now $a + (a + b) + b = 180$ {angles of △APB}
∴ $2a + 2b = 180$
∴ $a + b = 90$

So, $A\hat{P}B$ is a right angle.

EXERCISE 19C

1 In this question we prove the *chords of a circle* theorem.

  a For the given figure, join [OA] and [OB], and classify △OAB.

  b Apply the isosceles triangle theorem to triangle OAB. What geometrical fact results?

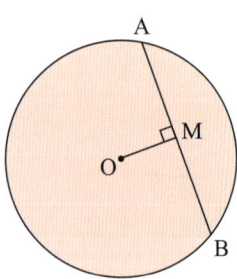

2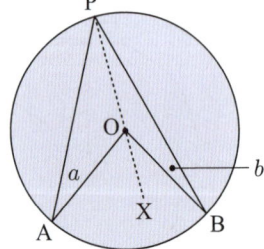

In this question we prove the *angle at the centre* theorem.

  a Explain why △s OAP and OBP are isosceles.
  b Find the measure of the following angles in terms of a and b:

   i $A\hat{P}O$ **ii** $B\hat{P}O$ **iii** $A\hat{O}X$
   iv $B\hat{O}X$ **v** $A\hat{P}B$ **vi** $A\hat{O}B$

  c What can be deduced from **b v** and **b vi**?

3 In this question we prove the *angles subtended by the same arc* theorem.

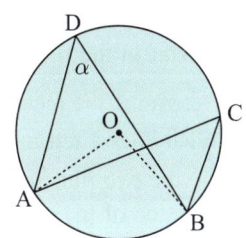

  a Using the results of **2**, find the size of $A\hat{O}B$ in terms of α.

  b Hence find the size of $A\hat{C}B$ in terms of α.

  c State the relationship between $A\hat{D}B$ and $A\hat{C}B$.

4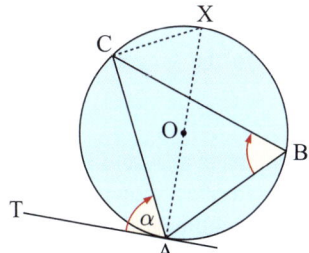

In this question we prove the *angle between a tangent and a chord* theorem.

  a We draw diameter [AX] and join [CX].

  Find the size of: **i** $T\hat{A}X$ **ii** $A\hat{C}X$

  b If $T\hat{A}C = \alpha$, find in terms of α:

    i $C\hat{A}X$ **ii** $C\hat{X}A$ **iii** $C\hat{B}A$

  c State the relationship between $T\hat{A}C$ and $C\hat{B}A$.

Example 6   ◀)) Self Tutor

$\triangle ABC$ is isosceles and is inscribed in a circle. [TC] is a tangent to the circle.

Prove that [AC] bisects $B\hat{C}T$.

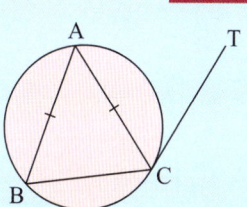

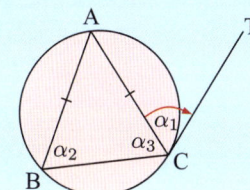

$\alpha_1 = \alpha_2$ {tangent and chord theorem}

and $\alpha_2 = \alpha_3$ {isosceles $\triangle$ theorem}

$\therefore \alpha_1 = \alpha_3$

So, [AC] bisects $B\hat{C}T$.

5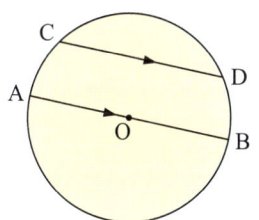

[AB] is a diameter of a circle with centre O. [CD] is a chord parallel to [AB].

Prove that [BC] bisects $D\hat{C}O$.

6 [AB] is the diameter of a circle with centre O. X is a point on the circle, and [AX] is produced to Y such that OX = XY.

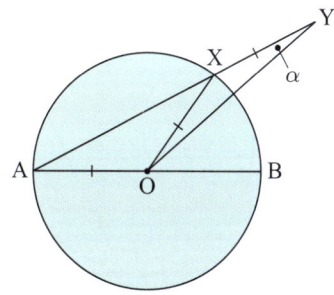

  a If $X\hat{Y}O = \alpha$, find in terms of α:

    i $X\hat{O}Y$ **ii** $A\hat{X}O$ **iii** $X\hat{A}O$

    iv $X\hat{O}B$ **v** $B\hat{O}Y$

  b What is the relationship between $B\hat{O}Y$ and $Y\hat{O}X$?

7 Revisit the **Opening Problem** on page **412**. Consider the two semi-circles in the figure alongside.

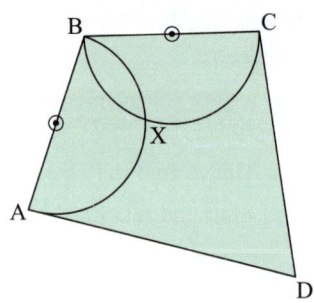

   a Determine the measure of $B\widehat{X}A$ and $B\widehat{X}C$.
   b What does **a** tell us about the points A, X, and C?
   c Do the two illustrated sprinklers water all of the area on one side of the diagonal [AC]?
   d Will Joe's four sprinklers water the whole garden? Explain your answer.

8 P is any point on a circle. [QR] is a chord of the circle parallel to the tangent at P. Prove that triangle PQR is isosceles.

9 Two circles intersect at A and B. Straight lines [PQ] and [XY] are drawn through A to meet the circles as shown. Show that $X\widehat{B}P = Y\widehat{B}Q$.

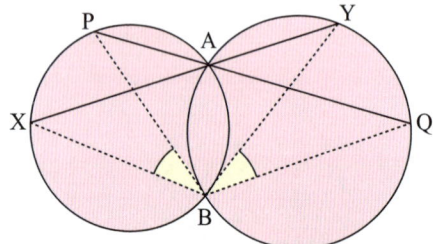

10 Two circles intersect at A and B. [AX] and [AY] are diameters as shown. Prove that X, B, and Y are collinear.

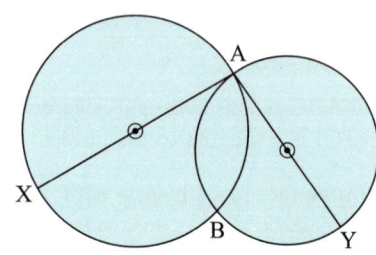

11 Triangle PQR is isosceles with PQ = PR.
A semi-circle with diameter [PR] is drawn to cut [QR] at X.
Prove that X is the midpoint of [QR].

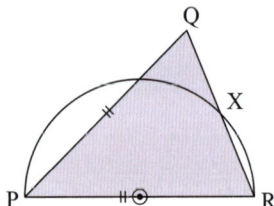

12 Brigitta notices that her angle of view of a picture on a wall depends on how far she is standing from the wall. When she is very close to the wall, the angle of view is small. When she moves backwards so that she is a long way from the wall, the angle of view is also small.

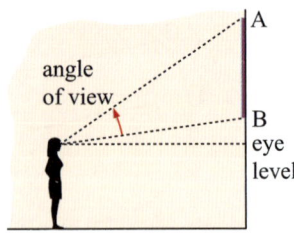

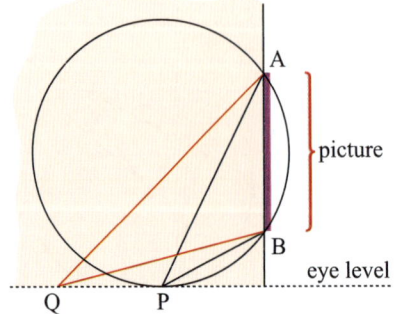

It becomes clear to Brigitta that there must be a point P in front of the picture at which her angle of view is greatest. The position of P can be found by drawing the circle through A and B which touches the 'eye level' line at P.

Prove this result by choosing any other point Q on the 'eye level' line, and showing that this angle must be less than $A\widehat{P}B$.

D CYCLIC QUADRILATERALS

Suppose we are given two points A and B, and we must draw a circle passing through these points. There are infinitely many circles that we can draw.

If we are given three points A, B, and C which are not collinear, there is a unique circle which passes through the points.

If we are given four points A, B, C, and D, no three of which are collinear, there may or may not be a circle which passes through the points. To see this, we draw the unique circle which passes through A, B, and C. The fourth point D may or may not lie on this circle.

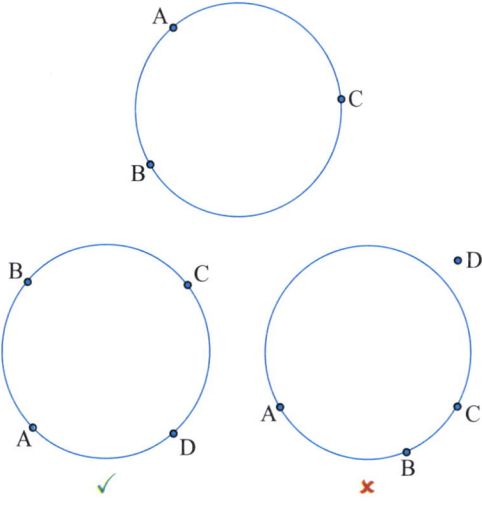

Four points are said to be **concyclic** if a circle can be drawn through them.

If four concyclic points are joined to form a convex quadrilateral, then the quadrilateral is called a **cyclic quadrilateral**.

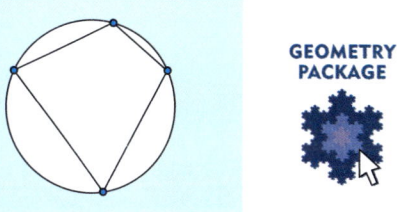

GEOMETRY PACKAGE

In the following **Investigation** we will discover an important property of cyclic quadrilaterals.

INVESTIGATION 2 CYCLIC QUADRILATERALS

This Investigation can be done using a compass, ruler, and protractor, or you can use the **geometry package** by clicking on the icon.

GEOMETRY PACKAGE

What to do:

1. Draw several circles, and on each circle draw a different cyclic quadrilateral with vertices A, B, C, and D. Make sure the quadrilaterals are large enough for you to measure the angles with a protractor.

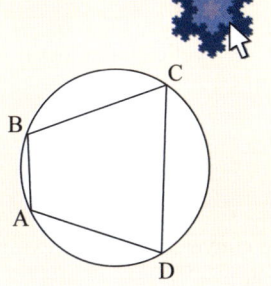

2 Measure all angles to the nearest degree, and record your results in a table like the one following.

Figure	$\hat{A}$	$\hat{B}$	$\hat{C}$	$\hat{D}$	$\hat{A} + \hat{C}$	$\hat{B} + \hat{D}$
1						
2						
⋮						

PRINTABLE QUADRILATERALS

3 Write a sentence to summarise your results.

From the **Investigation** you should have discovered the following theorem:

OPPOSITE ANGLES OF A CYCLIC QUADRILATERAL THEOREM

The opposite angles of a cyclic quadrilateral are **supplementary**.

$\alpha + \beta = 180°$ and $\theta + \phi = 180°$

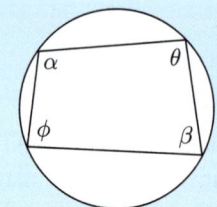

Example 7 ◀) Self Tutor

Find x given:

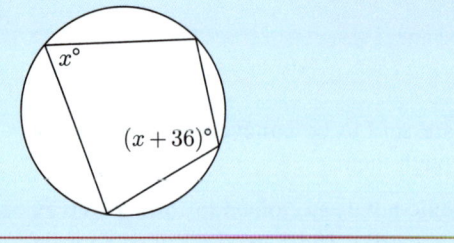

The angles given are opposite angles of a cyclic quadrilateral.

$\therefore\ x + (x + 36) = 180$
$\therefore\ 2x + 36 = 180$
$\therefore\ 2x = 144$
$\therefore\ x = 72$

We can use the *angles subtended by the same arc* theorem to discover another property of cyclic quadrilaterals.

For the cyclic quadrilateral ABCD, notice that $\widehat{DAC} = \widehat{DBC}$.

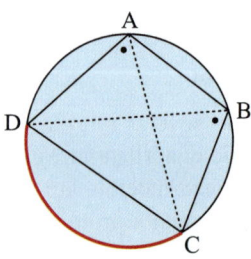

The converses of these two properties give us two useful tests for determining whether a quadrilateral is cyclic.

TESTS FOR CYCLIC QUADRILATERALS

A quadrilateral is a **cyclic quadrilateral** if one of the following is true:

- one pair of opposite angles is supplementary

If $\alpha + \beta = 180°$ then ABCD is a cyclic quadrilateral.

- one side subtends equal angles at the other two vertices

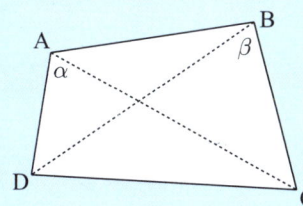

If $\alpha = \beta$ then ABCD is a cyclic quadrilateral.

Example 8 ◀)) Self Tutor

Triangle ABC is isosceles with AB = AC. X and Y lie on [AB] and [AC] respectively such that [XY] is parallel to [BC]. Prove that XYCB is a cyclic quadrilateral.

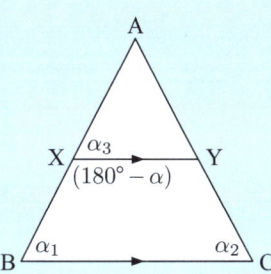

$\triangle$ABC is isosceles with AB = AC.

$\therefore \ \alpha_1 = \alpha_2$ {equal base angles}

Since [XY] $\parallel$ [BC], $\alpha_1 = \alpha_3$ {equal corresponding angles}

$\therefore \ Y\hat{X}B = 180° - \alpha$

$\therefore \ Y\hat{X}B + Y\hat{C}B = 180° - \alpha + \alpha$

$\qquad \qquad \qquad \quad = 180°$

$\therefore$ XYCB is a cyclic quadrilateral   {opposite angles are supplementary}

EXERCISE 19D

1 In this question we prove the *opposite angles of a cyclic quadrilateral* theorem.

   a For the given figure, find:

   i $D\hat{O}B$ in terms of a

   ii reflex $D\hat{O}B$ in terms of b.

   b Hence, show that $a + b = 180$.

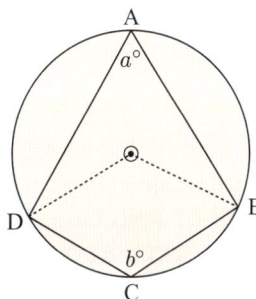

2 An alternative method for establishing the *opposite angles of a cyclic quadrilateral* theorem is to use the figure alongside. Show how this can be done.

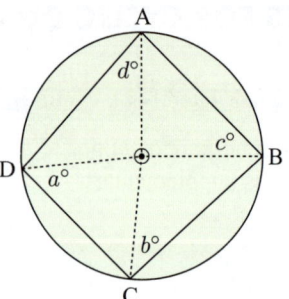

3 Find x, giving reasons:

a 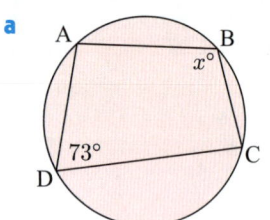 **b** 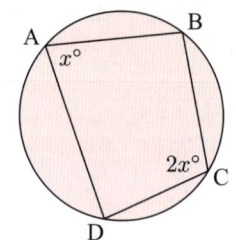 **c**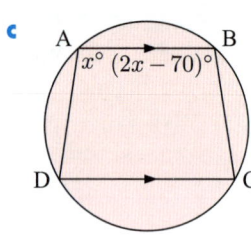

d 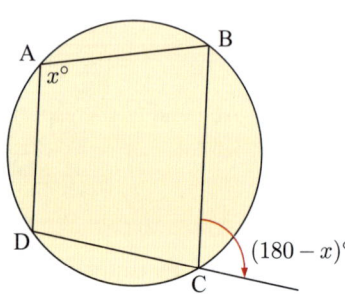 **e**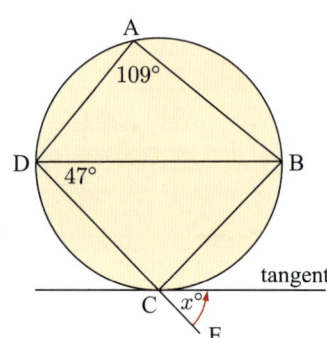

4 Is ABCD a cyclic quadrilateral? Explain your answer.

a 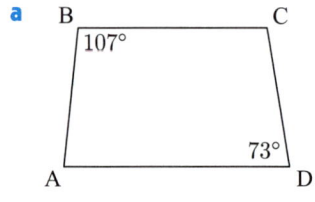 **b** 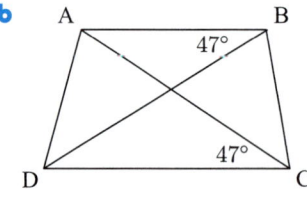 **c**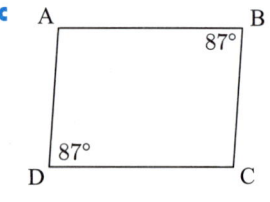

d A rectangle ABCD **e** 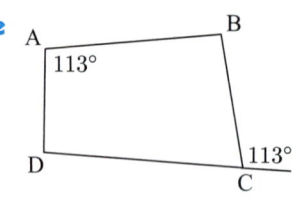 **f**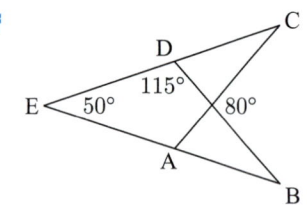

5 A parallelogram is inscribed in a circle. Prove that the parallelogram must be a rectangle.

6 OABC is a parallelogram.
A circle with centre O and radius [OA] is drawn.
[BA] produced meets the circle at D.
Prove that DOCB is a cyclic quadrilateral.

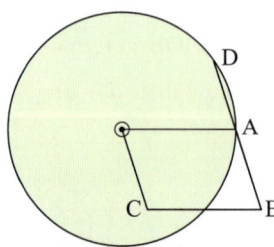

7 [AB] and [AC] are chords of a circle with centre O. X and Y are the midpoints of [AB] and [AC] respectively. Prove that OXAY is a cyclic quadrilateral.

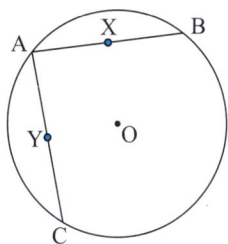

8 ABCD is a cyclic quadrilateral, and X is any point on diagonal [CA]. [XY] is drawn parallel to [CB] to meet [AB] at Y. [XZ] is drawn parallel to [CD] to meet [AD] at Z. Prove that XYAZ is a cyclic quadrilateral.

9 ABC is an isosceles triangle with AB = AC. The angle bisectors at B and C meet the sides [AC] and [AB] at X and Y respectively. Show that BCXY is a cyclic quadrilateral.

10 The non-parallel sides of a trapezium have equal length. Prove that the trapezium is a cyclic quadrilateral.

11 [AB] and [CD] are two parallel chords of a circle with centre O. [AD] and [BC] meet at E. Prove that AEOC is a cyclic quadrilateral.

12 [RX] is the bisector of angle QRT. Prove that [PX] bisects angle QPS.

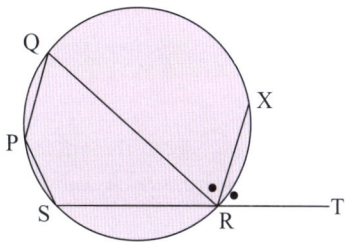

13 Two circles meet at points X and Y. Line segment [AXB] meets one circle at A and the other at B. Line segment [CYD] meets one circle at C and the other at D. Prove that [AC] is parallel to [BD].

INVESTIGATION 3 CIRCLES AND TRIANGLES

What to do:

1 Consider three points A, B, and C. Explain how to use a ruler and geometrical compass to locate the centre of the circle passing through A, B, and C. Clearly state any geometrical theorems you have used.
Check your construction by drawing the circle.

2 Draw any triangle PQR with sides between 6 cm and 10 cm. Label any points X, Y, and Z on [PR], [PQ], and [RQ] respectively.

   a Use **1** to accurately construct circles through:
      i P, X, and Y   **ii** Q, Y, and Z
      iii R, X, and Z.

   b What do you notice about the three circles?

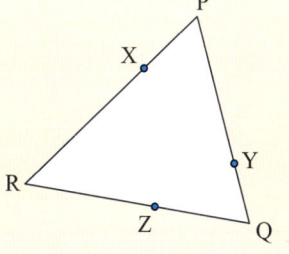

3 Repeat **2** with a different acute-angled triangle.

4 Use cyclic quadrilaterals to prove that the result you have found is always true.
Hint: Do **not** draw all three circles on your figure.

REVIEW SET 19A

1 Find the value of a:

a 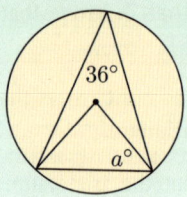   **b** 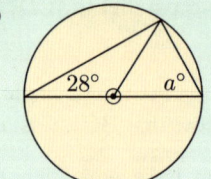   **c**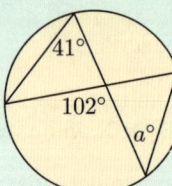

d 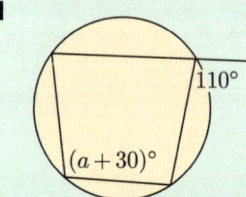   **e** 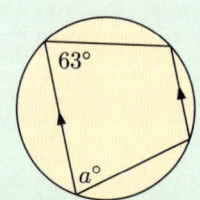   **f**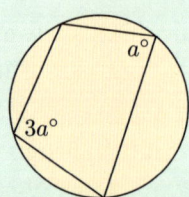

2 [AB] and [AC] are tangents to the circle.
Find an equation connecting α, β, and γ.

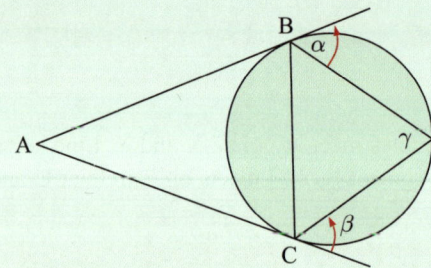

3 Find the value of x:

a 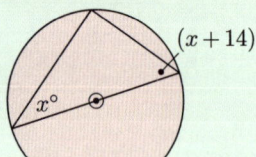   **b** 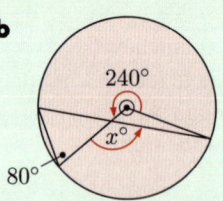   **c**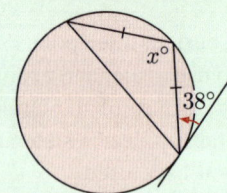

4 [AB] and [CM] are common tangents to two touching circles. Show that:
  a M is the midpoint of [AB]
  b $A\widehat{C}B$ is a right angle.

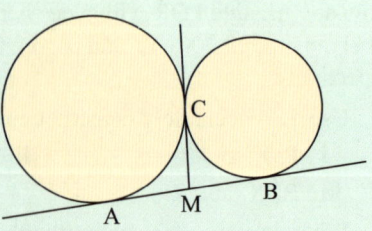

5 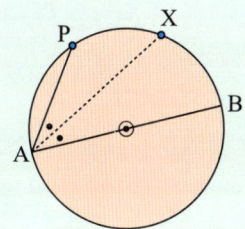 The circle alongside has diameter [AB], and P is another point on the circle. The angle bisector of $P\widehat{A}B$ meets the circle at X. Show that the tangent at X is parallel to [PB].

6 O is the centre of the circle alongside. The chords [AC] and [BD] are perpendicular.
Show that $\alpha + \beta = 180°$.
Hint: Join [BC].

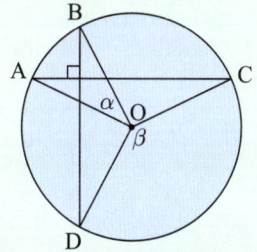

7 a Copy and complete: *"The angle between a tangent and a chord through the point of contact is equal to ......"*

b Two circles intersect at points P and Q. A line segment [APB] is drawn through P, and the tangents at A and B meet at C.

   i Let $A\widehat{B}C = \alpha$ and $B\widehat{A}C = \beta$.
Write expressions for $P\widehat{Q}B$, $P\widehat{Q}A$, and $A\widehat{Q}B$ in terms of α and β.

   ii Hence, show that ACBQ is a cyclic quadrilateral.

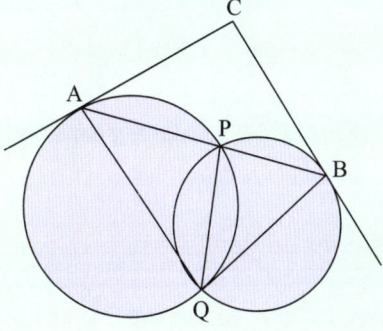

8 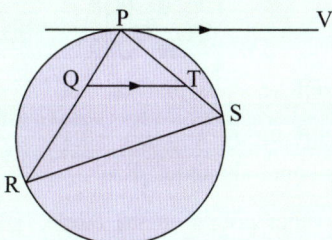 [PV] is a tangent to the circle, and [QT] is parallel to [PV]. Prove that QRST is a cyclic quadrilateral.

REVIEW SET 19B

1 Find the value of x:

a 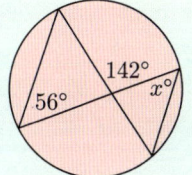 **b** 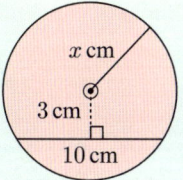 **c**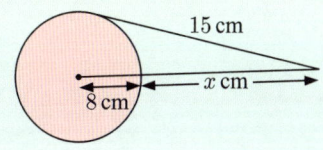

2 Find the value of x:

a 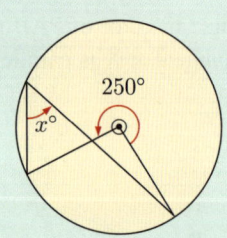   b 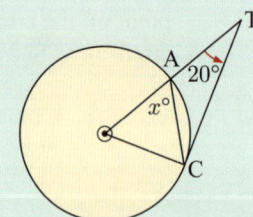   c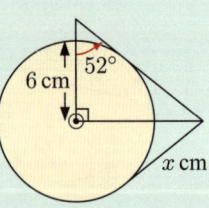

3 Find the length of the diameter of the circle below.

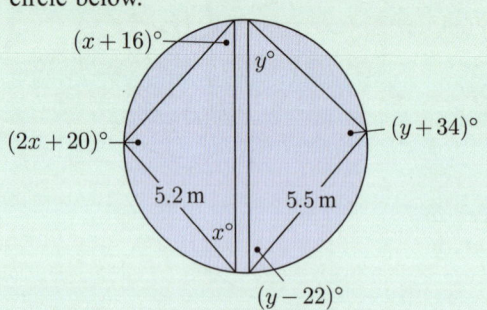

4 [AB] is the diameter of a circle with centre O.

[AC] and [BD] are any two chords.

Show that $B\hat{D}O = A\hat{C}D$.

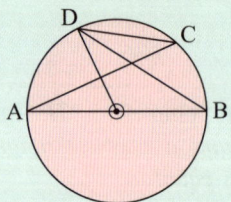

5 A, B, and C are three points on a circle. The bisector of angle BAC cuts [BC] at P, and the circle at Q. Prove that $A\hat{P}C = A\hat{B}Q$.

6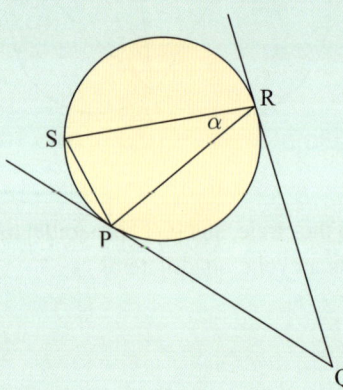

[QP] and [QR] are tangents to a circle. S is a point on the circle such that $P\hat{S}R$ and $P\hat{Q}R$ are equal, and both are double $P\hat{R}S$.

Let $P\hat{R}S$ be α.

a Find, in terms of α:
  i $P\hat{S}R$ ii $P\hat{Q}R$
  iii $P\hat{R}Q$ iv $Q\hat{P}R$

b Use triangle PQR to show that $\alpha = 30°$.

c Find the measure of $Q\hat{R}S$.

d What can you conclude about [RS]?

7 [AB] is the diameter of a circle, and C and D are two other points on the circle. [AC] and [BD] meet at E, and [AD] and [BC] meet at F. Show that points C, D, E, and F form a cyclic quadrilateral.

8 In the figure alongside, [XT] and [XP] are tangents.

Prove that:

a BTXP is a cyclic quadrilateral

b [PT] bisects angle CTX.

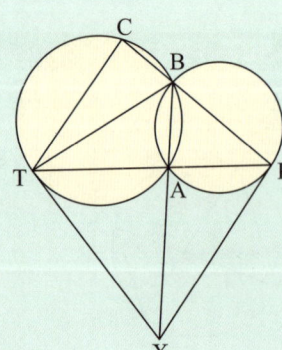

Chapter 20
Quadratic functions

Contents:
- **A** Quadratic functions
- **B** Graphs of quadratic functions
- **C** Axes intercepts
- **D** Axis of symmetry
- **E** Vertex
- **F** Quadratic optimisation

OPENING PROBLEM

Tennis player Bradley tosses the ball in the air before he serves it. The ball's height above the ground t seconds after it is tossed is given by the function $H(t) = -5t^2 + 6t + 2$ metres.

Things to think about:

a How high was the ball when it was released?

b What was the maximum height reached by the tennis ball?

c Bradley hits the ball when it is 3 metres above the ground, and on its way down. How long after Bradley releases the ball does he hit it?

In this chapter we consider relationships between variables which are **quadratic** in nature. These relationships can be described algebraically using **quadratic functions**.

A QUADRATIC FUNCTIONS

A **quadratic function** is a relationship between two variables which can be written in the form $y = ax^2 + bx + c$ where x and y are the variables, and a, b, and c are constants, $a \neq 0$.

Using function notation, $y = ax^2 + bx + c$ can be written as $f(x) = ax^2 + bx + c$.

FINDING y GIVEN x

For any value of x, the corresponding value of y can be found by substitution into the function equation.

Example 1

Suppose $y = 2x^2 + 4x - 5$. Find the value of y when:

a $x = 0$ **b** $x = 3$

a When $x = 0$,
$y = 2(0)^2 + 4(0) - 5$
$= 0 + 0 - 5$
$= -5$

b When $x = 3$,
$y = 2(3)^2 + 4(3) - 5$
$= 18 + 12 - 5$
$= 25$

FINDING x GIVEN y

When we substitute a value for y, we are left with a quadratic equation which we need to solve for x. Since the equation is quadratic, there may be 0, 1, or 2 possible values for x.

QUADRATIC FUNCTIONS (Chapter 20) 433

Example 2

Suppose $y = x^2 - 6x + 8$. Find the value(s) of x for which:
a $y = 15$ **b** $y = -1$

a When $y = 15$,
$$x^2 - 6x + 8 = 15$$
$$\therefore x^2 - 6x - 7 = 0$$
$$\therefore (x+1)(x-7) = 0$$
$$\therefore x = -1 \text{ or } x = 7$$

b When $y = -1$,
$$x^2 - 6x + 8 = -1$$
$$\therefore x^2 - 6x + 9 = 0$$
$$\therefore (x-3)^2 = 0$$
$$\therefore x = 3$$

Example 3

A stone is thrown into the air. Its height above the ground is given by the function $h(t) = -5t^2 + 30t + 2$ metres, where t is the time in seconds from when the stone is thrown.
a How high is the stone above the ground after 3 seconds?
b From what height above the ground was the stone released?
c At what times is the stone 27 m above the ground?

a $h(3) = -5(3)^2 + 30(3) + 2$
$\quad\quad = -45 + 90 + 2$
$\quad\quad = 47$
$\therefore$ the stone is 47 m above the ground.

b The stone was released when $t = 0$ s.
Now $h(0) = -5(0)^2 + 30(0) + 2 = 2$
$\therefore$ the stone was released from 2 m above ground level.

c When $h(t) = 27$,
$$-5t^2 + 30t + 2 = 27$$
$$\therefore -5t^2 + 30t - 25 = 0$$
$$\therefore t^2 - 6t + 5 = 0$$
$$\therefore (t-1)(t-5) = 0$$
$$\therefore t = 1 \text{ or } 5$$
$\therefore$ the stone is 27 m above the ground after 1 second and after 5 seconds.

EXERCISE 20A

1 Which of the following are quadratic functions?
   a $y = 15x - 8$ **b** $y = \frac{1}{3}x^2 + 6$ **c** $3y + 2x^2 - 7 = 0$ **d** $y = 15x^3 + 2x - 16$

2 For each of the following functions, find the value of y for the given value of x:
   a $y = x^2 + 5x - 14$ when $x = 2$
   b $y = 2x^2 + 9x$ when $x = -5$
   c $y = -2x^2 + 3x - 6$ when $x = 3$
   d $y = 4x^2 + 7x + 10$ when $x = -2$

3 State whether the following quadratic functions are satisfied by the given ordered pairs:
   a $y = 6x^2 - 10$ $(0, 4)$
   b $y = 2x^2 - 5x - 3$ $(4, 9)$
   c $y = -4x^2 + 6x$ $(-\frac{1}{2}, -4)$
   d $y = -7x^2 + 9x + 11$ $(-1, -6)$
   e $y = 3x^2 - 11x + 20$ $(2, -10)$
   f $y = -3x^2 + x + 6$ $(\frac{1}{3}, 4)$

4 For each of the following quadratic functions, find the value(s) of x for the given value of y:

   a $y = x^2 + 6x + 10$ when $y = 1$
   b $y = x^2 + 5x + 8$ when $y = 2$
   c $y = x^2 - 5x + 1$ when $y = -3$
   d $y = 3x^2$ when $y = -3$

5 Find the value(s) of x for which:

   a $f(x) = 3x^2 - 3x + 6$ takes the value 6
   b $f(x) = x^2 - 2x - 7$ takes the value -4
   c $f(x) = -2x^2 - 13x + 3$ takes the value -4
   d $f(x) = 2x^2 - 10x + 1$ takes the value -11

6 An object is projected into the air with a velocity of 80 m s^{-1}. Its height after t seconds is given by the function $h(t) = 80t - 5t^2$ metres.

   a Calculate the height of the object after:
       i 1 second   **ii** 3 seconds   **iii** 5 seconds.
   b Calculate the time(s) at which the height of the object is:
       i 140 m   **ii** 0 m.
   c Explain your answers in part **b**.

7 A cake manufacturer finds that the profit from making x cakes per day is given by the function $P(x) = -\frac{1}{2}x^2 + 36x - 40$ dollars.

   a Calculate the profit if   **i** 0 cakes   **ii** 20 cakes   are made per day.
   b How many cakes need to be made per day to achieve a profit of $270?

B   GRAPHS OF QUADRATIC FUNCTIONS

The graphs of all quadratic functions are **parabolas**. The parabola is one of the **conic sections**.

HISTORICAL NOTE

CONIC SECTIONS

Conic sections are curves which can be obtained by cutting a cone with a plane. The Ancient Greek mathematicians were fascinated by conic sections.

The name parabola comes from the Greek word for **thrown** because when an object is thrown, its path makes a parabolic arc.

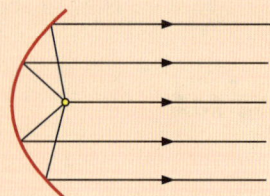

There are many other examples of parabolas in everyday life. For example, parabolic mirrors are used in car headlights, heaters, satellite dishes, and radio telescopes, because of their special geometric properties.

You may like to explore the conic sections for yourself by cutting an icecream cone. Cutting parallel to the side produces a parabola, as shown in the diagram.

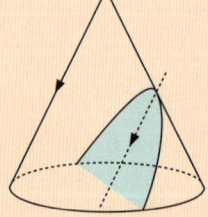

The simplest quadratic function is $y = x^2$. Its graph can be drawn from a table of values.

x	-3	-2	-1	0	1	2	3
y	9	4	1	0	1	4	9

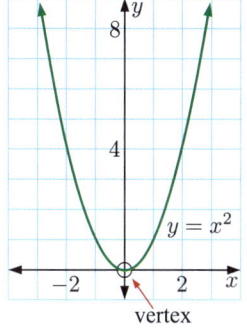

We can see that the graph has a minimum turning point at $(0, 0)$. We call this the **vertex** of the parabola.

Example 4   Self Tutor

Draw the graph of $y = x^2 + 2x - 3$ using a table of values from $x = -3$ to $x = 3$.

Consider $f(x) = x^2 + 2x - 3$

Now, $f(-3) = (-3)^2 + 2(-3) - 3$
$= 9 - 6 - 3$
$= 0$

We can do the same for the other values of x:

x	-3	-2	-1	0	1	2	3
y	0	-3	-4	-3	0	5	12

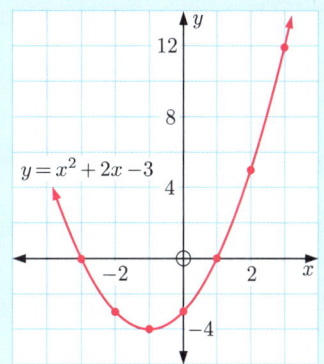

EXERCISE 20B.1

1. Using a table of values from $x = -3$ to $x = 3$, draw the graph of:
   a $y = x^2 - 2x + 8$
   b $f(x) = -x^2 + 2x + 1$
   c $y = 2x^2 + 3x$
   d $y = -2x^2 + 4$
   e $y = x^2 + x + 4$
   f $f(x) = -x^2 + 4x - 9$

   Use the **graphing package** or a **graphics calculator** to check your graphs.

    GRAPHING PACKAGE

    GRAPHICS CALCULATOR INSTRUCTIONS

2. a Use tables of values to graph $y = 2x^2 - x - 3$ and $y = -x^2 + 2x + 3$ on the same set of axes. *Hence* find the values of x for which $2x^2 - x - 3 = -x^2 + 2x + 3$.
   b Solve algebraically: $2x^2 - x - 3 = -x^2 + 2x + 3$.

USING TRANSFORMATIONS TO GRAPH QUADRATICS

By observing how a quadratic function is related to $f(x) = x^2$, we can transform the graph of $y = x^2$ to produce the graph of the function.

INVESTIGATION 1 — GRAPHS OF QUADRATIC FUNCTIONS

In this Investigation we consider different forms of quadratic functions, and how the form of the quadratic affects its graph. You can use either the graphing package or your graphics calculator to draw the graphs.

Part 1: Graphs of the form $y = x^2 + k$

What to do:

1. Graph the two functions on the same set of axes, and observe the coordinates of the vertex of each function.
    a $y = x^2$ and $y = x^2 + 2$
    b $y = x^2$ and $y = x^2 - 2$
    c $y = x^2$ and $y = x^2 + 4$
    d $y = x^2$ and $y = x^2 - 4$

2. What effect does the value of k have on:
    a the position of the graph
    b the shape of the graph?

3. What transformation is needed to graph $y = x^2 + k$ from $y = x^2$?

Part 2: Graphs of the form $y = (x - h)^2$

What to do:

1. Graph the two functions on the same set of axes, and observe the coordinates of the vertex of each function.
    a $y = x^2$ and $y = (x - 2)^2$
    b $y = x^2$ and $y = (x + 2)^2$
    c $y = x^2$ and $y = (x - 4)^2$
    d $y = x^2$ and $y = (x + 4)^2$

2. What effect does the value of h have on:
    a the position of the graph
    b the shape of the graph?

3. What transformation is needed to graph $y = (x - h)^2$ from $y = x^2$?

Part 3: Graphs of the form $y = (x - h)^2 + k$

What to do:

1. Graph the two functions on the same set of axes, and observe the coordinates of the vertex of each function.
    a $y = x^2$ and $y = (x - 2)^2 + 3$
    b $y = x^2$ and $y = (x + 4)^2 - 1$
    c $y = x^2$ and $y = (x - 5)^2 - 2$
    d $y = x^2$ and $y = (x + 1)^2 + 5$

2. Copy and complete:
    - The graph of $y = (x - h)^2 + k$ is the same shape as the graph of ......
    - The graph of $y = (x - h)^2 + k$ is found by translating $y = x^2$ ...... units horizontally and ...... units vertically. This is a translation through $\begin{pmatrix} ...... \\ ...... \end{pmatrix}$.
    - The vertex of the graph of $y = (x - h)^2 + k$ is at (......, ...).

Part 4: Graphs of the form $y = ax^2$, $a \neq 0$

What to do:

1 Graph the two functions on the same set of axes, and observe the coordinates of the vertex of each function.

    a $y = x^2$ and $y = 2x^2$ **b** $y = x^2$ and $y = 4x^2$ **c** $y = x^2$ and $y = \tfrac{1}{2}x^2$

    d $y = x^2$ and $y = -x^2$ **e** $y = x^2$ and $y = -2x^2$ **f** $y = x^2$ and $y = -\tfrac{1}{2}x^2$

2 These functions are all members of the family $y = ax^2$. What effect does a have on:

    a the position of the graph   **b** the shape of the graph

    c the direction in which the graph opens?

Part 5: Graphs of the form $y = a(x - h)^2 + k$, $a \neq 0$

What to do:

1 Graph the two functions on the same set of axes, and observe the coordinates of the vertex of each function.

    a $y = 2x^2$ and $y = 2(x - 1)^2 + 3$ **b** $y = -x^2$ and $y = -(x + 2)^2 - 1$

    c $y = \tfrac{1}{2}x^2$ and $y = \tfrac{1}{2}(x - 3)^2 - 2$ **d** $y = -3x^2$ and $y = -3(x + 1)^2 + 4$

2 Copy and complete:

- The graph of $y = a(x - h)^2 + k$ has the same shape and opens in the same direction as the graph of ......
- The graph of $y = a(x - h)^2 + k$ is found by translating $y = ax^2$ ...... units horizontally and ...... units vertically. This is a translation through $\begin{pmatrix} ...... \\ ...... \end{pmatrix}$.

From the **Investigation** you should have discovered the following important facts:

- Graphs of the form $y = x^2 + k$ have the same shape as the graph of $y = x^2$.

  The graph of $y = x^2$ is translated through $\begin{pmatrix} 0 \\ k \end{pmatrix}$ to give the graph of $y = x^2 + k$.

- Graphs of the form $y = (x - h)^2$ have the same shape as the graph of $y = x^2$.

  The graph of $y = x^2$ is translated through $\begin{pmatrix} h \\ 0 \end{pmatrix}$ to give the graph of $y = (x - h)^2$.

- Graphs of the form $y = (x - h)^2 + k$ have the same shape as the graph of $y = x^2$.

  The graph of $y = x^2$ is translated through $\begin{pmatrix} h \\ k \end{pmatrix}$ to give the graph of $y = (x - h)^2 + k$.

  The vertex is shifted to (h, k).

- If $a > 0$, $y = ax^2$ opens upwards.

  If $a < 0$, $y = ax^2$ opens downwards.

  If $a < -1$ or $a > 1$, then $y = ax^2$ is 'thinner' than $y = x^2$.
  If $-1 < a < 1$, $a \neq 0$, then $y = ax^2$ is 'wider' than $y = x^2$.

-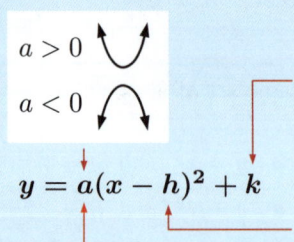

  vertical translation of k units:
  - if $k > 0$ it goes up
  - if $k < 0$ it goes down

  $$y = a(x - h)^2 + k$$

  horizontal translation of h units:
  - if $h > 0$ it goes right
  - if $h < 0$ it goes left

  $a < -1$ or $a > 1$, thinner than $y = x^2$
  $-1 < a < 1$, $a \neq 0$, wider than $y = x^2$

Example 5 ◀⎨ Self Tutor

Sketch each of the following functions on the same set of axes as $y = x^2$. In each case state the coordinates of the vertex.

a $y = x^2 + 3$ **b** $y = (x + 3)^2$

a We draw $y = x^2$, then translate it 3 units upwards.

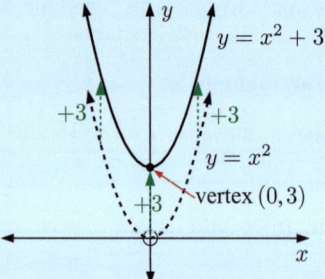

The vertex is at $(0, 3)$.

b We draw $y = x^2$, then translate it 3 units to the left.

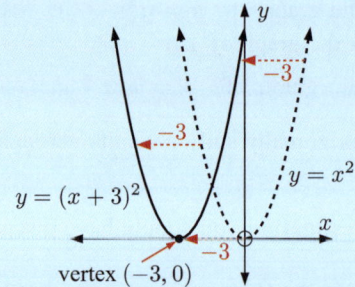

The vertex is at $(-3, 0)$.

EXERCISE 20B.2

1 Sketch each of the following functions on the same set of axes as $y = x^2$. Use a separate set of axes for each part, and in each case state the coordinates of the vertex.

GRAPHING PACKAGE

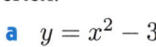

    a $y = x^2 - 3$ **b** $y = x^2 - 1$ **c** $y = x^2 + 2$
    d $y = x^2 - 5$ **e** $y = x^2 + 5$ **f** $y = x^2 - \frac{1}{2}$

Use a **graphics calculator** or **graphing package** to check your answers.

2 Sketch each of the following functions on the same set of axes as $y = x^2$. Use a separate set of axes for each part, and in each case state the coordinates of the vertex.

    a $y = (x - 3)^2$ **b** $y = (x + 1)^2$ **c** $y = (x - 2)^2$
    d $y = (x - 5)^2$ **e** $y = (x + 5)^2$ **f** $y = (x - \frac{3}{2})^2$

Use a **graphics calculator** or **graphing package** to check your answers.

Example 6

Sketch each of the following functions on the same set of axes as $y = x^2$. In each case state the coordinates of the vertex.

a $y = (x-2)^2 + 3$ **b** $y = (x+2)^2 - 5$

a We draw $y = x^2$, then translate it 2 units to the right and 3 units upwards.

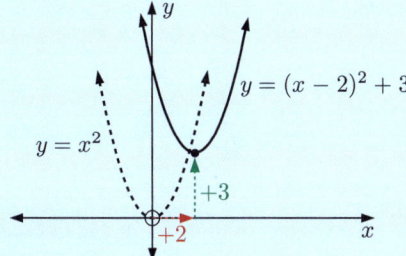

The vertex is at $(2, 3)$.

b We draw $y = x^2$, then translate it 2 units to the left and 5 units downwards.

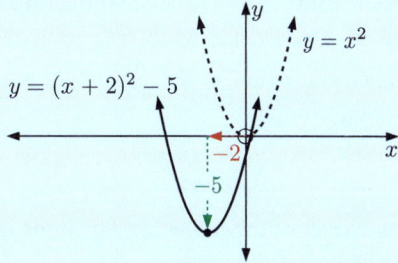

The vertex is at $(-2, -5)$.

3 Sketch each of the following functions on the same set of axes as $y = x^2$. Use a separate set of axes for each part, and in each case state the coordinates of the vertex.

     a $y = (x-1)^2 + 3$ **b** $y = (x-2)^2 - 1$ **c** $y = (x+1)^2 + 4$
     d $y = (x+2)^2 - 3$ **e** $y = (x+3)^2 - 2$ **f** $y = (x-3)^2 + 3$

Use a **graphics calculator** or **graphing package** to check your answers.

Example 7

Sketch $y = x^2$ on a set of axes and hence sketch:

a $y = 3x^2$ **b** $y = -3x^2$

a $y = 3x^2$ is 'thinner' than $y = x^2$.
b $y = -3x^2$ has the same shape as $y = 3x^2$, but opens downwards.

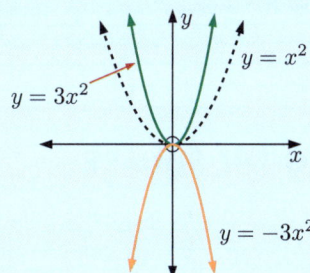

4 Sketch each of the following functions on the same set of axes as $y = x^2$. Comment on the shape of the graph, and the direction in which the graph opens.

     a $y = 5x^2$ **b** $y = -5x^2$ **c** $y = \frac{1}{3}x^2$
     d $y = -\frac{1}{3}x^2$ **e** $y = -4x^2$ **f** $y = \frac{1}{4}x^2$

GRAPHING PACKAGE

Use a **graphics calculator** or **graphing package** to check your answers.

Example 8

Sketch the graph of $y = -(x-2)^2 - 3$ from the graph of $y = x^2$, and hence state the coordinates of its vertex.

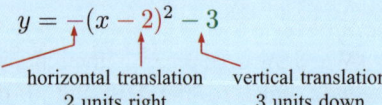

reflect in x-axis | horizontal translation 2 units right | vertical translation 3 units down

We start with $y = x^2$, then reflect it in the x-axis to give $y = -x^2$.

We then translate $y = -x^2$ 2 units to the right and 3 units down.

The vertex of $y = -(x-2)^2 - 3$ is $(2, -3)$.

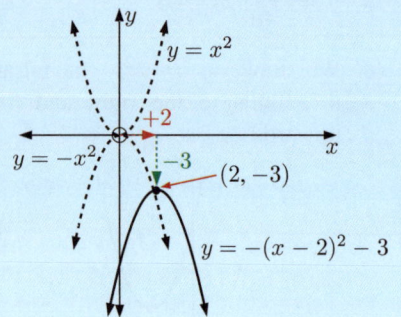

5 Sketch each of the following functions on the same set of axes as $y = x^2$. In each case, state the coordinates of the vertex.

- **a** $y = -(x-1)^2 + 3$
- **b** $y = 2x^2 + 4$
- **c** $y = -(x-2)^2 + 4$
- **d** $y = 3(x+1)^2 - 4$
- **e** $y = \frac{1}{2}(x+3)^2$
- **f** $y = -\frac{1}{2}(x+3)^2 + 1$
- **g** $y = -2(x+4)^2 + 3$
- **h** $y = 2(x-3)^2 + 5$
- **i** $y = \frac{1}{2}(x-2)^2 - 1$

Use a **graphics calculator** or **graphing package** to check your answers.

6 Match the following quadratic functions with their graphs:

- **a** $y = -(x+2)^2 - 3$
- **b** $y = (x-3)^2 + 2$
- **c** $y = 2(x+3)^2 + 2$
- **d** $y = -(x-3)^2 + 2$
- **e** $y = -\frac{1}{2}(x+2)^2 - 3$
- **f** $y = (x+3)^2 + 2$

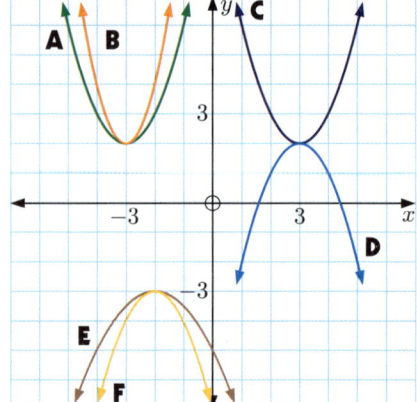

COMPLETING THE SQUARE

Suppose we want to graph the quadratic function $y = x^2 - 4x + 1$. This function is not written in the form $y = (x-h)^2 + k$, but we can convert it into this form by **completing the square**.

Consider
$$y = x^2 - 4x + 1$$
$$\therefore \quad y = \underbrace{x^2 - 4x + 2^2} + 1 - 2^2$$
$$\therefore \quad y = (x-2)^2 - 3$$

So, the graph of $y = x^2 - 4x + 1$ can be found by translating $y = x^2$ 2 units to the right and 3 units downwards.

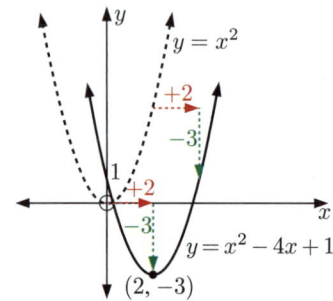

Example 9

Write $y = x^2 + 2x + 5$ in the form $y = (x-h)^2 + k$.
Hence sketch $y = x^2 + 2x + 5$, stating the coordinates of the vertex.

$y = x^2 + 2x + 5$
$\therefore y = x^2 + 2x + 1^2 + 5 - 1^2$
$\therefore y = (x+1)^2 + 4$

translate 1 unit left   translate 4 units up

The vertex is at $(-1, 4)$.

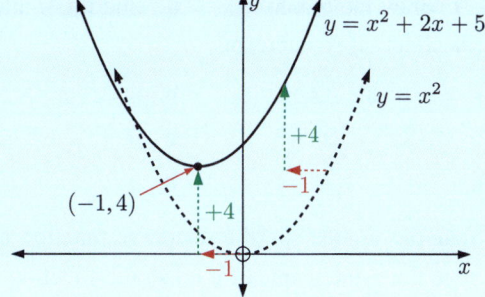

EXERCISE 20B.3

1 Write the following quadratics in the form $y = (x-h)^2 + k$.
Hence sketch each function, stating the coordinates of the vertex.

a $y = x^2 + 2x + 4$
b $y = x^2 - 6x + 3$
c $y = x^2 + 4x - 1$
d $y = x^2 - 2x + 5$
e $y = x^2 - 2x$
f $y = x^2 + 5x$
g $y = x^2 + 5x - 3$
h $y = x^2 - 3x + 3$
i $y = x^2 - 5x + 2$

GRAPHING PACKAGE

Use a **graphics calculator** or **graphing package** to check your answers.

2 Write the following quadratics in the form $y = a(x-h)^2 + k$.
Hence sketch each function, stating the coordinates of the vertex.

a $y = 2x^2 + 10x + 8$
b $y = -x^2 + x + 6$
c $y = 3x^2 - 6x - 24$
d $y = -2x^2 + 6x + 8$
e $y = 2x^2 - 8x - 3$
f $y = -3x^2 - 6x + 2$

Use a **graphics calculator** or **graphing package** to check your answers.

C AXES INTERCEPTS

- An **x-intercept** of a function is a value of x where its graph meets the x-axis.
  x-intercepts are found by letting y be 0 in the equation of the function.
- A **y-intercept** of a function is a value of y where its graph meets the y-axis.
  y-intercepts are found by letting x be 0 in the equation of the function.

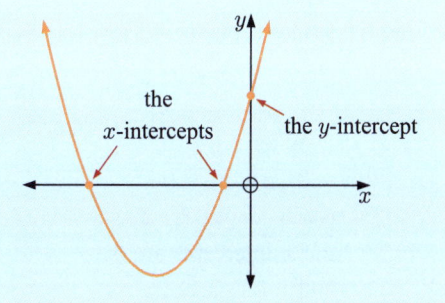

INVESTIGATION 2 — AXES INTERCEPTS

What to do:

1 For each of the following quadratic functions, use a **graphing package** or **graphics calculator** to:

    i draw the graph   **ii** find the y-intercept
    iii find any x-intercepts.

  a $y = x^2 - 3x - 4$ **b** $y = -x^2 + 2x + 8$ **c** $y = 2x^2 - 3x$
  d $y = -2x^2 + 2x - 3$ **e** $y = (x-1)(x-3)$ **f** $y = -(x+2)(x-3)$
  g $y = 3(x+1)(x+4)$ **h** $y = 2(x-2)^2$ **i** $y = -3(x+1)^2$

2 **a** State the y-intercept of a quadratic function in the form $y = ax^2 + bx + c$.
  b State the x-intercepts of a quadratic function in the form:
    i $y = a(x - \alpha)(x - \beta)$ **ii** $y = a(x - \alpha)^2$

THE y-INTERCEPT

For a quadratic function in the form $y = ax^2 + bx + c$, the y-intercept is the constant term c.

Proof:

If $x = 0$ then $y = a(0)^2 + b(0) + c$
$\therefore \ y = c$

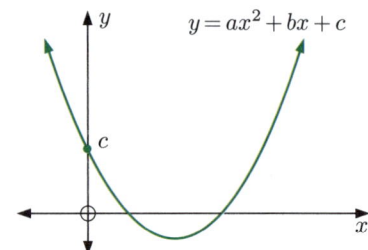

THE x-INTERCEPTS

For a quadratic function in the form $y = a(x - \alpha)(x - \beta)$, the x-intercepts are α and β.

Proof:

If $y = 0$ then $a(x - \alpha)(x - \beta) = 0$
$\therefore \ x = \alpha$ or β {since $a \neq 0$}

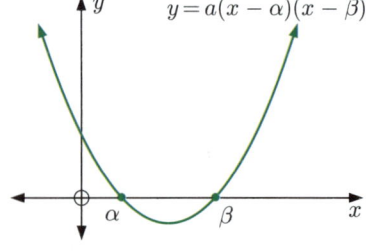

x-intercepts are therefore easy to find when the quadratic is in **factorised** form.

Example 10 — Self Tutor

Find the x-intercepts of:

  a $y = 2(x-3)(x+2)$ **b** $y = -(x-4)^2$

a When $y = 0$,
$2(x-3)(x+2) = 0$
$\therefore \ x = 3$ or $x = -2$
$\therefore$ the x-intercepts are 3 and -2.

b When $y = 0$,
$-(x-4)^2 = 0$
$\therefore \ x = 4$
$\therefore$ the x-intercept is 4.

If a quadratic function has only one x-intercept then its graph must **touch** the x-axis.

FACTORISING TO FIND x-INTERCEPTS

For any quadratic function of the form $y = ax^2 + bx + c$, the x-intercepts can be found by solving the equation $ax^2 + bx + c = 0$.

You will recall from **Chapter 11** that quadratic equations may have *two solutions, one solution,* or *no solutions*. These solutions correspond to the *two x-intercepts, one x-intercept,* or *no x-intercepts* found when the graph of the corresponding quadratic function is drawn.

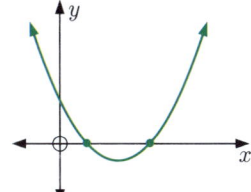
two x-intercepts

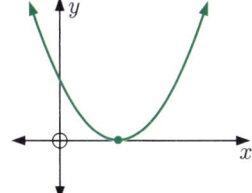
one x-intercept

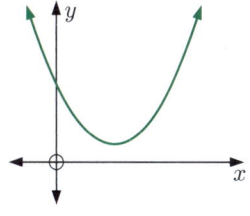
no x-intercepts

Example 11 ◀)) Self Tutor

Find the x-intercept(s) of the quadratic function:

a $y = x^2 - 6x + 9$ **b** $y = -x^2 - x + 6$

a When $y = 0$,
$x^2 - 6x + 9 = 0$
$\therefore (x - 3)^2 = 0$
$\therefore x = 3$
$\therefore$ the x-intercept is 3.

b When $y = 0$,
$-x^2 - x + 6 = 0$
$\therefore x^2 + x - 6 = 0$
$\therefore (x + 3)(x - 2) = 0$
$\therefore x = -3$ or 2
$\therefore$ the x-intercepts are -3 and 2.

EXERCISE 20C.1

1 For the following functions, state the y-intercept:
- **a** $y = x^2 + 3x + 3$
- **b** $y = x^2 - 5x + 2$
- **c** $f(x) = 2x^2 + 7x - 8$
- **d** $y = 3x^2 - x + 1$
- **e** $f(x) = -x^2 + 3x + 6$
- **f** $y = -2x^2 + 5 - x$
- **g** $y = 6 - x - x^2$
- **h** $f(x) = 8 + 2x - 3x^2$
- **i** $y = 5x - x^2 - 2$

2 For the following functions, find the x-intercepts:
- **a** $y = (x - 3)(x + 1)$
- **b** $f(x) = -(x - 2)(x - 4)$
- **c** $y = 2(x + 3)(x + 2)$
- **d** $y = -3(x - 4)(x - 5)$
- **e** $y = 2(x + 3)^2$
- **f** $f(x) = -5(x - 1)^2$

3 For the following functions, find the x-intercepts:
- **a** $y = x^2 - 9$
- **b** $y = 25 - x^2$
- **c** $y = x^2 - 6x$
- **d** $f(x) = x^2 + 7x + 10$
- **e** $y = x^2 + x - 12$
- **f** $y = 4x - x^2$
- **g** $y = -x^2 - 6x - 8$
- **h** $f(x) = -2x^2 - 4x - 2$
- **i** $y = 4x^2 - 24x + 36$

Example 12

Use the quadratic formula to find the x-intercepts of the quadratic function $y = x^2 - 2x - 5$.

When $y = 0$,

$x^2 - 2x - 5 = 0$

$\therefore x = \dfrac{2 \pm \sqrt{(-2)^2 - 4(1)(-5)}}{2(1)}$

$\therefore x = \dfrac{2 \pm \sqrt{4 + 20}}{2}$

$\therefore x = \dfrac{2 \pm \sqrt{24}}{2}$

$\therefore x = \dfrac{2 \pm 2\sqrt{6}}{2}$

$\therefore x = 1 \pm \sqrt{6}$

$\therefore$ the x-intercepts are $1 + \sqrt{6}$ and $1 - \sqrt{6}$.

4 Use the quadratic formula to find the x-intercepts of the following functions:

   a $y = x^2 - 4x + 1$ **b** $y = x^2 + 4x - 3$ **c** $y = -x^2 + 6x - 4$

   d $f(x) = 3x^2 - 7x - 2$ **e** $f(x) = 2x^2 - x - 5$ **f** $f(x) = -4x^2 + 9x - 3$

Example 13

Sketch the graphs of the following functions by considering:

   i the value of a **ii** the y-intercept   **iii** the x-intercepts.

   a $y = x^2 - 2x - 3$ **b** $y = -2(x+1)(x-2)$ **c** $y = 2(x-3)^2$

a $y = x^2 - 2x - 3$

   i $a = 1$ which is > 0, so the parabola opens upwards.

   ii When $x = 0$, $y = -3$
      $\therefore$ the y-intercept is -3.

   iii When $y = 0$,
      $x^2 - 2x - 3 = 0$
      $\therefore (x-3)(x+1) = 0$
      $\therefore x = 3$ or $x = -1$
      $\therefore$ the x-intercepts are 3 and -1.

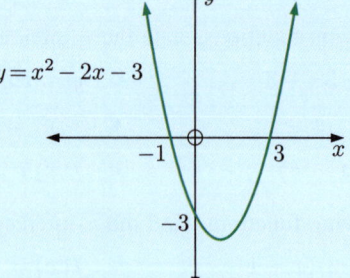

b $y = -2(x+1)(x-2)$

   i $a = -2$ which is < 0, so the parabola opens downwards.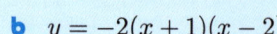

   ii When $x = 0$,
      $y = -2(0+1)(0-2)$
      $= -2 \times 1 \times -2$
      $= 4$
      $\therefore$ the y-intercept is 4.

iii When $y = 0$,
$-2(x+1)(x-2) = 0$
$\therefore x = -1$ or $x = 2$
$\therefore$ the x-intercepts are -1 and 2.

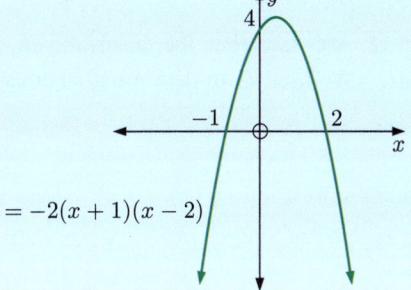

c $y = 2(x-3)^2$

i $a = 2$ which is > 0, so the parabola opens upwards.

ii When $x = 0$, $y = 2(0-3)^2 = 18$
$\therefore$ the y-intercept is 18.

iii When $y = 0$, $2(x-3)^2 = 0$
$\therefore x = 3$
$\therefore$ the x-intercept is 3.
There is only one x-intercept, which means the graph *touches* the x-axis.

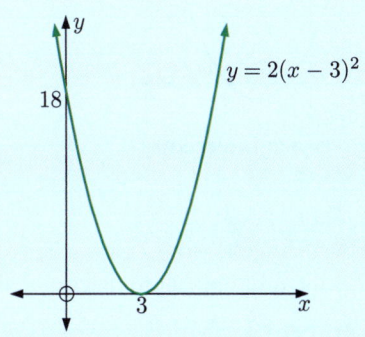

5 Sketch the graph of the quadratic function which has:
  a x-intercepts -1 and 1, and y-intercept -1
  b x-intercepts -3 and 1, and y-intercept 2
  c x-intercepts 2 and 5, and y-intercept -4
  d x-intercept 2 and y-intercept 4.

6 Sketch the graphs of the following quadratic functions by considering:
  i the value of a **ii** the y-intercept **iii** the x-intercepts.
  a $y = x^2 - 4x + 4$
  b $f(x) = (x-1)(x+3)$
  c $y = 2(x+2)^2$
  d $f(x) = -(x-2)(x+1)$
  e $y = -3(x+1)^2$
  f $y = -3(x-4)(x-1)$
  g $y = 2(x+3)(x+1)$
  h $y = -2x^2 - 3x + 5$
  i $f(x) = -x^2 + 8x - 10$

ACTIVITY

Click on the icon to practise matching a quadratic function with its graph.

QUADRATIC FUNCTIONS

THE DISCRIMINANT AND THE QUADRATIC GRAPH (EXTENSION)

In **Chapter 11**, we saw that the discriminant of the quadratic equation $ax^2 + bx + c = 0$ is $\Delta = b^2 - 4ac$. We used Δ to determine whether the equation has real solutions.

We can therefore use Δ to determine how many x-intercepts a quadratic function has.

For a quadratic function $f(x) = ax^2 + bx + c$, we consider the discriminant $\Delta = b^2 - 4ac$.

- $\Delta > 0$

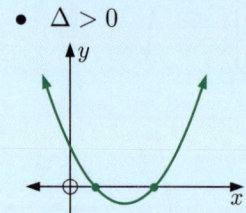

two x-intercepts

- $\Delta = 0$

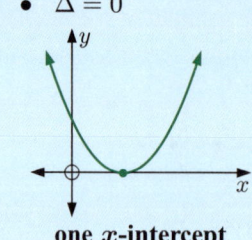

one x-intercept

- $\Delta < 0$

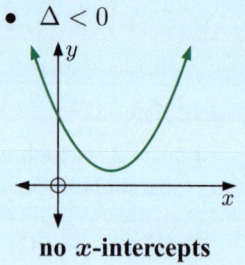

no x-intercepts

Example 14 ◀) Self Tutor

Use the discriminant to determine the relationship between the graph and the x-axis:

a $y = x^2 - 5x + 3$

b $y = -3x^2 + x - 2$

a $a = 1$, $b = -5$, $c = 3$
$\therefore \Delta = b^2 - 4ac$
$ = (-5)^2 - 4(1)(3)$
$ = 13$
Since $\Delta > 0$, the graph cuts the x-axis twice.

b $a = -3$, $b = 1$, $c = -2$
$\therefore \Delta = b^2 - 4ac$
$ = 1^2 - 4(-3)(-2)$
$ = -23$
Since $\Delta < 0$, the graph does not cut the x-axis.

EXERCISE 20C.2

1 Use the discriminant to determine the relationship between the graph and the x-axis:
   a $y = x^2 - 2x - 7$
   b $y = 2x^2 - 3x + 6$
   c $y = -x^2 + 4x - 2$
   d $y = x^2 - 10x + 25$
   e $y = 3x^2 + 2$
   f $y = -2x^2 + 12x - 18$

2 Consider the quadratic function $y = x^2 - 8x + 14$.
   a Write the function in the form $y = (x - h)^2 + k$.
   b Hence, sketch the function.
   c How many x-intercepts does the function appear to have?
   d Use the discriminant to check your answer to **c**.

3 Consider the quadratic function $y = x^2 + 2x + 5$.
   a Write the function in the form $y = (x - h)^2 + k$.
   b Hence, sketch the function.
   c How many x-intercepts does the function appear to have?
   d Use the discriminant to check your answer to **c**.

4 Match each description of a quadratic function $f(x) = ax^2 + bx + c$ with its graph:

  a $a = 1$, $\Delta = 7$
  b $a = -2$, $\Delta = 0$
  c $a = \frac{1}{2}$, $\Delta = -5$
  d $a = -1$, $\Delta = 11$
  e $a = -\frac{2}{3}$, $\Delta = -6$
  f $a = 2$, $\Delta = 0$

A 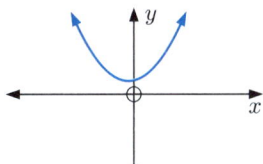 **B** 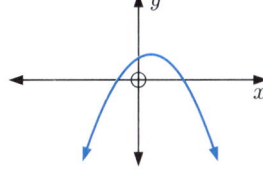 **C**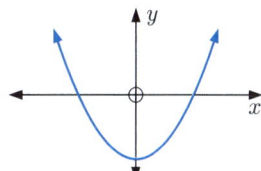

D 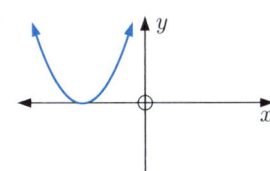 **E** 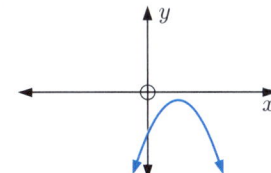 **F**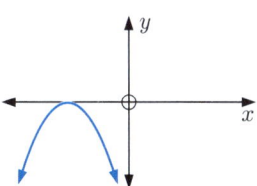

5 a Determine the relationship between $y = x^2 - 4x + c$ and the x-axis for the case where:

  i $c = 3$
  ii $c = 4$
  iii $c = 5$.

  b Using technology, sketch each of the graphs in **a** on the same set of axes.

6 Consider a quadratic function $y = ax^2 + bx + c$ where $a > 0$ and $c < 0$. Explain why the graph must cut the x-axis twice:

  a by considering the graphical significance of $a > 0$ and $c < 0$
  b using the discriminant.

D AXIS OF SYMMETRY

The graphs of all quadratic functions are symmetrical about a vertical line passing through the vertex. This line is called the **axis of symmetry**.

If the graph has two x-intercepts, then the axis of symmetry is midway between them.

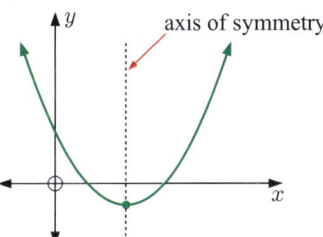

The equation of a vertical line has the form $x = k$.

Example 15 ◀)) Self Tutor

Find the equation of the axis of symmetry for the quadratic graph below.

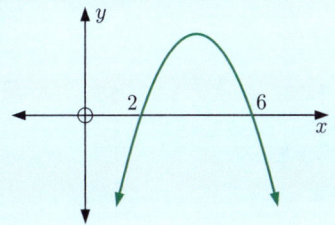

The x-intercepts are 2 and 6, and 4 is midway between 2 and 6.

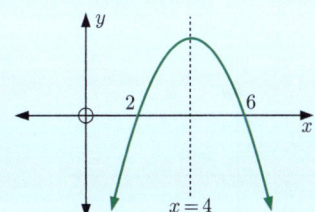

The axis of symmetry is $x = 4$.

If the quadratic does not have any x-intercepts, or if we do not know the x-intercepts, we can use the rule below to find the axis of symmetry:

The equation of the axis of symmetry of $y = ax^2 + bx + c$ is $x = \dfrac{-b}{2a}$.

Proof:

$y = ax^2 + bx + c$

$\therefore\ y = a\left(x^2 + \dfrac{b}{a}x\right) + c$

$\therefore\ y = a\left(x^2 + \dfrac{b}{a}x + \left(\dfrac{b}{2a}\right)^2\right) + c - a\left(\dfrac{b}{2a}\right)^2$

$\therefore\ y = a\left(x + \dfrac{b}{2a}\right)^2 + \left(c - \dfrac{b^2}{4a}\right)$

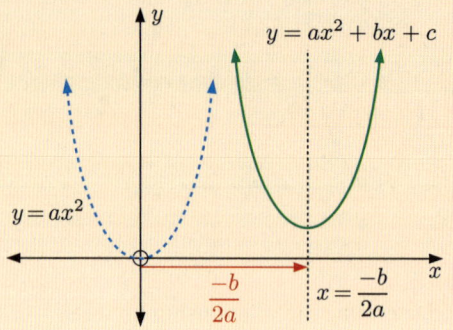

The horizontal shift from $y = ax^2$ to $y = ax^2 + bx + c$ is $\dfrac{-b}{2a}$ units.

$\therefore\ $ the axis of symmetry of $y = ax^2 + bx + c$ has equation $x = \dfrac{-b}{2a}$.

Example 16 ◀) Self Tutor

Find the equation of the axis of symmetry of $y = 2x^2 + 3x + 1$.

$y = 2x^2 + 3x + 1$ has $a = 2$, $b = 3$, $c = 1$.

Now $\dfrac{-b}{2a} = \dfrac{-3}{2 \times 2} = -\dfrac{3}{4}$

$\therefore\ $ the axis of symmetry has equation $x = -\dfrac{3}{4}$.

EXERCISE 20D

1 For each of the following graphs, find the equation of the axis of symmetry:

a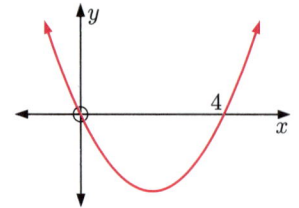

b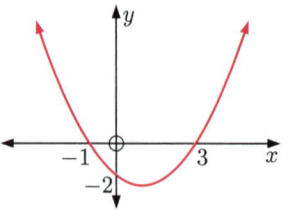

c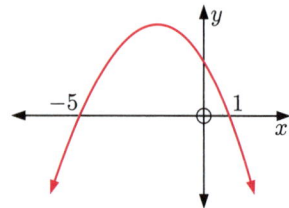

d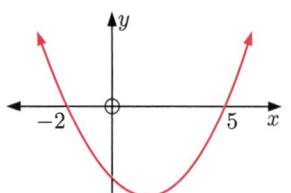

e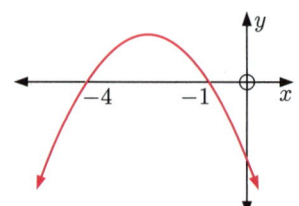

f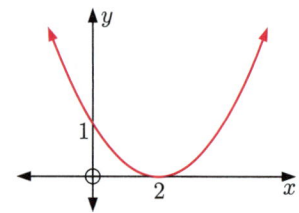

2 For each of the following quadratic functions, find the equation of the axis of symmetry:

  a $y = (x-2)(x-4)$ **b** $y = -(x+1)(x-5)$ **c** $y = 2(x+3)(x-3)$

  d $y = x(x+5)$ **e** $y = -3(x+4)^2$ **f** $y = 4(x+6)(x-9)$

3 Determine the equation of the axis of symmetry for the following quadratic functions:

  a $y = x^2 + 4x + 1$ **b** $y = 2x^2 - 6x + 3$ **c** $f(x) = 3x^2 + 4x - 1$

  d $y = -x^2 - 4x + 5$ **e** $y = -2x^2 + 5x + 1$ **f** $f(x) = \frac{1}{2}x^2 - 10x + 2$

  g $y = \frac{1}{3}x^2 + 4x$ **h** $f(x) = 100x - 4x^2$ **i** $y = -\frac{1}{10}x^2 + 30x$

E   VERTEX

The **vertex** or **turning point** of the quadratic function $y = ax^2 + bx + c$ is the point at which the function has:

- a **maximum value** for $a < 0$ ⌢, or
- a **minimum value** for $a > 0$ ⌣.

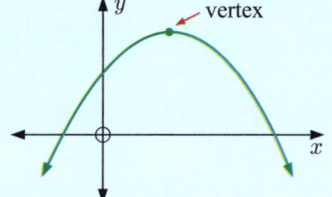

Since the vertex lies on the axis of symmetry, its x-coordinate will be $\dfrac{-b}{2a}$.

The y-coordinate can be found by substituting this value for x into the function.

Example 17   ◀)) Self Tutor

Consider the quadratic function $y = -x^2 + 2x + 3$.

  a Find the axes intercepts.
  b Find the equation of the axis of symmetry.
  c Find the coordinates of the vertex.
  d Sketch the function, showing all important features.

a When $x = 0$, $y = 3$
$\therefore$ the y-intercept is 3.
When $y = 0$, $-x^2 + 2x + 3 = 0$
$\therefore x^2 - 2x - 3 = 0$
$\therefore (x-3)(x+1) = 0$
$\therefore x = 3$ or -1
$\therefore$ the x-intercepts are 3 and -1.

b $a = -1$, $b = 2$, $c = 3$
$\therefore \dfrac{-b}{2a} = \dfrac{-2}{-2} = 1$
$\therefore$ the axis of symmetry is $x = 1$.

c When $x = 1$,
$y = -(1)^2 + 2(1) + 3$
$= -1 + 2 + 3$
$= 4$
$\therefore$ the vertex is $(1, 4)$.

d
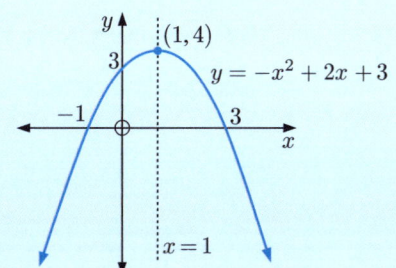

EXERCISE 20E

1 For each of the following quadratic functions:
  i Find the coordinates of the vertex.
  ii Determine whether the vertex is a maximum or minimum turning point.
  iii Find the range of the function.

> The vertex is called the **maximum turning point** or the **minimum turning point**, depending on whether the graph opens downwards or upwards.

  a $y = x^2 - 4x + 2$
  b $y = x^2 + 2x - 3$
  c $f(x) = 2x^2 + 4$
  d $y = -3x^2 + 1$
  e $y = -x^2 - 4x - 4$
  f $y = 2x^2 - 10x + 3$

2 For each of the following quadratic functions:
  i Find the axes intercepts.
  ii Find the equation of the axis of symmetry.
  iii Find the coordinates of the vertex.
  iv Hence, sketch the graph of the function.

  a $y = x^2 - 2x - 8$
  b $y = 4x - x^2$
  c $y = x^2 + 3x$
  d $f(x) = x^2 + 4x + 4$
  e $y = x^2 + 3x - 4$
  f $y = -x^2 + 2x - 1$
  g $y = 2x^2 + 5x - 3$
  h $f(x) = -3x^2 - 4x + 4$
  i $y = x^2 - 6x + 3$

Example 18 ◀)) Self Tutor

Consider the quadratic function $y = 2(x - 2)(x + 4)$.
  a Find the axes intercepts.
  b Find the equation of the axis of symmetry.
  c Find the coordinates of the vertex.
  d Sketch the function, showing all important features.

a When $x = 0$, $y = 2 \times -2 \times 4 = -16$
  $\therefore$ the y-intercept is -16.
  When $y = 0$, $2(x - 2)(x + 4) = 0$
  $\therefore$ $x = 2$ or $x = -4$
  $\therefore$ the x-intercepts are 2 and -4.

b The axis of symmetry is halfway between the x-intercepts, and -1 is halfway between 2 and -4.
  $\therefore$ the axis of symmetry is $x = -1$.

c When $x = -1$,
  $y = 2(-1 - 2)(-1 + 4)$
  $= 2 \times -3 \times 3$
  $= -18$
  $\therefore$ the vertex is $(-1, -18)$.

d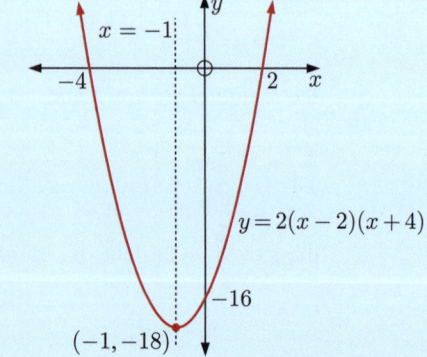

3 For each of the following quadratic functions:

    i Find the axes intercepts.
    ii Find the equation of the axis of symmetry.
    iii Find the coordinates of the vertex.
    iv Hence, sketch the graph of the function.

a $f(x) = x(x-2)$ **b** $y = 2(x-3)^2$ **c** $y = -(x-1)(x+3)$
d $y = -2(x-1)^2$ **e** $f(x) = -5(x+2)(x-2)$ **f** $y = 2(x+1)(x+4)$

F   QUADRATIC OPTIMISATION

The process of finding the **maximum** or **minimum** value of a function is called **optimisation**.

For the quadratic function $y = ax^2 + bx + c$:

- If $a > 0$, the **minimum** value of y occurs when $x = -\dfrac{b}{2a}$.
- If $a < 0$, the **maximum** value of y occurs when $x = -\dfrac{b}{2a}$.

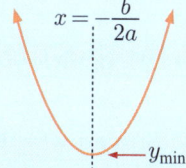
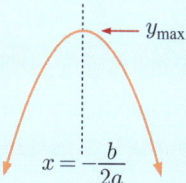

Optimisation is a very useful tool when looking at such issues as:

- maximising profits
- minimising costs
- maximising heights reached.

Example 19   🔊 Self Tutor

The height of a rocket t seconds after it is fired upwards is given by $H(t) = 100t - 5t^2$ metres, $t \geqslant 0$.

a How long does the rocket take to reach its maximum height?
b Find the maximum height reached by the rocket.
c How long does it take for the rocket to fall back to earth?

a $H(t) = 100t - 5t^2$
    $\therefore H(t) = -5t^2 + 100t$
    Now $a = -5$ which is < 0, so the shape of the graph is .

    The maximum height is reached when $t = \dfrac{-b}{2a} = \dfrac{-100}{2(-5)} = 10$

    $\therefore$ the maximum height is reached after 10 seconds.

b $H(10) = 100(10) - 5(10)^2$
             $= 500$

    $\therefore$ the maximum height reached is 500 m.

c The rocket falls back to earth when $H(t) = 0$
$$\therefore -5t^2 + 100t = 0$$
$$\therefore -5t(t - 20) = 0$$
$$\therefore t = 0 \text{ or } 20$$
$\therefore$ the rocket falls back to earth after 20 seconds.

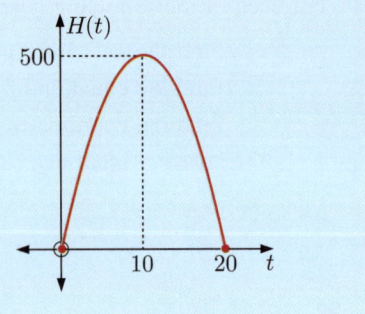

EXERCISE 20F

1. The height of a ball t seconds after it is kicked upwards is given by $H(t) = 20t - 5t^2$ metres.

   a How long does the ball take to reach its maximum height?

   b Find the maximum height reached by the ball.

   c How long does it take for the ball to hit the ground?

2. A manufacturer finds that the profit €P from assembling x bicycles per day is given by $P(x) = -x^2 + 50x - 200$.

   a How many bicycles should be assembled per day to maximise the profit?

   b Find the maximum profit.

   c What is the loss made if no bicycles are assembled in a day? Suggest why this loss would be made.

3. The driver of a car travelling downhill applied the brakes. The speed of the car, t seconds after the brakes were applied, is given by $s(t) = -6t^2 + 12t + 60$ km h^{-1}.

   a How fast was the car travelling when the driver applied the brakes?

   b After how many seconds did the car reach its maximum speed?

   c Find the maximum speed reached.

4. The hourly profit obtained from operating a fleet of n taxis is given by $P(n) = 120n - 200 - 2n^2$ dollars.

   a What number of taxis gives the maximum hourly profit?

   b Find the maximum hourly profit.

   c How much money is lost per hour if no taxis are on the road?

5. The temperature $T°$C in a greenhouse t hours after 7:00 pm is given by $T(t) = \frac{1}{4}t^2 - 6t + 25$ for $t \leqslant 20$.

   a Find the temperature in the greenhouse at 7:00 pm.

   b At what time is the temperature at a minimum?

   c Find the minimum temperature in the greenhouse for $0 \leqslant t \leqslant 20$.

6. Answer the questions posed in the **Opening Problem** on page **432**.

7 Infinitely many rectangles may be inscribed within the triangle ACE shown. One of them is illustrated.

Suppose $EF = x$ cm.

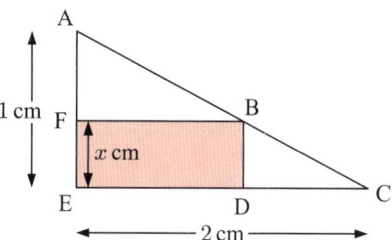

  a Show that triangles ABF and ACE are similar.
  b Show that $BF = 2(1 - x)$ cm.
  c Show that the area of rectangle BDEF is given by $A = -2x^2 + 2x$ cm^2.
  d **i** Find x such that the area of the rectangle is maximised.
      ii What is the maximum area?

REVIEW SET 20A

1 For the quadratic function $y = x^2 - 3x - 15$, find:
  a the value of y when $x = 4$
  b the values of x when $y = 3$.

2 Sketch each of the following functions on the same set of axes as $y = x^2$:
  a $y = 3x^2$
  b $y = (x - 2)^2 + 1$
  c $y = -(x + 3)^2 - 2$

3 **a** Write the quadratic $y = x^2 - 4x + 10$ in the form $y = (x - h)^2 + k$.
  b Hence sketch the function, stating the coordinates of the vertex.

4 Find the x-intercepts of:
  a $y = 5x(x + 4)$
  b $y = 2x^2 + 6x - 56$

5 Find the equation of the axis of symmetry for:
  a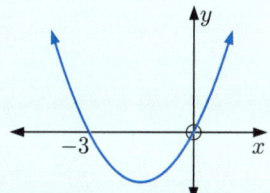
  b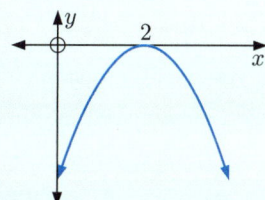

6 Consider the quadratic function $y = -2(x - 1)(x + 3)$.
  a Find the:
      i direction the parabola opens
      ii y-intercept
      iii x-intercepts
      iv equation of the axis of symmetry.
  b Sketch the function, showing all of the above features.

7 Find the vertex of each of the following quadratic functions:
  a $y = x^2 - 8x - 3$
  b $y = -4x^2 + 4x - 3$

8 Consider the function $y = x^2 - 2x - 15$.
  a Find the:
      i y-intercept
      ii x-intercepts
      iii equation of the axis of symmetry
      iv coordinates of the vertex.
  b Sketch the function, showing all of the above features.

9 A vegetable gardener has 40 m of fencing to enclose a rectangular garden plot where one side is an existing brick wall. Suppose the plot is x m wide as shown.

  a Show that the area enclosed is given by
  $A = -2x^2 + 40x$ m^2.

  b Find x such that the vegetable garden has the maximum possible area.

  c Find the maximum possible area.

10 Determine the relationship between the graph and the x-axis for:

  a $y = x^2 - 2x + 3$ **b** $y = -2x^2 + 5x - 3$ **c** $y = 5x^2 - 10x + 5$

REVIEW SET 20B

1 Find the values of x for which $f(x) = x^2 + x - 12$ takes the value 30.

2 Determine whether the ordered pair $(2, 5)$ satisfies the quadratic function $f(x) = x^2 - 3x + 8$.

3 Draw the graphs of $y = x^2$ and $y = (x + 2)^2 + 5$ on the same set of axes.

4 Use the quadratic formula to find the x-intercepts of:

  a $y = 3x^2 - x - 5$ **b** $y = -x^2 + 2x + 6$

5 Draw the graph of $y = 3(x - 2)^2$, showing the axes intercepts and the coordinates of the vertex.

6 Determine the equation of the axis of symmetry for the following quadratic functions:

  a $f(x) = (x + 3)(x - 5)$ **b** $f(x) = 3x^2 - 5x + 2$

7 **a** Find the vertex of the quadratic function $f(x) = -x^2 + 4x - 7$.

  b Hence, find the range of the function.

8 Consider the quadratic function $f(x) = (x - 1)(x - 4)$.

  a Find $f(-1)$.   **b** Find the axes intercepts.

  c Find the equation of the axis of symmetry.

  d Find the coordinates of the vertex.

  e Sketch the graph of $y = f(x)$, showing all of the above features.

9 Suppose $f(x) = (x + 2)(x + 6)$ and $g(x) = -x^2 - 8x - 20$.

  a Find the axes intercepts of each function.

  b Show that the two functions have the same vertex.

  c State the range of each function.

  d Sketch the functions on the same set of axes.

10 Suppose a quadratic function $y = ax^2 + bx + c$ has $c = 0$. Explain why the graph must cut the x-axis at least once:

  a by considering the graphical significance of $c = 0$

  b using the discriminant.

Chapter 21

Advanced trigonometry

Contents:
- **A** Radian measure
- **B** The unit circle
- **C** The relationship between $\sin \theta$ and $\cos \theta$
- **D** The multiples of $30°$ and $45°$
- **E** Trigonometric functions
- **F** Simplifying trigonometric expressions
- **G** Trigonometric equations
- **H** Negative and complementary angle formulae
- **I** Compound angle formulae

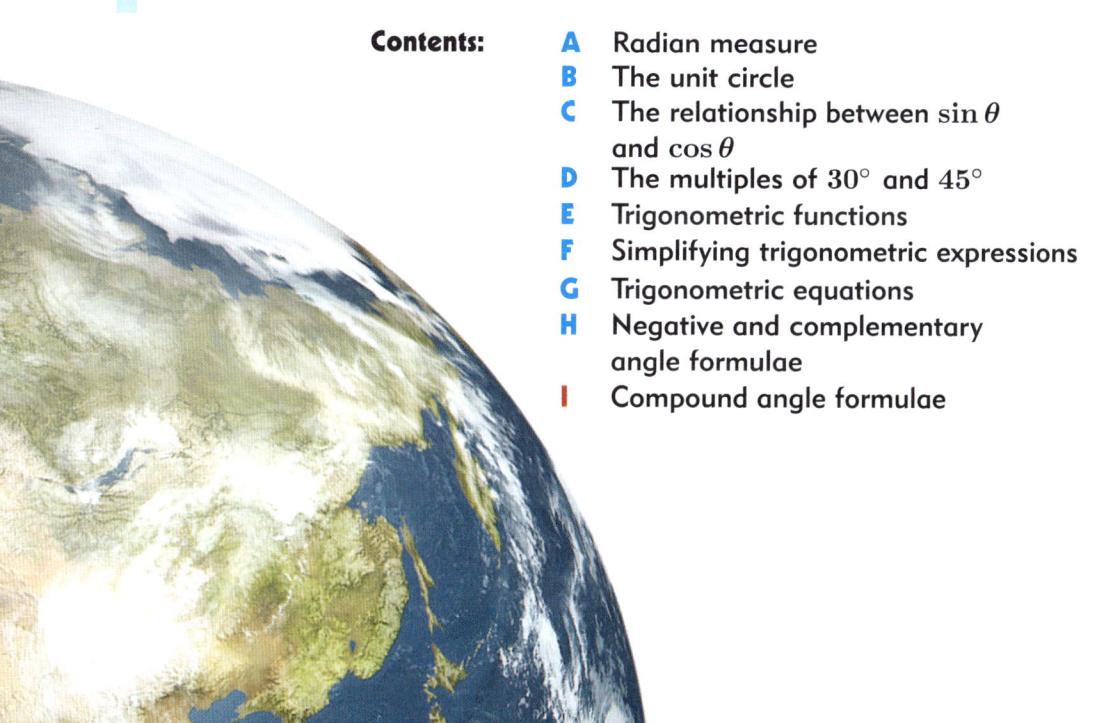

OPENING PROBLEM

A steamroller has a spot of paint on its roller. As the steamroller moves, the spot rotates around the axle.

Things to think about:

a How does the *height* of the spot above ground level change over time?
What would the graph of the spot's height over time look like?

b Suppose the roller has a radius of 1 metre. How would this be shown in the graph?

c Suppose the roller completes one full revolution every 10 seconds.
How would this be shown in the graph?

d Can we use a function involving a trigonometric ratio to determine the height of the spot over time?

DEMO

In this chapter we extend our knowledge of trigonometry. We will consider the trigonometric ratios of angles of any size, and we will see how the trigonometric ratios are used in **trigonometric functions** which model real world situations.

A RADIAN MEASURE

Instead of using degrees, there is another way of measuring angle size. We can use **radians** which relates to the arc length around a circle.

Suppose a sector of a circle has angle θ.

If the angle θ is small, then the arc length will be small compared to the radius.

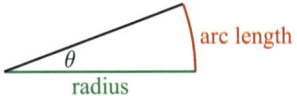

If the angle θ is large, then the arc length will be large compared to the radius.

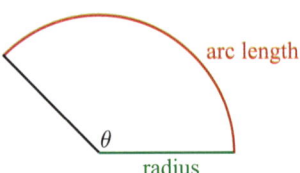

We can use the ratio $\dfrac{\text{arc length}}{\text{radius}}$ as a measure of an angle's size.

If the arc length is *equal* to the radius, then the ratio $\dfrac{\text{arc length}}{\text{radius}}$ is equal to 1.

We define the angle size in this case to be **1 radian**, written 1^c.

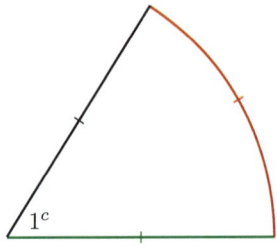

In the case of a complete circle, the ratio
$\dfrac{\text{arc length}}{\text{radius}} = \dfrac{2\pi r}{r} = 2\pi$.

So, a full revolution $= 2\pi$ radians

$\therefore\ 360° \equiv 2\pi^c$

$\boxed{180° \equiv \pi^c}$ is worth remembering.

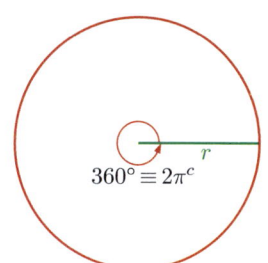

In general, we leave off the symbol for radians, so an angle of π radians is simply written as π.

In higher mathematics, only radian measure is used. It is more convenient, and formulae using radian measure are usually simpler.

For example:

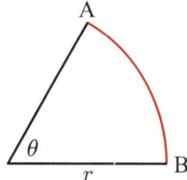

Using degrees,

arc AB $= \left(\dfrac{\theta}{360}\right) \times 2\pi r$.

Using radians,

arc AB $= r\theta$.

DEGREE-RADIAN CONVERSIONS

- To convert from degrees to radians, we multiply by $\dfrac{\pi}{180}$.
- To convert from radians to degrees, we multiply by $\dfrac{180}{\pi}$.

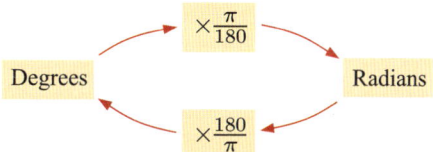

Example 1 ◀) Self Tutor

Convert:
  a $150°$ to radians, in terms of π
  b $131.8°$ to radians, rounded to 3 significant figures
  c $\dfrac{7\pi}{6}$ radians to degrees
  d 1.237 radians to degrees, rounded to 3 significant figures.

a $150° \equiv 150 \times \dfrac{\pi}{180}{}^c$
    $\equiv \dfrac{5\pi}{6}{}^c$

c $\dfrac{7\pi}{6} \equiv \dfrac{7\pi}{6} \times \dfrac{180°}{\pi}$
    $\equiv 210°$

b $131.8° \equiv 131.8 \times \dfrac{\pi}{180}$ radians
    ≈ 2.30 radians

d $1.237^c \equiv 1.237 \times \dfrac{180}{\pi}$ degrees
    $\approx 70.9°$

EXERCISE 21A

1 Convert to radians, giving your answer in terms of π:
  a $30°$ **b** $90°$ **c** $60°$ **d** $45°$ **e** $120°$
  f $135°$ **g** $10°$ **h** $225°$ **i** $210°$ **j** $315°$

2 Convert to radians, rounded to 3 significant figures.
   a $66°$ **b** $23°$ **c** $7°$ **d** $113.8°$ **e** $217.92°$

3 Convert the following radian measures into degrees:
   a $\frac{\pi}{4}$ **b** $\frac{\pi}{6}$ **c** $\frac{\pi}{5}$ **d** $\frac{2\pi}{5}$ **e** $\frac{\pi}{18}$
   f $\frac{5\pi}{18}$ **g** 3π **h** $\frac{\pi}{9}$ **i** $\frac{5\pi}{9}$ **j** 4π
   k $\frac{4\pi}{3}$ **l** $\frac{5\pi}{3}$ **m** $\frac{7\pi}{3}$ **n** $\frac{11\pi}{6}$ **o** $\frac{15\pi}{4}$

4 Convert the following radian measures into degrees, rounded to 3 significant figures.
   a 1^c **b** 3^c **c** 0.5^c **d** 0.78^c **e** 2.155^c

5 Copy and complete:

a

Degrees	0	45	90	135	180	225	270	315	360
Radians									

b

Degrees	0	30	60	90	120	150	180	210	240	270	300	330	360
Radians													

6 a Show that for θ in radians:
   i the arc length $l = r\theta$
   ii the sector area $A = \frac{1}{2}r^2\theta$.

b Find the arc length and area of a sector of radius 10 cm and angle 3 radians.

c A sector has radius 5 cm and arc length 7 cm. Find its area.

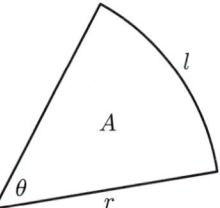

B THE UNIT CIRCLE

In **Chapter 12** we used the unit circle to find trigonometric ratios for angles from $0°$ to $180°$.

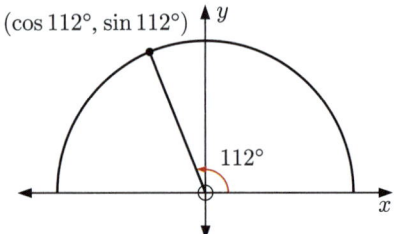

We can, in fact, use the unit circle to consider angles of any size.

For any point P on the unit circle which makes an angle θ with the positive x-axis:

- $\cos\theta$ is the x-coordinate of P
- $\sin\theta$ is the y-coordinate of P.

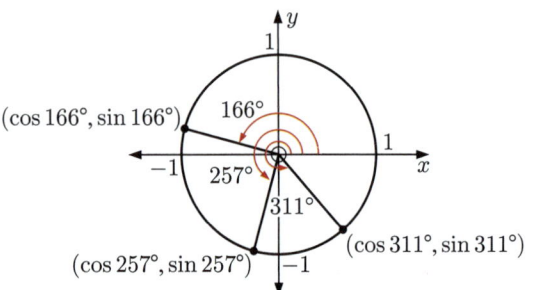

Note that:

- $-1 \leqslant x \leqslant 1$ and $-1 \leqslant y \leqslant 1$ for all points on the unit circle, so

$$-1 \leqslant \cos \theta \leqslant 1 \quad \text{and} \quad -1 \leqslant \sin \theta \leqslant 1 \quad \text{for all } \theta.$$

- θ is **positive** for anticlockwise rotations and **negative** for clockwise rotations.

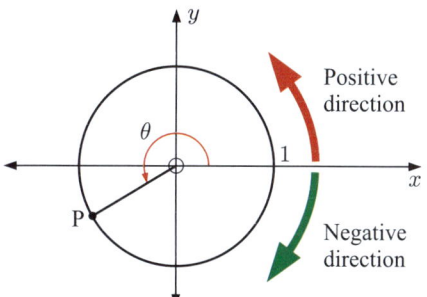

Example 2

From a unit circle diagram, find $\cos 270°$ and $\sin 270°$.

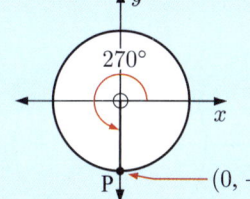

For an angle of $270°$, P is $(0, -1)$.

$\therefore \cos 270° = 0$ {the x-coordinate of P}

$\sin 270° = -1$ {the y-coordinate of P}

Example 3

Find the coordinates of P and Q, rounded to 3 decimal places.

P is $(\cos 212°, \sin 212°)$, which is approximately $(-0.848, -0.530)$.

Q is $(\cos(-51°), \sin(-51°))$, which is approximately $(0.629, -0.777)$.

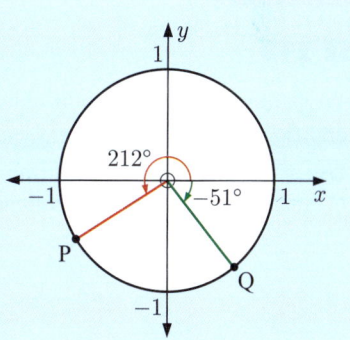

TI-*n*spire

TAN θ

Consider the point $P(\cos\theta, \sin\theta)$ on the unit circle, where θ is acute.

Using $\tan\theta = \dfrac{\text{OPP}}{\text{ADJ}}$ in $\triangle \text{OPQ}$, we observe that:

- $\tan\theta = \dfrac{\sin\theta}{\cos\theta}$
- $\tan\theta$ is the **gradient** of [OP].

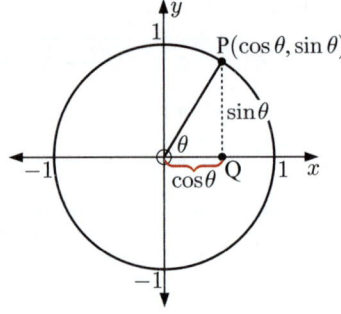

These facts are true for all angles θ.

By identifying the point P on the unit circle corresponding to angle θ, we can determine whether $\cos\theta$, $\sin\theta$, and $\tan\theta$ are positive or negative.

Example 4 ◀)) Self Tutor

For $\theta = 320°$, determine whether $\cos\theta$, $\sin\theta$, and $\tan\theta$ are positive or negative.

The point P on the unit circle corresponding to $\theta = 320°$ is in quadrant 4.

The x-coordinate of P is positive, so $\cos\theta$ is positive.

The y-coordinate of P is negative, so $\sin\theta$ is negative.

The gradient of [OP] is negative, so $\tan\theta$ is negative.

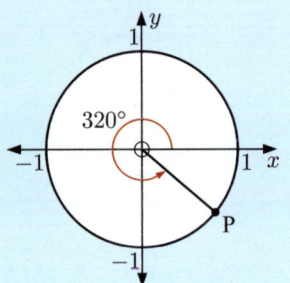

EXERCISE 21B

1   **a** Write down the exact coordinates of points A, B, C, and D.

b Use your calculator to state the coordinates of A, B, C, and D, rounded to 3 significant figures.

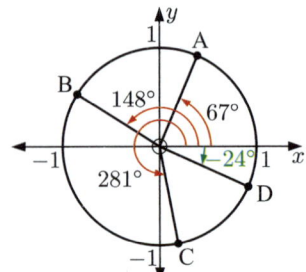

2   Use a unit circle to explain why:

    a $\cos 380° = \cos 20°$ **b** $\sin 413° = \sin 53°$

    c $\sin 160° = \sin 20°$ **d** $\cos 160° = -\cos 20°$

    e $\cos 310° = \cos 50°$ **f** $\tan 25° = \tan 205°$

3   Use a unit circle diagram to find the values of:

    a $\cos 0°$ and $\sin 0°$ **b** $\cos 90°$ and $\sin 90°$

    c $\cos 2\pi$ and $\sin 2\pi$ **d** $\cos 450°$ and $\sin 450°$

    e $\cos(-\frac{\pi}{2})$ and $\sin(-\frac{\pi}{2})$ **f** $\cos(-180°)$ and $\sin(-180°)$

4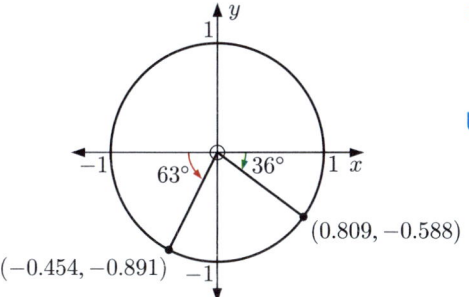

a Use the unit circle alongside to find the value of:
   i $\cos 243°$ ii $\sin 243°$
   iii $\cos 324°$ iv $\sin 324°$

b Hence, find the value of:
   i $\tan 243°$ ii $\tan 324°$

5 Determine whether $\cos \theta$, $\sin \theta$, and $\tan \theta$ are positive or negative for:

  a $\theta = 49°$ b $\theta = 158°$ c $\theta = 207°$ d $\theta = 296°$
  e $\theta = \frac{3\pi}{4}$ f $\theta = \frac{\pi}{6}$ g $\theta = \frac{5\pi}{3}$ h $\theta = \frac{7\pi}{6}$

Use your calculator to check your answers.

6 The diagram alongside shows the 4 quadrants.
They are numbered anticlockwise.

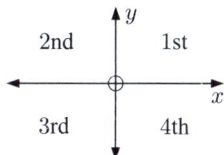

a Copy and complete:

Quadrant	Degree measure	Radian measure	$\cos \theta$	$\sin \theta$	$\tan \theta$
1	$0° < \theta < 90°$	$0 < \theta < \frac{\pi}{2}$	positive	positive	positive
2					
3					
4					

b Determine the quadrants in which:
   i $\sin \theta$ is negative   ii $\cos \theta$ is positive
   iii $\cos \theta$ and $\sin \theta$ are both negative   iv $\cos \theta$ is positive and $\tan \theta$ is negative.

7 Show that $\tan(180° - \theta) = -\tan \theta$.

C   THE RELATIONSHIP BETWEEN $\sin \theta$ AND $\cos \theta$

For any point $P(x, y)$ on the unit circle,
$x^2 + y^2 = 1$ {Pythagoras}.

Since $x = \cos \theta$ and $y = \sin \theta$, we find that for any angle θ, $(\cos \theta)^2 + (\sin \theta)^2 = 1$. We commonly write this as:

$$\cos^2 \theta + \sin^2 \theta = 1$$

If we are given one of the trigonometric ratios $\cos \theta$ or $\sin \theta$, we can use this relationship to find the possible values of the other ratio.

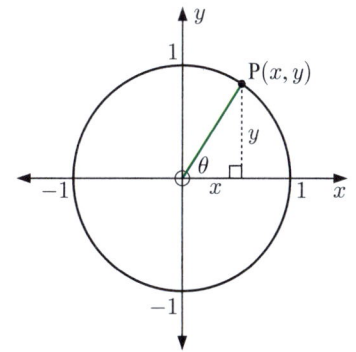

Example 5

Find the possible values of $\sin \theta$ when $\cos \theta = \frac{1}{2}$.
Illustrate your answers.

$\cos^2 \theta + \sin^2 \theta = 1$
$\therefore \left(\frac{1}{2}\right)^2 + \sin^2 \theta = 1$
$\therefore \frac{1}{4} + \sin^2 \theta = 1$
$\therefore \sin^2 \theta = \frac{3}{4}$
$\therefore \sin \theta = \pm \frac{\sqrt{3}}{2}$

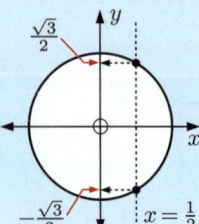

If we know the quadrant in which θ lies, we can determine the sign of the unknown ratio.

In the diagram alongside, the letters show which trigonometric ratios are positive in each quadrant. The 'A' stands for *all* of the ratios.

You might like to remember them using

All Silly Turtles Crawl.

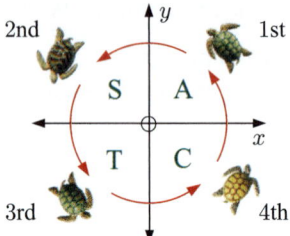

Example 6

Find the exact value of $\cos \theta$ if $\sin \theta = \frac{3}{4}$ and $\frac{\pi}{2} < \theta < \pi$.

$\cos^2 \theta + \sin^2 \theta = 1$
$\therefore \cos^2 \theta + \left(\frac{3}{4}\right)^2 = 1$
$\therefore \cos^2 \theta + \frac{9}{16} = 1$
$\therefore \cos^2 \theta = \frac{7}{16}$
$\therefore \cos \theta = \pm \frac{\sqrt{7}}{4}$

But θ lies in quadrant 2 where $\cos \theta$ is *negative*.

$\therefore \cos \theta = -\frac{\sqrt{7}}{4}$

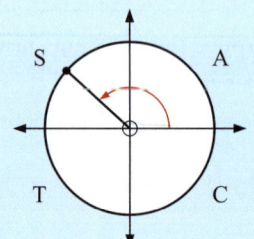

EXERCISE 21C

1 Using a unit circle to illustrate your answers, find the possible values of $\sin \theta$ when:

   a $\cos \theta = \frac{3}{5}$ **b** $\cos \theta = -\frac{1}{4}$ **c** $\cos \theta = 1$ **d** $\cos \theta = 0$

2 Using a unit circle to illustrate your answers, find the possible values of $\cos \theta$ when:

   a $\sin \theta = \frac{12}{13}$ **b** $\sin \theta = -1$ **c** $\sin \theta = 0$ **d** $\sin \theta = -\frac{3}{5}$

3 Find the exact value of $\cos \theta$ if:

   a $\sin \theta = \frac{2}{3}$ and $0 < \theta < \frac{\pi}{2}$ **b** $\sin \theta = \frac{4}{5}$ and $90° < \theta < 180°$

   c $\sin \theta = -\frac{1}{3}$ and $\pi < \theta < \frac{3\pi}{2}$ **d** $\sin \theta = -\frac{5}{13}$ and $270° < \theta < 360°$

4 Find the exact value of $\sin\theta$ if:

   a $\cos\theta = \frac{3}{5}$ and $0° < \theta < 90°$ **b** $\cos\theta = \frac{1}{4}$ and $\frac{3\pi}{2} < \theta < 2\pi$

   c $\cos\theta = -\frac{3}{4}$ and $\frac{\pi}{2} < \theta < \pi$ **d** $\cos\theta = -\frac{5}{13}$ and $180° < \theta < 270°$

5 Suppose $180° < \theta < 270°$ and $\sin\theta = -\frac{3}{8}$.

   a Find the exact value of $\cos\theta$.   **b** Hence, find the exact value of $\tan\theta$.

D   THE MULTIPLES OF 30° AND 45°

MULTIPLES OF 45° OR $\frac{\pi}{4}$

Consider $\theta = 45° \equiv \frac{\pi}{4}$.

Angle OPB also measures $45°$, so triangle OBP is isosceles.

$\therefore$ we let $OB = BP = a$

Now $a^2 + a^2 = 1^2$ {Pythagoras}

$\therefore a^2 = \frac{1}{2}$

$\therefore a = \frac{1}{\sqrt{2}}$ {since $a > 0$}

$\therefore$ P is $(\frac{1}{\sqrt{2}}, \frac{1}{\sqrt{2}})$ where $\frac{1}{\sqrt{2}} \approx 0.7$.

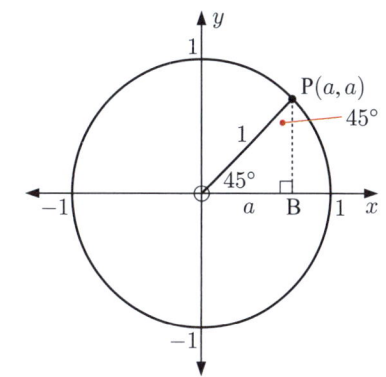

We can now find the coordinates of all points on the unit circle corresponding to multiples of $45°$ by using rotations and reflections.

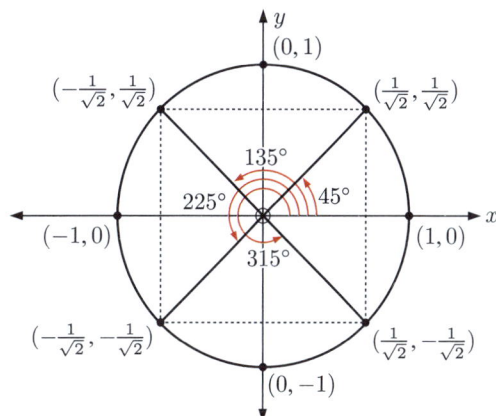

MULTIPLES OF 30° OR $\frac{\pi}{6}$

Consider $\theta = 60° \equiv \frac{\pi}{3}$.

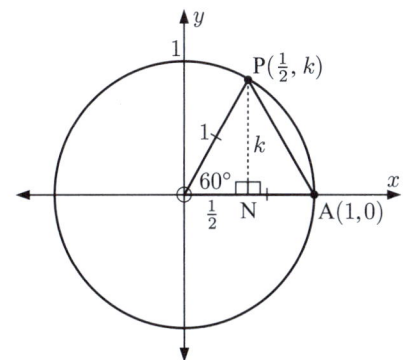

Since $OA = OP$, triangle OAP is isosceles.

Now $\widehat{AOP} = 60°$, so the remaining angles are therefore also $60°$. Triangle AOP is therefore equilateral.

The altitude [PN] bisects base [OA], so $ON = \frac{1}{2}$.

If P is $(\frac{1}{2}, k)$, then $(\frac{1}{2})^2 + k^2 = 1$

$\therefore k^2 = \frac{3}{4}$

$\therefore k = \frac{\sqrt{3}}{2}$ {since $k > 0$}

$\therefore$ P is $(\frac{1}{2}, \frac{\sqrt{3}}{2})$ where $\frac{\sqrt{3}}{2} \approx 0.9$.

We can now find the coordinates of all points on the unit circle corresponding to multiples of 30° by using rotations and reflections.

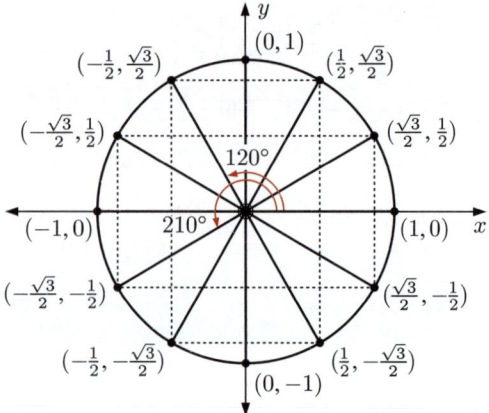

Summary:

- If θ is a **multiple of 90°** or $\frac{\pi}{2}$, the coordinates of the points on the unit circle involve 0 and ±1.
- If θ is a **multiple of 45°** or $\frac{\pi}{4}$, but not a multiple of 90°, the coordinates involve $\pm\frac{1}{\sqrt{2}}$.
- If θ is a **multiple of 30°** or $\frac{\pi}{6}$, but not a multiple of 90°, the coordinates involve $\pm\frac{1}{2}$ and $\pm\frac{\sqrt{3}}{2}$.

We can calculate the **tangent** of any angle θ using $\quad \tan\theta = \dfrac{\sin\theta}{\cos\theta}$.

Example 7 ◀)) Self Tutor

Use a unit circle diagram to find $\sin\theta$, $\cos\theta$, and $\tan\theta$ for:

a $\theta = 60°$ **b** $\theta = \frac{5\pi}{6}$ **c** $\theta = \frac{5\pi}{4}$

a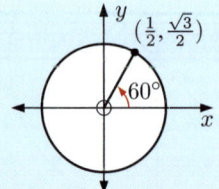

$\sin 60° = \frac{\sqrt{3}}{2}$

$\cos 60° = \frac{1}{2}$

$\tan 60° = \dfrac{\frac{\sqrt{3}}{2}}{\frac{1}{2}} = \sqrt{3}$

b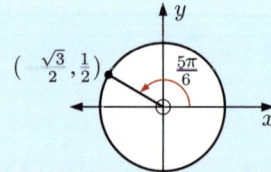

$\sin\frac{5\pi}{6} = \frac{1}{2}$

$\cos\frac{5\pi}{6} = -\frac{\sqrt{3}}{2}$

$\tan\frac{5\pi}{6} = \dfrac{\frac{1}{2}}{-\frac{\sqrt{3}}{2}} = -\dfrac{1}{\sqrt{3}}$

c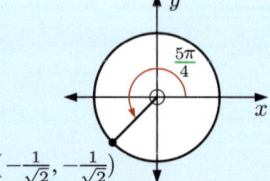

$\sin\frac{5\pi}{4} = -\frac{1}{\sqrt{2}}$

$\cos\frac{5\pi}{4} = -\frac{1}{\sqrt{2}}$

$\tan\frac{5\pi}{4} = 1$

EXERCISE 21D

1 Use a unit circle to find $\sin\theta$, $\cos\theta$, and $\tan\theta$ for:

- **a** $\theta = 30°$
- **b** $\theta = \frac{\pi}{4}$
- **c** $\theta = 0°$
- **d** $\theta = 135°$
- **e** $\theta = \frac{\pi}{2}$
- **f** $\theta = 120°$
- **g** $\theta = 270°$
- **h** $\theta = \pi$
- **i** $\theta = \frac{7\pi}{6}$
- **j** $\theta = 240°$
- **k** $\theta = \frac{11\pi}{6}$
- **l** $\theta = 2\pi$
- **m** $\theta = 300°$
- **n** $\theta = \frac{7\pi}{4}$
- **o** $\theta = \frac{5\pi}{2}$
- **p** $\theta = 3\pi$

2 Without using a calculator, find the exact value of:

    a $\sin^2 45°$ **b** $\cos^2(\frac{\pi}{3})$

    c $\tan^2(\frac{\pi}{6})$ **d** $\cos^3(-\frac{\pi}{6})$

    e $\sin^2 150°$ **f** $\tan^2 300°$

Check your answers using a calculator.

Make sure your calculator is in the correct angle mode.

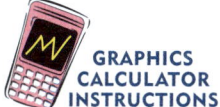

GRAPHICS CALCULATOR INSTRUCTIONS

Example 8

Use a unit circle diagram to find the angle between 0 and 2π which has a cosine of $\frac{1}{2}$ and a sine of $-\frac{\sqrt{3}}{2}$.

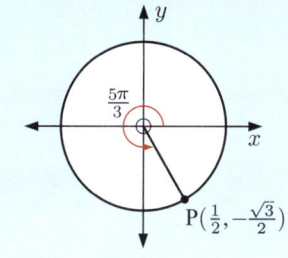

P is at $(\frac{1}{2}, -\frac{\sqrt{3}}{2})$.

Since $\frac{1}{2}$ and $-\frac{\sqrt{3}}{2}$ are involved, the angle is a multiple of $\frac{\pi}{6}$.

The angle is $\frac{5\pi}{3}$.

3 Use a unit circle diagram to find the angle between 0 and 2π which has:

    a a cosine of $-\frac{\sqrt{3}}{2}$ and a sine of $\frac{1}{2}$ **b** a cosine of $-\frac{1}{\sqrt{2}}$ and a sine of $-\frac{1}{\sqrt{2}}$

    c a cosine of $\frac{\sqrt{3}}{2}$ and a tangent of $\frac{1}{\sqrt{3}}$ **d** a sine of $-\frac{1}{\sqrt{2}}$ and a tangent of -1.

E   TRIGONOMETRIC FUNCTIONS

A **trigonometric function** is a function which involves one of the trigonometric ratios.

Consider the point $P(\cos\theta, \sin\theta)$ on the unit circle.

As θ increases, the point P moves anticlockwise around the unit circle, and the values of $\cos\theta$ and $\sin\theta$ change.

We can draw the graphs of $y = \sin\theta$ and $y = \cos\theta$ by plotting the values of $\sin\theta$ and $\cos\theta$ against θ.

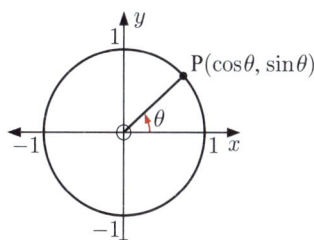

THE GRAPH OF $y = \sin\theta$

The diagram alongside gives the y-coordinates for all points on the unit circle at intervals of $\frac{\pi}{6}$.

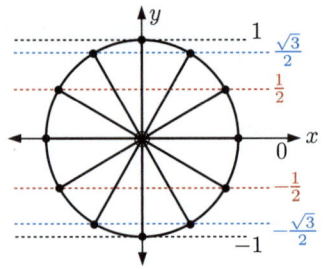

A table for $\sin\theta$ can be constructed from these values:

θ	0	$\frac{\pi}{6}$	$\frac{2\pi}{6}$	$\frac{3\pi}{6}$	$\frac{4\pi}{6}$	$\frac{5\pi}{6}$	π	$\frac{7\pi}{6}$	$\frac{8\pi}{6}$	$\frac{9\pi}{6}$	$\frac{10\pi}{6}$	$\frac{11\pi}{6}$	2π
$\sin\theta$	0	$\frac{1}{2}$	$\frac{\sqrt{3}}{2}$	1	$\frac{\sqrt{3}}{2}$	$\frac{1}{2}$	0	$-\frac{1}{2}$	$-\frac{\sqrt{3}}{2}$	-1	$-\frac{\sqrt{3}}{2}$	$-\frac{1}{2}$	0

Plotting $\sin\theta$ against θ gives:

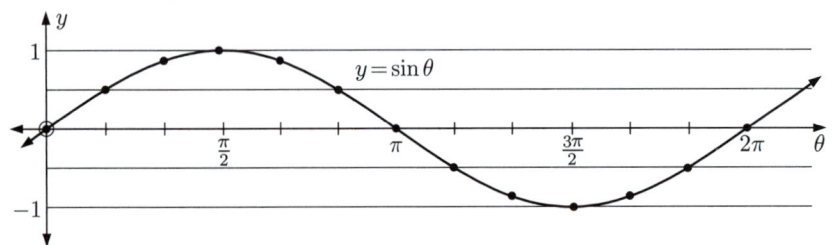

The graph of $y = \sin\theta$ shows the y-coordinate of the point P as P moves around the unit circle

Once we reach 2π, P has completed a full revolution of the unit circle, and so this pattern repeats itself.

DEMO

THE GRAPH OF $y = \cos\theta$

By considering the x-coordinates of the points on the unit circle at intervals of $\frac{\pi}{6}$, we can create a table of values for $\cos\theta$:

θ	0	$\frac{\pi}{6}$	$\frac{2\pi}{6}$	$\frac{3\pi}{6}$	$\frac{4\pi}{6}$	$\frac{5\pi}{6}$	π	$\frac{7\pi}{6}$	$\frac{8\pi}{6}$	$\frac{9\pi}{6}$	$\frac{10\pi}{6}$	$\frac{11\pi}{6}$	2π
$\cos\theta$	1	$\frac{\sqrt{3}}{2}$	$\frac{1}{2}$	0	$-\frac{1}{2}$	$-\frac{\sqrt{3}}{2}$	-1	$-\frac{\sqrt{3}}{2}$	$-\frac{1}{2}$	0	$\frac{1}{2}$	$\frac{\sqrt{3}}{2}$	1

Plotting $\cos\theta$ against θ gives:

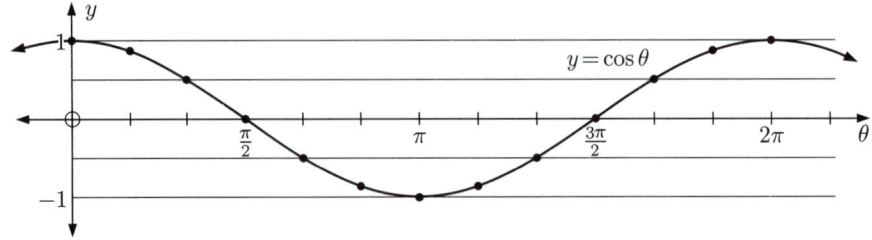

EXERCISE 21E.1

1 Below is an accurate graph of $y = \sin \theta$.

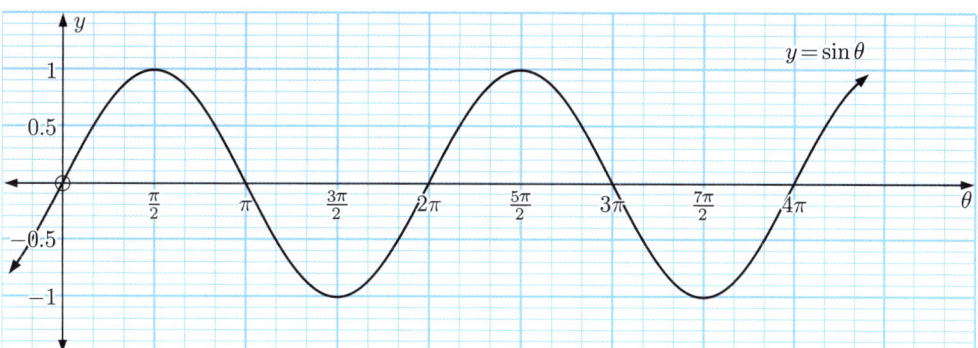

    a Find the y-intercept of the graph.

    b Find the values of θ on $0 \leqslant \theta \leqslant 4\pi$ for which:

        i $\sin \theta = 0$ **ii** $\sin \theta = -1$ **iii** $\sin \theta = \frac{1}{2}$ **iv** $\sin \theta = \frac{\sqrt{3}}{2}$

    c Use the graph to estimate the values of θ in terms of π on $0 \leqslant \theta \leqslant 4\pi$ for which $\sin \theta = 0.3$.

    d Find the intervals on $0 \leqslant \theta \leqslant 4\pi$ where $\sin \theta$ is:

        i positive   **ii** negative.

    e Find the range of the function.

2 Below is an accurate graph of $y = \cos \theta$.

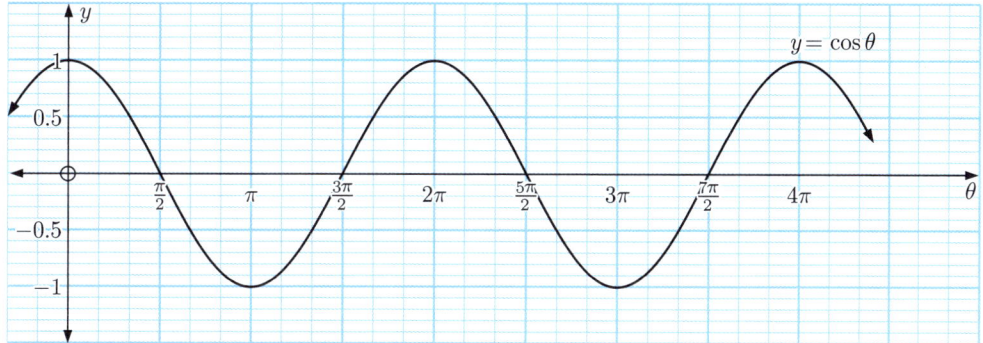

    a Find the y-intercept of the graph.

    b Find the values of θ on $0 \leqslant \theta \leqslant 4\pi$ for which:

        i $\cos \theta = 0$ **ii** $\cos \theta = 1$ **iii** $\cos \theta = -\frac{1}{2}$ **iv** $\cos \theta = -\frac{1}{\sqrt{2}}$

    c Use the graph to estimate the values of θ in terms of π on $0 \leqslant \theta \leqslant 4\pi$ for which $\cos \theta = 0.3$.

    d Find the intervals on $0 \leqslant \theta \leqslant 4\pi$ where $\cos \theta$ is:

        i positive   **ii** negative.

    e Find the range of the function.

USING TRANSFORMATIONS TO GRAPH TRIGONOMETRIC FUNCTIONS

Once we are familiar with the graphs of $y = \sin\theta$ and $y = \cos\theta$, we can use transformations to graph more complicated trigonometric functions.

Before we consider the graphs of these functions in detail, we need to learn appropriate language for describing them:

- A **periodic function** is one which repeats itself over and over in a horizontal direction.
- The **period** of a periodic function is the length of one repetition or cycle.
- The graph oscillates about a horizontal line called the **principal axis** or **mean line**.
- A **maximum point** occurs at the top of a crest.
- A **minimum point** occurs at the bottom of a trough.
- The **amplitude** is the vertical distance between a maximum or minimum point and the principal axis.

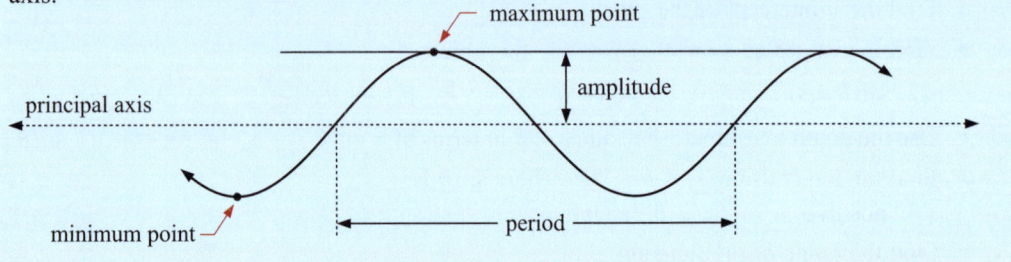

Instead of using θ, we will now use x to represent the angle variable. This is just for convenience, so we are dealing with the familiar function form $y = f(x)$.

For the graphs of $y = \sin x$ and $y = \cos x$:

- The **period** is 2π.
- The **amplitude** is 1.
- The **principal axis** is the line $y = 0$.

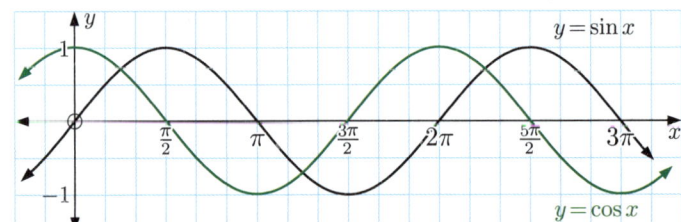

INVESTIGATION — FAMILIES OF TRIGONOMETRIC FUNCTIONS

In this Investigation, we will use technology to draw graphs related to $y = \sin x$.

GRAPHING PACKAGE

Before you begin, make sure your calculator is set to **radians**.

What to do:

1. **a** Use the graphing package to graph on the same set of axes:

   i $y = \sin x$ **ii** $y = 2\sin x$ **iii** $y = \frac{1}{2}\sin x$

   iv $y = -\sin x$ **v** $y = -\frac{1}{3}\sin x$ **vi** $y = -\frac{3}{2}\sin x$

b For graphs of the form $y = A\sin x$, comment on the significance of:

   i the sign of A **ii** the size of A, or $|A|$.

$|A|$ is the size of A, ignoring its sign. So, $|2| = 2$ and $\left|-\frac{1}{3}\right| = \frac{1}{3}$.

2 a Use the graphing package to graph on the same set of axes:

   i $y = \sin x$ **ii** $y = \sin 2x$

   iii $y = \sin\left(\frac{1}{2}x\right)$ **iv** $y = \sin 3x$

  b For graphs of the form $y = \sin Bx$, $B > 0$, what is the period of the graph?

3 a Graph on the same set of axes:

   i $y = \sin x$ **ii** $y = \sin(x - \frac{\pi}{3})$

   iii $y = \sin(x + \frac{\pi}{4})$

  b What translation moves $y = \sin x$ to $y = \sin(x - C)$?

Make sure your calculator is set to radians.

4 a Graph on the same set of axes:

   i $y = \sin x$ **ii** $y = \sin x + 2$

   iii $y = \sin x - 2$

  b What translation moves $y = \sin x$ to $y = \sin x + D$?

  c What is the principal axis of $y = \sin x + D$?

5 What sequence of transformations maps $y = \sin x$ onto $y = A\sin B(x - C) + D$?

From the **Investigation** you should have observed the following properties about the **general sine function** $y = A\sin B(x - C) + D$:

$$y = A\sin B(x - C) + D$$

affects **amplitude**   affects **period**   affects **horizontal translation**   affects **vertical translation**

- The amplitude is $|A|$.
- The period is $\dfrac{2\pi}{B}$ for $B > 0$.
- The principal axis is $y = D$.
- $y = A\sin B(x - C) + D$ where $A > 0$ is obtained from $y = \sin x$ by a vertical dilation with scale factor A and a horizontal dilation with scale factor $\dfrac{1}{B}$, followed by the translation $\begin{pmatrix} C \\ D \end{pmatrix}$.

Click on the icon to obtain a demonstration for the general sine function.   **DEMO**

The properties of the **general cosine function** $y = A\cos B(x - C) + D$ are the same as those of the general sine function.

Example 9 🔊 Self Tutor

Sketch the graph of the following for $0 \leqslant x \leqslant 4\pi$:

a $y = \sin x + 1$ **b** $y = 3\cos x$ **c** $y = \sin 2x$ **d** $y = \cos(x - \frac{\pi}{2})$

a We translate $y = \sin x$ 1 unit upwards.

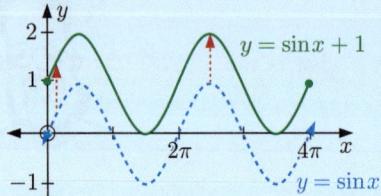

b We dilate $y = \cos x$ vertically with scale factor 3.

$\therefore$ $y = 3\cos x$ has amplitude 3.

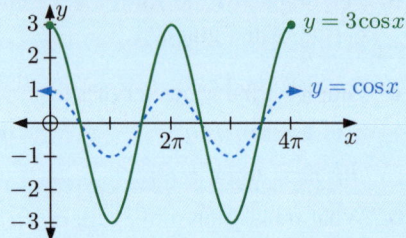

c We dilate $y = \sin x$ horizontally with scale factor $\frac{1}{2}$.

$\therefore$ $y = \sin 2x$ has period $\frac{2\pi}{2} = \pi$.

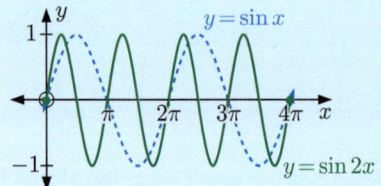

d We translate $y = \cos x$ $\frac{\pi}{2}$ units to the right.

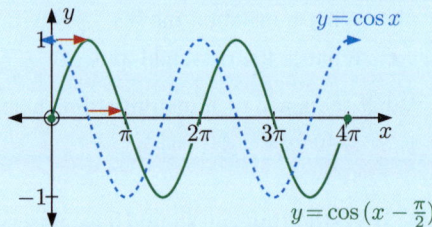

EXERCISE 21E.2

1 Find the amplitude of:
  a $y = 4\sin x$ **b** $y = -2\cos x + 1$ **c** $y = -\frac{1}{3}\sin(x - \frac{\pi}{6})$

2 Find the period of:
  a $y = \cos 3x$ **b** $y = 5\sin 4x + 2$ **c** $y = -\cos(\frac{x}{2})$

3 Find the principal axis of:
  a $y = \sin x - 3$ **b** $y = -2\cos x + 5$ **c** $y = \frac{1}{4}\sin(x + \frac{\pi}{3})$

4 Sketch the graph of the following for $0 \leqslant x \leqslant 4\pi$:
  a $y = 3\sin x$ **b** $y = \sin x - 2$
  c $y = -2\sin x$ **d** $y = \sin 3x$
  e $y = \sin(\frac{x}{2})$ **f** $y = \sin(x - \frac{\pi}{3})$

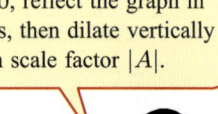

If $A < 0$, reflect the graph in the x-axis, then dilate vertically with scale factor $|A|$.

5 Sketch the graph of the following for $0 \leqslant x \leqslant 4\pi$:
  a $y = 2\cos x$ **b** $y = \cos x + 3$
  c $y = -\frac{1}{3}\cos x$ **d** $y = \cos 2x$
  e $y = \cos(x + \frac{\pi}{2})$ **f** $y = \cos(\frac{3x}{2})$

6 Sketch the graph of the following for $0 \leqslant x \leqslant 2\pi$:

   a $y = 2\cos x + 1$ **b** $y = \sin 2x + 3$ **c** $y = \frac{1}{2}\cos 3x$ **d** $y = 3\sin 4x + 7$

7 **a** Sketch the graph of $y = 6\sin x + 10$ for $0 \leqslant x \leqslant 4\pi$.

   b Find the value of y when $x = \frac{\pi}{6}$.

   c Find the maximum value of y, and the values of x at which the maximum occurs.

   d Find the minimum value of y, and the values of x at which the minimum occurs.

Example 10 ◀)) Self Tutor

The average daytime temperature for a city is given by the function
$D(t) = 5\cos(\frac{\pi t}{6}) + 20$ °C, where t is the time in months after January.

a Sketch the graph of D against t for $0 \leqslant t \leqslant 24$.

b Find the average daytime temperature during May.

c Find the minimum average daytime temperature, and the month in which it occurs.

a For $D(t) = 5\cos(\frac{\pi t}{6}) + 20$:

 • the amplitude is 5

 • the period is $\dfrac{2\pi}{\frac{\pi}{6}} = 12$ months

 • the principal axis is $D = 20$.

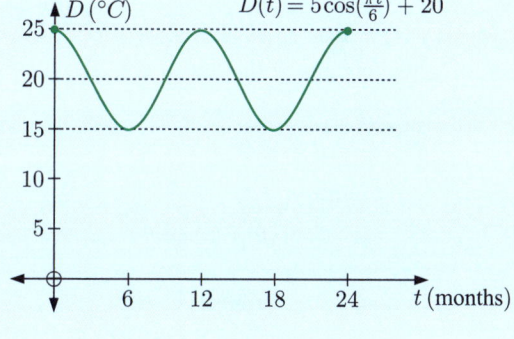

b May is 4 months after January.

When $t = 4$, $D = 5 \times \cos(\frac{4\pi}{6}) + 20$

$ = 5 \times (-\frac{1}{2}) + 20$

$ = 17.5$

So, the average daytime temperature during May is 17.5°C.

c The minimum average daytime temperature is $20 - 5 = 15$°C, which occurs when $t = 6$ or 18.

So, the minimum average daytime temperature occurs during July.

---

8 The temperature inside Vanessa's house t hours after midday is given by the function
$T(t) = 6\sin(\frac{\pi t}{12}) + 26$ °C.

   a Find the:

   i amplitude   **ii** principal axis   **iii** period of the function.

   b Sketch the graph of T against t for $0 \leqslant t \leqslant 24$.

   c Find the temperature inside Vanessa's house at:

   i midnight   **ii** 2 pm.

   d Find the maximum temperature inside Vanessa's house, and the time at which it occurs.

9 The depth of water in a harbour t hours after midnight is $D(t) = 4\cos(\frac{\pi t}{6}) + 6$ metres.

   a Sketch the graph of D against t for $0 \leqslant t \leqslant 24$.

   b Find the highest and lowest depths of the water, and the times at which they occur.

   c A boat requires a water depth of 5 metres to sail in. Will the boat be able to enter the harbour at 8 pm?

F SIMPLIFYING TRIGONOMETRIC EXPRESSIONS

We can simplify trigonometric expressions in the same way that we simplify algebraic expressions.
For example, just as $2x + 3x = 5x$, we can write $2\sin\theta + 3\sin\theta = 5\sin\theta$.

Example 11

Simplify:
a $2\cos\theta + 5\cos\theta$
b $2\sin\alpha - 7\sin\alpha$

a $2\cos\theta + 5\cos\theta = 7\cos\theta$
$\{2x + 5x = 7x\}$

b $2\sin\alpha - 7\sin\alpha = -5\sin\alpha$
$\{2x - 7x = -5x\}$

To simplify more complicated trigonometric expressions involving $\sin\theta$ and $\cos\theta$, we often use the result
$$\sin^2\theta + \cos^2\theta = 1.$$

Useful rearrangements of this result are $1 - \cos^2\theta = \sin^2\theta$ and $1 - \sin^2\theta = \cos^2\theta$.

Example 12

Simplify:
a $4\sin^2\theta + 4\cos^2\theta$
b $3 - 3\cos^2\theta$

a $4\sin^2\theta + 4\cos^2\theta$
$= 4(\sin^2\theta + \cos^2\theta)$
$= 4 \times 1$
$= 4$

b $3 - 3\cos^2\theta$
$= 3(1 - \cos^2\theta)$
$= 3\sin^2\theta$

Example 13

Expand and simplify if possible: $(\cos\theta + \sin\theta)^2$

$(\cos\theta + \sin\theta)^2$
$= \cos^2\theta + 2\cos\theta\sin\theta + \sin^2\theta$
$\qquad \{\text{using } (a+b)^2 = a^2 + 2ab + b^2\}$
$= \cos^2\theta + \sin^2\theta + 2\cos\theta\sin\theta$
$= 1 + 2\cos\theta\sin\theta$

We can expand and factorise in the same way as normal algebra.

EXERCISE 21F

1 Simplify:
    a $\cos\theta + \cos\theta$
    b $4\sin\theta + 3\sin\theta$
    c $4\sin\theta - \sin\theta$
    d $5\sin\theta - 3\sin\theta$
    e $2\cos\theta - 5\cos\theta$
    f $12\cos\theta - 7\cos\theta$

2 Simplify:

a $5\sin^2\theta + 5\cos^2\theta$ **b** $-3\sin^2\theta - 3\cos^2\theta$ **c** $-\sin^2\theta - \cos^2\theta$

d $2\cos^2\theta + 2\sin^2\theta + 1$ **e** $7 - 7\sin^2\theta$ **f** $6 - 6\cos^2\theta$

g $\sin^2\theta - 1$ **h** $6\cos^2\theta - 6$ **i** $7\sin^2\theta - 7$

3 Expand and simplify if possible:

a $\cos\theta(\cos\theta - 5)$ **b** $\sin\theta(4 - \sin\theta)$ **c** $(\cos\theta + 3)(\cos\theta - 1)$

d $(\sin\theta + 1)(\sin\theta - 1)$ **e** $(2 + \sin\theta)^2$ **f** $(\sin\alpha - 3)^2$

g $(\cos\alpha - 4)^2$ **h** $(\sin\phi - \cos\phi)^2$ **i** $-(1 - \cos\alpha)^2$

Example 14   ◀)) **Self Tutor**

Factorise:

a $\sin^2\alpha - \cos^2\alpha$ **b** $\sin^2\theta - 5\sin\theta + 4$

a $\sin^2\alpha - \cos^2\alpha$
     $= (\sin\alpha + \cos\alpha)(\sin\alpha - \cos\alpha)$ $\{a^2 - b^2 = (a+b)(a-b)\}$

b $\sin^2\theta - 5\sin\theta + 4$
     $= (\sin\theta - 4)(\sin\theta - 1)$ $\{x^2 - 5x + 4 = (x-4)(x-1)\}$

---

4 Factorise:

a $1 - \sin^2\phi$ **b** $\cos^2\theta - \sin^2\theta$ **c** $\cos^2\beta - 1$

d $3\sin^2\beta - \sin\beta$ **e** $6\cos\phi + 3\cos^2\phi$ **f** $4\sin^2\theta - 2\sin\theta$

g $\sin^2\theta + 6\sin\theta + 8$ **h** $\cos^2\theta + 7\cos\theta + 6$ **i** $8\cos^2\alpha + 2\cos\alpha - 1$

Example 15   ◀)) **Self Tutor**

Simplify:

a $\dfrac{3 - 3\sin^2\theta}{1 + \sin\theta}$ **b** $\dfrac{\cos^2\theta - \sin^2\theta}{\cos\theta - \sin\theta}$

a $\dfrac{3 - 3\sin^2\theta}{1 + \sin\theta}$
    $= \dfrac{3(1 - \sin^2\theta)}{1 + \sin\theta}$
    $= \dfrac{3(1 + \sin\theta)^1(1 - \sin\theta)}{(1 + \sin\theta)_1}$
    $= 3(1 - \sin\theta)$

b $\dfrac{\cos^2\theta - \sin^2\theta}{\cos\theta - \sin\theta}$
    $= \dfrac{(\cos\theta + \sin\theta)(\cos\theta - \sin\theta)^1}{(\cos\theta - \sin\theta)_1}$
    $= \cos\theta + \sin\theta$

---

5 Simplify:

a $\dfrac{1 - \cos^2\theta}{\sin^2\theta}$ **b** $\dfrac{2 - 2\cos^2\theta}{\sin\theta}$ **c** $\dfrac{\cos^2\theta - 1}{\sin\theta}$

d $\dfrac{1 - \cos^2\alpha}{1 - \cos\alpha}$ **e** $\dfrac{\sin^2\theta - 1}{\sin\theta + 1}$ **f** $\dfrac{\cos\alpha - \sin\alpha}{\cos^2\alpha - \sin^2\alpha}$

g $\dfrac{\cos^2\theta - \sin^2\theta}{\cos\theta + \sin\theta}$ **h** $\dfrac{\sin\phi + \cos\phi}{\cos^2\phi - \sin^2\phi}$ **i** $\dfrac{4 - 4\sin^2\theta}{2\cos\theta}$

6 By starting with the left hand side, prove the following identities:

a $(\cos\theta + \sin\theta)^2 - (\cos\theta - \sin\theta)^2 = 4\sin\theta\cos\theta$

b $(4\sin\theta + 3\cos\theta)^2 + (3\sin\theta - 4\cos\theta)^2 = 25$

c $(1 - \sin\theta)\left(1 + \dfrac{1}{\sin\theta}\right) = \dfrac{\cos^2\theta}{\sin\theta}$

d $\left(1 + \dfrac{1}{\cos\theta}\right)(\cos\theta - \cos^2\theta) = \sin^2\theta$

e $\dfrac{\cos\theta}{1+\sin\theta} + \dfrac{1+\sin\theta}{\cos\theta} = \dfrac{2}{\cos\theta}$

f $\dfrac{\cos\theta}{1-\sin\theta} - \dfrac{\cos\theta}{1+\sin\theta} = 2\tan\theta$

G TRIGONOMETRIC EQUATIONS

In this section we will solve equations involving the trigonometric ratios $\sin\theta$, $\cos\theta$, and $\tan\theta$.

To do this we recognise that:

- if two angles have the same **sine** they have the same y-coordinate
- if two angles have the same **cosine** they have the same x-coordinate
- if two angles have the same **tangent** they are located $180°$ or π apart.

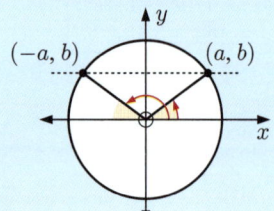
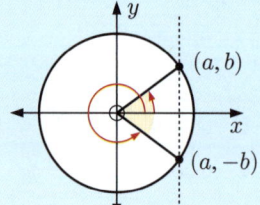
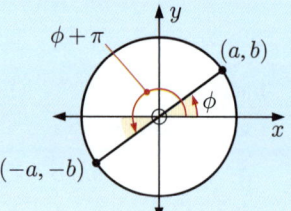

Example 16 ◀)) Self Tutor

Solve for θ on the interval $0 \leqslant \theta \leqslant 2\pi$:

a $\sin\theta = \dfrac{\sqrt{3}}{2}$ **b** $\sqrt{2}\cos\theta = -1$ **c** $\sqrt{3}\tan\theta - 1 = 0$

a $\sin\theta = \dfrac{\sqrt{3}}{2}$

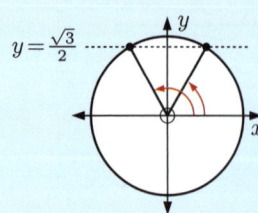

$\therefore \theta = \dfrac{\pi}{3}$ or $\dfrac{2\pi}{3}$

b $\sqrt{2}\cos\theta = -1$

$\therefore \cos\theta = -\dfrac{1}{\sqrt{2}}$

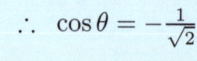

$\therefore \theta = \dfrac{3\pi}{4}$ or $\dfrac{5\pi}{4}$

c $\sqrt{3}\tan\theta - 1 = 0$

$\therefore \tan\theta = \dfrac{1}{\sqrt{3}}$

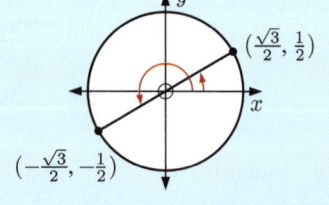

$\therefore \theta = \dfrac{\pi}{6}$ or $\dfrac{7\pi}{6}$

If you are required to solve equations over an interval larger than $0 \leqslant \theta \leqslant 2\pi$, you will need to add or subtract multiples of 2π to the solutions you read straight from the unit circle.

Example 17

Solve $2\cos\theta - 1 = 0$ on the interval $0 \leqslant \theta \leqslant 4\pi$.

$2\cos\theta - 1 = 0$

$\therefore \cos\theta = \frac{1}{2}$

On the interval $0 \leqslant \theta \leqslant 2\pi$, the solutions are $\theta = \frac{\pi}{3}$ or $\frac{5\pi}{3}$.

$\therefore$ on the interval $0 \leqslant \theta \leqslant 4\pi$, the solutions are

$\theta = \frac{\pi}{3}, \frac{5\pi}{3}, \frac{7\pi}{3},$ or $\frac{11\pi}{3}$.

$\uparrow \qquad \uparrow$
$\frac{\pi}{3}+2\pi \quad \frac{5\pi}{3}+2\pi$

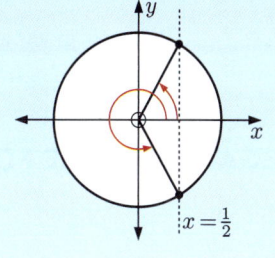

EXERCISE 21G

1 Solve for θ on the interval $0 \leqslant \theta \leqslant 2\pi$:

a $\cos\theta = \frac{\sqrt{3}}{2}$ **b** $\sin\theta = -\frac{1}{2}$ **c** $\tan\theta = \sqrt{3}$

d $\cos\theta = 0$ **e** $\tan\theta - 1 = 0$ **f** $2\sin\theta = -\sqrt{3}$

g $\sqrt{2}\sin\theta - 1 = 0$ **h** $2\cos\theta + 3 = 1$ **i** $\sqrt{3}\tan\theta + 1 = 0$

2 Solve the following equations on the intervals given:

a $\sqrt{2}\cos\theta = 1$, $0 \leqslant \theta \leqslant 4\pi$ **b** $5\sin\theta + 2 = 7$, $0 \leqslant \theta \leqslant 4\pi$

c $\sqrt{3}\tan\theta + 3 = 0$, $0 \leqslant \theta \leqslant 4\pi$ **d** $6\sin\theta + 8 = 11$, $-\pi \leqslant \theta \leqslant \pi$

e $4\cos\theta + 2\sqrt{3} = 0$, $-\pi \leqslant \theta \leqslant \pi$ **f** $\sin\theta + \cos\theta = 0$, $0 \leqslant \theta \leqslant 6\pi$

Example 18

Solve for θ on the interval $0 \leqslant \theta \leqslant 2\pi$:

a $\cos^2\theta = \frac{3}{4}$ **b** $2\sin^2\theta = \sin\theta$

a $\cos^2\theta = \frac{3}{4}$

$\therefore \cos\theta = \pm\frac{\sqrt{3}}{2}$

$\therefore \theta = \frac{\pi}{6}, \frac{5\pi}{6}, \frac{7\pi}{6},$ or $\frac{11\pi}{6}$

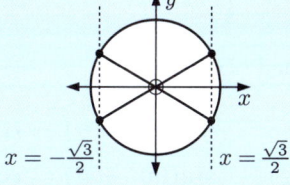

b $2\sin^2\theta = \sin\theta$

$\therefore 2\sin^2\theta - \sin\theta = 0$

$\therefore \sin\theta(2\sin\theta - 1) = 0$

$\therefore \sin\theta = 0$ or $\frac{1}{2}$

$\therefore \theta = 0, \frac{\pi}{6}, \frac{5\pi}{6}, \pi,$ or 2π

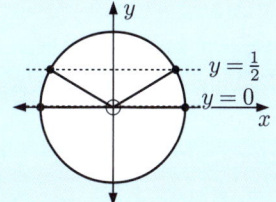

3 Solve for θ on the interval $0 \leqslant \theta \leqslant 2\pi$:

a $\sin^2\theta = \frac{1}{2}$ **b** $\tan^2\theta = 3$ **c** $\cos^2\theta + \cos\theta = 0$

d $2\sin^2\theta - \sqrt{3}\sin\theta = 0$ **e** $2\cos^2\theta - \cos\theta - 1 = 0$ **f** $\sin^2\theta - \cos^2\theta = 0$

H. NEGATIVE AND COMPLEMENTARY ANGLE FORMULAE

For any given angle θ:
- the **negative** of θ is $-\theta$
- the **complement** of θ is $\frac{\pi}{2} - \theta$.

NEGATIVE ANGLE FORMULAE

In the unit circle alongside, P′ corresponds to the angle $-\theta$.
∴ P′ is $(\cos(-\theta), \sin(-\theta))$ .... (1)

However, P′ is a reflection of P in the x-axis, so P′ has the same x-coordinate as P, and the negative y-coordinate to P.
∴ P′ is $(\cos\theta, -\sin\theta)$ .... (2)

Comparing (1) and (2) gives:
$$\cos(-\theta) = \cos\theta$$
$$\sin(-\theta) = -\sin\theta$$

COMPLEMENTARY ANGLE FORMULAE

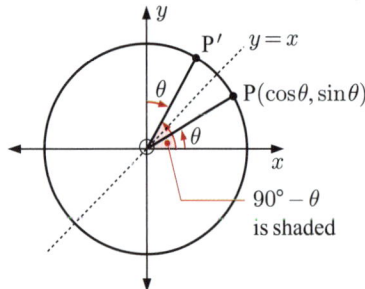

Consider P′ on the unit circle, which corresponds to the angle $(90° - \theta)$.
∴ P′ is $(\cos(90° - \theta), \sin(90° - \theta))$ .... (1)

But P′ is the image of P under a reflection in the line $y = x$. This transformation interchanges the coordinates of P.
∴ P′ is $(\sin\theta, \cos\theta)$ .... (2)

Comparing (1) and (2) gives:

$$\cos(90° - \theta) = \sin\theta \qquad \cos\left(\frac{\pi}{2} - \theta\right) = \sin\theta$$
$$\sin(90° - \theta) = \cos\theta \quad \text{or} \quad \sin\left(\frac{\pi}{2} - \theta\right) = \cos\theta$$

Example 19 ◀)) Self Tutor

Simplify:

a $5\sin\theta - 2\sin(-\theta)$ **b** $4\cos\theta - \cos(-\theta)$ **c** $4\cos\left(\frac{\pi}{2} - \theta\right) - 3\sin\theta$

a $5\sin\theta - 2\sin(-\theta)$
$= 5\sin\theta - 2[-\sin\theta]$
$= 5\sin\theta + 2\sin\theta$
$= 7\sin\theta$

b $4\cos\theta - \cos(-\theta)$
$= 4\cos\theta - \cos\theta$
$= 3\cos\theta$

c $4\cos\left(\frac{\pi}{2} - \theta\right) - 3\sin\theta$
$= 4\sin\theta - 3\sin\theta$
$= \sin\theta$

EXERCISE 21H

1 Simplify:

a $2\sin\theta + \sin(-\theta)$
b $3\sin(-\theta) - \sin\theta$
c $4\cos\theta + 2\cos(-\theta)$
d $8\sin\theta - 3\sin(-\theta)$
e $\cos^2(-\alpha)$
f $\sin^2(-\alpha)$
g $\cos(-\alpha)\cos\alpha - \sin(-\alpha)\sin\alpha$

2 Prove that $\tan(-\theta) = -\tan\theta$ for all θ.

3 Simplify:

a $4\cos\theta - 2\sin(90° - \theta)$
b $2\cos(-\theta) - 5\sin(90° - \theta)$
c $3\cos(90° - \theta) - \sin\theta$
d $2\sin(-\theta) - 7\cos(\frac{\pi}{2} - \theta)$
e $6\sin\theta + \cos(\frac{\pi}{2} - \theta)$
f $3\sin(\frac{\pi}{2} - \theta) + 4\cos\theta$

4 What is the relationship between $\tan(90° - \theta)$ and $\tan\theta$?

5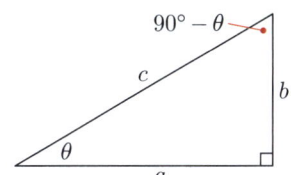

Consider the following 'proof' of the complementary angle formula $\sin\theta = \cos(90° - \theta)$:

In the triangle alongside, $\sin\theta = \dfrac{b}{c}$ and $\cos(90° - \theta) = \dfrac{b}{c}$

$\therefore\ \sin\theta = \cos(90° - \theta)$

Explain why this 'proof' is not acceptable in general.

I COMPOUND ANGLE FORMULAE

If A and B are **any** two angles, then:

$$\cos(A + B) = \cos A \cos B - \sin A \sin B$$
$$\cos(A - B) = \cos A \cos B + \sin A \sin B$$
$$\sin(A + B) = \sin A \cos B + \cos A \sin B$$
$$\sin(A - B) = \sin A \cos B - \cos A \sin B$$

These are known as the **compound angle formulae**.

Proof:

Consider the points $P(\cos A, \sin A)$ and $Q(\cos B, \sin B)$ on the unit circle, so $P\widehat{O}Q = A - B$.

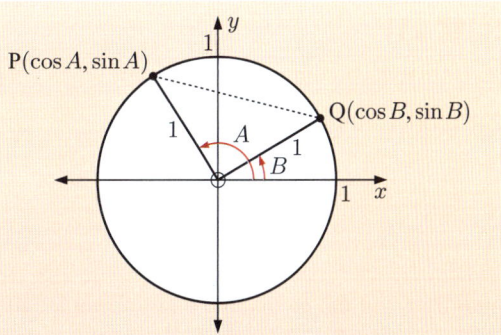

Now $PQ = \sqrt{(\cos A - \cos B)^2 + (\sin A - \sin B)^2}$ {distance formula}

$\therefore (PQ)^2 = \cos^2 A - 2\cos A \cos B + \cos^2 B + \sin^2 A - 2\sin A \sin B + \sin^2 B$
$= \cos^2 A + \sin^2 A + \cos^2 B + \sin^2 B - 2(\cos A \cos B + \sin A \sin B)$
$= 1 + 1 - 2(\cos A \cos B + \sin A \sin B)$
$= 2 - 2(\cos A \cos B + \sin A \sin B)$ .... (1)

But, by the *cosine rule* in $\triangle POQ$,

$(PQ)^2 = 1^2 + 1^2 - 2(1)(1)\cos(A - B)$
$= 2 - 2\cos(A - B)$ .... (2)

$\therefore \cos(A - B) = \cos A \cos B + \sin A \sin B$ {comparing (1) and (2)}

From this formula the other three formulae can be established:

$\cos(A + B) = \cos(A - (-B))$
$= \cos A \cos(-B) + \sin A \sin(-B)$
$= \cos A \cos B + \sin A(-\sin B)$ $\{\cos(-\theta) = \cos\theta$ and
$= \cos A \cos B - \sin A \sin B$ $\sin(-\theta) = -\sin\theta\}$

$\sin(A - B) = \cos(\frac{\pi}{2} - (A - B))$
$= \cos((\frac{\pi}{2} - A) + B)$
$= \cos(\frac{\pi}{2} - A)\cos B - \sin(\frac{\pi}{2} - A)\sin B$ $\{\sin(\frac{\pi}{2} - \theta) = \cos\theta$ and
$= \sin A \cos B - \cos A \sin B$ $\cos(\frac{\pi}{2} - \theta) = \sin\theta\}$

$\sin(A + B) = \sin(A - (-B))$
$= \sin A \cos(-B) - \cos A \sin(-B)$
$= \sin A \cos B - \cos A(-\sin B)$
$= \sin A \cos B + \cos A \sin B$

Example 20   ◀)) Self Tutor

Expand and simplify: $\cos(\alpha + 90°)$

$\cos(\alpha + 90°)$
$= \cos\alpha\cos 90° - \sin\alpha\sin 90°$
$= \cos\alpha \times 0 - \sin\alpha \times 1$
$= -\sin\alpha$

EXERCISE 21I

1 Check that each compound angle formula is correct for $A = 90°$ and $B = 30°$.

2 Expand and simplify:

   a $\sin(90° + \alpha)$ **b** $\cos(270° + \beta)$ **c** $\sin(180° - A)$ **d** $\cos(\alpha + \frac{\pi}{2})$

   e $\sin(\pi + \beta)$ **f** $\cos(\theta - \frac{3\pi}{2})$ **g** $\sin(\theta + \frac{\pi}{6})$ **h** $\cos(\frac{\pi}{3} - \alpha)$

   i $\sin(\theta + \frac{\pi}{4})$ **j** $\cos(\frac{\pi}{4} + \phi)$ **k** $\sin(\frac{3\pi}{4} + C)$ **l** $\cos(A - \frac{\pi}{6})$

3 Simplify using the compound angle formulae in reverse:

   a $\cos A \cos B + \sin A \sin B$ **b** $\sin\alpha\cos\beta - \cos\alpha\sin\beta$

   c $\cos M \cos N - \sin M \sin N$ **d** $\sin C \cos D + \cos C \sin D$

   e $2\sin\alpha\cos\beta - 2\cos\alpha\sin\beta$ **f** $\sin\alpha\sin\beta - \cos\alpha\cos\beta$

4 The **double angle** formulae are:
- $\sin 2A = 2\sin A \cos A$
- $\cos 2A = \cos^2 A - \sin^2 A$
- $\tan 2A = \dfrac{2\tan A}{1 - \tan^2 A}$

  a Use the compound angle formulae to prove the double angle formulae.

  b If $\sin\alpha = \tfrac{3}{5}$ and $\cos\alpha = -\tfrac{4}{5}$, find: **i** $\sin 2\alpha$ **ii** $\cos 2\alpha$ **iii** $\tan 2\alpha$.

5 Use the compound angle formulae to find the exact value of $\cos 15°$.

6 Illustrated is a unit circle diagram where $\overrightarrow{OP}$ and $\overrightarrow{OQ}$ make angles of B and A respectively.

  a Find $\overrightarrow{OP}$ and $\overrightarrow{OQ}$.

  b Use the scalar product of two vectors to establish that $\cos(A - B) = \cos A \cos B + \sin A \sin B$.

REVIEW SET 21A

1 Convert to radians in terms of π: **a** $15°$ **b** $22\tfrac{1}{2}°$

2 Convert to degrees: **a** $\tfrac{\pi}{10}$ **b** $\tfrac{7\pi}{9}$

3 Find the possible values of $\sin\theta$ if: **a** $\cos\theta = \tfrac{2}{3}$ **b** $\cos\theta = -\tfrac{3}{\sqrt{13}}$

4 Without using a calculator, find the exact value of:
  a $\cos^2 135°$ **b** $\tan^2\left(\tfrac{2\pi}{3}\right)$

5 Find the amplitude and period of:
  a $y = 5\cos 2x + 3$ **b** $y = -\tfrac{1}{4}\sin(x - 60°)$ **c** $y = -4\cos\left(\tfrac{x}{2}\right) - 1$

6 Simplify:
  a $4 - 4\cos^2\theta$ **b** $\dfrac{\cos^2\theta - 2\cos\theta}{\cos^2\theta - 4}$ **c** $\dfrac{\sin\theta}{\cos\theta} + \dfrac{\cos\theta}{\sin\theta}$

7 The fraction of the Moon which is illuminated each night is given by the function $M(t) = \tfrac{1}{2}\cos(\tfrac{\pi t}{15}) + \tfrac{1}{2}$, where t is the time in days after January 1st.

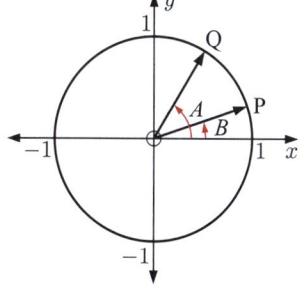

  a Sketch the graph of M against t for $0 \leqslant t \leqslant 60$.

  b Find the fraction of the Moon which is illuminated on the night of:
    i January 6th **ii** January 21st **iii** January 27th **iv** February 19th.

  c How often does a full moon occur?

  d On what dates during January and February is the Moon not illuminated at all?

8 Expand:
  a $\sin\theta(\sin\theta - 3)$
  b $(\cos\theta + 5)^2$

9 Solve for θ on the interval $0 \leqslant \theta \leqslant 2\pi$:
  a $\dfrac{\tan\theta}{\sqrt{3}} + 1 = 0$
  b $3\tan^2\theta = 1$
  c $6\cos\theta - 3\sqrt{3} = 0$

REVIEW SET 21B

1 Find:
  a the exact coordinates of P
  b the approximate coordinates of P, rounded to 3 significant figures.

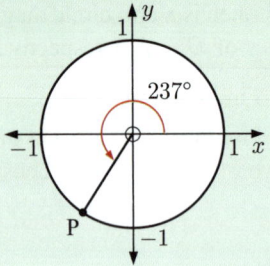

2 For $\theta = \dfrac{7\pi}{4}$, determine whether $\cos\theta$, $\sin\theta$, and $\tan\theta$ are positive or negative.

3 Find the possible values of $\cos\theta$ if:
  a $\sin\theta = -\dfrac{2}{\sqrt{5}}$ and $\pi \leqslant \theta \leqslant \dfrac{3\pi}{2}$
  b $\sin\theta = -\dfrac{3}{7}$ and $\dfrac{3\pi}{2} \leqslant \theta \leqslant 2\pi$.

4 Use a unit circle diagram to find the angle between $0°$ and $360°$ which has a sine of $\dfrac{1}{2}$ and a tangent of $-\dfrac{1}{\sqrt{3}}$.

5 Sketch the graph of the following for $0 \leqslant x \leqslant 4\pi$:
  a $y = 4\sin x$
  b $y = 2\cos x - 3$
  c $y = \sin(x - \dfrac{\pi}{2})$

6 Factorise:
  a $4\sin^2\theta - 12\sin\theta$
  b $\cos^2\theta - 3\cos\theta - 18$

7 As the tip of a windmill's blade rotates, its height above ground is given by $H(t) = 10\cos(\dfrac{\pi t}{6}) + 20$ metres, where t is the time in seconds.
  a Sketch the graph of H against t for $0 \leqslant t \leqslant 36$.
  b Find the height of the blade's tip after 9 seconds.
  c Find the minimum height of the blade's tip.
  d How long does the blade take to complete a full revolution?

8 Simplify:
  a $7\cos\theta - 4\cos(-\theta)$
  b $\sin^3(-\phi)$
  c $2\sin(-\theta) + 5\cos(\dfrac{\pi}{2} - \theta)$

9 Solve for θ on the interval $0 \leqslant \theta \leqslant 4\pi$:
  a $2\cos\theta = -1$
  b $\sqrt{3}\sin\theta - \cos\theta = 0$
  c $4\cos^2\theta - 2\cos\theta = 0$

10 Expand and simplify:
  a $\cos(\theta + \pi)$
  b $\sin(270° - \phi)$
  c $\tan(\alpha + \beta)$

Chapter 22
Inequalities

Contents:
- **A** Interval notation
- **B** Linear inequalities
- **C** Sign diagrams
- **D** Non-linear inequalities

482 INEQUALITIES (Chapter 22)

In this course so far, we have mostly dealt with **equations** in which two expressions are separated by the equality sign $=$.

In this chapter we consider **inequalities** in which two expressions are separated by one of the four inequality signs $<$, $\leqslant$, $>$, or $\geqslant$.

OPENING PROBLEM

To solve the inequality $\dfrac{2x}{x+3} < 1$, Trent performs these steps:

$\dfrac{2x}{x+3} < 1$

$\therefore \ 2x < x + 3$ {multiplying both sides by $(x+3)$}

$\therefore \ x < 3$ {subtracting x from both sides}

His friend Donna notices that $x = -4$ does not satisfy the inequality, since $\dfrac{2(-4)}{-4+3} = \dfrac{-8}{-1} = 8$, which is not < 1.

They concluded that there is something wrong with Trent's solution.

Things to think about:

a At what step was Trent's method wrong?

b Is there an algebraic method which gives the correct solution to this inequality?

A   INTERVAL NOTATION

In **Chapter 2**, we used **interval notation** to describe a set of numbers.

For example, the set of real numbers from 1 to 4 inclusive can be represented by

$\{x \mid 1 \leqslant x \leqslant 4, \ x \in \mathbb{R}\}$

the set of all   such that x is real.

The filled circle shows that 4 is included.

If it is not stated otherwise, we assume we are dealing with real x. So, the set can be represented simply as $\{x \mid 1 \leqslant x \leqslant 4\}$.

Example 1   🔊 Self Tutor

Draw a number line graph to display:

a $\{x \mid -2 \leqslant x < 3\}$ **b** $\{x \mid x < 2 \text{ or } x \geqslant 7\}$ **c** $\{x \mid x < 0 \text{ or } 1 \leqslant x < 4\}$

a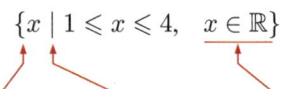

b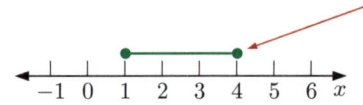

c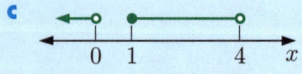

INEQUALITIES (Chapter 22)

SQUARE BRACKET NOTATION

An alternative to using inequality signs is to use **square bracket notation**.

The endpoints of the interval are written within square brackets. The bracket is reversed if the endpoint is not included.

- $[a, b]$ represents the interval $\{x \mid a \leqslant x \leqslant b\}$
- $[a, b[$ represents the interval $\{x \mid a \leqslant x < b\}$
- $]a, b]$ represents the interval $\{x \mid a < x \leqslant b\}$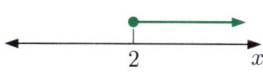
- $]a, b[$ represents the interval $\{x \mid a < x < b\}$

For intervals which extend to infinity, we use the symbol ∞. We always use an 'outwards' bracket for infinity. So, $[2, \infty[$ represents the interval $\{x \mid x \geqslant 2\}$.

In square bracket notation, we use the union symbol $\cup$ to replace 'or'.

So, for $\{x \mid 1 \leqslant x < 3 \text{ or } x \geqslant 5\}$ we would write $[1, 3[\cup [5, \infty[$.

Example 2 ◆) Self Tutor

Use square bracket notation to describe:

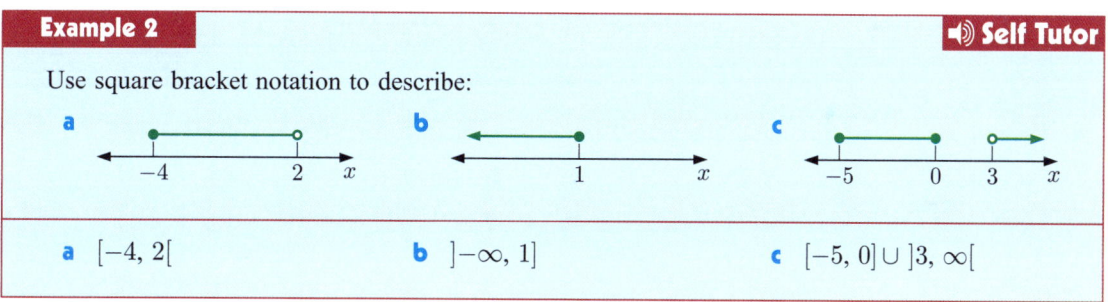

a $[-4, 2[$ **b** $]-\infty, 1]$ **c** $[-5, 0] \cup]3, \infty[$

EXERCISE 22A

1 Draw a number line graph to display:

     a $\{x \mid x > 4\}$ **b** $\{x \mid x \leqslant -5\}$ **c** $\{x \mid -2 \leqslant x \leqslant 3\}$

     d $\{x \mid 0 < x \leqslant 7\}$ **e** $\{x \mid x < 1 \text{ or } x > 3\}$ **f** $\{x \mid x \leqslant 2 \text{ or } x > 6\}$

     g $[-1, 6]$ **h** $]4, 9]$ **i** $[-5, 0[$

     j $]2, 8[$ **k** $[5, \infty[$ **l** $]-\infty, 6]$

     m $]-3, \infty[$ **n** $[0, 4] \cup [7, \infty[$ **o** $]-\infty, 2[\cup [5, 11[$

2 Use interval notation to describe:

a 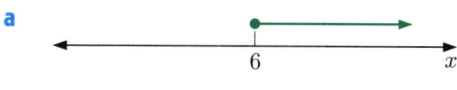   **b**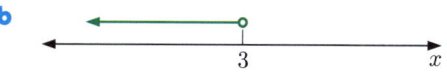

c    **d**

e 　　　　f

g 　　　　h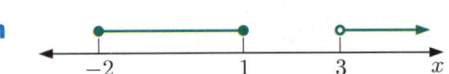

3 Write these number sets using square bracket notation:

   a $\{x \mid -1 \leqslant x \leqslant 6\}$ **b** $\{x \mid 0 < x < 5\}$

   c $\{x \mid -4 < x \leqslant 7\}$ **d** $\{x \mid 4 \leqslant x < 8\}$

   e $\{x \mid x > -7\}$ **f** $\{x \mid x \leqslant 0\}$

   g $\{x \mid x \leqslant 2 \text{ or } x \geqslant 5\}$ **h** $\{x \mid x < -3 \text{ or } x > 4\}$

   i $\{x \mid -1 < x \leqslant 1 \text{ or } x \geqslant 2\}$ **j** $\{x \mid x < -4 \text{ or } 2 \leqslant x < 7\}$

k 　　　　l

m 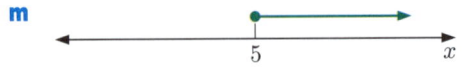　　　　n

o 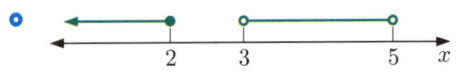　　　　p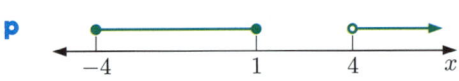

q 　　　　r

4 Display each set on a number line graph, and hence describe using a single interval:

   a $\{x \mid x > 3 \cup 0 < x < 7\}$ **b** $\{x \mid \tfrac{7}{2} \leqslant x < 9 \cup -1 \leqslant x < 4\}$

   c $\{x \mid x < 3 \cap 0 < x < 7\}$ **d** $\{x \mid \tfrac{7}{2} \leqslant x < 9 \cap -1 \leqslant x < 4\}$

B LINEAR INEQUALITIES

Linear inequalities take the same form as linear equations, except they contain an inequality sign instead of an 'equals' sign.

$2x < 7$ and $3x + 5 \geqslant -10$ are examples of linear inequalities.

RULES FOR SOLVING LINEAR INEQUALITIES

        Notice that $5 > 3$ and $3 < 5$,

        and that $-3 < 2$ and $2 > -3$.

This suggests that if we **interchange** the LHS and RHS of an inequality, then we must **reverse** the inequality sign. $>$ is the reverse of $<$, and $\geqslant$ is the reverse of $\leqslant$.

You may also remember from previous years that:

- If we **add** or **subtract** the same number to both sides, the inequality sign is *maintained*.
  For example, if $5 > 3$, then $5 + 2 > 3 + 2$.
- If we **multiply** or **divide** both sides by a **positive** number, the inequality sign is *maintained*.
  For example, if $5 > 3$, then $5 \times 2 > 3 \times 2$.
- If we **multiply** or **divide** both sides by a **negative** number, the inequality sign is *reversed*.
  For example, if $5 > 3$, then $5 \times -1 < 3 \times -1$.

The method of solving linear inequalities is thus identical to that of linear equations, with the exceptions that:

> - **interchanging** the sides **reverses** the inequality sign
> - **multiplying** or **dividing** both sides by a **negative** number **reverses** the inequality sign.

We should not multiply or divide both sides of an inequality by an expression involving the variable, unless we are certain that the expression is always positive or always negative. This is the mistake which Trent made in the **Opening Problem**.

Example 3 ◀)) Self Tutor

Solve for x and graph the solution:

a $3x - 4 \leqslant 2$ **b** $3 - 2x < 7$

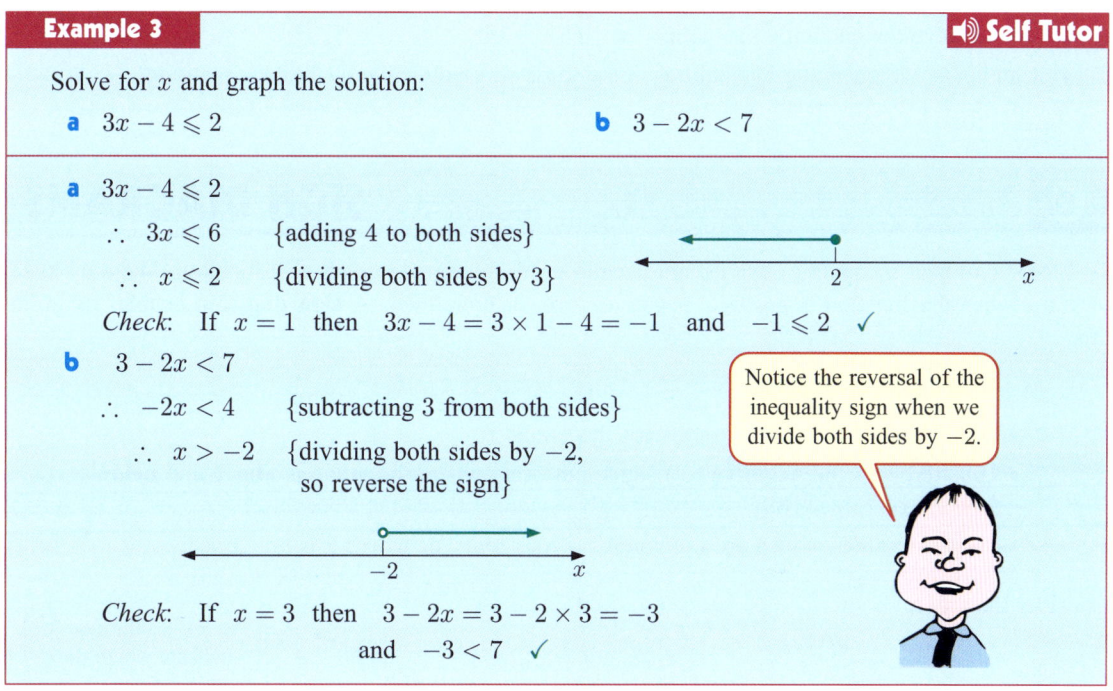

a $3x - 4 \leqslant 2$
  $\therefore \ 3x \leqslant 6$ {adding 4 to both sides}
  $\therefore \ x \leqslant 2$ {dividing both sides by 3}

Check: If $x = 1$ then $3x - 4 = 3 \times 1 - 4 = -1$ and $-1 \leqslant 2$ ✓

b $3 - 2x < 7$
  $\therefore \ -2x < 4$ {subtracting 3 from both sides}
  $\therefore \ x > -2$ {dividing both sides by -2, so reverse the sign}

> Notice the reversal of the inequality sign when we divide both sides by -2.

Check: If $x = 3$ then $3 - 2x = 3 - 2 \times 3 = -3$ and $-3 < 7$ ✓

EXERCISE 22B

1 Solve for x and graph the solution:

   a $3x + 2 < 0$ **b** $5x - 7 > 2$ **c** $2 - 3x \geqslant 1$
   d $5 - 2x \leqslant 11$ **e** $2(3x - 1) < 4$ **f** $5(1 - 3x) \geqslant 8$

2 Solve for x and graph the solution:

   a $7 \geqslant 2x - 1$ **b** $-13 < 3x + 2$ **c** $20 > -5x$
   d $-3 \geqslant 4 - 3x$ **e** $3 < 5 - 2x$ **f** $2 \leqslant 5(1 - x)$

Example 4

Solve for x and graph the solution: $3 - 5x \geqslant 2x + 7$

$3 - 5x \geqslant 2x + 7$
$\therefore \ 3 - 7x \geqslant 7$ {subtracting $2x$ from both sides}
$\therefore \ -7x \geqslant 4$ {subtracting 3 from both sides}
$\therefore \ x \leqslant -\frac{4}{7}$ {dividing both sides by -7, so reverse the sign}

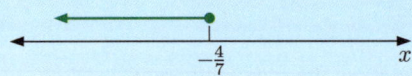

3 Solve for x and graph the solution:

a $3x + 2 > x - 5$ **b** $2x - 3 < 5x - 7$ **c** $5 - 2x \geqslant x + 4$
d $7 - 3x \leqslant 5 - x$ **e** $3x - 2 > 2(x - 1) + 5x$ **f** $1 - (x - 3) \geqslant 2(x + 5) - 1$

DISCUSSION

- Try to solve the quadratic inequality $x^2 + 5x < 14$.
- Can you solve quadratic inequalities in the same way you solve quadratic equations?

C   SIGN DIAGRAMS

To solve non-linear inequalities, we do not usually need a complete graph of a function. We only need to know when the function is positive, negative, zero, or undefined. A **sign diagram** enables us to do this.

A sign diagram consists of:
- a **horizontal line** which represents the x-axis
- **positive** $(+)$ and **negative** $(-)$ signs indicating where the graph is **above** and **below** the x-axis respectively
- **critical values**, which are the graph's x-intercepts, or where it is undefined.

Consider the graph:

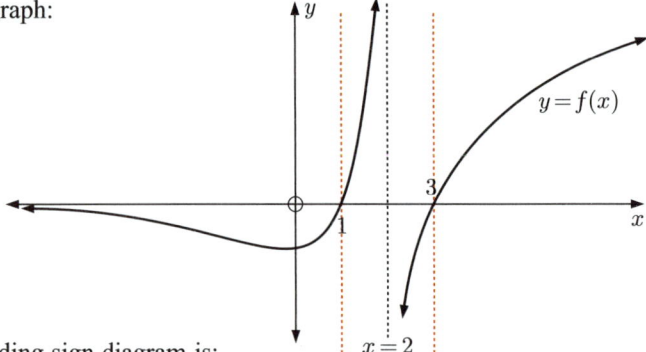

We use a solid line to indicate where the function is zero, and a dashed line to indicate where the function is undefined.

The corresponding sign diagram is:

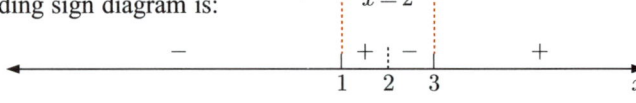

Further examples are:

Function	$y = (x+2)(x-1)$	$y = -2(x-1)^2$	$y = \dfrac{4}{x}$
Graph			
Sign diagram			

Notice that:

- A sign change occurs about the critical value for single factors such as $(x+2)$ and $(x-1)$, indicating **cutting** of the x-axis.
- No sign change occurs about the critical value for squared factors such as $(x-1)^2$, indicating **touching** of the x-axis.

Example 5 ◀)) Self Tutor

Draw a sign diagram for:

a $(x+5)(x-2)$ **b** $3(2x+1)(4-x)$

a $(x+5)(x-2)$ has critical values -5 and 2.

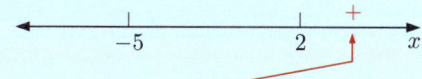

We try any number > 2:
When $x = 10$,
$(x+5)(x-2) = 15 \times 8 > 0$.

The factors are single so the signs alternate.
The sign diagram is

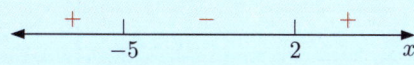

b $3(2x+1)(4-x)$ has critical values $-\tfrac{1}{2}$ and 4.

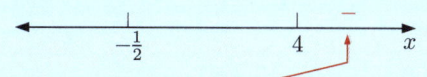

When $x = 10$,
$3(2x+1)(4-x) = 3 \times 21 \times -6 < 0$.

The factors are single so the signs alternate.
The sign diagram is

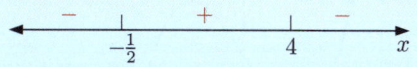

Example 6

Draw a sign diagram for:

a $-(x+2)^2$

b $\dfrac{x-3}{x+1}$

a $-(x+2)^2$ has critical value -2.

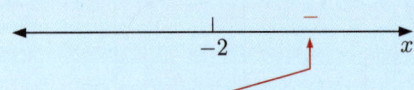

When $x = 10$, $-(x+2)^2 = -12^2 < 0$.

A squared factor indicates no change of sign about the critical value.
The sign diagram is

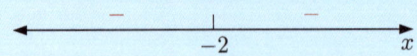

b $\dfrac{x-3}{x+1}$ is zero when $x = 3$ and undefined when $x = -1$.

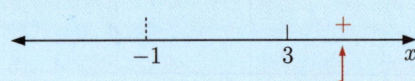

When $x = 10$, $\dfrac{x-3}{x+1} = \dfrac{7}{11} > 0$

Since $(x-3)$ and $(x+1)$ are single factors, the signs alternate.
The sign diagram is

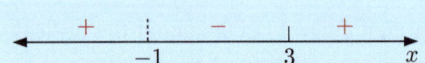

EXERCISE 22C

1 Draw a sign diagram for these graphs:

a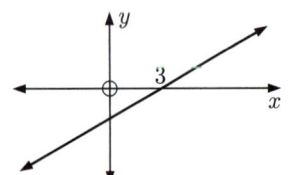

b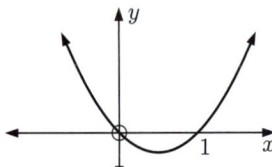

c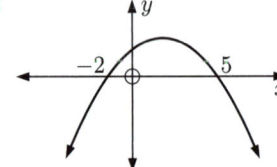

d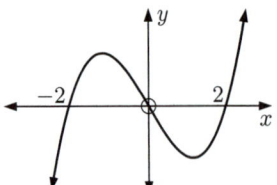

e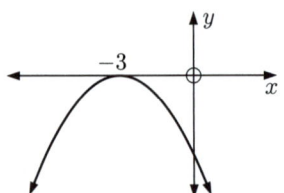

f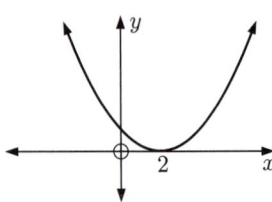

g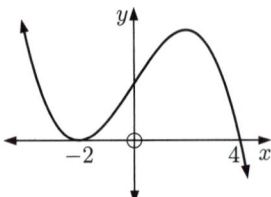

h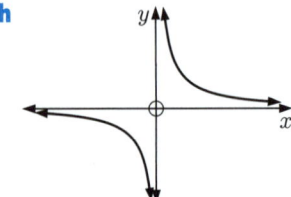

i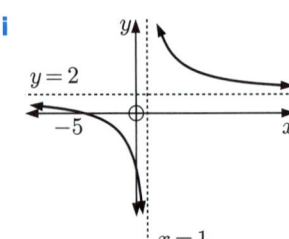

2 Draw a sign diagram for:

   a $(x+3)(x-1)$ **b** $x(x-4)$ **c** $x(x+5)$

   d $-(x+2)(x-3)$ **e** $(3x-1)(4-x)$ **f** $(3-x)(1-2x)$

   g $x^2 - 16$ **h** $1 - x^2$ **i** $2x - x^2$

   j $x^2 - 4x + 3$ **k** $2 - 18x^2$ **l** $-x^2 + 2x + 24$

   m $3x^2 - 8x - 3$ **n** $2 - 2x - 4x^2$ **o** $-10x^2 + 9x + 9$

3 Draw a sign diagram for:

   a $(x-1)^2$ **b** $(x+4)^2$ **c** $-(x+3)^2$

   d $-(x-2)^2$ **e** $(3x-1)^2$ **f** $x^2 - 6x + 9$

   g $-x^2 - 4x - 4$ **h** $-x^2 + 2x - 1$ **i** $-4x^2 - 4x - 1$

4 Draw a sign diagram for:

   a $\dfrac{x+1}{x-2}$ **b** $\dfrac{x-1}{x}$ **c** $\dfrac{2x+5}{2-x}$

   d $\dfrac{3x-1}{4-x}$ **e** $\dfrac{x+4}{3x-2}$ **f** $\dfrac{2x}{1-x}$

   g $\dfrac{(x-2)^2}{x+1}$ **h** $\dfrac{3x}{(x+3)^2}$ **i** $\dfrac{x(x+2)}{4-x}$

   j $\dfrac{(x-3)(x+4)}{2-x}$ **k** $\dfrac{5-x}{x^2-x-2}$ **l** $\dfrac{x^2-1}{-x}$

   m $\dfrac{x^2+2x-3}{x+1}$ **n** $\dfrac{x^2+1}{x^2-2x+1}$ **o** $\dfrac{x^2-6x+9}{2x^2-x-3}$

Example 7

Given the sign diagram alongside, use interval notation to describe where the function is:

   a > 0 **b** $\geqslant 0$

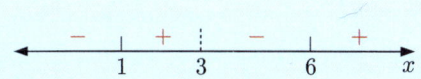

a The function is > 0 where $1 < x < 3$ or $x > 6$ which is $\{x \mid 1 < x < 3 \text{ or } x > 6\}$.

b The function is $\geqslant 0$ where $1 \leqslant x < 3$ or $x \geqslant 6$.

       We do not include 3 here because the function is undefined at $x = 3$.

Using interval notation, this is $\{x \mid 1 \leqslant x < 3 \text{ or } x \geqslant 6\}$.

5 Use interval notation to describe where the functions with these sign diagrams are:

   i > 0 **ii** $\geqslant 0$ **iii** < 0 **iv** $\leqslant 0$.

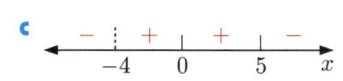

D NON-LINEAR INEQUALITIES

To solve non-linear inequalities, we use the following procedure:

- Make the RHS zero by shifting all terms to the LHS.
- Fully factorise the LHS.
- Draw a sign diagram for the LHS.
- Determine the values required from the sign diagram.

Example 8

Solve for x:

a $x^2 + 5x < 14$ **b** $x^2 + 4 \geqslant -4x$

a $\quad x^2 + 5x < 14$
$\therefore \ x^2 + 5x - 14 < 0 \quad$ {making RHS zero}
$\therefore \ (x + 7)(x - 2) < 0 \quad$ {fully factorising LHS}

Sign diagram of LHS is: $\quad \overset{+}{\underset{-7}{\mid}} \quad \overset{-}{} \quad \overset{+}{\underset{2}{\mid}} \longrightarrow x$

The inequality is true for $-7 < x < 2$.

b $\quad x^2 + 4 \geqslant -4x$
$\therefore \ x^2 + 4x + 4 \geqslant 0 \quad$ {making RHS zero}
$\therefore \ (x + 2)^2 \geqslant 0 \quad$ {fully factorising LHS}

Sign diagram of LHS is: $\quad \overset{+}{} \underset{-2}{\mid} \overset{+}{} \longrightarrow x$

The LHS is always $\geqslant 0$, so the inequality is true for all real x.

EXERCISE 22D

1 a Draw a sign diagram for $x^2 + x - 6$.

b Hence, solve for x:

    i $x^2 + x - 6 > 0$ **ii** $x^2 + x - 6 \geqslant 0$ **iii** $x^2 + x - 6 < 0$ **iv** $x^2 + x - 6 \leqslant 0$

2 Solve for x:

a $(x-1)(x-3) \leqslant 0$ **b** $(2x+3)(4-x) > 0$ **c** $(x+1)(x-2) > 0$

d $(x+5)^2 < 0$ **e** $x^2 - 2x \geqslant 0$ **f** $4x^2 + 2x < 0$

g $x^2 < 16$ **h** $3x^2 \leqslant 12$ **i** $x^2 + 4x - 5 > 0$

j $x^2 \leqslant x + 2$ **k** $x^2 - 4x + 4 < 0$ **l** $x^2 + 3x \leqslant 28$

m $3x^2 - 6x + 3 > 0$ **n** $2x^2 - 5 \leqslant 3x$ **o** $3x^2 \geqslant 2(x+4)$

p $4 < 5x^2 + 8x$ **q** $6(x^2 + 2) < 17x$ **r** $9x^2 \leqslant 12x - 4$

Example 9

Solve for x: **a** $\dfrac{3x+2}{x-4} \leqslant 1$ **b** $\dfrac{1}{x} \leqslant 10$

a
$$\dfrac{3x+2}{x-4} \leqslant 1$$
$$\therefore \dfrac{3x+2}{x-4} - 1 \leqslant 0$$
$$\therefore \dfrac{3x+2}{x-4} - 1\left(\dfrac{x-4}{x-4}\right) \leqslant 0$$
$$\therefore \dfrac{3x+2-(x-4)}{x-4} \leqslant 0$$
$$\therefore \dfrac{2x+6}{x-4} \leqslant 0$$

Sign diagram of LHS is

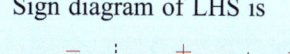

$\therefore -3 \leqslant x < 4$

b
$$\dfrac{1}{x} \leqslant 10$$
$$\therefore \dfrac{1}{x} - 10 \leqslant 0$$
$$\therefore \dfrac{1}{x} - 10\left(\dfrac{x}{x}\right) \leqslant 0$$
$$\therefore \dfrac{1-10x}{x} \leqslant 0$$

Sign diagram of LHS is

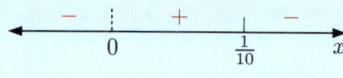

$\therefore x < 0$ or $x \geqslant \dfrac{1}{10}$

---

3 Solve for x:

a $\dfrac{x+2}{x-3} < 0$ **b** $\dfrac{x+3}{2-x} < 0$ **c** $\dfrac{x+4}{2x-1} \geqslant 0$ **d** $\dfrac{x-3}{2x} \leqslant 0$

e $\dfrac{x^2-4x}{x+3} > 0$ **f** $\dfrac{x}{x^2-1} \leqslant 0$ **g** $\dfrac{x-1}{x+3} \geqslant -1$ **h** $\dfrac{x+2}{2x-3} < 1$

i $\dfrac{1}{x} > 3$ **j** $\dfrac{x}{3x+1} \geqslant -2$ **k** $\dfrac{5-2x}{1-x} > 4$ **l** $\dfrac{4}{x} \leqslant x$

4 Find the domain of these functions:

a $f(x) = \sqrt{x(x-2)}$ **b** $f(x) = \sqrt{x^2-3x}$ **c** $f(x) = \sqrt{(x+1)(x-3)}$

d $f(x) = \dfrac{1}{\sqrt{x^2+x-2}}$ **e** $f(x) = \sqrt{\dfrac{x+3}{x-1}}$ **f** $f(x) = \sqrt{\dfrac{x+5}{x^2-4}}$

GRAPHING PACKAGE

Check your answers using the graphing package.

5 Find the values of m for which the quadratic function $f(x) = mx^2 + [m+3]x - 1$:

a does not cut the x-axis   **b** touches the x-axis   **c** cuts the x-axis twice.

REVIEW SET 22A

1 Draw a number line graph to display:

a $\{x \mid x > -3\}$ **b** $\{x \mid 5 \leqslant x < 10\}$ **c** $]0, 9]$

2 Solve for x and graph the solution:

a $5x - 11 > -7$ **b** $9 \leqslant 4 - 2x$

3 Solve for x:

a $4x - 1 > x + 9$ **b** $5(1-x) \leqslant 4(x+3)$

4 Draw a sign diagram for:

a $(x+4)(x-1)$ b $-x^2+2x+15$ c $\dfrac{2x-1}{(x-4)^2}$

5 Describe where the function with sign diagram alongside is:

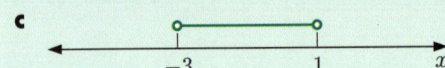

a >0 b $\geqslant 0$ c <0 d $\leqslant 0$

6 Solve for x:

a $(x+2)(x+6)<0$ b $x^2+5x \geqslant 36$ c $2x^2-15<7x$

7 Solve for x:

a $\dfrac{x+4}{x}<0$ b $\dfrac{(x-1)^2}{x+2} \geqslant 0$ c $\dfrac{3-x}{x+1}>2$

8 Solve the inequality in the **Opening Problem** on page **482**.

REVIEW SET 22B

1 Write these number sets using square bracket notation:

a $\{x \mid -2 \leqslant x < 8\}$ b $\{x \mid x \leqslant 1 \text{ or } 4 < x \leqslant 5\}$

c 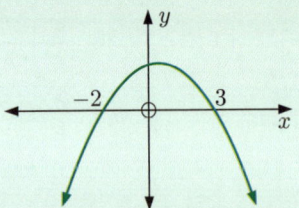   d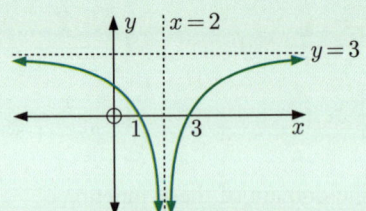

2 Draw a sign diagram for each graph:

a

b

3 Solve for x, and graph the solution:

a $3(2x+1)>4$ b $40 \leqslant 7-3x$

4 Draw a sign diagram for:

a $-x(x+9)$ b $2x^2-16x+32$ c $\dfrac{x^2+x-12}{x-1}$

5 Solve for x:

a $7x-2 \geqslant 2(x+3)$ b $-x^2-2x+35>0$ c $\dfrac{x+3}{2-x}<0$

6 Describe where the function with sign diagram alongside is:

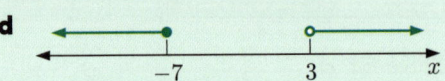

a >0 b $\geqslant 0$ c <0 d $\leqslant 0$

7 Solve for x:

a $(x+5)(6-x) \leqslant 0$ b $\dfrac{5}{x}>-1$ c $\dfrac{2x-3}{x+1}<4$

8 Find the domain of these functions:

a $f(x)=\sqrt{x(x-4)}$ b $f(x)=\dfrac{1}{\sqrt{3x^2+5x-2}}$

Chapter 23
Bivariate statistics

Contents:
- **A** Scatter plots
- **B** Correlation
- **C** Measuring correlation
- **D** Line of best fit

OPENING PROBLEM

The relationship between the *height* and *weight* of members of a football team is to be investigated. The raw data for each player is given below, with heights in cm and weights in kg.

Player	Height	Weight
1	203	106
2	189	93
3	193	95
4	187	86
5	186	85
6	197	92

Player	Height	Weight
7	180	78
8	186	84
9	188	93
10	181	84
11	179	86
12	191	92

Player	Height	Weight
13	178	80
14	178	77
15	186	90
16	190	86
17	189	95
18	193	89

Things to think about:

a Which is the *dependent* variable?

b How could we display this data?

c Does an increase in the *height* of a player generally cause an increase or a decrease in their *weight*?

d How can we indicate the strength of the linear relationship between the variables?

e How can we use this data to estimate the weight of a player who is 200 cm tall? How reliable will this estimate be?

We often want to know how two variables are **associated** or **related**. We want to know whether an increase in one variable results in an increase or a decrease in the other. We call this **bivariate statistics** because we are dealing with *two* variables.

To analyse the relationship between two variables, we first need to decide which is the **dependent** variable and which is the **independent** variable. The value of the dependent variable *depends* on the value of the independent variable.

Having made this decision, we can then draw a **scatter plot** to display the data. The independent variable is placed on the horizontal axis, and the dependent variable is placed on the vertical axis.

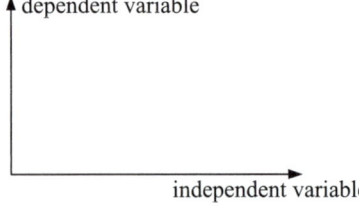

A SCATTER PLOTS

In the **Opening Problem**, we measured the *height* and *weight* of each football player.

We suspect that the weight of a footballer is dependent on his height, so we place height on the horizontal axis and weight on the vertical axis.

The data from each individual footballer is then displayed as a point on the scatter plot.

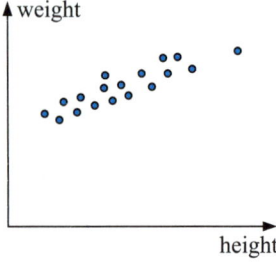

Example 1   🔊 Self Tutor

This scatter plot shows the ages and work done by 5 employees.

a Which person is the oldest?
b Who has done the most work?
c Who has done the least work?

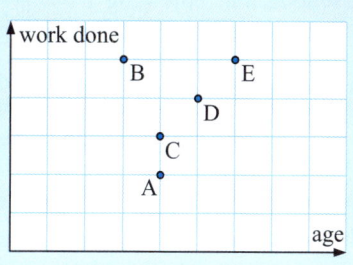

a E has the largest value on the *age* axis.
   ∴ E is the oldest.
b B and E have the highest values on the *work done* axis.
   ∴ B and E have done the most work.
c A has the lowest value on the *work done* axis.
   ∴ A has done the least work.

EXERCISE 23A

1 Liesl measured the height and weight of eight objects in her room. The results are shown in the scatter plot alongside.

  a Which object is the lightest?
  b Which object is the tallest?
  c Which two objects are the same height?

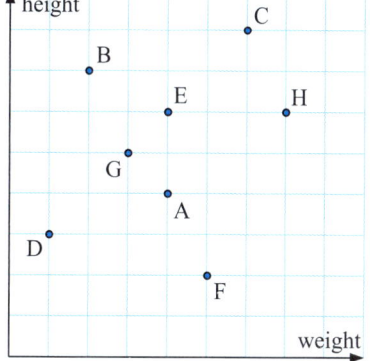

2 This scatter plot shows the productivity of five employees, and the number of hours of training they have received.

  a Who has received the most hours of training?
  b Who is the least productive?
  c Are there employees with equal productivity?
  d Do you think that the training given to the employees has been worthwhile? Explain your answer.

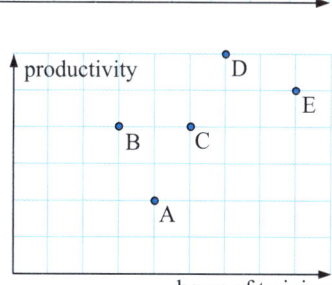

3 Peter's soccer team played seven games during an end-of-season carnival. The results of the games are displayed in the scatter plot.

  a In which game did the team score the most goals?
  b In which game did the team concede the least goals?
  c How many of the games ended in a draw?
  d How many games did Peter's team win?

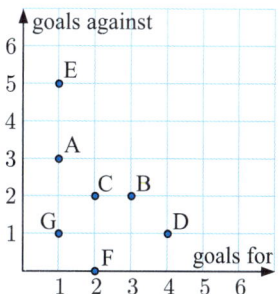

4 Six students were asked how far they lived from school, and how long it took them to travel to school. The results are shown in the table.

Student	P	Q	R	S	T	U
Distance to school (km)	8	5	2	12	6	4
Travel time (min)	10	5	20	15	15	7

    a Draw a scatter plot to display the data, with *distance* on the horizontal axis.
    b Which student lives furthest from the school?
    c Which student took the least time to travel to school?
    d One of the students walks to school. Which student do you think it is? Explain your answer.

In this case time is the *dependent* variable because the *travel time* depends on the *distance to school*.

B   CORRELATION

Correlation is a measure of the strength of the relationship or association between two variables.

We can use a scatter plot to describe the correlation between two variables.

Step 1: Look at the scatter plot for any **pattern**.

For a generally *upward* shape, we say that the correlation is **positive**.

As the independent variable increases, the dependent variable generally increases.

For a generally *downward* shape, we say that the correlation is **negative**.

As the independent variable increases, the dependent variable generally decreases.

For *randomly scattered* points with no upward or downward trend, we say there is **no correlation**.

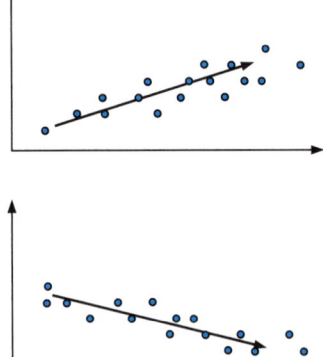

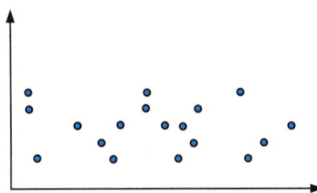

Step 2: Look at the spread of points to make a judgement about the **strength** of the correlation.
These scatter plots show strength classifications for positive relationships:

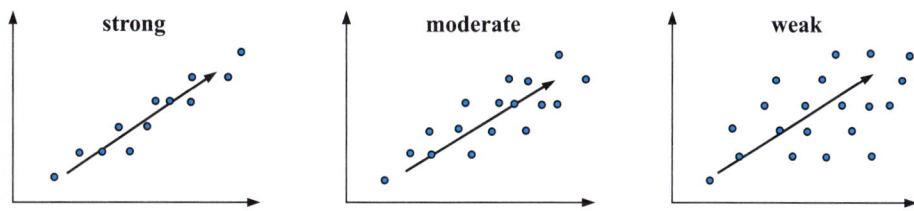

These scatter plots show strength classifications for negative relationships:

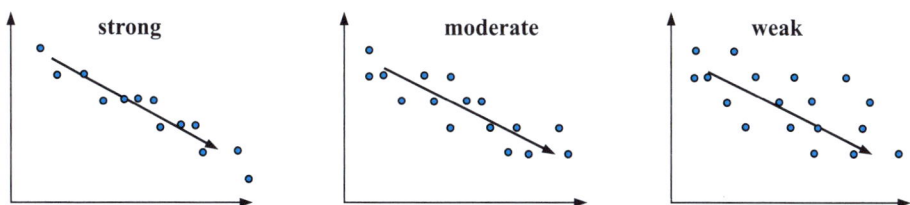

Step 3: Look at the pattern of points to see if the relationship is **linear**.

Example 2 ◀) Self Tutor

Alexander researched the elevation above sea level and mean annual temperature of 12 cities around the world. The results are given in this table.

Elevation (m)	600	850	150	300	100	200	500	450	750	30	300	50
Mean annual temperature (°C)	15	10	16	15	25	20	21	19	9	27	22	28

a Draw a scatter plot of the data.
b Describe the relationship between *elevation* and *mean temperature*.

a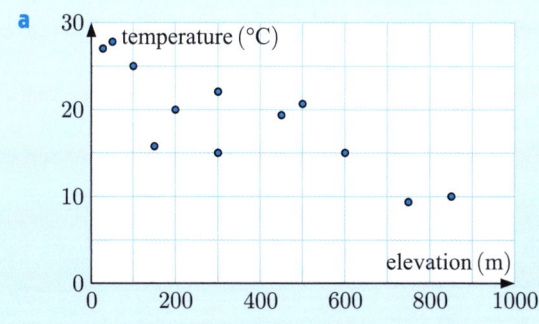

b There appears to be a moderate negative linear correlation between *elevation* and *mean temperature*.

What factors other than elevation affect the mean annual temperature of a city?

EXERCISE 23B

1. For each of the scatter plots below:
   i state whether there is positive, negative, or no association between the variables
   ii decide whether the relationship between the variables appears to be linear
   iii describe the strength of the association (zero, weak, moderate, or strong).

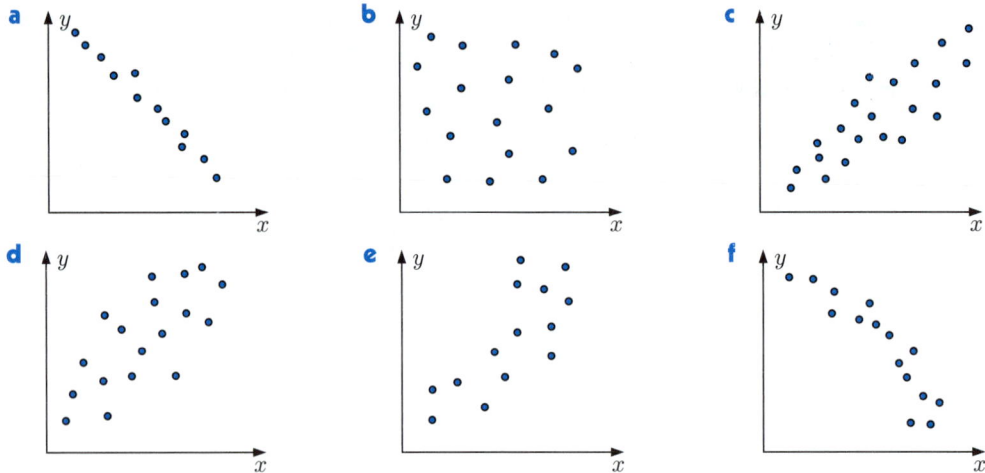

2. Copy and complete the following:
   a If there is a positive association between x and y, then as x increases, y ......
   b If there is a negative correlation between T and d, then as T increases, d ......
   c If there is no association between two variables then the points on the scatter plot are ....

3. A class of 15 students was asked how many text messages they had sent and received in the last week. The results are shown below:

Student	A	B	C	D	E	F	G	H	I	J	K	L	M	N	O
Messages sent	5	0	12	9	17	15	10	4	8	18	25	17	0	6	13
Messages received	8	0	15	7	19	11	8	7	12	15	21	16	4	6	16

   a Draw a scatter plot of the data.
   b Describe the relationship between *messages sent* and *messages received*.

4. a 10 students were asked for their exam marks in Physics and Mathematics. Their percentages are given in the table below.

Student	A	B	C	D	E	F	G	H	I	J
Physics	75	83	45	90	70	78	88	50	55	95
Maths	68	70	50	65	60	72	75	40	45	80

   i Draw a scatter plot of the data, with the Physics marks on the horizontal axis.
   ii Comment on the relationship between the Physics and Mathematics marks.

b The same students were asked for their Art exam results. Their percentages were:

Student	A	B	C	D	E	F	G	H	I	J
Art	75	70	80	85	82	70	60	75	78	65

Draw a scatter plot to see if there is any relationship between the Physics marks and the Art marks of each student.

5 The following table shows the sales of hot drinks in a popular cafe each month, along with the average daily temperature for the month.

Month	Jan	Feb	Mar	Apr	May	Jun	Jul	Aug	Sep	Oct	Nov	Dec
Temp (°C)	32	29	26	23	19	16	12	15	18	22	25	29
Sales ($ × 1000)	12	8	10	15	16	18	22	25	20	15	16	12

a Draw a scatter plot of the data, with the independent variable *temperature* along the horizontal axis.

b Comment on the relationship between the sales and the temperature.

C   MEASURING CORRELATION

Simple observation of the points on a scatter plot is a fairly inaccurate way to describe the strength of correlation between two variables. Instead, we can calculate **Pearson's correlation coefficient**. This gives us a numerical value between -1 and 1 which measures the strength of correlation between two variables.

> Consider a set of n data given as ordered pairs (x_1, y_1), (x_2, y_2), (x_3, y_3), ..., (x_n, y_n), where $\overline{x}$ and $\overline{y}$ are the means of the x and y data respectively.
>
> **Pearson's correlation coefficient** is $r = \dfrac{\sum(x - \overline{x})(y - \overline{y})}{\sqrt{\sum(x - \overline{x})^2 \sum(y - \overline{y})^2}}$
>
> where $\sum$ indicates the sum over all the data values.

You are not required to learn this formula, since we usually use technology to find the value of r.

The values of r range from -1 to $+1$.

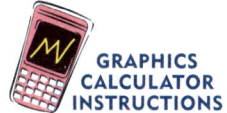
GRAPHICS CALCULATOR INSTRUCTIONS

> The **sign** of r indicates the **direction** of the correlation.

- A positive value for r indicates the variables are **positively correlated**.
  An increase in one of the variables will result in an increase in the other.
- A negative value for r indicates the variables are **negatively correlated**.
  An increase in one of the variables will result in a decrease in the other.

> The **size** of r indicates the **strength** of the correlation.

- A value of r close to $+1$ or -1 indicates strong correlation between the variables.
- A value of r close to zero indicates weak correlation between the variables.

Some examples of scatter plots with their corresponding values of r are given below.

POSITIVE CORRELATION

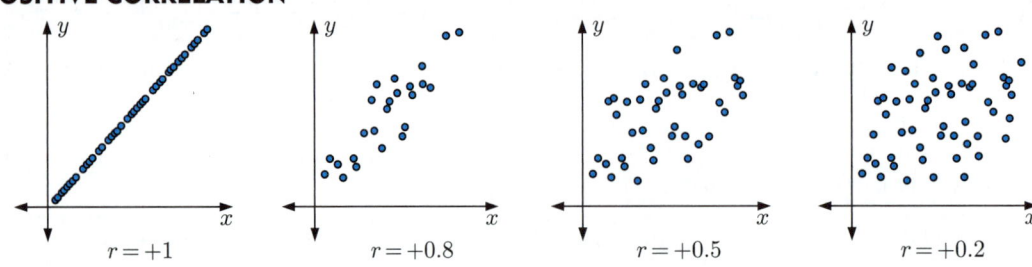

NEGATIVE CORRELATION

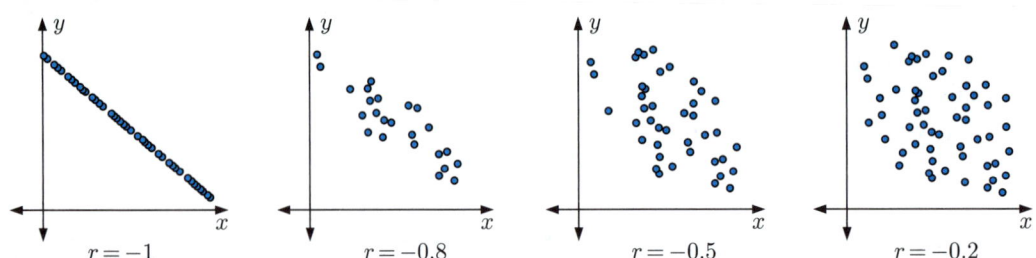

Example 3

Four students were asked how many children and pets were in their household. The results are shown in the table alongside.

Student	A	B	C	D
Number of children	1	4	2	1
Number of pets	1	6	3	2

a Draw a scatter plot for the data.
b Find the correlation coefficient r *without* using technology.
c Is the data positively correlated or negatively correlated?
d Describe the strength of the correlation between the variables.

a [scatter plot: number of pets vs number of children, points at (1,1), (1,2), (2,3), (4,6)]

b $\bar{x} = \dfrac{1+4+2+1}{4} = 2$ $\bar{y} = \dfrac{1+6+3+2}{4} = 3$

x	y	$x-\bar{x}$	$y-\bar{y}$	$(x-\bar{x})(y-\bar{y})$	$(x-\bar{x})^2$	$(y-\bar{y})^2$
1	1	-1	-2	2	1	4
4	6	2	3	6	4	9
2	3	0	0	0	0	0
1	2	-1	-1	1	1	1
			Total	9	6	14

$$r = \dfrac{\sum(x-\bar{x})(y-\bar{y})}{\sqrt{\sum(x-\bar{x})^2 \sum(y-\bar{y})^2}} = \dfrac{9}{\sqrt{6 \times 14}} \approx 0.982$$

c $r > 0$, so the data is positively correlated.
d r is close to 1, indicating a very strong correlation between the variables.

COEFFICIENT OF DETERMINATION r^2

Another commonly used statistic which describes the strength of the association between two variables is the square of Pearson's correlation coefficient r.

This value, r^2, is known as the **coefficient of determination**. Since $-1 \leqslant r \leqslant 1$, $0 \leqslant r^2 \leqslant 1$.

The following table is a guide for describing the strength of linear correlation using the coefficient of determination:

Value	Strength of correlation
$r^2 = 0$	no correlation
$0 < r^2 < 0.25$	very weak correlation
$0.25 \leqslant r^2 < 0.50$	weak correlation
$0.50 \leqslant r^2 < 0.75$	moderate correlation
$0.75 \leqslant r^2 < 0.90$	strong correlation
$0.90 \leqslant r^2 < 1$	very strong correlation
$r^2 = 1$	perfect correlation

Since $r^2 \geqslant 0$, it does not show the *direction* of correlation.

Example 4

At a father-son camp, the heights of the fathers and their sons were measured.

Father's height (cm)	175	183	170	167	179	180	183	185	170	181	185
Son's height (cm)	167	178	158	162	171	167	180	177	152	164	172

a Draw a scatter plot of the data.

b Calculate the coefficient of determination r^2 for the data, and interpret its value.

a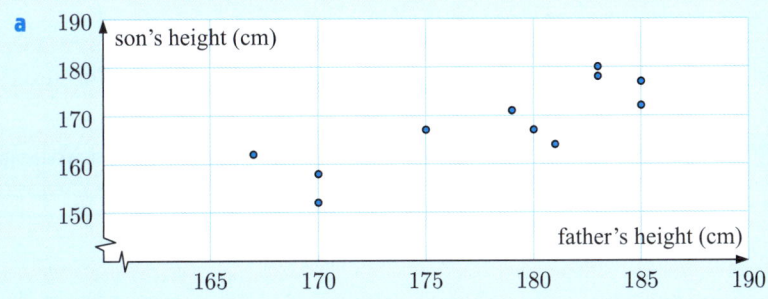

b Using technology, $r^2 \approx 0.683$.

GRAPHICS CALCULATOR INSTRUCTIONS

Casio fx-CG20   **TI-84 Plus**   **TI-*n*spire**

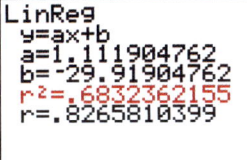
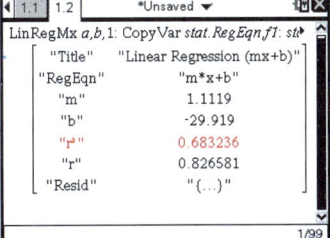

There is a moderate positive correlation between the *father's height* and the *son's height*.

EXERCISE 23C

1 The correlation coefficient for a set of bivariate data is $r \approx 0.812$.
   a Are the variables positively correlated or negatively correlated? Explain your answer.
   b Find the coefficient of determination r^2.
   c Describe the strength of the correlation between the variables.

2 Five students each took 10 shots at a netball goal. The table alongside shows how many times each student scored a goal, and how many times they missed.

Student	A	B	C	D	E
Scored	7	5	3	9	6
Missed	3	5	7	1	4

   a Draw a scatter plot of the data.
   b Find r using the formula $r = \dfrac{\sum(x-\overline{x})(y-\overline{y})}{\sqrt{\sum(x-\overline{x})^2 \sum(y-\overline{y})^2}}$.
   c Describe the correlation between the variables. Explain why this must be the case.

3 For each of the following data sets:
   i Draw a scatter plot of the data.
   ii Use technology to find r and r^2.
   iii Describe the linear correlation between X and Y.

   You can use your calculator to draw scatter plots.

   a
X	1	2	3	4	5	6
Y	3	2	5	5	9	6

   b
X	3	8	5	14	19	10	16
Y	17	12	15	6	1	10	4

   c
X	3	6	11	7	5	6	8	10	4
Y	2	8	8	4	7	9	11	1	5

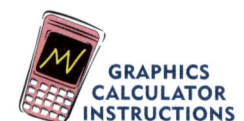

GRAPHICS CALCULATOR INSTRUCTIONS

4 Students were asked to measure their height in centimetres and their shoe size. The results are recorded in the table below:

Height (cm)	165	155	140	145	158	148	160	164	160	155	150	160
Shoe size	6.5	4.5	4	5.5	6	5.5	6	5.5	5.5	5	5	5.5

   a Construct a scatter plot of the data.
   b Calculate r and r^2.
   c Describe the relationship between height and shoe size.

5 The scores awarded by two judges at a diving competition are shown in the table.

Competitor	P	Q	R	S	T	U	V	W	X	Y
Judge A	5	6.5	8	9	4	2.5	7	5	6	3
Judge B	6	7	8.5	9	5	4	7.5	5	7	4.5

   a Construct a scatter plot of the data, with Judge A's scores on the horizontal axis, and Judge B's scores on the vertical axis.
   b Calculate r and r^2.
   c Describe the correlation between the judges' scores.

6 A basketballer takes 20 shots from each of ten different positions marked on the court. The table below shows how far each position is from the goal, and how many shots were successful:

Position	A	B	C	D	E	F	G	H	I	J
Distance from goal (m)	2	5	3.5	6.2	4.5	1.5	7	4.1	3	5.6
Successful shots	17	6	10	5	8	18	6	8	13	9

    a Draw a scatter plot of the data.
    b Will r be positive or negative?
    c Calculate r and r^2.
    d Describe the correlation between these variables.

7 Jane wanted to see whether there was any correlation between the length of a movie, and its performance at the box office. She selected 10 movies, and recorded their lengths and box office takings.

Length (min)	107	122	92	103	96	161	121	178	95	135
Takings ($ × 1 m)	100	336	47	1063	363	190	164	871	543	313

    a Draw a scatter plot of the data.
    b Does there appear to be a strong correlation between the variables? Explain your answer.
    c Calculate r and r^2.
    d Describe the relationship between the variables.

ACTIVITY — WHAT'S IN A NAME?

Do people with long surnames generally have long first names as well?

In this Activity we will investigate whether there is a relationship between the length of a person's first name and surname.

What to do:

1. Count the number of letters in your first name and surname.
2. As a class, predict the nature of the correlation between the *lengths of first names* and the *lengths of surnames*.
3. Use the names of each student in your class to create a scatter plot. Which is the independent variable?
4. Calculate r and r^2.
5. Describe the correlation between the *lengths of first names* and the *lengths of surnames*.

D   LINE OF BEST FIT

If there is a strong linear correlation between two variables x and y, then it is reasonable to draw a **line of best fit** through the data.

We can find the line of best fit:
- by eye
- using linear regression.

The line of best fit can be used to estimate y for any x.

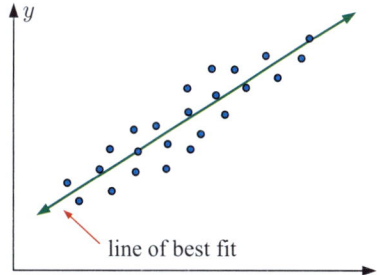
line of best fit

LINE OF BEST FIT BY EYE

For a bivariate data set involving x and y, we use these steps to find the line of best fit by eye:

Step 1: Find the means $\bar{x}$ and $\bar{y}$ of the x and y values respectively.

Step 2: Plot the **mean point** $(\bar{x}, \bar{y})$ on a scatter plot of the data.

Step 3: Draw a line through the mean point which fits the trend of the data and which has about as many points above the line as below it.

Example 5

On a hot day, six cars were left in the sun in a car park. The length of time each car was left in the sun was recorded, as well as the temperature inside the car at the end of the period.

Car	A	B	C	D	E	F
Time x (min)	50	5	25	40	15	45
Temperature y (°C)	47	28	36	42	34	41

a Calculate $\bar{x}$ and $\bar{y}$.

b Draw a scatter plot of the data.

c Plot the mean point $(\bar{x}, \bar{y})$ on the scatter plot. Draw a line of best fit through this point.

d Predict the temperature of a car which has been left in the sun for:

  i 35 minutes **ii** 75 minutes.

a $\bar{x} = \dfrac{50 + 5 + 25 + 40 + 15 + 45}{6} = 30$, $\quad \bar{y} = \dfrac{47 + 28 + 36 + 42 + 34 + 41}{6} = 38$

b, c

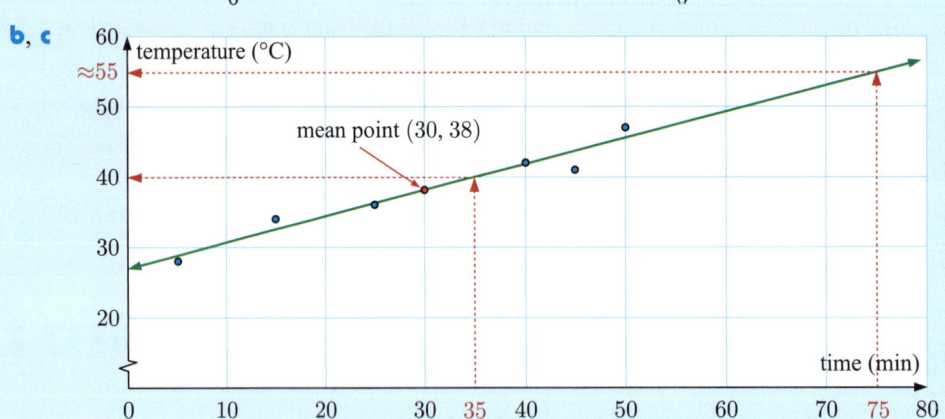

d **i** When $x = 35$, $y \approx 40$.

The temperature of a car left in the sun for 35 minutes will be approximately 40°C.

  ii When $x = 75$, $y \approx 55$.

The temperature of a car left in the sun for 75 minutes will be approximately 55°C.

INTERPOLATION AND EXTRAPOLATION

Given a bivariate data set, the data values with the lowest and highest values of x are called the **poles**.

If we use values of x **in between** the poles to estimate y, we say we are **interpolating** between the poles.

If we use values of x **outside** the poles to estimate y, we say we are **extrapolating** outside the poles.

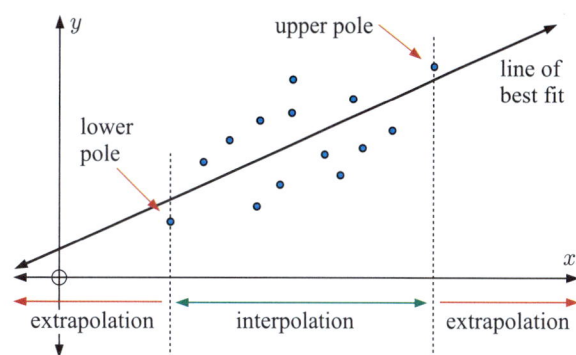

As a general rule, it is reasonable to interpolate between the poles, but unreliable to extrapolate outside them.

In **Example 5** above:

- The estimate in **d i** is an interpolation, so we would expect this estimate to be reliable.
- The estimate in **d ii** is an extrapolation, and therefore may not be reliable. We cannot assume that the linear trend shown in the data will continue up to a time of 75 minutes.

EXERCISE 23D.1

1 Consider the bivariate data alongside.

x	5	10	2	13	6
y	11	3	18	5	13

  a Find $\bar{x}$ and $\bar{y}$.
  b Draw a scatter plot of the data.
  c Does the data appear to be positively correlated or negatively correlated?
  d Plot the mean point $(\bar{x}, \bar{y})$ on the scatter plot, and draw a line of best fit through this point.
  e Estimate the value of y when $x = 8$.

2 The table alongside shows the *percentage of unemployed adults* and the *number of major thefts per day* in eight large cities.

City	Unemployment (%)	Thefts
A	7	113
B	6	67
C	10	117
D	8	88
E	9	120
F	6	38
G	3	61
H	7	76

  a Find the mean unemployment percentage $\bar{x}$ and the mean number of thefts $\bar{y}$.
  b Calculate r for this data.
  c Draw a scatter plot of the data.
  d Plot $(\bar{x}, \bar{y})$ on the scatter plot.
  e Draw the line of best fit on the scatter plot.
  f Another city has 15% unemployment.
    i Estimate the number of major thefts per day for that city.
    ii Comment on the reliability of your estimate.

3 Each month, an opinion poll shows the approval rating of the Prime Minister and the Opposition leader. The approval ratings for the last 10 polls are shown below:

Prime Minister (x%)	55	59	68	61	46	42	38	45	42	44
Opposition (y%)	37	35	31	35	43	40	42	37	41	39

a Calculate $\overline{x}$ and $\overline{y}$.

b Draw a scatter plot of the data. Plot the mean point $(\overline{x}, \overline{y})$ on the scatter plot, and draw a line of best fit through this point.

c In a new opinion poll, the Prime Minister's approval rating is 50%. Estimate the approval rating of the Opposition leader.

4 A café manager believes that during April the *number of people wanting dinner* is related to the *temperature at noon*. Over a 13 day period, the number of diners and the noon temperature were recorded.

Temperature (x °C)	18	20	23	25	25	22	20	23	27	26	28	24	22
Number of diners (y)	63	70	74	81	77	65	75	87	91	75	96	82	88

a Find the mean point $(\overline{x}, \overline{y})$.

b Calculate r^2 for this data, and interpret this value.

c Draw a scatter plot of the data. Plot $(\overline{x}, \overline{y})$ on the scatter plot, and draw a line of best fit through this point.

d Estimate the number of diners at the café when the temperature is:

   i 21°C   **ii** 14°C.

e Comment on the reliability of your estimates in **d**.

LINE OF BEST FIT USING LINEAR REGRESSION

The problem with drawing a line of best fit by eye is that the answer will vary from one person to another, and the line may not be very accurate. Instead, we can use a method called **linear regression**.

> **Linear regression** is a formal method of fitting a line which best fits a set of data.

This line of best fit is called the **least squares regression line**. It is the line which makes the sum of the squares of the distances $d_1^2 + d_2^2 + d_3^2 + ...$ as small as possible.

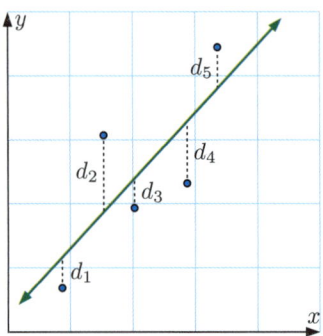

We use a **graphics calculator** or the **statistics package** to find the equation of the least squares regression line.

 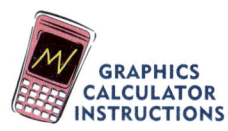

Once we have found the equation of the least squares regression line, we can estimate y for any x by substituting the value of x into the equation.

Example 6

The annual income and average weekly grocery bill for a selection of families is shown below:

Income (x thousand dollars)	55	36	25	47	60	64	42	50
Grocery bill (y dollars)	120	90	60	160	190	250	110	150

a Construct a scatter plot to illustrate the data.
b Use technology to find the least squares regression line.
c Estimate the weekly grocery bill for a family with an annual income of $95\,000$. Comment on whether this estimate is likely to be reliable.

a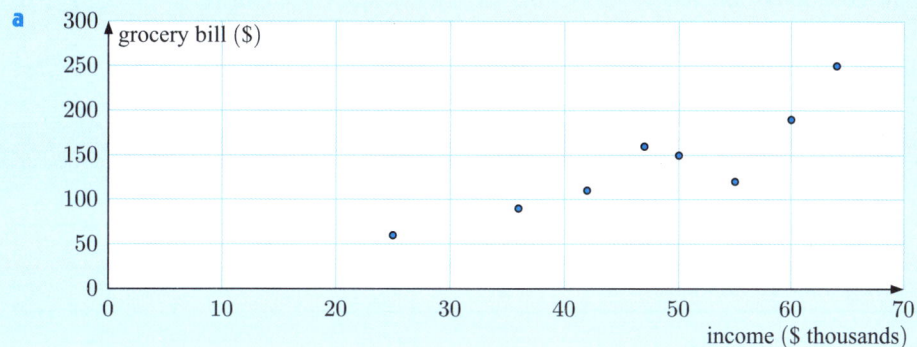

b

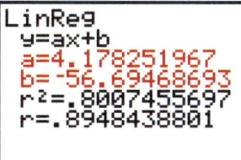 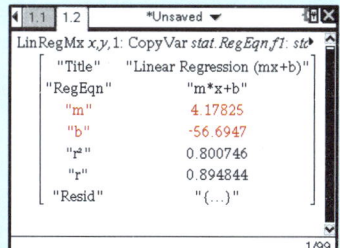

Using technology, the line of best fit is $y \approx 4.18x - 56.7$.

c When $x = 95$, $y \approx 4.18(95) - 56.7 \approx 340$

So, we expect a family with an income of $95\,000$ to have a weekly grocery bill of approximately $340.

This is an extrapolation, however, so the estimate may not be reliable.

EXERCISE 23D.2

1 For each data set:
  i draw a scatter plot of the data
  ii find the equation of the least squares regression line.

a

x	3	5	6	9	13	15	18	20
y	4	8	11	17	15	19	25	24

b

x	16	6	11	8	14	24	2	14	19	6
y	15	30	20	26	17	9	35	10	7	27

2 Tomatoes are sprayed with a pesticide-fertiliser mix. The table below gives the yield of tomatoes per row of bushes for various spray concentrations.

Spray concentration (x mL per 2 L)	2	4	6	8	10	12
Yield of tomatoes per row (y)	45	76	93	105	119	124

a Draw a scatter plot of the data.
b Find the equation of the least squares regression line.
c Interpret the y-intercept of this line.
d Use the equation of the line to predict the yield if the spray concentration was 7 mL.
Comment on whether this prediction is reasonable.

3 A group of friends competed in a fun-run. The table below shows how long each friend spent training, and the time they recorded for the fun-run.

Training time (x hours)	7	2	11	3	7	15	3	0	5	9	0
Fun-run time (y minutes)	60	75	47	70	52	37	72	75	60	62	80

a Draw a scatter plot of the data.
b Find r and r^2.
c Find the equation of the least squares regression line.
d Interpret the gradient of this line.
e Another friend of the group trained for 30 hours.
  i Use the least squares regression line to estimate his fun-run time.
  ii Comment on the reliability of your estimate.

4 The yield of cherries from an orchard each year depends on the number of frosty mornings. The following table shows the yield of cherries from an orchard over several years with different numbers of frosty mornings.

Frosty mornings (n)	18	29	23	38	35	27
Yield (Y tonnes)	29.4	34.6	32.1	36.9	36.1	32.5

a Produce a scatter plot of Y against n.
b Find the linear model which best fits the data.
c Estimate the yield from the orchard if there are 31 frosty mornings in the year.

d Copy and complete:

"The greater the number of frosty mornings, the ...... the yield of cherries."

5 Carbon dioxide (CO_2) is a chemical linked to acid rain and global warming. The concentration of CO_2 in the atmosphere has been recorded over a 40 year period. It is measured in parts per million or ppm found in Law Dome Ice Cores in Antarctica.

Year	1960	1970	1980	1990	2000
CO_2 concentration (ppm)	313	321	329	337	345

Let t be the number of years since 1960 and C be the CO_2 concentration.

a Draw a scatter plot of C against t.
b Describe the correlation between C and t.
c Obtain the linear model which best fits the data.
d Estimate the CO_2 concentration for 1987.
e If CO_2 emission continues at the same rate, estimate the concentration in 2020.

6 Paul researched the first 6 games of the 2012 Twenty20 Cricket World Cup. For the team which batted first, he recorded their score after 10 overs, and their final score.

Score after 10 overs (x)	76	46	68	51	75	74
Final score (y)	182	123	159	93	191	196

a Draw a scatter plot of the data.
b Describe the correlation between the variables.
c Find the equation of the least squares regression line.
d Predict the final score for a team which scores 60 runs in the first 10 overs. How reliable is your prediction?

Global context

click here

What is a dollar worth to you?

Statement of inquiry:	Using a model to represent relationships can help make predictions.
Global context:	Fairness and development
Key concept:	Relationships
Related concepts:	Model, Pattern
Objectives:	Communicating, Applying mathematics in real-life contexts
Approaches to learning:	Communication, Social, Research, Thinking

REVIEW SET 23A

1 The scatter plot shows the number of defective items made by each employee of a factory, plotted against the employee's number of weeks of experience.

Describe the correlation between the variables.

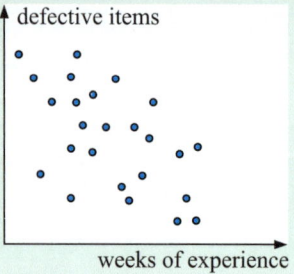

2 Five hockey clubs were surveyed on their players' average hours of general fitness training, and the number of injuries to players during matches.

   a Which club had the lowest number of injuries?

   b Which club's players had the lowest number of hours of fitness training?

   c Write a sentence describing the general trend of the graph.

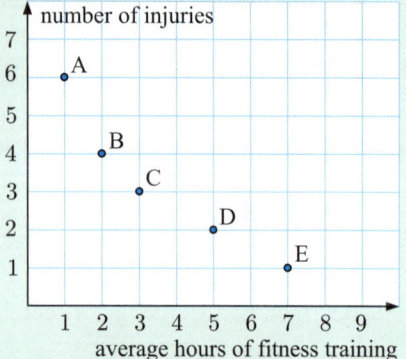

3 Sam and Richard competed in a series of 8 chess games. The table below shows how many pieces remained for each player at the end of each game.

Sam	4	2	6	2	4	1	5	7
Richard	2	1	3	7	4	8	3	5

   a Construct a scatter plot of the data.

   b Calculate r and r^2, and interpret these values.

4 Following an outbreak of the *Ebola* virus, a rare and deadly haemorrhagic fever, medical authorities begin taking records of the number of cases of the fever. Their records are shown below.

Days after outbreak (n)	2	3	4	5	6	7	8	9	10	11
Diagnosed cases (d)	8	14	33	47	80	97	118	123	139	153

   a Produce a scatter plot of d against n.

   b Plot the point $(\overline{n}, \overline{d})$ on the scatter plot, and draw the line of best fit by eye.

   c **i** Use the graph to predict the number of diagnosed cases on day 14.

       ii Is this predicted value reliable? Give reasons for your answer.

5 The whorls on a cone shell get broader as you go from the top of the shell towards the bottom. Measurements from a shell are summarised in the following table:

Position of whorl (p)	1	2	3	4	5	6	7	8
Width of whorl (w cm)	0.7	1.2	1.4	2.0	2.0	2.7	2.9	3.5

    a Obtain a scatter plot of the data.
    b Find Pearson's correlation coefficient for this data.
    c Find the linear regression model which best fits the data.
    d **i** If a cone shell has 14 whorls, what width do you expect the 14th whorl to have?
        ii How reliable is this prediction?

6 The table below shows the number of games won, and the final position on the ladder for the Liverpool football team from 2001-02 to 2012-13:

Games won (x)	24	18	16	17	25	20	21	25	18	17	14	16
Position (y)	2	5	4	5	3	3	4	2	7	6	8	7

    a Would you expect x and y to be positively or negatively correlated? Explain your answer.
    b Draw a scatter plot of the data.
    c Find r and r^2.
    d Use technology to find the equation of the line of best fit.
    e Suppose Liverpool wins 22 games next season. Predict their position on the ladder.

REVIEW SET 23B

1 This scatter plot displays the land area and population of 10 countries.

    a Which country has the smallest population?
    b Which country has the largest area?
    c Which two countries have the same population?
    d Which country is the most densely populated?

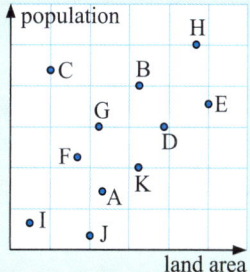

2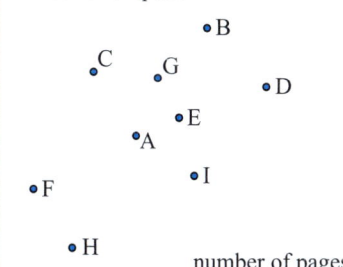

The scatter plot alongside shows the number of pages and chapters in the novels on Rashida's bookshelf.

    a Which book has the:
        i most pages   **ii** least chapters?
    b Copy and complete: As the number of pages increases, the number of chapters generally ......

3 Consider the relationship between a *number* and the *number of factors* it has.
   a Would you expect the correlation between these variables to be:
      i positive or negative
      ii strong, moderate, or weak?
   Explain your answers.
   b Copy and complete this table:

Number (x)	1	2	3	4	5	....	16	17	18	19	20
Number of factors (y)	1	2	2	3		....				2	6

   c Draw a scatter plot of the data.
   d Calculate the correlation coefficient r, and coefficient of determination r^2.
   e Describe the correlation between the variables.

4 Consider the bivariate data alongside.

x	11	7	13	3	12	8
y	17	14	20	5	26	8

   a Find $\overline{x}$ and $\overline{y}$.
   b Draw a scatter plot of the data.
   c Does the data appear to be positively correlated or negatively correlated?
   d Plot the mean point $(\overline{x}, \overline{y})$ on the scatter plot, and draw a line of best fit through this point.
   e Estimate the value of y when $x = 5$. How reliable is this estimate?

5 In a Los Angeles shopping mall, David asked 10 people how many coins they had in their wallet or purse, and the total value of those coins.

Number of coins	5	8	11	7	5	10	2	10	1	12
Value of coins	$1.10	$0.82	$1.56	$0.90	$0.51	$1.54	$0.30	$1.02	$0.10	$1.23

Let n be the number of coins, and v be the value of the coins.
   a Draw a scatter plot of the data.
   b Find the equation of the least squares regression line.
   c Interpret the gradient of this line.
   d Terese has 20 coins in her purse.
      i Estimate the total value of these coins.
      ii How reliable is your prediction?

6 The following table gives peptic ulcer rates per 1000 people for differing family incomes.

Income (I $1000s)	20	25	30	35	40	50	60	80	100
Peptic ulcer rate (R)	8.3	7.7	6.9	7.3	5.9	4.7	3.6	2.6	1.2

   a Draw a scatter plot of the data.
   b Find the equation of the line of best fit for the data.
   c Estimate the peptic ulcer rate in families with an income of $55 000.
   d Explain why the model is inadequate for families with an income in excess of $120 000.
   e Later it is realised that one of the figures was written incorrectly.
      i Which is it likely to be? Explain your answer.
      ii Repeat **b** and **c** with the incorrect data value removed.

Chapter 24

Polynomials

Contents:
- **A** Polynomials
- **B** Polynomial operations
- **C** The Remainder theorem
- **D** The Factor theorem

OPENING PROBLEM

To determine whether 7 is a **factor** of 56, we divide 56 by 7. The result is exactly 8. Since there is no remainder, 7 is a factor of 56.

Things to think about:

a Can we perform a similar test for *algebraic* factors?

b How can we divide $x^3 - 4x^2 + 2x + 3$ by $x - 3$?

c Can we determine whether $x - 3$ is a factor of $x^3 - 4x^2 + 2x + 3$ *without* performing a division?

A POLYNOMIALS

A **polynomial** is a function that can be written as the sum of terms using non-negative integer powers of the variable.

For example:

- $p(x) = 3x^2 + 5x - 4$ and $q(x) = -x^7 + \frac{1}{2}x^4 + 6x$ are polynomials.
- $f(x) = 3x + x^{\frac{1}{2}}$ is not a polynomial as the index in the second term is not an integer.
- $g(x) = 3^x + 6x$ is not a polynomial because one of the terms has x as the index.
- $h(x) = 2x^2 - x + 3x^{-1}$ is not a polynomial because the last term has a negative index.

The **degree** of a polynomial is the highest power of the variable.

The simplest polynomials are described in the following table:

Polynomials	Degree	Name
$ax + b$, $a \neq 0$	1	linear
$ax^2 + bx + c$, $a \neq 0$	2	quadratic
$ax^3 + bx^2 + cx + d$, $a \neq 0$	3	cubic
$ax^4 + bx^3 + cx^2 + dx + e$, $a \neq 0$	4	quartic

We have previously studied linear and quadratic functions in detail.

The term without the variable is called the **constant term**.

So, the polynomial $f(x) = 2x^3 - 7x^2 + 3x - 5$ has degree 3, and constant term -5.

EXERCISE 24A

1 State whether the following functions are polynomials. If they are not, give a reason.

a $f(x) = 3x^2 + 2$ **b** $g(x) = 3x + \frac{1}{3}x^2$ **c** $h(x) = 2^x - 4x^2 - 7$

d $p(x) = -8x^5 - 7x^4 + 1$ **e** $q(x) = 4x^3 + 2x^{\frac{3}{2}}$ **f** $r(x) = 5x^2 - x - 5x^{-2}$

2 Find the degree of the following polynomials:

a $f(x) = 3x^4 - x^2 + 7x - 2$ **b** $g(x) = 2 - x + \frac{1}{5}x^2$

c $p(x) = \frac{2}{3}x^4 - x^5 + 6$ **d** $q(x) = (x + 5)(x - 4)$

e $r(x) = (2x + 1)(x - 2)(x + 3)$ **f** $s(x) = (x^2 - 5)(x^2 + 2x - 7)$

3 Find the constant term in the following polynomials:

    a $f(x) = 9x^4 - 13x^2 + x - 4$ **b** $g(x) = 6 - x + 3x^2 - x^3$

    c $p(x) = (x - 3)(x + 4)$ **d** $q(x) = x(x + 6)(x - 2)$

B   POLYNOMIAL OPERATIONS

ADDING AND SUBTRACTING POLYNOMIALS

To add or subtract polynomials, we simply collect like terms.

Example 1

Let $p(x) = x^3 + 2x^2 - 4x + 3$ and $q(x) = 5x^2 + x - 2$.

Find:

  a $p(x) + q(x)$ **b** $p(x) - q(x)$

a $p(x) + q(x)$
$$= x^3 + 2x^2 - 4x + 3$$
$$ + 5x^2 + x - 2$$
$$= x^3 + 7x^2 - 3x + 1$$

b $p(x) - q(x)$
$$= x^3 + 2x^2 - 4x + 3 - [5x^2 + x - 2]$$
$$= x^3 + 2x^2 - 4x + 3 - 5x^2 - x + 2$$
$$= x^3 - 3x^2 - 5x + 5$$

Use brackets around subtracted expressions.

MULTIPLYING POLYNOMIALS

Multiplication of polynomials uses the same techniques as algebraic expansion.

- To multiply a polynomial by a constant, multiply each term by the constant.
- To multiply two polynomials, we multiply each term of the first polynomial by each term of the second polynomial, and then collect like terms.

Example 2

If $P(x) = x^2 + 4x - 5$ and $Q(x) = 3x^3 - 6x^2 - 2$, find:

  a $2P(x)$ **b** $-4Q(x)$ **c** $3P(x) + 2Q(x)$

a $2P(x) = 2(x^2 + 4x - 5)$
$$ = 2x^2 + 8x - 10$$

b $-4Q(x) = -4(3x^3 - 6x^2 - 2)$
$$ = -12x^3 + 24x^2 + 8$$

c $3P(x) + 2Q(x) = 3(x^2 + 4x - 5) + 2(3x^3 - 6x^2 - 2)$
$$= 3x^2 + 12x - 15 + 6x^3 - 12x^2 - 4$$
$$= 6x^3 - 9x^2 + 12x - 19$$

Example 3

If $p(x) = 2x^3 - x^2 + 6$ and $q(x) = x^2 - 3x + 4$, find $p(x)q(x)$.

$$\begin{aligned} p(x)q(x) &= (2x^3 - x^2 + 6)(x^2 - 3x + 4) \\ &= 2x^3(x^2 - 3x + 4) - x^2(x^2 - 3x + 4) + 6(x^2 - 3x + 4) \\ &= 2x^5 - 6x^4 + 8x^3 \\ &\quad\quad\ - x^4 + 3x^3 - 4x^2 \\ &\quad\quad\quad\quad\quad\quad + 6x^2 - 18x + 24 \\ &= 2x^5 - 7x^4 + 11x^3 + 2x^2 - 18x + 24 \end{aligned}$$

EXERCISE 24B.1

1 For each of the following pairs of functions, find: **i** $p(x) + q(x)$ **ii** $p(x) - q(x)$
  a $p(x) = x^2 + 1$, $q(x) = 2x^2 + 3x - 4$
  b $p(x) = x^3 - 4x^2 + 2x + 1$, $q(x) = 2x^3 - x^2 - x + 6$
  c $p(x) = -5x^4 - x^2 + x$, $q(x) = x^3 - 8x^2 - 2x - 4$
  d $p(x) = 2x^4 - x^3 + 7x - 3$, $q(x) = 8 - 5x - 3x^3$

2 If $p(x) = x^2 + 3x - 2$ and $q(x) = -2x^3 + x + 4$, find:
  a $3p(x)$
  b $4q(x)$
  c $-p(x)$
  d $p(x) + 4q(x)$
  e $2p(x) - 3q(x)$
  f $2q(x) - p(x)$

3 Find $f(x)g(x)$ for:
  a $f(x) = 3x - 1$, $g(x) = x + 2$
  b $f(x) = 2x^2 - x - 3$, $g(x) = x - 4$
  c $f(x) = 4x^3 - x^2 + 2$, $g(x) = x^2 - 5x + 4$
  d $f(x) = -2x^3 + x + 7$, $g(x) = x^4 + x^2 - 5x$

4 For $p(x) = x^4 - 3x^3 + 4x - 1$ and $q(x) = 2x^3 - 3x^2 + 6$, find:
  a $3p(x)$
  b $-5q(x)$
  c $2p(x) + 3q(x)$
  d $4q(x) - p(x)$
  e $4p(x) - 2q(x)$
  f $p(x)q(x)$

DISCUSSION

Suppose $f(x)$ is a polynomial of degree m, and $g(x)$ is a polynomial of degree n. What is the degree of:
- $f(x) + g(x)$
- $5f(x)$
- $f(x)g(x)$?

DIVIDING POLYNOMIALS

Polynomial division is a more complex operation than multiplication. We use a process similar to the long division of integers.

Consider the long division problem $\frac{5879}{13}$:

Step 1: Find the largest possible multiple of 13 less than or equal to 58. This is $4 \times 13 = 52$. Write the 4 above the line.

Step 2: Subtract 52 from 58 to get 6.

Step 3: Bring down the 7 to make 67.

Step 4: Go back to *Step 1*, finding the largest possible multiple of 13 less than or equal to 67. This is $5 \times 13 = 65$.
Repeat until all the digits have been used. The answer is 452 with remainder 3, or $452\frac{3}{13}$.

So, $\frac{5879}{13} = 452\frac{3}{13}$ ← remainder
                        ← divisor
        ↑
     quotient

Now consider the division $\frac{3x^3 + 10x^2 + 10x + 9}{x+2}$:

Step 1: Find the multiple of x equal to $3x^3$. This is $3x^2(x) = 3x^3$. Write the $3x^2$ above the line.

Step 2: Find $3x^2(x+2) = 3x^3 + 6x^2$. Subtract this from $3x^3 + 10x^2$ to get $4x^2$.

Step 3: Bring down the $+10x$ to get $4x^2 + 10x$.

Step 4: Go back to *Step 1*, finding the multiple of x equal to $4x^2$. This is $4x(x) = 4x^2$.
So, we find $4x(x+2) = 4x^2 + 8x$, and we subtract this from $4x^2 + 10x$ to get $2x$.
Repeat until all the terms have been used. The answer is $3x^2 + 4x + 2$ with remainder 5.

So, $\frac{3x^3 + 10x^2 + 10x + 9}{x+2} = \underbrace{3x^2 + 4x + 2}_{\text{quotient}} + \frac{5}{x+2}$ ← remainder
                                                                              ← divisor

> If $P(x)$ is divided by $ax + b$ until a constant remainder R is obtained, then
>
> $$\frac{P(x)}{ax+b} = Q(x) + \frac{R}{ax+b} \quad \text{where} \quad ax+b \text{ is the } \textbf{divisor},$$
> $$Q(x) \text{ is the } \textbf{quotient, and}$$
> $$R \text{ is the } \textbf{remainder.}$$

Notice that $P(x) = Q(x) \times (ax+b) + R$.

Example 4

Find the quotient and remainder of $\dfrac{2x^3 - 5x^2 + x + 7}{x - 3}$.

$$
\begin{array}{r}
2x^2 + x + 4 \\
x-3 \overline{\smash{)} 2x^3 - 5x^2 + x + 7 } \\
-(2x^3 - 6x^2) \\
\hline
x^2 + x \\
-(x^2 - 3x) \\
\hline
4x + 7 \\
-(4x - 12) \\
\hline
19
\end{array}
$$

$\therefore$ the quotient is $2x^2 + x + 4$, and the remainder is 19.

Check your answer by finding $(2x^2 + x + 4) \times (x - 3) + 19$.

In the long division process for integers, we only ever deal with *positive* multiples. By contrast, for polynomial division we sometimes need *negative* multiples.

Example 5

Find $\dfrac{x^4 - 17x^2 + 12x - 6}{x + 5}$.

$$
\begin{array}{r}
x^3 - 5x^2 + 8x - 28 \\
x+5 \overline{\smash{)} x^4 + 0x^3 - 17x^2 + 12x - 6 } \\
-(x^4 + 5x^3) \\
\hline
-5x^3 - 17x^2 \\
-(-5x^3 - 25x^2) \\
\hline
8x^2 + 12x \\
-(8x^2 + 40x) \\
\hline
-28x - 6 \\
-(-28x - 140) \\
\hline
134
\end{array}
$$

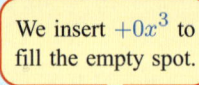

We insert $+0x^3$ to fill the empty spot.

The quotient is $x^3 - 5x^2 + 8x - 28$, and the remainder is 134.

$\therefore \dfrac{x^4 - 17x^2 + 12x - 6}{x + 5} = x^3 - 5x^2 + 8x - 28 + \dfrac{134}{x + 5}$

EXERCISE 24B.2

1 Find the quotient and remainder of:

a $\dfrac{x^2 + 5x + 6}{x + 4}$ b $\dfrac{2x^2 - 3x + 1}{x - 2}$ c $\dfrac{x^2 - x + 2}{x + 3}$

d $\dfrac{x^3 + 3x^2 + 5x + 11}{x + 2}$ e $\dfrac{x^3 + 2x^2 - 7x - 1}{x - 1}$ f $\dfrac{x^3 + 4x^2 - 2x + 3}{x + 4}$

2 Find:

a $\dfrac{x^2 - 4x + 5}{x - 3}$ **b** $\dfrac{3x^2 + x - 5}{x + 1}$ **c** $\dfrac{x^2 + 9}{x - 2}$

d $\dfrac{x^3 - 9x^2 + 6x - 7}{x - 4}$ **e** $\dfrac{x^3 + 5x - 4}{x + 2}$ **f** $\dfrac{2x^4 + 5x^3 + x^2 + 2x - 4}{x + 3}$

SYNTHETIC DIVISION (EXTENSION)

Division of a polynomial by the linear factor $x - k$ can be performed quickly by a process called **synthetic division**.

For example, consider the division of $2x^3 + x^2 + 3x + 5$ by $x - 3$.

Step 1:

Step 2:

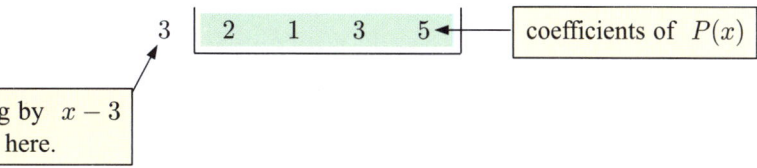

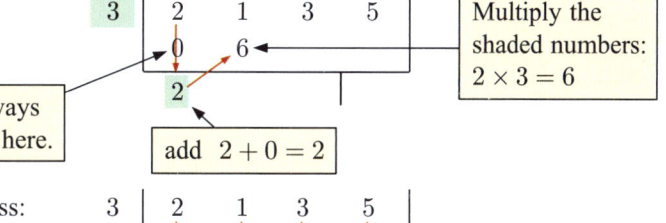

Step 3: Repeat the process: Continue adding then multiplying by 3 across the array.

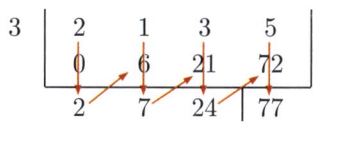

Step 4: The numbers along the bottom row are the coefficients of the quotient, and the remainder.

$$\dfrac{2x^3 + x^2 + 3x + 5}{x - 3} = 2x^2 + 7x + 24 + \dfrac{77}{x - 3}$$

Example 6   ◀) Self Tutor

Find $\dfrac{4x^3 + 5x - 3}{x + 1}$.

$$\begin{array}{r|rrrr} -1 & 4 & 0 & 5 & -3 \\ & 0 & -4 & 4 & -9 \\ \hline & 4 & -4 & 9 & -12 \end{array}$$

$\therefore \dfrac{4x^3 + 5x - 3}{x + 1} = 4x^2 - 4x + 9 + \dfrac{-12}{x + 1}$

$= 4x^2 - 4x + 9 - \dfrac{12}{x + 1}$

EXERCISE 24B.3

1 Find $\dfrac{3x^2 + 2x - 5}{x - 2}$ using:

a polynomial division **b** synthetic division.

2 Use synthetic division to find:

a $\dfrac{x^2 - 3x + 5}{x - 1}$

b $\dfrac{x^2 + 4}{x + 3}$

c $\dfrac{2x^3 - x^2 + 4x - 3}{x - 2}$

d $\dfrac{3x^3 + x^2 - 2}{x + 1}$

e $\dfrac{2x^3 - 8x + 10}{x + 5}$

f $\dfrac{x^4 - 5x^3 + 9x^2 - 7x}{x - 3}$

C   THE REMAINDER THEOREM

In **Example 4** we considered the polynomial $P(x) = 2x^3 - 5x^2 + x + 7$.

When $P(x)$ was divided by $(x - 3)$, the remainder was 19.

Notice that $P(3) = 2(3)^3 - 5(3)^2 + 3 + 7$
$= 54 - 45 + 3 + 7$
$= 19$, which is the remainder.

This result is explained by the **Remainder theorem**:

> When a polynomial $P(x)$ is divided by $(x - k)$ until a constant remainder R is obtained, then $R = P(k)$.

Proof: When $P(x)$ is divided by $(x - k)$, we have

$\dfrac{P(x)}{x - k} = Q(x) + \dfrac{R}{x - k}$ where $Q(x)$ is the quotient.

$\therefore \ P(x) = Q(x)(x - k) + R$

Letting $x = k$, $P(k) = Q(k)(k - k) + R$

$\therefore \ P(k) = Q(k) \times 0 + R$

$\therefore \ P(k) = R$

Example 7   ◀》 Self Tutor

Find the remainder when $2x^3 - x^2 + 15$ is divided by $(x + 3)$.

Let $P(x) = 2x^3 - x^2 + 15$.

We are dividing by $(x + 3)$, so we set $k = -3$.

Now $P(-3) = 2(-3)^3 - (-3)^2 + 15$
$= -54 - 9 + 15$
$= -48$

$\therefore$ when $2x^3 - x^2 + 15$ is divided by $(x + 3)$, the remainder is -48.
{Remainder theorem}

EXERCISE 24C

1 Use the Remainder theorem to find the remainder when:

a $3x^2 - 4x + 7$ is divided by $(x - 2)$

b $x^3 + 2x^2 - 5x + 2$ is divided by $(x + 4)$

c $2x^3 - 7x + 13$ is divided by $(x - 3)$.

2 Use the Remainder theorem to find the remainder when $3x^3 + 10x^2 + 10x + 9$ is divided by $(x+2)$. Check that your answer is the same as the corresponding result on page **517**.

Example 8   ◀)) **Self Tutor**

Find a given that $x^2 + ax + 7$ divided by $(x-5)$ has remainder 12.

Let $P(x) = x^2 + ax + 7$
Now $P(5) = 12$ {Remainder theorem}
$\therefore (5)^2 + a(5) + 7 = 12$
$\therefore 25 + 5a + 7 = 12$
$\therefore 5a = -20$
$\therefore a = -4$

---

3 Find a given that:

a $x^2 + 5x + a$ divided by $(x+1)$ has remainder -6
b $-2x^2 + ax + 8$ divided by $(x-3)$ has remainder 2
c $x^3 + ax^2 + 3x - 1$ divided by $(x+4)$ has remainder 3.

Example 9   ◀)) **Self Tutor**

When $2x^3 + 2x^2 + ax + b$ is divided by $(x+3)$, the remainder is -11.
When the same polynomial is divided by $(x-2)$, the remainder is 9.
Find a and b.

Let $P(x) = 2x^3 + 2x^2 + ax + b$
Now $P(-3) = -11$ and $P(2) = 9$ {Remainder theorem}
So, $2(-3)^3 + 2(-3)^2 + a(-3) + b = -11$
$\therefore -54 + 18 - 3a + b = -11$
$\therefore -3a + b = 25$ .... (1)
and $2(2)^3 + 2(2)^2 + a(2) + b = 9$
$\therefore 16 + 8 + 2a + b = 9$
$\therefore 2a + b = -15$ .... (2)
Solving simultaneously: $3a - b = -25$ $\{-1 \times (1)\}$
$\underline{2a + b = -15}$ $\{(2)\}$
Adding, $5a \quad = -40$
$\therefore a = -8$
Substituting $a = -8$ in (2) gives $2(-8) + b = -15$
$\therefore b = 1$

---

4 Find a and b given that:

a $x^2 + ax + b$ has remainder 4 when divided by $(x-3)$, and remainder 19 when divided by $(x+2)$

b $x^3 + 4x^2 + ax + b$ has remainder 20 when divided by $(x-2)$, and remainder 6 when divided by $(x+5)$

c $ax^4 + 2x^3 + bx - 8$ has remainder 0 when divided by either $(x-1)$ or $(x+2)$.

D   THE FACTOR THEOREM

The **Factor theorem** states that:

For any polynomial $P(x)$, $P(k) = 0 \Leftrightarrow (x-k)$ is a factor of $P(x)$.

Proof:

$P(k) = 0 \Leftrightarrow$ the remainder when $P(x)$ is divided by $(x-k)$ is 0
                                                       {Remainder theorem}

$\Leftrightarrow \dfrac{P(x)}{x-k} = Q(x) + \dfrac{0}{x-k}$, where $Q(x)$ is the quotient

$\Leftrightarrow P(x) = Q(x)(x-k)$

$\Leftrightarrow (x-k)$ is a factor of $P(x)$.

$\Leftrightarrow$ means 'if and only if'.

We can use the Factor theorem to determine whether $(x-k)$ is a factor of a polynomial, without having to perform the long division.

Example 10   🔊 Self Tutor

Determine whether:

a $(x-2)$ is a factor of $x^3 + 3x^2 - 13x + 6$
b $(x+3)$ is a factor of $x^3 - 8x + 7$.

a   Let $P(x) = x^3 + 3x^2 - 13x + 6$
$\therefore P(2) = (2)^3 + 3(2)^2 - 13(2) + 6$
$ = 8 + 12 - 26 + 6$
$ = 0$
Since $P(2) = 0$, $(x-2)$ is a factor of $x^3 + 3x^2 - 13x + 6$.   {Factor theorem}

b   Let $P(x) = x^3 - 8x + 7$
$\therefore P(-3) = (-3)^3 - 8(-3) + 7$
$ = -27 + 24 + 7$
$ = 4$

When $x^3 - 8x + 7$ is divided by $(x+3)$, a remainder of 4 is left over.

Since $P(-3) \neq 0$, $(x+3)$ is *not* a factor of $x^3 - 8x + 7$.
                                                {Factor theorem}

EXERCISE 24D

1 Use the Factor theorem to determine whether:

     a $(x-1)$ is a factor of $4x^3 - 7x^2 + 5x - 2$

     b $(x-3)$ is a factor of $x^4 - x^3 - 4x^2 - 15$

     c $(x+2)$ is a factor of $3x^3 + 5x^2 - 6x - 8$

     d $(x+4)$ is a factor of $2x^3 + 6x^2 + 4x + 16$.

Example 11

Find c given that $(x+2)$ is a factor of $x^3 + 7x^2 + cx - 12$.

Let $P(x) = x^3 + 7x^2 + cx - 12$

Now $P(-2) = 0$ {Factor theorem}

$\therefore (-2)^3 + 7(-2)^2 + c(-2) - 12 = 0$

$\therefore -8 + 28 - 2c - 12 = 0$

$\therefore 8 = 2c$

$\therefore c = 4$

2 **a** Find c given that $(x+1)$ is a factor of $5x^3 - 3x^2 + cx + 10$.
   b Find c given that $(x-3)$ is a factor of $x^4 - 2x^3 + cx^2 - 4x + 3$.
   c Find b given that $(x+2)$ is a factor of $x^6 + bx^5 - 2x^3 - 5x + 6$.

3 **a** Find a and b given that $(x-1)$ and $(x+2)$ are factors of $ax^3 - 4x^2 - 7x + b$.
   b Find p and q given that $(x+1)$ and $(x-3)$ are factors of $px^4 - 5x^3 - 5x^2 + qx + 9$.

4 Consider the cubic polynomial $f(x) = x^3 - 2x^2 - 23x + 60$.

   a Show that $(x-3)$ is a factor of $f(x)$.   **b** Find $\dfrac{x^3 - 2x^2 - 23x + 60}{x - 3}$.

   c Hence, write $f(x)$ in the form $f(x) = (x-3)Q(x)$, where $Q(x)$ is a quadratic polynomial.
   d By factorising $Q(x)$, write $f(x)$ in fully factorised form.

REVIEW SET 24A

1 State whether each of the following functions is a polynomial. If it is not, give a reason.

   a $f(x) = 5x^4 - \frac{1}{2}x^2 + \frac{2}{5}$ **b** $g(x) = 2x^3 - 5x + 4x^{-1}$ **c** $h(x) = 3x^5 + x^{\frac{1}{2}} - 7$

2 Given $p(x) = 5x^2 - x + 4$ and $q(x) = 3x^2 + 7x - 1$, find:

   a $p(x) + q(x)$ **b** $2p(x) - q(x)$ **c** $p(x)q(x)$

3 Use the Remainder theorem to find the remainder when:

   a $x^3 - 4x^2 + 5x - 1$ is divided by $(x-2)$
   b $2x^3 + 6x^2 - 7x + 12$ is divided by $(x+5)$.

4 For $f(x) = x^3 - 5x + 7$ and $g(x) = 2x^2 + 4x - 3$, find:

   a $f(x) - g(x)$ **b** $-5g(x)$ **c** $f(x)g(x)$

5 Find the quotient and remainder of:

   a $\dfrac{2x^2 + 11x + 18}{x + 3}$ **b** $\dfrac{x^3 - 6x^2 + 10x - 9}{x - 2}$

6 Use the Factor theorem to determine whether:

   a $(x+1)$ is a factor of $2x^4 - 9x^2 - 6x - 1$
   b $(x-3)$ is a factor of $x^4 - 2x^3 - 4x^2 + 5x - 6$.

7 $2x^2 + kx - 5$ has remainder 3 when divided by $(x+4)$. Find k.

8 $(x-2)$ and $(x+3)$ are factors of $ax^3 - 3x^2 - 11x + b$. Find a and b.

9 Suppose $f(x) = x^3 - 4x^2 + 3x - 1$ and $g(x) = 3x^2 + x - 5$.
  a Find:
    i $f(3)$ **ii** the degree of $g(x)$ **iii** $f(x) + g(x)$
  b Find the quotient and remainder when $f(x)$ is divided by $(x-3)$.
  Comment on the connection between your answer and the answer to **a i**.

10 Consider the cubic polynomial $f(x) = x^3 + x^2 - 17x + 15$.
  a Show that $(x+5)$ is a factor of $f(x)$.
  b Find $\dfrac{x^3 + x^2 - 17x + 15}{x+5}$.
  c Hence, write $f(x)$ in the form $f(x) = (x+5)Q(x)$, where $Q(x)$ is a quadratic polynomial.
  d By factorising $Q(x)$, write $f(x)$ in fully factorised form.

REVIEW SET 24B

1 State the degree of the polynomial $f(x) = (x-2)(x^2+5)$.

2 For $f(x) = x^3 - 4x + 5$ and $g(x) = x^2 - 6x + 1$, find:
  a $f(x) + g(x)$ **b** $f(x) - g(x)$

3 Find $\dfrac{x^4 - 6x^3 + 9x^2 - 22}{x - 4}$.

4 Find the constant term of the polynomial:
  a $f(x) = 3x^3 - 2x^2 + x - 5$ **b** $g(x) = (x+2)(x-3)(x-4)$

5 Use the Remainder theorem to find the remainder when $2x^3 - 3x^2 + 5x - 7$ is divided by $(x+3)$.

6 For $p(x) = 2x^4 - 3x^2 + 1$ and $q(x) = x^3 + 5x - 2$, find:
  a $5q(x)$ **b** $p(x)q(x)$

7 Find c given that $(x-2)$ is a factor of $x^5 - 2x^4 + cx^3 - 7x^2 + 5x - 6$.

8 Use the Factor theorem to determine whether $(x-5)$ is a factor of $x^3 - 3x^2 - 11x - 5$.

9 $ax^3 + 5x^2 - x + b$ has remainder 7 when divided by $(x-1)$, and remainder -11 when divided by $(x+2)$. Find a and b.

10 Suppose $f(x) = x^4 - 5x^3 + ax^2 + 4x - 8$.
  a $(x+1)$ is a factor of $f(x)$. Find a.
  b Show that $(x-2)$ is also a factor of $f(x)$.
  c Show that $f(x) = (x+1)(x-2)(x^2 - 4x + 4)$ by expanding the RHS.
  d Hence, write $f(x)$ in fully factorised form.

Chapter 25
Introduction to calculus

Contents:
- **A** Tangents
- **B** Limits
- **C** The derivative function
- **D** Rules for differentiation
- **E** Stationary points
- **F** Areas under curves
- **G** Integration
- **H** The definite integral

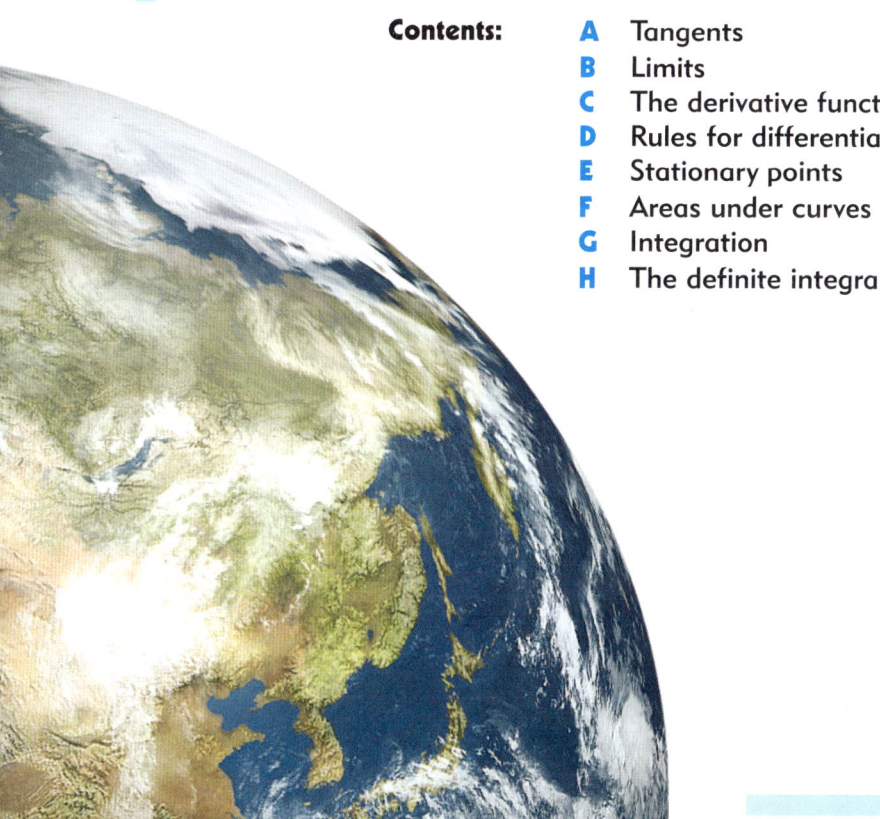

OPENING PROBLEM

A sheet of metal 30 cm by 20 cm has squares cut out of its 4 corners. The resulting shape is bent along the dashed lines to form an open rectangular dish.

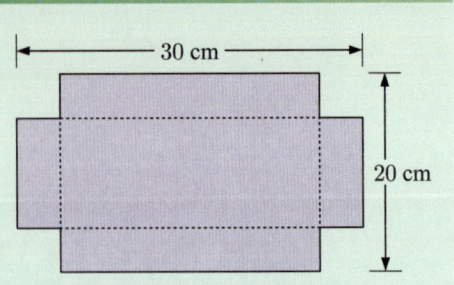

Things to think about:

a Can you write a function to describe the capacity of the dish?

b What size squares should be removed to maximise the capacity of the dish?

Calculus is the branch of mathematics which connects the equation of a function with the gradient of the tangent at any point on its graph. **Sir Isaac Newton** and **Gottfried Wilhelm Leibniz** were instrumental in developing this theory in the 17th century.

Calculus has two major branches called **differential calculus** and **integral calculus**. We use differential calculus to find special features of functions, find tangents to curves, and to solve optimisation and rates of change problems. We use integral calculus to find areas under curves and volumes of revolution.

TANGENTS

A **tangent** to a smooth curve at a given point is the straight line which best approximates the curve at that point.

In most cases, we say the tangent *touches* the curve at the *point of contact*.

For example:

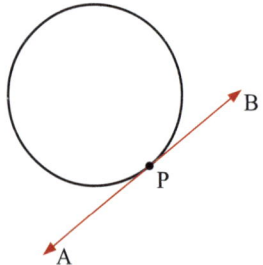

(AB) is the tangent to the circle at the point of contact P.

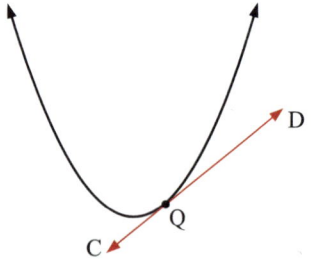

(CD) is the tangent to the parabola at the point Q.

For some curves, a tangent may:

- meet the curve again at some other point

- cross the curve at the point of contact

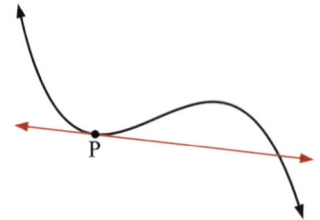

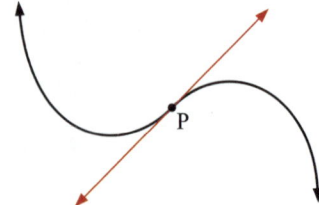

ESTIMATING THE GRADIENT OF A TANGENT

To estimate the **gradient** of a tangent to a curve, we can use this procedure:

Step 1: Draw an accurate graph of the curve on graph paper.

Step 2: Draw, as accurately as possible, a tangent to the curve at the given point.

Step 3: Construct a right angled triangle with legs parallel to the axes, and use it to estimate the gradient of the tangent.

Example 1

Consider the graph of $y = x^2$ for $x \geqslant 0$. Estimate the gradient of the tangent to the curve at the point $(1, 1)$.

We draw an accurate graph of $y = x^2$, and we draw on it the tangent to the curve at $(1, 1)$.

We draw a right angled triangle using the point $(1, 1)$ and an x-step of 1.

The y-step ≈ 2.

$\therefore$ the gradient of the tangent $\approx \frac{2}{1}$ or 2.

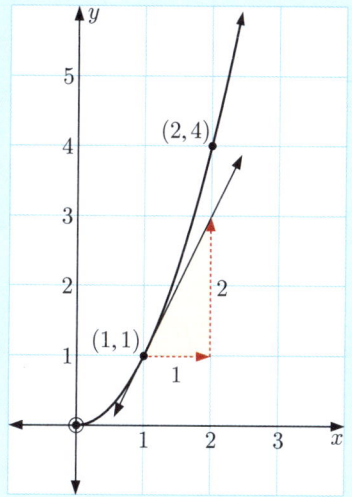

EXERCISE 25A.1

1 Consider the curve $y = -x^2$.
Estimate the gradient of the tangent to the curve at the point where:
   a $x = 1$ **b** $x = 2$ **c** $x = 1\frac{1}{2}$

2 Consider the curve $y = \dfrac{4}{x}$.
Estimate the gradient of the tangent to the curve at the point where:
   a $x = 1$ **b** $x = 2$ **c** $x = 3$

3 Consider the curve $y = 2^x$.
Estimate the gradient of the tangent to the curve at the point where:
   a $x = 1$ **b** $x = 2$ **c** $x = -\frac{1}{2}$

4 Consider the curve $y = \sqrt{x}$.
Estimate the gradient of the tangent to the curve at the point where:
   a $x = 1$ **b** $x = 4$ **c** $x = 6$.

To draw the tangent at a point, it helps to imagine a circle with the same curvature as the curve at that point. The tangent is perpendicular to the circle's radius at the point.

USING QUADRATIC THEORY TO FIND THE GRADIENT OF A TANGENT

For two types of functions we can use **quadratic theory** to find the gradients of tangents exactly:

- **quadratic functions** of the form $y = ax^2 + bx + c$, $a \neq 0$
- **reciprocal functions** of the form $y = \dfrac{a}{x}$, $a \neq 0$.

For these functions, the tangent and the curve meet only once. To find the gradient of a tangent, we first suppose the tangent has equation $y = mx + k$. Using the fact that the tangent and curve only meet once, we are left with a quadratic equation which we know has a repeated root. We use this property to find m.

Example 2

Use quadratic theory to find the gradient of the tangent to $y = x^2$ at the point $(1, 1)$.

Suppose the tangent has equation $y = mx + k$.
$y = x^2$ and $y = mx + k$ meet when $x^2 = mx + k$
$\therefore x^2 - mx - k = 0$

This is a quadratic in x with $a = 1$, $b = -m$, and $c = -k$.

The quadratic equation must have one solution as the tangent *touches* the curve.

$\therefore \Delta = 0$ and the only solution is $x = -\dfrac{b}{2a}$

But the solution is $x = 1$, so $1 = \dfrac{-(-m)}{2}$

$\therefore m = 2$

So, the gradient of the tangent at $(1, 1)$ is 2.

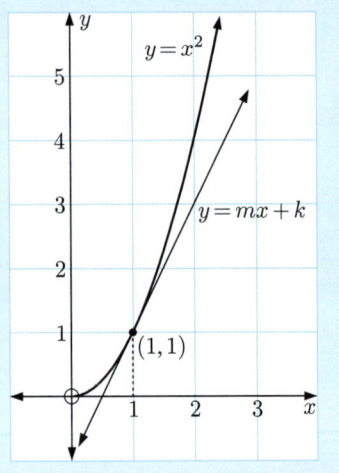

EXERCISE 25A.2

1 Use quadratic theory to find the gradient of the tangent to $y = x^2$ at the point:
  a $(2, 4)$ **b** $(3, 9)$

2 Using **Example 2**, question **1**, and arguments of symmetry, find the gradient of the tangent to $y = x^2$ at the point:
  a $(-1, 1)$ **b** $(-2, 4)$ **c** $(-3, 9)$

3 Use quadratic theory to find the gradient of the tangent to the curve:
  a $y = x^2 + 3x$ at the point $(0, 0)$
  b $y = x^2 - 2x + 1$ at the point $(2, 1)$
  c $y = \dfrac{4}{x}$ at the point $(1, 4)$
  d $y = \dfrac{6}{x}$ at the point $(2, 3)$.

4 Explain why the quadratic theory above cannot be used to find the gradient of the tangent to $y = x^3$ at the point $(1, 1)$.

B LIMITS

Sir Isaac Newton discovered a method for finding the gradients of tangents which can be used for all functions. To achieve this he used the idea of a **limit**.

> If $f(x)$ can be made as close as we like to some real number A by making x sufficiently close to (but not equal to) a, then we say that $f(x)$ has a **limit** of A as x approaches a, and we write $\lim_{x \to a} f(x) = A$.

For example, consider the function $f(x) = x^2$. As x approaches 3 from the left and the right, $f(x)$ gets closer and closer to 9.

So, $\lim_{x \to 3} x^2 = 9$.

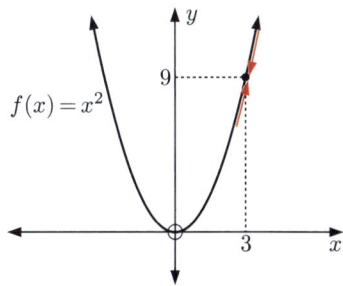

Even if the function $f(x)$ is undefined at $x = a$, we may still be able to find the limit as $x \to a$. We are only interested in the behaviour of $f(x)$ as x *gets closer* to a.

For example, consider the function $f(x) = \dfrac{x^2}{x}$.

For $x \neq 0$, we can write $f(x) = x$.

For $x = 0$, $f(x)$ is undefined. However, as x approaches 0 from the left and the right, $f(x)$ gets closer and closer to 0.

So, $\lim_{x \to 0} \dfrac{x^2}{x} = 0$.

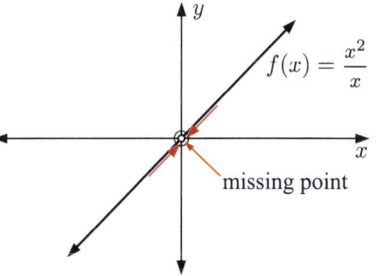

In practice, we do not need to graph functions each time to determine limits, and most can be found algebraically.

Example 3   ◀)) Self Tutor

Evaluate:

a $\lim_{x \to 2} (x^3 - 1)$ **b** $\lim_{x \to 0} \dfrac{x^2 - x}{x}$

a As $x \to 2$,
x^3 approaches 8
$\therefore x^3 - 1$ approaches 7
$\therefore \lim_{x \to 2} (x^3 - 1) = 7$

b $\lim_{x \to 0} \dfrac{x^2 - x}{x}$
$= \lim_{x \to 0} \dfrac{x(x-1)}{x}$
$= \lim_{x \to 0} (x - 1) \quad \{x \neq 0\}$
$= -1$

In **b**, we can divide the numerator and denominator by x, since we are only considering $x \to 0$, not $x = 0$.

EXERCISE 25B.1

1 Evaluate:

a $\lim_{x \to 3} (x^2 + 2)$ **b** $\lim_{x \to 5} (2x - 4)$ **c** $\lim_{x \to 0} (3x + 5)$

d $\lim_{h \to 0} (h - 3)$ **e** $\lim_{x \to 0} \dfrac{x + 4}{x + 1}$ **f** $\lim_{x \to 0} (x^2 + 4x + 2)$

2 Evaluate:

a $\lim_{x \to 0} \dfrac{x(x + 2)}{x}$ **b** $\lim_{x \to 0} \dfrac{x^2 - 5x}{x}$ **c** $\lim_{h \to 0} \dfrac{h^2 + 3h}{h}$

d $\lim_{x \to 0} \dfrac{4x}{x}$ **e** $\lim_{h \to 0} \left(-\dfrac{h}{h}\right)$ **f** $\lim_{x \to 0} \dfrac{x^2 + 6x}{2x}$

g $\lim_{h \to 0} \dfrac{3h^2 - 4h}{h}$ **h** $\lim_{x \to 0} \dfrac{x^3 - 2x}{x}$ **i** $\lim_{h \to 0} \dfrac{h^3 - 5h^2 + 8h}{h}$

GRADIENTS USING LIMIT THEORY

Suppose we wish to find the gradient of the tangent to a function $y = f(x)$ at a fixed point F. To do this, we consider a moving point M on the curve which is close to F, and examine the gradient of the line segment [FM] as M gets closer and closer to F.

In the diagram, the red line is the tangent to $y = f(x)$ at the point F where $x = 1$. F has coordinates $(1, f(1))$.

Let M be a point on the curve close to F. We let M have x-coordinate $1 + h$, so M is $(1 + h, f(1 + h))$.

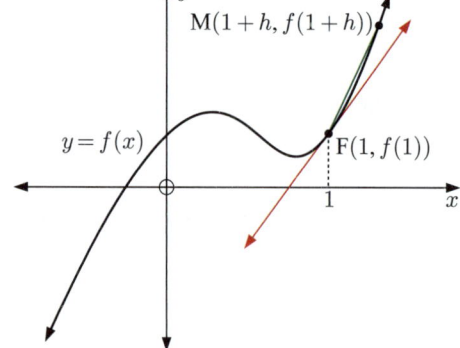

The gradient of [FM] $= \dfrac{f(1+h) - f(1)}{(1+h) - 1}$

$= \dfrac{f(1+h) - f(1)}{h}$

As $h \to 0$, M gets closer and closer to F. As this happens, the line segment [FM] becomes more and more like the tangent at F.

∴ the gradient of [FM] → the gradient of the tangent at F.

In fact, the gradient of the tangent at F $= \lim_{h \to 0}$ gradient of [FM]

$= \lim_{h \to 0} \dfrac{f(1+h) - f(1)}{h}$

More generally:

> The gradient of the tangent to the curve $y = f(x)$ at the point where $x = a$ is
>
> $\lim_{h \to 0} \dfrac{f(a+h) - f(a)}{h}$.

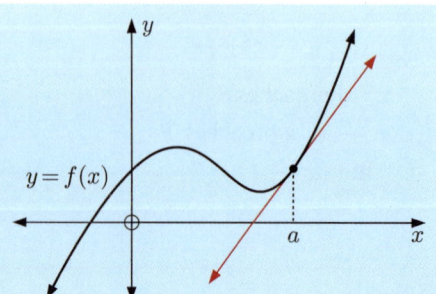

Example 4

Find the gradient of the tangent to $f(x) = x^2$ at the point $(2, 4)$.

Let F be the point $(2, 4)$ and M have the x-coordinate $2 + h$, so M is $(2 + h, (2 + h)^2)$.

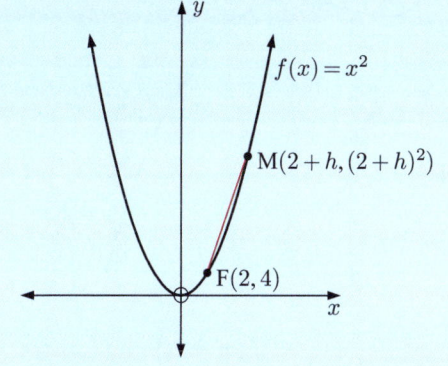

The gradient of the tangent at F

$$= \lim_{h \to 0} \frac{f(2+h) - f(2)}{h}$$

$$= \lim_{h \to 0} \frac{(2+h)^2 - 4}{h}$$

$$= \lim_{h \to 0} \frac{\cancel{4} + 4h + h^2 - \cancel{4}}{h}$$

$$= \lim_{h \to 0} \frac{\cancel{h}(4 + h)}{\cancel{h}}$$

$$= \lim_{h \to 0} (4 + h) \quad \{\text{as } h \neq 0\}$$

$$= 4$$

EXERCISE 25B.2

1 F(3, 9) lies on the graph of $f(x) = x^2$. M also lies on the graph, and has x-coordinate $3 + h$.
  a State the y-coordinate of M.
  b Show that the gradient of the line segment [FM] is $6 + h$.
  c Hence find the gradient of [FM] where M has coordinates:
    i (4, 16) **ii** (3.5, 12.25) **iii** (3.1, 9.61) **iv** (3.01, 9.0601)
  d Use limit theory to find the gradient of the tangent to $f(x) = x^2$ at the point $(3, 9)$.

2 Use limit theory to find the gradient of the tangent to:
  a $f(x) = x^2$ at the point $(4, 16)$
  b $f(x) = x^3$ at the point where $x = 1$
  c $f(x) = \frac{4}{x}$ at the point where $x = 2$
  d $f(x) = x^4$ at the point where $x = 1$.

3
  a Use limit theory to find the gradient of the tangent to $f(x) = x^2$ at the point where $x = 1$.
  b Use the previous results to copy and complete the table alongside for $f(x) = x^2$.
  c Predict the gradient of the tangent to $f(x) = x^2$ at the point (a, a^2).

x-coordinate	Gradient of tangent
1	
2	
3	
4	

C   THE DERIVATIVE FUNCTION

For a non-linear curve $y = f(x)$, the gradient of the tangent changes as we move along the curve.

We can therefore write a **gradient function** which gives the gradient of the tangent for any given value of x.

This gradient function is *derived* from $f(x)$, and is called the **derivative function**. It is labelled $f'(x)$.

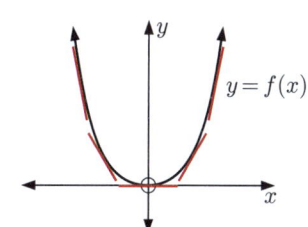

For example, in question **3** of the previous **Exercise**, you should have observed that for $f(x) = x^2$, the gradient of the tangent is always double the x-coordinate. So, for $f(x) = x^2$ we write $f'(x) = 2x$.

To find the gradient function $f'(x)$ for a function $f(x)$, we use limit theory to find the gradient of the tangent to the curve at a general point $(x, f(x))$.

The gradient of [FM] $= \dfrac{f(x+h) - f(x)}{(x+h) - x}$

$= \dfrac{f(x+h) - f(x)}{h}$

$\therefore$ the gradient of the tangent at $(x, f(x))$

$= \lim\limits_{h \to 0} \dfrac{f(x+h) - f(x)}{h}$

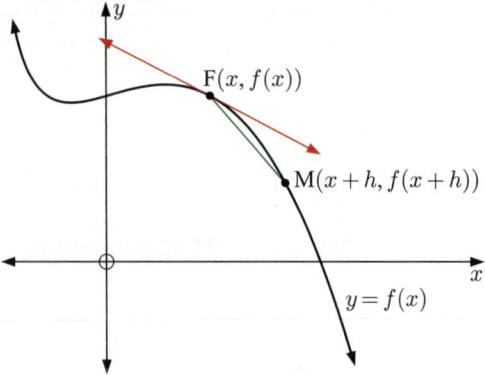

The **derivative function** of $y = f(x)$ is defined by $f'(x) = \lim\limits_{h \to 0} \dfrac{f(x+h) - f(x)}{h}$.

The process of finding the derivative function is called **differentiation**.

When we find the derivative using limit theory, we say we are performing **differentiation from first principles**.

Example 5   ◀)) Self Tutor

Find the derivative function of $f(x) = x^2$.

$f'(x) = \lim\limits_{h \to 0} \dfrac{f(x+h) - f(x)}{h}$

$= \lim\limits_{h \to 0} \dfrac{(x+h)^2 - x^2}{h}$

$= \lim\limits_{h \to 0} \dfrac{\cancel{x^2} + 2hx + h^2 - \cancel{x^2}}{h}$

$= \lim\limits_{h \to 0} \dfrac{\cancel{h}(2x + h)}{\cancel{h}}$

$= \lim\limits_{h \to 0} (2x + h)$ \qquad \{as $h \neq 0$\}

$= 2x$

Substituting a real number a into $f'(x)$ gives us $f'(a)$, which is the gradient of the tangent to $y = f(x)$ at the point where $x = a$.

Example 6   ◀)) Self Tutor

a Find $f'(x)$ given $f(x) = x^4$.
b Find $f'(-1)$, and interpret your answer.

a $f'(x) = \lim\limits_{h \to 0} \dfrac{f(x+h) - f(x)}{h}$

$= \lim\limits_{h \to 0} \dfrac{(x+h)^4 - x^4}{h}$

$$= \lim_{h \to 0} \frac{x^4 + 4x^3h + 6x^2h^2 + 4xh^3 + h^4 - x^4}{h} \quad \text{\{binomial expansion\}}$$

$$= \lim_{h \to 0} \frac{h(4x^3 + 6x^2h + 4xh^2 + h^3)}{h}$$

$$= \lim_{h \to 0} (4x^3 + 6x^2h + 4xh^2 + h^3) \quad \text{\{as } h \neq 0\text{\}}$$

$$= 4x^3$$

b $f'(-1) = 4(-1)^3$
$= -4$

The tangent to $f(x) = x^4$ at the point where $x = -1$, has gradient -4.

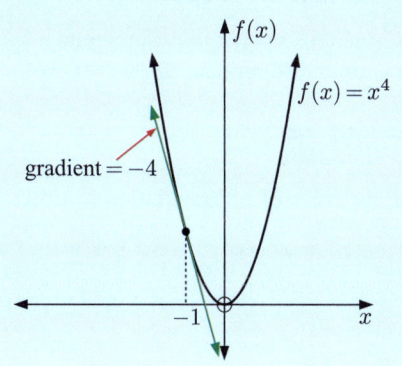

EXERCISE 25C

1 Find the derivative function of $f(x) = x$.

2 **a** Find $f'(x)$ given $f(x) = x^3$.   **b** Find $f'(2)$, and interpret your answer.

3 **a** Find $f'(x)$ given $f(x) = \frac{1}{x}$.

b Find $f'(-1)$ and $f'(3)$, and interpret your answers.

4 **a** Find $f'(x)$ for: **i** $f(x) = 7$ **ii** $f(x) = -4$

b What do you suspect is the derivative function of $f(x) = c$, where c is a constant?

5 **a** Find $f'(x)$ given $f(x) = 5x^2$.

b How does your answer compare to the derivative function of $g(x) = x^2$?

c Show that in general, if $f(x) = cg(x)$ where c is a constant, then $f'(x) = cg'(x)$.
Hint: $\lim_{h \to 0} cg(x) = c \lim_{h \to 0} g(x)$.

6 **a** Find $f'(x)$ for:
  i $f(x) = 2x^2$ **ii** $f(x) = 9x$ **iii** $f(x) = 2x^2 + 9x$

b Show that in general, if $f(x) = g(x) + h(x)$, then $f'(x) = g'(x) + h'(x)$.
Hint: $\lim_{h \to 0} (f(x) + g(x)) = \lim_{h \to 0} f(x) + \lim_{h \to 0} g(x)$.

7 **a** Use the previous results to copy and complete the table alongside.

b Copy and complete:
If $f(x) = x^n$, then $f'(x) = \ldots\ldots$

$f(x)$	$f'(x)$
x^1	
x^2	
x^3	
x^4	
x^{-1}	

D RULES FOR DIFFERENTIATION

There are a number of rules that we can use to differentiate functions. These rules allow us to find derivative functions without having to use the method of first principles.

Some of the rules are shown alongside.

The last rule tells us that to differentiate a sum or difference, we can simply differentiate *term by term*.

$f(x)$	$f'(x)$
c, a constant	0
x^n, $n \neq 0$	nx^{n-1}
$cg(x)$, c a constant	$cg'(x)$
$g(x) + h(x)$	$g'(x) + h'(x)$

Example 7   ◀)) Self Tutor

Use the rules of differentiation to find $f'(x)$ if:

a $f(x) = x^3 + 2x^2 - 3x + 4$ **b** $f(x) = \dfrac{x+4}{\sqrt{x}}$

a $f(x) = x^3 + 2x^2 - 3x + 4$
$\therefore f'(x) = 3x^2 + 2(2x) - 3(1) + 0$
$= 3x^2 + 4x - 3$

b $f(x) = \dfrac{x+4}{\sqrt{x}}$
$= \dfrac{x+4}{x^{\frac{1}{2}}}$
$= x^{\frac{1}{2}} + 4x^{-\frac{1}{2}}$
$\therefore f'(x) = \tfrac{1}{2}x^{-\frac{1}{2}} + 4(-\tfrac{1}{2})x^{-\frac{3}{2}}$
$= \tfrac{1}{2}x^{-\frac{1}{2}} - 2x^{-\frac{3}{2}}$

Example 8   ◀)) Self Tutor

Consider the curve $y = \sqrt{x}$ whose graph is drawn alongside.

a Find the gradient of the tangent at the point where $x = 1$.

b Find the point on the curve $y = \sqrt{x}$ at which the tangent has gradient $\tfrac{1}{4}$.

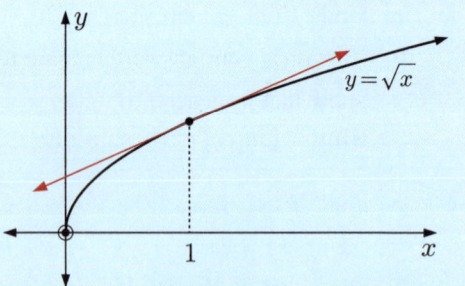

a $f(x) = \sqrt{x} = x^{\frac{1}{2}}$
$\therefore f'(x) = \tfrac{1}{2}x^{-\frac{1}{2}} = \dfrac{1}{2\sqrt{x}}$

Now $f'(1) = \dfrac{1}{2\sqrt{1}} = \tfrac{1}{2}$

$\therefore$ the tangent has gradient $\tfrac{1}{2}$.

b   If the gradient is $\tfrac{1}{4}$, then $f'(x) = \tfrac{1}{4}$
$\therefore \dfrac{1}{2\sqrt{x}} = \tfrac{1}{4}$
$\therefore \sqrt{x} = 2$
$\therefore x = 4$

When $x = 4$, $y = \sqrt{4} = 2$.
So, the point is $(4, 2)$.

EXERCISE 25D

1 Use the rules of differentiation to find $f'(x)$ for $f(x)$ equal to:

- **a** x^6
- **b** x^9
- **c** $5x^3$
- **d** $\dfrac{1}{x^2}$
- **e** $5x - x^2$
- **f** $\dfrac{1}{\sqrt{x}}$
- **g** $x^3 + 4x$
- **h** $\tfrac{1}{2}x^4$
- **i** $x^2 + 3$
- **j** $x + \dfrac{1}{x}$
- **k** $-\dfrac{2}{x}$
- **l** $\dfrac{x+1}{x}$
- **m** $\dfrac{x^2 + 5}{x}$
- **n** $\dfrac{10}{x^2}$
- **o** $6\sqrt{x}$
- **p** $(x+1)(x-2)$
- **q** $3 - \dfrac{4}{x^2}$
- **r** $\dfrac{4}{\sqrt{x}}$
- **s** $3x^3 - 2x - \dfrac{2}{x^2}$
- **t** $3 - x - \dfrac{2}{\sqrt{x}}$
- **u** $x(x+1)^2$
- **v** $(2x-1)^2$

2 Consider $f(x) = x^3 + 2x^2 - 3x + 1$.
- **a** Find $f'(x)$.
- **b** Find $f(2)$ and $f'(2)$.
- **c** Copy and complete:
  For $f(x) = x^3 + 2x^2 - 3x + 1$, the gradient of the tangent at $(2, \ldots\ldots)$ is $\ldots\ldots$.

3 Find the gradient of the tangent to:
- **a** $f(x) = 3x^2$ at $x = -1$
- **b** $f(x) = \dfrac{6}{x}$ at $x = 2$
- **c** $f(x) = x^3 + 2x + 1$ at $x = 1$
- **d** $f(x) = x^2 + 7x$ at $x = -2$
- **e** $f(x) = \dfrac{x^2 + 1}{x}$ at $x = 2$
- **f** $f(x) = \sqrt{x} + \dfrac{8}{x}$ at $x = 4$.

4 For the graph of $f(x) = x + \dfrac{4}{x}$ alongside, find the gradient of:
- **a** line 1
- **b** line 2
- **c** line 3.

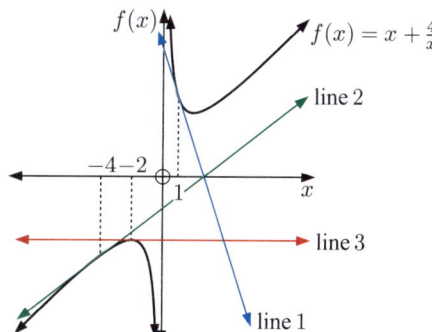

5 Find the coordinates of the point(s) on:
- **a** $f(x) = x^2 + 4x + 5$ where the tangent has gradient 0
- **b** $f(x) = \sqrt{x}$ where the tangent has gradient $\tfrac{1}{2}$
- **c** $f(x) = x^3 + x^2 - 1$ where the tangent has gradient 1
- **d** $f(x) = x^3 - 3x + 1$ where the tangent has gradient 9
- **e** $f(x) = x^3 - 6x^2 + 7$ where the tangent is horizontal.

E STATIONARY POINTS

A **stationary point** of a function is a point where $f'(x) = 0$. The gradient of the tangent to the function at any stationary point is zero. A stationary point could be a **maximum turning point**, a **minimum turning point**, or a **stationary inflection**.

TURNING POINTS

Consider the function $y = f(x)$ alongside.

We see there are two turning points at which the tangents are horizontal and $f'(x) = 0$.

The graph is increasing before the maximum turning point, decreasing between the turning points, then increasing after the minimum turning point.

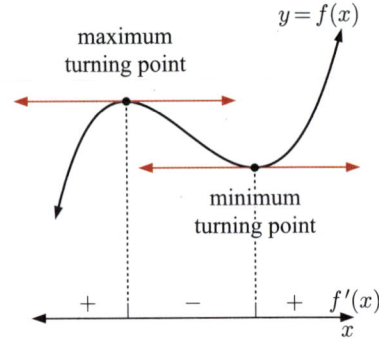

The sign diagram of $f'(x)$ is therefore:

STATIONARY INFLECTION POINTS

In the graph of $y = f(x)$ alongside, the tangent at A is horizontal, but A is not a turning point.

We say that A is a **stationary inflection**.

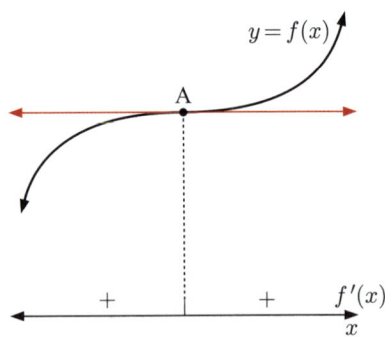

The graph is increasing either side of A, so the sign diagram of $f'(x)$ is:

Stationary point where $f'(a) = 0$	Sign diagram of $f'(x)$ near $x = a$	Shape of curve near $x = a$
maximum turning point	`+ — ` at a	peak at $x = a$
minimum turning point	`— +` at a	valley at $x = a$
stationary inflection	`+ +` at a or `— —` at a	increasing inflection at $x = a$ or decreasing inflection at $x = a$

Example 9

For each of the following functions:

   i Find $f'(x)$.   **ii** Draw the sign diagram for $f'(x)$.

   iii Find the position and nature of any stationary points.

   iv Use technology to help sketch the graph of $y = f(x)$.

  a $f(x) = -x^3 + 3x^2 - 3x + 5$ **b** $f(x) = x + \dfrac{9}{x}$

---

a **i** $f(x) = -x^3 + 3x^2 - 3x + 5$
$\therefore \ f'(x) = -3x^2 + 6x - 3$

   ii $f'(x) = -3(x^2 - 2x + 1)$
$= -3(x-1)^2$

$\therefore$ the sign diagram for $f'(x)$ is:

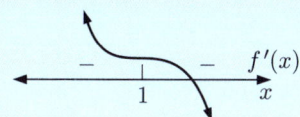

iii The stationary point occurs at $x = 1$.
Now $f(1) = 4$
$\therefore$ there is a stationary inflection at $(1, 4)$.

iv

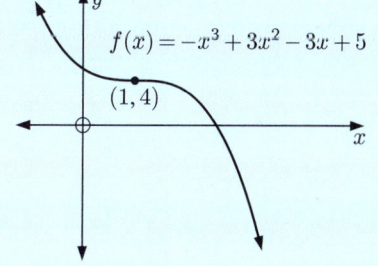

b **i** $f(x) = x + \dfrac{9}{x} = x + 9x^{-1}$
$\therefore \ f'(x) = 1 - 9x^{-2}$

   ii $f'(x) = 1 - \dfrac{9}{x^2}$
$= \dfrac{x^2 - 9}{x^2}$
$= \dfrac{(x+3)(x-3)}{x^2}$

$\therefore$ the sign diagram for $f'(x)$ is:

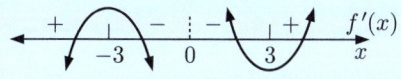

iii The stationary points occur at $x = -3$ and $x = 3$.
Now $f(-3) = -6$ and $f(3) = 6$
$\therefore$ there is a maximum turning point at $(-3, -6)$, and a minimum turning point at $(3, 6)$.

iv

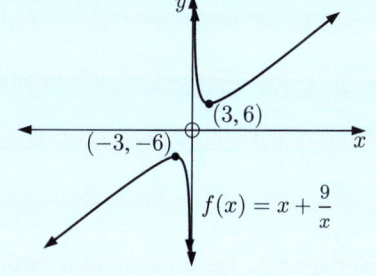

EXERCISE 25E

1 For each of the following functions:

   i Find $f'(x)$.   **ii** Draw the sign diagram for $f'(x)$.

   iii Find the position and nature of any stationary points.

   iv Use technology to help sketch the graph of $y = f(x)$.

  a $f(x) = x^2 - 4x + 6$ **b** $f(x) = x^3 + 3x^2 - 4$

  c $f(x) = x^3 - 6x^2 + 12x - 2$ **d** $f(x) = x^3 - 3x^2 - 24x + 5$

e $f(x) = 2x^3 - 3x^2 - 12x + 5$
  f $f(x) = -x^3 + 9x^2 - 27x + 20$
  g $f(x) = x + \dfrac{1}{x}$
  h $f(x) = 2x + \dfrac{32}{x}$
  i $f(x) = \dfrac{1}{x} + \dfrac{1}{x^2}$

2 a For the general quadratic function $f(x) = ax^2 + bx + c$, show that a stationary point occurs when $x = -\dfrac{b}{2a}$.
  b Under what conditions is this stationary point:
      i a maximum turning point
      ii a minimum turning point?

Example 10 ◀)) Self Tutor

Square corners are cut from a piece of 12 cm by 12 cm tinplate, which is then bent to form an open dish. What size squares should be removed to maximise the capacity of the dish?

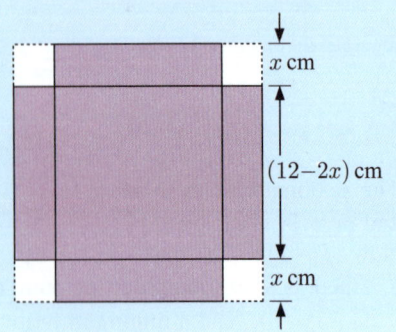

Suppose we cut out x cm by x cm squares, so $0 \leqslant x \leqslant 6$.

Capacity = length × width × depth
$\therefore\ V = (12 - 2x)^2 \times x$
$\therefore\ V = (144 - 48x + 4x^2) \times x$
$\therefore\ V = 144x - 48x^2 + 4x^3$
$\therefore\ V'(x) = 144 - 96x + 12x^2$
$ = 12(x^2 - 8x + 12)$
$ = 12(x - 2)(x - 6)$

$V'(x)$ has sign diagram:

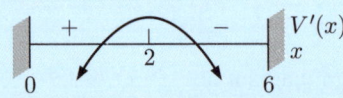

The maximum capacity occurs when $x = 2$ cm, so we should cut out 2 cm squares.

We use stationary points to identify the maximum and minimum values of functions. This process is called **optimisation**.

3 Two numbers have a sum of 10. Find the minimum value that the sum of their cubes could be.
4 Answer the **Opening Problem** on page 526.
5 A rectangle is positioned on the x-axis under the graph of $y = 9 - x^2$, as shown.
  a Find the coordinates of point P.
  b What domain of values can a have?
  c Write down a formula for the area of the shaded rectangle, in terms of a.
  d Find the maximum possible area of the rectangle.

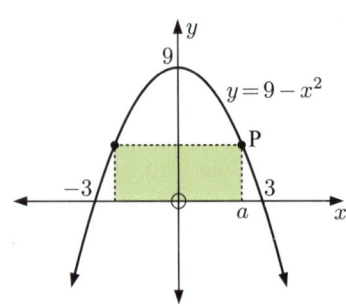

Global context — click here

Modelling population growth

Statement of inquiry: Discovering mathematical relationships can lead to a better understanding of how populations evolve.

Global context: Globalisation and sustainability

Key concept: Relationships

Related concepts: Model, Change

Objectives: Knowing and understanding, Communicating, Applying mathematics in real-life contexts

Approaches to learning: Thinking, Communication

F AREAS UNDER CURVES

In this section we consider areas of regions bounded by curves. These areas cannot be found using standard area formulae.

However, we can use limits to find these areas.

The branch of mathematics which deals with this is called **integral calculus**.

INVESTIGATION   THE AREA UNDER $y = x^2$ FROM $x = 0$ TO $x = 1$

Consider the area A between the curve $y = x^2$ and the x-axis from $x = 0$ to $x = 1$. The region is shaded in the diagram alongside.

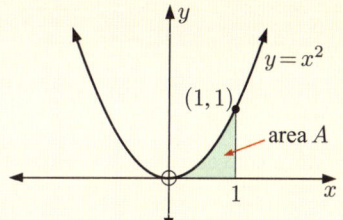

What to do:

1. Explain why $A < \frac{1}{2}$ units^2.

2. Use the graph alongside to explain why $A < \frac{3}{8}$ units^2.

3. Subdivide the interval $0 \leqslant x \leqslant 1$ into 3, 4, and then 5 equal parts, finding an upper bound for A in each case.

4. Consider the upper bounds for A found in **1**, **2**, and **3**. These numbers are approaching the actual value of A. Can you predict what this is?

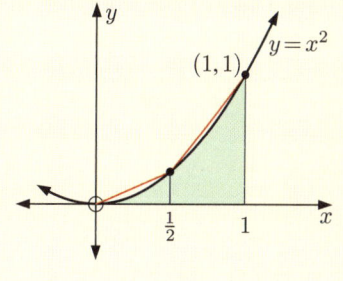

From the **Investigation** above, you may have guessed that the area between the curve $y = x^2$ and the x-axis from $x = 0$ to $x = 1$ is $\frac{1}{3}$ units^2.

To prove that this is the case, we use our knowledge of limit theory, and also a formula we saw in **Chapter 14**: $1^2 + 2^2 + 3^2 + \ldots + n^2 = \dfrac{n(n+1)(2n+1)}{6}$.

Consider a more general case where we want to find the area between $y = x^2$ and the x-axis from $x = 0$ to $x = a$.

We subdivide the interval $0 \leqslant x \leqslant a$ into n equal intervals of width h units, so $a = nh$.

We draw rectangular strips on each interval with height equal to the value of the function at the right hand side of the interval. The sum of the areas of the rectangles will therefore overestimate the required area. However, in the limit as h approaches zero, the rectangles will give the area exactly.

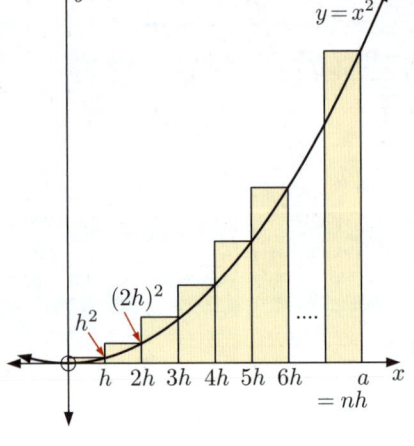

The sum of the areas of the rectangles is

$$S = h(h^2) + h(2h)^2 + h(3h)^2 + \ldots + h(nh)^2$$
$$= h^3(1^2 + 2^2 + 3^2 + \ldots + n^2)$$
$$= \left(\frac{a}{n}\right)^3 \frac{n(n+1)(2n+1)}{6} \quad \{\text{using formula}\}$$
$$= \frac{a^3}{6} \left(\frac{n+1}{n}\right) \left(\frac{2n+1}{n}\right)$$
$$= \frac{a^3}{6} \left(1 + \frac{1}{n}\right) \left(2 + \frac{1}{n}\right)$$

DEMO

Now $a = nh$, so $\dfrac{1}{n} = \dfrac{h}{a}$.

$\therefore$ as $h \to 0$, $\dfrac{1}{n} \to 0$ also.

$\therefore$ $\displaystyle\lim_{h \to 0} S = \dfrac{a^3}{6}(1)(2) = \dfrac{a^3}{3}$.

So, the area between $y = x^2$ and the x-axis from $x = 0$ to $x = a$, is $\dfrac{a^3}{3}$ units^2.

When $a = 1$, the area is $\frac{1}{3}$ units^2, as seen in the **Investigation**.

EXERCISE 25F

1 Use the known area formulae to find the shaded area:

a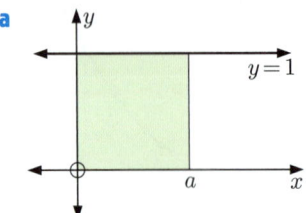

b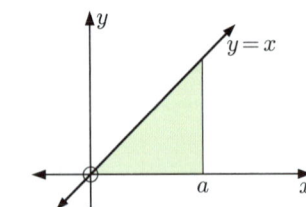

2 Consider the area between $y = x^3$ and the x-axis from $x = 0$ to $x = a$.

   a Sketch $y = x^3$ and divide the interval $0 \leqslant x \leqslant a$ into n equal intervals. Draw rectangular strips on each interval with height equal to the value of the function at the right hand side of the interval.

   b Write down the sum of the areas of the strips.

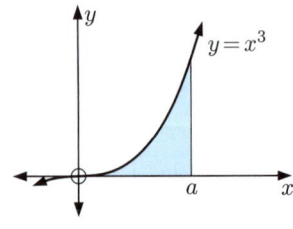

c Use the formula $1^3 + 2^3 + 3^3 + ... + n^3 = \dfrac{n^2(n+1)^2}{4}$ to show that the sum of the areas of the strips is $\dfrac{a^4}{4}\left(1 + \dfrac{1}{n}\right)^2$.

d Hence, find the exact area under the curve.

3 Use the previous results to predict these areas:

a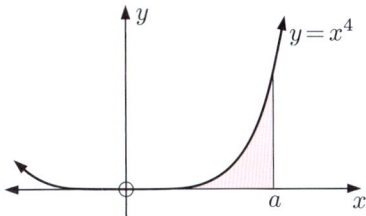

b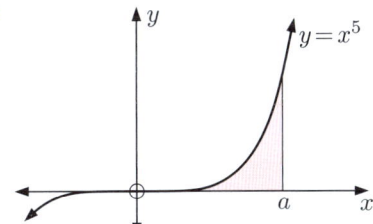

G INTEGRATION

The table summarises the results obtained in the previous **Exercise**.

Looking carefully at the results, you may be able to see a pattern.

For example, for the case $y = x^2$, the area is of the form $\dfrac{x^3}{3}$.

The derivative of $\dfrac{x^3}{3}$ is $\dfrac{3x^2}{3} = x^2$, which was the original function.

This pattern also holds for the other functions in the table.

Function	Area
$y = 1$	a
$y = x$	$\dfrac{a^2}{2}$
$y = x^2$	$\dfrac{a^3}{3}$
$y = x^3$	$\dfrac{a^4}{4}$

From this observation, we conclude that to make finding areas easier, we need a process that is the reverse of differentiation. We call such a process **anti-differentiation** or **integration**.

> **Integration** is the reverse process of differentiation.

Unlike differentiation, when we integrate we do not obtain a unique answer.

For example, we know the derivative of $\frac{1}{3}x^3$ is x^2, but the derivatives of $\frac{1}{3}x^3 - 1$, $\frac{1}{3}x^3 + 10$, and $\frac{1}{3}x^3 - 5$ are also x^2.

In fact, all functions of the form $\frac{1}{3}x^3 + c$ where c is any real constant, have the derivative x^2.

We say that $\frac{1}{3}x^3 + c$ is the **integral** of x^2 with respect to x, and write $\displaystyle\int x^2\,dx = \frac{1}{3}x^3 + c$.

> If $F(x)$ and $f(x)$ are functions such that $F'(x) = f(x)$ then:
> - $f(x)$ is the **derivative** of $F(x)$ and
> - $F(x)$ is the **integral** or **anti-derivative** of $f(x)$.
>
> $\displaystyle\int f(x)\,dx$ reads "the integral of $f(x)$ with respect to x".
>
> If $\boldsymbol{F'(x) = f(x)}$ then $\displaystyle\int \boldsymbol{f(x)\,dx = F(x) + c}$.

Example 11

a Find $F'(x)$ for $F(x) = \dfrac{x^4}{4}$, and hence find $\int x^3 \, dx$.

b Find $F'(x)$ for $F(x) = x^{\frac{3}{2}}$, and hence find $\int x^{\frac{1}{2}} \, dx$.

To find $\int f(x) \, dx$, we try to find a function $F(x)$ such that $F'(x) = f(x)$.

a If $F(x) = \dfrac{x^4}{4}$, then $F'(x) = \dfrac{4x^3}{4} = x^3$

$\therefore \int x^3 \, dx = \dfrac{x^4}{4} + c$.

b If $F(x) = x^{\frac{3}{2}}$, then $F'(x) = \tfrac{3}{2} x^{\frac{1}{2}}$

$\therefore$ if $F(x) = \tfrac{2}{3} x^{\frac{3}{2}}$, then $F'(x) = \tfrac{2}{3} \times \tfrac{3}{2} x^{\frac{1}{2}} = x^{\frac{1}{2}}$

$\therefore \int x^{\frac{1}{2}} \, dx = \tfrac{2}{3} x^{\frac{3}{2}} + c$.

EXERCISE 25G.1

1 a Find $F'(x)$ for $F(x) = \dfrac{x^2}{2}$, and hence find $\int x \, dx$.

b Find $F'(x)$ for $F(x) = \dfrac{x^5}{5}$, and hence find $\int x^4 \, dx$.

c Find $F'(x)$ for $F(x) = x^8$, and hence find $\int x^7 \, dx$.

d Find $F'(x)$ for $F(x) = x^{-2}$, and hence find $\int x^{-3} \, dx$.

e Find $F'(x)$ for $F(x) = x^{\frac{1}{2}}$, and hence find $\int x^{-\frac{1}{2}} \, dx$.

$\int x^4 \, dx$ reads "the integral of x^4 with respect to x".

2 a Use your previous results to predict a formula for $\int x^n \, dx$.

b Does this formula work for $n = -1$? Explain your answer.

3 a Find $F'(x)$ for $F(x) = 5x$, and hence find $\int 5 \, dx$.

b Predict an expression for $\int k \, dx$, where k is a constant.

4 a Find $F'(x)$ for $F(x) = 2x^3 + 5x^2$, and hence find $\int (6x^2 + 10x) \, dx$.

b Use your previous results to find $6 \int x^2 \, dx + 10 \int x \, dx$.

c Can you draw any conclusions from your results?

RULES FOR INTEGRATION

From the previous **Exercise**, we observe the following rules:

- $\int k\,dx = kx + c$ {k a constant}
- $\int x^n\,dx = \dfrac{x^{n+1}}{n+1} + c$ provided $n \neq -1$
- $\int k\,f(x)\,dx = k\int f(x)\,dx$ {k a constant}
- $\int [f(x) \pm g(x)]\,dx = \int f(x)\,dx \pm \int g(x)\,dx$

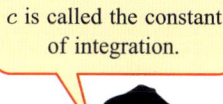 c is called the constant of integration.

Example 12   ◀)) Self Tutor

Integrate with respect to x:

a $x^3 + 3x + 4$ **b** $(x^2 - 4)^2$ **c** $\dfrac{4}{\sqrt{x}}$

a $\int (x^3 + 3x + 4)\,dx$
$= \int x^3\,dx + \int 3x\,dx + \int 4\,dx$
$= \dfrac{x^4}{4} + \dfrac{3x^2}{2} + 4x + c$

b $\int (x^2 - 4)^2\,dx$
$= \int (x^4 - 8x^2 + 16)\,dx$
$= \dfrac{x^5}{5} - \dfrac{8x^3}{3} + 16x + c$

c $\int \dfrac{4}{\sqrt{x}}\,dx$
$= \int 4x^{-\frac{1}{2}}\,dx$
$= \dfrac{4 \times x^{\frac{1}{2}}}{\frac{1}{2}} + c$
$= 8\sqrt{x} + c$

EXERCISE 25G.2

1   Integrate with respect to x:

    a x^{10} **b** $\dfrac{1}{x^4}$ **c** $3x^2$ **d** $x^2 + 3x - 2$

    e $x^3 - x$ **f** $5\sqrt{x}$ **g** $x^2 + \dfrac{1}{\sqrt{x}}$ **h** $2x^3 + 3x - \dfrac{4}{x^2}$

    i $\dfrac{x^4 - 3x + 4}{x^3}$ **j** $\dfrac{x^2 - 2}{\sqrt{x}}$ **k** $(2 - x)^2$ **l** $(2x + 1)^2$

2   Use the binomial expansion to help find:

    a $\int (x + 2)^3\,dx$ **b** $\int (x - 1)^4\,dx$

H THE DEFINITE INTEGRAL

We saw earlier that if $f(x) = x^2$ then the area between the curve and the x-axis from $x = 0$ to $x = a$ is $\dfrac{a^3}{3}$.

Similarly, the area between the curve and the x-axis from $x = 0$ to $x = b$ is $\dfrac{b^3}{3}$.

So, the area from $x = a$ to $x = b$ is $\dfrac{b^3}{3} - \dfrac{a^3}{3}$.

This can be written as $F(b) - F(a)$, where $F(x) = \dfrac{x^3}{3}$ is the anti-derivative of $f(x) = x^2$.

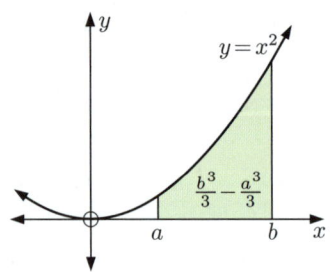

THE FUNDAMENTAL THEOREM OF CALCULUS

If $F(x) = \displaystyle\int f(x)\,dx$ then the **definite integral** of $f(x)$ on the interval $a \leqslant x \leqslant b$ is

$$\int_a^b f(x)\,dx = F(b) - F(a).$$

We often write $F(b) - F(a)$ as $[F(x)]_a^b$.

THE AREA UNDER A CURVE

If $f(x) \geqslant 0$ on the interval $a \leqslant x \leqslant b$, then the definite integral $\displaystyle\int_a^b f(x)\,dx$ will give the **area under the curve** and above the x-axis from $x = a$ to $x = b$.

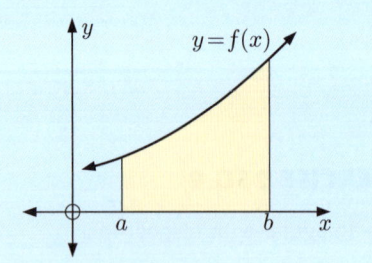

Example 13   ◀ੈ Self Tutor

Evaluate: $\displaystyle\int_1^2 x^2\,dx$

$$\int_1^2 x^2\,dx = \left[\dfrac{x^3}{3}\right]_1^2$$

$$= \left(\dfrac{2^3}{3}\right) - \left(\dfrac{1^3}{3}\right)$$

$$= \dfrac{7}{3}$$

$$= 2\tfrac{1}{3}$$

The constant c is not needed for definite integral calculations, as it cancels out anyway.

Example 14

Evaluate: $\int_1^4 (2\sqrt{x} + 5)\,dx$

$$\int_1^4 (2\sqrt{x} + 5)\,dx = \int_1^4 (2x^{\frac{1}{2}} + 5)\,dx$$

$$= \left[\frac{2x^{\frac{3}{2}}}{\frac{3}{2}} + 5x\right]_1^4$$

$$= \left[\tfrac{4}{3}x\sqrt{x} + 5x\right]_1^4$$

$$= \left(\tfrac{32}{3} + 20\right) - \left(\tfrac{4}{3} + 5\right)$$

$$= 24\tfrac{1}{3}$$

EXERCISE 25H

1 Evaluate:

a $\int_2^5 x\,dx$ **b** $\int_1^3 (2x+4)\,dx$ **c** $\int_{-1}^2 (x^2+3)\,dx$

d $\int_1^6 (2-x)\,dx$ **e** $\int_1^4 \sqrt{x}\,dx$ **f** $\int_4^9 \frac{4}{\sqrt{x}}\,dx$

2 Evaluate:

a $\int_1^4 \left(\sqrt{x} - \frac{1}{\sqrt{x}}\right)dx$ **b** $\int_0^2 (2x+3)^2\,dx$ **c** $\int_{-2}^{-1} \frac{x^2+4}{x^2}\,dx$

d $\int_{-1}^1 (x^3 - x)\,dx$ **e** $\int_4^9 \frac{\sqrt{x} - x^2}{x}\,dx$ **f** $\int_1^2 (x+2)^3\,dx$

Example 15

Find the area bounded by $y = x^4$, the x-axis, $x = 1$, and $x = 2$.

$x^4 \geqslant 0$ for all $x \in [1, 2]$

$\therefore$ Area $= \int_1^2 x^4\,dx$

$= \left[\dfrac{x^5}{5}\right]_1^2$

$= \tfrac{32}{5} - \tfrac{1}{5}$

$= 6\tfrac{1}{5}$ units^2

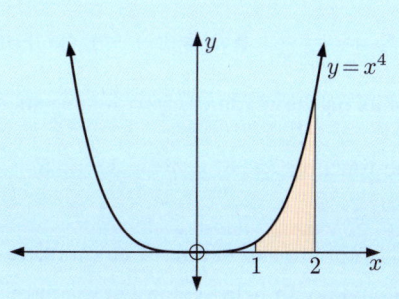

3 Find the area bounded by:

a $y = x^2$, the x-axis, $x = 1$, and $x = 3$

b $y = \sqrt{x}$, the x-axis, $x = 1$, and $x = 4$

c $y = x\sqrt{x}$, the x-axis, $x = 1$, and $x = 9$

d $y = x^3 + 1$, the x-axis, $x = 0$, and $x = 2$

e $y = 2x^2 + 3x + 1$, the x-axis, $x = 2$, and $x = 4$

f $y = \dfrac{1}{x^2}$, the x-axis, $x = \dfrac{1}{2}$, and $x = 2\dfrac{1}{2}$

g $y = \dfrac{4}{\sqrt{x}}$, the x-axis, $x = 1$, and $x = 4$.

4 The blue and red shaded areas are equal. Find k, giving your answer in the form $a + b\sqrt{2}$.

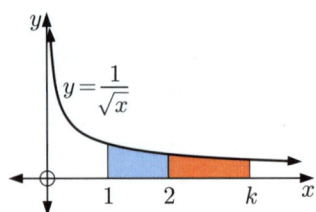

REVIEW SET 25A

1 a Draw an accurate graph of $y = x^2$.

b Use your graph to estimate the gradient of the tangent to the curve at the point $(2, 4)$.

c Use the rules of differentiation to check your answer.

2 Evaluate:

a $\lim\limits_{x \to 4} (x^2 + 5)$

b $\lim\limits_{x \to 0} (2x^2 - 5x + 3)$

c $\lim\limits_{h \to 0} \dfrac{3h^2 - 4h}{h}$

3 Find, using the limit method, the gradient of the tangent to $y = \dfrac{4}{x}$ at the point $(-2, -2)$.

4 Find, using the definition $f'(x) = \lim\limits_{h \to 0} \dfrac{f(x+h) - f(x)}{h}$, the derivative function of $f(x) = x^2 - 2x$.

5 Use the rules of differentiation to find $f'(x)$ for $f(x)$ equal to:

a $7x^3$

b $3x^2 - x^3$

c $(2x - 3)^2$

d $\dfrac{7x^3 + 2x^4}{x^2}$

6 Consider $f(x) = x^2 + \dfrac{1}{x}$.

a Find $f'(x)$.

b Find $f'(1)$, and interpret your answer.

7 Find the points on the graph of $y = \dfrac{2}{x}$ at which the tangent has gradient $-\dfrac{1}{2}$.

8 Consider the function $f(x) = x^3 + 3x^2 - 5$.

a Find $f'(x)$.

b Draw the sign diagram for $f'(x)$.

c Find the position and nature of any turning points.

d Use technology to help sketch the graph of $y = f(x)$.

9 Find $F'(x)$ for $F(x) = \sqrt{x}$, and hence find $\int \dfrac{1}{\sqrt{x}}\,dx$.

10 Integrate with respect to x:

   a $-\dfrac{1}{x^3}$ **b** $\sqrt{x}(1-x)$ **c** $(x^2 + 5)^2$

11 Evaluate:

   a $\displaystyle\int_{-1}^{2} (2x+1)\,dx$ **b** $\displaystyle\int_{1}^{2} \left(x - \dfrac{1}{\sqrt{x}}\right) dx$ **c** $\displaystyle\int_{1}^{2} \dfrac{(x+1)^2}{\sqrt{x}}\,dx$

12 Find the area of the region bounded by $y = x^2$, the x-axis, $x = 3$, and $x = 5$.

REVIEW SET 25B

1 **a** Use quadratic theory to find the gradient of the tangent to the curve $y = x^2 + x + 5$ at the point $(-2, 7)$.

   b Use the rules of differentiation to check your answer.

2 Evaluate:

   a $\displaystyle\lim_{x \to -2}(x^3 + 5)$ **b** $\displaystyle\lim_{h \to 0}\left(-\dfrac{2h}{h}\right)$ **c** $\displaystyle\lim_{h \to 0} \dfrac{4h^3 - 2h^2 + 5h}{h}$

3 Use the rules of differentiation to find $f'(x)$ for $f(x)$ equal to:

   a $6\sqrt{x}$ **b** $\dfrac{1}{x} - \dfrac{4}{x^2}$ **c** $\dfrac{2x+1}{\sqrt{x}}$ **d** $(2x-1)^3$

4 Find the equation of the tangent to $y = x^3 - 3x + 5$ at the point where $x = 2$.

5 Find all points on the curve $y = \dfrac{2x+1}{\sqrt{x}}$ where the tangent is horizontal.

6 Find the gradient of:

   a line 1
   b line 2.

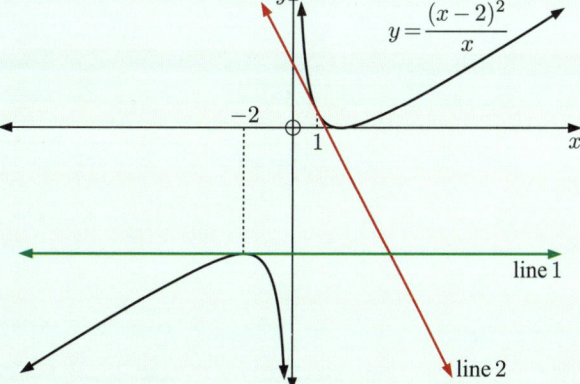

7 Consider $f(x) = 2x + \dfrac{2}{x}$.

   a Find $f'(x)$.   **b** Draw the sign diagram for $f'(x)$.

   c Find the position and nature of any stationary points.

   d Use technology to help sketch the graph of $y = f(x)$.

8 Find:

a $\displaystyle\int (-3)\,dx$
b $\displaystyle\int x^2(2x-1)\,dx$
c $\displaystyle\int (1-x)^3\,dx$

9 A 200 m fence is to be placed around a lawn which has the shape of a rectangle with a semi-circle on one of its sides.

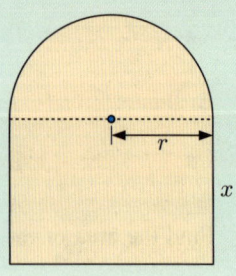

  a Write an expression for the perimeter of the lawn in terms of r and x.
  b Find x in terms of r.
  c Show that the area of the lawn A can be written as $A = 200r - r^2\left(2 + \frac{\pi}{2}\right)$.
  d Find the dimensions of the lawn which maximises its area.

10 Evaluate:

a $\displaystyle\int_{-1}^{0} x^2\,dx$
b $\displaystyle\int_{0}^{2} (x^2-x)\,dx$
c $\displaystyle\int_{4}^{9} \sqrt{x}\,dx$

11 Find the area bounded by $y = x^3 - x$, the x-axis, $x = 2$, and $x = 3$.

12 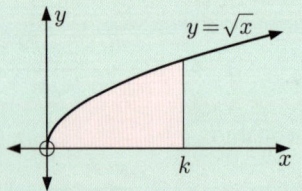 The shaded region has area 5 units^2. Find k correct to 3 decimal places.

Chapter 26

Counting and probability

Click on the icon to access this chapter

Contents:
- **A** The product and sum principles
- **B** Permutations
- **C** Factorial notation
- **D** Combinations
- **E** Probabilities using permutations and combinations

Chapter 27

CHAPTER

Click on the icon to access this chapter

Circles and ellipses

Contents: **A**   Circles
            B   Ellipses

Chapter 28

Matrices

Contents:
- **A** Matrix structure
- **B** Matrix operations and definitions
- **C** Matrix multiplication
- **D** The inverse of a 2×2 matrix
- **E** Simultaneous linear equations

Chapter 29
Linear programming

Click on the icon to access this chapter

Contents:
- **A** Feasible regions
- **B** Constructing constraints
- **C** Linear programming

ANSWERS

EXERCISE 1A

1 a 3^7 b x^9 c x^{5+n} d t^{12}
  e 7^4 f x^4 g t^{6-x} h t^{3m-1}
  i 5^6 j t^{12} k y^{3m} l a^{12m}

2 a 11^2 b 2^5 c 3^4 d 2^4
  e 5^4 f 7^{t+2} g 3^{a-2} h 2^{3p-2}
  i 7^2 j 3^{2-x} k 5^{4t} l 2^{3k-12}
  m 2^{2a-b} n 2^{3x-4y} o 5^{2x+4} p 3^6

3 a x^2y^2 b a^3b^3 c $x^2y^2z^2$ d $27b^3$ e $625a^4$
  f $100\,000x^5y^5$ g $\dfrac{p^2}{q^2}$ h $\dfrac{m^3}{n^3}$ i $\dfrac{x^4}{81}$
  j $\dfrac{125}{z^3}$ k $\dfrac{16a^4}{b^4}$ l $\dfrac{27x^3}{64y^3}$

4 a $8b^5$ b a^2b^2 c $6a^4b^2$ d $\dfrac{x^2y}{3}$
  e $\dfrac{a^6}{125b^3}$ f $\dfrac{8r^2}{5}$ g $16c^4d^3$ h $\dfrac{5k^2}{16}$

5 a 1 b $\dfrac{1}{6}$ c $\dfrac{1}{4}$ d 1 e 16 f $\dfrac{1}{16}$
  g 125 h $\dfrac{1}{125}$ i 49 j $\dfrac{1}{49}$ k 1000 l $\dfrac{1}{1000}$

6 a 1 b 1 c $2, t \neq 0$ d $1, t \neq 0$
  e 1 f 3 g $\dfrac{1}{25}$ h $\dfrac{1}{16}$ i $\dfrac{1}{x^5}$ j $\dfrac{8}{3}$
  k $\dfrac{3}{2}$ l 5 m 3 n $\dfrac{4}{5}$ o $\dfrac{11}{3}$ p 9
  q $\dfrac{27}{8}$ r $\dfrac{8}{27}$ s $\dfrac{25}{16}$ t $\dfrac{4}{25}$

7 a $\dfrac{1}{3b}$ b $\dfrac{3}{b}$ c $\dfrac{7}{a}$ d $\dfrac{1}{7a}$ e t^2
  f $\dfrac{y}{3x}$ g $\dfrac{1}{25t^2}$ h $\dfrac{t^2}{5}$ i $\dfrac{x}{y}$ j $\dfrac{1}{xy}$
  k $\dfrac{x}{y^3}$ l $\dfrac{1}{x^3y^3}$ m $\dfrac{1}{3pq}$ n $\dfrac{3}{pq}$ o $\dfrac{3p}{q}$
  p x^3y^5 q $\dfrac{125y^9}{x^6}$ r $\dfrac{4d^6}{c^2}$ s $\dfrac{r^6t^2}{9}$ t $\dfrac{125}{8p^3q^6}$

8 a $\dfrac{1}{a^{-n}} = \dfrac{a^0}{a^{-n}}$
      $= a^{0-(-n)}$
      $= a^{0+n}$
      $= a^n$
  b $\left(\dfrac{a}{b}\right)^{-n} = \left[\left(\dfrac{a}{b}\right)^{-1}\right]^n$
      $= \left(\dfrac{b}{a}\right)^n$
      $= \dfrac{b^n}{a^n}$

9 a m s^{-1} b $\text{m}^3\,\text{h}^{-1}$ c $\text{cm}^2\,\text{s}^{-1}$ d $\text{cm}^3\,\text{min}^{-1}$
  e g s^{-1} f kg m s^{-1} g m s^{-2}

10 $2^{125} = (2^5)^{25}$ and $3^{75} = (3^3)^{25}$
  $= 32^{25}$ $= 27^{25}$
  As $27^{25} < 32^{25}$, 3^{75} is smaller.

11 The indices have a common factor of 6.
  $2^{90} = (2^{15})^6 = 32\,768^6$
  $3^{60} = (3^{10})^6 = 59\,049^6$
  $5^{36} = (5^6)^6 = 15\,625^6$
  $10^{24} = (10^4)^6 = 10\,000^6$
  Order: $10^{24}, \, 5^{36}, \, 2^{90}, \, 3^{60}$

EXERCISE 1B

1 a 4 b $\dfrac{1}{4}$ c 5 d $\dfrac{1}{5}$ e 2 f $\dfrac{1}{2}$
  g -2 h $-\dfrac{1}{2}$ i 3 j $\dfrac{1}{3}$ k 2 l $\dfrac{1}{2}$

2 a not possible b -1 c $-\dfrac{1}{3}$ d not possible

3 a $10^{\frac{1}{2}}$ b $10^{-\frac{1}{2}}$ c $15^{\frac{1}{3}}$ d $15^{-\frac{1}{3}}$
  e $19^{\frac{1}{4}}$ f $19^{-\frac{1}{4}}$ g $13^{\frac{1}{5}}$ h $13^{-\frac{1}{5}}$

4 a 4 b 8 c 32 d 32 e 8 f 27
  g $\dfrac{1}{27}$ h $\dfrac{1}{2}$ i 2 j 4 k 8 l $\dfrac{1}{8}$
  m $\dfrac{1}{4}$ n $\dfrac{1}{81}$ o $\dfrac{1}{125}$

5 a $2^{\frac{3}{2}}$ b $2^{\frac{5}{3}}$ c $2^{\frac{1}{2}}$ d $2^{\frac{4}{3}}$ e $2^{-\frac{3}{4}}$ f $2^{-\frac{4}{3}}$
  g $2^{-\frac{3}{7}}$ h $2^{-\frac{6}{5}}$ i $2^{\frac{7}{2}}$ j $2^{\frac{9}{2}}$ k $2^{\frac{1}{3}}$ l $2^{\frac{3}{2}}$

6 a $3^{\frac{2}{3}}$ b $3^{\frac{3}{2}}$ c $3^{-\frac{3}{4}}$ d $3^{-\frac{4}{5}}$ e $3^{\frac{5}{2}}$ f $3^{\frac{5}{2}}$
  g $3^{\frac{9}{5}}$ h $3^{-\frac{2}{3}}$

7 a $5^{\frac{2}{3}}$ b $2^{\frac{5}{4}}$ c $5^{\frac{3}{5}}$ d $11^{\frac{2}{7}}$ e $7^{-\frac{2}{3}}$ f $2^{\frac{6}{5}}$
  g $5^{-\frac{4}{7}}$ h $3^{-\frac{5}{6}}$ i $2^{\frac{11}{2}}$ j $5^{\frac{7}{2}}$ k $13^{\frac{7}{3}}$ l $3^{\frac{5}{2}}$

8 a 125 b 9 c 128 d ≈ 2.41
  e ≈ 2.68 f ≈ 91.2 g ≈ 1.93 h ≈ 849
  i ≈ 2.13 j ≈ 9.16 k 0.0313 l $\approx 0.004\,12$
  m ≈ 0.339 n ≈ 0.182 o ≈ 0.215

9 3

EXERCISE 1C

1 a 2.3×10^2 b 5.39×10^4 c 3.61×10^{-2}
  d 6.8×10^{-3} e 3.26×10^0 f 5.821×10^{-1}
  g 3.61×10^8 h 1.674×10^{-6}

2 a 2300 b 0.023 c $564\,000$
  d $0.000\,793\,1$ e 9.97 f $60\,400\,000$
  g 0.4215 h $0.000\,000\,036\,21$

3 a $\approx 4 \times 10^6$ red blood cells b 8×10^{-4} m
  c 6.38×10^6 m d 4.3252×10^{19} arrangements

4 a $6\,990\,000$ m b 0.018 cm
  c $32\,000\,000$ bacteria d $0.000\,008\,2$ t

5 a 6×10^{10} b 2.8×10^9 c 5.6×10^{-8}
  d 5.4×10^{-6} e 9×10^{10} f 1.6×10^{15}
  g 1.6×10^{-11} h 1.25×10^{-7} i 1.2×10^0
  j 2.88×10^7 k 2.5×10^{-4} l 4×10^6

6 a 2×10^3 b 3×10^{-2} c 2×10^8
  d 1×10^{-19} e 3.2×10^3 f 8×10^8

7 a 1000 times b i 5×10^{-21} ii $100\,000$ times
  c 5×10^{10} times

8 a $\approx 4.01 \times 10^{13}$ b $\approx 2.59 \times 10^{12}$ c $\approx 7.08 \times 10^{-9}$
  d $\approx 4.87 \times 10^{-11}$ e $\approx 8.01 \times 10^6$ f $\approx 3.55 \times 10^{-9}$
  g $\approx 1.57 \times 10^{13}$ h $\approx 6.55 \times 10^{-22}$

9 a 5.84×10^7 b i 1.60×10^5 ii 5.84×10^8

10 a i 2.88×10^8 km ii $\approx 7.01 \times 10^{10}$ km **b** 0.9 s
   c ≈ 26.6 times **d** i Microbe C ii ≈ 32.9 times
11 As land areas are rounded to 2 significant figures, the answers should be rounded to 2 significant figures.
   a 9.1×10^6 km^2
   b Quebec > British Columbia > Ontario > Alberta > Saskatchewan > Manitoba > Newfoundland and Labrador > New Brunswick > Nova Scotia > Prince Edward Island
   c i ≈ 2.5 times ii ≈ 330 times **d** $\approx 0.58\%$

REVIEW SET 1A

1 a k^8 **b** p^5 **c** m^{48}
2 a $9w^2$ **b** $8x^6y^3$ **c** $\dfrac{a^6}{b^6}$ **d** $\dfrac{1}{125n^3}$
3 a $\frac{1}{7}$ **b** $\frac{3}{4}$ **c** $\frac{10}{11}$ **d** $\frac{16}{49}$
4 a 5.9×10^4 **b** 9×10^{-3} **c** 6.085×10^6 **d** 7.71×10^{-6}
5 a 7 **b** $\frac{1}{4}$ **c** 625 **d** $\frac{1}{9}$
6 a 623 000 **b** 0.000 300 8 **c** 4.597
7 a $2^{\frac{4}{5}}$ **b** $3^{-\frac{2}{3}}$ **c** $5^{\frac{7}{2}}$ **d** $2^{\frac{11}{2}}$
8 a ≈ 2.71 **b** ≈ 0.464 **c** ≈ 17.8 **d** ≈ 0.313
9 a $\dfrac{1}{m^2n^2}$ **b** $\dfrac{m}{n^2}$ **c** $\dfrac{125y^6}{x^3}$
10 a 1.8×10^{12} **b** 4×10^6 **c** 1.5×10^{-8} **d** 1.25×10^{-8}
11 a i $\approx 1.079 \times 10^{12}$ m ii $\approx 2.590 \times 10^{13}$ m
       iii $\approx 9.461 \times 10^{15}$ m
   b i $\approx 3.336 \times 10^{-9}$ s ii $\approx 3.336 \times 10^{-11}$ s
       iii $\approx 3.336 \times 10^{-12}$ s
   c $\approx 8.71 \times 10^5$ times faster

REVIEW SET 1B

1 a 2^6 **b** 5^{2x-3} **c** 7^{k+7}
2 a $15c^7$ **b** $7x^3y$ **c** $9p^2q^6$ **3** 81
4 a $\dfrac{b^2}{a^2}$ **b** $\dfrac{8a^3b^6}{27}$
5 a i $13^{\frac{1}{3}}$ ii $40^{-\frac{1}{5}}$ **b** ≈ 0.478
6 a 2.1×10^{15} **b** 6×10^{-12} **c** 4×10^{10}
7 a $2^{\frac{3}{4}}$ **b** $2^{-\frac{4}{5}}$ **c** $2^{-\frac{1}{2}}$ **8** 70 times
9 7^{20} as $2^{60} = (2^3)^{20} = 8^{20}$ and $8^{20} > 7^{20}$
10 a i 1.21×10^5 km ii 1.21×10^{10} cm
   b 6.05×10^6 m
   c Mercury < Mars < Venus < Earth < Neptune < Uranus < Saturn < Jupiter
   d i ≈ 10.5 times larger ii 20.6 times larger
11 a 7^9 **b** As $(\sqrt[5]{7} \times \sqrt[4]{7})^{20} = 7^9$ **d** $\sqrt[3]{11} \times \sqrt[5]{11}$
   then $\sqrt[5]{7} \times \sqrt[4]{7} = 7^{\frac{9}{20}}$ $= 11^{\frac{3+5}{3 \times 5}} = 11^{\frac{8}{15}}$

EXERCISE 2A

1 a $8 \in P$ **b** $k \notin S$ **c** $14 \notin \{\text{odd numbers}\}$
   d $n(Y) = 9$
2 a true **b** true **c** true **d** true
   e false **f** false **g** true **h** true
3 a rational **b** rational **c** rational **d** rational
   e irrational **f** neither **g** rational **h** rational
   i neither **j** rational

4 a i $A = \{1, 2, 3, 6\}$ ii finite iii $n(A) = 4$
   b i $B = \{6, 12, 18, 24, ...\}$ ii infinite
   c i $C = \{1, 17\}$ ii finite iii $n(C) = 2$
   d i $D = \{17, 34, 51, 68, ...\}$ ii infinite
   e i $E = \{2, 3, 5, 7, 11, 13, 17, 19\}$ ii finite
       iii $n(E) = 8$
   f i $F = \{12, 14, 15, 16, 18, 20, 21, 22, 24, 25, 26, 27, 28\}$
       ii finite iii $n(F) = 13$
5 a $0.\overline{7} = \frac{7}{9}$ **b** $0.\overline{41} = \frac{41}{99}$ **c** $0.\overline{324} = \frac{12}{37}$
6 0.527 can be written as $\frac{527}{1000}$, where 527 and 1000 are integers
7 $0.\overline{9} = 1$ and $1 \in \mathbb{Z}$
8 Note: There may be other answers.
   a $\sqrt{2}, -\sqrt{2}$ are irrational, but $\sqrt{2} + (-\sqrt{2}) = 0$ which is rational.
   b $\sqrt{2}, \sqrt{50}$ are irrational, but $\sqrt{2} \times \sqrt{50} = \sqrt{100} = 10$ which is rational.

EXERCISE 2B

1 a The set of all real x such that x is greater than 4.
   b The set of all integers x such that x is less than or equal to 5.
   c The set of all real y such that y lies between 0 and 8.
   d The set of all integers x such that x lies between 1 and 4 including 1 and 4.
   e The set of all real t such that t lies between 2 and 7.
   f The set of all real n such that n is less than or equal to 3 or n is greater than 6.
2 a $\{x \mid x > 3\}$ **b** $\{x \mid 2 < x \leqslant 5\}$
   c $\{x \mid x \leqslant -1 \text{ or } x \geqslant 2\}$ **d** $\{x \mid -1 \leqslant x < 5, \ x \in \mathbb{Z}\}$
   e $\{x \mid 0 \leqslant x \leqslant 6, \ x \in \mathbb{N}\}$ **f** $\{x \mid x < 0\}$
3 a number line: 4, 5, 6, 7, 8 **b** number line: −5, 0, 4
   c number line: −3 to 5 (open at −3) **d** number line: −5, 0
   e number line: ← 6 **f** number line: −5 to 0
4 a $\{x \mid x > 7\}$ **b** $\{x \mid -8 < x < 15, \ x \in \mathbb{Z}\}$
   c $\{x \mid 4 \leqslant x < 6, \ x \in \mathbb{Q}\}$

EXERCISE 2C

1 a $A \subseteq B$ **b** $A \nsubseteq B$ **c** $A \subseteq B$ **d** $A \nsubseteq B$
   e $A \subseteq B$
2 a true **b** true **c** false **d** true **e** false **f** true
3 $B \nsubseteq A, \ C \subseteq A$
4 a false **b** true **c** false **d** true
5 a $A' = \{1, 3, 4, 7, 8, 9\}$ **b** $B' = \{1, 4, 6, 8, 9\}$
   c $C' = \{2, 4, 6, 8\}$ **d** $D' = \{1, 2, 3, 5, 6, 7, 9\}$
   e $E' = \{1, 2, 3, 4, 5, 6, 7, 8, 9\}$ (or $E' = U$)
   f $F' = \{3, 4, 5, 6, 7, 8, 9\}$
6 a $P' = \{A, B, D, E, G, H, I, K, L, N, O, Q, R, S, T, V, W, X\}$
   b $Q' = \{\text{vowels}\}$
   c $R' = \{B, C, D, E, F, G, J, K, M, N, Q, R, U, V, W, X, Y, Z\}$
   d $S' = \{A, B, C, D, E, F, G, H, I, J\}$

7 a $A' = \{1, 2, 3, 4, 13, 14, 15\}$
$B' = \{1, 2, 3, 4, 5, 6, 10, 11, 12, 13, 14, 15\}$
b **i** false **ii** true **iii** true **iv** false

EXERCISE 2D

1 a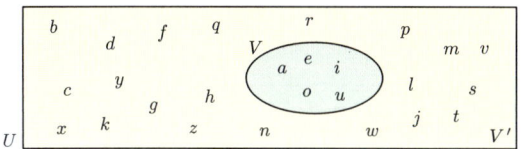
$A = \{2, 3, 5, 7\}$
b $A' = \{1, 4, 6, 8\}$
c **i** $n(A) = 4$
ii $n(A') = 4$
iii $n(U) = 8$

2 a

$$\begin{array}{l}U: b, d, f, q, r, p, m, v, c, y, g, h, z, n, w, j, s, t, V' \\ V: a, e, i, o, u, l\end{array}$$

b $V' = \{b, c, d, f, g, h, j, k, l, m, n, p, q, r, s, t, v, w, x, y, z\}$
c **i** $n(V) = 5$ **ii** $n(V') = 21$ **iii** $n(U) = 26$

3 a **i** $U = \{1, 2, 3, 4, 5, 6, 7, 8, 9, 10\}$
ii $N = \{3, 8\}$ **iii** $M = \{1, 3, 4, 7, 8\}$
b $n(N) = 2$, $n(M) = 5$ **c** No, $N \not\subseteq M$.

4 a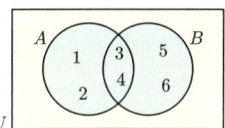
b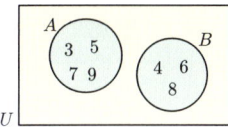

c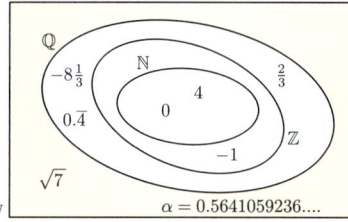

5 a, b, c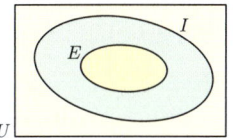

6 a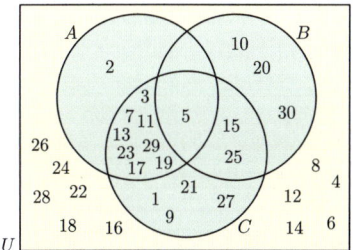

7 (three-set Venn diagram A, B, C with elements 2, 10, 20, 3, 7, 11, 13, 5, 30, 23, 29, 15, 17, 19, 25, 26, 24, 21, 8, 28, 22, 1, 27, 12, 4, 18, 16, 9, 14, 6)

EXERCISE 2E.1

1 a **i** $C = \{1, 3, 7, 9\}$ **ii** $D = \{1, 2, 5\}$
iii $U = \{1, 2, 3, 4, 5, 6, 7, 8, 9\}$ **iv** $C \cap D = \{1\}$
v $C \cup D = \{1, 2, 3, 5, 7, 9\}$
b **i** $n(C) = 4$ **ii** $n(D) = 3$ **iii** $n(U) = 9$
iv $n(C \cap D) = 1$ **v** $n(C \cup D) = 6$

2 a **i** $A = \{2, 7\}$ **ii** $B = \{1, 2, 4, 6, 7\}$
iii $U = \{1, 2, 3, 4, 5, 6, 7, 8\}$ **iv** $A \cap B = \{2, 7\}$
v $A \cup B = \{1, 2, 4, 6, 7\}$
b **i** $n(A) = 2$ **ii** $n(B) = 5$ **iii** $n(U) = 8$
iv $n(A \cap B) = 2$ **v** $n(A \cup B) = 5$

3 a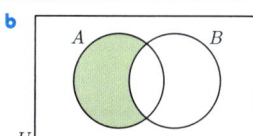
b **i** $A \cap B = \{2, 9, 11\}$
ii $A \cup B = \{1, 2, 7, 9, 10, 11, 12\}$
iii $B' = \{3, 4, 5, 6, 7, 8, 10\}$
c **i** $n(A) = 5$ **ii** $n(B') = 7$
iii $n(A \cap B) = 3$ **iv** $n(A \cup B) = 7$

4 a $A \cap B = \{1, 3, 9\}$
b $A \cup B = \{1, 2, 3, 4, 6, 7, 9, 12, 18, 21, 36, 63\}$

5 a $X \cap Y = \{B, M, T, Z\}$
b $X \cup Y = \{A, B, C, D, M, N, P, R, T, W, Z\}$

6 a **i** $n(A) = 8$ **ii** $n(B) = 10$
iii $n(A \cap B) = 3$ **iv** $n(A \cup B) = 15$
b $n(A) + n(B) - n(A \cap B) = 8 + 10 - 3$
$= 15 = n(A \cup B)$

7 a $\varnothing$ **b** U **c** $\varnothing$

EXERCISE 2E.2

1 a 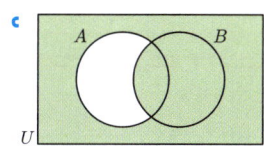 **b**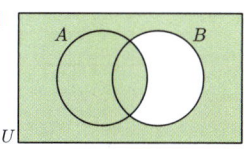

c 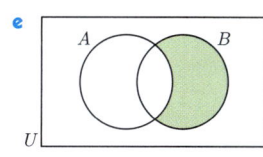 **d**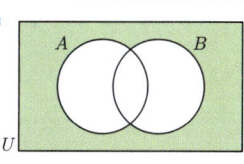

e (Venn diagram A, B) **f**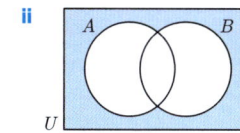

2 a in A but not in B
b the complement of 'in exactly one of A or B'

3 a **i** (Venn diagram A, B shaded) **ii** (Venn diagram A, B shaded)

iii

iv

v

vi

vii

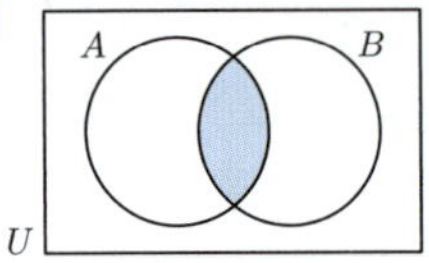

b **i** Since **a v** and **a vi** have the same regions shaded, $(A \cap B)' = A' \cup B'$.

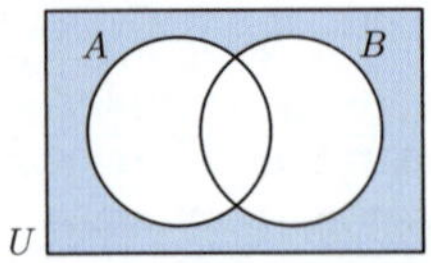

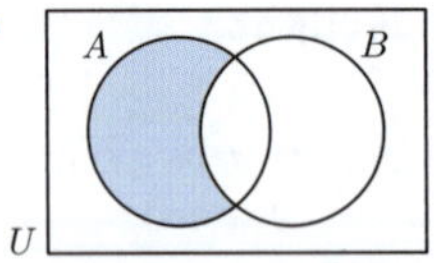

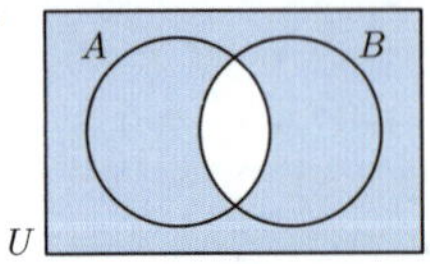

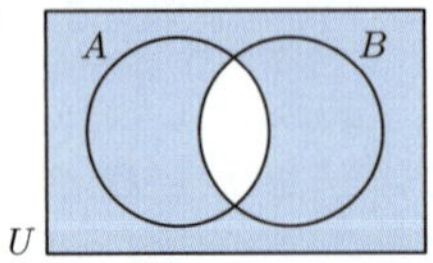

ii Since **a ii** and **a iii** have the same regions shaded, $(A \cup B)' = A' \cap B'$.

4 **a**

b

c

d

e

5 **a** **i**

ii

iii

iv

v

vi

vii

viii

ix

x

xi

xii

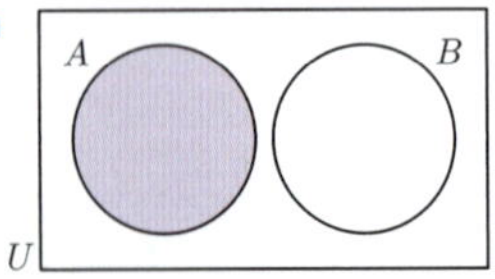

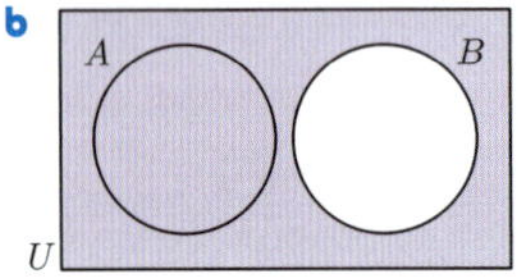

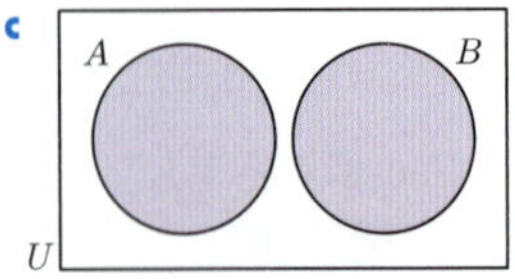

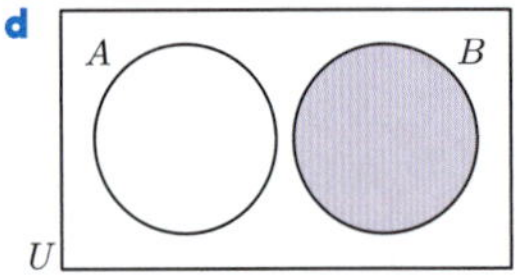

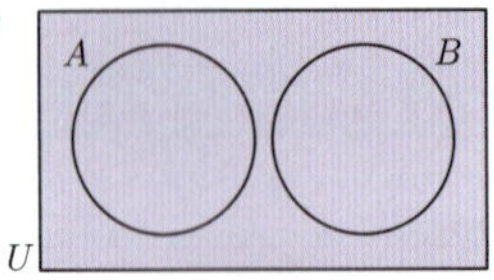

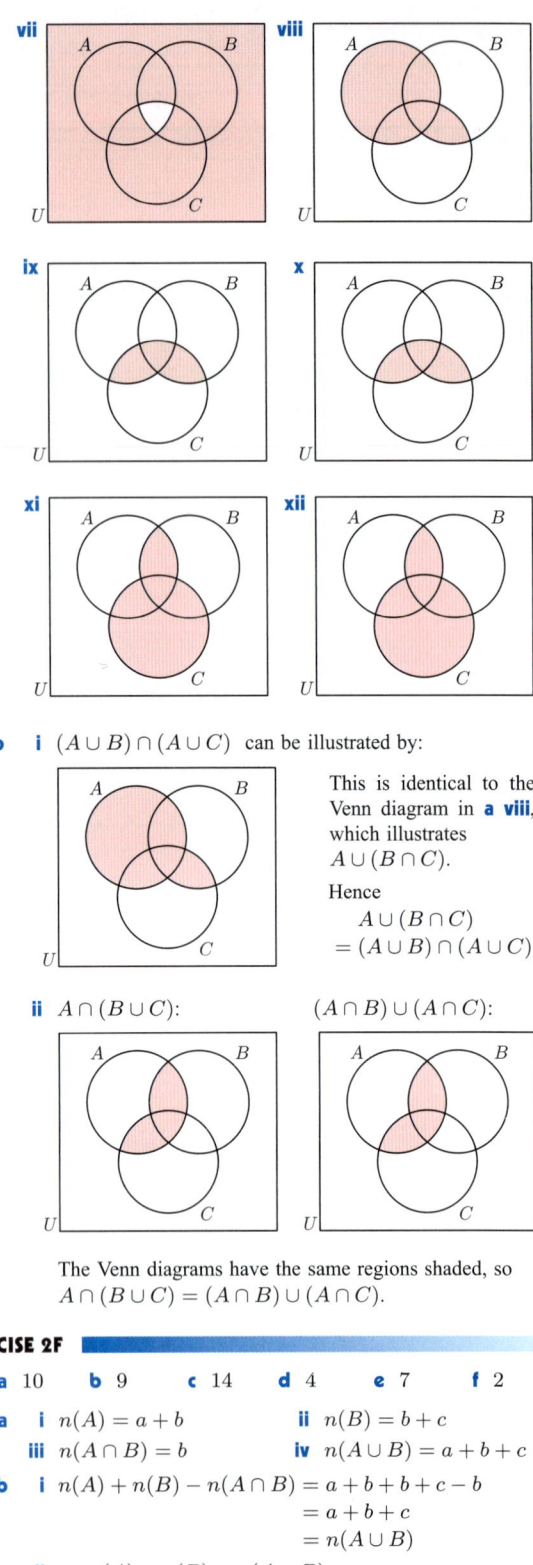

b **i** $(A \cup B) \cap (A \cup C)$ can be illustrated by:

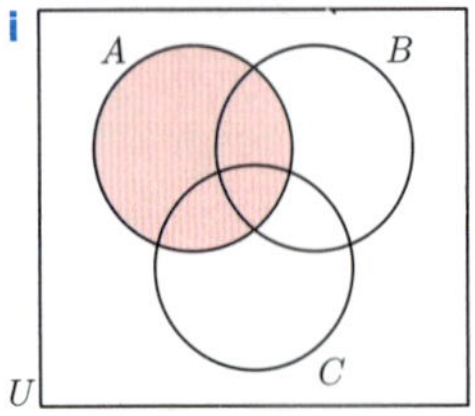

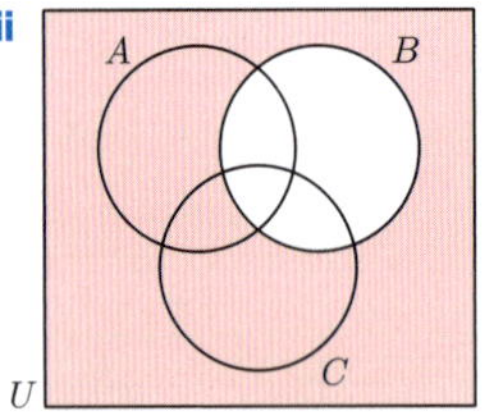

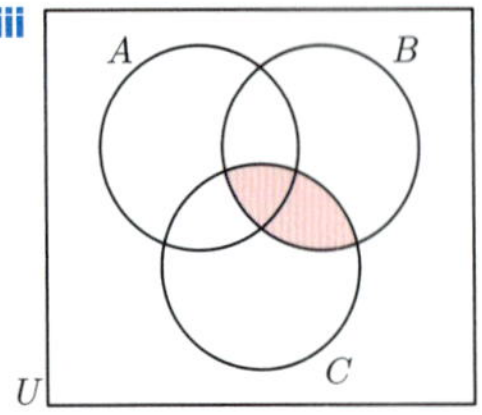

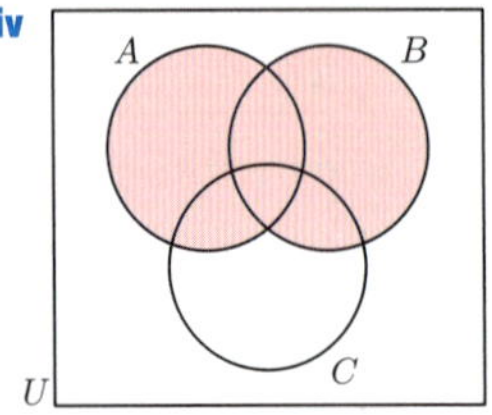

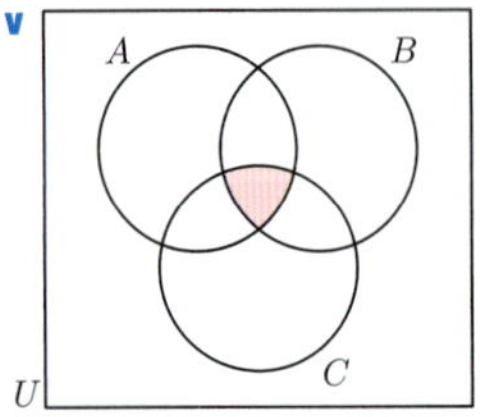

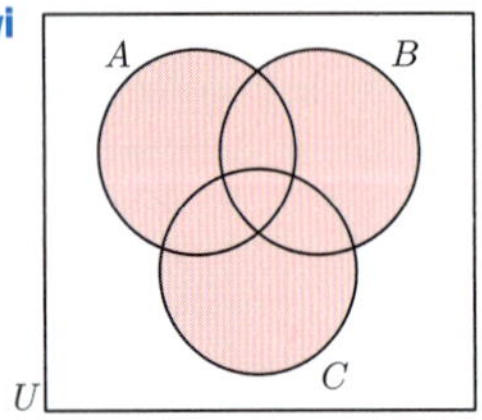

This is identical to the Venn diagram in **a viii**, which illustrates $A \cup (B \cap C)$.

Hence
$$A \cup (B \cap C) = (A \cup B) \cap (A \cup C)$$

ii $A \cap (B \cup C)$:

$(A \cap B) \cup (A \cap C)$:

The Venn diagrams have the same regions shaded, so $A \cap (B \cup C) = (A \cap B) \cup (A \cap C)$.

EXERCISE 2F

1 **a** 10 **b** 9 **c** 14 **d** 4 **e** 7 **f** 2

2 **a** **i** $n(A) = a + b$ **ii** $n(B) = b + c$

iii $n(A \cap B) = b$ **iv** $n(A \cup B) = a + b + c$

b **i**
$$\begin{aligned} n(A) + n(B) - n(A \cap B) &= a + b + b + c - b \\ &= a + b + c \\ &= n(A \cup B) \end{aligned}$$

ii
$$\begin{aligned} & n(A) + n(B) - n(A \cup B) \\ &= a + b + b + c - (a + b + c) \\ &= a + 2b + c - a - b - c \\ &= b \\ &= n(A \cap B) \end{aligned}$$

iii If A and B are disjoint then $n(A \cap B) = b = 0$.
So, $n(A \cup B) = a + b + c$
$= a + c$
and $n(A) + n(B) = a + b + b + c$
$= a + c$
$= n(A \cup B)$

3 a $n(A) - n(A \cap B) = (a + b) - b$
$= a$
$\therefore n(A \cap B') = n(A) - n(A \cap B)$
b $n(U) - n(A' \cap B) = (a + b + c + d) - c$
$= a + b + d$
$\therefore n(A \cup B') = n(U) - n(A' \cap B)$

4 a 17 **b** 5   **5 a** 7 **b** 10

EXERCISE 2G

1 a 18 **b** 2 **c** 17 **d** 12
2 a 75 **b** 9 **c** 24 **d** 42
3
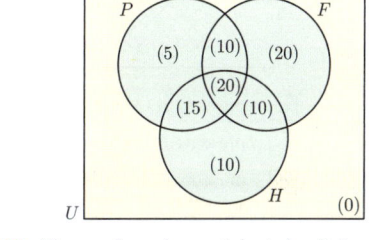
 a 21 **b** 4
 c 6   **d** 9

4 a 20 **b** 32 **c** 25 **d** 13   **5 a** 10 **b** 5
6 a 18 **b** 38   **7 a** 15 **b** 14 **c** 8
8 a
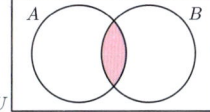
b i 45%
  ii 82%
  iii 11%
  iv 37%

9 11 violin players   **10** 43%   **11** 19 places
12 a
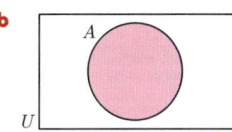
 b 15 students
 c 55 students

13 The number who participate in all three sports must be less than or equal to 30.

EXERCISE 2H

1 a
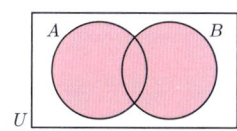

The shaded region could be either $A \cap B$ or $B \cap A$.
$\therefore A \cap B = B \cap A$

The shaded region could be either $A \cup B$ or $B \cup A$.
$\therefore A \cup B = B \cup A$

b

The shaded region is either $A \cap A$, A, or $A \cup A$.
$\therefore A \cap A = A$
and $A \cup A = A$

c
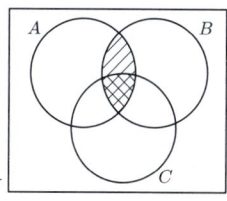

▨ represents $B \cap C$
▩ represents $A \cap (B \cap C)$

▨ represents $A \cap B$
▩ represents $(A \cap B) \cap C$

Region shaded is the same in each case.
$\therefore A \cap (B \cap C) = (A \cap B) \cap C$

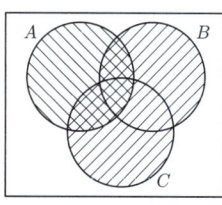
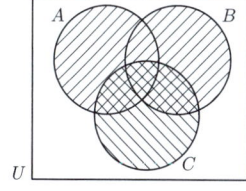

▨ represents A
▧ represents $B \cup C$
whole shaded region represents $A \cup (B \cup C)$

▨ represents C
▧ represents $A \cup B$
whole shaded region represents $(A \cup B) \cup C$

Total shaded region is the same in each case.

d
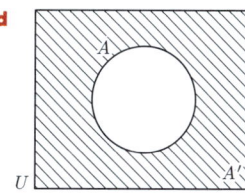

□ represents A
▨ represents A'

A' is the region outside A and is shaded.
$(A')'$ is the region not in A' and is unshaded.
$\therefore (A')' = A$

2 a $A \cup (B \cup A')$
$= A \cup (A' \cup B)$ {commutative law}
$= (A \cup A') \cup B$ {associative law}
$= U \cup B$ {complement law}
$= U$ {domination law}

b $A \cap (B \cap A')$
$= A \cap (A' \cap B)$ {commutative law}
$= (A \cap A') \cap B$ {associative law}
$= \varnothing \cap B$ {complement law}
$= \varnothing$ {domination law}

c $A \cup (B \cap A')$
$= (A \cup B) \cap (A \cup A')$ {distributive law}
$= (A \cup B) \cap U$ {complement law}
$= A \cup B$ {identity law}

d $(A' \cup B')'$
$= ((A \cap B)')'$ {De Morgan's law}
$= A \cap B$ {involution law}

e $(A \cup B) \cap (A' \cap B')$
$= (A \cup B) \cap (A \cup B)'$ {De Morgan's law}
$= \varnothing$ {complement law}

f $(A \cup B) \cap (C \cup D)$
$= ((A \cup B) \cap C) \cup ((A \cup B) \cap D)$ {distributive law}
$= (A \cap C) \cup (B \cap C) \cup (A \cap D) \cup (B \cap D)$
      {distributive law}
$= (A \cap C) \cup (A \cap D) \cup (B \cap C) \cup (B \cap D)$
      {commutative law}

REVIEW SET 2A

1 1.3 can be written as $\frac{13}{10}$, and 13 and 10 are integers

2 false

3 a yes **b** $P = \{23, 29, 31, 37\}$, $n(P) = 4$

4 S is the set of all real t such that t lies between -1 and 3, including -1.

5 $\{x \mid 0 < x \leqslant 5\}$ **6 a** $P \not\subseteq Q$ **b** $P \subseteq Q$

7 a $A' = \{1, 2, 4, 5, 6, 8, 10\}$ **b** $B' = \{1, 2, 3, 5, 7\}$

8 a

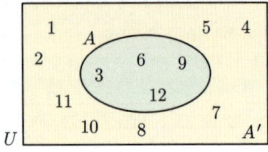

b $A' = \{1, 2, 4, 5, 7, 8, 10, 11\}$ **c** $n(A') = 8$

9 a False, as $0 \in \mathbb{N}$, but $0 \notin \mathbb{Z}^+$.
b False, as $\frac{1}{2} \in \mathbb{Q}$, but $\frac{1}{2} \notin \mathbb{Z}$.

10 a **i** $A = \{1, 2, 3, 4, 5\}$ **ii** $B = \{1, 2, 7\}$
iii $U = \{1, 2, 3, 4, 5, 6, 7\}$
iv $A \cup B = \{1, 2, 3, 4, 5, 7\}$ **v** $A \cap B = \{1, 2\}$
b **i** $n(A) = 5$ **ii** $n(B) = 3$ **iii** $n(A \cup B) = 6$

11 a

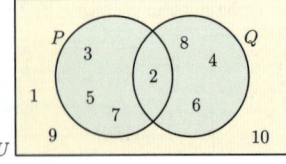

b **i** $P \cap Q = \{2\}$ **ii** $P \cup Q = \{2, 3, 4, 5, 6, 7, 8\}$
iii $Q' = \{1, 3, 5, 7, 9, 10\}$
c **i** $n(P') = 6$ **ii** $n(P \cap Q) = 1$ **iii** $n(P \cup Q) = 7$
d yes

12 a The shaded region is the complement of X, that is, everything that is not in X.
b The shaded region represents 'in exactly one of X or Y but not both'.
c The shaded region represents everything in X or in neither set.

13 a 11 **b** 14 **c** 21 **d** 2 **14** 200 families

REVIEW SET 2B

1 No **2** $0.\overline{51} = \frac{17}{33}$, and 17 and 33 are integers.

3

4 a **i** $A = \{1, 3, 5, 15\}$ **ii** finite **iii** 4
b **i** $B = \{8, 16, 24, 32, ...\}$ **ii** infinite
c **i** $C = \{31, 33, 35, 37, 39, 41, 43, 45, 47, 49\}$
ii finite **iii** 10
d **i** $D = \{2, 3, 5, 7, 11, 13, 17, 19, 23, 29\}$
ii finite **iii** 10

5 $Q \subseteq P$, $R \not\subseteq P$

6 $U = \{1, 2, 3, 4, 5, 6, 7, 8, 9, 10, 11, 12\}$
a $A = \{2, 3, 5, 7, 11\}$ **b** $A' = \{1, 4, 6, 8, 9, 10, 12\}$
c $n(A) = 5$ **d** $n(A') = 7$ **e** $n(U) = 12$

7

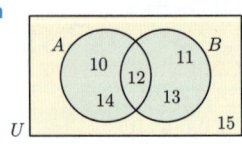 U is the set of all real numbers, $\mathbb{R}$.

8 a 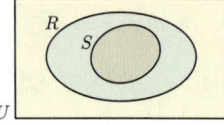 **b**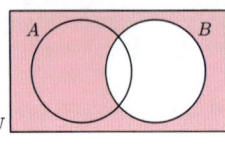

9 a $A \cap B = \{1, 2, 3, 6\}$
b $A \cup B = \{1, 2, 3, 4, 6, 8, 9, 12, 18, 24\}$

10 a **b**

c

11

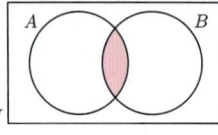

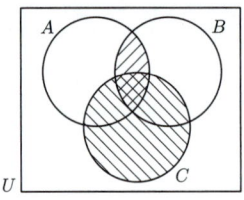

represents $A \cap B$
represents C
whole shaded region represents $(A \cap B) \cup C$

represents $A \cup C$
represents $B \cup C$
represents $(A \cup C) \cap (B \cup C)$

Area shaded is the same in each case.

12 a 18 **b** 4

13 a 65% **b** 35% **c** 22% **d** 28% **e** 9%

14 $A \cap (B \cup A') = (A \cap B) \cup (A \cap A')$ {distributive law}
$= (A \cap B) \cup \varnothing$ {complement law}
$= A \cap B$ {identity law}

EXERCISE 3A

1 a $6x + 15$ **b** $4x^2 - 12x$ **c** $-6 - 2x$
d $-3x^2 - 3xy$ **e** $2x^3 - 2x$ **f** $x^3 - x$
g $a^2 b - ab^2$ **h** $x^3 - 3x^2$ **i** $3a^2 + 9a + 3$
j $5x^2 - 15x + 10$ **k** $-8c^2 + 12c + 28$
l $6a^3 - 10a^2 + 2a$

2 a $7x - 14$ **b** $-5x - 6$ **c** $4x - x^2$ **d** $2x^3$
e $a^2 + b^2$ **f** $-x^3 + 9x^2 - 12x$

3 a $x^2 + 7x + 10$ **b** $x^2 + x - 12$ **c** $x^2 + 2x - 15$
d $x^2 - 12x + 20$ **e** $2x^2 - 5x - 3$ **f** $6x^2 - 23x + 20$

ANSWERS 559

    g $2x^2 - xy - y^2$ **h** $-2x^2 - 7x - 3$
    i $-x^2 - x - 2xy - 2y$
4 **a** $x^2 + 5x - 18$ **b** $2x^2 + 7x - 31$ **c** $x^2 - 8x - 12$
    d $-7t + 2$ **e** $2x^2 + 3$ **f** $10x^2 + 53x - 96$
5 **a** $x^2 - 49$ **b** $9 - a^2$ **c** $25 - x^2$ **d** $4x^2 - 1$
    e $16 - 9y^2$ **f** $9x^2 - 16z^2$
6 **a** 27 **b** $22p^2 + p - 4$ **c** $5y^2 + 8z^2$ **d** $8x^4$
7 **a** $x^2 + 10x + 25$ **b** $4x^2 + 12x + 9$
    c $x^2 + 14x + 49$ **d** $9x^2 + 24x + 16$
    e $x^4 + 10x^2 + 25$ **f** $9x^4 + 12x^2 + 4$
    g $25x^2 + 30xy + 9y^2$ **h** $4x^4 + 28x^2y + 49y^2$
    i $x^6 + 16x^4 + 64x^2$
8 **a** $x^2 - 6x + 9$ **b** $x^2 - 4x + 4$
    c $9x^2 - 6x + 1$ **d** $25p^2 - 60p + 36$
    e $4x^2 - 20xy + 25y^2$ **f** $a^2b^2 - 4ab + 4$
    g $x^4 - 10x^2 + 25$ **h** $16x^4 - 24x^2y + 9y^2$
    i $x^4 + 2x^2y^2 + y^4$
9 Hint: Area ① = total area − 2 × area ② − area ④
10 **a** $2x^2 + 14x + 85$ **b** $5x^2 + 18x - 8$ **c** $19x + 74$
    d $p^4 - 7p^2 - 10p + 41$ **e** $9x^4 - 10x^2 + 8x - 3$
    f $y^4 - x^5 + 2x^3y + 9xy^2 + 25x^2$

EXERCISE 3B

1 **a** $x^3 + 3x^2 + 6x + 8$ **b** $x^3 + 5x^2 + 3x - 9$
    c $x^3 + 5x^2 + 7x + 3$ **d** $2x^3 + x^2 - 6x - 5$
    e $2x^3 + 7x^2 + 8x + 3$ **f** $2x^3 - 9x^2 + 4x + 15$
    g $3x^3 + 14x^2 - x + 20$ **h** $8x^3 - 14x^2 + 7x - 1$
2 **a** $x^3 + 9x^2 + 26x + 24$ **b** $x^3 - x^2 - 14x + 24$
    c $x^3 - 10x^2 + 31x - 30$ **d** $2x^3 + x^2 - 12x + 9$
    e $12x^3 + 11x^2 - 2x - 1$ **f** $-3x^3 + 26x^2 - 33x - 14$
    g $-3x^3 + 16x^2 - 12x - 16$ **h** $x^3 + 9x^2 + 27x + 27$
    i $x^3 - 6x^2 + 12x - 8$
3 **a** $2 \times 2 = 4$ terms   **b** $3 \times 2 = 6$ terms
    c $2 \times 3 = 6$ terms   **d** $3 \times 3 = 9$ terms
    e $4 \times 2 = 8$ terms   **f** $4 \times 3 = 12$ terms
4 **a** $x^4 + 2x^3 + x^2 + 8x + 3$
    b $2x^4 + 7x^3 - 2x^2 - 5x + 2$
    c $6x^4 - 7x^3 - 8x^2 + 13x - 4$
    d $x^4 - x^3 - 19x^2 + 49x - 30$

EXERCISE 3C

1 **a** $x^3 + 3x^2 + 3x + 1$ **b** $x^3 + 9x^2 + 27x + 27$
    c $x^3 + 15x^2 + 75x + 125$ **d** $x^3 + 3x^2y + 3xy^2 + y^3$
    e $x^3 - 3x^2 + 3x - 1$ **f** $x^3 - 15x^2 + 75x - 125$
    g $x^3 - 12x^2 + 48x - 64$ **h** $x^3 - 3x^2y + 3xy^2 - y^3$
    i $8 + 12y + 6y^2 + y^3$ **j** $8x^3 + 12x^2 + 6x + 1$
    k $27x^3 + 27x^2 + 9x + 1$
    l $8y^3 + 36xy^2 + 54x^2y + 27x^3$
    m $8 - 12y + 6y^2 - y^3$ **n** $8x^3 - 12x^2 + 6x - 1$
    o $27x^3 - 27x^2 + 9x - 1$
    p $8y^3 - 36xy^2 + 54x^2y - 27x^3$

3 **a** $x^4 + 4x^3y + 6x^2y^2 + 4xy^3 + y^4$
    b $x^4 + 4x^3 + 6x^2 + 4x + 1$
    c $x^4 + 8x^3 + 24x^2 + 32x + 16$
    d $x^4 + 12x^3 + 54x^2 + 108x + 81$
    e $x^4 - 4x^3y + 6x^2y^2 - 4xy^3 + y^4$
    f $x^4 - 4x^3 + 6x^2 - 4x + 1$
    g $x^4 - 8x^3 + 24x^2 - 32x + 16$
    h $16x^4 - 32x^3 + 24x^2 - 8x + 1$
4 **a**   1 5 10 10 5 1
      1 6 15 20 15 6 1
    We start and finish each row with a 1. The other entries are obtained by adding the two adjacent numbers in the row above.
    b **i** $a^5 + 5a^4b + 10a^3b^2 + 10a^2b^3 + 5ab^4 + b^5$
        ii $a^5 - 5a^4b + 10a^3b^2 - 10a^2b^3 + 5ab^4 - b^5$
        iii $a^6 + 6a^5b + 15a^4b^2 + 20a^3b^3 + 15a^2b^4 + 6ab^5 + b^6$
        iv $a^6 - 6a^5b + 15a^4b^2 - 20a^3b^3 + 15a^2b^4 - 6ab^5 + b^6$
    c **i** $x^5 - 10x^4 + 40x^3 - 80x^2 + 80x - 32$
        ii When $x = 1$, $(x-2)^5 = (-1)^5 = -1$
        and $1^5 - 10 \times 1^4 + 40 \times 1^3 - 80 \times 1^2 + 80 \times 1 - 32$
        $= 1 - 10 + 40 - 80 + 80 - 32$
        $= -1$ ✓

EXERCISE 3D

1 **a** $x(x - 5)$ **b** $2x(x + 3)$ **c** $2x(2 - y)$
    d $3b(a - 2)$ **e** $2x^2(1 + 4x)$ **f** $6x(2 - x)$
    g $x^2(x + 1)$ **h** $3ab(b - 3a)$
2 **a** $(x + 5)(3 + x)$ **b** $(b + 3)(a - 5)$ **c** $(x + 4)(x + 1)$
    d $(x + 2)(2x + 5)$ **e** $(c - d)(a + b)$ **f** $(2 + y)(y - 1)$
    g $(x - 1)(ab + c)$ **h** $(x + 2)(a - 1)$ **i** $(x - 3)(x - 2)$
    j $(x + 5)(x + 8)$ **k** $2x(x - 2)$
    l $(x + y)(x + y + 1)(x + y - 1)$
3 **a** $(x + 4)(x - 4)$ **b** $(8 + x)(8 - x)$
    c $(3x + 1)(3x - 1)$ **d** $(7 + 2x)(7 - 2x)$
    e $(y + 2x)(y - 2x)$ **f** $(2a + 5b)(2a - 5b)$
    g $(9x + 4y)(9x - 4y)$ **h** $(2x^2 + y)(2x^2 - y)$
    i $(3ab + 4)(3ab - 4)$ **j** $(x + 5)(x + 1)$
    k $3(3x + 2)(x - 2)$ **l** $3(x - 3)(x - 1)$
4 **a** $2(x + 2)(x - 2)$ **b** $3(y + 3)(y - 3)$
    c $2(1 + 3x)(1 - 3x)$ **d** $x(2 + 3x)(2 - 3x)$
    e $ab(a + b)(a - b)$ **f** $2(5 + xy)(5 - xy)$
    g $b(3b + 2)(3b - 2)$ **h** $x(x^2 + y^2)(x + y)(x - y)$
5 **a** $(x + 2)^2$ **b** $(x - 5)^2$ **c** $(3x + 5)^2$ **d** $(x - 4)^2$
    e $(2x + 7)^2$ **f** $(x - 10)^2$
6 **a** $-(3x - 1)^2$ **b** $3(x + 3)^2$ **c** $-2(3x - 1)^2$
    d $2(x + 5)(x - 5)$ **e** $2(x - 4)^2$ **f** $-3(x + 3)^2$

EXERCISE 3E

1 **a** $(a + 1)(2 + b)$ **b** $(c + d)(a + 4)$ **c** $(a + 2)(b + 3)$
    d $(n + 3)(m + p)$ **e** $(x + 5)(2y - 1)$ **f** $(3 - c)(2a + b)$
2 **a** $(x + 4)(x + 2)$ **b** $(x + 3)(x + 7)$
    c $(x + 5)(x + 4)$ **d** $(2x + 1)(x + 3)$
    e $(3x + 2)(x + 4)$ **f** $(5x + 3)(4x + 1)$
3 **a** $(x - 4)(x + 5)$ **b** $(x - 7)(x + 2)$ **c** $(x - 3)(x - 2)$
    d $(x - 5)(x - 3)$ **e** $(x + 7)(x - 8)$ **f** $(2x + 1)(x - 3)$
    g $(3x + 2)(x - 4)$ **h** $(4x - 3)(x - 2)$ **i** $(9x + 2)(x - 1)$

EXERCISE 3F

1. **a** $(x+1)(x+2)$ **b** $(x+2)(x+3)$ **c** $(x+2)(x-3)$
   d $(x-2)(x+5)$ **e** $(x-3)(x+7)$ **f** $(x+4)^2$
   g $(x-7)^2$ **h** $(x-4)(x+7)$ **i** $(x-3)(x-8)$
   j $(x+4)(x+11)$ **k** $(x+7)(x-8)$ **l** $(x-9)^2$
   m $(x+4)(x-8)$ **n** $(x-5)(x+9)$
   o $(x+8)(x-12)$ **p** $(x-8)(x+12)$

2. **a** $2(x+1)(x+4)$ **b** $3(x-1)(x-6)$
   c $2(x+3)(x+4)$ **d** $5(x+2)(x-8)$
   e $4(x+1)(x-3)$ **f** $3(x-3)(x-11)$
   g $2(x+9)(x-10)$ **h** $3(x+2)(x-4)$
   i $2(x+4)(x+5)$ **j** $x(x+1)(x-8)$
   k $4(x-3)^2$ **l** $3(x-3)(x+9)$
   m $2(x-10)(x-12)$ **n** $x(x+4)(x-7)$
   o $x^2(x+1)^2$

3. **a** $-(x-6)(x+9)$ **b** $-(x+2)(x+5)$
   c $-(x+3)(x+7)$ **d** $-(x-1)(x-3)$
   e $-(x-2)^2$ **f** $-(x-1)(x+3)$

4. **a** $-(x+6)(x-8)$ **b** $-(x-3)^2$
   c $-3(x-3)(x-7)$ **d** $-2(x+7)(x-9)$
   e $-2(x-5)^2$ **f** $-x(x+1)(x-2)$

5. As $b = m + n$, $-b = -m - n$
   Since $c = mn$, $x^2 - bx + c = x^2 - mx - nx + mn$
   $= (x - m)(x - n)$

EXERCISE 3G

1. **a** **i** $3x^2 + 7x + 2$ **ii** $3x^2 + 7x + 2$
   $= 3x^2 + 6x + x + 2$ $= 3x^2 + x + 6x + 2$
   $= 3x(x+2) + 1(x+2)$ $= x(3x+1) + 2(3x+1)$
   $= (x+2)(3x+1)$ $= (3x+1)(x+2)$
   b Yes, as $ab = ba$.

2. **a** $(2x+3)(x+1)$ **b** $(2x+9)(x+2)$
   c $(7x+2)(x+1)$ **d** $(3x+1)(x+4)$
   e $(3x+2)(x+2)$ **f** $(3x+7)(x+3)$
   g $(4x+1)(2x+3)$ **h** $(7x+1)(3x+2)$
   i $(3x+1)(2x+1)$ **j** $(6x+1)(x+3)$
   k $(5x+1)(2x+3)$ **l** $(7x+1)(2x+5)$

3. **a** **i** $(2x+3)(2x-1)$ **ii** $(2x-1)(2x+3)$ **b** yes

4. **a** $(2x+1)(x-5)$ **b** $(3x-1)(x+2)$
   c $(3x+1)(x-2)$ **d** $(2x-1)(x+2)$
   e $(2x+5)(x-1)$ **f** $(5x-3)(x-1)$
   g $(11x+2)(x-1)$ **h** $(2x+3)(x-3)$
   i $(3x-2)(x-5)$ **j** $(5x+2)(x-3)$
   k $(3x-2)(x+4)$ **l** $(2x-1)(x+9)$
   m $(2x-3)(x+6)$ **n** $(5x+2)(3x-1)$
   o $(21x+1)(x-3)$

5. **a** $-(3x+7)(x-2)$ **b** $-(5x-1)(x-2)$
   c $-(4x-3)(x+3)$ **d** $-(3x-2)^2$
   e $-(4x+1)(2x+3)$ **f** $-(6x+1)(2x-3)$

6. **a** $(3x+5)^2 - (2x-3)^2$
   $= 9x^2 + 30x + 25 - [4x^2 - 12x + 9]$
   $= 9x^2 + 30x + 25 - 4x^2 + 12x - 9$
   $= 5x^2 + 42x + 16$

   b $(5x+2)(x+8)$
   $\{ac = 80, \ b = 42, \ \text{split is } +40x + 2x\}$

   c $(3x+5)^2 - (2x-3)^2$
   $= (3x + 5 + 2x - 3)(3x + 5 - 2x + 3)$
   $= (5x+2)(x+8)$

EXERCISE 3H

1. **a** $x(3x+2)$ **b** $(x+9)(x-9)$
   c $2(p^2+4)$ **d** $3(b+5)(b-5)$
   e $2(x+4)(x-4)$ **f** $n^2(n+2)(n-2)$
   g $(x-9)(x+1)$ **h** $(d+7)(d-1)$
   i $(x+9)(x-1)$ **j** $4t(1+2t)$
   k $(2x+1)(2x+5)$ **l** $2(g+5)(g-11)$
   m $(2a+3d)(2a-3d)$ **n** $5(a+1)(a-2)$
   o $2(c-1)(c-3)$ **p** $(x+7)(2x+3)$
   q $d^2(d+3)(d-1)$ **r** $x(x+2)^2$

2. **a** $7(x-5y)$ **b** $2(g+2)(g-2)$
   c $-5x(x+2)$ **d** $m(m+3p)$
   e $(a+3)(a+5)$ **f** $(m-3)^2$
   g $5x(x+y-xy)$ **h** $(x+2)(y+2)$
   i $(y+5)(y-9)$ **j** $(x+5)(2x+1)$
   k $3(y+7)(y-7)$ **l** $(6x+1)(x-5)$
   m $(2c+1)(2c-1)$ **n** $3(x+4)(x-3)$
   o $2(x-3)(b+5)$ **p** $(4x+3)(3x+1)$
   q $-2(x-1)(x-3)$ **r** $(4x+1)^2$
   s $-2x(x-1)^2$ **t** $(a+b+3)(a+b-3)$
   u $2(x-3)(6x-1)$

REVIEW SET 3A

1. Show that the total area equals the sum of the two smaller areas.

2. **a** $x^2 - x - 30$ **b** $6x^2 + 13x - 5$ **c** $18x - x^2$
3. **a** $x(7x-4)$ **b** $x(x-1)(x+6)$ **c** $(x-8)(x+5)$
4. **a** $x^3 + 4x^2 - 7x - 10$ **b** $2x^3 + 5x^2 - 8x - 6$
5. **a** $(4+3m)(4-3m)$ **b** $x(x+9)(x-9)$
   c $(x+12)(x+2)$
6. **a** $t^2 - 49$ **b** $4y^2 - 25$ **c** $4m^2 - 20mn + 25n^2$
7. **a** $2(x+5)^2$ **b** $(b+d)(2-c)$
8. **a** $8k^3 + 36k^2 + 54k + 27$ **b** $r^3 - 12r^2t + 48rt^2 - 64t^3$
9. **a** $(x-2)(x+9)$ **b** $3(x+2)(x-5)$ **c** $-2(x+4)(x-8)$
10. **a** $(4x+3)(2x+1)$ **b** $(5x-3)(x-2)$
    c $-(3x+1)(3x-2)$
11. **b** $3(x+2)(x+12)$
    c $(2x+9+x-3)(2x+9-x+3) = 3(x+2)(x+12)$
12. **a** **i** $a^2 + 2ab + b^2$ **ii** $a^3 + 3a^2b + 3ab^2 + b^3$
    iii $a^4 + 4a^3b + 6a^2b^2 + 4ab^3 + b^4$
    iv $a^5 + 5a^4b + 10a^3b^2 + 10a^2b^3 + 5ab^4 + b^5$
    b **i** 8 **ii** 16 **iii** 32 **c** 2^n
    d From **12 a**, we see that if $a = b = 1$ in these four expansions, we obtain results of $4 = 2^2$, $8 = 2^3$, $16 = 2^4$, and $32 = 2^5$.
    Letting $a = b = 1$ in $(a+b)^n$ we get $(1+1)^n = 2^n$.

REVIEW SET 3B

1. **a** $20x - 25$ **b** $12x - 4x^2$ **c** $3x^2 - 5x + 12$
2. **a** $x^3 + 2x - 20$ **b** $3b^2$

ANSWERS

3 a $2(x+7)(x-7)$ **b** $(4x-3)(2x+5)$
4 Show $(10a+b)(10c+d) = 100ac + 10(ad+bc) + bd$.
5 a $(x-6)(x+9)$ **b** $3(x+4)^2$ **6** 16 terms
7 a $9x^4 - 30x^2 + 25$ **b** $8a^3 - 12a^2b + 6ab^2 - b^3$
8 a $(x+6)(x-11)$ **b** $2(x-3)(x+13)$
  c $(2x+3)(2x-7)$
9 $x^4 + x^3 + 5x^2 + 5x + 12$
10 a $-(x+3)(x-4)$ **b** $-(3x+10)(2x-5)$
11 a We seek two numbers with product $6 \times 12 = 72$ and sum 17. These are 9 and 8.
$\therefore$ to factorise $6x^2 + 17x + 12$ we split the $17x$ into $9x + 8x$.
  b $(2x+3)(3x+4)$ **c** $(3x+4)(2x+3)$ ✓
12 a **i** $23^2 = 529, 27^2 = 729$ **ii** $18^2 = 324, 32^2 = 1024$
    iii $11^2 = 121, 39^2 = 1521$ **iv** $14^2 = 196, 36^2 = 1296$
  b From **a**, if $a+b=50$, it appears that the last two digits of a^2 and b^2 are the same. If this is always true then their difference will always be a multiple of 100.
  c As $a+b=50$, $b=50-a$
Show $a^2 - b^2 = 100(a-25)$ where $a-25$ is an integer
$\therefore a^2 - b^2$ is a multiple of 100.
$\therefore$ the last two digits of a^2 and b^2 are the same.

EXERCISE 4A

1 a 7   **b** 13   **c** 15   **d** 24   **e** $2\sqrt{2}$ **f** 4
  g $4\sqrt{2}$ **h** $\frac{1}{2}$ **i** $\frac{1}{3}$ **j** $\frac{4}{11}$ **k** $\frac{3}{17}$ **l** $\frac{2}{23}$
2 a 2   **b** -5 **c** $\frac{1}{5}$
3 a 12   **b** 6   **c** 30   **d** 24   **e** -30
  f -30 **g** 12   **h** 18   **i** $54\sqrt{2}$ **j** 48
  k $192\sqrt{3}$ **l** 64   **m** $45\sqrt{5}$ **n** $-150\sqrt{3}$ **o** -224
4 a $\sqrt{10}$ **b** $\sqrt{21}$ **c** $\sqrt{33}$ **d** 7
  e 6   **f** $-2\sqrt{10}$ **g** $6\sqrt{6}$ **h** $6\sqrt{15}$
  i $\sqrt{30}$ **j** $4\sqrt{3}$ **k** -12 **l** $162\sqrt{6}$
5 a 2   **b** $\frac{1}{2}$ **c** 3   **d** $\frac{1}{3}$ **e** 2   **f** $\frac{1}{2}$
  g 3   **h** $\sqrt{6}$ **i** $\frac{1}{\sqrt{10}}$ **j** 5   **k** 1   **l** 25
6 a $\frac{1}{5}$ **b** $\frac{4}{3}$ **c** $\frac{7}{4}$ **d** $\frac{9}{2}$
7 a $(\sqrt{a}\sqrt{b})^2 = \sqrt{a}\sqrt{b} \times \sqrt{a}\sqrt{b} = ab$
  $(\sqrt{ab})^2 = \sqrt{ab} \times \sqrt{ab} = ab$
  As $a \geqslant 0$, $b \geqslant 0$, $(\sqrt{a}\sqrt{b})^2 = (\sqrt{ab})^2$
  b Using **a**, $\sqrt{b} \times \sqrt{\frac{a}{b}} = \sqrt{b \times \frac{a}{b}} = \sqrt{a}$
  $\therefore \sqrt{\frac{a}{b}} = \frac{\sqrt{a}}{\sqrt{b}}$
8 a $\sqrt{9} + \sqrt{16} = 3 + 4 = 7$, whereas $\sqrt{9+16} = \sqrt{25} = 5$
  $\therefore \sqrt{9} + \sqrt{16} \neq \sqrt{9+16}$
  $\sqrt{25} - \sqrt{16} = 5 - 4 = 1$, whereas $\sqrt{25-16} = \sqrt{9} = 3$
  $\therefore \sqrt{25} - \sqrt{16} \neq \sqrt{25-16}$
  b No, as they are not true for all $a \geqslant 0$, $b \geqslant 0$.

EXERCISE 4B

1 a $2\sqrt{6}$ **b** $5\sqrt{2}$ **c** $3\sqrt{6}$ **d** $2\sqrt{10}$
  e $2\sqrt{14}$ **f** $3\sqrt{7}$ **g** $2\sqrt{13}$ **h** $2\sqrt{11}$
  i $2\sqrt{15}$ **j** $3\sqrt{10}$ **k** $4\sqrt{6}$ **l** $2\sqrt{17}$
  m $5\sqrt{7}$ **n** $9\sqrt{2}$ **o** $8\sqrt{2}$ **p** $10\sqrt{7}$

2 a $\frac{\sqrt{5}}{3}$ **b** $\frac{3\sqrt{2}}{2}$ **c** $\frac{\sqrt{3}}{2}$ **d** $\frac{5\sqrt{3}}{6}$
3 a $2+\sqrt{2}$ **b** $3-\sqrt{3}$ **c** $1+\frac{1}{2}\sqrt{5}$ **d** $2-\sqrt{2}$
  e $2+\sqrt{2}$ **f** $3+\frac{1}{2}\sqrt{3}$ **g** $\frac{7}{4}-\frac{1}{4}\sqrt{15}$ **h** $\frac{1}{2}-\sqrt{2}$

EXERCISE 4C

1 a $10\sqrt{2}$ **b** $3\sqrt{3}$ **c** $-\sqrt{5}$ **d** $\sqrt{10}$
  e $5\sqrt{6}$ **f** $-6\sqrt{15}$
2 a $6\sqrt{2} - 2\sqrt{3}$ **b** $7\sqrt{7} + 3\sqrt{6}$ **c** $8\sqrt{10} + 3\sqrt{5}$
  d $-2\sqrt{3} - 7\sqrt{13}$ **e** $6\sqrt{7} + 5\sqrt{11}$ **f** $\sqrt{14} - 2\sqrt{6}$
  g $11 - 2\sqrt{17}$ **h** $-21 + 6\sqrt{15}$
3 a $\frac{7\sqrt{5}}{12}$ **b** $\frac{5\sqrt{6}}{14}$ **c** $\frac{23\sqrt{3}}{24}$ **d** $-\frac{14\sqrt{11}}{45}$
  e $\frac{13\sqrt{10}}{12}$ **f** $-\frac{11\sqrt{2}}{28}$
4 a $\sqrt{20} + \sqrt{5}$ **b** $\sqrt{147} - \sqrt{75}$
     $= 2\sqrt{5} + \sqrt{5}$ $= 7\sqrt{3} - 5\sqrt{3}$
     $= 3\sqrt{5}$ $= 2\sqrt{3}$
     $= \sqrt{9} \times \sqrt{5}$ $= \sqrt{4} \times \sqrt{3}$
     $= \sqrt{45}$ $= \sqrt{12}$
5 a **i** 9 units^2 **ii** 4 units^2 **b** 5 units^2
  c $A = l^2 = 5$ units^2
  Since $(\sqrt{5})^2 = 5$, the side length is $\sqrt{5}$ units.
  d $4\sqrt{5}$ units

EXERCISE 4D

1 a $\sqrt{10} + 2$ **b** $3\sqrt{2} - 2$ **c** $3 + \sqrt{3}$
  d $\sqrt{3} - 3$ **e** $7\sqrt{7} - 7$ **f** $2\sqrt{5} - 5$
  g $22 - \sqrt{11}$ **h** $\sqrt{6} - 12$ **i** $3 + \sqrt{6} - \sqrt{3}$
  j $6 - 2\sqrt{15}$ **k** $6\sqrt{5} - 10$ **l** $30 + 3\sqrt{10}$
2 a $2 - 3\sqrt{2}$ **b** $-2 - \sqrt{6}$ **c** $2 - 4\sqrt{2}$
  d $-3 - \sqrt{3}$ **e** $-3 - 2\sqrt{3}$ **f** $-5 - 2\sqrt{5}$
  g $-3 - \sqrt{2}$ **h** $-5 + 4\sqrt{5}$ **i** $\sqrt{7} - 3$
  j $11 - 2\sqrt{11}$ **k** $\sqrt{7} - \sqrt{3}$ **l** $4 - 2\sqrt{2}$
  m $9 - 15\sqrt{3}$ **n** $-14 - 14\sqrt{3}$ **o** $4 - 6\sqrt{2}$
3 a $4 + 3\sqrt{2}$ **b** $7 + 4\sqrt{3}$ **c** $1 + \sqrt{3}$
  d $10 + \sqrt{2}$ **e** -2 **f** $3 - 3\sqrt{7}$
  g $-1 - \sqrt{5}$ **h** $1 - \sqrt{6}$ **i** $14 - 7\sqrt{2}$
4 a $3 + 2\sqrt{2}$ **b** $7 - 4\sqrt{3}$ **c** $7 + 4\sqrt{3}$
  d $6 + 2\sqrt{5}$ **e** $5 - 2\sqrt{6}$ **f** $27 - 10\sqrt{2}$
  g $9 + 2\sqrt{14}$ **h** $22 - 8\sqrt{6}$ **i** $8 - 4\sqrt{3}$
  j $13 + 4\sqrt{10}$ **k** $13 - 4\sqrt{10}$ **l** $44 + 24\sqrt{2}$
  m $51 - 10\sqrt{2}$ **n** $17 - 12\sqrt{2}$ **o** $19 + 6\sqrt{2}$
5 a $90 + 34\sqrt{7}$ **b** $9\sqrt{3} - 11\sqrt{2}$
6 a 13   **b** 23   **c** 1   **d** -9 **e** 14
  f 19   **g** -2 **h** -28 **i** -174
7 a 1   **b** -4 **c** $x - y$ **d** 15   **e** 20   **f** 2

EXERCISE 4E

1 a $\frac{\sqrt{2}}{2}$ **b** $\sqrt{2}$ **c** $2\sqrt{2}$ **d** $\frac{\sqrt{6}}{2}$ **e** $\frac{\sqrt{14}}{6}$
  f $\frac{\sqrt{3}}{3}$ **g** $\sqrt{3}$ **h** $\frac{4\sqrt{3}}{3}$ **i** $\frac{\sqrt{21}}{3}$ **j** $\frac{\sqrt{33}}{12}$
  k $\frac{\sqrt{5}}{5}$ **l** $\frac{3\sqrt{5}}{5}$ **m** $3\sqrt{5}$ **n** $\frac{\sqrt{15}}{5}$ **o** $\frac{25\sqrt{5}}{2}$
  p $\sqrt{5}$ **q** $\frac{\sqrt{3}}{6}$ **r** $\frac{2\sqrt{6}}{3}$ **s** $\frac{3\sqrt{5}}{2}$ **t** $\frac{\sqrt{2}}{4}$

2 a $\dfrac{3+\sqrt{5}}{4}$ b $\dfrac{2-\sqrt{3}}{1}$ c $\dfrac{4+\sqrt{11}}{5}$
  d $\dfrac{5\sqrt{2}-2}{23}$ e $\dfrac{\sqrt{3}-1}{2}$ f $\dfrac{10+15\sqrt{2}}{-14}$
  g $\dfrac{3\sqrt{5}-10}{11}$ h $\dfrac{-48+13\sqrt{7}}{59}$

3 a $4+2\sqrt{2}$ b $5-5\sqrt{2}$ c $-3+2\sqrt{2}$
  d $-\tfrac{4}{7}+\tfrac{1}{7}\sqrt{2}$ e $1+\sqrt{2}$ f $3+2\sqrt{2}$
  g $\tfrac{9}{7}+\tfrac{3}{7}\sqrt{2}$ h $\tfrac{10}{7}+\tfrac{6}{7}\sqrt{2}$

4 a -6 b $-14-2\sqrt{5}$ c $12+8\sqrt{2}-9\sqrt{3}+2\sqrt{6}$

5 a $(\sqrt{a}+\sqrt{b})(\sqrt{a}-\sqrt{b})$
   $=(\sqrt{a})^2-(\sqrt{b})^2$ {difference of two squares}
   $=a-b$ which is an integer since $a,b \in \mathbb{Z}^+$
  b i $\dfrac{4\sqrt{7}-4\sqrt{2}}{5}$ ii $\dfrac{10+2\sqrt{10}}{3}$ iii $\dfrac{-29-3\sqrt{39}}{10}$

6 $3+2\sqrt{2}$ **7** $\sqrt{6}=\dfrac{\sqrt{2}-\sqrt{3}}{p}$ (or $\sqrt{6}=\dfrac{12}{5-6p^2}$)

8 $x^2=8-2\sqrt{15}$ and so $2\sqrt{15}=8-x^2$
   Now square both sides.

9 $u_1=1$, $u_2=1$, $u_3=2$, $u_4=3$, $u_5=5$, $u_6=8$

EXERCISE 4F
1 a $x=3$, $y=2$ b $x=15$, $y=-4$
  c $x=-11$, $y=-3$ d $x=6$, $y=0$
  e $x=0$, $y=-3$ f $x=y=0$
2 a $x=2$, $y=\tfrac{3}{2}$ b $x=\tfrac{3}{7}$, $y=-\tfrac{1}{7}$
  c $x=-\tfrac{3}{7}$, $y=-\tfrac{1}{7}$ d $x=-\tfrac{8}{7}$, $y=-\tfrac{12}{7}$
3 a $a=3$, $b=1$ b $a=4$, $b=5$
  c $a=5$, $b=2$ or $a=-5$, $b=-2$
  d $a=3$, $b=-4$ or $a=-3$, $b=4$
4 Let $\sqrt{11-6\sqrt{2}}=a+b\sqrt{2}$; $a,b \in \mathbb{Q}$
   Show $a+b\sqrt{2}=3-\sqrt{2}$ or $-3+\sqrt{2}$
   But $11-6\sqrt{2}>0$
   $\therefore \sqrt{11-6\sqrt{2}}=3-\sqrt{2}$
5 a $\sqrt{11+4\sqrt{6}}=2\sqrt{2}+\sqrt{3}$
  b No. (Suppose it can and see what happens.)

REVIEW SET 4A
1 a 18 b -24 c $\sqrt{2}$ d -27 e $1500\sqrt{3}$ f $\tfrac{9}{16}$
2 a $4\sqrt{3}$ b $12\sqrt{6}$ **3** a $2\sqrt{5}-\sqrt{3}$ b $\tfrac{29\sqrt{6}}{60}$
4 a $8\sqrt{3}-6$ b $16-6\sqrt{7}$ c 1 d $\sqrt{5}-4$
  e $8+5\sqrt{2}$ f $79+12\sqrt{14}$
5 a $4\sqrt{2}$ b $5\sqrt{3}$ c $\dfrac{4\sqrt{3}-\sqrt{6}}{14}$ d $\dfrac{15+5\sqrt{3}}{12}$
6 $\tfrac{1}{7}\sqrt{7}$ **7** $155+77\sqrt{2}$ **8** a $7+4\sqrt{3}$ b 13
9 $\dfrac{-24+5\sqrt{35}}{23}$ **10** $x=-2$, $y=1$ or $x=-\tfrac{3}{5}$, $y=\tfrac{10}{3}$

REVIEW SET 4B
1 a $6\sqrt{15}$ b 20 c $-2\sqrt{2}$ d $2-2\sqrt{2}$ e 9 f 15
2 $5\sqrt{3}$ **3** a $\tfrac{3}{2}+\sqrt{6}$ b $2-\tfrac{3}{2}\sqrt{2}$

4 a 22 b $4\sqrt{5}-9$ c $6-4\sqrt{3}$ d $7\sqrt{2}-9$
5 a $7\sqrt{2}$ b $\dfrac{-\sqrt{6}-\sqrt{2}}{2}$ c $\dfrac{6-\sqrt{2}}{17}$ d $\dfrac{-25-10\sqrt{3}}{13}$
6 $49+20\sqrt{6}$
7 a $-\tfrac{1}{11}+\tfrac{1}{11}\sqrt{5}$ b $\tfrac{1}{2}-\tfrac{5}{2}\sqrt{5}$ c $\tfrac{3}{2}-\tfrac{1}{2}\sqrt{5}$
8 a $-1+5\sqrt{2}$ b $\dfrac{16+5\sqrt{3}}{11}$ **9** $\tfrac{3}{17}\sqrt{34}+\tfrac{1}{17}\sqrt{17}$
10 $p=2$, $q=-3$ or $p=-\tfrac{63}{5}$, $q=\tfrac{10}{21}$

EXERCISE 5A
1 a $\sqrt{65}$ cm b 10 cm c $\sqrt{233}$ km d $5\sqrt{2}$ cm
  e $2\sqrt{61}$ m f $\sqrt{481}$ mm
2 a $\sqrt{85}$ cm b 8 m c $6\sqrt{2}$ cm d $3\sqrt{13}$ cm
  e $\sqrt{26}$ m f 180 cm or 1.80 m
3 a ≈ 9.4 cm b ≈ 7.1 m c ≈ 8.8 cm d ≈ 5.9 cm
  e ≈ 5.2 m f ≈ 16.9 cm
4 a $x=\sqrt{11}$ b $x=\sqrt{2}$ c $x=\sqrt{5}$ d $x=\sqrt{19}$
  e $x=\tfrac{1}{\sqrt{2}}$ f $x=\tfrac{1}{2}$
5 a $x=3\sqrt{3}$ b $x=2\sqrt{13}$ c $x=2$
6 a $x=2\sqrt{2}$, $y=\sqrt{17}$ b $x=3\sqrt{5}$, $y=\sqrt{29}$
  c $x=\sqrt{5}$, $y=\sqrt{6}$
7 a $x=\sqrt{2}$ b $x=14$ c $x=12$
8 $AC=\sqrt{39}$ m ≈ 6.24 m

9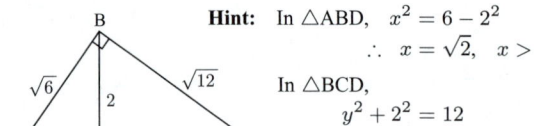
Hint: In $\triangle ABD$, $x^2=6-2^2$
   $\therefore x=\sqrt{2}$, $x>0$
In $\triangle BCD$,
   $y^2+2^2=12$
   $\therefore y=\sqrt{8}$, $y>0$
In $\triangle ABC$, $AC^2=(\sqrt{6})^2+(\sqrt{12})^2=18$ $\therefore AC=\sqrt{18}$

10 a $\sqrt{17}$ cm b $\sqrt{29}$ m c $\sqrt{41}$ m

EXERCISE 5B
1 a No {as $4^2+5^2=41$ and $7^2=49$}
  b Yes {as $9^2+12^2=225$ and $15^2=225$}
  c No {as $5^2+8^2=89$ and $9^2=81$}
  d No {as $3^2+(\sqrt{7})^2=16$ and $(\sqrt{12})^2=12$}
  e Yes {as $(\sqrt{27})^2+(\sqrt{48})^2=75$ and $(\sqrt{75})^2=75$}
  f Yes {as $8^2+15^2=289$ and $17^2=289$}
2 a As $(\sqrt{5})^2=1^2+2^2$, it is right angled at A.
  b As $8^2+12^2=208 \neq (\sqrt{218})^2$, it is not right angled.
  c As $7^2=49=(\sqrt{24})^2+5^2$, it is right angled at C.
  d As $4^2+(3\sqrt{2})^2 \neq (\sqrt{19})^2$, it is not right angled.
  e $5^2+(\sqrt{47})^2=72=(6\sqrt{2})^2$
   $\therefore$ it is right angled at A.
  f $(\sqrt{13})^2+(5\sqrt{2})^2=13+50=63$ and $(3\sqrt{7})^2=63$
   $\therefore$ it is right angled at B.
3 $x=\sqrt{101} \approx 10.0$
  Hint: Show right-most triangle to be right angled first.

EXERCISE 5C
1 a yes b no c yes
  d no {numbers must be integers} e yes
  f no {numbers must be positive}

2 **a** $k=20$ **b** $k=10$ **c** $k=48$ **d** $k=15$
  e $k=21$ **f** $k=11$
3 **a** As $\{a,b,c\}$ is a Pythagorean triple, $a^2+b^2=c^2$
  Hint: $(ka)^2+(kb)^2=k^2a^2+k^2b^2=k^2(a^2+b^2)$
  b **i** $\{6,8,10\}$, $\{9,12,15\}$, $\{12,16,20\}$, $\{15,20,25\}$
   ii $\{10,24,26\}$, $\{15,36,39\}$, $\{20,48,52\}$,
    $\{25,60,65\}$
4 **a** Show $(be-ad)^2+(bd+ae)^2=(cf)^2$
  b $\{36,77,85\}$
5 **a** **i** $\{3,4,5\}$, $3^2+4^2=5^2$
   ii $\{5,12,13\}$, $5^2+12^2=13^2$
   iii $\{7,24,25\}$, $7^2+24^2=25^2$
   iv $\{9,40,41\}$, $9^2+40^2=41^2$

EXERCISE 5D

1 $\sqrt{73}$ cm ≈ 8.54 cm
2 $3\sqrt{10}$ cm by $\sqrt{10}$ cm, or, ≈ 9.49 cm by 3.16 cm
3 **a** $24\sqrt{5}$ cm ≈ 53.7 cm **b** 160 cm²
4 $2\sqrt{11}$ cm ≈ 6.63 cm **5** $5\sqrt{2}$ cm ≈ 7.07 cm
6 $4\sqrt{41}$ cm ≈ 25.6 cm
7 $8^2+11.55^2=197.4025$ and $14.05^2=197.4025$
  $\therefore$ is right angled.
8 7.75 m **9** $\sqrt{89}$ km ≈ 9.43 km
10 $2\sqrt{445}$ km ≈ 42.2 km **11** ≈ 11.2 km/h and ≈ 22.4 km/h
12 **a** ≈ 115.4 m **b** 100 m **c** ≈ 15.4 m
13 D is 8 km from B. **18**
14 $6\sqrt{3}$ cm ≈ 10.4 cm
15 ≈ 22.2 cm²
16 8 cm
17 6.025 m

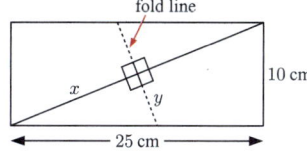

$x \approx 13.463$, crease ≈ 10.8 cm

EXERCISE 5E

1 BC = 6 cm **2** ≈ 6.26 cm **3** ≈ 3.71 cm
4 $3\sqrt{2}$ cm ≈ 4.24 cm **5** $2\sqrt{39}$ cm ≈ 12.5 cm
6 $6\sqrt{2}$ cm ≈ 8.49 cm **7** $4\sqrt{7}$ cm ≈ 10.6 cm
8 $(\sqrt{2}-1)$ m ≈ 41.4 cm **9** ≈ 717 km
10 AB = $4\sqrt{6}$ cm ≈ 9.80 cm **11** $\sqrt{101}$ m ≈ 10.050 m
12 AB = $2\sqrt{7}$ cm ≈ 5.29 cm **13** 5 cm
14 **a** **i** 6 cm **ii** 4 cm **b** $\frac{13}{18}$
15

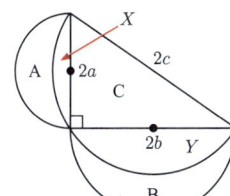

Hint:
$A + X = \frac{1}{2}\pi a^2$
$B + Y = \frac{1}{2}\pi b^2$
$C + X + Y = \frac{1}{2}\pi c^2$

EXERCISE 5F

1 15 cm **2** 10 cm **3** $\sqrt{10}$ cm ≈ 3.16 cm
4 $3\sqrt{3}$ cm ≈ 5.20 cm **5** ≈ 6.80 m **6** ≈ 4.12 cm
7 No, the maximum length would be about 8.06 m.

8 height = $\frac{100}{\sqrt{2}} \approx 71$ m
9 $5\sqrt{10}$ cm $\times 5\sqrt{10}$ cm ≈ 15.8 cm $\times 15.8$ cm
10 ≈ 42.9 m **11** ≈ 29.87 m
12 $L = \sqrt{50^2 + (20\pi)^2}$ m ≈ 80.30 m

REVIEW SET 5A

1 **a** $\sqrt{29}$ cm ≈ 5.39 cm **b** $\sqrt{33}$ cm ≈ 5.74 cm
  c $\sqrt{69}$ cm ≈ 8.31 cm
2 No, $5^2 + 11^2 = 146$ but $13^2 = 169$.
3 Yes, as $4^2 + 1^2 = (\sqrt{17})^2$. The right angle is at A.
4 **a** $x = \sqrt{113}$, $y = 2\sqrt{14}$ **b** $x = 4\sqrt{5}$, $y = 6$
5 **Hint:** Find the two lengths that make up the base of the triangle,
  then use Pythagoras in the largest triangle.
6 $30\sqrt{2}$ m ≈ 42.4 m
7 **a** $k = 36$
  b **i** **Hint:** Show $(4k)^2 + (k^2-4)^2 = (k^2+4)^2$
   ii $\{20, 21, 29\}$
8 ≈ 41.4 cm **9** $5\sqrt{2}$ cm ≈ 7.07 cm
10 **a** $x = 2\sqrt{5}$ **b** $x = 2\sqrt{14}$
11 **a** $\sqrt{61}$ m ≈ 7.81 m **b** $\sqrt{70}$ m ≈ 8.37 m
12 **b** **i** $a^2 + b^2$ **ii** c^2
  c Area of large square − areas of 4 triangles
   must be equal in both figures. $\therefore$ $a^2 + b^2 = c^2$
13 $h = \sqrt{\frac{2}{3}} \approx 0.816$ m

REVIEW SET 5B

1 **a** $x = 3\sqrt{2}$ **b** $x = \sqrt{2}$
2 $2^2 + 5^2 = 29$ and $AC^2 = 29$ $\therefore$ right angled at B.
3 $k = 35$ **4** 6 cm
5 **a** AB = $\sqrt{85}$ m ≈ 9.22 m **b** AB = $\sqrt{33}$ cm ≈ 5.74 cm
6 ≈ 1.431 m **7** $6\sqrt{5}$ m ≈ 13.42 m
8 Max. distance = $\sqrt{122}$ m ≈ 11.05 m which is > 10.5 m.
  $\therefore$ the beam will fit.
9 $\sqrt{99}$ cm ≈ 9.95 cm **10** AB ≈ 6.55 m
11 **a** AB = $\dfrac{s}{\sqrt{2}}$ **b** **i** $\dfrac{s^2}{4}$ **ii** $\dfrac{s^2}{2}$
  c $A = 4\left(\dfrac{s^2}{4}\right) + 4\left(\dfrac{s^2}{\sqrt{2}}\right) + s^2$, etc.
12 **a** **i** PQ = $\sqrt{a^2 + b^2}$ units **ii** $\frac{1}{2}$PQ $\times$ RN $= \frac{1}{2}ab$, etc.
  b ≈ 81.6 m
13 **a** radius = $\dfrac{r}{2}$
  b **i**

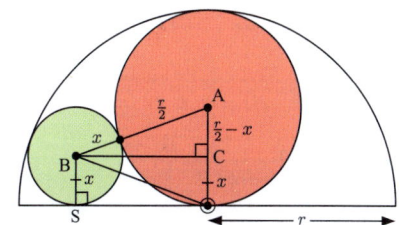

  Hint: Find expressions for BC^2 and OS^2.
   ii $\dfrac{r}{4}$

564   ANSWERS

EXERCISE 6A

1 a $2\sqrt{2}$ units   b 7 units   c $2\sqrt{5}$ units   d $3\sqrt{5}$ units
   e 7 units   f $\sqrt{5}$ units   g $\sqrt{10}$ units   h $\frac{\sqrt{5}}{2}$ units

2 a $10\sqrt{2} \approx 14.1$ km   b $20\sqrt{5} \approx 44.7$ km
   c $10\sqrt{26} \approx 51.0$ km

3 a isosceles with $AB = AC = \sqrt{85}$ units   b scalene
   c isosceles (and right angled at B) with $AB = BC$
   d isosceles with $BC = AC = \sqrt{7}$ units
   e equilateral, all sides $2\sqrt{3}$ units
   f isosceles ($AC = BC$) if $b \neq 2 \pm a\sqrt{3}$
      equilateral if $b = 2 \pm a\sqrt{3}$

4 a right angled at B   b not right angled
   c right angled at A   d not right angled

5 a $a = 2$

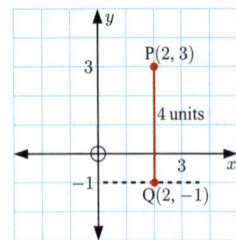

   b $a = 3$ or -5

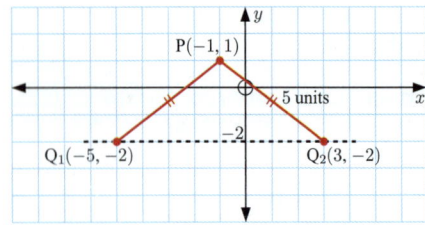

   c $a = \pm 2$ d $a = -1$

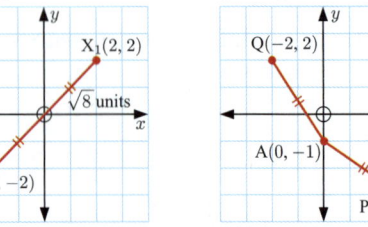

6 a i $x^2 + y^2 = 9$ ii $(x-1)^2 + (y-3)^2 = 4$
   b

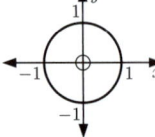

   This set represents a circle with centre $(0, 0)$ and radius 1 unit.

7 Let R be $(a, 0)$. Find PQ, PR, and RQ.
   Solve $PQ = PR$, $PQ = RQ$, $PR = RQ$.
   $(10, 0)$, $(-8, 0)$, $(-3, 0)$, $(-7, 0)$, and $(-\frac{101}{12}, 0)$.

EXERCISE 6B

1 a $(5, 3)$ b $(1, -1)$ c $(\frac{3}{2}, 3)$ d $(0, 4)$
   e $(2, -\frac{3}{2})$ f $(1, \frac{5}{2})$

2 a $B(0, -6)$ b $B(5, -2)$ c $B(0, 6)$ d $B(0, 7)$
   e $B(-7, 3)$ f $B(-3, 0)$

3 $C(1, -3)$ **4** $P(7, -3)$ **5** $X(\frac{3}{2}, \frac{3}{2})$, $S(-2, 0)$
6 $\frac{\sqrt{89}}{2}$ units ≈ 4.72 units   **7** $a = \frac{7}{3}$, $b = \frac{11}{2}$
8 Hint: Let the vertices be $A(a, b)$, $B(c, d)$, $C(e, f)$.
   Use the midpoint formula to find six simple equations and solve them simultaneously.
   Points are $(3, -1)$, $(7, 9)$, $(9, 1)$.

EXERCISE 6C.1

1 a $\frac{1}{3}$ b 0   c -3 d $\frac{2}{3}$ e $-\frac{3}{4}$
   f undefined   g -4 h $-\frac{2}{5}$

2 a 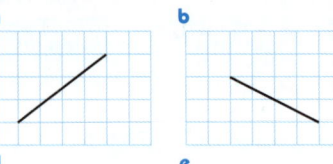   b   c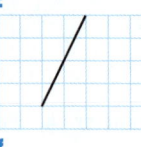

   d 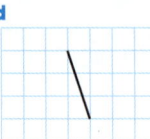   e 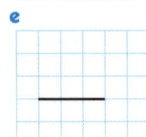   f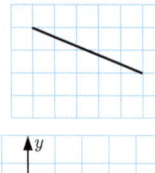

3 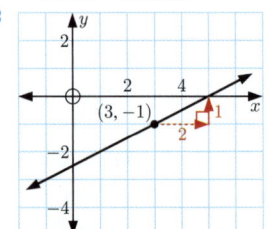   **4**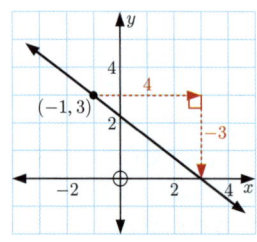

5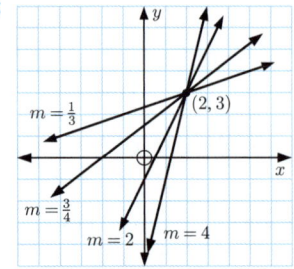

6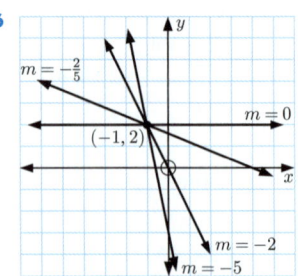

EXERCISE 6C.2

1 $\frac{4}{7}$

2 **a** $\frac{1}{5}$ **b** $\frac{1}{4}$ **c** 4 **d** 0 **e** undefined
 f $\frac{2}{7}$ **g** $-\frac{2}{7}$ **h** 1 **i** $-\frac{4}{3}$

3 **a** $t = 19$ **b** $t = \frac{29}{2}$ **c** $t = \frac{13}{3}$ **d** $t = \frac{2}{3}$
 e $t = 9$ **f** $t = 5$

4 $Q(0, 7)$, $R(\frac{28}{3}, 0)$ **5** **c** gradient of $[AC] = 2$

EXERCISE 6D.1

1 **a** -2 **b** $-\frac{5}{2}$ **c** $-\frac{1}{3}$ **d** $-\frac{1}{7}$ **e** $\frac{5}{2}$ **f** $\frac{2}{7}$
 g $\frac{3}{4}$ **h** 1

2 The line pairs in **c**, **d**, **f**, and **h** are perpendicular.

3 **a** [AB]: $\frac{3}{5}$, [BC]: -2, [CD]: $\frac{9}{2}$, [DE]: $-\frac{1}{2}$, [EF]: -2, [FA]: 2
 b **i** [BC] ∥ [EF] **ii** [DE] ⊥ [FA]

4 $k = -2$ **5** **a** $t = 4$ **b** $t = 4$ **c** $t = 14$ **d** $t = \frac{22}{7}$

6 **a** $PQ = PR = 2\sqrt{5}$ units **b** $M(4, 4)$
 c gradient of $[PM] = -\frac{1}{3}$, gradient of $[QR] = 3$, and their product is -1
 ∴ [PM] ⊥ [QR]
 d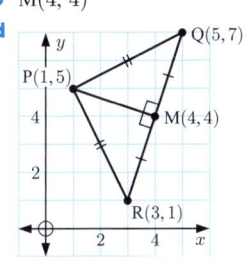

7 $M(0, 3)$ and $N(3, 3)$
 a gradient of $[MN] = 0$, gradient of $[AC] = 0$
 ∴ [MN] ∥ [AC]
 b $MN = 3$ units and $AC = 6$ units ∴ $MN = \frac{1}{2}(AC)$

8 **a** All sides have length 5 units. ∴ ABCD is a rhombus.
 b $(2, 1)$ and $(2, 1)$
 c gradient of $[AC] = -2$, gradient of $[BD] = \frac{1}{2}$ and their product $= -1$
 ∴ [AC] ⊥ [BD]
 d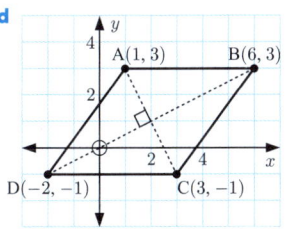

9 **a** **i** $P(0, 5)$ **ii** $Q(\frac{9}{2}, 2)$ **iii** $R(\frac{1}{2}, -\frac{5}{2})$ **iv** $S(-4, \frac{1}{2})$
 b **i** $-\frac{2}{3}$ **ii** $\frac{9}{8}$ **iii** $-\frac{2}{3}$ **iv** $\frac{9}{8}$
 c PQRS is a parallelogram.

10 **a** $s = 6$ **b** **i** $\frac{1}{2}$ **ii** -2
 c gradient of $[PS] \times$ gradient of $[SQ] = -1$
 ∴ $\widehat{PSQ} = 90°$

EXERCISE 6D.2

1 **a** gradient of $[AB] = \frac{4}{3}$, gradient of $[BC] = \frac{5}{4}$
 ∴ not collinear
 b gradient of $[PQ] =$ gradient of $[QR] = \frac{6}{5}$
 ∴ P, Q, R are collinear
 c gradient of $[RS] = -\frac{3}{11}$, gradient of $[ST] = -\frac{3}{2}$
 ∴ not collinear
 d gradient of $[AB] =$ gradient of $[BC] = 3$
 ∴ A, B, C are collinear

2 **a** $c = 3$ **b** $c = -5$

3 **a** $M(1, -4)$
 b gradient of $[AM] =$ gradient of $[MC] = 1$, ∴ collinear
 c gradient of $[AC] = 1$, gradient of $[BD] = -1$,
 ∴ perpendicular

EXERCISE 6E.1

1 **a** $y = 2x + 1$ **b** $y = -x + 1$ **c** $y = \frac{2}{3}x + 3$
 d $y = -\frac{4}{5}x + \frac{6}{5}$ **e** $y = -\frac{3}{4}x - \frac{1}{2}$

2 **a** $4x - y = 7$ **b** $3x + 5y = -1$ **c** $x - 3y = -11$
 d $3x + 4y = 24$ **e** $2x - 7y = 25$

3 **a** $y = x - 4$ **b** $y = -x + 4$ **c** $y = 6x + 16$
 d $y = \frac{1}{2}x + 8$ **e** $y = -\frac{1}{3}x - \frac{7}{3}$ **f** $y = -\frac{3}{5}x - \frac{14}{5}$

4 **a** $3x - y = -1$ **b** $2x + y = 3$ **c** $x + 4y = 1$
 d $5x - 3y = 10$ **e** $y = -3$ **f** $x = 2$

5 **a** $4x + 5y = 13$ **b** $4(12) + 5(-7) = 48 - 35 = 13$ ✓

6 **a** $2x - 5y = 10$ **b** $y = -2x - 2$ **c** $y = 2x + 6$
 d $4x + 3y = 20$ **e** $x - 2y = -8$

7 **a** $-\frac{3}{4}$ **b** $4x - 3y = 10$ **8** $7x - 5y = -42$

9 $y = \frac{3}{2}x - 3$ **10** **a** $y = \frac{2}{3}x - \frac{5}{3}$ **b** $-\frac{5}{3}$

11 $x + 3y = 13$

12 **a** **i** $y = -\frac{1}{2}x + 2$ **ii** $y = 2x - 3$ **iii** $y = -\frac{1}{2}x + \frac{19}{2}$
 b **Hint:** Solve $2x - 3 = -\frac{1}{2}x + \frac{19}{2}$.

13 **Hint:** P is $(a + b, c)$, Q is (b, c)
 a gradient of $[OP] = \dfrac{c}{a+b}$ etc.
 b gradient of $[AQ] = \dfrac{c}{b-2a}$ etc.
 c Solve the equations in **a** and **b** simultaneously.

EXERCISE 6E.2

1 **a** $x - 2y = 2$ **b** $2x - 3y = -19$ **c** $3x - 4y = 15$
 d $3x - y = 11$ **e** $x + 3y = 13$ **f** $3x + 4y = -6$
 g $2x + y = 4$ **h** $3x + y = 4$

2 **a** $-\frac{2}{3}$ **b** $\frac{3}{7}$ **c** $\frac{6}{11}$ **d** $-\frac{5}{6}$ **e** $-\frac{1}{2}$ **f** 3

3 **a** Parallel lines have the same gradient of $-\frac{3}{5}$.
 ∴ equations have the form $3x + 5y =$ a constant.
 b $3x + 5y = 2$ has gradient $-\frac{3}{5}$
 ∴ perpendicular lines have gradient $\frac{5}{3}$.
 ∴ equations have the form $5x - 3y =$ a constant.

4 **a** $3x + 4y = 10$ **b** $2x - 5y = 3$ **c** $3x + y = -12$
 d $x - 3y = 0$

5 **a** $\frac{2}{3}$ and $-\frac{6}{k}$ **b** $k = -9$ **c** $k = 4$

6 **a** $2\sqrt{34}$ km ≈ 11.7 km **b** $(6, -\frac{1}{2})$ **c** no
 d **i** $11x + 8y = 31$
 ii No, as $11(2) + 8(1) = 30 \neq 31$.

7 **a** $x - 3y = -16$ **b** $3x - 2y = 13$ **c** $2x - y = -3$
 d $x = 5$

8 **a** **i** $x - 7y = -12$ **ii** $x + y = 8$
 b $(\frac{11}{2}) - 7(\frac{5}{2}) = -\frac{24}{2} = -12$ ✓ $(\frac{11}{2}) + (\frac{5}{2}) = 8$ ✓
 c $PR = QR = \frac{5\sqrt{2}}{2}$ units

EXERCISE 6F

1. **a** $x - y = 4$ **b** $2x - y = -6$
   c $12x - 10y = -35$ **d** $y = 1$
2. **a** $2x + 3y = -1$ **b** $2(-5) + 3(3) = -1$ ✓
   c $AC = BC = \sqrt{65}$ units
3. $2x - 3y = -5$
4. **a** $x + 2y = 5$, $3x + y = 10$, $x - 3y = 0$ **b** $(3, 1)$
5. **Hint:** Start by finding the gradient and midpoint of [AB].
6. The perpendicular bisectors of [PQ] and [QR] are $x - 3y = -6$ and $2x - y = 3$. They meet at $(3, 3)$.
7. **a** $P(5, 3)$, $Q(4, 0)$, $R(2, 2)$
   b i $x - y = 2$ **ii** $3x + y = 12$ **iii** $x + 3y = 8$
   c $X(3\frac{1}{2}, 1\frac{1}{2})$ **d** Yes, $(\frac{7}{2}) + 3(\frac{3}{2}) = 8$ ✓
   e The perpendicular bisectors meet at a point.
   f X is the centre of the circle which could be drawn through A, B, and C.

EXERCISE 6G

1. **a** $2\sqrt{10}$ units **b** $3\sqrt{5}$ units **c** $3\sqrt{5}$ units
   d $2\sqrt{17}$ units **e** $2\sqrt{10}$ units **f** 5 units
2. **a** $\sqrt{10}$ units **b** 4 units
3. **a** $N(4.44, 0.92)$ **b** 3.8 km
4. **a** $A = \dfrac{ab}{2}$, $A = \dfrac{cd}{2} = \dfrac{d\sqrt{a^2 + b^2}}{2}$
   b i When $y = k$, $Ax + Bk + C = 0$
   $\therefore x = \dfrac{-Bk - C}{A}$
   $\therefore$ P is $\left(\dfrac{-Bk - C}{A}, k\right)$ etc.

EXERCISE 6H

1. **a**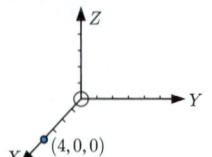
   b 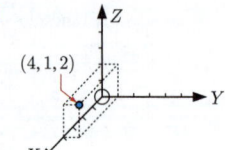 (0, 2, 0)
   c 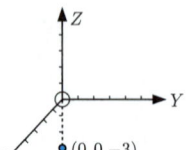 (0, 0, −3)
   d 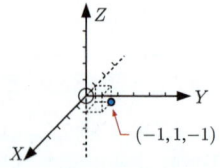 (1, 2, 0)
   e 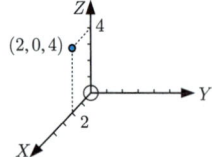 (2, 0, 4)
   f (0, 3, −1)
   g 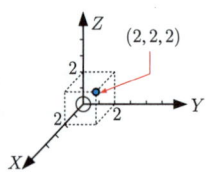 (2, 2, 2)
   h (2, −1, 3)

   i (4, 1, 2)

   j (−2, 2, 3)

   k (−1, 1, −1)

   l (−3, 2, −1)

2. **a i** $2\sqrt{14}$ units **ii** $M(1, 1, -1)$
   b i 6 units **ii** $M(1, -2, 2)$
   c i $2\sqrt{3}$ units **ii** $M(2, 2, 2)$
   d i $\sqrt{35}$ units **ii** $M(\frac{3}{2}, \frac{1}{2}, \frac{7}{2})$
3. **a** Isosceles with $AC = BC = \sqrt{14}$ units.
   b $\triangle ABC$ is right angled at A.
4. $k = 1 \pm \sqrt{19}$
5. **a** $x^2 + y^2 + z^2 = 4$ and must be the equation of a sphere, centre $(0, 0, 0)$, radius 2 units.
   b $(x-1)^2 + (y-2)^2 + (z-3)^2 = 16$ which is the equation of a sphere, centre $(1, 2, 3)$, radius 4 units.

6. **a**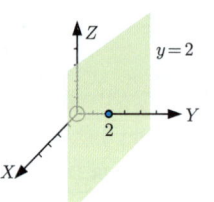
   A plane parallel to the XOZ plane passing through $(0, 2, 0)$.

   b A line parallel to the Z-axis passing through $(1, 2, 0)$.

   c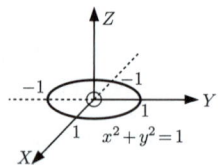
   A circle in the XOY plane, centre $(0, 0, 0)$, radius 1 unit.

   d A sphere, centre $(0, 0, 0)$, radius 2 units.

   e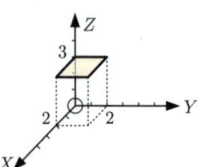
   A 2 by 2 square plane 3 units above the XOY plane (as shown).

   f All points on and within a $2 \times 2 \times 1$ rectangular prism (as shown).

REVIEW SET 6A

1. $(-3, 3)$ **2** $\sqrt{58}$ units **3** $-\frac{3}{2}$ **4** $m = 6$ or -2
5. $t = -11$

6 Gradient of [AB] and [BC] $= 2$.
∴ [AB] ∥ [BC] with B common.

7 **a** $y = -2x + 7$ **b** $2x + 3y = 7$ **c** $3x - 2y = 15$

8 $2x + 3y = 10$ **9** $a = 4$

10 **a** $AB = BC = 5$ units, $m_{AB} = \frac{3}{4}$, $m_{BC} = -\frac{4}{3}$
∴ right angle at B.
b $X(\frac{1}{2}, \frac{1}{2})$
c gradient of [BX] $= 7$, gradient of [AC] $= -\frac{1}{7}$
and $7 \times -\frac{1}{7} = -1$, ∴ [BX] ⊥ [AC].

11 **a** $x - 5y = -19$ **b** P(3, 7) **c** $5x + y = 22$
d **i** $(\frac{7}{2}, \frac{9}{2})$ **ii** $5(\frac{7}{2}) + \frac{9}{2} = \frac{44}{2} = 22$ ✓

12 **a** $y = 4x - 11$ **b** $6x - 16y = -11$ **13** $\sqrt{13}$ units

14 **a** $2\sqrt{14}$ units **b** M(0, 0, 0) **15** $k = 4$ or -6

REVIEW SET 6B

1 **a** $ST = \sqrt{73}$ units **b** $(3, -\frac{1}{2})$ **2** $x + 2y = 1$

3 **a** 2 **b** No, as $2x + y = 3$ has gradient -2.

4 $a = -1$ or -3 **5** $b = -3$

6 $x + 2y = 8$ **7** $5x + 6y = 29$ **8** $y = 3x - 5$

9 **a** **i** [AB]: $\frac{1}{5}$, [BC]: -2, [CD]: $\frac{1}{5}$, [AD]: -2
ii ABCD is a parallelogram.
b **i** $(\frac{1}{2}, \frac{1}{2})$ for both diagonals.
ii The diagonals of a parallelogram bisect each other.
c **i** [AC]: $-\frac{3}{7}$, [BD]: $\frac{5}{3}$
ii product $= -\frac{5}{7}$ ∴ not a rhombus

10 **a** N$(\frac{66}{13}, \frac{18}{13})$ **b** $\frac{7}{\sqrt{13}}$ units

11 **a** 5 units **b** $4x - 3y = -18$ **c** B(5, -4)
d $4x - 3y = 32$

12 **a** R is (b, c), [OB] has gradient $\frac{c}{b}$, etc.
c Hint: Show that the x-coordinate of T is a.

13 distance $= \frac{12}{\sqrt{5}}$ units **14** $\sqrt{30}$ units

EXERCISE 7A

1 **a** △ABC ≅ △FED {AAcorS}
b △PQR ≅ △ZYX {SAS}
c △ABC ≅ △EDF {AAcorS}
d △ABC ≅ △LKM {SSS}
e △XYZ ≅ △FED {RHS} **f** not congruent
g not enough information **h** not enough information
i △ABC ≅ △PQR {SSS} **j** △ABC ≅ △FED {AAcorS}

2 **a** B and D {SAS} **b** A and D {RHS}
c B and C {AAcorS} **d** A and D {SSS}

EXERCISE 7B

1 △ABC ≅ △EDC {AAcorS}

2 **a** △ABD ≅ △CBD {SSS} **b** **i** 47° **ii** 51°

3 **a** Join [AC].
Hint: Show △ABC ≅ △CDA {AAcorS}
b Now join [DB] and let the diagonals meet at M.
Hint: Show △AMD ≅ △CMB {AAcorS}

4 **a** Hint: Show △XYZ ≅ △ZWX {SSS}
b WẐX = YX̂Z so WZ ∥ XY
and WX̂Z = YẐX so WX ∥ ZY

5 Hint: Join [OA], [OB], and [OP], and
show △OAP ≅ △OBP. {RHS}

6 Hint: Join [AC], [BC], and [CX], and
show △ACX ≅ △BCX. {RHS}

7 Hint: Show △APB ≅ △AQC {AAcorS}

8 Hint: Join [AX], [BX], and [CX].
Show △AQX ≅ △BQX {SAS}
and △APX ≅ △CPX {SAS}

9 Hint: Join [WZ] and [ZY].
Show △WAZ ≅ △YDZ {SAS}

EXERCISE 7C

1 **e** Hint: Let NĴM be $\alpha°$; find all other angles in terms of α.
f Hint: Let AĈB $= \alpha$, then AB̂C $= \alpha$ and BD̂C $= \alpha$.

2 **a** $x = 1.2$ **b** $x = \frac{10}{3}$ **c** $x = \frac{20}{7}$ **d** $x = 7.5$
e $x = 10.8$ **f** $x = \frac{8}{3}$ **g** $x = \frac{4}{3}$ **h** $x = 4.8$
i $x = \frac{35}{3}$

3 7 m **4** ≈ 1.62 m **5** 10.625 km

6 ≈ 651 m **7** 8 cm

8 She is correct as the viewing region is always 20 m long no matter where the camera is located on [AB].

9 1.52 m **10** ≈ 35.7 m **11** ≈ 5.56 cm

EXERCISE 7D

1 **a** $x ≈ 14.2$ **b** $x ≈ 30.7$ **c** $x ≈ 41.5$
d $x ≈ 6.26$ **e** $x = 8$ **f** $x ≈ 10.7$

2 **a** $x = 96$ **b** $x = 432$ **c** $x ≈ 0.150$
d $x = 7.5$ **e** $x = 13.2$ **f** $x ≈ 6.94$

3 **a** 12.544 cm² **b** 6.144 cm²

4 **a** $x = 1.5$ **b** 17.6 m² **5** 30 cm

6 **a** **i** It is multiplied by 8. **ii** It is increased by 72.8%.
b **i** It is divided by 8. **ii** It is increased by 237.5%.
c **i** ≈ 48.8 cm³ **ii** 1310.72 grams

7 Length [RS] is the length of [PM] enlarged with scale factor $k = 2$.
∴ the area of the similar triangle will be enlarged by a factor of $k^2 = 4$.

8 **a** similar **b** not similar

9 **a** 10 cm **b** 30 cm² **c** 6 mm, 2.25 mm **d** 1.25 mL

10 B and F
Hint: Create a table for each pair of glasses.

	k	k^3	Calc. V	Actual V	
A, B	$\frac{10}{8.5}$	≈ 1.628	≈ 204	160	✗

REVIEW SET 7A

1 **a** B and C {AAcorS} **b** A and C {AAcorS}

4 **a** $x = \frac{13}{8}$ **b** $x = \frac{23}{3}$ **c** $x = \frac{40}{3}$

5 **a** 38.4 cm² **b** 28.8 cm²

6 Hint: Show △s APQ and ABC are similar, then △s PBC and QCB congruent, etc.

7 ≈ 117 m

8 Hint: Explain why △s ABI and CBI are congruent, etc.

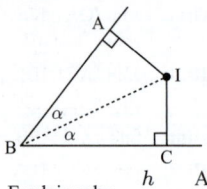

9 a Hint: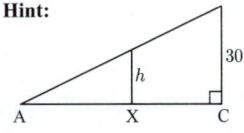
Explain why $\dfrac{h}{30} = \dfrac{AX}{AC}$.
Similarly find $\dfrac{h}{50}$.

b 18.75 m

10 a Hint: Consider △ADE, etc.
b Hint: Find the sizes of the interior angles of PQRST.

11 2 cm   **12 a** 5 : 4   **b** 25 : 16   **c** 125 : 64

REVIEW SET 7B

1 a yes {RHS}   **b** no   **c** no
2 a Hint: Use 'angle in semi-circle' theorem.
b BP = BQ, $P\hat{A}B = Q\hat{A}B$, $P\hat{B}A = Q\hat{B}A$
The triangles have equal area.
3 $x = 2.8$ **4 a** $x = 3$ **b** $x = 4$ **5** AE ≈ 4.74 m
6 Hint: Explain equally marked sides and angles, then consider △s MQR and NSR.

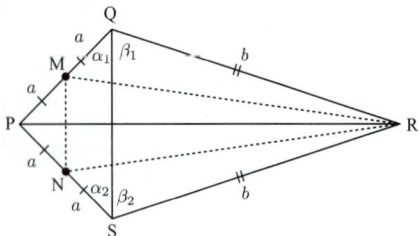

7 $x = 10$ **8** no   **10 a** ≈ 7.56 cm   **b** ≈ 5.24 cm

EXERCISE 8A.1

1 a (5, 3)   **b** (4, 6)   **2 a** $\binom{0}{3}$ **b** $\binom{5}{-5}$ **3** (0, 1)
4 a $\binom{8}{0}$ **b** $\binom{-8}{0}$ **c** $\binom{0}{-4}$ **d** $\binom{0}{4}$ **e** $\binom{4}{1}$
f $\binom{4}{6}$ **g** $\binom{-8}{-4}$ **h** $\binom{-4}{-6}$ **i** $\binom{0}{5}$ **j** $\binom{4}{-6}$
5 a P(−3, 1), Q(−1, 1), R(−1, −2), S(−3, −2)
b

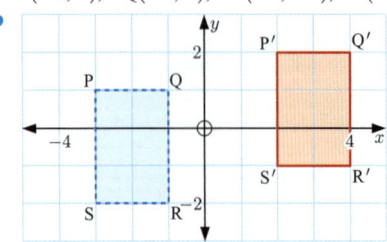

c P'(2, 2), Q'(4, 2), R'(4, −1), S'(2, −1)
6 a, b

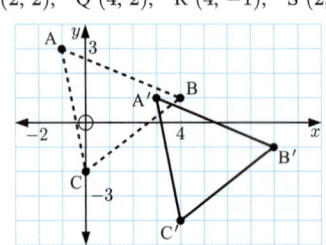

c A'(3, 1), B'(8, −1), C'(4, −4)   **d** $2\sqrt{5}$ units
7 a translation of $\binom{5}{5}$

EXERCISE 8A.2

1 a $y = 2x + 7$ **b** $y = \tfrac{1}{3}x + 1$ **c** $y = -x + 7$
d $y = -\tfrac{1}{2}x - 6$ **e** $3x + 2y = 11$ **f** $x = 6$
g $y = 2x$ **h** $y = 0$
2 a $y = x^2 + 3$ **b** $y = -2(x - 3)^2 + 2$
c $y = \dfrac{x + 9}{x + 4}$ **d** $y = \dfrac{-2x - 2}{x - 3}$ **e** $y = 2^x - 3$
f $y = 9 \times 3^{-x}$ or $y = 3^{2-x}$

EXERCISE 8B

1

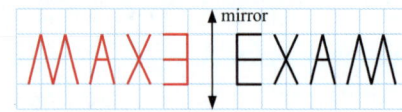

2 a (4, 1)   **b** (−4, −1)   **c** (−1, 4)   **d** (1, −4)
3 a (−1, 3)   **b** (1, −3)   **c** (−3, −1)   **d** (3, 1)
4

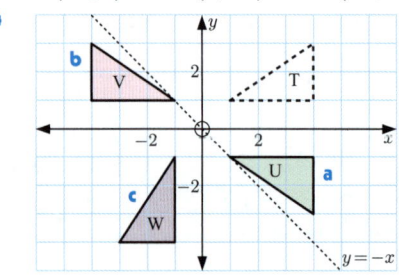

5 a $y = -2x - 3$ **b** $y = -x^2$ **c** $xy = -5$
d $x = 2^y$ **e** $3x + 2y = -4$ **f** $x^2 + y^2 = 4$
g $y = x^2$ **h** $2x + 3y = -4$ **i** $y = -3$ **j** $x = 2y^2$
6 a (1, −1)   **b** (5, −1)   **c** (3, −9)   **d** (1, 7)
e (5, 1)   **f** (−8, 3)
7 a $y = 2x - 5$ **c**
b $y = -2x + 5$

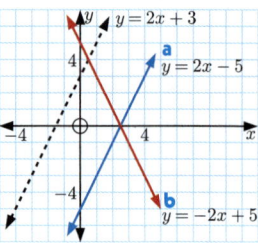

8 a $y = 3^{-x}$ **c**
b $y = \tfrac{1}{81} 3^{-x} + 1$

EXERCISE 8C

1 a (−3, −2)   **b** (3, 2)   **c** (2, −3)
2 a (1, 4)   **b** (−1, −4)   **c** (−4, 1)

3 a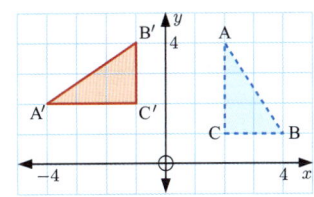
b $A'(-4, 2)$, $B'(-1, 4)$, $C'(-1, 2)$

4 a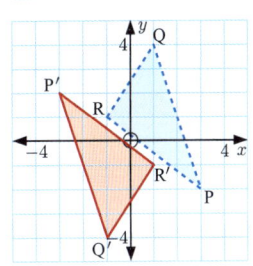
b $P'(-3, 2)$, $Q'(-1, -4)$, $R'(1, -1)$

5 a $4x + 3y = -7$ **b** $x = 3$ **c** $x = -7$
d $y = -x^2$ **e** $3x - 2y = 12$

6 a $(-3, -2)$ **b** $(2, 5)$ **c** $(1, 3)$ **d** $(0, 1)$

7 a $x - y = 13$ **b** $2x - y = 5$ **c** $y = x - 3$

EXERCISE 8D

1 a $(6, 9)$ **b** $(-\frac{1}{3}, \frac{4}{3})$ **c** $(3, -4)$ **d** $(4, 10)$
e $(-1, 1)$ **f** $(\frac{9}{2}, -4)$

2 a $y = 2x + 6$ **b** $y = -2x^2$ **c** $y = \frac{1}{8}x^2$
d $xy = 4$ **e** $y = -3x + 6$ **f** $y = 2^{x+1}$

3 a circle, centre O, radius 3 is $x^2 + y^2 = 9$
b ellipse, centre O, x-intercepts ± 2, y-intercepts ± 3

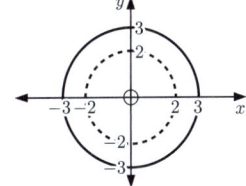 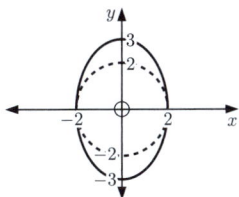

c ellipse, centre O, x-intercepts ± 3, y-intercepts ± 2

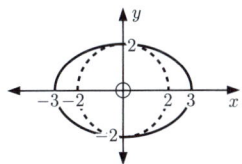

4 a Vertical dilation of factor $k = \frac{3}{4}$ with invariant x-axis.
b Horizontal dilation of factor $k = 2$, with invariant y-axis.
c Horizontal dilation of factor $k = 4$, with invariant y-axis.
d Dilation with centre O and scale factor $k = \frac{1}{2}$.

REVIEW SET 8A

1 a $(1, 0)$ **b** $(-3, -2)$
2 a $3x - 2y = -5$ **b** $y = 3$
    c $2x + y = 12$ **d** $y = 2(x - 2)^2 - 5$
3 a $(-2, -5)$ **b** $(6, -3)$ **c** $(5, 1)$ **d** $(5, 3)$
4 a $y = -3x + 2$ **b** $y = -3x^2$ **c** $x = 3^y$ **d** $xy = 6$
5 a $(-3, 2)$ **b** $(2, -4)$
6 a $x - 2y = -6$ **b** $x - 2y = -1$

c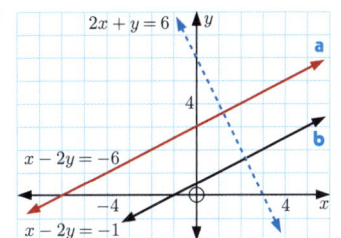

7 a $(4, -2)$ **b** $(3, 20)$ **c** $(-8, -7)$
8 Vertical dilation with scale factor $\frac{5}{3}$.
9 a $y = 3x + 6$ **b** $4x - 5y = 20$ **c** $y = -4x + 1$
   d $y = -x^2 + 3x - 5$ **e** $(x - 5)^2 + (y + 2)^2 = 4$
10 a **i** $\begin{pmatrix} -1 \\ -3 \end{pmatrix}$ **ii** $M_{y=x}$ **iii** R_{180}
       iv Horizontal dilation with scale factor $\frac{1}{3}$.
b Rotation of $180°$ about $(-\frac{1}{2}, -\frac{3}{2})$.
11 circle, centre O, radius 2 units, $x^2 + y^2 = 4$

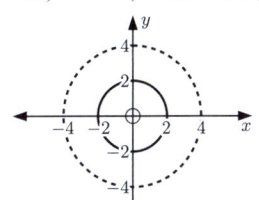

REVIEW SET 8B

1 a $(3, 2)$ **b** $(-3, -2)$ **c** $(2, -3)$
2 a $(-5, -11)$ **b** $(-7, -3)$
3 a $(5, 2)$ **b** $(-5, -2)$ **c** $(-2, 5)$
4 a $(3, 2)$ **b** $(4, -5)$ **c** $(2, 5)$ **d** $(7, 2)$
5 a $5x - 2y = 27$ **b** $y = -(x + 2)^2 + 5$
   c $y = -2 - \dfrac{4}{x - 1}$ **d** $(x + 3)^2 + (y + 4)^2 = 9$
6 a $4x - 3y = -8$ **b** $xy = -12$
   c $3x - 2y = -9$ **d** $y = 2x^2$
7 a $(-1, -13)$ **b** $(-3, -2)$
8 a $(9, 15)$ **b** $(-4, 3)$ **c** $(-5, -\frac{3}{2})$
9 Horizontal dilation with scale factor 3.
10 a $y = -6x + 3$ **b** $y = 2 - 15x$ **c** $x - 3y = 7$
    d $x = 1 + 3y - 2y^2$ **e** $(x + 3)^2 + (y + 4)^2 = 8$

EXERCISE 9A

1 a 45 shoppers **b** 18 shoppers **c** $\approx 15.6\%$
   d positively skewed
2 a 10 employees **b** $\approx 4.44\%$
   c positively skewed **d** It is an outlier.
3 a Number of TV sets in students' households
   b positively skewed, no outliers
   c 6 households
   d 15%

4 a

No. of toothpicks	Tally	Frequency
47	|	1
48	₩	5
49	₩ ₩	10
50	₩ ₩ ₩ ₩ |||	23
51	₩ ₩	10
52	₩ ||||	9
53				2
	Total	60

b Number of toothpicks in boxes

c approximately symmetrical   **d** ≈ 38.3%

5 a

No. of nights	Tally	Frequency
1						4
2	₩ |	6
3	₩ ||	7
4	₩ ||	7
5	₩ |	6
6						4
7						4
8				2
	Total	40

b Miami hotel data

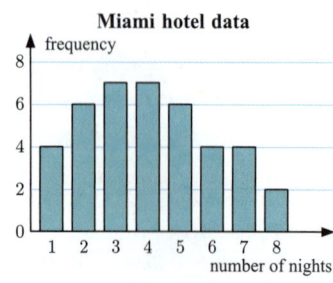

c no   **d** slightly positively skewed   **e** the Miami hotel

6 a

Test score	Tally	Frequency
20 - 29	|	1
30 - 39	||	2
40 - 49	|||	3
50 - 59	₩ ||||	9
60 - 69	₩ ₩ |||	13
70 - 79	₩ |||	8
80 - 89	₩ ₩	10
90 - 100	||||	4
	Total	50

b 28%   **c** 12%

d More students had a test score in the interval 60 - 69 than in any other interval.

e negatively skewed

7 a

Test score	Tally	Frequency
15 - 19	|	1
20 - 24		0
25 - 29	|||	3
30 - 34	₩	5
35 - 39	₩ |	6
40 - 44	₩ ₩ ₩	15
45 - 49	₩	5
50 - 54	₩ |	6
55 - 60	||||	4
	Total	45

b Students' test scores

c negatively skewed with no outliers   **d** 22.2%

EXERCISE 9B

1 a *Weight* can take any value in the given range, and is measured, not counted.

b Weights of volleyball squad

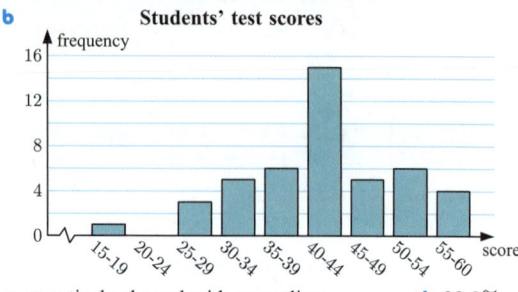

c $85 \leqslant w < 90$ kg.   More people in the volleyball squad have weights between 85 and 90 kg than in any other interval.

d approximately symmetrical

2 a 6 seedlings   **b** 30%

c Heights of seedlings in a nursery

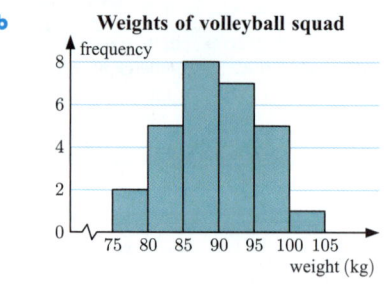

d $40 \leqslant h < 60$ mm   **e** positively skewed

f i ≈ 754 seedlings   **ii** ≈ 686 seedlings

3 a

Distance d (m)	Frequency
$10 \leqslant d < 12$	2
$12 \leqslant d < 14$	4
$14 \leqslant d < 16$	7
$16 \leqslant d < 18$	5
$18 \leqslant d < 20$	2

b
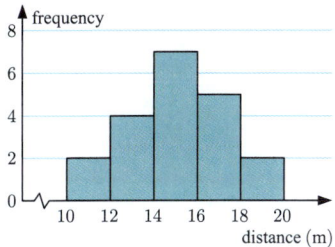

c $14 \leqslant d < 16$ m   **d** approximately symmetrical

4 a

Time t (s)	Frequency
$23 \leqslant t < 24$	3
$24 \leqslant t < 25$	4
$25 \leqslant t < 26$	7
$26 \leqslant t < 27$	10
$27 \leqslant t < 28$	11
$28 \leqslant t < 29$	5

b 17.5%

c
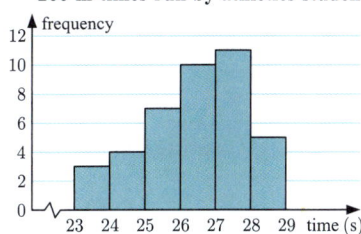

d $27 \leqslant t < 28$ s   **e** negatively skewed

EXERCISE 9C.1

1 a i 25   **ii** 24   **iii** 30
 b i ≈ 13.3 **ii** 11.5   **iii** 8
 c i ≈ 10.3 **ii** 10   **iii** 11.2
 d i ≈ 429 **ii** 428   **iii** 415, 427

2 a Data set A: $\bar{x} \approx 7.73$ Data set B: $\bar{x} \approx 8.45$
 b Data set A: 7   Data set B: 7
 c The data sets are the same except for the last value, and the last value of A is less than the last value of B, so the mean of A is less than the mean of B.
 d The middle value of both data sets is the same, so the median is the same.

3 a mean: $582 000,   median: $420 000,   mode: $290 000
 b The mode is the second lowest value, so does not take the higher values into account.
 c No, since the data is unevenly distributed, the median is not in the centre.

4 a mean: 3.11 mm,   median: 0,   mode: 0
 b i The data is very positively skewed so the median is not in the centre.
  ii The mode is the lowest value so does not take the higher values into account.
 Both median and mode indicate no rain for February if daily values are unknown.
 c 15 and 27

5 a 44 points   **b** 44 points   **c** ≈ 40.6 points
 d i increase   **ii** 40.75 points

6 a 1 head   **b** 1 head   **c** 1.4 heads

7 a

Donation ($)	Frequency
1	7
2	9
5	2
10	4
20	8
Total	30

b 30 donations
c i $\approx \$7.83$
  ii $2
  iii $2
d the mode

8 a i 4.25 ducklings   **ii** 5 ducklings   **iii** 5 ducklings
 b Yes, it is negatively skewed.
 c The mean is lower than the mode and median.

9 a i New York: 3.475 nights,   Miami: 4.075 nights
  ii New York: 2 nights,   Miami: 3 nights and 4 nights
  iii New York: 3 nights,   Miami: 4 nights
 b the Miami hotel

10 26 goals   **11** 7.875   **12** 48 trees
13 a $x = 12$ **b** $x = 8$ **14** 15   **15** 6

EXERCISE 9C.2

1 $\approx 32.1°C$
2 a $165 \leqslant s < 170$ km h^{-1}
 b i 76 serves   **ii** not possible   **iii** 73.5%
 c ≈ 167 km h^{-1}
3 a 23 times   **b** 16 times   **c** ≈ 24.1 runs
4 a

Male
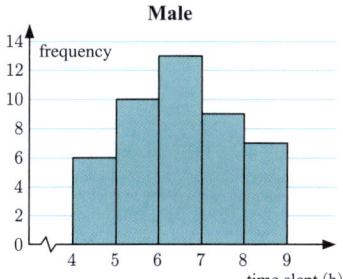

Female
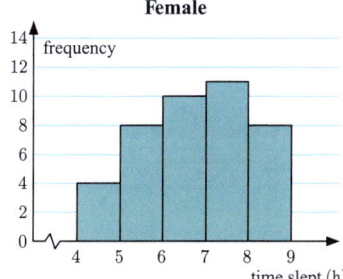

b Male: approximately symmetrical,
 Female: negatively skewed
c Male: ≈ 6.52 hours,   Female: ≈ 6.77 hours
d The female students. However the means are only estimates, and the difference in means is small, so the answer may not be reliable.

5 a $\bar{p} \approx 42.28$ litres
 b i

Petrol bought p (L)	Frequency
$20 \leqslant p < 30$	8
$30 \leqslant p < 40$	13
$40 \leqslant p < 50$	17
$50 \leqslant p < 60$	12

  ii $\bar{p} \approx 41.6$ litres

c **i**

Petrol bought p (L)	Frequency
$20 \leqslant p < 25$	2
$25 \leqslant p < 30$	6
$30 \leqslant p < 35$	6
$35 \leqslant p < 40$	7
$40 \leqslant p < 45$	9
$45 \leqslant p < 50$	8
$50 \leqslant p < 55$	3
$55 \leqslant p < 60$	9

ii $\bar{p} \approx 42.1$ litres

d The estimate found in **c ii** is closer to the actual mean found in **a**. However, both estimates are reasonable approximations.
e Using smaller intervals should produce a more accurate estimate of the mean. This is because as the intervals get smaller, the values in those intervals get closer to the interval midpoint used in estimating the mean.

EXERCISE 9D

1 a 50 trout **b i** ≈ 5 trout **ii** ≈ 15 trout
 c ≈ 26.8 cm

2 a

Score x (%)	Frequency	Cumulative frequency
$10 \leqslant x < 20$	1	1
$20 \leqslant x < 30$	3	4
$30 \leqslant x < 40$	6	10
$40 \leqslant x < 50$	15	25
$50 \leqslant x < 60$	14	39
$60 \leqslant x < 70$	28	67
$70 \leqslant x < 80$	18	85
$80 \leqslant x < 90$	11	96
$90 \leqslant x < 100$	4	100

b Cumulative frequency graph of examination scores

c i $\approx 64\%$ **ii** ≈ 52 students **iii** $\approx 74\%$ or more

3 a

Time t (min)	Frequency	Cumulative frequency
$30 \leqslant t < 35$	7	7
$35 \leqslant t < 40$	13	20
$40 \leqslant t < 45$	18	38
$45 \leqslant t < 50$	25	63
$50 \leqslant t < 55$	12	75
$55 \leqslant t < 60$	5	80

b Cumulative frequency graph of times

c i ≈ 45.4 min **ii** ≈ 14 runners **iii** ≈ 43 minutes
4 a ≈ 47.2 m
 b Baseball distances thrown

c i ≈ 46 m **ii** ≈ 4 students **iii** ≈ 53 m

EXERCISE 9E

1 a i 7 **ii** 9 **iii** $Q_1 = 7$, $Q_3 = 10$ **iv** 3
 b i 14 **ii** 18.5 **iii** $Q_1 = 16$, $Q_3 = 20$ **iv** 4
 c i 7.7 **ii** 26.9 **iii** $Q_1 = 25.5$, $Q_3 = 28.1$ **iv** 2.6
2 range = 12 seeds, IQR = 7 seeds
3 a ≈ 6.33 tows **b** 7 tows **c** 6 tows **d** 2.5 tows
4 a i Kylie: 11, Chris: 12.5 **ii** Kylie: 17, Chris: 9
 iii Kylie: 8, Chris: 4.5
 b Chris **c** Kylie
5 a i Year 6: 4 visits, Year 10: 2 visits
 ii Year 6: 4 visits, Year 10: 8 visits
 iii Year 6: 2 visits, Year 10: 3 visits
 b i the Year 6 class **ii** the Year 10 class
6 a ≈ 9.8 min **b** ≈ 6.3 min **c** ≈ 13 min **d** ≈ 6.7 min

EXERCISE 9F.1

1 a i 31 **ii** 54 **iii** 16 **iv** 40 **v** 26
 b i 38 **ii** 14
2 a i ...... 89 points **ii** ...... 25 points **iii** ...... 62 points
 iv ...... 73 points **v** ...... between 45 and 73 points
 b 64 **c** 28
3 a i min = 2, $Q_1 = 5$, median = 6, $Q_3 = 9$, max = 11
 ii

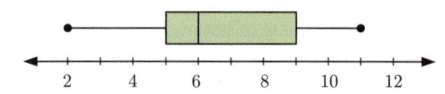

 iii range = 9 **iv** IQR = 4
 b i min = 0, $Q_1 = 4$, median = 7, $Q_3 = 8$, max = 9
 ii

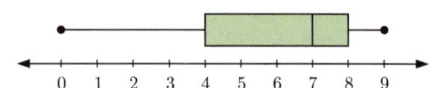

 iii range = 9 **iv** IQR = 4
4 a median = 20.2 kg, $Q_1 = 19.8$ kg, $Q_3 = 21.1$ kg, max. weight = 22.3 kg, min. weight = 18.8 kg
 b

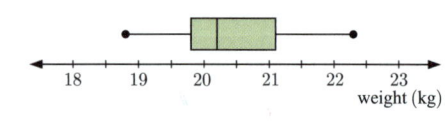

 c i IQR = 1.3 kg **ii** range = 3.5 kg

d i ...... 20.2 kg   **ii** 31.8% of the bags ......
  iii ...... 1.3 kg   **iv** ...... 19.8 kg or less
e positively skewed

EXERCISE 9F.2
1 a Year 10: min = 4 hours, Q_1 = 6.5 hours,
    med = 9 hours, Q_3 = 11 hours,
    max = 15 hours
  Year 12: min = 8 hours, Q_1 = 10 hours,
    med = 12 hours, Q_3 = 16 hours,
    max = 17 hours
  b i Year 10: 11 hours, Year 12: 9 hours
    ii Year 10: 4.5 hours, Year 12: 6 hours
2 a i Indonesia: 88 cm, Australia: 93 cm
  ii Indonesia: 43 cm, Australia: 41 cm
  iii Indonesia: 45 cm, Australia: 52 cm
  iv Indonesia: 15 cm, Australia: 20 cm
  b i 75% **ii** 50% **c i** Indonesia **ii** Australia
3 a New York: min = 1 night, Q_1 = 2 nights,
    med = 3 nights, Q_3 = 5 nights,
    max = 8 nights
  Miami: min = 1 night, Q_1 = 2.5 nights,
    med = 4 nights, Q_3 = 5.5 nights,
    max = 8 nights
b
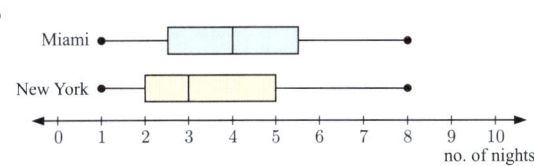
c New York: positively skewed,
  Miami: slightly positively skewed
d the Miami hotel
4 a Boys: min = 160 cm, Q_1 = 167 cm, med = 170.5 cm,
    Q_3 = 174 cm, max = 188 cm
  Girls: min = 152 cm, Q_1 = 162.5 cm, med = 166 cm,
    Q_3 = 170 cm, max = 177 cm
b
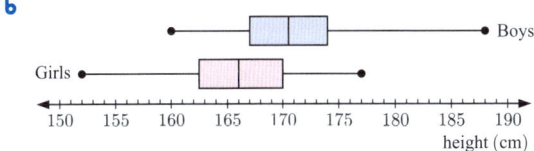
c The distributions show that in general, the boys are taller than the girls and are more varied in their heights.
5 a Bay 1: min = 2.3 pounds, Q_1 = 2.5 pounds,
    med = 2.6 pounds, Q_3 = 2.7 pounds,
    max = 2.9 pounds
  Bay 2: min = 2.6 pounds, Q_1 = 2.7 pounds,
    med = 2.75 pounds, Q_3 = 2.9 pounds,
    max = 3.2 pounds
b
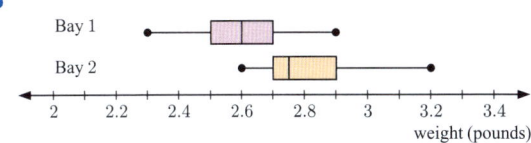
c Clearly Bay 2 catches weigh more than those from Bay 1. Median weight 2.75 pounds compared with 2.6 pounds. The range (0.6 pounds) and IQR (0.2 pounds) are identical for each bay indicating consistency of spread.

EXERCISE 9G.1
1 a ≈ 1.87   **b** ≈ 5.44
2 a ≈ 9.22   **b** ≈ 2.45
  c The outlier increases the standard deviation.
3 a Sample A **b** A: 7, B: 5
  c i A: 8, B: 4   **ii** A: 2, B: 1
    iii A: 1.90, B: 0.894
  d s takes all values into account, whereas the range and IQR each use only 2 values.
4 a Each brother was given the same number of eggs, and ate them over the same number of days, ∴ the mean is the same.
  b Kento: IQR = 2 eggs, Dongming: IQR = 9 eggs
  c Kento: s ≈ 1.41 eggs, Dongming: s ≈ 4.36 eggs
  d Dongming
5 a They both have mean = 3, range = 5   **b** Mickey's
  c Mickey: s ≈ 1.95 hits, Julio: s ≈ 1.26 hits
  d The standard deviation is better.
6 a Finnley: $\bar{x}$ = 23 people, Florence: $\bar{x}$ ≈ 17.4 people
  b Finnley: s ≈ 4.29 people, Florence: s ≈ 9.24 people
  c Finnley 332, Florence 244 ∴ Finnley
  d Florence, as s is greater.

EXERCISE 9G.2
1 1.5   **2** $\bar{x}$ = 28.8 chocolates, s = 1.64 chocolates
3 mean length = 38.3 cm, s = 2.66 cm
4 mean wage = €412.11, s = €16.35

EXERCISE 9H
1 a ≈ 68%   **b** ≈ 95%   **c** ≈ 99.7%
2 a
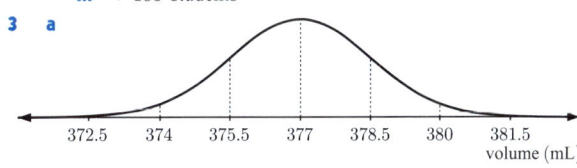
  b i ≈ 79 students   **ii** ≈ 11 or 12 students
    iii ≈ 409 students
3 a

  b i ≈ 286 bottles **ii** ≈ 252 bottles **c** ≈ 15.9%
4 a ≈ 2.28% **b** ≈ 84.1% **c** ≈ 97.6% **d** ≈ 84.1%
5 once

REVIEW SET 9A
1 positively skewed
2 a discrete **c**
  b no
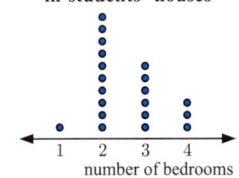
3 a i 14   **ii** 13.8   **iii** 14   **iv** 17
    v Q_1 = 10, Q_3 = 17   **vi** 7

b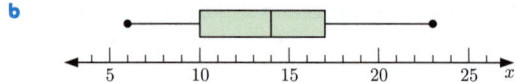

4 a Masses of eggs in a carton

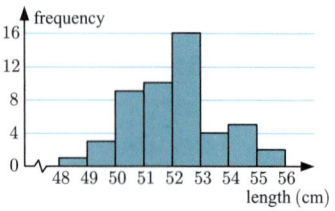

b $50 \leqslant m < 51$ g. This is the most common weight interval for the eggs.
c approximately symmetric
d ≈ 50.8 g

5 a i 48 **ii** 98 **iii** 15 **iv** 66 **v** 42
b i 83 **ii** 24

6 $x = 13$

7 a Comparing the median swim times for girls and boys shows that, in general, the boys swim 2.5 seconds faster than the girls.
b The range of the girls' swim times is 10 seconds compared to the range of 7 seconds for the boys.
c The fastest 25% of the boys swim as fast as or faster than 100% of the girls.
d 100% of the boys swim faster than 60 seconds whereas 75% of the girls swim faster than 60 seconds.

8 a 60 competitors **b** 25% **c** ≈ 207 points
9 a Davis: $\bar{x} = \$115.28$, $s \approx \$9.60$
    Douglas: $\bar{x} = \$102.37$, $s \approx \$20.42$
b the Davis family **c** the Douglas family

10 a $\bar{x} = 0.88$ kg, $s \approx 0.0980$ kg
b $\bar{x} = 1.76$ kg, $s \approx 0.196$ kg
c Both the mean and the standard deviation doubled when the individual scores were doubled.

11 a Histogram of lengths of newborn babies **b** 27 babies **c** 70%

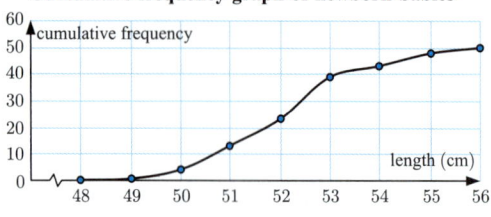

d Cumulative frequency graph of newborn babies

e i ≈ 52.1 cm **ii** ≈ 18 babies

12 336 or 337 apples

REVIEW SET 9B

1 a 32 students **c** Litter pieces picked up by students
b i ≈ 9.84 pieces
  ii 11 pieces
  iii 10 pieces
d negatively skewed

2 a $\bar{x} \approx 14.6$ **b** 14.5 **c** 14, 15 **3** $\bar{x} \approx 13.6$
4 a Number of people at judo class **b** negatively skewed

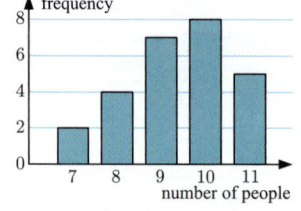

5 a

Number of people	Tally	Frequency
20 - 29	|||||	5
30 - 39	||||| |||||		11
40 - 49	||||| |||||		11
50 - 59	||||| ||||	9
60 - 69	||||	4
Total		40

b Number of people using the swimming pool

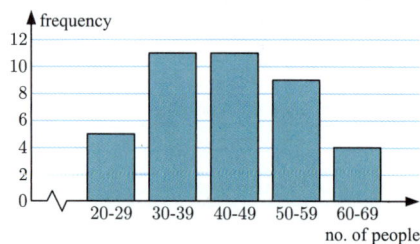

c 32.5%

6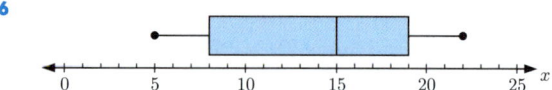

7 18 males **8** 19.5 **9 a** 32 houses **b** $\approx \$383\,000$
10 a ≈ 7.00 **b** ≈ 0.920
11 a Before: min = 25 words, Q_1 = 32 words,
           med = 37 words, Q_3 = 41 words,
           max = 52 words
    After: min = 42 words, Q_1 = 48 words,
           med = 52 words, Q_3 = 59 words,
           max = 67 words

b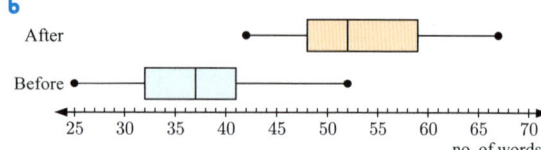

c Yes. Each value in the 5-number summary for the After data is greater than the corresponding value for the Before data.

12 a ≈ 79 batteries **b** ≈ 11 batteries **c** ≈ 239 batteries

EXERCISE 10A

1 a 3 **b** 2 **c** $\frac{1}{2}$ **d** -6 **e** $\frac{9}{2}$ **f** 1
  g $\frac{9}{2}$ **h** 12 **i** 2 **j** 6
2 a -2 **b** $-\frac{1}{2}$ **c** $\frac{1}{3}$ **d** 8 **e** 4 **f** -1
  g $\frac{1}{2}$ **h** -3 **i** $-\frac{2}{3}$ **j** -4

EXERCISE 10B.1

1. **a** $\dfrac{a}{2}$ **b** $2m$ **c** 6 **d** 3 **e** $2a$ **f** x^2
   g $2x$ **h** 2 **i** $\dfrac{1}{2a}$ **j** $2m$ **k** 4 **l** $\dfrac{2}{t}$
   m $2d$ **n** $\dfrac{b}{2}$ **o** $\dfrac{2b}{3a}$

2. **a** t **b** cannot be simplified **c** y
   d cannot be simplified **e** $\dfrac{a}{b}$ **f** cannot be simplified
   g $\dfrac{a}{2}$ **h** cannot be simplified **i** $\dfrac{7c}{4d}$

3. **a** 4 **b** $2n$ **c** a **d** 1
   e a^2 **f** $\dfrac{3n}{2}$ **g** $\dfrac{1}{2b^3}$ **h** $\dfrac{k^4}{2a^3}$

4. **a** $2(x+5)$ **b** $\dfrac{n+5}{6}$ **c** $\dfrac{b+2}{2}$ **d** $\dfrac{3(k-2)}{4}$
   e $\dfrac{5}{t-1}$ **f** $\dfrac{2}{5(k+4)}$ **g** $\dfrac{1}{3(x-3)}$ **h** $\dfrac{5(p+4)}{3}$

5. **a** $\dfrac{x+2}{9}$ **b** $\dfrac{12}{a+1}$ **c** $\dfrac{x+y}{3}$ **d** $x+y$
   e $\dfrac{2}{x+2}$ **f** $\dfrac{a+5}{3}$ **g** $\dfrac{y}{3}$ **h** $\dfrac{y-3}{3}$
   i $\dfrac{x+1}{3}$ **j** $\dfrac{1}{2(b-4)}$ **k** $\dfrac{2(p+q)}{3}$ **l** $\dfrac{8}{5(r-2)}$
   m $\dfrac{x}{x-1}$ **n** $\dfrac{(x+2)(x+1)}{4}$ **o** $\dfrac{(x+2)(x-1)^2}{4x}$

EXERCISE 10B.2

1. **a** $x+2$ **b** $x-2$ **c** $\dfrac{x+2}{2}$ **d** $\dfrac{x-5}{2}$
   e $\dfrac{y+3}{3}$ **f** $\dfrac{3x-15}{2}$ **g** $a+b$ **h** $\dfrac{a+b}{c+d}$

2. **a** $\dfrac{2x+3}{3}$ **b** cannot be simplified
   c cannot be simplified **d** $2a-1$ **e** $\dfrac{3a+1}{2}$
   f cannot be simplified **g** $\dfrac{b+3}{2}$ **h** $\dfrac{4b-6}{3}$

3. **a** $\dfrac{3}{4}$ **b** $\dfrac{5}{3}$ **c** x **d** $\dfrac{4}{5}$ **e** $\dfrac{1}{y}$ **f** $\dfrac{x}{y}$ **g** $4x$
   h $3x$ **i** $\dfrac{5x}{7}$ **j** $\dfrac{3b}{4}$ **k** $\dfrac{2x}{3}$ **l** $\dfrac{3(a+b)}{2a^2(2a+b)}$

4. **a** -2 **b** $-\dfrac{3}{2}$ **c** -1 **d** $-\dfrac{1}{2}$ **e** -3
   f $-\dfrac{2}{x}$ **g** $-\dfrac{ab}{2}$ **h** $-2x$

5. **a** $x+1$ **b** $x-1$ **c** $-(x+1)$ **d** $\dfrac{1}{x-2}$
   e $a-b$ **f** $-(a+b)$ **g** $\dfrac{2}{x-1}$ **h** $\dfrac{3+x}{x}$
   i $\dfrac{3(x+y)}{2y}$ **j** $-\dfrac{2(b+a)}{a}$ **k** $\dfrac{y}{4x+y}$ **l** $-\dfrac{4x}{x+4}$

6. **a** $x+1$ **b** $\dfrac{1}{x-5}$ **c** $\dfrac{2x}{x-5}$ **d** $\dfrac{x-2}{x+2}$
   e $\dfrac{x+3}{x-1}$ **f** $\dfrac{x+1}{1-x}$ **g** $\dfrac{x-5}{x+3}$ **h** $\dfrac{x+2}{x+3}$
   i $\dfrac{x+2}{2x-1}$ **j** $\dfrac{2x+1}{x-1}$ **k** $\dfrac{4x-3}{2x+1}$ **l** $\dfrac{3x+4}{x+2}$

EXERCISE 10C

1. **a** $\dfrac{xy}{10}$ **b** $\dfrac{3}{2}$ **c** $\dfrac{a^2}{2}$ **d** $\dfrac{1}{6}$ **e** $\dfrac{1}{5}$ **f** $\dfrac{c^2}{10}$
   g $\dfrac{ac}{bd}$ **h** 1 **i** $\dfrac{1}{2m}$ **j** 2 **k** $\dfrac{a}{b}$ **l** 4
   m $\dfrac{3}{m}$ **n** $\dfrac{a^2}{b^2}$ **o** $\dfrac{4}{x^2}$ **p** $\dfrac{1}{c}$

2. **a** $\dfrac{3}{2}$ **b** $\dfrac{3}{a}$ **c** $\dfrac{3x}{16}$ **d** $\dfrac{3}{4}$ **e** 2 **f** $\dfrac{c}{25}$
   g $\dfrac{1}{5}$ **h** $\dfrac{m^2}{2}$ **i** 2 **j** $\dfrac{n}{m}$ **k** $\dfrac{3}{4g}$ **l** $\dfrac{g}{3}$
   m $\dfrac{8}{x^3}$ **n** $\dfrac{x^2}{3}$ **o** $\dfrac{1}{a}$ **p** $\dfrac{3a}{5}$

3. **a** $\dfrac{5x}{2(x-2)}$ **b** $\dfrac{4}{3t}$ **c** $\dfrac{20}{a}$ **d** $\dfrac{4k}{3}$
   e $-\dfrac{x}{2}$ **f** $\dfrac{3m}{2(5m-1)}$

EXERCISE 10D

1. **a** $\dfrac{5a}{6}$ **b** $\dfrac{b}{10}$ **c** $\dfrac{7c}{4}$ **d** $\dfrac{5d-6}{10}$
   e $\dfrac{2x+15}{24}$ **f** $-\dfrac{5x}{14}$ **g** $\dfrac{4a+3b}{12}$ **h** $-\dfrac{2t}{9}$
   i $\dfrac{5m}{21}$ **j** $\dfrac{d}{2}$ **k** $\dfrac{11p}{35}$ **l** $\dfrac{22t}{45}$
   m $\dfrac{19k}{72}$ **n** m **o** $\dfrac{5a}{12}$ **p** $\dfrac{x}{12}$
   q $\dfrac{11z}{20}$ **r** $\dfrac{41q}{21}$

2. **a** $\dfrac{7b+3a}{ab}$ **b** $\dfrac{3c+2a}{ac}$ **c** $\dfrac{4d+5a}{ad}$ **d** $\dfrac{2an-am}{mn}$
   e $\dfrac{2a+b}{2x}$ **f** $\dfrac{5}{2a}$ **g** $\dfrac{4y-1}{xy}$ **h** $\dfrac{31}{5x}$
   i $\dfrac{35}{12z}$ **j** $\dfrac{ad+bc}{bd}$ **k** $\dfrac{6+a^2}{2a}$ **l** $\dfrac{3x+2y}{3y}$
   m $\dfrac{40-2p}{5p}$ **n** $\dfrac{7x}{18y}$ **o** $-\dfrac{19}{40t}$ **p** $\dfrac{5x+6}{2x^2}$

3. **a** $\dfrac{x+2}{2}$ **b** $\dfrac{y-3}{3}$ **c** $\dfrac{3a}{2}$ **d** $\dfrac{b-12}{4}$
   e $\dfrac{x-8}{2}$ **f** $\dfrac{6+a}{3}$ **g** $\dfrac{4x}{5}$ **h** $\dfrac{2x+1}{x}$
   i $\dfrac{5x-2}{x}$ **j** $\dfrac{a^2+2}{a}$ **k** $\dfrac{3+b^2}{b}$ **l** $\dfrac{1-2x^3}{x^2}$

4. **a** $\dfrac{5x+2}{6}$ **b** $\dfrac{-x-1}{4}$ **c** $\dfrac{11x+9}{12}$ **d** $\dfrac{5x+1}{6}$
   e $\dfrac{-2x-1}{12}$ **f** $\dfrac{10x+3}{6}$ **g** $\dfrac{7x+3}{12}$ **h** $\dfrac{5x+2}{4}$
   i $\dfrac{23x-6}{30}$ **j** $\dfrac{5b-a}{6}$ **k** $\dfrac{14x-1}{20}$ **l** $\dfrac{23-5x}{14}$
   m $\dfrac{11x-12}{30}$ **n** $\dfrac{3x-4}{20}$ **o** $\dfrac{3x-2}{8}$ **p** $\dfrac{3x-2}{10}$
   q $\dfrac{32-7x}{15}$ **r** $\dfrac{-17x-1}{12}$

5. **a** $\dfrac{7x+3}{x(x+1)}$ **b** $\dfrac{2x-6}{x(x+2)}$ **c** $\dfrac{x-7}{(x+1)(x-1)}$
   d $\dfrac{3x+7}{x+2}$ **e** $\dfrac{5x-4}{x(x-4)}$ **f** $\dfrac{-4x-10}{x+3}$
   g $\dfrac{2x^2+x+1}{(x+1)(x-1)}$ **h** $\dfrac{11x-10}{x(x-2)}$

i $\dfrac{-2x-6}{(x+1)(x+2)}$ j $\dfrac{2x^2+5x-4}{(x-1)(2x+1)}$

k $\dfrac{x^2+2x+17}{(x-1)(x+3)}$ l $\dfrac{-8x}{(x+5)(x-3)}$

m $\dfrac{3x^2+6x+2}{x(x+1)(x+2)}$ n $\dfrac{27x-24}{x(x+3)(x-4)}$

o $\dfrac{2x^3-x^2+1}{x(x-1)(x+1)}$

6 a $\$\left(\dfrac{210x+150}{x(x+1)}\right)$ b i $\$49.50$ ii $\$40$

7 a $\dfrac{2+x}{x(x+1)}$ b $\dfrac{2(x^2+2x+2)}{(x+2)(x-3)}$

c $\dfrac{x^2-2x+3}{(x-2)(x+3)}$ d $\dfrac{x+14}{x+7}$

8 a $\dfrac{-2}{x-2}$ b $\dfrac{2}{x+4}$ c $\dfrac{x-2}{x+2}$

d $\dfrac{x-6}{2-x}$ e $\dfrac{-(x+2)}{4x^2}$ f $\dfrac{12-x}{16x^2}$

9 a $\dfrac{2x}{x+1} - \dfrac{4}{(x-1)(x+1)} = \dfrac{2(x-2)}{x-1}$ is zero when $x = 2$, and undefined when $x = \pm 1$.

b $\dfrac{6}{(x+2)(x+5)} + \dfrac{x}{x+2} = \dfrac{x+3}{x+5}$ is zero when $x = -3$, and undefined when $x = -5$ or -2.

EXERCISE 10E

1 a $x = 15$ b $x = \tfrac{9}{2}$ c $x = \tfrac{35}{2}$ d $x = \tfrac{3}{8}$
e $x = -\tfrac{35}{12}$ f $x = \tfrac{15}{2}$ g $x = -\tfrac{25}{21}$ h $x = -\tfrac{3}{7}$

2 a $x = 2$ b $x = -9$ c $x = -\tfrac{4}{3}$ d $x = -27$
e $x = -\tfrac{7}{2}$ f $x = -1$

REVIEW SET 10A

1 a -2 b 4 c $\tfrac{1}{3}$ d $-\tfrac{13}{11}$

2 a $\dfrac{2t}{3}$ b $\tfrac{8}{3}$ c $\dfrac{x}{3}$ d $\dfrac{2}{x+2}$

3 a $\dfrac{2}{x-3}$ b $\dfrac{x+2}{x}$ c $\dfrac{3x}{3x+1}$

4 a -2 b $-\dfrac{5}{x}$ c $-\dfrac{x+4}{2}$

5 a $\dfrac{a}{3}$ b $\dfrac{3a}{b^2}$ c $\dfrac{3a+b^2}{3b}$ d $\dfrac{3a-b^2}{3b}$

6 a $\dfrac{21}{x}$ b $\dfrac{t}{24}$ **7** a $\dfrac{3}{2n}$ b $\dfrac{7x}{3(x+5)}$

8 a $\dfrac{11x}{12}$ b $\dfrac{14+x}{7}$ c $\dfrac{x-4}{4}$ d $\dfrac{5x}{12}$

9 a $\dfrac{7x-3}{12}$ b $\dfrac{3x+2}{6}$ c $\dfrac{3x+3}{10}$

10 a $\dfrac{3x}{(x+1)(x-2)}$ b $\dfrac{x+9}{(x-1)(x+1)}$ c $\dfrac{x^2+x+1}{x^2(x+1)}$

11 $x = 6$

12 a i $\dfrac{a^2-9}{a}$ ii $\dfrac{3-a}{3}$ b $-\dfrac{3(a+3)}{a}$
c i -12 ii undefined   iii $-\dfrac{24}{5}$

REVIEW SET 10B

1 a -6 b 0 c 2

2 a $\dfrac{3}{2x}$ b $a+2b$ c $\dfrac{x+2}{x}$

3 a $\tfrac{1}{3}$ b $2(x-2)$ c $\dfrac{x-3}{4}$

4 a $\dfrac{2m}{n^2}$ b $\dfrac{m}{2}$ c $\dfrac{m^3}{n}$

5 a $\dfrac{11}{2x}$ b $\dfrac{6b-ay}{by}$ c $\dfrac{35}{12x}$

6 a $\dfrac{5x}{14}$ b $\dfrac{4x+9}{3x^2}$

7 a $\dfrac{10+x}{2}$ b $\dfrac{3x-y}{x}$ c $\dfrac{6+3x+2y}{6}$

8 a $\dfrac{3y}{2(y+2)}$ b $-\dfrac{3}{4x}$

9 a $\dfrac{3x-2}{8}$ b $\dfrac{9x+27}{10}$ c $\dfrac{9-7x}{18}$

10 a $\dfrac{7-x}{(x-1)(x+2)}$ b $\dfrac{x^2-2x+2}{x^2(x-1)}$

c $\dfrac{2x^3+3x^2-10x-12}{x(x+3)(x+2)}$

11 a i 12 ii 50 b xy

c $(x+y) \div \left(\dfrac{1}{x}+\dfrac{1}{y}\right) = (x+y) \div \left(\dfrac{y+x}{xy}\right)$ d 420

$= \overset{1}{\cancel{(x+y)}} \times \dfrac{xy}{\underset{1}{\cancel{x+y}}}$

$= xy$

12 $x = \tfrac{1}{2}$

EXERCISE 11A

1 a $x = \pm 10$ b $x = \pm 5$ c $x = \pm 2$
d $x = \pm 3$ e no real solution   f $x = 0$
g $x = \pm 3$ h no real solution   i $x = \pm\sqrt{2}$

2 a $x = 4$ or -2 b $x = 0$ or -8 c no real solution
d $x = 4 \pm \sqrt{5}$ e no real solution   f $x = -2$
g $x = 2\tfrac{1}{2}$ h $x = 0$ or $-\tfrac{4}{3}$ i $x = \tfrac{8}{3}$ or $-\tfrac{10}{3}$
j $x = -\tfrac{1}{2} \pm 2\sqrt{3}$ k $x = \dfrac{3 \pm \sqrt{7}}{2}$ l $x = \dfrac{\pm\sqrt{6}-3}{2}$

3 a $x = \pm 2$ b $x = \pm\sqrt{10}$ c $x = \pm 4$

4 a $x = 1$ b $x = \tfrac{3}{5}$ or 1

EXERCISE 11B

1 a $x = 0$ or 7 b $x = 0$ or 5 c $x = 0$ or 8
d $x = 0$ or 4 e $x = 0$ or -2 f $x = 0$ or $-\tfrac{5}{2}$
g $x = 0$ or $\tfrac{3}{4}$ h $x = 0$ or $\tfrac{5}{4}$ i $x = 0$ or 3

2 a $x = -1$ or -2 b $x = 1$ or 2 c $x = 5$
d $x = -2$ or -3 e $x = 2$ or 3 f $x = -1$ or -6
g $x = -2$ or -7 h $x = -5$ or -6 i $x = -5$ or 3
j $x = -6$ or 2 k $x = 3$ or 8 l $x = 7$

3 a $x = -3$ or -6 b $x = -4$ or -7 c $x = -4$ or 2
d $x = -4$ or 3 e $x = 3$ or 2 f $x = 2$
g $x = 3$ or -2 h $x = -12$ or 5 i $x = 10$ or -7
j $x = \tfrac{1}{2}$ or 2 k $x = -3$ or $\tfrac{1}{3}$ l $x = -4$ or $-\tfrac{5}{3}$
m $x = \tfrac{1}{2}$ or -3 n $x = \tfrac{1}{2}$ or 5 o $x = -1$ or $-\tfrac{5}{2}$

ANSWERS

4 **a** $x = -\frac{1}{3}$ or -4 **b** $x = -\frac{2}{5}$ or 3 **c** $x = \frac{1}{2}$ or -9
  d $x = -1$ or $\frac{5}{2}$ **e** $x = \frac{4}{3}$ or -2 **f** $x = \frac{3}{2}$ or -6
  g $x = -\frac{1}{6}$ or 3 **h** $x = \frac{3}{2}$ or -4 **i** $x = \frac{3}{2}$ or $\frac{1}{3}$
  j $x = -\frac{8}{3}$ or 2 **k** $x = \frac{4}{7}$ or $-\frac{1}{2}$ **l** $x = \frac{1}{4}$ or $-\frac{4}{3}$

5 **a** $x = -4$ or -3 **b** $x = -3$ or 1 **c** $x = \pm 3$
  d $x = -1$ or $\frac{2}{3}$ **e** $x = -\frac{1}{2}$ **f** $x = \frac{5}{2}$ or 4
  g $x = 11$ or -3 **h** $x = -\frac{3}{4}$ or $\frac{5}{2}$

6 **a** $x = -2$ or 1 **b** $x = -6$ or 2 **c** $x = 2$ or -1
  d $x = 4$ or -1 **e** $x = 1$ or $-\frac{1}{3}$ **f** $x = \frac{1}{2}$ or -1

7 **a** $x = 4$ or -1 **b** $x = 15$ or 2 **c** $x = -9$ or -2
  d $x = 3$ or $-\frac{7}{2}$ **e** $x = 4$ or $\frac{4}{3}$ **f** $x = 1$ or $\frac{6}{5}$
  g $x = 0$ or $\pm\sqrt{11}$ **h** $x = 0$ or -3

8 **a** $x = \pm 1$ or ± 2 **b** $x = \pm\sqrt{3}$ or ± 2 **c** $x = \pm\sqrt{5}$

9 **a** $x = 0, 13$, or -3 **b** $x = 0$ or 4
  c $x = 0, \pm 2$, or $\pm\sqrt{11}$

10 **a** $x = 2$ **b** $x = 3$

EXERCISE 11C

1 **a** **i** 1^2 **ii** $(x+1)^2 = 6$
  b **i** 1^2 **ii** $(x-1)^2 = -6$
  c **i** 3^2 **ii** $(x+3)^2 = 11$
  d **i** 3^2 **ii** $(x-3)^2 = 6$
  e **i** 5^2 **ii** $(x+5)^2 = 26$
  f **i** 4^2 **ii** $(x-4)^2 = 21$
  g **i** 6^2 **ii** $(x+6)^2 = 49$
  h **i** $(\frac{5}{2})^2$ **ii** $(x+\frac{5}{2})^2 = \frac{17}{4}$
  i **i** $(\frac{7}{2})^2$ **ii** $(x-\frac{7}{2})^2 = \frac{65}{4}$

2 **a** $x = 2 \pm \sqrt{3}$ **b** $x = 1 \pm \sqrt{3}$ **c** $x = 2 \pm \sqrt{7}$
  d $x = -1 \pm \sqrt{2}$ **e** $x = -2 \pm \sqrt{3}$ **f** $x = -3 \pm \sqrt{6}$
  g $x = -1$ or -2 **h** $x = -4 \pm \sqrt{2}$ **i** $x = \dfrac{3 \pm \sqrt{13}}{2}$

3 **a** no real solution **b** $x = 3$ or 2 **c** no real solution
  d $x = \dfrac{-1 \pm \sqrt{5}}{2}$ **e** $x = \dfrac{-5 \pm \sqrt{33}}{2}$ **f** no real solution

4 **a** $x = \dfrac{-2 \pm \sqrt{6}}{2}$ **b** $x = \dfrac{6 \pm \sqrt{15}}{3}$ **c** $x = \dfrac{5 \pm \sqrt{10}}{5}$
  d $x = \dfrac{-6 \pm \sqrt{46}}{2}$ **e** no real solution **f** $x = \dfrac{-3 \pm \sqrt{21}}{6}$

5 **a** $x = \dfrac{-b \pm \sqrt{b^2 - 4c}}{2}$
  b **i** $b^2 - 4c > 0$ **ii** $b^2 - 4c = 0$ **iii** $b^2 - 4c < 0$

EXERCISE 11D

1 **a** **i, ii** $x = -2$ or -4 **b** **i, ii** $x = 5$
  c **i, ii** $x = -\frac{2}{3}$ or 3

2 **a** $x = \dfrac{-1 \pm \sqrt{21}}{2}$ **b** $x = \dfrac{5 \pm \sqrt{5}}{2}$ **c** $x = 2 \pm \sqrt{5}$
  d $x = \dfrac{-5 \pm \sqrt{37}}{6}$ **e** $x = \dfrac{1 \pm \sqrt{57}}{4}$ **f** $x = \dfrac{4 \pm \sqrt{11}}{5}$
  g $x = \dfrac{3 \pm \sqrt{5}}{2}$ **h** $x = \dfrac{1 \pm \sqrt{7}}{2}$ **i** $x = \dfrac{1 \pm \sqrt{2}}{3}$

  j $x = \dfrac{5 \pm \sqrt{53}}{14}$ **k** $x = \dfrac{-1 \pm \sqrt{7}}{3}$ **l** $x = \dfrac{2 \pm \sqrt{3}}{5}$

3 **a** $x = \dfrac{-1 \pm \sqrt{29}}{2}$ **b** $x = \dfrac{-1 \pm \sqrt{5}}{2}$ **c** no real solution
  d $x = 1 \pm 2\sqrt{2}$ **e** $x = \dfrac{7 \pm \sqrt{217}}{6}$ **f** $x = \dfrac{3 \pm \sqrt{13}}{2}$

EXERCISE 11E

1 -11 or 10 **2** -3 or 8 **3** $x = 3 + \sqrt{5}$ and $3 - \sqrt{5}$
4 The numbers are -2 and 5, or 2 and -5.
5 8 cm **6** 10 m **7** 18 m by 12 m
8 7.10 m or 16.90 m ; 8.45 m ; 3.55 m
9 17.9 cm **10** BC $= 16$ cm or 5 cm
11 **a** $x = 2$ **b** $x = 5$ **c** $x = 6$ **d** $x = \sqrt{31} - 1$
  e $x = \dfrac{3 + \sqrt{5}}{2}$ as $x > \dfrac{1}{2}$ **f** $x = 3 + \sqrt{34}$
12 BE $= 6$ cm **13** CD $= (1 + \sqrt{41})$ m **14** $n = 6$
15 $\frac{2}{5}$ or $\frac{-9}{-6}$ **16** 40 oranges **17** $\frac{4}{3}$ or $\frac{3}{4}$
18 The numbers are $\dfrac{4 + \sqrt{14}}{2}$ and $\dfrac{4 - \sqrt{14}}{2}$.
19 Cut out squares with sides 2 cm.
20 **a** $x + 2r = 10$ $\therefore$ $r = 5 - \dfrac{x}{2}$
  b Hint: Lawn area $= 4 \times$ total of flower bed areas
  $\therefore 2(\pi \times 5^2) = 4 \times \pi r^2$
  $\therefore 50\pi = 4\pi \left(5 - \dfrac{x}{2}\right)^2$ etc.
  c 2.93 m
21 $x = 5$
22 **a** Hint: Draw a diagram and show that
  area of pavement $= 2\left[x(12 + 2x) + 6x\right]$.
  b $4x^2 + 36x = \frac{7}{8}(6 \times 12) = 63$ **c** 1.5 m
23 3.2 cm

EXERCISE 11F

1 **a** $i\sqrt{2}$ **b** $5i$ **c** $i\sqrt{11}$ **d** $9i$
2 **a** $x = \pm i\sqrt{3}$ **b** $x = \pm 2i$ **c** $x = \pm i\sqrt{14}$
  d $x = \pm i\sqrt{7}$ **e** $x = \pm 4i$ **f** $x = \pm i\sqrt{6}$
3 **a** two real solutions **b** one real solution
  c imaginary solutions
4 **a** $x = \dfrac{-1 \pm i\sqrt{7}}{2}$ **b** $x = \dfrac{3 \pm i\sqrt{15}}{2}$ **c** $x = -2 \pm 3i$
  d $x = \dfrac{1 \pm i\sqrt{39}}{4}$ **e** $x = 1 \pm 4i$ **f** $x = \dfrac{3 \pm i\sqrt{51}}{6}$

EXERCISE 11G

1 **a** sum of the roots is $\frac{7}{3}$, product of the roots is $\frac{2}{3}$
  b roots are 2 and $\frac{1}{3}$, with sum $\frac{7}{3}$, product $\frac{2}{3}$
2 **a** sum of the roots is -2, product of the roots is -4
  b roots are $-1 \pm \sqrt{5}$, with sum -2 and product -4
3 **a** sum of the roots is 3, product of the roots is $\frac{1}{2}$
  b sum of the roots is $-\frac{4}{5}$, product of the roots is -2

c sum of the roots is $\frac{1}{4}$, product of the roots is $\frac{3}{2}$
4 $-\frac{2}{3}$
5 **a** sum of the roots is -4, product of the roots is 5
   b roots are $-2 \pm i$, with sum -4, product 5

REVIEW SET 11A
1 **a** $x = \pm\sqrt{11}$ **b** $x = \pm 4$
2 **a** $x = 9$ or -1 **b** $x = 0$ or -2
3 **a** $x = 7$ or -3 **b** $x = \pm\frac{5}{2}$ **c** $x = \frac{2}{3}$ or $-\frac{1}{2}$
4 **a** $x = 6$ or -4 **b** $x = -3$ **c** $x = \frac{1}{2}$ or 4
5 $x = -3 \pm \sqrt{5}$
6 **a** $x = -12 \pm \sqrt{155}$ **b** $x = 9$ or -2 **c** $x = -\frac{2}{5}$ or $\frac{3}{2}$
7 $\frac{2}{3}$ or $\frac{3}{2}$
8 **a** $x = 2$ or $-\frac{1}{2}$ **b** $x = \frac{-2 \pm \sqrt{19}}{3}$ **c** $x = \frac{13 \pm \sqrt{105}}{8}$
9 $x = 7$
10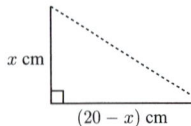
   a **i** $(10 + 2\sqrt{10})$ cm, $(10 - 2\sqrt{10})$ cm, and hypotenuse $2\sqrt{70}$ cm
        ii $(20 + 2\sqrt{70})$ cm
   b Hint: We require $\frac{1}{2}x(20-x) = 51$.

11 $x = 1$ or 5 12 **a** $x = \pm i$ **b** $x = \frac{-5 \pm i\sqrt{11}}{2}$
13 sum of the roots is 4, product of the roots is $\frac{1}{3}$

REVIEW SET 11B
1 **a** $x = \pm\sqrt{6}$ **b** $x = \pm 1$
2 **a** $x = -3 \pm \sqrt{19}$ **b** $x = \frac{1 \pm \sqrt{17}}{3}$
3 **a** $x = 11$ or -3 **b** $x = \frac{1}{2}$ or $-\frac{3}{4}$ 4 $x = 1 \pm \sqrt{101}$
5 **a** $x = 9$ or -5 **b** $x = \frac{2}{3}$ or -5
6 **a** $x = \pm\sqrt{35}$ **b** $x = -3$ or 1
7 8 cm, 15 cm, and 17 cm
8 **a** $x = \frac{-1 \pm \sqrt{3}}{2}$ **b** $x = \frac{2 \pm \sqrt{2}}{2}$
9 12 people, $\$40$ each   10 10 cm
11 **a** $x + \frac{1}{x} = 5$
   $\therefore\ x^2 - 5x + 1 = 0$ has solutions $x = \frac{5 \pm \sqrt{21}}{2}$
   b Hint: $\frac{5 + \sqrt{21}}{2} + \frac{2}{5 + \sqrt{21}} \left(\frac{5 - \sqrt{21}}{5 - \sqrt{21}} \right)$
12 **a** $x = \pm i\sqrt{5}$ **b** $x = -3 \pm 3i$ 13 $-\frac{3}{2}$

EXERCISE 12A.1
1 **a** $\tan 64° = \frac{c}{x}$ **b** $\sin 70° = \frac{a}{x}$ **c** $\cos 43° = \frac{x}{e}$
   d $\sin 35° = \frac{x}{b}$ **e** $\cos 61° = \frac{g}{x}$ **f** $\tan 30° = \frac{h}{x}$
2 **a** $x \approx 12.99$ **b** $x \approx 15.52$ **c** $x \approx 9.84$
   d $x \approx 6.73$ **e** $x \approx 3.31$ **f** $x \approx 20.01$
   g $x \approx 16.86$ **h** $x \approx 4.45$ **i** $x \approx 1.65$
   j $x \approx 26.75$ **k** $x \approx 7.53$ **l** $x \approx 9.61$

3 **a** $\theta = 22°$, $a \approx 8.09$, $b \approx 3.03$
   b $\theta = 59°$, $a \approx 13.0$, $b \approx 7.83$
   c $\theta = 65°$, $a \approx 5.42$, $b \approx 2.29$
4 ≈ 28.8 cm

EXERCISE 12A.2
1 **a** $\theta \approx 48.2°$ **b** $\theta \approx 45.6°$ **c** $\theta \approx 56.3°$
   d $\theta \approx 37.4°$ **e** $\theta \approx 42.2°$ **f** $\theta = 45°$
   g $\theta \approx 40.2°$ **h** $\theta \approx 35.3°$ **i** $\theta \approx 35.9°$
2 **a** $\phi \approx 45.6°$, $\theta \approx 44.4°$, $x \approx 7.14$
   b $\alpha \approx 53.9°$, $\beta \approx 36.1°$, $x \approx 5.94$
   c $a \approx 50.3°$, $b \approx 39.7°$, $x \approx 8.65$
3 **a** **i** $\sin\theta = \frac{3}{8}$ **ii** $\cos\theta = \frac{\sqrt{55}}{8}$ **iii** $\tan\theta = \frac{3}{\sqrt{55}}$
   b In each case, $\theta \approx 22.0°$.

EXERCISE 12B
1 ≈ 110 m   2 $\approx 32.9°$ 3 ≈ 238 m   4 ≈ 765 m
5 ≈ 280 m   6 $6.89°$ 7 ≈ 23.5 m   8 $\approx 21.8°$
9 ≈ 15.8 cm   10 $\approx 106°$ 11 No, ≈ 0.721 cm.
12 $\approx 41.4°$ 13 $\approx 53.2°$ 14 **a** ≈ 248 m   **b** ≈ 128 m
15 $\approx 14.3°$ 16 ≈ 729 m
17 **a** ≈ 1.66 units   **b** ≈ 1.66 units

EXERCISE 12C
1 **a** 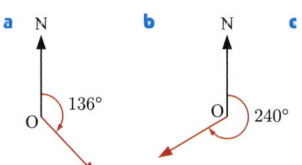 **b** **c** **d**

2 **a** $040°$ **b** $235°$ **c** $297°$ **d** $132°$ **e** $225°$
   f $337°$
3 **a** $041°$ **b** $142°$ **c** $322°$ **d** $099°$ **e** $221°$
   f $279°$
4 **a** $055°$ **b** $235°$ **c** $095°$ **d** $275°$ **e** $130°$
   f $310°$
5 $\approx 057.3°$ 6 $\approx 308°$
7 **a** 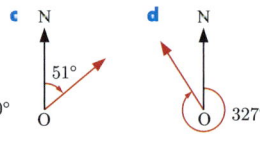   **b** 1.7 km
                                 c $061.9°$T

8 ≈ 7.81 km, $\approx 130°$ 9 ≈ 46.0 km
10 **a** 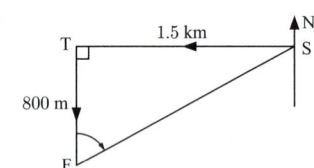   **b** 35 km
                                 c **i** ≈ 9.65 km
                                      ii ≈ 33.6 km

11 ≈ 2.44 km   12 ≈ 221 km

ANSWERS

13 a 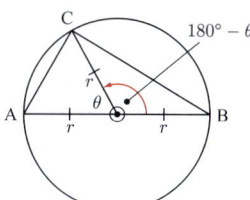 **b** 2.92 km **c** 159°

14 ≈ 3.61 km, ≈ 057.7°

15 a ≈ 33.5 km, ≈ 025.6° **b** ≈ 206°

EXERCISE 12D.1

1 a ≈ 21.2 cm **b** ≈ 35.3°
2 a HX ≈ 9.43 cm **b** ≈ 32.5°
 c HY ≈ 10.8 cm **d** ≈ 29.1°
3 a DF ≈ 8.94 cm **b** ≈ 18.5°
4 ≈ 69.2 cm **5 a** 45° **6** $\theta \approx 61.9°$

EXERCISE 12D.2

1 a i [GF] **ii** [HG] **iii** [HF] **iv** [GM]
 b i [MA] **ii** [MN]
 c i [CD] **ii** [DE] **iii** [DF] **iv** [DX]
2 a i $B\widehat{G}F$ **ii** $B\widehat{H}F$ **iii** $D\widehat{F}H$ **iv** $A\widehat{X}E$
 b i $P\widehat{Z}S$ **ii** $Q\widehat{Y}R$ **iii** $P\widehat{W}S$ **iv** $Q\widehat{W}R$
 c i $A\widehat{S}X$ **ii** $A\widehat{Y}X$
3 a i 45° **ii** ≈ 35.3° **iii** ≈ 63.4° **iv** ≈ 41.8°
 b i ≈ 18.4° **ii** ≈ 15.5° **iii** ≈ 17.5°
 c i ≈ 26.6° **ii** ≈ 22.6° **iii** ≈ 26.6°
 d i ≈ 61.9° **ii** ≈ 69.3°

EXERCISE 12E

1

θ	$\cos\theta$	$\sin\theta$	$\cos(180°-\theta)$	$\sin(180°-\theta)$
18°	0.9511	0.3090	−0.9511	0.3090
27°	0.8910	0.4540	−0.8910	0.4540
53°	0.6018	0.7986	−0.6018	0.7986
62°	0.4695	0.8829	−0.4695	0.8829
80°	0.1736	0.9848	−0.1736	0.9848
125°	−0.5736	0.8192	0.5736	0.8192

2 P(0.276, 0.961), Q(−0.906, 0.423)
3 a 154° **b** 135° **c** 111° **d** 94°
4 a 82° **b** 53° **c** 24° **d** 12°
5 a 154° **b** 135° **c** 111° **d** 94°
6 a 82° **b** 53° **c** 24° **d** 12°

EXERCISE 12F

1 a ≈ 55.2 cm² **b** ≈ 347 km² **c** ≈ 1.15 m²
2 In △PQR,
$\sin(180° - C) = \dfrac{h}{b}$
∴ $h = b\sin(180° - C)$
∴ $h = b\sin C$
But, area △PRS $= \tfrac{1}{2}ah$
$= \tfrac{1}{2}ab\sin C$
3 a ≈ 13.6 cm² **b** ≈ 58.6 m² **c** ≈ 5.81 m²

4 a ≈ 41.6 cm² **b** ≈ 36.7 m² **c** ≈ 7.70 cm²
5 50.0 cm² **6** $x \approx 21.9$ **7** ≈ 13.1 cm
8

Area △OBC
$= \tfrac{1}{2}r^2\sin(180° - \theta)$
$= \tfrac{1}{2}r^2\sin\theta$
$=$ area △OAC

9 a i Area $= \tfrac{1}{2}bc\sin A$ **ii** Area $= \tfrac{1}{2}ab\sin C$
 b From **a**, $\tfrac{1}{2}bc\sin A = \tfrac{1}{2}ab\sin C$
 Divide both sides by $\tfrac{1}{2}abc$, etc.

EXERCISE 12G.1

1 a $x \approx 11.05$ **b** $x \approx 11.52$ **c** $x \approx 5.19$
2 a $x \approx 9.43$ **b** $x \approx 11.9$ **c** $x \approx 6.37$
3 ≈ 10.2 cm²
4 a $\theta = 59°$, $x \approx 96.7$, $y \approx 90.1$
 b $\phi = 62°$, $x \approx 4.17$, $y \approx 5.62$
 c $\theta = \phi = 28.5°$, $x \approx 5.30$

EXERCISE 12G.2

1 a $A\widehat{C}B \approx 72.9°$ or ≈ 107° **b**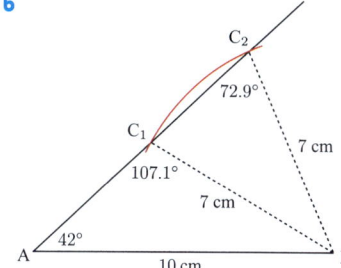

2 a Using the sine rule, $P\widehat{R}Q \approx 33.9°$ or 146.1°.
 In the case of 146.1°, 42° + 146.1° is already > 180°.
 ∴ $P\widehat{R}Q \approx 33.9°$ only.
 b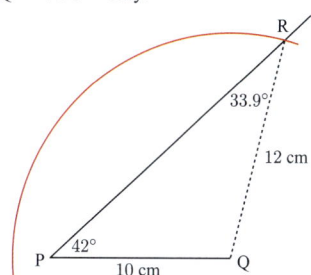

3 a $\theta \approx 31.4°$ **b** $\theta \approx 77.5°$ or 102°
 c $\theta \approx 43.6°$ or 136° **d** $\theta \approx 40.8°$
4 a $\widehat{A} \approx 49.1°$ **b** $\widehat{B} \approx 71.6°$ or 108° **c** $\widehat{C} \approx 44.8°$

EXERCISE 12H

1 a ≈ 2.66 cm **b** ≈ 9.63 m **c** 10.6 m
 d 27.5 cm **e** 4.15 km **f** 15.2 m
2 a $\theta \approx 36.3°$ **b** $\theta \approx 53.2°$ **c** $\theta \approx 115.6°$
3 a $\widehat{A} \approx 51.8°$, $\widehat{B} \approx 40.0°$, $\widehat{C} \approx 88.3°$
 b $\widehat{P} \approx 34.0°$, $\widehat{Q} \approx 96.6°$, $\widehat{R} \approx 49.3°$

4 **a** $\cos\theta = \dfrac{m^2 + c^2 - a^2}{2cm}$

b $\cos(180° - \theta) = \dfrac{m^2 + c^2 - b^2}{2cm}$

c Hint: $\cos(180° - \theta) = -\cos\theta$

d **i** $x \approx 9.35$ **ii** $x \approx 4.24$

5 **b** $x = 5 \pm \sqrt{6}$

c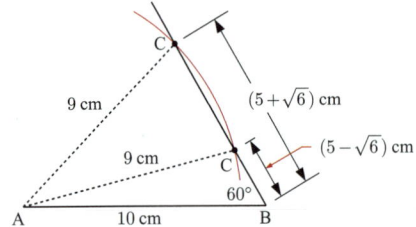

EXERCISE 12I

1 $AC \approx 14.3$ km **2** $AC \approx 1300$ m **3** $\theta \approx 13.4°$

4 **a** $\widehat{A} \approx 35.69°$ **b** ≈ 4 ha **5** ≈ 100 m

6 19.6 km in direction $106°$ **7** $\approx 214°$

8 **a**

b $XM_1 \approx 7.59$ km
$XM_2 \approx 23.0$ km

9 ≈ 63.4 m

10 $AB \approx 6.43$ m,
$BC \approx 9.85$ m,
$AC \approx 8.66$ m

11 ≈ 3.58 m,
≈ 1.95 m,
≈ 4.47 m

REVIEW SET 12A

1 **a** $x \approx 14.0$ **b** $x \approx 35.2$

2 $\theta = 36°$, $x \approx 12.4$, $y \approx 21.0$ **3** ≈ 55.2 m

4 **a** $157°$ **b** $281°$ **5** $\approx 201°$

6 **a** $\approx 56.3°$ **b** $\approx 33.9°$

7 $P(0.545, 0.839)$, $Q(-0.978, 0.208)$

8 **a** $29°$ **b** ≈ 117 m **c** ≈ 160 m

9 **a** ≈ 77 m^2 **b** ≈ 15.9 m

10 **a** $x \approx 223$ **b** $x \approx 99.4$

11 ≈ 337 m in the direction $\approx 138°$

12 **a** $DC \approx 10.2$ m **b** $BE \approx 7.00$ m **c** ≈ 82.0 m^2

13 $XR \approx 5.62$ cm

REVIEW SET 12B

1 **a** $\theta \approx 38.7°$ **b** $\theta \approx 37.1°$

2 **a** $x \approx 3.18$ **b** $x \approx 9.40$

3 $\alpha \approx 36.4°$, $\theta \approx 53.6°$, $x \approx 25.7$ **4** $\approx 32.2°$

5 187 m **6** **a** $230°$ **b** $165°$ **c** $140°$

7 **a** $45°$ **b** $60°$ **8** **a** 78.1 km **b** $\approx 051.2°$

9 **a** $142°$ **b** $128°$ **10** ≈ 69.3 m^2

11 $AC \approx 10.7$ m **12** $\widehat{ACB} \approx 50.5°$ or $129.5°$

13 **a** ≈ 185 m **b** $\approx 184°$

14 **a** $\cos\widehat{BQP} = \dfrac{2^2 + 5^2 - 4^2}{2 \times 2 \times 5} = \dfrac{13}{20}$

b $\cos(\widehat{BQR}) = \cos(180° - \widehat{BQP})$
$= -\cos\widehat{BQP}$
$= -\dfrac{13}{20}$

c $BR^2 = 2^2 + 5^2 - 2 \times 2 \times 5(-\dfrac{13}{20})$
$= 2^2 + 5^2 + 13$
etc.

EXERCISE 13A

1 $\dfrac{168}{200} = 0.84$ **2** $\dfrac{11}{123} \approx 0.0894$ **3** $\dfrac{169}{227} \approx 0.744$

4 $\dfrac{172}{417} \approx 0.412$

5 **a** $\dfrac{137}{200} = 0.685$ **b** $\dfrac{145}{200} = 0.725$

c We could combine Sam and Karla's results and estimate the chance of an end occurring using the combined data.

d Yes

EXERCISE 13B

1 **a** 407 people **b** **i** $\dfrac{93}{407} \approx 0.229$ **ii** $\dfrac{207}{407} \approx 0.509$

2 **a** 57 ice creams **b** **i** $\dfrac{17}{57} \approx 0.298$ **ii** $\dfrac{36}{57} \approx 0.632$

3 **a**

Councillor	Frequency
Mr Tony Trimboli	216
Mrs Andrea Sims	72
Mrs Sara Chong	238
Mr John Henry	74
Total	600

b **i** $\dfrac{74}{600} \approx 0.123$ **ii** $\dfrac{310}{600} \approx 0.517$

4 **a**

	Like	Dislike	Total
Junior students	87	38	125
Senior students	129	56	185
Total	216	94	310

b **i** $\dfrac{87}{310} \approx 0.281$ **ii** $\dfrac{129}{310} \approx 0.416$ **iii** $\dfrac{94}{310} \approx 0.303$

c The total is 1. This is because the three probabilities in **b** cover all possible outcomes that could occur.

5 **a** 100 students

b **i** $\dfrac{29}{100} = 0.29$ **ii** $\dfrac{8}{100} = 0.08$ **iii** $\dfrac{26}{100} = 0.26$

iv $\dfrac{68}{100} = 0.68$

6 **a** $\dfrac{69}{147} \approx 0.469$ **b** $\dfrac{26}{147} \approx 0.177$ **c** $\dfrac{43}{147} \approx 0.293$

7 **a** $\dfrac{3}{82} \approx 0.0366$ **b** $\dfrac{52}{82} \approx 0.634$ **c** $\dfrac{32}{82} \approx 0.390$

d $\dfrac{19}{82} \approx 0.232$

8 **a** $\dfrac{4822}{5038} \approx 0.957$ **b** $\dfrac{448}{5038} \approx 0.0889$

c $\dfrac{31}{5038} \approx 0.006\,15$ **d** $\dfrac{1864}{5038} \approx 0.370$

EXERCISE 13C

1 **a** {A, B, C, D} **b** {BB, BG, GB, GG}

c {ABCD, ABDC, ACBD, ACDB, ADBC, ADCB, BACD, BADC, BCAD, BCDA, BDAC, BDCA, CABD, CADB, CBAD, CBDA, CDAB, CDBA, DABC, DACB, DBAC, DBCA, DCAB, DCBA}

d {GGG, GGB, GBG, BGG, GBB, BGB, BBG, BBB}

e **i** {HH, HT, TH, TT}
ii {HHH, HHT, HTH, THH, HTT, THT, TTH, TTT}
iii {HHHH, HHHT, HHTH, HTHH, THHH, HHTT, HTHT, HTTH, THHT, THTH, TTHH, HTTT, THTT, TTHT, TTTH, TTTT}

ANSWERS 581

2 **a**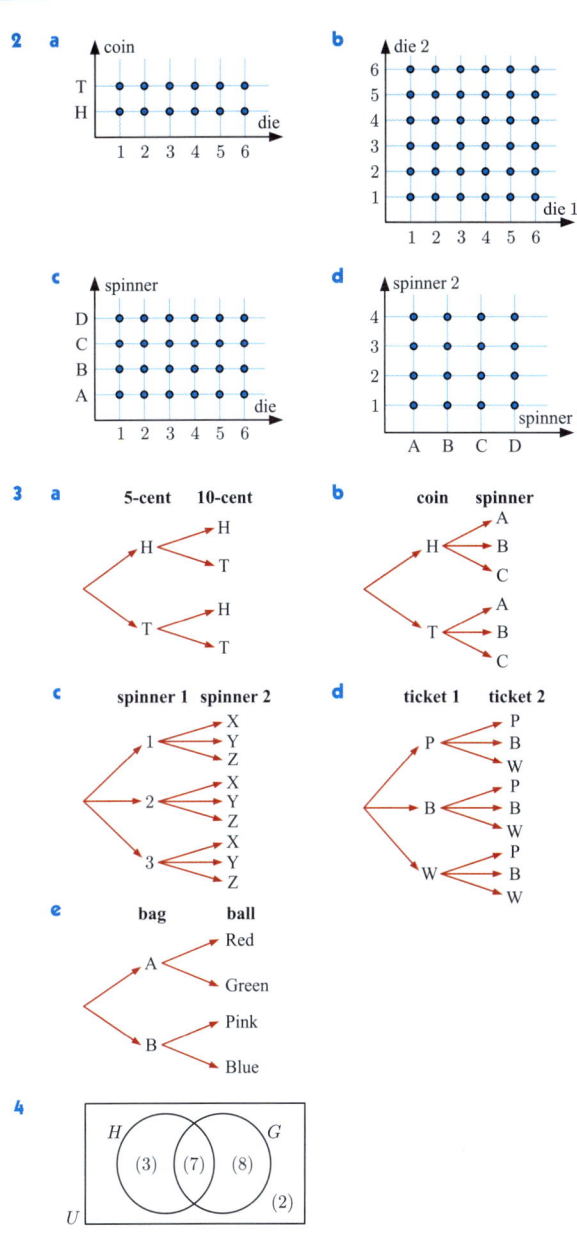

3

4

EXERCISE 13D

1 {ODG, OGD, DOG, DGO, GOD, GDO}
  a $\frac{1}{6}$ **b** $\frac{1}{3}$ **c** $\frac{2}{3}$ **d** $\frac{1}{3}$

2 {BBB, GBB, BGB, BBG, BGG, GBG, GGB, GGG}
  a $\frac{1}{8}$ **b** $\frac{1}{8}$ **c** $\frac{1}{8}$ **d** $\frac{3}{8}$ **e** $\frac{1}{2}$ **f** $\frac{7}{8}$

3 {ABCD, ABDC, ACBD, ACDB, ADBC, ADCB, BACD, BADC, BCAD, BCDA, BDAC, BDCA, CABD, CADB, CBAD, CBDA, CDAB, CDBA, DABC, DACB, DBAC, DBCA, DCAB, DCBA}
  a $\frac{1}{2}$ **b** $\frac{1}{6}$ **c** $\frac{1}{6}$ **d** $\frac{1}{2}$

4 **a**

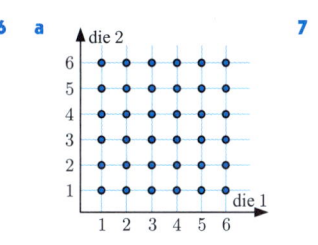

b **i** $\frac{1}{4}$ **ii** $\frac{1}{4}$ **iii** $\frac{1}{2}$ **iv** $\frac{3}{4}$

5 **a** 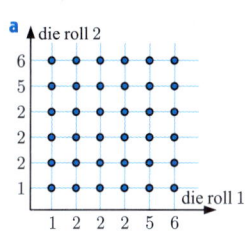 **b** **i** $\frac{1}{10}$ **ii** $\frac{3}{10}$ **iii** $\frac{2}{5}$ **iv** $\frac{3}{5}$

6 **a** **7** **a**

b **i** $\frac{1}{18}$ **ii** $\frac{1}{6}$ **iii** $\frac{11}{36}$ **b** **i** $\frac{1}{6}$ **ii** $\frac{2}{9}$ **iii** $\frac{1}{3}$
  iv $\frac{5}{9}$ **v** $\frac{1}{4}$ **vi** $\frac{1}{6}$ **iv** $\frac{11}{36}$ **v** $\frac{8}{9}$ **vi** $\frac{5}{9}$

8 **a** **i** $\frac{1}{15}$ **ii** $\frac{2}{15}$ **iii** $\frac{7}{15}$ **iv** $\frac{5}{15} = \frac{1}{3}$
  b P(odd) $= \frac{6}{15}$, P(even) $= \frac{9}{15}$ $\therefore$ even

9 **a** 33 students **b** **i** $\frac{17}{33}$ **ii** $\frac{5}{33}$ **iii** $\frac{8}{11}$ **iv** $\frac{19}{33}$

10 **a**

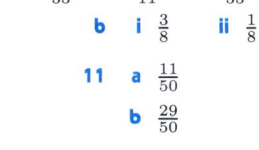

b **i** $\frac{3}{8}$ **ii** $\frac{1}{8}$

11 **a** $\frac{11}{50}$
   b $\frac{29}{50}$

EXERCISE 13E.1

1 **a** $\frac{1}{48}$ **b** $\frac{5}{16}$ **2** **a** $\frac{2}{9}$ **b** $\frac{4}{15}$

3 **a** $\frac{6}{625} = 0.0096 = 0.96\%$ **b** $\frac{506}{625} = 0.8096 \approx 81.0\%$

4 **a** $\frac{1}{49}$ **b** $\frac{10}{49}$ **c** $\frac{25}{49}$

5 **a** ≈ 0.0545 **b** ≈ 0.0584 **c** ≈ 0.441 **d** ≈ 0.0840

6 **a** **i** ≈ 0.405 **ii** ≈ 0.595
   b **i** ≈ 0.164 **ii** ≈ 0.354

7 **a** ≈ 0.366 **b** ≈ 0.0231

8 **a** **b** **i** $\frac{1}{4}$ **ii** $\frac{3}{4}$
    iii $\frac{5}{12}$

9 **a** 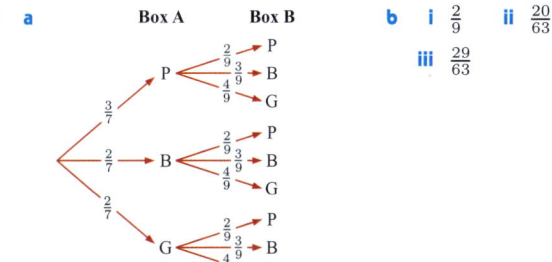 **b** **i** $\frac{2}{9}$ **ii** $\frac{20}{63}$
    iii $\frac{29}{63}$

c 1; this is because every possible outcome is covered by these three events.

10 a

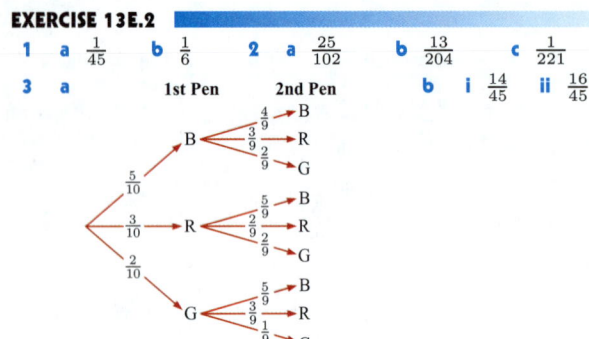

b 0.712

EXERCISE 13E.2

1 a $\frac{1}{45}$ **b** $\frac{1}{6}$ **2 a** $\frac{25}{102}$ **b** $\frac{13}{204}$ **c** $\frac{1}{221}$

3 a

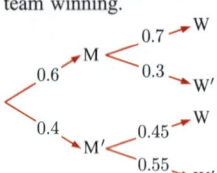

b i $\frac{14}{45}$ ii $\frac{16}{45}$

4 a M is the event of Matt playing in a game. W is the event of his team winning.

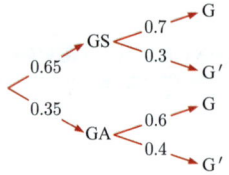

5

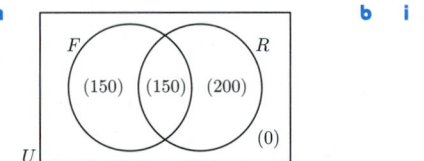

$P(G) = 0.665$

b 0.6

6

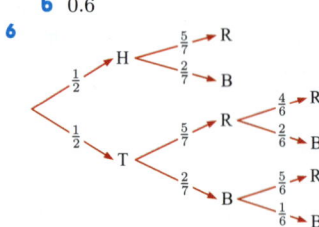

P(at least one red) $= \frac{5}{6}$

7

P(exactly one G) $= \frac{59}{120}$

8

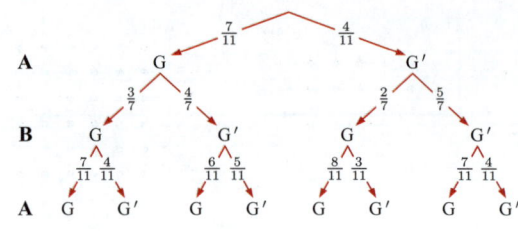

$P(\text{gold coin in A}) = \frac{519}{847} \approx 0.613$

9 0.448   **10 a** $\frac{13}{75}$ **b** $\frac{26}{75}$ **c** $\frac{12}{25}$

EXERCISE 13F

1 a $\frac{12}{25}$ **b** $\frac{12}{19}$ **2 a** $\frac{24}{25}$ **b** $\frac{1}{25}$
3 a $\frac{13}{14}$ **b** $\frac{5}{23}$ **c** $\frac{9}{10}$
4 a $\frac{1}{20}$ **b** $\frac{12}{19}$ **c** $\frac{17}{78}$ **d** $\frac{8}{31}$
5 a $\frac{17}{37}$ **b** $\frac{11}{19}$ **c** $\frac{11}{17}$
6 a $\frac{11}{37}$ **b** $\frac{14}{47}$ **c** $\frac{14}{29}$ **7 a** $\frac{3}{16}$ **b** $\frac{2}{5}$ **8** $\frac{3}{5}$
9 a $\frac{1}{4}$

  b i It increases the probability. In order for the sum to be 5, either the 3 or the 4 must be picked from bag A.
  ii $\frac{1}{2}$

EXERCISE 13G

1 A and B, A and D, A and E, A and F, B and D, B and F, C and D.

2 a

```
coin
 T  • • • • • •
 H  • • • • • •        die
    1 2 3 4 5 6
```

  b i No. It is possible to 'toss a head' *and* 'roll a 5'.
  ii $P(A \text{ or } B) = \frac{7}{12}$, $P(A \text{ and } B) = \frac{1}{12}$
  iii $P(A) + P(B) - P(A \text{ and } B) = \frac{1}{2} + \frac{1}{6} - \frac{1}{12}$
  $= \frac{7}{12} = P(A \text{ or } B)$ ✓

3 a No, since $P(A \text{ and } B) \neq 0$ **b** 0.75
4 $P(Y) = 0.4$ **5** $P(C) + P(D) > 1$ **6 a** 0 **b** 0.1
7 0.65   **8** $P(A) = 0.8$, $P(B) = 0.5$

REVIEW SET 13A

1 a 38 days   **b i** $\frac{1}{38}$ **ii** $\frac{11}{38}$ **iii** $\frac{19}{38} = \frac{1}{2}$

2
```
coin
 T  • • • • •
 H  • • • • •       spinner
    A B C D E
```

3 a $\frac{49}{81} \approx 0.60$ **b** $\frac{32}{81} \approx 0.40$
4 a $\frac{1}{20}$ **b** $\frac{3}{10}$ **c** $\frac{9}{20}$
5 a

```
    F           R
  (150)(150)(200)

                   (0)
U
```

b i $\frac{3}{10}$ **ii** $\frac{1}{2}$

6 a $\frac{2}{7}$ b $\frac{4}{7}$ **7** a $\frac{1}{9}$ b $\frac{2}{9}$

8

Injuries	0	1	2	3
Probability	0.336	0.452	0.188	0.024

∴ one injury is most likely.

9 0.66 **10** a 47 books b i $\frac{31}{47}$ ii $\frac{4}{47}$ iii $\frac{7}{16}$

11 $\frac{41}{90}$

12 a (graph: 2nd selection vs 1st selection, points at 5c, 10c, 20c, 50c, $1, $2)

b i $\frac{4}{9}$ ii $\frac{11}{36}$ iii $\frac{23}{36}$ c $\frac{20}{23}$

13 a 0 b 0.14

REVIEW SET 13B

1 a ≈ 0.364 b ≈ 0.551 c ≈ 0.814

2 a (tree diagram: bag A,B,C → ticket G,Y) b (tree diagram sets 1–5 with M,J branches)

3 a $\frac{318}{450} \approx 0.707$ b $\frac{132}{450} \approx 0.293$ c $\frac{21}{450} \approx 0.0467$

4 $\frac{1}{2}$ **5** a $\frac{1}{9}$ b $\frac{4}{9}$ c $\frac{4}{9}$

6 a $\frac{37}{50} = 0.74$ b ≈ 0.0176

7 a (tree diagram bag X,Y → 1st marble → 2nd marble R,W) b $\frac{9}{20}$

8 $\frac{7}{12}$ **9** 0.697 **10** $\frac{2}{7}$

11 P(A) = $\frac{3}{20}$, P(B) = $\frac{7}{20}$, P(C) = $\frac{2}{5}$

12 a $\frac{13}{55}$

b i Increases, as the number of tickets of the desired colour does not decrease with each draw.

ii $\frac{37}{121}$

13 a i 0.21 ii 0.28 iii 0.3

b P(Ihor wins) = 0.238 which is > 0.21
∴ the strategy increases his chance of winning.

EXERCISE 14A

1 a $A = 2000 + 150 \times 8$ b $A = 2000 + 150w$
c $A = 2000 + dw$ d $A = P + dw$

2 a $C = 40 + 60 \times 5$ b $C = 40 + 60t$
c $C = 40 + xt$ d $C = F + xt$

3 a $P = 3 \times 10 - 1(15 - 10)$
∴ $P = 3 \times 10 - 5$

b $P = 3 \times c - 1(20 - c)$ c $P = 3 \times c - 1(a - c)$
∴ $P = 4c - 20$ ∴ $P = 4c - a$

4 a $D = 4 \times 6 + 2(4 - 1)$ b $D = 5m + 3(5 - 1)$
c $D = 8m + b(8 - 1)$ d $D = mp + b(p - 1)$

5 a $G = 2 \times (3 - 1) + 3 \times (2 - 1)$
b $G = 3 \times (5 - 1) + 5 \times (3 - 1)$
c $G = 4 \times (4 - 1) + 4 \times (4 - 1)$
d $G = m(n - 1) + n(m - 1)$
∴ $G = 2mn - m - n$

6 a $A = 2ab + \dfrac{\pi a^2}{2}$ b $A = ar + \dfrac{\pi r^2}{2}$
c $A = aw + \dfrac{\pi w^2}{4}$ d $A = ab - \dfrac{\pi a^2}{8}$
e $A = 2ar - \pi r^2$ f $A = \dfrac{\pi(b^2 - a^2)}{8} + \dfrac{a\sqrt{b^2 - a^2}}{2}$

7 a $V = Al$ b $V = \dfrac{\pi d^2 h}{4}$ c $V = \dfrac{abc}{2}$

8 a $A = 2ab + 2bc + 2ac$ b $A = 6a^2 + 8ab$
c $A = \pi r^2 + 2\pi rh + \pi rs$

9 Hint: Area of end section $= \pi R^2 - \pi r^2$
$= \pi(R + r)(R - r)$

EXERCISE 14B

1 a ≈ 26.4 cm b ≈ 17.8 cm c ≈ 127 m
2 a 19.6 m b ≈ 4.52 s
3 a ≈ 129 cm² b ≈ 7.14 m
4 a ≈ 4260 cm³ b ≈ 1.06 cm c ≈ 4.99 mm
5 a ≈ 707 cm² b ≈ 39.9 cm
6 a ≈ 1.34 s b 81 cm

EXERCISE 14C

1 a $y = \dfrac{10 - 2x}{5}$ b $y = \dfrac{20 - 3x}{4}$ c $y = 2x - 8$
d $y = \dfrac{14 - 2x}{7}$ e $y = \dfrac{20 - 5x}{2}$ f $y = \dfrac{2x + 12}{3}$

2 a $x = r - p$ b $x = \dfrac{z}{y}$ c $x = \dfrac{d - a}{3}$
d $x = \dfrac{d - 2y}{5}$ e $x = \dfrac{p - by}{a}$ f $x = \dfrac{y - c}{m}$
g $x = \dfrac{s - 2}{t}$ h $x = \dfrac{m - p}{q}$ i $x = \dfrac{6 - a}{b}$

3 a $y = \dfrac{t - z}{5}$ b $y = \dfrac{c - p}{2}$ c $y = \dfrac{a - t}{3}$
d $y = \dfrac{n - 5}{k}$ e $y = \dfrac{a - n}{b}$ f $y = \dfrac{a - p}{n}$

4 a $z = \dfrac{b}{ac}$ b $z = \dfrac{a}{d}$ c $z = \dfrac{2d}{3}$
d $z = \pm\sqrt{2a}$ e $z = \pm\sqrt{bn}$ f $z = \pm\sqrt{m(a - b)}$

584 ANSWERS

5 **a** $a = \dfrac{F}{m}$ **b** $r = \dfrac{C}{2\pi}$ **c** $d = \dfrac{V}{lh}$
  d $K = \dfrac{b}{A}$ **e** $h = \dfrac{2A}{b}$ **f** $T = \dfrac{100I}{PR}$

6 $h = \dfrac{A - 2\pi r^2}{2\pi r}$ or $h = \dfrac{A}{2\pi r} - r$

7 **a** $r = \sqrt{\dfrac{A}{\pi}}$ **b** $x = \sqrt[5]{aN}$ **c** $k = \sqrt[3]{\dfrac{M}{5}}$
  d $x = \sqrt[3]{\dfrac{n}{D}}$ **e** $x = \pm\sqrt{\dfrac{y+7}{4}}$ **f** $Q = \pm\sqrt{P^2 - R^2}$

8 **a** $a = d^2 n^2$ **b** $l = 25T^2$ **c** $a = \pm\sqrt{b^2 + c^2}$
  d $d = \dfrac{25a^2}{k^2}$ **e** $l = \dfrac{gT^2}{4\pi^2}$ **f** $b = \dfrac{16a}{A^2}$

9 **a** $x = \dfrac{c-a}{3-b}$ **b** $x = \dfrac{c}{a+b}$ **c** $x = \dfrac{a+2}{n-m}$
  d $x = -\dfrac{a}{b+8}$ **e** $x = \dfrac{a-b}{1-c}$ **f** $x = \dfrac{e-d}{r+s}$

10 **a** $a = \dfrac{2-bP}{P}$ **b** $r = \dfrac{8-qT}{T}$ **c** $q = \dfrac{Ap-B}{A}$
  d $x = \dfrac{3-Ay}{2A}$ **e** $y = \sqrt{\dfrac{4-Mx^2}{M}}$

11 **a** $x = \dfrac{y}{1-y}$ **b** $x = \dfrac{2y+3}{1-y}$ **c** $x = \dfrac{3y+1}{3-y}$
  d $x = \dfrac{2y+1}{y+4}$ **e** $x = \dfrac{3y-7}{2y+3}$ **f** $x = \dfrac{3y-1}{y-1}$
  g $x = \dfrac{-4y-3}{y+2}$ **h** $x = \dfrac{2y}{y+3}$ **i** $x = \dfrac{y+12}{5}$

12 $p = \sqrt{1 - \dfrac{1}{N}}$ {as $p > 0$}

EXERCISE 14D

1 **a** $\theta = \dfrac{360A}{\pi r^2}$
  b **i** $\theta \approx 63.7°$ **ii** $\theta \approx 105°$ **iii** $\theta \approx 214°$

2 **a** $a = \dfrac{d^2}{2bK}$ **b** **i** $a \approx 1.29$ **ii** $a = 16.2$

3 **a** $t = (H-1)^2$
  b **i** 1 year **ii** 4 years **iii** $6\tfrac{1}{4}$ years

4 **a** $r = \sqrt[3]{\dfrac{3V}{4\pi}}$
  b **i** ≈ 2.12 cm **ii** ≈ 5.76 cm **iii** ≈ 62.0 cm

5 **a** $v = \sqrt{u^2 + 2as}$ **b** **i** ≈ 20.6 m/s **ii** ≈ 52.9 m/s

6 **a** $\approx 58.8\%$ **b** $w = \dfrac{Pl}{100-P}$ **c** 9 matches
  d 7 consecutive matches

7 **a** $c = \dfrac{A-2ab}{2(a+b)}$ **b** **i** $c = 3$ **ii** $c = 7$ **iii** $c = 7.5$

8 **a** $F \approx 2.01 \times 10^{20}$ Newtons **b** $d = \sqrt{\dfrac{Gm_1 m_2}{F}}$
  c **i** $\approx 1.50 \times 10^{11}$ m **ii** $\approx 1.43 \times 10^{14}$ m

9 **a** Hint: Use the diagram to show that the area of one triangle face
  $= \dfrac{s}{2} \times \dfrac{\sqrt{3}s}{2} = \dfrac{\sqrt{3}s^2}{4}$

  b $s^2 = \dfrac{A}{1+\sqrt{3}}\left(\dfrac{1-\sqrt{3}}{1-\sqrt{3}}\right)$ etc.
  c **i** ≈ 4.28 cm **ii** ≈ 7.41 cm **iii** ≈ 14.8 cm

10 **b** $p = \dfrac{3g}{g-1}$ **c** 0g 0p, 2g 6p, 4g 4p

11 **a** **i** $C \approx 0.816$ **ii** $C \approx 0.742$ **b** $h = C^2 H$
  c TB: ≈ 2.65 m, GB: ≈ 3.68 m, M: ≈ 2.16 m,
      SB: ≈ 3.99 m

12 **a** $v = \dfrac{c}{m}\sqrt{m^2 - m_0^2}$ **b** $v = \dfrac{2\sqrt{2}}{3}c$
  c $v \approx 3.00 \times 10^8$ m/s

EXERCISE 14E

1 **a** 6, 11, 16, 21, 26 **b** 51 **c** $5n+1$
2 **a** 7, 10, 13, 16, 19 **b** 34 **c** $3n+4$
3 **a** **i** 4 **ii** 9 **iii** 16 **iv** 25 **b** $S_n = n^2$
4 **a** **i** 3 **ii** 7 **iii** 15 **iv** 31
  b As $3 = 2^2 - 1$, $7 = 2^3 - 1$, $15 = 2^4 - 1$, etc.,
      $S_n = 2^n - 1$
5 **a** $S_1 = \tfrac{1}{2}$, $S_2 = \tfrac{2}{3}$, $S_3 = \tfrac{3}{4}$, $S_4 = \tfrac{4}{5}$, ...
  b **i** $S_{10} = \tfrac{10}{11}$ **ii** $S_n = \dfrac{n}{n+1}$

6 **a** $S_1 = \dfrac{1 \times 2 \times 3}{6} = 1$ and $1^2 = 1$ ✓
      $S_2 = \dfrac{2 \times 3 \times 5}{6} = 5$ and $1^2 + 2^2 = 5$ ✓
      $S_3 = \dfrac{3 \times 4 \times 7}{6} = 14$ and $1^2 + 2^2 + 3^2 = 14$ ✓
      $S_4 = \dfrac{4 \times 5 \times 9}{6} = 30$ and $1^2 + 2^2 + 3^2 + 4^2 = 30$ ✓
  b $S_{100} = \dfrac{100 \times 101 \times 201}{6} = 338\,350$

REVIEW SET 14A

1 **a** **i** $V = 6 \times 8$ litres **ii** $V = 8n$ litres **iii** $V = ln$ litres
  b $V = 25 + ln$ litres
2 **a** 90 km/h **b** 3900 km **3** $A = \tfrac{\sqrt{3}}{2}a^2 + 3ab$
4 **a** $x = \dfrac{3p-n}{m}$ **b** $x = \dfrac{5y}{7}$
5 **a** $k = T^2 + l^2$ **b** $k = -\sqrt{\dfrac{P+r}{2}}$
6 **a** 11 cm **b** $c = \sqrt{L^2 - a^2 - b^2}$ **c** 9 cm
7 $x = \dfrac{2y-3}{y-2}$
8 **a** 8 amperes **b** $r = \dfrac{E - IR}{I}$ **c** 0.15 ohms
9 **a** 4, 7, 10 **b** $M = 3n+1$
10 **a** **i** 3 **ii** 6 **iii** 10 **b** **i** 9 **ii** 36 **iii** 100
  c It seems that $C_n = S_n^2$.
11 **a** **i** ≈ 283.2 K **ii** ≈ 183.2 K **iii** ≈ 338.7 K
  b $F = \tfrac{9}{5}(K - 273.15) + 32$
  c **i** 104°F **ii** $-459.67°$F **iii** $-99.67°$F

REVIEW SET 14B

1 **a** $B = 15 + 25 \times 5$ **b** $B = c + 25 \times p$ **c** $B = c + mp$
2 **a** $E = 2 \times (3-2) + 2 \times (5-2) = 8$
  b $E = 2 \times (4-2) + 2 \times (8-2) = 16$
  c $E = 2(m-2) + 2(n-2)$

3 a $M = 37$ b $r = 8$ 4 $V = 4x^2 y$

5 a $a = \dfrac{B+f}{d}$ b $a = \dfrac{9Q^2}{t^2}$ 6 $h = \dfrac{5 - G^2}{G^2}$

7 a $b = \dfrac{a}{a-1}$ b $b = \frac{3}{2}$; $3 \times \frac{3}{2} = 3 + \frac{3}{2} = 4\frac{1}{2}$ ✓

8 $x = \dfrac{2y + 3}{4 - 3y}$ 9 8, 13, 18, ...   ∴ $M = 5n + 3$

10 a i 6   ii 12   iii 20   iv 30
    b $S_1 = 2 = 1 \times 2$
       $S_2 = 6 = 2 \times 3$
       $S_3 = 12 = 3 \times 4$
       $S_4 = 20 = 4 \times 5$
       $S_5 = 30 = 5 \times 6$ ∴ $S_n = n(n+1)$

11 a $E = 1000$ joules   b $v = \sqrt{\dfrac{2E}{m}}$ c 8 m/s

EXERCISE 15A

1 a Domain is $\{x \mid x > -4\}$. Range is $\{y \mid y > -2\}$.
   b Domain is $\{x \mid -3 \leqslant x \leqslant 4\}$. Range is $\{y \mid -5 \leqslant y \leqslant 2\}$.
   c Domain is $\{x \mid -3 < x < 4\}$. Range is $\{y \mid -5 < y < 6\}$.
   d Domain is $\{x \mid x = 2\}$. Range is $\{y \mid y \in \mathbb{R}\}$.
   e Domain is $\{x \mid -3 \leqslant x \leqslant 3\}$. Range is $\{y \mid -3 \leqslant y \leqslant 3\}$.
   f Domain is $\{x \mid x \in \mathbb{R}\}$. Range is $\{y \mid y \leqslant 0\}$.
   g Domain is $\{x \mid x \in \mathbb{R}\}$. Range is $\{y \mid y = -5\}$.
   h Domain is $\{x \mid x \in \mathbb{R}\}$. Range is $\{y \mid y \geqslant 1\}$.
   i Domain is $\{x \mid x \geqslant -5\}$. Range is $\{y \mid y \leqslant 7\}$.
   j Domain is $\{x \mid x \in \mathbb{R}\}$. Range is $\{y \mid y \leqslant 4\}$.
   k Domain is $\{x \mid x \geqslant -5\}$. Range is $\{y \mid y \in \mathbb{R}\}$.
   l Domain is $\{x \mid x \in \mathbb{R}, \ x \neq 1\}$.
      Range is $\{y \mid y \in \mathbb{R}, \ y \neq 0\}$.

2 a Domain is $\{x \mid 0 \leqslant x \leqslant 2\}$. Range is $\{y \mid -3 \leqslant y \leqslant 2\}$.
   b Domain is $\{x \mid -2 < x < 2\}$. Range is $\{y \mid -1 < y < 3\}$.
   c Domain is $\{x \mid -4 \leqslant x \leqslant 4\}$. Range is $\{y \mid -2 \leqslant y \leqslant 2\}$.

EXERCISE 15B

1 **a**, **b**, and **e** are functions as no two ordered pairs have the same x-coordinate.

2 **a**, **b**, **d**, **e**, **g**, **h**, and **i** are functions.

3 No, a vertical line is not a function as it does not satisfy the vertical line test.

EXERCISE 15C.1

1 a 3   b 7   c 1   d -7 e 2
2 a -2 b -17 c 13   d $5x + 3$ e $-5x - 17$
3 a 2   b 11   c 46   d $2x^2 + 3x + 2$
   e $2x^2 + x + 1$
4 a 45   b -3 c 0   d $4x^2 - 20x + 21$
   e $16x^2 + 8x - 3$
5 a i $-\frac{3}{2}$ ii $-\frac{1}{3}$ iii $-\frac{8}{3}$ b $x = -2$
   c $2 - \dfrac{7}{x}$ d $x = -1$

6 a $V(4) = 12\,000$. The value of the car after 4 years is $12\,000.
   b $V(t) = 8000$ when $t = 5$. 5 years after purchase the value of the car is $8000.
   c $28\,000

7 a i $f(2) = 1$ ii $f(3) = -1$ b $x = -4$
8 a i $f(4) = 2$ ii $g(0) = -6$ iii $g(5) = -1$

b $x = 0$ and $x = 3$ c $x = 2$
d g has gradient 1 and y-intercept -6.

9 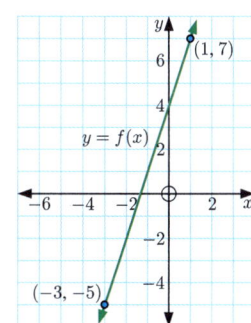   Other graphs are possible.

10 a

$f(-3) = -5$,
$f(1) = 7$
c $f(x) = 3x + 4$

EXERCISE 15C.2

1 a $\{x \mid x \in \mathbb{R}\}$ b $\{x \mid x \neq 0\}$
   c $\{x \mid x \neq 3\}$ d $\{x \mid x \neq -2 \text{ and } x \neq 1\}$
   e $\{x \mid x \neq 3 \text{ and } x \neq -3\}$ f $\{x \mid x \neq 1 \text{ and } x \neq 4\}$
2 a $\{x \mid x \geqslant 2\}$ b $\{x \mid x \leqslant 3\}$
   c $\{x \mid 0 \leqslant x \leqslant 2\}$ d $\{x \mid x > 0\}$
   e $\{x \mid x > 0\}$ f $\{x \mid x < 4 \text{ and } x \neq 0\}$

EXERCISE 15D

1 a $2 - 3x$ b $6 - 3x$ c $9x - 16$ d x
2 a $\sqrt{4x - 3}$ b $4\sqrt{x} - 3$ c 5   d 5
3 a $f(x) = \sqrt{x}$, $g(x) = x - 3$ b $f(x) = x^3$, $g(x) = x + 5$
   c $f(x) = \dfrac{5}{x}$, $g(x) = x + 7$ d $f(x) = 3 - 4x$, $g(x) = \dfrac{1}{\sqrt{x}}$
   e $f(x) = x^2$, $g(x) = 3^x$ f $f(x) = \dfrac{x+1}{x-1}$, $g(x) = x^2$
(Note: There may be other answers.)

4 a $f(g(x)) = 3x^2 + 6x + 1$ b $x = -3$ or 1
5 a $f(g(x)) = \dfrac{4}{x+2} + 1$ $\left(\text{or } \dfrac{x+6}{x+2} \right)$ b 5   c $x = 0$
6 a i 13   ii 4   iii 6   iv 17
   b $f(g(x)) = x$ and $g(f(x)) = x$ c i 3   ii -7

EXERCISE 15E

1 a i $f^{-1}(x) = x - 3$
      ii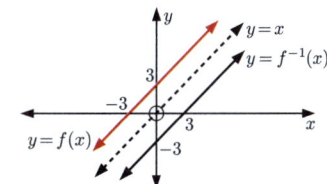

586 ANSWERS

b i $f^{-1}(x) = \dfrac{x-5}{2}$

ii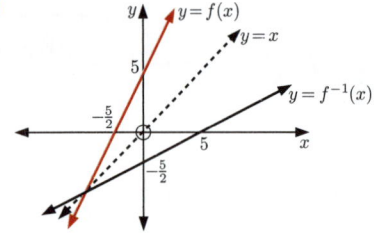

c i $f^{-1}(x) = -2x + \dfrac{3}{2}$

ii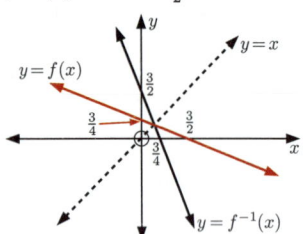

2 a, b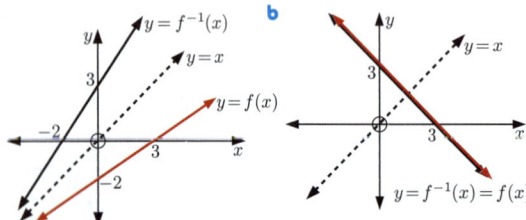

c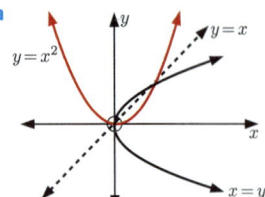

3 a $f^{-1}(x) = \dfrac{x-7}{2}$ **4 a** $f^{-1}(x) = \dfrac{1-3x}{x-2}$

5 a $g^{-1}(x) = \dfrac{5x}{x-1}$ **c** $g(6) = 6$, $g^{-1}(1)$ is undefined

6 a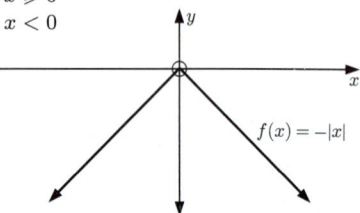

b No, as the vertical line test fails.

c Yes, it is $y = \sqrt{x}$ (not $y = \pm\sqrt{x}$).

7 b **i** and **iii** have inverse functions.

8 a Is a function as it passes the vertical line test, but does not have an inverse as it fails the horizontal line test.

b It passes both the vertical line and horizontal line tests.

EXERCISE 15F

1 a 2   **b** 10   **c** 5   **d** 11   **e** 11   **f** 40
  g 40   **h** −2

2 a 3   **b** 10   **c** 7   **d** 3   **e** 13   **f** 2
  g $\dfrac{5}{2}$ **h** $\dfrac{4}{5}$

3 a

x	9	3	0	−3	−9
x^2	81	9	0	9	81
$|x|^2$	81	9	0	9	81

b $x^2 = |x|^2$

4 a $f(x) = \begin{cases} -x & \text{if } x \geq 0 \\ x & \text{if } x < 0 \end{cases}$

$f(x) = -|x|$

b $f(x) = \begin{cases} 2x & \text{if } x \geq 0 \\ 0 & \text{if } x < 0 \end{cases}$

$f(x) = |x| + x$

c $f(x) = \begin{cases} x+2 & \text{if } x \geq 0 \\ -x+2 & \text{if } x < 0 \end{cases}$

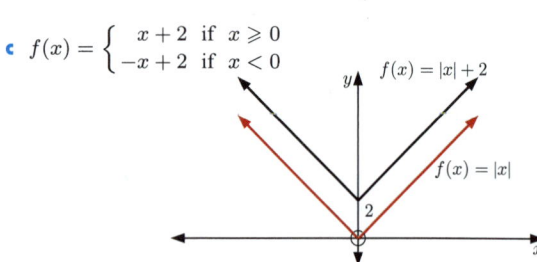

d $f(x) = \begin{cases} -x & \text{if } x \geq 0 \\ 3x & \text{if } x < 0 \end{cases}$

$f(x) = x - 2|x|$

e $f(x) = \begin{cases} 3x+1 & \text{if } x \geq 0 \\ -3x+1 & \text{if } x < 0 \end{cases}$

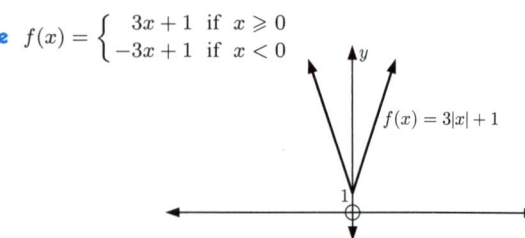

$f(x) = 3|x| + 1$

f $f(x) = \begin{cases} 5-x & \text{if } x \geq 0 \\ 5+x & \text{if } x < 0 \end{cases}$

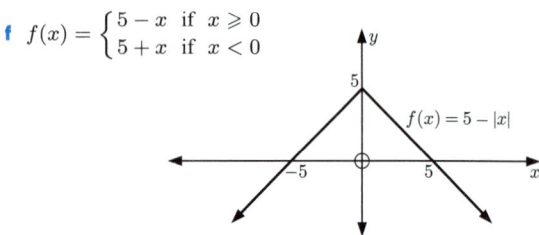

$f(x) = 5 - |x|$

g $f(x) = x^2 - 4$

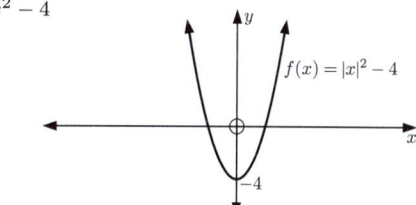

h $f(x) = \begin{cases} 1 & \text{if } x > 0 \\ \text{undefined} & \text{if } x = 0 \\ -1 & \text{if } x < 0 \end{cases}$

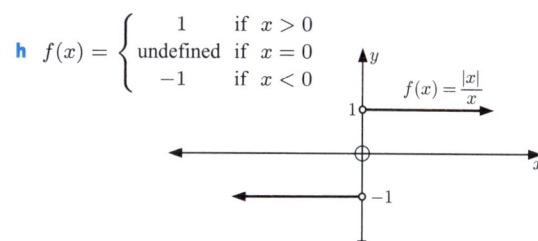

i $f(x) = \begin{cases} \sqrt{x} & \text{if } x \geq 0 \\ \sqrt{(-x)} & \text{if } x < 0 \end{cases}$

5 a i

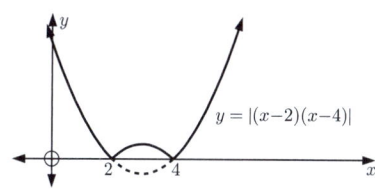

ii

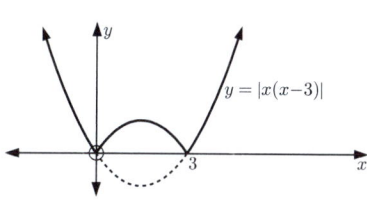

b The part of the graph $y = (x-2)(x-4)$ or $y = x(x-3)$ below the x-axis is reflected in the x-axis.

EXERCISE 15G

1 a $(2, 9)$ **b** $(\frac{5}{4}, \frac{43}{4})$ **c** $(5, \frac{1}{5})$ **d** $(1, 3)$

2 a at $(-3, 2)$ and $(2, 7)$ **b** at $(2, 1)$ and $(-1, -2)$
c at $(-\frac{1}{2}, -\frac{9}{4})$ and $(-3, 14)$ **d** at $(1, 1)$ and $(-\frac{1}{5}, -5)$

3 a at $(-1.62, -1.24)$ and $(0.62, 3.24)$ **b** at $(4.71, 0.64)$
c They do not intersect, $\therefore$ no solutions exist.
d at $(-0.75, -0.43)$

REVIEW SET 15A

1 a Domain is $\{x \mid x \in \mathbb{R}\}$. Range is $\{y \mid y \geq -2\}$.
b Domain is $\{x \mid x \geq 0\}$. Range is $\{y \mid y \in \mathbb{R}\}$.

2 a 2 **b** -4 **c** $-x^2 + 9x - 18$

3 a function **b** not a function

4 a 8 **b** $9x^2 + 6x$ **c** $x = -5$ or 3

5 a function **b** not a function

6

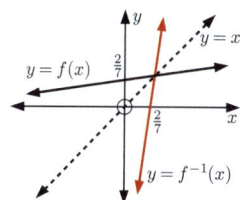

Note: There may be other answers.

7 a $0 \leq x \leq 15$ **b** $-5 \leq y \leq 15$
c When $x = 3$, $y = 10$, or $f(3) = 10$.
d When $y = 10$, $x = 3$, or $8 \leq x \leq 9$.

8 a $f(g(x)) = \sqrt{5x - 3}$ **b** $g(f(x)) = 5\sqrt{x} - 3$
c $g(g(x)) = 25x - 18$

9 a $f^{-1}(x) = 7x - 2$ **c**

10 a $g^{-1}(x) = \dfrac{4}{x - 1}$ **c** $g(2) = 3$, $g^{-1}(3) = 2$

11 a 7 **b** -1 **c** 0

12 a $f(x) = \begin{cases} 4x & \text{if } x \geq 0 \\ 2x & \text{if } x < 0 \end{cases}$ **b** $f(x) = \begin{cases} 2x - 4 & \text{if } x \geq 0 \\ -2x - 4 & \text{if } x < 0 \end{cases}$

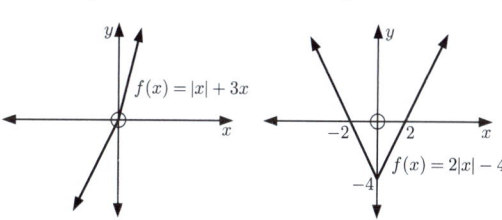

13 $(-3, -5)$ and $(1, 3)$

REVIEW SET 15B

1 a Domain is $\{x \mid x > -6\}$. Range is $\{y \mid y > -2\}$.
b Domain is $\{x \mid x \leq 1\}$. Range is $\{y \mid y \in \mathbb{R}\}$.

2 a function **b** not a function

3 a -24 **b** $-5x - x^2$ **c** $-x^2 + 3x + 4$

4 a Domain is $\{x \mid x \neq -4\}$.
b Domain is $\{x \mid x \neq -5 \text{ and } x \neq 1\}$.
c Domain is $\{x \mid 0 \leq x \leq 6\}$.

5 a

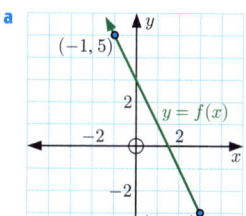

b $f(-1) = 5$, $f(3) = -3$
c $f(x) = -2x + 3$
d $f^{-1}(x) = \dfrac{3 - x}{2}$

6 a $f(g(x)) = 15 - 2x$ b $g(f(x)) = 6 - 2x$
   c $f(g(-2)) = 19$

7 a 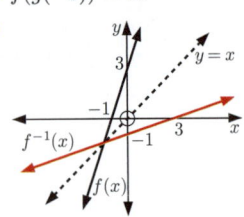 b

8 a 36 b 13 c $\frac{7}{4}$

9 a $f(g(x)) = \dfrac{7-x}{x-4}$ b 2 c $x = 10$

10 a $f^{-1}(x) = \dfrac{2x+1}{x-1}$ c 3

11 a $f(x) = \begin{cases} 7-x & \text{if } x \geq 0 \\ 7+x & \text{if } x < 0 \end{cases}$ b $f(x) = \begin{cases} 4 & \text{if } x > 0 \\ 2 & \text{if } x < 0 \\ \text{undef.} & \text{if } x = 0 \end{cases}$

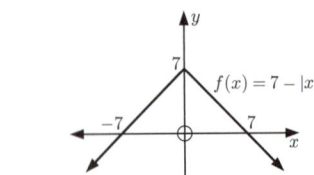 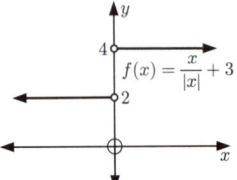

12 $(-1, -3)$ and $(\frac{3}{2}, 2)$

EXERCISE 16A

1 a 4 b 16 c 13
2 a 3, 7, 11, 15, 19, ... b 40, 35, 30, 25, 20, ...
   c 2, 3, 5, 7, 11, ...
3 a The sequence starts at 5 and increases by 3 each time.
   b $u_1 = 5$, $u_n = u_{n-1} + 3$ for $n \geq 2$
4 a The nth term of the sequence is n squared. b $u_n = n^2$
5 a 19 b 19 c 96 d 27
6 a $u_6 = 14$ b 136 c $u_8 = -14$
7 a 7, 10, 13, 16 b 25, 21, 17, 13 c 5, 15, 45, 135
   d 100, 50, 25, 12.5 e 3, 5, 9, 17
   f 4, 6, 4, 6 g 3, 4, 12, 48

EXERCISE 16B

1 a arithmetic b not arithmetic
   c not arithmetic d arithmetic
2 a $\square = 16$ b $\square = 34$ c $\square = 15$, $\triangle = 3$
   d $\square = 13$, $\triangle = -5$
3 a $u_1 = 41$, $d = 1$ b $u_1 = 1$, $d = 11$
   c $u_1 = 98$, $d = -10$ d $u_1 = 91$, $d = -9$
4 a common difference is 7 b $u_n = 7n - 3$
   c $u_{30} = 207$ d yes, the 49th term e no
5 a $d = -4$ b $u_n = 71 - 4n$ c $u_{60} = -169$
   d no e no
6 a $u_1 = 4$ and $d = 11$ b $u_{37} = 400$ c $u_{24} = 257$
7 a $k = 22$ b $k = 2\frac{1}{2}$ c $k = \frac{13}{3}$
8 a $k = 6$ b 29, 37
9 a $u_n = 5n + 17$ b $u_n = 10 - 4n$
   c $u_n = 3n - 16$ d $u_n = -\frac{17}{2} - \frac{3}{4}n$
10 a $u_n = 6n - 8$ b $u_{30} = 172$

EXERCISE 16C

1 a geometric b not geometric c geometric
   d not geometric
2 a 5 b $\frac{1}{2}$ c -2 d $-\frac{1}{10}$
3 a $b = 12$, $c = 24$ b $b = \frac{1}{2}$, $c = \frac{1}{8}$ c $b = \frac{5}{3}$, $c = -\frac{5}{9}$
4 a $r = 3$ b $u_n = 3^{n-1}$ c $u_{10} = 19\,683$
5 a $r = -\frac{1}{2}$ b $u_n = 40 \times (-\frac{1}{2})^{n-1}$ c $u_{12} = -\frac{5}{256}$
6 a $r = -\frac{1}{4}$ b $-0.000\,976\,562\,5$
7 $u_n = 3 \times 2^{\frac{n-1}{2}}$ or $3(\sqrt{2})^{n-1}$
8 a $k = \frac{2}{3}$ b $k = 9$ c $k = 2$ d $k = \pm 9$
   e $k = -7$ f $k = -\frac{8}{7}$ or 2
9 a $u_n = \frac{16}{9} \times 3^{n-1}$ b $u_n = 128 \times (-\frac{1}{2})^{n-1}$
   c $u_n = 2 \times 5^{n-1}$ or $u_n = (-2) \times (-5)^{n-1}$
   d $u_n = 6 \times (\pm \frac{1}{\sqrt{2}})^{n-1}$
10 $\pm \frac{3}{32}$

EXERCISE 16D

1 a $u_3 = 8$ b $S_3 = 16$ c $u_5 = 19$ d $S_5 = 46$
2 a i 5, 7, 9, 11 ii $S_4 = 32$ 3 $u_6 = 12$
   b i $-5, -2, 3, 10$ ii $S_4 = 6$
   c i 7, 14, 28, 56 ii $S_4 = 105$
   d i 3, 5, 11, 29 ii $S_4 = 48$
4 a $S_1 = \frac{1}{2}$, $S_2 = \frac{2}{3}$, $S_3 = \frac{3}{4}$, $S_4 = \frac{4}{5}$ b $\frac{100}{101}$

EXERCISE 16E

1 a, b, c 75 **2** $S_{12} = 450$ **3** $S_{20} = 220$
4 a 210 b 75 c 4075 d 6780
   e -2280 f -2400 g 275 h 387.5
5 2500 **6** a 24 b 1476
7 a 775 b 1705 c 969 d 1040 e -345 f 306
8 a $S_n = \dfrac{n}{2}(2u_1 + (n-1)d)$ where $u_1 = 4$, $d = 4$
   $= \dfrac{n}{2}(8 + 4(n-1))$ etc.
   b 840
9 a €65 b €1350
10 a $\dfrac{n(n^2+1)}{2}$ b $\dfrac{3(3^2+1)}{2} = \dfrac{3 \times 10}{2} = 15$ ✓ c 260

EXERCISE 16F.1

1 a, b 315
2 a 3280 b 4 882 812 c $\frac{1533}{32}$ d $63 + 63\sqrt{2}$
   e -1364 f $\frac{1640}{27}$ g ≈ 52.2 h ≈ 12.8
3 a $u_1 = 2$, $r = 3$ b 59 048
5 a i ≈ 158 mL ii ≈ 37.5 mL iii 8.91 mL
   b The amount of water Doug drinks is a geometric sequence with $r = \frac{3}{4}$.
   c i ≈ 1887.4 mL ii ≈ 1993.7 mL iii ≈ 1999.6 mL
   d If Doug followed the formula, the amount would eventually become too small to measure, and too small to sustain him. (In theory Doug would never run out of water.)

EXERCISE 16F.2

1 a diverge b converge c diverge d converge
2 a i ≈ 23.44 ii ≈ 26.53 iii ≈ 26.99
   b 27 c $S = \dfrac{9}{1 - \frac{2}{3}} = 27$

3 **a** 32   **b** $\frac{5}{4}$ **c** 27   **d** 128   **e** $\frac{432}{7}$ **f** $\frac{2}{3}$

4 **a** Start with $\frac{1}{3}$ unit^2 shaded blue. So $u_1 = \frac{1}{3}$.
  Each step shades $\frac{1}{3}$ of the previous area, so $r = \frac{1}{3}$.
  $\therefore\ S = \frac{1}{3} + \frac{1}{9} + \frac{1}{27} + ...$

  b At each step, the same amount is coloured blue as is coloured red.

  c If the process continues indefinitely, half the 1 unit^2 rectangle will be shaded blue and half will be shaded red. And from **a**, total blue area $= \frac{1}{3} + \frac{1}{9} + \frac{1}{27} + ...$
  $\therefore\ \frac{1}{3} + \frac{1}{9} + \frac{1}{27} + ... = \frac{1}{2}$

  d $S = \dfrac{\frac{1}{3}}{1 - \frac{1}{3}} = \frac{1}{2}$

5 **a** $(8 - 4) + (2 - 1) + (\frac{1}{2} - \frac{1}{4}) + ...$
  $= \ \ \ 4 \ \ \ + \ \ 1 \ \ + \ \ \frac{1}{4} \ \ + ...$

  b $\dfrac{8}{1 - \frac{1}{2}} = \dfrac{16}{3} = \dfrac{4}{1 - \frac{1}{4}}$ **6** $10 + 5\sqrt{2}$

REVIEW SET 16A

1 **a** 8, 13, 18, 23, 28   **b** 19, 12, 5, −2, −9
  c 1, 8, 27, 64, 125
2 2, 8, 20, 44   **3** **a** □ = 25   **b** □ = 21, △ = 9
4 $k = 6$ **5** **a** $\frac{4}{5}$ **b** −3   **6** $u_n = -3 \times (-2)^{n-1}$
7 **a** 3, 8, 15, 24   **b** 50   **8** **a** 1180   **b** −1410
9 **a** 1 747 625   **b** ≈ 11.08   **10** **a** $\frac{125}{4}$ **b** 16

REVIEW SET 16B

1 **a** $u_8 = 29$ **b** $u_8 = 54$
2 **a** $d = 4$ **b** $u_n = 4n - 10$ **c** $u_{100} = 390$
  d $u_{127} = 498$
3 **a** $r = -\frac{1}{2}$ **b** $u_{16} = -\frac{1}{512}$
4 **a** 5, 7, 5, 7, 5   **b** $u_{100} = 7$ **5** $S_{15} = 165$
6 $u_n = 39 - \frac{15}{2}(n - 1)$
7 **a** 1070   **b** 270   **c** −119   **d** $\dfrac{58\,025}{32} \approx 1813.3$
8 **a** $k = -5$ or 10
  b If $k = -5$, $r = -2$. If $k = 10$, $r = -\frac{1}{3}$.
9 **a** $u_1 = 6$, $r = -\frac{1}{2}$ **b** $S_{10} = \frac{1023}{256}$
10 **a** **i** 42 km   **ii** 58 km   **iii** 78 km
  b **i** 82 km   **ii** 490 km   **iii** 1180 km
  c yes, using $u_n = 2n + 38$ and $S_n = n^2 + 39n$
  d yes, $S_{30} = 2070$
11 12 cm

EXERCISE 17A

1 **a** Scale: 1 cm ≡ 10 km h^{-1}

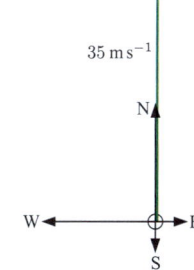

  b Scale: 1 cm ≡ 10 m s^{-1}

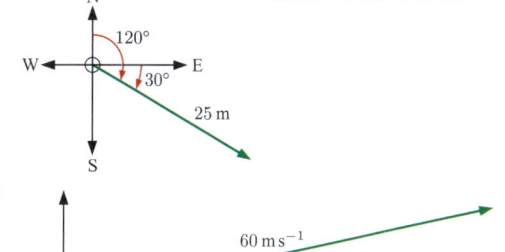

  c

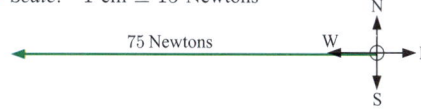

Scale: 1 cm ≡ 10 m

  d

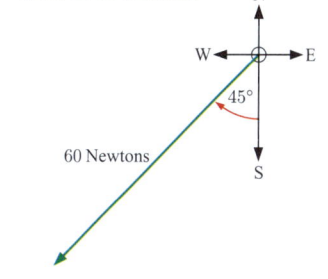

Scale: 1 cm ≡ 10 m s^{-1}

2 **a** Scale: 1 cm ≡ 15 Newtons

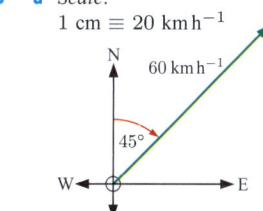

  b Scale: 1 cm ≡ 15 Newtons

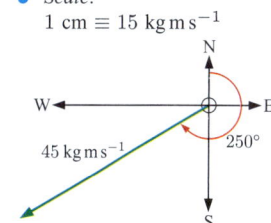

3 **a** Scale: 1 cm ≡ 20 km h^{-1}

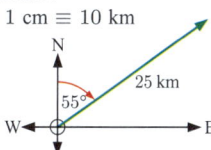

  b Scale: 1 cm ≡ 15 kg m s^{-1}

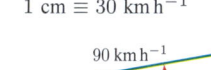

  c Scale: 1 cm ≡ 10 km   **d** Scale: 1 cm ≡ 30 km h^{-1}

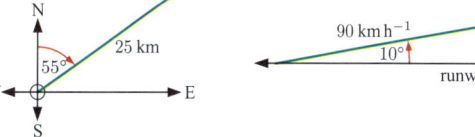

EXERCISE 17B

1 **a** **a**, **c**, and **e**; **b** and **d**   **b** **a**, **b**, **c**, and **d**
  c **a** and **b**; **c** and **d**   **d** none are equal
  e **a** and **c**; **b** and **d**
2 **a** false   **b** true   **c** false   **d** true   **e** true
3 Statements **a**, **d**, and **f** are true.

EXERCISE 17C

1 **a**

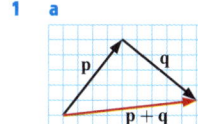

  b

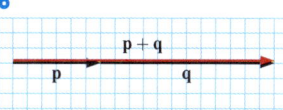

c 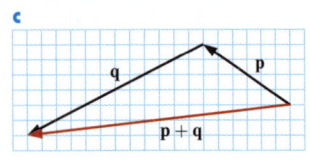   d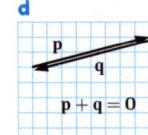

e 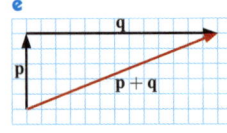   f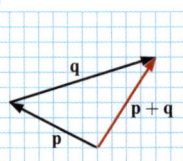

2 a $\overrightarrow{QS}$ b $\overrightarrow{PR}$ c $\overrightarrow{PQ}$ d $\overrightarrow{PS}$

3 a i 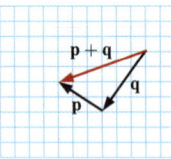 ii

 b $\mathbf{p}+\mathbf{q} = \mathbf{q}+\mathbf{p}$ for any two vectors $\mathbf{p}$ and $\mathbf{q}$

4 a 600 km h^{-1} due north   b 400 km h^{-1} due north
 c 510 km h^{-1} at a bearing of $011.3°$

5 a 0 km h^{-1} b 20 km h^{-1} east   c 14.1 km h^{-1} north east

6 The aircraft is travelling at a speed of 404 km h^{-1} at a bearing of $098.5°$.

7 The ship is travelling at a speed of 23.3 knots at a bearing of $134°$.

EXERCISE 17D

1 a, b, c, d, e, f (diagrams)

2 a $\overrightarrow{QS}$ b $\overrightarrow{PR}$ c $\mathbf{0}$ (zero vector)   d $\overrightarrow{RQ}$ e $\overrightarrow{QS}$ f $\overrightarrow{RQ}$

3 The plane must fly $4.57°$ west of north at 502 km h^{-1}.

4 a The boat must head $25.5°$ west of north.   b 28.3 km h^{-1}

5 a (diagram: 2 km h⁻¹, 3 km h⁻¹)   b The current will increase Ian's speed and push him to the right of the point he is swimming towards.

c Speed is $\approx 3.61 \text{ km h}^{-1}$, direction is $\approx 33.7°$ to the right.
d Ian should face $\approx 41.8°$ left of where he is aiming.

EXERCISE 17E.1

1 a 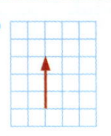   b   c 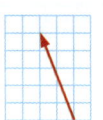   d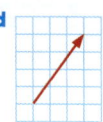

2 a $\begin{pmatrix} 4 \\ 2 \end{pmatrix}$ b $\begin{pmatrix} 0 \\ -3 \end{pmatrix}$ c $\begin{pmatrix} -3 \\ -4 \end{pmatrix}$ d $\begin{pmatrix} -6 \\ 0 \end{pmatrix}$ e $\begin{pmatrix} -6 \\ 4 \end{pmatrix}$
 f $\begin{pmatrix} 2 \\ -4 \end{pmatrix}$

3 a $\begin{pmatrix} 3 \\ 4 \end{pmatrix}$ b $\begin{pmatrix} -4 \\ -2 \end{pmatrix}$ c $\begin{pmatrix} -2 \\ 1 \end{pmatrix}$ d $\begin{pmatrix} 3 \\ -3 \end{pmatrix}$ e $\begin{pmatrix} 1 \\ 5 \end{pmatrix}$

4 a $k=2$ b $k=-1$ c $k=3$

5 a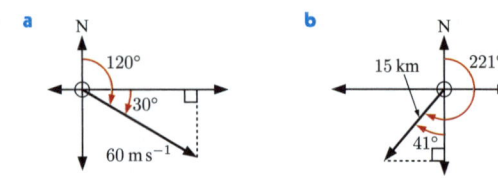

The vector is $\begin{pmatrix} 52.0 \\ -30 \end{pmatrix}$.   The vector is $\begin{pmatrix} -9.84 \\ -11.3 \end{pmatrix}$.

c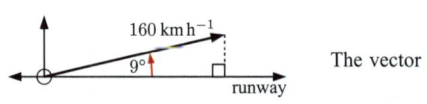

The vector is $\begin{pmatrix} 158 \\ 25.0 \end{pmatrix}$.

EXERCISE 17E.2

1 a $\begin{pmatrix} 5 \\ -4 \end{pmatrix}$ b $\begin{pmatrix} 5 \\ -4 \end{pmatrix}$ c $\begin{pmatrix} 1 \\ -4 \end{pmatrix}$ d $\begin{pmatrix} 1 \\ -4 \end{pmatrix}$
 e $\begin{pmatrix} 0 \\ -6 \end{pmatrix}$ f $\begin{pmatrix} 0 \\ -6 \end{pmatrix}$ g $\begin{pmatrix} 4 \\ -6 \end{pmatrix}$ h $\begin{pmatrix} 3 \\ -7 \end{pmatrix}$

2 a $\begin{pmatrix} 4 \\ 2 \end{pmatrix}$ b $\begin{pmatrix} -3 \\ -4 \end{pmatrix}$ c $\begin{pmatrix} -1 \\ 2 \end{pmatrix}$

3 a $\begin{pmatrix} 1 \\ 6 \end{pmatrix}$ b $\begin{pmatrix} -5 \\ 1 \end{pmatrix}$ c $\begin{pmatrix} -6 \\ 4 \end{pmatrix}$ d $\begin{pmatrix} -2 \\ 10 \end{pmatrix}$
 e $\begin{pmatrix} -4 \\ -2 \end{pmatrix}$ f $\begin{pmatrix} 2 \\ -10 \end{pmatrix}$

4 a $\begin{pmatrix} -3 \\ -3 \end{pmatrix}$ b $\begin{pmatrix} -4 \\ 9 \end{pmatrix}$

5 a $\sqrt{17}$ units   b 6 units   c $\sqrt{13}$ units
 d $\sqrt{26}$ units   e $\sqrt{20}$ units   f $\sqrt{37}$ units

6 a i $\begin{pmatrix} -2 \\ -3 \end{pmatrix}$ ii $\sqrt{13}$ units
 b i $\begin{pmatrix} 5 \\ -2 \end{pmatrix}$ ii $\sqrt{29}$ units
 c i $\begin{pmatrix} -3 \\ -4 \end{pmatrix}$ ii 5 units
 d i $\begin{pmatrix} -12 \\ 5 \end{pmatrix}$ ii 13 units

7 $\mathbf{a}+\mathbf{b} = \begin{pmatrix} a_1 \\ a_2 \end{pmatrix} + \begin{pmatrix} b_1 \\ b_2 \end{pmatrix} = \begin{pmatrix} a_1+b_1 \\ a_2+b_2 \end{pmatrix} = \begin{pmatrix} b_1+a_1 \\ b_2+a_2 \end{pmatrix} = \mathbf{b}+\mathbf{a}$

EXERCISE 17F

1 a i (diagram with r, 2r)   b i (diagram with -s, -3s)

 ii $2\mathbf{r} = \begin{pmatrix} 4 \\ 6 \end{pmatrix}$ ii $-3\mathbf{s} = \begin{pmatrix} -12 \\ 6 \end{pmatrix}$

ANSWERS 591

c i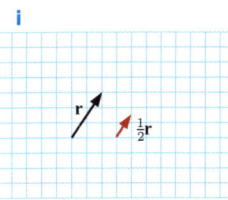

ii $\frac{1}{2}\mathbf{r} = \begin{pmatrix} 1 \\ \frac{3}{2} \end{pmatrix}$

d i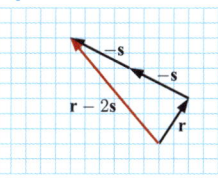

ii $\mathbf{r} - 2\mathbf{s} = \begin{pmatrix} -6 \\ 7 \end{pmatrix}$

e i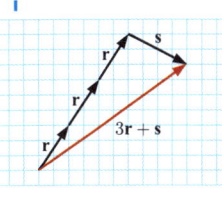

ii $3\mathbf{r} + \mathbf{s} = \begin{pmatrix} 10 \\ 7 \end{pmatrix}$

f i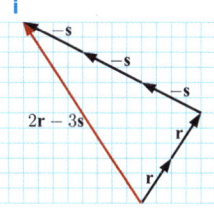

ii $2\mathbf{r} - 3\mathbf{s} = \begin{pmatrix} -8 \\ 12 \end{pmatrix}$

g i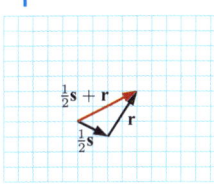

ii $\frac{1}{2}\mathbf{s} + \mathbf{r} = \begin{pmatrix} 4 \\ 2 \end{pmatrix}$

h i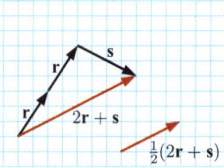

ii $\frac{1}{2}(2\mathbf{r} + \mathbf{s}) = \begin{pmatrix} 4 \\ 2 \end{pmatrix}$

2 a 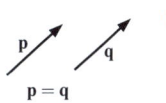 **b** $\mathbf{p}$ $\mathbf{q}$ **c** $\mathbf{q}$ $\mathbf{p}$

d $\mathbf{q}$ $\mathbf{p}$ **e**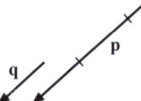

3 a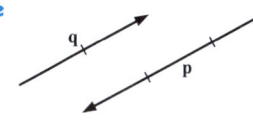
$|k\mathbf{a}| = \left|\begin{pmatrix} ka_1 \\ ka_2 \end{pmatrix}\right| = \sqrt{(ka_1)^2 + (ka_2)^2}$
$= \sqrt{k^2 a_1^2 + k^2 a_2^2}$
$= \sqrt{k^2(a_1^2 + a_2^2)}$
$= \sqrt{k^2}\sqrt{a_1^2 + a_2^2}$
$= |k||\mathbf{a}|$ {since $\sqrt{k^2} = |k|$}

b a has $|\mathbf{a}| = \sqrt{a_1^2 + a_2^2}$ so $\frac{1}{|\mathbf{a}|}\mathbf{a}$ has length
$\frac{1}{\sqrt{a_1^2 + a_2^2}} \cdot \sqrt{a_1^2 + a_2^2} = 1$ and $\frac{1}{|\mathbf{a}|}\mathbf{a}$ is of the
form $k\mathbf{a}$ where $k > 0$ (since $|\mathbf{a}|$ is always positive).
$\therefore \frac{1}{|\mathbf{a}|}\mathbf{a}$ is in the same direction as **a**.
$\therefore \frac{1}{|\mathbf{a}|}\mathbf{a}$ is a vector of length 1 in the direction of **a**.

EXERCISE 17G

1 a $t = -12$ **b** $t = 6$ **c** $t = 20$ **d** $t = -10$

2 $a = -\frac{12}{5}$ or 2   **3** $t = -1$

4 a $\mathbf{p} \parallel \mathbf{q}$ and $|\mathbf{p}| = 2|\mathbf{q}|$ **b** $\mathbf{p} \parallel \mathbf{q}$ and $|\mathbf{p}| = \frac{1}{2}|\mathbf{q}|$
  c $\mathbf{p} \parallel \mathbf{q}$ and $|\mathbf{p}| = 3|\mathbf{q}|$ **d** $\mathbf{p} \parallel \mathbf{q}$ and $|\mathbf{p}| = \frac{1}{3}|\mathbf{q}|$

5 $\overrightarrow{PQ} = \begin{pmatrix} 5 \\ -4 \end{pmatrix}$, $\overrightarrow{SR} = \begin{pmatrix} 5 \\ -4 \end{pmatrix}$ $\Rightarrow$ $\overrightarrow{PQ} \parallel \overrightarrow{SR}$ and $|\overrightarrow{PQ}| = |\overrightarrow{SR}|$
which is sufficient to deduce that PQRS is a parallelogram.

6 a C(2, 5) **b** D(9, 0)

EXERCISE 17H

1 a 17 **b** -15 **c** -14 **2** $\begin{pmatrix} 1 \\ -4 \end{pmatrix} \bullet \begin{pmatrix} 8 \\ 2 \end{pmatrix} = 0$

3 a i 5 **ii** $45°$ **b i** 10 **ii** $0°$
  c i 0 **ii** $90°$ **d i** 5 **ii** $\approx 70.3°$
  e i 33 **ii** $\approx 59.5°$ **f i** -11 **ii** $\approx 138°$

4 a $t = 6$ **b** $t = \pm 2\sqrt{3}$ **c** $t = -8$ **d** $t = -\frac{4}{3}$ or 2

5 a $\approx 37.9°$ **b** $\approx 121°$ **c** $\approx 14.5°$ **d** $\approx 4.40°$

6 $k = -\frac{11}{4}$

7 a $\widehat{P} \approx 8.13°$, $\widehat{Q} \approx 18.4°$, $\widehat{R} \approx 153.4°$
  b $\widehat{P} \approx 66.8°$, $\widehat{Q} \approx 31.3°$, $\widehat{R} \approx 81.9°$

EXERCISE 17I

1 a $\begin{pmatrix} 3 \\ 5 \\ 2 \end{pmatrix}$ **b** $\begin{pmatrix} -4 \\ -1 \\ -2 \end{pmatrix}$ **c** $\begin{pmatrix} 1 \\ 2 \\ 1 \end{pmatrix}$ **d** $\begin{pmatrix} -1 \\ -2 \\ 2 \end{pmatrix}$

2 a $\overrightarrow{PQ} = \begin{pmatrix} -2 \\ 6 \\ -9 \end{pmatrix}$ **b** S is $(-1, 5, -13)$

3 a $\begin{pmatrix} 8 \\ 0 \\ 12 \end{pmatrix}$ **b** $\begin{pmatrix} 2 \\ -10 \\ 4 \end{pmatrix}$ **c** $\begin{pmatrix} 1 \\ 5 \\ 1 \end{pmatrix}$ **d** $\begin{pmatrix} 3 \\ -5 \\ 5 \end{pmatrix}$

e $\begin{pmatrix} 5 \\ 5 \\ 7 \end{pmatrix}$ **f** $\begin{pmatrix} 7 \\ -25 \\ 13 \end{pmatrix}$

4 a 3 units **b** $\sqrt{65}$ units **c** $\sqrt{61}$ units

5 $\begin{pmatrix} 6 \\ -1 \\ 4 \end{pmatrix} \bullet \begin{pmatrix} 5 \\ 2 \\ -7 \end{pmatrix} = 0$ $\therefore$ **a** and **b** are perpendicular.

6 $t = -2$ **7** $\theta \approx 80.1°$

8 $\widehat{RPQ} \approx 57.1°$, $\widehat{PQR} \approx 84.1°$, $\widehat{QRP} \approx 38.8°$

REVIEW SET 17A

1 a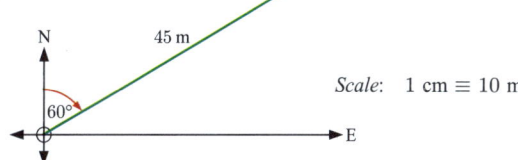

b

2 a 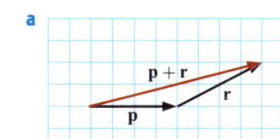 **b**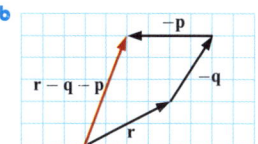

3 a $\overrightarrow{CA} = -\mathbf{c}$ b $\overrightarrow{AB} = -\mathbf{a} + \mathbf{b}$
  c $\overrightarrow{OC} = \mathbf{a} + \mathbf{c}$ d $\overrightarrow{BC} = -\mathbf{b} + \mathbf{a} + \mathbf{c}$
4 a $\overrightarrow{AD}$ b $\overrightarrow{BD}$ c $\mathbf{0}$ (the zero vector)
5 Speed is 12.3 km h^{-1} at a bearing of 145°.
6 $\mathbf{a} \parallel \mathbf{b}$ and $|\mathbf{a}| = \frac{1}{3}|\mathbf{b}|$
7 a $\binom{11}{1}$ b $\binom{1}{12}$ c $\sqrt{34}$ units
8 a $k = -4$ b $k = 9$ **9** $A(-2, -4)$
10 a -1 b $97.1°$ **11** $\approx 55.6°$
12 a $\overrightarrow{PQ} = \begin{pmatrix} -3 \\ -2 \\ -3 \end{pmatrix}$ b $PQ = \sqrt{22}$ units

REVIEW SET 17B

1 a They have the same length. b $\mathbf{p} \parallel \mathbf{q}$ and $|\mathbf{p}| = 2|\mathbf{q}|$
2 $\overrightarrow{BA} = -\overrightarrow{AB}$
3 a He must fly in the direction 11.3° south of east.
  b ≈ 204 km h^{-1}
4 a -23 b -21 **5** a $\binom{-1}{-9}$ b $\sqrt{34}$ units
6 a $t = \frac{3}{2}$ b $t = -\frac{8}{3}$ **7** $t = 6$
8 a $\binom{3}{-4}$ b 5 units **9** $k = 2$ **10** $\approx 26.6°$
11 a $2\mathbf{p}$ b $\mathbf{p} + \mathbf{q}$ c $\mathbf{q} - \mathbf{p}$
12 a $\begin{pmatrix} -20 \\ 5 \\ -5 \end{pmatrix}$ b $\begin{pmatrix} 8 \\ -15 \\ 7 \end{pmatrix}$ c $\approx 123°$

EXERCISE 18A

1 a, c, d, and f are exponential functions.
2 a 3 b 11 c $2\frac{1}{3}$ d $3^{2x} + 2$
3 a -2 b $-2\frac{4}{5}$ c 22 d $5^x - 3$
4 a $\frac{1}{9}$ b 9 c $\frac{1}{27}$ d 3^{x+3}

EXERCISE 18B.1

1 a 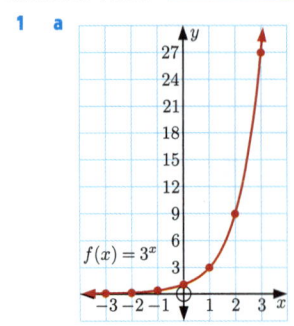 b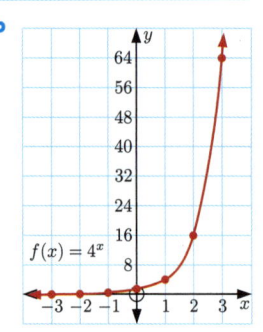
  c 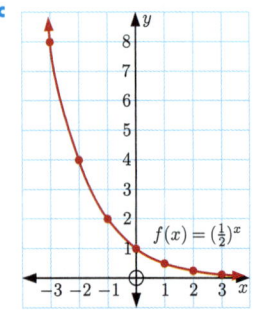 d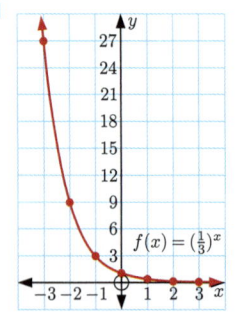

2 a, b, c, d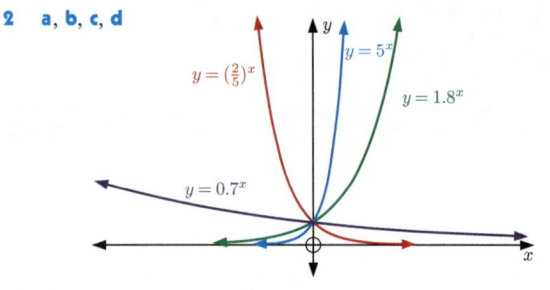

3 a D b A c F d C e B f E

EXERCISE 18B.2

1 a i 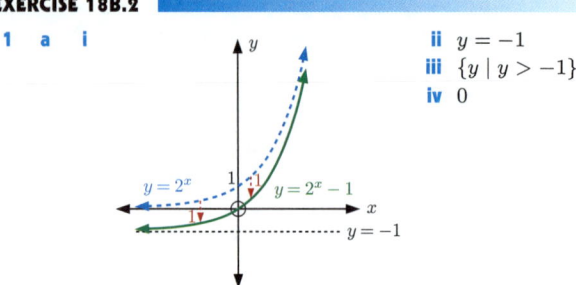 ii $y = -1$ iii $\{y \mid y > -1\}$ iv 0
  b i 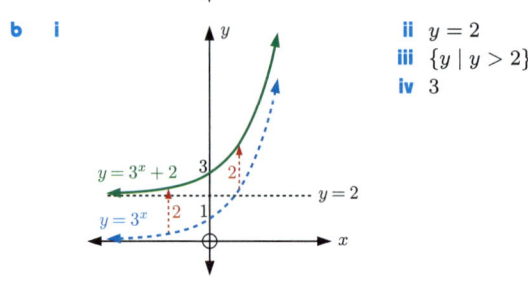 ii $y = 2$ iii $\{y \mid y > 2\}$ iv 3
  c i 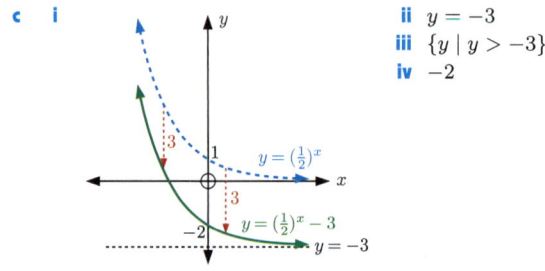 ii $y = -3$ iii $\{y \mid y > -3\}$ iv -2

2 a, b, c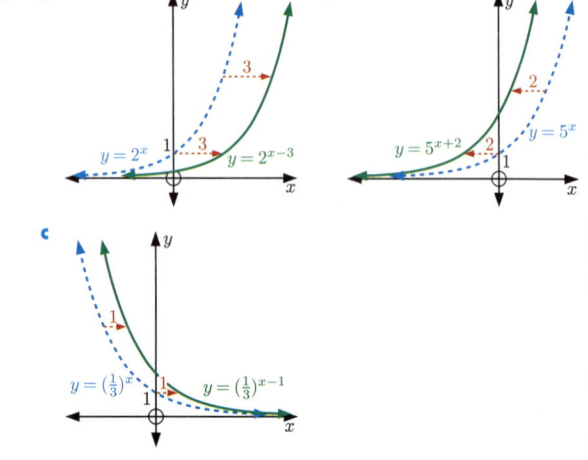

3 a 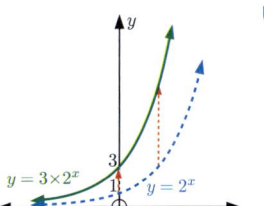 **b**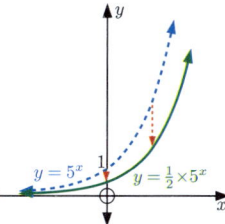

c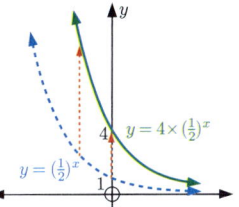

4 a 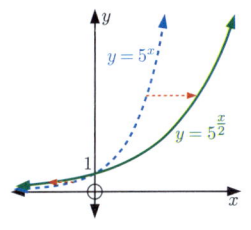 **b**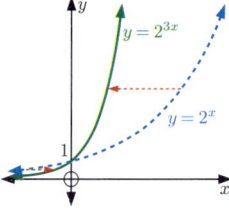

c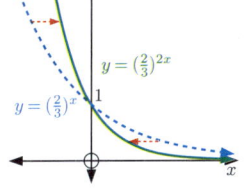

5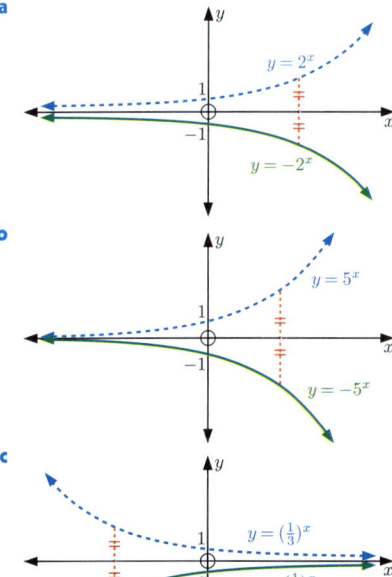

6 a 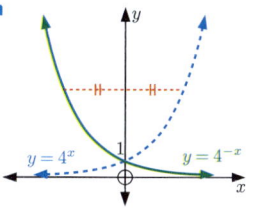 **b**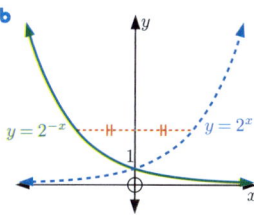

c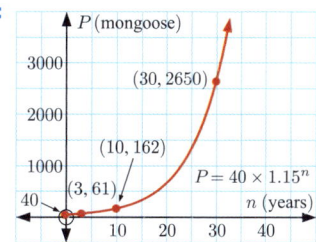

7 a $g(x) = f(x-1) = 3^{x-1} = \frac{1}{3} \times 3^x$
 b $h(x) = f(2x) = 3^{2x} = 9^x$
 c $j(x) = f(-x) = 3^{-x} = (\frac{1}{3})^x$

EXERCISE 18C.1

1 a 40 mongoose
 b i ≈ 61 mongoose   **ii** ≈ 162 mongoose
   iii ≈ 2650 mongoose
 c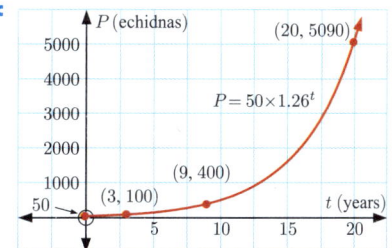

2 a 50 echidnas
 b i ≈ 100 echidnas   **ii** ≈ 400 echidnas
   iii ≈ 5090 echidnas
 c

3 a $G_0 = 28$ **c**
 b i ≈ 29
   ii ≈ 31
   iii ≈ 34

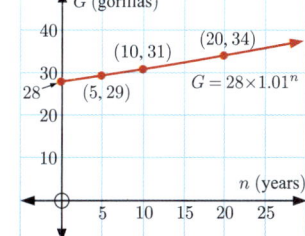

4 a The initial amount is 3000 tonnes, and the amount each year is 1.05 times the amount from the previous year.
 b i ≈ 3830 tonnes   **ii** ≈ 4890 tonnes

c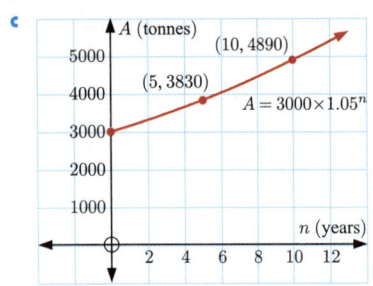

EXERCISE 18C.2

1. **a** $100°C$
   b **i** $\approx 70.6°C$ **ii** $\approx 17.5°C$ **iii** $\approx 3.06°C$
   c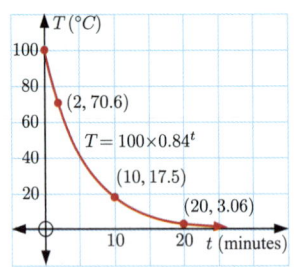

2. **a** 2.3 g
   b **i** ≈ 1.02 g   **ii** ≈ 0.449 g   **iii** ≈ 0.199 g
   d $\approx 55.8\%$ loss
   c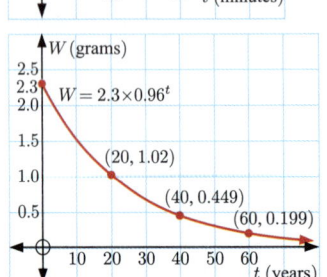

3. **a** $P = 500 \times 0.92^t$
   b **i** 460 **ii** ≈ 330 **iii** ≈ 217

EXERCISE 18D

1.
After year	Interest paid	Future Value
0	-	€8000
1	5% of €8000 = €400	€8400
2	5% of €8400 = €420	€8820
3	5% of €8820 = €441	€9261

2. **a** £53 240   **b** £13 240
3. **a** ¥62 985.60   **b** ¥12 985.60   **4** $14 976.01
5. €11 477.02   **6** $\approx 3.95\%$ **7 a** £1186   **b** $\approx 4.45\%$

EXERCISE 18E

1. $5684.29
2. **a**
Years owned	Depreciation or annual loss in value	Value after n years
0	-	£8495
1	£1019.40	£7475.60
2	£897.07	£6578.53
3	£789.42	£5789.10
4	£694.69	£5094.41

   b £694.69   **c** £3055.10

3. **a** $19 712   **b** $18 788   **4** 11.5%

EXERCISE 18F

1. **a** $x = 1$ **b** $x = 2$ **c** $x = 3$ **d** $x = 0$
   e $x = -1$ **f** $x = -1$ **g** $x = -4$ **h** $x = 0$
   i $x = -4$ **j** $x = -2$ **k** $x = 6$ **l** $x = 2$
   m $x = -\frac{3}{4}$ **n** $x = \frac{7}{2}$ **o** $x = 0$ **p** $x = 4$

2. **a** $x = 3$ **b** $x = 0$ **c** $x = -2$ **d** $x = 3$
   e $x = -5$ **f** $x = -2$ **g** $x = \frac{2}{7}$ **h** $x = \frac{1}{3}$
   i $x = 1$ **j** $x = 1$ **k** no solution   **l** $x = -1$ or 3

3. 5 months
4. **a** $x = 1$ **b** $x = 2$ **c** $x = 1$ **d** $x = \frac{5}{4}$
   e $x = 2$ **f** $x = -\frac{9}{7}$

EXERCISE 18G.1

1. **a** 2   **b** 5   **c** -2 **d** 1   **e** -4 **f** 0   **g** $\frac{1}{2}$ **h** $\frac{3}{2}$
2. **a** ≈ 1.447 **b** ≈ 0.699 **c** ≈ 2.477 **d** ≈ -0.398
   e ≈ 2.903 **f** ≈ 1.954 **g** ≈ -1.155 **h** ≈ 3.602
   i undefined
3. **a** $\log 70 \approx 1.845$ **b** $70 \approx 10^{1.845}$
4. 10^x is positive for all x.
5. **a** $\log x$ is positive if x is greater than 1.
   b $\log x$ is negative if x is between 0 and 1.

EXERCISE 18G.2

1. **a** $\log 30$ **b** $\log 5$ **c** $\log 11$ **d** $\log 12$
   e $\log(\frac{5}{4})$ **f** $\log 1 = 0$ **g** $\log 30$ **h** $\log 4$
   i $\log(\frac{1}{6})$ **j** $\log(\frac{1}{512})$ **k** $\log 2000$ **l** $\log(\frac{64}{125})$

2. **a** 3   **b** 2   **c** $\frac{5}{6}$ **d** -1 **e** -1 **f** $-\frac{3}{2}$
   g $\frac{b}{3}$ **h** $\frac{2}{a}$

3. **a** $\log \sqrt{5} = \log 5^{\frac{1}{2}} = \frac{1}{2} \log 5$
   b $\log \sqrt[3]{2} = \log 2^{\frac{1}{3}} = \frac{1}{3} \log 2$
   c $\log(\frac{1}{\sqrt{3}}) = \log 3^{-\frac{1}{2}} = -\frac{1}{2} \log 3$

4. **a** **i** ≈ 0.699 **ii** ≈ 3.699
   b $\log 5000 = \log 5 + \log 1000 = \log 5 + 3$

5. $\log 10^x = x \log 10 = x$

6. **a** $\log 600$ **b** $\log 5$ **c** $\log 8$ **d** $\log 250$
   e $\log 9$ **f** $\log 14 000$

7. **a** **i** ≈ 1.114 **ii** ≈ -1.114 **iii** ≈ 2.398
   iv ≈ -2.398
   b $\log\left(\frac{1}{x}\right) = \log x^{-1} = -\log x$

8. 3

EXERCISE 18G.3

1. **a** $x \approx 1.585$ **b** $x \approx 3.322$ **c** $x \approx 8.644$
   d $x \approx -4.454$ **e** $x \approx 4.292$ **f** $x \approx -0.099\,97$
   g $x \approx 6.511$ **h** $x \approx 4.923$ **i** $x \approx 49.60$
   j $x \approx 4.376$ **k** $x \approx 8.497$ **l** $x \approx 230.7$

2. **a** $x \approx 3.81$ **b** $x \approx 3.54$ **c** $x \approx 1.24$
   d $x \approx 6.58$ **e** $x \approx 2.74$ **f** $x \approx 18.1$

3. **a** 15.9 hours   **b** 60.6 hours
4. **a** $V = 125 \times (0.85)^t$ cm^3 **b** 90.3 cm^3
   c 5.64 minutes

5 a no
  b The area covered each week is 1.2 times greater than the area covered the previous week, and the initial area covered is 40 cm^2.
  d 69.12 cm^2
  e 5.03 weeks
  c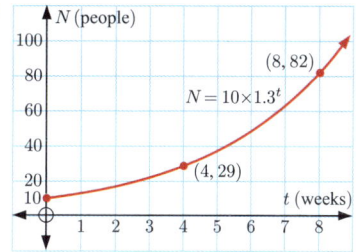

EXERCISE 18G.4

1 a $\log_2 8 = 3$ **b** $\log_3 9 = 2$ **c** $\log_5(\frac{1}{5}) = -1$
  d $\log_2 32 = 5$ **e** $\log_7 1 = 0$ **f** $\log_3(\frac{1}{81}) = -4$
  g $\log_2(\frac{1}{64}) = -6$ **h** $\log_2(\sqrt{2}) = \frac{1}{2}$

2 a $10^3 = 1000$ **b** $2^4 = 16$ **c** $3^{-1} = \frac{1}{3}$
  d $4^0 = 1$ **e** $7^{-2} = \frac{1}{49}$ **f** $(\frac{1}{7})^2 = \frac{1}{49}$
  g $10^2 = 100$ **h** $(\sqrt{5})^4 = 25$

3 $125 = 5^3$, $\log_5 125 = 3$
4 $\frac{1}{36} = 6^{-2}$, $\log_6(\frac{1}{36}) = -2$
5 a 2   **b** 6   **c** $\frac{1}{2}$ **d** $\frac{1}{4}$ **e** $\frac{3}{2}$ **f** 0
  g 1   **h** -1 **i** 1   **j** -1 **k** $-\frac{1}{2}$ **l** $-\frac{1}{6}$

REVIEW SET 18A

1 a 0
  b 26
  c $-\frac{2}{3}$
  d $3^{2x} - 1$

2 a, b, c

3 a   **b**

4 a 1000 g
  b i ≈ 817 g
    ii ≈ 364 g
    iii ≈ 133 g
  c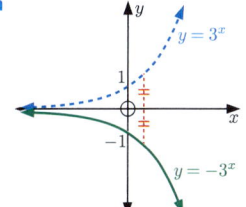

5 a £171 475.72   **b** £51 475.72
6 a $x = \frac{1}{3}$ **b** $x = \frac{13}{7}$ **c** $x = -\frac{2}{5}$ **d** $x = -2$
  e $x = \frac{5}{2}$ **f** $x = \frac{7}{11}$
7 a 450 seals   **b** 4 years
8 a $\log 80 \approx 1.903$ **b** $80 \approx 10^{1.903}$

9 a $-\frac{1}{2}$ **b** $\frac{5}{2}$ **10 a** $\log 8$ **b** $\log 5$ **c** 4   **d** $\frac{2b}{3}$
11 a i 10 people   **ii** ≈ 29 people   **iii** ≈ 82 people
  b   **c** ≈ 11.4 weeks

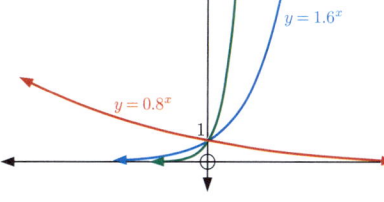

12 a $\frac{1}{\sqrt{5}} = 5^{-\frac{1}{2}}$ **b** $\log_5 \frac{1}{\sqrt{5}} = -\frac{1}{2}$

REVIEW SET 18B

1 a The variable x appears in the exponent.
  b Translate 2 units to the right.
2 a 2   **b** $\frac{2}{9}$ **c** $2 \times 3^{-x-4}$
3 a   **b**

4 $\{y \mid y > -2\}$
5 a i 2 words
    ii ≈ 14 words
    iii ≈ 50 words
  b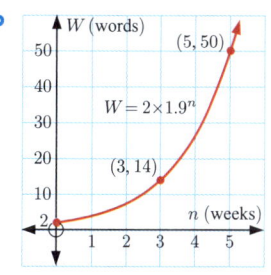

6 $6273.18   **7** ≈ 2.85
8 a $x = -2$ **b** $x = \frac{3}{4}$ **c** $x = \frac{2}{3}$
9 a $\log 55$ **b** $\log 400$ **c** $\log 25$
10 a 1
  b $(1 + \log 5)(1 - \log 5) = 1 - (\log 5)^2$ and
      $(1 + \log 5)(1 - \log 5) = (\log 10 + \log 5)(\log 10 - \log 5)$
      $= \log(10 \times 5) \times \log(\frac{10}{5})$
      $= \log 50 \times \log 2$
11 a $x \approx 5.42$ **b** $x \approx 5.86$ **12 a** $\frac{1}{2}$ **b** -4

EXERCISE 19A

1 a $x = 37$ {angle in a semi-circle, angles in a triangle}
  b $x = 30$ {angle in a semi-circle, angles in a triangle}
  c $x = 18$ {angle in a semi-circle, angles in a triangle}
2 a $a = b = 55$ {tangents from an external point, base angles of isosceles triangle}
  b $a = 3$ {chords of a circle}, $b \approx 36.9$
  c $a = 60$ {angle in a semi-circle}
      $b = 40$ {angles in a triangle, radius-tangent theorem}

3 **a** $x = 40$ {angles in a triangle} **b** ≈ 7.83 cm
4 **Hint:** AB + CD = (AP + PB) + (DR + CR)
     = AS + QB + DS + CQ, etc.
5 $(8 - 4\sqrt{3})$ cm ≈ 1.07 cm {chords of a circle}
6 10.25 cm   **7** 1 cm   **8** 40 cm

EXERCISE 19B

1 **a** $x = 64$ {angle at the centre}
   b $x = 94$ {angle at the centre}
   c $x = 70$ {angle at the centre, angles in an isosceles triangle}
   d $x = 45$ {angles in an isosceles triangle, angle at the centre}
   e $x = 66$ {angle at the centre}
   f $x = 25$ {angle at the centre, base angles of isosceles triangle}
2 **a** $x = 46$ {angles subtended by the same arc}
   b $x = y = 55$ {angles subtended by the same arc}
   c $a = 50$, $b = 40$ {angles subtended by the same arc}
   d $a = 55$, $c = 70$ {angles subtended by the same arc}
   e $a = 80$ {angles subtended by the same arc}
       $b = 200$ {angles at the centre, angles at a point}
   f $x = 75$ {angles subtended by the same arc}
       $y = 118$ {exterior angle of a triangle}
   g $x = 42$ {angles subtended by the same arc, exterior angle of a triangle}
   h $x = 25$ {angles in a semi-circle, base angles of isosceles triangle, angles subtended by the same arc}
   i $x = 25$ {angle in a semi-circle, angles in a triangle, angles subtended by the same arc}
3 **a** $x = 70$ {angle between a tangent and a chord, angles in an isosceles triangle}
   b $x = 40$ {angle between a tangent and a chord, angles in an isosceles triangle}
   c $x = 35$ {angles in an isosceles triangle, radius-tangent theorem}

EXERCISE 19C

1 **a** $\triangle$OAB is isosceles.
   b The perpendicular from the centre of a circle to a chord bisects the chord, and bisects the angle at the centre subtended by the chord.
2 **a** [OA], [OP], [OB] are radii of the circle, $\therefore$ are equal.
   b **i** $A\widehat{P}O = a$ **ii** $B\widehat{P}O = b$
       iii $A\widehat{O}X = 2a$ **iv** $B\widehat{O}X = 2b$
       v $A\widehat{P}B = (a + b)$ **vi** $A\widehat{O}B = (2a + 2b) = 2(a + b)$
   c The angle at the centre of a circle is twice the angle on the circle subtended by the same arc.
3 **a** $A\widehat{O}B = 2\alpha$ **b** $A\widehat{C}B = \alpha$ **c** $A\widehat{D}B = A\widehat{C}B$
4 **a** **i** $T\widehat{A}X = 90°$ **ii** $A\widehat{C}X = 90°$
   b **i** $90° - \alpha$ **ii** α **iii** α **c** $T\widehat{A}C = \widehat{CBA}$
5 **Hint:** Use alternate angles, 'angle at the centre' theorem, and isosceles triangle.
6 **a** **i** $X\widehat{O}Y = \alpha$ **ii** $A\widehat{X}O = 2\alpha$ **iii** $X\widehat{A}O = 2\alpha$
       iv $X\widehat{O}B = 4\alpha$ **v** $B\widehat{O}Y = 3\alpha$
   b $B\widehat{O}Y = 3 \times Y\widehat{O}X$

7 **a** $B\widehat{X}A = B\widehat{X}C = 90°$ {angles in a semi-circle}
   b A, X, and C are collinear.   **c** yes
   d yes (Repeat **a** to **c** using semi-circles with diameter AD and CD.)
8 **Hint:** Use the 'angle between a tangent and a chord' theorem.
9 **Hint:** Use vertically opposite angles and the 'angles subtended by the same arc' theorem.
10 **Hint:** Use the 'angle in a semi-circle' theorem.
11 **Hint:** Use the 'angle in a semi-circle' theorem.
12 **Hint:** Let [AQ] cut the circle at R. Find $A\widehat{R}B$. Use exterior angle of a triangle.

EXERCISE 19D

1 **a** $D\widehat{O}B = 2a°$, reflex $D\widehat{O}B = 2b°$
   b $2a + 2b = 360$ $\therefore$ $a + b = 180$
3 **a** $x = 107$ {opposite angles of a cyclic quadrilateral}
   b $x = 60$ {opposite angles of a cyclic quadrilateral}
   c $x = 70$ {co-interior angles, opposite angles of a cyclic quadrilateral}
   d $x = 90$ {angles on a line, opposite angles of a cyclic quadrilateral}
   e $x = 62$ {vertically opposite angles, opposite angles of a cyclic quadrilateral, angle between a tangent and a chord}
4 **a** Yes, one pair of opposite angles are supplementary.
   b Yes, AD subtends equal angles at B and C.   **c** No
   d Yes, opposite angles are supplementary.
   e Yes, one pair of opposite angles are supplementary.
   f Yes, AD subtends equal angles at B and C.
5 **Hint:** Use co-interior angles and 'opposite angles of a cyclic quadrilateral'.
6 **Hint:** Construct [OD]. Use opposite angles of a parallelogram, corresponding angles, base angles of an isosceles triangle.
7 **Hint:** Use 'chords of a circle theorem'.
8 **Hint:** Use corresponding angles.
9 **Hint:** Use 'one side subtends equal angles at the other two vertices'.
10 **Hint:** Use congruent triangles.
11 **Hint:** Use 'one side subtends equal angles at the other two vertices'.
12 **Hint:** Join [PX] and use 'angles subtended by the same arc'.
13 **Hint:** Use 'opposite angles of a cyclic quadrilateral'.

REVIEW SET 19A

1 **a** $a = 54$ {angle at the centre, angles in an isosceles triangle}
   b $a = 62$ {angle in a semi-circle, angles in a triangle}
   c $a = 61$ {angles subtended by the same arc, exterior angle of a triangle}
   d $a = 80$ {angles on a line, opposite angles of a cyclic quadrilateral}
   e $a = 63$ {co-interior angles, opposite angles of a cyclic quadrilateral}
   f $a = 45$ {opposite angles of a cyclic quadrilateral}
2 $\alpha + \beta + \gamma = 180°$ {angle between a tangent and a chord}
3 **a** $x = 38$ {angle in a semi-circle, angles in a triangle}
   b $x = 140$ {angle at the centre, exterior angle of a triangle}

ANSWERS 597

   c $x = 104$ {angle between a tangent and a chord, angles in an isosceles triangle}

4 a Hint: Use the 'tangents from an external point' theorem.
  b Hint: Let $A\widehat{C}M = \alpha$ and $B\widehat{C}M$ be β. Use the isosceles triangle theorem to show that $\alpha + \beta = 90°$.

5 Hint: Construct [PB] and [XB]. Use 'angle between a tangent and a chord' and 'angles subtended by the same arc' to show that alternate angles are equal.

6 Further hint: Use the 'angle at the centre' theorem (twice) and the 'angles in a triangle' theorem.

7 a The angle between a tangent and a chord through the point of contact is equal to the angle subtended by the chord in the alternate segment.
  b i $P\widehat{Q}B = \alpha$, $P\widehat{Q}A = \beta$, $A\widehat{Q}B = (\alpha + \beta)$
    ii Hint: Use the angles in a triangle theorem.

8 Hint: Use 'angle between a tangent and a chord', and alternate angles.

REVIEW SET 19B

1 a $x = 86$ {angles subtended by the same arc, exterior angle of a triangle}
  b $x = \sqrt{34} \approx 5.83$ {chords of a circle, Pythagoras}
  c $x = 9$ {radius-tangent, Pythagoras}

2 a $x = 55$ {angles at a point, angle at the centre}
  b $x = 55$ {angles in an isosceles triangle, radius-tangent, angles in a triangle}
  c $x \approx 7.68$ {tangents from an external point, angles in a triangle, radius-tangent}

3 ≈ 6.63 m

4 Hint: Use the isosceles triangle theorem and the 'angles subtended by the same arc' theorem.

5 Hint: Use the 'angles subtended by the same arc' theorem and the 'angles in a triangle' theorem (on $\triangle ABQ$ and $\triangle APC$).

6 a i $P\widehat{S}R = 2\alpha$ **ii** $P\widehat{Q}R = 2\alpha$ **iii** $P\widehat{R}Q = 2\alpha$
    iv $Q\widehat{P}R = 2\alpha$
  b Hint: Use the angles in a triangle theorem.
  c $Q\widehat{R}S = 90°$ **d** [RS] is a diameter of the circle.

7 Hint: Use angle in a semi-circle, and 'one side subtends equal angles at the other two vertices'.

8 a Hint: Let $X\widehat{T}A = \alpha$, $X\widehat{P}A = \beta$. Use 'angle between a tangent and a chord', and sum of angles of a triangle.
  b Show $\alpha = \beta$.

EXERCISE 20A

1 b and **c** are quadratic functions.
2 a $y = 0$ **b** $y = 5$ **c** $y = -15$ **d** $y = 12$
3 a no   **b** yes   **c** yes   **d** no   **e** no   **f** no
4 a $x = -3$ **b** $x = -2$ or -3 **c** $x = 1$ or 4
  d do not exist
5 a $x = 0$ or 1 **b** $x = -1$ or 3 **c** $x = -7$ or $\frac{1}{2}$
  d $x = 2$ or 3
6 a i 75 m   **ii** 195 m   **iii** 275 m
  b i At $t = 2$ s and $t = 14$ s.
    ii At $t = 0$ s and $t = 16$ s.
  c The object leaves the ground at $t = 0$ s. At $t = 2$ it is rising and at $t = 14$ it is falling. Height 0 m is ground level and the time of flight is 16 seconds.

7 a i $-\$40$, a loss of $\$40$ **ii** $\$480$ profit
  b 10 cakes or 62 cakes

EXERCISE 20B.1

1 a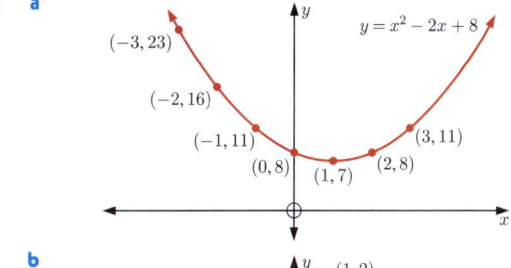

b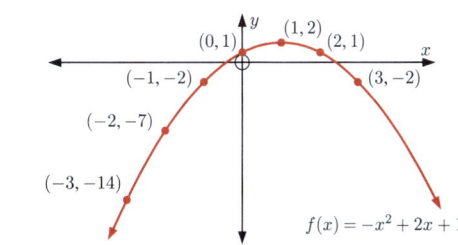

c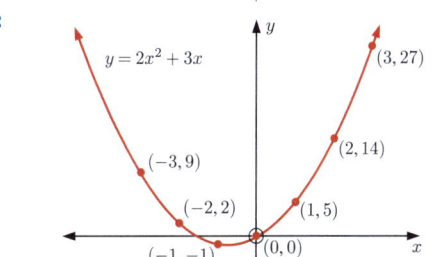

d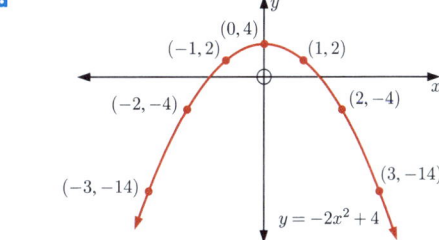

e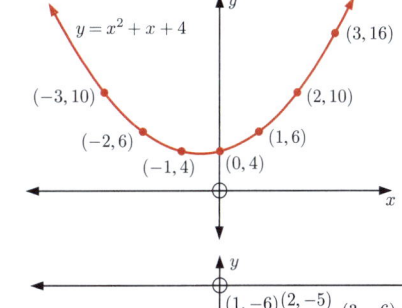

f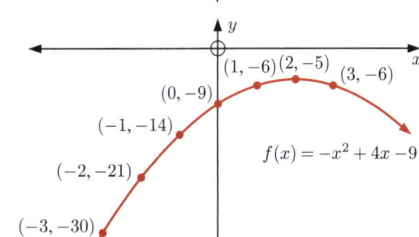

2 a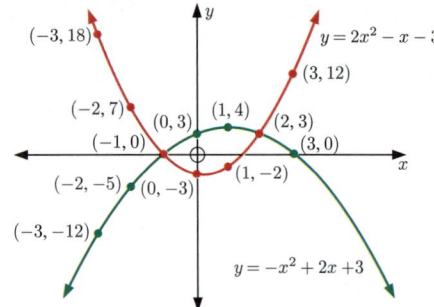

$x = -1$ or 2 (where they meet)

b $2x^2 - x - 3 = -x^2 + 2x + 3$ becomes
$3x^2 - 3x - 6 = 0$
$\therefore\ x^2 - x - 2 = 0$, etc.

EXERCISE 20B.2

1 a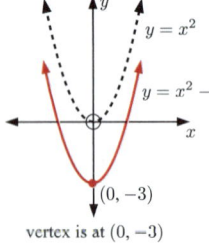
vertex is at $(0, -3)$

b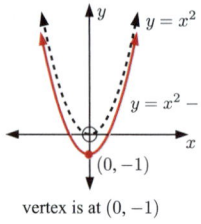
vertex is at $(0, -1)$

c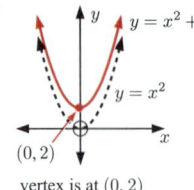
vertex is at $(0, 2)$

d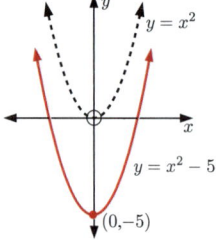
vertex is at $(0, -5)$

e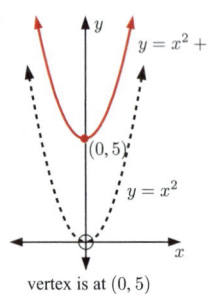
vertex is at $(0, 5)$

f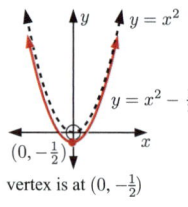
vertex is at $(0, -\tfrac{1}{2})$

2 a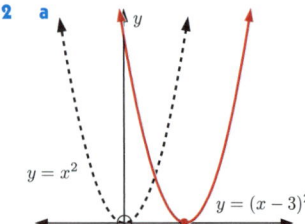
vertex is at $(3, 0)$

b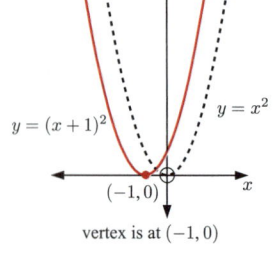
vertex is at $(-1, 0)$

c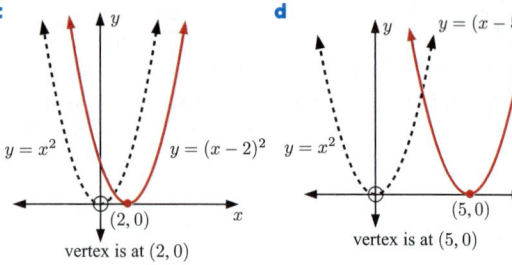
vertex is at $(2, 0)$

d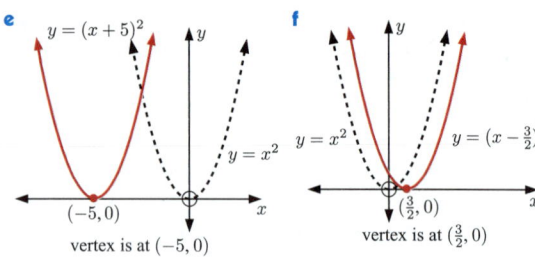
vertex is at $(5, 0)$

e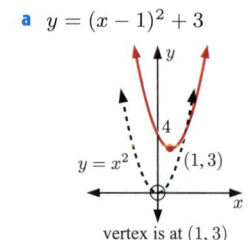
vertex is at $(-5, 0)$

f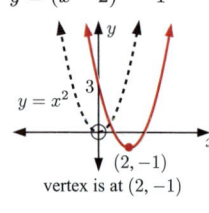
vertex is at $(\tfrac{3}{2}, 0)$

3 a $y = (x - 1)^2 + 3$
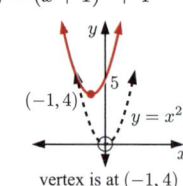
vertex is at $(1, 3)$

b $y = (x - 2)^2 - 1$
vertex is at $(2, -1)$

c $y = (x + 1)^2 + 4$
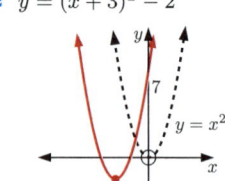
vertex is at $(-1, 4)$

d $y = (x + 2)^2 - 3$
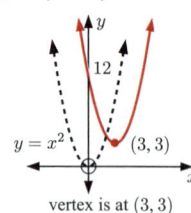
vertex is at $(-2, -3)$

e $y = (x + 3)^2 - 2$
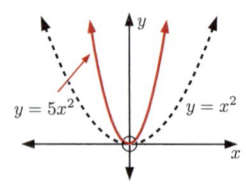
vertex is at $(-3, -2)$

f $y = (x - 3)^2 + 3$
vertex is at $(3, 3)$

4 a
$y = 5x^2$ is 'thinner' than $y = x^2$ and the graph opens upwards.

b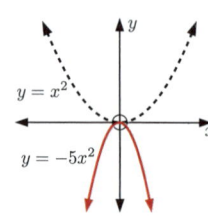
$y = -5x^2$ is 'thinner' than $y = x^2$ and the graph opens downwards.

c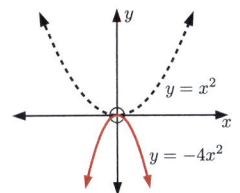

$y = \frac{1}{3}x^2$ is 'wider' than $y = x^2$ and the graph opens upwards.

d

$y = -\frac{1}{3}x^2$ is 'wider' than $y = x^2$ and the graph opens downwards.

e

$y = -4x^2$ is 'thinner' than $y = x^2$ and the graph opens downwards.

f

$y = \frac{1}{4}x^2$ is 'wider' than $y = x^2$ and the graph opens upwards.

5 a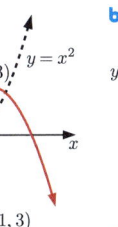
$y = -(x-1)^2 + 3$
vertex is at $(1, 3)$

b
$y = 2x^2 + 4$
vertex is at $(0, 4)$

c
$y = -(x-2)^2 + 4$
vertex is at $(2, 4)$

d
$y = 3(x+1)^2 - 4$
vertex is at $(-1, -4)$

e $y = \frac{1}{2}(x+3)^2$
vertex is at $(-3, 0)$

f
$y = -\frac{1}{2}(x+3)^2 + 1$
vertex is at $(-3, 1)$

g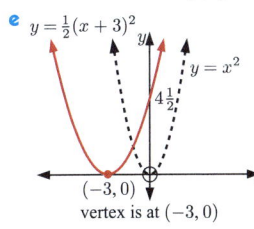
$y = -2(x+4)^2 + 3$
vertex is at $(-4, 3)$

h
$y = 2(x-3)^2 + 5$
vertex is at $(3, 5)$

i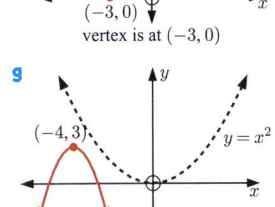
$y = \frac{1}{2}(x-2)^2 - 1$
vertex is at $(2, -1)$

6 a F **b** C **c** B **d** D **e** E **f** A

EXERCISE 20B.3

1 a $y = (x+1)^2 + 3$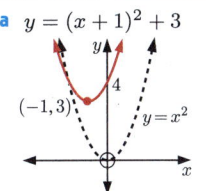
vertex is at $(-1, 3)$

b $y = (x-3)^2 - 6$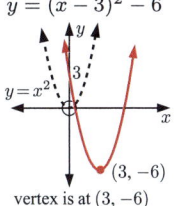
vertex is at $(3, -6)$

c $y = (x+2)^2 - 5$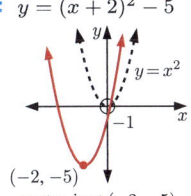
vertex is at $(-2, -5)$

d $y = (x-1)^2 + 4$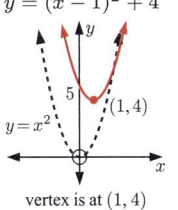
vertex is at $(1, 4)$

e $y = (x-1)^2 - 1$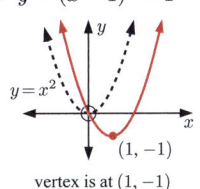
vertex is at $(1, -1)$

f $y = (x+\frac{5}{2})^2 - 6\frac{1}{4}$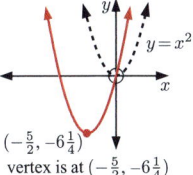
vertex is at $(-\frac{5}{2}, -6\frac{1}{4})$

g $y = (x+\frac{5}{2})^2 - 9\frac{1}{4}$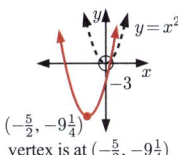
vertex is at $(-\frac{5}{2}, -9\frac{1}{4})$

h $y = (x-\frac{3}{2})^2 + \frac{3}{4}$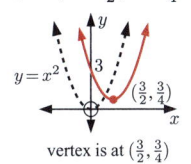
vertex is at $(\frac{3}{2}, \frac{3}{4})$

i $y = (x-\frac{5}{2})^2 - \frac{17}{4}$

vertex is at $(\frac{5}{2}, -4\frac{1}{4})$

2 a $y = 2(x+\frac{5}{2})^2 - \frac{9}{2}$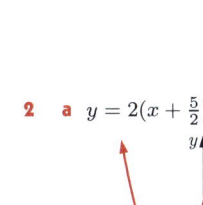
vertex is at $(-\frac{5}{2}, -\frac{9}{2})$

b $y = -(x-\frac{1}{2})^2 + \frac{25}{4}$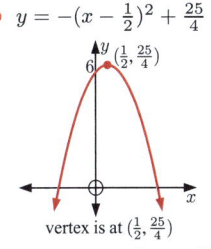
vertex is at $(\frac{1}{2}, \frac{25}{4})$

c $y = 3(x-1)^2 - 27$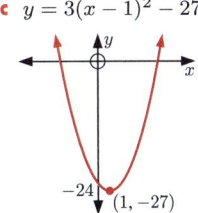
vertex is at $(1, -27)$

d $y = -2(x-\frac{3}{2})^2 + \frac{25}{2}$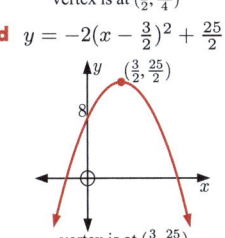
vertex is at $(\frac{3}{2}, \frac{25}{2})$

e $y = 2(x-2)^2 - 11$

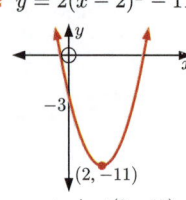

vertex is at $(2, -11)$

f $y = -3(x+1)^2 + 5$

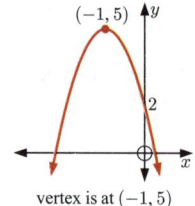

vertex is at $(-1, 5)$

EXERCISE 20C.1

1 **a** 3 **b** 2 **c** -8 **d** 1 **e** 6 **f** 5 **g** 6 **h** 8 **i** -2

2 **a** 3 and -1 **b** 2 and 4 **c** -3 and -2 **d** 4 and 5 **e** -3 (touching) **f** 1 (touching)

3 **a** -3 and 3 **b** -5 and 5 **c** 0 and 6 **d** -5 and -2 **e** -4 and 3 **f** 0 and 4 **g** -2 and -4 **h** -1 (touching) **i** 3 (touching)

4 **a** $2 \pm \sqrt{3}$ **b** $-2 \pm \sqrt{7}$ **c** $3 \pm \sqrt{5}$ **d** $\dfrac{7 \pm \sqrt{73}}{6}$ **e** $\dfrac{1 \pm \sqrt{41}}{4}$ **f** $\dfrac{9 \pm \sqrt{33}}{8}$

5 **a** 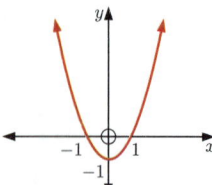 **b**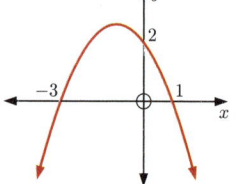

c 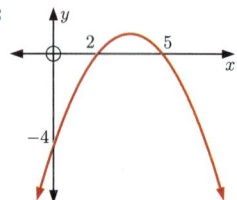 **d**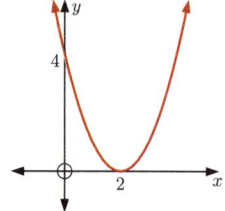

6 **a** **i** $a = 1$ **ii** 4 **iii** 2 (touching)

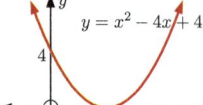

b **i** $a = 1$ **ii** -3 **iii** 1 and -3

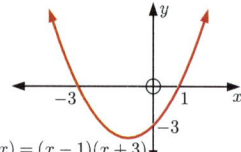

c **i** $a = 2$ **ii** 8 **iii** -2 (touching)

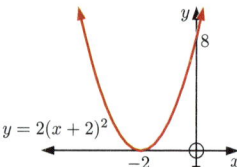

d **i** $a = -1$ **ii** 2 **iii** 2 and -1

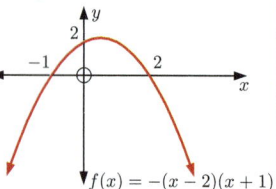

e **i** $a = -3$ **ii** -3 **iii** -1 (touching)

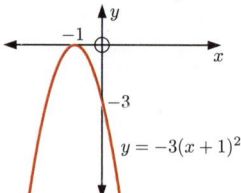

f **i** $a = -3$ **ii** -12 **iii** 4 and 1

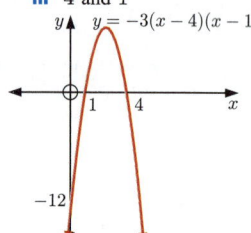

g **i** $a = 2$ **ii** 6 **iii** -3 and -1

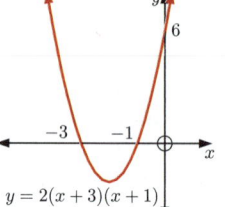

h **i** $a = -2$ **ii** 5 **iii** $-\frac{5}{2}$ and 1

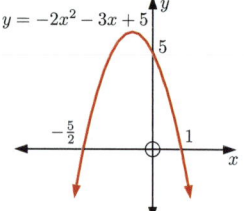

i **i** $a = -1$ **ii** -10 **iii** $4 \pm \sqrt{6}$

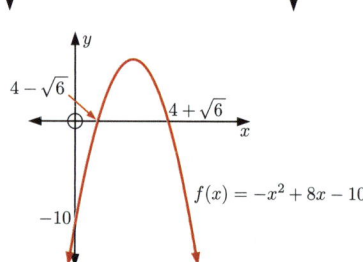

EXERCISE 20C.2

1 **a** $\Delta = 32$, $\Delta > 0$ $\therefore$ graph cuts x-axis twice.
b $\Delta = -39$, $\Delta < 0$ $\therefore$ graph does not cut the x-axis.
c $\Delta = 8$, $\Delta > 0$ $\therefore$ graph cuts x-axis twice.
d $\Delta = 0$, $\therefore$ graph touches x-axis.
e $\Delta = -24$, $\Delta < 0$ $\therefore$ graph does not cut the x-axis.
f $\Delta = 0$, $\therefore$ graph touches x-axis.

2 **a** $y = (x-4)^2 - 2$
b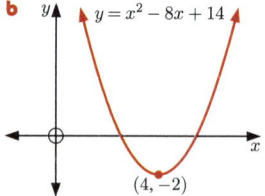
c two x-intercepts
d $\Delta = 8$ which is > 0

3 **a** $y = (x+1)^2 + 4$
b
c no x-intercepts
d $\Delta = -16$ which is < 0

4 **a** C **b** F **c** A **d** B **e** E **f** D

5 **a** **i** $\Delta > 0$, cuts the x-axis twice
ii $\Delta = 0$, touches the x-axis
iii $\Delta < 0$, does not cut the x-axis

b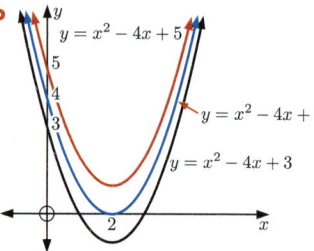

6 a If $a > 0$ the graph opens upwards.

A negative value for c means the graph has a negative y-intercept. ∴ the graph cuts the x-axis twice.

b If $a > 0$ and $c < 0$, then $-4ac > 0$. We know that $b^2 \geqslant 0$ and so $b^2 - 4ac > 0$. ∴ the graph cuts the x-axis twice.

EXERCISE 20D

1 a $x = 2$ **b** $x = 1$ **c** $x = -2$ **d** $x = \frac{3}{2}$
   e $x = -\frac{5}{2}$ **f** $x = 2$

2 a $x = 3$ **b** $x = 2$ **c** $x = 0$ **d** $x = -\frac{5}{2}$
   e $x = -4$ **f** $x = \frac{3}{2}$

3 a $x = -2$ **b** $x = \frac{3}{2}$ **c** $x = -\frac{2}{3}$ **d** $x = -2$
   e $x = \frac{5}{4}$ **f** $x = 10$ **g** $x = -6$ **h** $x = 12\frac{1}{2}$
   i $x = 150$

EXERCISE 20E

1 a i V(2, −2) **ii** minimum **iii** $\{y \mid y \geqslant -2\}$
   b i V(−1, −4) **ii** minimum **iii** $\{y \mid y \geqslant -4\}$
   c i V(0, 4) **ii** minimum **iii** $\{y \mid y \geqslant 4\}$
   d i V(0, 1) **ii** maximum **iii** $\{y \mid y \leqslant 1\}$
   e i V(−2, 0) **ii** maximum **iii** $\{y \mid y \leqslant 0\}$
   f i V($\frac{5}{2}$, $-\frac{19}{2}$) **ii** minimum **iii** $\{y \mid y \geqslant -9\frac{1}{2}\}$

2 a i x-intercepts −2 and 4, y-intercept −8
   ii $x = 1$ **iii** V(1, −9)
   iv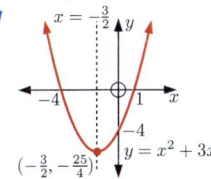

   b i x-intercepts 0 and 4, y-intercept 0
   ii $x = 2$ **iii** V(2, 4)
   iv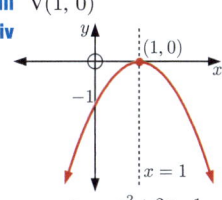

   c i x-intercepts 0 and −3, y-intercept 0
   ii $x = -\frac{3}{2}$
   iii V($-\frac{3}{2}$, $-\frac{9}{4}$)
   iv

   d i x-intercept −2, y-intercept 4
   ii $x = -2$
   iii V(−2, 0)
   iv

   e i x-intercepts −4 and 1, y-intercept −4
   ii $x = -\frac{3}{2}$
   iii V($-\frac{3}{2}$, $-6\frac{1}{4}$)
   iv

   f i x-intercept 1, y-intercept −1
   ii $x = 1$
   iii V(1, 0)
   iv

g i x-intercepts −3 and $\frac{1}{2}$, y-intercept −3
   ii $x = -\frac{5}{4}$
   iii V($-\frac{5}{4}$, $-\frac{49}{8}$)
   iv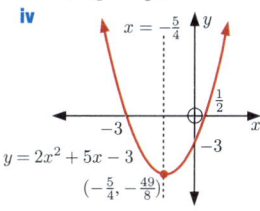

h i x-intercepts −2 and $\frac{2}{3}$, y-intercept 4
   ii $x = -\frac{2}{3}$
   iii V($-\frac{2}{3}$, $\frac{16}{3}$)
   iv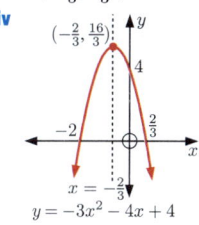

i i x-intercepts $3 \pm \sqrt{6}$, y-intercept 3
   ii $x = 3$
   iii V(3, −6)

iv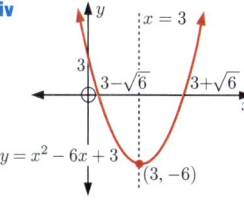

3 a i x-intercepts 0 and 2, y-intercept 0
   ii $x = 1$ **iii** V(1, −1)
   iv

   b i x-intercept 3, y-intercept 18
   ii $x = 3$ **iii** V(3, 0)
   iv

   c i x-intercepts −3 and 1, y-intercept 3
   ii $x = -1$ **iii** V(−1, 4)
   iv

   d i x-intercept 1, y-intercept −2
   ii $x = 1$ **iii** V(1, 0)
   iv

   e i x-intercepts −2 and 2, y-intercept 20
   ii $x = 0$
   iii V(0, 20)
   iv

   f i x-intercepts −1 and −4, y-intercept 8
   ii $x = -\frac{5}{2}$
   iii V($-\frac{5}{2}$, $-\frac{9}{2}$)
   iv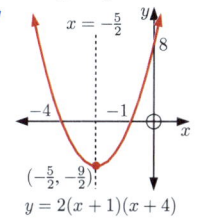

EXERCISE 20F

1 a 2 seconds **b** 20 m **c** 4 seconds
2 a 25 bicycles **b** €425
   c €200 (Due to fixed daily costs such as wages and electricity.)

3 **a** 60 km h^{-1} (when $t = 0$)   **b** $t = 1$ s   **c** 66 km h^{-1}
4 **a** 30 taxis   **b** $1600/hour   **c** $200
5 **a** 25°C   **b** 7:00 am the next day   **c** -11°C
6 **a** 2 m   **b** 3.8 m   **c** 1 s
7 **a** Hint: [FB] ∥ [EC]   **b** $\dfrac{BF}{2} = \dfrac{1-x}{1}$ etc.
  c Area $= x(2(1-x))$ etc.   **d** **i** $x = \tfrac{1}{2}$ **ii** $\tfrac{1}{2}$ cm^2

REVIEW SET 20A

1 **a** $y = -11$ **b** $x = 6$ or -3

2 **a** , **b**

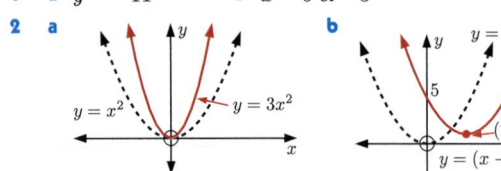

c

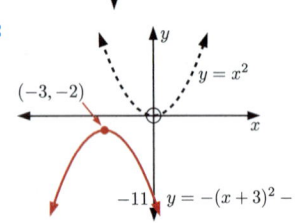

3 **a** $y = (x-2)^2 + 6$ **b**

(graph) $y = (x-2)^2 + 6$, vertex is at $(2, 6)$

4 **a** 0 and -4 **b** -7 and 4   **5** **a** $x = -\tfrac{3}{2}$ **b** $x = 2$

6 **a i** downwards   **ii** 6   **iii** -3 and 1   **iv** $x = -1$
  b (graph) $y = -2(x-1)(x+3)$, vertex $(-1, 8)$

7 **a** V$(4, -19)$ **b** V$(\tfrac{1}{2}, -2)$

8 **a i** -15 **ii** -3 and 5   **iii** $x = 1$ **iv** V$(1, -16)$
  b (graph) $y = x^2 - 2x - 15$, vertex $(1, -16)$

9 **a** unmarked side $= (40 - 2x)$ m
  ∴ $A = x(40 - 2x)$ m^2, etc.   **b** $x = 10$ **c** 200 m^2

10 **a** $\Delta < 0$, does not cut the x-axis
  b $\Delta > 0$, cuts the x-axis twice
  c $\Delta = 0$, touches the x-axis

REVIEW SET 20B

1 $x = -7$ or 6   **2** No, as $f(2) = 4 - 6 + 8 = 6 \ne 5$.

3

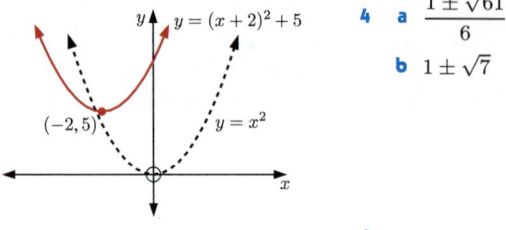

4 **a** $\dfrac{1 \pm \sqrt{61}}{6}$ **b** $1 \pm \sqrt{7}$

5 (graph) $y = 3(x-2)^2$, $x = 2$, point $(2, 0)$, y-intercept 12

6 **a** $x = 1$ **b** $x = \tfrac{5}{6}$

7 **a** V$(2, -3)$ **b** $\{y \mid y \leqslant -3\}$

8 **a** $f(-1) = 10$
  b x-intercepts 1 and 4, y-intercept 4
  c $x = \tfrac{5}{2}$
  d V$(\tfrac{5}{2}, -\tfrac{9}{4})$
  e

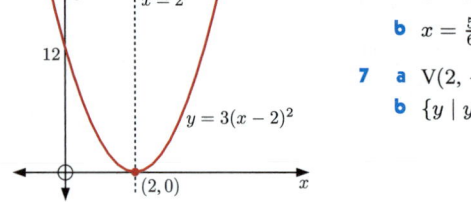

9 **a** $f(x)$ has x-intercepts -6 and -2 and its y-intercept is 12. $g(x)$ does not cut the x-axis and its y-intercept is -20.
  b Both $f(x)$ and $g(x)$ have axis of symmetry $x = -4$. Both $f(x)$ and $g(x)$ have vertex $(-4, -4)$.
  c Range of $f(x)$ is $\{y \mid y \geqslant -4\}$.
  Range of $g(x)$ is $\{y \mid y \leqslant -4\}$.
  d

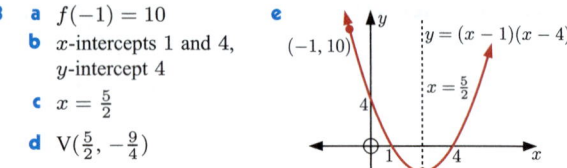

10 **a** If $c = 0$, the y-intercept of the graph is 0. This means the graph passes through the origin, or touches the x-axis at $(0, 0)$. So the graph cuts the x-axis at least once (it cuts twice if $b \ne 0$).
  b If $c = 0$, then $-4ac = 0$ also. That means the discriminant $b^2 - 4ac = b^2$, which is always $\geqslant 0$. Hence, the graph cuts the x-axis at least once. (It touches the x-axis if $b^2 = 0$.)

EXERCISE 21A

1 **a** $\tfrac{\pi}{6}$ **b** $\tfrac{\pi}{2}$ **c** $\tfrac{\pi}{3}$ **d** $\tfrac{\pi}{4}$ **e** $\tfrac{2\pi}{3}$
  f $\tfrac{3\pi}{4}$ **g** $\tfrac{\pi}{18}$ **h** $\tfrac{5\pi}{4}$ **i** $\tfrac{7\pi}{6}$ **j** $\tfrac{7\pi}{4}$

2 **a** $\approx 1.15^c$ **b** $\approx 0.401^c$ **c** $\approx 0.122^c$ **d** $\approx 1.99^c$
  e $\approx 3.80^c$

3 **a** 45°   **b** 30°   **c** 36°   **d** 72°   **e** 10°
  f 50°   **g** 540°   **h** 20°   **i** 100°   **j** 720°
  k 240°   **l** 300°   **m** 420°   **n** 330°   **o** 675°

4 **a** $\approx 57.3°$ **b** $\approx 172°$ **c** $\approx 28.6°$ **d** $\approx 44.7°$
  e $\approx 123°$

5 **a**

Deg	0	45	90	135	180	225	270	315	360
Rad	0	$\tfrac{\pi}{4}$	$\tfrac{\pi}{2}$	$\tfrac{3\pi}{4}$	π	$\tfrac{5\pi}{4}$	$\tfrac{3\pi}{2}$	$\tfrac{7\pi}{4}$	2π

b

Deg	0	30	60	90	120	150	180	210
Rad	0	$\frac{\pi}{6}$	$\frac{\pi}{3}$	$\frac{\pi}{2}$	$\frac{2\pi}{3}$	$\frac{5\pi}{6}$	π	$\frac{7\pi}{6}$

Deg	240	270	300	330	360
Rad	$\frac{4\pi}{3}$	$\frac{3\pi}{2}$	$\frac{5\pi}{3}$	$\frac{11\pi}{6}$	2π

6 a i $l = \left(\dfrac{\theta}{2\pi}\right) \times 2\pi r$ **ii** $A = \left(\dfrac{\theta}{2\pi}\right) \times \pi r^2$

b 30 cm, 150 cm² **c** 17.5 cm²

EXERCISE 21B

1 a A($\cos 67°$, $\sin 67°$), B($\cos 148°$, $\sin 148°$), C($\cos 281°$, $\sin 281°$), D($\cos(-24°)$, $\sin(-24°)$)
b A(0.391, 0.921), B(−0.848, 0.530), C(0.191, −0.982), D(0.914, −0.407)

2 a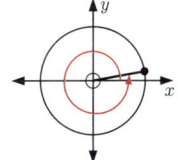
same point on unit circle
∴ same x-coordinate
∴ $\cos 380° = \cos 20°$

b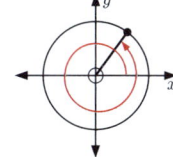
same point on unit circle
∴ same y-coordinate
∴ $\sin 413° = \sin 53°$

c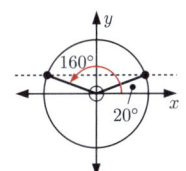
same y-coordinate on unit circle
∴ $\sin 160° = \sin 20°$

d
$\cos 160° = -a$
$= -\cos 20°$

e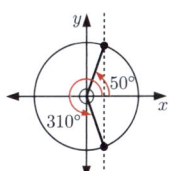
same x-coordinate on unit circle
∴ $\cos 310° = \cos 50°$

f
[OP] and [OP′] have the same gradient
∴ $\tan 25° = \tan 205°$

3 a $\cos 0° = 1$, $\sin 0° = 0$ **b** $\cos 90° = 0$, $\sin 90° = 1$
c $\cos 2\pi = 1$, $\sin 2\pi = 0$ **d** $\cos 450° = 0$, $\sin 450° = 1$
e $\cos(-\frac{\pi}{2}) = 0$, $\sin(-\frac{\pi}{2}) = -1$
f $\cos(-180°) = -1$, $\sin(-180°) = 0$

4 a i ≈ −0.454 **ii** ≈ −0.891 **iii** ≈ 0.809
 iv ≈ −0.588
b i ≈ 1.96 **ii** ≈ −0.727

5 a $\cos 49°$ is positive, $\sin 49°$ is positive, $\tan 49°$ is positive.
b $\cos 158°$ is negative, $\sin 158°$ is positive, $\tan 158°$ is negative.
c $\cos 207°$ is negative, $\sin 207°$ is negative, $\tan 207°$ is positive.
d $\cos 296°$ is positive, $\sin 296°$ is negative, $\tan 296°$ is negative.
e $\cos \frac{3\pi}{4}$ is negative, $\sin \frac{3\pi}{4}$ is positive, $\tan \frac{3\pi}{4}$ is negative.
f $\cos \frac{\pi}{6}$ is positive, $\sin \frac{\pi}{6}$ is positive, $\tan \frac{\pi}{6}$ is positive.
g $\cos \frac{5\pi}{3}$ is positive, $\sin \frac{5\pi}{3}$ is negative, $\tan \frac{5\pi}{3}$ is negative.
h $\cos \frac{7\pi}{6}$ is negative, $\sin \frac{7\pi}{6}$ is negative, $\tan \frac{7\pi}{6}$ is positive.

6 a

Quadrant	Degree	Radian measure
1	$0° < \theta < 90°$	$0 < \theta < \frac{\pi}{2}$
2	$90° < \theta < 180°$	$\frac{\pi}{2} < \theta < \pi$
3	$180° < \theta < 270°$	$\pi < \theta < \frac{3\pi}{2}$
4	$270° < \theta < 360°$	$\frac{3\pi}{2} < \theta < 2\pi$

Quadrant	$\cos \theta$	$\sin \theta$	$\tan \theta$
1	+ ve	+ ve	+ ve
2	− ve	+ ve	− ve
3	− ve	− ve	+ ve
4	+ ve	− ve	− ve

b i 3 and 4 **ii** 1 and 4 **iii** 3 **iv** 4

7 $\tan(180° - \theta) = \dfrac{\sin(180° - \theta)}{\cos(180° - \theta)} = \dfrac{\sin \theta}{-\cos \theta} = -\tan \theta$

EXERCISE 21C

1 a $\sin \theta = \pm \frac{4}{5}$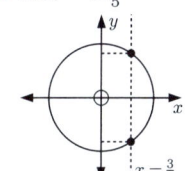
b $\sin \theta = \pm \dfrac{\sqrt{15}}{4}$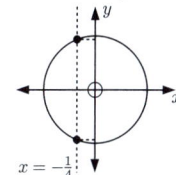

c $\sin \theta = 0$ **d** $\sin \theta = \pm 1$

2 a $\cos \theta = \pm \frac{5}{13}$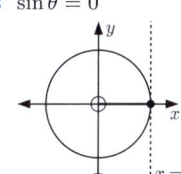
b $\cos \theta = 0$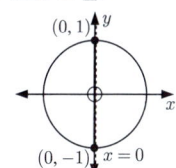

c $\cos \theta = \pm 1$ **d** $\cos \theta = \pm \frac{4}{5}$

3 a $\cos \theta = \dfrac{\sqrt{5}}{3}$ **b** $\cos \theta = -\frac{3}{5}$ **c** $\cos \theta = -\dfrac{2\sqrt{2}}{3}$
d $\cos \theta = \frac{12}{13}$

4 a $\sin \theta = \frac{4}{5}$ **b** $\sin \theta = -\dfrac{\sqrt{15}}{4}$ **c** $\sin \theta = \dfrac{\sqrt{7}}{4}$
d $\sin \theta = -\frac{12}{13}$

5 a $\cos \theta = -\dfrac{\sqrt{55}}{8}$ **b** $\tan \theta = \dfrac{3}{\sqrt{55}}$

EXERCISE 21D

1 **a** $\frac{1}{2}, \frac{\sqrt{3}}{2}, \frac{1}{\sqrt{3}}$ **b** $\frac{1}{\sqrt{2}}, \frac{1}{\sqrt{2}}, 1$ **c** 0, 1, 0
d $\frac{1}{\sqrt{2}}, -\frac{1}{\sqrt{2}}, -1$ **e** 1, 0, undefined **f** $\frac{\sqrt{3}}{2}, -\frac{1}{2}, -\sqrt{3}$
g $-1, 0$, undefined **h** $0, -1, 0$
i $-\frac{1}{2}, -\frac{\sqrt{3}}{2}, \frac{1}{\sqrt{3}}$ **j** $-\frac{\sqrt{3}}{2}, -\frac{1}{2}, \sqrt{3}$ **k** $-\frac{1}{2}, \frac{\sqrt{3}}{2}, -\frac{1}{\sqrt{3}}$
l 0, 1, 0 **m** $-\frac{\sqrt{3}}{2}, \frac{1}{2}, -\sqrt{3}$ **n** $-\frac{1}{\sqrt{2}}, \frac{1}{\sqrt{2}}, -1$
o 1, 0, undefined **p** $0, -1, 0$

2 **a** $\frac{1}{2}$ **b** $\frac{1}{4}$ **c** $\frac{1}{3}$ **d** $\frac{3\sqrt{3}}{8}$ **e** $\frac{1}{4}$ **f** 3

3 **a** $\frac{5\pi}{6}$ **b** $\frac{5\pi}{4}$ **c** $\frac{\pi}{6}$ **d** $\frac{7\pi}{4}$

EXERCISE 21E.1

1 **a** 0
 b **i** $\theta = 0, \pi, 2\pi, 3\pi, 4\pi$ **ii** $\theta = \frac{3\pi}{2}, \frac{7\pi}{2}$
  iii $\theta = \frac{\pi}{6}, \frac{5\pi}{6}, \frac{13\pi}{6}, \frac{17\pi}{6}$ **iv** $\theta = \frac{\pi}{3}, \frac{2\pi}{3}, \frac{7\pi}{3}, \frac{8\pi}{3}$
 c $\theta \approx \frac{\pi}{12}, \approx \frac{11\pi}{12}, \approx \frac{25\pi}{12}, \approx \frac{35\pi}{12}$
 d **i** $0 < \theta < \pi, \ 2\pi < \theta < 3\pi$ **e** $\{y \mid -1 \leqslant y \leqslant 1\}$
  ii $\pi < \theta < 2\pi, \ 3\pi < \theta < 4\pi$

2 **a** 1
 b **i** $\theta = \frac{\pi}{2}, \frac{3\pi}{2}, \frac{5\pi}{2}, \frac{7\pi}{2}$ **ii** $\theta = 0, 2\pi, 4\pi$
  iii $\theta = \frac{2\pi}{3}, \frac{4\pi}{3}, \frac{8\pi}{3}, \frac{10\pi}{3}$ **iv** $\theta = \frac{3\pi}{4}, \frac{5\pi}{4}, \frac{11\pi}{4}, \frac{13\pi}{4}$
 c $\theta \approx \frac{5\pi}{12}, \approx \frac{19\pi}{12}, \approx \frac{29\pi}{12}, \approx \frac{43\pi}{12}$
 d **i** $0 \leqslant \theta < \frac{\pi}{2}, \ \frac{3\pi}{2} < \theta < \frac{5\pi}{2}, \ \frac{7\pi}{2} < \theta \leqslant 4\pi$
  ii $\frac{\pi}{2} < \theta < \frac{3\pi}{2}, \ \frac{5\pi}{2} < \theta < \frac{7\pi}{2}$
 e $\{y \mid -1 \leqslant y \leqslant 1\}$

EXERCISE 21E.2

1 **a** 4 **b** 2 **c** $\frac{1}{3}$ 2 **a** $\frac{2\pi}{3}$ **b** $\frac{\pi}{2}$ **c** 4π

3 **a** $y = -3$ **b** $y = 5$ **c** $y = 0$

4 **a**
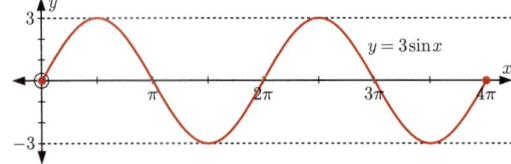

b
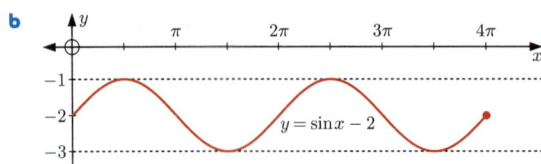

c
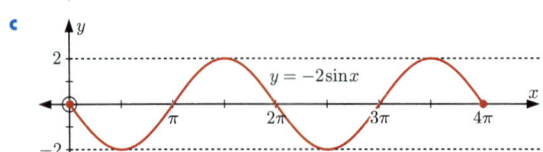

d
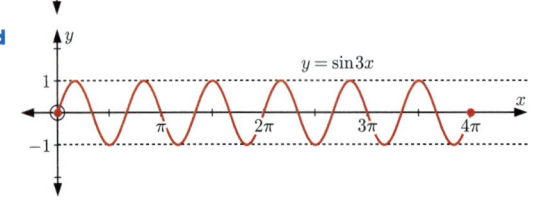

e
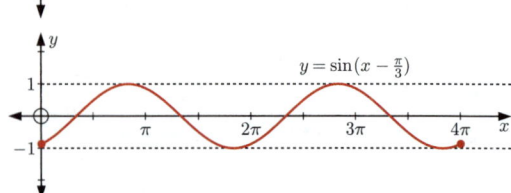

f
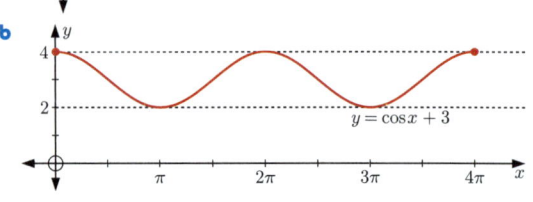

5 **a**
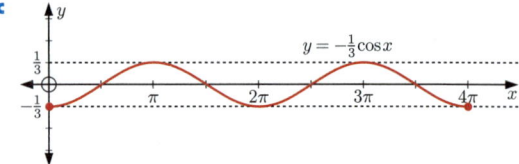

b
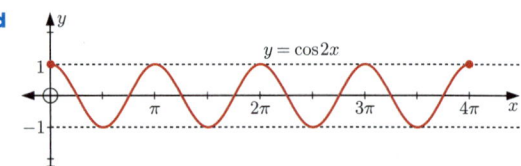

c
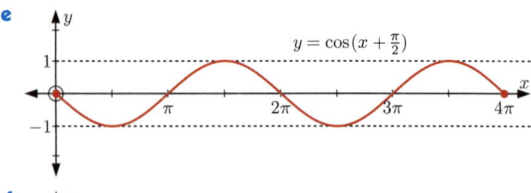

d
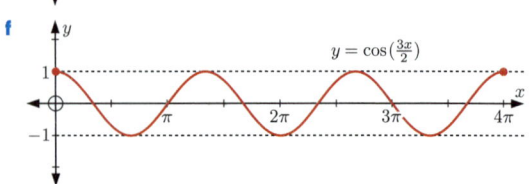

e

f

6 **a**
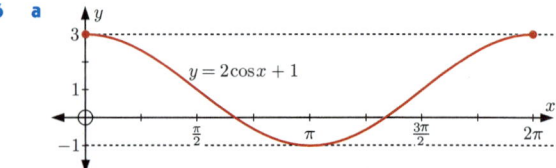

b

$y = \sin 2x + 3$

c

$y = \tfrac{1}{2}\cos 3x$

d

$y = 3\sin 4x + 7$

7 a

$y = 6\sin x + 10$

b $y = 13$ **c** maximum value $= 16$, when $x = \tfrac{\pi}{2}$ and $\tfrac{5\pi}{2}$

d minimum value $= 4$, when $x = \tfrac{3\pi}{2}$ and $\tfrac{7\pi}{2}$

8 a i 6 **ii** $T = 26$ **iii** 24

b

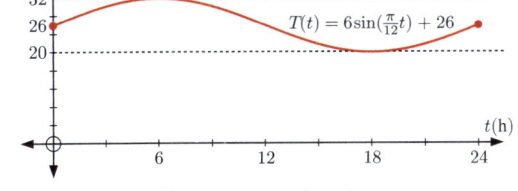

$T(t) = 6\sin(\tfrac{\pi}{12}t) + 26$

c i $26°$C **ii** $29°$C **d** $32°$C, at 6 pm

9 a

$D(t) = 4\cos(\tfrac{\pi}{6}t) + 6$

b highest $= 10$ m, at midnight, midday, and midnight the next day

lowest $= 2$ m, at 6 am and 6 pm

c no (water height is 4 m)

EXERCISE 21F

1 a $2\cos\theta$ **b** $7\sin\theta$ **c** $3\sin\theta$ **d** $2\sin\theta$
e $-3\cos\theta$ **f** $5\cos\theta$

2 a 5 **b** -3 **c** -1 **d** 3 **e** $7\cos^2\theta$
f $6\sin^2\theta$ **g** $-\cos^2\theta$ **h** $-6\sin^2\theta$ **i** $-7\cos^2\theta$

3 a $\cos^2\theta - 5\cos\theta$ **b** $4\sin\theta - \sin^2\theta$
c $\cos^2\theta + 2\cos\theta - 3$ **d** $-\cos^2\theta$
e $4 + 4\sin\theta + \sin^2\theta$ **f** $\sin^2\alpha - 6\sin\alpha + 9$
g $\cos^2\alpha - 8\cos\alpha + 16$ **h** $1 - 2\sin\phi\cos\phi$

i $-1 + 2\cos\alpha - \cos^2\alpha$

4 a $(1+\sin\phi)(1-\sin\phi)$ **b** $(\cos\theta+\sin\theta)(\cos\theta-\sin\theta)$
c $(\cos\beta+1)(\cos\beta-1)$ **d** $\sin\beta(3\sin\beta-1)$
e $3\cos\phi(2+\cos\phi)$ **f** $2\sin\theta(2\sin\theta-1)$
g $(\sin\theta+2)(\sin\theta+4)$ **h** $(\cos\theta+6)(\cos\theta+1)$
i $(4\cos\alpha-1)(2\cos\alpha+1)$

5 a 1 **b** $2\sin\theta$ **c** $-\sin\theta$
d $1+\cos\alpha$ **e** $\sin\theta-1$ **f** $\dfrac{1}{\cos\alpha+\sin\alpha}$
g $\cos\theta-\sin\theta$ **h** $\dfrac{1}{\cos\phi-\sin\phi}$ **i** $2\cos\theta$

EXERCISE 21G

1 a $\theta = \tfrac{\pi}{6}$ or $\tfrac{11\pi}{6}$ **b** $\theta = \tfrac{7\pi}{6}$ or $\tfrac{11\pi}{6}$ **c** $\theta = \tfrac{\pi}{3}$ or $\tfrac{4\pi}{3}$
d $\theta = \tfrac{\pi}{2}$ or $\tfrac{3\pi}{2}$ **e** $\theta = \tfrac{\pi}{4}$ or $\tfrac{5\pi}{4}$ **f** $\theta = \tfrac{4\pi}{3}$ or $\tfrac{5\pi}{3}$
g $\theta = \tfrac{\pi}{4}$ or $\tfrac{3\pi}{4}$ **h** $\theta = \pi$ **i** $\theta = \tfrac{5\pi}{6}$ or $\tfrac{11\pi}{6}$

2 a $\theta = \tfrac{\pi}{4}, \tfrac{7\pi}{4}, \tfrac{9\pi}{4}$, or $\tfrac{15\pi}{4}$ **b** $\theta = \tfrac{\pi}{2}$ or $\tfrac{5\pi}{2}$
c $\theta = \tfrac{2\pi}{3}, \tfrac{5\pi}{3}, \tfrac{8\pi}{3}$, or $\tfrac{11\pi}{3}$ **d** $\theta = \tfrac{\pi}{6}$ or $\tfrac{5\pi}{6}$
e $\theta = \tfrac{5\pi}{6}$ or $-\tfrac{5\pi}{6}$ **f** $\theta = \tfrac{3\pi}{4}, \tfrac{7\pi}{4}, \tfrac{11\pi}{4}, \tfrac{15\pi}{4}, \tfrac{19\pi}{4}$, or $\tfrac{23\pi}{4}$

3 a $\theta = \tfrac{\pi}{4}, \tfrac{3\pi}{4}, \tfrac{5\pi}{4}$, or $\tfrac{7\pi}{4}$ **b** $\theta = \tfrac{\pi}{3}, \tfrac{2\pi}{3}, \tfrac{4\pi}{3}$, or $\tfrac{5\pi}{3}$
c $\theta = \tfrac{\pi}{2}, \pi$, or $\tfrac{3\pi}{2}$ **d** $\theta = 0, \tfrac{\pi}{3}, \tfrac{2\pi}{3}, \pi$, or 2π
e $\theta = 0, \tfrac{2\pi}{3}, \tfrac{4\pi}{3}$, or 2π **f** $\theta = \tfrac{\pi}{4}, \tfrac{3\pi}{4}, \tfrac{5\pi}{4}$, or $\tfrac{7\pi}{4}$

EXERCISE 21H

1 a $\sin\theta$ **b** $-4\sin\theta$ **c** $6\cos\theta$ **d** $11\sin\theta$
e $\cos^2\alpha$ **f** $\sin^2\alpha$ **g** 1

3 a $2\cos\theta$ **b** $-3\cos\theta$ **c** $2\sin\theta$ **d** $-9\sin\theta$
e $7\sin\theta$ **f** $7\cos\theta$

4 $\tan(90° - \theta) \times \tan\theta = 1$

5 This proof is acceptable for θ being an acute angle only. Another method is required for a general proof.

EXERCISE 21I

2 a $\cos\alpha$ **b** $\sin\beta$ **c** $\sin A$ **d** $-\sin\alpha$ **e** $-\sin\beta$
f $-\sin\theta$ **g** $\tfrac{\sqrt{3}}{2}\sin\theta + \tfrac{1}{2}\cos\theta$ **h** $\tfrac{1}{2}\cos\alpha + \tfrac{\sqrt{3}}{2}\sin\alpha$
i $\tfrac{1}{\sqrt{2}}(\sin\theta + \cos\theta)$ **j** $\tfrac{1}{\sqrt{2}}(\cos\phi - \sin\phi)$
k $\tfrac{1}{\sqrt{2}}(\cos C - \sin C)$ **l** $\tfrac{\sqrt{3}}{2}\cos A + \tfrac{1}{2}\sin A$

3 a $\cos(A-B)$ **b** $\sin(\alpha-\beta)$ **c** $\cos(M+N)$
d $\sin(C+D)$ **e** $2\sin(\alpha-\beta)$ **f** $-\cos(\alpha+\beta)$

4 a Use the expansions of $\sin(A+B)$ and $\cos(A+B)$ letting B be A.

b i $-\tfrac{24}{25}$ **ii** $\tfrac{7}{25}$ **iii** $-\tfrac{24}{7}$

5 $\dfrac{1+\sqrt{3}}{2\sqrt{2}}$

6 a $\overrightarrow{OP} = \begin{pmatrix}\cos B\\\sin B\end{pmatrix}$, $\overrightarrow{OQ} = \begin{pmatrix}\cos A\\\sin A\end{pmatrix}$ **b** Use $\overrightarrow{OP}\bullet\overrightarrow{OQ}$.

REVIEW SET 21A

1 a $\tfrac{\pi}{12}$ **b** $\tfrac{\pi}{8}$ **2 a** $18°$ **b** $140°$

3 a $\sin\theta = \pm\tfrac{\sqrt{5}}{3}$ **b** $\sin\theta = \pm\tfrac{2}{\sqrt{13}}$

4 a $\tfrac{1}{2}$ **b** 3 **5 a** $5, \pi$ **b** $\tfrac{1}{4}, 2\pi$ **c** $4, 4\pi$

6 a $4\sin^2\theta$ **b** $\dfrac{\cos\theta}{\cos\theta+2}$ **c** $\dfrac{1}{\cos\theta\sin\theta}$

7 a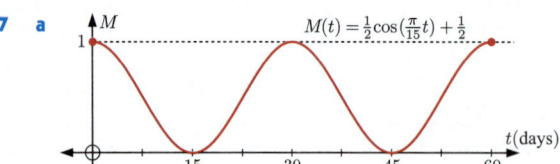

b i 0.75 **ii** 0.25 **iii** ≈ 0.835 **iv** ≈ 0.165
c Once every 30 days. **d** January 16, February 15

8 a $\sin^2\theta - 3\sin\theta$ **b** $\cos^2\theta + 10\cos\theta + 25$

9 a $\theta = \frac{2\pi}{3}$ or $\frac{5\pi}{3}$ **b** $\theta = \frac{\pi}{6}, \frac{5\pi}{6}, \frac{7\pi}{6}$, or $\frac{11\pi}{6}$
c $\theta = \frac{\pi}{6}$ or $\frac{11\pi}{6}$

REVIEW SET 21B

1 a P($\cos 237°$, $\sin 237°$) **b** P(-0.545, -0.839)

2 $\cos\frac{7\pi}{4}$ is positive, $\sin\frac{7\pi}{4}$ is negative, $\tan\frac{7\pi}{4}$ is negative

3 a $\cos\theta = -\frac{1}{\sqrt{5}}$ **b** $\cos\theta = \frac{2\sqrt{10}}{7}$ **4** 150°

5 a graph of $y = 4\sin x$

b graph of $y = 2\cos x - 3$

c graph of $y = \sin(x - \frac{\pi}{2})$

6 a $4\sin\theta(\sin\theta - 3)$ **b** $(\cos\theta - 6)(\cos\theta + 3)$

7 a graph of $H(t) = 10\cos(\frac{\pi}{6}t) + 20$

b 20 m **c** 10 m **d** 12 seconds

8 a $3\cos\theta$ **b** $-\sin^3\phi$ **c** $3\sin\theta$

9 a $\theta = \frac{2\pi}{3}, \frac{4\pi}{3}, \frac{8\pi}{3}$, or $\frac{10\pi}{3}$ **b** $\theta = \frac{\pi}{6}, \frac{7\pi}{6}, \frac{13\pi}{6}$, or $\frac{19\pi}{6}$
c $\theta = \frac{\pi}{3}, \frac{\pi}{2}, \frac{3\pi}{2}, \frac{5\pi}{3}, \frac{7\pi}{3}, \frac{5\pi}{2}, \frac{7\pi}{2}$, or $\frac{11\pi}{3}$

10 a $-\cos\theta$ **b** $-\cos\phi$ **c** $\dfrac{\tan\alpha + \tan\beta}{1 - \tan\alpha\tan\beta}$

EXERCISE 22A

1 a–o number line diagrams

2 a $\{x \mid x \geqslant 6\}$ **b** $\{x \mid x < 3\}$ **c** $\{x \mid -2 \leqslant x < 1\}$
d $\{x \mid x \leqslant 0 \text{ or } x > 1\}$ **e** $\{x \mid x < -1 \text{ or } x > 1\}$
f $\{x \mid 0 < x \leqslant 4\}$ **g** $\{x \mid x < -2 \text{ or } 1 < x \leqslant 4\}$
h $\{x \mid -2 \leqslant x \leqslant 1 \text{ or } x > 3\}$

3 a $[-1, 6]$ **b** $]0, 5[$ **c** $]-4, 7]$ **d** $[4, 8[$
e $]-7, \infty[$ **f** $]-\infty, 0]$ **g** $]-\infty, 2] \cup [5, \infty[$
h $]-\infty, -3[\cup]4, \infty[$ **i** $]-1, 1] \cup [2, \infty[$
j $]-\infty, -4[\cup [2, 7[$ **k** $[3, 8[$ **l** $[-2, 7[$
m $[5, \infty[$ **n** $]-\infty, -2[$ **o** $]-\infty, 2] \cup]3, 5[$
p $[-4, 1] \cup]4, \infty[$ **q** $]-\infty, -2] \cup]2, \infty[$
r $]-\infty, -3[\cup]10, \infty[$

4 a $\{x \mid x > 0\}$ **b** $\{x \mid -1 \leqslant x < 9\}$
c $\{x \mid 0 < x < 3\}$ **d** $\{x \mid \frac{7}{2} \leqslant x < 4\}$

EXERCISE 22B

1 a $x < -\frac{2}{3}$ **b** $x > \frac{9}{5}$ **c** $x \leqslant \frac{1}{3}$
d $x \geqslant -3$ **e** $x < 1$ **f** $x \leqslant -\frac{1}{5}$

2 a $x \leqslant 4$ **b** $x > -5$ **c** $x > -4$
d $x \geqslant \frac{7}{3}$ **e** $x < 1$ **f** $x \leqslant \frac{3}{5}$

3 a $x > -\frac{7}{2}$ **b** $x > \frac{4}{3}$ **c** $x \leqslant \frac{1}{3}$

d $x \geqslant 1$ **e** $x < 0$ **f** $x \leqslant -\frac{5}{3}$

EXERCISE 22C

1 (sign diagrams for parts **a**–**i**)

2 (sign diagrams for parts **a**–**o**)

3 (sign diagrams for parts **a**–**i**)

4 (sign diagrams for parts **a**–**o**)

5 a i $\{x \mid -3 < x < 6\}$ **ii** $\{x \mid -3 \leqslant x \leqslant 6\}$
  iii $\{x \mid x < -3 \text{ or } x > 6\}$ **iv** $\{x \mid x \leqslant -3 \text{ or } x \geqslant 6\}$
 b i $\{x \mid x < -1 \text{ or } x > 2\}$ **ii** $\{x \mid x \leqslant -1 \text{ or } x > 2\}$
  iii $\{x \mid -1 < x < 2\}$ **iv** $\{x \mid -1 \leqslant x < 2\}$
 c i $\{x \mid -4 < x < 0 \text{ or } 0 < x < 5\}$
  ii $\{x \mid -4 < x \leqslant 5\}$ **iii** $\{x \mid x < -4 \text{ or } x > 5\}$
  iv $\{x \mid x < -4 \text{ or } x = 0 \text{ or } x \geqslant 5\}$

EXERCISE 22D

1 a (sign diagram)
 b i $x < -3 \text{ or } x > 2$ **ii** $x \leqslant -3 \text{ or } x \geqslant 2$
   iii $-3 < x < 2$ **iv** $-3 \leqslant x \leqslant 2$
2 a $1 \leqslant x \leqslant 3$ **b** $-\frac{3}{2} < x < 4$ **c** $x < -1 \text{ or } x > 2$
 d no solutions   **e** $x \leqslant 0 \text{ or } x \geqslant 2$ **f** $-\frac{1}{2} < x < 0$
 g $-4 < x < 4$ **h** $-2 \leqslant x \leqslant 2$ **i** $x < -5 \text{ or } x > 1$
 j $-1 \leqslant x \leqslant 2$ **k** no solutions   **l** $-7 \leqslant x \leqslant 4$
 m $x \in \mathbb{R}, \ x \neq 1$ **n** $-1 \leqslant x \leqslant \frac{5}{2}$ **o** $x \leqslant -\frac{4}{3} \text{ or } x \geqslant 2$
 p $x < -2 \text{ or } x > \frac{2}{5}$ **q** $\frac{4}{3} < x < \frac{3}{2}$ **r** $x = \frac{2}{3}$
3 a $-2 < x < 3$ **b** $x < -3 \text{ or } x > 2$
 c $x \leqslant -4 \text{ or } x > \frac{1}{2}$ **d** $0 < x \leqslant 3$
 e $-3 < x < 0 \text{ or } x > 4$ **f** $x < -1 \text{ or } 0 \leqslant x < 1$
 g $x < -3 \text{ or } x \geqslant -1$ **h** $x < \frac{3}{2} \text{ or } x > 5$
 i $0 < x < \frac{1}{3}$ **j** $x < -\frac{1}{3} \text{ or } x \geqslant -\frac{2}{7}$
 k $-\frac{1}{2} < x < 1$ **l** $-2 \leqslant x < 0 \text{ or } x \geqslant 2$
4 a $\{x \mid x \leqslant 0 \text{ or } x \geqslant 2\}$ **b** $\{x \mid x \leqslant 0 \text{ or } x \geqslant 3\}$
 c $\{x \mid x \leqslant -1 \text{ or } x \geqslant 3\}$ **d** $\{x \mid x < -2 \text{ or } x > 1\}$
 e $\{x \mid x \leqslant -3 \text{ or } x > 1\}$
 f $\{x \mid -5 \leqslant x < -2 \text{ or } x > 2\}$
5 a $-9 < m < -1$ **b** $m = -9 \text{ or } m = -1$
 c $m < -9 \text{ or } m > -1 \text{ and } m \neq 0$

REVIEW SET 22A

1 a, b, c (number line diagrams)

2 a $x > \frac{4}{5}$ **b** $x \leqslant -\frac{5}{2}$

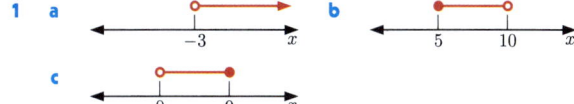

3 a $x > \frac{10}{3}$ **b** $x \geqslant -\frac{7}{9}$

4 a, b (sign diagrams)

c [number line with marks at $\frac{1}{2}$ and 4, signs $-,+,+$]

5 a $x < -1$ or $x > 6$ **b** $x \leqslant -1$ or $x > 6$
   c $-1 < x < 6$ **d** $-1 \leqslant x < 6$
6 a $-6 < x < -2$ **b** $x \leqslant -9$ or $x \geqslant 4$
   c $-\frac{3}{2} < x < 5$
7 a $-4 < x < 0$ **b** $x > -2$ **c** $-1 < x < \frac{1}{3}$
8 $-3 < x < 3$

REVIEW SET 22B

1 a $[-2, 8[$ **b** $]-\infty, 1] \cup]4, 5]$ **c** $]-3, 1[$
   d $]-\infty, -7] \cup]3, \infty[$
2 a [number line: $-,+,-$ at $-2, 3$]   **b** [number line: $+,-,-,+$ at $1, 2, 3$]
3 a $x > \frac{1}{6}$ **b** $x \leqslant -11$
   [number lines shown]
4 a [number line: $-,+,-$ at $-9, 0$]   **b** [number line: $+,+$ at 4]
   c [number line: $-,+,-,+$ at $-4, 1, 3$]
5 a $x \geqslant \frac{8}{5}$ **b** $-7 < x < 5$ **c** $x < -3$ or $x > 2$
6 a $1 < x < 3$ **b** $1 < x \leqslant 3$
   c $x < -6$ or $-6 < x < 1$ or $x > 3$
   d $x < 1$ or $x \geqslant 3$
7 a $x \leqslant -5$ or $x \geqslant 6$ **b** $x < -5$ or $x > 0$
   c $x < -\frac{7}{2}$ or $x > -1$
8 a $\{x \mid x \leqslant 0$ or $x \geqslant 4\}$ **b** $\{x \mid x < -2$ or $x > \frac{1}{3}\}$

EXERCISE 23A

1 a D   **b** C   **c** E and H
2 a E   **b** A   **c** B and C
   d Yes, generally more hours of training results in higher productivity (from the graph).
3 a D   **b** F   **c** 2   **d** 3
4 a 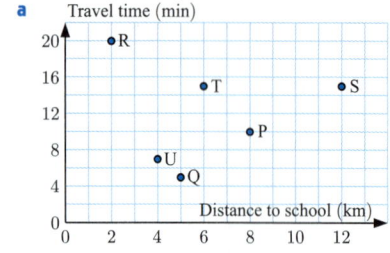   **b** S   **c** Q
   d Student R. They live the shortest distance from school, yet take the most time to get there.

EXERCISE 23B

1 a i negative association   **ii** linear   **iii** strong
   b i no association   **ii** not linear
   c i positive association   **ii** linear   **iii** moderate
   d i positive association   **ii** linear   **iii** weak
   e i positive association   **ii** not linear   **iii** moderate
   f i negative association   **ii** not linear   **iii** strong

2 a "...... as x increases, y increases"
   b "...... as T increases, d decreases"
   c "...... randomly scattered"
3 a 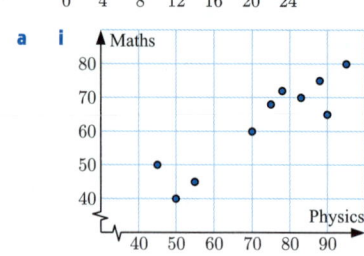   **b** A moderate, positive, linear correlation.
4 a i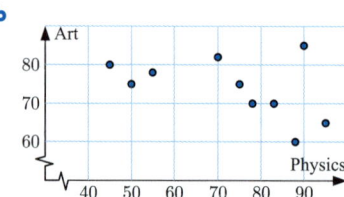
   ii A moderate, positive, linear correlation.
   b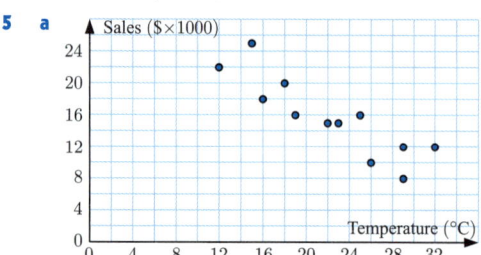
   A very weak, negative, linear correlation (virtually zero correlation).
5 a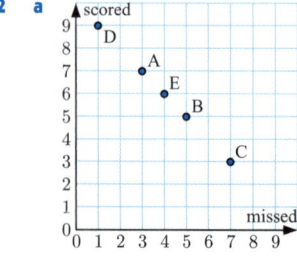
   b A moderate, linear, negative correlation.

EXERCISE 23C

1 a positive correlation as $r > 0$ **b** $r^2 \approx 0.659$
   c moderate positive linear correlation, $0.50 \leqslant r^2 < 0.75$
2 a [scatter plot: scored vs missed, points D, A, E, B, C]
   b $r = -1$
   c perfect negative linear correlation
   The number of shots scored is directly related to those missed. Out of 10 shots, each time the number of goals scored increases by 1, the number of misses decreases by 1.

ANSWERS 609

3 a i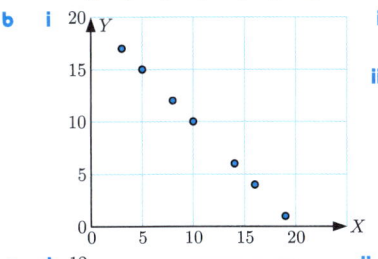
 ii $r \approx 0.786$, $r^2 \approx 0.617$
 iii moderate positive linear correlation

b i
 ii $r = -1$, $r^2 = 1$
 iii perfect negative linear correlation

c i
 ii $r \approx 0.146$, $r^2 \approx 0.0215$
 iii very weak positive linear correlation

4 a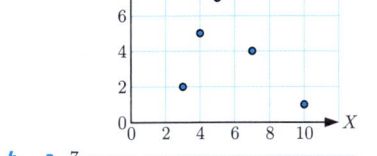
 b $r \approx 0.673$, $r^2 \approx 0.452$
 c A weak, positive, linear correlation exists between *Shoe size* and *Height*.

5 a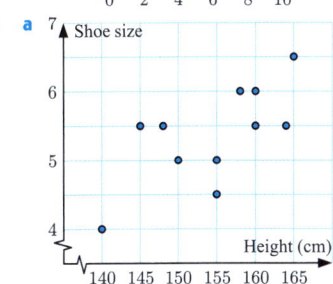
 b $r \approx 0.981$, $r^2 \approx 0.962$
 c A very strong, positive, linear correlation exists between Judge B's scores and Judge A's scores.

6 a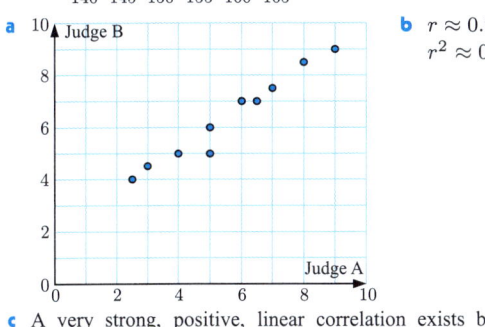
 b negative
 c $r \approx -0.911$, $r^2 \approx 0.830$
 d There is a strong, negative correlation between the number of successful shots and the distance from goal.

7 a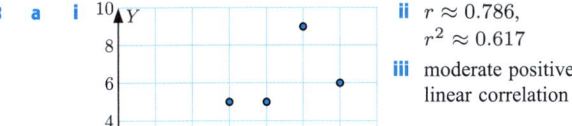
 b No, there appears to be almost no correlation between the variables.
 c $r \approx 0.191$, $r^2 \approx 0.037$
 d There is a very weak positive correlation (almost no correlation) between movie length and box office performance.

EXERCISE 23D.1

1 a $\bar{x} = 7.2$, $\bar{y} = 10$
 b, d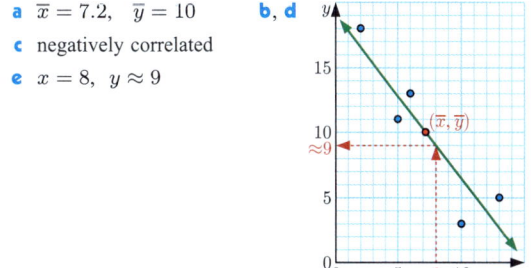
 c negatively correlated
 e $x = 8$, $y \approx 9$

2 a $\bar{x} = 7$, $\bar{y} = 85$
 b $r \approx 0.739$
 c, d, e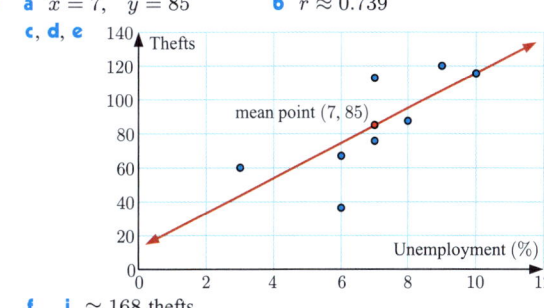
 f i ≈ 168 thefts
 ii Unreliable as it is an extrapolation well beyond the upper pole.

3 a $\bar{x} = 50$, $\bar{y} = 38$
 b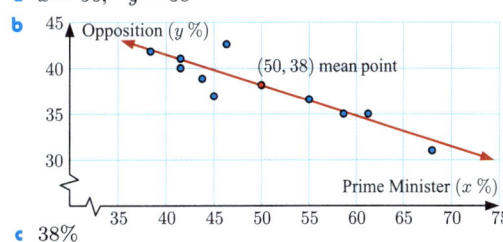
 c 38%

4 a $\bar{x} = 23.3$, $\bar{y} = 78.8$
 b $r^2 \approx 0.509$ There is a moderate correlation between *number of diners* and *noon temperature*.
 c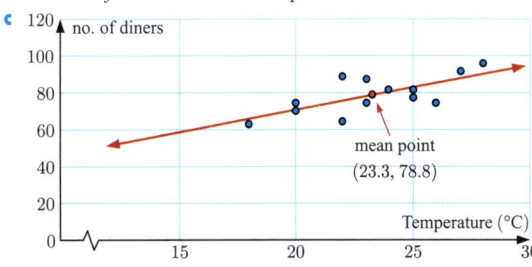
 d i 73 diners   **ii** 56 diners

e We expect the first estimate to be reliable as it is an interpolation, but the second may not be reliable as it is an extrapolation.

EXERCISE 23D.2

1 a i

ii $y \approx 1.12x + 2.90$

b i

ii $y \approx -1.34x + 35.7$

2 a

b $y \approx 7.66x + 40.1$

c The y-intercept indicates that a row can be expected to produce on average 40.1 tomatoes when no spray is applied.

d 94 tomatoes/row. Even though this is an interpolation, this seems low compared with the yield at 6 and 8 mL/2 L. Looking at the graph it would appear that the relationship is not linear.

3 a

b $r \approx -0.952$, $r^2 \approx 0.907$

c $y \approx -2.69x + 77.9$

d The gradient indicates that an increase in training time of 1 hour will decrease the fun-run time by ≈ 2.7 minutes.

e i -2.8 minutes

ii This value is clearly absurd as one cannot record a negative time for a fun-run. It is very unreliable as it is an extrapolation well beyond the upper pole.

4 a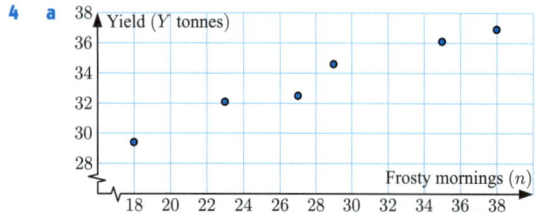

b $Y \approx 0.371n + 23.1$ **c** ≈ 34.6 tonnes

d "......, the *greater* the yield of cherries."

5 a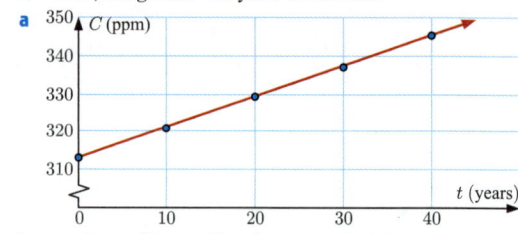

b $r = 1$, perfect positive linear correlation

c $C \approx 0.8t + 313$ **d** 335 parts per million

e 361 parts per million

6 a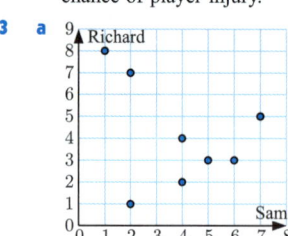

b $r \approx 0.922$, $r^2 \approx 0.851$, strong positive linear correlation

c $y \approx 2.90x - 30.9$

d ≈ 143 runs. This should be fairly reliable as it is interpolated.

REVIEW SET 23A

1 There is a weak, negative correlation between the variables.

2 a E   **b** A

c The greater the time spent on player fitness, the smaller the chance of player injury.

3 a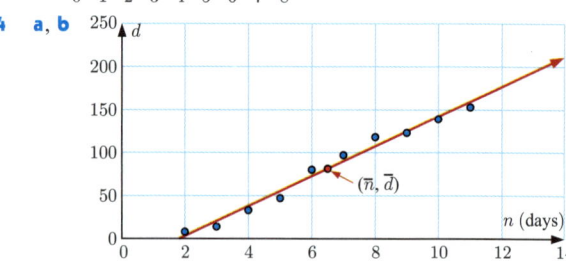

b $r \approx -0.334$

$r^2 \approx 0.112$

There is a very weak, negative correlation between the variables.

4 a, b

b $\overline{n} = 6.5$, $\overline{d} = 81.2$

c i About 210 diagnosed cases.

ii Very unreliable as 14 is outside the poles. The medical team have probably isolated those infected at this stage and there could be a downturn which may be very significant.

5 a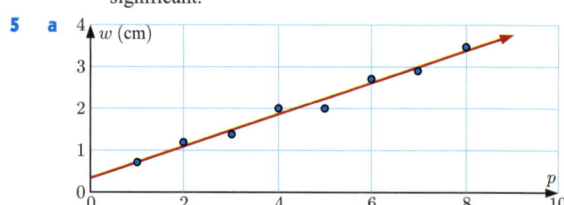

b $r \approx 0.990$ **c** $w \approx 0.381p + 0.336$
d **i** ≈ 5.7 cm
   ii As $p = 14$ is outside the poles, this prediction could be unreliable.

6 a Negatively correlated. The more games won, the higher the team's position on the ladder (and so the value for *Position* is smaller).

b 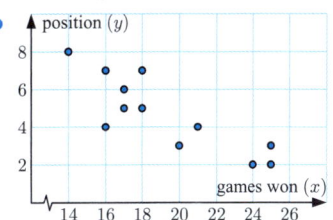   **c** $r \approx -0.843$, $r^2 \approx 0.711$

d $y \approx -0.454x + 13.4$ **e** 3rd

REVIEW SET 23B

1 a J   **b** E   **c** D and G   **d** C

2 a **i** D   **ii** H
b As the number of pages increases, the number of chapters generally increases.

3 a **i** Positive, as numbers get larger they have more possible factors.
   ii Weak, the larger the number, the more prime, square, cubic, etc. numbers you encounter that have very small numbers of factors.

b

Number	1	2	3	4	5	6	7	8	9	10
Number of factors	1	2	2	3	2	4	2	4	3	4

Number	11	12	13	14	15	16	17	18	19	20
Number of factors	2	6	2	4	4	5	2	6	2	6

c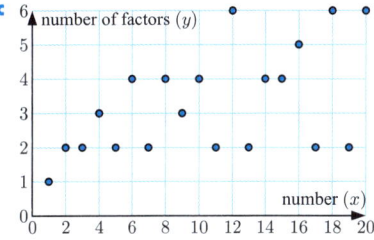

d $r \approx 0.531$, $r^2 \approx 0.282$
e weak, positive, linear correlation

4 a $\overline{x} = 9$, $\overline{y} = 15$
b, d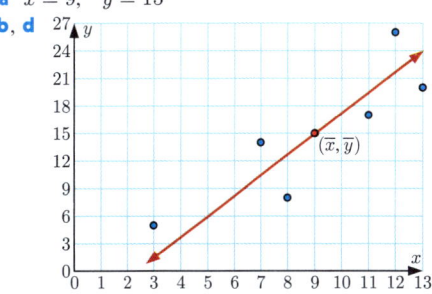

c positively correlated
e $y \approx 6$. Reasonably accurate by interpolation.

5 a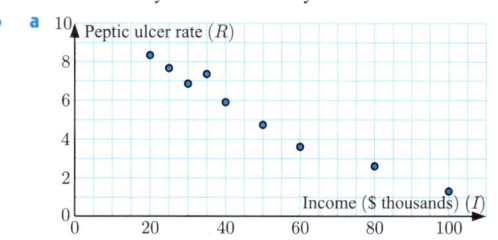

b $v \approx 0.114n + 0.100$
c Each coin added to a wallet or purse increases the value by 11.4 cents on average.
d **i** $\approx \$2.38$
   ii 20 coins is too far beyond the upper pole to extrapolate with any reliable accuracy.

6 a (graph: Peptic ulcer rate (R) vs Income (\$ thousands) (I))

b $R \approx -0.0907I + 9.79$ **c** when $I = 55$, $R \approx 4.80$
d \$120 000 gives a rate of -1.09 which is meaningless. So, \$120 000 is outside the data range of this model.
e **i** The point $(35, 7.3)$, as it does not follow the general trend of the data in that area.
   ii $R \approx -0.0887I + 9.61$; when $I = 55$, $R \approx 4.73$

EXERCISE 24A

1 a polynomial   **b** polynomial
c not a polynomial, one term has x as the index
d polynomial
e not a polynomial, the index in the second term is not an integer
f not a polynomial, the last term has a negative index

2 a 4   **b** 2   **c** 5   **d** 2   **e** 3   **f** 4
3 a -4 **b** 6   **c** -12 **d** 0

EXERCISE 24B.1

1 a **i** $3x^2 + 3x - 3$ **ii** $-x^2 - 3x + 5$
b **i** $3x^3 - 5x^2 + x + 7$ **ii** $-x^3 - 3x^2 + 3x - 5$
c **i** $-5x^4 + x^3 - 9x^2 - x - 4$
   ii $-5x^4 - x^3 + 7x^2 + 3x + 4$
d **i** $2x^4 - 4x^3 + 2x + 5$ **ii** $2x^4 + 2x^3 + 12x - 11$

2 a $3x^2 + 9x - 6$ **b** $-8x^3 + 4x + 16$
c $-x^2 - 3x + 2$ **d** $-8x^3 + x^2 + 7x + 14$
e $6x^3 + 2x^2 + 3x - 16$ **f** $-4x^3 - x^2 - x + 10$

3 a $3x^2 + 5x - 2$ **b** $2x^3 - 9x^2 + x + 12$
c $4x^5 - 21x^4 + 21x^3 - 2x^2 - 10x + 8$
d $-2x^7 - x^5 + 17x^4 + x^3 + 2x^2 - 35x$

4 a $3x^4 - 9x^3 + 12x - 3$ **b** $-10x^3 + 15x^2 - 30$
c $2x^4 - 9x^2 + 8x + 16$
d $-x^4 + 11x^3 - 12x^2 - 4x + 25$
e $4x^4 - 16x^3 + 6x^2 + 16x - 16$
f $2x^7 - 9x^6 + 9x^5 + 14x^4 - 32x^3 + 3x^2 + 24x - 6$

EXERCISE 24B.2

1 a quotient is $x + 1$, remainder is 2

b quotient is $2x + 1$, remainder is 3
c quotient is $x - 4$, remainder is 14
d quotient is $x^2 + x + 3$, remainder is 5
e quotient is $x^2 + 3x - 4$, remainder is -5
f quotient is $x^2 - 2$, remainder is 11

2 **a** $x - 1 + \dfrac{2}{x-3}$ **b** $3x - 2 - \dfrac{3}{x+1}$ **c** $x + 2 + \dfrac{13}{x-2}$
d $x^2 - 5x - 14 - \dfrac{63}{x-4}$ **e** $x^2 - 2x + 9 - \dfrac{22}{x+2}$
f $2x^3 - x^2 + 4x - 10 + \dfrac{26}{x+3}$

EXERCISE 24B.3

1 a, b $3x + 8 + \dfrac{11}{x-2}$

2 a $x - 2 + \dfrac{3}{x-1}$ **b** $x - 3 + \dfrac{13}{x+3}$
c $2x^2 + 3x + 10 + \dfrac{17}{x-2}$ **d** $3x^2 - 2x + 2 - \dfrac{4}{x+1}$
e $2x^2 - 10x + 42 - \dfrac{200}{x+5}$
f $x^3 - 2x^2 + 3x + 2 + \dfrac{6}{x-3}$

EXERCISE 24C

1 a 11   **b** -10 **c** 46   **2** 5 ✓
3 a $a = -2$ **b** $a = 4$ **c** $a = 5$
4 a $a = -4$, $b = 7$ **b** $a = -5$, $b = 6$ **c** $a = 2$, $b = 4$

EXERCISE 24D

1 a factor   **b** not a factor   **c** factor   **d** not a factor
2 a $c = 2$ **b** $c = -2$ **c** $b = 3$
3 a $a = 1$, $b = 10$ **b** $p = \frac{12}{7}$, $q = \frac{75}{7}$
4 a $f(3) = 0$ **b** $x^2 + x - 20$
c $f(x) = (x - 3)(x^2 + x - 20)$
d $f(x) = (x - 3)(x - 4)(x + 5)$

REVIEW SET 24A

1 a polynomial
b not a polynomial, the last term has a negative index
c not a polynomial, the index in the second term is not an integer
2 a $8x^2 + 6x + 3$ **b** $7x^2 - 9x + 9$
c $15x^4 + 32x^3 + 29x - 4$
3 a 1   **b** -53
4 a $x^3 - 2x^2 - 9x + 10$ **b** $-10x^2 - 20x + 15$
c $2x^5 + 4x^4 - 13x^3 - 6x^2 + 43x - 21$
5 a quotient is $2x + 5$, remainder is 3
b quotient is $x^2 - 4x + 2$, remainder is -5
6 a not a factor   **b** factor   **7** $k = 6$ **8** $a = \frac{8}{7}$, $b = \frac{174}{7}$
9 a **i** $f(3) = -1$ **ii** 2   **iii** $x^3 - x^2 + 4x - 6$
b quotient is $x^2 - x$, remainder is -1
By the Remainder Theorem, if $P(x)$ divided by $(x - k)$ has remainder R, then $P(k) = R$. In this case, $f(3) = -1$, and $f(x)$ divided by $(x - 3)$ has remainder -1.
10 a $f(-5) = 0$ **b** $x^2 - 4x + 3$
c $f(x) = (x + 5)(x^2 - 4x + 3)$
d $f(x) = (x + 5)(x - 1)(x - 3)$

REVIEW SET 24B

1 3   **2 a** $x^3 + x^2 - 10x + 6$ **b** $x^3 - x^2 + 2x + 4$
3 $x^3 - 2x^2 + x + 4 - \dfrac{6}{x-4}$ **4 a** -5 **b** 24   **5** -103
6 a $5x^3 + 25x - 10$
b $2x^7 + 7x^5 - 4x^4 - 14x^3 + 6x^2 + 5x - 2$
7 $c = 3$ **8** not a factor   **9** $a = 4$, $b = -1$
10 a $a = 6$ **b** $f(2) = 0$ **d** $f(x) = (x+1)(x-2)^3$

EXERCISE 25A.1

1 a -2 **b** -4 **c** -3 **2 a** -4 **b** -1 **c** ≈ -0.4
3 a ≈ 1.4 **b** ≈ 2.8 **c** ≈ 0.5
4 a ≈ 0.5 **b** ≈ 0.25 **c** ≈ 0.2

EXERCISE 25A.2

1 a 4   **b** 6   **2 a** -2 **b** -4 **c** -6
3 a 3   **b** 2   **c** -4 **d** $-\frac{3}{2}$
4 $y = x^3$ is not a quadratic function.

EXERCISE 25B.1

1 a 11   **b** 6   **c** 5   **d** -3 **e** 4   **f** 2
2 a 2   **b** -5 **c** 3   **d** 4   **e** -1 **f** 3
g -4 **h** -2 **i** 8

EXERCISE 25B.2

1 a $(3 + h)^2$ **b** $\dfrac{(3+h)^2 - 9}{(3+h) - 3} = 6 + h$ for $h \neq 0$
c **i** 7   **ii** 6.5   **iii** 6.1   **iv** 6.01   **d** 6
2 a 8   **b** 3   **c** -1 **d** 4
3 a 2   **b**

x-coordinate	Gradient of tangent
1	2
2	4
3	6
4	8

c $2a$

EXERCISE 25C

1 $f'(x) = 1$
2 a $f'(x) = 3x^2$ **b** $f'(2) = 12$, gradient of tangent to $f(x) = x^3$ at $x = 2$ is 12.
3 a $f'(x) = -\dfrac{1}{x^2}$
b $f'(-1) = -1$, gradient of tangent to $f(x) = \dfrac{1}{x}$ at $x = -1$ is -1.
$f'(3) = -\frac{1}{9}$, gradient of tangent to $f(x) = \dfrac{1}{x}$ at $x = 3$ is $-\frac{1}{9}$.
4 a **i** $f'(x) = 0$ **ii** $f'(x) = 0$ **b** $f'(x) = 0$
5 a $f'(x) = 10x$ **b** $f'(x) = 5g'(x)$
c $f'(x) = \lim\limits_{h \to 0} \dfrac{cg(x+h) - cg(x)}{h}$
$= \lim\limits_{h \to 0} c\left(\dfrac{g(x+h) - g(x)}{h}\right)$
$= c\left(\lim\limits_{h \to 0} \dfrac{g(x+h) - g(x)}{h}\right) = cg'(x)$
6 a **i** $f'(x) = 4x$ **ii** $f'(x) = 9$ **iii** $f'(x) = 4x + 9$
b $f'(x) = \lim\limits_{h \to 0} \dfrac{(g(x+h) + h(x+h)) - (g(x) + h(x))}{h}$
$= \lim\limits_{h \to 0} \dfrac{(g(x+h) - g(x)) + (h(x+h) - h(x))}{h}$
$= \lim\limits_{h \to 0} \dfrac{g(x+h) - g(x)}{h} + \lim\limits_{h \to 0} \dfrac{h(x+h) - h(x)}{h}$
$= g'(x) + h'(x)$

7 a

$f(x)$	$f'(x)$
x^1	1
x^2	$2x$
x^3	$3x^2$
x^4	$4x^3$
x^{-1}	$-x^{-2}$

b If $f(x) = x^n$, then $f'(x) = nx^{n-1}$.

EXERCISE 25D

1 a $6x^5$ **b** $9x^8$ **c** $15x^2$ **d** $-\dfrac{2}{x^3}$ **e** $5 - 2x$
f $-\dfrac{1}{2}x^{-\frac{3}{2}}$ **g** $3x^2 + 4$ **h** $2x^3$ **i** $2x$ **j** $1 - \dfrac{1}{x^2}$
k $\dfrac{2}{x^2}$ **l** $-\dfrac{1}{x^2}$ **m** $1 - \dfrac{5}{x^2}$ **n** $-\dfrac{20}{x^3}$ **o** $\dfrac{3}{\sqrt{x}}$
p $2x - 1$ **q** $\dfrac{8}{x^3}$ **r** $-\dfrac{2}{x\sqrt{x}}$ **s** $9x^2 - 2 + \dfrac{4}{x^3}$
t $-1 + \dfrac{1}{x\sqrt{x}}$ **u** $3x^2 + 4x + 1$ **v** $8x - 4$

2 a $3x^2 + 4x - 3$ **b** $11, 17$ **c** ...... at $(2, 11)$ is 17.
3 a -6 **b** $-\dfrac{3}{2}$ **c** 5 **d** 3 **e** $\dfrac{3}{4}$ **f** $-\dfrac{1}{4}$
4 a -3 **b** $\dfrac{3}{4}$ **c** 0
5 a $(-2, 1)$ **b** $(1, 1)$ **c** $(-1, -1)$ and $(\dfrac{1}{3}, -\dfrac{23}{27})$
 d $(2, 3)$ and $(-2, -1)$ **e** $(0, 7)$ and $(4, -25)$

EXERCISE 25E

1 a i $f'(x) = 2x - 4$
 ii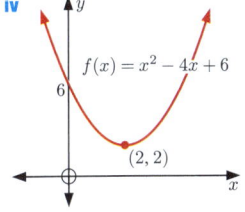
 iii minimum turning point at $(2, 2)$
 iv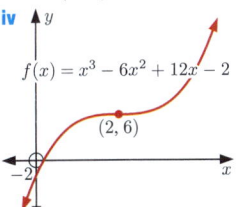

b i $f'(x) = 3x^2 + 6x$
 ii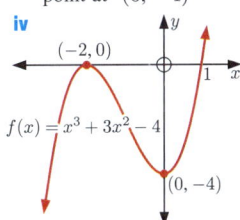
 iii maximum turning point at $(-2, 0)$ minimum turning point at $(0, -4)$
 iv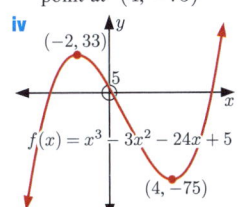

c i $f'(x) = 3x^2 - 12x + 12$
 ii
 iii stationary inflection at $(2, 6)$
 iv

d i $f'(x) = 3x^2 - 6x - 24$
 ii
 iii maximum turning point at $(-2, 33)$ minimum turning point at $(4, -75)$
 iv

e i $f'(x) = 6x^2 - 6x - 12$
 ii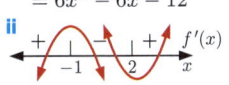
 iii maximum turning point at $(-1, 12)$ minimum turning point at $(2, -15)$
 iv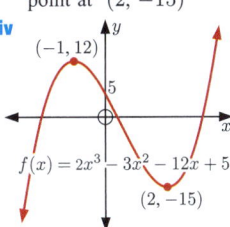

f i $f'(x) = -3x^2 + 18x - 27$
 ii
 iii stationary inflection at $(3, -7)$
 iv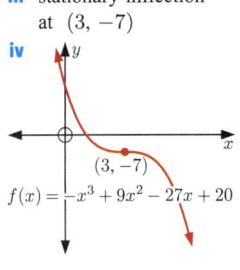

g i $f'(x) = 1 - \dfrac{1}{x^2} = \dfrac{x^2 - 1}{x^2}$
 ii
 iii maximum turning point at $(-1, -2)$ minimum turning point at $(1, 2)$
 iv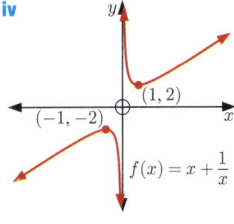

h i $f'(x) = 2 - \dfrac{32}{x^2} = \dfrac{2(x+4)(x-4)}{x^2}$
 ii
 iii maximum turning point at $(-4, -16)$ minimum turning point at $(4, 16)$
 iv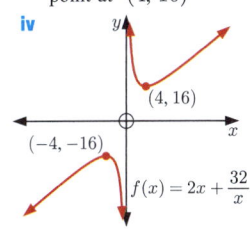

i i $f'(x) = -\dfrac{1}{x^2} - \dfrac{2}{x^3} = \dfrac{-(x+2)}{x^3}$
 ii
 iii minimum turning point at $(-2, -\dfrac{1}{4})$
 iv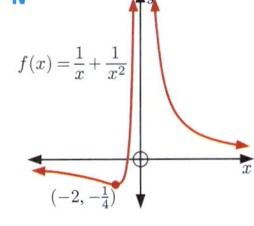

2 a $f'(x) = 2ax + b$ $\therefore$ $f'(x) = 0$ when $x = \dfrac{-b}{2a}$.
 b i $a < 0$ **ii** $a > 0$
3 250, when both numbers are 5
4 a $V(x) = x(30 - 2x)(20 - 2x)$
 $= 4x^3 - 100x^2 + 600x$ mL
 b Squares with sides about 3.92 cm.
5 a P is $(a, 9 - a^2)$ **b** $0 < a < 3$ **c** $A = 18a - 2a^3$
 d $12\sqrt{3}$ units^2 when $a = \sqrt{3}$

EXERCISE 25F

1 a $A = a$ units^2 **b** $A = \dfrac{a^2}{2}$ units^2

2 a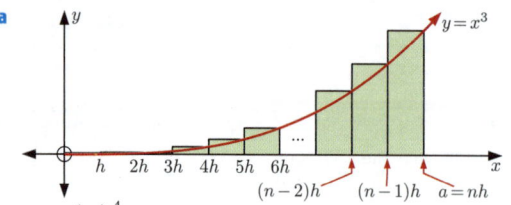

b $S = \left(\dfrac{a}{n}\right)^4 (1^3 + 2^3 + 3^3 + 4^3 + \ldots + n^3)$

c $S = \dfrac{a^4}{n^4}\left[\dfrac{n^2(n+1)^2}{4}\right] = \dfrac{a^4}{4}\left[\dfrac{n^2(n+1)^2}{n^4}\right]$ etc.

d as $n \to \infty$, $\dfrac{1}{n} \to 0$ ∴ $\left(1 + \dfrac{1}{n}\right)^2 \to 1$

∴ $\lim\limits_{n\to\infty} S = \dfrac{a^4}{4}$ So, the area is $\dfrac{a^4}{4}$ units².

3 a $A = \dfrac{a^5}{5}$ units²   **b** $A = \dfrac{a^6}{6}$ units²

EXERCISE 25G.1

1 a $F'(x) = x$ ∴ $\int x\,dx = \dfrac{x^2}{2} + c$

b $F'(x) = x^4$ ∴ $\int x^4\,dx = \dfrac{x^5}{5} + c$

c $F'(x) = 8x^7$ ∴ $\int x^7\,dx = \dfrac{x^8}{8} + c$

d $F'(x) = -2x^{-3}$ ∴ $\int x^{-3}\,dx = -\dfrac{x^{-2}}{2} + c$

e $F'(x) = \tfrac{1}{2}x^{-\frac{1}{2}}$ ∴ $\int x^{-\frac{1}{2}}\,dx = 2x^{\frac{1}{2}} + c$

2 a $\int x^n\,dx = \dfrac{x^{n+1}}{n+1} + c$ **b** no, cannot divide by 0

3 a $F'(x) = 5$ ∴ $\int 5\,dx = 5x + c$ **b** $\int k\,dx = kx + c$

4 a $F'(x) = 6x^2 + 10x$

∴ $\int (6x^2 + 10x)\,dx = 2x^3 + 5x^2 + c$

b $6\int x^2\,dx + 10\int x\,dx = 6\left(\dfrac{x^3}{3} + c_1\right) + 10\left(\dfrac{x^2}{2} + c_2\right)$
$= 2x^3 + 5x^2 + c$

c $\int kf(x)\,dx = k\int f(x)\,dx$, k is constant

EXERCISE 25G.2

1 a $\dfrac{x^{11}}{11} + c$ **b** $\dfrac{1}{-3x^3} + c$ **c** $x^3 + c$ **d** $\dfrac{x^3}{3} + \dfrac{3x^2}{2} - 2x + c$

e $\dfrac{x^4}{4} - \dfrac{x^2}{2} + c$ **f** $\dfrac{10}{3}x^{\frac{3}{2}} + c$ **g** $\dfrac{x^3}{3} + 2\sqrt{x} + c$

h $\dfrac{x^4}{2} + \dfrac{3x^2}{2} + \dfrac{4}{x} + c$ **i** $\dfrac{x^2}{2} + \dfrac{3}{x} - \dfrac{2}{x^2} + c$

j $\tfrac{2}{5}x^2\sqrt{x} - 4\sqrt{x} + c$ **k** $\dfrac{x^3}{3} - 2x^2 + 4x + c$

l $\tfrac{4}{3}x^3 + 2x^2 + x + c$

2 a $\dfrac{x^4}{4} + 2x^3 + 6x^2 + 8x + c$

b $\dfrac{x^5}{5} - x^4 + 2x^3 - 2x^2 + x + c$

EXERCISE 25H

1 a $10\tfrac{1}{2}$ **b** 16   **c** 12   **d** $-7\tfrac{1}{2}$ **e** $4\tfrac{2}{3}$ **f** 8

2 a $2\tfrac{2}{3}$ **b** $52\tfrac{2}{3}$ **c** 3   **d** 0   **e** $-30\tfrac{1}{2}$ **f** $43\tfrac{3}{4}$

3 a $8\tfrac{2}{3}$ units²   **b** $4\tfrac{2}{3}$ units²   **c** 96.8 units²   **d** 6 units²
e $57\tfrac{1}{3}$ units²   **f** $1\tfrac{3}{5}$ units²   **g** 8 units²

4 $9 - 4\sqrt{2}$

REVIEW SET 25A

1 a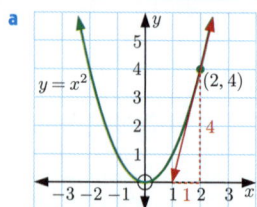

b 4

c $f'(x) = 2x$
∴ $f'(2) = 4$

2 a 21   **b** 3   **c** -4 **3** 1   **4** $f'(x) = 2x - 2$

5 a $f'(x) = 21x^2$ **b** $f'(x) = 6x - 3x^2$
c $f'(x) = 8x - 12$ **d** $f'(x) = 7 + 4x$

6 a $f'(x) = 2x - \dfrac{1}{x^2}$ **b** $f'(1) = 1$, the gradient of $y = f(x)$ at $x = 1$ is 1.

7 $(-2, -1)$, $(2, 1)$

8 a $f'(x) = 3x^2 + 6x$ **d**

b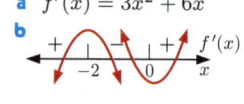

c maximum turning point at $(-2, -1)$
minimum turning point at $(0, -5)$

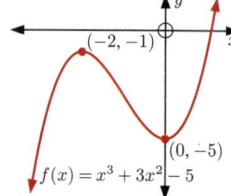

9 $F'(x) = \dfrac{1}{2\sqrt{x}}$ ∴ $\int \dfrac{1}{\sqrt{x}}\,dx = 2\sqrt{x} + c$

10 a $\dfrac{1}{2x^2} + c$ **b** $\tfrac{2}{3}x^{\frac{3}{2}} - \tfrac{2}{5}x^{\frac{5}{2}} + c$ **c** $\dfrac{x^5}{5} + \dfrac{10}{3}x^3 + 25x + c$

11 a 6   **b** $\tfrac{7}{2} - 2\sqrt{2}$ **c** $\dfrac{94\sqrt{2} - 56}{15}$ **12** $32\tfrac{2}{3}$ units²

REVIEW SET 25B

1 a -3 **b** $f'(x) = 2x + 1$ ∴ $f'(-2) = -3$

2 a -3 **b** -2 **c** 5

3 a $f'(x) = \dfrac{3}{\sqrt{x}}$ **b** $f'(x) = -\dfrac{1}{x^2} + \dfrac{8}{x^3}$

c $f'(x) = x^{-\frac{1}{2}} - \tfrac{1}{2}x^{-\frac{3}{2}}$ **d** $f'(x) = 24x^2 - 24x + 6$

4 $9x - y = 11$ **5** $(\tfrac{1}{2}, 2\sqrt{2})$ **6 a** 0   **b** -3

7 a $f'(x) = 2 - \dfrac{2}{x^2}$ **d**

b sign diagram for $f'(x)$

c maximum turning point at $(-1, -4)$
minimum turning point at $(1, 4)$

8 a $-3x + c$ **b** $\dfrac{x^4}{2} - \dfrac{x^3}{3} + c$ **c** $x - \dfrac{3x^2}{2} + x^3 - \dfrac{x^4}{4} + c$

9 a $P = 2r + \pi r + 2x$ m   **b** $x = 100 - r - \dfrac{\pi r}{2}$

c $A = 2xr + \tfrac{1}{2}\pi r^2 = 2r\left(100 - r - \dfrac{\pi r}{2}\right) + \tfrac{1}{2}\pi r^2$ etc.

d $r = 28.0$ m, rectangle has length 56.0 m, width 28.0 m

10 a $\tfrac{1}{3}$ **b** $\tfrac{2}{3}$ **c** $12\tfrac{2}{3}$ **11** $13\tfrac{3}{4}$ units²

12 $k \approx 3.832$ (to 3 decimal places)

INDEX

amplitude	468
angle at the centre	417
angle between a tangent and a chord	417
angle between two vectors	379
angle in a semi-circle	92, 412
angle of depression	250
angle of elevation	250
angles subtended by the same arc	417
arc	415
associativity laws	43
base	14
bell-shaped	200
bimodal	179
binomial	52
Cartesian plane	104
certain event	278
chords of a circle	92, 412
class intervals	174
coefficient of determination	501
collinear points	116
column graph	173
common difference	347
common ratio	350
commutative laws	43
complement of a set	32
complement laws	43
completing the square	440
complex number	238
concyclic	423
conic sections	434
constant term	514
continuous variable	177
cube root	64
cumulative frequency	185
degree	514
degree-radian conversion	457
DeMorgan's laws	43
dependent events	292
dependent variable	494
depreciation rate	400
difference of two squares expansion	49
difference of two squares factorisation	54
discriminant	233, 446
disjoint events	298
disjoint sets	37
distributive laws	43, 48
divisor	517
domain	325
domination laws	43
dot plot	173
dot product	379
empty set	28
enlargement	163
enlargement factor	139
equating indices	401
equidistant	123
evaluate	208
event	285
explicit formula	344
exponent	14
extrapolation	505
Fibonacci sequence	346
finite set	28
five-number summary	191
frequency	279
frequency histogram	177
future value	398, 400
general form	117
general term	344
gradient	460, 527
gradient formula	111
gradient-intercept form	117
horizontal asymptote	389
horizontal line	111
horizontal step	110
hypotenuse	80
idempotent laws	43
identity laws	43
image	154, 329
impossible event	278
independent events	289, 299
independent variable	494
index	14
infinite set	28
integer	29
interest rate	398
interpolation	505
interquartile range	188
inverse function	333
involution law	43
irrational number	29, 65
least squares regression line	506
length of a vector	363, 374
linear equation	224
linear regression	506
logarithm laws	404
logarithms in other bases	407
lower quartile	188
lowest common denominator	216
major arc	415
major segment	415
maximum point	468
maximum turning point	536
maximum value	449
mean	179
mean point	504
median	179
minimum point	468
minimum turning point	536
minimum value	449
minor arc	415
minor segment	415
mirror line	158
modal class	177
mode	179

...ier	397
...ually exclusive sets	37
natural number	28
negative vector	364, 373
negatively skewed	174
nth root	17
Null Factor law	226
number plane	104
object	154
ordered pair	105
outcomes	279
outliers	174
parallel box-and-whisker plots	193
Pascal's triangle	53
Pearson's correlation coefficient	499
perfect squares expansion	49
perfect squares factorisation	54
period	468
periodic function	468
position vector	363
positively skewed	174
power	14
present value	398, 400
principal axis	468
product rule	49
projection	257
proof by contradiction	74
quadrants	104
quotient	517
radical conjugate	72
radius-tangent	413
range	188, 325
rational number	17, 29, 65
real number	29
reciprocal	214
recursive formula	345
reduction	163
relative frequency	280
remainder	517
right angled triangle	80
root	224
scalar	362
sequences in finance	352
set identity	37
solution	224
square bracket notation	483
square root	64
stationary inflection	536
subject	312
surd	65, 74
symmetrical distribution	174
symmetry	154
synthetic division	519
tally and frequency table	173
tangent-radius property	93
tangents from an external point	413
terms of a sequence	344
test for cyclic quadrilaterals	425
transformation equations	156
transforming exponential functions	391
transforming quadratic functions	435
translation vector	155
two-way table	281
unit circle	260
universal set	32
upper quartile	188
vector addition	365, 373
vector between two points	371
vector equality	364, 372
vector subtraction	368, 374
vertical line	111
vertical line test	327
vertical step	110
x-intercept	441
y-intercept	117, 441
zero vector	364, 366, 374